I0004439

A System of Medicine

A SYSTEM OF MEDICINE.

A

YSTEM OF MEDICINE.

EDITED BY

J. RUSSELL REYNOLDS, M.D., F.R.S.

FELLOW OF THE ROYAL COLLEGE OF PHYSICIANS OF LONDON;
FELLOW OF THE IMPERIAL LEOPOLD-CAROLINA ACADEMY OF GERMANY;
FELLOW OF UNIVERSITY COLLEGE, LONDON;
PROFESSOR OF THE PRINCIPLES AND PRACTICE OF MEDICINE IN UNIVERSITY COLLEGE;
PHYSICIAN TO UNIVERSITY COLLEGE HOSPITAL.

N.Y. Academy of Medicine,
LIBRARY,

VOLUME THE FOURTH,

CONTAINING

DISEASES OF THE HEART.

LANE MEDICAL LIBRARY
16887
SAN FRANCISCO

Philadelphia:
J. B. LIPPINCOTT & CO.
1877.

B

R46
v. 4
1877

PREFACE.

It has been found necessary to divide into two volumes the remainder of the "System of Medicine," which I have the honour to edit; and this division has been determined mainly by the causes which have led to the delay in its appearance.

The Articles on Position and Malposition of the Heart, on Angina Pectoris, on Pericarditis, and Endocarditis, were begun by their respective authors some years ago, and several distinct portions of each of those articles were at once committed to the press. But both Dr. Gairdner and the late Dr. Sibson held that much new matter must be introduced into them; and by far the largest contributor to this volume, the late Dr. Sibson, found a mass of facts at his disposal, the analysis and representation of which occupied an amount of time and space that far exceeded his anticipation. The entire originality of his work, the subtlety of thought which it displayed, the carefulness of the observations upon which it was based, the catholicity of the views which it expressed, the honest, kind, although keen criticism that it contained of the opinions of other workers, and the intimate and important relations of all its parts, decided me not to reduce its magnitude beyond that which it now presents, and to wait for its completion. Those who know what it is to give a concise account of facts derived from their personal observation, and represented by the statistical method, will appreciate the years of labour that have been bestowed upon the articles, Position and Malposition of the Heart, upon Pericarditis and Endocarditis. Their Author, when he left England during this past autumn, had left one table uncorrected, and three pages on Carditis unwritten; I have endeavoured to correct the table, and Dr. Gowers has written the article on Carditis.

We have, in this volume, the results of many years of Dr. Sibson's ardent toil, and the last, and, as I think, the best production of that earnest, industrious, enthusiastic worker, and most kind and genial friend.

Another of the contributors to this volume has also passed away since his papers were printed, and happily in the main corrected by himself; I refer to the late Dr. Warburton Begbie, whose work was as good as his heart was large, and who never spared any pains to carry to the highest point of his ability even the smallest fragment of labour that he undertook to perform.

J. RUSSELL REYNOLDS.

38, Grosvenor Street,
December, 1876.

CONTRIBUTORS TO THE FOURTH VOLUME.

JAMES WARBURTON BEGBIE, M.D., F.R.C.P., Edinburgh; Professor of the Institutes of Medicine in the University of Edinburgh.

C. HILTON FAGGE, M.D., F.R.C.P., London; Senior Assistant Physician to Guy's Hospital.

WILLIAM TENNANT GAIRDNER, M.D., F.R.C.P., Edinburgh; Professor of the Practice of Physic in the University of Glasgow.

WILLIAM R. GOWERS, M.D., London; Assistant Physician to University College Hospital, and to the National Hospital for the Paralysed and Epileptic.

THOMAS BEVILL PEACOCK, M.D., Edinburgh, F.R.C.P., London; Physician to St. Thomas's Hospital.

FRANCIS SIBSON, M.D., F.R.C.P., F.R.S., London; formerly Lecturer on Medicine, and Physician to St. Mary's Hospital.

ERRATA.

Page 216, 5th line from bottom, *for* "10" *read* "19."
Page 216, 9th line from bottom, *for* "1 mitral aortic" *read* "5 mitral-aortic."
Page 216, 12th line from bottom, *for* "1" *read* "6"
Page 249, note 2, *for* "pages 250-253," *read* "pages 274-279."
Page 268, 15th line from top, *for* "In that case," *read* "In three cases."
Page 477, 5th line from top, *for* "30th," *read* "36th."
Page 485, 15th line from bottom, *for* "fixed" *read* "flexed."

LOCAL DISEASES (*continued*).

§ IV. Diseases of the Organs of Circulation.

A. The Heart.

Weight and Size of the Heart.

Position and form of the Heart and great Vessels.

Malpositions of the Heart.

Lateral or Partial Aneurism of the Heart.

Adventitious Products in the Heart.

Pneumo-Pericardium.

Pericarditis.

Adherent Pericardium.

Endocarditis.

Carditis.

Hydropericardium.

Angina Pectoris and Allied States; including certain kinds of sudden Death.

Diseases of the Valves of the Heart.

Atrophy of the Heart.

Hypertrophy of the Heart.

Dilatation of the Heart.

Fatty Diseases of the Heart.

Fibroid Disease of the Heart.

CONTENTS.

PART II. (*continued.*)

LOCAL DISEASES, OR AFFECTIONS OF PARTICULAR ORGANS, OR SYSTEMS OF ORGANS.

§ IV. DISEASES OF THE ORGANS OF CIRCULATION.

A. THE HEART :—

WEIGHT AND SIZE OF THE HEART, by Thomas B. Peacock, M.D., F.R.C.P.

PAGE

Of the Healthy Heart 3
Of the Diseased Heart 8

POSITION AND FORM OF THE HEART AND GREAT VESSELS, by Francis Sibson, M.D., F.R.S.

Front View after Death 14
Front View during Life 64
Side View after Death 89
Side View during Life 92
Back View after Death 99
Back View during Life 100
Notes from Pirogoff and Braun 109

MALPOSITIONS OF THE HEART. 125
Vertical Displacement 125
Lateral Displacement 135
Forward Displacement 148
Backward Displacement 148

LATERAL OR PARTIAL ANEURISM OF THE HEART, by
    Thomas Bevill Peacock, M.D., F.R.C.P.. . . . .
Aneurism of the Left Ventricle . . . .
Aneurism of the Left Auricle . . . .
Aneurism of the Valves . . . .

ADVENTITIOUS PRODUCTS IN THE HEART, by Thomas
    Bevill Peacock, M.D., F.R.C.P. . . . .
Tubercle in the Heart, and Tubercular Pericarditis . . . . . .
Cancer . . . .
Simple and other Cysts . . . .
Entozoa . . . .
Fibrinous Deposits: Syphilitic Affections of the Heart . . . . .
Fibro-Cartilaginous and Osseous Degeneration . . . .
Polypoid Growths . . . .

PNEUMO-PERICARDIUM, by J. Warburton Begbie, M.D. . .

PERICARDITIS, by Francis Sibson, M.D., F.R.S. . . . .
Clinical History of Pericarditis as it occurred in the Author's
    Practice in St. Mary's Hospital . . . .
Rheumatic Pericarditis . . . .
Sex, Age, and Occupation . . . .
The Affection of the Joints . . . .
The Degree of the Joint Affection during the Acme of Effusion .
Time in the Hospital . . . .
Occurrence of previous Attacks . . . .
Time of the first Observation of Friction-sound in relation to the
    Pericarditis and the Joint Affection . . . .
The Presence or Absence of Endocarditis . . . .
Progressive changes in the Organs . . . .
Over-Action of the Heart, and of the Limbs as Causes of
    Rheumatism with Heart Affection . . . .
Pain . . . .
Irregularity and Failure of the Heart . . . .
Difficult and Quickened Respiration . . . .
Difficulty in Swallowing . . . .
Loss of Voice . . . .
Effects on the Pulse . . . .
Fulness of the Veins . . . .
Appearance of the Face . . . .
Condition of Face when Effusion at its Acme . . . .

PERICARDITIS *continued*—

PAGE

    Affections of the Nervous System 249

        In Rheumatic Pericarditis with high Temperature 254

        In Endocarditis with high Temperature 262

        High Temperature without Inflammation 264

        In which Temperature was not Observed 273

        Coma 282

        Delirium 283

        Temporary Insanity, Melancholia, and Hallucinations . . . 283

        Chorea, Choreiform and Tetaniform Movements 292

        In Pericarditis without Rheumatism or Bright's Disease . . 295

    The Physical Signs of Rheumatic Pericarditis 304

        Percussion 309

        Prominence over the Region of the Pericardium 332

        Position of the Impulse 334

        Vibration or Thrill 343

        Auscultation 349

        The Character and Tests of Pericardial Friction Sound . . 388

        Physical Signs of Pericarditis in Bright's Disease 413

        Pericarditis, neither Rheumatic nor from Bright's Disease . . 419

    Treatment of Pericarditis 430

ADHERENT PERICARDIUM, by Francis Sibson, M.D., F.R.S. . 438

    Anatomical Description 438

    Physical Signs 442

    Clinical History 446

ENDOCARDITIS, by Francis Sibson, M.D., F.R.S. 456

    Anatomical Appearances 456

    Clinical History in Rheumatism 460

    Clinical History in Chorea 511

        „   „   Pyæmia 516

        „   „   Bright's Disease 517

        „   „   Valvular Disease 519

    Pathological Evidence of Endocarditis in Cases of Valvular Disease

        of the Heart 519

    Treatment 525

CARDITIS, by W. R. Gowers, M.D. 529

HYDROPERICARDIUM, by J. Warburton Begbie, M.D. 532

ANGINA PECTORIS AND ALLIED STATES; INCLUDING
    CERTAIN KINDS OF SUDDEN DEATH, by Professor
    Gairdner, M.D. . . . .
    General Description . . . .
    Diagnosis . . . .
    Causes . . . .
    Illustrations of sudden death without pain . . . .
    Pathology . . . .
    Treatment . . . .

DISEASES OF THE VALVES OF THE HEART, by C. Hilton
    Fagge, M.D., F.R.C.P. . . . .
    History . . . .
    Description and Anatomy . . . .
    Etiology . . . .
    Effects . . . .
    Diagnosis . . . .
    Prognosis . . . .
    Treatment . . . .

ATROPHY OF THE HEART, by W. R. Gowers, M.D. . . . . . .
    Definition and History . . . .
    Varieties : Causes . . . .
    Symptoms . . . .
    Diagnosis, Prognosis, Treatment . . . .

HYPERTROPHY OF THE HEART, by W. R. Gowers, M.D. . . .
    Synonyms, Definition, History . . . .
    Varieties, Causes, Pathology . . . .
    Pathological Anatomy . . . .
    Symptoms . . . .
    Diagnosis . . . .
    Prognosis . . . .
    Treatment . . . .

DILATATION OF THE HEART, by W. R. Gowers, M.D. . . .
    Synonyms, Definition, History . . . .
    Varieties, Causes . . . .
    Pathological Anatomy . . . .
    Consequences . . . .
    Symptoms . . . .
    Diagnosis . . . .
    Prognosis, Treatment . . . .

PAGE

FATTY DISEASES OF THE HEART, by W. R. Gowers, M.D. . 760
Fatty Overgrowth 760
History, Causes 761
Pathological Anatomy 762
Symptoms, Diagnosis, Treatment 763
Fatty Degeneration 764
Synonyms, Definition, History 764
Varieties 765
Etiology 766
Pathological Anatomy 771
Consequences, Symptoms 778
Course and Terminations 782
Diagnosis 783
Prognosis, Treatment 784
Rupture of the Heart 786
Symptoms, Diagnosis 789
Prognosis, Treatment 790

FIBROID DISEASE OF THE HEART, by W. R. Gowers, M.D. . 791
Synonyms, Definition, History 791
Etiology, Pathological Anatomy 792
Consequences, Symptoms 793
Diagnosis : Treatment 794

INDEX 797

LIST OF CHIEF AUTHORS REFERRED TO 809

DISEASES OF THE HEART.

WEIGHT AND SIZE OF THE HEART.

By Thomas B. Peacock, M.D., F.R.C.P.

1. *Of the Healthy Heart.*—From an early period pathologists have
felt the necessity of some standard by which the size of the heart
might be estimated, and its healthy and diseased conditions compared.
Corvisart was unable to suggest any such, and Laennec compared the
size of the healthy heart to the fist of the subject—a comparison too
indefinite to afford any satisfactory estimate. Meckel and Kerkring,
as quoted by Senac, were apparently the earliest writers who gave
any estimate of the normal weight of the heart; and Lobstein and
Bouillaud were the first to suggest the employment of the balance as
a means of comparison between the healthy and diseased organs.
The latter writer, in the first edition of his work, published in 1835,
gave some observations of the weight both of healthy and diseased
hearts, but they were too few in number to form the basis of
satisfactory conclusions. Bizot conceived that the dimensions of the
organ would furnish a better standard; and in 1837, in the Mémoires
of the "Société Médicale d'Observation," published a large series of
very careful measurements. Dr. Glendinning, in 1838, contributed
numerous observations of the weight of the heart in a paper in the
"Medico-Chirurgical Transactions;" and Dr. Ranking, in 1849, published in the *Medical Gazette* a series of measurements, both of
healthy and diseased organs. In 1843 the late Professor Reid appended to his paper on the weights of the different organs of the
human body, tables of the weight and dimensions of the heart; and
in 1854 I published a considerable number of observations of the
weight and size of the organ, under different circumstances of health
and disease; together with various tables compiled from them.
Both these sets of observations were published in the *Edinburgh
Monthly Journal.* More recently, Dr. Boyd has recorded in the "Phi-
losophical Transactions" a larger and more complete series of observations than had been published by any previous writer.

It is useless to refer to the estimates of the weight of the healthy
heart given by any of the earlier writers, for we have no means of
knowing the number of observations upon which they are based; the
age and sex of the subjects; the condition of the organs weighed, or the
precise weight employed. Of the more recent observers, M. Bouillaud

estimated the weight of the healthy heart in adults, not distinguishing the two sexes, as ranging from 8 oz. 10 drachms to 9 oz. 11 drachms imperial. Dr. Glendinning inferred that the mean weight of the healthy organ was in adult males 8¾ oz., and in females 7¾ oz. ; and Dr. Reid deduced the average in males as 11 oz. 12 drachms, and in females as 9 oz. These estimates are sufficient to show how wide the differences may be according to the mode in which the calculations are made. It is evident that the weight of the heart must vary considerably according to the cause producing death ; the organ being heavier when the patient dies suddenly or after only a short attack of illness, and lighter when death has taken place from lingering diseases, provided the diseases are not such as interfere with the functions of the organ, and so give rise to over-nutrition. Thus, while Dr. Reid, as just stated, estimated the average weight of the male heart at about 11 oz., he found that in twelve men who were killed the weight attained an average of 12 oz.; and, on the other hand, I have examined the hearts of persons who have died from cirrhosis of the liver and cancer of the pylorus, &c., which were only 5 or 6 oz. in weight. To form, therefore, an accurate estimate, not only must the age and sex be taken into consideration, but the weight of the organ must be given in acute and chronic diseases separately ; and the cases in which the nutrition of the heart may have been materially modified by the disease causing death must be excluded from the calculation. The size of the heart will also be similarly influenced, and especially the dimensions must vary with the degree of distension of the cavities at the time of death. To form a thoroughly satisfactory estimate, the weight and dimensions of the heart must therefore both be given, and the previous circumstances must be taken into consideration.

In the following tables I have endeavoured to carry out these views. In the first table the weight of the heart in the adult is given separately, for males and females, and for acute and chronic diseases. In the second, the dimensions of the organ, also in the adult and in males and females, are stated, in Paris lines, millimètres, and parts of English inches. The third table gives the average weight of the heart in males and females at different ages.

TABLE I.

Average Weight of the Healthy Heart in Males and Females, and in Acute and Chronic Diseases, from Twenty to Fifty-five Years of Age.

MALES—	
Mean weight	9 oz. 8 drs.
Ordinary range in acute cases . . .	9 oz. to 11 oz.
„ „ chronic cases . .	8 oz. to 10 oz.
FEMALES—	
Mean weight	8 oz. 13 drs.
Ordinary range in acute cases . . .	8 oz. to 10 oz.
„ „ chronic cases . .	7 oz. to 9 oz.

From the first table it will be seen that in adult males who have died from acute diseases, or from the effects of accident, the ordinary weight of the heart is from 9 to 11 oz.; and in those who have died from chronic diseases, 8 to 10 oz. In females, the ordinary weight of the heart in acute cases may be estimated at from 8 to 10 oz., and in chronic diseases from 7 to 9 oz. Occasionally, however, in persons of small and delicate frame, who have died from emaciating diseases, such as cancer of the stomach, bowels, or mesentery, or chronic affections of the liver, the heart will be found to weigh only 5 or 6 oz.; and in large and powerful men who have been killed or have died after short illnesses, the organ may weigh 12 oz. or even more, without exceeding the limit of health. Some writers have given calculations of the relation of the weight of the heart to that of the whole body, but the bulk of the body, and also, as before stated, the size of the heart, vary so greatly from the duration of illness and the mode in which death occurs, that such calculations do not possess much value. The height of the subject and the weight and size of the heart probably bear a more just relation.

From the second table it will be seen that the girth of the right ventricle, measured externally, exceeds that of the left, in males by about one-sixth, and in females by one-fifth. The length of the cavity of the right ventricle is greater than that of the left, in males by one-seventh, and in females by one-sixth. In both sexes the thickness of

TABLE II.

Dimensions[1] of the Healthy Heart (in French Lines, Millimètres, and English Inches) in Males and Females.

	MALES.			FEMALES.		
	Lines.	Milli-mètres.	Inches.	Lines.	Milli-mètres.	Inches.
Circumference of heart	103·7	233·92	9·209	104	234	9·236
Girth of right ventricle	55·4	123·85	4·919	58·4	131·4	5·184
„ left „	48·3	108·67	4·299	45·6	102·6	4·049
Length of cavity of right ventricle	43·3	96·42	3·821	44·3	99·67	3·925
„ „ left „	37·6	84·6	3·333	37·1	83·47	3·197
Thickness of walls of right ventricle, base . .	1·85	4·16	·164	1·85	4·16	·164
„ „ „ „ midpoint .	1·96	4·35	·176	2·0	4·5	·177
„ „ „ „ apex . . .	1·42	3·19	·125	1·3	2·92	·118
„ „ left „ base . . .	5·15	11·58	·425	4·9	11·02	·432
„ „ „ „ midpoint .	6	13·5	·532	5·6	12·6	·497
„ „ „ „ apex . . .	2·4	5·4	·214	2·5	5·62	·222
Thickness of septum	5·73	12·89	·51	4·7	10·57	·421
Circumference of right auriculo-ventricular aperture	53·4	120·15	4·74	51·4	115·65	4·562
„ left „ „ „	45·2	101·7	4	45	101·25	3·996
„ pulmonic aperture	40	90	3·552	39·3	88·42	3·493
„ aortic „	35·6	80·1	3·146	34	76·5	3·019

the walls of the right ventricle is about one-third that of those of the left. The thickness of the septum is intermediate between that of the

[1] The dimensions of the orifices are taken by balls, the first of which is 12 lines in circumference, which increase in circumference three Paris lines, and are numbered from 1 to 20.

external walls of the right and left ventricles. In males the pulmonic orifice is about one-eighth more in circumference than the aortic. The left auriculo-ventricular aperture is one-fourth more than that of the aorta, and the right auriculo-ventricular aperture one-half larger. In females the differences between the aortic and other orifices are some-what greater.

It has been generally supposed that the heart increases in weight with the progress of life; and this opinion is supported by the facts recorded relating to males, in the third table. It may, however, be doubted whether the result thus indicated is applicable to the heart in its strictly healthy state. It is well known that in advanced age there is a decided diminution in the weight of the brain, and there seems no reason why a similar decrease of weight should not occur in the heart, provided that organ be not the seat of disease inter-fering with its normal nutrition. As we well know, but few elderly persons, especially men, are entirely free from any form of disease which, by occasioning obstruction, might lead to over-action, and so

TABLE III.

Weight[1] of the Healthy Heart at Different Ages in Males and Females.

	MALES.		FEMALES.	
	oz.	drs.	oz.	drs.
Ages 10 to 14 inclusive —Mean weight	6	1·5	5	0
„ 15 „ 20　　„　　„　　„	8	2·66	8	1·66
From 20 „ 30　　„　　„　　„	8	0·14	8	10·42
„ 30 „ 40　　„　　„　　„	9	7·95	8	13·94
„ 40 „ 50　　„　　„　　„	9	11·11	9	3
„ 50 „ 60　　„　　„　　„	9	12	9	7·83
„ 60 „ 70　　„　　„　　„	10	13·33	7	0

Mean weight between 20 and 55 years of age—in 76 males . . . 9 oz 8·74 drs.
„　　„　　„　　„　　„　　„　 in 49 females . 8 oz. 13·16 drs.
Difference . . . . 11·58 drs.

to some degree of hypertrophy. And even if the heart be not itself diseased, there are few old persons who do not display some affec-tion of the lungs, kidneys, or other parts of the system, which might more or less interfere with the functions of the heart, and so lead to its enlargement. That this is the more correct view is supported by the diminution in the weight of the organ in elderly females, as also shown in the table.

2. The alterations in the weight of the heart in disease are illus-trated by Tables IV and V.

It was supposed by Dr. Glendinning, that the heart in cases of *phthisis*, contrary to what would à *priori* have been expected, acquires an increase of weight, while the rest of the body becomes emaciated. This idea appears to have arisen from a misapprehension of the facts which he collected. The effect of the pulmonary affection

[1] The weight employed is Avoirdupois or Imperial.

upon the nutrition of the heart appears to vary with the form of the disease. In cases of uncomplicated constitutional or tubercular phthisis, the progress of which is generally rapid and which is usually attended with great emaciation, the heart is found to weigh considerably below the healthy average, and the organ, on examination, often displays the appearance of atrophy. In cases of chronic phthisis, whether tubercular or inflammatory, on the other hand, and especially when one or both lungs are considerably contracted, or when there have been marked bronchitic symptoms, so that the blood has for a long time been transmitted with difficulty through the lungs, the heart is generally found to be enlarged, or, at least, not to have undergone any marked diminution in size; its weight equalling or exceeding the healthy standard. So also when, in cases of phthisis, there is any great impediment to the transmission of the blood from the heart

TABLE IV.

Range of Weight of Heart, in Different Forms of Disease, and when Diseased.

	MEAN.		EXTREMES.	
	oz. drs.		oz. drs.	oz. drs.
Phthisis. Males	9 3·4		6 4·5 to	11 0
" Females	8 6·06		5 9 „	11 0
Chronic Bronchitis. Males	14 8		11 8 „	21 0
" " Females	12 2·0		9 0 „	12 8
Morbus Renum.—Males.	9 12		7 4 „	14 8
" " Females.	10 5·4		7 4 „	15 8
Simple Hypertrophy.—Males	—		12 0 „	40 12
Aortic Disease. Males	—		10 0 „	24 0
" " Females	—		8 8 „	20 0
Aortic valvular obstruction.—Males	—		14 0 „	21 0
" " " Females	—		13 0 „	18 8
Aortic valvular regurgitation.—Males	—		14 0 „	34 0
" " " Females	—		16 0 „	23 0
Mitral valvular obstruction or regurgitation, or both.—Males	—		14 0 „	17 0
" " Females	—		13 0 „	18 8
Combined aortic and mitral valvular disease.—Males	—		14 8 „	21 0
" " " " " Females	—		7 8 „	23 0

from valvular or aortic disease, notwithstanding the general tendency to emaciation, the organ may exceed even very greatly the natural size.

Chronic Bronchitis.—When there is long-continued obstruction to the pulmonary circulation from chronic bronchitis, with or without deformity of the spine, the right side of the heart becomes hypertrophied; but, even a great increase in the thickness of the walls of the right ventricle does not very much augment the weight of the heart, and it is only after the left side has become implicated that the weight is found much to exceed the healthy standard. In some such cases, however, the organ may attain a weight considerably greater than the natural, amounting, in hearts I have weighed, to 15 or 16 oz.

Morbus Renum.—Dr. Bright noticed that the heart in cases of chronic disease of the kidneys was frequently found increased in size without there being any valvular disease to explain the enlargement ; and the occurrence of simple hypertrophy in such cases has been noticed by other pathologists. Of eighteen cases in which the organ was weighed by myself, in seven the weight was below the average of chronic diseases, while in eleven it exceeded it, attaining in some cases

TABLE V.

Extreme Dimensions of the Heart, with the Different Forms of Disease in which they occur.

	Lines.	Milli-mètres.	Inches	
Circumference.—Males	182	409·5	16 16	In simple hypertrophy.
„ Females	127	285 75	11·27	Mitral disease.
Thickness of walls of right ventricle.—Males .	5 75	12 93	·51	Mitral disease.
„ „ „ „ Females	7	15 75	·62	Congenital obstruction at pulmonic orifice.
„ „ left „ Males .	14	31·5	1 24	Aortic valvular disease.
„ „ „ „ Females	11	24·75	·97	Combined aortic and mitral disease.
Circumf. right auriculo-ventricular apert. Males	63	141 76	5·59	Simple hypertrophy
„ „ „ „ Fem.	60	135	5 32	Aortic valvular obstruction
„ left „ „ „ Males	60	135	5 32	Simple hypertrophy.
„ „ „ „ Fem.	45	101 25	3 99	Aortic valvular obstruction.
„ pulmonic aperture.—Males	54	121·5	4 79	Simple hypertrophy.
„ „ „ Fem.	39	87 78	3 46	Mitral valvular disease, chronic bronchitis, and deformed spine.
„ aortic „ Males	45	101·25	3 99	Aortic valvular disease.
„ „ „ Fem.	35	78·85	3 1	Aortic valvular disease and combined aortic and mitral disease.

in males the weight of upwards of 14 or 15 oz. In these cases the hypertrophy is doubtless due to the over-action of the heart from its efforts to overcome the obstruction to the transmission of the blood through the capillaries.

3.—WEIGHT AND DIMENSIONS OF THE DISEASED HEART.

Simple Hypertrophy.—The most remarkable case of increase in the weight and size of the heart which I have myself met with was in a case of hypertrophy, without any material valvular disease or any obvious source of obstruction in the aorta, to explain the condition. In this instance, which, however, is a very extreme one, the organ weighed 40 oz. 12 dr. ; but in various other cases I have found the weight considerably to exceed the average or extreme limit of health. In a heart which I examined with Mr. Hutchinson, the weight attained was 26 oz. ; and Dr. Bristowe exhibited one at the Pathological Society which weighed 27 oz. The ages of these patients were sixty-five, thirty-five, and forty-one respectively. It is difficult to explain the great enlargement which exists in some cases of this description. It may depend on some disease of the smaller arteries which may have escaped observation, or on obstruction in the capillaries ; but, in other instances, it is probably due to habitual over-action from athletic pursuits, and possibly in some cases to palpitation, at first originating in emotional causes. Enlargement unconnected with valvular disease is, however, rarely seen except in men, and in no instance have I found the heart much hypertrophied in females without there being some obvious source of obstruction to which the change was referable.

Aortic Obstruction and Aortic Valvular Disease.—The occurrence of obstruction in the aorta, and especially in the upper portion of that vessel, is generally attended by considerable increase of weight in the heart. In various cases of this description I have found the heart to range from near the natural standard to 24 oz. in males, 17 oz. in females. In the Transactions of the Medico-Chirurgical Society, a case is recorded by Dr. Risdon Bennett, in which the heart weighed 22½ oz. in a man fifty-three years of age, who died from rupture of the aorta, giving rise to dissecting aneurism and hemiplegia. The increase of size in the heart was apparently due to atheromatous disease of the aortic coats.

In aortic valvular disease still greater increase of weight is often met with. In cases of obstructive disease, I have weighed hearts ranging from 14 oz. to 21 oz. in males, and from 13 oz. to 18 oz. 8 drs. in females. In cases of aortic valvular incompetency, I have found the heart to weigh from 14 oz. to 34 oz. in males, and from 16 ozs. to 23 ozs. in females. Dr. Van der Byl, in a paper in the "Pathological Transactions," relates instances in which the heart weighed 36 oz. in a case of aortic valvular incompetency, in a man of twenty-eight; 30 oz. in a case of aortic disease with aneurism of the aorta, in a man of thirty-three; and 30 oz. in a case of aortic and mitral disease, in a man of sixty-two.

In the cases of incompetency of the aortic valves, it is often impossible to say how much of the great enlargement of the heart is due to the obstruction, and how much to the incompetency of the valves; for the latter condition is generally only the final stage of the former. In cases of rupture of the aortic valves during violent effort, we have, however, the opportunity of seeing the remarkable changes which may occur in the heart even during short periods of time, when, in organs previously healthy, the valves are rendered incompetent and the left ventricle rapidly becomes hypertrophied and dilated. Thus, in a case of this description which occurred to myself, the patient, a man of thirty-three years, survived the accident only twenty-seven months, yet the heart was found to weigh 17¾ oz. In a case related by Dr. Quain, the patient lived two years, and the heart weighed 22½ oz.; and in another case which I had the opportunity of examining after death, though the patient, a man thirty-six years of age, only survived three-and-a-half months, the weight was 23 oz. If, in this instance, the heart was sound at the time of the occurrence of the injury, the process of enlargement must have been most rapid; but it may be doubted whether the organ was not more or less hypertrophied before the accident, though the patient stated that he was previously quite well.

In some cases of disease, also, the enlargement must take place very rapidly. In a boy of eighteen, who died of aortic valvular disease originating in malformation, the duration of active illness was only three-and-a-half years, yet the heart weighed 28 oz. In a case of aortic valvular incompetency, with probably regurgitation through the left auriculo-ventricular aperture from maladjustment of the valves, described by Dr. Bristowe in the "Pathological Transactions," the heart weighed 46½ oz. avoirdupois, though the subject of the disease was only twenty-two years of age. In an instance of very great obstruction at the aortic valves, doubtless from malformation, which I have recently exhibited at the Pathological Society, the heart weighed 24 oz., the patient being only twenty-three years of age. These examples show that the heart may attain a very great increase of size even in comparatively young subjects; but, usually, those in whom the heart is very large are advanced in age. Probably, also, in most cases, the disease must be of long duration for the organ to become very greatly hypertrophied, and this great prolongation of life is only compatible with comparatively slight disease, or with disease which has been very slowly progressive, though at the time of death it may have become extreme.

In *mitral valvular disease*, whether consisting in obstruction and regurgitation, from contraction of the orifice and rigidity of the valves, or in free regurgitation from expansion of the aperture or maladjustment of the valves, the heart does not ordinarily attain by any means so great an increase of weight as in cases of aortic disease. In the former class of cases, the hypertrophy is chiefly limited to the right ventricle, and only affects the left ventricle secondarily, though in the latter the left ventricle also partakes of the change from the first. In cases of mitral disease, the weights have ranged from 14 oz. 8 drachms to 17 oz. 8 drachms in males, and from 12 oz. to 18 oz. in females.

As might be expected, in *combined aortic and mitral valvular disease*, the weight of the heart is intermediate between that which obtains in the two separate forms of disease, the organ being lighter than in aortic, heavier than in mitral disease. In males, in cases of this kind the heart was found to weigh 14 oz. 8 dr. to 21 oz. 8 dr., and in females from 17 oz. to 23 oz.

In cases of obstruction at the right side, consisting in *congenital contraction of the pulmonic orifice*, the effect produced on the nutrition of the heart is very similar to that which results from chronic bronchitis. In the first instance the right ventricle is chiefly hypertrophied, but subsequently the left also becomes involved; and similar changes ensue in the cases in which the aorta communicates with both ventricles, provided the life of the patient be sufficiently prolonged. In a male of twenty, in whom the pulmonary orifice was contracted from adhesion of the valves, the heart weighed 12 oz.; and in a female of nineteen, in whom there was similar disease of the pulmonic valves, and the aorta arose from both ventricles and the ductus arteriosus was open, the organ weighed 17½ oz.

The effect produced by *adhesions of the pericardium* on the functions and nutrition of the heart has been the subject of much discussion. On the one hand, adhesions have been supposed to interfere with the free movement of the heart, and so to give rise to hypertrophy; on the other, it has been thought that by the compression exercised upon the organ they might cause atrophy. The question is one which it is very difficult to decide, for there are few cases in which the pericardium is entirely adherent, in which the valves are not also more or less involved, and in which therefore the effects produced by the one condition may not be modified by the other. I find, however, that in three men in whom the pericardium was entirely adherent, while the valves were free from disease, the hearts weighed 16 oz., 17 oz. 4 dr., and 18 oz.; but I have examined other organs under similar circumstances in which the weight did not exceed the healthy standard. The general rule is, however, that in cases of adhesion the heart becomes hypertrophied.

General Remarks on the Weight of the Heart.—M. Bouillaud has collected some cases in which the heart otherwise healthy weighed considerably less than natural; and others in which in various states of disease it exceeded that point. The former are all cases in which the organ was reduced in weight with the progressive emaciation of cancer, consumption, &c. The lightest heart, that of a female of forty-five, weighed 4 oz. 5 dr. in a case of cancer; the heaviest organ weighed 24 oz. 4 dr. in a case of obstructive and probably also regurgitant disease of the aortic valves, in a female of fifty-three. From these observations, and his estimate of the average weight of the healthy organ as ranging from 8 oz. 10 drs. to 9 oz. 11 drs., he infers that the heart may attain when diseased three times the weight of the average healthy organ, and five times that of the most atrophied organ. These estimates are, however, considerably less than the variations of weight which actually obtain. I have found the heart to weigh only 5 oz. in a man fifty-three years of age who died of cirrhosis of the liver, and 6 oz. in a man of thirty-nine who had cancer of the pylorus. The average weights I have estimated in males at 9 oz. 8 drs., and the heaviest heart weighed was 40 oz. 12 drs. It follows therefore that in men the heart may attain a weight which is four times that of the healthy and eight times that of the atrophied organ. In females, the variations in the weight of the heart are sufficiently remarkable, though considerably less than in men. The average weight has been shown to be 8 oz. 13 drs.: the lightest hearts weighed 5 oz. 8 drs. in cases of phthisis in twenty-five and thirty years of age; the heaviest organ was 23 oz. The most enlarged heart was therefore three times the weight of the average, and four times that of the atrophied organ. It has also been mentioned that Dr. Bristowe has placed on record a case in which the heart of a man twenty-two years of age weighed 46¼ oz.; and Dr. Church has recently exhibited at the Pathological Society the heart of a female forty-seven years of age, who died of cancer of the pylorus, which weighed only 3 oz. 1 dr.

The heart described by Dr. Bristowe is, as far as I know, the heaviest on record. Dr. Hope says that he examined at St. George's a heart which weighed 2¼ lbs., which, if the weight employed were avoirdupois, would nearly equal the size of the largest heart which I have myself weighed—40 oz. 12 drs. M. Lobstein refers to a heart which weighed 34 oz., and Dr. Vanderbyl to one of 36 oz.

The dimensions of the heart in different forms of disease bear a general relation to the weights of the organ in similar conditions. Of the observations which I have myself made, the greatest weight was attained in cases of simple hypertrophy, obstruction in the course of the aorta, and obstructive, or obstructive and regurgitant disease of the aortic valves. It is equally in these forms of disease that the dimensions of the organ are most considerably enlarged, the cavities and orifices, especially those of the left side, being the most expanded, and the walls the most remarkably increased in thickness. There are, however, differences in the condition of the organ in these several forms of disease. In cases of obstruction, on whatever cause dependent, the heart is not generally so large as in cases of incompetency, and the form of the organ is also somewhat different. In the former class of cases the heart is peculiarly long and pointed at the apex, and the walls attain the greatest width near the base. In the latter the ventricle is usually of larger size and rounded at the apex, and the thickening is more equally diffused over the walls. In both forms of disease, the enlargement, though most marked on the left side of the heart, affects the right also very considerably.

In cases of mitral valvular disease, the size of the organ is considerably less than in the former class of cases, and the shape is very different, but the precise condition of the organ varies with the form of disease. In cases of great contraction of the left auriculo-ventricular aperture, the stress falls chiefly on the left auricle and the right cavities, and they are all found expanded and the walls increased in thickness, and much firmer than natural ; the orifices also being dilated; while the left ventricle is not much if at all enlarged, and its walls are not materially hypertrophied. It has, indeed, been supposed that the left ventricle becomes atrophied. In cases, on the other hand in which the defect consists chiefly or to a marked degree in incompetency of the valves, on whatever cause dependent, the left ventricle is found to be considerably dilated and hypertrophied, and the changes on the right side are less marked. In both these forms of disease, however, the alteration in the shape of the heart is very marked, the organ being wide and blunted at the apex—in the one case chiefly in consequence of the expansion of the right side, in the other of the dilatation of the left ventricle, and especially the widening of its apex. In cases of combined aortic and mitral valvular disease, the enlargement is intermediate, both in shape and extent, between the other two forms. In cases of chronic bronchitis, chronic phthisis, deformity of the chest, and pulmonic valvular obstruction, the hypertrophy and dilatation are at first limited to the right side, but subsequently, if life be much prolonged, involve the left also. Table V. shows some of the extreme dimensions which I have recorded in different forms of disease.

It will be observed that not only do the size of the cavities and the width of the walls vary greatly in different forms of disease, but the capacity of the orifices also undergoes remarkable change ; and this not only in cases of old disease, but even during comparatively short periods of illness. Thus it will generally be found in cases of acute bronchitis and very acute phthisis, that the pulmonic aperture, which ordinarily exceeds the aortic somewhat in capacity, is disproportionately larger than the aortic, and the right auriculo-ventricular aperture equally out of proportion with the left. I have also reason to believe that the apertures may not only expand in a short time, but may have their dimensions reduced without being otherwise diseased, and thus it is possible that in some forms of valvular defect the size of the orifice may be reduced and the incompetency diminished.

POSITION AND FORM OF THE HEART AND GREAT. VESSELS.

By Francis Sibson, M.D., F.R.S.

CONTENTS.

FRONT VIEW, AFTER DEATH	*Page* 14
FRONT VIEW, DURING LIFE	„ 64
SIDE VIEW, AFTER DEATH	„ 89
SIDE VIEW, DURING LIFE	„ 92
BACK VIEW, AFTER DEATH	„ 99
BACK VIEW, DURING LIFE	„ 100
NOTES FROM PIROGOFF AND BRAUN	„ 109

FRONT VIEW; AFTER DEATH.

The following observations on the position and anatomical relations of the healthy heart and great vessels after death are founded on the examination of a number of diagrams showing the position of the internal organs after death. This examination was restricted to those instances in which the heart was healthy and was not enlarged. The diagrams were made by drawing the outlines of the organs on a piece of lace or net, stretched upon a frame and placed over the body.

The heart and great vessels present great variety in form and position both after death and during life.

During the illness or injury that ends in death, at the time of death and after death, the heart and great vessels undergo a series of changes in position and form. According to the nature and direction of these changes, the heart after death may, in different instances, be (I.) higher or lower in position; or (II.) it may deviate more to the right or more to the left.

(I.) The Higher or Lower Position of the Heart and Great Vessels.

Three main conditions may influence the higher or lower position of the heart after death: (1). The contraction or expansion of the lungs: (2). The distension or flaccidity of the abdomen: and (3). The state of the heart itself.

(1). When death is associated with bronchitis, or pneumonia, or affections of a like nature, in which the lungs are large, and are expanded after death, the chest is broad and deep, the diaphragm is low, and the heart, which is charged with blood, especially in its right cavities, is large, and occupies a low position. As a rule, however, the lungs, when they are not thus affected, lessen in size and contract during the final expirations. The cage of the chest then becomes more flat and narrow; it lengthens downwards, and the sternum and costal cartilages and ribs in front are all lowered in position. The diaphragm at the same time is elevated. While the front of the chest is thus lowered, the heart, resting on the diaphragm, is raised, and the whole organ, and the great vessels occupy a higher position. We thus have a double and contrary movement in the descent of the bony framework of the front of the chest, and the ascent of the heart immediately behind that framework. As the heart within, and the sternum and cartilages without are both thus elevated by the distension of the abdomen, the actual elevation of the heart and great vessels is much greater than their apparent elevation, estimated as that usually is by the relation of those parts to the walls of the chest immediately in front of them.

(2). When the abdomen is distended, whether by fluid or air in the cavity itself, by an accumulation of gas in the stomach and intestines, or by other causes, the whole diaphragm is forcibly elevated, and the heart, resting as it does on the central tendon of the diaphragm, is lifted upwards. The sternum and costal cartilages in front of the heart are, at the same time, also raised in position, and the lower ribs on either side are pressed outwards. Although the actual elevation of the heart is, in these cases, often very great, its apparent elevation, which is measured by the relation of the heart to the walls of the chest in front of it, may be slight, owing to the simultaneous elevation of the heart and the sternum and cartilages in front of the heart caused by the distension of the abdomen.

When the abdomen is flaccid, owing to the stomach and intestines being empty, the reverse effects take place. The diaphragm descends, the heart drops downwards, the sternum and costal cartilages are lowered in position, and the inferior ribs fall inwards.

(3). During the final illness or injury that precedes death the heart may lessen or enlarge. Fatal hæmorrhage or wasting disease reduces the size of the heart and great vessels. On the other hand, the heart is swollen, especially on the right side, under the influence of suffocation or bronchitis; while its left ventricle may be thickened and enlarged in cases of Bright's disease with contracted kidney. Thus the right or the left side of the heart may be enlarged when the obstacle to the flow of blood is respectively in the lungs or the body.

At the time of death, the left ventricle usually closes firmly upon itself; while then or soon afterwards the right cavities of the heart become permanently swollen with blood.

After death the heart shrinks upwards to a greater or less extent.

This is owing partly to the diminution of the organ, but mainly, I believe, to the contraction of the arch of the aorta, for the shortening of that vessel draws the heart upwards, just as its lengthening pushes the organ downwards.

The exact extent to which the heart is thus raised, is measured by the space that is left between the lower boundary of the heart, and the lower boundary of the *front* of the pericardium. During life these two adjoining parts fit each other exactly; but after death they are separated by a space that varies according to the degree to which the heart shrinks upwards. Thus in the body of a youth who died from hæmorrhage after fever, and in that of a man who expelled two or three pints of blood from a cavity in the left lung, an inch of space intervened between the lower edge of the heart and that of the lower boundary of the *front* of the pericardium. In another instance that space was only the tenth of an inch. As a rule the space varied from a quarter to seven-tenths of an inch (in 38 of 44 instances) and its average measurement was nearly half an inch (0·46 inch). (Note 1, page 109.)

The heart and the great vessels mainly occupy the centre of the chest, being protected in front by the sternum and the adjoining costal cartilages. It is, however, my present object, not so much to describe the relative bearings of those parts after death, as to indicate the *variation* in the anatomical situation of the more important boundaries or landmarks of the healthy heart and great vessels observed by myself in different instances after death.

The lower Boundary of the Heart.—In one instance, a woman who died from starvation, the lower boundary of the heart was situated behind the ensiform cartilage an inch and a half below the lower end of the sternum (that term being restricted here and elsewhere to the manubrium and blade or osseous part of the sternum), while in another it was almost as much (1·4 inch) above that end of the bone. Between these two extreme points this boundary occupied every variety of position. In one-fifth of the instances observed (15 in 71) the lower boundary of the right ventricle was just behind the lower end of the sternum, while in two-fifths of them it was above (30 in 71), and in two-fifths of them it was below (26 in 71) that end of the bone. (Note 2, page 109.)

As we have already seen, the lower edge of the heart usually shrinks upwards after death for nearly half an inch, the extent varying from one inch to one-tenth of an inch. The position of the lower border of the *front* of the pericardium, which points out the position of the lower border of the heart at the time of death was indicated in four-fifths of the cases (55 in 71) in which the inferior boundary of the heart was observed after death. In one-fifth of these instances (11 in 55) the lower limit of the pericardium was on a level with the lower end of the sternum; while in two-thirds of them (37 in 55) it was below that point, being situated behind the ensiform cartilage; and in only one-eighth of them (7 in 55) was it above that point. We thus see that at the time of death, in the great majority of instances (40 in 59) the inferior border of the heart was below the lower end of the sternum, being situated behind the ensiform cartilage. (Note 3, page 110.)

The seat of the lower boundary of the apex in relation to the left fifth space is a more important landmark for the clinical observer than that of the lower boundary of the heart in relation to the lower end of the sternum.

The lower edge of the heart at the apex was on a level with the lower edge of the left fifth cartilage in one-seventh of the instances observed (9 in 69), it was below that edge in two-fifths of them (26 in 69), and it was above that edge in almost one half of them (34 in 69). In five instances the lower boundary of the apex was situated one inch above the lower edge of the fifth cartilage, and in four it was fully one inch below that edge. (Note 4, page 110.)

The lower border of the pericardium just below the apex, which corresponds with the seat of the lower border of the apex at the time of death, was on a level with the lower edge of the fifth cartilage in one-sixth of the instances observed (9 in 55), was situated below that edge in three-fourths of them (41 in 55), and was above that edge in only one eleventh of them (5 in 55). (Note 5, page 110.)

We thus see that there was a general, but not a constant correspondence between the relation of the inferior boundary of the right ventricle to the lower end of the sternum, and that of the inferior boundary of the apex to the lower edge of the fifth cartilage, both at the time of death, and after death when the examination of the body was made. This correspondence would have been more constant but for variation in (1) the comparative height of the fifth cartilage and the lower end of the sternum, (2) the degree of inclination from above downwards and from right to left of the lower boundary of the heart, and (3) the extent to which the right ventricle is situated to the right and to the left of the middle line of the sternum.

(1). In the great majority of instances (60 in 71) the inferior edge of the left fifth cartilage was lower in position than the inferior extremity of the sternum, to an extent varying from a quarter of an inch to an inch and a quarter; in five cases those two parts were on the same level; and in six the lower edge of the fifth cartilage was higher by from a quarter to three quarters of an inch than the lower end of the sternum.

The height of the fifth cartilage in relation to that of the lower end of the sternum is influenced by (1) respiration, (2) abdominal distension, and (3) natural and acquired formation. (1) Inspiration raises and expiration lowers both the sternum and the fifth cartilage attached to the sternum, but as the cartilage has an additional movement of its own, during the double act of breathing it is more lowered during expiration and more raised during inspiration than the sternum. The artificial distension of the lungs after death elevates the fifth cartilage from the sixth to the third of an inch more than the corresponding part of the sternum. If the chest is broad the left fifth cartilage is higher, and if the chest or the left side of it is narrow, the left fifth cartilage is lower in relation to the lower end of the sternum than it would have been otherwise. (2) Abdominal distension raises, and abdominal collapse lowers both the sternum and the fifth cartilage, but the raising or lowering of the fifth cartilage under these circumstances is greater than the respective raising or lowering of the sternum. (3) In some persons the fifth cartilage is naturally higher or lower than in others. Thus the fifth cartilage is sometimes integrally attached to the sixth cartilage and it is restrained by and shares its movements. When this is so the fifth cartilage tends to be lower in relation to the lower end of the sternum than when that cartilage is free. In robust persons with ample chests the fifth cartilage is higher relatively to the sternum than in thin persons with contracted chests, in whom the cartilage tends to be low in position in relation to the end of the sternum.

(2). In nearly all instances (67 in 70) the lower boundary of the heart inclined downwards from the auricle to the apex, in a direction from right to left. In one instance the lower boundary of the heart was an inch, and in another it was only the tenth of an inch lower at the apex than at the lower end of the sternum. Between these two extremes there was every variety, the average dip of the lower boundary of the heart from that point to the apex being about half an inch. (Note 6, page 110.)

The inclination or dip of the lower boundary of the right ventricle ceased at the apex, and thence the lower boundary of the heart curved gently upwards.

(3). The lower boundary of the heart usually extended from two inches to two inches and three quarters to the left of the middle line of the sternum, (in 43 instances in 65) but in one-third of the cases (20 in 65) it only extended from an inch and a quarter to an inch and three quarters, while in five instances it extended as much as three inches to the left of the middle line of the sternum. (Note 7, page 111.)

The Top of the Arch of the Aorta.—The top of the arch of the aorta, which is indicated by the adjacent origin of the innominate and left subclavian arteries, forms the upper limit of the system of the heart and great vessels. The position of the top of the arch, like that of the lower border of the heart, is subject to great variety.

In one instance the top of the arch was an inch and a half below the top of the manubrium, so that it was buried deep down in the chest and the innominate artery did not appear in the neck. In another, the top of the arch was seated in the neck, being half an inch above the top of the sternum, so that before the chest was opened the whole innominate artery was visible in the neck, coursing upwards and from left to right across the front of the trachea. The summit of the aorta occupied in different instances every variety of position between these two extreme limits. In five cases it was above, and in six it was on a level with the top of the manubrium; while in seven, instead of being thus almost or quite visible in the neck, it was situated quite an inch below the top of the manubrium and the whole of the innominate artery was shielded by that bone. In two-thirds of the instances, (30 in 48) however, the top of the aorta occupied an intermediate place behind the upper half of the manubrium, its average position being half an inch below the top of that bone. (Note 8, page 111.)

In forty-eight instances the position both of the lower boundary of the heart and the upper boundary of the arch of the aorta was observed, and, as might have been looked for, there was a general correspondence in the position of these two boundaries in those cases in which they occupied respectively a very high or a very low position. Thus, of the five cases in which the top of the arch of the aorta rose above the top of the sternum, the lower boundary of the heart was situated above the lower end of the sternum in three, at that point in one, and less than half an inch below it in one. Again, the top of the arch of the aorta was situated below the upper end of the manubrium in the whole of six cases in which the lower boundary of the heart was from half an inch to an inch and a quarter below the lower end of the sternum. Again, of seven instances in which the top of the arch was deep in the chest, being more than an inch below the top of the manubrium, in three the lower boundary of the heart was below the lower end of the sternum, in one at that point, and in three above it. Here the correspondence of the upper and lower boundaries is rather indicated than kept up, but this correspondence can scarcely be recognized when we compare these boundaries with each other in those cases in which they occupied a less extreme position. (Note 9, page 111.)

The Boundary-line between the Upper Border of the Heart and the Lower Limit of the Great Arteries.—The origin of the pulmonary artery and the top of the auricular portion of the right auricle may be regarded as the upper boundary of the heart and the lower boundary of the great arteries. The highest position of the origin of the pulmonary artery was at the top of the second cartilage, while that of the top of the auricle was a little higher or on a level with the first space. The lowest position of the origin of the pulmonary artery was the upper edge of the fourth cartilage, while that of the top of the auricle was a little less low, or on a level with the lower border of the third space. Between these two extreme limits the origin of the pulmonary artery and the top of the right auricle occupied every variety of position, but their favourite seat was at or on a level with the second space and the third costal cartilage, which was the situation of those parts in two-thirds of the instances (36 in 49 for the pulmonary artery; 43 in 63 for the top of the auricle).

In the majority of instances there was but little difference between the height of the origin of the pulmonary artery and the top of the right auricle, the height of the two being identical in one-fourth of

the instances (10 in 44), and the difference in their height
respectively less than the third of an inch or the third of the l
of a space or cartilage in one-half of them (21 and 20 in 44).
remaining instances, in twelve the difference of the height of tho
parts varied from one-third to two-thirds of an inch or two
of a space or cartilage, and in one the difference of their
amounted almost to an inch. As a rule, the origin of the puln
artery tended to be higher in position than the top of the
auricle, the former part being the higher of the two in t
instances, and the latter part being the higher of the two in fo
instances. (Note 10, page 111.)

The varying position, higher or lower, of (1) the pulmonary ;
(2) the aorta, (3) the right ventricle, and (4) the right auri
relation to the costal cartilages and the spaces between them, a
the sternum will next be considered.

The Pulmonary Artery.—A knowledge of the position of th
monary artery is important to the clinical worker, because it i
the surface of the chest, and because the signs afforded by it
the condition of the cavities and valves of the heart, and the e
difficulty with which the blood finds its way from and to those
ties, the lungs, and the body. Among those signs are, the cha
of the first sound, whether loud and sharp, or feeble and almost ;
or presenting a pulmonic murmur; the character of the second s
whether feeble or intense, blunt or sharp, or presenting a d
sound, giving in quick succession the aortic and the pulmonic s
sounds or the reverse, the later sound being the louder of the t

The trunk of the pulmonary artery varied in length from t
quarters of an inch to two inches and a half. In more than a
of the instances (17 in 46) the artery was from an inch to an
and a half in length, while in less than a third of them it was l
(15 in 46), and in less than a third of them (14 in 46) it was ;
that length.

The vertical measurement of the right ventricle, from the orig
the pulmonary artery to the lower boundary of the heart, vari
these instances from two inches and a half to a little over
inches. The length of the ventricle thus measured was from ;
inches to three inches and a half in less than one-half of the
(20 in 46).

The proportion between the length of the pulmonary artery
the length of the right ventricle, measured from above downw
presented great variety. In one instance the length of the a
was nearly equal to the length of the ventricle, that of the former b
two inches and a half, that of the latter scarcely three inches; w
in two others the vertical measurement of the ventricle was five tim
great as that of the artery, the length of the latter in one instance b
three-quarters of an inch, and that of the former being fully four inc
The average length of the ventricle in relation to that of the ar

was as three to one. As a rule, the length of the pulmonary artery regulated the proportion in length which that vessel bore to the ventricle; thus in the whole of the fifteen instances in which the length of the pulmonary artery was less than an inch, the length of the right ventricle was more than three times that of the artery; while in the whole of the fourteen in which the artery was an inch and a half in length and upwards, the length of the right ventricle was less than three times that of the vessel. (Note 11, page 112.)

As we have already seen, the origin of the pulmonary artery varied in position from the second to the fourth cartilage, its usual situation being the second space and the third cartilage. The top of the pulmonary artery was in one instance almost as high as the clavicle, and in almost one half of the cases (25 in 63) it was situated behind the manubrium or the first rib; while in one case it was so low as to be almost on a level with the upper edge of the third cartilage. In more than one half of the cases (33 in 63) it was seated behind the first space or the second cartilage. (Note 12, page 112.)

The situation of the pulmonary artery during its course is regulated by the length of the vessel and by the position of its starting-place and upper end. In one instance it was so high as to be entirely concealed by the manubrium, while in another it was so low as to be entirely covered by the third cartilage and third space. The artery was rarely limited in position to one space or one cartilage: thus in but one instance it only occupied the first space, and in but one it was quite covered by the second cartilage. The artery usually lay behind one space and one costal cartilage (35 times in 60), but in one-third of the instances (21 in 60) it extended to an additional space or cartilage. In two-thirds of the instances it was present behind the second cartilage (43 in 60); in more than half of them it lay behind the first space (35 in 60), and in nearly as many behind the second space (32 in 60); while in one-fourth it was covered by the third cartilage (15 in 60), and in one-sixth by the manubrium (9 in 60). (Note 12, page 112.)

When the pulmonary artery was long (it was so in 14 of 46 instances), its origin occupied, as a rule, a low position. Thus in sixteen instances the origin of the artery was entirely above the second space, and in only two of these was it long, while in seven it was short. On the other hand, in thirty instances the pulmonary artery at the first part of its course was at or below the second space, and in twelve of them the artery was long, while in eight it was short. (Note 12, page 112.)

The Arch of the Aorta.—The arch of the aorta is not, like the pulmonary artery, visible in its whole course from its root to its summit, being hidden at its root by the right auricle and ventricle. I shall, therefore, not speak here of the whole of the ascending aorta, but of that portion of it which comes into view above the right auricular appendix and between it and the beginning of the pulmonary artery and the arterial cone of the right ventricle.

The arch of the aorta, from the part in its course just spoken of where it first becomes visible, to its highest point at the origin of the innominate and left carotid arteries, varied much in length. In two female subjects, one aged nine the other a few years older, the arch was an inch and a half in length, but in the adult subject its length ranged from an inch and three quarters to three inches. The arch, measured from the lower to the higher points just named, was from just over two inches to two inches and a half in length in two fifths of the instances (19 in 47), that being about the average or standard length; from an inch and three quarters to two inches in more than one fifth (11 in 47), and from two inches and a half to three inches in less than two fifths of them (17 in 47). (Note 13, page 112.)

Viewed in proportionate relation to the length of the body, measured approximately from the chin to the pubes, the vertical measurement of the arch varied from one seventh to one fourteenth of the vertical measurement of the body thus taken, and in one half of the instances (23 in 45) the length of the aorta was one tenth of that of the body.

In three instances the vertical measurement of the arch of the aorta was the same as the vertical measurement of the right ventricle taken from the part at which the aorta was visible to the lower boundary of the organ. In two instances the arch was longer than the ventricle in the proportion of ten to nine, but in the remainder the length of the ventricle was greater than that of the aorta, the relative proportion varying from 10 to 10·1 to 10 to 19·17, so that in the last example the ventricle was nearly twice as long as the arch. The average length of the arch in proportion to that of the right ventricle was about 10 to 14 (14 in 47).

The variation in the proportionate length of the arch of the aorta and the right ventricle, although thus considerable, is not nearly so great as the variation in the proportionate length of the pulmonary artery and the right ventricle; since that artery varied in length from more than one half to less than one fifth of the vertical measurement of the ventricle, while the arch was about the same length as the vertical measurement of the ventricle at one end of the scale, and was of half that length at the other end.

There was some correspondence between the length of the aorta and that of the pulmonary artery. Thus the pulmonary artery was short, long, or of medium length in two fifths of the instances in which the aorta was respectively short, long, or of medium length (13 in 33). In the remaining instances (20 in 33) this strict proportion was not maintained, but in only two of them was the difference in the proportionate length of the vessels great, the aorta being long while the pulmonary artery was short.

The position of the lower boundary of the heart in relation to the lower end of the sternum, whether above, at or below that point is, as a rule, governed to a considerable extent by the length of the arch of the aorta. Thus in nine instances in which the arch was short, measuring two inches or less, the lower boundary of the heart was above the lower end of the sternum in seven instances and below that point in two. The other circumstances that regulate the position of the lower boundary of the heart in relation to the lower end of the sternum are (1) youth; (2) the distension or collapse of the right ventricle; (3) the length of the sternum; (4) the important influence of the higher or lower position of the sternum, higher when the chest is ample, being of an inspiratory type, and lower when the chest is narrow and flat, being of an expiratory type; (5) the higher or lower position of the top of the arch of the aorta which is often ruled by (4) the lower or higher position of the sternum; (6) the extent to which the heart shrinks upwards after death which is evinced by the space intervening between the lower boundary of the heart and the lower boundary of the *front* of the pericardium; and (7) the elevation or depression of the diaphragm, which is the most important influence in producing respectively the elevation or depression of the heart, and which may be caused by (*a*) the contraction or expansion of the lungs, or (*b*) the distension or collapse of the abdomen. These points are illustrated by the two exceptional cases just cited, in which, although the arch of the aorta was short, the lower boundary of the heart was below the level of the lower end of the sternum. Both of these cases were quite young (1); in both the vertical measurement of the right ventricle was long, while in one of them that cavity was distended and large (2); in both of them the sternum was short, its length being less than four inches in one, while in the other it was four inches and a half (3); again in one of them the sternum was high, the length of the neck being only two inches, that of the sternum four inches and a half, and that of the abdomen fourteen inches, while in the other instance in which the right ventricle was large, the sternum was low in position, the length of the neck being almost four inches, that of the sternum less than four inches, and that of the abdomen only ten inches and a half (4). In neither of these examples was the position of the lower boundary of the heart lowered owing to the low position of the top of the arch, for in one of them that point was above the top of the sternum and in the other is was a little way below it (5). In fact this influence, which tended to elevate the lower boundary of the heart in relation to the lower end of the sternum was more than counter-balanced by the combined influences of which I have just spoken, all working in the opposite direction so as to lower the inferior border of the heart.

In further illustration of this point, the influence, namely, of the shortness or length of the arch in respectively raising or lowering the lower boundary of the heart, we find that of seventeen cases in which the aorta was long, measuring two and a half inches and upwards, in ten the lower boundary of the heart was below the level of the lower end of the sternum, in four it was at that point, while in only three was it above the lower end of the sternum. The three exceptional cases in which the lower boundary of the heart was above the level of the lower end of the sternum were adults of full size (1) ; the right ventricle was narrow and contracted in two of them (2) ; and in two the heart deviated to the left so that the lower border of the right ventricle was situated to the left of the lower end of the sternum, instead of being to the right, as is usual. The sternum was long in two of them, measuring in one case over seven inches (3) ; in all of them the sternum was low in position, the length of the neck being five inches and a half, four inches, and three inches and a half respectively, while that of the abdomen was in each instance less than fourteen inches (4) ; in one of them the top of the arch was situated above the top of the sternum (5) ; in one of them the space between the lower limit of the heart and the lower limit of the front of the pericardium was nearly an inch, while in another it was fully half an inch in width, showing that the upward shrinking of the heart after death had been considerable (6) ; and finally one of them, that in which the space between the heart and the lower rim of the pericardium was small, the stomach was globose and much distended so as to push the heart upwards (7b).

In twenty-three cases the arch of the aorta was of intermediate length, or from a little over two inches to two inches and a half, and in these the lower boundary of the heart was in equal relative proportion above, at, and below the level of the lower end of the sternum.

It is evident and is illustrated by what has just been said that if we group the cases as I have just done, according to the actual length of the arch of the aorta without relation to age or the dimensions of the body, we shall include some instances in which the arch of the aorta is relatively short or long with those in which it is respectively actually long or short. I have therefore grouped the whole cases anew, and according to the proportional length of the aorta in relation to the length of the body. It will suffice here if I say that the results thus obtained are exactly confirmatory of those that I have just related, and show that the higher or lower position of the lower boundary of the heart in relation to the lower end of the sternum is to a considerable extent governed by the proportional shortness or length of the arch of the aorta. They show those results indeed more strikingly, for the conflicting element of (1) youth has been removed.

Two exceptional instances have been brought into the group in which the arch of the aorta was long in proportion to the length of the body, that were not included in the parallel group in which the arch was actually long. In these two examples the lower boundary of the heart was above the level of the lower end of the sternum, although the aorta was proportionally long. The heart was lifted directly upwards to a great extent in both of these instances, in one of them by very great enlargement of the liver, upwards, as well as downwards, owing to the presence of malignant disease in the organ, the sternum being in this case very long (6·8 inches); and in the other by excessive distension of the stomach and intestines owing to peritonitis, the sternum in this instance being short (4·7 inches) and the top of the aorta being situated in the root of the neck, a third of an inch above the level of the top of the sternum (7b).

The Right Auricle.—The right auricle is, as a rule, hidden from observation by the couch of lung that is interposed between it and the sternum and cartilages. It comes, however, to the surface in cases of pericarditis when the effusion into the sac accumulates in sufficient quantity to press aside that portion of lung with which the auricle is covered. With the exception of the important point just considered, the right auricle cannot be recognized locally by the clinical observer, the condition of that cavity being in fact best told by the state of the veins in the neck. The right auricle, measured from the top of its auricular portion to its lowest point, varied in length from one inch to four inches and a half. Its length was usually from two and a half to three and a half inches (in 41 of 62 instances). In one-fifth of the cases (12 in 62) its length was less than two and a half inches ; but one-half of these were youthful subjects (7 in 12). The vertical measurement of the right ventricle was longer than that of the right auricle in more than two-thirds of the cases in which the comparison was made (35 in 49) ; in one-fifth of them the two cavities were nearly or quite of equal length (10 in 49) ; and in one-twelfth of them the auricle was longer than the ventricle. (Note 14, page 112.)

The auricular portion of the auricle, which during life laps, like a tongue, to and fro, from right to left and back again, was usually nearly on the same level as the top of the right ventricle, the top of the auricle being of the same height as that of the ventricle in ten instances, higher than that of the ventricle in fourteen instances, and lower in twenty. It was at the lower boundary that the right auricle failed. In one case, in which there was fatal hæmorrhage, the auricle, which was quite insignificant in size, was only half as long as the ventricle. Usually, however, the auricle was shorter than the ventricle by from one-tenth to one-third of its vertical measurement (in 29 of 35 instances).

The right auricle, from the variable extent to which, on the one hand it receives blood, and on the other retains or parts with it before, during, and after death, and from its passive nature, is more variable in form and size than any other cavity of the heart. This point will be briefly illustrated when the lateral dimensions of the cavities are considered.

The Right Ventricle.—The vertical measurement of the right ventricle in relation to the pulmonary artery and the aorta has already been considered.

The right ventricle, measured from the origin of the pulmonary artery to the lower boundary of the cavity, varied in length from two inches and three quarters to four inches. In one-fifth of the instances (9 in 46) the length of the ventricle thus measured was less than two inches, the majority of these being youthful subjects (5 in 9) ; in nearly one-half of them (20 in 46) this measurement was from three inches to nearly three inches and a half ; and in the remainder it was three inches and a half and upwards, being fully four inches in six of them. The variable dimensions and form of the ventricle will be briefly noticed when its lateral measurements are considered. (Note 15, page 112.)

The extent of the vertical measurement or length of the right ventricle produces a marked influence on the position of the lower boundary of the heart in relation to the lower end of the sternum. Thus, of the nine cases in which the ventricle was short, its lower boundary was above the level of the end of the sternum in five instances, and below that level in only one; while of the sixteen instances in which the ventricle was long, in ten of them its inferior border was below the end of the sternum, while in only six of them was it above that point. It is, indeed, self-evident that the lower border of the ventricle must be lower in position when the cavity increases, and higher when it lessens in size.

The extent to which the upper part of the bony sternum covers the great arteries, and the lower part of it, the heart, is very variable. In one instance the great arteries occupied only the upper fourth of the sternum, while the heart occupied its lower three-fourths. In another instance this proportion was to a considerable extent reversed, for the vessels lay behind the upper five-eighths of the bone, the heart itself being limited to its lower three-eighths. In three-fourths of the instances (39 in 52) the greater share of the sternum lay in front of the heart, but in one-fourth the greater share of the bone was given to the great vessels. On an average, the position of the heart was behind the lower four-sevenths, and that of the great arteries was behind the upper three-sevenths of the sternum. (Note 16, page 112.)

(II.) The Position of the Heart and Great Vessels from Side to Side.

Relation of the Breadth of the Heart to the Breadth of the Chest.— The proportionate transverse diameter of the heart, compared with the transverse diameter of the chest, varied considerably. Thus in one instance, in which death was the result of hæmorrhage, the width of the heart was less than one-third of the width of the chest, on a level with the lower end of the ensiform cartilage (3·2 to 10 inches); while in another instance the measurement across the heart was nearly two-thirds of that across the chest (5·1 inches to 8·2 inches).

In a large number of the cases observed (39 in 65) the breadth of the heart was somewhat less than one-half of the breadth of the chest; the proportion varying from 10 to 4 to 10 to 5. In one-sixth of the instances (11 in 65) the width of the heart was less than two-fifths (10 to 3 to 10 to 3·9), and in one-third of them (15 in 65) it was more than one-half (10 to 5 to 10 to 6·2) of the width of the chest. The size of the chest from side to side did not appear to exercise any material influence on the proportional breadth of the heart, but the heart was more frequently of the average proportional width in those instances in which the chest was of medium breadth (9 to 9·9 inches) than in those in which it was either wide (10 to 12 inches) or narrow (6 to 8·9 inches). Thus, the heart was of the average proportional breadth in five-sixths of the instances in which the chest was of the medium breadth (10 in 12); in one-half of those in which the chest was wide (12 in 22); and in two-thirds of those in which the chest was narrow (19 in 31). The heart was comparatively wide and comparatively narrow in equal numbers in those instances in which the chest was wide (6 of each kind in 22); while the organ was more frequently comparatively wide than narrow, in those in which the chest was narrow (wide in 8, narrow in 4, of 31). Great distension and great collapse of the abdomen produced a marked effect on the proportionate width of the heart in relation to that of the chest. Thus, in fully two-thirds of the instances in which the heart was proportionally narrow, the abdomen was distended (8 in 11), and in one-half of these the distension was very great (4 in 11); while in one of the three remaining cases the abdomen was large, in one it was of moderate size, and in only one was it small. Then the reverse took place in those cases in which the heart was proportionally wide, since in only one-fifth of them was the abdomen distended (3 in 15), and in but one of these was the distension very great. Distension of the abdomen seemed to produce this effect by acting in two directions, one upon the chest, by widening it, the other upon the heart itself, by lessening it. The chest is widened because the distended abdomen pushes the ribs outwards on either side, and elevates the lower border of the chest in front and at each side; and the heart is lessened because the distended abdomen compresses the heart upwards into the contracting space of the higher part of the cone of the chest, and so lessens the amount of blood in the organ. (Note 17, page 113.)

The proportional size of the anterior transverse diameter of the combined right auricle and ventricle, compared with that of the left ventricle, exercises a marked effect on the proportional breadth of the heart in relation to the breadth of the chest. This might indeed be anticipated, for when the proportional width of the combined right auricle and ventricle is great in relation to the width of the left ventricle, the right cavities are distended with blood, and the whole heart is consequently large, measured from side to side. In more than one-half of the cases (7 in 12) in which the proportional breadth of the heart to that of the chest was great, the proportional breadth of the combined right auricle and ventricle to the left ventricle in front was very great, the former being about ten times wider than the latter; and in none of them was the proportional breadth of the right cavities small. Again, in almost one-half of the instances (5 in 11) in which the proportional width of the heart in relation to that of the chest was small, the proportional width of the right auricle and ventricle in relation to that of the left ventricle was also small, the ratio being about 10 to 4. (Note 18, page 113.)

Extent to which the Heart occupied the Right and the Left Sides of the Chest.—The extent to which the heart occupied respectively the right and the left sides of the chest varied much in different instances. Thus in one example, the heart extended one inch and a tenth to the right and four inches to the left of a vertical line drawn down the middle of the sternum; and in another the organ extended nearly two inches and a half to the right, and only two inches and a quarter to the left of that line; while in two other instances the heart occupied the right and the left sides of the chest in exactly equal proportions. Thus, taking the two extreme cases, in one of them one-fifth of the heart occupied the right side, and four-fifths of it the left side of the chest; while in the other fully one-half of the heart was lodged in the right side, and less than one-half of it in the left side of the chest.

There was every gradation of difference between these two extreme examples. In fully two-fifths of the instances (27 in 67) one-third of the heart or less was situated in the right side, and two-thirds of the heart or more, in the left side of the chest; while in fully two-fifths of them (28 in 67), three-fifths of the heart or less was seated in the left side, and two-fifths of it or more in the right side (literally 16 to 10).

In twelve intermediate and standard instances, the heart was distributed to the right and to the left of the middle line of the sternum in the proportion respectively of ten and eighteen, and this was the average position of the organ in sixty-seven bodies, so that nearly two-thirds of the organ lay in the left side, and more than one-third of it in the right side of the chest. (Note 19, page 113.)

The influences that cause the deviation of the heart towards the right or the left side of the chest, are (1) before all others, the difference in size of the right lung and the left; (2) the encroachment upwards of the liver or the stomach to an unusual extent on the right or the left side of the chest respectively; (3) the position of the patient before death on the right side or on the left, an occurrence that may take place in certain rare cases, such, for instance, as bed-sores and affections of one side of the chest; (4) the shrinking of the heart upwards after death, as evinced by the extent of the space intervening between the lower boundary of the heart and the lower boundary of the *front* of the pericardium; (5) the shortening of the aorta; (6) the relative size of the heart and of its cavities, measured from side to side. There are doubtless other influences at work to produce the effect in question, but I have not discovered them.

(1.) Of the small number of instances (6 in 66) in which the heart swerved very far to the left, so as to occupy that side of the chest to a greater extent by from three to four times than the right side of the chest, the two lungs were equal in size in one-third (2 in 6), while the right lung was greater than the left in the remaining two-thirds. On the other hand, of the cases in which the heart was lodged equally in the right and the left sides of the chest (3 in 66), and those in which it bore only a little more to the left than the right side of the chest (12 in 66), the two lungs were of equal size in one-fourth, and the left lung was larger than the right in the remaining three-fourths. Thus in none of the instances in which the heart deviated greatly to the left was the left lung larger than the right; and in none of those in which the heart tended towards the right side of the chest was the right lung greater than the left. In the whole of the remaining instances, with a few exceptions, an analogous condition obtained, the right lung being the larger when the heart was lodged to an unusual extent in the left side of the chest, and the left lung being the larger when the heart was lodged to an unusual extent in the right side of the chest. (Note 20, page 113.)

(2.) The position of the upper surface of the liver, covered by the diaphragm, was higher in the right side of the chest than that of the stomach in the left side of the chest in all but a fraction of the instances observed (57 in 61). On an average, the liver at this situation was higher than the stomach by more than half an inch (·6 inch). In two-fifths of the cases (25 in 61) the heart occupied the left side of the chest to an unusual extent; of these, in nearly two-thirds the height of the liver in relation to that of the stomach was above the average (14 in 25); in nearly one-third it was below the average (7 in 25); and in a fraction it was at the average (3 in 25). In all but one of the five instances in which the heart was very far to the left, the relative height of the liver was above the average. In one-fourth of the cases (14 in 61) the heart occupied the right side of the chest to an unusual extent, and in nearly three-fifths of these (8 in 14) the height of the liver was below the average, while in fully two-fifths of them (6 in 14) it was above the average. When the top of the liver encroached to an unusual proportional extent on the right side of the chest, it may be said that the unduly-elevated organ tended to displace the heart to the left. There were, however, a few remarkable exceptions to this rule. Thus, in one instance the heart occupied equally the right and the left sides of the chest, and yet the top of the liver rose higher by nearly an inch and a half into the right side of the chest than the stomach did into the left side of the chest. The reason of this was obvious. There was contraction of the right lung in this case, owing to phthisis, with the effect of drawing both the heart and the liver unduly into the space previously occupied by the right lung.

(3.) I have no after-death evidence to show that the position of the patient on the right side or the left during the period preceding death caused the heart to occupy unduly the right or the left side of the chest. We know, however, that during life the heart falls towards the side on which the person lies. At the same time that side of the chest expands less during inspiration than the opposite side, owing to the restraint offered to the movement of the ribs that bear the weight of the chest, while, to compensate for the deficient expansion of the restrained side, the free side of the chest expands to an increased extent. After death, the organs, as a rule, retain pretty nearly the place they occupied during life, and the effect of position during life in displacing the heart more towards the right side or the left, is retained after death.

(4.) When the heart shrinks upwards, so as to leave a considerable space between the lower boundary of the organ and the lower boundary of the *front* of the pericardium, the heart, as a rule, bears more towards the right than the left side of the chest. Thus the space below the heart was large in two-thirds of the cases in which that organ bore unusually to the right (8 in 12); and in only two-fifths of those in which it bore unusually to the left (8 in 19).

(5.) I am of opinion that in those cases in which the heart shrinks thus upwards, and bears unusually to the right, the contraction and shortening of the aorta is one of the principal agents that draws the apex and the body of the heart to the right as well as upwards.

(6.) The relative size of the heart and of its cavities, measured from side to side, exercised much less influence than the relative size of the right and left lung, and the relative height of the liver and stomach, on the extent to which the heart occupied after death the right and left sides of the chest respectively.

When the heart is large, the lungs necessarily make way for it, to the right and left equally if the development of the lungs is equal; but when one lung is expanded and the other is contracted, the heart when large encroaches more upon the contracted than the expanded lung, for that lung offers the least resistance. The stronger influence of the greater size of one lung overrides then the weaker influence of the size of the heart. But it is evident that the size of the heart must produce an influence supplementing and modifying the influence of the greater size of one lung. When the heart is large it enhances the influence of the greater size of one lung, and the heart encroaches more on the side containing the contracted lung; and when the heart is small it lessens the influence of the greater size of one lung, and the heart encroaches less on the side containing the contracted lung. Thus in the large group of cases in which the heart occupied the left side of the chest to an unusual extent (1 to 3·9 to 1 to 2, in 23 in 60), and in the equally large group in which the heart was distributed in the average proportion to the right and left sides of the chest (1 to 1·5 to 1 to 1·9 in 23 in 60), the heart was large in fully one-fourth of the respective instances (6 in 23 and 7 in 23), while in no instance was the heart large in the group in which that organ occupied the right side of the chest.

The heart was small in two of the three instances in which the organ occupied the right and the left sides of the chest to an equal extent. The heart is attached at the centre of the chest, behind, to the roots of the lungs by the pulmonary veins and pulmonary arteries; and above and in front, to the great arteries and the descending vena cava from which it is suspended. The heart, therefore, when it does not bear to the left or to the right owing to the greater or less size of the right or left lung, hangs directly downwards from the points of its suspension at the centre of the chest, and tends to occupy a central position, bearing equally to the right and to the left.

Breadth of the Combined Right Auricle and Ventricle in Relation to that of the Left Ventricle as seen in Front.—The breadth of the combined right auricle and ventricle in relation to the breadth of the left ventricle as seen in front, varied from 10 to 1 to 10 to 4½. Thus the right cavities occupied almost the whole front of the heart in some examples, and little more than two-thirds of it in others. Every shade of variation existed between these two extreme instances; but the average or standard proportion between the breadth of the right cavities and that of the left ventricle in front was as 4 to 1. (Note 21, page 114.)

Breadth of the Right Auricle.—The auricular portion of the right auricle varied in breadth from a little over half an inch (·55 inch) to two inches and a third (2·3 inch), its average breadth being one inch and a third (1·3 inch). (Note 22, page 114.)

The body of the right auricle[1] varied in breadth from a quarter of an inch to an inch and a half, its average breadth being four-fifths of an inch (8·1 inch). (Note 23, page 114.)

The left edge of the auricular portion of the right auricle extended to the left of the left edge of the sternum in four instances; it was placed nearer to the left than the right edge of the sternum in twenty-four cases; it was situated about midway between the left and the right edge of the sternum in eight instances; and it was nearer to the right than the left edge of that bone in fourteen. (Note 24, page 114.)

The right edge of the right auricle extended to the right of the right edge of the sternum to an extent varying from a quarter of an inch to an inch and three-quarters, so that to that extent the auricle lay behind the right costal cartilages. The right auricle extended on an average from half an inch to a little over an inch to the right of the sternum. (Note 25, page 114.)

The auricular portion of the right auricle was wider than the body of the auricle in all but two instances, in which instances their breadth was the same. As a rule, the auricular portion was wider than the body of the auricle in the proportion of ten to six and a half (10 to 6·4), but in two instances that portion was nearly three times as wide as the body of the auricle. (Note 26, page 114.)

The proportional breadth of the auricular portion of the right auricle varied from two-fifths to one-fifth of the breadth of the heart itself. The width of the heart was, on an average, nearly four times as great as that of the auricular portion of the right auricle. (Note 27, page 114.)

---

[1] The right auricle is about half an inch wider, and the right ventricle is about half an inch narrower than the measurements given in this article. Those measurements have been necessarily taken from the right auriculo-ventricular furrow, which is the apparent boundary-line between the right auricle and ventricle, but is situated half an inch to the right of the real boundary-line between those cavities.

The proportional breadth of the body of the right auricle varied from about a fourth (10 to 36) to a ninth (10 to 86) of the breadth of the heart. In one exceptional case in which death took place from hæmorrhage, the heart was twelve times as wide as the right auricle, that cavity being quite empty. The width of the heart was, on an average, nearly six times as great as the width of the right auricle. (Note 28, page 114.)

Breadth of the Right Ventricle.—The breadth of the right ventricle [1] varied from four-fifths (in 6 of 38 instances) to a little over one-half (in 11 of 38 instances) of the whole breadth of the heart. The average or standard breadth of the right ventricle was two-thirds of the breadth of the heart (10 to 15), and in one-half of the cases observed the proportional width of the right ventricle in relation to that of the heart was above (19 in 38), and in one-half of them it was below that average (19 in 38). (Note 29, page 114.)

The breadth of the arterial cone of the right ventricle a little way below the origin of the pulmonary artery varied from four-fifths to two-fifths of the breadth of the right ventricle at its middle, the average width of the arterial cone being nearly three-fifths of that of the body of the right ventricle. As a rule, when the body of the right ventricle was wide or narrow in relation to the heart, the arterial cone was respectively narrow or wide in relation to the body of the right ventricle. (Note 30, page 114.)

The vertical diameter or length of the right ventricle,[2] measured from the origin of the pulmonary artery to the lower boundary of that cavity, was somewhat shorter than the transverse diameter or breadth of the ventricle in one-sixth of the cases (5 in 30). In the rest of them the length of the right ventricle was greater than its breadth. In one instance the length of the ventricle was to its breadth as 17·3 to 10, but the average or standard measurement of the length to the breadth of that cavity was as 4 to 3. (Note 31, page 114.)

The breadth of the right ventricle in relation to that of the right auricle [1] below its auricular portion varied from 10 to 1·4 to 10 to 5·2, the average proportion being 10 to 3. (Note 32, page 114.)

The actual breadth of the right ventricle [2] in adults, without distinction of sex, varied from two to four inches. In three-fifths of them the width of the ventricle was from three to three and a half inches (in 14 in 24); in one-fifth of them it was above three and a half inches; and in two-fifths of them it was less than three inches. (Note 33, page 115.)

[1] The right ventricle is about half an inch narrower, and the right auricle is about half an inch wider than the measurements of those cavities given in this article, for the reason stated in the foot-note at page 31.

[2] As the breadth of the body of the right ventricle is about half an inch narrower than the measurements of that cavity given in this article, for the reason stated in the foot-note at page 31, the actual relation of the transverse diameter or width of the body of the right ventricle here stated to that of the *conus arteriosus*, and to the vertical diameter or length of the ventricle, is half an inch narrower than the proportional measurements here given.

In one instance the right ventricle extended further to the right than to the left of a vertical line drawn down the middle of the sternum, but in every other instance the ventricle extended more to the left than to the right of that line. In one case, nine-tenths of the right ventricle was situated in the left side of the chest, and only one-tenth of it in the right side; but, on an average, the ventricle extended nearly three times farther to the left than the right of the middle line (27 to 10). (Note 34, page 115.)

The limits of the body of the right ventricle and of its arterial cone are indicated, (1) to the left by the position of the longitudinal furrow between the ventricles; and (2) to the right by the position of the transverse furrow between the right ventricle, including the right edge of the origin of the pulmonary artery and the right auricle, including its auricular portion.

(1). As a rule, the inter-ventricular furrow takes an oblique direction outwards, or to the left from above downwards, so that the ventricle occupies a wider space below than above (in 26 of 39 instances). In a small number of cases (6 in 39) the reverse takes place, and the furrow tends inwards, and then outwards with a peculiar double curve as it descends. In these instances the right ventricle was in a state of contraction, and the left ventricle was exposed to a large extent, while in those in which the septum inclined markedly outwards during its descent, the right ventricle was distended so as to cover all but a small portion of the left ventricle. The greatest inclination of the longitudinal furrow to the left was one inch, and its greatest inclination to the right was half an inch (·45 inch). (Note 35, page 115.)

In one instance, a case in which the right ventricle was contracted, the longitudinal furrow in its descent curved to the right, and the body of the right ventricle towards its left border was completely shielded by the sternum; but in every other instance that cavity was covered in front to a greater or less extent by the cardiac costal cartilages, to the left of the lower half of the sternum. In a small proportion of the cases (6 in 36) the right ventricle lay behind the costal cartilages from end to end, from the sternum, namely, to the ribs to which they are united; and in half of these (3 in 6) the ventricle extended to the left, beyond the cartilages and behind the ribs. In the majority of the cases (19 in 36) the longitudinal furrow extended either up to the ends of the cartilages, a little beyond them, or half an inch or less to the right of them, so that in all these cases the cardiac cartilages covered the right ventricle almost or quite from end to end. In the remaining instances (17 in 36) a considerable portion of the cartilages, varying from less than an inch to more than an inch and a half (·7 to 1·7 inch) extended beyond the right ventricle. (Note 36, page 115.)

The body of the right ventricle, starting from a vertical line drawn down the middle of the sternum, extended to the left in all the cases, from a little over half an inch (·6 inch) to almost four inches (3·8 inch).

Between these two extreme instances there was every shade of differ-ence. In the great majority of the cases (35 in 52) the right ventricle extended from one inch and a half to two inches and a half to the left of the middle line of the sternum, and behind the cardiac carti-lages. (Note 37, page 115.)

(2).[1] The transverse or right auriculo-ventricular furrow was situ-ated to the right of the right edge of the lower portion of the sternum, and behind the right costal cartilages, in fully two-thirds of the cases (36 in 51), at that edge in a fraction of them (3 in 51), and to the left of that edge, and therefore behind the lower portion of the sternum, in one-fourth of them (12 in 51). In one instance the right auriculo-ventricular furrow extended an inch and a third (1·3 inch) to the right of the right edge of the sternum, so as to lie behind the right costal cartilages to that extent, and in five instances its right limit was situated behind the middle line of the sternum. Between these two extreme limits there was every gradation in the position of the right auriculo-ventricular furrow.

The left edge of the auricular portion of the right auricle gives, as a rule, very nearly the position of the right edge of the arterial cone of the right ventricle, where it is about to end in the pulmonary artery. The right edge of the arterial cone, starting from the triscupid orifice, invariably inclines, as it ascends, from right to left. There was con-siderable difference in the degree of its inclination, which was measured by the distance between the right limit of the auriculo-ventricular furrow and a line drawn downwards from the right edge of the pul-monary artery. The right edge of the arterial cone swerved as it ascended from right to left in one instance, a man, to the extent of two inches, and in another, also a man, to that of a little over half an inch (·6 inch). There was every variety of inclination between these extreme instances, but in the great majority of cases (34 in 51) the curved line of the right border of the arterial cone bent downwards, with an inclination from left to right of from an inch to an inch and a half, the boundary line starting above from the right border of the origin of the pulmonary artery, and ending below in the auriculo-ventricular furrow. (Note 38, page 115.)

Breadth and Position of the Pulmonary Artery.—As the origin of the pulmonary artery is the point of convergence towards which the right ventricle propels its blood, this is the natural place for examining the position of that artery. The pulmonary artery forms, indeed, the pointed apex of a triangle, the body of which is constituted by the front of the right ventricle, its base by the lower boundary of that cavity, resting on the central tendon of the diaphragm, its left side by the longitudinal furrow, and its right side by the auriculo-ventricular furrow.[2]

The breadth of the pulmonary artery varied from a little over half

---

[1] The transverse furrow, which is the apparent boundary-line between the right auricle and the right ventricle, is about half an inch to the right of the real boundary-line between those cavities. See note at page 31.

[2] Or rather by a line half an inch to the left of the furrow. See note at page 31.

an inch (·6 inch) to a little under an inch and a half (1·45 inch). Between these two extreme limits, both of which occurred in men, there was every kind of variation in the breadth of the artery. The width of the artery depended as much on the amount of blood that it happened to contain as on the natural size of the vessel. In one-third of the cases (18 in 45) the breadth of the artery varied from three-quarters of an inch to less than an inch, and of these three were boys and four were young people; and in one-third of them (17 in 45) the breadth varied from an inch to an inch and a quarter, and of these the youngest was a girl of 16, the rest being adults. The pulmonary artery was wider than the aorta in twenty-seven cases, narrower than the aorta in eleven, and of the same width as the aorta in six. (Note 39, page 115.)

In one instance the right border of the pulmonary artery at its origin lay two-thirds of an inch to the left of the sternum, and in another it was covered by the sternum to the extent of an inch, so that a mere rim of the artery (·25 inch) appeared in the second left space. Between these two extreme instances there was every degree of difference in the position of the origin of the pulmonary artery to the right or to the left.

In two-thirds of the cases (31 in 45) the pulmonary artery was situated partly behind the sternum, and partly behind the upper cartilages and spaces to the left of the sternum; but in one-third of them (14 in 45) the vessel lay entirely to the left of that bone, and behind the upper spaces and cartilages.

Of those instances in which the artery lay completely to the left of the sternum, in three-fourths (11 in 14) the right border of the vessel was on a line with or a little beyond the left border of the bone, and in the remainder (3 in 14) it was placed from one-third to two-thirds of an inch to the left of that bone. Of the instances in which the artery lay partly behind the sternum, partly behind the cartilages and their spaces, in all but one-fifth (6 in 31) the vessel was situated to a greater extent behind the spaces than the sternum. In no single instance was the artery entirely covered by that bone. In the large majority of the cases, therefore, the greater part (in 25 of 45 instances), or the whole (in 14 of 45 instances), of the artery bore to the left of the sternum and presented itself behind the upper costal cartilages and their spaces from the first cartilage to the third space. (Note 40, page 115.)

Breadth of the Left Ventricle.—The breadth of the left ventricle as it is seen in front where it extends from the septum between the ventricles to the left border of the heart, varied from almost half an inch (·4 inch) to almost an inch and a half (1·4 inch). The average width of the ventricle was four-fifths of an inch (·8 inch). The proportion that the width of the left ventricle at its anterior aspect bore to the width of the whole heart varied from less than one-tenth (·08 to 10) to more than three-tenths (3·2 to 10). As a rule, when the ventricle was actually narrow, it was also proportionally narrow in relation to the breadth of the heart; and when the ventricle was actually wide, it was also proportionally wide in relation to the breadth of the heart. The exceptions to this rule are so few that I need not give the details here. (Note 41, page 116.)

Position of the Apex of the Heart.—The line of junction of the fourth and fifth ribs to their cartilages is a landmark of some clinical importance, for, aided by knowledge, this line may be pretty nearly ascertained during life. A downward bow is made by the descending curves of those ribs and of their cartilages, and their junction usually corresponds to the deepest part of the bow. The left boundary of the heart at the apex was situated in one instance an inch to the left, and in another instance an inch to the right of the junction of the fourth or fifth rib to its cartilage; in five cases out of forty-two this left boundary was at that junction, in eighteen it extended to the left of it, and in six it was seated to the right of it.

The relation of the lower anterior edge of the upper lobe of the left lung to the apex of the heart is a point of clinical value. The septum between the upper and lower lobes is situated a little way to the left of the apex of the heart, and this portion of the upper lobe is detached as it were from the body of the lung and dips downwards and forwards, so that it may devote itself to the protection of the apex around which it is folded, being situated outside, behind and in front of, above and slightly below the apex. A small tongue of lung, the existence of which I pointed out in 1844, frequently interposes itself between the front and under surface of the apex and the walls of the chest. This tongue of lung and the adjoining structure of the lower portion of the upper lobe play backwards and forwards with the forward and backward play of the apex of the heart. When the apex comes forward towards the ribs and spaces during the contraction of the ventricle, the tongue of lung retracts; when the apex retracts, the tongue of lung expands; and thus those two structures interchange with and adapt themselves to each other during the movements of the heart and the lungs. This tongue of lung that thus laps round and in front of the apex was present in two-fifths of the series of cases under observation (24 in 61), was absent in one-half of them (31 in 61), and was just indicated in the form of an inward curve in one-tenth of them (6 in 61). This tongue was strongly marked in one-third of the instances in which it existed (8 in 24), was slightly marked in another third (9 in 24), and was of intermediate form in the remaining third (7 in 24). Besides these instances, this tongue was present in eighteen additional examples in my possession: in one-half of these it was large and pronounced (9 in 18), in four of them it was of medium size, and in four it was small.

During and after death the apex contracts in one direction, or upwards and to the right towards the centre of the heart, and the left lung retracts in another direction or to the left. The heart is therefore more exposed after death than during life. This especially applies to the apex of the heart. As a rule, however, in these cases, the apex and the adjoining portion of the heart are still covered to a certain extent by lung (in 34 instances out of 58). In two of these instances the lung covered the heart from the apex towards the sternum to the extent of two inches and a half, but in the rest of them the extent of lung in front of the apex varied in breadth from an inch and a quarter to the tenth of an inch. In one-sixth of the cases (9 in 58) the edge of the lung was on a line with or crossed the apex, and in one-fourth of them (15 in 58) it was situated to the left of the heart, so as to expose the apex. The space thus left between the lung and the apex varied from one inch to the eighth of an inch. (Note 42, page 116.)

The Breadth and Position of the Ascending Aorta.—The breadth of the ascending aorta varied from half an inch to an inch and-a-half (1·45), its average breadth being nearly one inch (.96 inch). (Note 43, page 116.)

The aorta was usually narrower than the pulmonary artery, (in 27 of 44 cases), but it was sometimes wider than that vessel (11 in 44), and in a few instances (6 in 44), the two arteries were of equal breadth. When the aorta was less than an inch in width, it was very seldom wider than the pulmonary artery (in 2 of 36 cases); but when the aorta was an inch or more in breadth, it was more often the wider of the two arteries, in the proportion of nine to eight. (Note 44, page 116.)

The ascending aorta was completely covered by the sternum in nearly one half of the cases (19 in 45), and of these instances, in one-third the artery was central (6), in one-third (6) it inclined to the right, and in one-third (7) it inclined to the left.

In one-third of the cases (15 in 45) the ascending aorta was visible to a greater or less extent to the right of the sternum, and in six of these the exposure of the artery to the right was great, the whole artery being brought into view in one case in which there was excessive distension of the abdomen.

In one-fourth of the cases (11 in 45), the ascending aorta was partially visible to the left of the sternum, but in only one instance did the breadth of the portion of the artery thus exposed amount to more than the third of an inch. (Note 45, page 116.)

The Position of the " Root of the Aorta," [1] *including the Orifice, Valve,* [2]

---

[1] I have adopted the term " root of the aorta " at the suggestion of Mr. Marshall and with the approval of Dr. Sharpey.

[2] Haller, writing in Latin, correctly designates the valves of the heart under the term "valvulæ," derived from " valvæ," folding doors, thus—" valvulæ semilunares," " valvulæ mitrales," "valvulæ in quas annulum venosum diviserunt." Senac (Structure du Cœur), speaking of the valves of the heart, uses the terms "valvules tricuspidales, mitrales, et sigmoides ;" and Douglas, in his translation of Winslow, describes the "tricuspid valves," the "mitral valves," and the " semilunar valves."

Portal was apparently the first to speak of the auriculo-ventricular valves in the singular number, under the name respectively of "valvule mitrale" and "valvule trigochine," on the ground, long previously recognised by anatomists, that the flaps of each of those valves are attached to a valvular ring.

The English word "valve" has been applied by engineers and in common use to the mechanism, as a whole, for preventing the back-flow of fluid, and not to one or other of the flaps composing that mechanism. I have therefore, here and elsewhere, spoken of the semilunar flaps of the aortic or pulmonic valve, and not of the semilunar valves.

and Sinuses of the Aorta.—I possess only seven illustrations of the position of the root of the aorta. They, however, show the aortic valve in a variety of situations, and as the anatomical relations of the "root of the aorta" to the root of the pulmonary artery, and to the visible portion of the ascending aorta are very definite, it is easy to infer the position of the aortic valve, when we know that of the pulmonic valve, and that of the ascending aorta.

The ascending aorta, as it mounts upwards, curves first to the right and then to the left. The upper and lower ends of the curve bear to the left, and the centre of the curve bears to the right. When, therefore, the visible portion of the ascending aorta is situated far to the left or far to the right, the sinuses and valve of the aorta are also situated far to the left or far to the right, their bearing being always more to the left than that of the ascending aorta. The lower boundary of the pulmonic orifice corresponds with the upper boundary of the aortic orifice at the junction of the anterior and the left posterior flaps of the aortic valve. Nearly one half of the root of the pulmonary artery is situated just above the left posterior aortic sinus, and more than one half of it extends to the left of the root of the aorta. The root of the aorta extends obliquely downwards to the extent of about one inch below, and fully half an inch to the left of the pulmonary artery, the extent being greater or less in accordance with the oblique diameter of the root of the aorta.

In one instance the greater part of the anterior aortic sinus was situated behind the second left space from its upper to its lower boundary, while the remainder of the root of the aorta was covered by the left border of the sternum. In this case the ascending aorta occupied the left half or three-fifths of the sternum, the right side of that bone being occupied by the descending cava, and the pulmonic valve was situated entirely to the left of the sternum behind the second cartilage and the upper third of the second space.

In another instance the right border of the right posterior sinus of the aorta was present in the third right space close to the right edge of the sternum, and the whole of the rest of the root of the aorta was covered by the right three-fifths of the sternum, its left two-fifths being occupied by the arterial cone of the right ventricle. In that case the whole heart lay more to the right than to the left of the median line, the ascending aorta extended four-fifths of an inch to the right of the right edge of the sternum, and four-fifths of the origin of the pulmonary artery, which was on a level with the third cartilage, was covered by the sternum.

In the first of these two cases, the situation of the ascending aorta, and that of the origin of the pulmonary artery were high and much to the left, and the situation of the root of the aorta was correspondingly also high and much to the left. In the second of them, the ascending aorta and the origin of the pulmonary artery were low in situation, and were placed very far to the right; and the root of the aorta was also low in situation, and was placed very far to the right.

Of the remaining five instances, in two the root of the aorta was situated for one-fifth of its breadth in the second left space, and for four-fifths of its breadth behind the sternum on a level with the second space and the third cartilage. In two other cases, the proportion of the root of the aorta behind the sternum and to the left of that bone was about the same as in the two cases just quoted; but in one of them it was situated behind the third left cartilage and the upper third of the third left space; while in the other instance it was still lower, being on a level with the lower border of the third cartilage, the third space, and the upper border of the fourth cartilage.

The root of the aorta, including as I have said, in that term the orifice, valve, and sinuses of the artery, was oblique in direction in all instances. Its longest or oblique diameter ranged from one inch to almost an inch and a half (1·4); its vertical diameter varied from ·8 inch to 1·05 inch; and its transverse diameter from ·8 inch to 1·2 inch. In three instances the transverse and vertical measurements were equal; in two the transverse diameter exceeded the vertical; and in two the vertical diameter exceeded the transverse.

Although the observation of the actual position of the root of the aorta in health has been limited to the seven cases just examined, yet we are able to infer its proximate position by the knowledge already obtained of the situation of the right edge of the ascending aorta, and of that of the origin of the pulmonary artery. The origin of the pulmonary artery was in one case as high as the upper border of the second cartilage, and in another it was as low as the upper border of the fourth cartilage. In the former case the root of the aorta must have been on a level with the second cartilage and the upper portion of the second space, while in the latter case it must have been on a level with the fourth cartilage and the upper portion of the fourth space. The usual position of the origin of the pulmonary artery was behind the second space or the third costal cartilage, and the usual position of the root of the aorta, following in the wake of its companion great artery, must have been on a level with the third cartilage and the third space. The average situation of the root of the aorta must therefore have been on a level with the lower portion of the third cartilage and the third space. In the seven cases just examined, the right edge of the ascending aorta was situated on a line to the right of the right edge of the root of the aorta, to an extent varying from the eighth of an inch to more than half an inch. In the same instances the left edge of the ascending aorta was situated on a line to the right of the left edge of the root of the aorta, to an extent varying from one-third (·3 inch) to three-fifths of an inch. The extent to which the ascending aorta bore to the right in relation to the root of the aorta was governed by two circumstances: (1) the degree to which the ascending aorta was situated to the right or to the left: and (2), the distension or collapse of the artery. (1) The root of the aorta was situated further to the left in relation to the ascending aorta, when the position of the ascending aorta was far to the left than when it was far to the right. (2) The root of the aorta was further to the left in relation to the ascending aorta when the breadth of the artery was great owing to distension, than when it was small owing to collapse.

In one instance, a case with great intestinal distension, the whole of the ascending aorta was situated to the right of the sternum, and in that instance the greater portion of the root of the aorta must have been also situated to the right of the sternum.   In another instance, the ascending aorta was situated to the extent of more than one half of its breadth to the left of the sternum, and in that instance, the greater portion of the root of the aorta must have been also situated to the left of the sternum.

Anterior aspect.

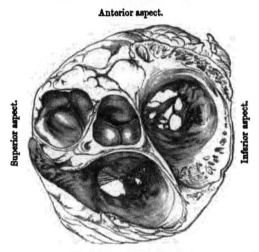

Posterior aspect of the heart.

Fig. 1.—Showing the pulmonic and aortic valves closed ; the tricuspid and mitral orifices open.   Period of the *diastole* of the ventricles.

In one half of the cases (19 in 45), the whole of the aorta was covered by the sternum, and in most of these the greater part of the root of the aorta must have been also covered by the sternum, but its left border must have usually passed a little to the left of that bone, being situated behind one of the cartilages or spaces close to the left edge of the sternum.

Under these circumstances the average or standard position of the root of the aorta must have been behind the left two-thirds or half of the sternum on a level with the third cartilage and the third space, its left border being placed behind and below that cartilage at its articulation to the sternum.   (Note 46, page 116.)

The Position of the Aortic Sinuses, and the Flaps of the Aortic Valve.[1] —The aortic orifice looks towards the apex of the ventricle in a direction to the left downwards, and slightly forwards. The aspect of the orifice is therefore oblique, its obliquity being usually quite as great from above downwards, as from left to right. When the heart bears unduly to the left, the downward obliquity of the aortic orifice is greater than when it bears unduly to the right.

The root of the aorta, including the aortic orifice, valve, and sinuses, projects forwards, in front of the mitral valve and the cavity of the left ventricle, so as to interpose itself between the orifice of the pulmonary artery above and the tricuspid orifice below. The root of the aorta thus separates those two openings from each other, the *conus arteriosus* being situated in front of it. When a section is

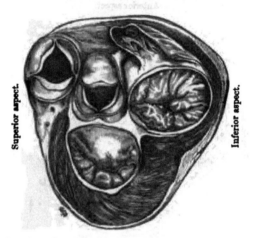

Fig. 2.—Showing the pulmonic and aortic orifices open; the tricuspid and mitral orifices shut. ⁂ Period of the *systole* of the ventricles.

made through the auricles across the base of the heart, so as to expose the four great openings of the heart, the pulmonic, the aortic, and the tricuspid orifices, viewed in their *natural position*, are seen to range themselves in a line from above downwards, the mitral orifice being situated behind the lower half of the aortic and the upper two-thirds of the tricuspid orifice. This line is not, however, straight, but is somewhat convex, the convexity looking backwards, so that the pulmonic and tricuspid orifices which are situated at the upper and lower portions of the line are somewhat in advance of the aortic orifice, which occupies the central position. When the line of the three orifices is looked at in front, it is seen to take an oblique direction from above downwards, and from right to left, the pulmonic orifice

[1] See Figs. 1, 2, and 3.

at the upper end of the line being situated partly behind and chiefly to the left of the left edge of the sternum at the second left cartilage and space, and the tricuspid orifice being situated behind the right half of the sternum at its lower portion.

The " Aortic Vestibule," or Intervalvular Space of the Left Ventricle. —When the semilunar flaps of the aortic valve meet together so as to shut the aortic aperture, they fall backwards into a short space that I have described in my " Medical Anatomy " under the name of the " intervalvular space of the left ventricle." I have here, however, at

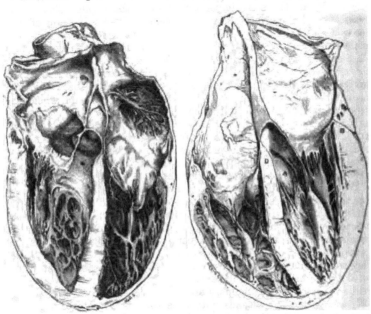

Fig. 3.—Aortic valve shut, seen in the aortic vestibule of the left ventricle, which parts are exposed by cutting a flap in the anterior cusp of the mitral valve and pinning it backwards.

Fig. 4.—Other half of the heart represented in Fig. 5, showing the mitral an l tricuspid valves and the fleshy septum (D) with its continuation in the form of a " fibrous septum," which is also seen in the companion figure.

the suggestion of Dr. Sharpey, adopted the appropriate name of the " aortic vestibule " for this space, which is well seen in the preparation from which Fig. 3 was taken, in which the semilunar flaps of the aortic valve are seen through an opening cut in the anterior flap of the mitral valve. The aortic vestibule bends forwards and to the right from the upper part of the left ventricle, and forms the channel between the cavity of that ventricle and its outlet at the aortic aperture. The walls of the aortic vestibule are rigid and unyielding, and it therefore retains its size during every stage of the action of the heart. These walls are muscular in front and to the left, where they are lined by rigid fibrous tissue, and where the space is situated immediately behind the *conus arteriosus* of the right ventricle; fibro-cartilaginous on the right, where they are formed by the central fibro-cartilage and "fibrous septum" of the heart; and fibrous behind, where they are formed by the base of the anterior flap of the mitral valve and the adjoining wall of the left auricle, upon which the posterior sinuses of the aortic valve are implanted.

The aortic vestibule occupies the centre of the heart, and is sur-rounded by all the more important parts of the organ. The *conus arteriosus* and the orifice of the pulmonary artery are in front of it; the tricuspid valve and right auricle are to the right of it; and the mitral valve and left auricle are behind it. During the ventricular diastole, when the left ventricle is of full size, the aortic vestibule is the narrowest portion or bent neck of the ventricle, and it then receives the flaps of the closed aortic valve which fall back into its cavity. During the ventricular systole, on the other hand, when the ventricle has completely contracted upon its contents so as to present an almost solid mass, the aortic vestibule moves downwards and to the left towards the apex, and becomes the widest part of the small remaining cavity, and the presence of this space then allows the mitral valve to remain closed up to the end of the systole by the pressure of the blood on its anterior flap.

The "aortic vestibule," as Mr. Marshall suggests, is a short *conus arteriosus*, since it corresponds in relative position and function, though not in shape or size, or in the structure of its walls, to the *conus. arteriosus* of the right ventricle, immediately behind which it is situated. These two analogous parts take opposite directions in relation to each other, and respectively to the ventricle from which they spring and the great artery to which they proceed. The right *conus arteriosus* ascends with a bearing to the left, and curves back-wards to end in the pulmonary artery; while the aortic vestibule or left *conus arteriosus* ascends with a bearing to the right and bends forwards to terminate in the root of the aorta. Those two great arteries, following the direction of the *conus arteriosus* from which they respectively spring, cross each other in their onward and up-ward course, so that the pulmonary artery proceeds backwards to the left and then to the right, while the ascending aorta proceeds for-wards to the right and then to the left. If the two cavities be looked at as a combined whole, each with its ventricle, its *conus arteriosus*, and its great artery, they resemble somewhat the curious double oil and vinegar flask that is met with so commonly in the most beautiful parts of South Germany.

The *central fibro-cartilage* and "*tendinous septum*" of the heart form, as I have just said, the right wall of the aortic vestibule. The fleshy septum terminates at its base in a strong tendinous aponeurosis or fibro-cartilage, which forms a part of great importance in the structure of the heart, and which is well seen in the preparation from which Figs. 3 and 4 have been taken. The muscular septum (D) is, in fact, converted at this region into a fibrous septum ; but while the muscular septum separates the two ventricles, the fibrous septum separates the left ventricle from the right auricle as well as from the top of the right ventricle. Higher up this fibrous septum is converted into the central fibro-cartilage, which corresponds to the central fibro-cartilage and bone of the heart of the ox (Fig. 6), and which is converted into bone in a human heart in my possession. The central fibro-cartilage, as may be seen in Fig. 2, forms a firm bond of connection between the tendinous rings of the mitral and tricuspid orifices, the central or inner angles of the mitral and tricuspid valves, the right posterior sinus of the aorta, and the aortic vestibule. It also gives insertion to muscular fibres from the left and the right ventricles (Fig. 5 A), which, sweeping round from the left and

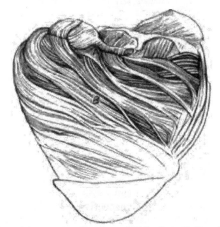

Fig. 5.—Showing the muscular fibres unravelled of the left and right ventricles. B, Fibres from the left and right ventricles going to the central fibro-cartilage of the heart, and forming a portion of the septum.

the right respectively, blend together toward the base of the posterior longitudinal furrow, so as to form short central bands of fibres, which dip forwards at right angles to the circular fibres, deepening as they advance, enter and go to form the septum and end in the central fibro-cartilage, which gives origin to numerous muscular fibres, to the inter-auricular septum, and the right and left auricles. During the ventricular systole the central fibro-cartilage, and with it the aortic vestibule and all the adjacent parts, are drawn downwards and to the left towards the apex by the contraction of the ventricular fibres inserted into the tendinous ring and especially into the central fibro-cartilage, which thus becomes the focus and movable pivot of the heart, which binds together all those important parts and gives to them a common movement.
The setting of the orifice of the aorta is muscular anteriorly and to

the left, and fibrous posteriorly and to the right. The muscular setting
is made by the anterior half of the base of the left ventricle, and the
fibrous setting by the anterior cusp of the mitral valve and its continuation towards the left auricle, and by the central fibro-cartilage. During the diastole the anterior cusp of the mitral valve
divides the ventricle into two portions, each with its own aperture,
an anterior or aortic portion, out of which the blood pours during the
systole through the aortic orifice, and a posterior or mitral portion, into
which the blood flows during the diastole through the mitral orifice.

There is one anterior, and there are two posterior and lateral aortic
sinuses. The right or anterior coronary artery springs from the anterior sinus, and the left or posterior coronary artery from the left
posterior sinus. The right posterior sinus is sometimes called the
intercoronary sinus. Owing to the obliquity downwards, forwards,
and to the right of the orifice of the aorta, the right posterior flap of
the aortic valve is much lower in position than the other flaps. Thus
the lower boundary of that flap was in two instances half an inch
lower than the lower boundary of either of the other flaps. In another
example, in which the aorta was far to the right, the lower edge of
the right posterior cusp was only a quarter of an inch lower than
that of the left posterior cusp, but it was half an inch lower than the
lower edge of the anterior cusp.

The root of the aorta is buried in the centre of the heart, and
is therefore incircled by all the cavities of the heart and the two
other great vessels. The crescentic edge of the anterior sinus is
attached throughout to the central fibro-cartilage which forms the
summit of the interventricular septum. The anterior sinus is
covered in front by the *conus arteriosus* and, higher up, on the right
side, to a varying extent, by the auricular portion of the right auricle,
and on the left side by the pulmonary artery.

The left and right halves respectively of the right and left
posterior flaps of the aortic valve are attached at their junction, and
along their lower border to the anterior cusp of the mitral valve,
and to the aponeurosis that is continuous with that cusp. At this
situation the two posterior sinuses of the aorta are in front of the
left auricle. (Figs. 3 and 4.)

The left half of the left posterior sinus is attached at its root to the
muscular base of the left ventricle, and is covered, going from right to
left, first by the auricular portion of the right auricle, and then by the
inner or right wall of the pulmonary artery. The junction of the
anterior to the left posterior flap of the aortic valve is usually a little
in front of the junction of the posterior and the left anterior flaps of
the pulmonary artery, so that a pin thrust through that artery at the
junction of the flaps in question into the aorta, appears about the
tenth of an inch behind the junction of those aortic flaps; but in
one instance the pin, thus inserted, pierced through the junction of
the aortic flaps as well as through that of the pulmonic flaps. The
left or posterior coronary artery at its origin is, in one of my prepara-

tions, ·25 inch from the left edge of the left posterior cusp, and ·4 inch from its right edge, and I believe it will be found that this represents the usual position of the origin of the artery.

The relations of the right posterior sinus of the aorta are of remarkable extent and importance. The centre and right side of the root of that sinus is firmly attached to or incorporated with the central fibro-cartilage and fibrous septum of the heart that crown the interventricular septum. To the left of this attachment to the fibro-cartilage, the right aortic sinus is united, as we have just seen, to the anterior cusp of the mitral valve, and it is seated in front of the left auricle. To the right and in front of this attachment, it is closely connected with the inner or left angle of the tricuspid valve. The right wall of the right posterior sinus, as it advances to join the right edge of the anterior sinus, is covered first by the inner or left wall of the right auricle, and finally by the inner or posterior wall of the arterial cone of the right ventricle.

This right aortic sinus is thus closely connected with every important part of the heart, except the pulmonary artery. The right and left ventricle, the right and left auricle, the mitral and tricuspid valves are all of them attached to or in contact with it; and the central fibro-cartilage of the heart, as we have seen, with which the base of this sinus is incorporated, acts as a tie that binds together the allied movements of those parts.[1] The descending vena cava also comes into contact with the upper portion of this sinus.

Mr. Thurnam brought into notice, thirty-three years ago, the extensive and important bearings of the sinuses of the aorta, in especial relation to aneurism of those parts.

It is customary for authors on anatomy, following the original error of the great Valsalva, unfortunately repeated by Mr. Thurnam, and more recently by that great anatomist, Henle, to describe the aortic sinuses as being two of them anterior, and one posterior. I have examined the heart *in situ* in many bodies, with regard to this point, and I have always found those sinuses and the corresponding flaps of the aortic valve in the position I have described, one being anterior, and two posterior. A little consideration as to the known relation of these sinuses to other parts, the position of which is well ascertained and admitted, will show that two of these sinuses are posterior and lateral, and that only one of them is anterior.

The right and left posterior flaps of the aortic valve are attached in about an equal degree to the anterior mitral cusp, as is shown in drawings and many hearts now around me, and in Dr. John Reid's figure.[2] The anterior cusp of the mitral valve is on a level with the posterior wall of the root of the aorta, and it is therefore impossible that either of the aortic sinuses that are attached to that flap can be situated at the anterior aspect of the aorta; they must, indeed, both be posterior in position. Again, while the right or anterior

[1] See Fig. 4.
[2] "Cyclopædia of Anatomy," vol. i. p. 588. See also Figs. 1, 2, and 3.

coronary artery arises from the anterior aortic sinus, the left or posterior coronary artery arises from the left posterior sinus; and while
the right artery advances to the right of the pulmonary artery, the
left artery passes to the left behind the pulmonary artery. Further,
the origin of the left coronary artery is nearer to the left or anterior
and lateral edge than to the right or posterior edge of the left posterior
sinus. I might adduce other points in illustration of what I have
advanced, but these facts, which speak for themselves, are sufficient.[1]

The error has, I believe, arisen and been perpetuated from the cus-
tom of examining these sinuses, not when the heart is *in situ*, but
after it has been removed from the body. If the right ventricle with
its arterial cone, and the ventricular septum are carefully removed
without disturbing the position of the heart, and without injuring the
anterior wall of the aorta at its origin, the true position of the aortic
sinuses and of the flaps of the aortic valve may be readily observed.

The right and left posterior aortic sinuses advance forwards on
either side, and finally curve gently inwards and forwards to complete
the circle of the aorta by uniting at either end with the anterior

[1] Valsalva's original drawing (V. Opera, tab. ii. fig. 1 ; see Fig. A), in which the
anterior and left posterior sinuses with their respective coronary arteries are represented
in front of the root of the aorta, gives not a front but a side view of the aortic arch.
The artery from which this drawing was taken shows the cut end of the vessel, and has
evidently been removed from the body and placed upon its right side. The effect of this
position would be to place the anterior and left posterior sinuses, each with its coronary
artery, on the same anterior plane. Fig. B is a reduced copy of a similar drawing of the
arch of the aorta after its removal from the body, given by Lower (Tractatus de Corde,
tab. i. fig. 4) in which the two coronary arteries, as in Valsalva's drawing, spring
from the front of the root of the aorta.
Nearly all the drawings of the root of the aorta that have been taken from the actual
body, the artery being *in situ* (reduced copies of several of which drawings are given
below), represent the sinuses in the position that I have described, two of them being
posterior in situation and one anterior, and the right posterior sinus being the lowest of the
three sinuses. I find it thus in Tiedemann's "Tabula Arteriarum," plate xix. (fig. E);
John Bell's "Anatomy," vol. ii. p. 283 (fig. F); Charles Bell's Engravings of the
Arteries, tab. ii. (fig. G); Mr. Quain's "Anatomy of the Arteries," anterior view, fig. 3,
and posterior view, fig. 4, plate xlviii. (figs. H I); Pirogoff's "Anatomia Topographica,"
in eleven different views (figs. K L M N); and Braun's "Topographisch-Anatomisch Atlas"
(figs. O P). Henle, in a much reduced figure of the aorta *in situ*, represents one anterior
and two posterior sinuses (fig. Q), but he gives a series of drawings of the heart and aorta
after their removal from the body (one of which I have given on a reduced scale, Fig. D),
in all of which the sinuses are represented and described as being two anterior and one
posterior.
Anatomists, including Morgagni and Senac in former times, and, as I have said above,
the respected names of Thurnam and Henle in our own day, have as a rule described
two of the sinuses of Valsalva and their corresponding coronary arteries as being anterior,
and one of them, or that which is destitute of a coronary artery, as being posterior.
On the other hand, Vesalius and P. Sylvius described the left coronary artery as arising
from behind the posterior valve. Some authors give contradictory descriptions of the
origin of the coronary arteries. Thus, Winslow in one passage says that there are two
coronary arteries, " one of which is situated anteriorly, the other posteriorly"(vol. ii. p. 3) ;
while elsewhere (p. 221) he says that "one of the vessels lies towards the right hand,
the other towards the left, of the anterior third part of the circumference of the aorta."
Portal ("Anatomie Medicale," vol. iii. p. 152) says that the left coronary artery arises from
the left posterior portion of the aorta ; but elsewhere (p. 51) he states that two of the
valves are anterior and lateral and the third is posterior, and that the right and left
coronary arteries are situated above the two anterior valves.
The accurate Haller, "Elementa Physiologiæ," iii. 345, speaking of the aortic valve,

sinus.   The anterior portion of the left posterior sinus is concea
the pulmonary artery, while the anterior portion of the right po

says : "Situs alequantum differt, duæ enim 'superiori loco ponuntur, altera s
posterior altera ; tertia inferior est. Earum eæ, quæ superiori loco ponuntur,
habent arterias coronarias, inferior nullum aortæ ramum vicinum habet." H
great anatomist has given a correct description of the situation of the flaps of th
valve and of the origin of the coronary arteries.

In our own day, Pirogoff and Mr. Heath describe the sinuses as being one
anterior and two of them posterior. Bourgery (fig. c) curiously figures the o
arteries and their sinuses as being both anterior ; but he describes the anterior c
artery as arising from the anterior sinus, and the posterior coronary artery fr
posterior sinus.

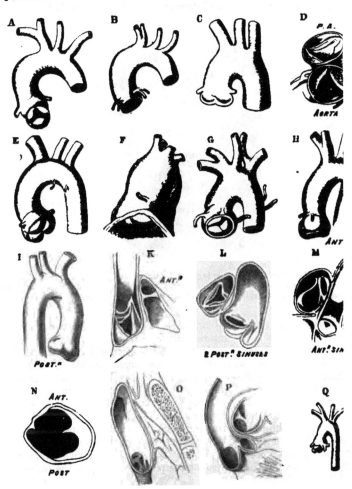

sinus is readily exposed by pressing aside the auricular appendix. It is rather difficult to say which of the two posterior sinuses comes forward to the greater extent at their points of attachment to the anterior sinus ; I think, however, that the right posterior sinus, which usually goes by the name of the posterior sinus, comes forward to a greater extent than the left posterior sinus, which usually goes by the name of the left anterior sinus. (Note 46, p. 116.)

The Position of the Mitral Valve.—In seven instances the size and position of the mitral valve are given, and in three of them accurate details of its structure are represented. These points are further illustrated by preparations and dissections. (Note 46, p. 118.)

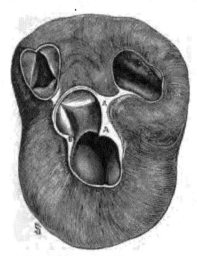

Fig. 6.—Calf's heart boiled, showing the aortic (c) and mitral (d) orifices thrown into one by the removal of the mitral valve, the lower A being the central fibro-cartilage, E the tricuspid orifice, and F the orifice of the pulmonary artery.

The setting of the mitral orifice is muscular in its two posterior thirds, and fibrous in its anterior third. In these respects the mitral and aortic orifices balance each other. The setting of the mitral orifice is muscular behind, while that of the aortic orifice is muscular in front, the two openings being separated by the interposed anterior flap of the mitral valve and its short fibrous continuation to the two posterior aortic sinuses, and by the central fibro-cartilage of the heart. When the heart is boiled for a sufficient length of time this interposed fibrous partition softens and separates from its attachments, and the aortic and mitral apertures are thrown into one large irregular opening (see Fig. 6). The base of the ventricles then presents not four but three great apertures, the tricuspid, the pulmonic, and the mitral-aortic.

The apparatus of the mitral valve occupies the whole of the
terior part of the left ventricle, and when its anterior wal
removed, the whole of this apparatus is brought into view.

The anterior cusp or flap of the mitral valve is alone visible i
of the three drawings giving the anatomical details of the valve,
in the two others the lower border of the posterior cusp is lik
brought into view.

The whole apparatus of the valve takes an oblique direction
right to left and downwards. The right end or base of the appa
of the valve corresponds with the junction of the left auricle wit
left ventricle, and its left end corresponds with the interior of the
of the left ventricle. The apparatus of the valve thus forms a
triangle, its base being at the base of the ventricle, its apex a
apex of the ventricle, its upper side being slightly curved up

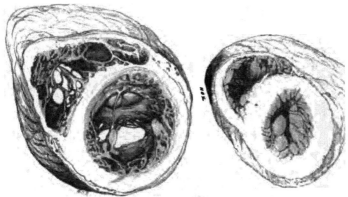

FIG. 7.—Showing the mitral orifice, the
anterior flap of the mitral valve, and
the right and left posterior flaps of the
aortic valve Diastole of the ventricles.

FIG. 8.—Systole of the left ventri

or outwards, and its lower side being slightly bent inwards or upw
at its middle. The flaps, the tendinous cords, and the papil
muscles, which are connected by the cords to the flaps, form
three component parts of the valve. (Figs. 7, 10, 11, 12, and "Med
Anatomy," Plate VI.)

The convex base of the anterior flap of the mitral valve is attac
on the one hand to the junction of the left ventricle to the left aur
and on the other to the roots of the right and left posterior flap
the aortic valve. This attachment of the mitral to the aortic va
is effected through the fibrous structure that extends from the bas
one valve to the base of the other, and by the central fibro-cartil
of the heart, which forms a triple bond of connexion that ties
mitral, the aortic, and the tricuspid valves to each other. (Fig. 2.

When the mitral valve is shut, the anterior flap of the valve presents a convex edge, shaped like a horseshoe, which falls back upon and fits like a lid into the posterior flap of the valve, which flap, being crescentic in shape, presents a concave edge.[1] Each flap adapts itself to the other by a notched lip, made up of small hemispherical eminences. The eminences of one lip fill up the notches of the other lip. These eminences, thus seen on the auricular surface of the valve, are cells when seen on its ventricular surface, and as these cells are distended with blood when the ventricle contracts, and are exactly maintained in their places by the tendinous cords and papillary muscles, the distended cells or eminences at the opposite lips of the valve adapt themselves to and press against each other during the systole, so as to shut the valve. (Figs. 2, 9, 10, 12.)

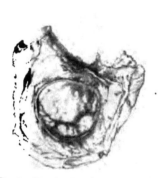 

Fig. 9.—Mitral valve shut; auricular surface; anterior or convex and posterior or crescentic flaps; ventricular systole.

Fig. 10.—Mitral valve shut; ventricular surface; anterior flap, with tendinous cords and papillary muscles; two posterior flaps of aortic valve; ventricular systole.

The anterior flap is simple, and when closed is shaped like a three-quarters moon. The posterior flap is compound, and when closed is shaped like a quarter or crescent-shaped moon. The compound posterior flap is usually made up of one central and two lateral sub-segments, the latter being sometimes subdivided. These sub-segments adapt themselves so to each other, that the concavity of the crescentic border of the posterior compound flap is preserved entire; for it would have been impossible, by means of one simple fold of membrane, to fill up without a break the whole of the crescentic border.

I need scarcely give a description of the arrangement of the tendinous cords in relation to the flaps of the valve, and of the papillary muscles in relation to the cords and the flaps. It will be sufficient if

[1] Figs 2, 9.

E 2

I here say that they are so arranged that when the muscular walls
of the ventricle contract, the papillary muscles, which are really semi-
detached portions of those walls, also contract with equal steps; that as
the walls shorten so as to approximate the base and the apex by
a double movement to each other, the papillary muscles shorten to an
exactly parallel degree; and that thus while they hold the flaps of the
valve, through the medium of the cords, in apposition, they steadily draw
the whole valve towards the apex, and the apex towards the valve, to
exactly the same extent that the base and apex of the ventricle are
drawn towards each other. The mechanical arrangements are complicated, for there are many parts to be adjusted to each other; but
the principle on which those parts are adjusted to each other is simple,
for it is by one single contraction of the whole single muscle of the
left ventricle, made up in its component parts of walls, columns, and

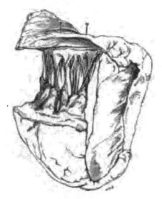

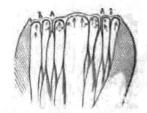

Fig. 11.—Mitral valve shut; posterior
flap, with tendinous cords and papillary
muscles.

Fig. 12. — Diagram of the shut mitral
valve, with the anterior cusp A A in close
contact with the posterior cusp (b, b).
The tendinous cords and papillary
muscles are shown, the direction of the
current and pressure of the blood being
indicated by arrows.

papillary muscles, that the base of the ventricle (including the mitral
aperture and valve and the aortic aperture and valve) and the apex of
the ventricle are approximated steadily to each other during the
systole.

When the convex anterior flap of the mitral valve falls back upon
and fills up the concave posterior flap of the valve, the anterior flap
and its membranous continuation to the left and right posterior aortic
flaps form a smooth scooped channel or hollow, along which the blood
flows noiselessly from the ventricle into the aorta during the systole.
(Fig. 7.)

The mitral orifice extends downwards, with an inclination to the
left, immediately behind and below the aortic orifice; and, like that

orifice, it looks towards the apex of the left ventricle, or to the left, downwards and slightly forwards. The line of direction of the mitral orifice, viewed from the front, is therefore from above downwards, with a slight obliquity from left to right. The upper and left boundary of the mitral orifice is about half an inch above the level of the lower edge of the right posterior flap of the aortic valve. The lower border of the mitral orifice is about three-quarters of an inch below the lower border of the aortic orifice. The upper or left edge of the mitral orifice is not so far to the left, while its lower or right edge is about as far to the right, as are the left and right edges respectively of the aortic orifice. The mitral orifice is situated deep behind the sternum, a little below the middle of that bone. Its upper or left boundary, in four instances, was on a level with the third cartilage, just within the left edge of the sternum; and its lower or right boundary was on a level with the fourth cartilage, behind a line drawn down the middle of the sternum. This is probably higher than the average position of the mitral orifice after death. In one other case the top of the mitral orifice was on a level with the lower border of the second space, its situation otherwise corresponding to that in the cases just described. In two other instances, the mitral orifice was comparatively low and was situated unusually to the right, its upper border being on a level with the lower edge of the third cartilage or upper border of the fourth space, behind the middle line of the sternum, and its lower or right border being on a level with the lower portion of the fourth space, or the top of the fifth cartilage behind the right edge of the sternum. As a rule, the mitral orifice occupied a space behind the left half of the sternum, extending downwards for more than one inch below the middle of the bone; but in occasional cases it was present behind the right half of the bone.

The tendinous cords and papillary muscles of the mitral valve, as they extended to the left with an inclination downwards, retained, as a rule, their situation behind the space or cartilage that was on a level with their starting-point from the valve.

Thus in the four instances in which the upper rim of the orifice was on a level with the third cartilage, the upper or left cords lay behind the third left cartilage, and the upper or left papillary muscle behind the third space; and in the same instances the lower rim of the orifice was in two of them on a level with the third space, and in two of them on a level with the fourth cartilage; and in these two sets of cases the lower or right cords and papillary muscle lay respectively behind the third space and the fourth cartilage, with a final dip to the space or cartilage below.

In the other cases in which the position of the upper and lower edges of the mitral orifice were higher or lower in relation to the spaces and cartilages than in those just quoted, the upper and lower cords and muscles retained their bearing throughout in relation to the space or cartilage on the level of which they started, until they also usually made a final dip so as to occupy a relatively lower position.

In two of the instances there was a space of half an inch between the right and left papillary muscles, the width of the interior of the ventricle being an inch and a half; and in the other instance, in which the systole of the ventricle was more pronounced, the space between the muscles was the fifth of an inch, the width of the cavity being a little over an inch (1·2 inch).

In one instance, in which the heart and all its parts lay unduly to the right, and in which the flaps, cords and muscles of the valve took a very oblique direction downwards, the right papillary muscle was situated behind the left border of the sternum and the sternal half of the fifth cartilage, and the left papillary muscle crossed the third cartilage and space midway between the sternum and the junction of the cartilages to their ribs.

This instance was throughout exceptional in the position of the heart and all its parts, and the great vessels; but the other instances offer fair average examples of the position of the mitral valve. I need not, therefore, further analyse additional cases. It is sufficient to bear in mind that when the origin of the pulmonary artery is high or low in position, the aortic and mitral valves are also correspondingly high or low in position; and that when the ascending aorta and the origin of the pulmonary artery are far to the right or far to the left of their usual situation, the aortic and mitral valves are also correspondingly far to the right or far to the left of their usual situation.

The Tricuspid Valve.—The apparatus of the mitral valve occupies the whole of the posterior part of the left ventricle, but the apparatus of the tricuspid valve fills up the whole body of the right ventricle, the narrowing *conus arteriosus* being the only portion of the ventricle unoccupied by it. (Note 46, page 119.)

The reason for this diffusion of the apparatus of the tricuspid valve and this concentration of that of the mitral valve is obvious. It depends on the form of the two ventricles and the relation to each other of their apertures of ingress and egress.

The left ventricle is the central cavity of the heart, and is flask-shaped; and its walls on a transverse section are shaped like a ring, and surround a circular space, the mitral valve being behind (see Fig. 3). The right ventricle is applied upon the anterior and inferior walls of the left ventricle, which project into the cavity of the right ventricle and form its inner or posterior wall. The right ventricle on a transverse section is crescent-shaped, its inner wall being convex, while the inner aspect of its outer wall is concave or angular, for it presents at its lower border and outer aspect a projecting angle. The whole cavity of the right ventricle looked at in front is triangular in form, the base of the triangle resting on the central tendon of the diaphragm, its apex pointing to the top of the pulmonary artery, its right side being formed by the junction of the right auricle to the right ventricle and by the tricuspid orifice, and its left side by the septum between the ventricles.

The three cusps of the tricuspid valve are visible when the cavity is opened, the anterior and inferior flaps being completely exposed while the posterior flap is partially concealed (Figs. 13, 14, 15).

The whole apparatus of the tricuspid valve, like that of the mitral valve, takes a direction from right to left; but while the apparatus of the mitral valve concentrates itself as it recedes from the flaps, the papillary muscles pointing towards the apex, and the whole structure forming a long triangle, the apparatus of the tricuspid valve spreads itself out as it recedes from the flaps, like the rays of a fan.

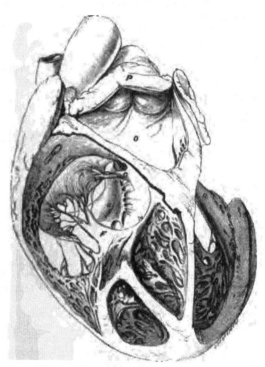

Fig. 13.—Showing the tricuspid valve open, during the complete dilatation (diastole) of the right ventricle.

Figs. 13, 14, and 15 are views of the interior of the right ventricle and of a portion of the left ventricle : A, anterior flap; B, posterior flap ; C, inferior flap ; and d, one of the long sub-segments of the inferior flap of the tricuspid valve. F, anterior papillary muscle ; O, superior papillary muscle ; H H, inferior papillary muscles ; s, sub-segment occupying the angle between the anterior and posterior flaps of the valve ; o, *conus arteriosus* ; P, pulmonary artery ; R, upper or left papillary muscle, and R, lower or right papillary muscle belonging to the left ventricle and mitral valve.

The anterior flap gives attachment at its upper edge to a group of cords which converge upon the small superior papillary muscle,

which is incorporated with the posterior wall of the cavity a
lower portion of the arterial cone. The cords from the lower e
the anterior flap converge upon the anterior papillary muscle,
muscle also sends a radiating series of cords that attach them
to the upper and anterior edge of the lower flap of the valve.
anterior papillary muscle is not immediately connected either
the front or the back wall of the ventricle, but is attached
mediately to both of them by fleshy columns. A strong and rathe
column curves backwards to be attached by outspreading roots t
posterior wall of the ventricle near the septum; while an interlace
of shorter and thinner columns advances forward and to the lef
tending from the base of the anterior papillary muscle to the an
wall of the ventricle, also near the septum (Fig. 13). Thus the

Fig. 14.—Showing the tricuspid valve shut during the early period of the contractic
the right ventricle.

of the anterior papillary muscle spread both backwards and forwa
the base of the muscle being, however, nearer to the front than
back of the ventricle. By this beautiful arrangement a purchase
given for this muscle to act upon the centre of the valve from t
middle of the cavity.

The inferior flap of the valve is not formed, like the anterior fl.
of one sheet of membrane, but is a compound flap, which is su
divided into four or five sub-segments, two of which are longer th
the rest, which, by meeting together and adapting themselves
each other, fill up the large rounded space of the tricuspid orifi
at its inferior portion. The cords from these sub-segments conver
upon a series of papillary muscles that are conveniently situat

around the lower portion of the ventricle, some, or one, being seated in front, some below, and some behind. The inferior papillary muscles are attached, like the anterior papillary muscle, not immediately to the walls of the ventricle, but intermediately by interlacing fleshy columns. The posterior papillary muscles of this group, which are thus connected with the inferior flap of the tricuspid valve, are immediately attached to the inner or convex wall of the ventricle.

The posterior flap is attached behind by a series of radiating cords to the inner walls of the ventricle, sometimes by means of small papillary muscles, sometimes by the immediate insertion of the cords into the walls.

The upper portion of the tricuspid orifice is narrow and angular, while its lower portion is wide and circular; and thus, therefore, the

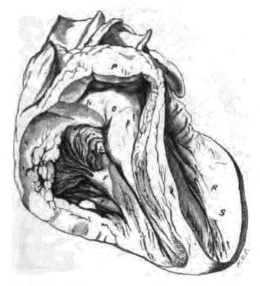

Fig. 15.—Showing the tricuspid valve shut during the period of the complete contraction of the right ventricle.

simple anterior and posterior flaps, with the intervention of one anterior and one superior sub-segment, fill up the upper and narrow part of the orifice; while the inferior and compound sub-segments adapt themselves to the large and rounded inferior portion of the orifice. (See fig. 2, p. 40.)

The whole of these segments of the valve meet together at the centre of the orifice, and hence arises the necessity for an array of papillary muscles, the points of which converge towards the centre of the valve, and that are attached at their roots by fleshy columns that connect them with both the outer and the inner walls of the ventricle.

The tricuspid orifice is situated behind the lower portion of the sternum and in front of the mitral orifice and the left ventricle. The direction of the tricuspid orifice is from above downwards with a slight inclination from left to right. The upper boundary of the tricuspid orifice is immediately below the orifice of the aorta, and in front of the mitral valve.

The four great orifices of the heart—the pulmonic, the aortic, the mitral, and the tricuspid—are situated in that order, one above another, the pulmonic orifice being the highest and the tricuspid the lowest. The lower portion of each of the first three orifices is lower than the upper portion of the orifice below it. Thus the pulmonic orifice, when looked at in front, covers the upper part of the orifice of the aorta on its left side; the lower border of the aortic orifice is lower than the upper border of the mitral orifice; and in like manner, the lower two-thirds, or three-fifths, of the mitral orifice lie behind the upper half of the tricuspid orifice, the lower half of which is below the level of the lower edge of the mitral valve.

The posterior aspect of the tricuspid orifice is attached to the anterior wall of the left ventricle, not on a level with the mitral orifice, but about half an inch nearer to the apex. The wall to which it is thus attached is convex, and the posterior surface of the tricuspid valve where it fits upon the left ventricle is therefore concave. The shape of the tricuspid orifice is, in consequence, angular above, concave behind, convex in front, and rounded and broad below. The tricuspid orifice thus maintains the crescentic form of the cavity of the right ventricle when a cross section is made through its walls.

In five of the cases, the upper and left boundary of the tricuspid valve was situated about the third of an inch to the left, and its lower and right boundary about a third of an inch to the right of a line drawn down the middle of the sternum. In two instances the lower and right boundary of the tricuspid valve extended to the right of the right edge of the sternum.

The right transverse or auriculo-ventricular furrow which corresponds with the right edge of the right ventricle, as I have already remarked, is situated about half an inch to the right of the right edge of the tricuspid valve, and when therefore we know the position of the furrow, we can infer the position of the right edge of the valve. As we have already seen (page 34) the transverse furrow was situated to the right of the right edge of the sternum in nearly three-fourths of the cases (36 in 51), at that edge in three of them, and to the left of that edge, behind the right half of the sternum, in one fourth of them (12 in 51); and it extended in one instance for an inch and a third to the right of the right edge, and was situated in five instances behind the middle line of the sternum. The transverse furrow occupied every variety of position between these two extreme points. We may therefore infer that the right border of the tricuspid valve occupied every range of position between a line three-quarters of an inch to the right of the right edge of the lower portion of the sternum, and a line half an inch to the left of its middle line; the average situation of the right border of the valve being behind the right edge of the sternum.

In like manner we can infer approximately the position of the lower border of the tricuspid valve if we know the position of the lower boundary of the right ventricle. We have already seen that the lower boundary of the right ventricle varied in situation from an inch and a half below, to an inch and a half (1·4 inch) above, the lower end of the sternum. The lower border of the tricuspid valve is from half an inch to nearly an inch above the level of the lower boundary of the right ventricle, and we may therefore infer that the lower border of the valve varies in position from a point nearly two inches above, to a point three-quarters of an inch below the lower end of the sternum.

The top of the tricuspid orifice and valve was situated on a level with the third cartilage in three cases, with the third space in one, and with the fourth cartilage in two; its lower edge being in those cases on a level respectively with the fourth cartilage, the fourth space, and the fifth cartilage. In each of those cases the upper edge of the tricuspid orifice and valve was lower, and its lower edge was much lower than the corresponding edges of the mitral orifice and valve.

The tendinous cords and papillary muscles of the tricuspid valve, as they radiated to the left, slightly upwards, downwards and outwards, retained, as a rule, their situation behind the space or cartilage that was on a level with their starting-point from the valve. Thus, the inferior cords and muscles maintained their relative position throughout, behind the fourth space or fifth cartilage, which was on a level with the lower edge of the tricuspid valve, while the anterior group of cords and the anterior papillary muscles lay behind the fourth cartilage or the fourth space. The upper group of cords retained its relation to the third cartilage or space, or the fourth cartilage, on a level with which the upper edge of the valve was situated, but the superior papillary muscle radiated upwards to a somewhat higher relative position than that from which it started, so that, as, for instance, in two cases, the top of the valve being on a level with the third or fourth cartilage, the superior papillary muscle was behind, respectively, the second or third space.

In the remaining instance, that in which the heart was placed to an unusual extent to the right, the flaps of the valve were situated behind and to the right of the right portion of the sternum, the valve extending from the level of the upper edge of the fourth cartilage to that of the lower edge of the fifth. The tendinous cords, and the papillary muscles took an oblique direction downwards, and they were seated almost entirely behind the right half of the sternum.

The position of the tricuspid valve corresponds with the position of the right ventricle, the valve occupying about the lower two-thirds of the cavity.

THE RELATION OF THE LUNGS TO THE HEART.

The extent to which the lungs covered the heart varied much in different examples. In two instances the heart was almost concealed by the lungs, the edges of which were separated over the lower portion of the right ventricle by a mere chink, which widened out to three-quarters of an inch at the inferior border of the heart. In other instances the lungs had receded from before the heart to such an extent that almost the whole organ and the great vessels were exposed to view, though in no instance were they entirely uncovered.

The space where the heart comes to the surface, which is bounded above and at the sides by the lungs, and below by the liver and stomach, was sometimes triangular in shape (in 10 of 60 cases), but was usually four-sided (50 in 60).

The superficial "cardiac space" was triangular in shape in the two instances just noticed in which that space was very small, the width at the lower boundary of the heart being three-quarters of an inch; and in an instance of an opposite kind in which the base of the triangle, which always corresponded with the lower boundary of the heart, was four and a half inches wide. In this instance the lower boundary or base of the superficial space of the heart was wider than in any other. The base of the triangular superficial cardiac space presented every intermediate gradation of breadth between the extreme instances just noticed. This triangular shape is favourable to the covering of every part of the heart with lung except the right ventricle, for, while the anterior wall of the right ventricle was laid bare to a greater or less extent in these cases, as it was in every case under observation, in but one of them was the apex of the heart exposed, while in only two of them the right auricle, the aorta and pulmonary artery were also somewhat uncovered.

The superficial cardiac space was in all these cases actually triangular in shape, the lower limit or base of the triangle being the lower border of the heart. If, however, the lower boundary of the heart had occupied a lower position in relation to the adjoining margins and the lower boundaries of the lungs, then that space would have been four-sided in shape in the majority of these instances (6 in 10); for in them the inner border of the left lung, after it had left the heart, curved in a downward direction. If, therefore, the heart had not shrunk upwards in these instances, the superficial cardiac space would, like the other cases, have been four-sided in shape.

When, as is usually the case, the superficial space of the heart is bounded by four sides,[1] the heart, which moulds for itself a place between and within the lungs, comes forwards to the surface at that part where the organ is massive and its walls are powerful. The

---

[1] I have grouped the remainder of the cases, amounting to fifty, under the common heading of those in which the superficial space of the heart was bounded by four sides, but in seven of these cases the space was almost triangular in shape, and in a few other instances irregularity in outline modified the typical four-sided form of the space.

inner edge of the right lung descends in a straight line behind the sternum, but the edge of the left lung leaves the right lung, and deviates to the left at a variable point. This deviating edge of the upper lobe of the left lung, which is suspended like a curtain above the upper margin of the superficial space of the heart, describes a double curve, first convex, where it leaves the right lung, and then concave, where it begins to dip downwards to form the outer edge of the space. It then, as I have already observed, again tends to curve inwards, and to form the tongue of lung that enfolds the apex of the heart. The breadth of the cardiac space, measured along its base at the lower boundary of the heart, varied from an inch and a half to four inches and a third (4·3 inch). The breadth of the lower boundary of the superficial cardiac space varied in three-fourths of the cases (37 in 50) from two to four inches ; it was less than two inches in one-fifth of them (9 in 50), two-thirds of these being youthful; and it was above four inches in four of them.

The superficial cardiac space was, as a rule, narrower at its upper than at its lower boundary (in 35 of 50 cases); but sometimes this was reversed, the space being narrower below than above (in 10 of 50 cases). In a few instances (5) the space was of equal breadth above and below.

The lower boundary of the superficial cardiac space measured less than three inches in all but one of those instances in which it was narrower than the upper boundary of that space.

The inner borders of the right and left lungs were in contact with each other behind the upper portion of the sternum so as to cover the great vessels in three-fifths of the cases under examination (in 35 of 59). In the remaining two-fifths of the cases (24 in 59) a space varying in width from the eighth of an inch to an inch and a half was interposed between the inner borders of the right and left lungs at the upper part of the front of the chest. In one-third of these instances (7 in 24) the space between the edges of the lungs was less than the third of an inch, so that, practically, these cases may be added to those in which the edges of the lung were in contact, which brings up their proportion to three-fourths of the total number of cases observed (42 in 59).

The point of separation and divergence of the left and right lungs in these cases, including those in which the lungs were nearly in contact, varied from the level of the first intercostal space to that of the fifth cartilage. In three-fourths of the cases this point of separation varied in position from the level of the second space to that of the fourth cartilage.

In the seventeen cases in which the lungs were separated from each other over the great vessels to an extent ranging from almost half an inch to an inch and a half, the position of the point of divergence of the right and left lungs varied from the level of the first cartilages to that of the third, the level of the second cartilages and second spaces being the more usual situation of the point of divergence in this group of cases.

There was much variation in the relative size of the right and left lungs. The two lungs were about of equal size in more than one-fourth of the cases (17 in 59), the right lung was larger than the left in nearly one-half of them (27 in 59), and the left lung was larger than the right in one-fourth of them (15 in 59).

Although the right lung was so often larger than the left, yet the base of the left lung was lower at the side than that of the right lung three times more often than the reverse, the bases of the two lungs being on the same level in one-fourth of the cases (14 in 57).

When the right and left lungs met together behind the upper half of the sternum to form a covering over the great vessels, the margin of the right lung extended to the left of a line drawn down the middle of the bone more often than that of the left lung extended to the right of that line in the proportion of 35 to 15, while in nine instances the edges of the two lungs lay in contact behind the middle line of the sternum.

Below the point of separation of the two lungs, while the left lung deviated, as we have seen, extensively to the left, the right lung usually (in 42 of 60 cases) deviated at first very slightly and then more definitely to the right, so that at its lower anterior border the left inner margin of the right lung at the level of the lower boundary of the heart was usually situated to the right of the middle line of the sternum, the extent to which it did so varying from the tenth of an inch to an inch and three-quarters. In less than one-third of the cases (18 in 60) the left margin of the right lung, at or a little above, the level of the lower boundary of the heart, extended to the left of the middle line of the sternum.

When the superficial cardiac space was small, measuring less than two inches across, the inner margin of the right lung extended to the left of the centre of the chest in three-fifths of the cases (10 in 18). When, however, the space was of medium size (2 to 3 inches wide), the right lung passed to the left of the middle line in less than one-fifth of the cases (4 in 21); and when the space was large (above 3 inches wide), the right lung extended thus to the left of the middle line over the superficial cardiac space in only one-tenth of the cases (2 in 21).

The upper boundary of the superficial cardiac space, which is an important landmark to the clinical worker, is formed by the lower anterior border of the upper lobe of the left lung after it deviates from its point of separation from the right lung. I have already described the direction and nature of this curve.

The margin of lung, which thus forms the upper boundary of the superficial cardiac space, lay immediately behind one or other of the left costal cartilages or their spaces, and it generally took the downward direction of the cartilage behind which it lay, or was somewhat more inclined. It generally lay behind one cartilage or space, from the point at which it left the sternum to the point where it curved downwards to form the left border of the superficial cardiac space.

It sometimes, however, took a more oblique direction downwards, and crossed from behind one cartilage to behind the next space below, and then, after crossing that space, it spent itself behind the next cartilage below. The upper boundary of the cardiac space varied in position from the level of the second left costal cartilage to that of the fifth, but it was most frequently present behind the third or fourth cartilage or the fourth space, being thus situated in three-fifths of the cases (35 in 60).

In three of the cases the surface of the heart exposed below the lower edge of the left lung was a mere belt composed of the lower boundary of the right ventricle, this belt being from two inches to two inches and a half in diameter from side to side, and from a fifth to a little over one-half of an inch from above downwards. The heart had been lifted upwards behind the lungs by great distension of the stomach and intestines in these three cases, and the front of the cage of the chest had been also lifted upwards by the same agency, while the lungs had expanded downwards under the influence of the forward movement of the ribs.

EXTENT TO WHICH THE SURFACE OF THE HEART IS EXPOSED.

In every instance more or less of the right ventricle was uncovered. A very small portion of the right ventricle was exposed in the two instances in which there was a narrow longitudinal chink over the front of the heart, and in the three in which the exposed surface of the organ was a very narrow belt extending from right to left along the lower border of the ventricle.

In nearly one-half of the cases (25 in 60) the right ventricle was the only part of the heart that was exposed at the superficial cardiac space. In five other cases the apex of the heart was the only additional part brought into view by the lateral withdrawal of the lung. In almost one-half of the cases (25 in 60) the apex of the heart was in contact with the walls of the chest, the pericardium intervening; and in one-third of them (19 in 60) the higher portion of the left ventricle was also exposed to a greater or less extent. In only one instance was the whole of the narrow anterior portion of the left ventricle laid bare. In the rest of the cases, more or less of the upper portion of the left ventricle was covered by the edge of the left lung where it overlaps the front of the heart.

The right auricle was uncovered to a greater or less extent in one-fifth of the cases (11 in 59,) and in all but three of these its auricular appendix was also apparent. In one instance the whole of the auricle was exposed. The tip of the auricle was just visible in eight additional cases.

The whole of the ascending portion of the aorta was exposed to view in nine instances, and it was visible on its right side in three, on its left side in four, and at its middle in one. Thus the aorta was more or less exposed in nearly one-fourth of the cases.

The whole of the pulmonary artery was laid bare in only one instance, but in eight other cases the right side of the vessel, and in five others the left side of the vessel, was respectively exposed. The arterial cone of the right ventricle was completely covered by the lungs in one-third of the cases (20 in 59). In certain cases (10) a very small portion of the cone was uncovered just below the point of separation of the right and left lungs. These cases may practically be added to those in which the cone was completely concealed, so that, with this reservation, it may be said that the cone was covered with lung in one-half of the cases (31 in 59). In several instances, only one-fourth of the arterial cone was exposed, while in one instance the whole of it was uncovered. Between these extreme cases there was every variety in the extent to which the cone was brought into view.

FRONT VIEW; DURING LIFE.

We have just seen that after death the healthy heart and great vessels, and the different parts composing them, present great variety in position; and that although perhaps in no two instances do those parts occupy precisely the same relative situation, yet in a considerable proportion of the cases, and within certain limits, they present a standard or average position.

During life in like manner the healthy heart and great vessels vary much in relative situation, yet those parts, within certain orderly limits, regulated and modified by the various demands of life, maintain a standard or average position.

It is evident that during life, when the heart is at work and in motion, sending blood to and receiving blood from the lungs and every part of the frame, the position of the heart and great vessels is different from what it is when observed in the dead body. A knowledge of the position of the heart and the great vessels during life, when in active motion, is essential to the clinical worker, and not merely that of the anatomy of the dead organ.

I shall here, therefore, endeavour to describe the average position of the heart and great vessels in the living frame, from the study of the situation of those parts after death and during life, and of the movements of the heart when in action, and when influenced by respiration.

When the exertions of the body are prolonged and powerful, the heart acts with corresponding power; it receives and distributes more blood than when the body is at rest, and its size, and that of its great vessels, become enlarged. When, however, the body is in repose the heart's action is weakened; it receives and sends out less blood, and its size and that of its great vessels are diminished. The used power and the size of the heart, and the supply of blood to and from the organ, strictly balance the actual demands of the body, whether in action or at rest.

Under the like circumstances the lungs, answering to the demands on respiration, enlarge or lessen in size, and the volume of the cage of the chest is correspondingly larger or smaller, while the pitch of the diaphragm is lower or higher, so as directly to depress or elevate the heart. As the result, therefore, of these changes, thus induced by respiration, the heart, when it enlarges during exertion, is low and deep, and when it lessens during rest, is high and superficial.

In a corresponding manner, and for the same reasons, the heart is large, low, and deep in strong labouring men, while it is small, high, and shallow in weak youths of sedentary habits. In women and in children the heart is proportionally smaller and higher than in adult men ; and in the scale of life, from infancy to old age, the heart tends proportionally to increase in size, and to become lower and deeper in position.

In order that we may have before us the movements of the heart and great vessels during the varied exercises of life, I shall, before describing the position of those parts in the living body, give a brief account of the action of the heart, of the currents of blood through the cavities of the heart, and of the movements of the heart caused by respiration.

MOVEMENTS OF THE HEART. (See Figs. 16, 17, 22, 23.)

I have observed, with the valuable assistance of Dr. Broadbent, the movements of the heart in the dog and the donkey, when under the influence of chloroform ; and from those observations, and the careful examination of the human heart in many subjects, I have constructed figures 16, 17, 22 and 23, representing the heart in man in the opposite conditions of complete ventricular contraction and dilatation. In figures 16 and 17, the direction and extent of the movements of the walls during the ventricular systole are represented by arrows.

The appearance of the heart in motion is very striking. The ventricles during their systole, contract from all sides upon their own centre and become wrinkled, and the arteries and veins on their surface are full and tortuous, while the auricles become purple, plump, and glistening. During the diastole, the aspect is reversed. The ventricles enlarge and become smooth, their superficial vessels almost disappearing, while the auricles shrink, and become pale and wrinkled.

The Systole of the Ventricles.—During the systole, the ventricles, when looked at in front, contract from all sides towards a given centre, which is situated on the right ventricle a little to the right of the septum, about midway between the origin of the pulmonary

artery and the lower boundary of the ventricle, where it rests up
diaphragm.   The contraction of the right ventricle, owing
position at the front of the heart, and its consequent complet
posure, is marked and vigorous.   The whole right margin of
ventricle, at its juncture to the auricle, moves extensively from
to left; while its left margin, at the longitudinal furrow or se
between the ventricles, moves to a comparatively slight degree
left to right.   At the same time the top of the ventricle, a
origin of the pulmonary artery, descends, while its lower b
where it rests on the diaphragm, ascends.

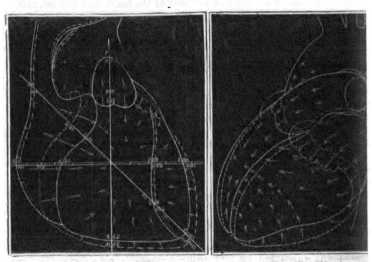

Fig. 16.—Front view.   Fig. 17.—Side view.

The *continuous* lines indicate the position of the outlines of the various parts
heart during the *systole* of the ventricles ; the *interrupted* lines indicate the po
of the same parts during the *diastole* of the ventricles ; the arrows point ot
direction and extent of the movements of the walls of the heart during the *s*
Fig. 16 shows the transverse, vertical, and oblique measurements in millin
during the systole and the diastole.

The point of rest towards which these various movements conv
corresponds closely with the attachment of the anterior papillary mu
The right auricle and superior vena cava are distended, and
pulmonary artery is enlarged and lengthened simultaneously with
contraction of the ventricle.   The auricle, which just before
wrinkled, becomes full; and its auricular portion and left edge n
rapidly inwards, and to the left, so as to replace the ventricle.
movement of the auricular portion is remarkable.   It suddenly
larges and becomes purple, and its tip moves from the right to
left edge of the sternum, at the level of the third costal cartilage.

The vigorous contraction of the left ventricle is only visible at its apex and along its left border, since the rest of the cavity is hidden by the right ventricle. The apex has a revolving movement, upwards, forwards, and to the right. The left border of the ventricle, like the apex, moves forwards and to the right; but while the portion of the ventricle near the apex ascends, the portion near the base descends. The appendix of the left auricle, which during the diastole of the ventricle is scarcely visible, descends during the systole, and moves rapidly forwards and downwards, so as to replace the retreating ventricles, and to fill up the angle between them and the pulmonary artery.

When we remove the left ribs and look at the heart from the left side so as to obtain a profile view, the animal lying upon the back, we see that the whole left ventricle moves forwards during the systole, the posterior wall advancing much more than the anterior; and that the base of the ventricle descends, while the apex ascends, so that apex and base approximate. It is difficult to fix upon the precise zone of rest of the ventricular walls towards which the apex ascends and the base descends, but it is somewhere about the middle of the ventricle, nearer, perhaps, to the apex than the base. This region of stable equilibrium corresponds to a similar point of rest in the papillary muscles. Owing to this arrangement, the ventricles and their valves adjust themselves to each other during the ventricular contraction.

The left auricle, like the right, enlarges during the systole, and as the base of the ventricle then descends and advances, the ventricular attachment of the swollen auricle descends likewise, apparently, as it were, pushing the base of the ventricle before it.

When the left ventricle propels its contents into the aorta, the arch of the aorta is distended and lengthened, and its root, like that of the pulmonary artery, descends. The arch of the aorta enlarges both in length and breadth, and becomes tense and rigid. Its lateral enlargement is small, but its elongation is considerable; and its orifice, like that of the pulmonary artery, descends during the systole.

During the systole, the auricles and great vessels enlarge, and descend into the place just left by the retreating ventricles; there is, therefore, more blood at the base of the heart at the end of the systole than at the end of the diastole. Since, however, during the systole, both ventricles contract, the increase of the blood at the base probably balances its diminution towards the apex. During the pause which follows the dilatation of the ventricles, the blood continues to flow into the auricle so that the amount of blood in the heart and great vessels is greater just before the ventricular systole than at any other period.

Movements of the Papillary Muscles.—That I might observe the action of the papillary muscles, I removed the anterior wall of the right ventricle when the heart was beating *in situ;* and I found that the tip of the anterior papillary muscle of the right ventricle contracted towards the septum during the systole.

I then removed the septum, so as to expose the two papillary muscles

F 2

of the left ventricle, and I noticed that both the muscles, which
during the diastole were wide apart, approximated and came close
together during the systole. At the same time the muscles shortened
towards their own centre, so that their tips and their tendinous cords
descended to the left towards the apex of the ventricle, while their
roots of attachment near the apex ascended to the right towards the
base of the ventricle. The fixed point towards which the two ends
approximated corresponded apparently to the zone of rest, or stable
equilibrium, in the walls of the ventricle, towards which the base
and the apex of the ventricle approximate during the systole.

Action of the Mitral and Tricuspid Valves.—In order that I might
see the movements of the mitral and tricuspid valves, I cut out the
heart when beating vigorously, and immersed it in water. The
ventricles contracted with force, and expelled the water from the
great arteries during each systole. The jet from the aorta was six
inches in length. The segments of the mitral and tricuspid valves
were seen to come together at their notched and bead-like margins,
so as to close the valves during the systole, and prevent the efflux
of a drop of liquid.

At the beginning of each diastole the margins of the valves
separated quickly from each other, so as to admit the flow of water
freely into the cavity.

DIRECTION OF THE CURRENTS OF BLOOD IN THE CAVITIES OF THE HEART. (See Figs. 18, 19.)

In the left ventricle, the aperture of entrance, the mitral orifice, is
contiguous to the aperture of exit, the aortic orifice, the two orifices
being separated by a membranous septum consisting of the anterior
flap of the mitral valve. In the right ventricle, the aperture of
entrance, the tricuspid orifice is at a distance from the aperture
of exit at the pulmonary artery, the two orifices being separated by the muscular channel of the *conus arteriosus.* In the left
ventricle the current of blood inwards, which descends during the
diastole behind the anterior segment of the mitral valve, is parallel in
direction to the current of blood outwards, which ascends during the
systole in front of that segment. (Fig. 18.) In the right ventricle
the current of blood inwards is at right-angles to the current of blood
outwards, since the blood enters the cavity from right to left, and
leaves it from below upwards (Fig. 19). During the systole the stream
of blood in the left ventricle takes a spiral direction towards the aortic
orifice, in accordance with the direction of the aorta itself. The stream
of blood in the right ventricle, as it ascends, mounts over the bulging
septum, being restrained by the concave anterior wall of the ventricle.
This upward stream, which narrows as it ascends, thus takes the
curved direction upwards, backwards, and inwards of the *conus arteriosus* and the pulmonary artery. In the left ventricle, the anterior
segment of the mitral valve and the right and left papillary muscles,

form a hollow channel for the stream of blood, which, as it ascends to the aorta, presses upon the under-surface of the valve. In the right ventricle the stream of blood, as it ascends, sweeps onwards at right angles to the under-surface of the tricuspid valve, and rushes between and across the papillary muscles, and through the tendinous cordage that connects the muscles to the flaps of the valve.

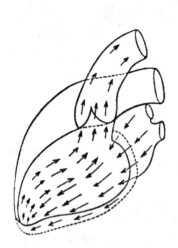 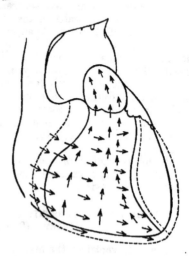

FIG. 18.—Showing the direction of the currents of the blood in the left side of the heart.

FIG. 19.—Showing the direction of the currents of the blood in the right side of the heart.

THE MOVEMENTS OF THE HEART CAUSED BY RESPIRATION.
(See Figs. 20, 21.)

During inspiration the diaphragm in its descent draws downwards the fibrous sac and floor of the pericardium, and the whole of its contents. The heart rests upon the central tendon of the diaphragm which forms the floor of the pericardium, and it therefore necessarily rises and falls with the rise and fall of the diaphragm. The descent of the diaphragm is accompanied by the advance of the anterior wall of the chest, which produces the corresponding expansion of the lungs anteriorly. The central tendon of the diaphragm forming the floor of the pericardium presents an inclined plane, upon which the heart glides forwards and downwards during inspiration, under the combined influence of the descent of the diaphragm and the forward movement of the ribs and sternum. Whatever be the cause of the altered level of the diaphragm, whether it contracts and descends, as in inspiration, or is pushed downwards by fluid or tumours in the chest — whether it is raised during expiration, or pushed upwards by distension of the stomach and intestines, by fluid in the abdomen, by abdominal tumours, or by abscess or other affections of the liver; whatever, in short, be the cause producing the ascent or descent of the diaphragm, a corresponding ascent or descent of the heart must ensue. The only exception is the displacement downwards of the central tendon of the diaphragm by means of effusion into the pericardial sac, when the fluid interposes itself between th

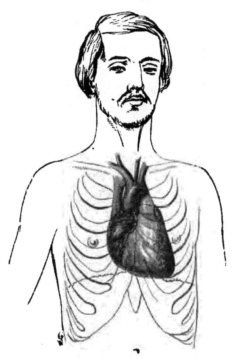

Fig. 20.—Showing the position of the heart and great vessels in relation to the walls of the chest, and the lungs in a healthy man *at the end of a forced expiration.*

heart and the diaphragm, with the effect of pushing the diaphragm downwards and the heart upwards. An important part is played by the pericardium in the influence of respiration on the position of the heart. The central tendon of the diaphragm forms the base of the pericardium, upon which the heart rests as upon a floor. The aponeurotic structure of the pericardium, which takes its origin from the central tendon, ascends so as to form a strong fibrous pouch which envelopes the whole heart, and gives off a fibrous investment to each of the great vessels as they enter or leave the pericardial sac. Through the medium of this aponeurotic structure, the diaphragm, during its descent, acts so as to draw downwards the great vessels simultaneously with the heart.

The respiratory movements of the heart are vertical. The organ and all its parts and great vessels move downwards during inspiration, and move upwards during expiration. While, therefore, the vertical relations of the heart and great vessels to the parietes of the chest

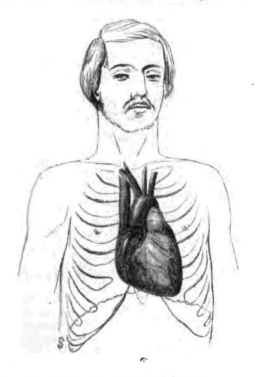

Fig. 21.—Showing the position of the heart and great vessels in relation to the walls of the chest, and the lungs in c healthy man *at the end of a deep inspiration.*
Note.—The lower boundary of the heart ought to have been somewhat lower in this figure.

are altered, the lateral relations of the various parts of the heart and great vessels to each other are unaltered, and their relative positions to the surrounding organs are not materially changed.

While the diaphragm descends during inspiration, carrying with it the heart, the front and sides of the cage of the chest, formed by the ribs and sternum, ascend. The change in the position of the heart in relation to the ribs and sternum is, therefore, doubled in extent by the twofold operation of the descent of the diaphragm and the heart simultaneously with the ascent of the cage of the chest.

Inspiration, besides causing the descent of the heart, produces also a lengthening and general enlargement of the organ and its great vessels. The lengthening of the heart and its vessels tells with decreasing effect from below upwards. The descent of the great vessels in the neck is much, but not completely, restrained by the attachments of those vessels. The innominate, the left carotid and the subclavian arteries, and the ascending aorta are elongated and straightened to a considerable extent, and as less blood is sent into those vessels during inspiration than during expiration, they are lessened in width at the same time that they are increased in length. The enlargement of the cavities of the heart is limited to the right side. The right auricle receives in increased quantity the blood which has been stored up in the hepatic and portal vessels and the great veins during expiration. The space in the vessels of the expanded lungs for the reception of blood is increased; the blood is sent with greater ease through the pulmonary artery from the right ventricle, in consequence of the enlargement of the pulmonary capillaries, and is at the same time sent in greater quantity from that cavity, because its supply of blood, derived from the auricle, is materially increased during inspiration. The venæ cavæ, the right auricle, the right ventricle, and the pulmonary artery are therefore enlarged both in length and width. The supply of blood to and from the right cavities of the heart, which is thus increased during inspiration, is then probably associated with a corresponding diminution in the supply of blood to and from the left cavities of the heart. The blood is retained in the pulmonary vessels in augmented quantity during inspiration. We may infer that less blood is sent then into the left auricle, and we know that less blood is sent then into the system through the arteries from the left ventricle, than during expiration.

The result of the various co-operating and contending forces which I have just considered are exhibited with, I believe, an approach to accuracy in Figs. 20 and 21, representing the position of the heart and great vessels in relation to the cage of the chest and the lungs at the end of a forced expiration, and at the end of a deep inspiration.

The greatest change in the relative position of the heart during inspiration takes place at its lower boundary, the descent of which is equal to that of the central tendon of the diaphragm, or at least one inch. The upward movement at the same time of the lower end of the sternum and the adjoining cartilages is about one inch also. The resulting change in the relative position of the lower boundary of the heart and the external walls ought to be, and I believe is, though I have not ascertained it by exact demonstration, about two inches. The ascertained change in the relative position of those parts is such, that the lower boundary of the right ventricle, at the end of expiration, is situated behind the lower end of the sternum, and at the end of inspiration, behind the lower end of the ensiform cartilage. The result during life, in a robust man, is that at the end of expiration, the impulse of the right ventricle may be perceptible to the left of the lower end of the sternum; while at the end of inspiration it is to be seen and felt beating with considerable force over, below, and to the left of the ensiform cartilage, or in other words, at the epigastrium. The heart has in fact descended into the space previously occupied by the liver and stomach, and instead of being protected at the part spoken of by a bony framework, is at the end of a deep inspiration only covered to each side of the ensiform cartilage by the abdominal muscles. The apex of the left ventricle descends to the same extent during a deep inspiration, or from the fifth rib to the seventh costal cartilage. The impulse at the apex, which at the end of expiration is often felt beating with force in the fourth intercostal space, is at the end of a deep inspiration quite imperceptible. I need not go through the whole of the details of the altered relative positions of the heart and great vessels in relation to the ribs and sternum during expiration, and at the end of a deep inspiration. They speak for themselves, and are exhibited in the accompanying figures. It will suffice, if I describe the altered bearings of the principal landmarks. A transverse boundary-line drawn across the top of the right auricle and right ventricle corresponds with the attachment of the great vessels to the heart. This transverse line, which marks the position of the aorta above the right auricle, and the commencement of the pulmonary artery, extends at the end of expiration across the second intercostal spaces, and the intervening portion of the sternum a little below the manubrium; while at the end of inspiration it crosses the lower boundary of the third intercostal spaces and the intermediate portion of the sternum. The pulmonary artery descends from the second to the third intercostal space, and the visible commencement of the aorta makes a corresponding descent behind the sternum. The top of the arch of the aorta which at the beginning of a deep inspiration is a little below the top of the manubrium, is, at the end of it, at or a little above the lower end of that bone.

The vertical and forward respiratory movements of the heart explain the difference in the position of the heart in relation to the walls of the chest in weak persons with flat chests on the one hand, and in those who are full-chested and robust on the other. The relations of the heart and great vessels to the cage of the chest follow the type of expiration in the feeble, and the type of inspiration in the strong.

FRONT VIEW OF THE HEART AND GREAT VESSELS IN A HEALTHY MAN WITH A WELL-FORMED CHEST. (See Figs. 22, 23.)

The heart and great vessels occupy the central region of the chest. The lower boundary of the right ventricle is situated behind the ensiform cartilage, and is about half an inch or more below the lower

end of the osseous sternum;[1] and the top of the arch of the a
at the origin of the innominate and left carotid arteries, is about
an inch or more below the upper end of the sternum.

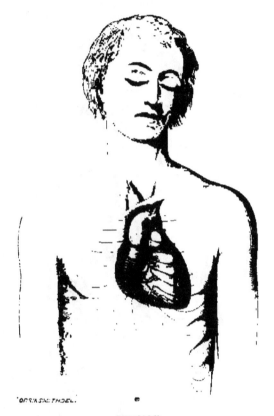

SYSTOLE.

FIG. 22.—Showing the position and relative size of the various cavities of the heart
of the great vessels during the ventricular systole in a healthy, well-formed man.

Note.—The fifth cartilages were unusually high in the body from which figures 22
23 were taken.

The breadth of the heart is about one-half of the breadth of t
chest. The heart, at its extreme limits, extends for a little more th

1 All the works on the diagnosis of the diseases of the heart with which I
acquainted, whether published in this country or in Germany, represent the lo
boundary of the heart as being situated above the lower end of the sternum. Severa
these works have evidently taken their figures from Luschka's well-known drawi
which gives undoubtedly an accurate view of the heart and the surrounding parts in t

one-third of its breadth into the right side of the chest, and for a little less than two-thirds of its breadth into the left side of the chest, or in that proportion to the right and left of a vertical line drawn down the middle of the sternum.

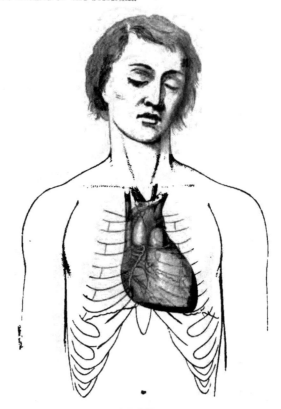

DIASTOLE.

Fig. 23.—Showing the position and relative size of the various cavities of the heart and of the great vessels during the diastole of the ventricles in a healthy, well-formed man.

During the systole of the ventricles the proportion of the heart in the left side of the chest lessens, owing to the inward contraction of

dead body from which it was taken. It gives, however, on that very account, an inaccurate view of the relative position of the heart in the living man.

I have just stated that the lower boundary of the heart is situated behind the ensiform cartilage, about half an inch or more below the lower end of the osseous sternum, and have done so on the following grounds :—

(1.) At the time of death the heart is raised by the elevation of the diaphragm during the final expiration. After death the heart contracts upwards towards its higher points the left border of the left ventricle, while that in the right side of the chest increases, owing to the outward expansion of the right border of the right auricle.

The boundary line across the sternum, between the upper border of the heart and the lower limit of the great vessels, is on a level with the third costal cartilages.

The lower boundary of the heart extends, with a slight inclination downwards, from about half an inch below the lower end of the sternum to the fifth left space, just above or on a level with the upper edge of the sixth left cartilage. The lower boundary of the heart ascends during the systole of the ventricle, and descends during its diastole; it descends also during ordinary inspiration, and ascends during ordinary expiration for about the third of an inch. A deep inspiration may bring down the lower border of the heart to the lower end of the ensiform cartilage, and a forced expiration may raise it to or above the level of the lower end of the sternum.

The left boundary of the heart at its apex is situated to the left of the junction of the fifth rib to its costal cartilage, and behind or to the left of a vertical line drawn downwards from the left nipple.[1] The right boundary of the heart extends about an inch to the right of the right edge of the sternum.

The Right Side of the Heart.—The right cavities occupy the whole front of the heart with the exception of its left portion, where the

---

of attachment, so as to leave an average space of half an inch between the lower boundary of the heart and the lower boundary of the *front* of the pericardium; that space being the exact measure of the upward shrinking of the heart after death. The lower boundary of the heart was situated behind the end of the osseous sternum in one-fifth, and below that point in two-fifths of my cases, while it was above that point in two-fifths of them. The lower boundary of the *front* of the pericardium, which marks the position of the lower boundary of the heart itself at the time of death, was behind the lower end of the sternum in one-fifth, and below that point (being situated behind the upper portion of the ensiform cartilage) in two-thirds of my cases, while it was above that point in only one-eighth of them.

(2). We have already seen (pp. 16, 17) that there is a general correspondence between the relation of the lower boundary of the right ventricle to the end of the osseous sternum, and the relation of the lower border of the apex of the heart to the inferior edge of the fifth costal cartilage and rib. The inferior edge of the junction of the fifth cartilage and rib was on a lower level than the end of the sternum by from a quarter of an inch to an inch and a quarter in 60 out of 71 cases, was on the same level in five, and was above that level in six instances. It is evident that, with few exceptions, the apex-beat could not be felt in the fifth space if the lower boundary of the heart were situated above the end of the sternum.

(3). The lower edge of the anterior portion of the right lung at its left border corresponds, as a rule, with the lower boundary of the heart at the same situation. In six cases the lower edge of that portion of the right lung was behind or on a level with the lower end of the sternum; in three it was above that point to the extent of half an inch; and in twenty it was below that point to an extent varying from a quarter of an inch to an inch and a half, or, in one exceptional case, two inches. We may therefore infer that the lower boundary of the heart was situated in two-thirds of these cases behind the ensiform cartilage, in one-fifth of them, behind the lower end of the osseous sternum, and in only one-tenth of them above that end of the bone.

[1] I have made comparatively few observations as to the position of the left nipple in relation to the junction of the adjoining ribs to their cartilages and the left boundary of the heart at its apex.

left ventricle comes into view from behind the right ventricle to the extent of an inch in breadth. The transverse or auriculo-ventricular furrow forms the external apparent separation between the right auricle and right ventricle. The auriculo-ventricular furrow sweeps backwards and forwards to so great an extent, to the left during the systole, and to the right during the diastole, that it presents no fixed position during life, but ranges to and fro between certain limits. The upper end of the furrow may be situated at the left edge or at the middle line of the sternum, on a level with the third cartilage; and its lower end may be placed a little below and to the right of the lower end of the sternum, being behind the sternal end of the seventh cartilage, but it may extend for fully half an inch to the right of this position. The transverse furrow thus crosses behind the lower half of the sternum obliquely from left to right, and from above downwards. The upper third of the transverse furrow forms a true line of separation between the auricular appendix and the arterial cone of the right ventricle; but the lower two-thirds of the furrow lie about half an inch to the right of the tricuspid orifice and the line of division between the right auricle and the right ventricle. The right transverse or "auriculo-ventricular" furrow is not therefore at this part of its course a true line of separation between the right auricle and ventricle, but is thrown half an inch to the right of that line by the presence there of the right coronary vessels, and the couch of fat in which they are embedded.

The Right Auricle—The right auricle is broad above, where it widens out into the auricular appendix, especially during the systole, and lies behind the middle of the sternum, reaching from its right often to its left edge, on a level with the third cartilages; and it is narrow below, where it appears to come to a point at the lower end of the transverse furrow, to the right of the lower end of the sternum. The real or internal breadth of the right auricle is, as I have just explained, greater than its apparent or external breadth along the line of the transverse furrow. When, therefore, the lower portion of that furrow is situated a little to the right of the sternum, the lower portion of the tricuspid orifice is covered by the lower end of the sternum, a little to the right of the middle line of that bone. The right boundary of the auricle extends behind the right costal cartilages for about an inch beyond the right edge of the sternum.

The right auricle undergoes more change in form during the action of the heart than any other portion of the organ. During the systole of the ventricles the auricle retains its length, but it becomes twice as wide, and its whole surface, instead of being pale and wrinkled, is purple, plump, and glistening. The ventricular border moves extensively to the left, so as to pass from the right margin to the middle line of the sternum, while its right border expands a little to the right. There is a slight descent of the upper and lower borders of the right auricle during the contraction of the ventricles. During the diastole of the ventricles these appearances and movements are reversed.

The Right Ventricle.—The right ventricle forms the solid muscular front of the heart, and is flanked to the right by the right auricle, and to the left by that small portion of the left ventricle that comes into view in front of the heart, and forms its left border.

The right ventricle, when exposed to view in front of the heart, presents a pyramidal shape. The base of the pyramid is formed by the lower boundary of the ventricle, which rests on the central tendon of the diaphragm, and extends, with a slight obliquity downwards and from right to left, from the right auricle to the apex of the left ventricle; its upper border is crowned by the pulmonary artery, which forms the apex of the pyramid; its left border is formed by the longitudinal furrow, which divides the right from the left ventricle; and its ostensible right border by the transverse furrow which apparently separates the right auricle from the right ventricle, the actual separation of those two cavities at the tricuspid orifice being situated, as I have just stated, about half an inch to the left of the transverse furrow.

The right ventricle, in its vertical diameter or length, extends from the third left cartilage to the sixth, which are the cardiac cartilages. In its transverse diameter, or breadth, the right ventricle extends from the transverse furrow, at or to the right of the right edge of the sternum below, and somewhat to the right of the left edge of the sternum above, to the anterior longitudinal furrow, which is situated behind or a little to the right of the junction of the left costal cartilages to their ribs from the third to the fifth.

The length or vertical measurement of the ventricle is greater than its breadth or transverse measurement, in the proportion of about four to three. The body of the ventricle forms about the lower two-thirds of the cavity extending from the fourth left cartilage to the sixth, and the *conus arteriosus* forms about the upper third of the cavity extending from the third left cartilage to the fourth. The arterial cone of the right ventricle narrows from below upwards until it ends in the pulmonary artery, and the breadth of the cone a little below the origin of the pulmonary artery in relation to that of the body of the right ventricle, is in the proportion of nearly three to five, or in other words, the width of the cone is nearly three-fifths of the width of the body of the right ventricle.

Owing to the arterial cone being so much narrower than the body of the right ventricle, especially at its right border, the transverse furrow extends further to the left at its upper than at its lower border by more than an inch. In consequence of this great deviation towards its upper end the transverse furrow presents a double curve, which, looking to the right, is concave above, where the rounded auricular appendix fits into the hollow profile of the arterial cone; and convex below, where it is situated half an inch to the right of the tricuspid orifice.

The longitudinal furrow takes a downward direction, with a slight inclination to the left, this inclination to the left increasing rapidly towards the lower end where it approaches the apex. In consequence of this, the longitudinal furrow also presents a double curve, which, looking to the left is convex above, concave below. The deviation to the left of the lower end of the longitudinal furrow is caused by the deviation to the left of the cavity of the right ventricle as it approaches the apex of the heart. The furrow between the ventricles turns to the left at its inferior extremity, and, so to speak, cuts through the apex of the heart. The apex of the heart is thus composed of the apex of the left ventricle and the adjoining left end of the lower border of the right ventricle.

During the contraction of the right ventricle its four sides approximate towards a point of rest or stable equilibrium, which is situated on the anterior wall of the cavity, over or close to the attachment of the anterior papillary muscle, a little to the left of the longitudinal furrow, and slightly nearer to the lower than the upper border of the ventricle. The movement of the transverse furrow to the left is extensive, and that of the longitudinal furrow to the right is slight; the downward movement of the upper border at the origin of the pulmonary artery is considerable, and the upward movement of the lower border of the ventricle is somewhat less. The right border of the *conus arteriosus* moves less to the left than the right border of the ventricle at the tricuspid orifice. At the same time the surface of the ventricle becomes wrinkled, and its coronary vessels start out from the surface and become tortuous. During the dilatation of the ventricle the reverse movements take place, its surface becomes smooth, glistening, and rounded, and the vessels on its surface cease to be prominent. (See Fig. 16, page 66.)

The Left Ventricle.—The left ventricle, where seen in front, comes into view to the left of the right ventricle, and forms the convex left border of the heart. The left ventricle forms here a comparatively long, narrow slip, extending from the third left space down to the fifth, and from the longitudinal furrow behind or to the right of the junction of the corresponding ribs to their cartilages, to the left border of the heart, which reaches up to or just beyond the left nipple. This visible anterior portion of the left ventricle is of the greatest width at and below its middle, behind the fourth space and the fifth cartilage. Above and below this region the ventricle narrows, coming to a point at the apex below, and above bearing to the right, where it is finally hidden by the appendix of the left auricle. The breadth of the anterior visible portion of the ventricle at its widest part is about one-fifth of the breadth of the heart.

The apex of the heart occupies the fifth space, its lower border being situated just above or behind the upper edge of the sixth cartilage and rib, and its left border being at or a little beyond a vertical line drawn down from the nipple.

During the contraction of the left ventricle the right and left borders of its visible anterior portion both move a little to the right, its base and upper portion descend, and its lower portion and apex ascend, both portions moving forwards and to the right. (See Fig. 17, page 66.)

The Appendix of the Left Auricle is situated behind the third left cartilage close to its junction with the third rib, and fills up the angle or space between the upper end of the left and right ventricles, at the top of the longitudinal furrow, and the left boundary of the origin of the pulmonary artery.

The left auricular appendix is much more prominent and extensive during the contraction of the ventricles, when its right and lower borders move respectively considerably to the right and downwards, and its left and upper borders move obliquely to the right and slightly downwards, than it is during the dilatation of the ventricles, when the auricular appendix shrinks inwards upon itself.

The Great Vessels.—The great vessels lie side by side, the ascending aorta being in the centre, the pulmonary artery to the left, and the superior vena cava to the right, behind the upper portion of the sternum and the adjoining costal cartilages, at and above the level of the third cartilage.

The Arch of the Aorta.—The root of the aorta, including the aortic orifice, valve, and sinuses, is hidden in the centre of the heart. The ascending aorta comes into view just above the appendix of the right auricle, on a level with the third costal cartilages, and is covered by the sternum, the right border of the artery being situated behind or a little to the left of the right edge of the sternum ; and its left border, which is partially covered by the right border of the pulmonary artery, being about a quarter of an inch or less to the right of the left edge of the sternum. As the arch of the aorta ascends, it bears to the left, and at the point where it gives origin to the innominate artery, it is exactly behind the middle line of the sternum. From this point the transverse aorta ascends slightly until it gives origin to the left carotid artery, whence it curves backwards and slightly downwards, with an inclination to the left, and gives off the left sub-clavian artery, the last of its three great branches. The left carotid arises just within a line drawn downwards from the sternal end of the left clavicle, and the left subclavian just without that line. The part at which the innominate and left carotid arteries take their origin is the highest point of the arch, and is situated about three quarters of an inch or rather less below the top of the manubrium, as far as the breadth of the innominate artery to the left of a line drawn down the middle of that bone, and in front of the lower portion of the body of the third or the upper portion of that of the fourth dorsal vertebra, which corresponds with the third dorsal spine, which is situated mid-way between the spines of the scapulæ. The transverse aorta, as it curves backwards, to the left and downwards, rests first on the front and left side of the trachea, and then upon the left side of the œsophagus, and is situated between the manubrium, just to the left of the middle line, from three-quarters of an inch or less below the top of the bone down to its lower end in front; and the left side of the body of the fourth and the upper portion of the fifth dorsal vertebra behind. The relations of the transverse aorta to the manubrium in front are very variable, but those to the dorsal vertebræ behind are less so.

The deep left border of the descending portion of the arch may be seen in a front view, and this border is situated in succession behind the left and lower portion of the manubrium, near its junction to the first rib, the first space and the sternal portion of the second left costal cartilage, and the adjoining portion of the sternum. The relations of this important portion of the arch will be considered when the side and back views of the heart and great vessels are described.

The ascending aorta just above the right auricular appendix descends slightly during the contraction of the ventricles; but the top of the arch, at the origin of the innominate and left carotid arteries, is scarcely moved during the contraction of the heart. Inspiration causes the descent of the ascending and transverse aorta and its great branches. This descent is slight during ordinary breathing, but is considerable on a deep inspiration. The inspiratory descent of the arch of the aorta is much less than that of the root of the aorta and heart.

The Pulmonary Artery.—The origin of the pulmonary artery is situated behind the upper portion of the third left cartilage, and its top lies behind the second left cartilage. As the artery ascends to the left of the ascending aorta, it occupies the second left space and cartilage for four-fifths of its breadth, and is covered by the left border of the sternum for the remaining fifth. The pulmonary artery, at its origin, is situated just above and within the appendix of the left auricle; and, as it proceeds on its course, it makes for the hollow of the arch of the aorta, through which it sends its right branch. Its direction is therefore much more from before backwards than from below upwards. The remaining course of the artery cannot be seen in front, and will be considered when the side and back views of the heart and great vessels are described.

During the contraction of the right ventricle the pulmonary artery descends at its origin to a considerable extent, and the higher parts of the artery also descend, but less and less from below upwards. At the same time the whole artery enlarges and lengthens. The pulmonary artery descends also during inspiration, but to a less extent than the body of the right ventricle, and less at its upper part than at its origin.

The Superior Vena Cava.—The superior vena cava receives the right and left innominate veins a little below the level of the top of the arch of the aorta, behind the right portion of the manubrium, midway between the upper and lower end of the bone. The right innominate vein descends behind the sternal end of the right clavicle, and the left innominate vein crosses in front of the three great arteries, just at or above their origin from the arch of the aorta. The superior vena cava descends immediately to the right of the sternum behind the first space, the second cartilage and the second space, and it opens into the right auricle behind the third right costal cartilage.

The superior vena cava descends slightly at its point of entrance into the right auricle during the contraction of the ventricle. It descends also during the inspiration, but to a greater extent.

The Relation of the Lungs to the Heart in Front.—The lungs cover the great vessels and the whole of the heart except the more prominent portion of the right ventricle which is behind the cardiac cartilages.

The inner margins of the right and left lungs in front meet together behind the upper two-thirds of the sternum, the right lung, as a rule, passing to the left of the centre of the sternum, so as to encroach somewhat on the left side of the chest. The inner margin of the left lung separates from that of the right lung, and diverges to the left on a level with the fourth left costal cartilage. Thence the lower border of this portion of the lung extends to the left, lying behind the lower edge of the fourth cartilage or the upper border of the fourth space, and in front of the body of the right ventricle. Before this border of the lung reaches the longitudinal furrow and the junction of the cartilages to the ribs, it curves downwards, crossing within the fourth space and the fifth cartilage, where it again curves to the right so as to form a hollow space for the lodgment of the apex of the heart. After crossing the fifth space the inner margin ends in the lower border of the upper lobe, which is situated behind the upper edge of the sixth cartilage and rib, where it soon ends in the septum that divides the upper from the lower lobe of the left lung. Owing to the outward and inward curve thus made by the inner margin of the left lung where it crosses the heart to form the left and lower border of the superficial cardiac space, a remarkable tongue of lung is formed by the inner and lower borders of the upper lobe of the left lung. This tongue of lung, owing to its free position just in front of the interlobular septum, wraps round the apex of the heart, being above, below, outside and in front of it, so as to adapt itself to every movement of the apex. When the apex advances it recedes, when the apex recedes it advances, and thus it allows free play to the apex at the same time that it softens the impulse of the apex upon the walls of the chest, and shields it, when it becomes again flaccid, and retires within its nest.

The inner margin of the right lung, after that of the left lung has deviated to the left, continues its course downwards, behind the sternum, being nearer to the left than the right edge of that bone. It thus completely covers the transverse furrow, the right border of the right ventricle, and the tricuspid orifice. This inner margin of the right lung inclines to the left before it reaches the lower boundary of the heart, where it soon ends in the lower margin of the right lung; which margin lies at first behind the upper part of the ensiform cartilage, then crosses behind the sternal portion of the seventh and sixth right cartilages, and afterwards takes its course to the right, behind or just above the sixth cartilage.

It is evident, from what has just been stated, that the lungs are moulded by a natural adaptation to the form and structure of the heart and great vessels. They thus cover the soft and yielding right auricle, which requires the additional protection of the soft covering in which it is thus imbedded; they thus cover the great vessels, which do not advance so far forwards as the body of the heart; they thus cover the circuit of the ventricles around the three sides of the superficial cardiac space; and they thus leave uncovered the most prominent and powerful portion of the right ventricle. Obeying this law of adaptation, the inner margin of the right lung extends inwards and to the left along its whole length, more than that of the left lung extends to the right; for the greater prominence of the pulmonary artery, of the *conus arteriosus*, and of the centre of the right ventricle, parts that are situated to the left of the middle line of the sternum, offers resistance to the free inward expansion to the right of the margin of the left lung. On the other hand, the less prominence of the ascending aorta, the soft and yielding character of the right auricle and its appendix, and the less prominence of the right border of the right ventricle, parts that are situated behind and to the right of the sternum, allow and even invite the more free inward expansion to the left of the inner margin of the right lung. The inner margins of the lungs, in short, advance freely where they meet with the least resistance, and stop or even recede where they meet with the greatest resistance.

The Orifices and Valves of the Heart and the Great Arteries.—The orifices and valves of the heart may be considered in two orders: (1) As they are superficial or deep in situation, when the pulmonic and tricuspid orifices and valves would come first, and then the aortic and mitral orifices and valves; and (2) as they are ranged from above downwards when the pulmonic orifice and valve come first in order, then the aortic, then the mitral, and last the tricuspid orifice and valve. I shall consider them in detail according to the first and most natural of those orders, namely, the superficial and deep orifices and valves, which are also the orifices and valves of the right or anterior and the left or posterior cavities. After doing so, I shall briefly indicate them, for the sake of their common connexion, in their order, from above downwards.

The orifice of the pulmonary artery is the highest of the four orifices, and its anterior portion is situated mainly behind the third left cartilage, its right border being covered by the adjoining edge of the sternum. During the systole of the ventricles the anterior portion of the orifice of the pulmonary artery descends into the third space.

The root of the pulmonary artery consists of two anterior sinuses and one posterior sinus, and its valve consists of two flaps in front and one behind, each in its own sinus. The position of the anterior flaps is higher than that of the posterior flap. The anterior or superficial convex wall of the right ventricle is much longer than its posterior or internal convex wall, owing to its outer wall being a section of a much larger sphere than its inner one. When, therefore, the right ventricle contracts, its anterior and outer wall shortens and draws downwards the anterior flaps of the pulmonic valve to a much greater extent than the posterior and inner wall shortens and draws downwards the posterior flap. The result is that when the right ventricle is in a state of complete contraction, the anterior and posterior flaps of the pulmonic valve are nearly on the same level; and that when the ventricle is in a state of distension the anterior flaps may be an inch higher than the posterior flap. This is well seen in several of Pirogoff's vertical sections.

The tricuspid orifice, is the lowest as well as the most superficial of the four orifices, and is separated from the orifice of the pulmonary artery by the *conus arteriosus* of the right ventricle. In a healthy active man with a well-formed chest, the tricuspid orifice is situated behind the lower fourth of the sternum to the right of the middle line of that bone, its upper border being on a level with the lower edge of the fourth cartilage, and its lower border being behind the lower end of the sternum, and the articulation to it of the right sixth cartilage.

The tricuspid orifice is situated about half an inch to the left of the right transverse auriculo-ventricular furrow. It is impossible to assign accurately a fixed position to the tricuspid orifice, owing to its extensive movement to the left during the contraction, and to the right during the dilatation of the right ventricle. The limits of the range of this movement may, however, be defined to the right by a line a little to the right of the sternum, and to the left by a line a little to the left of the middle line of that bone, the orifice playing backwards and forwards behind, and to the right of the right half of the lower portion of the sternum.

The position of the flaps, the tendinous cords, and the papillary muscles of the tricuspid valve have been already described in detail.[1] It will, therefore, be sufficient to say here that the papillary muscles radiate like a fan upwards, outwards, and downwards from the cords and flaps of the valve; that the superior papillary muscle, when present, ascends behind the fourth cartilage; that the anterior papillary muscle takes the direction outwards of the fifth cartilage; and that the inferior papillary muscles descend behind the sixth cartilage.

The root of the aorta,[2] including its orifice, valve and sinuses, occupies the space between the pulmonic and tricuspid orifices. The root of the aorta, and the aortic vestibule, which is the channel or chamber with rigid walls that leads to it from the cavity of the left ventricle, project forwards in front of that cavity and of its mitral orifice, so that the orifice of the aorta, covered by the posterior wall of the *conus arte-*

---

[1] See pages 54–59.
[2] I have already described the anatomical relations of the root of the aorta. (See pages 37–42).

riosus, interposes itself, as has just been stated, between the pulmonic and tricuspid orifices. By this arrangement the aortic orifice advances more nearly to the front of the chest, the shallow *conus arteriosus* being in front of the orifice, and the deep cavity of the right ventricle being below it. Hence the murmur of aortic regurgitation, and an intensified aortic second sound, and coincident doubling of that sound, are heard loudly over and to the left of the middle third of the sternum in front of the arterial cone and the root of the aorta; and feebly over and to the left of the lower third of the sternum, in front of the cavity of the right ventricle. The root of the aorta is somewhat overlapped above and to the left by the root of the pulmonary artery, and is situated accordingly below and to the right of the pulmonic orifice, behind the left half or three-fifths of the sternum, on a level with the third space, the left portion of the aortic orifice extending beyond the sternum so as to lie within that space. The upper and left border of the aortic orifice, especially during the diastole, is seated behind the lower portion of the third cartilage, near the sternum; and its lower and right border, especially during the systole, is situated behind the middle line of the sternum, on a level with the upper portion of the fourth cartilage.

The root of the aorta descends considerably and moves to the left, so as to approach towards the apex during the contraction of the left ventricle, and at the same time the apex moves to a less degree upwards, and to the right, so as to approach towards the aortic orifice.

The mitral orifice is situated partly behind, and partly below the level of the aortic orifice, its upper third or upper two-fifths being behind, and its lower two-thirds or three-fifths below the level of that orifice; and partly behind, and partly above the level of the tricuspid orifice, its lower two-thirds or three-fourths being behind, and its upper third or fourth being above the level of that orifice. The mitral orifice is seated behind the left half of the sternum, at the upper two-thirds of the lower third of that bone, on a level with the fourth cartilage, the fourth space, and the upper portion of the fifth cartilage. It is impossible to assign a fixed position to the mitral orifice, for it, like the tricuspid orifice, plays to and fro during the contraction and dilatation of the ventricles. The limits of its movement may, however, be approximately defined by a line a little to the right of the middle line of the sternum on the one hand and a line corresponding to the left edge of the sternum on the other. I have already described the anatomical relations of the mitral valve,[1] and it will therefore be sufficient to state here that the left or upper and the right or lower papillary muscles, starting from their attachments through their tendinous cords to the flaps of the valve, concentrate themselves towards their roots at the apex, instead of radiating from the flaps upwards, outwards, and downwards, as in the instance of the tricuspid valve. The left or superior papillary muscle usually follows the course of the fourth

[1] See pages 49–54.

cartilage and space, and the right or inferior papillary muscle that of the fifth cartilage, both muscles dipping downwards towards the lower cartilage or space as they approach the apex.

It may be gathered, from what has just been said, that each of the higher orifices overlaps in position the orifice immediately below it. Thus the pulmonic orifice at its lower and right edge is situated to a slight extent in front of the upper and left edge of the aortic orifice; the right posterior or lower flap of the aortic valve is situated in front of the upper third or two-fifths of the mitral orifice; and the lower two-thirds or three-fourths of the mitral orifice is behind the corresponding upper portion of the tricuspid orifice.

The position of the orifices and valves of the heart in relation to the deeper parts of the heart and of the chest, and to the spinal column, will be considered when the side and back views of the heart and great vessels are described.

THE POSITION OF THE HEART AND GREAT VESSELS IN ROBUST AND FEEBLE PERSONS.

(See Figs. 20, 21, 22, 23, 24.)

We have just seen that respiration materially alters the position of the heart and the great vessels, and that at the end of a deep inspiration the lower boundary of the heart may be two inches lower in relation to the walls of the chest than at the end of a forced expiration. Thus, the lower boundary of the heart is situated behind or even above the lower end of the sternum at the completion of a forced expiration; while it may be situated at the lower end of the ensiform cartilage at the termination of a deep inspiration. Again, the top of the arch of the aorta may be situated behind the upper end of the manubrium at the end of a forced expiration, and behind its lower end on the completion of a deep inspiration.

This great change is produced by a double agency, acting in opposite directions: one, the descent of the diaphragm which lowers and lengthens the heart and great vessels, and lengthens the lungs by lowering their base; the other, the ascent and advance of the walls of the chest in front. This combined downward movement of the heart and arteries, and upward movement of the sternum and cartilages, doubles the effect on the position of the organ in relation to the cartilages and sternum.

In robust persons, who lead an active and laborious life, the amount of reserved air constantly in the lungs is great, the chest is high, deep and broad, and the heart and arteries are low in position in relation to the anterior walls of the chest. In such persons the chest and its organs present the form and position of inspiration, and they have therefore the *inspiratory* type of chest. (See Figs. 20, 21, 22, 23.)

In feeble persons, on the other hand, who lead an indoor sedentary life, the amount of reserved air constantly in the lungs is small, the chest is flat and narrow, and the heart and arteries are high in position in relation to the anterior walls of the chest. In such persons the chest and its organs assume the form and position of expiration, and they present the *expiratory* type of chest. (See Fig. 24.)

In robust persons, such as sailors, miners, labourers and smiths, the lower boundary of the heart may be situated quite an inch below the lower end of the sternum, so that the heart may be felt beating in the epigastrium to the left of the ensiform cartilage and the apex of the heart may be situated behind the sixth left cartilage or space. The lungs at the same time enlarge forwards and downwards, so as to interpose themselves between the heart and the walls of the chest, all but a small space bounded above by the fifth cartilage, on the right by the ensiform cartilage, and on the left by the sixth and seventh cartilages near their attachment to the sternum. The heart's impulse is, therefore, quite imperceptible over the front of the chest, that of the right ventricle being sometimes transferred, as I have just said, to the epigastrium, and the apex beat is lost, being enveloped in the folds of the enlarged lung. In such persons, also, the top of the arch of the aorta is low in position, being perhaps situated quite an inch below the top of the manubrium.

The position of the lower boundary of the heart and the summit of the arch of the aorta being unusually low, the position of every part of the heart and the great arteries is also correspondingly low. It is not necessary to describe the situation of the various anatomical points in detail, but it will be well to name that of the leading landmarks of the heart and great arteries.

The boundary-line across the third cartilage that indicates the upper border of the right auricle and ventricle and the lower limit of the great arteries may be shifted downwards to the level of the fourth cartilages. The position of the origin of the pulmonary artery in front being thus given, that of the aperture and valve of the aorta, being a degree lower and to the left, may be inferred, it being situated behind and a little to the left of the left half of the sternum, on a level with the fourth cartilage and the fourth space. The mitral and tricuspid orifices in their descending order take each of them a lower position the mitral orifice being situated behind the lower fourth of the sternum, its upper boundary being on a level with the fourth space and its lower border, a quarter of an inch above the lower end of the sternum; and the tricuspid orifice being behind the lower sixth of the sternum and the upper portion of the ensiform cartilage.

In feeble, thin persons, of sedentary occupation, or in those who have only recently recovered from illness, the lower boundary of the heart may be situated behind the lower end of the sternum, or somewhat higher, and its apex may be present behind the fifth left cartilage, and may be felt, therefore, beating, not in the fifth, but in the fourth space. Each lung at the same time lessens at its base, and shrinks away from before the body of the heart, uncovering the apex and the left ventricle, the whole of the right ventricle, and a portion of the auricular appendix, of the pulmonary artery, and even of the ascending aorta. The heart's impulse is, therefore, diffused to an unusual extent over the front of the central part of the chest, from the second space to the fourth, and from the right of the lower portion of the sternum to the apex, being felt not only over the apex, but with considerable force over the right ventricle, where it is usually feeble or absent. A double pulsation may also be often felt over the pulmonary artery, feeble and soft with the first sound, but sharp and sudden with the

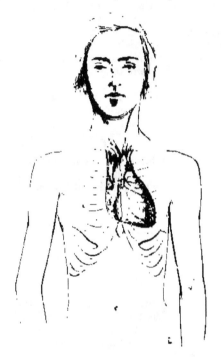

FIG. 24.—Showing the heart and great vessels in relation to the front of the chest and the lungs in a slender youth with a small chest.

second sound. In such persons also the top of the arch of the aorta is high, being situated behind or even above the top of the manubrium.

The position of the other parts of the heart and great vessels is correspondingly high. The boundary-line between the upper border of the right auricle and ventricle and the lower limit of the great arteries may be on a level with the middle of the second space, behind which the origin of the pulmonary artery may be seated. The orifice and valve of the aorta, being a stage lower and to the left, may be on a level with the lower portion of the second space and the third cartilage, behind the left half of the sternum. The mitral orifice may be situated behind the left half of the sternum, behind and just below the central portion of the bone, its upper border being on a level with the upper edge of the third cartilage, and its lower border with that of the upper edge of the fourth cartilage; and the tricuspid orifice may be situated behind the right half of the sternum just below the centre of the bone, so that its upper border may be on a level with the lower edge of the third cartilage or the upper portion of the third space, while its lower border may be on a level with the fourth space.

In many well-formed women of active, healthy habits, the heart and great vessels maintain their proper position. But this is not so in the large class of women who work indoors with the needle, and in whom the chest is wont to be flat, the position of the heart being high.

The effect of tight stays is to lessen the descent of the diaphragm, and to increase, for the sake of compensation, the expansion and elevation of the upper part of the front of the chest. In such persons a double and opposite effect may be produced. The lower boundary of the heart in relation to the lower end of the sternum may be high, but the top of the aorta in relation to the higher costal cartilage may be low.

In children of both sexes the position of the heart in relation to the walls of the chest is high.

SIDE VIEW; AFTER DEATH.

LEFT SIDE. (Fig. 25.)

The ninth plate of my Medical Anatomy represents a side view, looked at from the left side, taken from the body of a robust well-formed man. In this body the lower boundary of the heart was situated behind the ensiform cartilage, an inch and a half below the lower end of the sternum.

In this instance the top of the manubrium was on a level with the middle of the body of the third dorsal vertebra, and the lower end of the sternum was on a level with the upper border of the ninth vertebra. The middle of the sternum corresponded in level to the lower portion of the body of the fourth vertebra; the lower end of the manubrium, to the lower portion of the fifth vertebra; and the top of the lower third of the sternum, to the middle of the body of the seventh dorsal vertebra. The ensiform cartilage was of great length, measuring nearly 3 inches (2·8 inches), and its lower end was about on a level with the upper border of the body of the twelfth dorsal vertebra.

This drawing and Plate X. of the same work show well the great anatomical importance of the somewhat neglected ensiform cartilage, especially to the clinical worker. The front of the diaphragm, and the floor of the pericardium, which is formed by the central tendon of the diaphragm, take their origin in part from the tip of the ensiform cartilage by means of a strong slip of muscular fibres. The lower boundary of the pericardium and of the heart, and the lower boundary of the diaphragm, and with it that of the cavity of the right side of the chest and the right lung, may be brought down on a deep inspiration almost to the extremity of the ensiform cartilage, when that point forms the lower boundary of the chest. In this drawing, the lower boundary of the pericardium and the lower margin of the right lung were situated an inch above the end of the ensiform cartilage, and nearly two inches below the lower end of the sternum, and the lower boundary of the heart at the apex, as I have already remarked, was an inch and a half below the level of the lower end of the sternum.

The top of the arch of the aorta at the adjacent origin of the innominate and left carotid arteries was in this instance four-fifths of an inch (·8 inch) below the top of the manubrium, and was on a level with the upper portion of the body of the fourth dorsal vertebra.

The lower end of the descending portion of the arch of the aorta was in front of the upper portion of the body of the sixth dorsal vertebra, and was on a level with a point a little below the lower end of the manubrium.

The top of the pulmonary artery was a little higher in position than that of the lower end of the descending portion of the arch of the aorta just described; the origin of the pulmonary artery was three-quarters of an inch below the centre of the sternum, and within the third space, and was on a level with the lower portion of the body of the seventh vertebra; and the pulmonary artery occupied in its ascent the upper portion of the third space, the third cartilage, and the second space.

The top of the appendix of the right auricle was nearly half an inch below the centre of the sternum, and on a level with the cartilage between the sixth and seventh vertebræ. The top of the appendix of the left auricle, and the upper boundary of the left ventricle, which would be a little above the lower boundary of the orifice of the aorta, were about on a level with the middle of the body of the seventh dorsal vertebra behind, and the top of the lower third of the sternum, or about the fourth costal cartilage in front. The lower boundary of the left auricle, which would nearly correspond with the lower boundary of the mitral valve, was in front of the top of the ninth vertebra, and on a level with a point a quarter of an inch above the lower end of the sternum. The lower boundary of the posterior part of the left ventricle was in front of the top of the tenth dorsal vertebra, and about on a level with a point four-fifths of an inch below the lower end of the sternum; while the lower boundary of the left ventricle at the apex was on a level with the lower portion of the body of the tenth dorsal vertebra, and with a point about an inch and a half below the lower end of the sternum.

RIGHT SIDE.

The tenth plate of my Medical Anatomy represents a side view, looked at from the right side, taken from the body of a strong man with a well-formed chest of the inspiratory type. In this body the heart was distended with water, and the lower boundary of the swollen right ventricle was situated behind the ensiform cartilage, three quarters of an inch (·7 inch) above the tip of that cartilage, and an inch and a half (1·4 in.) below the lower end of the sternum.

The top of the manubrium in this instance corresponded in level with the lower border of the body of the second dorsal vertebra; the lower end of the sternum, with the lower border of the ninth vertebra; the middle of the sternum at the level of the third cartilage, with the body of the sixth vertebra; the lower end of the manubrium, with that of the fifth vertebra; and the upper border of the lower third of the sternum corresponded in level with the body of the seventh dorsal vertebra.

The commencement of the superior vena cava in this instance was on a level with a point below the middle of the manubrium in front, and with the body of the fourth dorsal vertebra behind; and the termination of the vein in the right auricle was in front of the cartilage between the sixth and seventh vertebræ, and on a level with a point half an inch below the middle of the sternum, and with the third space.

The top of the appendix of the right auricle was on a level with the middle of the sternum and the third cartilages in front, and the body of the sixth dorsal vertebra behind; the attachment of the lower boundary of the appendix to the body of the right auricle, at the transverse furrow, which corresponds closely to the upper boundary of the tricuspid valve, was on a level with a point an inch and a quarter above the lower end of the sternum in front, and the upper border of the eighth dorsal vertebra behind; and the lower boundary of the right auricle, which corresponds closely to the lower boundary of the tricuspid orifice, was on a level with a point half an inch below the lower end of the sternum in front, and the upper portion of the tenth dorsal vertebra behind.

The origin of the pulmonary artery and the upper boundary of the right ventricle were on a level with a point half an inch below the centre of the sternum and the third space in front, and with the lower border of the sixth vertebra behind; and the lower boundary of the right ventricle in front was situated behind the ensiform cartilage, an inch and a half (1·4 in.) below the lower end of the sternum, and three quarters of an inch above the tip of the ensiform cartilage in front, and about on a level with the lower border of the body of the tenth dorsal vertebra behind. The lower boundary of the right ventricle was about three-quarters of an inch higher behind than in front.

The lower boundary of the pericardium was about an inch and three-quarters below the lower end of the sternum, and about half an inch above the tip of the ensiform cartilage.

Although I possess other drawings showing a side view of the heart and the other internal organs, these are the only ones that give the relation of the heart and its various parts to the walls of the chest in front and the spinal column behind. Both of these drawings were taken from the bodies of men of a robust frame, with a chest of the inspiratory type, and with a heart well developed and low in position. The relations of the heart to the front of the chest in all their variety have been already abundantly illustrated, and its relations to the spinal column will be further described when the position of the heart and great vessels looked at from the back is considered. Pirogoff gives numerous sections, both vertical and horizontal, showing the position of the various parts of the heart and great vessels in relation to the anterior walls of the chest and the spinal column, and I therefore refer the reader to the notes describing those sections and two others that are figured in Braun's work. (Note 46, page 116 ; Note 47, page 121.)

SIDE VIEW; DURING LIFE.

IN A HEALTHY MAN WITH A WELL-FORMED CHEST.

LEFT SIDE. (Fig. 25.)

The heart and great vessels occupy the space in the centre of the chest, between the sternum in front and the bodies of the dorsal vertebræ behind. The margins of the lungs fill up the unoccupied spaces in front of the great vessels and the heart ; and the œsophagus and descending aorta are interposed between the heart and the bodies of the vertebræ behind.

It is evident that in the recumbent posture and during the ventricular systole, the heart would press backwards upon the œsophagus and the descending aorta so as to render swallowing difficult, and to interfere with the flow of blood to the lower part of the body, unless the heart were supported by some special contrivance. Such support is to be found in the walls of the pericardial sac. The floor of the pericardium is formed by the central tendon of the diaphragm, which is suspended in its place, in the middle of the partition between the chest and the abdomen, by means of the great converging circuit of the muscular fibres of the diaphragm, arising from the ensiform cartilage and the ribs ; and is supported firmly from below by the liver and stomach. The heart rests upon the floor of the pericardium, formed by the central tendon of the diaphragm, and this supplies a smooth inclined plane, upon which the heart glides forwards and downwards during inspiration, and backwards and upwards during expiration, so as to adapt itself to the various modulations of respiration. The strong fibrous walls of the pericardium arise from the cen-

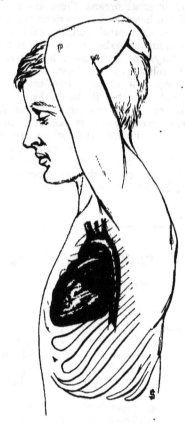

FIG 25. - Side view, looked at from the left side, showing the heart and great vessels in relation to the walls of the chest and the spinal column.

tral tendon of the diaphragm. Those walls are endowed with a fibrous structure which is of especial strength posteriorly, where it is firmly incorporated with the coats of the pulmonary veins as they enter the pericardium. A fibrous covering is also contributed by the pericardium to the inferior and superior venæ cavæ where they enter the sac, and to the pulmonary artery and ascending aorta where they leave the sac. In virtue of this arrangement the posterior wall of the pericardium supports the heart forwards and prevents it from making pressure upon the aorta and œsophagus, where they are situated immediately behind the left auricle and the base of the left ventricle. By the distribution also of the fibrous pericardium to the veins entering, and the arteries leaving the sac, and to the branches of those arteries in the neck, the central tendon of the diaphragm, when it descends during inspiration, draws intermediately upon the whole of those vessels so as to save them from dragging immediately upon the heart itself.

The lower boundary of the heart is on a level with the lower end of the upper third of the ensiform cartilage and the upper edge of the sixth costal cartilage in front, and with the upper edge of the tenth dorsal vertebra behind. The top of the arch of the aorta, at the origin of the innominate and left carotid arteries, is on a level with the top of the middle third of the manubrium in front, and the lower edge of the body of the third or the upper edge of that of the fourth dorsal vertebra behind. The horizontal boundary-line that divides the upper border of the heart from the origin of the pulmonary artery and the ascending aorta, is on a level with the third cartilage in front, and the body of the sixth dorsal vertebra behind. The heart therefore extends downwards from the body of the sixth dorsal vertebra to that of the tenth, and from the third costal cartilage to the sixth; and the great arteries extend upwards from the body of the seventh to that of the third or fourth dorsal vertebra behind, and from the level of the third cartilage to the top of the middle third of the manubrium in front.

The left auricle and ventricle occupy fully as great a proportionate amount of space at the left side of the heart as the right auricle and ventricle do at the front of the heart. The left ventricle occupies by much the largest share of the left side of the heart, and its double-convex cone-shaped outline is completely exposed to view from its base to its apex when the left side of the chest is looked at. The transverse furrow, which divides the left ventricle from the left auricle, follows a direction from above downwards and somewhat backwards. The left auricle rests behind on the descending aorta and the œsophagus; and that auricle, the transverse groove, and the mitral orifice are situated in front of the seventh and eighth dorsal vertebræ and the upper border of the ninth; and on a level with the sternal end of the third and fourth costal cartilages, the fourth space, and the upper edge of the fifth cartilage in front. The upper border of the left ventricle is nearly as high as that of the left auricle, but the lower boundary of the left ventricle which extends down almost or quite to the upper border of the body of the tenth dorsal vertebra, is considerably lower than that of the left auricle, which reaches down to the lower border of the eighth or upper border of the ninth vertebra. The left auricle and ventricle take a direction from behind forwards, to the left and downwards, and as they have a similar inclination to that of the ribs, they, as well as the transverse furrow between them, are covered throughout by the fourth, fifth, and sixth ribs. The left auricle and ventricle start from the back of the centre of the chest in front of the bodies of the seventh, eighth, and ninth dorsal vertebræ, and the left ventricle crosses from the back to the front of the chest with a definite leaning to the left, so that its apex points at the left fifth space. The left auricular appendix and the left pulmonary veins, where they enter the auricle at its higher part, are situated in front of the adjoining portions of the bodies of the seventh and eighth dorsal vertebræ and their intervening cartilage, and on a level with the third and fourth costal cartilages and the third space in front.

The anterior longitudinal furrow presents a convex outline, looking forwards towards the pulmonary artery at its upper third, and towards the right ventricle at its lower two-thirds; and a concave outline looking backwards and downwards towards the left auricular appendix and the left ventricle. The upper end of this furrow is in front of the body of the seventh dorsal vertebra and behind the third costal cartilage or space, and the lower end of the furrow at the apex of the heart is situated behind the lower border of the fifth space, and is on a level with the body of the tenth dorsal vertebra behind.

During the ventricular systole, the left ventricle and auricle change remarkably in form, size, and position (Fig. 17). The ventricle contracts and shortens, and the auricle expands and lengthens to a great extent. The base of the ventricle and the adjoining edge of the auricle, the transverse furrow and the mitral orifice advance to a considerable extent forwards, to the left and downwards away from the spinal column and towards the apex of the left ventricle. The apex at the same time moves forwards, upwards and to the right, towards the base, so that the base and apex of the ventricle both approximate towards each other, and towards a zone of rest in the walls of the ventricle, situated nearer to the apex than the base. The anterior wall of the ventricle, at the anterior longitudinal furrow, advances forwards and becomes more convex; while the posterior wall of the ventricle also advances forwards, but to a much greater extent, especially at its middle, where it becomes hollow, the apex pointing downwards; so that the posterior wall of the ventricle, previously convex, becomes concave towards the apex and convex at the base, thus presenting a double curve. All the systolic movements of the left ventricle converge forwards, towards the point of rest on the surface of the right ventricle, about its middle and near the septum.

During the ventricular systole the left auricle becomes greatly distended and expands upwards, forwards and downwards, along its upper, anterior and lower borders respectively, the amount of movement of the auricular appendix being greater than that of the transverse furrow. The posterior wall of the auricle which rests on the back of the pericardium remains stationary.

The right ventricle extends in front from the third cartilage to the sixth, and from the middle of the sternum to the lower portion of the upper third of the ensiform cartilage, and is on a level behind with the body of the seventh dorsal vertebra at its upper boundary, and with the upper portion or middle of the body of the tenth dorsal vertebra at its lower boundary.

During the systole of the ventricles, the right ventricle advances, while the upper portion of its walls contracts downwards and the lower portion of its walls contracts upwards, those movements converging towards a point situated near the longitudinal furrow and the attachment of the anterior papillary muscle.

The pulmonary artery conceals the ascending aorta in the first half of its course, when we look at the left side of the heart. By removing the fat between the pulmonary artery and the left auricular appendix, the left posterior sinus of the aorta and the left or posterior coronary artery are brought into view, deep behind and beyond the posterior surface of the pulmonary artery. The mode in which the pulmonary artery in its progress backwards, and the ascending aorta in its progress upwards, cross each other, is now well seen. When the arch of the aorta is looked at in front, it does not present the appearance of an arch, since the left border of the ascending aorta is situated almost in front of the deep right border of the descending aorta; and the pulmonary artery covers the left edge of the ascending and almost the whole of the descending aorta, the deep left edge of which is alone visible in front. When, however, the left side of the arch of the aorta is looked at, its arched form is at once apparent, the ascending aorta forming the front, the descending aorta the back, and the transverse aorta the top of the arch.

The pulmonary artery as it ascends makes for the hollow of the arch of the aorta, through which it sends its right branch, and its direction is therefore much more from before backwards than from below upwards.

The origin of the pulmonary artery is situated just behind the third left cartilage, and is on a level with the body of the seventh dorsal vertebra. The upper boundary of the pulmonary artery, at the top of its point of bifurcation, which is also its most posterior portion, is situated in front of the lower portion of the body of the fifth, or the upper portion of that of the sixth dorsal vertebra, and on a level with the second costal cartilage; and the left and right branches of the pulmonary artery are situated in front of the body of the sixth dorsal vertebra, on a level with the second space.

The pulmonary artery in its course from before backwards and upwards presents a convexity on its anterior and upper surface, and a concavity on its posterior and lower surface, and is on a level with the third left cartilage and the second space. The posterior sinus of the pulmonary artery is somewhat lower in position than the two anterior sinuses, and is situated behind the upper portion of the third space. The left bronchus separates the left pulmonary artery from the left pulmonary veins.

During the systole of the ventricles, the whole pulmonary artery lengthens and enlarges. The origin of the artery moves to a considerable extent downwards and forwards, the higher parts of the artery sharing this movement, but to a less and less extent from below upwards. The two anterior sinuses of the pulmonary artery descend more during the systole than its posterior sinus, so that the anterior or higher valves are then more nearly on a level with the posterior or lower valve than during the diastole.

The arch of the aorta, like the pulmonary artery, lengthens and enlarges during the systole, so that the whole arch widens. The orifice of the aorta, which is situated at the centre of the heart, moves to a considerable extent downwards and to the left, the direction of its movement, like that of the mitral valves, being towards the apex. The walls of the ascending aorta also move downwards, but to a less and less extent from below upwards.

The position of the ascending, transverse and descending portions of the arch of the aorta in relation to the sternum, the adjoining parts, and the spinal column has already been described.

The pulmonic, the aortic, and the mitral orifices and valves are situated in their relative position on an inclined plane, each being one above and behind the other in the order named, the orifice of the pulmonary artery being the highest and most anterior, the mitral orifice the lowest and most posterior, and the aortic orifice holding an intermediate position. The upper and anterior boundary of the pulmonic orifice and valve is behind the third costal cartilage and on a level with the lower third of the body of the sixth dorsal vertebra; and the lower boundary of the mitral valve is on a level with the fifth cartilage and is situated in front of the lower border of the body of the eighth or the upper border of that of the ninth dorsal vertebra. The aortic orifice, being a stage lower than the pulmonic orifice, by which it is overlapped, is in front of the body of the seventh dorsal vertebra, and the intervertebral cartilage just below it. The mitral orifice is in front of the same intervertebral cartilage, the body of the eighth and the upper border of the body of the ninth dorsal vertebra. The position of the sternum and costal cartilages in relation to those valves need not be here repeated.

The position that I have assigned to the various parts of the heart and great arteries, is that which usually exists in a healthy, well-formed man, but those parts change in position during the systole and diastole of the ventricles, and during inspiration and expiration, in the manner and to the extent that I have already described. In those who are robust and possess a broad and deep chest of the inspiratory type, the position of the heart and arteries and of all their parts are lower, while in those who are slender and possess a narrow and flat chest of the expiratory type, the position of those parts is higher, than in the average man whom I have taken as an example. During inspiration the whole of the anterior walls of the chest ascend considerably, but the spinal column, owing to the

H

deepening of the dorsal arch, descends to a small but definite degree, the descent of the upper being greater than that of the lower dorsal vertebræ, some of the lowest of which are stationary. While, therefore, during respiration, the change in the position of the cartilages and sternum in relation to the heart and arteries is doubled by the inspiratory ascent of those cartilages during the descent of the heart, and by the expiratory descent of those cartilages during the ascent of the heart; the slight respiratory movement of the dorsal vertebræ is in the same direction as the movement of the heart, that of both of them being downwards during inspiration, and upwards during expiration. The result is, that the position of the heart and great arteries in relation to the bodies of the dorsal vertebræ during respiration is more stable than their position in relation to the sternum and cartilages. For a twofold reason, the position of the great arteries in relation to the superior dorsal vertebræ changes less during respiration than the position of the heart in relation to the lower dorsal vertebræ. The first reason is the greater respiratory movement downwards and upwards of the higher than of the lower vertebræ. The second reason is the attachment of the descending aorta by means of the intercostal arteries to the spinal column, as well as that of the great branches of the arch to the head, neck, and arms, which hold the movements of the great arteries in check. The heart itself, on the other hand, is suspended so freely in the centre of the chest that it yields without restraint to every definite influence, being thus moved readily upwards and downwards by respiration, and by the distension and collapse of the abdomen, and from side to side by changes in position, or by effusion into or tumours in the chest, or by contraction or expansion of either lung singly.

RIGHT SIDE.

The position of the heart and great vessels viewed from the right side is much more simple than that of their position viewed from the left side. When the right side of the heart is looked at, the right auricle and ventricle, the descending vena cava, the ascending aorta, and the pulmonary artery are visible, but every other part is concealed. The relative position of the lower boundary of the heart, of the top of the arch, and of the boundary-line separating the great vessels from the heart is necessarily the same on the right side of the chest as on the left side. The upper boundary of the right ventricle is on a level with the body of the seventh, and its lower boundary with that of the tenth dorsal vertebra. The right ventricle occupies the anterior portion of the space between the sternum and the spinal column; and the right auricle, including its appendix, occupies the posterior portion of that space; so that its posterior surface is situated in front of the right side of the bodies of the dorsal vertebræ from the seventh to the upper portion of the tenth, the right pulmonary arteries and pulmonary veins and the right portion of the left auricle being interposed.

The tricuspid orifice is the most anterior and the lowest in position of the four orifices of the heart and great vessels, and is separated from the spinal column by the left ventricle and auricle. The tricuspid orifice is situated, as we have already seen, behind the right half of the lower fourth of the sternum, and is on a level with the bodies of the eighth and ninth dorsal vertebræ.

The descending vena cava is situated to the right of the ascending aorta and on a deeper plane. The commencement of the vein, at the confluence of the two innominate veins, is on a level with the body of the fourth dorsal vertebra, and it enters the right auricle behind its appendix in front of the body of the seventh dorsal vertebra, the right pulmonary artery being just above its termination, the superior right pulmonary vein just below it, and the œsophagus just behind it or to its left. The vein, as it descends, rests upon the right side of the trachea near and at its bifurcation, and upon the right bronchus.

BACK VIEW; AFTER DEATH.

I made observations some years ago on the position of certain parts of the heart and great vessels in relation to the spines of the dorsal vertebræ in eleven different bodies.

The top of the arch of the aorta was situated in front of a point below the spine of the second dorsal vertebra in one instance, just above the spine of the third dorsal vertebra in seven instances, and below the spine of that vertebra in three instances. In other words, in one instance the top of the arch was in front of the upper portion of the body of the third dorsal vertebra, in seven cases it was in front of its lower portion, and in three it was in front of the body of the fourth dorsal vertebra. The lower boundary of the left ventricle was on a level with the spine of the ninth dorsal vertebra in one instance, with a point just above that spine or below that of the eighth vertebra in eight cases, with the spine of the eighth vertebra in one, and above it in one. In other words, the lower boundary of the left ventricle varied in position from the level of the lower edge of the body of the eighth to that of the upper third of the tenth dorsal vertebra. In five instances the upper boundary of the left auricle was on a level with the spine of the fifth dorsal vertebra (in one), or just above that spine (in one), or just below that spine (in three); and its lower boundary was on a level with (in one), above (in one), or below (in three) the spine of the seventh dorsal vertebra. In other words, the upper border of the left auricle was situated in front of the upper part of the seventh dorsal vertebra, or just above it, and its lower border in front of the body of the eighth vertebra.[1]

[1] Note 46, p. 116; Note 47, p. 21.

H 2

BACK VIEW; DURING LIFE.

In a Healthy Man with a well-formed Chest. (See Fig. 26.)

When the back of the heart and great vessels is exposed, the left cavities of the heart are brought into view, the lower boundary of the left ventricle resting upon the floor of the pericardium, which conceals the under surface of the heart. When the floor of the pericardium is withdrawn, the under surface of the heart is visible from behind. The under surface of the heart inclines from behind downwards and forwards, and it presents posteriorly, the lower border of the left ventricle from base to apex ; anteriorly, the lower surface of the right ventricle ; and intermediately, the posterior longitudinal furrow.

The lower boundary of the left ventricle is on a level with or higher than the spine of the ninth and the upper portion of the body of the tenth dorsal vertebra ; the top of the arch of the aorta at the origin of the innominate and left carotid arteries is in front of the spine of the third and the lower edge of the body of the third or the upper edge of that of the fourth dorsal vertebra or it may be somewhat higher ; and the boundary line between the heart and the great arteries, at the lower border of the division of the right and left pulmonary arteries and the upper border of the left auricle, is in front of the spine of the fifth and the lower border of the body of the sixth dorsal vertebra. The level of the boundary-line between the heart and the great arteries is somewhat higher behind, where it follows the line of the lower border of the division of the pulmonary artery, than it is either in front or at the sides, where it follows the line of the origin of the pulmonary artery or that of the top of the right auricle.

The Left Auricle and Ventricle.—The left auricle and ventricle maintain the same relation to each other and to the spinal column at the back of the chest that the right auricle and ventricle do to each other and to the sternum at the front of the chest, but each portion of the left side of the heart bears more to the left behind, than the corresponding portion of the right side of the heart does in front.

The left auricle at its upper and posterior portion, which includes the auricular appendix, is central, being situated in nearly about equal proportions to the right and left of the middle line of the spinal column. The auricular appendix, which is a semi-detached wing of the auricle, leaves the body of the auricle at its left upper corner and advances forwards and to the left, so as to fill up the deep furrow between the pulmonary artery and the base of the left ventricle. The lowest portion of the left auricle lies entirely to the right of the middle line of the spine, while the left ventricle lies almost completely to the left of it, and the transverse furrow where it separates the two cavities occupies an intermediate position, its upper portion lying considerably to the right, and its lower portion slightly to the left of the middle line of the spine. The left auricle at its anterior aspect lies, when at rest, almost entirely to the right of the middle line of the chest, but its left boundary moves to the left of the middle line when the ventricles contract, and to the right of that line when they dilate. The transverse furrow takes an oblique direction from above downwards and from right to left, and as it sweeps to and fro, from one side to the other and back again, during the contraction and dilatation of the ventricle, it occupies a position in front of the spines of the fifth, sixth, and seventh, and the bodies of the seventh and eighth dorsal vertebræ, and the upper part of that of the ninth.

The heart is attached to the roots of the lungs by the entrance of the right and left pulmonary veins into the upper part of the left auricle at either side of the spine. The left pulmonary veins are as a rule higher in position, and enter the auricle nearer to the centre of the spine than the right, while the right lower pulmonary vein is larger and lower in position than the left, the right lower vein being sometimes double. The greater size of the lower lobe of the right lung compared with that of the left, evidently accounts for the greater size of the right lower pulmonary veins. The higher position of the left side of the auricle owing to the presence on that side of the base of the ventricle, and the general inclination downwards of the heart, its longitudinal parts following the line of the longitudinal furrows from right to left, and its transverse parts following the oblique direction of the transverse furrow from left to right, explain, I consider, the lower position of the right than the left pulmonary veins. The pulmonary veins have, in short, more room to deploy on the right side of the left auricle, where no object interferes with their freedom, than on the left side of the auricle at its upper angle, where the veins and the auricular appendix are pushed up into a corner by the close proximity of the upper border of the left ventricle. The downward inclination from left to right of the upper boundary of the left auricle, between the left and right pulmonary veins, although quite definite, is very much less than the downward inclination from left to right of the posterior transverse furrow. The right pulmonary veins are on a level with the spines of the fifth and sixth dorsal vertebræ, and the two left pulmonary veins, holding a higher position, are respectively just above the level of those two spines.

The left ventricle lies to the left of the spinal column, and extends in a direction to the left, downwards and forwards, from its base at the back of the chest where it is in front of the spinal column, on a level with the sixth and seventh dorsal spines, to its apex at the front of the chest where it is behind the fifth left intercostal space. The upper boundary of the left ventricle is more rounded and more inclined from above downwards than ts lower boundary along the line of the posterior longitudinal furrow, where it is in nearly straight and horizontal.

The posterior and left border of the mitral orifice is situated ab or fully half an inch to the left of the posterior transverse furro This orifice looks towards the apex of the left ventricle, or in a dii tion to the left, forwards and slightly downwards. Its superior or

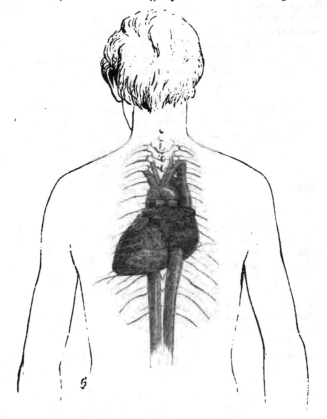

Fig. 26.—Back view, showing the heart and great vessels in relation to the spi column, the ribs, and the diaphragm.

angle is a little behind the auricular appendix, on a level with point above the spine of the sixth, and with the middle of the bo of the seventh dorsal vertebra, and about half an inch, more or le to the left of the middle line of the spine. Its inferior or rig boundary is on a level with the spine of the seventh, and the low portion of the body of the eighth dorsal vertebra, and with a poi between the scapulæ, just above their lower angles, and a litt to the left or right of the middle line of the spine. The space between the mitral orifice and the apex of the left ventricle is occupied by the flaps of the mitral valve, their tendinous cords, and the papillary muscles, the apparatus of the mitral valve occupying the space at the back of the left ventricle between its base and its apex. The apparatus of the mitral valve is always in action. The transverse furrow and the mitral orifice oscillate to and fro extensively, moving to the left, forwards, and slightly downwards towards the apex during the contraction of the ventricle, and in the reverse direction during the dilatation of the ventricle (see Fig. 17, p. 66). The mitral portion of the left auricle and the base of the left ventricle necessarily share in the movements of the mitral orifice and of the transverse furrow in extent and direction, but the movements of the walls of both cavities, as they recede from the orifice, gradually lessen, and at a zone or transverse circuit of stable equilibrium around each cavity, the walls both of the auricle and ventricle maintain a state of rest. This zone of rest in the left ventricle is probably more near to its apex than its base, while the position of the zone of rest in the left auricle is probably to the left of and just below the termination of the right and left inferior pulmonary veins. The apex moves towards the zone of rest of the ventricle during the contraction of that cavity, but the upper and right boundary of the left auricle moves away from, or to the right of, the zone of rest of the auricle during the dilatation of that cavity. Thus during the systole of the ventricle there is a movement, both of the base and the apex of the cavity towards a common centre, tending to its complete contraction; while during the same period the auricle dilates in all directions, and its left and right portions both diverge from the zone of rest of the cavity. The movement of expansion to the left, forwards and downwards, of the mitral portion of the auricle, is much greater than the movement of expansion to the right and upwards of the right portion of the auricle. During the contraction of the left auricle and the expansion of the left ventricle, the reverse movements take place at the mitral orifice, the transverse furrow, and both cavities at all points. The play of all these parts is constant, and they are always undergoing a series of regulated and co-ordinate changes in position. For this reason, although the range of movement of each part, so far as we know it, can be assigned within certain limits, yet the exact position of each part cannot be stated.[1]

The position of the mitral orifice, which is oblique in direction from above downwards, and from left to right, is, as I have just said, in front and to the left of the spines of the sixth and seventh dorsal vertebræ, and between the scapulæ, a little above their lower angles. This region forms a landmark for the position of the

[1] I have frequently observed the movements of the heart in animals at the front and the side but never at the back of the organ, so that the movements of the left auricle described above have been derived from inference and not from observation.

mitral orifice and valve over the dorsum. The left ventricle is situated to the left of this region, and extends below its level. During the diastole of the ventricle, the stream of blood from the auricle into the ventricle pours across this region in a direction from right to left, forwards and somewhat downwards. To the right of, and rather above this region, is situated the left auricle; and in cases of mitral incompetence, the reversed stream of blood pours across this region from left to right and somewhat upwards, as it regurgitates from the left ventricle into the left auricle.

In cases of mitral regurgitation, one might be led, *à priori*, to expect that the mitral murmur would be always audible over the back at the region of the mitral orifice, or midway between the scapulæ, just above the level of their lower angles. This is, however, not usually the case, and especially when the mitral murmur is soft in character, the lungs and chest are of full size, and respiration is free. This is, I believe, to be explained by the great space that intervenes, owing to the presence of the vertebræ, between the mitral orifice and the ear when applied over that region, by the extent to which the lungs envelope the heart and fill the chest backwards, and by the position of the descending aorta and the œsophagus between the mitral orifice and left auricle in front and the spinal column behind. When, however, the mitral murmur is grave, vibrating or musical in character and loud, and when the lungs and chest are contracted and respiration is limited, then the mitral murmur is audible over the back at the region of the mitral valve, and in many cases with great intensity.

The Right Auricle and Ascending Vena Cava.—The inferior and posterior portion of the right auricle, and the entrance of the ascending vena cava into that portion of the auricle are situated at the back of the heart. The right auricle is here separated at its upper boundary from the left auricle below the entrance of the lower right pulmonary vein by a septum, which often makes but little mark externally. The lower boundary of the right auricle is defined by the continuation backwards of the posterior transverse furrow between the base of the left ventricle and the right auricle, until it reaches the posterior longitudinal furrow. The posterior and inferior portion of the right auricle thus fills up the angle formed between the lower border of the left auricle and the base of the left ventricle posteriorly. This angle is formed by the downward prominence and thickness of the muscular wall of the left ventricle at its base.

The ascending vena cava penetrates the diaphragm on a level with the eighth or ninth dorsal spine, where it is situated nearly half an inch to the right of the descending aorta, and of the middle line of the spine; and after ascending to the extent of an inch or less, it enters the right auricle on a level with the seventh dorsal spine, about three-quarters of an inch to the right of the descending aorta.

The Under Surface of the Heart; the Longitudinal Furrow and the Right Ventricle.—The posterior longitudinal furrow divides the left ventricle behind from the right ventricle in front, on the under surface of the heart, and when that organ rests upon the floor of the pericardium, the transverse furrow and the right ventricle are hidden. When, however, the floor of the pericardium is lowered so as to bring into view the under surface of the heart, which inclines from behind, forwards and downwards, the posterior longitudinal furrow, and the under surface of the right ventricle beyond and in front of it, are rendered visible. The posterior longitudinal furrow, resting upon and adapting itself as it does to the floor of the pericardium, is comparatively horizontal in direction; but it is slightly convex near the base of the ventricle, owing to the shoulder formed there by the muscular walls. During the contraction of the ventricle, when its base and apex approximate, the transverse furrow changes in direction both toward the base and the apex. The furrow then becomes more convex than before at the base, because the base of the ventricle itself becomes more convex, and it turns or twists downwards in a peculiar manner towards the apex, because the apex itself twists downwards, so as to form a concavity towards that end. The longitudinal furrow then presents, therefore, an outline with a double curve.

The posterior longitudinal furrow at its auricular extremity comes very close to the posterior border of the heart, and I think that it is visible from behind at that point, even when the heart rests upon the floor of the pericardium. Thence the furrow advances forwards and to the left to the apex of the heart, where it divides the left ventricle from the right, and where it joins the anterior longitudinal furrow.

The under surface of the heart contracts gradually from its auricular portion or base, where it is wider than at any other part, to its apex, where it is narrower than at any other part. The under surface of the right ventricle is thus triangular in form, the base of the triangle being at the auriculo-ventricular furrow, and its apex at the apex of the heart. The posterior longitudinal furrow which is straight, forms the posterior side of the triangle, and the lower boundary of the right ventricle, which is somewhat convex, forms its anterior side. This lower boundary of the right ventricle at the front of the heart, which is on a level with the body of the tenth and the spine of the ninth dorsal vertebra, is lower in position than the lower border of the left ventricle at the back of the heart, which is situated in front of the cartilage between the bodies of the ninth and tenth dorsal vertebræ, or a little lower, and is on a level with the space between the eighth and ninth dorsal spines.

The apex of the heart is lower in position than the lower boundary of the right ventricle, and is on a level with the body of the tenth, and with a point above the spine of the ninth dorsal vertebræ, and with the lower angle of the left scapula.

The Great Vessels.—The position of the boundary line between the upper border of the heart and the lower limit of the great vessels is, as I have already stated, higher at the back than at either side or in front. The boundary-line dividing the upper border of the left auricle from the lower border of the right and left pulmonary arteries is situated in front of the cartilage below the body of the sixth and the spine of the fifth dorsal vertebra; and the lower end of the descending portion of the arch of the aorta and of the vena cava, where it is lost behind the right pulmonary vein, are nearly on the same level.

The great arteries of the neck, the descending portion of the arch of the aorta, through the medium of the transverse and ascending portions of the arch, the right and left pulmonary arteries, and the right and left pulmonary veins, form in succession a series of central attachments for the heart, which are situated, so to speak, in tiers one below the other. To these must be added, but on a different plane, the descending vena cava. The heart is suspended forwards and downwards from these various attachments. Two of them, those formed by the pulmonary veins and the pulmonary arteries, connect the heart intimately with the roots of the lungs, so that the roots of the lungs and the heart at that position enjoy a common movement of descent during inspiration, and of ascent during expiration, a degree of movement that is measured by the respiratory movements of descent and ascent of the larynx.

The descending portion of the arch is maintained at its lower end in a fixed position in relation to the spinal column by the sixth intercostal arteries. The higher intercostal arteries, those which go to the third, fourth, and fifth intercostal spaces, arise in succession from the descending portion of the arch, in front, in their descending order, of the fifth and sixth dorsal vertebræ. These vessels all ascend from their point of origin to the spaces they respectively supply, the higher arteries making a greater ascent than the lower ones, because they have to reach a higher point in relation to their respective origins; and the right arteries mounting upwards to a greater extent than the left arteries, because they arise from a lower part of the aorta, owing to the right side of the descending portion of the arch being otherwise occupied by the passage behind it of the œsophagus, and under and in front of it, of the right bronchus. The intercostal arteries to the sixth spaces pass directly to the right and left from their point of origin. It is evident, therefore, that the lower end of the descending portion of the arch, which is braced down to the spinal column by the direct origin of the sixth intercostal arteries, is more fixed in position than its upper part, the intercostal arteries from which have a free ascent, and where the œsophagus is interposed between the artery and the spine; that the descending portion of the arch has less range of movement than the transverse portion, the great arteries from which are comparatively long and capable of being put on the stretch; and that the ascending portion of the arch enjoys a still more free play of movement than the transverse portion, for it is weighted at its root by the heart, and it is long, curved, and free from vascular connexions.

The descending portion of the arch lies in front of the left half of the bodies of the fourth and fifth dorsal vertebræ, and that of the upper border of the sixth, on a level with the third and fourth, and the space between the fourth and fifth dorsal spines, and with the inter-scapular space at and below the spines of the scapulæ. This region forms a landmark at the back for the position of the descending portion of the arch of the aorta; over this region direct and even regurgitant aortic murmurs, especially if they are loud, grave, and musical, are often audible, and that with great intensity; and in this region, the signs of aneurism of the descending aorta most frequently betray themselves. It is sufficient if I allude here to the effect in such cases of the pressure of aneurism affecting this artery on the left recurrent laryngeal nerve, which winds underneath this portion of the arch on its way to the larynx; on the œsophagus, where it passes behind the artery; on the left bronchus, where it passes underneath it; on the left pulmonary artery, which is situated in front of the artery; on the bodies of the vertebræ, upon which it rests; and on the intercostal nerves that pass between and to the left of those vertebræ.

I have already described the position of the transverse aorta. The right and left pulmonary arteries are situated in front of the body of the sixth and the spine of the fifth dorsal vertebra, and they, as I have just said, form one of the two great points of attachment of the heart to the roots of the lungs. The principal points of clinical interest with regard to those arteries is the one I have just alluded to in relation to the pressure of aneurism of the descending aorta on the right or left pulmonary artery, which interferes with the supply of blood to the lungs; of the analogous effect of aneurism of the transverse aorta, below which the division of the pulmonary artery is situated; of aneurism of the ascending aorta on the right pulmonary artery, which often leads to secondary affections of the right lung; and on the effects of the pressure of an intra-thoracic tumour or enlarged bronchial glands on either of those arteries.

The right pulmonary artery is somewhat lower in position than the left pulmonary artery, in the same way and for the same reasons that the right pulmonary veins are lower than the left pulmonary veins.

The descending vena cava is seen from behind, winding round the right side of the ascending aorta; and its great affluent, the left innominate vein, lies in front of the upper border of the transverse aorta and the great arteries that spring from it. Aneurisms of the ascending aorta tend therefore to make pressure on the descending vena cava so as to impede or arrest the flow of flood through that vein to the heart, and the same may be said with regard to the effects of the pressure of aneurisms of the transverse aorta in impeding or arresting the flow of blood through the left innominate vein.

The descending aorta, being attached by the intercostal arteries to the spinal column, is situated in front of the bodies of the dorsal vertebræ at their centre and left side, and it is therefore interposed

between the mitral orifice and the base of the left ventricle in fro
and the spine behind.   The œsophagus lies in front of the right si
of the spinal column until it reaches the bodies of the eighth, nin
and tenth dorsal vertebræ, which are on a level with the seven
eighth, and ninth dorsal spines, where it gradually passes over t
front of the aorta.   It is thus interposed between the left auric
and the right side of the spinal column, and finally between the ba
of the left ventricle in front and the aorta and spinal column behin

The right and left lungs at the back of the chest fill up the de
hollow in front of the angles of the ribs, and their inner margi
overlap respectively the right and left borders of the bodies of t
dorsal vertebræ.

The lungs at the back and both sides completely envelop tl
heart and great vessels, with the exception of those parts that lie
the very centre of the chest, in front of the anterior portion of t
bodies of the dorsal vertebræ.

NOTES.

Note 1.—Pirogoff, in his valuable "Anatomia Topographica," Braun, in his beautiful "Topographisch-Anatomischer Atlas;" and Le Gendre, in his "Anatomie Chirurgicale Homolographique," give drawings taken from sections of the frozen dead body representing the position of the internal organs. In this and the following notes I shall briefly describe the position of the heart as it is represented in those various drawings. I may remark that many of these drawings are evidently not of the size of nature.

Pirogoff represents vertical sections of twelve different bodies, the section being made either through the centre of the sternum in front and the spinal column behind or to the right or left of the centre. In these instances the front of the pericardium was lower in position than the front of the heart to an extent varying from ·8 or ·9 inch to ·02 inch. Between these two extreme instances there was every variety of difference from ·2 inch to ·7 inch, the average extent to which the front of the pericardium was lower than the front of the heart being ·4 inch, or less than half an inch.

These drawings of Pirogoff represent, which mine do not, the relation of the whole under surface of the heart to the floor of the pericardium. In two of them, the whole lower surface of the heart, including both ventricles and the longitudinal furrow between them, rested upon the pericardium; while in one of these, with healthy organs, the front of the pericardium was ·7 inch, and in another with ascites it was ·35 inch below the front of the right ventricle. In the latter case the fluid in the abdomen pressed the pericardium upwards into close contact with the heart, and elevated that organ. In four other cases the right ventricle rested upon the pericardium, while in all of these the interventricular furrow was separated by fluid from the pericardium from ·2 in. to ·65 in., and in three of them the left ventricle was higher than the pericardium from ·3 in. to ·4 in. In the six remaining cases, a film of fluid, varying from ·1 in. to ·5 in., separated both ventricles and the longitudinal furrow from the pericardium; in two of those cases the separation of the two surfaces was equal throughout: in two it was greater at the furrow than the ventricles, and greater below the left ventricle than the right; and in two it was greater below the right ventricle than the left.

Note 2.—Pirogoff represents the exact position of the lower boundary of the front of the heart in relation to the lower end of the bony sternum in five instances in which a vertical section was made through the centre of the sternum in front and the spinal column behind. In two of these instances the lower boundary of the heart was above the lower end of the sternum to an extent varying from ·8 in. to ·7 in., and in three of them it was below the lower end of the sternum to an extent varying from one inch to half an inch. He also gives thirteen cross sections of the body that show whether the lower boundary of the heart was higher or lower than the lower end of the sternum. In three of these cases the heart was below, in four it was above, and in six it was either at, a little above, or a little below the lower end of the sternum. In one instance the lower border of the heart was very much below, and in another it was very much above the lower end of the sternum. The latter case stood alone. The

section was made through the lower margin of the nipples and the middl
the third space, and only a small piece of the ventricles towards the apex
mained frozen in the pericardial fluid; the heart being absent from behind
centre of the sternum.   The stomach and the œsophagus were enormously
tended with food, and both the stomach and the liver rose high into the cavit
the chest, above the level of the section.   In eight other cases the section
made, as in this one, through the third cartilage, in nine others thro
the fourth, and in four others through the fourth space; and in all of th
amounting to twenty-one, the heart was present in the section of full size.

Braun gives vertical sections of the body through the centre of the stern
and the spine in two instances, in one of which the lower boundary of the h
is half an inch above, and in the other is an inch and a third below the leve
the lower end of the sternum.

NOTE 3.—The position of the lower boundary of the pericardium in rela
to the lower end of the sternum is represented by Pirogoff in the two group
sections, vertical and transverse, referred to in Note 2.   In two of the vert
sections the lower boundary of the front of the pericardium was above the l
of the lower end of the sternum from the tenth to the third of an inch, and
three of them it was below the lower end from 1·2 in. to ·88 in.   In
thirteen cross sections the lower border of the pericardium was above the l
of the lower end of the sternum in only one case, and below it in twelve cas

NOTE 4.—Pirogoff represents the position of the apex in relation to
fourth, fifth, and sixth spaces and cartilages in the two groups of vertical
transverse sections.   In one of the vertical sections, a case of ascites, the a
was situated in the fourth space; in another, it was situated behind the f
rib, and in a third behind the sixth rib; while of the cross sections, in five
apex was situated in the fifth space, in five behind the fifth cartilage, and in
behind the fourth cartilage or the third space.   Five vertical sections also re
sent the relation of the lower boundary of the right ventricle to the cartilages
spaces, at a point intermediate between the lower boundary of the sternum
the apex; in two of these the inferior margin of the right ventricle was beh
the seventh cartilage, in one behind the sixth cartilage, in one behind the
space, and in one behind the fifth cartilage.

NOTE 5.—Pirogoff, in the three vertical and eleven cross sections referre
in Note 4, shows the relation to the cartilages and spaces of the lower bound
of the pericardium below the apex.   In two of the three vertical sections re
senting the apex, the inferior border of the pericardium was lower than
inferior border of the apex from two-thirds of an inch (·7 in.) to half an i
(·4 in.); and in the remaining one the pericardium fitted close upon the a
In two of these cases the lower boundary of the pericardium below the a
was behind the sixth cartilage, and in the third, that affected with ascites, beh
the fifth cartilage.   In three of the cross sections the lower boundary of
pericardium below the apex was situated behind the sixth cartilage, in five
them it was behind the fifth space, in two behind the second cartilage, and
the remaining one behind the fourth cartilage.   In two of the five vertical
tions in which the relation of the lower border of the right ventricle to the
tilages and spaces is shown, the lower boundary of the pericardium below
ventricle was situated behind the seventh cartilage, in two behind the sixth sp
and in one behind the sixth cartilage.

NOTE 6.—Pirogoff gives a series of deepening sections made downwards
from side to side, presenting a front view of the organs.   In two of the more sup
ficial of these sections there was an inclination of two-thirds of an inch (·7

from right to left extending from the lower boundary of the right auricle to the apex of the heart. In a third section, a case of ascites, there was no inclination, the apex being on the same level as the lower border of the right auricle. When the sections deepened, the inclination was still maintained, but the dip from auricle to the apex was less great. Thus in three sections in which the lower border of the left ventricle was exposed, the dip from auricle to apex was respectively one-half (·4 in.), one-third (·3 in.), and one-sixth (·15 in.) of an inch, the latter section being progressively deeper than the former. In like manner, but with a different effect, in two other sections of the case of ascites, the lower boundary of the apex was higher than that of the auricle, in one section by the fifth of an inch (·2 in.), and in a deeper section by half an inch (·5 in.)

NOTE 7.—Pirogoff shows the extent to which the heart extends to the left of the middle line of the sternum in four (or five) vertical, and in eighteen (or seventeen) cross sections. The heart extended to the left of the centre of the sternum from two inches to two and three-quarters (2·8 in.) in two-thirds of these cases (14 in 22); from an inch and a third (1·4 in.) to an inch and three-quarters (1·85 in.) in one-third of them (7 in 22); and three inches and a third (3·4 in.) in one additional instance.

NOTE 8.—Pirogoff indicates approximately the position of the top of the arch in five vertical and four cross sections. In two of the vertical sections the top of the arch appeared to be respectively a quarter and a tenth of an inch above the top of the manubrium, on a level in one with the top of the second, and in the other with the top of the third dorsal vertebra. In the three other vertical sections the top of the arch was three-quarters of an inch (·6 to ·8 in.) below the top of the manubrium, and on a level with the lower portion of the third dorsal vertebra. In one of the four cross sections the top of the arch at the origin of the innominate and left carotid arteries was on a level with the lower edge of the sterno-clavicular articulation, and with the lower border of the second or upper border of the third dorsal vertebra; while in three of them it was on a level with the first space, and in the individual cases respectively with the lower border of the second, the lower border of the third, and the upper border of the fourth dorsal vertebra. Braun gives two vertical sections, in one of which the top of the arch of the aorta was from a quarter to half an inch below the top of the manubrium and on a level with the third dorsal vertebra, while in the other it was more than an inch below the top of the sternum and on a level with the fourth vertebra.

NOTE 9.—The lower boundary of the heart was from two-thirds of an inch (·6 in.) to an inch below the lower end of the sternum in Pirogoff's three vertical sections in which the top of the aorta was three-quarters of an inch (·6 in. to ·8 in.) below the top of the manubrium; and was an inch and a quarter below the end of the sternum, reaching, indeed, to the tip of the ensiform cartilage in Braun's case, in which the top of the aorta was more than an inch below the top of the sternum. On the other hand, the lower boundary of the heart was three-quarters of an inch (·8) above the lower end of the sternum in one of Pirogoff's cases, in which the top of the aorta was above the top of the sternum, and was fully half an inch above that bone in Braun's case, in which the top of the aorta was from a quarter to half an inch below the top of the sternum.

NOTE 10.—Pirogoff shows in his vertical sections the position of the origin of the pulmonary artery in eight instances, and that of the top of the auricular portion of the right auricle in seven. The origin of the pulmonary artery was situated behind the second cartilage in one instance, and behind the fourth cartilage in another; in three cases it lay behind the third cartilage, and in one behind the second space ; while in two it lay from two to two-and-a-half inches below the top of the manubrium. The top of the right auricle was seated behind the second cartilage in two cases, behind the third cartilage in two, and below the top of the manubrium from an inch and a half to an inch and three-quarters in three. In one of the instances in which it lay behind the third cartilage, it was three inches below the top of the manubrium.

NOTE 11.—In five of Pirogoff's vertical sections referred to in Note 10 the vertical length of the pulmonary artery and the right ventricle is shown. In two cases the vertical length of the pulmonary artery was about half an inch, and in these two cases the vertical length of the right ventricle was respectively three inches (3·2 in.) and two and a third (2·3 in.). In the three other cases the vertical length of the pulmonary artery was about one inch (·9 in., 1·05 in., 1·2 in.), that of the right ventricle in those cases being about three inches (2·8 in., 3·1 in., 3·5 in.). In the three latter cases, in which the pulmonary artery was relatively long, the length of the ventricle to that of the artery was as three to one ; while in the two others in which the vessel was short, the ventricle was from four-and-a-half to six times the length of the artery.

NOTE 12.—In one of Pirogoff's transverse sections, referred to in Note 11, the top of the pulmonary artery was situated just above the second cartilage, and the artery, in its short upward course (·4 in.), was covered by the second cartilage ; in another, the top of the artery lay behind the third cartilage, and the artery ascended within the third space. In the three other cases the artery took an intermediate and average position within the second space, its top being seated behind the second cartilage, and its origin behind the third cartilage, or, in one instance, the second space.

The origin of the pulmonary artery was the lowest in position, being behind the fourth cartilage, in the one among these five cases in which the vessel took the longest upward course (1·2 in.) ; while on the other hand, the origin of the artery was the highest, being behind the second cartilage, in the one in which the vessel was the shortest (·4 in.)

NOTE 13.—The arch of the aorta, measured from the point at which it came into view above the right auricle to the adjacent origin of the innominate and left carotid arteries, in Pirogoff's vertical sections, varied in approximate vertical length from about one inch to more than two inches (about 2·2 in.), its average length being about an inch and a half. In two cases, in which the vessel was short (about 1 in.), the vertical length of the arch, from the point at which it came into view, was less than that of the heart, measured from the same point, in the proportion of 10 to 25 ; while in three cases, in which the vessel was long (1·8 in., 2 in., 2·2 in.), the ratio of the length of the vessel to that of the heart was about 10 to 18.

NOTE 14.—Pirogoff shows the vertical length of the right auricle in six sections. In three of these the length of that cavity was two inches and three quarters (2·6 in., 2·7 in., 2·8 in.) ; and in three it was from three inches and third to almost four inches (3·3 in., 3·4 in., 3·8 in.)

NOTE 15.—Pirogoff represents the vertical length of the right ventricle in eleven cases. In two of these the cavity was two inches and a third (2·3 in. and in one it was four inches in length. There was considerable variation in the other cases between these limits, the average length of the cavity in the eleven cases being three inches.

NOTE 16.—The great vessels occupied the upper half of the sternum, and the heart its lower half, in two of Pirogoff's and in one of Braun's sections In one of Braun's sections the great vessels lay behind the upper third of the bone, and the heart behind its lower two-thirds; in three of Pirogoff's sections the great arteries were covered by the upper three-sevenths of the sternum, and the heart by its lower four-sevenths (1·5 in. to 2·1 in.; 2·7 in. to 3in.; 1·4in. to 2·3 in.); while in one of Pirogoff's the great vessels occupied the sternum to a greater extent than the heart in the proportion of eight to seven (3·1 in. to 2·7 in.).

NOTE 17.—The width of the healthy heart was one-half of the width of the chest in two of Pirogoff's cross sections (7·8 in. to 3·9 in. and 7·2 in. to 3·5 in.); it was one-third of that of the chest in four of them (7·4 in. to 2·4 in., 9·4 in. to 3·2 in., 9·2 in. to 3·2 in., 7·2 in. to 2·6 in.), and in six of them the proportion between the width of the heart and that of the chest varied from 10 to 3·9 to 10 to 4·6. In no instance was the breadth of the healthy heart greater in proportion than one-half of that of the chest. In this respect Pirogoff's cases differ from mine, for, as I have said above, in one-third of my cases the width of the heart was greater than one-half of that of the chest (10 to 5 to 10 to 6·2). This may partly be accounted for that in Pirogoff's drawings the section was not as a rule made across the widest part of the heart, and that the breadth of the heart was measured from precisely opposite points; whereas in mine the measurement was taken from the point of the heart furthest to the left, which was near the apex, to the point of the heart furthest to the right, which was about the middle of the right auricle; and I need scarcely say that these points were never precisely opposite to each other.

NOTE 18. — In some of Pirogoff's sections the right ventricle and auricle were proportionally broad in relation to the front of the left ventricle when the heart itself was wide in relation to the width of the chest, while the right cavities were relatively narrow when the heart itself was relatively narrow. In other instances, however, it was the reverse, the heart being relatively narrow or wide, when the right cavities were respectively relatively wide or narrow.

NOTE 19.—In one of Pirogoff's cross sections the heart extended one inch and a tenth into the right side of the chest, and nearly three inches (2·8 in.) into its left side; while in another of them the heart occupied the right side of the chest for a little less than two inches (1·85 in.), and its left side for a little more than two inches (2·15 in.). In one of these extreme instances nearly three-fourths of the heart occupied the left side, and over one-fourth of it the right side of the chest; while in the other more than one-half of the organ lay in the left side, and less than one-half of it in the right side.

In twenty-five cross sections nearly two-fifths of the heart occupied, on an average, the right side, and fully three-fifths of it the left side of the chest (10 to 17). These sections were made across the heart at all levels, from just below the origin of the great vessels to a little above the lower boundary of the organ. In at least four instances more sections than one were made through the same body at different heights, and in these instances the heart, as a rule, lay more to the right in the higher than in the lower sections. This was due to the greater proportionate prevalence of the right auricle in the higher and middle sections; and of the right and left ventricles in the lower sections of the heart. There were, however, three marked exceptions to this rule, which seemed to be due to the greater extension of the right auricle to the right at its middle than at its higher region.

NOTE 20.—The right lung was more developed in front than the left in eight out of nine cases, in which two-thirds of the heart or more occupied the left side, and one-third of it or less the right side of the chest; and the development of the two lungs was about equal in seven out of eight cases in which two-fifths of the heart or more lay in the right side, and three-fifths of it or less in the left side of the chest, the right lung being, however, larger than the left in the two exceptional cases.

NOTE 21.—The breadth of the combined right auricle and ventricle in relation to that of the left ventricle as seen in front in fifteen of Pirogoff's cross sections, varied from 10 to 1·4 to 10 to 4·4, the average proportion being 10 to 3·3.

NOTE 22.—The auricular portion of the right auricle varied in breadth in Pirogoff's cases from nearly an inch and a half (1·4 in.) to four-fifths of an inch (·8 in.), its average breadth in ten cases being one inch.

NOTE 23.—The body of the right auricle varied in breadth in Pirogoff's cases from nearly an inch and a half (1·4 in.) to the fifth of an inch (·2 in.), its average breadth in twenty-one cases being two-thirds of an inch (·66 in.).

NOTE 24.—The left edge of the auricular portion of the right auricle extended almost to the left edge of the sternum (·1 in. from left edge) in one instance ; almost or quite to the centre of the sternum, so as to lie behind its right half, in four instances ; and in one instance it was covered by the right third of that bone.

NOTE 25.—The right edge of the right auricle extended to the right of the right edge of the sternum from the third of an inch to an inch, and, on an average, for two-thirds of an inch in sixteen of Pirogoff's cross sections.

NOTE 26.—The auricular portion of the right auricle was from one-third to two-thirds wider than the body of the auricle in five hearts represented by Pirogoff.

NOTE 27.—The width of the heart in ten of Pirogoff's sections varied from a little more than twice (22 to 10) to almost four times as great as that of the auricular portion of the right auricle ; the heart being on an average fully three times as wide as the auricular appendix.

NOTE 28.—The heart was from three to nine times wider than the exposed portion of the body of the right auricle in twenty of Pirogoff's cases ; the heart being on an average nearly six times as wide as the auricle.

NOTE 29.—The breadth of the right ventricle varied from four-fifths (10 to 12·5) to a little less than one-half (10 to 20·5) of the breadth of the heart in twenty-one of Pirogoff's drawings, sixteen of which were from cross sections of the body, and five from front views of the heart. The average breadth of the right ventricle in these drawings was two-thirds of the breadth of the heart (10 to 15), and in one-half of them (10 in 21) the proportionate width of the heart was at or above, and in one-half of them (11 in 21) it was below that average. The average proportionate breadth of the right ventricle in relation to that of the heart was 10 to 16 in the sixteen cross sections, and 10 to 14 in the five front views of the heart.

NOTE 30.—The breadth of the upper part of the *conus arteriosus* varied from one-half (10 to 20) to four-fifths (10 to 17·2) of the breadth of the right ventricle at its middle, in Pirogoff's five front views of the heart ; the average width of the *conus arteriosus* being in those cases fully three-fifths of that of the right ventricle (10 to 18·6).

NOTE 31.—The length of the right ventricle was equal to that of its breadth in one, and was greater than that of its breadth in four of Pirogoff's five front views of the heart, the average proportion of the length to the breadth of the right ventricle being in those four cases as 5 to 6 (10 to 11·75).

NOTE 32.—The breadth of the right ventricle in relation to the right auricle in Pirogoff's five front views of the heart varied from 10 to 1·3 to 10 to 3·4, the average proportion being 10 to 2·2.

NOTE 33.—The breadth of the right ventricle varied from an inch and two-thirds (1·65 in.) to nearly three inches (2·9 in.) in sixteen of Pirogoff's cross sections, its average breadth being just over two inches (2·1 in.); while in his five front views of the heart, its breadth varied from two inches and a half to three and a third, its average breadth being almost three inches (2·9 in.). The cross sections were somewhat reduced in size, while the front views appeared to be of the natural dimensions.

NOTE 34.—In one of Pirogoff's sections the right ventricle extended further to the right than the left of the middle line of the sternum (1·4 in. to 1· in. to left); in one it occupied the right and left sides of the chest in equal proportions (1·2 in. to 1·2 in.); but in fourteen other sections the right ventricle extended more to the left than the right of the vertical centre of the sternum. In two instances six-sevenths of the ventricle lay to the left, and one-seventh of it to the right of the central line; but on an average, two-thirds of the ven tricle occupied the left, and one-third of it the right side of the chest.

NOTE 35.—In three of Pirogoff's five front views of the healthy heart, the longitudinal furrow during its descent took a direction slightly to the left or outwards during its whole course, so that it was about half an inch more to the left at its lower than its upper portion; but in two of them the furrow curved first to the right for the third of an inch (·3 in.), and then to the left for, in one instance, the same, and in the other for a greater extent (·5 in.)

NOTE 36.—In one of Pirogoff's cross sections the right ventricle extended for only a quarter of an inch to the left of the sternum; but in every other instance that ventricle was covered to a greater or less extent by the costal cartilages. The exact extent to which they were so is not indicated, but I judged that in one-fifth of the cases (3 in 16) the right ventricle extended almost as far to the left as the junction of the cartilages to their ribs; that in one-fourth of them (4 in 16) the ventricle was covered by the two sternal thirds of the cartilages; that in two of them it extended to midway between the sternum and the ribs; and that in one-third of them (6 in 16) it was only covered by the sternal third of the cardiac costal cartilages.

NOTE 37.—The body of the right ventricle extended to the left of the middle line of the sternum from four-fifths of an inch (·85 in.) to two inches (2·1 in.), and on an average for an inch and a half (1·45 in.), in sixteen of Pirogoff's cross sections.

NOTE 38.—The right auriculo-ventricular furrow, starting from the right edge of the origin of the pulmonary, as it descended, extended to the right to an amount varying from one inch to one inch and four-fifths, and on an average for an inch and a half (1·45 in.), in Pirogoff's five front views of the healthy heart.

NOTE 39.—The breadth of the pulmonary artery at its origin varied from an inch to an inch and a half, and was on an average an inch and a quarter, in Pirogoff's five front views of the healthy heart; and in the same cases the breadth of the pulmonary artery a little above its origin varied from three-quarters of an inch to an inch and a quarter, and was on an average about one inch. The pulmonary artery was wider than the aorta in four of these instances, and narrower than the aorta in one of them.

NOTE 40.—The right edge of the pulmonary artery was covered by the sternum to the extent of the third of an inch in one instance, and the tenth of an inch in another, and the remainder of the artery, amounting to three-fourths of its diameter in one instance (·8 in., ·11 in.), and six-sevenths of its

I 2

diameter in the other, occupied the second left space or the second costal cartilage.

NOTE 41.—The *approximate* breadth of the left ventricle as seen in front of the heart varied from almost half an inch (·4 in.) in two instances to an inch and one-fifth (1·2 in.) in three cases, and was on an average three-quarters of an inch in nineteen of Pirogoff's cross sections and five of his front views of the heart. The proportion that the width of the left ventricle at its anterior aspect bore to that of the whole heart in those cases varied from one-eighth (10 to 1·25) to one-third (10 to 3·2).

NOTE 42.—The apex was covered by the inner margin of the left lung to the extent of from half an inch to three-quarters in three of Pirogoff's cross sections, and to the extent of the tenth and the fifth of an inch respectively in two of them; while in two others the outer edge of the lung was not covered by the lung, which, however, was close to it; and in one other instance the apex was completely exposed, the left edge of the lung being ·6 in. to the left of the apex and ·3 in. to the left of the outer left border of the pericardium.

NOTE 43.—The ascending aorta varied in breadth from three-quarters of an inch (·7 in.) to an inch and a fifth (1·2 in.) in Pirogoff's five front views of the healthy heart, its average breadth being one inch.

NOTE 44.—The aorta was narrower than the pulmonary artery in four and wider in one of Pirogoff's cross sections.

NOTE 45.—The ascending aorta was covered by the sternum in four of Pirogoff's five cross sections showing that vessel, and of these instances, in three the artery was central and in one it inclined to the right. In the remaining case the ascending aorta extended a quarter of an inch to the left of the sternum, being present to that extent within the left second space.

NOTE 46.—Pirogoff, whose work is rich in illustrations of the root of the aorta, including its valve and sinuses, represents those parts in eight cross sections, five vertical sections, made through the sternum or cartilages in front, and the spinal column or adjoining ribs behind, and two vertical sections made from side to side. In the eight cross sections the root of the aorta, including its sinuses and the flaps of its valve, was in part covered to a very varying extent by the sternum, and was in part situated behind the corresponding cartilage or space to the left of the sternum. In one of them four-fifths of the artery lay behind the sternum (·8 in.), and one-fifth of it extended to the left of that bone (·2 in.); while in one of them only one-fifth of the vessel (·8 in.) was covered by the sternum, while four-fifths of it occupied the adjoining third left space. There was every gradation between these two extreme instances; and, on an average, less than three-fifths of the root of the aorta lay behind the left portion of the sternum, and more than two-fifths of it behind the corresponding left cartilage or space.

The upper part of the root of the aorta, including its sinuses and the flaps of its valve, was situated in two of the cross sections on a level with the second space, its lower portion being on a level with the third cartilage; in three of them its upper portion was on a level with the middle or lower edge of the third cartilage, its lower portion extending to a greater or less extent to the level of the third space; in one of them its lower border was on a level with the upper half of the third space; and in two of them its upper portion was on a level with the third space, at and above its middle, while its lower portion extended to the level of the upper part of the fourth cartilage. In an additional cross section made through the third space the lowest portion of the right posterior flap of the aortic valve remained, showing its attachment to the anterior flap of the mitral valve.

Pirogoff shows the root of the aorta, including its sinuses and the flaps of its valve, in five vertical sections, of which, (1) two sections were made through the left costal cartilages in front, close to their articulation to the sternum, and the ribs behind near their attachment to the transverse processes of the vertebræ; (2) one through the left side of the sternum and the fifth and sixth cartilages near their attachment in front, and the bodies of the vertebræ behind; and (3) two through the centre of the sternum and ensiform cartilage in front, and that of the spinal column behind.

The relations of the anterior and left posterior flaps of the aortic valve were shown in three of those sections (1, 2), and those of the three flaps, including in addition the right posterior flap, in two others (3). In one section the top of the angle of junction of the anterior and left posterior flaps was situated behind the left third cartilage, in one of them the tenth of an inch (·1 in.) below its upper edge, and in another of them the third of an inch (·3 in.) above its lower edge. In two of them the lower boundary of the section of the aortic valve was half an inch (·5 in. and ·45 in.) below the lower edge of the third cartilage or about the middle of the third space. As, however, in these instances the right posterior flap had been removed, the lower boundary of the valve and of the origin of the aorta must have been about half an inch lower than the lowest point of the section, or behind the upper portion of the fourth left costal cartilage. In the third instance (2), in which also the inferior flap had been removed, the top of the angle of junction of the two superior flaps lay behind the sternum, three-quarters of an inch (·7 in.) below the lower end of the manubrium, or about on a level with the lower border of the second space; and the lowest portion of the section through the aortic valve was situated behind the sternum an inch and a half (1·5 in.) below the lower end of the manubrium, or about on a level with the top of the third space, so that in this instance the lower boundary of the aortic valve would be about on a level with the lower border of the third space. In these three cases the measurement of the section of the aortic valve, the lower portion of those valves being removed, varied from two-thirds of an inch in one instance (·6 in.) to almost an inch (·9 in.) in two instances. In the two remaining sections, however, in which the whole valve was exhibited, its measurement from above downwards amounted to a little over an inch (1·1 in.) in one instance, and to an inch and a half (1·5 in.) in the other. In one of these cases, in which the lower boundary of the heart was four-fifths of an inch (·8 in.) above the lower end of the sternum, the upper boundary of the aortic valve was situated about half an inch (·4 in.) above the middle of the sternum, or about on a level with the second space, and its lower boundary about three-quarters of an inch (·7 in.) below the middle of the sternum, or about on a level with the lower edge of the third cartilage or upper border of the third space. In another case, in which the lower boundary of the heart was situated behind the ensiform cartilage, about an inch (·95 in.) below the lower end of the sternum, the upper boundary of the aortic valve was situated behind the sternum four-fifths of an inch (·8 in.) below the middle of the bone, or about on a level with the lower edge of the third cartilage or upper border of the third space, and the lower boundary of the valve was situated behind the sternum, fully two inches (2·2 in.) below the middle of the bone, and two-thirds of an inch (·65 in.) above its lower end, or about on a level with the fifth cartilage. Keeping out of view this unusual case, it may be said that in Pirogoff's sections, on an average, the root of the aorta, including its sinuses and the flaps of its valve, was situated on a level with the third cartilage and the third space.

MITRAL VALVE.—In one of Pirogoff's vertical sections the top of the mitral valve was fully half an inch (·55 in.) and in another of them it was a third of an inch (·3 in.) above the lower border of the right posterior flap of the aortic valve. In three other sections, the right inferior flap of the aortic valve had been removed, the other flaps being retained; and in one of these sections the top of the mitral valve was the third of an inch, in another it was the fifth of an inch (·2 in.), and in the third it was about the tenth of an inch above the lower edge of the left posterior flap of the aortic valve.

The lower border of the mitral valve was about an inch below the lower border of the left posterior or the anterior flap of the aortic valve in the three instances in which the right posterior flap had been removed; and it was from fully half an inch to fully three-quarters of an inch below the lower edge of the right posterior flap in the two other instances. In one of Pirogoff's front vertical sections the top of the mitral valve was fully half an inch (·6 in.) above the level of the lower border of the right posterior flap of the aortic valve.

In two of Pirogoff's vertical sections, and probably in a third, the top of the mitral valve was about half an inch (·6 in.) below the level of the middle of the sternum, but it was an inch and three-quarters below that point in another instance in which the lower boundary of the heart was an inch below the lower end of the sternum.

In one of Pirogoff's vertical sections the top of the mitral valve was on a level with the lower edge of the third cartilage; and in three of them it was behind the third space, these occupying respectively the upper, the middle, and the lower portion of that space. If we combine the cases in which the vertical section was made through the cartilages with those in which it was made through the sternum, and estimate in the latter cases the approximate relative position of the valve to the cartilages by its position in relation to the sternum, we find that in two cases the top of the mitral valve was on a level with the lower portion of the third cartilage; in three, with the upper third of the third space; in two, with the middle or lower portion of the third space; and in one, with the fourth space.

In one of Braun's vertical sections (a woman aged 25), in which the lower boundary of the heart was half an inch above the lower end of the sternum, the top of the mitral valve was half an inch (·4 in.) below the centre of the sternum; and in another section (a soldier aged 21), the lower boundary of the heart was an inch and a fifth (1·2 in.) below the lower end of the sternum, and the top of the mitral valve was nearly an inch and a half (1·4 in.) below the middle of the sternum.

The lower border of the mitral valve was situated an inch and a half above the lower end of the sternum in one vertical section, and in two it was as low as half an inch above that point; while in three other vertical sections it was on a level with the fourth space, and in two with the fifth cartilage. If we group the two sets of cases together, it may be estimated that in four of them the lower end of the valve was behind the fourth space, and in four behind the fifth cartilage.

In one of Braun's vertical sections, from a woman aged 25, in which the lower boundary of the heart was half an inch above the lower end of the sternum, the lower boundary of the mitral valve was an inch and a half (1·4 in.) above that end of the bone; and in another, from a soldier aged 21, in which the lower boundary of the heart was an inch and a fifth below the lower end of the sternum, the lower border of the mitral valve was less than half an inch (·4 in.) above the end of the bone.

Pirogoff represents nine cross sections through the second space, the whole of which were above the mitral valve; four through the third cartilage, two of which were above the mitral valve, and two were made through the upper part of the valve; eight through the third space, one of which was above and one below the mitral valve, while five were made through the upper portion of the valve, and one through the middle of the mitral orifice; nine through the fourth cartilage, of which two were made through the upper portion and two through the middle of the valve, while five were made below the valve; six through the fourth space, of which one was made through the top of the valve, and three through its middle, while two were made below the valve; and seven through the fifth cartilage, of which six were below the valve, and one was made through the middle of the mitral orifice.

It is self-evident that, in these cases, the top of the mitral valve occupied the space or cartilage above that in which the section passed through the middle of the mitral orifice, and that the top of the valve was relatively still higher in those cases in which the section was made below the mitral valve.

Estimating the position of the top of the mitral valve approximately in these sections on this view, I consider that the upper boundary of the valve was situated in one case on a level with the second space; in nine, on a level with the third cartilage; in two, with the third cartilage or third space; in nine, with the third space; in two, with the third space or fourth cartilage; in three, with the fourth cartilage; in six, with the third cartilage or space or the fourth cartilage; and that in one instance the top of the mitral valve was on a level with the fourth space.

In these cases, on the basis of the calculation just made, it may be approximately estimated that the average position of the top of the mitral valve was about on a level with the upper half of the third intercostal space.

In the same transverse sections, on a similar approximate calculation, the lower border of the mitral valve was situated about on a level with the third cartilage in one instance; the third space in six instances; the fourth cartilage in two; the fourth space in four; the third space, fourth cartilage, or fourth space in six; the fifth cartilage in four instances; and below that cartilage in one.

The average position of the lower boundary of the mitral valve in these cases appears to me, from as close an estimate as I can make, to be about on a level with the lower edge of the fourth cartilage and the upper border of the fourth space.

Pirogoff represents the mitral valve or orifice in seven cross sections, and in all of them the anterior wall of the mitral orifice was situated more to the right than its posterior wall to an extent varying from one-third (·35 in.) to four-fifths (·8 in.) of an inch.

In four of these sections the mitral orifice was situated behind the left half of the sternum; and in three of them it was placed partly behind the left portion of the sternum, partly behind the cartilages and spaces to the left of that bone. In no instance was the anterior wall or border of the mitral valve seated to the right of the middle line of the sternum.

TRICUSPID VALVE.—In two of Pirogoff's vertical sections the top of the tricuspid valve was nearly the third of an inch (·3 in.), and in two others it was nearly half an inch (·4 in. and ·45 in.) below the level of the top of the mitral valve.

The lower border of the tricuspid valve was below the level of the lower border of the mitral valve from half an inch, in the first two cases noted above, to three-quarters of an inch (·65 in. and ·75 in.) in the other two cases

The top of the tricuspid valve was situated, in one of Pirogoff's vertical sections, half an inch, and in two of them one inch, below the centre of the sternum ; in another instance it was an inch above the lower end of that bone. In one of Braun's vertical sections, in which the lower boundary of the heart was high, the top of the tricuspid valve was on a level with the centre of the sternum.

The top of the tricuspid valve was on a level with the top of the third space in one vertical section, with the fourth space in another, and with the fifth cartilage in a third instance.

The lower border of the tricuspid valve was one inch above the lower end of the sternum in two of Pirogoff's vertical sections, and an inch and a half above that point in one of Braun's vertical sections, in which the lower boundary of the heart was above the lower end of the sternum ; and it was a third of an inch (·3 in.) below the lower end of that bone in two of Pirogoff's sections, in which the inferior boundary of the heart was behind the middle of the ensiform cartilage. The lower border of the valve was on a level with the fourth space in one of Pirogoff's sections, and with the sixth cartilage in two of them.

Pirogoff represents four cross sections through the third cartilage, all of which were above the tricuspid valve ; eight through the third space, four of which were above that valve, three were made through its upper portion, and one below it ; nine through the fourth cartilage, of which three were above the valve, one was made through its middle, three through its lower portion, one through the bottom of the valve, and one below it ; six through the fourth space, of which one was above the valve, three through its upper portion, one through its lower portion, and one below it ; and seven through the fifth cartilage, of which one was made through the middle of the tricuspid orifice and six below it.

Estimating approximately the position of the top of the tricuspid valve in these cross sections, I consider that the upper boundary of the valve was situated on a level with the second space, or third cartilage in one instance; with the third cartilage or space in two ; with the third space in seven ; with the third space or fourth cartilage in ten ; with the fourth cartilage in three ; with the fourth cartilage or space in four ; and with the fourth space in two.

I think that we may estimate that in these sections the top of the tricuspid valve was on an average situated behind the lower portion of the third space, or the upper edge of the fourth cartilage.

In the same cross sections, and on a similar approximate calculation, the lower border of the tricuspid valve was about on a level with the third cartilage in one instance; with the third space in one ; with the third space or fourth cartilage in one ; with the fourth cartilage in one ; with the fourth cartilage or space in six ; with the fourth space in seven ; with the fifth cartilage in three ; and with the fifth cartilage or space or lower in ten.

The approximate average position of the lower boundary of the tricuspid valve in these transverse sections appears to me to be about on a level with the lower portion of the fourth space, or upper portion of the fifth cartilage.

Pirogoff represents the tricuspid orifice in eleven cross sections, and in all of them the anterior edge of the tricuspid orifice was more to the right than its posterior edge to an extent varying from a quarter (·25 in.) to four-fifths (·85 in.) of an inch.

The left edge of the tricuspid valve was situated more to the right than the right edge of the mitral valve in six of seven instances in which the section went through both valves, to an extent varying from the tenth to the third (·3 in.) of an inch ; while in the seventh instance the left edge of the tricuspid was immediately in front of the right edge of the mitral valve.

In five of the eleven sections the tricuspid valve was situated behind the right half of the sternum ; in one of them it was behind the right third of that bone ; in one it lay partly behind the right portion of the sternum and partly to the right of it ; in two it was central, occupying equally the right and left sides of the sternum, and in the remaining two it lay to the left of the middle line of that bone.

NOTE 47.—Pirogoff shows the relation of the sternum and costal cartilages in front to the vertebræ behind in twelve antero-posterior vertical sections and in sixty-two cross sections.

In five of the vertical sections the top of the sternum was on a level with the lower border of the body of the second or the upper border of the third dorsal vertebra, or the cartilage between these two vertebræ ; in one of them it was on a level with the top of the fourth dorsal vertebra ; and in one of them, an instance that stands alone, it was according to Pirogoff's description, on a level with the upper portion of the first dorsal vertebra. This description is however evidently an accidental error, and I, therefore, for the first, read the second vertebra. In Braun's two vertical sections the top of the sternum was on a level with the cartilage between the second and third dorsal vertebræ.

I examined eleven human skeletons in the Museum of the Royal College of Surgeons, with the valuable assistance of Mr. Wright, of the Museum, and I found that in eight of them, including one in the Hunterian Museum, the top of the manubrium was on a level with the second dorsal vertebra,[1] the point varying from its upper to its lower border ; and that in three of them it was on a level with the first dorsal vertebra.

In two of Pirogoff's vertical sections the top of the sternum was on a level with the lower border of the third rib, near the spine, in one of them it was on a level with the upper border of the fourth rib, and in one it was above the level of the first rib. In this last instance there was evidently an accidental error.

The lower end of the osseous sternum was on a level with the middle of the eighth dorsal vertebra in two of Pirogoff's vertical sections, in one of which the sternum and ribs had been elevated by a large accumulation of fluid in the abdomen ; in one of them it was on a level with the middle of the ninth vertebra, and in one with the cartilage between the ninth and tenth vertebræ.

In Braun's two sections the lower end of the sternum was on a level respectively with the middle and lower border of the ninth vertebra.

In one of the skeletons in the Museum of the Royal College of Surgeons the lower end of the sternum was on a level with the seventh dorsal vertebra, in one with the cartilage between the seventh and eighth vertebræ, in three with the middle of the eighth vertebra, in two with the cartilage between that vertebra and the ninth, and in three with respectively the top, middle, and lower border of the ninth vertebra, the last instance being the skeleton in the Hunterian Museum.

The middle of the sternum which corresponds with its articulation to the third costal cartilages was on a level with the middle of the fifth dorsal vertebra in one of Pirogoff's vertical sections, with the cartilage between the fifth and sixth vertebræ in two of them, and with the middle of the sixth vertebra in another of them, and in Braun's two sections.

The bottom of the manubrium which corresponds with the second cartilage and with the lower end of the upper third of the sternum was on a level with the lower half of the body of the fourth dorsal vertebra in two of Pirogoff's vertical sections, and in two of them and in Braun's two sections with the middle of the fifth vertebra.

[1] The body of the dorsal vertebra is referred to here and elsewhere, unless it is otherwise specified.

in four instances in front of the middle or top of the seventh vertebra or the cartilage above it, and in one in front of the middle of the eighth vertebra.

The upper boundary of the mitral valve was situated in six of Pirogoff's vertical sections in front respectively of the middle of the sixth dorsal vertebra, the cartilage between the sixth and seventh vertebræ, the seventh vertebra, and in one instance the eighth; and its lower boundary was situated in three of his vertical sections in front of the eighth, and in one it extended down to the top of the lower third of the ninth vertebra. In one of Braun's vertical sections the mitral valve extended from the level of the cartilage below the sixth vertebra down to that of the upper third of the eighth, and in the other it extended from the cartilage below the seventh vertebra down to the upper third of the ninth vertebra.

The mitral valve was situated in front of the cartilage above the seventh dorsal vertebra in two of Pirogoff's cross sections, the seventh vertebra in probably nine of them, the cartilage between that vertebra and the eighth in two of them, and in front of the eighth vertebra in four of them.

The upper boundary of the tricuspid valve was situated in seven of Pirogoff's vertical sections on a level respectively with the upper and (in a case of ascites) lower borders of the sixth dorsal vertebra, the cartilage between that vertebra and the seventh, and the upper border of the seventh vertebra, the lower portion of the eighth vertebra, and the cartilage below it. The tricuspid valve in one of Braun's sections extended from the level of the top of the seventh vertebra to that of the middle of the eighth.

The tricuspid valve was on a level with the eighth vertebra in five instances, with the cartilage below it in two, and with the ninth vertebra in two.

MALPOSITIONS OF THE HEART.

THE displacements of the heart may be conveniently divided into the Vertical, Lateral, Forward, and Backward displacements.

THE VERTICAL DISPLACEMENTS OF THE HEART.

CASES IN WHICH THE HEART IS LOWERED.—The cause of the vertical lowering of the healthy heart is in all cases, with the exception of aneurisms of the arch of the aorta, an unusual lowering of the diaphragm. Pulmonary emphysema, bronchitis, and spasmodic asthma; croup, laryngitis, and laryngismus stridulus; collapse of the stomach and intestines; and aneurism of the arch of the aorta—all tend to lower the heart. To these may be added certain cases of mediastinal tumour, and pleuritic effusion into the left side during the middle period of its increase.

Pulmonary Emphysema, Bronchitis, and Spasmodic Asthma.—In Pulmonary Emphysema the right cavities of the heart and the pulmonary artery are greatly enlarged. The right ventricle often completely covers the left ventricle. The diaphragm is remarkably low, its standard position being often lower than it is in health at the end of the deepest possible inspiration. The enlargement of the lungs is so extensive that they cover the heart within the chest; and they are consequently everywhere interposed between the heart and the walls of the chest, with the exception of the border of the seventh costal cartilage (Fig. 27). The heart is invariably enlarged, the enlargement being almost limited to the right side. The venæ cavæ and right auricle are usually distended and of great size; the right ventricle is so much increased in volume that it almost or altogether conceals the left ventricle, its walls being hardened and hypertrophied; and the pulmonary artery is greatly increased in length and breadth. Notwithstanding the enlargement of the heart, its impulse is imperceptible over the walls of the chest; and in some cases its sounds are so muffled that they are scarcely audible over the usual cardiac region owing to the great development of the lungs in front of the heart. In no instance, however, is the heart absolutely covered by the dilated lungs. The central tendon of the diaphragm descends almost or quite to the level of the lower end of the ensiform cartilage, and necessarily draws downwards the enlarged heart. It is customary to speak of the displacement of the heart downwards as being caused by

the expansion of the lung. This may be so in some cases, but as
rule the unusual descent of the heart, like that of the base of t
lungs, is caused by the unusual descent of the diaphragm. T
lower boundary of the right ventricle is brought downwards into t
epigastrium, so that it is situated behind and to each side of the en
form cartilage. In that position, and to the left of it, the heart is r
covered with lung, and it is therefore in contact with the ensiform can
lage, with the neighbouring margin of the seventh left costal cartila

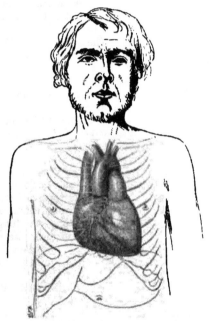

F⍺. 27.—Position of the heart and great vessels in *Pulmonary Emphysema.* T
    heart is displaced downwards, and is covered with the over-developed lungs. T
    apex-beat is imperceptible, but the impulse of the right ventricle is seen and felt
    the epigastrium.

and with the intermediate abdominal muscles, the pericardium inte
vening. The result is that, as Dr. Stokes has pointed out, the impul
of the right ventricle may be felt in the epigastrium; and as tl
right ventricle is hypertrophied, "the heart may be felt pulsatir
with a violence that we would not expect from the examination
the pulse at the wrist, which is often small and feeble, while tl
impulses of the right ventricle are given with great strength." *   Tl
form of the chest, the great expansion of the lungs, the low positio

* Dr. Stokes on the Diseases of the Chest, p. 178.

of the diaphragm, and the enlargement, elongation, and lowering of the heart and great vessels, all correspond, though to an exaggerated degree, with the condition of those parts at the end of the deepest possible inspiration in health. The presence of the impulse and sounds of the heart over the epigastrium, and their absence over the walls of the chest, are the signs that often first direct attention to the morbidly enlarged condition of the lungs.

In cases of severe bronchitis, the diaphragm is invariably lowered, the right cavities of the heart are enlarged, and the lungs are amplified. In those cases, therefore, as in emphysema, the heart is lowered, its impulse is obliterated over the intercostal spaces by the interposition of the lung, and the beat of the right ventricle is felt and seen in the epigastrium. The extent to which the heart is enlarged, lowered, and covered by lung is by no means so great in bronchitis as in emphysema.

When, as is often the case, the patient affected with emphysema is attacked by bronchitis, the extent to which the heart is lowered, and enveloped by the lungs is increased.

During an attack of spasmodic asthma, the diaphragm descends, the lungs are expanded to the utmost, and the impulse of the right ventricle is lowered into the epigastrium, just as in cases of true pulmonary emphysema. After the seizure is over, its effect upon the size of the lungs and the position of the heart does not immediately disappear. Gradually, however, the organs resume their healthy size and position. The asthmatic seizure that often attacks those affected with emphysema, is accompanied by an excessive amplification of the lungs and descent of the impulse; but in such patients the lungs and heart do not regain their normal size and position after the cessation of the attack, and in this important respect true spasmodic asthma is to be distinguished from the asthmatic seizure of a person affected with true pulmonary emphysema.

Croup, Laryngitis, Laryngismus Stridulus.—In all those cases in which there is excessive narrowing of the fauces, larynx, or trachea so as to contract the channels through which air is admitted into the lungs and render inspiration exceedingly difficult, the inspiratory efforts are laborious but ineffectual. Every muscle of respiration is brought into powerful action. The diaphragm descends as low as possible. The lungs are consequently lengthened and the heart is drawn downwards. As air, in spite of the laboured breathing, can scarcely enter the air tubes, the lungs, being lengthened downwards, instead of expanding, collapse during inspiration, and the walls of the chest fall inwards. The lungs recede from before the heart, which is in immediate and extensive contact with the walls of the chest as well as with the ensiform cartilage. The heart is, therefore, in such cases to be felt beating with force over and to the left of the lower sternum and in the epigastrium.

Collapse of the Stomach and Intestines.—When the abdomen is un-usually spare, the stomach and intestines being comparatively or quite empty, the abdominal organs shrink downwards, and th

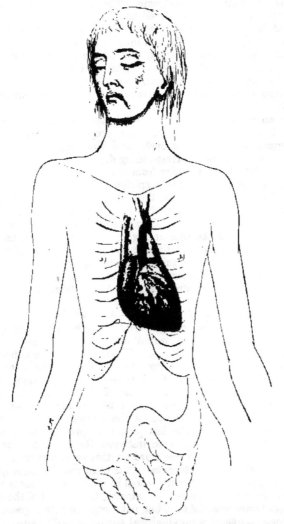

Fig. 28.—Position of the heart and great vessels in a case with *Collapse of the Stomach and Intestines.* The heart is displaced downwards, and covered with lung to the fifth cartilage. The apex-beat is present in the fifth space, and perhaps in the sixth, and the impulse of the right ventricle is seen and felt in the epigastrium.

diaphragm is permanently lowered. This was well seen in the poor woman from whom fig. 28 was taken. She had been unable to swallow owing to cancer of the œsophagus for a fortnight before her death. Her emaciation was extreme. The stomach and intestines were absolutely empty of gas as well as of food. The liver, though not enlarged, had dropped downwards, so that its lower border rested on the bones of the pelvis. The diaphragm necessarily followed the liver and stomach in their descent, and as the result, the lungs at their base, and the heart where it rested on the diaphragm, were unusually lowered, and both organs were remarkably lengthened. The elongation of the ascending aorta and the pulmonary artery was very marked.

This was an extreme case, but in all instances of abdominal collapse, the diaphragm descends in exact proportion to the descent of those organs upon which it rests, and the lungs and heart are lengthened downwards to a corresponding degree. In some of those cases the transfer of the impulse from the intercostal spaces to the epigastrium may give rise to the suspicion of pulmonary emphysema on the one hand, or aneurism of the abdominal aorta on the other. In emphysema the chest is unduly developed, and the abdomen, instead of being retracted, is usually of more than average size. In aneurism of the lower thoracic or higher abdominal aorta, the impulse or pulsation in the epigastrium is strong during expiration, but it lessens and even disappears during a deep inspiration. In cases of abdominal collapse, it is the reverse, for the impulse in the epigastrium becomes lower and stronger when the patient takes a deep breath.

Aneurism of the Arch of the Aorta.—One would have expected *à priori* that aneurisms affecting the arch of the aorta, especially when they are of large size, would cause considerable displacement of the heart downwards. Dr. Townshend saw an instance of aneurism of the arch thrusting the heart downwards, so that it pulsated in the epigastrium.[1] I possess drawings taken from thirteen cases of aneurism of the arch of the aorta. In one of these the lower boundary of the right ventricle was situated more than an inch below the lower end of the sternum. In four there was effusion of blood into the left pleura, displacing the heart to the right. In the remaining seven instances the lower boundary of the right ventricle was from one-third to three-quarters of an inch below the lower end of the sternum. It is clear that in the majority of these cases, although the aneurism was in nearly all of them large, varying from three to five inches in diameter, the descent of the heart into the epigastrium was definite, but not proportionately great. In two of the instances there was cylindrical aneurism or dilatation of the ascending aorta. In these the transverse diameter of the aorta was only two inches, while its vertical measurement was four inches. They must, therefore, be included with the others in estimating the influence of aneurism of the arch of the aorta in displacing the heart downwards. The aneurismal sac displaces not so much the

[1] Cyclopædia of Medicine, ii. 391.

whole heart as those parts of it upon which it makes immediate pressure, and which are subjected thereby to compression. This applies especially to the aneurisms of the ascending aorta, which amount to nine among my cases. In all of these the right ventricle, and in most of them the right auriole, were compressed from above downwards, the compression starting from a point at the top of the transverse furrow between those cavities, where the aorta comes into view. The difference in the vertical diameter of the right ventricle below the part in question and just below the pulmonary artery, amounted in one instance to two inches, the actual measurements being respectively three and five inches. As a rule the difference was much less, but this was mostly due to the right ventricle being compressed downwards in its whole breadth by the sac. In five of the cases the auricular appendix was displaced downwards and to the right.

The downward displacement of the apex in aneurism of the arch of the aorta is not considerable, being in fact mainly due to co-existing hypertrophy of the left ventricle. That condition, however, is not usual, except in those cases of cylindrical aneurism or dilatation of the ascending aorta, in which there is free aortic regurgitation, when the left cavity is greatly enlarged, and when the descent of the apex is much more due to that cause than to the aneurism.

Mediastinal Tumours.—Dr. Bennett gives a case of mediastinal tumour, which will be more fully noticed at page 144, in which there was considerable displacement downwards and to the right of the heart, which was seen and felt beating in the epigastrium.

Pleuritic Effusion into the Left Side.—In the middle period of these cases, when the fluid is steadily increasing, but has not yet reached to its height, there is displacement downwards and to the right of the heart, which may be felt beating in the epigastrium. A full account of such cases, and an explanation of their phenomena, will be found at page 136.

CASES IN WHICH THE HEART IS RAISED.—Abdominal enlargement from gastro-intestinal distension, ascites, the presence of gas in the cavity of the abdomen, abdominal tumours, ovarian dropsy, aneurism of the abdominal aorta at the cœliac axis, and enlarged liver and spleen, all tend to elevate the heart. To these may be added certain cases of mediastinal tumours.

We have just seen that when there is collapse of the abdomen the diaphragm descends, drawing after it the heart and lungs. When there is distension of the abdomen, whatever be the cause, the reverse of this takes place. The diaphragm is raised, the cavity of the chest is shortened, and the heart and lungs are elevated and compressed upwards.

Distension of the Stomach and Intestines.—By far the most frequent distressing, and often fatal cause of the elevation of the diaphragm and compression upwards of the heart and lungs, is the distension of the stomach and intestines with gas. The effect of this condition is well shown in fig. 29, which was taken from a youth affected with diabetes, who, for months before his death, suffered from great abdominal distension. The cavity of the chest was materially lessened. The lower ribs, especially on the left side, were pressed outwards so

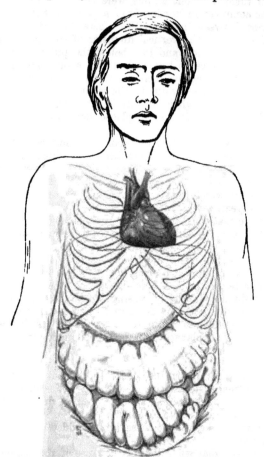

FIG. 29.—Position of the heart and great vessels in cases with *Distension of the Stomach and Intestines.* The heart is displaced and compressed upwards, its impulse being present in the second and third spaces, and perhaps in the fourth.

as to restrain their movements, and the whole cage of the chest was elevated in front and at the sides. The heart and lungs were compressed upwards and lessened in size, so as to impede respiration and circulation.

K 2

When the abdomen is enlarged, it is enlarged in two directions, one outwards and downwards by the expansion of the walls of the abdomen, the other upwards by the elevation of the diaphragm. When the abdomen is extremely distended, the whole cavity becomes oval in form, or shaped like a balloon; the outer part of it presses outwards, and the upper part of it presses upwards. The cage of the chest is raised by this double movement of distension upwards and outwards. The wide irregular cone formed by the upper part of the swollen oval abdomen, acting upon the lower ribs, forces them asunder to the right and to the left, and lifts up the whole front of the cage of the chest. The more important effect of this distension of the abdomen is to lift up the diaphragm, and with it the heart at the centre of the chest, and the right and left lung on each side of it. When these organs are thus raised, as the walls of the chest in front of them, by which their relative position is measured, are raised also, the apparent elevation of the heart is much less than its real elevation. The heart and great vessels are compressed upwards, and displaced somewhat to the right, so that the heart takes a central position in the chest, while the great vessels often bear unduly to the right. The shape of the heart is altered. It is shortened from below upwards, and is proportionally though not actually widened. Its apex is especially tilted upwards, and instead of being, as in health, lower than the inferior boundary of the right ventricle at the end of the sternum, is higher than that point by from a third to one-half of an inch. It is to be observed that the heart and lungs are compressed upwards into the highest part of the cavity of the chest, and as that cavity is a cone narrowing from below upwards, those organs, to their great additional inconvenience, are pushed up into the narrowest part of the space that they naturally occupy.[1]

Intestinal distension is usually present in peritonitis, and it becomes in many cases the most distressing symptom. As Dr. Stokes has shown, muscles are paralysed by inflammation. The inflamed muscular coat of the intestines, being paralysed, yields before the gaseous distension, which is no longer restrained by the peristaltic contraction of the intestines. In peritonitis, abdominal respiration is suspended and the diaphragm is passive. It therefore yields without resistance to the upward pressure exerted upon it by the distended intestines, and the heart and lungs are compressed upwards to a greater degree than in those cases of abdominal distension in which the diaphragm retains its power. Distension of the stomach and intestines is very frequent in the dying. It was present to an excessive degree in either the stomach or intestines, or both, in 63 out of 122 dead bodies observed by me indiscriminately; and in 28 of these the stomach and intestines were very much distended. In such cases the abdominal distension, which is usually one of the secondary

[1] For additional details as to this subject, see a lecture by the author on the "Influence of Distension of the Abdomen on the Functions of the Heart and Lungs," in the *British Medical Journal* for August 2, 1873, p. 108.

effects of the original disease, produces compression of the heart and lungs, and thereby often hastens death or becomes its immediate cause. The introduction of the œsophagœal tube from above, or of O'Beirne's tube from below, or the insertion of a small aspiration tube through the abdominal walls into the stomach, will in some of these cases give vent to the flatus and so produce material relief.

Many persons, especially those who have become stout, are subject to habitual distension of the stomach and intestines, with the effect of compressing the diaphragm upwards, curtailing its power to descend freely during inspiration, and so encroaching on the cavity of the chest. Those so affected do not, in many instances, suffer when they are at rest, but on any exertion respiration becomes hurried and difficult and the circulation of the blood is impeded. Such persons generally present themselves in two classes. One class, complain of shortness of breath, the other, of pain or distress in the heart when they make exertion, especially after a full meal. In many cases of angina pectoris, the distress is most easily excited after food. Some stout people are unusually subject to distress in breathing or in the heart or both from comparatively slight distension of the abdomen. In these persons the cavity of the abdomen is naturally incapable of great expansion owing to its walls being firm and resisting. The abdominal fulness, when it passes certain limits, cannot make way forwards and outwards, and the result is that the diaphragm is pushed upwards and the lungs and heart are soon subjected to a distressing amount of pressure.

In dyspeptic persons, the most distressing symptoms induced by the fulness of the stomach after food are often referred to the heart. This is apt to be the case also whenever the stomach is greatly distended. The reason is obvious: the stomach is immediately subjacent to the heart, the diaphragm being interposed, so that the heart, in fact, rests upon the stomach. Whenever, therefore, the stomach is greatly swollen by an accumulation of gas and food, the heart is compressed upwards in an especial manner, and the distress experienced is often, therefore, almost limited to the heart. I do not of course lose sight of the additional physiological influence exerted by the stomach upon the heart through the medium of the eighth pair of nerves.

Ascites.—In ascites, the accumulation of the fluid is gradual. The patient is usually in bed, and the distress in breathing and in the heart experienced by the patient, owing to compression of the heart and lungs, is by no means proportionate to the amount of the distension. Indeed, those cases of ascites that suffer great distress in the organs of the chest usually have in addition distension of the stomach and intestines as well as enlargement of the liver. When this is so, a small amount of fluid in the peritoneal cavity will produce serious discomfort, and the removal even of a little of it by tapping will give immediate and unusual relief. Some years ago I had a patient in St. Mary's Hospital who was affected with aortic and mitral regurgitation. The heart was enlarged and the pericardium was adherent. He breathed with difficulty, owing to the great size of the abdomen, which was produced by the triple combination of great enlargement of the liver, distension of the stomach and intestines, and ascites. The quantity of urine was scanty, being about eleven ounces daily. The amount of fluid in the peritoneal cavity was small, but with the view of affording relief, tapping was resorted to. The intestines were so near the surface that an incision was made in the parietes of the abdomen, and the trochar and canula were introduced in a downward direction. At first only half a teaspoonful of fluid escaped, but by passing a female catheter through the canula, so as to press the intestines gently away from the end of the tube, about ninety ounces of serum were withdrawn. The relief to breathing was complete. The urine, before so scanty, now began to flow freely, and from fifty to eighty ounces were passed daily. By drawing off the fluid the extreme distension was relieved, and the ligature, so to speak, on the circulation, caused by the compression of the heart, was removed. Ultimately the fluid reaccumulated, and the patient died. The result was unfavourable, but the case was none the less instructive, for it demonstrated that the encroachment of the abdomen upon the chest checked the circulation of the blood and so prevented the free secretion of urine.

In all cases of abdominal distension the seat of the impulse of the heart is a ready and exact measure of the extent to which the cavity of the abdomen encroaches upwards on the cavity of the chest. The progress of such distension, whether on the ascending or descending scale, may be exactly ascertained by noticing the varying position, upwards or downwards, of the impulse of the heart. It must however be borne in mind that, when the heart and lungs are raised by distension of the abdomen, the walls of the chest in front of those organs is raised also, and that the apparent elevation of the heart, measured by its relation to the walls of the chest, is much less than its real elevation.

Escape of Gas into the Cavity of the Abdomen.—The escape of gas into the cavity of the abdomen, owing to perforation of the stomach or intestines, produces rapid distension of that cavity and great elevation of the diaphragm and the heart and lungs, with the effect of inducing great distress in breathing and difficulty in the action of the heart.

Abdominal Tumours, even when they are of considerable size, rarely produce any material disturbance either in the action of the heart or in the performance of respiration.

Ovarian Dropsy.—The same may be said of cases of ovarian dropsy even when the sac is of very large size, and rises upwards so as to encroach on the chest, unless that affection be accompanied by intestinal distension. In the female the walls of the abdomen are capable of great forward expansion, and the result is that large ovarian cysts as well as the gravid uterus at the full time tend rather to protrude forwards so as to distend the abdominal parietes anteriorly, than to rise upwards so as to elevate the diaphragm and encroach upon the heart and lungs.

Simple Enlargement of the Liver and Spleen.—When the liver is universally enlarged, even when it assumes a very great size, it does not rise upwards, so as to raise the diaphragm and compress the heart and lungs, but it tends to grow downwards, so as to displace the stomach and intestines. The same may be said of the spleen in cases of leucocythemia, even when that organ attains to a very large size.

The result is, that simple enlargement of the liver or spleen does not as a rule encroach upon the chest so as to produce serious disturbance in the functions of the heart or lungs.

It is quite otherwise when the upper part of the right lobe of the liver is occupied by large abscesses or hydatid cysts or malignant growths. These morbid conditions produce a peculiar displacement of the heart upwards and towards the left subclavicular region, and I shall therefore consider them under the lateral displacements of the heart.

Mediastinal Tumour.—Dr. Bennett[1] gives a case of mediastinal cancer involving the bronchial glands and spinal column, in which the heart was found displaced, being drawn upwards. During life there was very little impulse to be felt or seen immediately to the left of the sternum just above the nipple.

THE LATERAL DISPLACEMENTS OF THE HEART.

Pleuritic effusion, empyema, and pneumo-thorax of one side of the chest; hæmorrhage into either cavity of the chest from the rupture of an aneurism of the aorta; thoracic tumours; aneurisms of the arch of the aorta; aneurisms of the abdominal aorta at the cæliac axis; and large abscesses or hydatid cysts or malignant tumours in the upper part of the liver; all tend to displace the heart towards the side of the chest opposite to that which is affected. Contraction or cirrhosis of one lung with adhesions of the pleura tends to displace the heart towards the affected side. To these may be added lateral curvature of the spine and congenital transposition of the viscera.

The lateral or transverse displacements of the heart, which are sometimes called dislocations, unlike the displacement of the heart upwards by the encroachment of the cavity of the abdomen upon that of the chest, do not as a rule produce much distress in the heart itself or disturbance of the circulation. The lateral displacements of the heart are, however, valuable and decisive indications of disease, since by the evidence they afford they often render our diagnosis accurate and certain.

Pleuritic Effusion, Empyema, Pneumo-thorax.—The effusion of serum into either cavity of the chest, owing to pleuritis, acute or chronic, is the usual cause of the lateral displacement of the heart.

[1] Intrathoracic Tumours, p. 127.

When extensive effusion takes place into the left side, the heart is pushed over towards or into the right side of the chest, as may be seen in fig. 30. This figure, unlike the others, does not represent an actual case, but is a diagram, made from drawings of six cases, one

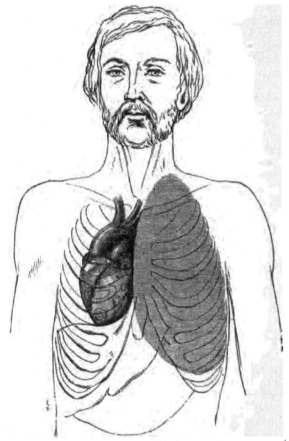

Fig. 30.—Position of the heart and great vessels in cases of *Pleuritic Effusion into the Left cavity of the Chest.* The heart is displaced into the right side of the chest, its impulse being felt in the third, fourth, and fifth spaces.

of effusion of serum into the pleura, one of empyema, and the four others of extensive effusion of blood into the left pleura from the rupture of a thoracic aneurism. In one of these the clot measured three pints and a half.

The displacement of the heart from the increasing effusion of fluid into the pleura is usually gradual. It may, however, be rapid, and Dr. Walshe states that thirty-six hours will sometimes suffice for the heart's impulse to find its way beyond the right nipple. When the quantity of fluid is so small as to occupy only the back part of the left side of the chest, the heart is scarcely displaced. When the fluid increases the left ventricle and its apex are at first thrown a little forwards, and towards the centre of the chest. The pressure of the effused fluid is not made directly upon the heart, but upon the strong fibrous sac of the pericardium, and, through its medium, upon the heart. If the heart had no sac of its own, and was present without restraint in, say, the left cavity of the chest, it would not be forced forward and to the right when the left cavity of the chest is filled with fluid, but it would, I consider, gravitate backwards owing to its own dead weight, and sink to the back of the cavity, just as the liver sinks to the back of the fluid in cases of ascites. The presence of the pericardium completely prevents such a state of things. The accumulated fluid distending the left cavity of the chest presses equally in every direction. It displaces the ribs backwards, forwards, and especially outwards, so that they draw the lower end of the sternum somewhat to the left; it displaces the left wing of the diaphragm, the spleen, stomach, and left lobe of the liver downwards and to the right; and it displaces the pericardium and the heart and great vessels inwards and to the right. The lower end of the pericardium at its attachment to the central tendon of the diaphragm is stretched downwards by the traction upon it of the lowered left wing of the diaphragm, to which it is attached by its central tendon.

The apex forms throughout the lowest part of the heart, and it describes a segment of a circle or arc as it sweeps round from its natural position in the left side of the chest to the position of extreme deviation to which it may attain in the right side of the chest. When the apex describes this curve, instead of being raised by the resistance offered by the abdominal organs, it is lowered during the first two-thirds of its course. The reason for this is obvious. The fluid in the left pleura, which displaces the pericardium and the heart to the left, displaces at the same time, as I have just explained, the left wing of the diaphragm and its central tendon and the subjacent organs downwards, forwards, and to the right. Under these circumstances, as the central tendon forming the base of the pericardium is lowered, there is a free space downwards into which the apex of the heart, suspended from the arch of the aorta, necessarily drops, so that it may be felt beating in the epigastrium over, beyond, and even below the ensiform cartilage. At length, however, the heart, as it advances further into the right side, meets with increasing resistance from the solid convexity of the liver; and the heart, consequently, again rises, so that it is at length about as high on the right side as it is in health on the left. The displaced heart may indeed attain to a higher position if it deviate still farther to the right, when, as in a case of Wintrich's,[1] it may approach the axilla, and be felt beating from the second to the fourth spaces.

Information of some diagnostic value is to be obtained by observing the position of the heart in comparatively early stages in cases of pleuritic effusion, at a time when the impulse of the apex has already moved from its natural position and is on its way towards the central line. To quote Dr. Stokes, we observe, first, that the apex strikes in a situation about midway between its natural position and the upper portion of the ensiform cartilage.[2] It is not, however, until the apex beat presents itself in the epigastrium that much notice is taken of the altered position of the heart. In four of my cases of displacement of the heart towards the right from effusion into the left side of the chest, the apex presented itself in the epigastrium, being in one of these behind the lower end of the ensiform cartilage, and in two behind its middle. As Dr. Townshend remarks, in speaking of empyema in the left side, the heart is thrust from its natural position down into the epigastrium, where it may be seen and felt beating. There is no difficulty in distinguishing the impulse of the apex from that of the right ventricle in the epigastrium. When the latter is present the whole heart has been lowered, owing to the lowering of the diaphragm. This may occur, as we have already seen, in cases either of pulmonary emphysema, or croup, or with collapse of the stomach and intestines. when the presence of *pulmonary* resonance over the left side will at once enable us to distinguish the case. In cases of pleuritic effusion the existence of dulness, and in those of pneumothorax the presence of amphoric resonance, over the whole of the left side, and the absence of impulse to the left of the sternum, will generally suffice to make the case clear. Cancerous tumours occupying the whole of the left side may also give rise to displaced impulse and to general dulness on percussion, when that disease cannot be distinguished from pleuritic effusion or empyema on those grounds alone. In cases of pneumonia of the whole of the left lung, it is possible that owing to the enlargement of the pneumonic lung from consolidation and the development of the right lung to compensate for the disablement of the left lung, the impulse of the apex may disappear from the walls of the chest, while that of the right ventricle may descend into the epigastrium. In such cases, however, the impulse is comparatively slight, and it always extends rather to the left than the right of the ensiform cartilage, while in cases of pleuritic effusion the impulse is usually strong and marked, and tends rather to the right than the left side of that cartilage. As soon as the seat of the impulse disappears from the left side of the chest and extends to the right of the sternum, every difficulty of the kind just stated vanishes.

As the heart passes over from the left to the right side of the chest it gradually and necessarily turns over upon itself, hinging, so to speak,

[1] Krankheiten der Respirationsorgane.
[2] Dr. Stokes on the Diseases of the Heart and Lungs, p. 500.

upon the vessels by which the heart is attached to the lungs and the system, so that the right auricle is hidden, all but the top of its appendix, and instead of the right ventricle being in front of the left ventricle, all but its left border, it is the reverse, for the left ventricle hides a large portion of the right ventricle (see Fig. 30). The part of the right ventricle exposed is, however, not that near the apex, but that near the pulmonary artery. The ascending aorta and pulmonary artery change their direction; they move to the right at their respective origins, but higher up they are retained in their places, the arch of the aorta at the end of its transverse portion, and the pulmonary artery at its bifurcation. The aorta and pulmonary artery, therefore, present not a front but a profile view, with a direction to the right.

I published a case with a diagram showing the position of the internal organs in the "Provincial Medical Transactions" for 1844 (p. 162), in which effusion in the left side of the chest was limited to the lower two-thirds of the cavity, owing to the upper lobe of the left lung being adherent down to the third rib. In this case the heart was simply displaced to the right, the front of the organ being still occupied by the right ventricle, and its right and left sides by the right auricle and the left ventricle. This case shows that the heart does not turn over upon itself so as to present the left ventricle instead of the right in front, unless the fluid presses upon the left side of the pericardium for its whole length, so as to bear upon the great vessels as well as upon the body of the heart.

The impulse to the right of the sternum is sometimes limited to the fourth and fifth intercostal spaces, while sometimes it is also present over the third and even the second space. In the latter case the impulse is double, and is due to the pulsation, followed by the second beat coincident with the second sound of the pulmonary artery or aorta, or both. When pulsation is present in the first, second, and third right spaces, and also in the normal position to the left of the sternum, the case is one of aneurism of the aorta; and the distinction of this impulse or pulsation from that of displaced heart presents therefore no difficulty.

Wintrich[1] states that sometimes, when the effusion is in the left side, the heart is displaced backwards (and to the right) being covered by lung, when the displacement of the heart can by no means be discovered. He saw one such case in which an able clinical physician mistook the disease for pericarditis with very great effusion.

When effusion of fluid takes place into the right cavity of the chest, the heart is displaced towards the left side. As the impulse, however, is already seated on that side, the change in position of the impulse of the heart is not nearly so marked or diagnostic as in cases in which the heart is displaced to the centre or right side of the chest, owing to effusion into the left side. Important information, however, is to be obtained in such cases from the position of the impulse on the left side.

In a patient under my care who had extensive effusion into the

[1] Krankheiten der Respirationsorgane, p. 255.

right pleura, the impulse was felt in the sixth space, two inches farther to the left, and somewhat lower than the natural position. In two cases of seropurulent effusion in moderate quantity into the right pleura, of which I possess drawings, the heart was displaced to the left, and lowered to a slight extent. In one the apex of the heart was situated behind the seventh rib, more than an inch to the left of the natural site, and nearly an inch lower. In the other, the displacement of the heart downwards and to the left also existed, but to a less degree.

Since the above was in type I have seen three cases of extensive effusion of fluid into the right side of the chest. In two of these cases the apex-beat was felt as far to the left as about the seventh rib, the position of the impulse being somewhat lower than natural. In the third case, a young woman, whom I saw through the kindness of Dr. Wane, the amount of fluid in the right side of the chest was very great. The impulse of the heart was not perceptible to the right of the mamma, but prevailed along its upper left border from the third or fourth to the seventh space where it was unusually low in situation. There was a double impulse over the great arteries at the left upper border of the mamma, and doubling of the second sound, the second of the two sounds being that made in the pulmonary artery. There was also a loud mitral murmur around the region of the apex. A large quantity of fluid was drawn off, by means of a glass syringe through a fine tube, by Mr. James Lane, who performed the same operation for the two other cases. I watched the position of the impulse when the fluid was being withdrawn, and noticed that it soon disappeared from the seventh space, and more slowly from the sixth, the beat moving steadily to the left and somewhat upwards. When the full amount of fluid had been withdrawn, the impulse was present in the fourth and fifth spaces, and perhaps in the third, being situated to the right of the mamma. The doubling of the second sound at once disappeared, and later I believe that the mitral murmur also vanished. In the drawing of an instance of great cylindrical dilatation or aneurism of the ascending aorta, in which there was considerable effusion of fluid in the right side of the chest, the heart, which was greatly enlarged and lowered in position, was displaced to the left as far as the ribs would allow, the apex extending to the seventh space, fully two inches below the level of the lower end of the sternum.

In two cases related by Dr. Gairdner[1] of effusion into the right pleura, the apex-beat in both was displaced to the left; in one (p. 329) the impulse probably retained its usual level, being displaced about one inch to the left. In the other (p. 354), before paracentesis, the apex-beat was felt in the fifth space, one inch and a half to the left of the normal site; after the operation it was present in the fourth space. In this case the impulse was probably lowered. Dr. Townshend, who was the first to observe the displacement to the left in such cases, felt the apex striking against

[1] Clinical Medicine.

the stethoscope between the fourth and fifth ribs in the axilla in two cases of empyema of the right side.[1] It is evident, then, that when considerable effusion takes place into the right side the apex-beat is always pushed further to the left, and that it is usually lower, sometimes on the same level as, and sometimes higher than the natural position. I attribute the lowered position of the impulse to two causes, the displacement downwards of the central tendon of the diaphragm by the effusion, and the inspiratory lowering of the diaphragm to enlarge the left lung, and so to compensate for the disuse of the right lung.

I do not find that the displacement of the heart from empyema differs in any respect from that caused by the effusion of serum into the pleura.

In pneumo-thorax of the left side, the displacement of the heart is the same as in cases of fluid effusion into the pleura. In general, fluid is combined with the air in those cases, but air without fluid will produce displacement of the heart, and it must do so when it is in sufficient quantity to distend the sac of the pleura, press down the diaphragm, and so push the pericardium and the heart over to the opposite side. Dr. Douglas Powell[2] relates a case in which the right side of the chest was filled with air, and the right border of the heart was situated to the left of the left sterno-clavicular line.

Wintrich[3] states that displacement of the heart takes place in pneumothorax as in pleuritic effusion; the only difference being that in pneumothorax the heart is more frequently displaced from before backwards.

Hæmorrhage into either Cavity of the Chest from the rupture of an aneurism of the aorta displaces the heart, as a rule, to the opposite side, in the same manner, and to the same extent, the quantity of fluid being alike, as in cases of pleuritic effusion. Two circumstances, however, tend to modify this result, one, the size and position of the aneurismal sac; the other, the lessening of the size of the heart that may be induced by the hæmorrhage. Mr. Sidney Coupland[4] gives a case in which a diffuse aneurism of the thoracic and abdominal aorta ruptured into the left cavity of the chest, which contained twenty-four ounces of clot. During life the apex was tilted upwards, and was felt beating in the fourth space, one inch within, and on a line with the left nipple.

Contraction or Cirrhosis of the Lung with Adhesion of the Pleura.— When pleuritis with effusion, whether chronic or acute, ends in the permanent condensation of the lung, fibroid thickening of the pleura, and binding adhesions, the whole of the affected side contracts and the ribs are crowded together. That side of the chest, however, is not obliterated; it is still much larger than the condensed lung, and the result is that if, for instance, the right be the affected side, the heart is permanently drawn over into the right side.

[1] Cycl. of Med. vol. ii. p. 38.
[3] Krankheiten der Respirationsorgane, p. 344, 347.
[2] Path. Trans. xix. 77.
[4] Path. Trans. xxiv. 54.

Dr. Stokes was the first to draw attention to the displacement of the heart to the right side, in consequence of the absorption of an effusion into the right pleura.[1]

When the left is the affected side, the heart may be drawn quite over into the left side, the right auricle being situated to the left of

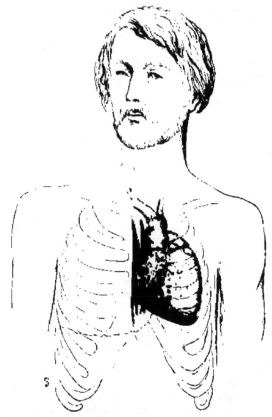

FIG. 31.—Position of the heart and great vessels in a case with *Contraction of the Left Lung.* The heart and great vessels are drawn completely over into the left side of the chest, so that it is much farther to the left and higher in situation than in the healthy chest. They are partially covered by the right lung, but not at all by the left, and the impulse of the heart is present in the second, third, and fourth spaces, and perhaps in the fifth.

the median line. This is well seen in fig. 31, which was taken from a man in whom, owing to the complete contraction of the left lung, the heart entirely occupied the left side of the chest in front, no

[1] On the Diseases of the Chest, p. 501.

portion of the left lung being interposed between the heart and the walls of the chest. The heart is raised towards the infra-clavicular region and the axilla, and the ribs fit closely upon the heart from the second to the fifth. In this man the impulse must have extended from the first intercostal space to the fourth.

It may be observed that here also, as in displacement of the heart into the right side, the heart revolves upon itself and turns over, but in the reverse direction. In displacement into the right side, the left ventricle and auricle are situated in front, the right ventricle being partially and the right auricle all but its tip being wholly concealed. In displacement to the left, the right ventricle entirely hides the left side of the heart. The aorta and pulmonary artery are twisted to the left, both venæ cavæ are completely exposed when the right lung is turned aside, and are situated behind the sternum, and the whole heart seems to turn to the left upon the two venæ cavæ as upon a hinge or pivot.

In cirrhosis of either lung the heart is drawn towards the affected side. Dr. Hilton Fagge[1] relates a case of cirrhosis of the right lung in which the impulse was seen and felt two inches below and one inch to the left of the right nipple. The heart deviated more to the right during life than after death, when the apex was two inches to the left of the middle line, being situated between the fifth and sixth (cartilages); and one-half of the heart was to the left, and one-half of it was to the right of the middle line. Dr. Greenhow[2] gives a case of contraction of the right lung, the precise condition of which was unknown, observed by him during life, in which the heart was displaced very far to the right and upwards, and was felt beating in the third and fourth spaces over an area of three inches by three and a half, of which the right nipple formed the central point.

Dr. Wilks[3] communicates a case of cirrhosis of the left lung, in which that lung was contracted and hard, and had to be cut out. The right lung was enlarged, and was the only organ observable on removing the sternum. The heart was drawn towards the left side, "owing to the pericardium being firmly united to the pleura."

Dr. Bastian[4] gives an analysis of thirty cases of cirrhosis derived from various sources. The heart was much displaced towards the affected side in twelve of these, and slightly in three; while in three of them there was no displacement, and in the remaining twelve there was no notice of the position of the heart.

When the left bronchial tube is obliterated by compression, by its own contraction, or by the admission of a foreign body, the left lung shrinks, the left side contracts, and the heart is displaced towards the clavicle and axilla, exactly as in cases of complete contraction with adhesions of the left lung. Dr. Stokes publishes a case of Dr. Mayne's of aneurism arising from the front of the transverse portion of the arch of the aorta, which extended downwards towards

[1] Path. Trans. xx. 35.   [2] Ibid. xix. 159.
[3] Ibid. viii. 39.   [4] Ibid. xix. 47.

the left lung, compressing and flattening the left bronchial tube. The left side of the chest was less than the right by two inches, the ribs were crowded together, and the heart was displaced towards the left axilla.[1]

There are many cases of partial contraction of a portion of the upper lobe of the left lung, whether from phthisis, cirrhosis of the lung, gangrene of the lung, or other cause, in which the upper part of the heart and the great vessels, especially the pulmonary artery, are drawn upwards and to the left towards or into the former seat of the contracted portion of the lung. In such cases the presence of the pulmonary artery, elevated in position and drawn to the left, may be immediately ascertained by its peculiar double impulse. I cannot say that I have strictly observed the analogous displacement of the ascending aorta towards the seat of the upper lobe of the right lung, in cases of contraction of that lobe, but I have noticed cases of this class in which the vessel evidenced itself by very loud superficial first and second sounds, which communicated themselves to the ear, if not to the hand, like a double shock or impulse. Dr. Stokes has given an interesting account of the displacements of the heart from the diminished volume of the lung, in his work on Diseases of the Heart, p. 458.

Intra-thoracic Tumours.—Large cancerous growths in the cavity of the chest, when they press upon the heart without penetrating into its structure, necessarily displace it in the direction of the pressure. The heart is simply pushed aside by the tumour, and its displacement is in no way influenced by the relation of the heart to the central tendon of the diaphragm.

"In the year 1856 I saw," writes Dr. Cockle, in his paper on intra-thoracic cancer, "a case of intra-thoracic cancer occupying the whole of the left side of the chest, and encroaching slightly on the right side, in which the tumour carried the heart before it as far as the right nipple. The impulse was felt pulsating between the second and third ribs, and down to, and at a later period beyond, the right nipple."

Dr. Bennett[2] relates the case, communicated to him by Dr. Sutton, of a little girl, in whom the entire left side was occupied by a mass of medullary cancer which had pushed the heart considerably to the right. During life the heart was displaced and was felt beating at the right nipple. The diagnosis was "*very great effusion into the left pleural cavity,*" and the chest was twice punctured.

In a case published by Dr. Andrew,[3] in which a large malignant growth occupied the upper lobe of the left lung, the heart was displaced downwards and to the right. Dr. Bennett[4] gives a case of cancer of the anterior and posterior mediastinum involving the anterior portion and root of the right lung on which the heart was pushed downwards and towards the right side, so that rather more than half

[1] Dr. Stokes on Diseases of the Heart and Aorta, p. 566.
[2] Intra-thoracic Growths, p. 100.   [3] Path. Trans. xvi. 51.   [4] *Loc. cit.* p. 92.

of the organ was to the right of the median line. A fortnight before death there was manifest and considerable displacement of the heart, which was beating in the epigastrium. Dr. Douglas Powell[1] relates a case in which the left cavity of the chest was occupied by a solid mass, displacing the heart to the right, and the lung posteriorly. After death it was found that this tumour was intimately connected with the heart at its left and posterior aspects. I might cite other cases of intra-thoracic tumour, published by Dr. Townsend, Boerhaave, quoted by him, and others, in which the heart was displaced.

On the other hand, cases are recorded in which there was little or no marked displacement of the heart, although the extent of the disease was great.

Dr. Graves and Dr. Stokes[2] have published a well-known instance of this disease, in which there was found, in place of the right lung, a solid mass, weighing more than six pounds. It encroached upon the left side of the chest, enveloping and nearly concealing from view the pericardium, great vessels, and trachea. Notwithstanding the extent and position of the disease, the heart pulsated in its natural situation.

Dr. Wilks describes a case in which the whole right lung was converted into one mass of medullary cancer, which protruded into the pericardium, ran along the great vessels at the base of the heart, and pierced the auricles of the organ itself. The superior cava was almost destroyed by the cancer, the inferior vena cava was closely surrounded by it but was free, the right pulmonary artery was a mere slit in the midst of it, and it had entered the heart through the pulmonary veins. There is no notice of displacement of the heart, although it is stated that the sounds of the heart were very feeble.

Dr. Quain[3] exhibited before the Pathological Society an encephaloid mass of the size of a large cocoa-nut, which was situated between the root of the left lung and the heart. When the patient was first seen, six weeks before his death, the heart was little displaced. Afterwards effusion took place into the left side, and the heart became much displaced towards the right side.

It is evident from these cases, that a large intra-thoracic tumour occupying one side of the chest may in some instances displace the heart into the opposite side, while in other instances, in which the tumour is equally large, there may be no displacement of the heart whatever. The reason is obvious. In those instances in which there is no displacement, the cancer penetrates into or surrounds the organ, without pushing it aside.

It is evident, then, that the displacement or non-displacement of the heart, and the mode and extent of its displacement, in instances in which there is complete dulness of one side, may sometimes help us to discover whether the case is one of intra-thoracic cancer or of simple effusion into the pleura.

[1] Path. Trans. xxiv. 28.   [2] Dr. Stokes on the Diseases of the Chest, p. 371.
[3] Path. Trans. viii. 54.

Large abscesses, hydatid cysts, or malignant tumours in the upper or convex portion of the Liver.—The patient from whom fig. 32 was taken was affected with jaundice.   On post-mortem examination several large abscesses were found in the upper portion of the liver,

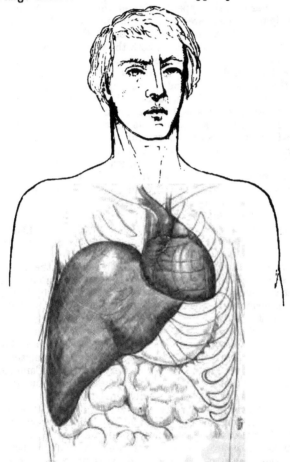

Fig. 32.—Position of the heart and great vessels in a case with *Large Abscesses in the Upper portion of the Liver.*   The heart and great vessels are displaced extensively upwards and to the left towards the left axilla, so as completely to occupy the left side of the chest.   The impulse is present in the second and third left spaces.

where it ascends into the right side of the chest.   He also had peritonitis, and excessive intestinal distension.   The whole diaphragm was raised, and with it the heart was pushed upwards and to the left in a remarkable manner.   The liver encroached upon the right side of the chest to such an extent that its highest point was on a level with the lower edge of the second rib. The convexity of the liver consequently encroached on the left side of the chest as well as the right, and carried the heart, resting upon its upper surface, completely over into the upper portion of the left side of the chest.

If this figure be compared with fig. 29, in which the diaphragm is excessively raised by means of distension of the stomach and intestines, it will be seen that while in both the diaphragm is raised to an excessive degree, there are important points in which they differ materially from each other. In that figure as well as in this we find that the abdomen is distended, the diaphragm is pushed upwards, the lower ribs are prominent, and the heart and lungs are pressed upwards and lessened in size, being encroached on by the abdominal organs. In universal distension of the abdomen, the heart, while it is compressed upwards, retains a central position, as it rests on the central tendon of the diaphragm. It deviates rather to the right than to the left. But in those cases in which there are large abscesses or hydatid cysts, or cancerous growths in the upper portion of the liver, the heart, as it is pushed upwards, deviates extensively to the left, and occupies a space to the left of the upper half of the sternum, behind the first, second, third, and fourth ribs. It is to be remembered that in this case there was peritonitis and great intestinal distension, consequently the compression of the heart upwards was effected by a double cause.

The deviation of the heart to the left side of the chest from extensive abscesses in the upper portion of the liver, differs thus from the deviation caused by effusion of fluid into the right side of the chest—in effusion into the right side of the chest, the heart and the impulse at the apex are either lowered or only slightly raised; while in cases with abscesses in the upper portion of the liver they are pushed upwards, being above the fourth rib. The position of the heart in enlargement of the liver from abscess, and in great contraction and adhesions of the left lung, corresponds very closely. (Compare figs. 31 and 32.) In both the heart and great vessels are situated behind the second and two or three upper ribs, in both the heart is pushed entirely into the left side, the venæ cavæ being behind the sternum. But in the following respects they differ. In enlargement of the liver from abscesses, the anterior aspect of the heart is unchanged; the left upper ribs are widened apart and the ribs on both sides are raised and pushed outwards; the dulness on percussion is more extensive on the right side than the left, especially behind, and the heart and its impulse scarcely appear below the fourth rib. In contraction of the left lung, these conditions are reversed. The heart turns upon the venæ cavæ as upon a hinge over towards the left, the right auricle and both venæ cavæ being completely exposed, and the left ventricle being hidden by the right; the ribs are crowded together, the whole of the left side of the chest being contracted; there is dulness on percussion over the whole left lung, while the

ɪ 2

whole right side of the chest is very resonant, the area of resonance being increased, owing to the encroachment of the right lung upon the left side of the chest to the left of the sternum ; and the impulse of the heart is felt down to the fifth rib.

Extensive effusion in the pericardium in *acute* pericarditis is an additional cause of displacement of the heart towards the axilla. Of this displacement I shall speak in the article on pericarditis.

DISPLACEMENT OF THE HEART FORWARDS.

Dr. Hope relates a case in which the thoracic aorta, extending from an inch below the left subclavian artery down to the diaphragm, was enlarged into an aneurismal sac which lay across the spine, and projected on the right side three inches beyond the vertebræ without reaching the ribs, while on the left it extended to the ribs, causing destruction of three and caries of two or more of them, and at last formed a considerable tumour on the back. This tumour necessarily compressed the heart forwards against the front of the chest. The impulse of the heart was exceedingly vigorous, and was double, consisting of a diastolic as well as a systolic impulse, each of a jogging character. It was agreed that there must be considerable hypertrophy of the heart to account for so strong an impulse, and yet the organ was found by Mr. Cæsar Hawkins, who drew up the autopsy, only "slightly enlarged and thickened."[1] Dr. Hope quotes without reference, a case mentioned by Dr. Todd, in which the heart was pushed forward and outwards, and, as it were, compressed against the ribs by an enormous aneurism of the thoracic aorta. The sounds of the heart were so modified by this compression as to lead to the erroneous diagnosis of concentric hypertrophy.

I possess a drawing taken from a case of extensive aneurism of the abdominal aorta at the cœliac axis, in which the aneurismal sac extended upwards, behind the diaphragm, in front of the lower dorsal vertebræ, so as to displace the heart forwards and probably somewhat upwards.

DISPLACEMENT OF THE HEART BACKWARDS.

When abscesses or tumours form in the anterior mediastinum, behind the lower portion of the sternum, the heart must be displaced backwards.

The displacement of the heart backwards is also induced by the very extensive effusion that gradually takes place into the pericardium in cases of chronic pericarditis.

Wintrich states, as we have already seen, that sometimes when there is pleuritic effusion in the left side, the heart is displaced backwards and to the right, so that its displacement can by no means be discovered.

[1] Dr. Hope on the Diseases of the Heart, p. 447.

LATERAL OR PARTIAL ANEURISM OF THE HEART.

By Thomas Bevill Peacock, M.D., F.R.C.P.

Under this term it is proposed to treat of the partial or lateral sacculated dilatations, in contradistinction to the general enlargements of the cavities of the heart, to which, and especially in France, the term aneurism has also been applied. The partial aneurisms differ, however, from the latter forms of the disease, not only because they involve only a portion of the parietes of the cavity, but also in that the structure of the muscular walls is always more or less altered in the seat of disease.

The real aneurismal tumours affect only the left cavities of the heart, the left ventricle and auricle, or the corresponding arterial and auriculo-ventricular valves. The immunity thus possessed by the right cavities has been variously explained by different writers. Breschet, who thought that the aneurismal dilatation was almost always, if not invariably, situated near the apex of the left ventricle, and that its production was due to the laceration of the inner portions of the ventricular walls, supposed that the non-occurrence of the disease in the right ventricle was owing to the greater relative power of its walls at the apex. Dr. Thurnam referred the freedom of the right ventricle from disease to the peculiar action of the valves at the right auriculo-ventricular orifice, by which, when the ventricle becomes distended, the aperture is incompletely closed so as to allow the reflux of the blood into the right auricle. He also contended that the term aneurism should be restricted to the dilatations of the cavities of the heart through which arterial blood circulates; while the term varix should be applied to the similar enlargements of the venous cavities, so as to maintain the analogy between the affections of the two sides of the heart and those of arteries and veins. Rokitansky considers the dilatations of the right side of the heart as not truly aneurismal, and ascribes the occurrence of the real aneurisms only on the left side to the greater frequency of endocarditis in that situation. There seems good reason to believe that the proneness to inflammation of the lining membrane of the left cavities, is mainly influential in causing the occurrence of aneurism on the left and not on the right side of the heart; but it is also probable that the greater tension to which the walls of the left ventricle are exposed, with the variations of pressure exerted by the column of blood in the arteries, materially conduces to the disease. Certainly when from any cause any portion of the parietes is rendered less resistant and more readily expansible, the pressure of the blood will tend rapidly to expand the weaker part so as to form a distinct sac.

In the following notice I shall treat first of aneurisms of the left ventricle, then of those of the left auricle, and lastly of valvular aneurisms.

ANEURISM OF THE LEFT VENTRICLE.

The occasional occurrence of partial aneurismal dilatations of the heart similar to those which are of such frequent occurrence in the arteries, was first shown by the case recorded by Galeatti in 1757; and it is a curious coincidence that in the same year the condition was brought to the knowledge of John Hunter by the occurrence of a case, the preparation of which is contained in the Museum of the Royal College of Surgeons, and of which the description was found by Dr. Thurnam[1] in his MS. Catalogue. In 1759 a case of the kind occurred to Walter, which was published in 1785,[2] and in 1793 another specimen preserved in Dr. Hunter's Museum, was described by Dr. Baillie and figured by him in the plates which appeared in 1799. Corvisart met with a case in 1796, which was published in 1806. Hodgson described one in 1815,[3] Zannini in 1816,[4] Rostan in 1820,[5] and Shaw in 1822,[6] Sir A. Cooper, in his Lectures published by Tyrrell in 1825, said that he had met with three cases, of which two were contained in the Museum of St. Thomas's Hospital. In 1827 the first memoir on the subject was published by Breschet,[7] in which the particulars of ten cases were collected, including one communicated to him by Cruveilhier in 1816, two by the Berards which first appeared in a Paris Thesis, and one by Dance, together with the case of the celebrated Talma and the description of a specimen in the museum of the Faculty by Breschet himself. In the same year two other cases of the kind were described by Adams in Dublin,[8] and by Johnson in this country.[9]

In 1830, Dr. Elliotson, in his Lumleian Lectures, described another case, of which the preparation is now in the Museum at St. Thomas's, and referred to sixteen cases as on record at that time. In 1829 two additional cases were narrated by Bignardi and Reynaud,[10] in 1832

[1] Med.-Chir. Trans. vol. 21. 1838.
[2] Nouv. Mém. l'Acad de Berlin.
[3] Diseases of Arteries and Veins, p. 84.
[4] Italian Translation of Baillie's Morbid Anatomy.
[5] Sur les Rupt. du Cœur, Obs. v.
[6] Manual of Anatomy, vol. i. p. 251.
[7] Rep. Gén. d'Anat. tome 3me p. 181.
[8] Dublin Hospital Reports, vol. iv.
[9] Med.-Chir. Rev. vol. xv.
[10] Journal Hebd. de Méd.

a third was published by Hope, and in 1833 a fourth by Lobstein. In 1834 a notice of the subject was given by Ollivier,[1] in which he referred to the cases collected by Breschet, together with those of Adams, Bignardi, and Reynaud. In 1835, Dr. Thomas Davies referred to the disease, and stated that there were two specimens in the Museum of the late Mr. Langstaff. In the same year, Bouillaud treated of the subject in a section of his work, detailing the more important observations recorded by Breschet and Ollivier, with two more recently published cases by Choisy and Petigny. In 1838 Dr. Thurnam contributed a memoir to the Medical and Chirurgical Society,[2] which was then completely exhaustive of the subject and still leaves little to supply, and affords the best description of the pathology of these affections which has appeared. In this memoir he related seven new cases, of which three were drawn from the MSS. of John Hunter in the possession of the Royal College of Surgeons. He further referred to five other specimens previously undescribed, which he had found in different museums. In 1842 a short notice of the subject was published by Rokitansky, in his work on Pathological Anatomy; and in 1843, Dr. Craigie contributed to the Edinburgh Medical and Surgical Journal a valuable memoir,[3] detailing the particulars of twenty-two of the cases up to that time recorded, all of which had, however, been previously referred to by Dr. Thurnam, together with a very interesting example which had occurred in his own practice. In 1846 a case was described by myself;[4] in 1850, Dr. Halliday Douglas[5] related the particulars of four cases; and in 1852, M. Cruveilhier discussed the subject in his Pathological Anatomy, illustrating his views by reference to various examples which had fallen under his own notice.

Since the publication of Dr. Thurnam's memoir, numerous observations have been placed on record, so that I have had no difficulty in collecting forty-three fresh cases, together with brief notices of others not fully reported. Of this number fourteen are contained in the Bulletins of the Société Anatomique of Paris, two in the Mémoires of the Société de Biologie, and sixteen in the Transactions of the Pathological Society. With the cases collected by Dr. Thurnam, fifty-eight in number, those on record must at present exceed one hundred, and I have seen references to several others the particulars of which I have not been able to obtain.

Nature and Mode of Origin.—Breschet, as the name, *false consecutive aneurism,* which he gave the affection, indicates, regarded the real aneurisms of the heart as originating in rupture or ulceration of the lining membrane of the ventricle and some portion of the muscular walls, the result of softening from inflammation or atheroma. Reynaud showed that in his case the dilatation originated in disease of the endocardium; and Cruveilhier pointed out that in some cases the

[1] Dict. de Méd. tome viii. p. 303.
[2] Transactions, vol. xxi. In Dr. Thurnam's paper references will be found to all the cases here named, published up to the period of its appearance.
[3] Vol. lix. p. 381.
[4] Edin. Med. and Surg. No. 169   [5] Monthly Jour. of Med. Sc.

whole of the structures of the ventricular walls were dilated,—and apparently in consequence of the muscular fibres having undergone conversion into a fibroid structure, which was less resistant to pressure and more readily admitted of expansion.

Dr. Thurnam to some extent adopted the views of the pathologists who had preceded him, and contended, that, while the aneurisms did in some cases originate in rupture or softening of the lining membrane and muscular walls of the ventricle, they more frequently were connected with the changes in the endocardium and muscular substance pointed out by Reynaud and Cruveilhier, and consisted in dilatations of the whole of the structures constituting the parietes of the ventricle. He also thought that these changes were probably often referable to inflammation, and that in some cases the formation of coagula in the cavity of the ventricle might cause the expansion of the ventricular wall in the seat of deposition. He further contended that the aneurisms of the heart presented all the several forms which are met with in similar affections of arteries. Rokitansky regards the aneurisms of the heart as always depending upon inflammatory processes, either of an acute or chronic character. In the first or acute form of the affection, the disease originates in recent inflammation of the endocardium and probably also of the contiguous muscular substance, and the consequent laceration or breaking down of the inflamed surface under the pressure of the blood. In the other variety, the dilatation is the more remote result either of inflammation of the endocardium and a somewhat thick layer of the muscular substance, or of the whole thickness of the wall of the ventricle during endo- and peri-carditis. In this form the muscular fibres become replaced by fibroid structure, the endo- and peri-cardium are blended with the altered tissue, and the parietes become expanded under the pressure of the blood. The first of these forms corresponds therefore with the false consecutive aneurism of Breschet; the second with the true aneurism of Reynaud, Cruveilhier, and Thurnam. While adopting Rokitansky's views as to the inflammatory origin of the cardiac aneurisms, there is no reason to deny the correctness of the analogy contended for by Dr. Thurnam, between their various forms and the different varieties of arterial aneurisms. It is, however, very doubtful how far the coagulation of the blood in the cavities of the heart gives rise to partial dilatation. Such coagula form, it is well known, chiefly on the right side, in which the aneurismal dilatation does not occur; and the clots which Dr. Thurnam has described and figured, might as probably have originated in the already dilated part as have given rise to the dilatation.

It is obviously only by the examination of incipient aneurismal sacs, or those of small size, that we can form a correct judgment as to their original modes of development. Confining his assertion only to such cases, Dr. Thurnam states that of twenty-eight out of the fifty-eight cases which he collected, twenty-two originated in dilatation of the structures entering into the composition of the walls of the heart;

while in six there was solution of continuity of the endocardium
and inner stratum of muscular fibres. Of the forty-three cases
which I have myself collected, in thirteen the data are imperfect or
the disease is very far advanced ; of the remaining thirty, in twenty-
five the sac was lined by endocardium, which is stated to have been
opaque, thickened, indurated or ossified in eleven cases ;—and in four
the lining membrane was destroyed. In sixteen of these cases the
subjacent muscular structure had undergone the fibroid degeneration
and was more or less attenuated, in one of them to such an extent as
to present only a trace of the altered tissue ; in five the muscular
substance was thinned but not otherwise altered; and in seven cases it
was wholly wanting and the sac was only bounded by the endo- and
peri-cardium. Both series of facts, therefore, show that in the cases
in which satisfactory opinions as to the mode of origin of the sacs
can be formed, they are usually at first of the true form, or that in
which all the structures are expanded.

From several specimens which I have had the opportunity of
examining, either in the recent state or as preparations, the following
may be stated to be the progressive changes in the development of the
true aneurisms.

1. In the earliest stage in which the affection can be recognised,
we observe thickening and opacity of the endocardium, with slight
dilatation of the corresponding portion of the walls of the ventricle,
and attenuation of the muscular substance without any marked
alteration of its texture.

2. In a more advanced stage there is thickening and opacity of the
endocardium, and conversion of a more or less thick stratum of the
muscular substance into a dense, yellowish or whitish coloured fibroid
tissue intermixed with the muscular structure. The parietes of the
ventricle in the seat of disease have become more atrophied, and the
cavity presents a more marked dilatation.

3. At a still later period, together with the thickening and opacity
of the endocardium, this membrane becomes intimately blended with
the subjacent tissue, so as to be no longer separable from it. The
muscular substance throughout the whole or the greater part of the
thickness of the ventricular parietes, is converted into dense, pale-
coloured fibroid tissue. The attenuation of the walls of the ventricle is
greater, and the dilatation of the corresponding portion of the cavity,
if occupying the outer surface of the heart, occasions a more or less
marked prominence externally.

While these changes are in progress in the parietes of the ventricle,
others are proceeding in its interior. The dilated portion of the cavity
becomes, especially if it be somewhat circumscribed and bounded by a
tolerably defined margin, the seat of coagula. These are at first thin,
loose, and dark coloured, subsequently they become more firm and
paler ; and at length the sac is found more or less completely filled
by coagula, of which the outer portions are distinctly laminated and
decolorized, and often adherent to the altered endocardium. As the

partial dilatation of the ventricular cavity increases and forms a more or less decided prominence externally, the visceral pericardium becomes implicated in the disease. At first it is only slightly opaque and presents a rough surface, from the existence of small granular concretions of fibrine; these become thicker and coalesce, and finally constitute a distinct layer of false membrane; and at length adhesions are formed between the visceral and reflected pericardium over the seat of the aneurism, or more rarely uniting the whole or a large portion of the membranes; often also, when there are not entire adhesions, the surface of the heart displays large white patches. In the cases in which there are evidences of the existence of more general pericarditis, it seems probable that the alterations in the ventricular walls upon which the aneurismal dilatation depends, have, as stated by Rokitansky, proceeded from without, and have involved the inner portions of the parietes secondarily.

With the gradual expansion of the aneurismal sac, the lining membrane and part or the whole of the muscular layers may be eroded or destroyed, so that the cavity may come to be bounded by the pericardium, with or without a portion of altered muscle; the aneurism thus assuming the "*false consecutive*" form.

Pathologists have within the last few years described the occurrence of fibrinous deposits in the walls of the heart. The Pathological Transactions contain various instances of the kind, originating either in acute inflammatory action, or resulting from an altered condition of the blood. In some cases this fibrinous material may undergo imperfect organization, giving rise to the fibroid degeneration of the muscular tissue which, as above shown, so frequently precedes the formation of the true aneurisms. In other cases the deposit breaks down and destroys the involved tissue, so as to give rise, under the pressure of the blood, to a kind of sac, to which the term "*false aneurism*" may be applied.

It should, however, be stated that Rokitansky regards the acute, or originally false form of aneurism, as of decidedly less common occurrence than that in which the whole of the tissues are expanded, and his conclusions are confirmed by the observations of others. Various cases originating in the former mode are, however, on record. One such was reported by Dr. Pereira, in which the cavity was situated at the base of the septum of the ventricle; and another is related by Mr. Shillitoe and myself in the Pathological Transactions. In both these cases there was considerable disease of the adjacent parts and the patients rapidly sank; and such is probably generally the case in similar instances. It is by no means uncommon in connexion with endocarditis of the aortic valves to find smaller or larger excavations in the ventricular walls at the base of the septum, which, were life sufficiently prolonged, might probably become aneurismal sacs. Cases of the kind have at different times been exhibited at the Pathological Society by the late Mr. Avery,[1] Dr. Bennett,[2] and myself.[3]

In some cases it has been supposed that an extravasation of blood, or

[1] Path. Trans. i. p. 72.   [2] Ibid p. 59   [3] Ibid. ii. p. 49.

the formation of an abscess in the substance of the ventricular walls, producing a laceration or erosion extending into the cavity, may give rise to the formation of an aneurismal sac; and instances affording examples of aneurisms probably so originating have been referred to by Cruveilhier. I have also myself described a case in which, in connection with general pericarditis, an abscess had formed in the septum of the auricles, which opened into the base of the left ventricle and origin of the aorta. In this instance the aortic valves were also extensively involved and the patient died rapidly, but it apparently formed an instance in which an abscess in the cardiac walls might have been followed by aneurism. The case is more fully reported by Dr. Craigie, in whose practice it occurred. It is also highly probable that in some cases lacerations of the internal portions of the muscular walls of the ventricle connected with fatty degeneration, may lead to the formation of the false consecutive aneurisms.

I have already mentioned the conclusions deduced from the cases analysed as to the parts constituting the walls of the sacs. Dr. Thurnam has also given particulars of their contents. He states that in twenty-three cases they contained a greater or less amount of laminated coagulum; in nineteen simple amorphous clots; and in twenty-three cases they had been found empty. Of my own series of cases, nineteen contained old coagula, which were more or less decolorized, laminated, and in some cases adherent to the lining membrane of the sac; three displayed old and recent clots combined: and seven contained only recent coagula. The condition of the sac has not been reported in most of the remaining cases. In twenty-one of the first collection of cases the aneurismal walls, and especially when the sacs formed distinct tumours, had been strengthened by adhesions of the pericardium; in other instances there were loose false membranes on the pericardium without adhesions; and in seven cases the layers of pericardium were universally adherent. In the second series, eleven out of thirty in which the condition of the pericardium is named in the reports, displayed adhesions over the projections of the aneurisms; in five there were white patches and adhesions in the seat of disease or elsewhere; in one the adhesions were almost entire; and in three instances the two layers of pericardium were universally attached.

Seat of Disease.—M. Breschet supposed that the aneurismal sacs were nearly always situated at the apex of the left ventricle. Dr. Thurnam was led to qualify this opinion, and showed by the analysis of the cases which he collected, that, while the partial dilatations are of more frequent occurrence at the apex than elsewhere, they do occur in all parts of the ventricular walls. Of fifty-seven cases in which the description was complete, in twenty-seven the sac was situated at or near the apex; in twenty-one in different parts of the base; in fifteen in the intermediate parts of the ventricle; and in three in the septum. Of forty-two of the more recent cases, in fourteen the sacs were situated at the apex; in eleven near the base; in eight in the middle of the ventricle, at the anterior, outer, or posterior part; and in six in the septum.   In three instances there were two or more sacs in the same case. In one of them one sac was situated at the apex, and another on the left side; in a second, one aneurism was at the apex, the other in the septum; in the third, one sac was situated partly in the septum and partly in the anterior wall, another was situated posteriorly in the septum, and a third occupied the middle of the external wall.   Both these enumerations concur in showing that the most frequent situations for the aneurismal sacs are first the apex, then the base, and lastly the external wall and septum.

The greater liability to the occurrence of aneurisms at the apex of the ventricle is supposed by M. Breschet to be owing to the relative thinness of the parietes in that situation, exposing them to rupture during the active contraction of the heart. It is, however, more probably owing to the tissues being readily involved in inflammatory action, extending from the peri- or endo-cardium, when, as at the apex, those membranes are more nearly in contact, than when the layer of muscular structure is of greater width. The portions of the ventricle near the base are probably commonly affected, from the frequency of endocarditis of the aortic valves, leading to induration and thickening, and so to more or less obstruction to the flow of blood from the ventricle. Under these circumstances there is a tendency to excavation beneath the aortic valves, which may proceed to the extent of forming a distinct aneurismal sac.   In some cases the disease is situated in what has been termed the "*undefended space*," the space which intervenes between the base of the ventricular septum and the convex sides of the left and posterior semilunar valves.   This ordinarily is only closed by the endocardium of the left ventricle, and by a layer of fibrous tissue, a thin layer of muscle, and the endocardium of the right ventricle. Being thus imperfectly protected, the space is readily expanded under any unduly distending force, and a sac is formed which will protrude into the right cavities about the auriculo-ventricular aperture. When in Vienna a year ago Rokitansky showed me one or two cases of the kind; one was exhibited at the Pathological Society during the last session, by Dr. Hare, and I have found the condition myself. In some cases portions of the ventricular wall in this situation may be congenitally deficient, and a column of blood flowing from the left ventricle may distend and dilate the folds of the tricuspid valves, as shown in a specimen in the Museum of the Royal College of Surgeons.   In other cases, the excavation may occupy some other portion of the base of the ventricle beneath the aortic valves, and a channel may be formed leading into a small aneurismal sac, situated external to the origin of the aorta; and such sac may be still further prolonged so as to open above into the aorta. Cases of this kind were first described and figured by Dr. Hope, though he supposed that the aneurisms originated in connexion with the aorta and only opened into the ventricle. I have described two cases of the kind in the Pathological Transactions, and a similar one is also related by Dr. Bristowe. Aneurism at the base of the ventricle may also rupture into the right auricle or pericardium. Rokitansky mentions having seen a case in which both these results occurred. When the sacs form in the external wall of the ventricle, they may open into the left auricle or may burst into the left pleura, as in a case referred to by Sir A. Cooper. When seated in the septum they may press upon the right auricle and ventricle and open into one or other of those cavities, especially the right ventricle, as in the case related by Dr. Pereira, one existing in the Museum of St. Thomas's Hospital, and one referred to by Rokitansky. In cases of this kind a form of aneurism results, which, as pointed out by Dr. Thurnam, is analogous to the "*spontaneous varicose aneurisms*" of authors.

Form and Size.—Aneurisms of the heart may be either circumscribed or diffused ; or, in other words, the apertures by which they communicate with the ventricle may be more or less constricted ; or the cavity of the aneurism may gradually extend from that of the ventricle without any obvious line of separation. The sacs, when situated at the apex, are more generally of the diffused form ; those at the base, and in other parts of the ventricle, are more commonly circumscribed. In the first series of cases the sacs are inferred to have been circumscribed in twenty-five cases, and diffused in nineteen. As far as can be ascertained from the reports of the more recently published cases, it appears that of thirty-seven cases, twenty-five were circumscribed and twelve diffused.

The size of the sacs also varies according to the seat and duration of the disease. At the base and in the septum the sacs rarely attain any great size ; on the contrary, when developed in the external wall or at the apex, they may form tumours of considerable magnitude or may even equal the dimensions of the heart itself. The acute forms of aneurism also appear, as might be expected, not to attain the dimensions of the more chronic cases. Dr. Thurnam states that in his cases the sacs might, in nine instances, be compared to nuts, in twenty to walnuts, in seven to fowls' eggs, in fourteen to oranges, and in nine their size almost or quite equalled that of the healthy heart itself. In thirty of the cases which I have myself collected, in four the aneurisms are simply stated to have been small; in five they are compared to hazel nuts or filberts ; in two to walnuts ; one is said to have been large enough to hold a plover's egg, one to hold a pigeon's egg, and six are compared to bantam's or smaller or larger fowl's eggs. One sac is said to have been as large as a nutmeg, another as a plum ; one is reported to have been capable of holding the whole end of the thumb, another to have been as large as an apple, and a third as a small orange. Two are described as being large. In one case, in which there were two distinct cavities, both were the size of walnuts ; in a second one was as large as a hen's egg, the other as a walnut. In a third there were three cavities, the largest the size of a nut. In several cases the cavities contained one or more loculi, and in one there were three large pouches projecting from the main cavity.

State of other parts of the Pericardium and Heart.—The frequency of alterations in the pericardium and endocardium and in the walls of the ventricle in the seat of the aneurismal swellings, has already been referred to. It must also be mentioned that the occurrence of thickening, opacity, and induration and ossification of the endocardium and pericardium, and the fibroid transformation of the muscular substance, are by no means confined to the immediate seat of disease. These changes often involve a considerable portion of the heart, and especially of the left auricle and ventricle. In addition to these morbid conditions, also, the effects of more recent inflammation are frequently found. Hæmorrhagic pericarditis occurred in one of the first collection of cases; and in the recent series, pericarditis, with or without old adhesions and white patches, is recorded to have been found in four cases. In two also of the cases, blood was found in the pericardium, and in a large proportion of both series there was serous effusion in conjunction with general dropsy. In two cases also of the later collection there were evidences of recent endocarditis, and in several instances fatty degeneration of the muscular structure had occurred in different parts of the heart.

In five of Dr. Thurnam's cases there is stated to have been disease of the mitral valves, in three of the aortic valves, and in one of both sets, and in only eight cases are the valves expressly stated to have been healthy. In my own cases, the valves are stated to have been healthy in only five cases. The aortic valves are reported to have been diseased in seven instances, the mitral in two, and both sets in three, and in two or three other instances the aneurismal sacs were so situated as to have interfered with the action of the auriculoventricular valves. It must necessarily follow that the state of the whole heart is affected to a greater or less extent in these conditions, which necessarily lead to alterations in the size of the cavities and in the thickness of the walls. From the first series of cases it was inferred that there was general dilatation of the organ in three cases, dilatation with hypertrophy in three, dilatation of the left ventricle only in two, hypertrophy in two, and dilatation with hypertrophy of both ventricles in nine. In only ten cases was the heart reported to have presented no other lesion than the aneurisms, and in three only was it stated to have been positively healthy. In the more recent collection the heart appears to have been greatly enlarged in seven cases; there was great enlargement, but especially hypertrophy and dilatation of the left ventricle in twenty cases; dilatation of the left ventricle in two; and dilatation of the right ventricle in one. In two cases the separation of the two sides of the heart was imperfect from the apertures having formed in the fold of the foramen ovale. In three cases the coronary arteries were diseased; and in six there existed more or less atheroma, calcification, dilatation, or aneurism of the ascending portion of the aorta. Of the whole number of cases, excluding from consideration six in which the reports are imperfect as to the general condition of the heart, there is not one in which there was not some alteration in the state of the heart or pericardium, in addition to the aneurism. In one case the heart is indeed said to have been of natural size, but in that instance there was recent pericarditis and an acute aneurism.

The shape of the heart is stated to have been frequently altered by the presence of the aneurismal swellings. In some it had an unusually wide or globular form; in others there was a bulging of the aneurismal sac, separated by a more or less distinct furrow from the other portion of the ventricular wall; and in yet other cases there were obvious tumours projecting from the surface of the organ. These were sometimes only of small size so as to be compared to a small nut or thimble; in others they were of considerable magnitude, and were separated from the walls of the heart by a distinct constriction or neck. In one specimen contained in the Museum of St. Thomas's Hospital, probably one of those referred to by Sir A. Cooper, there is a tumour with thin parietes as large as an ordinary heart projecting from the anterior surface of the organ, and separated from it by a neck which is not half the circumference of the tumour itself.

The existence, however, of an obvious tumour or irregularity on the surface of the heart depends upon the seat and size of the aneurismal sac. At the base the tumours are generally, if not always small, and do not form projections which can be detected till the parts around are dissected away. Aneurisms in the septum also can produce no marked alteration in the general form of the organ; but those on the anterior, outer, and posterior walls, if at all of large size, necessarily occasion either some general bulging or form a distinct tumour. Of fifty-four aneurisms it is inferred that only thirty-five were attended by tumour.

State of other Organs of the Body.—The condition of the other organs of the body is not recorded by Dr. Thurnam, probably from the histories of the cases which he collected being defective in these particulars. I regret also that I am not able to supply satisfactory information from the reports of the more recent cases. I find, however, that in a large proportion of them there was more or less general dropsy, and that serous effusion had occurred in one or both pleural cavities and in the peritoneal sac. In one of the cases the fluid in the pleura was bloody, the lungs being also engorged in the same case. In two cases there were signs of recent pleurisy, and in eight the visceral and parietal pleuræ were attached by old adhesions. In eight cases there was pulmonary apoplexy, emphysema, bronchitis, or pneumonia, and in one of the latter cases the lung was gangrenous. In one instance there were tubercles in the lungs, and in another old syphilitic disease of the larynx.

The liver is reported to have been small and pale in one case; fatty in one; and congested, enlarged, granular or indurated in eight cases. The spleen was large in two cases, small in one, and softened and containing fibrinous or purulent deposits in one. The kidneys were engorged in four cases; granular, atrophied, cystic, or otherwise diseased in six: and contained purulent deposits in one.

Symptoms and Cause of Death.—It is impossible to point out any symptoms which can, in the present state of our knowledge, be regarded as characteristic of the lateral or partial aneurisms of the heart ; and, indeed, it is doubtful whether any such symptoms will hereafter be ascertained. This will readily be understood when the frequency with which the affection is associated with valvular diseases and with alterations in the size of the cavities and thickness of the walls of the heart is considered. On analysing the reports which have been published, it appears that in several cases the condition was only detected on postmortem examination, in the bodies of persons who were not known to be suffering from any form of cardiac disease, and were supposed to be previously in good health. In by far the largest proportion of cases, however, twenty-two out of twenty-seven, there is a history of prolonged indisposition, not unfrequently commencing with acute rheumatism or in some inflammatory affection of the thoracic organs, and characterised by the usual symptoms of cardiac disease. Difficulty of breathing, and sense of suffocation and oppression at the chest ; pain in the region of the heart, at the sternum, and at the epigastrium ; palpitation and tumultuous action of the heart, and irregularity of the pulse ; with cough, expectoration, and dropsical symptoms, are generally mentioned as having been present. Not unfrequently, also, the sounds of the heart are stated to have been replaced by morbid murmurs, but these appear to have been chiefly, if not wholly, referable to coincident valvular affections. The only symptoms, indeed, which can be regarded as at all of a specific character are pain and sense of weight in the region of the heart, which appear to be more constant attendants on these forms of disease than on any other kind of organic affection of the heart. It must, however, be concluded, that, at the present time, the diagnosis of these affections cannot be effected during life, and it is indeed doubtful whether it will be ever possible, with any exactitude, to diagnose them.

The cause of death is also often not clearly stated in the reports which have been published. It appears, however, that of the cases collected, in three the patients died suddenly, and probably from syncope, without any obvious reason being detected for the occurrence. In two, death resulted from cerebral congestion and convulsions. In one, from more acute disease supervening upon old laryngeal affection. In one from bronchitis, two from pneumonia, one from pleurisy, and in one from phthisis. In two cases the patients sank from coma and other symptoms connected with disease of the kidneys. In four instances death resulted from the rupture of the sac and the escape of blood into the cavity of the pericardium ; in four from the rupture of an aneurism of the ascending aorta into the pulmonary artery. In two cases the patients died from extensive disease of the aortic valves connected with endocarditis ; combined in one with the opening of an acute aneurism into the left auricle and very nearly externally, and in the other with purulent deposits in different organs. In the remaining seventeen, out of the twenty-five cases in which the particulars are given, it appears that death resulted from the progress of the general and dropsical symptoms and the affections of different organs super-induced by the cardiac defects. Of the cases previously analysed, the cause of the death was assignable in twenty-four. In twelve of them death was sudden: in three from syncope, in six from rupture of the sac into the pericardium, in one into the left pleura, and in one from rupture of the heart itself. In four, the patients died of apoplexy or paralysis, and in one from epistaxis. In nine cases death ensued from the progress of the cardiac symptoms, and six from other coincident complications. Rokitansky mentions the case of a boy of twelve years of age, in whom a small aneurism at the base of the ventricle, after having first formed a connection with the right auricle, opened into the pericardial sac.

It thus appears that there are on record eleven cases in which the aneurismal cavities have terminated by rupture. In most of them the affection proved suddenly fatal. Such was the result in the instance of General Kidd, a gentleman of seventy-three years of age, whose case is related by Dr. Johnson, and who was found dead in his bed. Here the aneurism was of small size, and was situated near the base of the ventricle. In a case related by Dr. Wilks, a girl twelve years of age, died suddenly when playing, and an aneurism about the size of a walnut was found about the middle of the anterior wall of the left ventricle near the septum. In other instances, however, life has been prolonged for some short time after the occurrence of the rupture. Thus, in the case related by Galeatti, the symptoms indicating the rupture appeared about a week before the fatal termination; and in one which I have myself related, blood appears to have escaped into the cavity of the pericardium, not, however, by a distinct rupture, five days before death; more rapid extravasation having been prevented by adhesions between the layers of pericardium at the seat of disease.

In some cases the aneurism may be regarded as having undergone a partial natural cure. M. Cruveilhier has described cases in which the process of dilatation seems to have been arrested and the sac had been converted into bone, or more properly speaking, in which cretaceous matter had been deposited in its walls. In a case recorded by Dr. Wilks[1] the cure appears indeed to have been almost complete. A man, fifty-two years of age, of very intemperate habits, died of phthisis, and on examination after death, the heart and pericardium were found adherent to the diaphragm at the apex. In this situation there existed a hard calcified tumour, about the size of a pigeon's egg, which contained layers of decolorized coagulum. The cavity communicated with that of the ventricle by an aperture of about the same size as the sac itself. The edges of this aperture were smooth, and the membrane lining the sac was continuous with the endocardium of the ventricle. No history of the case could be obtained; but there is no doubt that the sac was

[1] Path. Trans. vol. viii. p. 103.

aneurismal, and that the progress of the disease had been entirely arrested some time before the death of the patient.

Age and Sex of the Subjects of the Disease.—Dr. Thurnam found the sex assigned in forty of the cases which he collected, and of them thirty were males and ten females, and he points out the difference which this proportion displays to the frequency of aneurismal affections of the arteries in the two sexes. The facts which I have brought together show a still larger proportion of cases in females—the numbers being thirty-nine—twenty-five males and fourteen females. The ages of the patients in the first series of cases ranged from eighteen to eighty-one, and were pretty evenly distributed throughout the middle and later periods of life, though somewhat more frequent between twenty and thirty, and in advanced life. The more recent cases display a tolerably equal distribution from early to advanced age, and are given in the following table:—

Age.	Males.	Age.	Females.
14 and 16	2	12 and 15	2
21 to 30	4	21 to 30	4
31 to 40	4	31 to 40	0
41 to 50	4	41 to 50	0
51 to 60	3	51 to 60	0
61 to 70	3	61 to 70	4
71 to 77	2	71 to 77	2
Between 60 and 70	1	Between 60 and 70	0
Not stated	2	Not stated	2
	25		14

The most noticeable circumstance in this enumeration is the very early age at which the cardiac cases occur as compared with different forms of arterial aneurism ; this being explained by the frequent origin of the disease in endocarditis, and the frequency of endocarditic affections, as complications of rheumatism, in early life. It would have been interesting to have given some more satisfactory information as to the influence which rheumatism exercises, either immediately or more remotely, in the production of the partial aneurisms of the heart. The reports of the cases are, however, very imperfect on this point ; but they clearly indicate that the aneurisms are not unfrequently connected with rheumatism. They appear also to be very commonly predisposed to by habits of dissipation and intemperance, both causes which we know are very influential in the causation of other forms of cardiac disease.

Aneurism of the Left Auricle.—An instance of dilatation of the left auricle with deposition of coagula in the dilated part, the result of an injury, was related by Dionis in 1716.[1] With this exception, however, the condition does not appear to have been noticed till the

[1] L'Anat. de l'Homme, p. 713.

beginning of the present century, when cases of the kind were related by Abernethy, Burns, and Hodgson, and, more recently, others have been placed on record by Sir A. Cooper, Elliotson', Hope, Chassaigniac, and Virchow, &c. Dr. Thurnam refers to eleven cases, including a further notice of one previously mentioned by Dr. Thomas Davies. Since the date of his memoir there have been four or five other cases published. Of these one is related by Dr. Fenwick,[1] another by Mr. Prescott Hewitt,[2] a third by Dr. Bristowe,[3] and one by myself.[4]

The so-called aneurisms of the auricle consist of dilatations containing coagula and fibrinous deposits of the sinus and auricular appendix, or both. They may either involve a considerable portion of the walls of the cavity and pass gradually from the undilated part without any obvious constriction or separation; or they may form distinct sacculated expansions. In the largest proportion of instances the sinus has been the seat of the disease, and the aneurism has been of the diffused form. In the cases, however, of M. Chassaigniac and Virchow, and in that of Dr. Fenwick, the cavity was distinctly circumscribed. Most generally, also, the disease has been found in connection with some, and often very marked, obstruction at the left auriculo-ventricular aperture; but in the instances named the valves were free from disease. The case of Dr. Fenwick was further interesting from there having existed during life a loud systolic sound audible at the apex, which was clearly due to the obstruction caused by the aneurismal swelling.

In two of the cases referred to, those of Mr. Prescott Hewitt and Dr. Bristowe, the right auricle was greatly dilated as well as the left, and the cavity contained coagula; in the former instance, apparently of similar character to those in the left auricle—in the latter, however, only the usual amorphous clots. Partial expansions of this kind should not, however, have the term aneurism applied to them; but to maintain the analogy between the similar affections of the arteries and veins, the dilatations of the right side of the heart should be termed varicose.

ANEURISMS OF THE VALVES.—A dilatation of the mitral valve, to which the term aneurism may properly be applied, was described by Morand in 1729; another was mentioned by Laennec and Fizeau at the beginning of this century. Sir A. Cooper, also, in 1825, referred to a case then and still existing in the Museum of St. Thomas's Hospital, and two other instances of the kind have been more fully related by Dr. Thurnam though previously noticed by others, of which one occurred in the practice of Sir Thomas Watson at the Middlesex Hospital. More recently specimens have been described by Cruveilhier, by Mr. Prescott Hewitt,[5] Dr. Habershon,[6] Dr. Ogle,[7] and myself;[8] and the affection has been noticed by Rokitansky in his Pathological Anatomy.

[1] Lancet, Feb. 1846.
[2] Path. Trans. 1848-50, vol. ii. p. 194.
[3] Ibid. xi. 1859-60. p. 65.
[4] Ed. Med. and Surg. Journal, 1846.
[5] Path. Trans. vol. iii. p. 78.
[6] Vol. ix. p. 117.
[7] Ibid. vol. vi. p. 156
[8] Vol. iii. p. 71.

M 2

Aneurisms may occur both in the aortic and mitral valves. Of their mode of origin in the former situation a very interesting example is contained in the Museum of St. Thomas's Hospital. In one of the aortic valves there exists a small distinctly-marginated sac, which would have contained a small bean ; in a second, there is one of somewhat less size, and in the third there is simply a deposit of fibrine in one part of the fold and a very slight dilatation in the same seat. It is evident that the last is the result of inflammatory action, and indicates the first stage in the production of the small aneurisms which exist in the other valves. Dr. Chevers has shown that in cases of contraction of the outlet of the ventricle and expansion of the inlet, whether relative or absolute, the aortic valves have a tendency to bulge at their most dependent parts. If this be unattended by any deposit of fibrine, the fold ultimately gives way in the weakened portion; if, however, the valve be strengthened by a deposit of fibrine the bulging may increase till a distinct sac is produced. A very characteristic example of the kind was exhibited by myself at the Pathological Society.

In the mitral valve the disease is, I believe, always found in the free fold. The dilatation may occupy merely a small part of the valve, or may be of large size, so as to involve a large portion of the fold. In some cases the disease seems to originate in the protrusion of the endocardium of the left ventricle, through the fibrous structure of the valve, so as to come in contact with the lining membrane of the left auricle. In other cases all the coats are dilated. In both instances the sacs generally project into the cavity of the left auricle, and sometimes the base of the sac gives way, and an opening is produced in the valve as if a piece of the fold had been punched out. The sacs may vary in size from one which would lodge a pea or bean or filbert, to one capable of holding a pigeon's egg. Of the former size the cases of Mr. Prescott Hewitt and myself afford instances. Of the latter, the specimen in the Museum of St. Thomas's, referred to by Sir A. Cooper, is a most remarkable example. In several cases two or more sacs have been found in the same valve. These small aneurisms of the mitral valve not unfrequently occur in cases of aortic valvular obstruction, and I have described one which was found in a case of rupture of the aortic valves. The sacs may contain laminated coagula, and in one of the cases described by Mr. Keith, a portion of the valve was entirely wanting, and a small sac was produced by a fibrinous coagulum being attached on the auricular side.

These affections are not only interesting pathologically, but may be of practical importance, as both at the aortic and mitral valves they may give rise to the symptoms and signs of incompetency.

I have before referred to a specimen which exists in the Museum of the Royal College of Surgeons, in which the current of blood flowing through a congenital aperture existing at the base of the ventricular septum has expanded portions of the tricuspid valves, so as to form small sacs or aneurisms; and I have seen a similar condition of the tricuspid valve in a recent case of malformation of the same kind.

ADVENTITIOUS PRODUCTS IN THE HEART.

By Thomas Bevill Peacock, M.D., F.R.C.P.

TUBERCLE IN THE HEART AND TUBERCULAR PERICARDITIS.

Laennec [1] when alluding to accidental products says, that he had only three or four times met with tubercles in the substance of the heart; and when speaking of chronic pericarditis, he remarks, that a tuberculous eruption may sometimes be developed in the false membrane and may thereby convert the acute into chronic disease, as frequently happens in pleurisy and peritonitis, and he states that he had met with two cases of the kind. In this passage, Laennec indicates the forms in which tuberculous deposits are found in the heart; in one of these they take place in the substance of the organ; in the other on the surface, in connection with inflammation of the pericardium. The former is certainly a very rare condition. Louis [2] says that in 112 dissections of phthisical persons he did not meet with a single instance of the existence of tubercle in the substance of the heart. Rokitansky [3] also speaks of the extreme rarity of the affection; and in the records of 116 post-mortem examinations of persons who had died of phthisis which I have analysed, I do not find more than two or three cases in which tubercle is said to have been found in the heart. The recorded instances of such deposits being at all of serious importance are also very few in number. The first writer who alludes to cases of the kind is, I believe, Dr. Baillie,[4] who in his "Morbid Anatomy" says that he "once saw two or three scrofulous tumours growing from the cavity of the pericardium, one of which was nearly as large as a walnut. They consisted of white soft matter, somewhat resembling new cheese," and he adds that "the pericardium is a very unusual part for any scrofulous affection;" and in his "Dissections,"[5] in alluding to the same case, he further says that both lungs were studded with tubercles, and the right in a state of suppuration in places. The subject of the dissection was a man twenty-one years of age

---

[1] Diseases of the Chest, Forbes's trans. 4th edit. 1834, pp. 586 and 623.
[2] Sydenham Society's Trans. 48–50.   [3] Ibid vol. iv. p. 210.
[4] Morbid Anatomy, and works by Wardrop, 1825, vol ii. p. 9.
[5] Works by Wardrop, vol. i. p. 220.

Dr. Macmichael,[1] in 1826, detailed the history of a man of thirty-five, who died at the Middlesex Hospital with dropsy and other symptoms of cardiac disease, and in whom the lungs and bronchial glands were found tuberculous, and the pericardium, especially at the base, studded with tuberculous deposits. In 1834, M. Sauzier. as quoted by Bouillaud,[2] found in a man thirty-four years of age, who died with abscess from caries of the sternum after accident, the lungs, pancreas, and pleura tuberculous, and in the substance of the auricles there were two tubercles, and around them the pericardium was adherent. The most remarkable case of the kind is, however, that related by Dr. Townsend in 1852.[3] In this instance a large mass described as tuberculous was connected with the left auricle, and had compressed that cavity and the entrances of the pulmonary veins, so as to give rise to extreme distension throughout their course; tubercles existed in the bronchial glands but not apparently in the lungs. The subject of the disease was a man sixty-two years of age, who died after an illness of twelve months. Since this time a case has been recorded by the late Dr. Baly in the Pathological Transactions.[4] It occurred in a prisoner at Millbank, sixteen years of age, who died with symptoms of sub-acute fever and head affection, after an illness of about ten days, and tubercular masses were found in the substance of the brain, and small tubercles in the lungs, bronchial glands and intestines. A yellow rounded mass, the size of a man's thumb, projected from the inter-auricular septum into the cavities of the right and left auricles, the two projections being parts of the same tuberculous mass which was situated in the septum. Dr. Quain also mentions that there were tubercular deposits in the pericardium in a Bosjesman girl, who died of tuberculosis.[5]

The second form of tuberculous deposit which occurs in connection with inflammation of the pericardium, is by no means so rare as that which has just been mentioned. The first instance of the kind that is recorded is probably that by Corvisart,[6] and another was figured by Cruveilhier, and is further alluded to in the General Pathology more recently published. The pericardium adhered intimately to the heart, and in these adhesions a thick and continuous layer of tuberculous matter was deposited, and this enveloped the vessels and had destroyed the muscular structure of the auricle. M. Fauvel, as quoted by Aran,[7] and by Rilliet and Barthez in their work on diseases of children, met with a case of tubercular pericarditis in a child six years and a half old, who died with dropsy and symptoms of disease of the heart. The pericardium was entirely adherent, the heart was considerably enlarged, and its surface was studded by whitish-yellow friable nodules, some of them the size of a nut, and as numerous

---

[1] London Medical and Physical Journal, vol. lvi. (N.S. vol. i.) p. 119.
[2] Maladies du Cœur, 2me edit. tome ii. p. 442.
[3] Dublin Journal, vol. i. 1852, p. 176.
[4] Path. Trans. vol. iii. 1850-51, 1851-2, p. 34.
[5] Path. Trans. vol. ii. 1848-49, 1849-50, p. 182.
[6] 3me édit. Paris, 1818, p. 26.
[7] Aran, Arch. Gén. de Méd. 4me série, 1846, tome xi. p. 181.

behind as in front. The internal surface of the right ventricle displayed similar depositions everywhere except at the septum. Since this time the occurrence of tuberculous deposits in connection with pericarditis has been made the subject of a special memoir by Sir G. Burrows,[1] in which he details three cases which he supposes to be examples of the affection; and in two of them—one of which occurred in his own practice, the other under the care of the late Dr. Baly—the inference was confirmed by post-mortem examination. More recently, Dr. Bristowe has described three other cases in the Pathological Transactions,[2] and such instances cannot indeed be very uncommon. Cruveilhier says that he has many times met with tubercles, in connection with false membranes, in children with tuberculous lungs.[3] Louis also refers to such cases, and details the particulars of one in his memoir on pericarditis.[4] Otto[5] mentions having twice seen the condition in children, and Dr. Walshe[6] states that it is displayed in one of Dr. Carswell's drawings contained in the collection to illustrate morbid anatomy at University College. I have myself met with three cases of the kind, two while Pathologist of Edinburgh Infirmary and one at the Victoria Park Hospital.

Tubercular deposits in the pericardium bear a close resemblance to the similar disease of the arachnoid, pleura and peritoneum. They may be of very small size, mere specks, or may attain the dimensions of a cherry-stone, filbert, or walnut. In consistence they are generally soft, and they are usually of a greyish or yellowish colour. In one of my own cases, the tubercles, which were thickly spread over the attached and reflected pericardium, varied in size from that of a pin's head to a cherry-stone. In another, while there were very small masses of yellowish tubercle thickly studded over the surface of the heart, there were also laminated false membranes, in some places a quarter of an inch, in other parts fully half an inch in thickness, and the middle layers of this deposit were of a yellowish colour, soft and granular, and closely resembled what is commonly called tuberculous infiltration. In the third case the tuberculous deposit assumed the form of small granulations of a greyish colour, the two layers of pericardium being entirely attached by cellular adhesions. The affection in two of Dr. Bristowe's cases consisted of small miliary granulations, in one with patches more closely set together in places; in the other there were both separate tuberculous masses and laminæ of considerable size.

In the cases which have fallen under my own notice the deposits were situated beneath the serous membrane, and in one of them there were masses which were more deeply embedded in the substance of the ventricles and which were only exposed on section. One of these cases also, it will be observed, displayed tubercle in the centre of a thick layer of false membrane covering the heart, thus corresponding

---

[1] Med.-Chir. Trans. vol. xxx. 1847, p 77.   [2] Vol. xii. 1860-61, p. 63.
[3] Traité d'Anat. Path. tome iv. série 1862, p. 684.
[4] Revue Médicale, 1826.   [5] Path. Anat. by South, 1831, p. 258.
[6] Diseases of Heart, 1862, p. 357.

with the observations of Laennec and Cruveilhier. The different writers who have alluded to this subject have agreed in asserting that tuberculous affections of the heart are only met with in connection with similar deposits in other parts of the body, and the cases which have been recorded entirely confirm that view. The most frequent co-existence is with tubercle in the bronchial glands, or in the lymphatic glands of the mediastinum. In two of the cases which I have myself seen, though occurring in persons twenty-eight and sixty-seven years of age, there was tuberculous deposit only in the bronchial glands and heart; though the general rule is, as is well known, that, after early life, if tubercle be found in any part of the body it also exists in the lungs. In the third case, the subject of which was a girl thirteen years of age, no tubercle was found anywhere else. In this instance there was also slight mitral valvular disease. In Sir G. Burrows' case the lungs, pleura, bronchial glands, peritoneum, and spleen were tuberculous; and in Dr. Baly's there were tubercles and ulcers in the intestines and lungs. In one of Dr. Bristowe's patients there was tuberculous perforation of the intestines; in a second, there was tubercle in the mediastinum; and in the third, in the brain, lungs, pleura, spleen, and mesentery. The occasional occurrence of tuberculous deposits in the heart with similar affections of the bronchial glands and mediastinum, and in some cases when the lungs are entirely free, led Cruveilhier to suggest that possibly the affection of the glands might be secondary to that of the heart; but this supposition is scarcely in accordance with the advanced disease of the lungs which is reported to have existed in other instances. Laennec supposed that the tubercles in cases of this description were the result of the inflammation, and were situated in the false membrane; the latter is, however, certainly not usually the seat of the deposit, and Sir G. Burrows is much more probably correct in regarding the pericarditic affection as the effect of the irritation set up by the deposit under the membrane. Indeed, the first class of cases, in which the tubercles are situated deeply in the substance of the heart or under the endocardium and assume the form of separate tumours, cannot be regarded as essentially distinct from the second, in which the tubercles are more superficial. The absence of adhesions in some of the latter class of cases seems conclusively to show that the inflammatory exudation is at least generally secondary.

The tuberculous deposits in the heart occur under the same circumstances as those which attend similar affections in other parts of the body; they may be found in both sexes, and at all ages, but they are more common in comparatively early life.

The age and sex of the subjects of some of the cases referred to are as follows:—

Males						6½ years.	Females						14 years.
,,	.	.	.	.	.	13 ,,	,,	.	.	.	.	.	20 ,,
,,	.	.	.	.	.	16 ,,	,,	.	.	.	.	.	28 ,,
,,	.	.	.	.	.	19 ,,							
,.	.	.	.	.	.	21 ,,							
,,	.	.	.	.	.	24 ,,							
,,	.	.	.	.	.	34 ,,							
,.	.	.	.	.	.	36 ,,							
,,	.	.	.	.	.	62 ,,							
,,	.	.	.	.	.	62 ,,							
,,	.	.	.	.	.	67 ,,							

In several of the cases of tubercular pericarditis the evidences of effusion in the pericardium had been observed during life. When such signs arise in persons who are obviously tuberculous, and especially if they assume the sub-acute form and are not attended by any large amount of liquid effusion, they may be suspected to be connected with tubercular deposits. It must however be borne in mind that pericarditis, having no connection with tubercle, may occur during the progress of phthisis. The inference as to the tubercular origin of such cases is therefore by no means decisive.

CANCER.

Cancerous deposits in the heart are of more common occurrence than tubercle. Dr. Walshe,[1] writing in 1846, says that he had readily found twenty-five cases recorded; and more recently, in a paper in the Pathological Transactions,[2] I collected the particulars of forty-five, including in this number two which had fallen under my own notice. The earliest published examples of the disease were, I believe, those of Andral and Bayle in 1824.[3]

The cases of cancerous deposit in the heart may be classed into four series: First, Cases of primary cancer, in which the disease exists only in some part of the organ. These are of extremely rare occurrence; of the forty-five cases referred to, only two were expressly stated to have been instances of the kind,[4] though in the reports of seven others, no mention was made of the existence of cancer in any other part of the body.

Secondly, Cases in which the disease occurred coincidently and probably simultaneously, in the heart and in different parts of the body, and especially in parts adjacent to the heart. This form, though still rare, is more common than the other.

Thirdly, Instances in which the disease first appears in parts adjacent to the heart,—the bronchial or mediastinal glands, the lungs, or the glands around the larynx and in the neck,—and thence spreads so as to involve the pericardium and the large vessels at the base of

[1] Nature and Treatment of Cancer, p. 368.   [2] Vol. xvi. p. 99, 1864, 1865.
[3] Revue Médicale, 1824, tome 1ᵉ, p. 268.
[4] Ollivier, Traité de la Moëlle Epinière, 3ᵐᵉ edit., 1837, tome ii. p. 164; Segalas, Rev. Méd. tome iv. 1825, p. 247.

the heart or the auricles. Cases of this kind are not uncommon, though less frequent than those of the next series.

Fourthly, By far the largest proportion of cases of cancerous disease of the heart occur secondarily to the deposit of cancer in some distant organ. Of the forty-five cases, twenty-one were of this description; the primary disease being seated in different cases in the eye, the cheek and bones of the face, the lower lip, the breast and axillary glands, the ribs and pleura, the abdominal organs, the inguinal glands, the uterus, vagina, labia, the penis and testes, and the upper and lower extremities.

The heart may be affected by cancer in different forms. Thus, of the cases collected seven are reported to have been cases of scirrhus, four of melanosis, and twenty-five of encephaloid. The deposit also may assume either the form of distinct masses or tubera, or it may be infiltrated into the tissue, or occur on the surface.

The first form is the most common, especially when the deposits are secondary. The masses in different published cases are compared in size to peas or beans, to almonds or chestnuts, or to hen's eggs or oranges; and they may be only one, two, or three in number, or they may amount to a dozen or more [1] and in one very remarkable case it is stated that they were so numerous that the examiner ceased counting them after enumerating six hundred.[2] The most frequent seat of the disease seems to be the right auricle and ventricle, though the tumours may also occur, either alone or otherwise, in other parts of the organ. Generally they are situated beneath the attached pericardium; more rarely beneath the endocardium; and still more rarely in the substance of the auricles and ventricles or in the septa. The deposits may only slightly project above the adjacent surface, or they may form distinct and nearly separate tumours, the mass being only attached to the part from which it projects by a narrow pedicle. In the Museum of St. Thomas's Hospital there is a specimen of medullary growth from the left auricle, which is almost entirely detached from the lining membrane. In some cases the masses are reported to have pressed upon the cardiac cavities or apertures, so as to interfere with the transmission of the blood or with the action of the valves.

More rarely the disease assumes the form of infiltration, and when this is the case, the structure of the heart may be only slightly affected, or it may be extensively and completely destroyed. In one instance it is stated that not more than a twelfth of the organ was free from the deposit.[3]

In the third form of disease the heart is found enveloped in a

[1] Exposition d'un cas remarkable de Maladie Cancereuse (Paris, 1825), quoted by Dr. Churchill in London Med. and Phys. Journal, vol. lvii. (N.S. vol. ii), 1827, p. 280.
[2] Case of Dupuytren, quoted by Cruveilhier in Essai sur l'Anat. Path. Paris, 1816, vol. i. pp. 86–87.
[3] Rilliet; Bullet. de la Soc. de Méd. 1813, No. 5, tome iii. p. 357. A very marked case of cancerous infiltration with masses in the mediastinum, which occurred in a patient of Dr. Barker's, at St. Thomas's Hospital, is described by Dr. Bristowe in the Path. Reports, vol. vii. The specimen is preserved in the Museum, x. 67.

cancerous mass, which produces entire adhesion of all parts of the pericardium. This is, I believe, of very unfrequent occurrence. A case of the kind has, however, been described and figured by Dr. Bright in the Medico-Chirurgical Transactions.[1] A second is related by Dr. Kilgour,[2] in the " London and Edinburgh Journal of Medical Science;" and a third was described by myself in the paper in the Pathological Transactions before referred to.[3]

In only two or three of the recorded cases is the cancer stated to have been softened or ulcerated, and the nature of one of them may be doubted. In one instance, however, a cancerous mass situated near the origin of the anterior coronary artery had softened and caused perforation of the arterial coats and the escape of blood into the cavity of the pericardium.[4]

Cancerous deposits in the heart do not appear to be generally productive of any special symptoms by which their presence can be detected during life. In some cases, when there was disease of the adjacent organs, there were signs of pressure on the large vessels and of interference with the circulation of the blood ; and in three or four other instances the formation of the deposits on the surface of the heart occasioned inflammation of the pericardium which was recognised by the usual signs during life. Of this I have myself seen two instances. Most usually, however, there are no symptoms by which the affection of the heart is indicated, and the condition is only detected on post-mortem examination. In the case under my own care which has been mentioned—notwithstanding that the existence of a tumour in the chest was ascertained a considerable time before the patient's death, and that the patient's father was said to have died of cancer of the heart, and thus attention was particularly directed to the state of the organ—no symptoms indicating the heart to have been involved were detected.

SIMPLE AND OTHER CYSTS.

Lancisi mentions having seen a cyst containing thick matter (meliceris) in the substance of the heart, and other writers describe the occasional occurrence of cysts of different kinds in the heart or pericardium. Thus Cruveilhier refers to hæmatoid cysts as occurring in the pericardium and other serous surfaces, but does not detail any instance of the kind; and I do not know any recorded case except that reported by Dr. Ogle in the Pathological Transactions for 1857 and 1858.[5] In this instance a large cyst was found beneath the pericardium covering the posterior surface of the right ventricle. It had firm and thick walls, and contained laminated coagulum with brownish

---

[1] Vol. xxii. 1839, p. 15.   [2] Vol. iv. 1844, p. 828.
[3] Vol. xvi. 1864-1865, p. 100, Case 1. The specimen is preserved in the Victoria Park Hospital Museum.
[4] M. Broca, Bullet. de la Soc. Anat. 25ᵐˢ, année, 1850, p. 253.
[5] Vol. ix. p. 165.

granular material The layers of pericardium were adherent, and there were old and thick adhesions of the right pleura, with some similar coagulum in its sac. No connection could anywhere be traced between any of the cavities of the heart and the cyst; and Dr. Ogle supposes that probably the blood had escaped from one of the branches of a coronary artery; and that having first lodged in the pericardium, it had subsequently ruptured into the pleura. The cavities of the heart were rather large, the lining membrane of the right auricle was thickened and opaque, and the coronary arteries were in various places rigid. The specimen was removed from a man fifty-five years of age, who died with symptoms of cardiac disease and dropsy, and who had been ill for two years; but no decided history of any attack to which the condition of the heart could be ascribed appears to have been obtained. The condition of the coronary arteries is in favour of Dr. Ogle's supposition, but it may be open to question whether the cysts might not have originated in acute hæmorrhagic inflammation of the pericardium and right pleura.

Certainly in some cases the appearance of a cyst is produced by the remains of a pericarditic effusion; the two layers of serous membrane becoming adherent, except in one portion, where a cavity containing pus or serum still exists. A specimen of this kind was exhibited at one of the meetings of the Pathological Society.

ENTOZOA.

In the works of the earlier writers on morbid anatomy, cases are referred to in which the heart is stated to have contained worms. Such reports are, however, generally entitled to little credit, though of late years hydatid cysts, have, in various cases, been found in different parts of the heart. Probably the earliest recorded instance of the kind is that mentioned by Morgagni,[1] of a man seventy-four years of age, who died in the hospital at Padua; but of whose previous state no further history was obtained than that he had not suffered from any of the usual symptoms of cardiac disease. A tumour about the size of a cherry was found at the posterior surface of the heart near the apex. It was half embedded in the substance of the organ, and "on puncturing it a small quantity of clear fluid escaped, but a more turbid humour remained, and was only evacuated on laying it open. In so doing a small piece of membrane escaped. This displayed white, and, as it were, mucous particles, and a particle of tendinous hardness." The whole was included in a dense sheath. Dupuytren,[2] at the beginning of the present century, placed a similar case on record. It occurred in a female forty years of age, who died in one of the Paris hospices, whose body was dissected in the anatomical school. No history of the

[1] Alexander's Translations, vol. i. p. 583. Letter xxi. Art. 4. See also Letter iii. Art. 26, p. 60, where it is said a white membrane protruded like a hydatid.
[2] Journal de Corvisart et Leroux, tome v. année xi. p. 139.

case during life was obtained. The right auricle was very greatly dilated, and on its inner surface, under a smooth membrane, were found numerous cysts which nearly filled the cavity. About the same time a third case was related by Dr. Trotter ;[1] it occurred in a boy fourteen years of age, on board one of her Majesty's ships, who had been very livid and subject to dyspnœa and palpitation : a large cyst, containing several loose hydatids, was found in the right auricle, and two similar bodies were also contained in the ventricle. Two cases of the kind are contained in the Transactions of the Medical and Chirurgical Society ; one of these, which was published in 1821, occurred in a boy of ten, who died suddenly without having been previously ill, and the case is imperfectly related by Mr. David Price.[2] The other was communicated by Mr. Evans[3] in 1832. The subject of the disease was a delicate female, forty years of age, who was suddenly seized with pain in the præcordia and difficulty of breathing, and died in a few days. The pericardium displayed an effusion of lymph and serum ; and a considerable tumour was situated at the apex of the heart and projected into the right ventricle, filling a fourth of the cavity. The tumour proved to be a cyst containing numerous hydatids, varying in size from a pea to a pigeon's egg. A plate is given of the specimen, which is stated to be preserved in the Museum of St. Bartholomew's Hospital. In 1838, Mr. Smith of Bristol published a somewhat similar case, which occurred in the practice of a surgeon at Warminster. The subject of the disease was a female, whose age is not stated, and who died after an illness of three hours. A large hydatid was found in the right ventricle, and must have obstructed the entrance of the blood into the pulmonary artery.

The more recent writers on cardiac diseases and on pathological anatomy very generally refer to cases of hydatid cysts found in some portion of the heart. Andral[5] says that he has seen three instances of the kind. In one a tumour, the size of a walnut, was embedded in the substance of the left ventricle; in another a cyst, as large as a nut, was attached by a small pedicle to the lining membrane of the right ventricle ; and in the third, three cysts, the size of nuts, were embedded in the substance of the heart. The cysts were transparent except at one point which was white and could be made to protrude like a head from the centre, and he was thus led to regard them as cysticerci. Rokitansky[6] relates the case of a woman, twenty-three years of age, who died suddenly, and a tumour the size of a hen's egg was found at the upper part of the interventricular septum, and protruded into both ventricles. On the right side the cyst had burst, and the contained hydatid had become impacted in the conus arteriosus, so as to obstruct the entrance into the pulmonary artery. In another instance, in a soldier thirty-five years of age, who also

[1] Medical and Chemical Essays, 1795, p. 123. Case of a Blue Boy.
[2] Vol. xi. p. 274.   [3] Vol. xvii. p. 507.   [4] Lancet, vol. ii. p. 628.
[5] Path. Anat. by Townsend and West, vol. ii. p. 348.
[6] Path. Anat., Sydenham Society's Trans. vol. iv. p. 208.

died suddenly, a tumour of the size of a duck's egg was found in the upper part of the septum and corresponding portion of the left ventricle behind. The sac contained fibrinous coagula mixed with portions of acephalocyst. The surfaces of pericardium were adherent in the seat of the tumour. M. Aran,[1] in a paper on these and other forms of tumour of the auricles, published in 1846, relates a case which occurred to M. Dupaul, in a female twenty-three years of age, who died suddenly after her confinement, and on examination a hydatid cyst iu the left auricle was found to have ruptured on both sides, so as to allow of the escape of blood from the auricle into the pericardiac cavity. It was evident that the tumour had been developed under the endocardium of the auricle. Mr. H. Coote, in 1854,[2] found a large cyst in the walls of the left ventricle of a subject under dissection at St. Bartholomew's Hospital, and he refers to a second specimen as existing in the museum, doubtless the case of Mr. Evans before referred to. In addition to the cases now mentioned several will be found reported in the Pathological Transactions by Dr. Budd,[3] Dr. Wilks,[4] Dr. Habershon,[5] &c., and one which occurred in a patient of my own at St. Thomas's Hospital, is related by Dr. Hicks and myself.[6] I have also had the opportunity of examining a specimen exhibited by the late Mr. Ward, at one of the earlier meetings of the society.[7] In Mr Ward's case the subject of the disease was a man, twenty-two years of age, who died shortly after having sustained an accident: the cyst was about the size of a French walnut, and was situated at the posterior and upper part of the left ventricle, beneath the superficial muscular fibres. My own patient was a boy of eighteen, who died after an illness of about thirteen months: the cyst, about the size of a walnut, was partially embedded in the muscular substance of the right ventricle, but did not project into the cavity. In the sixth volume of the Transactions,[8] there is a description of a case in which a patient at the Colney Hatch Asylum died suddenly when under excitement, and after death two cysts, one of which had ruptured, were found beneath the attached pericardium.

The precise nature of the cyst in some of the above cases is not clear. The description given of that related by Morgagni is supposed by Laennec conclusively to indicate the hydatid to have been a cysticercus; and both Andral and Rokitansky speak of having met with cysticerci in the substance of the heart. Most generally, however, the cysts appear to be those of the echinococcus. Such is stated to

---

[1] Arch. Gén. de Méd. 4me série, tome xi. p. 187.
[2] Med. Times and Gazette, xxix. p. 156.   [3] Vol. x. p. 80.
[4] Vol. xi. p. 71.   [5] Vol. vi. p. 108.   [6] Vol. xv. p. 247.
[7] Vol. i. p. 225. Dr. Walshe mentions in his work on Diseases of the Heart, &c. (3rd. edit. 1862, p. 65), that a specimen is figured in one of Dr. Carswell's drawings, and that a hydatid, the size of a pigeon's egg, situated in the interventricular septum, is contained in University College Museum. In the Museum of St. Thomas's Hospital there is in addition to the specimen described by Dr. Hicks and myself (x. 68) another (x. 64) in which the cyst, as large as a duck's egg, is situated at the apex.
[8] P. 114. See Report on the case by Dr. Wilks.

have been the case in the instances related in the Pathological Transactions, though the bodies were not always met with. The Trichina, on the other hand, is usually considered not to be found in the heart. This is, however, denied by Dr. Cobbold,[1] who says that all the different forms of larvæ occur in the heart, but they do not stay there, the firmness of the muscular texture interfering apparently with the development of the worm in that situation. The same writer gives some calculations of the relative frequency with which the echinococcus is found in the heart and in other organs. Thus he states that Droaim, of 373 cases in which these cysts were found in some part of the body, met with them in the heart in ten cases; and Dr. Cobbold, of 136 cases, found echinococci in the heart or pericardium in nine instances. The most common situations for the cysts appear to be the right auricle and ventricle, but no part of the organ is free from them; cases being recorded in which the walls of the left ventricle were affected; and, it will be observed also, the interventricular septum. The cysts may be developed beneath the pericardium or endocardium, or in the substance of the muscle. According to the situation which they occupy is their tendency to grow, so as to protude externally or internally; and they may ultimately rupture into the pericardium or into one of the cavities of the heart. In the former situation they may give rise to acute pericarditis, or to adhesion of the surfaces of the membrane covering the projecting portion. In the latter the loose hydatids may escape into the cavity and produce fatal obstruction to the circulation of the blood. In one case, it will be observed that a cyst ruptured both externally and internally, and so allowed of hæmorrhage into the cavity of the pericardium.

The hydatids in the heart appear frequently to be solitary, not occurring in any other structure of the body. Such seems to have been the case in the instances related by Morgagni, Dupuytren, Dr. Trotter, Mr. Smith, and Mr. Coote, in one of those by Rokitansky, and in the cases described in the Pathological Transactions by Dr. Budd and Dr. Habershon, and probably also in that of Mr. Ward. On the other hand, in the second case of Rokitansky there were three separate cysts in the liver. In the case of Dr. Wilks, there was also a cyst in the liver; and in my own case, in addition to the cyst in the right ventricle, there were numerous hydatids in the liver, spleen, omentum, right kidney, and lungs; and portions of cysts were expectorated during life.

It will be seen that in the cases referred to the hydatids occurred in persons of both sexes and of all ages. It may also be observed that there are no certain signs by which their presence in the heart can be detected during life. In some cases they have been found without having been preceded by any indications of defect in the circulatory organs; in other instances they have occurred in persons who have died after longer or shorter illnesses, with symptoms clearly pointing to some cardiac disease. In cases of the latter description,

[1] Entozoa, 1864, p. 275.

if there were evidences of hydatids in some other part of the system the suspicion might be entertained that the cardiac symptoms were due to the development of hydatid cysts in some part of the heart. In my own case there was nothing observed during life which at all indicated that the heart was the seat of disease.

FIBRINOUS DEPOSITS ; SYPHILITIC AFFECTIONS OF THE HEART.

The substance of the heart is not unfrequently the seat of fibrinous deposits. These may occur either as the result of acute inflammation of the muscular structure, myocarditis, with or without peri- and endo-carditis ; or they may be connected with an altered condition of the blood, leading to the effusion of fibrine into the muscular structure, in the same way as such effusions occur in other organs, the spleen or kidneys, or as the blood coagulates in the vessels themselves. When deposited the fibrinous material may soften and allow of the partial destruction of the walls of the heart, so as to constitute a false lateral or partial aneurism ; or it may undergo an imperfect organization being converted into fibroid tissue, and this, being less resistant than the natural muscle, may yield to the pressure of the blood, and a true partial aneurism be formed. Closely allied to these deposits are those which occur in the substance of the heart in connection with constitutional syphilis. Corvisart, struck with the remarkable resemblance sometimes presented by vegetations on the valves of the heart to syphilitic warty growths on the external organs of generation, suggested that in some such cases the vegetations might have a syphilitic origin; and he detailed several cases which he regarded as supporting this idea. His views have not, however, been generally adopted ; and Laennec in particular, considering the frequency of venereal affections and the comparative rarity of such vegetations, expressed his decided dissent from the supposition. More recently, however, writers have attached more importance to the suggestions of Corvisart. Dr. Julia, of Cazeres,[1] has published several cases in which vegetations on the endocardium were found in persons who were known to have recently had syphilis and presented other indications of the disease ; and in two of these cases there were small patches of ulceration on the surface or in the substance of the heart. He also refers to a case published in 1778, which, though often quoted as an example of ulcerated cancer of the heart, is doubtless an instance of syphilitic ulceration. The case was reported by M. Carcassone to the Académie de Médecine, and occurred in a female of dissipated habits, twenty-two years of age, who was an inmate of the House of Refuge at Perpignan. Her illness, which followed upon chancres, was characterized by weight

---

[1] Gaz. Méd. de Paris, 1845, No. 52, p. 845.

and pain in the region of the heart, and rapidly proved fatal; after death a large ulcer with indurated base was found on the anterior surface of the heart. More recently cases have been recorded by Ricord, Lebert, and especially by Virchow.[1] The latter writer has indeed made the syphilitic affections of the heart the subject of a special memoir, of which a translation has been published as a separate work in French.[2] In this country several communications of a similar kind have recently appeared in the Pathological Transactions, chiefly by Dr. Wilks.

The syphilitic affections of the heart resemble the similar degeneration of muscular structure in general. They consist of fibrinous exudations into the connective tissue, which may either soften and suppurate, forming ulcers or small abscesses; or they may be converted into masses of hardened fibroid tissue, causing a puckered appearance resembling a cicatrix on the surface, and are generally combined with thickening and induration of the covering and lining membranes. In the first case described by Virchow, it is stated that a portion of the organ near the base of the posterior fold of the mitral valves, for the space of about an inch and a half, was occupied by a whitish-coloured hard mass, and the intra-ventricular septum was also similarly degenerated to the depth of from a quarter to half an inch. The endocardium was nearly cartilaginous, and tendinous cords passed deeply into the substance of the heart; the muscular structure had undergone the fatty degeneration, and the surface of the ventricle was marked by callous tuberosities. Under the microscope in the points of a white colour and tendinous structure, the muscular fibres had disappeared and were replaced by fibrous tissue. At the apex of the heart there was a slight dilatation, indicating the commencement of an aneurism.

FIBRO-CARTILAGINOUS AND OSSEOUS DEGENERATION.

Under these terms, authors have described changes which are not of uncommon occurrence. Corvisart has related a case in which he states that the walls of the left ventricle were at least an inch in width, and much hardened. "At the apex, up to a certain point and throughout its thickness, the muscular structure was cartilaginous. The fleshy bodies also had acquired a remarkable hardness, approaching that of cartilage."[3] This occurred in a man sixty-four years of age, who died after an illness of about two years' duration characterized by dyspnœa, dropsy, and other cardiac symptoms. The state of the pericardium is not mentioned, but the mitral valve was

[1] Archiv. für Path. Anat. und Phys. etc. 1864, p. 468.
[2] Le Syphilis Constitutionelle, par M. Rudolphe Virchow, traduit de l'Allemand par le docteur Paul Picard, Paris, 1860.
[3] 3me éd. 1818, p. 171, obs. 28.

also cartilaginous. The condition here described was alluded to by Laennec, and has been more fully illustrated by Cruveilhier.[1]

The transformation may either be general or diffused, extending over a considerable portion of the heart; or it may be partial and limited to a small part. The diffused or more general change is chiefly seen in the parietes of the right ventricle, occurring in cases where the orifice of the pulmonary artery, the pulmonic circulation, or the left auriculo-ventricular aperture is obstructed, so as to subject the affected part to long-continued distension. This condition, which is well known to all pathologists, has recently been made the subject of a paper by Sir W. Jenner.[2]

The other or partial form is seen in the walls of the left ventricle, and especially at the apex or outer wall. When existing to a marked degree, it is generally combined with some dilatation of the cavity in the seat of the transformation, and not unfrequently with bulging of the walls; and it has been regarded by Cruveilhier as the first step towards the formation of the true lateral or partial aneurisms. A view somewhat similar is also maintained by Rokitansky.

In the slighter forms of the degeneration, such as occur in cases where the change is diffused, the structure of the heart is much coarser than usual, the altered parts have a yellowish colour and a peculiarly hard leathery feeling, and resist when cut by the knife. The more advanced degrees of the transformation are only seen in cases in which the disease is limited in extent, and under such circumstances the muscular structure may be almost entirely replaced by dense white fibrous material. This, as before mentioned, is generally only found at the apex of the left ventricle, but it may occur over a large portion of the outer wall, or in the interventricular septum and fleshy bodies; and Cruveilhier says that he has seen the change affecting fully a third of the muscular substance of the organ.

The mode in which the transformation is effected probably varies in different cases. Cruveilhier supposed that it was a slow change, by which the cellular tissue in the muscular substance became thickened and indurated, and replaced the atrophied contractile tissue. Rokitansky refers the change to inflammation; and there can be no doubt that inflammatory action, affecting the peri- and endo-cardium or both these membranes, and involving to a greater or less extent the interjacent muscular substance, does in some cases give rise to the alteration. This is shown by the very general occurrence of thickening and induration of the investing membranes, or of adhesion of the visceral and reflected layers of the pericardium, in cases in which the muscular structure is transformed. The relative thinness of the muscular substance of the heart at the apex affords apparently the explanation of the greater frequency of the change in that situation; and the proneness to endocarditis on the left side accounts for the more marked changes being only found in the walls of the left ventricle.

[1] Traité d'Anat. Path. Gén. tome iii. 1856, p. 601.
[2] Med.-Chir. Trans. vol. xliii. 1860, p. 199.

In other cases the change is probably due, as pointed out by Sir W. Jenner, to long-continued congestion of the substance of the heart, causing slow hypertrophy and induration of the connective tissue and secondary atrophy of the muscular fibres. This seems the mode in which the diffused and general induration of the walls of the right ventricle is produced, though there does not appear to be any adequate reason why it should be so frequently confined to the right side. In yet other cases the transformation is probably the result of the imperfect organization of fibrinous material, which, in connection with an altered condition of the blood, is effused beneath the investing membranes or in the substance of the heart. These effusions are not of unfrequent occurrence and generally co-exist with similar depositions in the spleen, kidneys, &c. Whatever be the mode in which the disease commences, the subsequent changes correspond, the connective tissue becomes greater in quantity and more solid, and by its contraction compresses the muscular structure and so leads to its atrophy, and in some instances to its entire disappearance. It is not, properly speaking, a degeneration or transformation of the muscular substance, but the replacement of the muscle by fibrous tissue.

The older writers frequently speak of the conversion of portions of the heart into bone, or of bones being found in the substance of the heart, and most pathologists have met with cases of the kind. When such formations do not occur in connection with chronic pericarditis or in old false membranes, and are not traceable to the calcification of the fibrous structures around the orifices or in the valves, they take place in portions of the muscular substance which have undergone the changes now described. Such formations are not, however, to be regarded as truly bony, though they may be very hard, thick, and of large size. They consist indeed only of granules of calcareous matter, deposited in the altered tissue, without any of the elements of true bone structure.

POLYPOID GROWTHS.

Most writers on cardiac pathology mention polypoid growths as occurring in the different cavities of the heart. There can, however, be no doubt that many of the cases which have been described as of this description were only instances in which decolorized coagula were adherent to the lining membrane. Such may be concluded to have been the nature of the bodies described by Dr. Ryan[2] and Mr. Stewart,[3] which have been frequently referred to by authors. In other instances, however, it may be inferred that the formations observed were new growths. Such apparently

[1] Case of M. Renauldin; Corvisart, p. 175.
[2] Med. Gaz. vol. iii. 1829, p. 336.
[3] Ed. Med. and Surg. Jour. vol. xii 1317, p. 182.

were the polypi described by Mr. Reeves, Mr. Mayo,[1] and Mr. Wilkinson King,[2] and by MM. Puisaye,[3] Dubreuil,[4] Choisy,[5] and Bouillaud.[6] Most of these cases have been collected by M. Aran, in a memoir published in 1846.[7] Two other similar cases are described by Dr. Wilks[8] and Mr. Birkett,[9] in the Pathological Transactions, and one has fallen under my own notice.

The true polypoid growths appear generally to occur in the left auricle, and to be most usually attached to the fibrous zone of the auriculo-ventricular valves. Sometimes they are connected with some other part of the walls of the cavity, or are found in the right auricle or either ventricle. When in the former situation, they frequently project through the auriculo-ventricular aperture into the cavity of the left ventricle. They vary considerably in size in different instances. Some have been compared to partridge's or pigeon's eggs or to walnuts; others to hen's eggs; and yet others are stated to have filled the cavity from which they sprang. Most usually they assume a pyriform or cordate shape, and are attached to the walls of the cavity by a more or less constricted pedicle. The surface of the growths is sometimes smooth, sometimes nodulated or studded with vegetations; and most generally they are covered wholly or in part by the endocardium, this, especially at the root, being thickened and indurated. They may consist of a simple growth, or, on the contrary, may be composed of different portions. The precise nature of the bodies is not clear in the accounts of several of the published cases. Mr. Burns says, in reference to that which he has described, that it was dense, laminated and fully organized, and closely resembled the polypi of the nose. Mr. Mayo is in doubt whether the specimen he mentions was to be regarded as a slowly growing polypus, or a medullary sarcomatous growth. In the case which occurred at the Middlesex Hospital,[10] the structure of the tumour is compared to the spleen; in that of M. Puisaye the growth is stated to have been fungous, and to have had the aspect and consistence of gelatine; and in those of M. Dubreuil, the tumours are called fibrous or albugineous. Dr. Wilks and the reporters on his case described the tumour as fibrous, and Mr. Birkett regards the specimen he exhibited as fibroid. The growths are included by M. Aran under the general term of "Tumeurs fongeuses sanguines." The specimen which fell under my own notice was about the size of a walnut; it was attached to the auricular surface of the mitral valve, was of a rounded form with a short and thin pedicle, and

[1] Outlines of Human Pathology, 1836, p. 472.
[2] Lancet, 1842, vol. ii. p. 428.
[3] Gaz. Méd. de Paris, 1843, p. 270.
[4] Ibid. p. 512. Two cases, one of which is quoted by Bouillaud.
[5] Revue Médicale, 1833, tome ii. p. 425, quoted by Aran, p. 278.
[6] Vol. ii. p. 170. Obs. 105.
[7] Arch. Gén. de Méd. 4me série, tome xi. 1846, p. 274.
[8] Vol. viii. p. 150.   [9] Vol. i. p. 224.
[10] Lond. Med. Gaz. vol. xv. (1834-35), vol. i. p. 671.

was studded on its upper surface with vegetations or granulations. It was apparently covered by endocardium throughout, and was of a pearly white colour and obviously fibrous structure. The subject of the disease was a young woman who was insane and died of gangrene of the extremities, but had not during life presented any symptoms attracting attention to the heart.

The mode of origin of these growths probably varies in different cases. In some instances they may be simply adherent clots which have become organized; in others they probably originate in inflammatory exudations in the subserous cellular tissue. Indeed, this would appear to be the most usual mode of origin of the polypoid growths, for, as before stated, they generally spring from the fibrous tissue of the left auriculo-ventricular aperture and valves, and are usually covered by the endocardium. As might be expected, the cavities in which these bodies are developed are ordinarily considerably dilated; and similar effects are produced on other parts of the heart to those which would result from obstructions of any other kind in the same situation.

The polypoid growths have been met with at various ages and in both sexes, and generally in persons, who, for a longer or shorter time, have presented obvious symptoms of cardiac disease. When, as in most of the cases on record, the bodies obstruct the orifices of the heart or interfere with the action of the valves, they give rise to the ordinary effects of valvular disease which manifest themselves, by the usual signs. In one very interesting case, quoted by M. Aran from the "Annali Universali" for 1844,[1] a pulsating tumour was observed for a considerable period before the death of the patient, on the left side of the upper part of the sternum, between the cartilages of the second and third ribs; and this ultimately attained a considerable size. After death a tumour was found to occupy the upper and anterior part of the heart, and proved to be connected with the left auricle. The pericardium was inflamed and covered with recent exudation. The precise situation and character of the tumour is not clear from the description. M. Aran[2] also quotes from Schmidt, a case in which a hollow body was found filling the right auricle, passing through the auriculo-ventricular aperture, and communicating with the cavity of the aorta by an opening between the sigmoid valves.

[1] Supra, Obs. x. p. 275.　　　　[2] Obs. xviii. p. 287.

PNEUMO-PERICARDIUM.

BY J. WARBURTON BEGBIE, M.D.

THIS is the term employed to designate the presence of air in the cavity
of the pericardium, and may be applied to that condition, whether or
not the signs of inflammatory action in the sac are present. There
exist three different ways in which an accumulation of air in the
pericardial sac may be determined :—1st. Such may be the direct
product of the irritated membrane itself. It is admitted that occasionally, air is produced in the cavities of the pleura and peritoneum.
when these are the seat of inflammatory action, and if this be the
case, there can be no reason why the same formation should not occur
within the pericardium. Dr. Stokes has recorded an instance of this
nature, in which, although recovery happily occurred, and the diagnosis
must therefore be regarded as inferential rather than demonstrative,
the opinion expressed by him seems alone tenable. " I could form,"
he says, " no conclusion but that the pericardium contained air in
addition to an effusion of serum and coagulated lymph." [1] 2d. Air
may result from the decomposition of fluid in the pericardium.
Laënnec and other observers have not only pointed out the physical
signs which in their opinion indicate the existence of this lesion, but
the former more particularly, has in all probability greatly exaggerated the frequency of its occurrence. The effusion of fluid and
air into the pericardial sac, in the opinion of Laënnec, is a phenomenon likely to occur in the last stages of all diseases, and its existence he believed himself able to recognise both by percussion and
auscultation. " L'épanchement liquide et aëriforme à la fois du
Péricarde peut avoir lieu dans l'agonie de toutes les maladies. Il
m'est arrivé quelquefois de l'annoncer à une résonnance plus claire
du bas du sternum, survenue depuis peu de jours, ou à un bruit de
fluctuation déterminé par les battements du cœur et par les inspirations fortes."[2] In a case recorded. by M. Bricheteau, to which reference is made in Bouillaud's work, " Traité des Maladies du Cœur", as
well as in a note by Andral to his edition of Laënnec's Treatise, and
which is also alluded to by Dr. Stokes and Dr. Walshe, the diagnosis
of air as well as fluid existing in the sac of the pericardium was made
during the life of the patient, and depended chiefly on the presence

---

[1] Diseases of the Heart and Aorta, p. 21.
[2] Traité de l'Auscultation médiate : Des Maladies du Cœur—Du Pneumo-Péricarde,
chap. xxiii.

of a peculiar sound with the heart's action, a sound compared by Bricheteau to that produced by a water-wheel ("l'eau agitée par la roue d'un moulin"), while on examination after death the pericardium was found to be occupied by a peculiar fluid of very fetid character, air escaping with a whistling sound when the sac was opened. Acknowledging, however, the occasional occurrence during life of Pneumo-pericardium, as the result of decomposition in fluid occupying the sac, it is manifest that this source of the lesion is of much greater frequency as a post-mortem occurrence. Laënnec, indeed, has acknowledged this, for after alluding to Pneumo-pericardium as of common existence in autopsies, he adds, " Et surtout de ceux (cadavres) qui ont été gardés pendant un certain temps." 3rd. Air may reach the pericardium from a distance, through perforation, and the establishment of a communication between its cavity and that of any hollow organ normally containing air. Thus the sources of the air may be various, and the event may further be the result of direct injury or of disease. A very remarkable illustration is mentioned by Dr. Walshe, in which a communication was established between the œsophagus and pericardium, in an attempt to swallow a long blunt instrument, a juggler's knife—the case terminated fatally.[1] A case of traumatic Pneumo-pericardium, unattended by inflammation and resulting in complete recovery, is given by Dr. Austin Flint, to whom it was related by Dr. Knapp of Louisville. " The patient was stabbed with a knife, which penetrated the pleural cavity and perforated slightly the pericardium. A splashing sound with the heart's action was immediately heard, which continued for a few days and disappeared. The symptoms and signs, subsequently, did not denote pericarditis, but the patient had pleurisy, which was followed by considerable contraction of the left side. The splashing sound in this case," continues Dr. Flint, " was fairly attributable to the presence of air and probably a little blood within the pericardium."[2] Whether the inference that no inflammation of the Pericardium succeeded the injury in this instance be correct or not, there can be no doubt that the ordinary result of a perforation of the sac, whether by wound or by communication established between it and any organ containing air, is pericarditis. Dr. Walshe observes in regard to the latter :—" Now Pneumo-pericarditis must exist temporarily, be it for ever so few minutes, as the sole result of perforative communication between the pericardial sac and any hollow viscus containing gas ; but in this isolated state *it has never been observed, pericarditis having supervened before clinical examination has been made.*

After the operation of Paracentesis Pericardii and injections of iodine into the sac, physical signs have been discovered precisely similar in character to those met with in traumatic cases. Such

[1] Diseases of the Heart. See pp. 46 and 271.
[2] A Practical Treatise on the Diagnosis, Pathology, and Treatment of Diseases of the Heart. By Austin Flint, M.D. See p. 357.

resulted in the memorable instance recorded by the late M. Aran under the title, "Pericardite avec épanchement, traitée avec succès par la ponction et l'injection iodée."

Of communication established between the Pericardium and neighbouring organs through the progress of disease, and permitting the entrance of air into the cavity of the former, several instances have been recorded by different writers. Dr. Graves has furnished a remarkable example of communication by fistulous opening between the stomach and an hepatic abscess, on the one hand, and the pericardium on the other.[1] Dr. M'Dowel exhibited to the Pathological Society of Dublin the morbid appearances in a case of communication established between a cavity in the left lung and the pericardium.[2] The writer has placed on record the history of a very interesting case, in which disease of a cancerous nature primarily affecting the œsophagus, subsequently involved adjacent organs, giving rise to pericarditis with effusion, and ultimately by perforation led to Pneumo-pericardium. When the close anatomical relationship of œsophagus to the pericardium, the former lying in the posterior mediastinum in contiguity with the posterior portion of the pericardium for nearly two inches, is considered, it will be seen how, in their conditions of disease likewise, the one is very apt to influence the other. In the instance now specially referred to, a careful scrutiny had led to the opinion that rupture of the œsophagus where in contact with the pericardium, and affected by cancer, had taken place, and, as a result of the perforation, that the passage of air into the pericardial sac had occurred. Post-mortem examination confirmed the correctness of the diagnosis. On opening the chest, the pericardium, marked by the pressure of the ribs, bulged forwards, and on being punctured air escaped. Several ounces of dark-brown fetid fluid existed in the sac: lymph, recent in its deposition, and of yellowish colour, coated the inner surface of the membrane. Cancerous ulceration, and destruction to a considerable extent of the wall of the œsophagus existed, corresponding to its usual point of contact with the pericardium.[3]

In the diagnosis of Pneumo-pericardium, of Pneumo-hydropericardium, and Pneumo-pericarditis, reliance may reasonably be placed on the physical signs as determined by percussion and auscultation. Laënnec, who, as already observed, exaggerated the frequency of the occurrence of air in the pericardial sac before death, speaks of three signs to be expected when air and fluid exist in the pericardium. 1. Unusual resonance over the lower part of the sternum: 2. Fluctuation sound ("bruit de fluctuation") audible with the action of the heart, and on deep inspiration. 3. This specially relating to the diagnosis of simple Pneumo-pericardium, that is, without fluid

---

[1] Clinical Lectures, edited by Dr. Neligan. Edition of 1864, page 616.
[2] See Dr. Stokes's work, p. 23, also p. 35 ; and Dr. Walshe's work, p. 271.
[3] Observations in Clinical Medicine, by J. Warburton Begbie, M.D. Edinburgh Medical Journal, 1862.

effusion, or inflammatory product; the heart's sounds being heard at
a distance from the chest. Upon this sign the distinguished inventor
of auscultation placed very great reliance. Dr. Stokes, whose entire
observations on the subject of Pneumo-pericarditis are most instructive, noticed the fact of the heart's sounds being heard at a distance
in a case which he has recorded; he remarks, however, that this
indication did not exist in the instances of Dr. Graves and Dr.
M·Dowel, already alluded to. Auscultation over the region of the
heart, when practised by the writer in the case which fell under his
own observation, revealed the probable existence of air and fluid
in the pericardial sac, by the extraordinary guggling sound which
accompanied the heart's action—a sound which cannot, he thinks, be
better described than as a churning splash. Dr. Stokes gives the
following description of the sounds which he observed :—"They were
not the rasping sounds of indurated lymph, or the leather creak of
Collin, nor those proceeding from pericarditic with valvular murmurs,
but a mixture of various attrition murmurs with a large crepitating
and guggling sound, while to all these phenomena was added a
distinct metallic character. In the whole of my experience I never
met so extraordinary a combination of sounds. The stomach was not
distended by air, and the lung and pleura were unaffected, but the
region of the heart gave a tympanitic *bruit de pot fêlé* on percussion,
and I could form no other conclusion but that the pericardium contained air in addition to an effusion of serum and coagulable lymph."
The phenomena on auscultation and percussion thus graphically
described by Dr. Stokes, will receive a farther value as indicating the
existence of Pneumo-pericarditis, if in addition there be noticed, as
was done by Dr. Walshe in the singular case of traumatic communication between the œsophagus and pericardium, a dull or tympanitic
sound over the precordial region, according to the position assumed
by the patient. Even without this indication, and in default of a
metallic character attaching itself to the cardiac sounds, as noticed by
Dr. Stokes, the diagnosis of Pneumo-pericarditis, or, to be still more
explicit, of Hydropneumo-pericarditis, may be made from observing a
guggling or churning splash sound with the heart's action limited to
the cardiac region, with which more or less of tympanitic precordial
resonance on percussion is associated. These signs will be still more
available, if the guggling sound has been noticed to succeed a distinct
friction sound, and the tympanitic has replaced a dull percussion
note.

It is satisfactory to note that the phenomena to which attention
has now been called, and which serve to indicate the existence of a
very serious lesion, are not necessarily of a fatal import. In Dr.
Stokes's case, as already noticed, recovery resulted, and in the instance
of Pneumo-pericardium, traumatic in origin, noticed by Dr. Knapp,
and recorded by Dr. Flint, the termination was equally gratifying.
We may indulge the hope that the records of medicine may yet
contain other examples of a similar nature.

PERICARDITIS.

By Francis Sibson, M.D., F.R.S.

CLINICAL HISTORY OF PERICARDITIS AS IT OCCURRED IN THE AUTHOR'S PRACTICE IN ST. MARY'S HOSPITAL.

INFLAMMATION of the surface of the heart and the lining of the pericardial sac occurs so very rarely by itself, and is so generally one of the attendant affections of a general disease, such as acute rheumatism, Bright's disease, and pyæmia or the secondary inflammations; or of a local affection, such as aneurism of the aorta or cancer; or of a local injury; that we cannot practically regard it as a distinct disease. Pericarditis is indeed, with very rare exceptions, one of the inflammations attendant upon those diseases or injuries.

Pericarditis occurs so much more frequently in acute rheumatism than in any other disease, that I shall first consider the affection as it exists in connexion with that disease; and in so doing shall examine the proportion of my cases of acute rheumatism that were affected with Pericarditis, and shall describe the progress of that affection in those cases.

RHEUMATIC PERICARDITIS.

I possess notes of 326 cases of acute rheumatism that were admitted under my care into St. Mary's Hospital during the fifteen years ending in the autumn of 1866. This number does not include fourteen patients in whom it was doubtful whether the affection was acute rheumatism or acute gout.

One-fifth of those cases [1] (63) were attacked with Pericarditis, which was accompanied in all but nine instances (54) by endocarditis, and fully one-third of them with simple endocarditis (108), while in only one-fourth of them was there no evidence of either endocarditis or pericarditis (79). There was, however, an intermediate group, amounting nearly to one-fourth of the whole number (76), in which

---

[1] In two of those cases (59, 61) the evidence of pericarditis was slight and perhaps doubtful, but I am of opinion that in both of them the affection existed though in a slight and transient form. The numbers thus given here and elsewhere refer to the individual cases of Pericarditis as they occur in my records, so that the reader may trace for himself each of those cases as it appears from part to part of this analysis.

endocarditis, though not established, was either threatened or probable, the signs of that affection being either transient or imperfect. I think that we may class this intermediate group arbitrarily into two divisions, and consider that in one-half of them there was endocarditis, and that in the other half there was no endocarditis.

If we add the cases of pericarditis that were also affected with endocarditis (54), and half of those in which endocarditis was threatened or probable (38), to those in which simple endocarditis was present (108), we shall find that in my patients inflammation of the interior of the heart (200) was fully three times as frequent as inflammation of the exterior of the heart (63).

This summary, otherwise stated, stands thus :—

Cases of acute rheumatism with Pericarditis . .	63
Cases in which the Pericarditis was accompanied by endocarditis	54
Cases of simple endocarditis	108
Cases of threatened or probable endocarditis . .	76
Cases in which there was no sign of endocarditis	79
Total number of cases of acute rheumatism .	326

I.—Sex, Age, and Occupation in Acute Rheumatism in especial relation to Pericarditis.

Sex.—Acute rheumatism affected the female sex somewhat more frequently than the male sex in the proportion of 168 to 158.

Pericarditis attacked 35 male and 28 female patients, so that nearly one in four of the former (35 in 154), and only one in six of the latter (28 in 166) were affected by it. Endocarditis was also present in 31 of the male and 23 of the female patients affected with pericarditis.

Simple endocarditis, on the other hand, attacked 47 male and 61 female patients, while, in addition, endocarditis was threatened or probable in 32 male and 41 female patients.

The cause of the greater proportional frequency of Pericarditis, usually accompanied by endocarditis, in the male sex, and of simple endocarditis in the female sex in these cases, will, I think, be in part explained by the influence of age and occupation on acute rheumatism and its complications.

Age.—One-half of the male (17 in 34)[1] and more than one-half of the female patients (17 in 27)[1] affected with Pericarditis, were below the age of 21: while two-fifths of the male (13 in 34) and only one-seventh of the female patients (4 in 27) were above the age of 25.

If we group these two classes of cases separately in relation to age,

---

[1] The age of one of the 35 male patients and that of one of the 28 female patients was not stated.

and compare them with each other, we find that acute rheumatism attacked 70 male and 77 female patients *below the age of* 21, and that of these 17 of each sex were affected with Pericarditis, combined with endocarditis in all but one or two cases, and 25 of the males and 32 of the females with simple endocarditis; that in 12 of the males and 20 of the females endocarditis was threatened or probable, and that in 15 of the males and in only 8 of the females there was no sign of inflammation of the heart, within or without.

On the other hand, we find that acute rheumatism affected 53 men and 53 women *above the age of* 25, and that of these 13 men (13 in 53 or one-fourth) and only 4 women (4 in 53 or one-thirteenth) were affected with Pericarditis which was usually accompanied by endocarditis, and 13 men and 17 women with simple endocarditis; that in 11 men and 11 women endocarditis was threatened or probable; and that the residue, or 16 men and 21 women, gave no sign of inflammation of the heart.

The accompanying Table shows the proportion in which endocarditis and Pericarditis were absent or present in the cases of acute rheumatism, and the influence of age and sex in the proportionate production of those affections of the heart in that disease.

	No Endocarditis.		Endocarditis threatened or probable.										Endocarditis.			Pericarditis.			Total.		
			Threatened.			Probable.			Total.												
Male . Female.	42}79 37}		26}63 37}			8}13 5}			34}76 42}				47}108 61}			35}63 28}			158}326 168}		
Ages.	Male.	Female.	Total.	Male.	Female.	Total.	Male.	Female.	Total.	Male.	Female.	Total.	Male.	Female.	Total.	Male.	Female.	Total.	Male.	Female.	Total.
10 to 15	5	3	*	2	1	3	0	1	1	2	2	4	10	9	19	6	3	9	23	17	40
16 to 20	11	5	16	9	14	23	1	4	5	10	18	28	15	23	38	11	14	25	47	60	107
21 to 25	10	8	18	6	9	15	4	0	4	10	9	19	8	11	19	4	6	10	32	34	66
26 to 30	8	13	21	3	5	8	2	0	2	5	5	10	8	6	14	5	1	6	26	25	51
31 to 40	5	4	9	6	5	11	0	0	0	6	5	11	4	10	14	6	2	8	21	21	42
41 to 50	3	3	6	0	1	1	0	0	0	0	1	1	1	0	1	2	0	2	6	4	10
51 and –	0	1	1	0	0	0	0	0	0	0	0	0	0	1	1	0	1	1	0	3	3
? . . .				0	2	2	1	0	1	1	2	3	1	1	2	1	1	2	3	4	7
Total .	42	37	79	26	37	63	8	5	13	34	42	76	47	61	108	35	28	63	158	168	326

We thus see that in these cases of acute rheumatism, inflammation of the heart, grouping together those in which it attacked the interior and the exterior of the organ, affected the young below 21 (91 in 147) more frequently than the adult above 25 (47 in 106); that the heart was more frequently free from signs of inflammation in the adult above 25 (37 in 106), and especially in women (21 in 53), than in the young below 21 (24 in 147), and especially in girls (8 in 77); that endocarditis was threatened or probable as often in the young below 21 (32 in 147) as in the adult above 25 (22 in 106); and, this being the point to which I would especially call attention, that Pericarditis—

while it affected the two sexes in nearly equal proportions below the age of 21, the male patients (17 in 70) a little more frequently than the female patients (17 in 77)—attacked men above the age of 25 (13 in 53) three times more frequently than women above that age (5 in 53).

Occupation.—The study of the influence of occupation on the occurrence of acute rheumatism and on the production of inflammation of the heart, both outside and in, throws light in two directions, one on the influence of sex, the other on that of age in producing those affections.

The accompanying Tables show (I. pages 190–3) the influence of occupation in acute rheumatism in relation to age; the presence or absence of endocarditis and Pericarditis; the degree of the affection of the joints, and that of the heart; and (II. pages 194–7), for the sake of comparison, of ages (1) of 1,000 patients, taken consecutively, with an occasional break, from my hospital books, affected with all other internal diseases besides acute rheumatism and acute gout, and (2) of 326 cases of acute rheumatism with its attendant Pericarditis and Endocarditis, in relation to occupation.

I take female domestic servants first, since they formed nearly one-third (101 in 326) of the whole number of those of both sexes, and nearly three-fifths of those of the female sex (101 in 168) who were affected with acute rheumatism. Among those patients affected with other diseases than acute rheumatism, female servants formed one-fifth of the whole number (204 in 1,000) and two-fifths of the female patients (204 in 453). Nearly two-thirds of the female patients affected with acute rheumatism were below the age of 21 (57 in 100), while of those affected with other diseases, only one-third were below that age (64 in 195, or 33 per cent.) Table II. p. 12.

The influence of that employment in causing Pericarditis and endocarditis in acute rheumatism, especially below the age of 21, is remarkable. Of the whole number of 101 servants only 13—one-eighth—presented no sign of inflammation of the heart, while one-fifth of them (19) were attacked with Pericarditis, accompanied in all but one instance with endocarditis also, and two-fifths of them (43) with simple endocarditis, while in the remaining fourth part (26) endocarditis was either threatened or probable. Servants formed fully two-thirds of the whole of the female patients affected with Pericarditis complicated usually with endocarditis (19 in 28), and with simple endocarditis (42 in 60); and three-fifths of those in whom endocarditis was threatened or probable (26 in 42): while they formed only one-third of those who gave no sign of affection of the heart (13 in 37).

The influence of age in inducing inflammation of the heart in servants affected with acute rheumatism is still more remarkable. Of the whole number of servants (101) attacked with that disease, 57 were below the age of 21. In only 3 of these was there no mark of affection of the heart, but one-fourth of them (14) were attacked

TABLE I., *See p.* 189.—OCCUPATION IN RELATION TO AGE, THE DEGREE

| MALE PATIENTS. | PATIENTS IN WHOM | | | | |
| | There was no indication of Endocarditis. | | Endocarditis was threatened or probable. | | |
	Number.	Years.	Joint affection.	Number.	Years.	Joint affection.
Out-of-door Employments.						
Engaged in *laborious employments in the open air,* including labourers (17), gardeners (5), bricklayer, brickmaker, sawyer (in twice), mason, dustman, carter, plasterer, seaman, smiths (4), butchers (6), carpenters (4) . .	9	2 æt. 20 / 1 ,, 24 / 2 ,, 26 to 27 / 2 ,, 32 ,, 37 / 2 ,, 42 ,, 46	1 + / 6 — + / 2, ○ +	11	3 æt. 20 / 4 ,, 22 to 25 / 1 ,, 26 ,, 29 / 3 ,, 31 ,, 38	6 + / 4 — + / 1 ○, +
Engaged in *employments chiefly on foot, in the open air,* including porters (4), watchman, errand boys (4), milkmen (2), hawker, cowkeeper, out of work—"on tramp" (1)	7	2 æt. 10 to 12 / 3 ,, 16 ,, 20 / 1 ,, 28 / 1 ,, 38	1 + / 3 — + / 1, ○ + / 1 — / 1 ?	2	1 ,, 14 / 1 ,, 21	2 — +
Employed *with horses and in stables,* including grooms (6), riding-master, horsekeeper, coachmen (9), cabmen (5)	7	2 æt. 19 / 1 ,, 23 / 2 ,, 26 / 1 ,, 38 / 1 ,, 43	3 + / 4 — +	7	4 ,, 16 ,, 19 / 2 ,, 21 ,, 24 / 1 ,, 27	4 + / 3 - +
TOTAL of those employed in the above laborious out-of-door employments . .	23	2 æt. 10 to 12 / 7 ,, 16 ,, 20 / 2 ,, 23 ,, 24 / 5 ,, 26 ,, 28 / 4 ,, 32 ,, 38 / 3 ,, 42 ,, 46	5 + / 13 — + / 3 ○ + / 1 — / 1	20	1 ,, 14 / 7 ,, 16 ,, 20 / 7 ,, 21 ,, 25 / 2 ,, 26 ,, 29 / 3 ,, 31 ,, 38	10 + / 9 — + / 1, ○ +
Painters (3), plumber, gas-fitter .	2	1 æt. 17 / 1 ,, 26	1 — + / 1 ○ +	2	1 ,, 16 / 1 ,, 21	1 + / 1 - +
Commercial traveller	...		...	...		...
In-door Employments. Including servants (12), bakers (3), paperhanger, french-polishers (4), boot and shoemakers (3), "shopman," greengrocer, drapers (4), cheesemonger, slop cutter, tailor, teacher, silversmith, chairmaker, bath-attendant, and 2 others	7	1 æt. 14 / 2 ,, 16 to 18 / 2 ,, 25 / 2 ,, 27 ,, 28	3 + / 2 — + / 1, ○ + / 1 —	9	2 ,, 19 / 1 ,, 25 / 3 ,, 29 / 3 ,, 33 ,, 37	1 + + / 4 + / 4 — +
Waiters (6), potmen and barmen (5)	8	1 æt. 19 / 6 ,, 21 to 23 / ,, 40	2 + / 5 — + / 1, ○ +	1	1 ,, 21	1 — +
Schoolboys (5)	...		...	...		...
Had no employment, including one discharged from the Navy (1?)		2 æt. 14 to 15	1 — + / 1 —	2	1 ,, 14 / 1 not stated	1 + / 1 —
Occupation not stated	...		...	...		...

OF JOINT AFFECTION AND THAT OF HEART AFFECTION.

			PATIENTS IN WHOM THERE WAS						
Simple Endocarditis.			Pericarditis, usually with Endocarditis (54 in 63).				Total		Joint affection.
Number.	Years	Jnt-aff.	Number.	Years.	Jt.-affe.	Heart-aff.	Number.	Years.	
6 æt. 16 to 20 4 ,, 21 ,, 24 3 ,, 26 ,, 29 2 ,, 35 ,, 38	10 + 5 -- +		1 æt. 17 to 19 1 ,, 22 ,, 24 4 ,, 27 ,, 28 3 ,, 31 ,, 39 1 ,, 42	4 + + 4 + + 2 -- +	10	1 ♡ 3 + 2 + 3 -- + 1 ○ +	45	12 æt. 17 to 20 10 ,, 21 ,, 24 10 ,, 26 ,, 30 10 ,, 31 ,, 40 3 ,, 42 ,, 46	4 very severe + + 21 severe + 17 rather severe - + 3 not severe ○ +
1 ,, 12 1 ,, 17 1 ,, 22	1 + 1, ○ + 1 --	3	2 { 1 ,, 17 1 ,, 25 }	1 + 1 ○ +	2 +		14	4 ,, 10 ,, 14 5 ,, 16 ,, 20 3 ,, 22 ,, 25 1 ,, 28 1 ,, 38	3 severe + 5 rather severe - + 8 not severe ○ + 2 slight — 1 doubtful ?
3 ,, 18 ,, 20 2 ,, 21 1 ,, 26 1 ,, 33 ,, 38 1 ,, 42	2 + 5 -- + 1, ○ +	5	1 ,, 22	1 +	1 +		23	9 ,, 16 ,, 20 6 ,, 21 ,, 24 4 ,, 26 ,, 28 2 ,, 33 ,, 38 2 ,, 42 ,, 43	10 severe + 12 rather severe -- + 1 not severe ○ +
1 ,, 12 10 ,, 16 ,, 20 7 ,, 21 ,, 24 4 ,, 26 ,, 29 3 ,, 33 ,, 38 1 ,, 42	13 + 10 -- + 2, ○ + 1 —	18	2 ,, 17 ,, 19 3 ,, 22 ,, 25 4 ,, 27 ,, 28 5 ,, 31 ,, 39 1 ,, 42	4 + + 6 + 2 -- + 1 ○ +	1 ♡ 3 + + 3 -- + 3 -- + 1 ○ +	82	4 ,, 10 ,, 15 26 ,, 16 ,, 20 19 ,, 21 ,, 25 15 ,, 26 ,, 30 13 ,, 31 ,, 40 5 ,, 41 ,, 46	4 very severe + + 34 severe + 34 rather severe -- + 7 not severe ○ + 2 slight — 1 doubtful ?
...	...		1 ,, 35	1 + +	1 +	♡	5	2 ,, 16 ,, 18 1 ,, 21 1 ,, 26 1 ,, 35	1 very severe + + 1 severe + 2 rather severe - + 1 not severe ○ +
...	...		1 ,, 18	1 +	1 + +	♡	1	1 ,, 18	1 severe +
5 ,, 18 ,, 19 1 ,, 22 2 ,, 29 ,, 30 1 ,, 38	4 + 3 -- + 2, ○ +	13	2 ,, 14 8 ,, 17 ,, 20 1 ,, 23 1 ,, 38 1 ,, 50	6 + 2 ○ + 1 —	1 ♡ 2 + + 4 + + 4 -- + 2 ○ + 1 —	38	3 ,, 14 17 ,, 16 ,, 20 8 ,, 21 ,, 25 7 ,, 27 ,, 30 5 ,, 33 ,, 38 1 ,, 50	1 very severe + + 17 severe + 13 rather severe — + 5 not severe ○ + 2 slight —
2 ,, 27 ,, 30	1 -- + 1 ○ +		1 ,, 39	1 —	1 ♡ +		12	1 ,, 19 7 ,, 21 ,, 23 2 ,, 27 ,, 30 1 ,, 39 1 ,, 40	3 severe + 7 rather severe — + 2 not severe ○ +
3 ,, 9 ,, 15	2 -- + 1 ○ +		2 ,, 11 ,, 15	1 -- + 1 ○ +	1 + 1 — +		5	5 ,, 9 ,, 15	3 rather severe — + 2 not severe ○ +
6 ,, 9 ,, 15	3 + 3 -- +		2 ,, 14 ,, 15	2 — +	1 ♡ 1 — + 1 —		12	11 ,, 9 ,, 15 1 not stated	4 severe + 6 rather severe — + 2 slight —
1 not stated	1 — +		2 { 1 ,, 26 1 not stated }	2 — +	1 ♡ 1 — + 1 —		3	1 ,, 26 2 not stated	3 rather severe — +

FEMALE PATIENTS.	PATIENTS IN WHOM					
	There was no indication of Endocarditis.			Endocarditis was threatened or probable.		
	Number.	Years.	Joint affection.	Number.	Years.	Joint affection.
Active In-door Employments. Servants	13	3 æt. 19 to 20 4 ,, 21 ,, 25 6 ,, 26 ,, 30	4 + 5 — + 4 O +	26	1 æt. 15 14 ,, 16 to 20 4 ,, 22 ,, 23 3 ,, 26 ,, 30 3 ,, 31 ,, 40 1 not stated	9 + 11 — + 6 O +
Cooks (5), charwomen (2), nurses (5), laundresses (9), washer-woman	6	2 æt. 26 to 28 1 ,, 36 2 ,, 42 ,, 50 1 ,, 52	2 + 1 — + 3 O +	7	3 ,, 19 ,, 20 2 ,, 21 ,, 24 1 ,, 26 1 ,, 40	3 + 4 — +
Sedentary In-door Employments. Needlewomen (3), milliners, dress-makers (3), tailoress, shoebinder, shoemaker	4	1 æt. 20 2 ,, 26 1 ,, 49	1 + 2 — + 1 O +		1 ,, 44	1 — +
Kept a stall		...	—		1 ,, 21	1 +
Married women, without spe-cial occupation, including two widows	8	3 æt. 25 2 ,, 28 to 30 3 ,, 36 ,, 40	4 + 2 — + 2 O +	5	2 ,, 25 1 ,, 30 1 ,, 32 1 not stated	2 + 3 — +
Of no occupation	5	3 æt. 13 to 15 1 ,, 16 1 ,, 25	1 + 1 — + 2 O + 1 —	2	1 ,, 6 1 ,, 18	1 + 1 — +
Occupation not stated . . .	1 æt. 29		1 — +	..		...
MALE PATIENTS. TOTAL .	42	5 æt. 10 to 15 11 ,, 16 ,, 20 10 ,, 21 ,, 25 8 ,, 26 ,, 30 5 ,, 31 ,, 40 3 ,, 41 ,, 46	10 + 22 — + 6 O + 3 — 1 ?	34	2 æt. 14 10 ,, 16 to 20 10 ,, 21 ,, 25 5 ,, 26 ,, 30 6 ,, 31 ,, 38 1 not stated	1 + + 16 + 15 — + 1, O + 1 —
FEMALE PATIENTS TOTAL	37	3 æt. 13 to 15 5 ,, 16 ,, 20 8 ,, 21 ,, 25 13 ,, 26 ,, 30 4 ,, 31 ,, 40 3 ,, 42 ,, 50 1 ,, 52	12 + 12 — + 12 O + 1 —	42	2 æt. 6 to 15 13 ,, 16 ,, 20 9 ,, 22 ,, 25 5 ,, 26 ,, 30 5 ,, 31 ,, 40 1 ,, 44 2 not stated	16 + 20 — + 6, O +
GRAND TOTAL of the Male and Female Patients . . .	79	8 æt. 10 to 15 16 ,, 16 ,, 20 18 ,, 21 ,, 25 21 ,, 26 ,, 30 9 ,, 31 ,, 40 6 ,, 41 ,, 50 1 ,, 52	22 + 34 — + 18, O + 4 — 1 ?	76	4 æt. 6 to 14 23 ,, 16 ,, 20 19 ,, 21 ,, 25 10 ,, 26 ,, 30 11 ,, 31 ,, 40 1 ,, 44 3 not stated	1 + + 32 + 35 — + 7, O + 1 —

4 of these cases died.

PATIENTS IN WHOM THERE WAS

Simple Endocarditis.		Pericarditis, usually with Endocarditis (54 in 68).			Total.		Joint affection.
Number. Years.	Jt-aff.	Number. Years.	Jt. aff.	Heart aff.	Number. Years.		
43 { 4 æt. 12 to 15 21 „ 16 „ 20 10 „ 21 „ 25 4 „ 26 „ 30 3 „ 31 „ 40 1 „ 55	2 + + 19 + 13 — + 7 O + 1 — 1 ?	19 { 1 æt. 25 13 „ 16 to 20 4 „ 21 „ 25 1 „ 26	6 + + 9 + 3 — + 1 . +	2 8 + + 6 + 2 — + 1 O +	101 { 6 æt. 12 to 15 51 „ 16 „ 20 22 „ 21 „ 25 14 „ 26 „ 30 6 „ 31 „ 40 1 „ 55 1 not stated		8 very severe + + 41 severe + 32 rather severe — + 18 not severe O + 1 slight — 1 doubtful ?
4 { 1 „ 21 1 „ 27 2 „ 33 „ 40	2 + 2 —	5 { 1 „ 20 1 „ 21 1 „ 35 1 „ 60 1 not stated	1 + 2 — + 1 O 1 ?	1 + 2 — + 1 O + 1 —	22 { 4 „ 19 „ 20 4 „ 21 „ 25 4 „ 26 „ 30 5 „ 31 „ 40 2 „ 42 „ 50 2 „ 52 „ 60 1 not stated		8 severe + 9 rather severe — + 4 not severe O + 1 doubtful ?
4 { 1 „ 18 3 „ 31 „ 38	3 — + 1 O +	…	…	…	9 { 2 „ 18 „ 20 2 „ 26 3 „ 31 „ 38 2 „ 44 „ 49		1 severe + 6 rather severe — + 2 not severe O +
1 „ 33	1 +	…	…	…	2 { 1 „ 21 1 „ 33		2 severe +
2 { 1 „ 30 1 „ 40	1 + 1 — +	2 { 1 „ 24 1 „ 34	1 + + 1 — +	1 + 1 —	17 { 6 „ 24 „ 25 4 „ 28 „ 30 6 „ 34 „ 40 1 not stated		1 very severe + + 7 severe + 7 rather severe — + 2 not severe O +
7 { 5 „ 13 „ 15 1 „ 18 1 not stated	3 + 3 — + 1 O +	2 „ 13 „ 14	1 + 1 —	1 + + 1 —	16 { 11 „ 6 „ 15 3 „ 16 „ 20 1 „ 25 1 not stated		6 severe + 6 rather severe — + 3 not severe O + 1 slight —
…	…	…	…	…	1 „ 29		1 rather severe — +
34 { 10 æt. 9 to 15 15 „ 16 „ 20 5 „ 21 „ 25 8 „ 26 „ 30 4 „ 32 „ 38 1 „ 42 1 not stated	20 + 20 — 6 O + 1 —	35 { 6 æt. 11 to 15 11 „ 16 „ 20 4 „ 22 „ 25 5 „ 27 „ 28 6 „ 31 „ 39 2 „ 41 „ 50 1 not stated	5 + + 14 + 11 — + 4 O + 1 —	2 6 + + 12 + 11 — + 2 O + 1 —	158 { 23 æt. 9 to 15 47 „ 16 „ 20 32 „ 21 „ 25 26 „ 26 „ 30 21 „ 31 „ 40 6 „ 41 „ 50 3 not stated		6 very severe + + 60 severe + 68 rather severe — + 17 not severe O + 6 slight — 1 doubtful ?
67 { 9 æt. 12 to 15 23 „ 16 „ 20 11 „ 21 „ 25 6 „ 26 „ 30 10 „ 31 „ 45 1 „ 55 1 not stated	2 + + 26 + 22 — + 9 O + 1 — 1 ?	28 { 3 „ 13 „ 14 14 „ 16 „ 20 6 „ 21 „ 25 1 „ 26 2 „ 34 „ 35 1 „ 60 1 not stated	7 + + 11 + 7 — + 2 O + 1 ?	2 9 + + 9 + 4 — + 2 O + 1 — 1 ?	168 { 17 „ 6 „ 15 60 „ 16 „ 20 34 „ 21 „ 25 25 „ 26 „ 30 21 „ 31 „ 40 4 „ 42 „ 50 3 „ 52 „ 60 4 not stated		9 very severe + + 65 severe + 61 rather severe — + 29 not severe O + 2 slight — 2 doubtful ?
162 { 19 æt. 9 to 15 38 „ 16 „ 20 19 „ 21 „ 25 16 „ 26 „ 30 14 „ 31 „ 41 1 „ 42 1 „ 55 2 not stated	2 + + 46 + 42 — + 15 O + 2 — 1 ?	63 { 9 æt. 11 to 15 25 „ 16 „ 20 10 „ 21 „ 25 6 „ 26 „ 30 8 „ 31 „ 40 2 „ 41 „ 50 1 „ 60 2 not stated	12 + + 25 + 18 — + 6 O + 1 —	4 15 + + 21 + 15 — + 4 O + 3 — 1 ?	326 { 40 æt. 6 to 15 107 „ 16 „ 20 66 „ 21 „ 25 51 „ 26 „ 30 42 „ 31 „ 40 10 „ 41 „ 50 3 „ 55 „ 60 7 not stated		15 very severe + + 125 severe + 129 rather severe — + 46 not severe O + 8 slight — 3 doubtful ?

[1] 1 of these cases died.   [2] 5 of these cases died (1 from Bright's disease).

Ages of I.—1,000 Patients affected with all other Internal Diseases except Acute Rheumatism Pericarditis and Endocarditis, and III.—58 Patients

MALE PATIENTS.		BELOW THE AGE OF 21.	FROM 21 TO 25 YEARS.
Workers out of doors.	Other diseases except acute rheumatism and acute gout	21, or 10 per cent. of those whose ages are stated.	31, or 15 per cent.
Laborious employments	Acute rheumatism . . .	12, or 26·6 per cent.	10, or 22·2 per cent.
	Ditto with pericarditis . .	{1, or 8·3 per cent. at that age.[1] {1, or 10 per cent. of whole.[2]	1, or 10 per cent. at that age. 1, or 10 per cent. of whole.
	Ditto with simple endocardit	{6, or 50 per cent. at that age. {6, or 40 per cent. of whole.	4, or 40 per cent. at that age. 4, or 27 per cent. of whole.
	Acute gout	0	2
Workers on foot	Other diseases except acute rheumatism and acute gout	6, or 17·7 per cent.	4, or 11·7 per cent.
	Acute rheumatism . . .	9, or 64 per cent.	3, or 21·4 per cent.
	Pericarditis	{1, or 11 per cent. at that age. {1, or 50 per cent. of whole.	1, or 33·3 per cent. at that age. 1, or 50 per cent. of whole.
	Endocarditis	{2, or 22 per cent. at that age. {2, or 66·7 of whole.	1, or 33·3 per cent. at that age. 1, or 33·3 per cent. of whole.
	Acute gout	0	0
Workers among horses . . .	Other diseases except acute rheumatism and acute gout	1, or 1·5 per cent.	4, or per cent.
	Acute rheumatism . . .	9, or 39 per cent.	6, or 26 per cent.
	Pericarditis	0	{1, or 16·6 per cent. at that age. {1, or 100 per cent. of whole.
	Endocarditis	{3, or 33·3 per cent. at that age. {3, or 37·2 per cent. of whole.	2, or 30·9 per cent. at that age. 2, or 25 per cent. of whole. .
	Acute gout	0	1
Painters, plumbers . . .	Other diseases besides acute rheumatism and acute gout	2, or 5 per cent.	9, or 22 per cent.
	Acute rheumatism . . .	2, or 40 per cent.	1, or 20 per cent.
	Pericarditis	0	0
	Endocarditis	0	0
	Acute gout	0	0
In-door employments . . .	Other diseases besides acute rheumatism and acute gout	20, or 16·3 per cent.	20, or 16·3 per cent.
	Acute rheumatism . . .	20, or 52·5 per cent.	5, or 13·5 per cent.
	Pericarditis	{10, or 50·6 per cent. at that age. {10, or 77 per cent. of whole.	1, or 20 per cent. at that age. 1, or 7·7 per cent. of whole.
	Endocarditis	{5, or 25 per cent. at that age. {5, or 55·2 per cent. of whole.	1, or 20 per cent at that age. 1, or 11 per cent. of whole.
	Acute gout	0	2
Waiters, barmen, and one commercial traveller . .	Other diseases besides acute rheumatism and acute gout	2, or 16·6 per cent.	2, or 16·6 per cent.
	Acute rheumatism . . .	2, or 15·3 per cent.	7, or 54·1 per cent.
	Pericarditis	{1, or 50 per cent. at that age. {1, or 50 per cent. of whole.	0
	Endocarditis	0	0
	Acute gout	0	0
Of no occupation and at school . . .	Other diseases except acute rheumatism, &c.	37, or 100 per cent.	0
	Acute rheumatism . . .	16, or 100 per cent.	0
	Pericarditis	4, or 25 per cent. at that age.	0
	Endocarditis	9, or 56·6 per cent. at that age.	0
TOTAL OF MALE PATIENTS. .	Other diseases except acute rheumatism and acute gout	89, or 17 per cent.	70, or 13·4 per cent.
	Acute rheumatism . . .	70, or 45 per cent.	32, or 20·8 per cent.
	Pericarditis	17, or 24·3 per cent. at that age. 17, or 51·5 per cent. of whole.	4, or 12 per cent at that age. 4, or 12 per cent. of whole.
	Endocarditis	25, or 35·7 per cent. at that age. 25, or 54·3 per cent. of whole.	8, or 24·2 per cent. at that age. 8, or 17·4 per cent. of whole.
	Acute gout	0	5

[1] Here and elsewhere in these columns add after "age" of those with acute rheumatism who were so affected and who were engaged in the class of employments indicated in the column headed "Male Patients."

[2] Here and elsewhere in these columns "whole" applies to the whole number of all ages of those with acute

*tcute Gout, and II.—326 Patients affected with Acute Rheumatism, with its attendant
d with Acute Gout, in relation to Occupation.*

ABOVE 25 YEARS.	AGE AND OCCUPA-TION NOT STATED.		TOTAL.	
ɪ 73 per cent.	Age not stated 14		221	or{40·4 per cent. of the males. {22·1 per cent. of the whole.²
ɪ 51 per cent.	...	...	45	or{29 per cent. of the males. {14 per cent. of the whole.
ɪ 35 per cent. at that age.	...	...	} 10	{Or 22 per cent. of those with acute rheumatism.
ɪ 50 per cent of whole.	...	...		
ɪ 21 per cent. at that age.	...	...	} 15	{Or 33·3 per cent. of those with acute rheumatism.
ɪ 33 per cent. of whole.	...	...	15	
er 70·6 per cent.	...	... 4	38	Or{6·9 per cent. of the males. {3·8 per cent. of the whole.
ɪ 14·3 per cent.	...	...	14	Or{9 per cent. of the males. {4·8 per cent. of the whole.
	...	... }	2	{Or 14 per cent. of those with acute rheumatism.
	...	...		
	...	... }	3	{Or 21·4 per cent. of those with acute rheumatism.
	...	...	2	
or 93 per cent.	...	... 3	69	Or{12·6 per cent. of the males. {6·9 per cent. of the whole.
ɪɪ 35 per cent.	...	...	23	Or{14·8 per cent. of the males. {7·1 per cent. of the whole.
	...	...	1	{Or 4·3 per cent. of those with acute rheumatism.
ɪ 37 per cent. at that age.	...	... }	8	{Or 35 per cent. of those with acute rheumatism.
ɪ 37·5 per cent of the whole.	...	...	15	
ɪ 73 per cent.	...	...	41	Or{9·5 per cent. of the males. {4·1 per cent. of the whole.
ɪ 40 per cent.	...	...	5	Or{3·2 per cent. of the males. {1·5 per cent. of the whole.
ɪ 50 per cent. at that age.	...	...	1	Or 20 per cent. of those with ac. rh.
	...	...	0	
	...	...	4	
ɪɪ 67·4 per cent.	...	... 6	129	Or{23·6 per cent. of the males. {12·9 per cent. of the whole.
ɪ 54 per cent. !	...	...	38	Or{24·5 per cent. of the males. {11·4 per cent. of the whole.
ɪ 15·3 per cent. at that age.	...	... }	13	{Or 35 per cent. of those with acute rheumatism.
ɪ 15·3 per cent. of whole.	...	...		
ɪ 23 per cent. at that age.	...	... }	9	{Or 24·3 per cent. of those with acute rheumatism.
ɪ 33·3 per cent. of whole.	...	...	13	
or 66·6 per cent.	...	...	12	Or{2·2 per cent of the males. {1·2 per cent. of the whole.
or 30·6 per cent.	...	...	13	Or{8·4 per cent. of the males. {4 per cent. of the whole.
er 25 per cent. at that age.	...	... }	2	{Or 8·3 per cent. of those with acute rheumatism.
or 50 per cent. of whole.	...	...		
or 50 per cent. at that age.	...	... }	2	{Or 16·6 per cent. of those with rheumatism.
er 100 per cent. of whole.	...	...	3	
	...	...	38	Or{6·9 per cent. of the males. {3·8 per cent. of the whole.
	...	... 1	17	Or{11 per cent. of the males. {5·3 per cent. of the whole.
	...	...	4	Or 24 per cent. of those with ac. rh.
	...	...	9	Or 53 per cent. of those with ac. rh.
or 69·4 per cent.	Age not stated 27		547	
er 33·7 per cent. + 1 occu-ation not stated.	{Age (?) 1 + 2 occ.} not stated		{155 + 3 occ.} not stated	
or 25 per cent. at that age.	{Age (?) 1 + 1 occ.} not stated		{33 + 2 occ.} not stated	
or 36·2 per cent. of whole.				
or 25 per cent. at that age.	{Age (?) and occ. not} stated 1		{46 + 1 occ.} not stated	
or 28·2 per cent. of whole.				
+ 1 occupation not stated.	{Age (?) — 3 occ.} not stated		52	

*...... whose ages were stated, and who were so affected, who were engaged in the class of occupations
.... in the column headed "Male Patients."*
.... and elsewhere in this column "whole" applies to the whole number of patients of both sexes.

o 2

TABLE II.—

FEMALE PATIENTS.		BELOW THE AGE OF 21 YEARS.	FROM 21 TO 25 YEARS.
Servants . . .	Other diseases except acute rheumatism	64, or 32·8 per cent. of those whose ages are stated.	60, or 30·8 per cent.
	Acute rheumatism	57, or 57 per cent.	22, or 22 per cent.
	Pericarditis	{14, or 24·5 per cent. at that age.[1] {14, or 73·7 per cent. of the whole.[2]	4, or 18·2 per cent. at that age. 4, or 22·2 per cent. of the whole.
	Endocarditis	{25, or 44 per cent. at that age. {25, or 58·5 per cent. of whole.	10, or 45·5 per cent. at that age. 10, or 23·2 per cent. of the whole.
Other in door active employments	Other diseases except acute rheumatism and acute gout	1, or 1·4 per cent.	9, or 12·5 per cent.
	Acute rheumatism	4, or 18·2 per cent.	4, or 18·2 per cent.
	Pericarditis	0	{1, or 25 per cent. at that age. {1, or 25 per cent. of the whole.
	Endocarditis	0	1, or 25 per cent.
	Acute gout	0	0
Sedentary indoor employments . . .	Other diseases except acute rheumatism	1, or 2·7 per cent.	5, or 13·8 per cent.
	Acute rheumatism	2, or 22·3 per cent.	0
	Pericarditis	0	0
	Endocarditis	{1, or 50 per cent. at that age. {1, or 25 per cent. of whole.	0
Married women without special employment . . .	Other diseases except acute rheumatism	3, or 4·3 per cent.	9, or 12·6 per cent.
	Acute rheumatism	0	6, or 37·5 per cent.
	Pericarditis	0	{1, or 16·6 per cent. at that age. {1, or 50 per cent. of the whole.
	Endocarditis	0	
Out-of-door employment. Kept a stall .	Other diseases except acute rheumatism	0	0
	Acute rheumatism	0	1, or 50 per cent.
	Pericarditis	0	0
	Endocarditis	0	0
Of no occupation, including girls at school . . .	Other diseases except acute rheumatism	57, or 100 per cent.	0
	Acute rheumatism	14, or 93 per cent.	1, or 7 per cent.
	Pericarditis	2, or 14·4 per cent. at that age.	0
	Endocarditis	6, or 43 per cent. at that age.	0
Total of female patients . .	Other diseases except acute rheumatism and acute gout	126, or 29 per cent.	83, or 19 per cent.
	Acute rheumatism	77, or 47·2 per cent.	34
	Pericarditis	{17, or 22 per cent. at that age. {17, or 63·3 per cent. of the whole.	6, or 17·6 per cent. at that age. 6, or 22·2 per cent. of the whole.
	Endocarditis	{32, or 41·5 per cent. at that age. {32, or 53·3 per cent. of the whole.	11, or 32·3 per cent. at that age. 11, or 18·3 per cent. of the whole.
	Acute gout	0	
Grand Total of Male and Female Patients . . .	Other diseases except acute rheumatism and acute gout	215, or 22·5 per cent. of the whole with ages stated	153, or 16 per cent. of whole, with ages stated
	Acute rheumatism	147, or 46·7 per cent.	66, or 20·8 per cent.
	Pericarditis	{34, or 33 per cent. at that age. {34, or 56·6 per cent. of the whole.	10, or 15 per cent. at that age. 10, or 16·6 per cent. of the whole.
	Endocarditis	{57, or 38·8 per cent. at that age. {57, or 53 per cent. of the whole.	19, or 28·8 at that age. 19, or 18 per cent. of the whole.
	Acute gout	0	4

[1] Here and elsewhere in these columns add after "age" of those with acute rheumatism who were so affected, and who were engaged in the class of employments indicated in the column headed "Male Patients."
[2] Here and elsewhere in these columns "whole" applies to the whole number of all ages of those with acute

ABOVE 25 YEARS.	AGE AND OCCUPATION NOT STATED.		TOTAL.	
1, or 36·4 per cent.	Age not stated 9		204	Or {42 per cent. of the females. 20·4 per cent. of the whole.
1, or 21 per cent.	...	 1	101	Or {60·5 per cent. of the females. 31·3 per cent. of the whole.
1, or 4·7 per cent. at that age. 1, or 5·2 per cent. of whole.	...	...	19	Or 18·8 per cent. of those with acute rheumatism.
5, or 33 per cent. at that age. *, or 18 per cent. of whole.	...	...	43	Or 42·5 per cent. of those with acute rheumatism.
2, or 86·1 per cent.	...	 5	77	Or {15 per cent. of the females. 7·7 per cent. of the whole.
1, or 62 per cent.	...	 1	22	Or {13·7 per cent. of the females. 6·8 per cent. of the whole.
1, or 37·7 per cent. at that age. 1, or 75 per cent. of whole.	...	 1	5	Or 22·7 per cent. of those with acute rheumatism.
1, or 75 per cent.	...	...	4	Or 18 per cent. of those with acute rheumatism.
1	...	...	3	
1, or 34·5 per cent.	...	.... 1 .	38	Or {8·4 per cent. of the females. 3·8 per cent. of the whole.
*, or 77·7 per cent.	...	...	9	Or {5·4 per cent. of the females. 2·8 per cent. of the whole.
1	...	...	0	
1, or 43 per cent. at that age. 1, or 75 per cent. of whole.	...	...	4	Or 44·4 per cent. of those with acute rheumatism.
1, or 83 per cent.	...	 4	75	Or {16·3 per cent. of the females. 7·5 per cent. of the whole.
1, or 62·5 per cent.	...	 1	17	Or {10·2 per cent. of the females. 5·3 per cent. of the whole.
·, or 10 per cent. at that age. ·, or 50 per cent. of whole.	...	...	2	Or 11·8 per cent. of those with acute rheumatism.
·, or 20 per cent. at that age. ·, or 100 per cent. of whole.	...	...	2	Or 11·8 per cent. of those with acute rheumatism.
·, or 100 per cent.	...	...	2	Or {3·4 per cent. of the females. 0·2 per cent. of the whole.
·, or 50 per cent.	...	...	2	Or {1·2 per cent. of the females. 0·6 per cent. of the whole.
·, or 100 per cent. at that age.	...	...	0	
	...	...	1	Or 50 per cent. of those with ac. rh.
	...	...	57	Or {12·5 per cent. of the females. 5·7 per cent. of the whole.
	...	 1	16	Or {9·6 per cent. of the females. 5 per cent. of the whole.
	...	...	2	Or 12·5 per cent. of those with ac. rh.
	...	 1	7	Or 44 per cent. of those with ac. rh.
1, or 51·8 per cent.	...	 19	453	
1 + 1 occupation not stated.	...	 3	{167 + 1 occ.} not stated	
1, or 7·5 per cent. at that age. 1, or 15 per cent. of whole.	...	 1	28	
·, or 33·7 per cent. at that age. 1, or 28·3 per cent. of whole.	...	 1	61	
1	...	...	3	
M, or 61·4 per cent. of those with ages stated.	...	 46	1,000	
M + 2 occupation not stated, or 32·9 per cent.	{Age (?) 5 + 2 occ.} not stated		{322 + 4 occ.} not stated	
1 + 1 occupation not stated, or 13·4 per cent. at that age, or 26·8 per cent. of the whole.	{Age (?) 1 + 2 occ.} not stated		{61 + 2 occ.} not stated	
1, or 29·4 per cent. at that age. 1, or 28·3 per cent. of whole.	{Age (?) 1 + 1 occ.} not stated		{107 + 1 occ.} not stated	
1	{Age and occ. not stated 3}		{55 + 3 occ.} not stated	

matism whose ages were stated, and who were so affected, who were engaged in the class of occupation named in the column headed " Male Patients."
Here and elsewhere in this column " whole " applies to the whole number of patients of both sexes.

with Pericarditis, all of whom had endocarditis also, and nearly one-half of them (25) with simple endocarditis, while endocarditis was either threatened or probable in the remaining 15. Three-fourths of the servants attacked with Pericarditis and endocarditis (14 in 19), and three-fifths of those with simple endocarditis (26 in 42) were below the age of 21, while only one-fourth of those who were quite free from symptoms of heart affection were below that age (3 in 13).

Girls engaged in the hard labour of a servant, at work, at a tender age, from morning to night, when attacked with this disease to which they are so subject, are all but certain to have inflammation of the heart without or within. Servant-girls below the age of 21, keeping in view their time of life and constitution, are more exposed to the causes of acute rheumatism and its attendant inflammation of the heart than persons of any other class. They are growing, their frame is not yet knit, they are sensitive to cold and wet, and they are subject to palpitation. Before all, in these young women their joints are not yet perfected, the ends of the bones forming them being still united to their shafts by cartilage; their growth is active so that the blood circulates in them freely; their structures are sensitive; and while they are supple, and their play is free and lively, they are tender and do not bear undue pressure; they are liable to strains, are unequal to labour and fatigue, and are easily affected by draughts, and by exposure to wet and cold, especially after undue and prolonged exertion. Then the labour of these poor girls, especially in hard places of service, is great and constant; they carry weights up and down stairs, often in lofty houses; they are constantly on foot, standing rather than walking, so that full pressure is continuously made on the joints; or what is worse, they are kneeling sometimes on cold and even wet stone floors, hard at work, scrubbing and brushing.

The joint affection was, as a rule, more severe in servants suffering from acute rheumatism than in the rest of those so affected, the joints being attacked with severity in one-half of the servants (49 in 101), and a little over one-third of the rest (91 in 225). Among those servants who suffered from Pericarditis, the joint affection was severe in fully three-fourths (15 in 19), and in a large proportion of these (6) it was very severe. If we compare these cases with the rest of the servants affected with acute rheumatism, we find that the severity of the joint affection rose in the scale in exact proportion to the severity of the heart affection. The joint affection was severe in less than one-third (4 in 13) of those servants who presented no sign of inflammation of the heart, while it was so in a little over a third (9 in 26) of those in whom endocarditis was threatened or probable, and in one-half of those who were attacked with simple endocarditis (21 in 42); while, as I have just said, it was severe in three-fourths of the cases with Pericarditis (15 in 19).

In the servants who were attacked with Pericarditis, the severity of the joint affection bore a strict relation to the severity of the heart affection in the great majority of the cases.

In one-third of them (6 in 19) the joint affection was very severe; and in the whole of these the heart affection was very severe, while in one of them it was fatal.

In nearly one-half of these patients (9 in 19) the joint affection was severe in the second degree, and in two-thirds of these (6 in 9) the heart affection was severe; in two cases it was rather severe; and in one it was slight. In three patients the joint affection was rather severe, and of these the heart affection was severe in one, rather so in a second, and not so in a third.

The last case is a notable exception to this rule. The attack in the joints was slight, but the attack at the heart was very severe, and proved fatal.

The accompanying Tables show (1) the proportion in which female domestic servants affected with acute rheumatism were attacked by endocarditis and Pericarditis, and the influence of age in the proportionate production of those affections of the heart in that disease; and (2) the relation of the degree of the joint affection to the degree of the heart affection in those cases.

1. Degree of the Joint Affection in Servants affected with Acute Rheumatism, in relation to Age and Heart Affection.

Joint Affection.	No Endocarditis.				Endocarditis threatened or probable.					Endocarditis.				Pericarditis.				Total.				Grand Total.
	Below 21.	21 to 25.	Above 25.	Total.	Below 21.	21 to 25.	Above 25.	? age.	Total.	Below 21.	21 to 25.	Above 25.	Total.	Below 21.	21 to 25.	Above 25.	Total.	Below 21.	21 to 25.	Above 25.	? age.	
severe + + .	0	0	0	0	0	0	0	0	0	2	0	0	2	5	1	0	6	7	1	0	0	8 + +
re + ...	1	0	3	4	5	0	4	0	9	10	5	4	19	7	1	1	9	23	6	12	0	41 +
her severe — + .	1	3	1	5	7	3	1	1	12	7	4	1	12	2	1	0	3	17	11	3	1	32 — +
severe o + .	1	1	2	4	3	2	1	0	6	5	0	2	7	0	1	0	1	9	4	5	0	18 o +
t —	0	0	0	0	0	0	0	0	0	1	0	0	1	0	0	0	0	1	0	0	0	1 —
tiful	0	0	0	0	0	0	0	0	0	0	0	1	1	0	0	0	0	0	0	1	0	1 ?
Total . . .	3	4	6	13	15	5	6	1	27	25	9	8	42	14	4	1	19	57	22	21	1	101

2. Degree of the Joint Affection in Servants in relation to the degree of the Heart Affection in the cases of Rheumatic Pericarditis.

Degree of the Joint Affection.	Degree of the Heart Affection.						Total Degree of the Joint Affection.
	Fatal.	Very Severe. + +	Severe. +	Rather Severe. — +	Not Severe. o +	Slight. —	
ry severe + + . .	1	5	0	0	0	0	6 + +
rere + ...	0	1	5	2	0	1	9 +
ther severe — + .	0	0	1	1	1	0	3 — +
t severe o + . . .	1	0	0	0	0	0	1 o +
Heart Affection .	2	6 + +	6 +	3 +	1 o +	1 —	19

I will now briefly consider the occupations of the remaining *female patients* who were attacked with acute rheumatism. I have thrown into one group the cooks, charwomen, nurses, and laundresses, who numbered altogether 22. Of these 5 had Pericarditis, 4 of whom had endocarditis also, and 4 had simple endocarditis; in 7 endocarditis was threatened or probable; and in 6 the heart gave no evidence of being affected. Of the whole number less than a fifth were younger than 21 (4 in 21 [1]). Of the five cases with Pericarditis, in one the attack was severe but transient, and in that patient the joint affection was severe. In two others the heart affection was rather severe, and in the remaining two it was slight, while in none of these was the joint affection severe.

Nine of the women followed sedentary employments, using chiefly the needle; and in none of these was there Pericarditis; four of them, however, had endocarditis.

The married women numbered 17, and of these only two had Pericarditis and endocarditis, one severely, the other slightly. In both the joint affection was rather severe. Of the remainder, 2 had simple endocarditis, and 5 were threatened with it, while one-half (8) gave no sign of heart affection. These patients were all older than 23.

Sixteen of the female patients had no occupation, only one of whom was above the age of 20. Only two of them had Pericarditis, one of whom had endocarditis also; in one of these the heart affection was fatal, in the other it was severe; and in one of them the joint affection was severe, while in the other that ended fatally it was so only to a moderate degree. Seven of these cases had simple endocarditis and 2 were threatened with it; while 5 of them presented no indication of endocarditis.

These cases, taken as a whole, show that those women who followed at a mature age occupations as laborious as the young servants, were affected in but a moderate proportion with Pericarditis, and that in a comparatively mild form. They also show that those of tender age who followed no occupation were not attacked with inflammation of the heart with anything like the same frequency as young female servants. We thus see, in brief, that in acute rheumatism affecting the female sex, youth with labour is nearly always attacked or threatened with endocarditis or Pericarditis, or both; that youth without labour is thus attacked with comparative infrequency; and that mature age with labour is attacked less frequently and much less severely with inflammation of the heart than youth with labour.

The *male patients* give us two great illustrations. One of these is supplied by those working *in-doors*, and they naturally run in the same grooves as the female patients, who were, all but two, occupied in-doors. The other is supplied by those following *out-of-door* occupations; and they stand completely apart in kind of labour, age, and character of disease, as well as in sex, from the female patients, whose cases have just been considered.

---

[1] In one of the 22 cases belonging to this group the age of the patient is not stated.

I have brought the male patients working *in-doors* including ten servants, into one group, numbering 37. In several features this group presents a remarkable agreement as regards age and the frequency of heart affection, and especially of Pericarditis, with the important and large analogous group of female servants. Thus in each group more than half of the patients were below the age of 21 (of the male patients 19 in 37, of the female servants 57 in 100);[1] in each, the proportion of cases with Pericarditis was great, amounting among the males to one-third (13 in 37), among the female servants to one-fifth (19 in 101); in each three-fourths of those thus affected with Pericarditis were below the age of 21, (10 of the 13 male patients, and 14 of the 19 female servants); in each the proportion of those in whom the heart presented no sign of inflammation was small, amounting to one-sixth of those male patients (6 in 37), and one-eighth of the female servants (12 in 101); and in each few of the patients whose hearts were thus unaffected were below the age of 21, amounting to fully one-third of those male patients (3 in 7), and to one-fourth of the female servants (3 in 13). Here, however, this close parallel ends, since among the patients affected with acute rheumatism above the age of 25, Pericarditis attacked the men working in-doors more frequently (2 in 13) than the female servants (1 in 22), and among those with Pericarditis, less than one-half of the males (6 in 13), and almost as many as three-fourths of the females (15 in 19) were attacked with severity; while the proportion of cases affected or threatened with simple endocarditis was much smaller among the male patients (9 and 9 respectively in 37) than the female servants (42 and 26 in 101).

Looking at these two sections of the patients in their larger and more vital relations, it is evident that in both sexes the same causes produce, under like conditions, the same effects; and that a very large proportion of the young persons who work on foot in-doors during many hours daily, are attacked with inflammation of the heart when affected with acute rheumatism, while a very small proportion are thus attacked of the men and women of mature age who are engaged in the same manner.

If we looked solely to the kind of employments just considered it would be natural to infer that overwork in-doors in young people of both sexes was the main cause of acute rheumatism and of its attendant Pericarditis and endocarditis. While, however, as we have just seen, the whole of the female patients with occupations were engaged in-doors, save two poor women who each kept a stall, only about one-fourth of the male patients worked in-doors.

The larger proportion of the male patients affected with acute rheumatism, amounting nearly to three-fifths (82 in 154), excluding those working with lead, worked *out-of-doors.* More than one-half of these (45 in 84) were engaged in hard labour. Pericarditis attacked

[1] In one of the 99 female servants affected with acute rheumatism, the age of the patient is not stated.

nearly one-fourth of these patients (10 in 45). We here find, what is at first sight an unexpected result, that of these laborious workers out of doors thus attacked with Pericarditis only one in ten was below the age of 21; whereas of the male in-door workers thus affected, fully three-fourths (10 in 13) were below that age. If we look at those of older age, we find the scale exactly reversed; since of those labouring out of doors four-fifths (8 in 10) were above the age of 25; while of those working in-doors only one-sixth (2 in 13) were above that age. We here, I consider, find the explanation, that I promised when considering age, of the twofold fact, that the male cases of Pericarditis usually combined with endocarditis outnumber the female cases by one-fifth (35 to 28); and that the number of the men so affected above the age of 25 is three times as great as that of the women so affected (men with Pericarditis 13 in 53, women 4 in 53). I think we may infer from these facts that excessive labour in the open air in men of mature age is a frequent cause of acute rheumatism having a strong tendency to Pericarditis.

Male patients with acute rheumatism, whose occupation was chiefly on foot, such as watchmen and porters; and those employed with horses and in stables, whose habits make them liable to gout, including coachmen, cabmen, and grooms; did not suffer from Pericarditis so frequently as those who were engaged in hard labour: since of those working on foot only one-seventh (2 in 14) and of those employed with horses only one-twenty-third (1 in 23), while of those whose work was laborious, nearly one-fourth (10 in 45), were thus attacked.

These facts support the view that Pericarditis tends to attack men of mature age affected with acute rheumatism when their work is hard, but not when it is comparatively easy.

It remains to me to speak of two other classes of employments, painters and plumbers on the one hand, and waiters and barmen on the other, who tend to have gout much more frequently than acute rheumatism. I find, however, that 11 waiters and barmen and 5 of those working with lead were attacked with acute rheumatism. One of each of those classes was attacked with Pericarditis, both of whom were above 30 years of age. Seven of the waiters and barmen and two of the workers in lead presented no sign of heart affection. These were all but one below the age of 24, and in none of them was the great toe affected.

It would thus appear that when barmen, painters, or workers among horses, whose employments tend to induce gout, are attacked with acute rheumatism, especially when young, they do not tend to have Pericarditis or endocarditis.

II.—The Affection of the Joints in Rheumatic Pericarditis.

The inflammation of the joints and the inflammation of the heart in acute rheumatism form one disease. We know that in a certain proportion of the cases the heart shows no sign of being touched by the disease, and here and there perhaps in a very rare instance the heart is attacked with inflammation when the joints are free from it. The unity of the two phases of the disease, the external phase, in the joints, and the internal in the fibrous structures of the exterior and the interior of the heart being established, we have to inquire what was the relative intensity of the inflammation of the joints and the inflammation of the heart in my cases of acute rheumatism, and especially in those affected with Pericarditis.

We have just seen that in servants attacked with acute rheumatism, the joint affection was, as a rule, only of moderate severity when the heart gave no sign of being affected; that the joint affection was more severe when the heart was threatened or probably attacked with endocarditis; and that the severity of the joint affection increased in a direct ratio with the increased certainty and severity of the heart affection; the joint affection being greater when simple endocarditis was actually present than when it was threatened or probable, and much greater when the heart was attacked with both endocarditis and Pericarditis.

I find that the same rule applies to the whole body of the cases of acute rheumatism; as may be seen in the accompanying Table, showing the degree of intensity of the joint affection in relation to the absence or presence of endocarditis and Pericarditis in cases of acute rheumatism.

Degree of intensity of the Joint Affection in relation to the absence or presence of Endocarditis and Pericarditis in cases of Acute Rheumatism.

Joint Affection.	No Endo-carditis.	Endocar-ditis threatened or probable.	Endocar-ditis.	Pericar-ditis.	Total.	Female servants.	Other em-ployments.
Very severe	0	1	2	12	15 —	8 =	7
Severe	22	32	46	25	125 —	41 =	84
Rather severe	84	35	42	18	129 —	32 =	97
Not severe	18	7	15	6	46 —	18 =	28
Slight	4	1	2	1	8 —	1 =	7
Doubtful	1	0	1	1	3 —	1 =	2
Total	79	76	108	63	326 — 101 = 225		

Thus the joint affection was severe in one-fourth (22 in 78)[1] of those patients in whom the heart gave no sign of inflammation; in two-fifths (32 in 76) of those in whom endocarditis was threatened or probable; in more than two-fifths (48 in 107)[2] of those affected with simple endocarditis, and in three-fifths (37 in 62)[3] of those who were attacked with Pericarditis, all but 9 of whom (54) had endocarditis also.

[1] The degree of the joint affection was not stated in one of the 79 cases belonging to this group.
[2] The degree of the joint affection was not stated in one of the 108 cases belonging to this group.
[3] The degree of the joint affection was not stated in one of the 63 cases belonging to this group.

TABLE GIVING THE ACTUAL NUMBER OF THE JOINT AFFECTION IN RELATION TO THE DEGREE OF HEART AFFECTION IN 62[1] CASES OF RHEUMATIC PERICARDITIS.

JOINT AFFECTION.	HEART AFFECTION.					Total.
	Fatal ⊙	Very severe ++	Severe +	Rather severe -+	Not severe O +, or slight -	
The *joint affection* was very severe (+ +) in **12** cases						12
Of these the *heart affection* was fatal(⊙) in . . .	1 ···	···	···	···	···	
,, ,, very severe (+ +) in . .	···	6 + +	3 +	2 — +[3]	···	
,, ,, severe (+) in . .	···	···	···	···	···	
,, ,, rather severe (— +) in . .	···	···	···	···	···	
The *joint affection* was *severe* (+) in **25** cases						25
Of these the *heart affection* was fatal (⊙) in . . .	2 ···	···	···	···	···	
,, ,, very severe (+ +) in . .	···	7 + +	11 +[3]	3 — +[4]	2 ⊙ +[4]	
,, ,, severe (+) in . .	···	···	···	···	···	
,, ,, rather severe (— +) in . .	···	···	···	···	···	
,, ,, not severe (O +) in . .	···	···	···	···	···	
The *joint affection* was *rather severe* (— +) in **18** cases . . .						18
Of these the *heart affection* was fatal (⊙) in . . .	0 ···	···	···	···	···	
,, ,, very severe (+ +) in . .	···	2 + +	5 +	6 — +[4]	5 {2 O +, 3 — }	
,, ,, severe (+) in . .	···	···	···	···	···	
,, ,, rather severe (— +) in . .	···	···	···	···	···	
,, ,, not severe 2 (O +) or slight 3 (—) in	···	···	···	···	···	
The *joint affection* was *not severe* 6 (O +) or slight 1 (—) = 7 . .						7
Of these the *heart affection* was fatal (⊙) in . . .	1 ⊙[2]	···	···	···	···	
,, ,, very severe (+ +) in . .	···	0 + +	2 +	4 — +	···	
,, ,, severe (+) in . .	···	···	···	···	···	
,, ,, rather severe (— +) in . .	···	···	···	···	···	
,, ,, not severe (O +) or slight (—) in	···	···	···	···	···	
The *joint affection* was not described (?) in **1**						1
In this case there were no signs of Endocarditis.	···	···	···	···	···	
Of the total of the above **63** cases of Pericarditis, the heart affection was fatal (⊙) in	4 ⊙	···	···	···	···	
The heart affection was very severe (+ +) in . . .	···	15 + +	21 +	15 — +	7 {3 O +, 4 — }	
,, ,, severe (+) in . . .	···	···	···	···	···	
,, ,, rather severe (— +) in . . .	···	···	···	···	···	
,, ,, not severe (O +) or slight (—) in . .	···	···	···	···	···	
TOTAL NUMBER OF cases						64

[1] In 1 of the 63 cases of Rheumatic Pericarditis the condition of the joints is not described.
[2] In 2 of these cases there were no signs of Endocarditis.
[3] In these 2 cases the signs of Endocarditis were absent or doubtful.
[4] In 1 of these cases the signs of Endocarditis were absent or doubtful.
[5] In this case Endocarditis was absent or doubtful.

The inflammation of the joints was very intense in 12 of the 37 patients with Pericarditis, usually coupled with endocarditis, in whom the inflammation of the joints was severe, whereas in only 3 of the 184 patients in whom simple endocarditis was present or threatened, and in none of the 79 in whom the heart gave no evidence of being affected, was the joint affection of this great degree of intensity.

In the cases of Pericarditis, there was a close correspondence in severity between the inflammation of the joints and the inflammation of the heart. The accompanying Table [see opposite page] shows in detail the degree of the joint affection in relation to the degree of the heart affection in sixty-two cases of Rheumatic Pericarditis.[1] The joint affection was very severe in 12 cases, and in three-fifths of those cases (7) the heart affection was very severe, being fatal in one; in one-fourth of them (3) it was severe; and in only one-sixth of them (2) was it of moderate severity. The joint affection was severe in 25 cases, and in one-third of those cases (9) the heart affection was very severe; in less than one-half of them (11) it was severe, and in one-fifth of them (5) it was of moderate severity, or slight. If we combine these two groups of cases, amounting to 37, that were marked by the severity of the joint affection, we find that in four-fifths of them (30) the affection of the heart was severe, while in one fifth of them (7) it was not severe or only moderately so. Endocarditis was present in all but two of the 30 cases in which the affection both of the joints and the heart was severe; while the signs of endocarditis were either absent or doubtful in 4 of the 7 cases in which the affection of the joints was severe, while that of the heart was either of moderate severity or slight.

If we examine those cases, amounting to 25, or two-fifths of the whole number, in which the degree of the joint affection was below the line of severity, we find that in 18 of them the affection of the joints was only of moderate severity, while in 7 of them it was slight; and that in two-fifths of these (10) the heart affection was severe, while in three-fifths of them (15) it was either slight or of moderate severity. We find, then, that in the 37 cases of Pericarditis in which the joint affection was more severe, the heart affection was more severe in four-fifths (30) and less severe in one-fifth (7); while in the 25 cases of Pericarditis in which the joint affection was less severe, the heart affection was more severe in two-fifths (10) and less severe in three-fifths (15).

III.—THE DEGREE OF THE JOINT AFFECTION DURING THE ACME OF THE EFFUSION INTO THE PERICARDIUM.

When the exterior of the heart is attacked by inflammation in cases of acute rheumatism, the distress and oppression in the region of the heart and in the chest is often so great as to call the patient's

---

[1] In one of the 63 cases of Pericarditis the joint affection was not described.

attention away from the seat of suffering in the joints. At the same time the physician or the clinical clerk is so much interested in the state of the central organ that he readily overlooks that of the joints. I find that in 12 of the 45 cases given in the accompanying plans (see pages 190, 191), the condition of the joints was not reported during the acme of the pericardial effusion, and in one other case the joint affection was not noted until the attack of Pericarditis had declared itself.

The state of the joints during the period of the acme of the inflammation of the exterior of the heart, marked by the extent of fluid in the pericardium being then at its height, is shown in 32 of the 45 patients under examination. These cases divide themselves naturally into two groups; in one of these, amounting to 12, the Pericarditis was at its acme at the time of admission, or on the following day; while in the remaining 20 cases the effusion into the pericardium reached its acme after the admission of the patient. In the latter set of cases, the intensity of the joint affection had been, as a rule, modified and lessened by rest and soothing treatment, and, especially in four-fifths of the cases, by opium given at repeated intervals; while in the former set of cases in which the pericarditis was at its height at the time of admission, the joint affection had been, as a rule, somewhat aggravated by the removal of the patient from home to the hospital. The set of cases, therefore, that were admitted with pericarditis at its height show the natural relation of the degree of the joint affection to that of the heart affection during the period of the acme of the disease, in a manner less affected by other influences than the set in which the pericarditis came on and reached its height after admission.

The inflammation of the joints was severe at the time of admission in more than one-half of the patients (7 in 12) who came in with the Pericarditis at its height, and in six (16, 18, 12, 51, 55, 35,) of these seven cases the joint affection was of about equal severity before admission and at the time of the acme of the effusion into the pericardium; while in one of them (56) the joints were less severely affected before than during the period of the height of the Pericarditis.

In two-fifths of this group of cases (5 in 12) the joint affection was not severe when the Pericarditis was at its height, at the time of admission or on the next day, and in three (6, 43, 40) and perhaps in four (42) of these the inflammation of the joints was more severe before admission than after it and during the period of the acme of the effusion into the pericardium. The remaining case (13) stands alone, since in it, although the affection of the heart proved fatal, that of the joints was but slight, both before and after admission.

The second group consists of twenty cases in which the effusion into the pericardium reached its acme after admission; and it will be seen that the relation of the joint affection to the heart affection was very different in this group from what it was in the former one in which the patients came in when the Pericarditis was at its height.

The inflammation of the joints was more severe at the period of the acme of the pericardial effusion than before that period in one-fifth of these cases (4 in 20) (3, 4, 30, 49), and it was of equal severity during the two periods in one other case (19).

The affection of the joints became less severe during the period of the acme of Pericarditis than before that period in three-fourths of these cases (15 in 20).[1] Four-fifths of these patients (12 in 15) took repeated doses of opium, with lessening joint affection during the acme of Pericarditis, while only one of the four patients with increasing joint affection during the acme was placed under the influence of opium.

It is evident that if we looked only to the first group, or only to the second group of these cases, we should arrive at opposite conclusions with regard to the relation of the degree of the joint affection to that of the heart affection during the acme of Pericarditis. Thus the joint affection lessened during the acme of the disease in one-third of the first group (4 in 13) and in three-fourths of the second group (15 in 20). The influence of repeated doses of opium evidently told on the second group of cases, and the movement of the patients from their homes to the hospital, on the first group of cases, to modify the relation of the joint affection to the heart affection.

I think that we may safely draw an inference midway between these two extreme illustrations, and consider that in about one-half of the cases of Pericarditis the joint affection was of equal severity during the period of the acme of the disease, and before that period; and that in about one-half of them the joint affection became less severe when the Pericarditis was at its height. The general conclusion may be drawn from this inference, that the joint affection tends to lessen in severity when Pericarditis is at its height in about one-half of the cases.

IV. Time in the Hospital.

The accompanying Table shows the average time that the patients remained in the hospital in relation to the absence or presence of endocarditis or pericarditis in acute rheumatism :—

Time in the Hospital in relation to the absence or presence of Endocarditis and Pericarditis in cases of Acute Rheumatism.

In the Hospital.	No Endo-carditis.	Endocarditis threatened or probable.	Endocar-ditis.	Pericarditis.	Total.
From 6 to 20 days	33	22	14	7	76
,, 21 ,, 30 ,, ...	23	21	31	8	83
,, 31 ,, 50 ,, ...	15	21	37	16	89
Over 50 days	3	3	21	28	60
An uncertain number of days . .	2	3	3	4	11
Total	76	74*	106*	63	319*

* Since this Table was drawn up, seven cases have been added, making the total number 326.

[1] 8, 15, 20–22, 24, 26, 28, 31, 33, 34, 36, 44a, 50, 54.

The time that the patient remained in the wards measures the duration and severity of the disease. Two-fifths of the patients in whom the heart gave no sign of being affected, left the hospital before the end of the third week (33 in 76), three-fourths of them during the first month (56 in 76), and one-fourth of them after the first month (20 in 76). Those who had Pericarditis usually accompanied by endocarditis remained in the wards for a much longer period, since only one-ninth. of them (7 in 63) left the hospital before the end of the third week, and one-fourth of them (15 in 63) during the first month, while three-fourths of them remained in the hospital longer than a month (48 in 63), and one-half of them more than fifty days. Those with simple endocarditis remained in the house much longer than those whose hearts were healthy, but not nearly so long as those with Pericarditis usually combined with endocarditis.

V.—Occurrence or Non-Occurrence of one or more Previous Attacks of Acute Rheumatism.

The accompanying Table shows the proportion in which the patients affected with acute rheumatism had been previously attacked by that disease in fully three-fourths of the patients (243 in 319 cases). Less than one-third of those who gave no sign of endocarditis (23 in 76) and nearly one-half of those who were affected with endocarditis (48 in 106,) had suffered from one or more previous attacks of acute rheumatism ; so that in my cases the occurrence of a previous attack evidently favoured the presence of endocarditis. This did not, however, appear to be the case with pericarditis, for only one-third of the cases with that affection had been previously attacked by acute rheumatism. The previous occurrence of acute rheumatism implies in a certain proportion of the cases the presence of valvular disease of the heart, a condition that promotes the occurrence of endocarditis in acute rheumatism. It is open to inquiry why valvular disease should have more frequently influenced the production of endocarditis than of pericarditis in my cases.

Occurrence or Non-Occurrence of Previous Attacks of Acute Rheumatism in relation to the Absence or Presence of Endocarditis and Pericarditis.

Joint Affection.	No Endo-carditis.	Endocarditis threatened or probable.	Endocar-ditis.	Pericarditis.	Total.
No previous attack	37	23	31	26	117
No note of previous attack . .	16	17	27	16	76
One previous attack	17	24	35	15	91
More previous attacks than one .	6	10	13	6	35
Total	76	74*	106*	63	319*

* Since this Table was drawn up, seven cases have been added, making the total number 326.

VI.—The Time of the First Observation of Friction Sound and of the Beginning of Rheumatic Pericarditis in Relation to the Beginning or Relapse of the Affection of the Joints.

In a large proportion of the cases of acute rheumatism affected with Pericarditis, friction sound was heard over the heart either at the time of admission or very soon after it. Thus in more than one-third of the total number of the cases, the rubbing noise was noticed on the day that they entered the hospital (22 in 63); in all but one-half of them (29 in 63) it was heard on that or the following day; and in fully two-thirds of them (41 in 63) it was observed either at the time of admission or during the three days following it. In nine-tenths of the whole number of cases affected with Pericarditis (55 in 63) the frottement was distinguished during the first nine days of the patient's residence in the hospital.

These facts do not, however, point out how soon Pericarditis occurred after the commencement of the attack of acute rheumatism. To ascertain this, we must add the number of days from the commencement of the attack to the time of admission, to the number of days from that time to the period at which the to-and-fro sound was heard. This plan answers with those cases in which the friction sound was observed on or after the third day from the date of admission, since in all but four of them the heart had been previously examined. It does not, however, apply to those patients in whom the frottement was detected during the day of admission or on the next day, since in those cases we do not know how long the rubbing sound may have been in existence before the patient came in. This applies to one-half of the patients affected with rheumatic Pericarditis, since they had suffered from acute rheumatism for a period varying from two days to three weeks before entering the wards. These cases are, however, of use in showing how early in the disease, and how late, Pericarditis may declare itself by friction sound in full play. Thus out of the twenty-nine cases in which frottement was heard during the first two days, more than one-fourth (8 in 29) had been affected with acute rheumatism for a period of from two to four days; while on the other hand one-fifth of them (6 in 29) had been ill for from two to three weeks before admission.

If we bring together the whole of the 63 cases of Pericarditis, we find that in one-sixth of them (10 in 63) the rubbing sound was audible as early as from the third to the sixth day after the commencement of the disease; while in one-half of them (30 in 63) that sound was audible on or before the eleventh day of the illness.

In only seven of the cases did the heart affection show itself so late as the twenty-fifth day and from that to the sixty-third after the onset of the acute rheumatism.

These facts point, I think, to the conclusion that in a certain small proportion of the cases, amounting perhaps to one-eighth (8 in 63) the onset of the inflammation both of the exterior and the interior of the heart took place at the very commencement of the disease, and at the same time with the onset of the inflammation of the joints.

It is scarcely needful to say that the first appearance of the rubbing sound is later than the beginning of the inflammation of the surface of the heart. In this respect, the inflammation of the outside of that organ corresponds with the inflammation of the joints, since, as in inflammation of the joints, pain and tenderness precede exudation and swelling, so in Pericarditis, in at least some instances to which I shall now refer, pain and exquisite sensitiveness over the heart preceded the notable increase of effusion into the pericardium and the existence of a rubbing sound.

In five of the cases in which friction sound was heard on the day of admission (13, 15, 44a, 53, 61), pain had existed over the region of the heart, or in the left side, or in the chest, for one or more days before the patient entered the hospital. In one of these cases (44a) pain was present over the heart from about the beginning of the illness, the precise time of which is not stated.

In nearly one-half of the patients in whom the frottement was heard for the first time from one to fifty-three days after admission (16 in 39), there was pain over the region of the heart or in the chest from one to seven days before the rubbing noise was observed. In seven (51, 8, 26, 28, 50, 29, 5) of them the pain was noticed one day; in three (57, 56, 23), two days; in one, three days (14); in two, four days (55, 36); in two, six days (123, 30); and in one, seven days (20) before the first observation of the friction sound.

The patient (24), in whom friction sound was heard on the fifty-third day after admission, presented a chain of symptoms interesting in two points of view, one, that the attack of Pericarditis was immediately preceded by a relapse of the joint affection; the other, that pain over the heart preceded the frottement. The patient was a labourer, aged 27, and had almost passed through a severe attack of acute rheumatism with endocarditis, resulting in permanent injury to the mitral and aortic valves. On the 36th day, he being stronger and of better colour, was allowed to get up. On the 42nd his general health was good, his pains were diminished, and he walked about. On the 45th he felt stiffness in the right hip-joint on walking, that joint having been affected for eight months previously; and on the 48th the pain in the hip was worse, though he was otherwise free from complaint, and his appetite was good. On the 50th day, however, his neck was stiff, and he had flying pains about the knees; and on the next day his face was flushed, he perspired copiously, and complained of great pain over the region of the heart and palpitation. On the 52nd he suffered from a terrible pain in the neck and head, the wrists were swollen and painful, and the heart's action was so loud that the mitral and aortic murmurs were inaudible; and on the following day a loud and harsh double friction sound was heard over the heart. Here the attack of Pericarditis immediately followed the relapse in the joint affection, and the pain over the heart preceded the rubbing sound by two days.

In four other cases in which the friction sound appeared some time after admission, the Pericarditis followed closely upon a *relapse* of the joint affection. In one of these (36), a woman, aged 20, who was motionless on admission from the affection of the joints, the pain was worse on the 6th day, she was still powerless on the 7th from the pain in the joints, and on the 8th a harsh grating frottement, chiefly systolic, was heard over the apex of the heart. In another patient (3), a man, aged 26, who was re-admitted with a severe relapse of the affection of the joints six days after leaving the hospital, the hands and hips were better on the 5th day after his readmission, but on the 8th there was again pain in the hip, and on the 9th there was excessive pain and tenderness in the fascia of the thigh. On the next day (the 10th) there was pain, and increased dulness on percussion over the heart, and a double friction brush was audible at the apex. In a third case (30), a man, aged 31, all the joints were swollen and painful when he came in, but were so much better on the 8th day that they only pained him when he moved. The pain in the joints returned, however, on the 9th, being better next day, when a harsh double friction sound was audible over the heart.

In the last case of this group (17), a female servant, aged 20, the joints were painful and swollen on admission, they were less so on the 4th day, and on the 7th they were almost of the natural size. On the 9th a little pain returned in the joints and there was oppression over the heart. On the 13th the pain had increased and she suffered much in the chest, the first sound being rough and prolonged. On the 16th there was a murmur all over the heart, which was the seat of pain; and on the 17th a soft double friction sound was established over the region of the pericardium.

To these cases must be added one of a series that were treated by rest during the years 1866–68. In this patient, a man, aged 20, the pain in the joints, which was considerable on admission and which lessened on the 4th day, again increased in the arms and neck on the 5th, when a pain, beginning at the lower portion of the breast bone, shot through the region of the heart to the back. This symptom and pain in the region of the apex were relieved by leeches. The joints also improved, but on the 10th, after he had been using his hand, pain returned in the finger, and on the 14th, the next report, Pericarditis had fully declared itself.

VII.—The Presence or Absence of Endocarditis in Rheumatic
Pericarditis.

Cases where Endocarditis was present.—There was evidence of
inflammation in the interior of the heart in all the cases excepting
nine (54 in 63).

The heart was healthy at the time of the attack in 46 of the cases
with endocarditis, and the mitral, or mitral and aortic valves were
crippled by previous disease in the remaining 8 cases, including one
just alluded to (24) in which Pericarditis followed a relapse of the
affection of the joints, the aortic and mitral valves having become
affected during the earlier part of the attack of acute rheumatism.

A tricuspid murmur was alone present in three of the 46 cases
of endocarditis : in two of these cases that murmur was persistent,
and in one of them it disappeared. These cases were comparatively
free from serious symptoms, the heart affection being severe in only
one instance, and the inflammation of the joints being very severe in
another. The proportion of cases of this class with simple tricuspid
murmur, was much smaller in these cases of combined endocarditis
and Pericarditis than in those of simple endocarditis; 1 in 18 of
the former, as we have just seen (3 in 54), and 1 in 8 of the latter
(13 in 108) being thus affected.

The mitral valve was affected in 42 of the 46 patients with Pericarditis in whom endocarditis attacked the heart when previously
healthy, in 6 of whom the aortic valve was affected as well as the
mitral. The aortic valve was attacked in one other case in which the
mitral valve was not involved.

I have divided these 43 cases with mitral (36), aortic (1), and
mitral and aortic (6) incompetence into three groups; in the first
group, containing 16 cases (11 mitral, 5 mitral and aortic incompetence), valvular disease was finally established, or, in two instances,
the disease proved fatal when the murmur was in full play ; in the
second group, which numbered 8 cases with mitral regurgitation, the
murmur was lessening when the patients were discharged; while in
the third group, amounting to 19 (17 mitral, 1 aortic, and 1 mitral
and aortic incompetence), the murmurs disappeared on the recovery of
the patients from acute rheumatism, and the heart was restored to a
healthy condition.

The accompanying Table shows the relation of the degree of the
affection of the joints and that of the affection of the heart to the
occurrence and degree of endocarditis in cases of acute rheumatism
affected with Pericarditis.

If we compare the cases of endocarditis thus combined with Pericarditis, with the cases of uncomplicated or simple endocarditis, we
find that valvular disease was finally established, that the murmur
lessened in intensity, and that the murmur finally disappeared in
nearly the same proportion in the two sets of cases. Thus in 70 cases

of simple endocarditis, either mitral (53), aortic (10), or mitral and aortic (7) incompetence was present. If we divide these cases, like those with Pericarditis and endocarditis, into three groups, we find that in the first group containing 28 cases (16 mitral, 5 aortic, and 5 mitral and aortic incompetence), valvular disease was finally established, or, in two instances, the disease proved fatal; in the second group, which numbered 11 cases (11 mitral incompetence), the murmur was lessening when the patients were examined for the last time; while in the third group, amounting to 31 cases (24 mitral, 5 aortic, and 2 mitral and aortic incompetence), the murmur had disappeared on the recovery of the patients from acute rheumatism, and the heart became again healthy. A tricuspid murmur was alone audible in 13 additional cases of simple endocarditis: in 7 of these the murmur disappeared, but in 6 of them it was still audible when the heart was listened to for the last time.

I am of opinion, notwithstanding the remarkable correspondence in the effects of the inflammation of the valves in the three parallel groups of each of these two sets of cases, that when inflammation attacks the interior of the heart alone, it is less likely to induce permanent valvular disease, than when the heart is inflamed both without and within. This, I think, is *à priori* self-evident, and it is supported by two pieces of clinical evidence that I shall now adduce. (1) Disease of both the mitral and aortic valves, which is the most extensive form of valvular disease, was established in 5 of the 43 cases affected with both endocarditis and Pericarditis, and in 5 only of the 70 cases affected with simple endocarditis. (2) Simple endocarditis was present in 28 out of 74 cases of acute rheumatism that were treated by me in St. Mary's Hospital on a careful and rigid system of *rest*. Valvular disease of old standing existed in 7 of those patients, and a recent mitral murmur, accompanied in one instance by aortic incompetence, affected the remaining 21 cases. The heart regained its healthy condition in 14 of these patients, the murmur was lessening or doubtful in 4 of them on their recovery from acute rheumatism, and valvular disease was established in 3 only of the whole series of 21 cases.

The inflammation both of the joints and the heart was more often severe in those cases in which the valves became permanently diseased, than in those in which the recovery of their function was complete. The heart affection was severe in 12 of the 16 cases in which the valves were permanently disabled, being fatal in two and very severe in six of them; while it was severe in 13 of the 19 in which the valves were restored to health, being very severe in four of them. The relative intensity of the joint affection was even greater than that of the heart affection; since, in the former class of cases, it was severe in 12 of the 16 in which the organ became diseased, and in only 10 of the 19 in which its recovery was perfect.

There was mitral regurgitation in the whole of the group of cases, amounting to 8, in which there was previous valvular disease, in three

PERICARDITIS WITH AND WITHOUT ENDOCARDITIS.

RELATION OF THE DEGREE OF THE HEART AFFECTION AND OF THE JOINT AFFECTION TO THE OCCURRENCE AND DEGREE OF ENDOCARDITIS.

	Fatal	Very severe ++	Severe +	Rather severe -+	Not severe O+	Slight -	Doubtful	Total
With Endocarditis,								
Tricuspid murmur permanently established {Heart affection / Joint affection} 2	...	...	1 +	1 +	...	...	...	9, 2
Tricuspid murmur disappearing on recovery {Heart affection / Joint affection} 1	...	...	... 1 +	2 +	1 O +	...	...	1, 1
Tricuspid murmur Total number {Heart affection / Joint affection} 8	...	...	1 +, 1 +	1 ++, 2 +	1 O +	...	...	8, 8
Mitral regurgitation, ending in mitral valve disease 11 {Heart affection / Joint affection}	1 O	5 ++, 4 ++	1 ++, 4 +	2 +, 3 +	...	2 -	...	11, 11
Aortic and Mitral regurgitation, ending {Heart affection} 5	1 O	1 +	3 +	1 +	...	...	...	5
In established disease of both valves {Joint affection}	...	1 +	3 +	...	...	...	...	5
Mitral and Mitral-aortic regurgitation {Heart affection} 16	3 O	6 +	4 +	3 +	...	3 -	...	16
ending in established valve disease {Joint affection}	...	5 +	7 +	4 +	...	...	...	16
Mitral regurgitation ceasing on recovery {Heart affection / Joint affection} 8	...	1 ++	3 ++, 8 +	3 ++, 2 +	1 O O, 2 O	1 -, 1 -	...	8, 8
Mitral regurgitation disappearing on recovery 17 {Heart affection / Joint affection}	...	4 ++, 2 ++	8 ++, 7 ++, 1 +	4 +, 6 +	1 O O, 2 O	...	...	17, 17, 1
Aortic regurgitation {Heart affection} 1	...	1 +	...	...	...	...	...	1
disappearing on recovery {Joint affection}	...	...	...	...	...	...	...	1
Mitral-aortic regurgitation {Heart affection} 1	...	...	...	1 +	...	...	...	1
disappearing on recovery {Joint affection}	...	...	...	1 +	...	...	...	1

	○	+ +	+	− +	O +	−		Total
Mitral, Aortic, and Mitral-aortic regurgitation disappearing on recovery **19** — Heart affection △	…	4 +	9 +	5 −	1 O +	…	…	19
— Joint affection ☩	…	3 +	7 +	7 −	2 O +	…	…	19
Mitral valve-disease of old standing **5** — Heart affection △	1	1 +	2 +	1 −	… C	…	…	5
— Joint affection ☩	…	1 +	2 +	1 −	1 O +	…	…	5
Mitral-aortic valve-disease of old standing (1 recent) **3** — Heart affection △	1	3 +	…	1 −	…	…	…	3
— Joint affection ☩	…	1 +	1 +	1 −	…	…	…	3
Mitral and Mitral-aortic valve-disease of old standing **8** — Heart affection △	1	4 +	2 +	1 −	1 O +	…	…	8
— Joint affection ☩	…	2 +	3 +	2 −	1 O +	…	…	8
TOTAL Number of cases of Pericarditis accompanied by Endocarditis **54**	3	15 +	19 +	11 −	3 O +	8 −	…	54
	…	10 +	21 +	17 −	5 O +	1 −	…	54
Endocarditis absent or doubtful. Cases without sign of Endocarditis — Heart affection △	1	…	2 +	1 −	1 O +	1 −	…	6
— Joint affection ☩	…	1 +	3 +	…	1 O +	1 −	…	5
Cases in which the signs of Endocarditis were doubtful — Heart affection △	…	…	…	3 −	…	…	…	3
— Joint affection ☩	…	1 +	1 +	1 −	…	…	…	3
TOTAL Number of cases in which Endocarditis was absent or doubtful — Heart affection △	1	…	2 +	4 −	1 O +	1 −	…	9
— Joint affection ☩	…	2 +	4 +	1 −	1 O +	…	1 ?	9
GRAND TOTAL of cases of Pericarditis — Heart affection △	4	15 +	21 +	15 −	4 O +	4 −	…	63
— Joint affection ☩	…	12 +	25 +	18 −	6 O +	1 −	1 ?	63

of which the aortic valves were also incompetent. The heart affection was severe in the whole of these cases save one, and the joint affection was so in five of them. The all but universal presence of inflammation within the heart in patients of this class, supports the inference that in acute rheumatism, old standing valvular disease, by throwing additional labour on the organ, tends to produce endocarditis and pericarditis, and to increase the severity of the inflammation of the heart, both within and without.

II. *Cases in which Endocarditis was absent or doubtful.*—The signs of endocarditis were absent or uncertain in only 9 of the 63 cases of Pericarditis. In five of these patients no murmur was audible; in one there is no note that a murmur could be heard, and in the remaining three the existence of a murmur was doubtful. One of these cases proved fatal, and the affection of the heart was severe in two and of moderate severity or slight in the remaining six patients. The joint affection was severe in six of these cases.

Classification of the cases of Pericarditis.—I have classified the cases according to the presence or absence of endocarditis, and subdivided those with endocarditis into the groups which have just been described and which are specified in the following scheme:

I. Cases of Pericarditis in which Endocarditis was present 54

  A.—Cases with Endocarditis attacking the healthy heart . . . 46

    1.—Cases with tricuspid regurgitation ← 3

      a.—Cases in which the regurgitation became permanent } ← 2
      after recovery from acute rheumatism. . . . } ←

      c.—Cases in which the regurgitation disappeared on re- } ← 1
      covery . . . . } ←o

    2.—Cases with mitral (36 →), aortic (1 ↓), and mitral-aortic
    (1 ↓→) regurgitation 43

      a.—Cases in which the regurgitation became permanent
      after recovery from acute rheumatism (mitral 11,→, 16
      mitral-aortic ↓→↓→) . . . .

      b.—Cases in which the regurgitation lessened after recovery
      (mitral 8→) 8

      c.—Cases in which the regurgitation disappeared after recovery
      (mitral 17 →, aortic 1 ↓↓, mitral-aortic 1 ↓o→) 10

  B.—Cases with Endocarditis attacking a heart already affected with
  mitral (5 ↓→), or mitral-aortic (3 ↓↓ ↓→), valve-disease . . 6

II.—Cases of Pericarditis in which Endocarditis was absent (6) or doubtful (3) 9

        TOTAL number of cases of Pericarditis 63

VIII.—SKETCH OF THE PROGRESSIVE CHANGES THAT TAKE PLACE IN THE
HEART AND PERICARDIUM DURING THE PROGRESS OF PERICARDITIS.

We cannot rightly understand the symptoms and signs of Pericarditis unless we keep in the mind's eye the changes that are going
on in the heart and pericardium, and the surrounding organs during
the periods of the beginning, increase, and *acme*, the decline and ending of the disease. I shall, therefore, before discussing the symptoms
and signs of the disease that were present in my cases, give here a
slight sketch of the more important morbid changes, in so far as they
make themselves appreciated during life, and shall afterwards describe
some of those changes more fully when the consideration of the
symptoms and signs of the affection seems to call for it.

When the surface of the heart becomes inflamed, a blush of fine
vessels, consisting of a velvety network, appears on the surface of the
organ, and especially over the larger coronary vessels at the base and
septum of the ventricles. The inner surface of the pericardial sac,
wherever it rests upon the inflamed heart, kindles also into a blush
of fine vessels. The inflammation caught from the heart on the inner
lining of the sac, spreads rapidly to the fibrous structure of the pericardium, and through it may even often extend to the surface of the
pleura covering the sac. The inflammation of those parts tells upon
the nerves distributed to them. The surfaces of the heart and sac,
instead of being smooth and glistening, become dull and velvety;
and fluid is poured out and lymph exudes from the inflamed surfaces.

The liquid in the pericardium increases rapidly. At first it falls
into the back part of the sac, but as it increases in quantity it makes a
space for itself between the floor of the pericardium, which it depresses,
and the lower surface of the heart, which it elevates, and it gradually
distends the pouch in every direction, displacing the lungs to each side
in front, pushing the central tendon of the diaphragm, the stomach,
and the liver downwards, and pressing backwards, when the distension
from the fluid becomes great, upon the bifurcation of the trachea, the
left bronchus, the œsophagus, and the aorta. The fluid at the same
time re-acts upon the heart so as to compress the auricles, the venæ
cavæ, the pulmonary veins, and the ascending aorta; and to displace
the apex and body of the organ and its great arteries upwards and
forwards, owing to the extensive interposition of the fluid between the
lower surface of the heart and the floor of the pericardium.

The lymph is poured out upon the surfaces of the heart and the
sac. Where those two surfaces touch each other, the soft lymph is
drawn into threads and little pointed ridges and prominences, and
wrought into a network, so that when ridges or prominences are
present on the heart, ridges or prominences are present on the inner
surface of the pouch lying upon it, and when a network of lymph
covers the heart, a network of lymph lines the corresponding sac.
The constant play of expansion and contraction of the heart alter-

nately stretches and relaxes its coating of lymph, so that its surface resembles a honeycomb in structure.

The heart, elevated by the fluid between the under surface of the ventricles and the base of the pericardium to a degree proportioned to the amount of the fluid, leaves the broader part of the chest below, and ascends into the narrower part of the chest above. The lungs, and especially the left lung, are consequently displaced from before the swollen sac and the heart, and the front of the right and left ventricles, including the apex and the great arteries, beat with some force against the higher costal cartilages and intercostal spaces, and the adjoining portion of the sternum, with which they come into close contact. Owing to the narrowing compass of the portion of the chest in which the heart is then situated, and the withdrawal of the lung from before the organ, its impulse is both elevated and widened outwards, so that it is felt beating strongly in the second and third, or third and fourth left spaces, according to the amount of the effusion, the apex-beat being felt above, and beyond the nipple ; instead of the impulse, as in health, being felt gently in the fourth and fifth spaces, the apex-beat being within the nipple line. When the pericardium is distended to the utmost, its sac becomes pyramidal or pear-shaped, the apex or narrowest part of the pyramid pointing upwards, behind the lower portion of the manubrium and to the left of it, the base of the pyramid bearing downwards and extending across the ensiform cartilage from the sixth right costal cartilage to the lower border of the sixth left cartilage at its attachment to the rib. The fluid rapidly fills the sac, and often reaches its acme in two, three, or four days ; but it soon begins to lessen, and in from four to six additional days it usually returns to its healthy amount. At the same time the heart descends and comes again in contact with the lower end of the sternum and the top of the ensiform cartilage, the fifth space, the sixth costal cartilage, and the diaphragm. In most instances slight threads of adhesion form between the sac and portions of the right auricle, and often also between the sac and the apex and interventricular septum, that being the portion of the front of the heart that presents the least movement during the action of the ventricles. These soft threads of adhesion are generally drawn out, by the oscillating movements of the heart, until they at length yield, and break away, but sometimes permanent adhesions form, which may be partial or universal.

IX.—Over-Action of the Heart in Acute Rheumatism as a Cause of Endocarditis and Pericarditis ; and (in illustration), Over-Action of the Limbs, Local Injury, and other Influences, as Causes of Acute Rheumatism with Affection of the Heart.

In a small number of my cases of rheumatic Pericarditis the inflammation of the heart commenced soon after laborious, or violent, action of the organ

A woman (12), aged 26, a servant, was attacked, seven days before admission, with great pain in the soles of her feet. On the following day the pain continued, and proceeded up the legs to the knees and hips, so as to confine her to bed. On the third day she was seized with violent palpitation of the heart, and pain below the lower part of the sternum. On admission her countenance was flushed and anxious, the pulse was 160, and there was pain on pressure over the region of the heart, which was beating with great force. A friction sound was perceptible at the apex with each beat, but indistinctly, owing to the violent action of the organ. The breathing was hurried. Eight leeches were applied over the region of pain, and next day her aspect was better, the action of the heart was natural, the area of dulness on percussion over the region of the pericardium was greatly enlarged, reaching as high as the second cartilage, and friction sound was audible over the whole front of the heart, where the pain was only slight. After this the heart's action became feeble, irregular, and intermittent, but it regained its regularity in eighteen days. The friction sound lasted for about three weeks, and a mitral murmur became permanently established.

Another patient (24), already referred to, a labourer, aged 27, came in with acute rheumatism and endocarditis, presenting first mitral and then aortic regurgitation, both of which became established. He was allowed to get up on the 36th day. On the 48th he looked well, but pain in the hip, a trouble of old standing, had increased in severity. On the 50th the right side of his face was swollen and flushed, and he complained much of stiffness in the muscles of the neck, and next day of great præcordial pain and palpitation, the heart acting strongly and rapidly. On the 52nd he was seized with terrible pain in the neck and head, and the heart's action was so loud that the endocardial murmurs were rendered inaudible, and on the 53rd he suffered from acute pain about the præcordia, the left cartilages were arched, præcordial dulness extended up to the third space, and a loud and harsh double friction-sound was heard over the front of the heart. His attack was of unusual severity, but the rubbing sound had disappeared on the 68th day after his admission, and on the 83rd he was walking about.

A third case (17), a servant girl, aged 20, who was affected with permanent mitral disease owing to a previous attack, was admitted on the fifth day of her illness with severe joint affection, the heart being rapid and its sounds loud. Next day its action was very tumultuous, its impulse was strong, and its sounds were ill-defined, loud, and harsh. Leeches were applied to the chest, and the bleeding from one of the bites could not be restrained. On the 3rd the sounds of the heart were softer; on the 13th the first sound was more rough, on the 16th the impulse was very much diffused, and a murmur was audible over the front of the heart, and next day friction sound was heard over that region and Pericarditis in a severe form was fully established. After this the heart's action became irregular and intermittent, and she looked and felt anxious and depressed. A long, severe and varying illness followed. On the 55th day she seemed to be sinking, though she thought herself better. On the 58th day she kept nothing on her stomach, but on the 59th she felt better and looked much brighter. Small-pox, however, then in the wards, declared itself on the 62nd day, and on the 63rd she died.

In the first and second of these cases the heart continued to act with increased force during the period of the onset of the Pericarditis; but in the first of them this condition gave way after the application of leeches to irregular action of the heart, which lasted for eighteen days. In seven or eight other cases the impulse of the heart was strong during the early period of the inflammation of the exterior of the heart. As a rule, however, the impulse of the heart was feeble when first observed during the attack of Pericarditis. The condition of the impulse of the heart during Pericarditis will, however, be considered under its proper heading.

If we look at these cases, and especially the first and second of them; combine with them the six others already given in which Pericarditis followed closely upon a relapse in the joint affection, brought on often by getting up too soon; and add to these the relation that existed in my cases of acute rheumatism, between the severity of the joint affection and the presence, character, and severity of the heart affection, the joint affection being slight in the majority of cases without signs of endocarditis, severe in the majority of cases with simple endocarditis, and still more severe in the great majority of cases with Pericarditis and endocarditis; the severity of the heart affection corresponding, as a rule, with the severity of the joint affection; we must, I consider, conclude that we have here not a mere lifeless chain of passive links, but a living succession of active events, one giving birth to the other. Exposure to cold and wet, combined with undue labour or exertion, give the first impulse,—the start, to the affection of the joints. When the joint affection is severe, it may call forth excessive labour or even tumultuous action of the heart. In acute rheumatism, inflammation attacks the fibrous structures, especially if those structures are unduly strained, and the increased action of the heart may therefore, I consider, induce inflammation of the fibrous tissues of that organ, such inflammation being proportioned in severity to the augmented action of the heart.

This interesting subject derives larger illustration from the influence, already considered, of *sex, age, and occupation* in the production of acute rheumatism, accompanied, in proportion to the severity of the affection of the joints, by inflammation of the heart within and without. I need only here again refer to the large number of young female servants, in whom the ends and shafts of the bone are as yet only united by cartilage, who are attacked by acute rheumatism in a severe form; and the very large proportion in which those cases have endocarditis or Pericarditis, or both, the heart being subject, in those overworked young women, to undue action and palpitation.

In illustration of the influence of over-action of the heart in producing inflammation of the interior and the exterior of that organ, I
shall give here a brief summary of the influence of local injury,
scarlet fever, chorea, abscess, and general illness in the production of
acute rheumatism with endocarditis and Pericarditis, including those
cases of acute rheumatism in which a relapse of the joint affection,
followed by Pericarditis, was induced by the too early use of the
limbs, when the recovery was almost but not quite perfect.

Two influences usually combine to produce acute rheumatism; one,
exposure to wet and cold; the other, the *over-use* of certain limbs and
joints. The part immediately in use is usually the part first attacked,
while the joints that take the greatest share in the permanent
labour of the patient are generally those visited by the disease with
the greatest severity and duration. Thus, among the coachmen
admitted under my care, one was first attacked in the right thumb,
the knees being afterwards affected; another was seized badly in the
right arm, and then in the left; a third in the wrist and hands; and
a fourth in the hands, and especially the middle finger, the arms, and
then the knees, the affection of the fingers being obstinate; in a fifth
the back and hips were the seat of pain; and in the sixth the ankles,
knees, hands, and hips were all involved. If we take the carpenters,
we find that one of them was attacked in the arms, wrists, and
elbows; another, who was in search of work, in the arms, back,
ankles, and knees; and a third was seized, when walking, with pain in
the knees, the ankles, shoulders and arms being afterwards affected.
Young female servants, for to them I must here again refer, who
usually work too hard, whose joints are not yet perfect, being still
in a state of active growth, are for the most part first attacked in
the feet and ankles, that is to say, the parts that more immediately
tread the ground. The knees usually then suffer, or perhaps earlier,
at the same time as the feet and ankles; and afterwards the wrists,
hands, arms and shoulders, in succession, share in the affection. The
knees, which generally bear not only the internal pressure of standing,
but also the external pressure of kneeling when at work, are, as a
rule, more constantly and deeply affected, and for a longer period,
than any other joint. The effect of past labour is, so to speak,
stored up in the knees, which are therefore in these cases more affected
in acute rheumatism than any other joint.

Under the combined influence, then, of exposure and overwork,
rheumatic inflammation is set up in the joints, and under the combined influence of the disease thus established, and overwork of the
heart, rheumatic inflammation is established in that organ.

In a small but important group of my cases, acute rheumatism
followed *local injury.* The first of these, a stonemason, fell from a
scaffold on his back. He had pain in his back and legs, and could
not stand. On the 5th day he had a profuse sour perspiration, and
his finger and elbow-joints were red, swollen, and painful. The hips,
knees, and shoulders were afterwards attacked, and he probably had

endocarditis, the first sound being prolonged, while the second was followed by a soft murmur. The second patient was admitted under Mr. Lane's care for a slight injury, and was attacked on the fourth day with pain in the chest and inflammation of the wrist and ankles. On the 7th he was transferred to my charge with acute rheumatism, mitral murmur, and Pericarditis. A third patient, a dustman, hurt his back by carrying a sack of flour. The pain in the back was increased by his getting wet; and this was followed by acute rheumatism. A fourth patient was attacked with the disease in the wrists 32 days after breaking his leg. A fifth came in with acute rheumatism five days after leaving the surgical ward; and a sixth, who was admitted with endocarditis and transient Pericarditis, had received a kick in the groin five weeks previously, and since then had been subject to pain in the loins. In some of these cases the disease appeared to be directly, and in others to be indirectly, caused by local injury.

These cases and others given below are allied to those previously given, in which the *too early use of a limb*, during the period of convalescence from acute rheumatism, produced inflammation in the used joint, a *relapse* of the affection in the other joints, endocarditis and Pericarditis, ending in permanent crippling of the valves of the heart. The whole of these results, the latter of them so permanently injurious, started from the renewed focus of the disease in the single joint thus affected for the second time.

Through what means is this diffusion and transmission of the disease effected? Is it by a blood poison? Is it by a change in the fibrous structures of the limbs and the heart? Or is it by reflex influences, transmitted through the afferent nerves, locally acted upon in the inflamed joint or injured part, and sent back through the vaso-motor or other nerves distributed to the fibrous structures of the joints and the heart? The local character of the injury inducing this general effect, and the quickness with which the effect is induced, would appear to forbid the material agency of either blood poison or change in the tissues; and would tend to throw us upon the transmission of influences through the nerves for an explanation of these remarkable effects,—effects not less remarkable, but rather more so, that they are open to daily observation; or must we look for some other explanation than any of these here suggested?

We cannot, however, limit ourselves to the points of view just sketched in our inquiry into that many-sided disease, acute rheumatism, with its attendant inflammation of the heart; and I would here briefly state the other influences that have been apparently at work in the origin of the disease, besides overwork and exposure on the one hand, and local injury on the other.

In three of my patients the disease was associated with *scarlet fever*, one of whom had Pericarditis in the hospital, one out of it. The latter was the son of a medical friend, who detected symptoms of acute rheumatism just as the scarlet fever was declaring itself, and by which the acute rheumatism was suspended. When, however, the eruption had ceased and desquamatiou was going on, endocarditis and Pericarditis, the offspring of the original rheumatism, declared them-selves. This case did well, and though a mitral murmur existed for some time, it at length disappeared. In the two other cases, acute rheumatism followed a chill caught by too early exposure after the scarlet fever had disappeared.

In several of my cases, *chorea* has given place to acute rheumatism or the reverse. In one patient, a girl, acute rheumatism passed into chorea, for which she was admitted. After a time the choreal move-ments were for a period suspended by the renewal of acute rheumatism. I do not here speak of that terrible complication, the occurrence of serious local choreal and tetaniform symptoms in connection with rheumatic endocarditis and Pericarditis, complications to which I shall soon refer.

In three patients the acute rheumatism was preceded by recent *abscess,* in one of them in the axilla, in another in the perineum, and in a third in the tonsil; and in a fourth case, abscess in the neck existed sometime before the supervention of the rheumatism.

Sore throat appeared for from one day to three weeks before the occurrence of acute rheumatism in thirteen cases, including the case of abscess in the tonsil just quoted. Two of these patients had Pericarditis; three had simple endocarditis; in three endocarditis was threatened; and five gave no sign of heart affection.

In eleven patients, *pain in the chest,* sometimes accompanied by cough, existed for from one day to two or even three weeks before the developement of acute rheumatism.

I refrain from pursuing this important collateral subject farther in this place.

X.—PAIN.

I.—PAIN OVER THE REGION OF THE HEART AND PERICARDIUM.

Pain over the region of the heart and pericardium showed itself in six different ways: 1. Over the front of the organ; 2. On pressure at the same place; 3. In the Epigastrium, chiefly on pressure; 4. Over the back of the heart, when it was excited by swallowing and by eructation; 5. After eating; and, 6. Pain shooting through the heart, evidently anginal in character.

1. The pain over the front of the heart extended usually from the right of the sternum at its lower two-thirds to the left nipple; it was more or less continuous, and was complained of in three-fourths of the cases (48 in 63). This pain came on in one-fourth of the patients affected with it (9) before the friction sound was heard, and in a greater number (16, including 5 in which the pain and the friction sound were both present on the day of admission) at the time that the sound was first audible. In a few instances (7) it was felt soon after the appearance of the rubbing sound. It was either relieved, suspended, or removed by the application of leeches. It

was complained of in about one-fourth of the cases (8) at the time the effusion was at its height, but usually relief, which was permanent, came at that time. In two instances (15, 51) of relapse, the second, and in one (44*a*) even a third, wave of increase of pericardial effusion was preceded by a second, and in one even a third attack of pain over the heart ; but in three cases the pain came late in the period of the relapse, and when the effusion was declining. In scarcely any instance did the pain over the heart continue during the whole period of the duration of the friction sound, and in only two or three of the cases did it last over the first half of that period. When the pain comes on with the first blush of the inflammation on the surface of the heart, before it has spread to the inner surface of the pericardial sac, and before friction sound is audible, it may be inferred that it is seated in the sentient nerves distributed to the surface of the heart. When, however, the pain strikes over the heart at the same time as the appearance of the friction sound, and still more when it comes on at a later period, it is generally, I believe, seated in the pericardial sac, and especially in the pleura covering the sac.

The accompanying table gives a *résumé* of the period of the occurrence of pain over the region of the heart in relation to the time of the appearance of friction sound in the cases of Pericarditis (see page 225).

2. If the pain over the heart is increased or excited by pressure over the region of the organ, it may, with an approach to certainty, be attributed to inflammation of the pleura, especially if the pain on pressure is complained of, not before, but at the time of or after the first presence of friction sound.

Pain on pressure over the heart occurred in one-fourth (14 in 63) of the whole number of cases affected with acute rheumatism, and in one-third of those who suffered from continuous pain in the region of the heart (11 in 38). In two only of these cases was the pain excited by pressure before the friction sound was audible, and in these the pain was probably excited over the surface of the inflamed heart. In one-half of the patients the pain on pressure and the rubbing sound appeared on the same day, and in the rest the pain was preceded by the friction sound. In most or all of these cases, the pleura covering the pericardial sac, or the fibrous structure of the sac itself, was the probable seat of the suffering (see Tables, pages 225, 226).

In one-half of those patients (7 in 14) the skin over the region of the pericardium was tender and sensitive, so much so indeed, in some instances, as to forbid the slightest manipulation over the chest, and to make a proper examination of the heart impossible until this exquisite sensibility was subdued by the application of leeches or of belladonna liniment with chloroform.

In the majority of the cases the pain was deeper than the skin, and was not excited unless actual pressure was made. In three of the patients the pain was only felt when pressure was made over the region of the heart; but in all the others continuous pain already existed over that region, and was intensified by the pressure. In one or two instances the suffering and distress over the heart were so great as to drown all other complaints; but in three others, as I have just said, the pain was only brought into play when pressure was exerted. Between these two opposite extremes, there was every shade in the extent, variety, and constancy of the pain.

Period of the occurrence of Pain over the region of the Heart and Pericardium in relation to the time of the appearance of Friction Sound in cases of Rheumatic Pericarditis.

Pain over the region of heart and pericardium, including pain over the epigastrium.	Cases.
Pain over heart ♡ and friction sound on day of admission	5
Pain over epigastrium and friction sound on day of (in one day after) admission, included above . .	4
Pain over heart ♡ before admission, friction sound on admission . .	4
Pain over heart ♡ before appearance of friction sound	9
Pain over epigastrium before appearance of friction sound, included above	2
Pain over heart ♡ and friction sound occurring on same day . . .	11
Pain over epigastrium, and friction sound occurring on same day, *not* included above	3
Pain over heart ♡ coming on after friction sound had been observed	7
Pain over epigastrium coming on after friction sound had been observed, *not* included above . .	2
Ditto, included above	8
Pain over heart ♡ appearing shortly before relapse (renewed increase of fluid in the pericardium) *not* included above . .	1
Ditto, included above	1
Pain over epigastrium before relapse .	1
Pain over heart ♡ late in period of relapse, *not* included above . .	1
Ditto, included above	2
Pain over heart ♡ at the time of acme of Pericarditis	8
Pain over heart ♡ shortly before time of acme of Pericarditis . . .	2
Pain of epigastrium at time of acme of Pericarditis	6
Ditto before acme of Pericarditis . .	4
Ditto after acme of Pericarditis . .	4

Pain on pressure over the region of the heart ♡	→⇉	→	↓ or ⇊	No Endocarditis.	Total.
Appearing before friction sound .	1	...	1	...	2
Appearing same time as friction sound	4	2	...	1	7
Appearing after first indication of friction sound	2	1	1	...	4
Appearing after friction sound had ceased . .	1	...	...	...	1
	8	3	2	1	14

Explanation of Symbols.

← tricuspid regurgitation.
→ mitral regurgitation.
↓ aortic regurgitation.
→↓ { mitral-aortic regurgitation.

Table showing the proportion in which Pain was present over the region of the Heart ♡, in the Side, and in the Chest, in 326 cases of Acute Rheumatism.

(This table is continued on the following two pages.)

CASES WITH PERICARDITIS.

Explanation of Symbols.	Cases with tricuspid murmur, valves previously healthy.	Cases with mitral, aortic, and mitral-aortic murmur.			Cases with previous valve-disease.	Cases in which Endocarditis was absent, or doubtful.	Total cases of Pericarditis.	Total cases with special conditions.
		I. Murmur established on recovery from acute rheumatism.	II. Murmur lessening on recovery.	III. Murmur disappearing on recovery.				
Total of each class of cases	3	16 ...	8 ...	19 ...	8 ...	9 ...	63 ...	...
Cases with pain over the region of the heart ♡	2	12 ...	3 ...	11 ...	5 ...	5 ...	38 ...	38
Pain on pressure over the heart {included above	...	... 5	... 1	... 3	1 ...	... 1	... 11}	14
{not included above	1	1 ...	...	...	1 ...	...	3 ..}	
Pain shooting through the heart, included above	...	... 2	...|...	... 1	... 3	...	6	6
Pain in the epigastric space {included above	...	... 9	...|...	... 4	... 1	...	... 14}	16
(Pain seated in pericardium) {not included above	...	1 ...	...|...	...	...	1...	2 ...}	
Pain in the abdomen. Pain not noted in epigastrium {included above	...	... 1	...|...	... 1	... 2	2	5 ...	5
Pain at back of pericardium, from swallowing {included above	...	... 2	... 1	... 3	... 1	...|...	... 7}	14 or 13
Difficulty in swallowing, with out note of pain {included above	...	... 3	... 1	... 2 or 1	...|...	... 1	... 7 or 6}	
Pain in back of pericardium, from retching {included above	...	... 1	...	...	...|...	...	... 2	1
Pain in back of pericardium, from eructation {not included above	...	...	...	...	1...	...|...	1 ...	1
TOTAL cases with pain in the region of the heart ♡ and pericardium, including the epigastrium	3	14 ...	3 ...	11 ...	7 ...	6 ...	44 ...	...
Pain of side {included above	...	... 10	... 1	... 8	7 ...	... 1	... 27}	31
{not included above	...	1 ...	1 ...	1 ...	...|...	1...	4 ...}	
Of these the pain was in the left side in	...	7 ...	2 ...	4 ...	4 ...	2 ...	19 ...	
„ „ right side in	...	1 ...	...|...	3 ...	1 ...	...|...	5 ...	31
„ „ both in right and left sides in	...	3 ...	...|...	2 ...	1 ...	...|...	6 ...	
„ „ of uncertain situation in	...	...	...|...	...	1...	...|...	1 ...	
Pain of chest {included above	...	... 9	... 1	... 9	... 5	... 4	... 28}	30
{not included above	...	...	...|...	1 ...	1 ...	...|...	2 ..}	
Leeches to region of heart, without note of pain {included above	...	... 2	...|...	...	... 1	...|...	... 3}	6
{not included above	...	...	1 ...	2 ...	...|...	1...	4 ..}	
Tightness of chest, without note of pain over the heart {included above	...	...	...|...	... 1	...|...	...|...	... 1}	2
{not included above	...	...	...|...	1 ...	...	...|...	1 ..}	
TOTAL of the above	...	15 ...	5 ...	16 ...	8 ...	8 ...	55 ...	...
No note of pain over heart, side, or chest {not included above	...	1 ...	3 ...	3 ...	...|...	1...	8 ...	...
GRAND TOTAL	3	16 ...	8 ...	19 ...	8 ...	9 ...	63 ...	...

Symbols in the explanation of symbols column:
← tricuspid regurgitation.
→ mitral regurgitation.
↓ aortic regurgitation.
→↓ mitral-aortic regurgitation.
⇢ mitral valve-disease.
⇢↓ mitral-aortic valve-disease.

ble (continued from p. 226) showing the proportion in which Pain was present over the

	Cases with prolonged first sound.	Cases with tricuspid murmur.	CASES WITH ENDOCARDITIS.						
			Cases with mitral, aortic, and mitral-aortic murmurs.						
			Cases in which the valves were previously healthy.						
			Cases with mitral murmur.			Cases with aortic murmur.		Cases with mitral-aortic murmur.	
			I. Murmur established on recovery from acute rheumatism.	II. Murmur lessening on recovery.	III. Murmur disappearing on recovery.	I. Murmur established on recovery.	III. Murmur disappearing on recovery.	I. Murmur established on recovery.	III. Murmur disappearing on recovery.
Total of each class of cases . . .	2	13	18	11	24	5	5	5	2
a over the region of the heart . .	1	4	7	2	4	...	2	1	1
a on pressure included above . .	...	...	...	1	...	...	...	...	...
ver the heart { not included above	...	...	...	1	...	...	...	...	...
in shooting } included above . .	...	...	...	...	2	...	...	...	...
rough heart									
n in epigas- { included above. .	...	...	2	...	...	...	...	...	...
rium . . . . { not included above	...	...	...	...	1	...	...	...	...
a in abdomen included above. .	...	...	...	...	...	...	...	...	...
ot noted in									
pigastrium . . } not included above	...	...	...	1	...	...	...	...	...
a in pericardium } included above	...	...	...	...	...	...	...	...	...
rom swallowing . .									
allowing difficult, } included above	...	...	...	...	...	...	...	...	...
a note of pain . .									
a in pericardium } included above	...	...	...	...	...	...	...	...	...
rom retching . .									
a in pericar-									
ium from eruc- } not included above	...	...	...	...	...	...	...	...	...
tion									
TOTAL cases with pain over heart } and pericardium	1	4	7	3	5	...	2	1	1
la of side. . . { included above .	...	2	1	3	2	1	2	2	...
{ not included above	...	...	...	...	3	...	...	...	...
these, pain in left side in . . .	...	3	...	1	4	2	2	2	...
" " right side in . . .	...	1	...	1	1	...	...	1	...
" " right and left sides in	...	...	...	...	...	...	...	...	...
" " of uncertain situation in	...	...	...	...	1	...	1	...	...
ia of chest . . { included above	...	1	5	...	2	...	...	...	...
{ not included above	1	1	2	2	3	1	...	...	...
aches over heart included above .	...	...	1	2	...	...	...	...	...
to note of pain { not included above	...	...	1	...	1	...	...	...	...
ptness of chest, included above .	...	...	...	...	...	...	...	...	...
a note of pain } not included above	...	...	...	...	...	...	...	...	...
ver heart . .									
Total of the above	2	7	11	5	11	2	4	3	1
a note of pain } not included above	0	6	7	6	13	3	1	2	1
ver heart . .									
AND TOTAL	2	13	18	11	24	5	5	5	2

region of the Heart ♡, in the Side, and in the Chest in 326 cases of Acute Rheumatism.

CASES WITH ENDOCARDITIS.									Cases with Endocarditis threatened or probable.	Cases with no indication of Endocarditis.	GRAND TOTAL of cases of Acute Rheumatism. (For cases of Pericarditis see p. 226).
Cases with mitral, aortic, and mitral-aortic murmurs.								Total cases of Endocarditis.			
Cases in which the valves were previously healthy.				Cases with previous valve-disease.							
Combined cases with mitral, aortic, and mitral-aortic murmurs.			Total cases with valves previously healthy.	Cases with			Total with previous valve-disease.				
I. Murmur established on recovery.	II. Murmur lessening on recovery.	III. Murmur disappearing on recovery.		Mitral valve-disease.	Aortic valve-disease.	Mitral-aortic valve-disease.					
28	11	31	70	9	3	11	23	108	76	79	326
8	2	7	17	3	2	3	8	30	14	...	82
1	1	...	2	...	...	...	...	2	...	...	5
...	1	...	1	...	...	...	...	1	1	...	7
...	...	...	...	...	...	...	...	1	...	...	7
1	...	1	1	...	...	1	...	1	4	1	8
...	...	...	...	...	...	...	...	...	3	...	8
...	...	...	...	...	...	...	...	...	...	2	3
...	...	...	...	...	...	...	...	...	...	...	7
...	...	...	...	...	...	...	...	...	...	...	7 or 6
...	...	...	...	...	...	...	...	...	...	...	1
...	...	...	...	...	...	...	...	...	...	...	
8	3	8	19	3	2	3	8	32	19	1 or 0	96
4	3	4	7	1	1	1	5	12	12	2	30
4	1	5	10	...	...	1	1	14	6	1	46
1	1	1	3	2	...	2	2	6	7	...	18
...	...	...	2	...	...	1	3	3	2	2	11
...	1	1	7	...	1	...	3	3	2	...	8
3	2	3	8	2	1	5	8	18	2	2	24
1	...	1	2	...	...	...	...	2	...	...	6
...	...	...	...	...	...	...	...	...	...	...	1
...	...	...	...	...	...	...	...	...	...	...	
16	5	16	37	6	3	9	18	64	33	5	157
12	6	15	33	3	0	2	5	44	43	74	169
28	11	31	70	9	3	11	23	108	76	79	326

100 90 80 70 60 50 40 30 20 10

GRAND TOTAL cases of Acute Rheumatism. 46

Total cases without sign of Endocarditis. 7

Total cases of Endocarditis threatened or probable. 44

Total cases of Simple Endocarditis. 57

Total cases of Pericarditis. 79

Cases with pain of heart, side, and chest.

326 cases.	152 pain ▽. side, chest, side, chest.
79 cases.	7 pain ▽. side, chest, side, chest.
76 cases.	33 pain ▽. side, chest, side, chest.
106 cases.	62 pain ▽. side, chest, side, chest.
63 cases.	50 pain ▽. side, chest, side, chest.

Proportion per cent. of cases with pain of heart, side, and chest.

GRAND TOTAL cases of Acute Rheumatism. 30

Total cases without indication of Endocarditis. 1·3 or 0

Total cases of Endocarditis threatened or probable. 25

Total cases of Simple Endocarditis. 30

Total cases of Pericarditis. 70

Cases in which Endocarditis was absent or doubtful. 90·6

326 cases.	96 pain ▽.
79 cases.	1 pain epi-gastrium.
76 cases.	19 pain ▽.
106 cases.	32 pain ▽.
63 cases.	44 pain ▽.
9 cases.	6 pain ▽.

Proportion per cent. of cases with pain over the region of the heart.

Cases of Pericarditis.

Cases with Endocarditis.

Cases with mitral, aortic, or mitral-aortic murmur.

Cases in which heart was previously healthy.

Cases with quiescene valve-disease.	87·3	8 cases. / 7 pain ▽.
III. Cases in which murmur diminished or appeared on recovery.	58	19 cases. / 11 pain.
II. Cases in which murmur les-sened on re-covery.	41	8 cases / 3 pain ▽.
I. Cases in which murmur was established.	87·5	16 cases. / 14 pain ▽.

100 90 80 70 60 50 40 30 20 10

3. Pain was present over the epigastric region, frequently increased and sometimes induced by pressure, in one-fourth of the patients with rheumatic pericarditis (16 in 63), and in nearly two-fifths of those who suffered from pain over the region of the heart (14 in 38). It would appear curious, at first sight, that pain over the pit of the stomach should be a marked feature in so many cases of pericarditis. When, however, we consider that in health the lower boundary of the heart is situated behind the upper third of the ensiform cartilage, and that the pericardial sac, when distended with fluid in Pericarditis, dips downwards so that its lower boundary may be on a level with the point of that cartilage, or perhaps even below it, we see how natural it is that pain should be excited by pressure over the epigastric region (see Tables, pages 225–229).

This epigastric pain appeared in only two cases before the supervention of friction sound. Those two patients, however, suffered from a renewal of the pain after the commencement of the rubbing sound, consequently in every case the suffering over the pit of the stomach was complained of either at the time of the first observation of the friction sound (7 in 16, including 4 in which the pain and the friction sound were both present on the day of admission), or from one to several days later (9 in 16).

In one-third of the cases (6) the epigastric pain appeared at the time when the effusion into the pericardium was at its height, and when the sac bulged downwards into the epigastric space; and in four of them it was complained of before, and in four of them after, the effusion had reached its acme.

In all these cases the disease had reached a stage in which the heart was separated by the intervention of fluid from the floor of the pericardial sac, which is formed by the central tendon of the diaphragm. The pain in the epigastric region in these cases, especially when it is increased or excited by pressure, is therefore seated not in the surface of the heart, but in the lower portion of the pericardial sac. It is natural to suppose that the branches of the phrenic nerve must be the immediate seat of the pain, but the exact anatomical distribution of the phrenic nerve has not yet been ascertained. These questions suggest themselves: is this pain seated in the fibrous tissue, the pericardial surface, or the peritoneal surface of the affected diaphragmatic portion of the sac?

Peritonitis affecting the central tendon of the diaphragm has been noticed in few or no fatal cases of Pericarditis, but indirect evidence of its existence has been supplied in rare instances by the discovery of partial adhesions of the spleen and liver to the diaphragm in cases with adherent pericardium. We may, however, I think, fairly infer that the pain on pressure below or at the side of the ensiform cartilage is in these cases due, not to peritonitis, but to inflammation of the fibrous structure and pericardial or inner surface of the central tendon of the diaphragm, where it forms the floor of the pericardial sac, and the lower and anterior portion of that sac.

The distribution of the nerves to the pericardium, like that of the phrenic nerve, has not yet been ascertained, and this interesting clinical question therefore invites the attention of the physiologist.

4. In three of the patients affected with rheumatic Pericarditis deep pain was felt between the shoulder-blades, and in one of them this pain was increased by the act of swallowing. Pain in the chest was excited in three cases by swallowing, and in two others it was complained of there after eating. Another patient complained that the ascent of wind from the stomach gave much pain over the posterior region of the heart. In all these instances, amounting to nine, the suffering must have been seated in the back of the inflamed pericardium, being either constant or induced by local pressure, due to swallowing or eructation. In several other cases it is stated that pain was seated in the back, but it is impossible to say, from this description, whether the pain was situated in or near the pericardium or lower down.

5. Pain and fulness after eating was complained of by one patient, and I think it likely that the suffering in this instance was excited by the pressure made by the distended stomach over the lower and back part of the pericardium.

We thus see that in a large proportion of my cases affected with rheumatic Pericarditis, pain was felt over the heart, frequently in front of the pericardial sac, and occasionally behind and below it, the pain being usually fixed, sometimes increased by pressure, and less often excited by it.

6. The heart itself was attacked with a shooting pain, more or less violent, associated either with faintness or failure in the action of the organ, and evidently anginal in character, in four of my patients affected with rheumatic Pericarditis.

In two of these cases the heart, already crippled by valvular disease, was attacked with inflammation within and without, but in the others the Pericarditis and endocarditis seized upon the virgin heart, the valves being previously healthy; one of these two cases proved fatal, and in the other valvular disease became established.

In the fatal case (4), a man, aged 27, a carpenter, a darting pain passed now and then from the heart to the right side on the day of his admission. This pain was relieved by leeches, the application of which was followed by faintness. On the 3rd his limbs started when he fell asleep; on the 6th he was seized with delirium and trembling; and on the 7th, the day of his death, he was noisy and restless, and was continually moving his lower jaw.

Another patient (15), a servant girl, suddenly became very faint on the evening of the 10th day, when she was suffering from a relapse of Pericarditis, and was attacked with great pain over the heart. This pain returned on the evening of the 12th, when it was also felt between the shoulders.

One (3) of the two remaining patients had old standing aortic and mitral disease, and suffered from pain over the region of the heart on the 10th day, when friction-sound appeared. On the 16th day, when the Pericarditis was at its height, when I was examining him, he cried out as if from pain, beginning over the stomach, and begged to be raised up, the dyspnœa becoming extreme, the face being flushed, the perspiration pouring off it, the lips somewhat livid, and his countenance being expressive of extreme anxiety. He was immediately raised up, and, having a towel placed behind him, was as it were slung in it, when he took a little port wine and fell asleep.

The other patient (17), a young woman, affected with old mitral disease, was attacked on the 17th day, when the Pericarditis was at its acme, with great pain over the sternum and the whole front of the chest, the pain passing through to the back. She ultimately died on the 63rd day, with small-pox, which attacked her when in a state of extreme exhaustion.

If we add to the cases in which there was continuous pain over the region of the heart (38), those others not so affected in which a, there was pain on pressure over the heart (3) ; b, pain over the epigastric region (2) ; and c, pain at the back of the pericardium on eructation (1); we find that in 44 of the 63 cases of Pericarditis, or in 70 per cent., there was pain over the heart or pericardium.

II.—Pleuritic Pain in the Side.

Pain in the side was complained of in one-half of the cases of rheumatic Pericarditis (31 in 63). Pain was present over the region of the heart and pericardium also in all but 4 of these patients. The pain was limited to the left side in 19 cases, and to the right in only 5, while it attacked both sides in 6 instances. There were, besides the pain, other symptoms or physical signs of pleurisy in all but seven of the patients thus affected.

Pleuritic friction sound was heard in nearly one-half of those cases (15 in 31) and in five others there was tenderness on percussion over the seat of pain. In a large proportion of the cases the pain was increased or excited by a deep breath (18 in 31), and in four of these it was catching. The pain was induced by coughing or laughing, stooping or moving in fourteen instances, and in three it was " pleuritic" or cutting.

The first complaint of pain in the side was made after the appearance of the friction sound in 19 of the 31 cases that suffered in this manner ; the pain and the friction sound appeared together in seven patients ; and the pain occurred before the friction sound in five. In one, of the five, and three of the seven patients just spoken of, the pain affected both sides, having appeared at a late period in one side, and at a period actually or comparatively early in the other.

The pleurisy that induced the pain in the side which came into play either with or after the friction sound, was due to two causes ; one the extension of the inflammation through the fibrous structure of the pericardium to the pleura covering it; the other, the occurrence of pulmonary apoplexy with its attendant pleurisy.

The more frequent appearance of the pain, and the greater spread of the pleurisy on the left side of the chest than the right, is, I conceive, due in many instances to the greater extent to which the inflamed pericardium occupies the left side of the chest than the right, and the great displacement backward of the left lung, and especially its lower lobe, by the distension of the pericardial sac. Perhaps the pressure of the distended pericardium on the left bronchus increases the tendency of the left lung to inflammation.

In one of the five patients that were seized with pain in the side before the supervention of the friction sound, the pain came on at the first onset of the disease, and at the same time as the affection of the joints three days before admission. I think it likely that this case was attacked with pleurisy and acute rheumatism affecting the joints at the same time , the pleurisy being, however, rheumatic in its nature, like the joint affection in this instance, and like the Pericarditis in the other cases. We may have, in short, in these cases, rheumatic pleurisy, just as we may have rheumatic Pericarditis.

In another of these cases (20), the patient, a married woman, aged 24, was attacked with pain in the joints the day after being wet through, and a week before admission. She came in with very severe pain in the left side, which had existed for some days, and which was somewhat reduced by leeching. On the 6th day after admission she suffered much in the left side, and a pleuritic friction sound was audible just below the seat of pain. Friction sound from Pericarditis was heard over the region of the heart for the first time on the same day. In this case the pleurisy preceded the Pericarditis by ten days.

Pain in the side was, in proportion, twice as frequent in Pericarditis usually accompanied with endocarditis as in simple endocarditis; one-fourth of the latter (26 in 108), and as we have just seen, one-half of the former (31 in 63) being thus affected. A similar proportion of such cases existed among the patients who were threatened with endocarditis, of whom rather more than one-fourth were affected with pain in the side (17 in 63). None of the thirteen cases classed under the heading of "probable endocarditis" suffered from pain in the side, and only three of those who were attacked with acute rheumatism and had no endocarditis, complained of pain in that region (3 in 71). The pain more frequently attacked the left side than the right in the cases of endocarditis in the proportion of 14 to 6 ; but among those threatened with endocarditis, the two sides were affected in nearly equal numbers, the right side being rather more often attacked than the left in the proportion of 7 to 6.

III.—"Pain in the Chest."

"Pain in the chest" was present in 30 of the 63 cases of rheumatic Pericarditis. The pain thus described is so indefinite in situation—that it may be seated either at the centre of the chest or at its sides, either over the pericardium or the pleura. Fortunately, to guide us to the actual seat of suffering, the "pain in the chest" was attended in all but two instances with other pain, either over the heart, or in the side, or in both regions. Thus in all but four of the thirty cases, pain was present over the region of the heart or the epigastrium; in all but nine, in the side; and in one-half of them (16 in 30) it was situated both over the heart and in the side.

In fully one-half of the cases (17 in 30) the pain in the chest was itself associated with symptoms of pleurisy, in the way of being increased or caused by deep breathing, or coughing, or moving, or it was a cutting pain, or it was accompanied, in two instances only, by pleuritic friction sound. There were symptoms of pleurisy in eight of the nine cases in which pain of the chest was not associated with pain of the side, and I think those eight cases may be added to the 31 in which pain in the side was actually present, thus bringing their number up to 39 in 63 cases of rheumatic Pericarditis. On the other hand, there were four cases with pain in the chest in which there was no notice of pain in the heart, and I think that these four cases may probably be added to those in which the presence of cardiac pain is stated; thus bringing the total number so affected up from 44 to 48 in 63.

Eleven patients suffered from pain in the chest, either previously to admission or before friction sound was audible. In the greater number of these I think that the pain was seated over the region of the heart, and was not due to pleurisy. And I find, giving strength to this view, that in all of these but two, pain was described as being present over the heart.

It would be futile to compare the relative frequency of pain in the chest in Pericarditis, and in the other various groups of cases in acute rheumatism, since to do so would be to compare unlike conditions under the same name. But it will be instructive to compare the proportion of cases attacked with pain over the heart, in the side and in the chest, combined together, with those in which there was no such pain, in cases of acute rheumatism with Pericarditis and endocarditis, and with and without simple endocarditis. The accompanying table, and graphic scheme, will show this comparison, the one by study, the other at a glance (see pages 225–229).

In those affected with Pericarditis, most of whom had endocarditis also, four-fifths had pain in the heart, chest, or side, and one-fifth had no such pain; in those with endocarditis nearly six-tenths had such pain and over four-tenths had none; in those threatened with endocarditis, less than one-half had pain, and more than one-half had none ; and in those who gave no sign of endocarditis only one-tenth suffered from this kind of pain, and nine-tenths had no internal pain, thus nearly reversing the proportion that we find in cases affected with Pericarditis.

XI. Irregularity and Failure of the Action of the Heart. Faintness.

We have already seen that in two of the patients, in whom the action of the heart, which was powerful and tumultuous before the occurrence of Pericarditis, became at a later period feeble, irregular, and intermittent, this state being accompanied by a look of great anxiety and depression. We have also seen that the four patients who were attacked with pain shooting through the heart, experienced faintness or failure in the action of the organ (p. 231).

In the following case (13) death took place from syncope. A female servant, aged 25, came in on the 7th day of her illness, with difficult, hurried breathing, which was relieved when she was raised, great pain in her chest, cough, which had continued from the 2nd day of the attack, mucous rattle, slightly rusty phlegm, a sensation of choking, difficulty in swallowing, and great anxiety. The joint affection was slight, and apparently limited to the shoulder. Pericarditis, with friction sound and great effusion, was at its height. She was very ill throughout, perspiration being profuse, the voice husky, the face flushed and anxious, and breathing laborious. Her face was brighter, and she breathed with ease from the 7th day to the 13th, when her appetite was improving ; but at two hours after midnight, in the early morning of the 14th, when attempting to turn on her side, she became quite pulseless, her face turned livid, and she frothed at the mouth. After taking some wine she gradually recovered. An hour later the sounds of the heart were muffled, and the rubbing noise, which had been harsh, loud and dry on the previous day, could not be detected. In another hour she had a similar attack, in which she died. There were 18 ounces of fluid in the pericardium, the heart was covered with honeycomb lymph, and there were patches of pulmonary apoplexy in the left upper lobe.

Faintness occurred as a symptom in several of the cases, but in none, besides those alluded to and that just given, did it appear in a threatening form.

Although, as we have already seen, in a few cases the action of the heart was unusually strong during the early period of Pericarditis, yet even then, or rather when the attack was first observed, the impulse of the heart was more frequently feeble than strong, and this was especially the case during the remaining course of the affection.

Feebleness, irregularity, and even failure of the heart's action, may evidently be induced in these cases by several influences working separately or together, and by the exhaustion of the nervous and general forces induced by the accumulated effect of those influences, all tending to lower and exhaust the power of the heart, and even, as in the case just told, to arrest its action. Among such influences are, the pain and inflammation of the joints when severe, extensive, and prolonged ; the pain in the heart and pericardium, the side, and the chest; the existence of endocarditis with its immediate and remote consequences; the presence of previous valvular disease ; the grave influences exerted by great distension of the pericardium, which,—by compressing the venæ cavæ, the pulmonary veins, both auricles, and the aorta, impedes the supply of blood through the venæ cavæ and pulmonary veins to both sides of the heart, and through the aorta to the system, and causes the accumulation of blood in the lungs,—by pressing upon the bifurcation of the trachea and the left bronchus, and by lessening the size of the lungs, seriously embarrasses respiration—and by compressing the œsophagus, renders deglutition difficult ; and the existence of congestion of the lungs, of pulmonary apoplexy and pleurisy, due to one or more of the causes just named.

Besides these, there are two important influences that may induce feebleness, irregularity, and perhaps even failure of the action of the heart ; one, the inflammation of the superficial muscular fibres of the heart ; the other, the inflammation of the nerves situated at the surface of the heart and great vessels. Inflammation of the superficial muscular fibres of the heart, which sometimes occurs in pericarditis, paralyses the affected fibres. This paralysis of the inflamed fibres must in itself embarrass the action of the heart, especially when we consider that those superficial fibres turn inwards by a double entrance at the apex, to become the innermost fibres of the left ventricle, where they end in the papillary muscles of the mitral valve. But this influence cannot be limited to those fibres, but must extend in a varying degree to the other muscular structures of the organ so as to interfere with the exercise of their power ; just as inflammation of certain limited fibres of a voluntary muscle, say the biceps, while it paralyses those fibres, interferes with the exercise of the whole muscle.

The many and important nerves situated at the surface of the heart and great vessels may be more or less involved in the inflammation affecting those parts in Pericarditis. That accurate physiologist, Dr. Burdon Sanderson, remarks, "that nothing is known either as to the anatomical distribution of nervous elements in the hearts of mammalia, or as to the functions which they perform." [1] When, however, we consider that electrical or other excitation of the vagus retards the contractions of the heart, and if it is strong enough, arrests the organ in diastole, and in the dog, lessens arterial pressure, while division of the vagi produces acceleration of the contractions of the heart, and in the dog, increased arterial pressure ; that the lower cervical ganglion of the sympathetic exercises an accelerating influence, not always in action, on the contractions of the heart ; and that in the frog, the ganglion cells contained in the heart are the springs of its automatic

[1] Handbook for the Physiological Laboratory, p. 263.

movement; and that the surface of the heart is rich in nerves connected with the vagi, the sympathetic and the intrinsic ganglia of the heart, and that those nerves are therefore locally affected by the inflammation in Pericarditis; we must, I consider, conclude that this affection exercises in such cases an important influence, either to stimulate or to injure those nerves and so to accelerate or retard the contractions of the heart, to excite or, more frequently, depress the powers of the organ, and to increase or diminish arterial pressure. It is for the physiologist to ascertain, by direct experiment, the effect of the inflammation or irritation of those nerves on the functions of the heart.

It is right that I should mention another depressing influence on the action of the heart in Pericarditis, accidentally due, in the case about to be referred to, to treatment. In one case (17) already given at page 219, the loss of blood due to irrepressible hæmorrhage from a leech-bite seemed to produce serious irregularity of the action of the heart.

XII. Difficult and Quickened Respiration.

Respiration was disturbed to a marked degree in 49 of the 63 patients affected with rheumatic Pericarditis; it was slightly or not at all affected in 3, and in 11 its character was not recorded. The Pericarditis was severe in 2 only of the 11 cases in which the state of the respiration was not noticed, and in none of the 3 in which the breathing was but slightly affected; but the attack was severe in 37 of the 49 patients in whom the respiration was markedly disturbed.

The respiration was rendered difficult and quick by three or four local causes: first, in order of time, the inflammation of the heart, without and within, and of the pericardial sac, including the central tendon of the diaphragm, and the accompanying pain in the heart, the sac, and the diaphragm, with the consequent restraint imposed upon the movements of the latter; after this, the distension of the pericardial sac with fluid, which greatly enhanced the severity of the symptoms; and, at a later period, the supervention of pleurisy with its attendant permanent pain and stitch in the side, or of pulmonary apoplexy, often accompanied by pleurisy. The breathing is hurried, and rendered laborious by distension of the pericardium, often so as to demand a raised posture, owing to two causes, one, the encroachment of the swollen sac upon both lungs, and especially upon the lower lobe of the left one; the other, the direct pressure, backwards and upwards, exerted by the fluid in the tense pericardium on the trachea at its bifurcation, and on the left bronchus, a pressure that is materially relieved by the erect posture, and still more by the forward attitude which throws the volume of the liquid forwards and downwards towards the diaphragm and away from the trachea.

There was great distress, difficulty, and rapidity of respiration in 24 of the cases of rheumatic Pericarditis, and in one-half of them it is recorded that the patient was raised or propped up. The attack was fatal in 4 of those patients, and severe in 18, being very severe in 11.

One of those cases (3), a sawyer, aged 26, who had aortic and mitral valve-disease of old standing, came in feeling low and anxious, and was delirious at night. On the 5th day he was better, the respirations being 20 in the minute; but on the 10th he had pain and friction sound over the heart, and the respirations rose to 30 in the minute. The dulness over the pericardium increased, and reached its acme on the 19th. On the 16th he was seized with extreme and urgent dyspnœa, which was relieved when he was raised. The respirations were 70 during the attack, and fell after it to 35; on the 18th they varied from 36 to 44, and on the 21st, when the pericardial dulness had greatly lessened, they had fallen to 28 in the minute.

A man (24), whose case I have already given, had Pericarditis with rubbing sound, on the 53rd day, the pericardial effusion being at its height on the 57th. On the 55th the respirations were 44 in the minute, and he had extreme difficulty in breathing, which was relieved by the upright posture. On the 58th the pericardial effusion had lessened, the respirations had fallen to 24, and he breathed easily in the recumbent posture.

Another patient (36), a servant girl, breathed 32 times in a minute on admission, as well as on the 7th day when leeches were applied over the region of the heart. On the 8th friction sound appeared, and the effusion was at its height next day, when the respirations were 52, and on the 10th her head and shoulders were propped up. On the 11th the effusion had lessened, and her breathings numbered 40. On the 14th there was pleuritic pain, followed by friction sound, and the respirations rose to 48; but on the 20th, when there was no pain in the chest, they had fallen to 24.

In the following case (38), a female servant, the breathing rose in frequency a second time during a second wave of increased pericardial effusion. On the 6th the respirations were 28 in the minute; on the 7th they were 40; on the 9th friction sound was heard over the heart, and on the 10th the pericardial dulness was at its height. On the 12th the effusion had lessened; she was in a raised position breathing more freely, 40 times in a minute; but on the 17th the fluid in the pericardium had again attained to the full; she had pulmonary apoplexy and pleurisy, and the respirations mounted up to 66; but next day, with a renewed diminution of the fluid, there was a renewed lowering of the respirations to 44.

I would gladly illustrate this point by additional cases, but shall limit myself to one more instance (55) that shows the effect on the breathing of pulmonary apoplexy and pleurisy in cases of rheumatic Pericarditis. A young man was admitted with pain in the chest and shortness of breath. On the second day friction sound was heard, and pericardial effusion had already reached its acme; leeches gave relief, and the breathing was more free; but on the

6th he had a stitch in the side, and the respirations numbered 60 in the minute; on the 8th, when he was easier, they were 46; but on the 13th pulmonary apoplexy was established, and they had risen to 72. On the 17th he had diphtheria, the respirations being 50; on the 28th this was nearly well, and he raised little phlegm, the respirations being 36, and on the 35th they were 28.

We thus see that with pain over the heart and pericardium, the breathing is hurried and distressed, while it is slackened and relieved with the relief of the suffering; that with the rise and fall of Pericarditis, with the increase, the acme, and the decline of pericardial effusion, we have an increase, an acme, and a decline in the number of the respirations; that a second wave of increase in the amount of pericardial effusion, leads to a second wave of increase in the number of the respirations; and that the respirations are also again accelerated, if, in the later progress of the case, pleurisy should spring up from the spreading of the pericardial inflammation; or if pulmonary apoplexy should declare itself, especially if combined, as it usually is, with notable pleurisy.

XIII. DIFFICULTY IN SWALLOWING.

There was difficulty or pain in swallowing in 13 of my cases of rheumatic Pericarditis.

I have already spoken of cases in which the act of deglutition caused pain over the back of the inflamed pericardium, generally complained of, however, in the chest, by the pressure of the morsel of food upon the inflamed structures during its descent along the œsophagus, where it passes behind the affected region.

The difficulty in swallowing, of which I now speak, occurs when the pericardial sac is distended to the full with fluid, and is caused by the compression of the œsophagus between the swollen sac and the spinal column. When the effused fluid lessens, the pressure diminishes, and swallowing becomes easy; but it becomes again difficult when a relapse takes place and the effusion again increases.

When the patient lies flat, the weight of the fluid in the pericardium falls backwards with full pressure upon the œsophagus, and deglutition becomes more difficult; when, however, he is raised into the sitting posture, and especially if he leans forwards, the volume of the liquid tends forwards and downwards, and swallowing is more easy.

A servant girl (15), aged 16, who had been ill about 3 weeks, came in suffering much both in the joints and the chest. Her breathing was laborious and very rapid; she looked anxious; dulness was increased over the pericardial region, and a soft friction sound was audible over the heart on pressure. On the 3rd day the amount of effusion in the pericardium had reached to its acme; swallowing was difficult, breathing was accelerated, her face was livid and anxious, she had pain in the epigastrium increased by pressure, and the veins of the neck were full. On the 5th she still had much difficulty in deglutition, but on the 8th the pericardial dulness had lessened all round, and she swallowed much more easily. On the 9th she was more bright and lively, the pericardial dulness had lessened much, but pain came in catches over the heart. On the evening of the 10th she had a relapse, she became suddenly faint, her lips turned blue and dusky, and she had great pain over the heart, which was soon relieved, but difficulty in swallowing returned. Next day the dulness over the pericardium had again increased, and the difficulty in swallowing was very great. On the 12th she was still very ill, but she could swallow more easily, and on the 15th the effusion into the pericardium had again lessened, and she was better. The friction sound was audible until the 17th day. She improved daily and gained strength.

The poor female servant (13), who died from sudden failure in the action of the heart, whose case I have just related, on the day of her admission, when the amount of effusion into the pericardium was great, swallowed more easily when the shoulders were raised than when she was lying flat.

One patient (44 a), a female servant, had a four-fold attack of difficulty of swallowing; on the second day after admission, from great distension of the pericardium, the effect being heightened by shortness of breath; on the 4th from diphtheria; on the 7th from a renewed increase in the effusion owing to a relapse, there being great distress in the chest; and on the 11th to a slighter degree from a second relapse with increase of the pericardial effusion. This case recovered perfectly without valvular mischief, after passing through an attack of pneumonia or rather pulmonary apoplexy and pleurisy.

Each patient presents some peculiarity in the way in which deglutition is affected; but I shall only allude here specially to two more cases; one of them (40), a youth, could not swallow solids readily, but could drink freely; the other (50), a coachman, aged 22, sometimes when drinking had a spasm which stopped his breath before he could swallow.

The possibility that diphtheria may be the cause of the difficulty of swallowing must not be overlooked. It was, as we have seen, the intervening cause, in my case (44 a), with double relapse, and it was the cause of dysphagia in another patient (55), a young man of 18, a commercial traveller, who had diphtheria on the 6th day after the cessation of friction sound, and the 16th after admission.

XIV. Loss of Voice.

In the case fatal from syncope (13), a female servant, to whom I have several times alluded, on the 5th day after admission the voice was husky, and she spoke in a whisper, but she could, with a great effort, speak aloud. She was less husky on the 5th, and on the 8th her voice was more natural. This case tends to support the view that the left laryngeal recurrent nerve may become so affected by the contiguous inflammation as to paralyze the larynx.

XV. EFFECTS ON THE PULSE OF RHEUMATIC PERICARDITIS.

The pulse obeys the same law as the respiration under the influence of the disease; it rises in number, like the respirations, as the disease rises in intensity, is at its greatest rapidity when the disease is at its acme, and falls in number as the disease declines. The increase in the rate of the pulse is not as a rule in proportion to the increase in the number of the respirations. During the early stage of the inflammation of the heart, when pain is generally felt and friction sound is audible over the organ, the pulse usually mounts up to 90, 100, or even 120, while the respirations increase to from 30 to 40 in the minute, so that at this early period the ratio of the pulse to the breathing is in number as about three to one, instead of maintaining the healthy standard of about four to one.

When the amount of the effusion into the pericardium reaches its height, the pulse is usually quicker than it is during the early stages, and on rare occasions it becomes very much quickened, reaching even to 160. More often, however, the pulse is not more rapid at this the stage of the acme of the disease than it is during its early period. The breathing, as we have just seen, is almost always more quickened and laborious at the time the fluid in the pericardium has reached to its height than at any previous period, so that then the ratio in number of the pulse to the respiration is often two or two and a half to one, instead of maintaining the healthy ratio of four to one.

At a later period, when the effusion is lessening, and the inflammation of the pericardium is coming to an end, the pulse, like the respiration, falls in number. At this stage, however, in severe cases, one or other, or even both of the two secondary affections, pleurisy and pulmonary apoplexy, that quicken the respirations quicken also the pulse, when the numbers of both, and the proportion that they bear to each other, are as a rule nearly the same that they were during the early period of the attack, the ratio of pulse to respiration being usually three to one.

In considering the effects of rheumatic pericarditis on the pulse and respiration, I have separated from each other the advance, the acme, and the decline of the disease, and the two secondary influences, pleurisy and pulmonary apoplexy. In nature, however, those stages melt into each other, and those various causes combine and operate together to produce the hurry and distress of breathing and the quickening of the pulse of which I have just spoken.

XVI. Fulness of the Veins of the Neck from Distension of the Pericardial Sac.

In several of the cases of rheumatic pericarditis there was fulness of the veins of the neck, sometimes with pulsation, during the period that the effusion into the pericardium was at its height, and the sac was distended to the utmost.

The fulness of the veins of the neck present at this period must, I consider, be mainly due to the resistance offered to the return of the blood through the venæ cavæ into the right auricle, owing to the yielding inwards of the thin walls of that cavity before the pressure of the fluid contained in the swollen pericardium. The fluid exerts also direct pressure upon the thin walls of the descending vena cava, which carries on the latter part of its course for the extent of an inch within the pericardial sac. The ascending cava on the other hand sustains this pressure to a considerable extent by being short and very large, and by possessing walls thickened by fibrous structure derived from the central tendon of the diaphragm. We may, indeed, measure the degree of the distension of the pericardial sac by the degree of the distension of the veins of the neck. This compression inwards of the right auricle must be looked upon as one of the most serious consequences of pericardial distension, for it materially lessens, or in extreme cases may almost tend even to cut off the supply of blood to the right side of the heart, the lungs, the left side of the heart and the system. The walls of the left auricle, being thicker, do not yield so readily as those of the right, but the compression of the left auricle and of the pulmonary veins by the fluid in the distended pericardium produces its own special mischief by impeding the flow of blood from the lung, thus often inducing pulmonary apoplexy. From this joint compression of the sister auricles flows a succession of consequences to which I need not here allude in detail, but which in their turn tend to produce weakening and intermission of the heart, a feeble irregular pulse, and even death from syncope. I shall have occasion by-and-by to speak of the support that the thin walls of the auricles and veins derive from the coating of lymph with which they are covered, and which enables them to bear much of the pressure to which they are then subjected.

One patient (16), a servant girl, after being ill for a week and affected severely in the joints for two days, came in breathing hurriedly, suffering from pain over the region of the heart, and in great distress. There was dulness over the pericardium from the second space to the sixth, and a loud, harsh friction sound was heard over all that region. The left jugular vein was distended and did not empty during inspiration ; next day the amount of effusion had lessened, she improved rapidly, and the friction sound ceased on the ninth day, when a mitral murmur declared itself.

In another servant (13), whose case, already referred to, proved fatal, the veins on the right side of the neck pulsated strongly, while those on its left side did so to a less extent, as they did not fill or empty themselves so completely. She died in a fit of syncope on the 14th day. Eighteen ounces of fluid were found in the pericardium, and several patches of pulmonary apoplexy were diffused through the upper lobe of the left lung.

Another fatal case (4), a carpenter, who died delirious on the eighth day, presented pulsation in the neck on the second day after admission, when the pericardial effusion had reached its acme. This pulsation was partly in the carotids but was chiefly venous and was more marked on the right side of the neck, the veins on that side being fuller than those on the left. On the third day the upper boundary of the region of pericardial dulness was lower, having descended from the third to the fourth costal cartilage, and the venous pulsation was not so perceptible. I will name two other cases of this class: one (29), a man who came in with an anxious expression of face: on the fifth day friction sound was heard over the heart, and on the seventh he presented extensive double venous pulsation in the neck: the other (15), already related, a girl who came in with rheumatic pericarditis, and in whom the veins of the neck were full during expiration on the third day when the pericardial effusion was at its height and deglutition was difficult.

There was visible pulsation of the jugular veins in three of the patients who had been affected with valvular disease of some standing before being attacked with rheumatic pericarditis. In these cases, the venous pulsation was evidently due to the valvular affection.

XVII. APPEARANCE AND EXPRESSION OF THE FACE DURING THE COURSE OF PERICARDITIS.

The face was flushed, dusky or very pallid, or its expression was one of anxiety or depression, in 43 of the 63 patients affected with rheumatic pericarditis. In six other cases it is stated that the aspect had improved, although there is no previous description of the face. There was thus a marked change in the appearance of the patient in four-fifths of the cases (49 in 63). The face is not mentioned in the remaining thirteen cases, and in one only of these was the attack severe, while it was so in thirty-six of the patients in whom its appearance was notably altered. The face was similarly affected in three-fifths of the patients attacked by endocarditis (60 in 108), in less than one-half of those who were threatened with endocarditis (27 in 59), and in one-fourth only of those who presented no sign or symptom of endocarditis. The appearance of the face was less and less profoundly altered in these patients, as the class to which they belonged became less and less affected in the heart, and still less in the class made up of those who gave no evidence of affection of that organ.

The face was flushed in 19 of the 63 cases of rheumatic pericarditis. Perspiration was copious in all but three of these, the perspiration often standing in beads upon the face. The flush, instead of being limited to the cheeks, was diffused over those parts that are usually white even in persons of the most rosy hue, the forehead, namely, the eyelids, the nose, the white skin of both lips, and the chin. I never noticed the colour spread at the first blush from feature to feature, but it seemed to tint them all at once. Thus the face was pallid on the day of admission in a fatal case already quoted by me, and on the following day it was flushed all over. But the flush which at first seemed to suffuse the whole face usually vanished step by step; the pink skin of the upper and lower lips first becoming white, then the nostrils and, in succession, the eyelids, the chin, the brow, and the cheeks in several of my cases.

The face was pale during the period of the friction sound in nine cases. One of these (13), a female servant, was very pallid and sallow, the features being pinched, when admitted with pericarditis; while on the following day, the face was rather flushed, and the fever seemed to be greater. Another case, (44a) a servant girl, aged 20, admitted with pericarditis, was flushed on the second day, but on the third, when the fluid in the pericardium had reached its acme, deglutition was difficult, and she was depressed, pallid, and weak. The face was twice as often flushed (19 times), as pale (9 times), during the attack of pericarditis. I have been unable to discover clinical reasons for the difference in these cases of the hue and colour of the face. The clinical history of the pallor of the face induced by rheumatic pericarditis is illustrated by a case, the physical features of which I published in 1844;[1] a youth, aged 16, was admitted into the General Hospital near Nottingham, on the 17th of November, 1842, under the care of Dr. Williams, suffering from acute rheumatism, with pericarditis. His countenance was pale, and his surface generally was also pale. On the third day after admission, the general symptoms were milder, although the extent of pericardial dulness had not lessened, and the face was less pallid, the lips being red. On the sixth, the following is my report: "The gums are slightly tender, his general appearance improves, the hue of the skin is clear, and rather red; the reflex influence of disease in contracting the capillaries being removed." He made a complete and rapid recovery. In this case, the general surface was pale as well as the face; but in the cases under analysis, my notes do not, as a rule, describe the hue of the body.

The aspect was dusky, muddy, or glazed in sixteen, and the expression of the face was anxious or depressed in thirty-five of the patients affected with pericarditis.

---

[1] Prov. Med. Trans., vol. xii., 1844, p. 532.

I would here briefly compare these numbers with the numbers of those thus affected in the other cases of acute rheumatism.

The face was notably flushed in one-fifth of the cases with simple endocarditis (19 in 108), one-eighth of those threatened with endocarditis (8 in 63), and in one-twentieth of those giving no sign of endocarditis (4 in 79). The aspect was dusky or muddy in one-tenth of those with simple endocarditis (10 in 108), in one of those threatened with endocarditis (1 in 63), and in one of those who gave no evidence of endocarditis (1 in 79). The expression was anxious or depressed in one-fourth of those with simple endocarditis (25 in 108), in one-sixth of those threatened with that affection (10 in 63), and in one-twelfth of those who presented no sign of inflammation of the heart (6 in 79).

I have drawn up these numbers from a careful examination of my case books, and they present an accurate return of the symptoms there recorded. These cases are however necessarily reported with varying degrees of minuteness, and the more severe cases, attracting the greatest interest, are naturally observed and related with greater care than those that present no unusual features. These must therefore be taken not as the actual, but the approximate numbers.

Keeping this in view, it must be felt, from what I have said, that rheumatic pericarditis with endocarditis, and to a less degree simple endocarditis, produce a remarkable change on the complexion, aspect, and expression of the face. The attention is at once drawn to the heart by the altered countenance. When the inflammation of the heart is established, the varying hue and expression of the face tell, with remarkable accuracy, the varying state of the powers of the heart, and of the double inflammation with which the organ is affected.

When the tide of the effusion into the pericardium has reached its height, as I shall illustrate in the next section, the hue of the face is . usually more dusky and livid, and its expression more anxious than at any other time; but when the tide has fairly turned, and, the effusion having lessened, the inflammation ceases to be active, the face becomes often quite suddenly cheerful, while its hue becomes clear; the eye at the same time, instead of being heavy and charged with blood vessels, becomes bright and clear. After this, if there is no relapse, the powers rally with remarkable quickness and freedom, and the appetite returns. This state is very different from the convalescence of fever, which passes through its period of improvement slowly and with scarcely perceptible steps.

In a patient, to whom I have already alluded, whose heart acted strongly and rapidly at the time of the first onset of the inflammation, the right side of the face was swollen and flushed, evidently under the influence of the attack of pericarditis.

What are the causes of this remarkable influence of inflammation of the exterior and interior of the heart on the face ?

There are probably more causes than one at work to produce the flushing or pallor present in pericarditis. The moderate elevation of

temperature present in all cases of inflammation is probably connected
with flushing of the face, either as a cause, or rather as a common
effect. The question must here be put, what is the cause of the
moderate elevation of temperature in cases of inflammation ? Is it
from general relaxation of the arteries, with elevation of temperature,
owing to the influence of the inflammation on the afferent nerves of the
part affected? such influence being conveyed to the vaso-motor centre
in a manner analogous to that in which relaxation of arteries and
elevation of temperature is produced on one side of the head and
face by the division of the sympathetic on that side of the neck, or
by the pressure of that nerve by an aneurism of the arch of the aorta.
This influence would, of course, only account for the moderate rise of
temperature in local inflammation, and does not touch the question of
the cause of the increased heat in fevers or in cases of acute rheumatism with delirium.

Putting this cause aside, which applies to every case of inflammation, I would suggest that one great cause of the flushing or pallor of
the face in pericarditis is the influence of the inflammation on the
afferent nerves at the surface of the heart and great vessels, which,
being depressed or stimulated, may induce reflex dilatation of the
arteries of the head, with flushing of the face, or reflex contraction of
the arteries of the head with pallor of the face. I suggested this
in principle as the cause of the pallor in the Nottingham case in my
note-book in 1842, and am still disposed to do so. In aneurism of
the arch of the aorta, pressure on the branches of the sympathetic
of one side causes relaxation of the arteries and elevation of temperature on the corresponding side of the head and face. I consider
that a parallel effect would result from the excitation or the injury of
the sympathetic and sensory nerves, and perhaps of other nerves
having, say, a vaso-inhibitory property distributed to the seat of the
inflammation of the heart and great vessels in pericarditis ; contraction
of the arteries of the head and face with pallor being produced on the
one hand, and relaxation of those arteries with flushing and perspiration on the other. In one case only, just referred to, was there
flushing and perspiration notably limited to one side of the face. It
is natural, however, to expect that as the inflammation affects the
nerves of both sides in pericarditis, both sides of the face should be
equally affected, as it was indeed in all but one of my cases of pericarditis affected with pallor or flushing of the face.

I would here remark that as the reflex contraction or dilatation of the arteries with pallor or flushing, from excitation or
injury of the sympathetic or sensory nerves is *continuous*, it differs
essentially from the reflex movements of the muscles caused by the
excitation of an afferent nerve, such movements being necessarily short
and *intermittent*, the withdrawal and renewal of the stimulus to the
afferent nerve being needful for their reproduction. In short, the
reflex vaso-motor current is continuous, while the reflex excito-motor
current (of the muscle) is interrupted.

The increased contraction of the arteries caused by the excitation of a sensory or sympathetic nerve appears to be due to the increased discharge of nervous force directly from the vaso-motor centre when that centre is thus stimulated by the excitation of those nerves. That centre would indeed seem to require, for the exercise of its proper functions, to be reinforced and stimulated through the sympathetic nervous system, and probably by the blood circulating in the arteries, when we consider that the division of the left splanchnic in the rabbit may lower the arterial pressure from 90 millimetres to 41, that excitation of the divided nerve may raise the pressure to 115 millimetres, and that division of the other splanchnic may further lower it to 31 millimetres.[1]

I would here remark that similar effects are produced by analogous causes in pneumonia, and especially in pneumonia of the upper lobe, when the face, besides being congested, presents a dusky hue and a powerless expression that speak of the profound influence exercised upon it by the disease. In this disease also, as in pericarditis, with the turn of the tide of the inflammation and with the removal of its products, the veil is as it were lifted away from the countenance ; and a patient, one day, under the weight of the inflammation, with an aspect dark depressed and anxious, presents on the next day, with the removal of the exudation from the affected air cells, and the renewal of their respiration, a face clear, and clean, and an expression bright and cheerful.

The eye is every now and then reported to have been dull, and heavy in appearance during the attack of pericarditis, its minute vessels being congested; but it is more frequently described as becoming bright and clear when the effusion into the pericardium was lessening, and the inflammation was becoming inactive and only present in the shape of its results. I had not, until quite recently, made any close observation of this organ, but in one of the last cases of acute rheumatism with endocarditis treated by me in St. Mary's Hospital, I found that during the acme of the disease, when the face was flushed, dusky and anxious, the conjunctiva was crowded with small vessels which ended a very short distance from the cornea, so that round the clear of the eye there was a white zone or ring edged by fine converging vessels. When the inflammation ceased to be active, and the face, in keeping with this improvement, became clear and cheerful, the eye became bright, and the vessels crowding the conjunctiva lessened in number, so that the ball of the eye became again white. This organ requires careful observation in cases of rheumatic pericarditis and endocarditis.

[1] Ludwig and Cyon, quoted by Dr. Burdon Sanderson : Handbook for the Physiological Laboratory," p. 249.

XVIII. Condition of the Face when the Pericardial Distension
was at its Height.

When the pericardium is distended to the full with fluid, under the
three-fold influence of (1) what may be termed the "fluid" pressure,
induced by the distension of the sac bearing with varying force, outwards upon the œsophagus and trachea, the left bronchus, the lungs,
especially the left, and the diaphragm; and inwards on the descending
vena cava, the right and left auricles, and the pulmonary veins;
(2) inflammation involving the nerves distributed to the surface of
the heart and the great vessels; and (3) inflammation of the superficial
muscular fibres of the heart itself; as we have seen, point by point,
pain may be present around and within the heart, over the pericardial
sac and the pleura; swallowing may be difficult; the voice may be
hoarse or reduced to a whisper; the action of the heart, which at the
beginning of the attack is often forcible, may become feeble and intermitting, or even altogether fail; the respirations may be hurried and
laborious, often so as to compel the raised and forward posture; the pulse
may be rendered weak and irregular and be quickened, though not in
the same proportion, as the breathing, the ratio of the pulse to respirations being two or three and a half to one, instead of, as in health,
four to one; and the veins of the neck may be swollen and pulsating.
The last effect of the over distension of the pericardium that I shall
illustrate is that upon the circulation of the head and face.

A female servant whose case (15) has already been alluded to was
admitted with acute rheumatism and pericarditis of great severity. On
the third day, I found that the pericardium was distended to the
full, she complained of a sensation of choking, swallowing was
difficult, the countenance was anxious, the face was livid and
perspiring profusely, and the veins of the neck were full. On the
sixth day the pericardial dulness had lessened all round, her face was
less dusky, and her aspect had improved. On the tenth, in the
evening, she suddenly came over faint, the lips being blue, and the face
dusky; but in a few hours the face, though still anxious, lost its dark
hue and the lips became again red. Next day it was found that the
pericardial effusion had again increased. The fluid, however, soon
again diminished. On the twelfth her aspect had again improved, on
the fifteenth her face was flushed, and on the sixteenth it was of good
colour, and its expression was no longer anxious. Here, twice over,
the effusion in the pericardium reached its acme, and under the influence of its pressure and the inflammation of the organ, the heart
faltered, the venous blood was delayed in its passage, the arterial
blood was with difficulty supplied, the face and neck became charged
with venous blood, and the lips became livid; and here, twice over, the
pressure was removed by the lessening of the fluid, when the colour
returned to the face and the expression of anxiety disappeared.

XVII. Affections of the Nervous System in Rheumatic Pericarditis.

Dr. Davis, of Bath, in the year 1808 [1] published three cases of acute rheumatism, two of them being affected with pericarditis, and one with endocarditis. One of the cases of pericarditis, which was observed in 1785 by Dr. Haygarth—who curiously does not mention this important case in his "Clinical History of the Acute Rheumatism," published in 1806—was affected with moaning, restlessness, and delirium ending in death. The other case of pericarditis, a young lady, who was under the care of Dr. Davis, had great heats, with perspiration, screaming, and the most violent jactitation of the body, "occasioned by the extreme anguish which she felt in the region of the heart." She was perfectly sensible throughout, and died after the disease had lasted twenty-six days. The patient with endocarditis was affected with want of sleep and violent delirium, for nine days, at the end of which time she died.

In a series of important clinical contributions, Corvisart, Mr. Stanley, Dr. Abercrombie, Dr. Macleod, Andral, Dr. Latham, Dr. Bright, Dr. Mackintosh, M. Bouillaud, Sir Thomas Watson, Sir George Burrows, and Dr. Kirkes,[2] have described cases of pericarditis, some connected with acute rheumatism, but many not so, in which delirium, coma, convulsions, temporary insanity, chorea and choreiform movements, or tetaniform symptoms and rigidity, and even actual tetanus were present.

These observations suggested to several of those authors, including Andral and Dr. Bright, a close connection amounting even to cause and effect, between pericarditis and the affections of the nervous system associated with it.

The affections of the nervous system in cases of rheumatic pericarditis, and acute rheumatism are always serious, often fatal, and comparatively rare. Recent observations have shown in many of those cases the presence of a very high temperature, delirium and coma, ending in death. I shall therefore, in inquiring into the clinical history of those associated affections, examine those cases admitted into St. Mary's Hospital under my care during the twenty years that I have held office, and all the published cases that I can find of this class.

I have brought together from various sources, 180 cases of acute rheumatism with affections of the nervous system, more than one half of which had pericarditis (92 in 180). The temperature of the body was recorded in one-third of the total number of cases (61 in 180); and although these cases were observed at a much more recent period than those in which the temperature was not recorded, I shall examine the more recent series of cases first, for they throw light upon the older series of cases. (See tables on the following pages.)

[1] "An Inquiry into the Symptoms and Treatment of Carditis," by John Ford Davis, M.D.
[2] For references to these authors, see the note given in the appendix to the table at pages 250–253, of cases of acute rheumatism with affection of the nervous system, in which the temperature of the body was not observed.

CASES OF ACUTE RHEUMATISM WITH AFFECTION OF THE NERVOUS SYSTEM, IN WHICH THE TEMPERATURE WAS OBSERVED.

CASES WITH PERICARDITIS.

TOTAL PATIENTS OF BOTH SEXES, 27.

SEX AND AGE . . {
MALE PATIENTS. Total 14.—Below 21 years, o; 21 to 25 years, 5 (3, 14, 20, 26, 27); above 25 years, 9 (6, 7, 9, 12, 13, 17, 21, 22, 23).
FEMALE PATIENTS. Total 13.—Below 21 years, 5 (2, 4, 10, 24, 25); from 21 to 25 years, 1 (18); above 25 years, 7 (1, 5, 8, 11, 15, 16, 19).
}

OCCUPATION, HABITS, AND PREVIOUS CONDITION . . {
MALE PATIENTS. Total 13.—*Workers out of doors,* 6—*laborious,* 4; gardener, 1 (6, never ill); smiths, 2 (22, 26); bargeman, 1 (27); on foot, 1; policeman, 1 (inexcusious after kick in month ten years before); among horses, 1; coachman, 1 (7, lived well, not a drunkard). *Workers in-doors,* 5—servants, 2 (17; 21, well-nourished, heavy drinker, much exposed); coachman, 1 (20, poorly nourished, arsenic); shoemaker, 1 (23, poorly nourished, pale); shopman, 1 (in easy circ.); 1 (13; gentleman in business), 1 (13, muscular, intellectual, nervous, took beer, took chloral for sleep). Occupation not stated, 2 (3; 9, had epistaxis a month before admission).

FEMALE PATIENTS. Total 13.—*Active in-door Workers,* 7—servants, 2 (1, 18); married 5 (5, lived badly till year before attack; 8, had child three months old, badly off, no milk; 15, rubican, stout; 16, in great trouble; 19, had child ten weeks old, subject to palpitation). No occupation, 1 (24, a dim, passionate, nervous child.) Occupation not stated, 5 (2, 4, 10, 11, 25).
}

CHARACTER OF AFFECTION OF THE NERVOUS SYSTEM {
[extensive faded handwritten clinical notes describing cases 4—, 4—Had Coma not preceded by delirium, 1—5, coma at temp. of 108·4°-110° &c.; bath, lowered to 68°, &c.; at 106·7° some consciousness, at 100·9° could speak; Recovery. For cases of semi-consciousness and no temporary coma see below.; various delirium, coma, and temperature readings]

43—Had Delirium, followed by deep Stupor, 1—13 (very delirious, temp. ...)

B—Had Delirium, without coma or other important complication, 9 [with numerous temperature and clinical readings]

*Semi consciousness, 1—18, kind of 24, frothing at lips, semi-conscious for four hours at night, temp. 99·3°-100·9°, albumen in urine, ⌢.
C—3—Had Choreal Movements and continuous muscular contraction 1—34, temp. 101·5°.
}

THE DURATION AND DELIRIUM AND COMA, AND THEIR RELATION TO PERICARDITIS AND ENDOCARDITIS.

AFFECTION OF JOINTS.

PERSPIRATION.

CONVULSIVE, CHOREI-FORM, OR TETANI-FORM SYMPTOMS.

Restlessness, before delirium or coma, 1, 4, 25; during delirium or coma, 3, 9, 20. *Want of Sleep*, 8, 12, 13, 18, 14, 16, 20, 21. *Tremulousness*, 5, 12, 13, 14, 20, 21, 22

Violent spasmodic movements of whole body, 12; convulsive movements of limbs, arms, or legs, 1, 4, 5, 9 to chatlation, 11, 20; distortion of face, 4, 14; rolled violently about bed, 3; rolled head from side to side, 4, 14; spasms of rigidity of muscles of lips, 5, lips pointing and rubbing teeth, 6; *risus sardonicus*, 22, 23, 27; trismus, 1, 27 (could not separate teeth); spasms of rigidity of muscles of neck, 3; jaw finger flexed, 14.

Military Eruption Sudamina, 3, 8, 12, 13, 14, 16, 17, 19, 21, 22, 23.

Face.—Flushed, usually dusky, glazed, or anxious, 22; (before delirium), 3, 7, 16, 17; purple dusky, 5; flushed at 110·8°, pale livid at 109·6°, 4; flushed, later death-like pallor, temp. 106·3–69, very pale, livid, 8. *Diarrhœa* during delirium or coma, 1, 7, 14, 19, 21, 22, 23. *Urine very abundant* during delirium or coma, 7, 13, 21. Evacuations in bed, 1, 8, 9, 14, 21.

EXPLANATION.—The numbers (1–27) refer to the different cases analysed in this table. Throughout the table each number refers to the same case. Reference to the sources from which the cases have been obtained will be found in the appendix.

TOTAL PATIENTS OF BOTH SEXES, 13.

SEX AND AGE.
- MALE PATIENTS. Total 7.—Below 21 years, 3 (3, 5, 12); 21 to 25 years, 1 (7); above 25 years, 3 (4, 4, 10.)
- FEMALE PATIENTS. Total 6. 21 to 25 years, 1 (1); above 25 years, 5 (6, 8, 9, 11, 13.)

OCCUPATN., HABITS, PREV. CONSTITN.
- MALE PATIENTS.—Total 7.—Worker out of doors, 1; on foot, 1; porter, 1 (4). Worker in-doors, 1; laundryman, 1 (12). Occupation not stated, 5 (3, drank beer freely; 3, 5, 7, 10).
- FEMALE PATIENTS. Total 8.—Servants, 3 (1, 6, 11). cook, 1 (9). married, 2 (8, always ailing; 13, sixth attack).

CHARACTER OF AFFECTION OF NERVOUS SYSTEM.

A3—Had Delirium, followed by coma 4 —10, {morbid delirium, temp. 109°}; 7, {delirium violent, temp. 106°, then muttering delirium {coma, temp. 110°2° , end of bath 100·8°, 1 hour later 96·5°, maniacal (2nd bath), tetaniform symptoms.

8 {delirium slight, temp; 102°.
8 {coma, temp. 109·5°–10·5° (bath 80°–62° 45 minutes), 109·8° rectum
2 {delirium slight 1 night, temp. 104·4° morning, then muttering delirium
2 {coma, temp. (?).

Had Delirium, followed by Convulsive movements, 1.— {delirium, temp. 102°–106·2°.
{face convulsed, threw arms about: died, temp. 111·9°

B1—Had Delirium, without coma or other important modification, 1.—
5, del. violent, temp. 107·5°–104·8°, general collapse, temp. 111·4°
11, uninterrupted del., temp. 104°–109·4°
1, del. (sensorium much disordered), ice 5° (cold applied inside and out), after it temp. 98·6° no del.—Recovered.
3, del. 1 night, temp. 108·9°, later, 102°, no del.—Recovered.
6, del. 1 night, temp. 99·6°–102·2°.

B2—Had Delirium with cerebral Embolism and Hemiplegia, 1.—13, after acute rheumatism, del., left hemiplegia, imperfect speech, temp. 103°, cessation of del., —Old mitral-aortic valve disease, endocarditis.

B3—Had Delirium and Chorea, and minute cerebral embolism, 1.—12, del., speech indistinct, twitching, especially of right side, screamed, left bed, temp. 103°–102·3°.

Had High Temperature, without note of delirium, 1.—9, head heavy, giddiness, great heat, temp. 105·9° (ice-bag to head and precordia), in half an hour temp. 103·2—Recovered.

Delirium and Coma.—8, del. about 3 days and 8 nights, coma short time—duration (?), (3 baths); 7, del. 3 hours, coma short; 2, slight del. 1st night; no del., 2nd night, violent del. ½ hour, coma 1½ hour.

Delirium, Convulsive Movements—4, del. about 3 nights.

DURATION OF DELIRIUM AND COMA.
Delirium.—5, del. 1 hour, exhaustion 1 hour; 1, del., duration (?) shortened by bath—Recovered: 8, del. 2 nights—Recovered: 6, del. 1 night.
Delirium Embolism.—13, del. 3–4 days.
Delirium Chorea.—12, del. 8–9 days.

AFFECTION OF JOINTS.
Before Delirium or Coma} —8 {severe+: 7{+: 8 {+: 4{+:
During Delirium or Coma} —none O; 1{(?): 1{O none, and – slight: 1{+: = or – + O +: 3{+: + rather severe; 9{+ or – +: 10{+: 13{+: O +.

PERSPIRATION.
Before Delirium or Coma,}—8 {very profuse + +: 7{+: 2{+ 4{+:
During Delirium or Coma} —8 {(?)+: 1{(?): 1{O or – : 1{O, after bath +: 3{+: O +, after bath +: 3{+: 6, del. on admission +.

Miliary Eruption or Sudamina, 4, 7, 9.

Diarrhœa during delirium or coma, 5, 5, 7, 8. Urine very abundant during delirium or coma, 4, 5, 7. Evacuations involuntary, 4, 8: probably, 5, 7.

Restlessness usually before delirium, 4, 8, 11, 7 (during delirium).

CONV. CHOREITT. OR TETANIFM. SYMP. Twitchings of legs and arms, 2; of right side, 12; threw arms about, 1; convulsions of face just before death, 4; much convulsed, tonic spasms, teeth closing firmly on lower lip—drawing blood, risus sardonicus, opisthotonos, 8.

CASES IN WHICH THERE WAS NO PERICARDITIS, ENDOCARDITIS BEING ABSENT OR DOUBTFUL.

TOTAL PATIENTS OF BOTH SEXES, 21.

SEX AND AGE.
- MALE PATIENTS. Total 12.—Below 21 years, 3 (3, 17 beer drinker, 16); 21 to 25 years, 1 (21); above 25 years, 8 (5, 6, 7, 12, 13,16, 19, 20).
- FEMALE PATIENTS. Total 9.—Below 21 years, 2 (10); 21 to 25 years, 5 (4, 8, 11, 14, 15); sex and age not stated, 1 (9).

OCCUPATN., HABTS, PREV. CONSTN.
- MALE PATIENTS. Total 12.—Workers out of doors, 6; laborious, 6—laborious, 2 (5, 6, nervous); smith, 1 (7, bad lich); carpenter, 3 (16 free liver, 19, 21). Workers in-doors, 1—carver, 1 (20); no occupation, 1 (18); occupation not stated, 4 (3, 12 nervous, 13 nervous, 17 had ague twice, 19)
- FEMALE PATIENTS. Total 9.—Servant, 1 (14); married, 1 (9); no occupation, 1 (15). Occupation not stated, 3 (1, 3, 4 had neuralgia, 10, 11).

4 { slight delirium (?)
  { coma at temp. 109°4-110°8 } .

6 { violent delirium, out of bed, like del. treun at temp. 107° } () .

{ violent delirium, would leave bed, temp. (?) () };
18 { coma at temp. 108°-109°6'
  { coma at temp. 110°

7 { 1st, slight delirium.
  { 2nd, coma. 3 violent delirium at temp. 106°8'.

Had Delirium, followed by Somnolence, 9—11 { mutering del. at temp. 104°5'-105°3'
  { coma at temp. 106°, in bath at temp. 90°-91° for 20 minutes, then temp. 102°, comfortable—Recovered

8 { noisy delirium at temp. 102°9'
  { drowsy at temp. 100°-101° () .

CHARACTER OF AFFECTION OF THE NERVOUS SYSTEM

Had Delirium without coma or other important complication, 10.—
1, noisy del., sank rapidly, temp. 110° ()
3, muttering del., temp 107°8'-108°2' (bath at 71°-82° for ¼ hour) when removed from bath temp. 101°8'. 35 minutes later, temp. 98°8', asleep, temp. 105°8', slight del. (second bath)—Recovered.
15, del. temp 107° (bath at 42°, after bath, temp 97°, mind clear—Recovered.
16, slight del. at 104°2', noisy del 104°5' (ice-bag to head, bath at 87°-90°), after it temp. 101°4', wandering (highest temp. 106°, had 20 baths, bath lowered temp, restored reason for a time) ()
18, del at temp. 102°8'-104°5' ()

17, noisy del. at temp. 108°4', followed by paraplegia—Recovered.
18, del. temp. 101°5'—Recovered.

20, del. sometimes muttering, temp. 100°4'-101°:5'—Recovered.
9, del. somewhat violent, temp. 101°16' (albumen in urine)—Recovered.
21, slight and violent del., hallucination, sprang through open window, killed, Bright's disease, temp. 100°4° ()

Had very High Temperature, without delirium, 2—12, very restless, talked in sleep, deaf, temp. 102°8'-106°3° (bath 90°-83° for 33 minutes), after bath temp. 101°, later 99°8', deafness left him—Recovered. 2, vomiting, dyspnœa, no note of delirium, temp. 110°8' ()

Twitching of limbs, 1—19, no sleep, general muscular twitchings at temp. 101°-102°, later repetition of twitching at 98°4°, albumen in urine—Recovered.

Delirium and Coma, 6—8, wandering, one day, then better, muttering del. ¼ hour, coma 1 hour ; 4, del. 1½ hour, coma about 1 hour () ; 14, del. and
coma combined, 1½ hour () ; 6, del 6 days, coma 1½ hour () ; 13, del 4 hours, coma 4 hours ; 7, del. about 2 days, del. and coma alternately 2 days ()

DURATION OF DEL. AND COMA

Delirium and Somnolence, 2—11, del. about 1 day (bath)—Recovered ; 8, del. about 10 days, drowsy about 1 day ()

Delirium, without coma or other important complication, 10—1, del. about 1 day () ; 2 hrs. ; 3, del. ¾ hr., bath, sleep, slight del., second bath—Recovered ; 16, del.
about 16 days (?), 20 baths () ; 18, del. 3 baths () ; 17, del 19 nights, several days—Recovered ; 20, del. 3 nights, muttering 1 morning—Recovered ;
10, del. if diarrhœa checked, duration (?)—Recovered. 9, del. especially during nights—Recovered ; 21, del. about 2 days ()

Before Delirium   → Delirium and Coma, 5 { mod. severe – +; 4 {O – +; 14 { +; – +; 6 { +; –
During Delirium or Coma   (?) { +; 20 { + +; 20 { – +; later – +; 18 { + +; +; 7 { +; +; Delirium and Somnolence, 11 {– +
                                                                                                                   (?);

AFFECTION OF JOINTS

Before Delirium
During Delirium or Coma → Delirium and Coma, 5 { mod. severe – +; 4 { O – +; 14 { +; – +; 6 { +; +; Delirium and Somnolence, 11 { – +
8 { O – + or +;   Delirium, 3 { – +; 16 { +; 18 { + +; 20 { – +; Very High Temp., no Del., 12 { +; Twitchings, 19 { O + or – +
  { O + or much better;   (?);   (?);
21 { +;
  { O;

PERSPIRATION

Before very High Temperature or Delirium → Delirium and Coma, 5 { +; 4 { +; 14 { +; 6 { +; 18 { perspiring ; 7 { +; Delirium, 3 { +; 16 { O then +;
During very High Temperature or Delirium →   { O;   { O;   { (?)   { (?).   { –;   { +;
20 { +; Very High Temperature, no delirium, 12 { +;
  { O +   { (?).

Had Miliary Eruption or Sudamina, 3, 5, 6, 7, 12, 13, 14, 16.

Face during period of excessive heat, delirium, or coma—red, V; red and then livid, 18; flushed during delirium, pallid, cadaverous during coma, 6;
pale, 4, 5; livid, 5; cyanosed, 14.
Diarrhœa during delirium or coma, 3, 13, 16, 18, 19.   Urine abundant during delirium or coma, 3, 13. Evacuations involuntary, 3, 16, 17, 18. Vomiting, 13.
Restless, 3, 7, 11, 12, 13, 14, moved his arms about, 16, 17, 20, 21.   Tremulousness, 16, 17.

CONVULSIVE CHOREIFORM AND TETANIFORM SYMPTOMS.—Twitchings of limbs and body, 19 ; of limbs and features, 5 ; of face, 6 (sardonic grin), 16, especially of lips.

EXPLANATION.—The numbers 1–13 and 1–21 refer to the different cases analysed in these tables. Throughout each table, each number refers to the same
case. Reference to the sources from which the cases have been obtained will be found in the appendix.

CASES OF ACUTE RHEUMATISM WITH AFFECTIONS OF THE NERVOUS
SYSTEM, IN WHICH THE TEMPERATURE OF THE BODY WAS OBSERVED.

Dr. Sydney Ringer, published in the year 1867, three cases of acute
rheumatism with pericarditis, in which the temperature rose before
death respectively to 109·2°, 110·8°, and 110·0°.[1] These three patients
had delirium, followed by coma and death, and one of them was
under the care of Dr. Reynolds as early as May 1862.

Dr. Kreuser related in 1866 [2] three fatal cases, of acute rheumatism
in which the temperature rose respectively to 109·4°, 110·2°, and
110·4°, and these three patients were affected with delirium, and one
of them with coma also.

More recently an important series of cases of this class have been
communicated by Dr. Hermann Weber in an important paper, Dr.
Murchison, Dr. Burdon Sanderson, Dr. Greenhow, Dr. Southey, Dr.
Henry Thompson, Dr. Meding, Mr. Anderson, Dr. Wilson Fox, whose
work on the treatment of hyperpyrexia is of great value, and Dr.
Andrews.[3]

I have brought together from these and other sources, sixty-one
cases of acute rheumatism, affected with coma, delirium, chorea,
or convulsive choreiform, or tetaniform symptoms, in which the
temperature was observed during the progress of the illness. See
table, pp. 250—253.

Of the sixty-one cases in which the nervous system was affected,
and the temperature was ascertained—I. twenty-seven had pericarditis; II. thirteen had simple endocarditis; and, III. twenty-one
were free from pericarditis, endocarditis being absent or doubtful.

I.—CASES WITH PERICARDITIS IN WHICH THE NERVOUS SYSTEM WAS
    AFFECTED, AND THE TEMPERATURE, GENERALLY VERY HIGH, WAS
    OBSERVED.

SUMMARY.

A^1 Had *coma* without *delirium*, maximum temp. 110° . . 1
A^3 Had *delirium* followed by *coma*, temp. 110·8°—104·6° . 11
A^4 Had *delirium* followed by *stupor*, temp. 106°—103° . . 1
   Had *delirium* and *convulsive movements*, temp. 107°—110·2° 1
B^1 Had uncomplicated *delirium*, temp. 110·4°—103° . . . 9
   Had *delirium* with general stiffness, temp. 103·2°—102·2° 1
   Had *temporary* or *partial coma*, temp. 101·8°—99·3° . . 2
C^1 Had *chorea*, temp. 101·5° 1

                                     —
                              TOTAL . . . 27
                                     =

[1] "Medical Times and Gazette," 1867, II. 378.
[2] "Medicinisches Correspondenz-Blatt des Württembergischen ärztlichen Vereins,"
band xxxvi. p. 105.
[3] For references to these authors, see the note given in the appendix to the table, at
pages 250-253, of cases of acute rheumatism with affection of the nervous system, in
which the temperature of the body was observed.

The temperature of the body was observed in twenty-seven cases of rheumatic pericarditis with affection of the nervous system, and was very high in three-fifths of them (15 in 27), their highest temperature varying respectively from 106·8° to 115.8°. Five of these cases were placed in a cooling bath, when their temperature, then at the highest, was ascending rapidly, with the effect of arresting its rise, cooling the body, and, in four instances, leading to the recovery of the patient. The bath was employed also in two cases in which the temperature was 105° and 105·5° respectively, with the effect of cooling the body; but as the ascent of the thermometer was neither rapid nor very high, those cases can scarcely be included with those of hyperpyrexia. The temperature was 104·6° and 105·3° respectively in two cases during the period of delirium, but was not observed during that of coma, and I therefore think that both those cases may be included with those of hyperpyrexia—which bring their number up to seventeen, or two-thirds of the total number of cases with pericarditis.

Seven of the remaining ten cases, or one-fourth of the total number, had a high, but not very high, temperature, varying from 103° to 106°, so that these cases would rank, as regards the heat of the body, with fever or pyrexia. The temperature was only moderately high in the three remaining cases, or one-eighth of the total number, varying from 99·3° to 101·8°.

A^1 Profound coma, without delirium, was present in one case; A^3, ^{4}, delirium that passed into coma in eleven cases, into stupor in one case, and into convulsive movements in one case; B, uncomplicated delirium was present in nine cases, one of which had Bright's disease; and delirium with stiffness of jaws, neck and limbs occurred in one case. Temporary coma occurred in one case, and semi-consciousness in another, both with albumen in the urine; and C^1 chorea and slight continuous contraction of certain muscles existed in one case.

A^1.The case of coma without delirium, a woman, was under the care of Dr. Wilson Fox,[1] with acute rheumatism and pericarditis. The temperature was about 102° on the morning of the fourteenth day of illness, and had risen to 108·4° at 9.15 P.M., when she became entirely unconscious, and to 109·1′ at 9.50 P.M., when she was put into a bath at 96°, and ice was applied to her body. She was unconscious, pulseless and cyanotic, her respirations were irregular, gasping and stertorous, and she appeared to be dying. In half-an-hour, her temperature had fallen to 106·2°, when the pulse became perceptible, and she showed signs of consciousness. In ten more minutes, the temperature was 103·6°, and she was taken out of the bath, and twenty minutes later it had fallen to 100·1°, when she could speak, and had imperfect consciousness. After various oscillations, this patient recovered. I relate this case here briefly not to illustrate the treatment, but to show that profound coma became established when the

[1] " Treatment of Hyperpyrexia," by Dr. Wilson Fox, p. 2.

temperature was excessively high, and that consciousness was restored when the body was cooled.

A^3. Ten cases, in which delirium was followed by coma, and in which the bath was not used, proved fatal, but one such case recovered after the employment of the bath.

Delirium appeared at a temperature of from 103° to 104·8° in eight of the eleven cases in which coma was preceded by delirium, the temperature in six of these being at or above 104° when the disturbed state of mind was first noticed. In three of these cases delirium was still present when the thermometer was as high as from 107° to 108°, and in one of them when it was as low as 99·6°.

Profound coma declared itself when the temperature had risen from 109° to 109·4° in five of the eleven cases in which complete unconsciousness followed delirium, when the thermometer stood at 108·4° in one of them, at 106·8° in another, and at 106·6° to 107·6° in another, in which the coma, not profound, was transient.

In several of these cases it was noticed that the temperature rose between the supervention of coma and death.

The delirium was violent in five of those eleven patients who passed from delirium into coma, two of whom got out of bed; was active in three of them; and resembled delirium tremens in two, while in another the manner was strange and excited, and the sentences were disconnected and incoherent.

The transition from a state of violent or active delirium to coma was usually gradual. Muttering replaced active delirium in three instances, the muttering delirium being accompanied by restlessness in two of them. A state of semi-consciousness, accompanied by moaning in one and by restlessness in the other, intervened in two cases between the period of delirium and that of coma; and two other cases passed from delirium to a state almost of unconsciousness, and from that to coma. Violent delirium ceased abruptly after venesection in one patient, who was quiet for a short time, but soon passed into a state of perfect unconsciousness.

The duration of the delirium was very various in the different cases, lasting in one case about three-quarters of an hour, and in another, eight days. The delirium was more frequent by night than by day, and lasted from one to four nights in four cases in which it was scarcely observed during the day.

The period of coma varied much less than that of the delirium, lasting from a quarter of an hour to seven hours in nine of the eleven cases with delirium and coma. In one of the remaining cases, the duration of the coma was prolonged, death being delayed, and in another of them consciousness was restored, and recovery was established, by the use of the bath.

The two cases were fatal in which delirium preceded semi-stertorous breathing, with violent spasmodic movements of the whole body in one instance, and profound stupor in the other. The temperature in the former case rose to 110·2° before death, but in the latter it was never higher than 106°. Dr. Murchison favoured me with the leading features of that case.

B[1] Delirium without coma or other important modifications affected nine cases of acute rheumatism with pericarditis. These cases divide themselves naturally into two groups; in the first group, consisting of four, the delirium was of the usual character, and the temperature was very high, varying from 107·3° to 110·5°, and was kept in check in two of them by the cooling bath; while in the second group, containing four cases, the temperature was not so very high, varying from 103·3° to 105·3°. The delirium was accompanied by tremor, and usually by hallucinations, and a general condition resembling delirium tremens. The remaining case of delirium belongs to neither of these groups, since the delirium was slight, and gave way to general emaciation, ending in death.

Delirium was present throughout in one of the four cases with very high temperature, and in that patient it ranged from 103° to 105·6°, and ascended to 107·4° during the last ten hours. Death was sudden. The second case, a coachman who had lived well, was under the care of Dr. Wilson Fox.[1] His temperature was 107°, his pulse 100—108, respiration 44—45. At 2 A.M. he was put for twenty-five minutes into a bath at 89° to 86°, when his temperature fell from 107° to 103·1°, and he became perfectly conscious. Fifteen minutes after the bath his temperature had fallen to 98°, when his pulse was 84, respiration 20, and he was perfectly rational and conscious. The pericarditis in this case was of unusual duration and severity. The bath, the wet-pack, or the ice-bag was employed during the next six days to keep down the temperature, which had a strong tendency to rise. This patient recovered. In another case, a man, the temperature was lowered by the bath from 108·2°, when he was delirious, to 103·8°, when he could answer questions rationally. A second bath lowered his temperature from 105° to 102°, and thirty-five minutes after his removal from it, to 98·7°, when he was quiet. He recovered slowly.[2]

One of the four patients with tremor, hallucinations, a state resembling delirium tremens, and a temperature not excessively high, who was under the care of Dr. Southey, was an intellectual, nervous man, and a drinker of beer. His tongue and hands were at a temperature of 105°; he was placed in a bath at 71° for ten minutes, when he felt cold, talked rationally, and thought it the queerest treatment for rheumatism. He was wet-sheeted whenever his temperature rose to 104°, when he was always delirious. He died with bronchial symptoms. Sir William Gull saw the case, and suggested that it indicated the association of acute rheumatism with delirium tremens.[3]

The next case resembling delirium tremens was a poorly nourished, pale man. The bath lowered his temperature on the first occasion

---

[1] " Treatment of Hyperpyrexia," p. 10.
[2] Dr. Andrews, " St. Bartholomew's Hospital Reports," x. 338.
[3] *Lancet*, 1872, ii. 562.

from 104·3° to 99·8°, and on the second from 105·3° to 101·6°, when he was rational, and after the second bath he had *risus sardonicus,* his limbs were tremulous, and he remained delirious until the fourteenth day (temp. 103·4° to 100·2°). After this he steadily improved.[1] Dr. Southey favoured me with the notes of another case of this class, a poorly nourished, anæmic man, a coachmaker, who had been ill ten days. When admitted (temp. 103°), his tongue was tremulous, and he perspired profusely. On the fifth day he had pericarditis ; on the seventh night, constant muttering delirium; and next day an abrupt manner. On the ninth, after a delirious night, his hands were tremulous. On the seventeenth day his skin was hot and dry, temp. 103·8° ; and the activity of his mind resembled what is observed in delirium tremens, but he had no horrors. The ice-bag was applied to his head on the eighteenth, and as he was sleepless, he had 30 grains of chloral, after which he slept for four hours. On the following day he was conscious, had pain in the knees and shoulders, perspired less, and looked better, but still had some tremulousness and jactitation. His respiration and temperature steadily fell, and he gradually recovered.

The fourth case was a constable, who ten years before had been unconscious after a kick. His highest temperature was 103·3°, but it rarely exceeded 102°. In the course of his illness he had delirious nights, choreal movements of the left hand, on one occasion tremor of the right hand, hallucinations, and frequent rolling of his head from side to side. He improved slowly, but remained for some days incoherent, and childish in manner.[2]

B[4] Delirium with stiffness of jaws, neck, back and limbs, occurred in a patient of Dr. Bristowe's, a bargeman, aged 21, with slight acute rheumatism, pericarditis, and endocarditis.[3]

Two cases, one affected with temporary unconsciousness, the other with stridor and semi-consciousness, were under my care in St. Mary's Hospital. They had albumen in the urine, and were both fatal. The first case had previous aortic and mitral valvular disease. The second had a presystolic murmur, and mitral and tricuspid systolic murmurs, and the inspection after death showed pericarditis, button-hole contraction of the mitral valve, and acute Bright's disease of the kidneys.

C[1] Choreal and continuous contraction of some muscles occurred in the following case, a delicate, excitable girl, aged eleven, for observing which I am indebted to Mr. Saunders. When I first saw her, about the tenth day of her illness, a loud pericardial friction sound prevailed over the whole front of the chest, extinguishing all other heart-sounds. Ten days later, temp. 101·5°, she took little notice, bent and extended her right arm and hand irregularly, but bent the hand backwards on the fore-arm, flexed the fingers, and pointed the right great toe downwards, by the continuous, but not

[1] Dr. Andrews, " St. Bartholomew's Hospital Reports," x. 350.
[2] Dr. Greenhow, Clin. Soc. Trans. vii. 172.　　　　　[3] Path. Trans. xxiv. p.

constant, contraction respectively of the flexors and extensors of the fore-arm and the muscles of the calf. The face was still, the tongue protruded itself steadily and for long; her body was quiet, and speech was limited. During the night she alarmed her mother by screaming violently, throwing herself about the bed, and tossing her head from side to side. After about twenty minutes she became quiet and fell asleep. Four days later she had a return of pain and swelling in the right knee, friction sound was barely audible over the heart, and the movements of the right arm had lessened and were more simply those of ordinary chorea.

The *affection of the joints* during the early period of the attack of acute rheumatism was severe in three-fifths (15 in 27), and of moderate severity in one-third of the patients (8 in 27), not severe in two instances, and in one, the condition of the joints was not described. The affection of the joints disappeared,, or was much lessened in severity at the time of the delirium, coma or chorea in all those cases (20 in 27) in which the condition of the joints is described. In thirteen cases the affection of the joints was well at the period in question; in four it was slight, and in three it was not severe.

The invariable subsidence of the inflammation of the joints in these cases, when affection of the nervous system takes place, shows that there is some connection between the appearance of the one affection and the disappearance of the other. The improvement of the inflammation of the joints generally coincides with improvement of the general symptoms, unless the heart is inflamed. We may therefore, I think, infer that the presence of trouble in the nervous system, whether accompanied or not by a very excessive rise in temperature, has a distinct association with the lessening of the affection of the joints.

The *perspiration,* before the nervous system was affected, in these cases was noted in ten of the fourteen cases with coma, stupor or convulsions preceded in all but one instance by delirium, and during that early period it was profuse in seven, and moderate or slight in three of those ten cases. The perspiration was observed in eleven of the fourteen cases just noticed during the period of delirium or coma, when it was absent in three, slight in four, moderate or considerable in two, and profuse in two of these eleven cases.

The perspiration was noted both before and during the period of the delirium or coma in nine of those fourteen cases. In eight of those nine patients, the temperature was excessively high at the time of the delirium or coma, and perspiration was then absent or lessened. In one case with delirium, the highest temperature observed was only 103·8°, and perspiration, previously moderate, was then profuse.

The perspiration was observed during both periods in four of the nine cases in which delirium was present without coma or stupor, and was profuse in those four cases during the early period of the disease. One of those patients had on previous days perspired

s 2

freely, but the skin became dry when the temperature rose to 107·3°. In another of them, the skin previously perspiring, felt hot and dry when delirium appeared at a temperature of 103·8°. The perspiration remained profuse in two cases during the period of delirium with hallucinations and tremor, the temperature being then respectively 105° and 102°. Both of those patients were predisposed to affections of the nervous system. Dr. Wilson Fox justly regards the cessation of perspiration while the temperature is still high as a symptom of very great gravity. It would appear from what I have just stated, that the cooling influence of the perspiration may have kept down the temperature in the three latter cases, while in the ten former cases the want of that cooling influence may have allowed the temperature to rise unchecked when heat was supplied from within by the rapid combustion of the tissues of the body during the disease.

The presence of a *miliary eruption* or sudamina was noticed in nearly one-half of the cases (12 in 26).

The *Pericarditis* was of average intensity or severe in eleven and slight in three of the fourteen cases with coma, stupor, or convulsions, in all of which but one the more grave affection of the nervous system was preceded by delirium. In seven of the nine cases with uncomplicated delirium, the pericarditis was of average severity, and in two of them it was slight. The pericarditis was of average severity in the remaining three patients, in none of whom was the temperature above 101·5°, one of them having transient coma, one of them coma, and the other choreal symptoms.

We shall be better able to consider whether the presence of pericarditis had any influence in producing the excessive rise of temperature in cases with "hyperpyrexia" when we have inquired into the whole chain of cases, those namely without as well as those with that affection.

Endocarditis was present in nearly one-half of these cases, with pericarditis and affection of the nervous system (11 in 26), was absent in almost as many (9 in 26), and was doubtful or not noted in the few remaining cases (5 in 26).

Convulsive, Choreiform and Tetaniform Movements.—Movements of a convulsive, choreiform or tetaniform kind affected nine of the twenty-four patients with acute rheumatism and pericarditis in whom the temperature was observed, including the case just related, in which choreal symptoms were present without delirium. Besides these, two patients affected with delirium had distinct *risus sardonicus.*

One of these patients, a shopman in a cigar shop, aged 28, had in the morning muttering delirium, and a temperature of 107°. In the afternoon he had violent spasmodic movements of the whole body, his respirations were semistertorous, his temperature was 110·2°, and an hour later he died.[1] Another of them, a female servant,

[1] Dr. Murchison, Clin. Soc. Trans. i. 32.

being violently delirious, temp. 107·8° F., was bled, and became, as I have already stated, abruptly unconscious. Then succeeded a peculiar series of irregular muscular movements of the hands and arms, with chattering and grinding of the teeth, and convulsive movements of the jaw, or trismus. Fully two hours later, after being in the bath, when she had cooled down to 104°, she had an attack of clonic spasms of the muscles of the arms, lasting some minutes.[1] There were muscular twitchings of the limbs in three patients when in a state of unconsciousness.

One patient, a police-constable, aged 23, who, ten years previously, had been unconscious from a kick in the mouth, after little sleep, had wandering, much jactitation, constant movement of the fingers of the left hand, tremors of the right hand, and subsultus. Two days later there was also frequent rolling of the head from side to side. His temperature was not above 102°.[2] Another patient, a woman aged 29, also rolled her head from side to side, contracted her brows, and distorted her face into various grimaces. Her temperature was 107·8°.[3] One patient, a man aged 23, on the evening before he died, temp. 105·4°, was very delirious, and rolled violently about the bed, so that he required to be held down. This violence quickly passed away, and he then lay half unconscious and moaning loudly.

Symptoms of a more or less tetaniform character, that is to say, with continuous rigidity or contraction of muscles, appeared in five of the cases.

Dr. Wilson Fox's patient, already sketched at page 257, after the bath, temp. 100·6°, had at times spasms of rigidity of the muscles of the lips and neck, but not of the limbs. Another patient, a gardener, seven hours before death, became incoherent, and within ten minutes, unconscious; his lips pouted and rubbed incessantly over the teeth, and his whole voluntary muscles twitched constantly.[4] The third is that of Dr. Wilson Fox just referred to, with chattering and grinding of the teeth, and convulsive movements of the jaw, or "trismus."[5] The fourth case is Dr. Greenhow's, already noticed, with choreal movements of the left hand. When that hand was turned on to its back,[6] there were constant twitching movements of the hand and fingers, and the forefinger became flexed towards the palm. The fifth case is my own, already related at page 258, with choreiform movements of the right arm. Her right hand was bent backwards, her right fingers were flexed, and her right toe pointed downwards, owing to the continuous contraction of the corresponding sets of muscles, which offered steady resistance when put on the stretch. These five cases seem to suggest a combination of convulsive, choreiform and tetaniform movements.

The question naturally arises, were the cases presenting choreiform

---

[1] Dr. Fox. " Treatment of Hyperpyrexia," 44.
[2] Dr. Greenhow, Clin. Soc. Trans. vii. 175.
[3] Dr. Sydney Ringer, *Medical Times and Gazette*, 1867, ii. 380.
[4] Mr. Anderson, *British Medical Journal*, 1871, i. 529.
[5] Loc. cit. p. 48.   [6] Loc. cit. p. 174.

movements associated with endocarditis? The answer to that is, however, as regards these cases, definitely in the negative, for endocarditis was absent, or not observed, in those cases, excepting to a slight and doubtful degree in one of those with muscular twitching. Endocarditis was, however, present in Dr. Wilson Fox's case with spasms of rigidity of the muscles of the lips and neck. I shall again briefly consider these cases when I return to the important question of the association of pericarditis with tetaniform and choreiform movements.

Tremor was present in seven of the cases, all of which have been already alluded to.

II.—CASES WITH SIMPLE ENDOCARDITIS IN WHICH THE NERVOUS SYSTEM WAS AFFECTED AND THE TEMPERATURE, GENERALLY VERY HIGH, WAS OBSERVED.

SUMMARY.

A^3 Had *delirium* followed by *coma*, temp. 104·4°—110·2°   .   4
A^2 Had *delirium* and *convulsive movements*, temp. 111·6°   .   1
B^1 Had uncomplicated *delirium* in three, temp. 108·5°—
    111·4°; in two, temp. 102·8°—103·9°   5
B^2 Had *delirium*, cerebral embolism and hemiplegia, t. 103°   1
B^3 Had *delirium* and *chorea* (minute cerebral embolism)
    temp.   1
Had high temperature without notice of delirium, temp.
    105·8° (ice-bag)   1
                               Total   13

The nervous system was affected in thirteen cases of simple endocarditis in which the temperature was observed. The majority of these cases, like that of those affected with pericarditis, presented an excessively high temperature; and in three of the whole number the temperature, when undergoing a rapid ascent, was arrested in its rise, lowered, and kept down by the use of the cooling bath or the external application of the wet sheet and ice. The temperature was as high as from 108·5° to 111·6° in three-fifths of the cases (7 in 13); and in the one of those cases in which the temperature was the lowest, 108·5°, the vigorous use of ice-cold water within and without arrested the rise of temperature and induced its permanent lowering, followed by the recovery of the patient. In one patient the temperature was checked at 105·8°, and brought down by the bath; and in another the thermometer was at 104·4° during the period of delirium, but was not employed during that of coma. In four of the cases the temperature was only of a moderate height, being from 103·9° to 102·3°; and we may therefore infer that fully two-thirds of the cases with simple endocarditis (9 in 13) in which the nervous system was affected, had "hyperpyrexia."

$A^{2\cdot3}$ Twelve of the thirteen cases had delirium, which passed into coma in four instances, ended in convulsive movements in one, B^1 was without complication in five, was associated with B^2 cerebral embolism and hemiplegia in one patient, and with B^3 minute cerebral embolism and chorea in another. In one instance, in which the temperature was high (105·8°), there was no note of delirium.

A^3 One of the four cases in which delirium passed into coma was a delicate, ailing woman. On the seventh day her temperature in the morning was 102°, but it rose in the evening to 109·5°, when she was comatose. For want of a bath, she was taken downstairs, placed, doubled up, in a washing-tub containing water at 80° cooled to 62°, and cold water was ladled over her body. Spasms soon came on, which were more and more continuous until she was taken out of the bath in one of them after being there for forty-five minutes, while her temperature had fallen to 100·3°. Towards midnight she was much convulsed, the teeth closing firmly on the lower lip and drawing blood. On the tenth day the temperature rose to 105·1°, she was again put into the tub for fifty-eight minutes, and at the end of that time was taken out in a state of well-marked opisthotonos, which passed off gradually in about two hours. She died on the twelfth day.[1]

B^1 Three of the four cases with delirium without coma had high temperatures, 111·4°—108·5°; while in two the temperature was comparatively low, 103·9°—102·8°. One of the patients with delirium and high temperature was a female servant, aged 22. On the eighth day of treatment, temp. 108·5°, her sensorium was much disturbed, and her skin, which hitherto had been moist and sometimes covered with sweat, was dry. Cold was used energetically. Ice-cold water and cloths were applied freely to the body, and ice-water enemata were given every half-hour. In an hour's time she breathed more freely, her head was relieved, and the pulse fell. At half-past six in the evening her temperature was 98·6°, skin perspiring, mind clear, and she felt like a new-born person. Two days later she sat up in bed, and took food with appetite.[2]

In the two cases with comparatively low temperature the delirium was only present during the night. The temperature was 103·9° in the daytime in one of these patients, and 100·4° in the other. Convulsive movements affected four of the thirteen patients belonging to this group with endocarditis.

The *affection of the joints* was severe in eight and was rather severe in one of the thirteen cases with simple endocarditis before the period of delirium or coma; while it was absent in two and not severe in three; and its condition was doubtful in four of those cases during that period.

[1] Dr. Andrews, "Bartholomew's Hospital Reports," x. 346.
[2] Dr. Meding, Archiv der Heilkunde, xi. 467.

Perspiration was profuse in five and absent in one of the cases of simple endocarditis before delirium set in; and it was absent in two, slight in one, probably profuse in one, and doubtful in two of those cases after the appearance of delirium, while it was profuse in another patient who was delirious when admitted and whose temperature never rose above 102·8°.

III.—Cases in which there was no Pericarditis, Endocarditis being absent or doubtful, in which the Nervous System was affected, and the Temperature, generally very high, was observed.

SUMMARY.

A^3 Had *delirium* followed by *coma*, temp. 111·1°—105·8° .		6
A^4 Had *delirium* followed by *somnolence*, temp. 106° . . .		2
B^1 Had *delirium* uncomplicated, temp. 110° to 100·4°. . .		10
Very high temperature without *delirium*, temp. 110·8°—106·3°		2
Twitching of limbs, temp. 102°		1
	Total	21

Twenty-one cases had no pericarditis, endocarditis being absent or doubtful; and the majority of these cases, like that of those with pericarditis and with simple endocarditis, presented an excessively high temperature; and in five of the whole number the temperature, when undergoing a rapid ascent, was arrested in its rise, lowered, and kept down by the use of the cooling bath, the wet sheet, or ice. The temperature was as high as from 106° to 111·2° in three-fifths of the cases (12 in 21), being kept down in the one of those in which it was the least high by the use of the cooling bath. In one-fifth of the cases (4 in 21), the highest ascertained temperature varied from 106° to 103·4°, and in these the cooling bath was not employed. In one-fourth of the cases (5 in 21), the highest temperature varied from 102° to 100·4°. From this summary it would appear that three-fifths of these cases of acute rheumatism without pericarditis, endocardititis being absent or doubtful, in which the nervous system was seriously affected, had hyperpyrexia.

Pericarditis was absent and endocarditis was absent or doubtful, as we have just seen, in twenty-one cases of acute rheumatism in which there was affection of the nervous system and the temperature was ascertained. A^3 In six of those cases delirium gave place to coma, and in one of these the delirium reappeared: A^4 in two delirium passed into somnolence. B^1 Delirium without coma was present in ten cases. Two patients had very high temperature without delirium, one of whom was restless and talked when asleep, and the other had vomiting and dyspnœa; and in one there was twitching of the limbs and body without delirium, the temperature not rising above 102°.

A[3] The whole of the six cases in which delirium passed into coma were fatal. The delirium was present in these patients when the temperature varied from 102·2° to 108·4°, and coma replaced the delirium in five of them at a temperature ranging respectively from 108° to 110°. The highest temperatures observed in these cases towards or at the time of death was from 109·5° to 111·1°. In a case in which delirium gave place to coma and that again to delirium, the temperature about the period of coma was 104°, but eight hours before death it was 105·8°.[1]

The delirium was violent or active in four of these six patients, three of whom got out of bed or tried to do so; and in two of them it was muttering or quiet.

The duration of the delirium varied much in these cases. In one patient the delirium continued for four days, in another two; in one it lasted four hours, and in another, the most interesting of the series, after it was slight for one day, it became muttering for half an hour. The duration of the coma was more constant. It lasted for from an hour to an hour and a half in four cases, and in one for four hours, while in one there was alternate delirium and coma for two days.

A[4] In two cases delirium passed into drowsiness. One of these, a dull, corpulent woman, aged 32, was strange in manner (temp. 103·4°) on the eighth day after admission, and had low muttering delirium. At 2 A.M. on the following night (temp. 105·3°) she awoke restless; and at 5 A.M. (temp. 106°) she was dull and somnolent. She was put for twenty minutes into a bath at 90° to 81°. When in the bath she felt comfortable, but at length she complained of cold (temp. 102°). After this her temperature never rose above 104·7°, she had bronchitis and pneumonia for some days, and finally recovered.

I was favoured by Dr. Murchison with notes of the other case of this class. A lady, aged 35, stout, was attacked with acute rheumatism. At the end of ten days her joints were better, but she became sleepless and delirious. Opium, chloral, and bromide of potassium only made her worse. Her pulse was 108, weak; temp. 102·5°. She gave no signs of peri- or endo-carditis, and had headache. The following is the report of her case ten days later:—" The temperature has been as high as 106°, but is now only 101°. She is heavy and drowsy, but has been very noisy and delirious. Respiration is quick and irregular—cerebral. She swallows well. Pulse 64. Heart seems still sound. Urine is made in bed. There are bedsores, and she has some pains in the joints." She died next day.

B[1] There was delirium without coma in ten cases. In three of these the temperature was very high, being 110° in a fatal case; and 108·2° and 107° respectively in two that recovered after the use of the cooling bath; in one of these the temperature, rarely above 104·6°, once rose to 105°, and this case died in spite of the repeated use of the bath; while the remaining six cases had the comparatively low maximum temperatures respectively of 104·5°, 103·4°, 101·2°, 101·1°,

---

[1] Lebert, " Klinik des acuten Gelenkrheumatismus," p. 55.

101·1°, and 100·4°; and of these the first case (temp. 104·5°) and that in which the temperature was the lowest (100·4°), a case with Bright's disease, died, while the four others recovered.

The duration of the delirium was very various in different cases, having ended in death in one instance in two hours and a half, and being prolonged with interruptions in another for twenty-nine days, the high temperature being kept down and lowered and the delirium from time to time suspended by the cooling effects of a succession of twenty baths.

As I have just said, in two of the three cases with delirium and very high temperature, the temperature was kept in check by the cooling bath. One of these cases, a youth, on the morning of the fourth day of treatment, muttered to himself but could be roused, temp. 107·8°, and at 7.45 temp. 108·2°. After being half an hour in a bath at 76°, his temperature was 101°, and half an hour later 98·8°, when he fell asleep, and awoke in a perfectly conscious state. In the evening, a second bath again lowered the temperature from 105·8° to 98°, when he perspired freely and slept. After this the temperature never rose above 99·8°, and he recovered.[1] The second case, a woman, with a temperature of 107°, was put into a bath at 90° cooled to 42°. Her temperature was lowered to 97·5°, and her mind became clear.[2]

One patient, a man, who had been a free liver, presented throughout from time to time profuse sweating, variable delirium, tremor of hands, subsultus, and twitchings of the face, and a temperature varying from 104·4° to 106·4°. The use of the cooling bath invariably lowered the temperature, restored the patient from a state of delirium to one of consciousness, and caused a subsidence of the other nerve-symptoms, tremor, subsultus, and facial spasms. This condition lasted for twenty-nine days, during which time twenty baths were employed, five of them in one day for a combined period of over five hours, and the patient finally died, the temperature at the instant of death being 104·2°.[3]

Among the six cases with delirium in which the temperature was not very high, varying from 104·5° to 100·4°, two died and four recovered.

One of these cases, with a temperature of 103·5°, was a great beer-drinker. His hands were tremulous, he wandered during the day, was very noisy towards the evening, when he screamed out much, continued in a state of variable delirium for fourteen days, and finally recovered.[4]

The highest temperature observed in the four remaining cases with delirium was 101·4° and 100·4° respectively. Two of them had albumen in the urine, and the other one had obstinate diarrhœa, and was delirious when the diarrhœa was checked.

There were three cases of hyperpyrexia in which there was no

[1] Dr. Weber, Clin. Soc. Trans. v. 186.
[2] Sir William Gull, *Lancet*, 1872, ii. 562.
[3] Dr. Greenhow, Clin. Soc. Trans. vi. 7.
[4] Dr. Johnson, *Lancet*, 1867, i.

delirium. One of these was a man whose temperature rose to 106·3°. He had previously been deaf and very restless. Under the influence of a cooling bath his temperature fell to 101·8°, and later to 99·8°. After the bath his deafness left him, and he did well.[1] Another case, a woman aged 24, was suddenly seized with dyspnœa and vomiting, which continued until death; a short time before which event her temperature was 110·8°.[2]

Convulsive, Choreiform and Tetaniform Movements.—Twitchings were present in four of the twenty-one cases that form this group, in which there was no pericarditis and endocarditis was absent or doubtful. The twitchings affected the body in one instance, the limbs and features in another, the muscles of the face for a long period in another, whenever the temperature rose; and in a fourth, the features occasionally twitched with a sardonic grin. In one case the patient was restless and moved his arms about; but, perhaps with this exception, there were no notable choreiform or tetaniform movements in any of the cases. In two cases there was tremor—in one, of the trunk and limbs, in the other, of the hands.

Twitching movements were present in four of the twenty-six cases with pericarditis, in one of the eleven cases with simple endocarditis, and as we have just seen, in four of the twenty-one cases in which there was no pericarditis and endocarditis was absent or doubtful. Twitching movements were therefore distributed in nearly equal proportion in those three groups of cases, and were therefore not due to pericarditis. Twitchings were present in eight cases with hyperpyrexia, and it is therefore probable that they were associated with the very high temperature. This is borne out by a case of Dr. Greenhow's, in which twitchings came on, and were again and again renewed when the temperature became very high, and were again and again almost or quite suspended by the cooling bath.

In the remaining case with twitchings, a man who was under my care, the temperature was never above 102°. On the fifth day, temp. 100·2°, he had muscular twitchings all over the body, which continued for several days, and reappeared on the twenty-eighth day. There was albumen in the urine on both occasions when the twitchings were present. His recovery was slow.

There were choreiform or tetaniform symptoms—or both—in seven of the twenty-four cases with pericarditis, but in only one of the eleven cases with simple endocarditis, and in none of the twenty cases in which there was no pericarditis, endocarditis being absent or doubtful. The question how far the choreiform and tetaniform movements observed in these cases was connected with pericarditis will be considered when we review the larger series of cases of acute rheumatism with and without pericarditis in which the temperature was not observed.

The *affection of the joints* during the early period of the disease

[1] Dr. H. Thompson, *Medical Times and Gazette*, 1873, i. 269.
[2] Dr. Ogle, *Lancet*, 1870, ii. 154.

was severe in ten, and moderately so in five of the twenty-one cases in which there was no pericarditis and endocarditis was absent or doubtful. The affection of the joints was more severe before than during the delirium or other affection of the nervous system, in all but three cases, in which the joint-affection was equally severe during the two periods. In two of these three exceptional cases the temperature never rose above 102°, in one of these the delirium was only present during the night, and in the other there was no delirium, but twitchings were present for a short time during the early days of the illness.

Perspiration.—The state of the skin is described in one-half of the cases belonging to this group (10 in 21), and all of these had profuse perspiration before the nervous system became affected. In seven of those cases there was either no perspiration, or it was much lessened during the period of delirium. In that case, perspiration was equally copious during the two periods. In three of these cases the skin, which had been perspiring profusely before the excessive rise of temperature, and the occurrence of delirium, was hot and dry when the temperature was 110° to 111·1°; coma was present, and death approached. These clinical facts correspond with those which, as we have already seen, occurred in the analogous cases affected with pericarditis. One of the cases in which there was no affection of the heart was observed by Mr. Anderson night and day. This patient, of a nervous, excitable temperament, a labourer, aged 29, had a hot, dry skin, and rambled during the night for four succeeding nights; but during the three intervening days his skin was covered with a profuse acid perspiration, and his mind was unaffected. On the morning of the fourth day his manner was wild and excitable, not unlike that of a patient in the early stage of delirium tremens, and his skin was hot and dry, and covered with a miliary eruption. After a bath, he sprang out of bed, ran into the grounds, and struggled violently. His temperature at that time was 107°, and later in the evening, ten minutes before his death, it was 110·3°.

Dr. Greenhow's case, already referred to at page 261, offers a contrast in some respects, but not in others, to Mr. Anderson's case. In this man, perspiration was absent with delirium at a temperature of 104·8°, and was absent without delirium after the bath at 100·2°, and was present afterwards with obscured intellect and intermediate temperatures.

Perspiration, which is not present at ordinary temperatures, is indeed an index of the internal production of great heat, and a safety-valve for carrying away a large portion of that heat. When perspiration takes place from an exposed skin in a dry air—in motion —its evaporation tends to keep down the heat. In these patients, however, lying, as they do, in their own perspiration, covered by bed-clothes, in a still air saturated with moisture, evaporation can do comparatively little towards cooling the body.

We must look, then, to some other influence than evaporation to account for the cooling effect of perspiration in acute rheumatism. Such an influence we find in the welling out of hot liquid from every part of the body—a liquid charged with a portion of the surplus heat generated by the rapid combustion or disintegration of the internal structures in that disease. It is self-evident, that if the temperature of the body be 103° or 104°, the fluid poured out from the body must likewise have a temperature of 103° or 104°, and that this fluid during its steady universal expulsion must carry away with it a corresponding proportion of the heat generated within, and so tend to keep down the temperature of the whole of the structures that compose the body.

If, on the other hand, the skin is dry, the chemical heat generated in the rapidly-changing tissues tends not to escape, and may be stored up in accumulating quantities in the blood and the tissues, with the effect of producing an excessively high temperature, or " hyperpyrexia."

Respiration.—I have not made an analysis of the rate of respiration in cases of acute rheumatism with affection of the nervous system, with and without high temperature. One well-observed and well-treated case of hyperpyrexia is sufficient for our present purpose, which is to illustrate the influence of an excessively high temperature of the body on the one hand, and of the cooling of that body on the other, on the frequency of respiration. In Dr. Wilson Fox's case, already related at page 257, when the temperature of the body was 107°, the patient was delirious, and the respiration was 45 in the minute, but when the patient's body had been cooled down by the bath to 98°, the mind was clear, and the respiration was 20 in the minute.

It is evident, therefore, that during hyperpyrexia, the cooling effect of respiration is stimulated to its highest degree by the excessive heat of the body, but that this cooling effect is quite inadequate to keep down the temperature of the body below that of hyperpyrexia.

There were some conditions common to the three sets of cases— those namely with: 1, pericarditis; 2, simple endocarditis; 3, without pericarditis, endocarditis being absent or doubtful—and I shall now briefly notice those conditions.

Restlessness affected a considerable proportion of the patients before the occurrence of delirium. Six of the twenty-seven cases with pericarditis; three of the thirteen cases with simple endocarditis; and ten of the twenty-one cases that had no pericarditis, endocarditis being absent or doubtful, were thus affected with restlessness.

A *miliary eruption* or *sudamina* appeared in a considerable number of the cases, being noticed in twelve of the twenty-seven cases with pericarditis; in three of the thirteen cases with simple endocarditis; and in eight of the twenty-one cases in which there was no pericarditis and endocarditis was either absent or doubtful.

An *abundant secretion of urine* took place in a few of the cases, at the time of the great rise in temperature. The urine was very abundant under those circumstances in three of the twenty-seven cases with pericarditis; in three of the thirteen cases with simple endocarditis; and in two of the twenty-one cases in which there was no pericarditis, endocarditis being either absent or doubtful.

Diarrhœa, sometimes profuse and offensive, was present when the temperature was very high in seven of the twenty-seven cases with pericarditis; in four of the thirteen cases with simple endocarditis; and in five of the twenty-one cases in which there was no pericarditis, and endocarditis was either absent or doubtful.

Excessively high temperature or "hyperpyrexia" in acute rheumatism with and without pericarditis. We have just seen that in sixty-one cases of acute rheumatism in which the temperature of the patient was observed, the nervous system was affected, and we shall now enquire how many of them presented an excessively high temperature, and what was the influence of pericarditis in those cases of hyperpyrexia. The temperature was excessively high, ranging from 106·8° to 111·1° in thirty-one of those sixty-one cases, and was arrested during its rise when it was at from 105° to 106·3° by the use of the cooling bath, or cold externally, in six cases. In three of those six cases, the tendency of the temperature to rise was great, but in three of them it was not so. The temperature was not observed during the period of coma or the last hours of life in three fatal cases in which the temperature was 104·6°, 104·8°, and 105·8° respectively at the time of the last observation, and I consider that these three cases and three of the six in which the high temperature was kept in check by the bath, ought to be added to the thirty-one cases in which the temperature was very high, thus bringing up the number of those with "hyperpyrexia," to thirty-seven of the total number of sixty-one cases. Thus estimated, we find that seventeen of the twenty-seven cases with pericarditis, nine of the thirteen with simple endocarditis, and eleven of the twenty-one without pericarditis, endocarditis being absent or doubtful, either had, or were threatened with, "hyperpyrexia." Among these thirty-seven cases of hyperpyrexia, one had coma without delirium, twenty-one, delirium followed by coma, or, in one instance, stupor, two, delirium with convulsive movements, ten, uncomplicated delirium, and three had neither coma nor delirium.

The case of simple coma, and all but one of the twenty-one cases in which delirium passed into coma, were affected with actual (18) or threatened (3) hyperpyrexia. The temperature observed soon rose above 106° in three cases with delirium and stupor, but in one of these it was kept down and lowered by the cooling bath, while in both the cases which ended fatally with convulsive movements, the temperature was very high. Of the twenty-four cases with uncomplicated delirium, only two-fifths had hyperpyrexia (10 in 26).

Coma preceded by delirium is, as we have just seen, the typical effect of rheumatic hyperpyrexia, and one-half of those with hyperpyrexia and coma preceded by delirium, had pericarditis (10 in 20). From these clinical facts it would appear that hyperpyrexia attacked cases of acute rheumatism almost as frequently when they had pericarditis, as when they were not so affected (17 in 27 with pericarditis, 20 in 37 without pericarditis). When we consider that pericarditis usually attacks only one in every five or six cases of acute rheumatism, we must multiply the cases of pericarditis with hyperpyrexia by five or six if we would make a parallel comparison between those cases with pericarditis and those without it. It would appear from this that the presence of pericarditis in a case of acute rheumatism increases the chance of the occurrence of hyperpyrexia with delirium and coma, in the proportion of four or five to one. An important case successfully treated by Dr. Wilson Fox by the cold bath had pericarditis in its worst form. The dulness or percussion over the region of the pericardium filled the whole left front of the chest from apex to base. In that case the tendency to the renewed excessive rise of temperature after it had been brought down again and again by the cold bath, the ice-bag, or the wet-pack, continued until the seventh day; when the pericardial dulness fell to the first rib mid-sternum, and the tendency to the increase of temperature lessened. It is a clinical fact that here the renewed rise of temperature continued so long as the pericarditis was severe, and gave way when the pericarditis gave way, and it is probable that the continued severity of the pericarditis had an influence in keeping up the tendency to the rise of temperature. It must however not be lost sight of that as a rule, cases of acute rheumatism with pericarditis are in all respects worse than those without it, and that, not only at the time of the pericardial inflammation, but usually also before it. It becomes therefore a question whether or not the same severity of the acute rheumatism itself that brought the pericarditis into existence, brought also the excessively high temperature, with its attendant delirium and coma into existence, the two affections being affiliated, and due to a common cause.

The occurrence of a high temperature of the body in cases of acute rheumatism, corresponds in essential features with the high temperature observed in sun-stroke, in certain exceptional cases of tetanus, and in injuries to the cervical portion of the spinal marrow. In sun-stroke the temperature varies from 112° to 105·5°, the skin is hot and dry, coma supervenes, preceded occasionally by delirium, and death tends to ensue unless the temperature of the body is lowered by cold.[1]

The temperature in tetanus, though variable, does not as a rule rise to a very great height. Wünderlich, however, gives a case in which it attained to 44·75° C. (112·55° F.) before death.[2] This instance resembled in all its main features the cases of hyperpyrexia in acute rheumatism. The patient, before the time of the fatal rise of heat, was very restless; had profuse perspiration and an abundant miliary rash; then came on delirium, night trembling, contracted pupils, and

---

[1] Dr. Levick, "Pennsylvania Hospital Reports," 1868, p. 371; Dr. Gee,'Gulstonian Lectures on Pyrexia, Brit. Med. Journal, 1871, I. 302; Dr. Maclean on Sunstroke, Reynolds' "System of Medicine," II. 128.
[2] Wünderlich, Archiv der Heilkunde, II.

death.   Wünderlich, without giving any reason for it, gives the name
of rheumatic tetanus to another but less extreme case of the same
kind.

Injury of the spinal cord from the fourth to the sixth cervical
vertebra from fracture or caries of the spinal column has induced an
excessively high temperature in several cases published since the
first observation to that effect by Sir Benjamin Brodie.[1]   The symptoms
in these cases closely resemble those of hyperpyrexia in acute rheumatism, but in only one of them was it stated that the final and fatal
coma was preceded by delirium.   One of Dr. Hermann Weber's two cases
was a youth, who could walk supported, but like a drunken man, and
could move his arms twenty minutes after the accident, which caused
fracture and incomplete dislocation of the third, fourth, and fifth cervical vertebræ.   He voided urine frequently and in great quantities.   An
hour after admission his temperature was 100·4°.   Two hours and
a-half after the accident he passed liquid motions unconsciously, had
occasional convulsive twitches in the arms and legs, his skin was
slightly moist and hot, and his temperature was 109·58°.   Four and
a-half hours after the accident there was complete coma, and his
temperature was 111°, and it was 111·2° at the time of death, eight
hours after the accident.[2]

Dr. Burdon Sanderson, who has favoured me with the use of the
manuscript notes of his lectures delivered at Manchester, gives an
account of experiments made by him in which the cervical portion
of the spinal cord was injured.   He found that there was no increase
of temperature for two hours after the injury to the cord, but that at
the end of that time it began to rise and to rise rapidly, attaining
a very great elevation, 42° C. or 107·6° F., or higher than that of fever.
Dr. Burdon Sanderson considers that this experiment shows conclusively that the process of which the higher temperature is the outcome,
must consist in a gradual modification of those processes on which
heat production depends, must have as wide a localisation as they,
and cannot therefore be attributed to any sudden interruption of the
relation between the centre and the periphery of the nervous system.
These experiments correspond remarkably with Dr. Hermann Weber's
case just reported.

*Cases in which the temperature of the body was below that of hyper-
pyrexia.*—We have just seen that of the sixty-one cases of acute rheumatism associated with affection of the nervous system in which the
temperature was observed, in thirty-seven there was actual (31) or
threatened (6) "hyperpyrexia."   In the remaining twenty-four cases,
the maximum temperature of the body observed in the different
instances varied from 99·3° to 106·3° temp.   Ten of the twenty-seven
cases with pericarditis, four of the thirteen with simple endocarditis,
and ten of the twenty-one without pericarditis, and in which endo-

[1] Sir Benjamin Brodie, Med. Chir. Trans. **xx.** 118 ;   Reineke, Berliner Klinische
Wörterbuch, 1869, 113, 301 ;   Billroth, Archiv für Klin. Chirurgie Langenbeck, ii. 482.
[2] Dr. Hermann Weber, Clin. Soc. Trans. I. 163.

carditis was absent or doubtful, belong to this group in which the temperature was not excessively high. In twelve of these twenty-one cases, the maximum temperature varied in the different cases from 103° to 106°, and in nine of them from 99·3° to 102·8°.

A considerable proportion of those who were attacked with delirium at comparatively low temperatures were either habitual drinkers, or of a nervous temperament, or had been subject to anxieties and privation, or to lowering diseases, or had received injuries affecting the nervous system, and in several of those cases the affection was closely allied to delirium tremens; several such cases occurred among those affected with pericarditis. This was so in Dr. Southey's two cases with pericarditis, referred to at pages 257, 258, in Dr. Greenhow's case, given at page 258, in Dr. Murchison's two patients, quoted at page 265, and in a patient of my own.

To these must be added the case with which Dr. Southey favoured me since the above was written, given at page 258, and two of Dr. Andrew's cases.

Most of these cases had pericarditis.

CASES OF ACUTE RHEUMATISM WITH AFFECTIONS OF THE NERVOUS SYSTEM IN WHICH THE TEMPERATURE OF THE BODY WAS *not* OBSERVED.

There were 119 cases of acute rheumatism with affections of the nervous system in which the temperature was not observed. Of these 65 had pericarditis; 16 had simple endocarditis; and 38 were free from pericarditis, endocarditis being absent or doubtful.

TEMPERATURE WAS *NOT* OBSERVED.

I.—CASES WITH PERICARDITIS.

TOTAL PATIENTS OF BOTH SEXES, 65.

SEX AND AGE . . .

    MALE PATIENTS. Total **37**.—Below 21 years, 15 (1, 2, 3, 20, 23, 24, 25, 32, 42, 43, 49, 50, 55, 60, 65); 21 to 25 years, 10 (9, 12, 13, 31, 48, 52, 56, 61, 63, 7); 64; above 25 years, 12 (5, 6, 10, 11, 14, 15, 16, 40, 47, 54, 58, 62).

    FEMALE PATIENTS. Total **27**.—Below 21 years, 19 (17, 19, 21, 22, 26, 27, 28, 29, 30, 33, 34, 36, 37, 38, 41, 45, 46, 51, 57); 21 to 25 years, 1 (4); above 25 years, 7 (7, 18, 35, 39, 44, 53, 59). SEX AND AGE NOT STATED, 1 (8).

OCCUPATION, HABITS, AND PREVIOUS CONDITION . .

    MALE PATIENTS, **37**.—*Workers out of doors*, **12** : labourers, 5 (6, 10, 40, 43, 54); gardener, 1 (32, excitable, not under control); sawyer, 1 (62); carpenters, 2 (16 drinker, 38, 61); butcher-boy, 1 (35). Painter, 1 (5). *Workers in-doors*, **3** : greengrocer, 1 (60); sealmaker, 1 (11); copperworker, 1 (13). Schoolboy, 1 (2). Potman, &c., **2** : potman, 1 (56); brewer's worker, 1 (64). *No occupation*, **5** (1, 3, 23 chorea four years before, 42, 49). *Occupation not stated*, **14** (9, 12, 14 strong, 15 rather intemperate, 20, 24, 25, 31, 47, 48, 50, 52, 63, 65).

    FEMALE PATIENTS, **27**.—*Active in-door Workers*, **3** : Servants, 6 (7, 19, 41, 44, 46, 57); cook, 1 (59); married, 1 (39); *Sedentary in-door Workers*, **2**, sempstress, etc., 2 (4, 21). *No occupation*, **4** (22 chorea two years before, 30, 45, 51) *Occupation not stated*, **13** (17, 18, 26, 27, 28, 29 often had rheumatism, 33, 34, 35, 36, 37, 38, 53, 66 anæmic.

CHARACTER OF AFFECTION OF THE NERVOUS SYSTEM .

A¹.—Had *Coma* not preceded by delirium, **3**—12, died ◡.   44, consciousness restored after bath, ⌒ exudation on pia mater.
  47, became unconscious in vapour bath, died in twenty minutes ◡.

A².—Had *Coma* ending in convulsions and death, **2**—10, ◡.   11, ◡.

A³.—Had *Delirium* followed by *Coma*, **5**—8, ◡.   5, ◡.   6, ◡.   31, del, convulsions, tetaniform spasms, coma, ◡.
  33, del. choreiform and tetaniform movements, coma, ◡.   Had *semi-consciousness for some days*, 1 57.—*Recovered.*

B¹.—Had *Delirium* without coma or other important complication, **21**.—1, del. during nights, ◡.   2, del., incoherent, ◡.
  would get out of bed, maniacal—*Recovered.*   7, sudden loud del., wet packing, better—*Recovered.*   9, strong del. ◡.
  10, del. nights—*Recovered.*   14, violent del., convulsive movements, ◡.   15, violent del.—*Recovered.*
  16, troubling agitation, fastened down, confused—*Recovered.*   17, violent del., out of bed, agitation, ◡.
  18, del., jactitation—*Recovered.*   49, occasional del. ◡.   30, severe del. ◡.   52, tremor, furious del. ◡.
  19, transient del.—*Recovered.*   39, occasional del., albumen in urine—*Recovered.*   63, transient del.—*Recovered.*
  25, furious del. ◡.   59, weak, tremor, violent del., hallucination as in del. trem.—*Recovered.*
  58, del., agitation, pyæmia, injected arachnoid.   "Symptoms of inflammation of brain," probably delirium, 2 8 ◡.

B².—Had *Delirium* passing into temporary insanity, taciturn melancholy, lasting three weeks to three months, **11**—19, despondent, speech confused
  continued twelve days, improved by wet sheet—*Recovered.*   36, dejected, hallucination, taciturn, ill fully six weeks—*Recovered.*
  37, del., taciturn and rational by turns, ill two months—*Recovered.*   38, reason gave way—*Recovered.*
  39, del., confused, hallucinations, speech obscure, ill three months ◡.   41, mind confused, duration doubtful—*Recovered.*
  40, silent, melancholy, hallucinations, ill about a month (?)—*Recovered.*
  46, melancholy taciturn, cried out (wet sheet), silent, ill about one month—*Recovered.*
  54, mollism, aphasia, taciturn, ill about three weeks—*Recovered.*
  56, depressed, taciturn, refused food, evacuations in bed, ill about two months—*Recovered.*

B³.—Had *Delirium* passing into temporary insanity with *Chorea, choreiform or tetaniform movements*, **5**—29, choreic movements of right arm and leg,
  childish manner—sometimes irritable, sometimes rational, 7th day, less chorea, better, 10th day more rational, 35th day well—*Recovered.*
  30, violent chorea, incoherent, utterance difficult, died 10th day.   31, taciturn, violent chorea, noisy del., died 8th day ◡.
  3, del., better, stupor, stubborn, hallucinations, choreiform movements, speech varied, convulsed, 23rd day ◡.
  33, eyes rolled, carried, tetanic spasm, del., idiotic and violent by turns till 26th day—*Recovered.*

THE DURATION OF DELIRIUM AND COMA, AND THEIR RELATION TO PERICARDITIS AND ENDOCARDITIS

A¹—*Coma*, 12 {sudden short coma.
{peric. and endoc.

44 {sudden coma, restored by bath
{pericarditis and endocarditis

47 {coma twenty minutes
{slight pericard., no endocard.

A²—*Coma, Convulsions,* 10 {coma 1 hour
{pericard., no endoc

11 {convulsions, speedy death
{pericard., endocard (?)

A³—*Delirium and Coma,* 3 {del. 1 night, coma short
{peric., no endoc.

33 {del. 9 days, coma short (?)
{peric. and endoc.—*Recovered*

5 {del. 1 night, coma
{pericarditis, no endocarditis

6 {del. 1 night, coma short
{pericarditis, no endocarditis

81 {del. 7-8 nights. occ. days
{pericarditis and endocarditis

2 {del. 2 nights and 1 day
{peric. no endoc. (?)

Semi-Conscious, 57 {almost unconscious 2-3 days
{pericard. (?), endocard —Rec.

B—*Delirium,* 1 {del. 1 or 2 nights, later 2 or 3 days
{pericarditis, no endocarditis (?)

9 {del. 12 hours in night
{peric., no endoc.

14 {del. 5 nights, remission in night
{slight peric. and endoc

4 {del. several nights and 2 days
{peric. and endoc.—*Recovered*

7 {del. 1 night and day (wet pack)
{pericarditis, endocarditis (?)—*Recovered*

17 {del. 1 day, remission, coma 4 hours
{pericarditis, no endocarditis (?)

18 {del. 2 or 3 days
{per., no end. (?)

15 {violent. del. 2 hours, del. about 4-5 days)
{pericarditis (?). endocarditis—*Recovered*

16 {del. 3 or 4 days
{peric., no endo.—*Recovered*

49 {del. occasionally
{per. and end.

50 {slight del. before death
{peric. and endoc.

52 {del. 3 days
{slight per., no end.

55 {del. about 1 night
{per. and end.—*Recovered*

59 {del. 1 or 2 nights
{slight peric, endoc. (?)

63 {del. 2 or 3 nights
{per. and end.

68 {del. a few hours
{per., no end. (?)

64 {del. trem. 2-3 days
{per., no end—*Recovered*

53 {del. 1 day
{per. and end

B²—*Delirium passing into temporary insanity.* (For duration see above). Presence of pericarditis and endocarditis—19, per. and end.; 35, per. no end (?); 36, per. and end.; 37, per. and end.; 38, per. and end.; 39, per. and end.; 40, per. and end.; 41, per. and end.; 46, per. and end.; 64, per. and end.; 56, per and end. *Delirium passing into temporary insanity, with chorea.*—29, per. and end.—*Recovered;* 30, per. and end.; 21, per. and end. 43, per. and end.—*Recovered.*

B³—*Delirium, Chorea, and choreiform movements,* 24 {del. chorea, 7 days
{per. and end.

45 {childish, chorea, after peric., 3 weeks)
{pericard. and endocard.—*Recovered*

51 {occ. del., chorea 3 days
{pericard. and endocard

Jactitation, 61 {mutteriug, movement of hand 3-4 days}
{pericard. and endocard.—*Recovered*

Choreiform and Tetaniform Movements, 68 {conv. mort. 4 days
{peric. and endoc.

65 {opisth. 2 days
{peric. & endo.

C¹—*Chorea, choreiform movements,* no delirium, 22, peric. and endoc.—*Recovered;* 23 {chorea 3 weeks
{peric. and end.

25 {chorea and pericarditis simultaneous
{peric. and endoc —*Recovered*

26 {Chorea in course of pericarditis
{pericard., endocard. not named}

27 {chorea 5 days
{per. and end

28 {chorea 6 days
{per. and end.—*Recovered*

42, per., end. (?).

C² {jactitation a few days
{peric. and end

C²—*Jactitation,* 80 {peric. and endo.

C³—*Choreiform and tetaniform movements,* 32 {choreif. movement 19 days, tot. movement 7 days
{pericarditis and endocarditis

60 {chorea 1 day, choreif. and tet. movement
{30 days pericarditis and endocarditis

4a, medial manner, twitchings of face and arm.—*Recovered.*

Had *Delirium* and *jactitation* with *choreiform movements,* (excluding 1 (43) that is included among those with temporary insanity), 1.—61, muttered, needless movements with hands.—*Recovered.*

B³—Had *Delirium* with *tetaniform movements* (excluding 1 (34) that is included among those with temporary insanity), 2.—68, trembles, not quite rational, continual movement of lower jaw and biting of lip, knocks about; 65, occasional del., slight opisthotonos.

C¹—Had *Chorea* without Delirium, 7.—22, first chorea, then pericarditis, then acute rheumatism (usual order reversed)—*Recovered.* 23, chorea and pericarditis on admission; 25, endocarditis, pericarditis, ... at same time—*Recovered* 26, chorea came on in course of acute rheumatism and pericarditis; 27, involuntary movement of limbs, with chorea; 28, Involuntary movement of ... arm, jerking of trunk, chorea ... in six days, apparently sane and ... with pericarditis—*Recovered* 42, violent chorea, symptoms of pericarditis improved.—*Recovered*

C²—Had *Jactitation* in course of pericarditis, 1.—80, screaming and most violent jactitation of body for short time in course of illness.

C³—Had *choreiform* and *tetaniform movements,* 2.—32, twitchings of face, movement of head from side to side, convulsions like tetanus and opisthotonon, rolled eyes, smacked lips; 60, choreiform movements, later rigid bending of left hand on forearm, and forearm on arm.

D—Had *slight Fit,* with ptosis of one eye, few hours before death, 1.—43.

01, occasional del., choreiform twitching three days

1.—CASES WITH PERICARDITIS—*Continued.*

AFFECTION OF JOINTS

A^1—*Coma.* Convulsion {before coma or delirium} $10\{-+(?);\ 11\{\begin{smallmatrix}++\\-.\end{smallmatrix}$ A^3—*Delirium Coma,* $5\{\begin{smallmatrix}+\\\text{prob.}\end{smallmatrix}\ O(?);\ 6\{\begin{smallmatrix}+:+\\-;\end{smallmatrix}\ 33\{\begin{smallmatrix}+\\(?).\end{smallmatrix}$ B^1—Delirium, $12\{\begin{smallmatrix}++\\-+\end{smallmatrix}$ {during coma or delirium}

$14\{\begin{smallmatrix}+:\\(?).\end{smallmatrix}\ 15\{\begin{smallmatrix}+:\\O.\end{smallmatrix}\ 16\{\begin{smallmatrix}+:\\(?).\end{smallmatrix}\ 17\{\begin{smallmatrix}+\\-\text{ or }O.\end{smallmatrix}\ 49\{\begin{smallmatrix}+:\\(?).\end{smallmatrix}\ 55\{\begin{smallmatrix}+:\\(?).\end{smallmatrix}\ 59\{\begin{smallmatrix}+\\\text{coc.}+.\end{smallmatrix}\ 62\{\begin{smallmatrix}+:\\(?).\end{smallmatrix}\ 64\{\begin{smallmatrix}+.\\O.\end{smallmatrix}$ B^2—Temporary insanity, $35\{\begin{smallmatrix}+:+\\-:.\end{smallmatrix}\ 39\{\begin{smallmatrix}(?)\\+:\end{smallmatrix}\ 40\{\begin{smallmatrix}+:\\(?).\end{smallmatrix}\ 64\{\begin{smallmatrix}+:\\+:.\end{smallmatrix}$

$56\{\begin{smallmatrix}+.+\\-+\text{ or }O+.\end{smallmatrix}$ B_3—*Delirium Chorea* {before chorea} $21\{\begin{smallmatrix}+:\\(?).\end{smallmatrix}$ {during chorea} $43\{\begin{smallmatrix}+:\\-+:\end{smallmatrix}\ 6,\ -+.$ B—*Chorriform and islaniform movements,* $34\{\begin{smallmatrix}+:\\(?)\end{smallmatrix}$ $58\{\begin{smallmatrix}+:\\-.\end{smallmatrix}$

C—*Chorea, no Delirium,* $28\{\begin{smallmatrix}+:\\(?)\end{smallmatrix}\ 60\{\begin{smallmatrix}-+:\\-+.\end{smallmatrix}$

PERSPIRATION

{Before affection of nervous system} A^3—*Coma, convulsion,* $11\{\begin{smallmatrix}+.\\(?).\end{smallmatrix}$ A^3—*Delirium coma,* $5\{\begin{smallmatrix}+:\\-.\end{smallmatrix}$ B—*Delirium,* $2\{\begin{smallmatrix}(?)\\O\end{smallmatrix}\ 9\{\begin{smallmatrix}+:\\+.\end{smallmatrix}\ 14\{\begin{smallmatrix}+:\\(?).\end{smallmatrix}\ 16\{\begin{smallmatrix}+:\\(?).\end{smallmatrix}\ 40\{\begin{smallmatrix}+:+\\-(?).\end{smallmatrix}$ {After affection of nervous system}

$55\{\begin{smallmatrix}+:\\(?).\end{smallmatrix}\ 59\{\begin{smallmatrix}+:\\\text{coc.}+.\end{smallmatrix}\ 62\{\begin{smallmatrix}O\ 1\text{st day};\\+\ 2\text{nd day}.\end{smallmatrix}\ 64\{\begin{smallmatrix}+:\\+.\end{smallmatrix}$ B—*Temporary insanity,* $54\{\begin{smallmatrix}+:\\(?).\end{smallmatrix}$ *Chorea,* $21\{\begin{smallmatrix}+:\\(?).\end{smallmatrix}\ 60\{\begin{smallmatrix}+:\\\text{cold sweat.}\end{smallmatrix}$

Miliary Eruption, Sudamina, 5, 6, 9, 16, 44, 53, 58.

Face.—Flushed, 6, 34, 53; pale 1, 7, 27 (before del.), 81 (before del.), 32, 40; flushed, then pale (when worse), and again flushed (when better), 58; clouded, 5; dusky, 6; anxious, 2, 14, 31, 34, 54, 58, 60, 61, 64.

AFFECTIONS OF NERVOUS SYSTEM

Restlessness, 1, 2, 3, 4, 6, 16, 17, 18, 21, 31, 33, 34, 43, 45, 46, 54, 58, 60, 61, 62, 64. *Trembling,* 16, 52, 58, 64. *Moaned,* 2, 35. *Noisy,* 21. *Shrieked,* screamed, or cried out loud, 6, 7, 21, 30, 31, 43, 46. *Agitation,* 14, 16, 52, 53, 55.

Diarrhœa, 5, 16, 44, 56, 58, 61, 62. *Motions involuntary,* 7, 16, 44, 56.

CONVULSIVE CHOREI-FORM OR TETANI-FORM SYMPTOMS.

Convulsive movements, 3. Subsultus, 64. Twitching of muscles of mouth, 32; of face, 64; of voluntary muscles, 51. Jactitation of joint and movement of body, 30; of limbs, 5, 16: of face, 18: of left arm, 30: of right arm and leg, 33. 17, Involuntary movements of limbs, 37. Objectless movement with fingers, 61. Head thrown from side, to side, 20, 21, 32.

AFFECTIONS OF IN-TELLECT

Would get out of bed, 4, 17, 21, 33, 35, 43. Hallucinations, 19, 36, 39, 40, 43, 55 (?)

SEX AND AGE . . .
{ TOTAL PATIENTS, 16.
MALE PATIENTS. Total 9.—Below 21 years, 3 (3, 6, 12); 21 to 25 years, 2 (4, 14); above 25 years, 3 (2, 5, 9).
FEMALE PATIENTS. Total 8.—Below 21 years, 2 (1, 8); 21 to 25 years, 3 (14, 15, 16); above 25 years, 3 (7, 10, 13). }

OCCUPATION, HABITS, AND PREVIOUS CONDITION . .
{ MALE PATIENTS. Total 9.—Workers out of doors, 2: laborious, 1: laborer, 1 (2): among horses, 1: post-boy, 1 (5). Plumber's labourer, 1 (11). Workers in-doors, 3: servant, 1 (14, nervous, not robust); shoemaker, 1 (10); upholsterer, 1 (3). Occupation not stated, 2 (6, 9).
FEMALE PATIENTS. Total 8.—Active in-door Workers 4: Servants, 4 (4, 7, 13, 15). No occupation, 2 (1, 8, 12). Occupation not stated, 1 (16). }

CHARACTER OF AFFECTION OF THE NERVOUS SYSTEM
{
A¹—Had Convulsions and Coma, 1.—15, 43rd day—rigors, restless, convulsions, impaired consciousness; 44th day—violent convulsions, coma, urine bloody ○.
A²—Had Delirium followed by Coma, 1.—16, muttering delirium, depressed, drowsy, active delirium, coma, death. Had embolism of minute cerebral arteries ○.
B¹—Had Delirium uncomplicated, a., 7.—1, sleepless, continuous agitation, del. often loud (9 days) ○—; 2, violent del. (about 1 day,) agitation ○—; 14, del. (2 nights and 1 day) (?), somnambulism, much agitatel—Recovered; 10, restless, quite del. (1 night) ○—; 14, violent del. (4 days)—Recovered; 12, del., left bed 1st night, 3rd night lay muttering—Recovered; 13, wandering del. (1 day and several nights)—Recovered.
B²—Had Delirium passing into temporary insanity, taciturn melancholy, 3.—5, del., left bed, dogged silence (3 weeks) ○—; 4, restless, hallucinations, apathetic, slowly recovered; 3, melancholy, spoke low, hallucinations, ill about 2 months—Recovered; 6, taciturn, hallucinations, imbecility. Ill 2 months ○—; 7, violent del., taciturn, hallucinations, melancholy, pendulum movement of head, ill about 3 months—Recovered.
C—Had Choreal movements, 1.—3, apparently no del., choreal movements, violent restlessness ○.
E—Had Embolism and Hemiplegia, 1.—2, headache, agitation, right hemiplegia, apoplectic symptoms, clot in basilar artery ○.
}

AFFECTION OF JOINTS
{
A⁴—Convulsions, Coma {before coma}15{−.+. {during coma} {+ (very severe)
14{+.+. 10{+.+. 11{−.+. or +(?) 12{(del on admission) 1{O + (not severe) {before delirium →} 2{+.+. 3{+.+. s{−.+.
−. (?); −.+ or +(?); −. (del on admission). O or −.(none or slight); {during delirium →} −.; (?); (?).
7{O + or − +. C—Embolism, delirium − 16{ (del. −. B—Delirium and Temporary Insanity, 3{+.(?); 4{+.+. Embolism, hemiplegia, 14{+.+.
O during del. −. Choreal Movements, 8{−.+. O or −.
}

PERSPIRATION . . . .
{ B¹—Delirium (a) with agitation, 2{+.+. (b) Uncomplicated delirium, 10{+. 11{+.+. 11′.O + (del. on admission). }

Sudamina, 11.

Face.—Red, 2 (before del.); pale, 3, 6, 12; dusky, 12, 13.

Diarrhœa, 3, 5, 11 (?). Involuntary evacuations, 16.

AFFECTIONS OF NER-VOUS SYSTEM . .}
{ Restless, 3, 4, 6, 8, 10, 15, 16. Agitation, 1, 2, 9, 14. Pendulum movement of head, from side to side, backwards and forwards, 7. }

CASES OF ACUTE RHEUMATISM, WITH AFFECTIONS OF THE NERVOUS SYSTEM, IN WHICH THE TEMPERATURE WAS *NOT OBSERVED—Continued.*

III.—CASES WITHOUT PERICARDITIS, ENDOCARDITIS BEING ABSENT OR DOUBTFUL.

TOTAL PATIENTS, 38.

SEX AND AGE . . . .

MALE PATIENTS. Total **25**.—Below 21 years, 2 (15, 27): from 21 to 25 years, 6 (3, 7, 17, 22, 28, 38); above 25 years, 12 (5, 6, 8, 9, 14, 18, 20, 21, 27, 30, 35, 36). Age not specified, **5** (10, 11, 16, 23, 26).

FEMALE PATIENTS. Total **12**.—Below 21 years, 2 (24, 25); 21 to 25 years, 5 (1, 2, 13, 19, 33); above 25 years, 3 (4, 29, 34). Age not specified, 2 (31, 32). Sex and age doubtful, 1 (12).

OCCUPATION, HABITS, AND PREVIOUS CONDITION . . .

MALE PATIENTS. Total **25**.—*Workers out of doors*, **8** : laborious, 2 (5, 20 drunkard); among horses, 1 : groom 1 (17). Gentleman, 1 (26). *Workers in-doors*, **12** : servants, 4 (7, 15, 21, 23, robust); clerk, 1 (18); baker, 1 (14); tailor, 1 (28); shoemaker, 1 (6); typographic worker, 1 (16); barmen, brewer's servant, 3 (36, 38, 3). *Occupation not stated*, **8** (8, 9, 10, 11, 22, 27 formerly drunkard, 30, 35).

FEMALE PATIENTS. Total **12**.—*Active in-door Workers*, **8** : servants, 4 (2, 13, 19, 29); nurse, 1 (31); married, 3 (33, 34, 4 widow of landlord). *No occupation*, **2** (24, 25). *Occupation not stated*, **2** (1, 33). Sex and occupation not stated, 1 (12).

CHARACTER OF AFFECTION OF THE NERVOUS SYSTEM.

A¹—Had *Coma* not preceded by delirium, **2**.—14, suddenly lost consciousness, soon dead ⌒; 34, agitation, coma about 2 hours ⌒.

A²—*Convulsions and Coma*, without delirium, **2**.—22, sudden convulsions, coma, speedy death ⌒; 29, sudden convulsions, coma 12 hours ⌒.

A³—Had *Delirium* followed by *Coma*, **8**.—3, sudden violent del. (about 12 hours ?), sopor, coma (2-3 hours) ⌒; 1, wandering (2 nights), tremor, violent del. (few hours ?), quiet, coma, death ⌒; 19, restless, del. (1-2 nights), tremor, violent del. (few hours ?), coma (few hours) ⌒; 16, minurua), heavy, coma (3 nights) ⌒; 17, del., coma (strangulated intestine 6th day) ⌒; 37, wandering, trembled (albuminuria), heavy, coma (3 nights) ⌒; 17, del., coma (strangulated intestine 6th day) ⌒; 8, del. (1½ day), coma (pyæmia ?) ⌒.

A⁴—*Delirium* followed by *Stupor*, **2**.—15, inarticulate cries, accompanied by imperfect consciousness (37 hours, including del.); 5, del. (1 night and day), left bed, stupor, del. (about 24 hours)—*Recovered.*

B¹—Had uncomplicated *Delirium*, **14**.—6, restless, very del. (3 nights) ⌒; 7, restless, left bed, del. (1 night) ⌒; 13, restless, del. (1 day) ⌒; 18, del., restless, violent del., out of bed (2 nights, 1 day) ⌒; 22, sudden struggling del. (½ hour) ; 33, violent del. (3 days, and nights) ⌒; 4, del., quick, return of recollection, restless, collapse (1 day and night) ⌒; 38, restless, hurried in speech (1 nuch) ⌒; 9, excessive agitation, del. (2 days), sleep, rational—*Recovered*, 36, violent del. (about 4 days ?), out of bed, quiet, sept. rational—*Recovered*, 12, cerebral symptoms, del. (4 days), trembling, agitation, purt. diffusion pia mater ⌒; 10 and 11, "brain symptoms"—both recovered.

B²—Had *Delirium* passing into temporary insanity, tacitum melancholy, 1 or 2 months. 3.—20, during mornings, morose; tacitum ; during nights, lively del., hard to keep in bed, ill about 1 month ⌒—*Recovered*; 21, hallucinations, despondent, trembled, stammered, ill 1-2 months—*Recovered*. 27, sudden night and day, violent fits of noisy del. tacitum, sulky, ill about 1 month—*Recovered*. Had *Delirium, temporary insanity, choreiform* movements, 2—35, speech slow, hallucinations, del. in paroxysms, choreic and convulsive movements, del. continuous, ill about 2 months—*Recovered*.

B³—Had *Delirium* and *choreiform* movements, **1**.—24, speech very indistinct, choreiform movements in arm and face, noisy screaming del. at night, 25, very restless, moved arm but not in jerks, did not answer questions, movements more violent, constant del.—*Recovered*.

B⁴—Had *Delirium* and *tetaniform* movements, **1**.—26, tetanic spasms, opisthotonos, violent del.—*Recovered*.

F—Had *paraplegia*, **2**.—31, pain in back, lower limbs paralyzed (some time)—*Recovered*; 32, stupor 2 days ill, then paraplegia, case incomplete (ill some time).

G—Had agitation and prostration, 1.—35, agitation, prostration, death rapid ⌒

AFFECTION OF JOINTS {

Before delirium
During delirium or coma

A^1—Coma, 14 {+: ℧: ; 34{+. +. A^4—Convulsions, coma, 28{+: ℧: ; 29{+: ℧. A^5—Delirium, coma, 3{+ or − +: ; 1{+: ; 19{+: ℧:.

2{+: +: ; 8{O. +. A^4—Delirium, stupor, 18{+: ℧: ; 5{O + or −+. B^1—Delirium, 6{−: +: ; 7{O + ℧; 18{+: +:; 38{−: +:; 9{O + +.

36{+: ; 30{+: O + ℧. B^2—Delirium, temporary insanity, 20{+ or −+; 21{O: +:; 37{O + ℧. Delirium, temp. insanity, 22{−+ ℧; 23{−: O +: ℧. choreiform movements

C^3—Delirium, choreiform movements, 24{−+: . Agitation, prostration, 35{−+.
}

PERSPIRATION {

Before delirium or coma
During delirium or coma

A^1—Coma 14{+: ℧: ; 34{+. +. A^4—Convulsions, coma, 28{+: ℧:. 29{+: ℧. A^5—Delirium, coma, 3{+: ; 1{+: ℧:; 19{+: ℧.

A^4—Delirium, stupor, 15 {O +. 5{O. + B^2—Delirium, 18{+: +: ; 28{+: ℧:; 4{+: O. 30{O: +. B^3—Delirium, temporary insanity, 20 {+: ℧:; 21{−+: +.
}

Miliary Eruption, Sudamina, 5, 9, 19, 29, 34.

Face.—Flushed, 1, 8, 19 (before delirium); pale, 4, 9, 15; dusky, 1, 37; livid, congested, heavy, anxious, 37. Pain of neck, 21. Stiffness of neck early in illness, 24.

Diarrhœa, 4, 6, 6, 9, 15, 37. Motions involuntary, 4, 9, 15, 37. Urine abundant, 9.

AFFECTIONS OF NERVOUS SYSTEM { Restlessness, movement of various muscles of hands and feet during sleep, 5, 4, 6, 7, 13, 18, 19, 25, 38. Sleepless, 24, 27. Trembling, 1, 19, 30, 37. Inarticulate cries, 15. Screaming, 24. Agitation, 9, 15, 30, 34, 35.

CONVULSIVE, CHOREI-FORM OR TETANI-FORM SYMPTOMS. { Startings on falling asleep or during sleep, 36, 37. Very violent movements of arms and legs, 25. Rolling of head from side to side, 24. Constantly flexed and extended fingers, 22.

AFFECTIONS OF IN-TELLECT. { Would get out of bed, 5, 7, 18, 20, 21, 22, 24. Had hallucinations, 21, 22, 23.

CASES OF PERICARDITIS, NEITHER RHEUMATIC NOR FROM BRIGHT'S DISEASE, ACCOMPANIED BY AFFECTIONS OF THE NERVOUS SYSTEM.

TOTAL PATIENTS, 26.

SEX AND AGE. — MALE PATIENTS, **19.**—Below 21 years, 7 (2, 6, 7, 10, 20, 22, 26); 21 to 25 years, 2 (4, 18); above 25 years, 10 (3, 11, 14, 15, 16, 17, 21, 23, 24, 25).
FEMALE PATIENTS, Total **7**.—Below 21 years, 3 (8, 9, 19); 21 to 25 years, 1 (16); above 25 years, 2 (5, 12). Age not stated, 1 (1).

OCCUPATION, HABITS, AND PREVIOUS CONDITION. — MALE PATIENTS, Total **19**.—*Workers out of doors*, **3** ; coachman 1 (24 drunkard); shoe-black, 1 (14). *Workers in-doors*, **3** ; paper-stainer, 1 (22); printer, 1 (4); schoolboy, 1 (6). *No occupation*, **3** (2, 7, 20). *Occupation not stated*, **8** (3, 10, 15, 16 creole, 17, 19, 21, 23, 25 gin drinker, 26).
FEMALE PATIENTS. Total **7**.—*Active in-door Worker*, **1** ; married, 1 (12). *No occupation*, **1** (8). *Occupation not stated*, **5** (1, 5, 9, 11, 12, 18 creole).

DISEASE (IF ANY) WITH WHICH PERICARDITIS WAS ASSOCIATED. — Uncomplicated Pericarditis, **9**—(1, 3, 4, 5, 7 granulations on surface of heart, 9, 10, 11, 12 after miscarriage). Pericarditis with chorea, 2 (8, 19). Pericarditis probably with Bright's disease, 1 (13). Pericarditis with pleurisy, 3 (14 left, 15 left, 16 right). Pericarditis with pyæmia, 4 (2, 6, 17, 20, 21). Pericarditis with pleuro-pneumonia, 3 (4, 18, 24 left). Phthisis, 1 (25 vast cavity right lung).
Empyema, 2 (22, 26 both left).

CHARACTER OF AFFECTION OF THE NERVOUS SYSTEM.

A¹—Had Coma not preceded by Delirium, **1**—1, 2nd day coma, 4th day ◡

A²—Had Delirium followed by Coma, **2**—2, 2nd day, del., watchful; 3rd day, convulsive fit; 4th day, coma ◡; 12, on admission, obstinate taciturnity, lips trembled convulsively; 3rd day, convulsive movement of body, incoherent; 4th day, no delirium, convulsive agitation of face, tetaniform stiffness of arms from time to time; 5th day, delirium, coma ◡

Had Coma followed by Delirium, **2**—3, 11th day, coma ; 12th day, loquacious del.; 13th day ◡; 13 (painter, probably Bright's disease), 12th day, confused, coma; 13th day, eyes turned up, foaming, limbs relaxed; 17th day, slight del.; 19th day, sterior ◡

Had Delirium and Convulsions, **1**—6, great heat, del., convulsions, pain forehead

B¹—Had Delirium uncomplicated, **11**—23, 22nd day, del.; 25th day, never quiet, maniacal ◡; 5, 1st day, slight del.; 7th day ◡; 21, 14th day, 10 P.M. del., wandered, tried to get out of bed; both day ... ... both day, wandered ◡; 24, 3rd day of illness, del.; 5th day, admitted, had little sleep, lamb. frequent ... morbled ... ; ... av. mid-day 12th of illness, del. previous night, wished to get out of bed; 3rd day ◡; 14, 6th day of illness, lay down ◡; 17, 26th day, del.; 26th day, ... 4, 5th day, slight del.—Recovered.
del., bathed in sweat ◡; 26, 3rd day, restless; 4th day, wandered ◡

B²—Had Delirium and Choreiform Movements, **1**—9, first 2 weeks very restless, scarcely slept, del.; 3rd week, convulsive agitation of limbs, constant motion of head, wild rolling of eyes, del., cold to head.—Recovered. (Second illness fatal.)

Had Delirium and Jactitation, **1**—16, head affected, extreme agitation of body, jactitation, head more and more affected ◡

C¹—Had Chorea without delirium, **2**—8, had chorea 6 weeks before admission; on 27th day slight convulsion, soon ◡; 19, 3rd day, choreic symptoms ; 5th day, chorea established; 7th day less chorea; 9th day ◡

C²—Had Choreiform movements without delirium, **2**—18, extreme jactitation ◡; 15, 3rd day, convulsive movements of face; nights of 13th and 14th, agitation, del. ◡

C³—Had modified Tetanus without delirium, **2**—10, relapse; 1st day, fingers bent convulsively, later and successively ... of suffocation, cramps in legs, fingers, forearm, and arm ; feet and legs strongly bent, muscles of limbs, abdomen, and jaw ... hard ... state, skin hot, sweating, cold effusion, great relief; 3rd day, return of cramps; 4th day, no rigidity, joints slightly ... in drinking; ... cold bath, relapse ; 5th day, intense spasmodic contraction, death in paroxysm of choking ◡; 11, last day, violent spasmodic contraction of limbs; 5th day, occasional spasmodic rigidity of whole body, opisthotonos during night spasms so severe could scarcely be kept in bed ; 6th day ◡

D—Had slight Convulsions without delirium, **1**—7, 20th day, slight convulsions, exhausted, died in half an hour ◡

SUMMARY OF CASES OF ACUTE RHEUMATISM, WITH AFFECTIONS OF
THE NERVOUS SYSTEM, IN WHICH THE TEMPERATURE WAS NOT
OBSERVED.

	With Pericarditis.	Simple Endocarditis.	No Peric., Endocard. absent or doubtful.	TOTAL.
A¹—Coma without delirium or convulsions	3	0	2	5
A²— „ with convulsions	2	1	2	5
A³— „ preceded by delirium	5	0	8	13
A⁴—Stupor preceded by delirium	0	0	2	2
A— Had Coma or Stupor. TOTAL . . .	10	1	14	25
Had Semi-consciousness	1	—	—	1
B¹—Delirium, uncomplicated	21	8	14	42
B²— „ passing into temporary insanity	11	5	3	20
„ with chorea or choreiform or tetaniform symptoms	5	0	2	7
„ TOTAL	16	5	5	27
B³—Delirium, with chorea and choreiform movements, not including those with temporary insanity . . .	4	0	1	5
B⁴—Delirium with tetaniform movements, not including those with temporary insanity	2	0	1	3
B—Delirium without Coma. TOTAL . .	43	13	21	77
Delirium. TOTALS (including those with coma)	48	13	31	92
C¹—Chorea without delirium	7	--	—	7
C²—Choreiform movements (jactitation), without delirium	1	1	—	2
C³—Tetaniform symptoms, without delirium	2	—	—	2
D—Had slight fit	1	—	—	1
E—Had Embolism, hemiplegia	—	1	—	1
F—Had Paraplegia	—	—	2	2
G—Had agitation and prostration . . .	—	—	1	1
TOTAL	65	16	38	119

I.—CASES AFFECTED WITH PERICARDITIS.

There were sixty-five cases of acute rheumatism with pericarditis,
in which the nervous system was affected. (*A.*) Ten of these had
coma, of which (A¹,) three had uncomplicated coma; (A²,) two had
coma with convulsions; and (A³,) in five the coma was preceded
by delirium. (*B.*) Forty-three cases had delirium without coma;
of these (B¹,) twenty-one had uncomplicated delirium, one of which
had "symptoms of inflammation of the brain," and one apparently
had pyæmia; (B²,) sixteen, of which five had choreal or tetaniform
symptoms, had temporary insanity, lasting from two weeks to three

months, or, in three instances, insanity was cut short by death; (B³,) four had chorea or choreiform movements, and (B⁴,) two had tetaniform symptoms without temporary insanity. (C¹.) Eight of the cases had chorea or choreiform movements, and (C²,) two had tetaniform symptoms without delirium. (D.) One of them had a slight fit with ptosis.

II.—Cases affected with Simple Endocarditis.

There were sixteen cases of acute rheumatism with simple endocarditis, in which the nervous system was affected, excluding cases of ordinary chorea, but including cases of chorea rapidly fatal, or with delirium.
(A².) One of these cases had coma with convulsions, associated with acute Bright's disease from embolism. (A³.) One had delirium ending in coma, with embolism of the minute cerebral arteries. (B.) Twelve of them had delirium without coma, of these (B¹,) seven had uncomplicated delirium; and (B²,) five passed into a state of temporary insanity, lasting from three weeks to four months. (C¹.) One had chorea ending rapidly in death. (E.) One had embolism with hemiplegia.

III.—Cases in which there was no Pericarditis and Endocarditis was absent or doubtful.

There were thirty-eight cases of acute rheumatism without pericarditis, endocarditis being absent or doubtful, in which the nervous system was affected, exclusive of cases of ordinary chorea. (A.) Twelve of these had coma or stupor, of which, (A¹,) two had uncomplicated coma, (A²,) two had coma with convulsions, (A³,) in eight the coma was preceded by delirium; and there were also (A⁴,) two cases in which delirium passed into stupor. (B.) Twenty of the cases had delirium including two with "cerebral rheumatism," and one that had pus in the pia mater; of these (B¹,) fourteen had uncomplicated delirium; (B²,) five passed into temporary insanity, two of which had chorea also; (B³,) one had chorea; and (B⁴,) one had tetanic spasms. (F.) Two of the cases had paraplegia. (G.) One of the cases had agitation and prostration ending in rapid death.

A.—Coma.

I.—*Cases with Pericarditis.* A¹.—*Uncomplicated Coma.*—Three cases with Pericarditis had coma without convulsions or delirium, all of which proved fatal.
A².—*Coma with Convulsions.*—In the two cases of coma with convulsions, death was speedy.
A³.—*Coma preceded by Delirium.*—Four of the five cases in which delirium passed into coma, died; and one recovered. One of the cases passed rather into stupor than coma. The duration of the

coma in these cases was variable and uncertain, and that of the delirium lasted for from one or two nights to nine or ten days.

II.—*Cases with Simple Endocarditis.* A².—*Coma with Convulsions.*—One fatal case of coma preceded by convulsions had simple endocarditis with embolism of the spleen and kidneys, the coma and convulsions being evidently associated with acute Bright's disease.[1]

III.—*Cases without Pericarditis, Endocarditis being absent or doubtful.* A¹·²·—*Coma without and with Convulsions.*—There were four fatal cases of coma without delirium among the cases without pericarditis, endocarditis being absent or doubtful, two of them having convulsions. In three of them death was very rapid, and in one coma, coming on after convulsions, lasted for twelve hours before death.

These cases did not differ materially in character and history from those with coma and pericarditis.

A³.—*Coma and Delirium.*—Coma was preceded by delirium in eight fatal cases that presented no sign of affection of the heart.

The delirium was more frequent by night than by day, being present in three of the cases from two to five or six nights, while it was absent in the daytime, and it lasted in the other five cases from two to four or five days.

The coma, as a rule, soon ended in death. In one half of the cases, or four, the delirium became violent, and in the other half, its character was not described.

These cases do not differ materially in essential character from those with pericarditis that were affected with delirium and coma. There were, however, nervous symptoms in the form of agitation, twitchings, and choreiform and tetaniform movements in a much greater proportion of those with pericarditis than of those not so affected.

A⁴.—*Delirium and Stupor.*—One of the two cases in which delirium preceded stupor recovered after the employment of the wet sheet, and the other died.

B.—DELIRIUM.

B¹.—*Uncomplicated Delirium.*—1. *Cases with Pericarditis.*—Twenty-one of the sixty-five cases with rheumatic pericarditis had uncomplicated delirium, including one with "symptoms of inflammation of the brain," and one with probable pyæmia. Eleven of these cases died and ten recovered.

The duration of the delirium varied much. The delirium was more active by night than by day, and in five cases was present from one to three or four nights, but was absent during the day. In the rest of the cases it lasted from for a few hours to four or five days. The delirium was noisy or violent in eleven instances, moderate in four, and slight in five cases.

[1] Frerichs, "On the Diseases of the Liver," New Sydenham Soc. Edition, vol. i. p. 164.

One case, a female servant, felt much better at the evening visit, but a quarter of an hour later became delirious, with loud continuous cries. A varied treatment, includiug wet packing, was employed, and she recovered.

Another case, a workman in Messrs. Guinness's Brewery, drank largely of their XX porter besides whisky. He had pericarditis, and "delirium tremens," and recovered after taking opium.[1]

2. *Cases with Simple Endocarditis.*—Seven of the sixteen cases with simple rheumatic endocarditis had uncomplicated delirium. Three of these cases died and four recovered.

The duration of the delirium varied from, for a single night in one patient, to at least nine days in another. It was present more often, and, as a rule, with greater violence by night than by day. In four of the cases the delirium was active or violent, in one the delirium was wandering, and in another, it was accompanied by somnambulism.

One of these cases was observed by Dr. Boisragon and Mr. Tudor, and reported by Dr. Davis, and is, so far as I have discovered, the first case in which endocarditis was well described.

Three of the cases of endocarditis with delirium were under my own care, and of these, one died and two recovered.

3. *Cases without Pericarditis, Endocarditis being absent or doubtful.*— Fourteen of the thirty-eight cases without pericarditis, endocarditis being absent or doubtful, had uncomplicated delirium. Ten of the fourteen cases died, and four recovered.

The duration of the delirium varied much in the different cases. It prevailed more during the night than the day. In three instances it was only present during the night for from one to three nights. In one case the delirium was only present for a quarter of an hour before death, in four cases it existed for one day, and in four others from two to five or six days. The delirium was violent or lively in five of the cases, and five were simply "delirious."

These cases corresponded in essential features with those that had delirium with pericarditis.

"Hyperpyrexia" in cases of acute rheumatism without and with Pericarditis in which the temperature was not observed.—The ten fatal cases belonging to the last group of fourteen with delirium, the twelve with coma and the two with stupor, all of which had neither pericarditis nor endocarditis, evidently belong to the important group of cases of acute rheumatism with hyperpyrexia. All of those twenty-four cases except one with stupor, died, and that patient recovered after the external use of the wet sheet. The ten cases with coma, and the eleven fatal cases and one case that recovered under the use of wet packing that had uncomplicated delirium among the patients with pericarditis, and three fatal cases of delirium with simple endocarditis, may also be ranked among the cases of hyperpyrexia. According to this

---

[1] Dr. Graves, " Clinical Lectures on the Practice of Medicine," vol. i. p. 531.

estimate, twenty-two of the sixty-five cases with pericarditis, three of the sixteen with simple endocarditis, and twenty-four of the thirty-eight without pericarditis or notable endocarditis, in which the temperature was not observed, were affected with "hyperpyrexia."

These forty-nine cases corresponded in their broad features as regards coma, delirium, and death with those cases of "hyperpyrexia" in which the temperature was observed. As in those also so in these, in the few cases where these conditions were observed, the affection of the joints ceased when the delirium appeared, and the perspiration, copious during the earlier stages, was absent or much lessened during the stage of delirium or coma, when the skin was usually dry and hot.

Convulsive, choreiform, and tetaniform movements in the cases with hyperpyrexia.—There was an important difference in the two sets of cases with and without pericarditis, as regards the presence of convulsive, choreiform, and tetaniform symptoms in combination with the far more important symptoms of "hyperpyrexia."

Convulsive movements, jactitation, agitation, choreiform movements without actual chorea, and tetaniform symptoms, appeared more frequently in the cases of coma or delirium with pericarditis, than in those without pericarditis. Involuntary movements of the muscles occurred in one, and general agitation in three of the twenty-five cases of hyperpyrexia that had neither pericarditis nor notable endocarditis. A convulsive fit occurred in one, jactitation of the limbs or body in two, tetaniform symptoms in two, and great general agitation in three, of the twenty-two cases with hyperpyrexia that had pericarditis. Besides these eight instances of convulsive, choreiform or tetaniform affections among the fatal cases of coma and delirium with pericarditis, there were two with jactitation, and one with twitchings of the muscles of the face, among the cases of delirium with pericarditis that were not fatal. Four of the eleven cases with pericarditis thus affected with convulsive, choreiform, or tetaniform movements had endocarditis, three had no endocarditis, and in four the presence of endocarditis was doubtful.

We have already seen that among the cases of "hyperpyrexia," in which the temperature was observed, choreal and tetaniform symptoms occurred much more frequently among those with, than among those without, pericarditis; while on the other hand twitching movements were as frequent among those without, as among those with, pericarditis.

Delirium resembling Delirium Tremens.—Among the cases of delirium in acute rheumatism without pericarditis or evident endocarditis as among those previously analysed with pericarditis, there are several that present symptoms partly allying them to delirium tremens—partly to the delirium of rheumatic hyperpyrexia, and that are associated with previous habits of drinking, or with some affection of the nervous system. One of these patients, a hard drinker, complained of being unable to see, called out "thief," rushed out of bed and fell down. After this he struggled with two attendants, and then dropping back, died. All this took place in less than a quarter of an hour.[1]

Two of my own patients belong to this class, one of whom recovered, the other died. One was a stout florid waiter, aged 40, who perspired profusely, slept but little, and became very violent. On the seventh night he slept with an opiate. He recovered rapidly.

The patient who died was a barman, aged 23, who was rather restless, and hurried in speech on the day after admission, became more restless on the third day, and died suddenly.

B[2].—Temporary Insanity with Taciturn Melancholy and Hallucinations.

B[2]. I.—*Cases with Pericarditis.*—The series of cases that I have now to consider present a remarkable succession of symptoms. In eleven cases of acute rheumatism with pericarditis, delirium, usually desponding and taciturn, often with hallucinations, came on when the heart was inflamed; but instead of passing away quickly, this sombre delirium lasted for from two or three weeks to three months. Of these eleven cases of temporary insanity, ten recovered, and one died; eight of those cases were females, six being below the age of twenty, and three were males. All but one of these patients were affected with endocarditis as well as pericarditis.

The duration of the insanity varied considerably, and the return to a healthy state of mind was gradual, and never sharp. The temporary insanity lasted for above a fortnight in three cases; for about a month in three; for two months in one; for ten weeks in one patient, whose mind was not yet clear at the end of that time; and one died with her intellect still confused at the end of two months.

The prevailing feature of the delirium was a state of taciturn melancholy. Only one patient, a young woman, the fatal case, was at times in wild delirium, at times taciturn and almost idiotic, and at times quiet and rational.[2] Eight of the patients were taciturn, and two others were confused in mind or speech. Four of them had hallucinations; one saw her mother at her side; one a knife and poison; one was followed and insulted, and then reached out his hand as to an old friend; and one complained of vermin. Another patient had delusions.

Two of my patients belong to this series of cases. One of these, a potman, aged 21, on the seventeenth night after his admission was in a state of partial stupor and delirium. On the following day he answered no questions, and as he would not take food, stimulants were given by enemata. On the twenty-sixth day he again took food, but he continued to be taciturn. On the thirty-ninth day he recovered the powers of nature, was up on the forty-seventh, and left on the seventy-fifth day, his heart-sounds being healthy.

[1] Trousseau, " Lectures on Clinical Medicine," (New Sydenham Soc.) vol. i. p. 513.
[2] Sir Thomas Watson, loc. cit. ii. 307.

The other case, a labourer, with endo-pericarditis, had a vacant, torpid, and wandering mind for three weeks, which followed an attack of hemiplegia from embolism affecting the right side, with loss of speech, which was apparently a mixture of aphasia and a taciturn character of mind. On the tenth day his face was paralysed on the right side, and the pupils were irregular. On the thirteenth he would not or could not speak, but muttered slightly, and tried to get out of bed. He improved daily and his speech returned, but his expressions were incoherent. On the thirty-eighth day he had more command over his articulation, and on the forty-second had almost regained the use of his right side. He improved steadily, and on the seventy-second day he went out well, the heart-sounds being healthy.

Besides the eleven cases just spoken of with temporary insanity of a taciturn melancholic type, there were five others in which a similar condition was associated with chorea or choreiform movements (in 4) or with tetaniform symptoms (in 1). Three of these cases were fatal, and two of them recovered. The whole of the five cases were below the age of twenty-one, and two of them were male and three were female patients. All of them had endocarditis as well as pericarditis. The affection lasted in one of the two that recovered about a month, and in the other for a shorter period. The three fatal cases died respectively in about twenty-three, sixteen, and nine days after the beginning of the mental trouble. One of those patients was taciturn, then delirious, and finally had the most violent choreiform movements, ending in death. Another fatal case had difficult utterance, incoherence, tossing of the head from side to side, and choreiform spasms which put on the character of the most violent convulsions. A third case spoke loud and low, after, in succession, being excited and stubborn, weeping, seeing a dead man, and grimacing as in chorea: death took place an hour after an attack of universal convulsions. One of the two cases that recovered had a rather childish appearance; her answers were sometimes irrelevant, sometimes rational, and she had choreal movements of the right arm and leg.

The last case had delirium with tetanic spasms; at first he had an excited manner, with wild rolling of his eyes, then furious delirium, followed by firm clenching of the hands, sleep, and a more tranquil state. After this he was idiotic and violent by turns, until the twenty-eighth day after the first disturbance of the mind, when he became tranquil.

These sixteen cases with taciturn melancholy, often with hallucinations, lasting for from three weeks to three months, and then usually getting well, present a group of conditions that seems to separate them from the twenty-one cases of delirium that were not followed by coma, and the five that were so. In those cases the delirium was often violent, generally active, sometimes muttering; in these it was melancholic and taciturn. In those cases the delirium was often exclusively by night and was then almost always most noisy; in these it was present day and night, though it was usually more active by night. In those cases the delirium lasted for from one or more hours to five or six nights and five days; in these it lasted for from three weeks to three months. In those cases perspiration was generally profuse before the appearance of the delirium, the skin usually becoming hot and dry as the temperature rose to the fatal height; in these perspiration was only noted as being profuse in two cases, and slight in one. In those cases death was the natural result; in these, all but one of the eleven without chorea recovered, while three of the five with chorea died. In those endocarditis was absent in three-fifths of the cases (11 in 32) with coma and delirium, but three more of those cases probably had endocarditis; in these endocarditis was present in all but one.

We saw that in the two sets of cases, in one of which the temperature was, and in the other, was not observed, delirium presented itself in two forms: (1) one, and the leading form, of delirium with hyperpyrexia, ending in death; (2) the other, the secondary form, with a less high temperature in which a condition resembling delirium tremens associated itself with and modified the delirium of hyperpyrexia, often occurring in persons who had been intemperate, anxious, nervous, or in want, and ending generally in recovery.

In these cases of temporary insanity with taciturn melancholy we have clinical evidence of a third kind of delirium, differing from the two other kinds of which we have just spoken.

These cases resemble in some of their symptoms, cases of insanity with settled taciturn melancholy; but from those they differ in this essential point, that while in those the insanity is obstinate, often indeed for life; in these the insanity comes definitely to an end in from two or three weeks to three or even four months.

The features, then, that characterize these cases of temporary insanity are youth and previous good health; or in a few cases intemperate habits; the absence of hyperpyrexia; the existence of endocarditis; the settled though varying and even intermittent character of the taciturn delirium, which is present, though modified, by day as well as by night; and the dying out of the affection in a limited period. These conditions point, not to a rapidly progressive and varying cause, which marks hyperpyrexia, which is kept in check or suspended by a perspiring skin, or the external use of cold, and is promoted by a hot dry skin; but to a continuous cause, that is excited during the height of the disease, but that varies in operation for from two weeks to three months after the acute rheumatism and the acute stage of the endocarditis have passed away. In one of my own cases there was embolism, evidenced by the loss of power in the right side, and taciturn aphasia, in combination with endocarditis; and it appears to me that in embolism of the minute cerebral arteries of the convolutions, we have a series of conditions that correspond with those occurring in the whole of these remarkable cases. Embolism of the cerebral arteries comes on with endocarditis, and arrests for a time the circulation of the blood through the parts of the brain sup-

plied by the affected vessels ; its effects remain after the acute stage of
the originating endocarditis has passed away ; and, if death does not
cut short the clinical history of the case, those effects usually gradually
lessen and disappear in from two or three weeks to several months,
unless the extent of the plugging of the vessels be such as to cause
extensive softening of the part of the brain supplied by those vessels.
I therefore consider that to embolism we may have to look for the
explanation of these cases. We shall find other instances of a like
nature among the cases without pericarditis, in which endocarditis
was present, and in those also in which it was doubtful or absent.

B². —II. *Cases with Simple Endocarditis.*—Five of the sixteen cases
that had endocarditis without pericarditis were affected with delirium
of a desponding type with taciturn melancholy. Two of these died
and three recovered.   In addition to these five cases with taciturn
melancholy, there was another analogous case of embolism of the
basilar artery, with headache and agitation, and in the evening
apoplectic symptoms, right hemiplegia, and difficulty of speech.[1] As
this case did not survive the first great attack, I shall not add it to
the rest. The length of time that the mind was disturbed varied in the
different cases from three weeks to four months ; one of the fatal cases
lasted twenty-three days, and another two months ; while those that
recovered were affected for one, two, and four months respectively.
Four of them were restless ; three were taciturn, especially during the
night; another answered slowly; and the fifth case in a low voice ; three
had hallucinations, including one of those that were also taciturn, and
two would get out of bed.   Three of them were desponding or melancholy ; one was apathetic ; and the remaining one, a fatal case, was
for ten days in a state of quiet delirium, and afterwards preserved a
dogged silence. Two of them were confused ; and one of them was
violent. If we compare these five cases of temporary insanity, with
simple endocarditis ; with the sixteen cases of the same class with
pericarditis and endocarditis, we find that the two sets of cases
correspond in their main features. Both had disorder of mind, by
day as well as by night, though with greater accentuation at night
in those with simple endocarditis ; in both early restlessness, obstinate
silence, melancholy, apathy, and hallucinations prevailed ; and in both
the affection of the intellect commenced during the attack of acute
rheumatism, and of the accompanying endocarditis, and lasted for a variable period after the acute affections had ceased.

As we have just seen, five out of the sixteen cases, or one-third, with
simple endocarditis, not including the fatal case of embolism, difficult
speech, and right hemiplegia, and another case with embolism of the
minute cerebral arteries and delirium that died on the eleventh day; and
sixteen of the sixty-five with pericarditis, all but one of them having
endocarditis also, or one-sixth, were thus affected with taciturn melancholy lasting for a limited period after the cessation of the acute

---

[1] Bouillaud, " Maladies du cœur," vol. i. p. 405.

affection. We may, I think, consider that the existence of endocarditis in so large a proportion of such cases adds to the probability of embolism being the cause of the temporary insanity.

Since the above was written Dr. Broadbent has favoured me with his notes of an important case of acute rheumatism and endocarditis, with chorea and delirium, in which there was capillary cerebral embolism. I have also met with a case observed by Dr. Dickinson of acute rheumatism and endocarditis with delirium and minute cerebral embolism, and red softening of some of the convolutions; and with another case of chorea and endocarditis with delirium and minute cerebral embolism. These three cases afford direct evidence of the association of embolism of the minute arteries of the convolutions of the brain with delirium.

Dr. Broadbent's patient, a laundryman, aged 17, when attacked, had severe affection of the joints, and was light-headed; two days later his right limbs twitched and jumped, and he was delirious. On admission, after being ill a week, he seemed stupid, had to be spoken to loudly, his answers were confused, his articulation was indistinct, and his limbs still twitched, but especially on the right side. T. 103°. During the two following nights he had no sleep, was very delirious, talked, screamed, and jumped out of bed. He slept after a dose of chloral, but was soon pale and prostrate, and died on the fourth day after his admission. Recent loose clots were found in the minutest arteries and capillaries of the *corpora striata* and of some of the convolutions.

B². —III. *Cases without Pericarditis, Endocarditis being absent or doubtful.*—Five of the thirty-eight cases in which there was no pericarditis, and endocarditis was absent or doubtful, or one in eight of the whole number, became delirious during the acute stage of the disease, and remained of unsound mind for two months and a half in one, and for about a month in four instances. Two of these patients were also affected with choreiform movements. Four of these were men, and one was a girl, aged 16. Two of the men had been at one time drunkards, one of them had suffered in health from losses and excesses, and the other man was a servant, and probably lived generously. The speech was affected in all of them. One stammered, one answered slowly, one was taciturn, one refused to answer, and the girl did not reply to the question put to her, but spoke of something else. Two of them had hallucinations; one was despondent; another, after being noisy, became sulky; one was morose by day, and had lively delirium. One, with choreal movements, after being confused and delirious in paroxysms, became so continuously; and the fifth, also having chorea, was strange in manner.

In none of these five cases was there any notable sign of endocarditis, and the disturbed state of mind and speech could not therefore be attributed to embolism.

B². *Temporary Insanity—General Summary.*—There were altogether twenty-one cases of acute rheumatism with temporary insanity; and six of delirium, usually of the low melancholy type, in which the insanity was cut short by death. Of these twenty-seven cases, sixteen had pericarditis, six simple endocarditis, and five had apparently neither pericarditis nor endocarditis.

Four-fifths of the cases had endocarditis (21 in 27), and one-fifth of them gave no evidence of endocarditis (6 in 27).

I have already given clinical reasons for thinking that the temporary insanity may have been due to embolism of the minute cerebral arteries in those cases with endocarditis, and direct evidence that in two cases that condition coincided with delirium.

In six of those cases with endocarditis the temporary insanity delirium, or melancholy was associated with chorea, and their clinical history would seem to suggest that in those cases the temporary insanity and the chorea were due to a common cause acting perhaps on different parts of the nervous centre. This view is strengthened by Dr. Tuckwell's important remarks on Muscular Chorea and its probable connection with Embolism. This memoir is illustrated by a case [1] in which there were two large patches of red softening affecting the cortex, and in one of them the white substance also, of the right hemisphere of the brain. The arterial branches leading to one if not both of these softened patches were occluded by coagula, and very fine granular particles were dotted along the small bloodvessels in the softened cerebral grey matter. This patient, a boy, was attacked with chorea nine days before admission, and became delirious during the first night after it. On the third day he had wild maniacal delirium, and furious choreic movements. This wild state soon quieted itself, but was renewed on the eighth night, and on the ninth day he became comatose and died.

More than one-half of the cases were below the age of twenty-one (14 in 27) and of these all but one had endocarditis, while one-third of them were above the age of twenty-five (9 in 27) and of these nearly one-half (4 in 9) presented no sign of endocarditis.

Although the majority of these cases, and especially those with endocarditis, were young people of previously good health, yet a small but definite group of the cases form an important exception to this typical series. Six of the cases, all men, were either known to be of habits of intemperance, or were of occupations in which such habits are possible. Three of those male patients were drunkards or given to excess, and of the rest, one was a policeman, one a man-servant, and the sixth was a postboy. Four of these patients, all of whom recovered, presented no sign of endocarditis, and the two others had endocarditis.

The question arises here, whether the temporary insanity in these four men who had not endocarditis, one of whom had chorea also, may have been due to thrombosis or the spontaneous collection of fibrine in the minute arteries of the convolutions? I simply put this as a question, but in support of the possibility of

[1] British and Foreign Medico-Chirurgical Review, xl. p. 506.

this condition I find an important case that was closely observed by Dr. Charlton Bastian during life and after death. The patient was a strong man, a gate porter, who had been accustomed to drink a great deal of late, and was attacked with erysipelas of the head and face following a fall, when he cut his head on the kerb-stone. He became violently delirious, was then quieter, became comatose at night, and died early on the following morning. The heart was healthy; the pia mater and brain were abnormally vascular; the consistence of the brain was good. Minute embolic masses were present in the small arteries and capillaries of the brain in every specimen looked at.[1]

B³ & C ¹, ², ³.—Chorea and Choreiform and Tetaniform Movements, with and without Delirium, in Cases of Acute Rheumatism, with especial reference to Pericarditis.

The occurrence of chorea without delirium in cases of acute rheumatism when connected with endocarditis will be considered when we enquire into that affection. The present enquiry will be limited to (1) cases of chorea and of choreiform movements with delirium, or ending in sudden death, occurring in acute rheumatism with or without pericarditis; and (2) cases of chorea and choreiform movements without delirium, occurring in acute rheumatism with pericarditis; and in inquiring into these cases, I shall briefly include the cases of combined chorea and temporary insanity that have already been considered.

B³ & C¹,².—I. *Cases with Pericarditis.*—Chorea occurred as a definite accompanying affection in six instances with delirium, and in seven without delirium; and choreiform movements not amounting to definite chorea occurred in two instances with delirium and in one instance without delirium among the sixty-five cases of acute rheumatism affected with pericarditis now under examination. In addition to these cases so affected, there were six patients with pericarditis who had delirium, or coma, or both, as the principal affections, and who had choreiform movements as a subsidiary affection. There were thus twenty-two cases of rheumatic pericarditis with chorea or choreiform movements, not including several who had also tetaniform symptoms.

The thirteen cases with chorea, and two of the three with limited choreiform movements, were below the age of twenty-one, nine of these being girls and six youths. The remaining case with limited choreiform movements was a man aged 22. Nine of these sixteen choreal cases died and seven recovered.

Thirteen of these cases, including the whole of those with delirium, had endocarditis as well as pericarditis; in two cases endocarditis was probable, and in one it was absent or doubtful.

In eight of the cases the chorea appeared after the commencement of the pericarditis; in seven of them the two affections probably

---

[1] Path. Trans. xx. 3.

came into existence about the same time; and in one exceptional case, recorded by Dr. Ormerod, the chorea appeared first, then the pericarditis, and finally the affection of the joints, thus reversing the usual order of succession of those affections.

The chorea appears to have continued up to the time of death in most of the fatal cases when the pericarditis was active; but the reports of several of them are, in this respect, imperfect.

The relation of the termination of the chorea to that of the pericarditis varied much in the cases that recovered. In one case the choreic movements were violent on the day that the frottement diminished, and were absent four days later. In another case the chorea improved with the improvement of the state of the heart.[1] A patient of my own made objectless movements with his hands when the pericarditis was at its acme; and two days later those movements ceased. In a boy with pericarditis, violent chorea appeared when the rheumatic and cardiac affections rather suddenly disappeared. Six days later with return of pain in the joints the chorea ceased.[2] In another patient, a girl, chorea appeared four days after the disappearance of friction sound.[3]

Partial choreiform movements, usually of short duration, appeared in six of the cases that were affected with delirium with and without coma, and in all of them the movements appeared when pericarditis was present.

The character of the choreiform movements was peculiar in some of the cases. Two of the patients rolled the head from side to side; one smacked his lips, another pursed his mouth, a third snapped, grimaced, and cried out; two moved the left hand and arm constantly; and in five the spasmodic movements of the body were very violent, so that in three of them personal restraint was demanded. In one of those five patients, on the second and third days, the spasms put on the character of the most violent convulsions. The cases of chorea with delirium presented considerable variety; and several of them, as we have already seen, had temporary insanity.

Five of the eight cases with delirium were fatal, and three recovered. The duration of the cases varied considerably. The five fatal cases died at various periods from the fourth to the sixteenth day of the delirium. Of the three that recovered, one had delirium for a month, one had chorea for three weeks, and in one, a man under my care, quick and needless movements of the hands, and occasional muttering, lasted two or three days.

B³.—II. *Cases with Simple Endocarditis.*—No case of chorea with delirium, and only one with rapid death, occurred among the cases of acute rheumatism with endocarditis.

B³.—III. *Cases without Pericarditis, Endocarditis being absent or doubtful.*—I have already given two cases of this class with chorea

[1] Guy's Hospital Reports, vi. 1841, pp. 420, 421.
[2] Mr. Land, *Lancet*, 1873, i. 38.
[3] Dr. Kirkes, Trans. of the Abernethian Society, 1850, p. 57.

and delirium that were affected with taciturn melancholy of limited duration. The third case, a girl, aged 14, also had chorea and delirium.[1]

B³. *Cases with Choreiform Movements* in which those movements were partial and of secondary importance, and occurred in patients already included among those with delirium or coma. B³.—I. *Cases with Pericarditis.*—Six cases with delirium, one of which had coma also, among the sixty-five cases of rheumatic pericarditis had movements of a choreiform character for a single day in the course of the disease. Three of these patients died and three recovered. Four of them were male and two were female patients, and of these, five were above the age of twenty-five, and only one below that of twenty-one.

B⁴, C³.—*Cases with Tetaniform Movements sometimes associated with Choreiform Movements.*—I. *Cases with Pericarditis.*—In a small but important group of cases tetaniform symptoms occurred in connection with rheumatic pericarditis. Seven of the sixty-five cases of pericarditis had tetaniform movements, or continuous contraction or rigidity of muscles, of greater or less intensity. Some of these affections approached in their severity and characteristic form to tetanus, others could only be indistinctly associated with that disease.

The first case was an excitable man, aged 19, a gardener, who had, when first seen, twitching of the muscles, and of the right side of the face, increased by speaking. He had increasing agitation, indistinct articulation, and a difficulty in opening his mouth, which he closed with a snap. After this he threw his head from one side of the bed to the other, his convulsions resembled tetanus and opisthotonos, and his distress in swallowing was like that in hydrophobia. Four days later he rolled his eyes, ground his teeth, and smacked his lips; and he died exhausted by laborious spasm and probably by want of sustenance. His brain was vascular, and there was questionable softening around a vascular spot in the spinal cord opposite the first dorsal vertebra. There was pericarditis and endocarditis.[2] The next case, an over-worked girl, aged 19, at a late period of its history, seemed to plunge almost at once into the tetaniform condition. She rolled her eyes wildly, had furious delirium, and violent tetanic spasms with firm clenching of the fingers. After a week the delirium subsided, but she talked incessantly and incoherently, and was half maniacal, half idiotic up to the forty-sixth day, but from that time her progress to recovery was steady.[3] The third case, a youth, had pericarditis, but no endocarditis, inflammation of the kidney, occasional delirium, and slight opisthotonos; and on the eleventh day he died.[4]

The two following cases, both of which were fatal, were under my own care. The more important case was a youth aged 17. On the eighteenth day, the left side and the tongue were affected with

---

[1] Tüngel, loc. cit. 1860, p. 125.
[2] Dr. Yonge; Dr. Bright, Guy's Hospital Reports v. (1840) p. 276.
[3] Dr. Fuller, loc. cit. 201.　　　　　[4] Dr. Fuller, loc. cit. 289.

choreiform movements, which extended, with stiffness, to both arms. On the thirty-eighth the left arm, which still jerked and shook about, was rigid, the fore-arm being bent on the arm, the hand on the fore-arm. On the forty-seventh day, stiffness of the neck appeared, and he moved his arm with difficulty; and on the following day he died. He had both pericarditis and endocarditis. In this case the rigidity of the limb points to an affection of the nervous centre, probably due to embolism.

The other case, a man aged 27, a carpenter, came in with pericarditis at its acme, and endocarditis. On the third day he frequently slumbered and, as the eyes were half-closing, the arms and legs started. On the evening of the seventh day he was restless, and not quite rational, trembled, and kept moving his lower jaw and biting his lips. Half an hour later he was more noisy, and knocked about, still shaking his jaw. His pupils were dilated and very sluggish, and at eleven o'clock he died. I can find no notes of his *post mortem* examination.

The two remaining cases with tetaniform symptoms belong to the group of cases of endo-pericarditis with delirium and coma. One of these, a young man, had pain in his right temple, followed by wild delirium. During the night general convulsions came on in occasional spasms of a tetanic character, and in the intervals he lay in a state of coma. He remained in this condition for three more days, when he died.[1] The remaining case, a young woman, became restless and flighty on the sixth day of her illness, and next day pericarditis and endocarditis declared themselves. She then became very violent. The right arm and leg were never still; at times, however, this state became aggravated into one of general convulsions of a tetanic character. She continued thus for nine days, the convulsions being incessant. On the twelfth day she became comatose, after jumping up and falling out of bed with her forehead on the floor. She finally recovered.

PERICARDITIS—NEITHER RHEUMATIC NOR FROM BRIGHT'S DISEASE—ACCOMPANIED BY AFFECTIONS OF THE NERVOUS SYSTEM.

An important series of cases of pericarditis in which there was neither acute rheumatism nor, so far as was directly ascertained, Bright's disease, have been published from time to time by Rostan, Dr. Abercrombie, Dr. Bright, Bouillaud, Andral, and Sir George Burrows.

The cases of this class that I have gathered together from the records of various observers, and from the note-books of St. Mary's Hospital amount to twenty-six. See Analytical Table at page 280.

These cases present examples of the whole series of affections of the nervous system that have been observed in cases of rheumatic peri-

[1] Sir Thomas Watson, loc. cit. ii. 306.

carditis, with the exception of those with temporary insanity, and these were possibly represented by one fatal case that had obstinate taciturnity.

Among these twenty-six cases, (A[1]) one had coma without delirium; (A[3]) four had delirium and coma, the delirium in two of them preceding, and in two of them following the coma; one had delirium and convulsions; (B[1]) eleven had uncomplicated delirium which was slight and of short duration in seven of them; and of those without delirium, (C[1, 2]) three had chorea or choreiform movements; (C[3]) two had tetanus, and (D) one had slight convulsions. The affections of the nervous system in these cases of pericarditis, instead of being similar in character were thus very various.

A[1]. *Coma.*—The patient with coma was a woman who was suddenly seized with complete loss of consciousness, remained in this state four days, and died. Pericarditis was the only appreciable lesion.

A[3]. *Coma with Delirium.*—Among the four cases with coma associated with delirium, in two instances the delirium, as usual, preceded the coma, while in two the delirium followed the coma. One of the former class, a boy, aged 12, affected with pyæmia, was delirious, and after a night without sleep, became unconscious and died in the afternoon. Pericarditis was associated with small deposits of pus in the walls of the heart, the fibres of which were soft and almost black.[1] The other case in which delirium was followed by coma, presented tetaniform symptoms. A woman aged 26, was admitted soon after a false conception in a state of delirium and obstinate taciturnity. After this she frequently reversed her head backwards, had convulsive movements of the face, and the arms presented from time to time a rigidity almost tetanic. On the fifth day the arms when raised fell as if paralysed, she became comatose, and died in the evening. Pericarditis was the only morbid state discovered after death.[2]

Three of these cases may have been affected with " hyperpyrexia." There is, however, no indication that their temperature was raised.

In the other patient, a house-painter, in whom the coma preceded the delirium, I think that Bright's disease, not noticed after death, when the kidneys were not examined, was the probable cause of the fatal conditions spoken of.[3]

The patient with delirium and convulsions was a schoolboy with evident pyæmia, who had, in the opinion of all who saw him, severe inflammation of the brain. His brain was healthy, but his pericardium was inflamed, and innumerable small patches of pus oozed from among the muscular fibres of the heart.[4] The case with convulsions without delirium was also a boy, aged 7, who had pain in the left side and the epigastrium, and on awaking next morning was seized

---

[1] Mr. Stanley, Med. Chir. Trans. vii. 322.
[2] Andral, Clinique Medical, i. 25.
[3] Bouillaud, loc. cit. i. 319.
[4] Dr. Latham, London Medical Gazette, iii. 1829, p. 209.

with slight convulsions, sank into a low exhausted state, and died in half an hour. There was universal pericarditis, and when the heart was cleared from its soft gelatinous envelope, it was covered with small irregular granulations.[1]

B[1]. *Delirium* without coma or other complications was present in eleven cases of pericarditis not occurring in acute rheumatism or Bright's disease.

The most important of these cases was a man aged 36, under the care of Sir James Alderson. Three and a quarter pounds of dark amber-coloured fluid were found in his pericardium, the heart being covered and the sac lined with a thick honeycombed layer of new membrane. The supra-renal capsules, especially the right one, were enlarged with tubercular deposit. He had excessive distress and pain over the heart, the whole front of the chest was dull on percussion, and the impulse and sounds of the heart were absent. From the presence of these signs Sir James Alderson concluded that his patient was affected with pericarditis. On the twenty-second day after admission he became delirious, and on the twenty-fifth he was maniacal, and died.

Another case of this class was a shoe-black, aged 67, who had delirium, with great loquacity. He raised himself suddenly, went to the window to breathe, returned to bed, lay down and soon died. There was extensive pleurisy on the left side, spreading to the pericardium, which contained a pound of purulent liquid; the walls of the heart being soft and its fleshy substance yellow.[2] A third case, a man, had pericarditis associated with pyæmia, following an operation for stricture.

Seven of the remaining cases of this series presented only slight delirium and may be conveniently grouped together. One, who had pleuro-pneumonia and pericarditis, recovered.[3] Another had slight delirium and fever, and pericarditis. One, had empyema and pericarditis. Two cases under my care were delirious the day before death. One had pyæmia, and purulent dots were scattered through the fleshy substance of the heart; the other had empyema of the left side, and pericarditis. In the two remaining cases the delirium appeared a short time before death; one had extensive phthisis of the right lung and a vast cavity, the other had empyema of the left side, the pericardium being inflamed and thickened. In all these cases the delirium appeared to be quite as much connected with the disease upon which the pericarditis had grafted itself as upon the pericarditis itself, and in most of them it was little more than the wandering of mind incident to illness of so lowering and fatal a character.

The remaining patient of this group, a coachman, aged 51, and a drunkard, who was under the care of Dr. Chambers, presented a condition resembling delirium tremens. He had extensive pleuro-pneumonia of the left lung, and pericarditis. Two of these cases with

---

[1] Dr. Abercrombie, Trans. Edin. Med. Chir. Soc. i. 1821–4.
[2] Corvisart, loc. cit. p. 239.   [3] Bouillaud, loc. cit. i. 367.

brief delirium, were under the care of Sir James Alderson, and two under that of Dr. Chambers.

C[1], [2]. *Chorea and Choreiform Movements.*—Two cases of non-rheumatic pericarditis had chorea, and four presented movements of a choreiform character.

C[1]. *Chorea.*—One of the cases, a well-grown girl of 15, had chorea for six weeks before admission, and on the twenty-seventh day after it, was suddenly seized with obstructed respiration followed by a convulsive fit, and died. There was pericarditis, and the mitral valve was somewhat thickened, but the presence of endocarditis was not noted. The other case, a little girl, was under my own care. She was brought to the hospital in her mother's arms, in great distress. She presented prominence over the region of the pericardium, dulness on percussion extending up to the clavicle, and a pericardial friction sound. There was evidence also of pleurisy of the left side. Choreal symptoms appeared in the face, beginning in the corrugator supercilii, on the third day after admission, and chorea was established on the fifth day. On the ninth day she was much quieter; her face was pale, her lips were blue, and the veins of the neck pulsated, being full during expiration and during the ventricular systole; and a loud mitral murmur was audible at the apex. She died on that day, but I have found no notes of the examination after death.

C[2]. *Choreiform Movements.*—Four cases of non-rheumatic pericarditis presented in the course of their illness movements of a choreiform character. These cases hold an intermediate place between those with well-developed chorea, and those with regularly repeated local convulsive movements. The most important case ought perhaps to be included among those with chorea, but it developed certain characteristic symptoms of the choreiform type that are rarely or never present in uncomplicated chorea. This patient, a young lady, after a fortnight of extreme restlessness, and a good deal of delirium, fell into a state resembling chorea with convulsive agitation of the limbs, constant motion of the head, and wild rolling of the eyes. Cold was applied to the head, her symptoms subsided in a few days, and she gradually recovered. Three months and a half after the commencement of her illness she took cold, became suddenly worse, and died on the seventh day. The pericardium was universally adherent to the heart by lymph, and a deposit of lymph covered its outer surface.[1]

The other three cases, all fatal, of non-rheumatic pericarditis were reported by Corvisart, and the most remarkable symptom was a state of extreme agitation amounting to jactitation. They all had pleurisy as well as pericarditis, and one had pneumonia also. One of them had delirium, in another the mind was affected, and in the third disturbance of the intellect was not noted.

C[3]. *Tetaniform Symptoms and Tetanus.*—Two of the cases of non-rheumatic pericarditis were affected with tetaniform movements, or

---

[1] Dr. Abercrombie, Trans. of Med. Chir. Soc. of Edin. i. 1.

rather with actual tetanus, some of the symptoms of which were unusual. One of these cases was a boy who when admitted had cramps, and a threat of suffocation. His fingers, arms and forearms, his legs and feet were strongly bent, and the muscles of his limbs and abdomen and his masseters were so hard that they felt like touching a stone, especially during the paroxysms. A warm bath and cold affusion gave great relief, and the paroxysms of suffocation ceased half-an-hour later. After this the jaws were slightly closed, he had a return of the suffocation, especially when he drank, and occasional cramps. On the fifth day he had a cold bath by accident, and was seized with cramp when in the bath. He had spasmodic contractions of great intensity on the following day, and died in a paroxysm of suffocation. There were two ounces of pus in the pericardium, the surface of which was injected.[1]

The other patient with tetanus was a gentleman of middle age who, when first seen, was suffering from a violent spasmodic contraction of his limbs. On the fifth day he had cramps of his extremities and occasional spasmodic rigidity of the whole body, which was sometimes bent backwards, being supported by the occiput and the heels in a state of complete opisthotonos. During the night his spasms were so severe that he could scarcely be kept in bed, and he died suddenly on the following day. He had pericarditis, and the brain and spinal cord were healthy.[2]

I have ranked these cases with those of tetanus because they presented universal rigidity of the limbs and body; which, in the first case, extended to the masseters; and in the second, caused, during the paroxysms, complete opisthotonos. There were, however, certain conditions in which they both differed from ordinary tetanus. In neither of them did the affection commence with trismus, and in the second case its presence is not mentioned. In both of them at the outset of the attack the muscles of the extremities were involved; and in the first of them, besides cramps of the legs, the fingers, arms and forearms were strongly bent. In tetanus I need scarcely say that the reverse conditions prevail, for trismus is usually the earliest symptom, and the affection of the limbs is comparatively late, while that of the hands and arms is usually slight, the extensor muscles being more affected than the flexors. In tetanus the advance of the disease is steadily progressive, but there was a suspension of the spasmodic contraction of the limbs in both of these cases.

Dr. Bright describes a case of tetanus occurring in a man affected with inflammation of the pleural surface of the right side of the pericardium, involving the phrenic nerve, in which there was no pericarditis. In this instance the tetanus advanced rapidly through its usual progressive course. On the first evening he complained of difficulty in opening his mouth, and swallowed with a convulsive catch. During that night his teeth were completely closed, and

[1] Bouillaud, loc. cit. i. 333. [2] Dr. Mackintosh, Practice of Physic, ii. 25.

next morning he could get nothing into his mouth, and could not even swallow his saliva. There were slight indications of opisthotonos, and spasmodic action of the muscles of the back. In the afternoon there was no relaxation of the spasm; he had several epileptiform seizures, during which his face was purple, his eyes stared, and his whole body was convulsed. He rambled occasionally, and died twenty-fours hours after the first seizure of dysphagia. Dr. Bright suggests that in this case tetanus may have been caused by the phrenic nerve being involved in the seat of the inflammation.[1]

Convulsive Movements, Chorea, and Choreiform and Tetaniform Symptoms in Cases of Acute Rheumatism with and without Pericarditis, and in cases of Non-Rheumatic Pericarditis, in which Bright's Disease was Absent. Summary. Convulsive Movements.—I do not consider here cases of coma with convulsions, of which there were five, three with and two without pericarditis, one with and three without endocarditis, which was probably present in the remaining instance; nor those with convulsions associated with albuminous urine, of which there was but one patient, affected with both pericarditis and endocarditis.

There were altogether nineteen patients with convulsive movements among the whole series of 180 cases of acute rheumatism with affection of the nervous system; twelve of whom had pericarditis and seven had no pericarditis, while eight or perhaps nine of them had endocarditis. Fourteen of these cases had twitchings of the limbs or face, and of these, eight had pericarditis, and five endocarditis.

From this *résumé* it is evident that although these convulsive movements are probably influenced, and may in some instances have been caused by the co-existence of pericarditis or endocarditis; yet they may, and often do occur quite independently of either of those affections, and in the absence of both of them.

Hyperpyrexia (actual in seven cases, inferred in four), was present in eleven of the nineteen cases with convulsive movements or twitchings. In Dr. Greenhow's important case, given at page 266, twitchings of the face were generally present when the temperature ranged from 102·1° to 106·2°, but they were suspended by the cooling bath, and returned after removal from the bath.

The general affection of the nervous system varied in the different cases with convulsive movements and twitchings. In one patient a convulsive fit preceded coma without delirium. In seven cases there was delirium followed by coma. In four of these, twitchings occurred during the delirium; while in two of them, twitchings, and in one, convulsive movements, accompanied the coma. Convulsive movements of the whole body in one instance, and of the face in another, followed delirium and preceded death. There were general convulsive movements in one, and twitchings of the face in two cases of uncomplicated delirium.

[1] Med. Chir. Trans. xxi. 4.

There were twitching movements in four cases with chorea and delirium, in one of which there was also a state resembling tetanus and opisthotonos. In these four cases the twitchings were probably choreiform in character.

In one of the two remaining cases, a slight fit with ptosis preceded death by a few hours; and in the other twitching was present with albuminuria.

Convulsions were present in three, and convulsive agitation of the limbs in one, and of the lips or face in two of the twenty-six cases of non-rheumatic pericarditis, in which there was no Bright's disease.

Chorea, and Choreiform, and Tetaniform Symptoms. Chorea.—
Twenty-one of the 180 cases of acute rheumatism with affections of the nervous system had chorea. Fifteen of those patients with chorea had pericarditis, six had no pericarditis; while fourteen of them had endocarditis; three had no endocarditis; and in three of them, endocarditis was probable or doubtful. Pericarditis and endocarditis attacked three-fifths of these patients conjointly (13 in 21). It would appear from this, at first sight, as if pericarditis favoured or influenced the production of chorea, thus apparently supporting the view of Dr. Bright that the more frequent cause of chorea in conjunction with rheumatism is inflammation of the pericardium, the irritation being probably communicated thence to the spine through the phrenic nerve.[1] This view is apparently strengthened by the history of several of the cases in which the chorea and the pericarditis appeared, improved, and disappeared simultaneously. On the other hand, in one case, chorea preceded pericarditis, and in at least two others it came into play when the pericarditis was vanishing. The united presence of inflammation without and within the heart in so many of these cases, complicates the question as to the influence of pericarditis on the production of chorea; and these clinical statistics favour the view that endocarditis may be the cause of the chorea, quite as much as that pericarditis may be its cause. I will not pursue this question in this place farther, excepting to repeat that in Dr. Broadbent's and Dr. Tuckwell's important cases of chorea and delirium, there was embolism of the most minute cerebral arteries, associated with endocarditis. These two cases seem to show that it is possible that in some of the above cases also, chorea may have been associated with minute cerebral embolism due to endocarditis. I have already illustrated the possible or probable connection of temporary insanity in cases of acute rheumatism with endocarditis and minute cerebral embolism, or with minute cerebral thrombosis, the convolutions being affected; and five of these cases of chorea had also temporary insanity, in three of which there was endocarditis, while in two there was no endocarditis.

Chorea was present in two cases of non-rheumatic pericarditis

---

[1] Med. Chir. Trans. xxii. 15.

without Bright's disease. In one of these the onset of the chorea preceded, and in the other followed, that of the pericarditis. In one of those cases endocarditis was also present, and in the other it was doubtful.

Choreiform Movements. Jactitation.—Chorea, as we have just seen, affected twenty-one of the 180 cases of acute rheumatism with affection of the nervous system. Besides these there were fourteen cases that had choreiform movements without definite chorea. One patient moved automatically, as in chorea, and another made objectless movements with his hands. Both of these cases had endo-pericarditis. Eight patients were affected with jactitation, which was general in six instances, and limited to the right or left side in two. The whole of these patients had pericarditis, while endocarditis was present in three of them, was absent in one, and probably absent in four.

There was extreme jactitation of the whole body in three cases of non-rheumatic pericarditis, probably without endocarditis, observed by Corvisart; two of these had pleurisy, and the other one pleuro-pneumonia; those affections in two of the cases being the probable cause of the pericarditis.

The invariable presence of pericarditis and the frequent apparent absence of endocarditis in these cases of general jactitation, would appear to point to pericarditis as a possible cause of that condition, and perhaps by inducing reflex movements.

Agitation.—Fourteen of the cases with affection of the nervous system in which the temperature was not observed had agitation, which is a condition allied to general jactitation, which was also present in two of them. I find no express mention of agitation in the sixty-one cases in which the temperature was observed. Five of the fourteen cases with agitation had pericarditis; eight of them had endocarditis; while five of those cases had neither endocarditis nor pericarditis.

Ten of the cases with agitation died and four recovered.

Rolling of the Head from side to side.—A peculiar, regularly repeated rolling of the head from side to side occurred in eight of the 180 cases of acute rheumatism with affection of the nervous system. Five of these cases had well-developed chorea, and two others had limited choreiform movements. Six of these cases had pericarditis, while five of them had endocarditis, and in one its presence was doubtful. All of them had either endocarditis or pericarditis. This peculiar oscillating movement of the head, though generally connected in these cases with chorea or choreiform movements, is not, so far as I know, ever present in ordinary chorea, and it forms, therefore, a feature of difference between those cases and these. One patient, who had endo-pericarditis, delirium, and coma, rolled violently about the bed so that he required to be held down.

Choreiform movements were present in four cases of non-rheumatic pericarditis without Bright's disease. In one of these the state resembled chorea, there being convulsive agitation of the limbs and

constant motion of the head, with delirium ; in another patient there
was slight convulsive agitation of the face ; and in two other cases
there was violent general jactitation.

Tetaniform Symptoms and Tetanus.—Thirteen, or if the presence
of "risus sardonicus" alone be included, fifteen cases presented
symptoms of a tetaniform nature.

In eight of those cases the tetaniform symptoms were general.
Some of these had also chorea, or choreiform movements. In one such
case the choreal convulsions put on a character resembling tetanus
and opisthotonos, and the distress in swallowing was not unlike that
in hydrophobia. Another case had opisthotonos and tetanic spams ;
and a third had slight opisthotonos. Three other cases had spasms
or convulsions of a tetanic character, which were accompanied in one
instance by firm clenching of the hands. One patient under my care
had stiffness of the neck ; and rigid jerking and shaking about of the
left arm ; the forearm, at a later period, being bent on the arm, the
hand on the forearm. The eighth case, a woman, had a temperature
of 109·5, and after being put into a tub of cold water was attacked
with tonic spasms. Two cases had spasms of rigidity of the muscles
of the neck, in one after being cooled in the bath from t. 109°
to 103·6°, and two had stiffness of the neck, one of which has
been already alluded to.

One patient who was violently delirious at a temperature of 107·8°
to 109°, after being bled, immediately passed into a state of unconsciousness, and was attacked with trismus, and convulsive movements
of the jaws, hands and arms. Two cases were affected with stiffness
of the jaw ; which was accompanied in one of them by swelling
of the temporo-maxillary articulation ; this being the patient just
spoken of who was seized with tonic spasms after the bath ; and
who closed her teeth firmly over her lips, drawing blood. Another
patient, a man, was continually moving his lower jaw and biting his
lip ; and another, also a man, kept incessantly pouting his lips and
rubbing them over his teeth. One patient, spoken of above, with
spasms of rigidity of the neck after the bath, had also spasms of
rigidity of the lips. Another case with opisthotonos and tetanic
convulsions, closed the lips in snaps before, and smacked the lips
after having convulsions.

" Risus sardonicus " was observed in five cases, in three of which
there were, and in two there were not, other tetaniform symptoms.

Of the above thirteen cases with tetaniform symptoms, not including
the two with simple "risus sardonicus," ten had endo-pericarditis, one
had pericarditis, endocarditis being absent, in one both of those
affections were doubtful, and in one they were both absent. These
clinical facts make it probable that pericarditis or endocarditis, or
both, may sometimes be concerned in the production of tetaniform
symptoms. Other influences were, however, at work connected with
hyperpyrexia in some of the cases. Thus trismus appeared in one

patient just alluded to who became unconscious after being bled, the temperature rising from 107·8° to 109°; and in three cases the tetaniform symptoms came into play after the excessive temperature had been cooled down by the bath.

We have already seen that in one case of non-rheumatic pericarditis ending in coma, the arms presented occasionally a rigidity as of tetanus; and that in two other cases of the same kind, there was actual tetanus of a peculiar type. These three fatal cases had no endocarditis.

Andral, in commenting on the first of these cases, or that with occasional rigidity of the arm, and delirium ending in coma, asks whether the cause of the affection of the nervous system in these cases is not in the inflammation of the pericardium itself? We have already seen that Dr. Bright looks to the communication of an influence from the inflamed pericardium, through the phrenic nerve to the spine, as a cause of choreal and tetaniform affections. I would here remark that tetanus may be caused by a wound and by exposure to cold, and there is nothing therefore inconsistent, so far as I can see, in the idea that it may be caused also by an internal inflammation affecting local nerves, and through their channel acting on the spinal marrow.

Tetanus is not, so to speak, an intermittent contraction of the muscles of the reflex type, but a continuous contraction of the muscles, due to the direct continuous action of the spinal cord. In tetanus, as Dr. Lockhart Clarke has shown, there are areas of disintegration in the spinal cord. In traumatic tetanus, the cause of the affection is the injury to the nerve, and in these cases the nerve must carry from its periphery to its centre an influence that sets into action the disintegration of the cord. If the inflammation of the peripheral ends of the nerves of the pericardium excites tetanus, it would perhaps do so in some such manner as that just suggested. The cases of tetanus and tetaniform affection associated with pericarditis, though striking are very rare, and we may fairly ask whether in those cases in which the two affections coincided, some other cause may not have been at work to induce the tetanus. I know of no instance in which tetanus was induced by any other internal inflammation, and if this be so, it is not easy to see why pericarditis or pleurisy affecting the phrenic nerve should be the only internal inflammations capable of inducing that affection in its typical or modified form.

THE PHYSICAL SIGNS OF RHEUMATIC PERICARDITIS.

In every case of rheumatic pericarditis there is an increase in the amount of fluid in the pericardium, and a layer of ridged, roughened, or honeycombed lymph is spread over the opposing surfaces of the heart and the pericardial sac. The amount of the fluid poured into the sac is made known by the extent of dulness on percussion, the prominence of the sternum and costal cartilages, and the widening of the intercostal spaces over the region of the pericardium, and by the position of the impulse; while the presence of lymph covering the heart and lining the sac is told by a friction sound.

Effusion of Fluid into the Pericardium in Rheumatic Pericarditis.—Although in the prescribed order, the examination of the chest by the

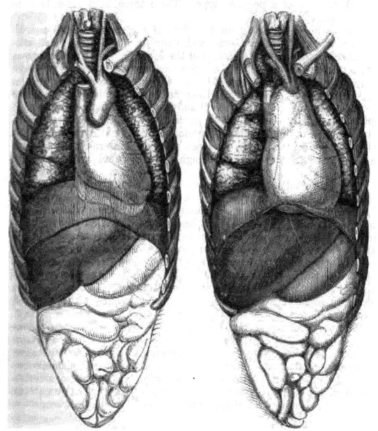

FIG. 33.—Pericardium not distended. FIG. 34.—Pericardium artificially distended with fifteen ounces of fluid.

eye and the application of the hand rightly precede that by percussion I shall here reverse this order, and begin with percussion, for by it we really judge of the extent of the fluid in the sac.

The pericardium of an adult man with a healthy heart is capable of holding from fourteen to twenty-two ounces of fluid, and that of a boy of from 6 to 9 years old, about six ounces, when the sac is distended to the full by injecting water into it by a syringe, through an opening made in the anterior wall of the pericardium.

The effect of this artificial distension of the pericardium on the size, form, and position of the sac and on the situation of the surrounding parts is shown in the accompanying figures (33, 34). The pericardium, thus distended, is pyramidal or pear-shaped. It is formed, so to speak, of a larger and a smaller sphere, the smaller one resting on the top of the larger. The larger and lower sphere contains the heart, the ascending vena cava, and the pulmonary veins; and the smaller sphere holds the great vessels. The distended sac occupies the whole centre of the chest, filling up the space between the sternum in front and the spinal column behind; and extending across the chest from a little within the right nipple to a little beyond the left nipple. The whole sac is lengthened; its smaller end reaches upwards almost to the top of the sternum; and its floor, being formed by the central tendon of the diaphragm, presents a large spherical prominence that bulges downwards into the abdomen, occupies the epigastrium, and reaches as low as the tip of the ensiform cartilage and the lower edge of the sixth costal cartilage. The enlarged and swollen sac displaces all the organs and parts surrounding it. In front it separates the two lungs from each other, so as to uncover the pericardium in front of the heart and great arteries. It pushes forwards the two lower thirds of the sternum, the ensiform cartilage, and the adjoining costal cartilages, especially the left, from the third to the sixth; and by counter-pressure backwards it compresses the œsophagus, the descending aorta, the bifurcation of the trachea, and the left bronchus between itself and the bodies of the vertebræ upon which those parts rest. It displaces the lungs to either side and backwards; and the central tendon of the diaphragm where it forms the floor of the pericardium, the stomach, and the left lobe of the liver downwards.

The artificial distension of the pericardium closely corresponds in general form with its natural distension from pericarditis, when the amount of the effusion has reached its acme. I have already sketched at page 217 what I believe to be the usual course of the increase of the effusion from the beginning of an attack of pericarditis to the period of its acme. When, however, the inflammation of the pericardium has existed for some time, the walls of the sac, so thin, tough, and firm in health, become comparatively thick, soft, and yielding; and as the sac cannot expand to a material degree either upwards towards the neck, or downwards towards the abdomen, it yields sideways and backwards, and widens to the right and especially to the left, so as to encroach on both lungs, but more seriously on the left lung; as may be seen in the accompanying figure, which is taken from a case of chronic pericarditis of long standing, in which the sac contained three pounds and a quarter of fluid (fig. 35). When thus distended, the sac seems to occupy the whole front of the chest; and it completely conceals the left lung, which is pushed backwards and compressed by it so that comparatively little air is admitted into that lung at its lower and posterior part; this effect being increased by the compression of the left bronchus.

There is another effect of this distension of the pericardium to which I have already alluded, its inferred effect namely upon the heart itself. The muscular walls of the ventricles are so thick, and their action is so powerful, that the direct effect of the fluid pressure upon them cannot be very great. But the pressure of the fluid tells inwards upon the weak and unresisting walls of the auricles, the vena cava descendens within the pericardium, and the pulmonary veins, so as to compress and lessen those vessels and the auricles, and to resist and impede the currents of blood, on the one hand from the system along the cava, and on the other from the lungs along the pulmonary veins. This partial blocking of the double stream from the system and the lungs to the heart lessens the contents of the organ, and tends to diminish the size of its cavities. At the same time the supply of blood to the aorta is lessened, and the ascending aorta is therefore also compressed by the fluid. The pulmonary artery, however, owing to the obstacle to the flow of blood through the lungs, tends to resist the pressure of the fluid in the swollen sac, and to remain distended.

Fig. 35.—Case of pericarditis in which one sac contained 3¼ lbs. of fluid. The patient was under the care of Sir James Alderson.

While, however, this influence on the part of the fluid pressure of the distended pericardium is at work compressing the auricles and veins; a second influence is at work, also set up by the inflammation, to counteract the first influence, and to shield to some extent the weaker parts of the heart. The auricular appendices shrink at an early stage, and the walls of the auricles and veins are thickened and somewhat protected from the pressure of the effused fluid by a leathery coat of mail in the shape of the roughened and honeycombed coating of lymph that clothes and strengthens the feeble natural walls of those parts. Thus the double march of the inflammation supplies at the same time a compressing fluid, and a sustaining covering of lymph

The distension of the pericardium with fluid produces two other effects on the heart. 1. The heart is heavier than the fluid in which it plays, and its ventricles consequently tend to sink backwards so that the left ventricle rests upon the posterior wall of the pericardium, just as the liver sinks backwards when the abdomen is distended with fluid in cases of ascites. 2. The other effect of pericardial distension on the heart is the lifting or tilting upwards of the organ within the sac. The heart is attached by its great vessels to the posterior and upper parts of the sac, and the whole organ, therefore, tends to shrink upwards and gravitate backwards towards its points of attachment. At the same time the accumulating fluid which occupies in volume the space between the lower surface of the heart and the central tendon of the diaphragm, displaces the organ upwards into the higher part of the pericardium.

The natural effect of this gravitation, shrinking, and upward displacement of the heart, owing to the great accumulation of fluid in the sac, would be, I conceive, if not modified by other agencies, to cause a layer of fluid to be interposed between the front of the heart and the anterior walls of the chest. Practically however we find that this is not usually the case over the mass of the ventricles; for with one or two rare exceptions we can always feel the impulse of the heart beating sometimes with force, sometimes with a thrill, in the second and third, or third and fourth left spaces, extending from the edge of the sternum to above and beyond the nipple. A layer of fluid is, however, evidently interposed between the lower portion of the front of the heart and the anterior walls of the chest.

The reasons for the presence and pulsation of the heart in the upper intercostal spaces when the pericardium is distended, I believe to be, firstly, the distension of the pulmonary artery, and to a less extent, of the right ventricle, owing to the difficulty with which the blood flows through the lungs; and, secondly, the raised position of the heart, which having left the broader space of the chest below, where it enjoyed free play, occupies its narrower space above, where the heart and pericardium are as it were grasped between the walls of the chest in front and the bodies of the vertebræ behind. The result is that under the combined influence of the elevation of the heart; the distension of the pericardium; and the contracted area of the upper part of the chest in which the heart is lodged, the left lung is displaced from before the organ and the right and left ventricles, and the apex and the great arteries beat against the higher intercostal spaces with which they come into direct contact. In consequence of the withdrawal of the lung from before the heart, and the narrowing compass of the portion of the chest in which the organ is situated, its impulse besides being raised, is also widened outwards, so that the apex beats against the third or fourth space, at or above the level of the left nipple, where it extends beyond the nipple line.

Although the upper portion of the right ventricle is in immediate contact with the walls of the chest, I am satisfied that a portion of the fluid effused into the sac is interposed between those walls and the lower portion of the right ventricle over its anterior surface.

We shall afterwards see that the impulse is raised in position when the fluid in the pericardium increases, and is lowered in position when that fluid diminishes, so that under these circumstances the varying amount of the fluid is told by the varying position of the impulse.

Cases, included in the following tables, that form the subject of this inquiry into the physical signs of pericarditis.—I possess notes of 44 of my 63 cases of rheumatic pericarditis, of the increase, acme, and diminution of the quantity of fluid in the pericardium, as shown by the enlarging and lessening area of the dulness on percussion over that region; the progressive changes in the position of the impulse; and the variations in the tone, intensity, and area of the friction sound; all of which signs are at once the effects and the witnesses of the advance and decline of the inflammation. I have arranged these 44 cases in columns in the accompanying tables (see pages 313—327), so that day by day each of those parallel effects of the disease may be seen either singly or in comparison with each other; and have combined with them the co-existing endocardial murmurs, the presence of pain over the region of the heart and elsewhere in the chest, and the affection of the joints; and I shall now briefly analyse point by point, these parallel effects in those cases.

PERCUSSION.

The enlarged Area of Dulness on Percussion over the Pericardium, caused by the Increase of Fluid in the Sac.—In 22 of the 44 cases under examination, the increased amount of fluid in the pericardium, as indicated by the extended area of dulness over that region, had already at the time of its first observation reached its acme, and from that time, the amount of fluid with its area of dulness steadily declined. One of these cases had a relapse and proved fatal on the 14th day. In the remaining 22 cases the period of the greatest distension of the sac was preceded by a gradual increase, and was followed by a more gradual decrease, in the amount of the fluid; the periods of increase, acme, and decrease of the amount of fluid, being shown by the corresponding gradual enlargement, greatest area, and lessening of the region of dulness on percussion over the pericardium. In 11 of these 22 cases there was a single rise and fall of the tide of the effusion; but in the 11 remaining cases there was a relapse, and the amount of effusion, after lessening considerably, again increased and attained to a second acme. In five of those cases, indeed, there was a second relapse, so that the fluid in the pericardium presented a third, and in one of them even a fourth wave of increase.

The duration of the whole period of increase of dulness on percussion over the region of the pericardium varied much in different patients. Of the 22 cases in which the region of dulness had attained to its greatest area at the time of the first observation, the average duration of the increased dulness from the effusion into the pericardium was eight days, the extreme duration varying from three days on the one hand, to seventeen on the other. The average duration of the period of increased dulness in the 11 cases in which there was a gradual increase, single acme, and a decrease in the amount of fluid effused into the pericardium, amounted to fully eight days, the extreme variation ranging from four to thirteen days. The average duration of the whole period of increased pericardial dulness was more than twice as long in the 11 cases of relapse, as in the cases with a single acme, since in them it amounted to eighteen days, the extremes varying from fourteen to twenty-four days.

The increase of fluid in the early stage was usually rapid. In one half of the cases in which this increase was watched, the area of dulness had reached its maximum on the second or third day after the first observation (11 in 22), and in all but two or perhaps three of the remainder, on the fourth or fifth day. The early advance of the dulness was, as a rule, more slow in those patients who suffered from a relapse than in those who did not do so.

The time during which the effusion into the pericardium remained at its height was, as a rule, very short. In 39 of the 44 cases the region of dulness extended over its greatest area for about a single day. It may have lasted longer, but on the next examination, made usually on the following day, but sometimes later, the tide had turned and the extent of dulness had lessened. The acme of the pericardial dulness lasted two days in three of the remaining cases, and three days in two of them.

The period of the decrease of the effusion in the pericardium was much longer than that of its increase, its average duration having been, as we have already seen, eight days in the 22 cases in which the effusion was at its acme on the first examination.

We thus see that the period of the advance of the effusion, dating from the time of its first observation in the early stage, usually lasted about three days; that the period of the acme of the effusion was usually observed during only one day; and that the period of the decline of the effusion generally lasted about eight days.

The fluid in the pericardium begins to increase on the first day of the inflammation; but, as it necessarily gravitates backwards during the early stages, the effusion does not appear in front until it has accumulated so as to occupy the natural hollow at the back of the sac, and the space between the lower surface of the heart and the floor of the pericardium. Dulness on percussion over the region of the pericardium therefore does not declare itself until the inflammation has lasted for a day or two. I have no exact indications telling how soon the fluid advances to the front of the heart in sufficient quantity to push aside the lungs. That it must, however, have been rapid in certain cases is I think shown by the following instances :—

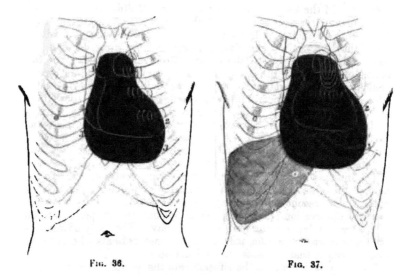

FIG. 36.   FIG. 37.

Figure 36, from a youth aged 17, affected with rheumatic pericarditis, who recovered in nine days from the time of his admission.

Period of the rapid increase of the effusion into the pericardium, just before the occurrence of its acme. The effusion completely distended the sac.

Day of admission.

The pericardial effusion distends, lengthens, and widens the sac, to the same extent and with the same effect as when the healthy pericardial sac is artificially distended with fluid (see figs. 33, 34, p. 305). The swollen pericardium is pyramidal or shaped like a pear, as in figure 34. Its smaller and higher portion (1, 1,) contains the great arteries ; and its larger portion is occupied above (2, 2,) by the heart, and below (3, 3,) by the great volume of fluid which accumulates between the under surface of the heart and the floor of the pericardium. The distended pericardium displaces the lungs upwards, and to each side ; and the diaphragm, liver, and stomach downwards : and the fluid in the sac compresses the auricles ; and that in the lower portion of the sac, between the under surface of the heart and the floor of the pericardium, elevates the heart. Owing to the displacement of the lungs from before the pericardium, the whole of the anterior surface of the heart and great arteries is exposed, including the right auricle and ventricle, the apex and front of the left ventricle, the ascending aorta within the pericardium and the pulmonary artery ; and, owing to the elevation of the heart by the fluid, that organ presses and rubs with increased force against the walls of the chest in front of it ; the anterior surface of the heart at its lower portion is, however, separated from the sternum and cartilages by a thin layer of interposed fluid.

This explanation, and that which follows, given once for all, will apply to figures 37 ; 40, p. 338 ; 42, p. 342 ; 45, p. 356 ; and 48, p. 395, which represent, each of them, the single, or first or second acme of the pericardial effusion.

There is *prominence over the region of the pericardium*, the left costal cartilages and ribs from the third to the eighth being raised and moved outwards.

The region of dulness on percussion over the distended pericardium, ("pericardial dulness," see the black space,) indicates the extent of the pericardial effusion ; has the pyramidal or pear-shaped form of the distended sac ; and extends from a little above the lower end of the manubrium, where it displaces the lungs, down almost to the tip of the ensiform cartilage, where it intrudes on the epigastrium. The lower and larger portion of the region of pericardial dulness over the heart and the great body of the effusion is more than twice the width of its upper and smaller portion over the arteries. This narrow upper portion forms therefore a peak which gives to the region of pericardial dulness its pear-shaped form, and which rises high behind the sternum, and occupies the lower portion of the manubrium. The wider portion of the region of pericardial dulness bears chiefly to the left ; and its upper border, starting from the foot of its narrower portion, is on a level with one of the higher left costal cartilages or spaces. The upper and left boundary of the region of pericardial dulness is therefore indented ; and its upper border is much higher behind the manubrium, than behind the adjoining left costal cartilage or space that may form its higher limit. The higher and narrower region of pericardial dulness (1, 1,) over the ascending aorta and pulmonary artery, is about two inches in width, and is situated behind the sternum, on a level with the first and second spaces, and for about half an inch to the left of it in those spaces. The lower, larger and wider region of pericardial dulness that extends over the heart itself (2, 2) and over the accumulated fluid that occupies the depending portion of the sac below the heart, and that bulges downwards into the epigastric space (3, 3,), extends from the upper edge of the third left costal cartilage, and the corresponding portion of the sternum, down to the lower edge of the sixth left cartilage, and almost to the tip of the ensiform cartilage ; and from about an inch to the right of the lower half of the sternum, to half an inch or more to the left of the nipple. The lower border of the fifth cartilage, and a line running thence across the sternum to the fourth right space, *probably* forms the lower boundary of the heart (2, 2), and the upper boundary of the depending space (3, 3,) occupied by the volume of the fluid distending the pericardial sac.

The *impulse of the heart* occupies the third and fourth left spaces, (see the curved lines in those spaces,) and extends in the latter space to just beyond the nipple ; and the pulsation of the pulmonary artery is felt in the first and second spaces to the left of the sternum ; where the first impulse is followed by a sharp second stroke, which is synchronous with the loud second sound of the pulmonary artery, and which gives the effect of a double impulse, one systolic and gradual, the other diastolic and sharp.

Figure 37, from the same patient as figure 36.
Period of the acme of pericardial effusion.
Third and fourth days after admission.
The explanation of pericardial effusion and dulness given with figure 36, applies also to this figure.

The pericardial effusion, which distended the sac on the day of admission (see fig. 36,) has steadily increased in quantity since then, so that the whole pericardium has become enlarged, and has yielded sideways, and especially to the left ; but it has not lengthened from above downwards. In this patient, therefore, the *region of pericardial dulness* (see the black space) during the acme is unusually wide, and especially along its left border ; this increased width being fully as great above over the great vessels (1, 1), as lower down over and below the heart (2, 2, 3, 3). The left boundary of the region of pericardial dulness over the great arteries (1, 1), extends about an inch to the left of the sternum, in the first and second spaces ; while the left boundary of the large region of pericardial dulness over and below the heart, extends fully half an inch to the left of the mammary line (2, 2, 3, 3). In all other respects, except the increase of the dulness to the left, the region of pericardial dulness corresponds with figure 36, taken on the day of admission. The apex of the left ventricle seems in this case to be behind the fourth left rib or space, and the lower boundary of the heart *probably* extends along the upper edge of the fifth left cartilage, and across the corresponding portion of the sternum ; the heart having been much elevated by the increase of the fluid, which interposes itself between the anterior surface of the heart at its lower border and the walls of the chest.

The prominence over the region of the pericardium has increased.

The impulse is peculiar ; it is felt beating (4th day) from the first to the third left costal cartilages, while the third and fourth spaces are retracted during the systole (see the curved and straight lines in those spaces). These movements give to the impulse the appearance of an undulation. The interposition of the fluid between the apex and lower border of the front of the heart and the walls of the chest has combined with the elevation of the organ to raise the impulse.

For later views of this case see figures 38, 39, p. 335.

The effusion had reached its acme in one patient three days after the beginning of the attack of acute rheumatism ; and the increased cardiac dulness was observed for the first time on the fifth or from that to the seventh day after the beginning of the illness in nine cases. Pain attacked the heart in three cases the day before, and in one

CASES OF RHEUMATIC PERICARDITIS.

EXPLANATION.

1.— ———— means the upper boundary of the region of pericardial dulness, and is placed on a line with the space or cartilage that formed the upper limit of the dulness.

2.— ᴧᴧᴧᴧ means the upper or lower boundary, according to its position, of the region of pericardial friction sound over the sternum, and is placed on a level with the part of the sternum that forms the limit of the region of friction sound. The whole space between these upper and lower boundaries is occupied by the friction sound.

3.— ᴧᴧᴧ means the upper or lower boundary, according to its position, of the region of pericardial friction sound over the costal cartilages and their spaces, and is on a line with the space or cartilage forming the limit of the friction sound. The whole space between these upper and lower boundaries is occupied by the friction sound.

4.— ∪ means the position of the heart's impulse, and is on a level with the space where the impulse was felt.

5.—Murmur →, means mitral murmur; ←, tricuspid murmur; ↓, aortic regurgitant murmur; ↑, aortic systolic murmur; ↖, pulmonic murmur; ○→ means absence of such murmur.

The thin lines merely connect the successive observations with each other, and show that no examination as to the point in question was made on that day.

M., Male : F., Female.

I.—CASES WITH A THRILL OVER THE REGION OF THE HEART OR GREAT VESSELS DURING THE ACME OF PERICARDIAL EFFUSION. (See pp. 358—365.)

(1.)—*Cases with a creaking friction sound during the acme. (See p. 354.)*

	Sternum.	Left costal cartilages.	Spaces between cartilages.	Days.							
				1	2	3	4	5	6	7	
	Manu-brium.	2nd cartil.	1st space								
			2nd space								
	Middle	3rd cartil.	3rd space								
	Third	4th cartil.	4th space								
	Lower	5th cartil.	5th space						○		
	Third Ensiform cartil.	6th cartil.	6th space								
		7th cartil.									
		8th cartil.									
		9th cartil.									

Murmur
Pain in region of heart ♡

Affection of Joints — Very severe / Severe / Rather severe / Not severe

For references in the letter-press with regard to this case, see pp. 331, 339, 343, 354, 369.

	Sternum.	Left costal cartilages.	Spaces between cartilages.	Days.																
				1	2	4	5	6	7	8	9	10	11	12	13	14	15	16	17	18	19	23
	Manu-brium.	2nd cartil.	2nd space																			
	Middle	3rd cartil.	3rd space																			
	Third	4th cartil.	4th space																			
	Lower	5th cartil.	5th space																			
	Third Ensiform cartil.	6th cartil.	6th space																			
		7th cartil.																				
		8th cartil.																				

Murmur
Pain

Affection of Joints — Severe / Rather severe / Slight

See pp. 340, 342.

For Explanation see p. 313.

Cases with a thrill.—Cases with a creaking friction sound during the acme (continued).

13 F. æt. 25.	Sternum.	Left costal cartilages.	Spaces between cartilages.	Acme		Days.												
				1	2	3	4	5	6	7	8	9	10	11	12	13	14
o→	Manu- brium	1st cartil. 2nd cartil.	1st space 2nd space														
	Middle	3rd cartil.	3rd space														
	Third	4th cartil.	4th space														
	Lower	5th cartil.	5th space														
	Third Ensiform cartil.	6th cartil. 7th cartil. 9th cartil.	6th space														

Pain ... ...

Affection of Joints } ... { Severe ... ... / Rather severe / Slight ... ...

See pp. 206, 235, 240, 243, 244.

7 M. æt. 14.	Sternum.	Left costal cartilages.	Spaces between cartilages.	Acme		Days.								
				1	2	3	4	5	6	7	8	9	10	11	12
→ o→	Manu- brium	1st cartil. 2nd cartil.	Clavicle... 1st space 2nd space												
	Middle	3rd cartil.	3rd space												
	Third	4th cartil.	4th space												
	Lower	5th cartil.	5th space												
	Third Ensiform cartil.	6th cartil. 7th cartil.	6th space												

Murmur ... ...

Affection of Joints } ... { Very severe ... / Severe ... ... / Rather severe / Slight ... ...

43 M. æt. 17.	Sternum.	Left costal cartilages.	Spaces between cartilages.	Acme		Days.																		
				1	2	3	4	5	6	7	10	11	12	13	14	15	16	17	18	19	20	24	25	27
	Manu- brium	2nd cartil.	2nd space																					
	Middle	3rd cartil.	3rd space																					
	Third	4th cartil.	4th space																					
	Lower	5th cartil.	5th space																					
	Third Ensiform cartil.	6th cartil. 7th cartil.	6th space																					

Murmur ... ...
Pain ... ...

Affection of Joints } ... { Very severe ... / Severe ... ... / Rather severe / Slight ... ...

For Explanation see p. 313

Cases with a thrill (continued).   (2.)—Cases with a grating friction sound during the acme. (See p. 354.)
(Cases with a treble acme.)

31 M. æt. 22.	Sternum.	Left costal cartilages.	Spaces between cartilages.	Acme				Acme	Days.		Acme									
				1	2	3	4	5	6	7	8	9	10	11	12	13	14	15	16	17	18	19	20
	Manu- brium	1st cartil. 2nd cartil.	1st space 2nd space																		
	Middle	3rd cartil.	3rd space																		
	Third	4th cartil.	4th space																		
	Lower	5th cartil.	5th space																		
	Ensiform cartil.	6th cartil. 7th cartil. 8th cartil.	6th space																		
Murmur	...	...	...																		
Pain	...	...	...																		
Affection of Joints	...	Severe ... Rather severe Slight																			

See pp. 334, 339, 342, 354.

(3.)—Cases with a harsh double friction sound during the acme. (See pp. 354, 355.)

14 F. æt. 17.	Sternum.	Left costal cartilages.	Spaces between cartilages.	Acme									Days.	
				1	2	3	4	5	6	7	8	9	11	
	Manu- brium	1st cartil. 2nd cartil.	2nd space											
	Middle	3rd cartil.	3rd space											
	Third	4th cartil.	4th space											
	Lower	5th cartil.	5th space											
	Third Ensiform cartil.	6th cartil. 7th cartil.	6th space											
Murmur	...	...	...											
Pain														
Affection of Joints	...	Very severe... Severe ... Rather severe Slight ...												

See p. 354.

6 F. æt. 22.	Sternum.	Left costal cartilages.	Spaces between cartilages.	Acme									Days.	
				10	11	12	13	14	15	16	17	18	19	24
	Manu- brium	2nd cartil.	1st space 2nd space											
	Middle	3rd cartil.	3rd space											
	Third	4th cartil.	4th space											
	Lower	5th cartil.	5th space											
	Third Ensiform cartil.	6th cartil. 7th cartil.	6th space											
Murmur	...	...	...											
Affection of Joints	...	Very severe ... Severe ... ... Rather severe Slight												

Y 2

For Explanation see p. 313.

Cases with a thrill.—Cases with a harsh double friction sound during the acme (continued).

36 F. æt. 20.	Sternum.	Left costal cartilages.	Spaces between cartilages.	Days. Acme.
				1 2 3 4 5 6 7 8 9 10 11 12 13 14 15 16 17 18 19 20
→ o→	Manubrium	2nd cartil.		
	Middle ...	3rd cartil.	2nd space	
	Third ...	4th cartil.	3rd space	
	Lower ...	5th cartil.	4th space	
	Third Ensiform cartil.	6th cartil. 7th cartil. 8th cartil.	5th space 6th space	
Murmur Pain ...	... ...	... ...	... ...	
Affection of Joints	...	Very severe ... Severe ... Rather severe Slight ...		
See pp. 211, 238.				

II.—CASES IN WHICH NO THRILL WAS OBSERVED OVER THE REGION OF THE HEART DURING THE ACME OF PERICARDIAL EFFUSION. (See pp. 355–361.)

(1.)—*Cases with a creaking friction sound during the acme. (See pp. 355–356.)*

28 F. æt. 19.	Sternum.	Left costal cartilages.	Spaces between cartilages.	Days. Acme.
				1 3 4 5 6 7 8 9 10 11 12 13 14 15 16 17 18 19 21 23 24 25
→ o→	Manubrium	2nd cartil.		
	Middle ...	3rd cartil.	2nd space	
	Third ...	4th cartil.	3rd space	
	Lower ...	5th cartil.	4th space	
	Third ...	6th cartil.	5th space	
		7th cartil.	6th space	
Murmur Pain ...	... ...	... ...	... ...	
Affection of Joints	...	Very severe ... Severe ... Rather severe Not severe ...		

34 M. æt. 15.	Sternum.	Left costal cartilages.	Spaces between cartilages.	Days. Acme.
				1 2 3 4 5 6 7 8 9 10 11 12 16 20 23
	Manubrium	2nd cartil.		
	Middle ...	3rd cartil.	2nd space	
	Third ...	4th cartil.	3rd space	
	Lower ...	5th cartil.	4th space	
	Third ...	6th cartil.	5th space	
Murmur Pain ...	... ...	... ...	... ...	
Affection of Joints	...	Severe ... Rather severe		

For Explanation see p. 313.

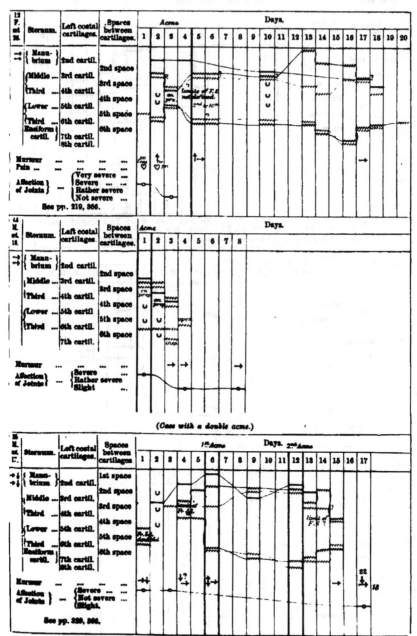

(*Case with a double acme.*)

For Explanation see p. 313.

Cases in which the friction sound was almost creaking during the acme.

6 M. æt. 11.	Sternum.	Left costal cartilages.	Spaces between cartilages.	Acme									Days.
				1	2	3	4	5	6	7	8	9	
	Manubrium	2nd cartil.	1st space										
			2nd space										
	Middle ...	3rd cartil.	3rd space										
	Third	4th cartil.	4th space										
	Lower ...	5th cartil.	5th space										
	Third	6th cartil.	6th space										
	Ensiform cartil.	7th cartil. 8th cartil.											
Murmur	...	...	...										
Affection of Joints }	...	Very severe ... Severe ... ... Rather severe Not severe ...											

31 M. æt. 28.	Sternum.	Left costal cartilages.	Spaces between cartilages.				Acme						Days.	
				1	2	3	4	5	6	7	8	9	10	11
	Manubrium	2nd cartil.	2nd space											
	Middle ...	3rd cartil.	3rd space											
	Third ...	4th cartil.	4th space											
	Lower ...	5th cartil.	5th space											
	Third	6th cartil.												
Affection of Joints }	...	Very severe ... Severe ... ... Rather severe Slight												

(2.)—Cases with a grating friction sound during the acme. (See p. 356.)

47 F. æt. 20.	Sternum.	Left costal cartilages.	Spaces between cartilages.			Acme						Days.		
				1	5	6	7	8	9	10	11	12	13	14	15
	Manubrium	2nd cartil.	2nd space											
	Middle ...	3rd cartil.	3rd space											
	Third ...	4th cartil.	4th space											
	Lower ...	5th cartil.	5th space											
	Third ...	6th cartil.												
Murmur ... Affection of Joints }	...	... ... Severe ... Rather severe												

See p. 396.

For Explanation see p. 313.

49 F. æt. 14.	Sternum.	Left costal cartilages.	Spaces between cartilages.	Acme. Days.																					
				1	2	3	6	7	8	9	10	11	12	13	14	15	16	17	18	19				
	Manubrium	2nd cartil.	2nd space															U						
	Middle ...	3rd cartil.	3rd space							U								U						
	Third ...	4th cartil.	4th space										U					U						
	Lower ...	5th cartil.	5th space										U					U						
	Third ...	6th cartil.	6th space										U											
	Ensiform cartil.	7th cartil. 8th cartil.																						
Murmur																								
Pain																								

(5.)—*Cases in which there was a definite double friction sound, usually harsh, during the acme.* (See pp. 357–359.)
Cases in which there was a creaking friction sound on pressure.

30 M. æt 31.	Sternum.	Left costal cartilages.	Spaces between cartilages.	Days. Acme.																					
				1	2	3	4	5	6	7	8	9	10	11	12	13	14	16	17	19	20	21	22	
	Manubrium	2nd cartil.	2nd space																					
	Middle ...	3rd cartil.	3rd space																					
	Third ...	4th cartil.	4th space																					
	Lower ...	5th cartil.	5th space																					
	Third ...	6th cartil.	6th space																					
		7th cartil. 8th cartil.																						
Pain																								
Affection of Joints } ...	Very severe ... Severe ... ... Rather severe Slight																							

(*Case with a treble acme.*)

F. æt.	Sternum.	Left costal cartilages.	Spaces between cartilages.	1st Acme					2nd Acme					3rd Acme								
				3	4	5	6	7	8	9	10	11	12	13	14	15	16	17	18	19	20	21	22
	Manubrium	2nd cartil.	2nd space																		
	Middle ...	3rd cartil.	3rd space																		
	Third ...	4th cartil.	4th space																		
	Lower ...	5th cartil.	5th space																		
	Third ...	6th cartil.	6th space																		
		7th cartil. 8th cartil.																			
Murmur																				
Pain																				
Affection of Joints } ...	Very severe ... Severe ... ... Rather severe... Slight																			

See pp. 329. 349. 371. 377–379.

* See figs. 44, 45, p. 350; figs. 46, 47. p. 377; and fig 48. p 374

For Explanation see p. 313.

Cases with a thrill.—Cases with a creaking friction sound during the acme (continued).

13 F. æt. 25.

Sternum.	Left costal cartilages.	Spaces between cartilages.	Acme	Days.													
			1	2	3	4	5	6	7	8	9	10	11	12	13	14	
Manu- brium	1st cartil.	1st space															
	2nd cartil.	2nd space															
Middle ...	3rd cartil.	3rd space															
Third ...	4th cartil.	4th space															
Lower ...	5th cartil.	5th space															
Third Ensiform cartil.	6th cartil.	6th space															
	7th cartil. 9th cartil.																

Pain ... ...
Affection of Joints } ... { Severe ... ... / Rather severe / Slight ... ...

See pp. 206, 235, 240, 243, 244.

7 M. æt. 14.

Sternum.	Left costal cartilages.	Spaces between cartilages.	Acme	Days.											
			1	2	3	4	5	6	7	8	9	10	11	12	
Manu- brium	1st cartil.	Clavicle... 1st space													
	2nd cartil.	2nd space													
Middle ...	3rd cartil.	3rd space													
Third ...	4th cartil.	4th space													
Lower ...	5th cartil.	5th space													
Third Ensiform cartil.	6th cartil. 7th cartil.	6th space													

Murmur ... ...
Affection of Joints } ... { Very severe ... / Severe ... ... / Rather severe / Slight ... ...

45 M. æt. 17.

Sternum.	Left costal cartilages.	Spaces between cartilages.	Acme	Days.																			
			1	2	3	4	5	6	7	10	11	13	14	15	16	17	18	19	20	24	25	27	
Manu- brium	2nd cartil.	2nd space																					
Middle ...	3rd cartil.	3rd space																					
Third ...	4th cartil.	4th space																					
Lower ...	5th cartil.	5th space																					
Third Ensiform cartil.	6th cartil. 7th cartil.	6th space																					

Murmur ... ...
Pain ... ...
Affection of Joints } ... { Very severe ... / Severe ... ... / Rather severe / Slight ... ...

For Explanation see p. 313

Cases with a thrill (continued). (2).—*Cases with a grating friction sound during the acme.* (See p. 354.)
(Case with a treble acme.)

51 M. æt. 22. Sternum.	Left costal cartilages.	Spaces between cartilages.	*Acme* 1	2	3	4	5	6	7	*Acme* 8	9	**Days** 10	11	12	*Acme* 13	14	15	16	17	18	19	20
Manu- 1st cartil.		1st space																				
brium 2nd cartil.		2nd space																				
Middle ... 3rd cartil.		3rd space																				
Third ... 4th cartil.		4th space																				
Lower ... 5th cartil.		5th space																				
hird 6th cartil.		6th space																				
Ensiform cartil. 7th cartil. 8th cartil.																						
Murmur ...	...	...																				
Pain ...	...	...																				
Affection of Joints } — { Severe ... ... Rather severe ... Slight																						

See pp. 354, 329, 342, 354.

(3).—*Cases with a harsh double friction sound during the acme.* (See pp. 354, 355.)

16 F. æt. 17. Sternum.	Left costal cartilages.	Spaces between cartilages.	*Acme* 1	2	3	4	5	6	7	8	9	**Days.** 11
Manu- 1st cartil.												
brium 2nd cartil.		2nd space										
Middle ... 3rd cartil.		3rd space										
Third ... 4th cartil.		4th space										
Lower ... 5th cartil.		5th space										
Third Ensiform cartil. 6th cartil. 7th cartil.		6th space										
Murmur ...	...	...										
Pain ...	...	...										
Affection of Joints } — { Very severe... Severe ... ... Rather severe Slight												

See p. 354.

55 F. æt. 21. Sternum.	Left costal cartilages.	Spaces between cartilages.	*Acme* 10	11	12	13	14	15	16	17	18	**Days.** 19	24
Manu- 2nd cartil.		1st space											
brium		2nd space											
Middle ... 3rd cartil.		3rd space											
Third ... 4th cartil.		4th space											
Lower ... 5th cartil.		5th space											
Third Ensiform cartil. 6th cartil. 7th cartil.		6th space											
Murmur ...	...	...											
Affection of Joints } — { Very severe ... Severe ... ... Rather severe Slight													

For Explanation see p. 313.

Cases with a thrill.—Cases with a harsh double friction sound during the acme (continued).

56 F. æt. 20.	Sternum.	Left costal cartilages.	Spaces between cartilages.	Acme Days.																	
				1	2	3	4	5	6	7	8	9	10	11	12	13	14	15	16	17	18	19	20
→ o→	Manu- brium	2nd cartil.																					
			2nd space																				
	Middle ...	3rd cartil.	3rd space																				
	Third ...	4th cartil.	4th space																				
	Lower ...	5th cartil.	5th space																				
	Third Ensiform cartil.	6th cartil. 7th cartil. 8th cartil.	6th space																				
Murmur Pain ...	... ...	... ...	... ...																				
Affection of Joints	...	Very severe ... Severe ... Rather severe Slight ...																					

See pp. 211, 238.

II.—CASES IN WHICH NO THRILL WAS OBSERVED OVER THE REGION OF THE HEART DURING THE ACME OF PERICARDIAL EFFUSION. (See pp. 355–361.)

(1.)—*Cases with a creaking friction sound during the acme.* (See pp. 355–356.)

28 F. æt. 19.	Sternum.	Left costal cartilages.	Spaces between cartilages.	Acme Days.																	
				1	3	4	5	6	7	8	9	10	11	12	13	14	15	16	17	18	19	21	23	24	25
→ o→	Manu- brium	2nd cartil.																					
			2nd space																				
	Middle ...	3rd cartil.	3rd space																				
	Third ...	4th cartil.	4th space																				
	Lower ...	5th cartil.	5th space																				
	Third ...	6th cartil.	6th space																				
		7th cartil.																					
Murmur Pain ...	... ...	... ...	... ...																				
Affection of Joints	...	Very severe ... Severe ... Rather severe Not severe ...																					

34 M. æt. 15.	Sternum.	Left costal cartilages.	Spaces between cartilages.	Acme Days.													
				1	2	3	4	5	6	7	8	9	10	11	12	16	20	23
	Manu- brium	2nd cartil.															
			2nd space														
	Middle ...	3rd cartil.	3rd space														
	Third ...	4th cartil.	4th space														
	Lower ...	5th cartil.	5th space														
	Third ...	6th cartil.															
Murmur Pain ...	... ...	... ...	... ...														
Affection of Joints	...	Severe ... Rather severe															

For Explanation see p. 318.

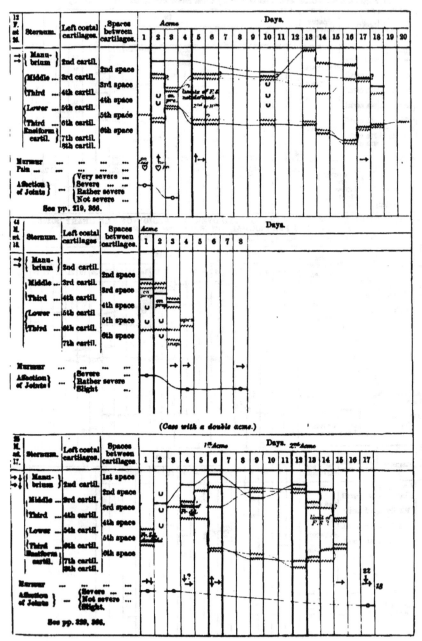

(*Case with a double acme.*)

For Explanation see p. 313.

Cases in which the friction sound was almost creaking during the acme.

6 M. æt. 11.	Sternum.	Left costal cartilages.	Spaces between cartilages.	Acme		Days.							
				1	2	3	4	5	6	7	8	9	
	Manu-brium	2nd cartil.	1st space										
			2nd space										
	Middle ...	3rd cartil.	3rd space										
	Third ...	4th cartil.	4th space										
	Lower ...	5th cartil.	5th space										
	Third ...	6th cartil.	6th space										
	Ensiform cartil.	7th cartil.											
		8th cartil.											
Murmur ...	...	...	...										
Affection of Joints	...	Very severe ... Severe ... ... Rather severe Not severe ...											

31 M. æt. 28.	Sternum.	Left costal cartilages.	Spaces between cartilages.			Acme			Days.				
				1	2	3	4	5	6	7	8	9	10	11
	Manu-brium	2nd cartil.											
	Middle ...	3rd cartil.	2nd space										
	Third ...	4th cartil.	3rd space										
	Lower ...	5th cartil.	4th space										
	Third ...	6th cartil.	5th space										
Affection of Joints	...	Very severe ... Severe ... ... Rather severe Slight											

(1.)—Cases with a grating friction sound during the acme. (See p. 356.)

47 F. æt. 20.	Sternum.	Left costal cartilages.	Spaces between cartilages.		Acme			Days.					
				1	5	6	7	8	9	10	11	12	13	14	15
	Manu-brium	2nd cartil.	2nd space										
	Middle ...	3rd cartil.	3rd space										
	Third ...	4th cartil.	4th space										
	Lower ...	5th cartil.	5th space										
	Third ...	6th cartil.											
Murmur ...	...	...	...										
Affection of Joints	...	Severe ... Rather severe See p. 356.											

For Explanation see p. 313.

68 F. st. 14.	Sternum.	Left costal cartilages.	Spaces between cartilages.	Days. Acme.

(Chart — Days 1–19)

Manu-brium	2nd cartil.	2nd space
Middle ...	3rd cartil.	3rd space
Third ...	4th cartil.	4th space
Lower ...	5th cartil.	5th space
Third ...	6th cartil.	6th space
Ensiform cartil.	7th cartil. / 8th cartil.	

Murmur ... ...
Pain ... ...

(3.)—*Cases in which there was a definite double friction sound, usually harsh, during the acme. (See pp. 357–359.)*
Cases in which there was a creaking friction sound on pressure.

38 M. st. 51.	Sternum.	Left costal cartilages.	Spaces between cartilages.	Days. Acme.

(Chart — Days 1–22)

Manu-brium	2nd cartil.	2nd space
Middle ...	3rd cartil.	3rd space
Third ...	4th cartil.	4th space
Lower ...	5th cartil.	5th space
Third ...	6th cartil.	6th space
Ensiform cartil.	7th cartil. / 8th cartil.	

Pain ... ...

Affection of Joints } ... { Very severe ... / Severe ... ... / Rather severe / Slight ... ...

(*Case with a treble acme.*)

F. st. 30.	Sternum.	Left costal cartilages.	Spaces between cartilages.	1st Acme.	2nd Acme.	3rd Acme.

(Chart — Days 3–22)

Manu-brium	2nd cartil.	2nd space
Middle ...	3rd cartil.	3rd space
Third ...	4th cartil.	4th space
Lower ...	5th cartil.	5th space
Third ...	6th cartil.	6th space
Ensiform cartil.	7th cartil. / 8th cartil.	

Murmur ... ...
Pain ... ...

Affection of Joints } ... { Very severe ... / Severe ... ... / Rather severe ... / Slight ... ...

See pp. 339, 340, 371, 377–379.

* See figs. 44, 45, p. 340; figs. 46, 47, p. 377; and fig 48, p. 379

For Explanation see p. 313.

Cases in which there was a definite double friction sound, usually harsh (continued).

Other cases belonging to this class.

50 M. æt. 22.	Sternum.	Left costal cartilages.	Spaces between cartilages.	Acme															Days.
				1	2	3	4	5	6	7	8	9	10	11	12	13	14	15	16	17

Manu-brium — 2nd cartil.
Middle — 3rd cartil. — 2nd space
Third — 4th cartil. — 3rd space
Lower — 5th cartil. — 4th space
Third Ensiform cartil. — 6th cartil. — 5th space — 6th space

Murmur
Pain
Affection of Joints — Very severe / Severe / Rather severe / Slight.

See p. 240.

54 M. æt. 35.	Sternum.	Left costal cartilages.	Spaces between cartilages.	Acme														Days.			
				1	2	3	4	5	6	7	8	9	10	11	12	13	14	15	16	17	18	19

Manu-brium — 2nd cartil.
Middle — 3rd cartil. — 2nd space
Third — 4th cartil. — 3rd space
Lower — 5th cartil. — 4th space
Third Ensiform cartil. — 6th cartil. 7th cartil. — 5th space — 6th space

Murmur
Affection of Joints — Very severe / Severe / Rather severe / Not severe

32 M.	Sternum.	Left costal cartilages.	Spaces between cartilages.	Acme						Days.		
				1	2	3	4	5	6	7	15	23	27

Manu-brium — 2nd cartil.
Middle — 3rd cartil. — 2nd space
Third — 4th cart. — 3rd space
Lower — 5th cartil. — 4th space
Third Ensiform cartil. — 6th cartil. 7th cartil. — 5th space — 6th space

Murmur

. For Explanation see p. 313.

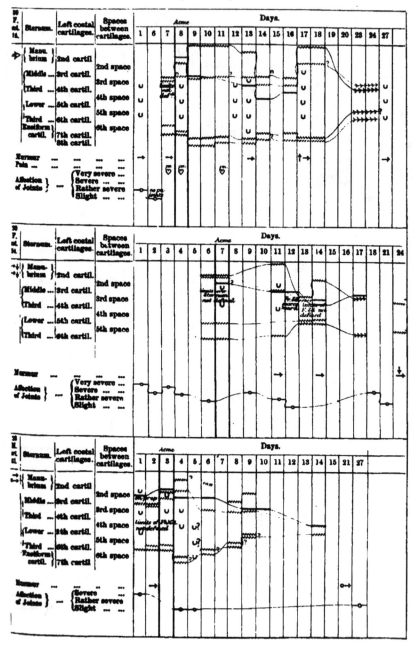

For Explanation see p. 312.

Cases in which there was a definite double friction sound, usually harsh, during the acme (continued).

41 M. ret. 50.	Sternum.	Left costal cartilages.	Spaces between cartilages.							Acme		Days.									
				1	2	22	33	34	35	36	37	38	39	40	41	42	43	44	45	46	47	51
→ →| Manubrium	2nd cartil.																				
	Middle ...	3rd cartil.	2nd space																			
	Third ...	4th cartil.	3rd space																			
	Lower ...	5th cartil.	4th space																			
	Third ...	6th cartil.	5th space																			
	Ensiform cartil.	7th cartil.	6th space																			
Murmur																					
Pain ...																					
Affection of Joints } ...		Rather severe Slight																				

21 M. æt 17.	Sternum.	Left costal cartilages.	Spaces between cartilages.						Acme		Days.									
				1	2	3	4	5	6	7	8	9	10	11	12	13	14	15	16	17	20
→ →	Manubrium	2nd cartil.																				
	Middle ...	3rd cartil.	2nd space																			
	Third ...	4th cartil.	3rd space																			
	Lower ...	5th cartil.	4th space																			
	Third ...	6th cartil.	5th space																			
Murmur																					
Affection of Joints } ...		Very severe ... Severe ... ... Rather severe Slight																				

See p. 329.

55 M. æt. 18.	Sternum.	Left costal cartilages.	Spaces between cartilages.	Acme					Days.						
				1	2	3	4	5	6	7	8	9	10	11	12
→ →	Manubrium	2nd cartil.													
	Middle ...	3rd cartil.	2nd space												
	Third ...	4th cartil.	3rd space												
	Lower ...	5th cartil.	4th space												
	Third ...	6th cartil.	5th space												
	Ensiform cartil.		6th space												
Murmur															
Pain															

See p. 733.

For Explanation see p. 313.

(Cases with a double acme.)

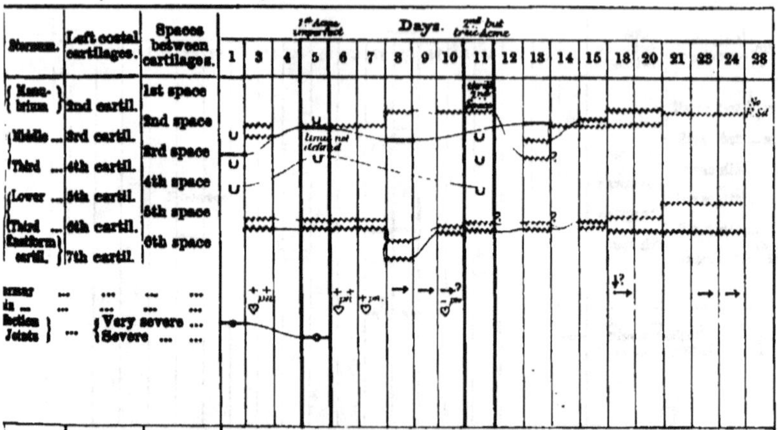

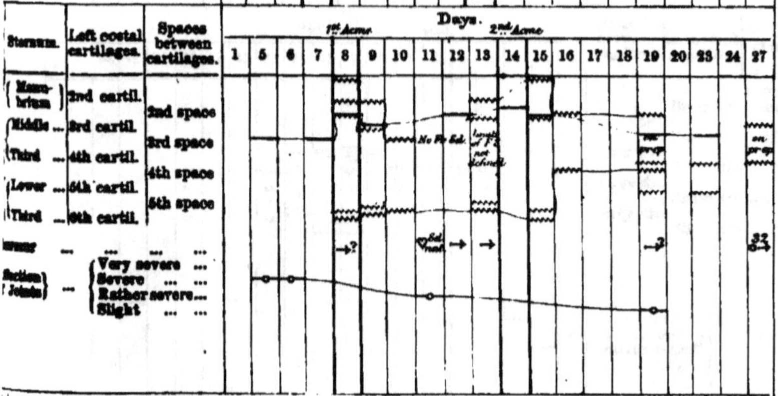

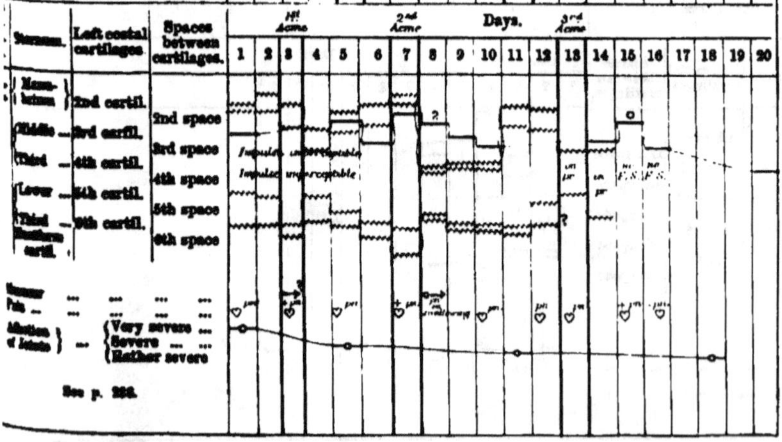

See p. 288.

For Explanation see p. 313.

Cases in which there was a definite double friction sound, usually harsh, during the acme (continued).
(Case with a treble acme.)

(4).—*Cases in which the friction sound was soft, and was rendered harsh by pressure, during the acme.*
(See p. 359.)

For Explanation see p. 313.

(Case with a double acme.)

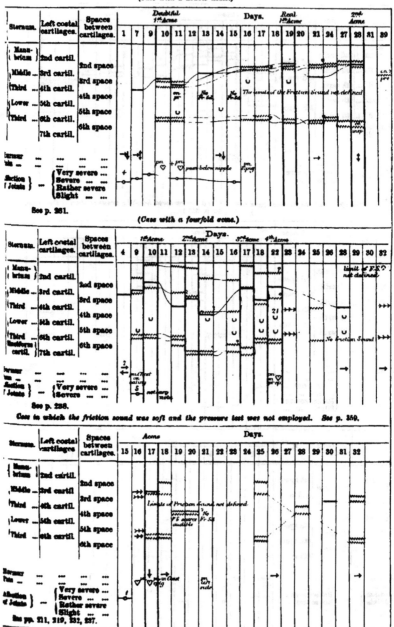

See p. 261.

(Case with a fourfold acme.)

See p. 228.

Case in which the friction sound was soft and the pressure test was not employed. See p. 359.

See pp. 211, 219, 232, 227.

For Explanation see p. 315.

(5.)—Cases in which pressure brought out a friction sound that was not otherwise present during the acme.
(See pp. 359–360.)

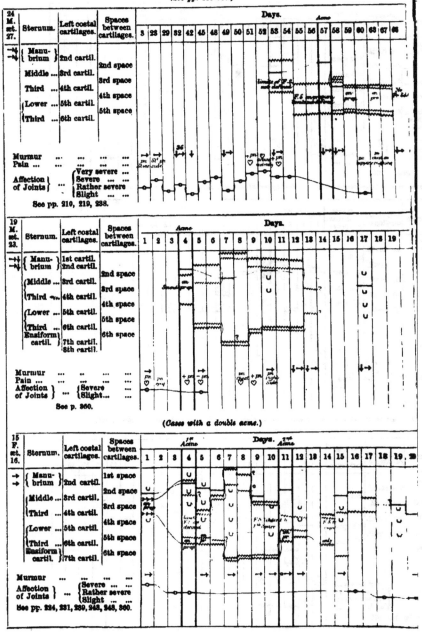

(Cases with a double acme.)

For Explanation see p. 313.
(*Case with a double acme.*)

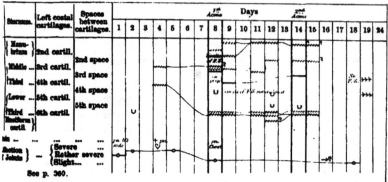

See p. 360.

)—*Case in which friction sound was absent during two of the three days that the acme lasted.* (*See pp. 360–361*).

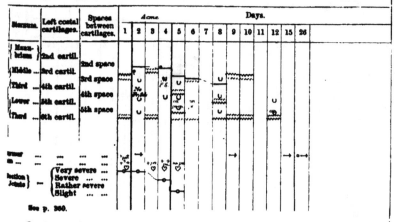

See p. 360.

(7.)—*Case in which a double friction murmur was present during the acme.* (*See p. 361.*)
(*Case with a double acme.*)

INFLUENCE OF PRESSURE IN (I.) EXCITING AND (II.) INTENSIFYING A
FRICTION SOUND WHEN APPLIED WITH THE STETHOSCOPE OVER THE
REGION OF THE HEART IN CASES OF RHEUMATIC PERICARDITIS.

*I.—Influence of Pressure over the Region of the Heart in Exciting a Friction Sound when not
previously audible.*

(For the explanation of this part of the Table, see page 392.)

The figures refer to the cases in the preceding Tables, see pp. 313-327. The repetition of the figure shows that the sign was again audible.	During advance of effusion	During acme of effusion.	During decline of effusion.
Friction murmur excited by pressure—			
Systolic friction murmur	15, 28	—	16, 40, 47, 50, 50, 50.
Double friction murmur	49	—	34, 35, 47, 47, 49.
Time or rhythm of friction murmur not specified . . . . }	7, 24	—	28, 30, 30, 43.
Smooth or feeble friction sound—			
Systolic friction sound	8	—	16, 49 (faint friction sound).
Double friction sound	21	—	6, 12, 58.
Time or rhythm of friction sound not specified . . . . }	24	19	8
Friction sound—			
Systolic friction sound	23	—	28, 30, 30, 43.
Double friction, or to and fro sound . .	8, 21	8, 15, 32	8, 32, 34, 44, 45, 48.
Time or rhythm of friction sound not specified . . . . }	24, 24	12, 24 ; 15 (2nd acme).	8, 26, 35, 36, 44.
Creaking or grating sound—			
Systolic creaking friction sound	21	—	30, 31 : 42 (grating).

*II.—Influence of Pressure over the Region of the Heart in Intensifying a Friction Sound
already present.*

(For the explanation of this part of the Table, see page 392.)

The large figures indicate the cases given in the preceding tables (see pp. 313-327). The small figures show the
days on which the observation was made.

Instances in which it was doubtful whether the sound modified by pressure was a friction sound	Loud ringing sound, increased by pressure, 25 2nd day after admission. Murmur, more distinct on pressure, 20, 18th day. Soft double sound (? friction), rendered louder by pressure, 20, 35th day.
Instances in which an endocardial murmur was replaced, on pressure, by a friction murmur or sound,	Feeble murmur, replaced, on pressure, by double friction murmur, 54, 12th day. Mitral murmur to right of, or above, nipple (→); replaced, on pressure, by a friction sound, 36, 8th day ; 17, 35th (→). Double endocardial murmur, beginning with accent: on pressure, a double friction murmur, not beginning with accent, 39, 22nd day.
Friction murmur modified by pressure	Systolic friction murmur ; intensified by pressure, 4, 7th day ; 6, 5th ; 39, 39th. Systolic friction murmur ; on pressure, a double friction murmur, 6, 7th. Systolic friction murmur ; replaced, on pressure, by a to-and-fro friction sound 23, 21st ; 54, 8th. Double friction murmur ; intensified by pressure, 24, 50th ; 33, 21st ; 39, 17th ; 39, 18th ; 49, 11th-29th. Double friction murmur ; converted by pressure into a double friction sound, 26, 15th ; 28, 14th ; 45, 3rd ; 51, 19th.
Friction sound resembling a murmur, changed by pressure to definite friction sound	Friction sound, like a bellows murmur ; much harsher on pressure, 33, 4th day. Friction sound, of murmuring character ; rendered grating by pressure, 42 12th. Friction sound, almost a murmur ; changed, by pressure, to a harsh double friction sound, 26, 18th.
Systolic friction sound modified by pressure . . .	Friction sound, scarcely audible ; on pressure, a harsh double friction sound, 26, 17th Systolic friction sound ; intensified by pressure, 6, 1st ; 21, 9th ; 40, 7th ; 46, 12th. Systolic friction sound ; followed, on pressure, by a diastolic murmur, 21, 5th. Systolic friction sound ; changed, by pressure, to a double friction sound, 15, 5th ; 39, 18th ; 42, 15th ; 45, 30th.
Friction sound intensified and altered in character by pressure	Smooth, soft, or grazing double friction sound ; intensified by pressure, 4, 3rd day 4, 17th ; 25, 4th ; 35, 5th ; 28, 5th ; 32, 4th ; 33, 9th ; 36, 35th ; 39, 17th 40, 14th ; 45, 4th ; 47, 11th ; 54, 4th ; 56, 21st. Smooth or soft "friction sound" probably double, intensified by pressure, 4, 3rd 25, 1st ; 26, 12th ; 39, 14th. Double friction sound ; intensified or altered in character by pressure, 2, 21st day 6, 1st ; 7, 4th ; 5, 9th ; 8, 14th ; 3, 15th ; 12, 1st ; 15, 5th ; 16, 6th ; 19, 2nd 20, 11th ; 29, 18th ; 33, 3rd ; 34, 4th ; 36, 22nd ; 42, 7th ; 51, 6th ; 53, 1st 50, 4th ; 51, 1st ; 51, 2nd ; 56, 15th ; 56, 9th ; 56, 16th. "Friction sound," probably double ; intensified or altered in character by pressure, 7, 9th day ; 20, 6th ; 24, 58th ; 32, 5th ; 39, 9th ; 39, 12th ; 44, 10th ; 44, 12th ; 45, 14th ; 45, 17th ; 45, 18th ; 54, 7th ; 55, 2nd ; 56, 3rd. Harsh or rough double friction sound ; harsher on pressure, 7, 5th ; 12, 5th ; 7th ; 19, 8th ; 22, 14th ; 33, 4th ; 36, 9th ; 39, 10th ; 39, 8th ; 40, 5th ; 10th ; 42, 11th ; 44, 3rd ; 56, 5th ; 56, 9th. Harsh or rough "friction sound," probably double, intensified by pressure, 10th ; 21, 6th ; 33, 12th. Friction sound scarcely audible, grating on pressure, 42, 9th.
Grating friction sound excited or intensified by pressure.	Double friction sound ; rendered almost grating by pressure, 42, 15th. Double friction sound ; rendered grating by pressure, 26, 6th ; 44, 1st ; 44, 2nd 51, 4th. Grating friction sound; increased or rendered harsher by pressure, 26, and 47, 7th.

three days before the first appearance of increased dulness over the pericardium ; and from one to four days before the effusion had reached its acme in eight other cases.

Friction sound, like increased pericardial dulness, is not present at the first blush of pericarditis, and in my cases the two signs usually appeared at the same time. Thus they did so in 16 of the 22 cases in which the dulness on percussion was detected in the early stage ; while in only one of those cases did the first brush of the friction sound precede, and in the remaining five it followed the onset of the increased pericardial dulness.

The upper boundary of the pericardial dulness when first observed, was limited by the space between the third and fourth left cartilages in 11 out of 22 cases, by the fourth cartilage in three cases, and by the third cartilage in seven cases. In one patient only did the dulness on its first observation reach as high as the second space.

The increase of the region of dulness over the pericardium was sometimes gradual, sometimes rapid. In rare instances the gradual ascent was slow and irregular. As a rule, however, the ascent was rapid.

The contour of the area of dulness on percussion over the pericardium when swollen with fluid in acute rheumatism corresponds very closely with the outline of the sac when distended with water after death. (See figures 33, 34, p. 305.) In a paper in the Provincial Medical Transactions I gave illustrations of the area of pericardial dulness in which the boundary lines of the effusion were ascertained with care, and I here give figures of those cases (figs. 36, 37, p. 311 ; 38, 39, p. 335 ; 40, 41, p. 338 ; 42, 43, p. 340); and elsewhere, views taken from a case of pericarditis in St. Mary's Hospital, which show the same point during various stages of the affection. (See figures 44, 45, p. 356 ; 46, 47, p. 394 ; 48, p. 395.)

The form of the region of pericardial dulness changes as its area increases, its upper boundary being then on a higher level over the sternum than over the costal cartilages, instead of being, as in health, on the same level. The pericardial dulness, at the same time, extends further downwards in the manner shown in the figures just referred to, so as to intrude on the abdomen, and to replace the liver and stomach to a degree proportionate to the amount of the effused fluid.

When the increase of fluid in the pericardium reaches its height, and the sac is completely distended, the area of dulness over the affected region is pyramidal, or, more exactly, pear-shaped, and it extends over and beyond the heart, and in front of the great vessels. The inner borders of the right and left lungs are pushed to each side by the distended sac, so as to expose the whole of the heart and the great vessels.

The region of dulness over the great vessels extends upwards from the level of the third cartilages, sometimes as high as across the middle of the manubrium, or within an inch of the top of the sternum, but more usually to a little above the junction of the manubrium with the long bone of the sternum, or about two inches below the upper end of the bone. This space of dulness over the aorta and pulmonary artery extends across the whole width of the sternum and reaches some distance to the left of it, in the first and second spaces.

The area of the region of dulness over the heart itself and the lower portion of the distended pericardium, may extend across the chest from an inch or more to the right of the lower portion of the sternum to an inch beyond the left nipple; and from above downwards from the second cartilage to the lower edge of the sixth cartilage. The extreme measurement from side to side of the whole region of pericardial dulness may vary from four and a half to six inches, and somewhat diagonally from above downwards, from five and a half to seven inches.

The lower portion of the region of dulness, from side to side, for the extent of about two inches from above downwards, is situated below the lower boundary of the heart; and is entirely occupied by the effused fluid, which here, as I have before shown, displaces the heart upwards, and the diaphragm, stomach, and liver downwards to an extent corresponding to the amount of the effusion.

The width of the region of pericardial dulness in front of the great arteries is usually about two inches, and this region usually ascends above the upper boundary of the heart to an extent varying from one inch to an inch and a half.

This upper region of pericardial dulness, over the great arteries, which is two inches wide, is much narrower than the great region of dulness over the heart itself, which at its upper portion is above four inches wide, the greater width of the cardiac portion of the region of dulness being gained chiefly to the left. This sudden widening of the area of pericardial dulness from distension of the sac gives that area a peaked form above, and an indented outline along its left upper border, that distinguish it from the equally high and extensive area of cardiac dulness due to adherent pericardium and valvular disease, when the heart is enlarged in all directions and especially upwards and to the left, and when the upper left border of the region of cardiac dulness presents a very gradual inclination downwards and to the left without a break. (Compare figure 42 with figure 43, p. 340.) This pear-shaped outline of the region of dulness over the pericardium is quite characteristic, and indicates with certainty the presence of extensive effusion into the sac.

Among the forty-four cases, the upper boundary of the region of dulness when the effusion had reached its acme was over the first space or second cartilage in ten cases, over the second space in twenty-two, and over the third cartilage in twelve. In those cases that suffered a relapse, the first acme was as a rule higher, and the second, and still more the third acme were lower than the single acme in cases that had no relapse.

If the position of the upper boundary of the pericardial dulness over the cartilages and their spaces is known, the whole area of the region of dulness over the pericardium may be inferred with considerable accuracy; since the whole outline of that area shrinks when its upper boundary is lowered, and widens when it is raised. In this respect with certain definite reservations, the upper border of the region of pericardial dulness over the cartilages and spaces to the left of the upper half of the sternum, serves to measure the whole area of dulness and to define its complete outline; just as the ebb and flow of the tide, or the rise and fall of a flood indicated on a measuring post, will tell anyone accurately acquainted with the coast, or the contour lines of the country, the exact area over which the land is covered by water.

If the upper boundary of pericardial dulness reach to the second space, the contour line defining the dulness extends—to within an inch of the top of the sternum; an inch beyond the right edge of the lower half of that bone; and more than an inch below its lower end, where it may descend as far as the tip of the ensiform cartilage; to the lower edge of the left sixth cartilage; and about an inch beyond the left nipple. (See figures 42, p. 340; 45, p. 356.) If the upper margin of dulness be limited by the third space, the boundary line extends— across the sternum on a level with the third costal cartilages; to the right edge of that bone; and to fully half an inch below its lower end; to the upper edge of the sixth cartilage; and to the left nipple. (See figures 38, p. 335; 44, p. 356.) The lungs, the diaphragm, the liver, and stomach are all correspondingly displaced, to a greater degree all round when the upper limit of dulness is over the second cartilage; and to a lesser degree all round when that limit is over the third space. The intermediate position of the upper edge of dulness over the other cartilages and spaces gives an intermediate outline of the whole area.

The restrictions to this rule are due to age and sex, to previous affections of other organs, to valvular disease of the heart of old standing, to coinciding affections of the lungs, especially the left lung, to the duration of the attack of pericarditis and the occurrence of relapses, to accompanying endocarditis, to the progress of the disease, and to its terminations, whether in complete restoration to health, the valves being intact, in valvular disease, or in pericardial adhesions. These restrictions are numerous in appearance, but practically they seldom interfere with the rule just stated of the correspondence of the whole area of dulness with the boundary of a particular part of it.

The rule that the region of pericardial dulness in rheumatic pericarditis enlarges over corresponding areas in different cases, holds good in young persons of both sexes, and in women. In men, however, the bony frame-work of the chest is larger, the lungs are more ample and cover the heart to a greater extent, and the diaphragm is lower than in boys, youths, or women. The result is, that in men both the upper and lower boundaries of the region of pericardial dulness are lower than in the classes just spoken of. Thus the upper boundary of dulness during the acme was over the third cartilage in 8 out of 14 cases of rheumatic pericarditis in men; while in the whole

z 2

of those of the female sex so affected, except one, that boundary was above the third cartilage. In nearly one-third, or 3 in 11 of the male youths with rheumatic pericarditis, the upper boundary of the region of dulness during the acme was over the third cartilage. This is due to the fact that in the male sex, the lungs at a comparatively early period are more largely developed than in the female sex.

When rheumatic pericarditis attacks a heart enlarged from previous valvular disease, the pericardial sac, being more ample, is capable of containing a larger amount of fluid, and the region of pericardial dulness is of greater relative width than when the affection attacks the virgin heart.

If the lower lobe of the left lung shrinks, owing to the combined effect of the compression of that lobe and of the left bronchus by the swollen sac, and of pleurisy with or without pulmonary apoplexy, a condition of things by no means unusual, the whole area of pericardial dulness tends towards the left, and its left border comes into direct contact with the ribs at the side.

Changes in the Form of the Outline of Pericardial Dulness caused by Variations in the Progress and Termination of the Affection.—If the attack lasts long, the pericardial sac, as I have already stated, becomes softened, it yields sideways, and becomes widened to the left and right, while it is not proportionally lengthened above and below (see figure 35, p. 307). This is especially to be noted when relapses take place, and when the effusion, after lessening in quantity, again increases. (See figure 48, p. 378.)

If the affection passes quickly through its stages, and the recovery is perfect, the heart being restored to health, the changes of the increase, the acme, and the decline of the pericardial effusion and of the area of pericardial dulness pass through the course I have described. (See figures 36, 37, p. 311 ; 38, 39, p. 335.)

If, however, the heart becomes enlarged owing to the establishment of valvular disease, the lessening and disappearance of the effusion are delayed, and the area of dulness is somewhat widened and lowered, especially towards the left.

If along with valvular disease, adhesions of the heart are established, the whole organ is enlarged, upwards, downwards, and sideways. The outline of the area of dulness loses its characteristic pear-shaped form, and its peaked outline over the great vessels gives place to a gradual widening of that area from above downwards, that corresponds with the enlarged outline of the heart itself. (Compare figure 42 with figure 43, p. 340.)

PROMINENCE OVER THE REGION OF THE PERICARDIUM.

Increased dulness on percussion over the region of the pericardium is the only reliable sign of the increase of fluid in the sac. Increased prominence of the costal cartilages over the heart, with widening of the spaces between them, form, however, a secondary sign of some interest and value.

In my paper before alluded to, I state that the distension of the pericardial sac by fluid, besides displacing the surrounding organs, pushes forward the sternum, elevates the costal cartilages from the second to the seventh, widens the spaces between the cartilages and ribs from the second to the sixth or seventh, pushes outwards the sixth left rib, and causes some degree of prominence over the left side.

This condition was observed with care in one or more of the cases of pericarditis examined by me in the Nottingham Hospital. I find that prominence over the region of the pericardium was noticed by me in 19 of 63 cases of rheumatic pericarditis under my care in St. Mary's Hospital. More than three-fourths of those patients (15 in 19) were males, while only 4 were females. The cardiac prominence is obscured in women by the mamma; that sign having been observed in only one-seventh of the female cases of rheumatic pericarditis (4 in 27), while it was noticed in nearly one-half of the male cases (15 in 36).

The increased prominence over the region of the heart was usually noticed when the effusion into the pericardium was at its height, and it lessened when the effusion declined. In the greater number of the cases (12 in 19), the prominence over the region of the heart is described in general terms, but in seven its area was specified. In one of these it extended from the second cartilage to the sixth; in two, from the third to the sixth; in three, from the third to the fifth; and in the remaining one, from the fourth cartilage to the sixth.

In these cases the cartilages yielded to the distension of the sac, and were displaced by it forwards and upwards; with the good effect of somewhat relieving the pressure exerted by the swollen sac on those important structures, the bifurcation of the trachea, the left bronchus, the œsophagus, and the aorta, that are situated between the back of the pericardium and the bodies of the dorsal vertebræ. The prominence over the cardiac region caused by the forward pressure of the enlarged pericardium, points out that a serious counter-pressure backwards is exerted at the same time on the three vital tubes that I have just named, which convey air to the lungs, and especially the left lung, food to the stomach, and blood to the lower half of the frame. Indeed, the true value of this sign is that its presence reveals to us at the surface, the existence of deep and serious pressure on important internal parts, a pressure that is augmented when the superficial prominence increases, and that is relieved when that prominence lessens.

It is to be remarked that at the same time that the sternum and cartilages over the region of the distended pericardium are rendered prominent with the effect of somewhat lessening the pressure of the swollen sac upon the bifurcation of the trachea, the left bronchus, the œsophagus and the aorta—the dorsal portion of the spinal column deepens itself and curves backwards so as to afford increased space for the swollen sac, and those important tubes that are compressed by it. At the same time the patient sits up, and even leans forward, so as to allow of the gravitation downwards and forwards of the fluid in the pericardium. By this attitude, and the deepened spinal curvature, indeed, the pressure of the distended sac upon those vital parts is materially lessened, breathing and swallowing are rendered less difficult, and blood is supplied through the descending aorta with greater freedom to the body and lower limbs.

THE POSITION OF THE IMPULSE OF THE HEART IN CASES OF PERICARDITIS.

When the amount of fluid in the pericardium has increased so as to enlarge the area of dulness on percussion over the region of the heart, the seat of the impulse is raised and extended outwards.

I gave figures of three cases of pericarditis with great increase of fluid in the sac, in my paper on the position of the internal organs, in which the impulse was present in the third and fourth spaces, instead of occupying its usual position in the fourth and fifth spaces. In that paper, attention was I believe called for the first time to the elevation of the impulse in cases of pericarditis with effusion into the sac.

In thirty-seven of the forty-four cases of rheumatic pericarditis, daily details of which are given in columns in the accompanying tables, the exact position of the impulse during successive visits is stated, in five others the impulse is described, but its situation is not specified, and in the remaining two the impulse was almost or quite imperceptible (see pp. 313—327).

In examining these cases I shall study the position of the impulse from two points of view, (1) the elevation of its lower boundary; (2) its diffusion into the higher intercostal spaces during the period of the increase of fluid in the pericardium.

(1) *The Elevation of the* Lower Boundary *of the Impulse.*—In fourteen cases, the extent of dulness on percussion over the region of the pericardium increased, and the effusion attained to its acme after the first observation; and in twelve of these the impulse occupied a higher position at the time of the acme than at that of the first observation, while in two its position was unchanged.

In twenty-two of the patients the amount of fluid in the pericardium was at its greatest height or acme at the time of the first observation; and as the effusion lessened, in eighteen of these the lower boundary of the impulse fell, in three it was stationary, and in one it became higher in position.

We thus see that in thirty of these thirty-seven cases of rheumatic pericarditis, the lower boundary of the impulse was raised in position when the amount of effusion in the pericardium was at its acme.

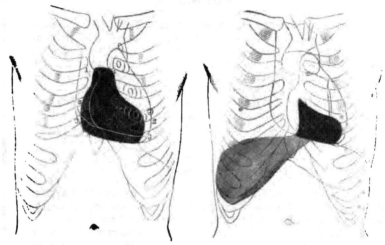

Fig. 38.   Fig. 39.

For previous views of this case, see figures 36, 37, page 311.

Figure 38, from a youth aged 17, affected with rheumatic pericarditis.

Period of the decline of the pericardial effusion.

Sixth day after the acme of pericardial effusion, eighth day after admission.

The pericardial effusion has diminished to a great extent, and the sac, no longer distended, has contracted, so that it has lost its pear-shaped form, and resumed more nearly that of the heart itself, a little modified and enlarged by undue fulness above.   The lower border of the heart is much lower than during the acme, being situated behind the fifth cartilage, and the lower boundary of the pericardium is much higher ; it no longer protrudes into the epigastric space, but has shrunk upwards, being situated behind the upper third of the ensiform cartilage, and behind or above the upper edge of the sixth left cartilage.   The right ventricle and the apex of the left ventricle are exposed ; but the upper part of the conus arteriosus and of the front of the left ventricle, the pulmonary artery, and the ascending aorta, are covered with lung.

The prominence over the pericardium has almost disappeared and the left side has nearly resumed its natural shape.

The region of pericardial dulness (see the black space) corresponds with the lessened amount of the pericardial effusion, and instead of being pear-shaped, or longer than it is broad, as it was during the acme, it has now more nearly the contour of the natural region of cardiac dulness, and is broader than it is long.   It still, however, presents a peaked form at its upper border behind the sternum, where that border is on a level with the third cartilage, and where it is still much higher than its upper border to the left of the sternum, which is situated at the third left space.   Its lower border is situated behind the upper third of the ensiform cartilage ; and its right and left borders are respectively behind the right margin of the sternum, and within the left nipple.

The impulse is felt in the first, second, third, and fourth left spaces, being feeble in the fourth space.   (See the curved and circular lines in those spaces.)

Figure 39, from the same patient as figures 36, 37, 38.

Period of the disappearance of the pericardial effusion and restoration of the heart to its natural position, which is however still rather high.

Eighth day after the acme of pericardial effusion, tenth day after admission.

There is no pericardial effusion, and the chest has resumed its natural shape.

The region of cardiac dulness (see the black space) has regained its natural form, and is no longer preternaturally higher behind the sternum than to the left of it.   Its upper boundary is situated behind the fourth cartilage, and the adjoining portion of the sternum, its lower boundary, is behind the fifth space and the upper end of the ensiform cartilage ; its right margin is a little to the left of the middle line of the sternum, and its left border is fully half an inch within the mammary line.

In one-fifth of the cases (7 in 37) the lower boundary of the impulse was pushed up as high as the third space, and in three-fifths of them it was present in the fourth space (21 in 37). In two patients, one with disease of the aortic and mitral valves, the other with that of the mitral valve alone, of some standing, the impulse was seated in the sixth space, in three cases it occupied the fifth space, and in three it was felt over the third cartilage.

The existence of previous valvular disease, owing to the increased size of the heart in such cases, exercised a marked influence on the position of the lower boundary of the impulse, and as a rule lessened or prevented its ascent during the acme of the effusion. Thus, of five patients of this class, all of whom had affection of the mitral valve, and one of them of the aortic valve also, in two the lower boundary of the impulse occupied the sixth space, in two the fifth space, and in one it was seated in the fourth space.

If we deduct from the thirty-seven cases these five with valvular disease, which are exceptional both in their nature and as regards the influence of the effusion on the seat of the impulse, we find that in only one of the remaining thirty-two patients was the lower boundary of the impulse as low as the fifth space during the acme of the effusion.

These cases of previous valvular disease are exceptional in another point of view. In three of these five patients the position of the lower boundary of the impulse was not higher during the acme of the effusion than at other times. If we deduct these five cases from the thirty-seven under review, we find that in only three of the remaining thirty-two cases was the position of the lower boundary of the impulse unchanged during the acme of the effusion, while in twenty-nine of them it was definitely higher than in health.

Extent to which the Lower Boundary *of the Impulse was Raised, when the Effusion into the Pericardium was at its Height or Acme.*— In the twelve patients in whom the acme of the effusion was reached after the first observation of increased dulness on percussion, and in whom the lower boundary of the impulse was then elevated, the impulse at its lower boundary ascended two spaces in two instances (compare figure 44 with figure 45, p. 356), a space and a half in one, one space in six, and less than a space in three cases ; and it descended after the acme two spaces in five instances, one space in five, less than a space in one, and in the remaining case its descent was not observed.

In the eighteen cases in which the effusion had attained to its acme at the time of the first observation, the lower boundary of the impulse subsequently descended two spaces in three patients, one space in thirteen, one rib's breadth in one, and half a space in one case.

If we combine these thirty cases in one group, we find that the lower boundary of the impulse was higher during the acme of the effusion than in the natural state by two spaces in eight cases, by one space in nineteen, and by less than a space in three cases.

Time occupied during the Ascent and the Descent of the Lower Boundary of the Impulse in connection respectively with the Increase, the Acme, and the Decline of the Fluid in the Pericardium.—In the twelve cases in which the impulse at its lower boundary ascended to its highest point after the first observation, and during the period of the increase of the pericardial effusion, the time occupied by its ascent was from one to two days in nine cases, and from four to six days in three cases.

The lower boundary of the impulse fell from its highest position to its natural one in from one to two days in ten cases, in from three to nine days in eighteen, and in sixteen days in two out of a total of thirty cases. The ascent of the lower boundary of the impulse was therefore more rapid than its descent.

Relation between the Extent of the Effusion in the Pericardium, and the Height of the Lower Boundary of the Impulse.—The clinical facts just given show that the lower boundary of the impulse was raised by the increase of the fluid in the pericardium; and we find, therefore, as a rule, a relation between the extent of the effusion and the height of the impulse in these cases of pericarditis. But this rule is reversed in a small group of exceptional cases, amounting to seven, in which the upper limit of the effusion was as high as the first space or the second cartilage; while the lower boundary of the impulse was present in the sixth space in one, in the fifth space in two, in the fourth space in three, and in the third space in only one of these cases. Three of these patients in whom the impulse was low had valvular disease of old standing, a condition that, as I have already shown, prevents or lessens the ascent of the impulse.

(2) *The Diffusion of the Impulse over the* Higher *Intercostal Spaces during the Acme, and Decline of the Fluid in the Pericardium.*—In three-fifths of the cases (22 in 37) the impulse, at the time of the acme of the effusion, extended upwards above its lower boundary to the extent of one or more of the higher intercostal spaces. In more than one-half of these cases the impulse was felt beating as high as the second space (12 in 22), while in less than one-half of them its upper limit was the third space (10 in 22). The extent to which the impulse was felt in the higher spaces was naturally regulated by the position of its lower boundary. Thus, the impulse was bounded below by the fourth space in ten cases, and in eight of these it extended up to the third space or cartilage, and to the second space in only two; while in eight other patients the impulse, which was bounded below by the third space or cartilage, spread upwards to the second space. According, therefore, to the degree to which the impulse was raised by the increased amount of fluid in the pericardium, it was felt beating in the second and third spaces, or the third and fourth spaces, instead of, as in health, the fourth and fifth spaces.

In these cases there were two agencies at work: one, the increase of fluid in the pericardium, which elevated the heart and its impulse

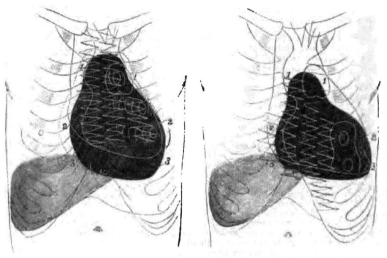

Fig. 40.   Fig. 41.

Figure 40 from a housemaid aged 17, affected with rheumatic pericarditis.
Period of the first acme of pericardial effusion, fifth day after admission.
The explanation of pericardial effusion and dulness given with figure 36, page 311, applies also to this figure.
The *pericardial effusion* extends less to the left and more to the right than in figure 37, page 311 (acme of pericardial effusion), and is of about equal extent in the two figures from above downwards. The heart, which is enlarged, is elevated by the fluid, but to a less degree than in figure 41, its lower boundary being *probably* situated behind the lower border of the fifth cartilage, and just above the lower end of the sternum.
The whole front of the heart is exposed, including the right auricle and ventricle, the apex and front of the left ventricle, the ascending aorta within the pericardium, and the pulmonary artery.
The region of pericardial dulness (see the black space) extends from a little above the lower end of the manubrium and the second left space, down to the tip of the ensiform cartilage, and the middle of the sixth cartilage ; and from a little over an inch to the right of the lower half of the sternum, to a little beyond the left mammary line.   The area of dulness includes (1, 1,) the region of the great arteries ; (2, 2,) that of the heart ; and (3, 3,) that of the volume of the effused fluid below the heart, and projecting downwards into the epigastric space.
The impulse is less elevated than in figure 37 (acme), being situated in the second, third, and fourth spaces.   (See the curved and circular lines in those spaces.)
The *friction sound* (represented by zigzag lines, the systolic lines being thick, the diastolic thin), is heard, double, over the whole length of the sternum, being audible, with pressure over its upper third (the great arteries), and without pressure over its lower two-thirds ; and is also audible with pressure from the third to the fifth left cartilages (right ventricle) ; and over, but not beyond the apex of the left ventricle.
A loud mitral murmur ➔ is audible extensively to the left of the heart.

Figure 41 from the same patient as figure 40.
Period of the decrease of the pericardial effusion after the first acme.
Eighth day after admission, third after the acme—for the sounds.   Eleventh day after admission, sixth after the acme—for the pericardial effusion and dulness, and impulse.
The pericardial effusion has lessened considerably, but is still present in considerable quantity.   The right ventricle and the apex and front of the left ventricle are completely exposed ; and the left border of the right auricle, and the lower portions of the ascending aorta and pulmonary artery, are also brought into view.   The heart, (2, 2,) which is

enlarged, has dropped down into its natural place, and even extends beyond that place, at its lower and left boundaries.' The amount of effusion between the under surface of the heart and the floor of the pericardium (3, 3,) is very small.

The region of pericardial dulness (see the black space) has lessened considerably in area ; it extends from between the second spaces, behind the sternum, down to the lower third of the ensiform cartilage ; from the third left space to the upper border of the sixth cartilage ; and from the right edge of the sternum to a point an inch beyond the left mammary line. There is reason to believe that adhesions have formed at the apex, so that the latter boundary is not pericardial but cardiac. The region of dulness over the great arteries (1, 1,) is still very marked but has materially lessened ; that over the heart (2, 2,) being still extensive ; and that over the depending portion of the pericardial effusion between the under surface of the heart and the floor of the pericardium (3, 3,) being very narrow, indeed a mere strip.

The impulse of the apex is felt in the sixth space, considerably to the left of the nipple. The position of the impulse elsewhere is not mentioned in the report, but I have given it in the figure as being present in the fourth and fifth spaces, because three days later, at the time of the second acme, it was felt in those spaces, as well as in the second and third spaces. (See the circles and curved lines in those spaces.)

The friction sound (see the zigzag lines, systolic thick, diastolic thin) on the seventh day had increased considerably below and to the right, and lessened above and to the left. It was audible over the sternum from below, but not above, the level of the second spaces, and thence down to the tip of the ensiform cartilage ; to the right of the lower half of the sternum ; and over the left cartilages, from the third to the seventh, where it extended about two inches below the heart ; but it was inaudible over the region of the apex, where there were probable adhesions.

For the later views of this case, see figures 42, 43, p. 340.

both at their lower and upper boundaries into the contracted space at the higher part of the chest, and caused the heart to beat against the left upper spaces ; the other, the enlargement from distension of the right ventricle and especially of the pulmonary artery, owing to the difficulty with which the blood passes through the lungs from the combined effect of the pressure upon the auricles by the fluid in the swollen sac, and the existence of endocarditis with mitral regurgitation. The enlarged right ventricle and pulmonary artery displace the lungs, and pulsate, the former against the third, the latter usually against the second space ; and in that space the double beat of the artery is then felt, the first being feeble, the second sudden and like a shock, coinciding with a feeble first and intensified second sound heard over the same situation. When the heart is much raised, it is evident that the conus arteriosus must sometimes occupy the second space, the pulmonary artery being elevated into the first space.

After the acme, when the amount of the fluid in the pericardium lessened, the position of the impulse, as we have just seen, as a rule descended at its lower boundary, but it generally retained its place at its upper boundary. Sometimes, indeed, the impulse extended upwards as well as downwards during the period of the lessening of the effusion.

The clinical facts that I have just related as to the extension of the impulse into the upper region during the successive periods of the increase, the acme, and the decrease of the effusion into the pericardium ; while its lower boundary steadily rose during the increase, and fell during the decrease of the fluid, are to be traced I consider to a succession of causes. I have just considered the two agencies that are at work to extend the impulse into its higher region during

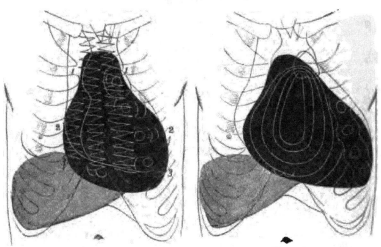

FIG. 42.   FIG. 43.

For previous views of this patient see figures 40, 41, page 338.

Figure 42, from a housemaid aged 17.

Period of the second acme of pericardial effusion owing to a relapse of pericarditis.

From the fourteenth to the eighteenth day after admission, from the tenth to the fourteenth day after the first acme (figure 40), and from the third to the seventh day after the period of decrease of the effusion illustrated in figure 41. The period of the acme lasted four days.

The explanations of pericardial effusion, prominence and dulness, given with figure 36, at page 311, apply also to this figure.

The pericardial effusion has increased again to a very great extent. The heart is considerably enlarged, and is probably adherent at the apex; its lower boundary is therefore much lower than during the first acme, figure 40, and apparently reaches down to the sixth cartilage, and the middle of the ensiform cartilage. The effusion has increased very much, especially upwards, downwards, and to the right; but owing probably to adhesions at the apex, it has been stationary or has lessened in area at the left side—compared with its amount and area during the period of decrease of the effusion after the first acme shown in figure 41. The effusion extends much higher and more to the right than during the first acme (figure 40), but it is of the same extent at its lower and left boundaries in this as in the first acme. The area of the effusion was much wider in relation to its length, and especially towards the left, in the single acme shown in figure 37, owing to the enlargement of the sac from long-continued distension, than it is in this instance, in which the expansion of the sac to the left has been apparently stopped by the probable adhesion of the apex and front of the left ventricle.

The whole front of the heart and great arteries is exposed, including the right auricle and ventricle, the apex and front of the left ventricle, and the ascending aorta and pulmonary artery.

The region of pericardial dulness (see the black space), corresponding to the pericardial effusion, extends very high, or to within an inch of the episternal notch; far to the right, or nearly two inches to the right of the sternum; low down, or below the tip of the ensiform cartilage; and owing probably to adhesions at the apex, proportionally less far to the left, or fully half an inch to the left of the mammary line. The region of dulness over the arteries is unusually high and narrow. Its width on the first day of the acme was little more than one inch; but it had increased to about two inches on the fourth day, when its upper border was not quite so high as on the first day of the acme at its upper part.

The impulse is extensive but not strong, the double pulsation over the pulmonary artery being felt over the second and third spaces; and the impulse of the heart, over the third, fourth and fifth spaces, where it extends beyond the nipple (see the curved lines and circles in those spaces). The lower boundary of the impulse has therefore been elevated from the sixth space to the fifth since the period of the decrease of the effusion following the first acme, shown in figure 41 : it is, however, lower in this second acme than it was in the first acme, when it occupied the fourth space. '

The friction sound (see the zigzag lines, the systolic lines being thick, the diastolic thin) is scarcely audible anywhere without pressure, but with pressure it is heard, double, over the whole region of the pericardial dulness except over the apex and front of the left ventricle, where there are probably adhesions, and where a loud mitral murmur → prevails. The rubbing sounds are louder over the two lower thirds of the sternum and to each side of it, than higher up.

Figure 43, from the same patient as figures 40, 41, 42.
Period of complete adhesion of the pericardium to the heart.
For pericardial dulness—fifty-two days after admission, thirty-nine to forty-three days after the second acme.
For the impulse—eighty-eight days after admission, when the dulness, tested by post-mortem examination, was about the same as on the fifty-third day after admission.

The region of pericardial dulness (see the black space) is very extensive, measuring about seven inches from left to right, with a slight downward inclination, and nearly five inches from above downwards. Its upper boundary was behind the lower border of the manubrium ; its lower boundary, behind the lower end of the ensiform cartilage, the sixth left space and the seventh left rib ; its right boundary was situated midway between the right nipple and the edge of the sternum ; and its left boundary extended to the sixth and seventh ribs at the outer side of the chest.

The impulse on the fifty-third day was present in the fourth, fifth and sixth spaces from two inches within, to two inches without, the nipple line, and was quite absent from the sternum and the spaces between the cartilages ; since that time the patient has been getting gradually worse ; and the impulse has been becoming gradually stronger and more extensive, and is now, on the eighty-ninth day, felt over the whole sternum, the epigastrium, and the cartilages to each side, and on the left side down to the seventh left rib, where it beats against the outer side of the chest (see the curved lines occupying all that region). The impulse heaves up rather slowly during the systole, and immediately after it, falls suddenly backward. The impulse in the first and second spaces, over the pulmonary artery, is double, protruding slightly during the systole, and going back with a flapping rapid movement during the diastole, conveying the impression of a sharp impulse or shock, synchronously with the second sound. Ninety-first day. The impulse is still felt over the sternum, but feebler than two days ago, similar in character, but not felt.

the periods of the increase and acme of the effusion; the increase namely of the pericardial fluid elevating the heart into the contracted space of the chest above ; and the enlargement of the right ventricle and pulmonary artery from obstruction to the flow of blood through the lungs. During the decline of the fluid the first of these influences is reversed, for the heart descends into its natural place, where it beats with comparative freedom; but the second influence, the enlargement of the right ventricle and pulmonary artery from obstruction through the lungs, often remains in full force to retain the impulse in its higher position; and this influence is frequently added to by other causes that have a like effect. These additional influences include the thickening and matting of the inflamed pericardium ; the possible adhesion from pleurisy of the left lung to the pericardium at its upper border; and the deficient or absent expansion of this portion of the lung from adhesion and other causes, such as pulmonary apoplexy, and the imperfect general use of the left lung. These views derive additional confirmation from the fact that in all the cases save one in which the impulse extended over the higher spaces during both the acme and the decline of the effusion, there was endocarditis with mitral incompetence, and in several of them, aortic incompetence also.

Position of the Impulse after the Decline of the Pericardial Effusion during the Later Stages of Rheumatic Pericarditis; and after its Cessation.—When the effusion disappears and the heart resumes its natural position, and when the lungs again cover the great vessels and the upper part of the organ in front, the impulse as a rule descends into its natural position, and is again felt in the fourth and fifth spaces.

In those patients in whom the heart becomes again healthy after the attack, the size, position and customary beat of the organ are restored: but in those in whom valvular disease is established, the nature and extent of the disease are made apparent by the force, extent, and position of the impulse. When the resulting mitral disease is severe, the impulse of both the right and left ventricles is extended, and is felt beating from the lower half of the sternum to the left nipple. When, however, the mitral affection is slight, and such as scarcely or not at all to interfere with the function of the organ, then the impulse resumes its natural boundary and strength; and thus the impulse becomes a true measure of the extent of the valvular disease. When both the aortic and mitral valves are affected, the apex-beat and the impulse generally of the left ventricle become more markedly developed, the action of the right ventricle being still unduly strong. In those comparatively rare cases in which the aortic valve is alone affected, the right ventricle is untouched; but the size and force of the left ventricle are increased in exact proportion to the increased labour thrown upon that cavity by the degree of the crippling of the valve. The apex-beat and general shock of the left ventricle become extended outwards beyond the left nipple, and downwards into the sixth space, when the valvular affection is great; but they are held almost within the natural limits when it is slight. When the heart becomes adherent and there is disease of one or more of its valves, the impulse of the organ becomes extended in every direction—to the right, over and beyond the sternum; to the left beyond the line of the nipple; downwards, over the ensiform cartilage, and even below it in the epigastrium; and especially upwards, to the second space and to the adjoining portion of the sternum. In some cases the whole impulse bears at first forwards during the systole, and then drags the walls of the chest in a characteristic manner backwards; while in other cases, in which there is complete fibrous attachment of the adherent pericardium to the sternum, that bone and the adjoining costal cartilages are steadily drawn inwards during the systole, and spring forwards with a shock during the diastole. An essential difference is also established between the influence of respiration on the area of the impulse of the adherent and the non-adherent heart. When the heart is not adherent, a deep inspiration, by drawing down the heart and covering it with the expanded lungs, causes a complete transfer of the impulse from the fourth and fifth spaces to the epigastrium and the sixth and seventh cartilages; but when the heart is adherent, the outspread dragging impulse almost retains its position during a deep inspiration, neither materially lessening its area over its upper borders, nor materially increasing it below. There is, in short, no transfer, such as occurs when there are no adhesions, of the impulse during a deep breath from the intercostal spaces to the ensiform cartilage and epigastrium and the adjoining left costal cartilages. Thus in a patient who has recovered from rheumatic endo-pericarditis we are enabled to judge by the position and force of the impulse, whether the valves, if affected, are seriously or only slightly affected; and, by the extent to which the play of the impulse is influenced by respiration, whether the valvular affection is combined or not with extensive and binding adhesions of the heart.

VIBRATION OR THRILL FELT BY THE HAND OVER THE REGION OF PERICARDIAL FRICTION.

A sense of vibration or thrill was felt over the seat of the friction sound at the region of its greatest intensity in fully one-fifth of the patients with rheumatic pericarditis (13 in 63).

In seven of the cases, or more than one-half of them, the thrill was felt over the whole region of the impulse, extending in two instances over the second and third left spaces, in one, over the spaces from the second to the fifth, in three, over those from the third to the fifth, and in one, from the fourth to the sixth spaces.

In two other instances the thrill was confined to the second space, apparently over the pulmonary artery, in three to the region of the apex, and in the remaining case it was present both over the second space and the apex. In all these patients the friction sound was harsh and grating, vibrating, or creaking in character.

In those cases in which the vibration was felt over the whole region of the impulse, the thrill was present at the time of the acme of the effusion, or in one instance two days after it (see pp. 313-315); and the same may be said, with one exception, of those in which the vibration was felt in the second space.

The duration of the thrill was short. It was observed for only one day in seven cases, for two days in three, for three days in two cases, and for four consecutive days in the remaining one. In two cases (51, see p. 315; 40, see p. 313), the thrill, after being absent from its previous seat over the body of the heart for several days, returned over a limited space when the surfaces were comparatively dry, the effusion having disappeared.

The character of the friction thrill or vibration is peculiar, and differs from the thrill due to altered blood-currents, chiefly in the following points. The blood-thrill presents a succession of equal vibrations, often like those made by a vibrating musical cord; is diffused; has a focus of greatest intensity, from which it lessens and fades away all round; gives the impression to the hand of being deeply seated as well as superficial; begins, when diastolic after the impulse ends, and often continues, when systolic, for a short period after the cessation of the beat of the ventricle; retains its character, position, focus of intensity, and general outspread, unchanged or with only slight modifications from day to day; and finally, has a long previous history pointing to an affection of the heart, and probably dating from an attack of acute rheumatism. The friction thrill or vibration, on the other hand, is shallow, giving a sensation as if it were made just under the hand by the rubbing together of two rough surfaces; has often a grating, rasping or irregularly vibrating character; presents no focus of intensity, but is spread, with varying force, over the region of the impulse; begins and ends rather abruptly, being limited to the period of the impulse and not passing beyond or preceding it; does not end with an abrupt shock; is short-lived and transient, and, if felt on one or two following days, it always changes in extent, and perhaps in position, and alters in character; and finally has a short previous history of local pain, extended dulness on percussion, increased prominence over the region of the pericardium, and elevated impulse. Sometimes, however, the blood-thrill and the friction-thrill are so much alike that they cannot be distinguished by the hand. The character of the thrill is, however, at once cleared up by the ear; the friction-thrill being accompanied by a friction sound which is in all cases increased by pressure, and is most vibrating, grating, or creaking and harsh at the very seat of the vibration; while the blood-thrill is accompanied by the murmur, usually musical, that distinguishes the valvular affection.

The thrill of presystolic murmur is distinguished by the position of the thrill over and to the left of the interventricular septum, the peculiar large vibrating character of the murmur; the abrupt shock with which the thrill and murmur terminate; the persistency of the thrill, murmur, and shock from day to day; and the long previous history.

The character of the friction sound presented in the various cases a close approximation to the character of the thrill or vibration.

The sensation conveyed to the hand when applied over the seat of thrill in the thirteen cases under examination was not always of the same character. Thus, under these circumstances the hand felt a sense of grating or rasping in two, of vibration in four, and of thrill in seven of the cases.

On listening over the region of the thrill or vibration in these cases a loud harsh friction sound was heard in seven patients, in five of whom the sound was described as being " to and fro ; " in five others of them there was a noise resembling the creaking of leather; in three the sound was grating, in one rasping, in two vibrating, in one grazing, and in one " churning." In several of these cases the friction sound presented, as we have already seen, different phases at different periods of their progress. In all of them the friction sound became less harsh and extensive when the vibration or thrill over the region of the pericardium ceased to be perceptible.

It is to be remarked that when the thrill was perceptible in these cases, especially if it extended over the ventricles, and was not limited to the region of the apex or that of the pulmonary artery, the area of the friction sound was increased as well as the intensity. In one of the cases the rubbing sound was audible over the whole front of the chest, and in several of the patients it spread downwards to the ensiform cartilage and to the left and right seventh and eighth costal cartilage.

The character of the friction sound, associated with the presence of a thrill over the heart and great vessels, whether creaking or grating, vibrating or rustling, or to and fro, will be considered in the next section.

AUSCULTATION.

Position and Character of the Sounds heard over the Heart and Pericardium during the Early Stages of Pericarditis.—In more than one-half of my cases of rheumatic pericarditis (33 in 63), I observed the character of the sounds of the heart at or soon after the commencement of the attack, and before the effusion into the pericardium had arrived at its height. I was frequently surprised by the rapidity with which the affection attained to its acme. In twenty-three of these patients friction sound was heard for the first time before the fluid in the pericardium had reached its greatest amount; and in fifteen of these the rubbing sound was detected only one day, and in four two days before the time of the acme.

Modification of the Sounds of the Heart at the Commencement of Pericarditis, before the Occurrence of Friction Murmur or Friction Sound.—There were five cases in which the sounds of the heart were modified before the occurrence of a friction sound, or the period of the acme. In one of them the heart sounds were muffled two days before the occurrence of the friction sound and the acme; in three of them those sounds were ringing in character from three to four days before the acme; and in one of these the systolic sound was rough and unduly prolonged four days before that period. All the cases of this group but one presented on pressure either a single or double murmur or a rubbing sound subsequently to this modification of the heart sounds, and before the occurrence of the acme.

Position and Character of the Friction Murmur, influenced by Pressure, heard at the Beginning of Pericarditis.—A murmur, which was excited or rendered more intense by pressure, was heard over the region of the heart before the period of the acme of effusion into the pericardium in eight cases.

Pain was felt directly over the seat of the pericardial inflammation in seven of the cases, being excited by pressure on the surface of the chest in three of them. In five of the cases the pain was present at the same time as the appearance of a murmur on pressure, and in two the pain preceded the murmur by a day or two.

In four cases the friction murmur was single and systolic. In four cases a double murmur, excited or intensified by pressure, preceded the friction sound and the acme of pericardial effusion. In the last case of this group (49, see p. 327), a youth aged 17, a fatal case, the friction murmur prevailed more or less through the whole of the illness until the heart became adherent.

The double friction murmur, heard during the early period of pericarditis, is thus distinguished from the double murmur caused by aortic incompetence, combined as it usually is with mitral regurgitation. It is accompanied, and often preceded, by pain over the heart, usually increased by pressure; it comes into play suddenly; its area is limited to the middle, or lower half of the sternum, and the adjoining left, and, on rare occasions, right cartilages; it is accompanied by the natural heart sounds, but is not rhythmical with them, the heart sounds and the murmur being heard as it were side by side; it does not begin with a double accent or shock, the double accent or shock of the natural heart sounds, but is of equal intensity throughout; it is invariably rendered more intense by pressure, which often converts it into a true to-and-fro *frottement*, and which always obscures or silences the natural heart sounds. It is not accompanied by marked visible pulsation of the great arteries in the neck, or by the sudden pulse at the wrist of aortic regurgitation, audible when the arm is raised; it is accompanied by extended dulness on percussion over the region of the pericardium; and as a rule it speedily gives place to a friction sound, with which, however, it may co-exist, being audible beyond the circumference of the friction sound especially below, and on either side.

In all these respects the double friction murmur contrasts notably with the double aortic murmur; which is not usually accompanied by pain over the heart; does not come into play suddenly; is not limited in its area to the middle or lower half of the sternum and the adjoining cartilages—but extends also to the upper portion of the sternum and to its right; is rhythmical with the natural heart sounds; commences with a double accent or shock; is not rendered to a material degree more intense by pressure, which never converts it into a friction sound, and which never abolishes the double accent with which the double murmur begins; is accompanied by marked visible pulsation of the carotid and radial arteries, the pulse of the latter becoming audible as a shock when the arm is raised; is not accompanied by extension of dulness over the region of the pericardium; and does not give place suddenly to friction sound, but is persistent.

The single systolic friction murmur is not so easily distinguished from the tricuspid murmur as from other systolic blood murmurs, but their differences are sufficiently marked. The systolic friction murmur is accompanied or preceded by pain over the heart, usually increased by pressure; comes into existence suddenly; is limited usually to the base of the right ventricle, being heard over the middle or lower sternum, or over the fourth left space; is accompanied by the natural first sound, but is not rhythmical with it, the heart sound and the murmur being distinctly heard side by side; does not begin with an accent or shock, the accent or shock of the natural first sound, but begins and ends with a single note of equal intensity throughout; extends rarely beyond the period of the systole into that of the diastole; is usually produced, and invariably rendered more intense by pressure, so that it obscures or masks the natural first sounds; is accompanied by extended dulness on percussion over the region of the pericardium; and speedily gives place to a double friction murmur or a friction sound.

The several systolic blood murmurs may be thus distinguished from the single or systolic friction murmur.

The tricuspid murmur is more likely to be taken for a friction murmur than any other systolic murmur, for it is situated over the front of the right ventricle—over and to the left of the lower half of the sternum—and, like the friction murmur, it is a shallow sound, and it may appear and vanish quickly. It differs, however, in these respects; it is rarely accompanied by pain and tenderness over the heart; is never accompanied by the natural first sound over the right ventricle, for that sound is converted into the murmur; always commences with an accent, the accent or shock of the first sound of the right ventricle; may be intensified, but is not changed in character by pressure, which, however, brings the ear more close to the murmur; is not accompanied by extended dulness on percussion over the pericardium; and does not give place to a double friction murmur or a friction sound.

The systolic mitral murmur is readily distinguished from the friction murmur by the intensity with which it is heard to the left of and below the apex; and its great relative feebleness, or silence over the right ventricle—to the left of the lower portion of the sternum; and by its persistence. When the mitral murmur is audible in the situation just spoken of it is feeble, and is accompanied by the natural sounds of the right ventricle. The heart sounds and the murmur are rhythmical and go well together; and pressure, though it makes the mitral murmur somewhat more clear, does not mask or obliterate the healthy sounds of the right side of the heart.

The direct aortic, and pulmonic systolic murmurs are distinguished at once from the systolic friction murmur by their situation above the level of the third cartilage; the pulmonic murmur, which is often scratching in character, and is therefore apt to be mistaken, when first heard, for a friction sound, being limited to the second left space; and the direct aortic murmur being heard over the upper sternum, and to the right of it, and in the neck over the carotid.

The essential features of difference between the friction murmurs

A A 2

1 A SYSTEM OF MEDICINE.

and the blood murmurs are these:—The friction murmurs do not begin with an accent, but usually maintain the same tone and pitch throughout; while the blood murmurs begin with an accent or shock: the friction murmurs are intensified and altered by pressure, becoming sometimes rubbing in character; while the valve murmurs are only intensified by pressure: the friction murmur and the natural heart sounds are heard at the same time, but they do not play together or in unison, being audible as it were side by side, each having its own rhythm; and on pressure the friction murmur becomes so loud and even rubbing in character as to mask and extinguish the heart sounds; while the blood murmurs are in perfect accord with the heart sounds: the friction murmurs come suddenly, with pain and increased pericardial dulness, and, are transient; the blood murmurs come gradually, without pain or increased dulness, and are permanent.

Friction Sound in Pericarditis before the Occurrence of the Acme of the Effusion into the Pericardium.—Friction sound was heard during the early stage of Pericarditis, in every gradation from a sound scarcely to be distinguished from a murmur up to a grating, vibrating, or creaking noise.

In a few of the cases, the early friction sound was not audible until pressure was made over the heart. In nearly all the cases, the friction sound was double from the first, but in two, and perhaps three patients the sound was single and systolic when first heard. In a small group of four patients, a smooth or feeble double friction sound, intensified by pressure, came into play from one to four days before the occurrence of the acme of the affection, when the friction sound became louder and more harsh.

In the last great division of cases of pericarditis with friction sound before the acme, the double friction sound, as a rule, was loud and harsh, was intensified by pressure, and set in suddenly; and the effusion into the pericardium speedily attained to its acme after the first observation of the friction. This set of cases divides itself into three groups; in the first group (1), the friction sound became inaudible during the acme; in the second (2), the friction sound became less loud and harsh during the acme; and in the third group (3), the friction sound remained during the acme with little or no change.

(1) In two cases, the friction sound, harsh at the onset, disappeared during the acme. It is difficult to explain the disappearance of the friction sound at the time of the acme of the effusion in these two remarkable cases on physical grounds, but the following circumstances show that it was mainly due to lowering of the power of the heart. It is natural to expect that when the fluid increases, it should interpose itself between a portion of the right ventricle and the anterior wall of the chest, and so limit the area of the friction sound, and lessen its intensity. This will not, however, account for the disappearance of the rubbing sound at the period of

the acme, since the impulse was then still perceptible, though higher in position and less forcible.

(2) The second group of this division, in which a loud double friction sound appeared suddenly before the acme of the effusion, and became less loud during the acme, consists of five patients.

The case of this group (33, see p. 319) that I shall relate, is illustrated by the accompanying figures (44, 45, p. 350); during its later stages, by figures 46, 47, 48, pp. 377, 378. A housemaid, aged 20, came in on the fifth day of her illness, the heart sounds being natural. On the third day there was increased dulness on percussion over the region of the heart; and a to-and-fro friction sound over the whole of the region of cardiac dulness, to which it was exactly limited. The impulse was present, as before, in the fifth space, but was higher in position. The dulness and the friction sound extended from the sternum almost to the nipple, and from the third left cartilage to the sixth, but did not pass beyond the sternum to the right, so that the rubbing sound was limited to the right ventricle. It was stronger over the sternum than the cartilages, and became everywhere much harsher on pressure. On the fourth, the double friction sound was heard over the greater part of the sternum, and was audible over the manubrium during expiration only. The friction sound had somewhat the character of a bellows murmur over the fourth space. It was not quite rhythmical with the sounds of the heart, which were also audible. It was harsher and louder during the systole than the diastole, and was rendered more intense by pressure. On the fifth day, the effusion into the pericardium was at its acme—reaching up to the second space and the manubrium. The impulse was raised from the fifth to the third space. The area of the friction sound was more extensive upwards, but more limited below. It was heard over the whole sternum, being louder over the manubrium on expiration, over the lower portion of that bone on inspiration, and was most harsh and strong over the middle third of the sternum. The rubbing sound was heard from the second to the fourth cartilage, but not apparently below it, and was harsh in the third space. A bellows murmur was audible over the fourth cartilage on the light application of the stethoscope; but when pressure was made, a creaking noise was heard there during the systole, and a rubbing sound during the diastole.

I believe that this group and this case represent the natural progress of the friction sound from the commencement of pericarditis to its acme when the effusion is at its height. During the first blush of inflammation, the surfaces of the heart and the sac are crowded with vessels, but are as yet scarcely coated with lymph. A single or double friction murmur, induced or intensified by pressure, may then be the only sound excited by the rubbing of the heart against the pericardium. Speedily their surfaces become coated with a finely honey-combed rugose covering; and the amount of fluid in the sac increases so as to enlarge the area of dulness over the

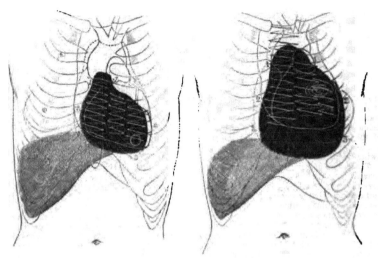

Fig. 44.   Fig. 45.

Figure 44, from a housemaid aged 20, affected with rheumatic pericarditis (33, see p. 319).

Early period of the increase of the pericardial effusion.

First day of the friction sound ; third day after admission.   The sounds of the heart were natural when she was admitted.

The pericardial effusion probably already occupies to some extent the space between the under surface of the heart and the floor of the pericardium, and elevates the heart to a slight degree, and, to a moderate extent, displaces the lungs upwards and to each side ; and the centre of the diaphragm, where it forms the base of the pericardium, and the subjacent portions of the liver and stomach downwards.   Owing to the displacement of the lungs upwards and to each side from before the heart, the whole of the right ventricle except the upper portion of the conus arteriosus, the inner or left border of the right auricle, and the apex and a portion of the front of the left ventricle are exposed.

Probable region of pericardial dulness on percussion (see the black space).   The outlines of the region of pericardial dulness, which is increased in extent, are not described on this occasion, but the extent of the friction sound and the position of the impulse are given ; and I have assigned to the region of dulness an outline corresponding to the region of friction sound and the position of the impulse.   The region of pericardial dulness has not yet acquired the pyramidal or pear-shaped form that it presents during the acme of the pericardial effusion, but still retains the general form of the healthy region of cardiac dulness, but its outline is considerably enlarged in all directions, and is higher behind the sternum than over the cartilages.   It extends across from the right edge of the sternum to the left nipple ; its upper boundary probably crosses the sternum on a level with the upper edges of the third costal cartilages, and occupies the third space ; and its lower boundary is probably situated a little above the middle of the ensiform cartilage, and the upper edge of the sixth cartilage.

Third day.   *The impulse of the heart* is felt at the fifth space below the nipple.   (See the circle in that space.)

Fourth day.   The impulse is feeble, being slightly perceptible below the nipple.

Friction sound (see the zigzag lines, systolic thick, diastolic thin).   Third day.   A loud but soft to-and-fro friction sound is heard over the sternum from below the manubrium to its lower end, and up to but not beyond its right border ; and over the fourth and fifth cartilages and intermediate spaces, where it extends almost, but not quite to the nipple, where it is feebler than it is over the sternum.   The friction sound is rendered much harsher by pressure.   Fourth day.   The friction sound is nearly the same in extent, character and area as it was yesterday, but it is now audible over the manubrium during expiration; it is lower and louder below during inspiration than expiration; and it is louder generally during the systole than the diastole.

Figure 45 from the same patient as figure 46, affected with rheumatic pericarditis.

Period of the first acme of pericardial effusion. Third day of the friction sound and of the increase of pericardial dulness, fifth day after admission.

The explanations of pericardial effusion and dulness given with figure 36, page 311, apply also to this figure.

The pericardial effusion completely distends the sac, which is pyramidal or pear-shaped, as in figures 34, p. 305 ; 36, 37, p. 311 ; 40, p. 338 ; 42, p. 340. The extent of the effusion, and of the displacement upwards and to each side of the lungs, and downwards of the diaphragm, liver and stomach may be inferred from the description given below of the extent of the region of pericardial dulness on percussion. The whole front of the heart is exposed, including the right auricle and ventricle, the apex and front of the left ventricle, the pulmonary artery, and the ascending aorta within the pericardium, owing to the extensive displacement of the lungs from before those parts.

The region of pericardial dulness (see the black space) on percussion is pyramidal or pear-shaped, like the distended pericardium. The upper and narrower region of dulness over the great vessels (1, 1) is situated behind and below the lower half of the manubrium and extends a little way into the adjoining first and second spaces ; the larger portion of pericardial dulness, which includes the heart itself and the volume of fluid effused into the space between its under surface and the floor of the pericardium (2, 2 ; 3, 3), extends from the second space down to the lower border of the sixth cartilage, and almost to the end of the ensiform cartilage, and from an inch to the right of the sternum to about half an inch to the left of the nipple. The lower boundary of the heart (2, 2) is probably situated behind the lower border of the fifth cartilage ; and the heart (2, 2) extends from this boundary up to the third cartilages : and the volume of effused fluid between the under surface of the heart and the floor of the epicardium extends from the lower boundary of the heart down into the epigastric space, almost to the end of the ensiform cartilage, and the lower edge of the sixth left cartilage.

The impulse has been elevated from the fifth to the third space, and extends outwards to the nipple line. (See the concentric curves in that space.)

The friction sound (see the zigzag lines—systolic thick, diastolic thin) is double, and extends from the nipple to the lower end of the sternum. It is most harsh about the middle of the sternum, and is louder at the upper end of that bone during expiration, and at its lower end during inspiration ; and is more intense during the systole than the diastole. The frottement is also audible over the left second, third, and fourth cartilages ; and is soft without pressure, but with pressure it is creaking over the fourth cartilage.

A mitral murmur → is audible at the apex.

For the later views of this case see figures 46, 47, 48, pp. 377, 378.

pericardium, and to expose the whole of the right ventricle and the apex, but neither the right auricle nor the great vessels. The heart is slightly raised and the apex beat ascends from the lower to the higher part of the fifth space. A double friction sound is audible over the whole region of pericardial dulness, to which it is exactly limited, louder and more continuous during the systole than the diastole, and rendered more intense by pressure, which brings into full play both sounds, exciting a to-and-fro rustle or *frou-frou*.

When the effusion has increased to its utmost limits, the heart is elevated, its impulse being raised from the fifth to the fourth or third space ; the increased effusion displaces the lungs and so exposes the whole surface of the heart and great vessels ; and depresses the central tendon of the diaphragm downwards towards the abdomen, fluid being alone present below the fourth space. The whole region of actual friction is shifted upwards, and with it the whole region of the friction sound ; which is no longer audible below the fourth or fifth cartilage, but spreads outwards over the right auricle and the left

ventricle, as well. as the right ventricle; and upwards over the great
vessels and to the top of the sternum. The friction sound silenced
below is intensified and extended above; so that there is a transfer
upwards of the friction sound; while the dulness on percussion increases in all directions, upwards as well as downwards.

Four cases differed from the rest in this, that while the friction
sound spread upwards at the time of the acme, it also either
increased downwards, or, retaining its hold below, increased extensively to the left side.

*The comparative relative Area and Intensity of the Friction Sound just
before*[1], *and during the Acme of the Effusion into the Pericardium.*—In
twenty-nine cases the comparative area and intensity of the friction
sound were observed both before, and at the time when, the effusion
into the pericardium was at its height.

Area.—When the effusion into the pericardium increases, the
heart is raised, and the lungs are displaced upwards, and to the left
and right by the increased fulness of the sac and the greater elevation
of the heart itself; for the organ is then pushed upwards from a wider
into a narrower space. It is natural to expect that, under these
circumstances, the area of the friction sound should steadily increase
upwards and to each side with the increase of the area of pericardial
dulness. This was found to be so in the great majority of instances.
Thus the area of friction sound was greater at the time of the acme
than before it in twenty out of the twenty-nine cases; while it was
less under the same circumstances in only two of them. In six
patients, the area of the friction sound was equal before and during
the acme; and in one case the friction sound was absent before, but
present at the time of the height of the disease.

These clinical facts show that when the curtain of lung in front of the
heart and great vessels is displaced by the distended pericardium and
the elevated heart, the friction sound spreads upwards, and to the
right and left; so as to be audible over the whole front of the right
ventricle, the great vessels, the right auricle, and the apex.

The lower boundary of the friction sound, while it retains its
place, at the time of the height of the effusion, becomes softened in
character. The focus of intensity of the rubbing sound is shifted
upwards, with the upward shifting of the heart and its impulse; and
the intensity of the sound is toned and graduated downwards, from
the seat of its focus to that of its inferior limit.

Intensity.—In nearly three-fifths (16 in 29) of the cases, the friction
sound was more intense; and in fully one-third of them (10 in 29), it
was less intense, when the effusion into the pericardium was at its
height, than just before that time. The tendency, then, is for the
friction sound to increase both in intensity and area, during the acme.
The exceptions to this rule are, however, much more frequent as regards

[1] At the time of the last observation, made before the effusion had reached its height.

intensity than area; for the area lessened at the time of the acme, in only two instances, while the intensity did so at that time, in ten instances out of twenty-nine.

The area of the friction sound, then, is, as a rule, larger, and its intensity greater at the time of the acme of the pericardial effusion, than at that of the last previous observation, made from one to two days before the acme. The exceptions to this rule are rare as regards the area, but rather frequent as regards the intensity of the friction sound, which is greater in one-third of the cases on the day before, than at the time of the acme. The change, both in area and intensity, is often notably rapid and great; the character of the friction sound being sometimes altogether altered, and its area remarkably enlarged in the course of one or two days.

The Character and Area of the Friction Sound at the Time of the Acme of the Effusion into the Pericardium. — The friction sound, audible over the region of the heart and arteries and the pericardium during the acme of the pericardial effusion, presented great variety of character, intensity, and area in the forty-four cases under examination. I. In nine of those cases the friction sound was accompanied during the acme by a thrill over the region of the heart and great vessels; and II. in thirty-five of them the presence of a thrill was not observed. I. Of the nine cases with a thrill, (1) in five a sound resembling the creaking of new leather; (2) in one a grating sound; and (3) in three a harsh friction sound was respectively audible over the region of the pericardium. II. Of the thirty-five cases in which a thrill was not observed, (1) in seven a creaking sound was heard; (2) in two the sound was grating in character; (3) in fifteen a definite friction sound, intensified by pressure, which in two instances excited a creaking noise, usually harsh, but sometimes not so, was audible; (4) in five the friction sound was soft in character, but was rendered harsh or more intense by pressure, except in one instance, in which pressure was not employed; (5) in four a friction sound, previously absent, came into play when pressure was made over the region of the heart; (6) in one friction sound, present during one, was absent during two of the three days during which the acme lasted; and finally (7), in the remaining case a double friction murmur, intensified by pressure, was audible over the region of the pericardium during the acme. The cases in the tables at pages 313-327 are classified according to this arrangement.

I.—*Cases with Thrill and* (1) *a Creaking,* (2) *Grating, or* (3) *Harsh Friction Sound over the Heart* (see pp. 313-316).—In nine of the forty-three cases under review, a systolic thrill was felt over the heart, and (1) in five of those cases a creaking; (2) in one of them a grating; and (3) in three of them a harsh friction sound was audible at the seat of thrill at the time of the height or acme of the disease. In six of these cases the thrill was present over the right ventricle, and, in some of those, but not in all, it was probably situated over the left ventricle also; in another of them it was present over the apex and the second space, but not over the right ventricle; in one of the two remaining cases it was felt over the apex; and in the other one over the second space alone.

(1.) *Creaking Friction Sound* (see pp. 313, 314).—In three of the cases with a thrill over the right ventricle, and in one of those with a thrill over the apex alone, a creaking sound was audible over the seat of thrill.

One of these patients (4, see p. 313), a man aged 27, came in with extensive pericardial dulness; a thrill over the right ventricle extending from the fourth left cartilage to the sixth; a loud systolic creaking friction sound consisting of five vibrations, the diastolic sound being much smoother than the systolic, over the seat of the thrill; and a double *frottement* extending widely over the front of the chest from the second cartilage down to the ninth on both sides, and audible at the epigastric space. The pericardial dulness on that day extended upwards to the third space, and on the following day to the third cartilage, when it reached its greatest height. The region of thrill had increased upwards, and extended from the third cartilage to the sixth. A creaking sound was audible apparently over the whole seat of the thrill, but over the fifth cartilage there was a vibrating, grating, systolic friction sound of a churning character, which was creaking towards the end of the systole, the diastolic sound being short and smooth.

(2.) *Grating Friction Sound* (see p. 315).—A grating friction sound without a creak was present on the presumed day of the acme in one case (51, see p. 315).

(3.) *Harsh Friction Sound* (see pp. 315, 316).—A harsh friction sound was present with a thrill in three cases. One of these cases (16, see p. 315) a girl, aged 17, came in with an extensive impulse, a double thrill, and a loud, double scraping sound over, but not below, the heart. On the second day, there was less dulness, and no note of thrill, and the friction sound was less harsh and extensive: but, on the third day, there was less effusion, the impulse was lower and more diffused, and the friction sound was much more intense and extensive.

We may, I think, say, on reviewing these cases, that at the time of the acme of the disease, when a thrill is present over the right ventricle, a creaking noise is audible over the seat of the thrill; and that from this noise, as from a focus, a to-and-fro sound radiates in all directions over the front of the chest, reaching far beyond the limits of the region of actual friction, becoming more feeble towards its outlying margins, and spreading almost up to the clavicles, out to or beyond the nipples, and down to the eighth or ninth cartilages; and that when the effusion lessens and the thrill disappears, the creak vanishes, and the friction sound softens, and limits its area to the region of actual friction, being bounded below by the sixth cartilage. The reason for the great extension during the acme of the friction sound upwards, outwards, and downwards beyond the region of actual friction in these cases is obvious. The heart, surrounded by the distended pericardial sac, is displaced upwards into the higher and narrower portion of the cone of the chest. It works in a confined space, and rubs with its roughened surface against the roughened surface of the pericardium; and, the lungs being pushed aside, it presses against the sternum and cartilages, and excites vibrations and a creaking or grating friction sound over the walls of the chest in front of the heart. The play of the two roughened surfaces of the pericardium upon each other induces vibrations, sensible to the hand, that excite consonant vibrations in the superimposed sternum and cartilages; and these parts, acting as a sounding-board, transmit the sound to a distance over the front of the cage of the chest in all directions, and especially downwards. When the thrill is limited during the acme to the second space, over the pulmonary artery, or to the apex of the heart, or is felt both over the apex and the second space, the creaking or grating noise is limited to the seat of the thrill; and the friction sound does not extend beyond the region of actual friction, excepting perhaps to a small extent over the circuit of the apex. When in such a case the effusion lessens, the heart descends, and the thrill disappears, the friction sound may spread downwards, so as to reach the eighth cartilage.

II. *Cases in which a Thrill was not observed over the Region of the Heart or Great Vessels* (see pp. 316-327).

(1.) *Cases in which a Sound like the Creaking of New Leather was audible at the time of the Acme of the Effusion, no Thrill being present* (see pp. 316-318).—In seven of the forty-four cases under examination, a creaking noise, usually systolic, was heard without a thrill at the seat of the impulse of the heart at the time of the acme.

In all of these cases, and in several of those in which a thrill over the heart was accompanied by a creaking or grating noise, as soon as the fluid in the pericardium lessened and the heart descended, the creaking noise was replaced by a comparatively smooth friction-sound. This occurred on the day after the acme of the effusion in four of the seven cases. This sudden disappearance of the creaking noise with the diminution of the fluid and the descent of the heart, appears to me to show that the presence or absence of the creaking noise depended more on the position of the heart and on the degree and kind of pressure exerted by it during its contraction; than on the character of the roughened coat of lymph covering the heart and lining the pericardial sac, since that lining cannot have changed materially in one day when the disease was at its height. At the time of the acme of the effusion into the pericardium, the heart is elevated so as to occupy the upper and narrower part of the cone of the chest; and beats with force in its contracted space against the cartilages and sternum which confine its movements. When the heart pulsates thus against the walls of the chest, the movements of the former are resisted by the pressure of the latter. The accumulated force of the heart overcomes the resistance of the walls of the chest, and the accumulated resistance of those walls then overcomes the force of the heart; these two opposite forces by turns arrest and overcome each other and give rise to a series of fine jerks or vibrations that may give birth to a thrill, and a vibrating creaking noise. In one case, this creaking noise consisted of five distinct vibrations; and such a succession of vibrations forms, indeed, the essential nature of the thrill and its attendant creaking sound.

The creaking sound, and the main varieties of friction sound, may be imitated by rubbing the forefinger on the thumb with varying degrees of force when the back of the thumb rests upon the ear. When the finger and thumb rub gently or with moderate force upon each other, to and fro, the rubbing sound is smooth or harsh in proportion to the gentleness or force employed. When, however, the pressure exerted by the finger on the thumb is great, the resistance to their onward movement on each other causes them to stop in a succession of jerks, which produce a creaking noise.

When the fluid decreases, the heart descends into the ampler space of the chest; the organ moves with freedom; and, as it no longer presses with a resisted force against the walls of the chest, the thrill, vibrations, and creak give place to a moderated friction sound; which may be so harsh as to sound like the rubbing of sand-paper; or so soft as to resemble a murmur.

(2.) *Vibrating, Grating Friction Sound* (see pp. 318, 319).—The grating, vibrating friction sound ranks next to the creaking noise in intensity. It is, in fact, a sister-sound to the creaking noise, with which it is closely allied. Thus, it may be audible when there is a thrill, when it may be heard alone, or associated with a creak; or it may by pressure be converted into a creak; or it may precede or follow, displace or be displaced, by that sound; or it may, like it, be produced by pressure. The grating sound, like the creaking sound, is the combined effect of pressure and friction, but the pressure is usually less, while the rubbing surfaces are, I believe, more invariably rough, when the sound is grating than when it is creaking. A grating sound was audible during the acme of effusion in two or three cases in which there was a thrill, and in two in which there was no thrill; and it was excited by pressure in two. It was, therefore, observed in one-seventh of the cases (6 or 7 in 44).

We have already seen that the creaking sound is usually single, but it is the reverse with the grating sound, which is usually double. The grating friction sound is a jarring, grating, vibrating noise, rough and to-and-fro in character, made in a succession of jerks, each jerk being separately audible, and varying slightly, and the whole series not combining to form one note like the creaking sound, but, as I have just said, a jarring, grating, vibrating noise. I made out, as I have already stated, that in one case the creak was composed of five vibrations, or at the rate of twenty-two vibrations in a second; but, as I took no special note of it, I do not know what number of vibrations were made in a second by the grating noise. I believe, as I have already hinted, that the grating noise is always associated with the rubbing of the two harsh and roughened surfaces of the heart and pericardium upon each other, but I have no direct proof of this at present.

(3.) *Harsh To-and-Fro Friction Sound, intensified by Pressure, at the Time of the Acme of the Pericardial Effusion* (see pp. 319-324).— Résumé, *including the whole of the preceding cases, whether with or without a thrill.*—We have just seen that a creaking noise, usually systolic, was present over the heart at the time of the acme of the disease in one-fourth of the cases in which the dulness was observed at or about the period when the effusion was at its height (12 in 44); while in four other cases it was then excited by pressure, and in two it was heard just before the acme of the effusion. Creaking, therefore, was present as a primary sound in twelve cases; as a secondary sound, or from pressure, in four cases; and in two others it was audible just before the acme. We have also seen that a grating friction sound, usually double, was present over the heart when the effusion was at or about its height, as a primary sound in three cases in which there was no creaking, and in one or more in which there was creaking; and as a secondary sound in two in which it was excited by pressure; while in four others it was present just before or after the period of the acme of the disease.

If we combine the two sounds, we find that during the acme the creaking and grating sounds were primary in fifteen cases, and secondary, or excited by pressure, in six; while they were associated with each other in one or more. Besides these fifteen cases, in which creaking or grating sounds were primary, there were nineteen cases in which there was a definite friction sound, which was usually harsh; in all of these it was double, or to-and-fro in character, being audible both during the systole and the diastole of the ventricle, and in all but two it was intensified by pressure. Three-fourths, therefore, of the patients (34 in 44) in whom the pericardial dulness was observed when at or near its height presented either a systolic creaking noise, or a double grating, or a definite to-and-fro friction sound, usually harsh in character.

Besides the nineteen cases in which there was a double *frottement,* usually harsh, at the time of the acme; there were seven cases in which that sound was associated with a creaking noise; and in one it accompanied a grating noise. In these cases the creaking or grating noise was limited to that part of the right ventricle, or the apex, that was pressing with the greatest force upon the costal cartilages or sternum, while the double *frottement* pervaded and often overstepped the rest of the heart and the great vessels.

If we group together the eight cases with harsh double *frottement,* in seven of which the *frottement* was associated with a creaking sound and in one with a grating noise, and the nineteen cases not so associated, we find that in one-half of those twenty-seven cases the character of the sound is definitely specified (13 in 27); while in twelve it is described as a harsh double friction sound; and in two as a to-and-fro sound.

Of the thirteen cases in which the character of the double sound was specified, in four it was described as being like that made by rubbing with sand-paper; in seven as being either rasping, or musical planing, scraping, scratching, grazing or rustling, the latter sound being a genuine *frou-frou;* while in the remaining two the sound resembled that made by sharpening a scythe.

In the whole of the twenty-seven cases except two, pressure with the stethoscope intensified the double *frottement;* it sometimes altered or modified the character of the sound; and in five instances it transformed the double *frottement* into a creaking sound. When the creaking sound was thus brought into birth by pressure, or secondary, it was usually double; but when the creak was always present, or primary, it was, as I have already shown, usually and essentially single or systolic.

In all these cases the double *frottement* was essentially a to-and-fro sound. The character and volume of the sound, and the relative intensity of the to-and-fro, or the systolic and diastolic friction sounds, varied over the different parts of the heart. As a leading principle, the greater the pressure exerted by the heart, or any portion of it, during its action upon the cartilages or sternum against which it beat, the more intense was the friction sound.

The friction sound in the remaining cases of this group was limited to a comparatively small area.

In two of the nineteen cases, in both of which there was a thrill over the right ventricle, the rubbing noise as I have already stated, extended over the front of the chest, far beyond the region of actual friction. These two cases, however, stand apart, for in the remaining seventeen the area of the friction sound was limited to the region of actual friction; with, however, this slight exception, that in six of the patients the to-and-fro sound spread upwards to the top of the sternum, and in one of them it was diffused outwards as far as the left arm-pit. The upper limit of the distended pericardial sac and of actual friction is rarely higher than the transverse centre of the manubrium, which is about an inch below the top of the sternum; therefore in the six patients just spoken of, the friction sound extended itself upwards for from an inch to fully two inches above the actual seat of friction over the great vessels, which, at their higher portion, are partly covered by lung.

The explanation of this extension of the friction sound upwards beyond the immediate seat of friction is the same as that of the diffusion of the friction sound over the front of the chest far beyond the region of the distended pericardium and of actual friction, when a thrill and a corresponding creaking noise are present over the heart. The to-and-fro movements of the heart upon the pericardial sac, both being covered with lymph, excite a to-and-fro sound which is audible over the region of those movements. The vibrations that produce the sound are communicated to the sternum, which is played upon by the rubbing surfaces; and the sternum, which acts as a sounding-board, propagates the sound to its own upper end, which is at some distance from the seat of the parent vibrations. The extension of the friction sound beyond the region of actual friction depends on the loudness and intensity of the rubbing noise, and the force with which the heart, when it is rubbing to and fro, presses against the sternum and cartilages. Of the six cases in which the to-and-fro sound mounted to the top of the sternum, in three there was a creaking sound over the heart, with a thrill also in two of those; in two others a creaking sound was excited by pressure; and in the remaining one a loud, harsh, double friction sound was present over the region of the pericardium. Although a creaking friction sound was audible over the apex in four instances, in only one of them did the to-and-fro sound spread to the left beyond the apex, but in that one the rubbing sound extended outwards into the left arm-pit. In that case there was dulness over the left lower lobe, and bronchial breathing between the left axilla and the spine. It is, therefore, evident that the heart and pericardium were displaced towards the left side owing to the condensation of the left lung, and that this circumstance facilitated the extension of the friction sound to the left axilla.

With these few exceptions, the region of friction sound coincided in these cases with the actual region of friction at the time when the effusion into the pericardium was at its height.

(4.) *Cases in which a Soft Friction Sound, audible over the Heart at the Time of the Acme of the Effusion into the Pericardium, was converted by Pressure into a Harsh Rubbing Noise* (see pp. 324, 325).—Four cases with a soft friction sound, in which pressure rendered the sound harsh, come under this heading, and in one of these the friction sound elicited by pressure resembled the noise made by sharpening a scythe. In a fifth case, with a similar friction sound, the pressure test was not employed.

In these four cases a comparatively soft double friction sound was intensified and altered by pressure, becoming converted in one instance into a sound like that made by sharpening a scythe, and in one into a rasping, grating noise. Here pressure expelled any interposed fluid; brought the opposite roughened surfaces of the pericardium more closely into contact; and aroused counter-pressure on the part of the heart against the cartilages and sternum during its to-and-fro rubbing movements. These effects spoke out not only in a louder and more diffused, but also in an altogether altered sound; so that the soft sounds, sometimes so murmur-like as to be almost doubtful in quality, became instantly transformed into a loud double and broken noise, like that made by sharpening a scythe, or into a rasping, grating, almost creaking sound.

(5.) *Cases in which a Double Friction Sound, not otherwise audible, came into play when Pressure was made over the Heart during the time of the Acme of Pericardial Effusion* (see pp. 326, 327).—In four cases during the acme, on listening without making pressure, the healthy sounds of the heart were alone audible; but on making pressure those sounds were either replaced or accompanied by a double rubbing noise.

In three of these cases, at the time the effusion into the pericardium was at its height, when the stethoscope was applied lightly over the heart, the natural heart sounds were alone heard, friction sounds being everywhere inaudible. When, however, pressure was made with the stethoscope, a double friction sound was immediately brought into play, which could be suspended or renewed at will by withdrawing or replacing the pressure. In one case the friction sound thus generated was limited to the region of the right ventricle, and in another to the base of that ventricle; but in a third case it was diffused over the whole space occupied by the heart and great vessels. The impulse was feeble in one of these patients, and was felt over the right ventricle in another. It is difficult to say why friction sound was absent without pressure over the seat of the impulse; but it is self-evident that if we press the cartilages or sternum inwards upon the walls of the heart moving to and fro, those walls will work with increased counter pressure against the resisting walls of the chest; and may thus elicit a friction sound when previously absent, or intensify a friction sound already existing, owing to the increased friction of the two roughened surfaces. In two of the cases a to-and-fro sound was audible without pressure over the apex, and in one of them over the lower border of the right ventricle also; but it was brought into play by pressure over the whole region of the heart and great vessels.

The subsequent history of these cases illustrates with great clearness the cause of the absence of friction sound without pressure, and its presence with pressure during the acme of the disease. In three of them (15, 8, 19), as soon as the effusion into the pericardium lessened, the heart descended, and its impulse became stronger and lower; the fluid interposed between the front of the heart at its lower border and the pericardial sac disappeared; and the friction sound came into spontaneous play where it was before absent without pressure. That sound, indeed, gradually augmented in loudness and intensity, and increased in area upwards, sideways, and especially downwards.

(6) *Case in which Friction Sound was Absent for Two of the Three Days during which the Acme of Pericardial Effusion lasted* (35, see p. 327).— This patient (35), a woman aged 21, came in with great pain and a double friction sound all over the region of the heart. The pain was relieved by leeches. Next morning the effusion was at its height, but the friction sound had vanished and could not be brought back even by pressure. That evening there was a return of pain, and a renewal of the friction sound which lasted until next day, but again vanished on the fourth day, when the effusion was still at its acme. She was in great distress from pain over the heart, but the impulse was faint in the third and fourth spaces. Next day there was less effusion, a lowered impulse, and no distress, and friction sound was rendered audible by moderate pressure over the right ventricle. Why was the friction sound absent in this case of pericarditis? When we consider that the impulse was perceptible, it must be allowed that the answer is difficult. The loss of blood on the second day and the great distress on the fourth

day may in some measure, however, account for the exit of the friction sound.

(7) *Case in which a Friction Murmur was audible over the Heart at the Time of the Acme of the Disease* (see p. 327).—This case (49) of a youth æt. 17, presented a long history, and proved fatal on the forty-eighth day. On examination after death, the heart was found to be universally adherent by means of recent lymph. Throughout the whole period, with rare and doubtful exceptions, the inflammation of the pericardium was made evident, not by the ordinary friction sound, but by a true friction murmur.

The Area of the Friction Sound during the Acme of the Effusion.— The area of the friction sound when the effusion into the pericardium is at its height may, on the one hand, be so extensive as to cover the whole front of the chest, extending from the clavicles down to the ninth right and left costal cartilages; or, on the other, be so limited as to be confined to the middle or lower portion of the sternum. This great diffusion, or narrow limitation of the friction sound at the period of the acme of disease, is, however, comparatively rare; and, as a rule, the area of the friction sound corresponds either with the area of actual friction, or with that of dulness on percussion over the pericardium.

The friction sound was audible over a great extent in all those cases, amounting to nine, in which a thrill was felt over the heart or great vessels, and especially in those in which it was perceptible over the front of the right ventricle.

In all the cases with thrill the friction sound was audible over the right auricle and ventricle, the outlying portion and apex of the left ventricle, and the great vessels; in all but one of them, also, it extended to the top of the sternum, beyond the region of the distended pericardium over the great vessels. In these cases, as I have already explained, the friction sound was most intense over the region of the thrill, and it radiated thence over a wide area, becoming gradually less intense from its focus to its extreme limits, being conducted by the sternum and cartilages acting as a sounding-board.

In six of the twelve cases in which a creaking sound was heard over the heart, the area of the friction sound extended down to the seventh, eighth, or ninth costal cartilages; but in five of these the creak accompanied a thrill. In the remaining six cases the frottement extended to the sixth cartilage, or occupied an unspecified space to the right and left of the sternum. It is evident, therefore, that the great diffusion of the sound in these cases was due more to the thrill, than to the creaking sound that was audible at the seat of the parent thrill.

I need not here specify the exact limits of the friction sound in the remaining cases.

These clinical facts show that, when the effusion into the pericardium is at its height, if we put out of view those cases in which a thrill is felt over the right ventricle, the friction sound is, with a slight exception, practically limited to the region of pericardial dulness,

or rather of the heart and great arteries. This exception applies to
the presence of the friction sound over the upper end of the sternum,
which is fully an inch higher than the uppermost limit of that region.
This was observed in nineteen cases, and in ten of these no thrill
was noticed over the region of the heart or great vessels. In all
these cases the friction sound was conducted to the top of the manubrium, from the actual seat of friction by the sternum itself, acting
as a sounding-board.

When the lower boundary of the friction sound reaches to the lower
end of the sternum and the sixth cartilage, that limit is still within
the lower boundary of the region of pericardial dulness, which is situated, when the pericardium is completely distended, behind the
ensiform cartilage and along the lower margin of the sixth cartilage.
As I have already shown, however, the lower boundary of the heart,
and consequently of the region of actual friction, is, in the great
majority of cases, above the lower end of the sternum and the sixth
cartilage; for the fluid in the pericardium presses the heart upwards,
and interposes itself between the lower border of the heart and the
walls of the chest in front of that border. The position of the impulse
is a good practical test of the position of the actual seat of friction.
In three of the seven cases in which the friction sound was audible as
low as from the seventh to the ninth cartilages, the impulse was felt
in the fifth space, and in one of them, a case of established valvular
disease with enlarged heart, in the sixth space. But with one single
exception, in which the beat of the heart was felt in the fifth space,
in all the rest of the cases the impulse was not present below the
fourth space, and in nine instances its lowest position was in the third
space. In the nature of things, the seat of the actual friction behind
the sternum, except at its upper portion, corresponded, as a rule,
pretty closely with its seat at the intercostal spaces.

In all the cases save one the friction sound was audible down to
the lower end of the sternum at the time of the height of the effusion,
and in twelve of them it was heard over the sixth cartilage. In all
these cases, therefore, it is evident that the friction sound was audible
below the actual seat of friction. The sternum is an excellent
sounding-board, and the conduction of the friction sound to the
lower end of that bone, by its own resonant vibrations, at once explains the presence of the sound at its lower end. The presence of
the *frottement* over the sixth cartilage, an inch below the actual seat
of friction, appears to me to call for a different explanation. The
observed facts are indeed different in these two cases. The sound
heard at the lower end of the sternum is, like that at its upper
end, usually of the same harsh to-and-fro quality, and of about the
same intensity as that audible over the two rubbing surfaces at the
middle of the bone. But this, as a rule, is not so with regard to
the friction sound audible over the sixth cartilage, for that is softer,
smoother, and less loud than the sound over the seat of the impulse,
from one to two spaces higher up. The presence of the soft mus-

cular space cuts off the direct connection between the fifth cartilage and the sixth. The sixth cartilage is, however, directly attached
to the sternum, and that bone, acting as a sounding-board, doubtless
conveys some of its own resonant vibrations to the cartilage. But it
is to be noted that the sound over the fifth space, though softer and
feebler than that over the fourth space, is harsher and louder than that
over the sixth cartilage. It is self-evident that the sound over the
space can scarcely be conducted from the sternum ; and I think, therefore, that we must look to the fluid within the pericardium, and to the
inner surface and structure of the roughened and thickened pericardium itself, as the principal media by which the sound is conducted
in these cases to the sixth cartilage.

If we except those cases in which a thrill is felt over the right
ventricle or at the apex, we find that when the sac is filled with
fluid the friction sound stops quite suddenly along the left and
right margins of the region of dulness over the pericardium. This
sudden arrest of the rubbing sound at its outer border is less
marked along the right than the left margin. This is, I consider,
explained, firstly, by the softer, smoother, and more equal character
of the to-and-fro sound over the right auricle than over the right
and left ventricles ; and, secondly, by the presence of fluid between
the compressed right auricle and the walls of the chest in front
of it, along its outer border. If, on the other hand, we look at the
left border of the distended pericardium, we find that there the solid
ventricles by their own pressure and action against the ribs and spaces,
displace the fluid and completely occupy the ground. Here we pass
suddenly from the loud double *frottement* made by the two rubbing solid
surfaces of the ventricle and the rib lined with roughened pericardium,
to the silent, soft, non-conducting surface of the lung.

We may, I think, conclude, with the qualifications just stated, that
when the effusion is at its height, as well as when it is increasing in
quantity, the friction sound is limited to the region of pericardial
dulness ; and, though with less rigour, to the region of actual friction ;
and that the law originally stated by Dr. Stokes, that the area of the
friction sound is usually limited to the region of the heart, is correct in
the great majority of cases, during the period of the acme of the effusion.

Before concluding what I have to state with regard to the area of
the friction sound, I would here estimate, as nearly as I can, the
extent to which the sound was heard over the various chambers of
the heart and the great vessels during the acme of the pericardial
effusion in the forty-four cases now under examination.

In one-half of the cases (21 in 44) the friction sound was audible
over the whole front of the heart, including the right auricle and
ventricle, the apex and a portion of the left ventricle, and the great
vessels. In seven or eight other cases it was heard over the right
auricle and ventricle, in four or five of which it was also present
over the apex, and in one over the great vessels. In fifteen other
cases the *frottement* was audible over the right ventricle, in nine of

which it was also heard over the apex, and in four or five over the great vessels. In six of these cases the friction sound was limited to the right ventricle. If, upon this estimate, we take each portion of the heart separately, we find that the friction sound was present during the acme over the right ventricle in the whole of the forty-four cases under notice; over the apex of the left ventricle in thirty-four or perhaps thirty-five of those cases; over the right auricle in twenty-eight or twenty-nine of them; and over the great vessels in twenty-six or twenty-seven of them.

Intensity and Character of the Friction Sound over the different parts of the Heart and Great Vessels during the acme of the Effusion.— When inquiring into the relative intensity and character of the friction sound over the different cavities of the heart, except the right ventricle, and the great vessels at the time of the acme of the effusion, I shall take into account the forty-four cases now under examination; but as regards the right ventricle I shall limit myself to the twelve cases with primary creaking sound, the two with grating friction sound, and the nineteen cases in which there was a harsh friction sound intensified by pressure, which form a total of thirty-three cases. Although the left ventricle forms the pivot of the heart's action, and does its work with three-fold more power than the right ventricle, I shall first examine the friction sound as it presented itself over the right ventricle, because it forms the front of the heart; covers the left ventricle except at its left border and apex; and is the main seat of actual friction.

*Right Ventricle.—*As the right ventricle forms the front of the heart, it is always in contact to a greater or less degree with the anterior walls of the chest. Owing to the distension of the pericardium during the acme, and the elevation of the heart into the contracted space at the upper part of the chest, the heart and great vessels are stripped of the lung that covered them, and press directly forward upon the middle and upper part of the sternum and the higher costal cartilages and intercostal spaces, from the second to the fifth.

The to-and-fro movements of the right ventricle, by rubbing against the opposed surface of the sac, give birth to the to-and-fro friction sound audible in front of the ventricle. Those movements play from right to left during the contraction of the ventricle, and from left to right during its dilatation (see Figs. 16, 17, p. 66). The sweep of the walls is very extensive behind the sternum, at the junction of the auricle to the ventricle; thence it gradually lessens; and comes to a stand-still near the septum. The friction movements are therefore greater, and the friction sounds are louder, at the sternal than the costal halves of the cartilages. As the position of the ventricle is raised from the fourth and fifth spaces to the third and fourth spaces, the *frottement* is usually louder over the sternal portions of those spaces, and the adjoining portion of the sternum, than elsewhere.

As the movements made during the emptying of the ventricles are active, and those made during the filling of the ventricle are passive, the increased pressure made by it upon the cartilage and sternum during the systole often intensifies the *frottement*, and, as I have already shown, may even transform it into a reaking noise. Thus, of the thirty-three cases under examination, in six there was a systolic creak over the right ventricle; in thirteen the systolic friction sound was louder than the diastolic; in two the systolic and diastolic sounds were equal; and in twelve it is not stated whether there was any difference between the two sounds.

From these clinical facts it is evident that the active friction sound made during the contraction of the ventricle is, as a rule, louder than the passive friction sound made during its dilatation. In a small minority of cases, however, the two sounds are equal, and a true to-and-fro sound is produced, the diastolic portion of which speaks with the same intensity, length, and continuousness as the systolic portion. In these cases I believe that the impulse is feeble, and that the systolic friction sound, like the diastolic, is, so to speak, passive, and is not intensified by the greater pressure from within of the anterior wall of the ventricle upon the walls of the chest.

The *conus arteriosus* of the right ventricle calls for special notice. It is situated behind the third space and the two adjoining cartilages, and as it enjoys extensive play during the systole, when its movements are twofold, from above downwards, and from left to right, the friction sound is often notably harsh, loud, and to-and-fro in that situation. Sometimes it is there creaking or grating, when it may be accompanied by a thrill. It sometimes resembles the sound made by rubbing together two opposite surfaces of emery paper, of stuff or of silk; or it is rasping, or scratching, or rustling when it may present a true *frou-frou ;* or it may, though less frequently, be soft in character. A friction murmur is, however, rarely or never present in this situation. Pressure readily intensifies and alters the friction sound over the conus arteriosus, and sometimes converts it into a creaking sound. As the conus arteriosus is covered in health by a thin layer of lung, it is not usually the early seat of friction sound ; but as the lung, when once displaced from before it, does not readily replace itself, the rubbing sound is often heard in this position up to a late period in the history of the case. The friction sound is notably double or to-and-fro over the conus arteriosus, and this may be accounted for by the ready completeness with which the right ventricle spontaneously fills itself during the ventricular diastole.

The Apex and Outlying Portion of the Left Ventricle.—The apex and outlying portion of the left ventricle are in health covered by the lung. The extent to which the lung thus affords a protection for the apex depends upon the vigour of the individual, the size of the chest, and the amplitude of the lungs. The portion of left lung immediately covering the apex is a thin tongue, the lowermost protruding angle of its upper lobe, which laps round the apex of the organ, and interposes itself between that part and the ribs. During the diastole, when the ventricle is inactive, the covering of lung is complete; but when the ventricle contracts, owing to the combined muscular rigidity of the organ, and the outward pressure of the blood that is compressed by the contracting cavity, it pushes aside the tongue of lung in front of it, so that the apex sweeps against the ribs and their interspaces. It is thus in young persons and those who are not robust; but in strong adults, inured to exercise, the average size of the lung is increased, and the apex is so embedded in the lung, that its proper beat cannot be felt, except perhaps at the end of a forcible expiration, or when they lie on the left side. In one instance (12, see p. 317) and in one only an obscure friction sound was heard over and limited to the apex before it was audible elsewhere. This was on the day of admission, but on the following day it had left the apex, and transferred itself to the whole right ventricle and right auricle. I can offer no explanation of this exceptional sign.

As a rule, the friction sound was, as I have said, limited at first to the right ventricle; but as the disease advanced, the increased fluid in the pericardium displaced the left lung and laid bare the apex, so that the friction sound spread itself from the right ventricle to the left.

When the effusion was at its height the heart was raised, and the apex-beat was felt in the fourth, or even the third space, at or just above and beyond the nipple. Friction sound was probably audible over the apex during the acme in thirty-four of the forty-four cases now under notice; it was absent from that point in nine; and its presence there was doubtful in one case.

The movement of the apex is, in its nature, the reverse of that of the right ventricle at its junction with the right auricle; for while, during the systole, that part moves from right to left, the apex moves from left to right, and from below upwards. As the active sweep of the apex takes place during the contraction of the ventricles, it is natural to expect that the friction sound at the apex should be mainly systolic, and the examination of my cases shows that this is so. Of the thirty-four cases in which a friction sound was audible over the apex, in six it was heard during the systole only; in ten the *frottement* was double, but was more intense and prolonged during the systole than the diastole; and in none was it stated that the two sounds were of equal intensity during the two periods. In six cases there was a creaking friction sound, usually systolic, at the apex.

When the lower lobe of the left lung shrinks under the double effect of pulmonary apoplexy within the lung, and pleurisy on its exterior, on the one hand; and of compression of that portion of the lung and of the left bronchus, by the great distension of the pericardium, on the other, the apex becomes completely exposed, and extends far to the left. In one such case (25, see p. 317), a youth, aged 17, a systolic creaking sound was audible over and beyond the apex, and the friction sound extended far to the left, ceasing suddenly in the axilla.

Right Auricle.—The right auricle is in health completely screened from the anterior wall of the chest by the middle lobe of the right lung, which separates it from the middle of the sternum and the costal cartilages to the right of the lower half of that bone. Friction sound is therefore never audible over the right auricle until the portion of lung that is interposed between it and the right cartilages is pushed aside by the advancing tide of effusion, so as to lay bare the auricle. When the effusion into the pericardium was at its height, a friction sound was audible over the right auricle in three-fifths of the cases (28 or 29 in 44).

The expansion of the right auricle is quite passive, and its contraction is made with so little exercise of force, that its movement to the right during its period of filling, and its movement to the left during its period of emptying, are made so quietly, that it exerts no pressure on the cartilages during its to-and-fro movements. It is natural to expect that the to-and-fro *frottement*, the *frou-frou* produced by the passive double friction of the right auricle, should be made up of two equal sounds, and as a rule those two sounds were equal over that cavity.

In twelve of the twenty-nine cases in which friction sound was audible over the right auricle, the systolic and diastolic sounds were equal; in eleven the *frottement* was double, but the relative intensity of the two sounds was not described; and in one a systolic sound, almost creaking in character, was audible over the right auricle. In this last exceptional case a similar almost creaking noise was heard over the base of the right ventricle at the lower portion of the sternum, and that was evidently the source of the rubbing sound over the auricle.

The two sounds made respectively over the right auricle during the two alternate movements of its dilatation, with contraction of the ventricle, and its contraction with dilatation of the ventricle; are not only equal in character, intensity, and continuousness; but they are also more soft and smooth in tone than they are over the ventricle; this contrast being most remarkable in some of those cases that present a thrill and a creaking sound over the right ventricle, and the diffusion of a harsh double friction sound over the whole front of the chest extending downwards even to the eighth or ninth right and left cartilages.

The question here arises whether under these circumstances the soft double friction sound audible over the cartilages to the right of the lower sternum is due to the immediate friction of the subjacent right auricle; or to that of the right ventricle, transmitted through the fluid and softened in its transmission? I think that we must infer that the latter is the usual source of this sound, when we consider that the yielding right auricle is compressed by the fluid in the pericardium at the time of the acme. Why under these circumstances, the two sounds are usually equal, I cannot say.

The Ascending Aorta and Pulmonary Artery.—In health the two great arteries lie behind the upper half of the sternum and the spaces to the left of it, above the level of the third cartilages. They not only have the bony protection thus afforded them, but they are additionally sheltered by a thin covering of lung that is interposed between them and the bony shield in front, and is made up of the inner adjoining margins of both lungs. The aorta is guarded by the strongest portion of the sternum, and the pulmonary artery lies behind the second space and cartilage, and the adjoining margin of the sternum. In the early stages, therefore, of pericarditis, friction sound is never audible over the great vessels. When the fluid increases, the distended pericardium and the elevated heart and great vessels push the double curtain of lungs to each side, so as to bring the great arteries into contact with the sternum and the first and second spaces and cartilages. The heart and great vessels then, as I have already said, occupy the narrower space in the upper portion of the cone of the chest, and there is now no longer room both for them and for the portion of lung superficial to them in health, which is therefore displaced.

In considering the character of the friction sound over the two great arteries, we must distinguish the aorta from the pulmonary artery. The roots of those arteries, including under that term their apertures, valves, and sinuses, descend and ascend fully half an inch during the successive periods of the systole and diastole of the ventricles; the movement of the systole being more active than that of the diastole.

The root of the pulmonary artery is situated at the front of the heart, and when the lung is displaced from before it, the artery lies immediately behind the second, and sometimes also the first, left intercostal space, the second costal cartilage, and the adjoining border of the sternum. The movement of the pulmonary artery, like that of the conus arteriosus from which it springs, is downwards and from left to right during the systole, and the reverse during the diastole. The friction sound over the pulmonary artery, is not, therefore, so far as I know to be distinguished from that over the conus arteriosus. The to-and-fro sound caused by those two adjoining and connected parts must resemble and blend with each other; but while that of the pulmonary artery is situated over and above the second space and the adjoining border of the sternum; that of the conus arteriosus extends downwards from that point to the fourth cartilage, but widening to the right, so as to occupy the whole breadth of the centre of the sternum.

A peculiar systolic scratching noise, that somewhat resembles a friction sound, is sometimes audible over the pulmonary artery during the course of acute rheumatism, and is generally associated with endocarditis. This sound is evidently caused by the vibration of the blood advancing during the systole along the artery when not in a state of tension; and is to be distinguished from a friction sound by its limited area, the sound being confined to the second space, and not accompanied by friction sound elsewhere over the heart; its restriction to the period of the systole and its consequent total want of a to-and-fro character; its freedom from change when pressure is made over it; its unaltering character on successive days; and the absence of pain over the heart or other symptoms or signs of pericarditis.

The root of the aorta instead of being exposed in front, like that of the pulmonary artery, is buried deeply in the centre of the heart, being covered by that artery, the conus arteriosus, and the left border of the right auricle. The root of the aorta cannot therefore cause a friction sound. The ascending aorta, where it comes into view above the right auricle and behind the lower half of the manubrium, is in health deep in situation, being covered by the adjoining margins of the opposite lungs. When, however, the heart and great vessels are lifted upwards by the advancing invasion of the fluid in the pericardium, the lungs are displaced from before the ascending aorta, which may possibly be pressed against the back of the manubrium. Even then, however, it can only excite a partial friction sound, for its movements, which are downwards and upwards, are very slight.

Friction sound was audible at the manubrium over the ascending aorta and the adjoining portion of the pulmonary artery at the time of the acme of the effusion into the pericardium, and especially during expiration, in twenty-six or perhaps twenty-seven of the forty-four cases under review; but this friction sound was evidently not generated by the double movement of those vessels, but was conducted upwards by the sternum, acting as a sounding-board, from the harsh double friction sound over the right ventricle. This was shown by that sound reaching with full intensity to the top of the sternum, which is a little above the transverse aorta, in twenty-six or perhaps twenty-seven of the forty-four cases; and by the close correspondence between the character of the double *frottement* over and above the great vessels at the upper half of the sternum, and that over the right ventricle, at the lower half of the sternum.

At the time of the acme of the effusion into the pericardium the whole heart is raised, and the lungs are separated from each other in front, so that the pulmonary artery, the conus arteriosus and the rest of the right ventricle, the apex and outlying portion of the left ventricle, and the right auricle are uncovered, and brought into immediate contact with the walls of the chest in front of them.

The whole front of the right ventricle bears upon the sternum and left cartilages with varying force. Sometimes it produces a thrill during its contraction, which may extend over its surface from the third to the sixth cartilages, and is often accompanied by a systolic creaking sound. At other times, sometimes with, but generally without a thrill, a double grating sound or a harsh friction sound of various tones, the systolic sound being usually louder than the diastolic, springs up over the whole right ventricle. In rare instances the two sounds are equal. More rarely a soft friction sound, rendered harsh by pressure, or a to-and-fro sound, excited by pressure but absent without it, is present over the right ventricle.

A friction sound is heard over the apex during the acme in about three-fourths of the cases. The apex may, like the right ventricle, present a thrill and a creaking sound during the systole; or a loud, prolonged systolic friction sound, and a short, feeble diastolic one. In no instance are the systolic and diastolic friction sounds equal over the apex.

During the acme the right auricle in two-thirds of the cases presents over its surface, to the right of the lower half of the sternum, a double, smooth, to-and-fro murmur or friction sound, equally loud during its dilatation and contraction. This double smooth *frottement* over the right auricle is probably transmitted, softened in its transit, through the fluid, from the noisy and active right ventricle.

The friction sound, if any, that may be made during the acme by the ascending aorta and the adjoining portion of the pulmonary artery behind the manubrium, is almost always masked by the friction sound of the right ventricle, which is conducted by the sternum acting as a sounding-board, the sound being thus conducted in more than half of the cases to the upper end of the bone.

The double *frottement* proper to the pulmonary artery when covered with lymph is undoubtedly audible during the acme over the second space, where it must resemble and blend with the double *frottement* proper to the conus arteriosus.

In every instance pressure intensifies the two friction sounds; and it sometimes transforms an ordinary *frottement* into a creaking or grating sound; or a soft friction sound into a harsh rubbing noise; or it excites a friction sound when one was previously absent.

Second Acme.—*Renewed Increase of Effusion into the Pericardium owing to Relapse.*—In eleven cases the effusion into the pericardium, after it had reached its height and commenced to decline, again increased in quantity, and attained to a second acme. Another case that had a relapse and a second acme, that was admitted during the period of the first acme, has not been included in the inquiry that is about to follow. In five of those eleven patients under consideration the fluid, after declining for a second time, again increased so as to present a third acme of pericardial effusion, and in one of the five there was a fourth wave of increase.

I shall examine in these cases with relapse and renewed acme, the comparative height of the pericardial effusion; the extent of the heart's impulse; the area and intensity of the friction sound; the severity of the general illness; and the intensity of the accompanying endocarditis, and its permanent effect on the functions of the valves of the heart during the period of the later acme.

Extent of the Effusion into the Pericardium.—In five of the cases the effusion into the pericardium was equal in extent during the first and the second acme; while in five it was greater, and in one it was less, during the first than the second acme. In six of the cases, from two to five days, and in five of them from six to eight days, elapsed between the end of the first period and the beginning of the second period of the height of the effusion.

Position of the Impulse.—In six of the cases, and probably in a seventh, the impulse at its inferior boundary occupied a lower position by from one to two intercostal spaces during the second acme of the effusion than the first (compare Figs. 48, p. 378; and 42, p. 340 respectively with Figs. 45, p. 350; and 40, p. 338); in two cases the impulse occupied the same position during the two periods; in one instance it was imperceptible throughout; and in one it was very feeble.

We thus find that in the great majority of the cases the impulse of the heart was lower during the second acme of effusion, or the period of relapse, than during the first acme. The reason is, I think, evident. When the fluid in the pericardium begins to increase during the early period of pericarditis, the heart, which is then yielding in structure and usually of the natural size, is steadily floated upwards by the increasing tide of effusion into the pericardium, which may indeed compress the auricle, and lessen the size of the heart. The heart, under the double influence of the inflammation on its exterior, and the resulting thick coating of lymph, on the one hand; and the inflammation on its interior, and the resulting crippling of valves, enlargement of cavities, and thickening of walls, on the other, becomes increased in size. The whole organ is, in fact, enlarged, and it is often unyielding in its position owing to its tough new covering, and perhaps to partial adhesions that may have already connected the double surfaces of the thickened pericardium and the heart, especially along and near the septum; and although the renewed increase of fluid elevates the heart to a certain extent, this second elevation of the impulse is not usually so great as the first elevation.

Thrill.—A thrill was felt over the heart for the first time during the second acme in three of the cases. In two of them the thrill was present over the apex, and this was the natural effect of the lowered position, greater prominence, and increased force of that portion of the heart during the second acme than the first. In the other case the thrill was present over the second left space, but in this patient the second acme was the true one, for the effusion was considerably higher during the second than the first acme. A thrill is, in fact, more frequently present over the second space during the first acme than the second, and over the apex during the second acme than the first, for the reasons that I have just stated.

Area and Intensity of the Friction Sound during the Second Acme of Increased Effusion into the Pericardium.—During the second acme of the pericardial effusion a creaking friction sound was audible over the heart in four cases, and a grating noise in one; a to-and-fro sound in five patients, and a double friction murmur increased by pressure in one.

In five of the cases the area of the friction sound was greater, and in four it was less during the second than the first acme of the effusion into the pericardium, and in two it was of equal extent during both periods. In five of them the friction sound was audible over a lower position during the second acme than the first, and in none of them was the friction sound lower during the first acme than the second.

In like manner, the friction sound was more intense in six cases, and less intense in four, during the second acme than the first; and in one it was of equal intensity during both periods. In four of the patients both the area and the intensity of the *frottement* were greater, and in three they were both less, during the second than the first acme.

The following agencies, on the one hand, tend to increase the area and intensity of the friction sound during the second acme as compared with the first:—The greater size of the heart; the increased thickness and force of its walls; the lowered position of the organ and its impulse; and the greater roughness and toughness of the lymph covering the heart and lining the pericardium.

The following, on the other hand, tend to lessen the area and intensity of the friction sound during the second acme as compared with the first:—The greater extent to which the lungs sometimes cover the heart; the restraint placed on the movements of the heart, and especially of the right auricle, by the thickness and toughness of its envelope of lymph; and the adhesions that have often already taken place between the pericardium and the heart; and especially along the septum, between the ventricles, and at the apex. Vital influences blend with and counteract these physical influences in producing the result.

My analysis of the cases does not enable me to assign to each of those causes its proper share in the production of these effects.

In the one fatal case the heart was universally adherent, and in that patient the friction sound was less in extent and intensity during the second acme than the first, owing, I consider, to adhesions that had already begun to form between the heart and the pericardium.

The friction sound, as we have seen, was lower in extent during the second acme than the first in one-half of the cases (5 in 11), owing to the lower position of the heart and its impulse during that period.

In five of the cases the friction sound maintained the same character during the second acme as during the first, but in six others it was altered. Thus, one that had a friction sound on pressure, one that had a smooth friction sound harsher on pressure, and one that had a harsh friction sound creaking on pressure during the first acme, presented, all of them, a creaking friction sound during the second acme; while one with a to-and-fro sound during the first, gave a grating noise during the second acme.

From what I have just said, it is evident that the influences tending to increase the area and intensity of the friction sound during the second acme were in greater force than the influences tending to lessen them; and that the friction sound was usually more intense and more extensive, especially downwards, during the second acme than the first.

Comparative Area and Intensity of the Friction Sound just before, during, and soon after the Second Acme of Effusion into the Pericardium.—The friction sound is, as a rule, louder and more extensive during the second acme of pericardial effusion than either just before or soon after that period. At this stage, therefore, the *frottement* increases with the advance, and decreases with the decline of the fluid.

Degree of the General Illness during the Second Period of Increased Pericardial Effusion.—In five of the cases the illness was extreme, in three it was severe, and in three it was slight or probably so during the second acme.

Of the five cases in which the illness was extreme, the face was anxious in four; there were choreal movements and rigidity, chiefly of the left arm, in one; breathing was laborious in one and quick in four, the respirations ranging from 32 to 48; pain was present over the heart in one, and in another pain was felt, apparently in the side, on a deep breath; swallowing was difficult in two; one had diphtheria; and one raised phlegm tinted with blood.

The patients who were thus affected with relapse of the inflammation of the pericardium suffered more frequently with symptoms of great severity during the first than the second period of the increase of the effusion into the sac. Thus during the first acme in seven patients the illness was extreme, including the five in which it was so during the second acme, and in three it was severe. In one case the symptoms were not described.

Of the seven cases in which the illness was extreme during the first acme, perspiration was very profuse in three; the face was anxious, pallid, livid, or of a leaden hue, in four; there were slight choreal movements in one; breathing was quick in five, the respirations ranging from 40 to 48; pain was present over the heart in four of those seven patients and in two others in whom the symptoms were less severe; and swallowing was difficult or painful in three.

We thus see that pain attacked the region of the heart in six cases during the first acme, and in only one case during the second acme. The breathing also was more urgently affected during the first acme, when they numbered from 40 to 48 in the minute; than during the second acme, when they ranged from 32 to 48.

On the other hand, depression and anxiety were more marked during the second acme than the first.

The general illness was much more often extremely severe during the first acme in those cases that suffered from a relapse, than during the single acme in those that had no relapse. Thus of those patients in whom there was a renewal of the acme, the illness was extreme during the first acme of the effusion in two-thirds (7 in 10 or 11), and severe in one-third (3 in 10 or 11); while of those who had no renewal of attack, the illness was extreme in only one-third of the cases (10 in 30 or 32), severe in one-half (14 in 30 or 32), and not severe in one-fifth (6 in 30 or 32). In one case of the series with a relapse, and in two cases of the series without a relapse, the symptoms were not recorded.

Intensity of the Endocarditis accompanying the Pericarditis during the Second Acme of the Effusion; and Permanent Effect of the Endocarditis on the Valves.—All the cases that had a relapse of pericarditis were affected with endocarditis in an intense degree. One of the patients had old-standing disease of the mitral and aortic valves; and in seven of them valvular disease was established when they left the hospital, the mitral valve being affected in all of them, and the aortic valve also in three. In three cases the mitral valve, which was incompetent during the attack, owing to inflammation of the valve, completely regained its function.

The proportion of cases in which the valves were permanently crippled among those who were affected with relapse of the pericarditis was much greater than among those who were not so affected. Thus the valvular incompetence became permanent in two-thirds of the patients with relapse of the affection (7 in 10), three of them being affected with both aortic and mitral disease; and in only about one-fourth or one-third of those who had no relapse (11 in 52 and 7 others who left with lessening murmur.)

These clinical facts tend to make it probable that when there is a relapse of the inflammation of the exterior of the heart, there is a relapse also of the inflammation of the interior of the heart and its valves; and that the inflammation when thus prolonged tends to cripple the valves for life.

Second Relapse of Pericarditis with a Third Acme *of Pericardial Effusion.*—In five of the eleven cases with relapse and a renewed increase of effusion into the pericardium, after the fluid began to decline, there was a second relapse, and the fluid increased in quantity for a third time. In one of those cases there was indeed a third relapse followed by a fourth acme of pericardial effusion.

In one of the cases the effusion into the pericardium was equal in amount during the first acme, the second, and the third, the wave of increase rising on each occasion to the same height. In two of them the fluid was equal in quantity during the first acme and the third, but was less during the intermediate period of renewed increase; and in the two remaining cases the wave of increased effusion lessened on each repetition, the effusion being less during the third acme than the second, and less during the second acme than the first.

In those five cases from three to five days elapsed between the second acme and the third.

The impulse, at its inferior boundary, was lower during the third acme than the first in three of the cases; and it was lower in one case and higher in another during the third acme than the second; while its position was unchanged during those two periods in a third. In one of the cases the impulse was imperceptible throughout, and in another it became so at the period of the third acme.

The presence of a thrill was not observed in any of the cases during the third acme.

The friction sound is in a declining state during the third acme. The *frottement* was of a definite rubbing to-and-fro character, intensified by pressure, in only one of the four cases during the final acme. In one of those patients the friction sound was double and smooth in character; in another it was single and systolic; in a third it was almost like a bellows murmur; and in the remaining case it was absent with light pressure, but firm pressure brought a to-and-fro sound into existence.

Four of the five patients belonging to this group were affected with great general illness during the final acme; their breathing was distressed and rapid, numbering respectively from 36 to 60 in the minute; while two of them had pain in the chest, and the remaining two pain in the region of the heart.

The Area and Intensity of the Friction Sound during the Decline *of the Pericardial Effusion.*—In forty-three cases the comparative area and intensity of the friction sound were observed both when the effusion into the pericardium was at its height, and during the period of its decline.

(1) The friction sound spread downwards to a greater extent during the decline than the acme of the effusion into the pericardium, in three-fifths of the cases (26 in 43.) (2) In less than one-fourth of the cases (10 in 43) the reverse took place, the friction sound being more extensive, and especially downwards, during the acme of the effusion than when the fluid diminished. (3) The area of the friction sound extended downwards to an equal extent during the acme and the decline of the effusion in a still smaller proportion of the cases (7 in 43).

(1) *Cases in which the Friction Sound spread downwards to a greater extent during the Decline than the Height of the Effusion into the Pericardium.*—I shall consider (1) the time of occurrence; and (2) the duration of the downward extension of the friction sound in these cases; (3) the area; and (4) the character of the sound; and the position of the heart and its impulse and thrill; and (5) the degree of the general illness during the period in question.

1. *Time of the Occurrence of the Downward Extension of the Friction Sound.*—The friction sound spread rapidly downwards soon after the fluid in the pericardium began to decline in all but a very small proportion of these cases. Thus the rubbing sound had already extended downwards to its lowest position in four-fifths of the patients (21 in 26) during the first three days after the acme. During the three following days the descent of the rubbing sound appeared in four more of the cases; but in the last of these this condition came into play quite

suddenly on the twelfth, and still more on the fourteenth day after the fluid began to lessen.

2. *Duration of the Extreme Downward Extension of the Friction Sound.* —The downward extension of the friction sound lasted in these cases for a very short period. In two-thirds of them (17 in 26) it was observed during only one day, and in but two cases, or rather one, did it last over three days. This extension downwards of the friction sound during the decline of the fluid was therefore short and transitory.

3. *Area of the Downward Extension of the Friction Sound.*—When the fluid in the pericardium, after having reached its height, lessens in quantity, the heart descends, its impulse is lowered by from one to two intercostal spaces, and the friction sound extends downwards. The area of the rubbing noise is, as a rule, by no means limited to the area occupied by the heart itself; but spreads downwards to an extent varying from one to four inches below the lower boundary of the heart. The friction sound does not, in these cases, diffuse itself downwards over the whole breadth of the region below the heart; for it is usually silent over the front of the abdomen in the epigastric space; while it is present along the right and left seventh and even eighth costal cartilages that bound that space to the right and left; and over the ensiform cartilage that dips downwards from the lower end of the sternum at the centre of that space.

The rubbing noise is usually heard with equal intensity over the right and the left seventh and eighth cartilages. Sometimes indeed the sound was louder and more extensive over the right seventh and eighth cartilages than the left; and it appeared as if in those cases the cartilages that rested on the liver conducted the sound better than the cartilages that covered the stomach. The contrast between the harsh rubbing noise heard in some cases over those cartilages, and the complete silence present over the intervening epigastric space was very remarkable.

The friction sound, besides travelling downwards, extended also upwards in one half of these cases (14 in 26) when the fluid in the pericardium lessened, and the heart and its impulse descended. In one third of the patients (8 in 26) the area of the friction sound was equally high over the front of the chest during the period of the acme of the effusion into the pericardium, and that of its decline.

In four instances the whole area of the friction sound shifted bodily downwards when the pericardial effusion lessened, and the heart and its impulse descended; so that the upper and lower borders of that area were then simultaneously lowered. In these four cases while the lower boundary of the region of friction sound descended from the sixth to the seventh cartilages; its upper boundary descended in two of them from the second left cartilage to the third, and in the other two from the third cartilage to the fifth.

In two-thirds of those cases (16 in 26) in which the friction sound extended much downwards after the acme, it was also audible up to the top of the sternum. In three of those cases the friction sound so

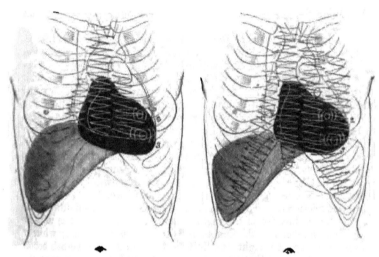

FIG. 46.   FIG. 47.

For previous views of this case, see Figs. 44, 45, page 350.

Fig. 46, from a housemaid aged 20, affected with rheumatic pericarditis (33, see p. 319). *Period of the decline of the pericardial effusion* after the first acme.

Fifth day after the acme of pericardial effusion, seventh day after the first observation of the friction sound and increased pericardial dulness, and ninth day after admission.

The pericardial effusion has lessened much since the period of the acme, its upper boundary (1, 1) having descended from the middle of the manubrium to the middle of the sternum ; and its lower boundary having probably ascended from a little above the end to about the middle of the ensiform cartilage. The heart (2, 2) is lower, and the amount of fluid between the under surface of the heart and the floor of the pericardium (3, 3), though still considerable, has evidently lessened by at least one half. The right ventricle, the inner or left half of the right auricle, and the apex and front of the left ventricle are exposed ; but the great arteries are covered with lung.

The region of pericardial dulness (see the black space) probably extends from the middle of the sternum between the third cartilages, and from the fourth left cartilage, down to the middle of the ensiform cartilage, and the lower third of the sixth cartilage ; and from a little to the right of the lower half of the sternum to the nipple line. The lower boundary of the heart is behind the upper edge of the sixth rib, and the top of the ensiform cartilage.

The impulse has descended from the third space during the acme, to the fourth and fifth spaces. (See the circular and curved lines in those spaces.)

A double friction sound (see the zigzag lines—systolic lines thick, diastolic thin), which is more harsh on making pressure, is heard over the whole length of the sternum ; which is most intense at the middle of the bone, and is louder at its lower end during inspiration, and over the manubrium during expiration ; a creaking sound is audible during systole over the third, fourth, and fifth left spaces ; and a friction sound is heard to the right of the lower portion of the sternum. (The nipple is too far to the left in this figure.)

Fig 47, from the same patient (33) as Figs. 44, 45 (page 350), 46, and 48.

Period of the decline of the pericardial effusion ; second view, taken the day after a slight and transient second acme, when the fluid was again declining.

Remarkable extension of the friction sound over the greater part of the front of the chest, and especially downwards.

Tenth day after the first acme of pericardial effusion ; twelfth day after the first observation of the friction sound and of pericardial dulness ; fourteenth day after admission ; and four days before the occurrence of a second acme.

The pericardial effusion has diminished. There is therefore less fluid between the under surface of the heart and the floor of the pericardium (3, 3); the roughened front of the heart is more dry, and is closer to the corresponding roughened surface of the pericardial sac; the heart (2, 2), which is somewhat enlarged, is lower in position; and the upper boundary of pericardial effusion (1, 1) is lower, and its inferior boundary is somewhat higher than when Fig. 46 was taken five days previously. The whole right ventricle, the left border of the right auricle, and the apex and front of the left ventricle are exposed; while the great arteries and part of the conus arteriosus are covered with lung.

The region of pericardial dulness (see the black space), which is bounded above by the fourth cartilage, and below by the sixth cartilage, is probably rather less extensive above, below, and to the right, than in Fig. 46, taken on the ninth day after admission.

The impulse is lower, stronger, and more extensive than in Fig. 46, and is present from the third to the fifth spaces, and up to or beyond the mammary line (see the circular and curved lines in those spaces); and gives therefore direct evidence that the heart is lower in position, and that the effusion has lessened.

The friction sound (see the zigzag lines—systolic lines thick, diastolic thin) has gained a very great extension, being audible over a great part of the front of the chest, from the first costal cartilage to the seventh left and the eighth right cartilages; and from the top of the sternum to the bottom of the ensiform cartilage. This extension of the friction sound is especially marked downwards, where it extends for about four inches below the heart, and is lower on the right than on the left side, reaching over the right eighth cartilage in front of the liver, and the seventh left cartilage in front of the sternum. This is the reverse above, when the rubbing sound extends four inches to the left, and only about two inches to the right of the sternum.

The friction sound is harsher than it was yesterday; over the midsternum it is louder during the systole than the diastole; and it is intensified by pressure; over the manubrium, the to-and-fro sounds are equal; over the ensiform cartilage, friction sound is present during inspiration; it is creaking during systole over the second and first spaces; and it becomes louder below the mamma during inspiration.

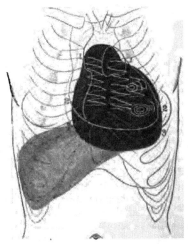

FIG. 48.

For previous views of this case, see Figs. 44, 45, page 350, and 46, 47 on the preceding page.

Fig. 48, from a housemaid affected with rheumatic pericarditis (33, see p. 319).

Third acme of pericardial effusion (the second acme was very slight and transitory). Thirteenth day after the first acme; eighteenth day after admission.

The pericardial effusion is greatly increased, but its extent and limits are not definitely described. If we compare this third acme with the first acme (Fig. 46, page 377), we find that the distended pericardium, though it contains less fluid, is wider in relation to its length ; that the heart is larger ; and that the lower boundary of the heart is lower, in this the later and renewed, than in that the earlier and original acme. In the first acme the heart was not yet enlarged, or, being compressed by the fluid in the distended sac, was possibly lessened in size ; and the walls of the pericardium were still unyielding, so that the swollen sac took the form that it would naturally take if artificially distended with fluid (see Figs. 33, 34, page 305). In this, the third acme, the heart has become enlarged both by pericarditis and by mitral endocarditis ; the lower boundary of the heart, although elevated by the accumulated fluid, is lower than in the first acme ; and the walls of the pericardium have become thicker, softer, and more yielding than in health, so that the distended sac yields to the right and left, where it meets with no resistance, to a greater extent than it does upwards and downwards, where it meets with much resistance ; and is therefore wider in relation to its length than it was during the first acme, when its form was more purely pear-shaped. The whole front of the heart and great vessels is exposed, including the right auricle and ventricle, the apex and front of the left ventricle, the pulmonary artery, and the ascending aorta within the pericardium. The fluid has evidently interposed itself to a greater extent between the surface of the lower portion of the front of the heart and the walls of the chest during this, the third acme, than during the first acme.

The region of pericardial dulness (see the black space), the limits of which are not described, corresponds in general form and outline to the pericardial effusion, and evidently extends more to the right and left, and less upwards and downwards than it did during the first acme.

The impulse has again been elevated at its lower boundary, and this time from the fifth space, as in Fig. 47, page 377, to the fourth space, where it is feeble ; and it is felt over the third space during expiration. (See the concentric circles in those spaces.) The lower boundary of the impulse is therefore lower by one space than it was during the first acme, when it occupied the third space (see Fig. 45, page 350).

The friction sound (see the zigzag lines—systolic lines thick, diastolic thin) is softened, and is limited in area, being heard over the middle region of the sternum, where it is double, and although frictional in character is almost like a bellows murmur ; and is audible over the second and third spaces during the systole.

Later progress of this case.—On the following day, the nineteenth after admission, the friction sound was almost creaking, or like the sound made by rubbing with sand-paper, over the second and third left spaces. On the twenty-first day, or the fourth after the third acme, the extent of dulness over the pericardial region had lessened ; and a double friction murmur, which was not rhythmical with the sounds of the heart, was audible over the base of the right ventricle, and became harsh on pressure. The friction murmur was still heard on the following day, but after this it was scarcely audible.

covered the front of the chest as to be audible up to the clavicles, while in one of them it reached the first cartilage. In the whole of these cases the friction sound extended from two to nearly four inches above the actual seat of friction. The region of pericardial dulness was limited above in all but three of the patients by the third intercostal space or the fourth cartilage ; and the space between this limit and the top of the sternum nearly measures the extent to which the *frottement* extended above the seat of the friction

When the fluid in the sac declines, the roughened heart rubs against the roughened pericardium, and in doing so bears directly upon the lower half of the sternum with which it is almost in contact ; owing to the removal of the anterior layer of the fluid, and the descent of the heart and its impulse. The sonorous vibrations excited by the movements of the heart are directly conveyed to the sternum, and that bone and the costal cartilages attached to it act as a sounding-board and transmit the rubbing noise in all directions.

c c 2

In three of the cases the sound was audible over the whole front of the chest. Usually, however, it extended only slightly to the right, and over a greater extent to the left of the lower half of that bone. As a rule, therefore, the rubbing noise extended in a straight line from the top to the bottom of the sternum, and there it divided into two diverging lines, one along the right, the other along the left seventh cartilage, where they form the boundaries of the intervening epigastric space. The area of friction sound thus extending along the sternum and the right and left seventh cartilages closely resembles in shape the inverted letter Λ. Since however the friction sound also extends downwards over the ensiform cartilage, its area is somewhat like a trident with a short central prong.

In one-fifth of the cases (5 in 26) the area of the friction sound dwindled during a short period after the time of the acme, and then suddenly expanded, and especially downwards, at a later date during the decline of the effusion.

In one case the friction sound alternately lessened and increased in area and intensity during the ten days that intervened between the termination of the acme, and the time at which the frottement had a remarkable downward development.

4. *Character and Intensity of the Friction Sound ; and Position of the Heart and of its Impulse and Thrill.*—At the time that the friction sound spread downwards when the effusion lessened, the sound was intense, loud, and of a marked character in all but three or four of the twenty-six cases that belong to the group under consideration.

In nine of those cases the friction sound was creaking (6), or grating (3); in thirteen it was harsh and loud; and in four its intensity was not specified.

The friction sound in the twenty-six cases under review, as a rule, gained in intensity as it gained in area ; and lost in intensity as it lost in area. Thus in all but six of the cases, the rubbing noise became more harsh when it increased in extent ; and in all but two of them it became softer when it lessened in extent.

When the effusion lessened, the impulse, while it descended at its lower boundary, was still felt beating in the higher spaces into which it had been forced during the acme in fully one-fourth of the cases (5 in 19): while, curiously, the impulse ascended to a higher space than it had occupied during the acme in six other patients.

A thrill was felt over the heart in five of these twenty-six cases during the acme of the effusion. In four of these the thrill disappeared when the effusion lessened, and in one it remained, though with lessened intensity. In three other patients a fresh thrill came into play during the decline of the fluid ; in two of them over the apex, and in the other case at the second space.

In these twenty-six cases, when the effusion into the pericardium lessened, the heart, relieved from the pressure of the fluid, descended into its natural space, and even below and beyond it. The heart thus relieved, beat with increased force ; its right cavities were enlarged, owing to the increased supply of blood from the system, and the continued resistance offered to the flow of blood through the compressed lung and the incompetent mitral valves; and, as the general result, its anterior walls played with greater power and noise upon the sternum and cartilages, and the friction sound was heard over a largely increased area.

5. *Degree of the General Illness.*—At the time that the area of the friction sound was most extensive, especially downwards, when the fluid in the pericardium lessened, twenty of these twenty-six cases were less ill or in better health, three of them were probably better, and three were worse in health than they were during the acme.

In a large proportion of the cases under review, when the fluid in the pericardium lessened, the heart descended and gained freedom of movement and power, and the general health improved; and as a natural result the friction sound increased in extent, and especially downwards. The comparatively dry roughened surface of the heart rasped to and fro upon the roughened surface of the pericardium. These influences combined to cause the increased harshness and extension of the friction sound; which, starting from its focus of greatest intensity over the right ventricle, radiated in all directions over and beyond the region of the heart and the great vessels, outwards to the right and left, upwards to the summit of the sternum, and especially downwards over the ensiform cartilage and the diverging right and left seventh and eighth cartilages.

(2) *Cases in which the Friction Sound was audible downwards to a greater extent during than after the Acme of the Effusion.*—In ten cases the friction sound was audible to a greater extent downwards when the effusion was at its height than during its decline.

Two series of influences are at work in these cases, acting at different times, to enlarge the area of friction sound during the acme, and to lessen it during the decline of the effusion.

1. When, during the acme, the friction sound is creaking or grating, being sometimes associated with a thrill, over the right ventricle, and when it radiates thence in all directions, softened in character, beyond the region of actual friction, the heart, raised by the increased effusion into the narrower space at the upper part of the cone of the chest, beats with increased force directly against the sternum, the higher cartilages, and their spaces, and so excites an intense and widely diffused friction sound.

When the fluid lessens the heart descends and is again partially covered with lung; and as it beats over a smaller extent, and with less pressure against the sternum and cartilages, the friction sound lessens in intensity and area.

2. When the friction sound is of moderate intensity and extent during the acme, it sometimes lessens during the decline of the effusion. In these cases the impulse at its inferior boundary is not notably lowered, while it disappears from the upper spaces. In some of these cases the action of the heart is throughout feeble; and probably

in others of them slight adhesions take place at the apex and septum which restrain and lessen the descent of the heart, the rubbing movements of the right ventricle, and the area and intensity of the friction sound over the higher intercostal spaces.

(3) *Cases in which the Friction Sound extended Downwards to an equal extent during and after the Acme of the Effusion.*—In seven cases the friction sound was of equal extent during the two periods, when the fluid in the pericardium was at its height and was declining.

Character and Intensity of the Friction Sound during the Decline of the Effusion, and the Relation of the Intensity to the Area of the Friction Sound.—I shall examine these conditions during three periods in the order of time of the decline of the effusion, (1) the beginning of the decline of the effusion; (2) the gradual and the interrupted progress of the decline of the effusion; and, (3) the final dying away of the friction sound; and (4) shall then inquire into cases in which the ordinary friction sound gave place to a friction murmur towards the end of the attack.

1. *Character and Intensity of the Friction Sound at the Beginning of the Decline of the Effusion.*—When the amount of fluid in the pericardium began to lessen, if the friction sound increased or diminished in intensity, it usually increased or diminished also in area.

As a rule, the friction sound increased in intensity and area in those cases in which the *frottement* extended further downwards after than during the acme; while it lessened in intensity and area in those in which the friction sound spread more downwards during the acme than after it.

When the friction sound spread downwards during the decline of the effusion, the sound gained in area in nearly every case (25 cases in 26), and in intensity in two-thirds of the cases (18 in 26). We thus see that while an increase in the intensity of the *frottement* almost invariably leads to an extension of its area—for I find only one exception to this rule—and while a diminution of its intensity likewise generally causes a diminution of its area; yet, in certain cases, the friction sound gains in extent, though it lessens (4 cases in 43) or remains unchanged (3 cases in 43) in intensity. This is explained by the lowering of the heart, and the consequent descent of its impulse during the decline of the effusion in all the cases—the surface of the roughened organ being thus brought into more extensive contact with the sternum at its lower half, and with the corresponding costal cartilages: while in the small number of cases in which, although the friction sound gains in area, it is lessened or not increased in intensity, the heart, released from its confinement in the contracted space of the chest above, where it rubbed with force and noise against the sternum and cartilages in front of it, finds itself moving with ease in its proper place in the lower and wider part of the chest, and so presses with less force and less noise than before on the sternum and cartilages in front of it. The causes of the increased intensity as well as area during the decline of the effusion, which, as we have just seen, occur in the great majority of the cases under examination, have been already considered at page 381.

2. *The Gradual and Interrupted Progress of the Decline of the Effusion.* —In thirty-one of the forty-three cases now being examined, the effusion in the pericardium steadily and gradually declined, and, as we have already seen, in twelve of them, owing to relapse, the effusion after beginning to decline, again increased in quantity generally once, sometimes twice, and on one occasion even a third time.

The progress of the friction sound during the decline of the effusion was rarely uniform. It was in several of the cases silenced and suspended for a time (6 in 43); it more frequently, however, when in full play, became feebler during a short period, and then again louder (13 in 43). In a larger number of the cases the *frottement*, after attaining to its greatest intensity, more or less steadily lessened in loudness and extent until it finally disappeared (23 in 43).

In one case the friction sound suddenly and permanently disappeared after an attack of syncope. In this patient, a girl, the friction sound vanished when the action of the heart became enfeebled; and she died in a second attack of syncope a few hours after the first attack.

Cases in which the Friction Sound vanished and reappeared during the Decline of the Effusion.—In six of the forty-three cases under review and in one other patient the friction sound disappeared and reappeared during the decline of the effusion. In five of these cases the *frottement* was absent for from two to three days, and in one of them for about seven days.

In three of the patients the friction sound, as in the case just referred to, vanished for a time after the application of leeches for the relief of pain.

If we view these cases as a whole, and take into the survey the case of the female servant who died from a second attack of syncope, the first attack having permanently quenched a loud and pervading friction sound, we shall, I think, see that when the force of the heart's action and the volume of the blood in circulation are lessened—either by immediate syncope, by loss of blood from leeching, by diarrhœa, sickness, or other exhausting influences, by pain in or over the organ, by extreme distress in breathing, or more often by a combination of several of these lowering agencies—then the rubbing sound, when in full play, may gradually or suddenly vanish, and may suddenly rekindle into full volume after a longer or shorter period of silence.

Cases in which the Friction Sound lessened and then increased in Area and Intensity during the Decline of the Effusion.—In thirteen of the forty-three cases under examination, and in three other cases, the friction sound, when in full play, lessened in extent and intensity, and after a longer or shorter interval again resumed more or less nearly its full sway.

In one of these sixteen cases the diminution of the *frottement* was associated with sudden faintness; in two with loss of blood from leeching; in eight with increase of the general illness—in seven of which as the health improved the friction sound resumed its extent and intensity—in two with an amelioration of the symptoms; in two with irregularity and intermission of the pulse and the action of the heart; and in two the state of the health is not described.

In eight cases the diminution of the friction sound corresponded with an increase of the general illness, which showed itself generally by an anxious expression, accelerated and difficult breathing, and pain over the heart; sometimes with cough and rusty phlegm; and sometimes with abundant perspiration. With the renewed increase of the rubbing sound there was in all these cases, save perhaps one, a marked improvement in the health; manifested usually by a comparatively cheerful expression, more easy respiration, lessening or absent pain over the heart, and assuaging of cough with diminution of phlegm.

(1) *Duration* and (2) *Progress of the Friction Sound during the Decline of the Effusion.*—(1.) *Duration.*—The friction sound lasted for a very variable period during the decline of the disease.

In the group of thirty-one cases that had no relapse and no return of the effusion into the pericardium, the friction sound lasted from three to nineteen days, its average duration being ten days.

In the group of twelve cases that suffered from relapse with return of the effusion into the pericardium, the friction sound lasted from eleven to twenty-two days, its average duration being fifteen days.

(2) *Progress.—Cases in which the Maximum Development of the Friction Sound took place during the Decline of the Effusion.—Period between the Maximum Development and the Cessation of the Friction Sound.* —In thirteen of the nineteen cases under examination the area of the friction sound steadily lessened from the day of its maximum extension to that of its final disappearance. It contracted gradually from right to left and from left to right, from above downwards and from below upwards, towards the centre or focus of actual friction. It thus died away from beyond and over the great vessels, the right auricle, and the apex, and from the region that it had previously occupied below the lower boundary of the heart. Towards and over the region of actual friction it step by step concentrated itself, and after lingering over the right ventricle with softening tones for a shorter or longer period, it quietly died away. In about one-half of the cases (6 in 13) this subdued sound outlived the period of its greatest intensity and extent for from one to two days; in the remainder, for from three to seven days; and in only one did it exist for nine days.

The front of the right ventricle was, as I have just said, the last home of the friction sound, as it had been indeed the seat of its birthplace. As the position of that ventricle varied in different patients accordingly as the heart was larger or smaller in size, higher or lower in situation, the final seat of the softened friction sound varied in different cases, from the left third and fourth cartilages to the fifth or sixth; and from the middle third of the sternum to the ensiform cartilage.

There was a general but by no means invariable correspondence between the area of the friction sound on its last observation, and the position of the impulse.

In only three of the nineteen cases now under review did the impulse occupy the same position when the friction sound was heard for the last time, as when it was most extensive. In four cases it had descended at its lower boundary from the fourth space to the fifth; and in four cases it had disappeared from the upper space at the time of the last observation of the friction sound, when compared with the time at which it was predominant. There was therefore in these patients a tendency for the heart and its impulse to take up a lower position, and to be covered to a greater extent with lung as the friction sound was about to disappear, and the case advanced towards its termination. On the other hand, in two other cases the impulse gained ground above, and appeared in the second space for the first time when the *frottement* was heard for the last time.

The descent of the impulse both above and below when the case advances to recovery and the friction sound is dying out, appears to me to be the natural bias in these cases when the heart is not adherent, and descends into its natural situation; when the right ventricle and pulmonary artery are not greatly enlarged; and when the upper lobe of the left lung expands in front so as to cover the pulmonary artery and the upper portion of the right ventricle.

When, however, the heart becomes more or less adherent; when the pulmonary artery and right ventricle become enlarged owing to mitral regurgitation; when mitral incompetence is combined with adherent pericardium; when the walls of the pericardium are thickened; or when the left lung does not expand in front of the upper border of the heart so as to cover the pulmonary artery and the conus arteriosus; and notably when two or more of these conditions combine their influence, then the impulse tends to remain in or attain to the higher intercostal spaces, and especially the second space.

In one remarkable case belonging to the group of nineteen now under review, the friction sound was lost on the fifth day after the acme, and reappeared on the twelfth day with greater intensity and over a larger area than at any previous time. In three other cases the friction sound, after gradually diminishing in intensity and area, became suddenly reinforced; and in two others a similar diminution and increase of the *frottement* took place but to a comparatively slight degree.

3. *The final dying away of the Friction Sound.*—The friction sound offered greater variety in different cases just before the time of its extinction than at any other period of its existence.

(1) In a very small number of the cases (4 in 43) the friction sound, when in full play, suddenly disappeared; (2) in two-fifths of them (16 in

43) the *frottement*, after being more or less loud up to a certain date, rapidly declined, and vanished in one or two days; (3) in a fifth of them (8 in 43) the decline of the friction sound was gradual; (4) and in two-fifths of them (16 in 43) the ordinary rubbing sound gave place towards the end of the case to a friction murmur sometimes double, and increased by pressure (8), sometimes double and excited by pressure (5), sometimes single and systolic and intensified by pressure (2), and in one case a single friction murmur was excited by pressure.

4. *Cases in which the ordinary Friction Sound gave place to a Friction Murmur towards the end of the attack.*—In fifteen patients, and possibly in a sixteenth, a friction murmur was audible in lieu of the ordinary friction sound towards the end of the attack of pericarditis.

We have already seen that in a certain number of cases, at the beginning of the attack, the ordinary friction sound was preceded by a friction murmur: and that in one remarkable case a friction murmur prevailed throughout the whole course of the disease to the exclusion of the usual rubbing sound. I would here refer to what has already been said as to the friction murmur as it was observed during the beginning of the attack, at pages 345-348.

In one case a systolic friction murmur audible on making pressure, and in another case a systolic friction murmur increased by pressure, was respectively the final sign of pericarditis.

In six cases a double friction murmur was audible on pressure towards the close of the affection. One of the cases of this group (47, see p. 318), a servant girl aged 20, presented on the seventh day, when the effusion was at its height, an extension of the *frottement*, when there was a double grating friction sound. On the eleventh, when the effusion was declining, there was a feeble murmur-like friction sound over the right auricle, to the right of the lower sternum; and later in the day the heart sounds were natural over the lower sternum, but pressure brought out a double friction murmur not quite rhythmical with the sounds of the heart. A systolic friction sound was audible over the left fifth cartilage. On the fourteenth day a faint double murmur was still excited by pressure over the lower sternum. This was the last day of undoubted pericardial friction sound, but on the eighteenth day a double grating friction sound burst out on pressure at the end of a deep breath, that was probably pleuritic.

In several of these cases a friction murmur either prevailed over the right ventricle during the early stages, or was limited to certain favourite spots, such as the right auricle, when the friction sound was at its height. Later, the friction murmur gradually again developed itself as the harsher friction sounds became softened, and at length spread itself over the heart. Soon, however, this disappeared as a constant sound, but for one or two final days of the disease it could be again awakened by making pressure over the right ventricle. Several of these cases ended with a double friction murmur that was intensified by pressure.

In addition to these cases in which the friction murmur prevailed exclusively towards the termination of the disease, there were others in which, while the friction sound was harsh, and even creaking or grating over the focus of its greatest intensity, it was yet so toned down towards the lower margins of the area of rubbing sound, especially at and below the ensiform cartilage, that a double friction murmur was audible there, when a loud double grating noise was heard over the right ventricle. In some of the cases also, when a creaking, or grating, or rasping sound prevailed with a thrill over the right ventricle, a double friction murmur was audible over the right auricle. Here the stormy noises prevailed over the forcible ventricles, and the soft murmuring sounds over the passive auricle.

The occurrence of a creaking, grating, or harsh friction sound depends on the force with which the heart contracts and presses against the cartilages and sternum, and on the roughness of the lymph-covered rubbing surfaces; the creaking sound being mainly excited by pressure, the grating noise by the roughness of the two surfaces when the one rubs actively upon the other. The friction murmur, on the other hand, is due to the gentle or restrained movements of the heart, and the comparative smoothness of the rubbing surfaces all over the heart, that occur towards the end of the attack. It may also be present in its softest and most murmur-like tones over the comparatively smooth and feeble right auricle, and below the heart over the epigastrium, when the attack is at its height, and is speaking with the greatest harshness and noise over the more vigorous parts of the organ; and when the harsh friction sound is evidently softened and rendered murmur-like during its transmission through the fluid intervening between the seat of active friction, and the comparatively distant surface of the chest over the right auricle or the epigastrium.

I have already given the distinctions between the friction murmur and the valvular murmur when inquiring into the occurrence of the former during the first blush of the affection. The rules that apply to the distinction of the friction murmur during the early period of the attack apply also to its distinction during the later period. These rules have been already given at pages 346-348, but the following is a *résumé* of the more important distinctions between the friction murmur and the valvular murmur :—

The friction murmur is not rhythmical with the natural heart-sounds, but the two sounds are heard side by side; the valve murmur is rhythmical with the natural heart-sounds, and the two sounds are in perfect unison. The friction murmur does not begin with an accent or shock, but is of equal tone throughout; the valvular murmur begins with an accent or shock, the accent or shock of the corresponding first or second sound which serves as the starting-point for the murmur. The friction murmur is greatly intensified, and is often altered in tone on pressure; the valvular murmur is brought nearer to the ear by pressure, but is not altered in tone.

There are certain differences between the early and the late friction murmur, although their characters in the main correspond.

In situation the early and late friction murmurs for the most part correspond, being generally seated over the base or body of the right ventricle. The early friction murmur was situated to the left of the sternum in six cases (6 in 8), in four of which it was also heard over the sternum; and it was present over the sternum alone in two cases (2 in 8). The late friction murmur was audible over the sternum alone in four cases; over that bone and to the left of it in five; to the left of the sternum alone in four; and to the right of the sternum in three cases, including one case in which it was also audible to the left of the sternum. From these figures it would appear that the early friction murmur is always situated over the right ventricle; but that while the late friction murmur is present over the right ventricle in seven-eighths of the cases, it is audible over the right auricle in one-fifth of the cases.

The late friction murmur is smoother and more equal in tone; more prolonged; less rustling and more murmur-like; more alike in tone and intensity during the systole and the diastole; varies less from day to day; and lasts much longer than the early friction murmur. Pressure intensifies both of them and often modifies their tone, but I think that the early friction murmur is more frequently converted by pressure into a true rubbing sound than the late friction murmur.

The complication of a co-existing aortic murmur with the friction murmur is more frequent during the late than the early period of the affection.

THE CHARACTER AND TESTS OF PERICARDIAL FRICTION SOUND.

I shall, before concluding the subject of pericardial friction sound, briefly consider the characteristic nature and tests of that sound, including its character and rhythm; its position and extent; the influence exercised over it by respiration; its variation from day to day in character, intensity, rhythm, position and extent; and finally, the effect upon it of external pressure over the region of the pericardium during pericarditis, or the *pressure test* of friction sound.

Character of the Pericardial Friction Sound.—The friction sound when in full play, and of its usual to-and-fro character, speaks for itself. I have already illustrated, in the preceding pages, the clinical history of the forms and variations, the growth, ripening, and decline of the friction sound. When the friction sound is smooth and soft, almost resembling a murmur, or when a friction murmur is present, the sound no longer declares itself, from its very nature, to be of a rubbing quality, and requires for its distinction that other points shall be considered besides the tone, nature, and to-and-fro quality of the sound. The clinical history and distinguishing characters of the friction murmur during the early advance and the late decline of the attack of pericarditis have been given respectively at pages 345 and 387.

The Rhythm of the Friction Sound.—In a large proportion of my cases it was noticed that when the friction sound was not of its completely developed to-and-fro and rubbing character, that is, during both the advance and the decline of the pericarditis, the healthy sounds of the heart were heard along with the double or single friction sound. The natural sounds of the heart and the friction sounds were never welded or incorporated together, but were each of them heard separately, and, so to speak, side by side. They did not seem to begin or end together; and although they were both sounding at the same time, they yet appeared to be completely separate and apart. They were not, therefore, rhythmical with each other. That the natural heart sounds are in play within the period of the to-and-fro friction sound is evident, for when that sound becomes sufficiently loud and continuous, whether by the natural advance of the disease, or by pressure made from without, the sounds of the heart are overwhelmed, being masked by the predominant rubbing noises.

When the to-and-fro friction sound is loud, harsh, and in full play, the systolic and diastolic sounds being equal in duration—though rarely in loudness, the systolic sound being the louder—each sound seems almost to fill up its respective space, leaving two very short intervals of silence between the two sounds. These two friction sounds never begin with an accent or shock, but they commence, continue, and end as a rule with the same tone throughout. In these respects they differ from the natural heart sounds. The first sound always ends in a shock, followed by a short but definite space between itself and the second sound; and the second sound consists in a short shock, followed by a prolonged space between itself and the first sound. The mitral murmur always begins with a shock or accent, the shock of the first sound, and the murmur fills up the space more or less completely between that shock and the second sound. The diastolic aortic murmur also commences with a shock or accent, the shock of the second sound, and it usually fills up the space but not always completely, between that shock and the first sound. The absence of a commencing shock or accent from the friction sound or friction murmur and the presence of a commencing shock or accent with the valve murmurs distinguish those two classes of sounds from each other.

The first contraction of the ventricles precedes by an appreciable period the flow of blood from them into the great arteries; and after that flow has ceased, the exterior of the heart is still in motion. The play of the surface of the heart against that of the pericardium therefore precedes, accompanies, and follows the natural first sound of the heart, and precedes and accompanies the coinciding valvular murmur if present. The closure of the aortic valve precedes the second sound by the tenth of a revolution of the heart's action. The diastolic frottement therefore both precedes and follows the second sound; and accompanies a diastolic murmur, if present, throughout its whole period. The friction sound being made by the moving exterior of the heart, is in relation to the healthy heart sounds and the valvular murmur, which spring from the interior of the heart, as if it were made, so to speak, by an instrument playing outside the room, while they are made as if by an instrument playing inside the room. The friction sound is therefore a surface noise, working apart from, and often over-riding the healthy heart sounds and the valvular murmurs. The healthy heart sounds and the valvular murmurs are, on the other hand, internal noises made simultaneously and by the same parts, and playing together inseparably and in unison.

When listening to the two sounds, the frictional and the natural heart sounds, playing together but not in concert or unison, I have found it very difficult to say whether the systolic friction sound commenced before the first sound of the heart or not. For the reasons just given, however, and that a considerable space of time intervenes between the beginning of the systole and its final shock, amounting to about two-fifths of the healthy revolution of the heart's action, it is evident that the commencement of the systolic friction sound must precede the final shock of the first sound. In one case I heard a short brush at the beginning of the systole, and this no doubt represents the natural beginning of the prolonged systolic friction sound. As a rule the systolic friction sound is of equal tone throughout, whether it is creaking, grating, rubbing, or rustling; but in one instance that sound became suddenly less loud about the middle of its course, and remained so to the end of the systole, the second half of the sound being weaker than its first half.

In one instance a systolic brush, excited by pressure, occupied the latter two-thirds of the systole; in another a systolic whiff, excited by pressure, extended into the diastolic period; and in a third, a double brush was excited by pressure, the systolic being the longer, and each brush occupied a part of the systole and a part of the diastole. I state these signs as I heard them, but cannot account for them.

The diastolic friction sound presents much greater variety in character and rhythm than the systolic friction sound. While the systolic sound is usually continuous through the whole of its proper period, the diastolic friction sound is often of short duration; when it is, I believe, usually present about the beginning of the diastole, and when it accompanies but is separate from the natural second sound : in one instance, however, the natural second sound was followed by a diastolic graze. Sometimes there was a double graze or rub during the diastole; when the entire friction sound resembled the noise made by sharpening a scythe, having one forward or systolic, and two backward or diastolic strokes. When the friction sound was to-and-fro, the second sound appeared generally to be equal in duration, but not in loudness, to the first. When a creaking sound was present it was mostly limited to the systole : this was not so, however, with the grating noise, which was usually a double sound.

The diastolic sound was usually equal in intensity and length to the systolic over the right auricle, both sounds being in all but one instance soft in character. This double soft to-and-fro sound over the right auricle was evidently transmitted, softened during its transit, from the loud speaking right ventricle, through the fluid, to the cartilages in front of the right auricle.

The diastolic friction sound was often absent, and, relatively to the systolic friction sound, was always short and feeble over the apex. In more than one instance, in adults, the diastolic friction sound at the apex appeared to have in it a peculiar twist.

Respiration exercised in many of my cases a definite and speaking influence upon the area, and in a few of them upon the intensity of the friction sound. The friction sound became more loud or harsh in three cases during expiration, and in four during inspiration; and in one the frottement disappeared at the end of a deep breath.

The area of the friction sound increased below during inspiration in a large number of cases, or thirty-one, while in a much smaller number of instances, or eight, it increased above during expiration.

The Friction Sound varied in character, intensity, rhythm, and position from day to day. The clinical history contained in the previous pages of the friction sounds during pericarditis is pervaded throughout with instances of the great daily variability of the friction sound in all its relations. This changing condition of the friction sound during the successive phases of the disease is one of the important characteristic features of that sound. This feature has been already abundantly illustrated.

Position and Extent of the Pericardial Friction Sound.—Dr. Stokes[1] in 1834 stated that the friction sounds in pericarditis are audible generally only over the region of the heart. I stated independently, in 1843, that I had never heard the friction sounds beyond the region of the heart.[2] We have seen in the previous pages that during the advance of the effusion, and usually during its acme, the friction sound is limited to the region of the heart, but that in certain cases with a thrill, the friction sounds spread during the acme from the seat of the thrill as from a focus, in all directions, over the front of the chest, and especially downwards.

During the period of the decline of the effusion, the friction sound, as we have seen, also often extends beyond the region of the heart, over the front of the chest, and especially downwards to the seventh and eighth, and even the ninth cartilages (see pp. 376, 380). The various changes in the area of the friction sound are given in the previous pages, and to those I refer for the more extended study of this subject.

The position, limitation, and extension of the pericardial friction sound supply characteristic differences between pericardial friction sounds and endocardial murmurs.

The Effect of Pressure with the Stethoscope *over the region of the Pericardium during Pericarditis on the Friction Sound ; or the* Pressure Test *of Pericarditis.*—I called attention in 1843, in my paper on the

---

[1] Dublin Journal, iv. 60.
[2] Situation of the Internal Organs. Prov. Med. Trans., xii. 52.

situation of the internal organs,[1] to the effect of pressure made with the stethoscope over the region of the pericardium in rheumatic pericarditis, in intensifying or even bringing into play a pericardial friction sound. Since then Dr. Walshe—who, in the *British and Foreign Medical Review*, very kindly reviewed my paper just referred to, soon after its publication, and Dr. Stokes, independently observed this sign. This effect of pressure is thus spoken of by Friedrich. " Sehr brauchbar is das von Sibson, Walshe, und Stokes, angegebene Zeichen, das nämlich Reibungs geräusche bei Druck mit dem stethoskop stärker werden, was allerdings Endocardiale Geräusche nicht thun."[2]

The pressure test shows itself in two ways, (I.), when pressure over the region of the heart elicits a friction sound that was previously absent; and the other, (II.), when pressure made over the seat of a friction sound intensifies, changes, or modifies that sound.

I. *Influence of Pressure over the region of the Heart in exciting a Friction Sound not previously audible* (see Table I. at p. 328).—Pressure made with the stethoscope over the region of the heart elicited a friction sound not otherwise audible in twenty-nine of the forty-four cases that are included in the tables of cases of pericarditis given at pages 313—327, and in the special Table at page 328, in all of which cases the acme of the pericardial effusion was observed. As might be expected, it was usually (1) during the period of the commencement of the attack or (2) that of its decline that this sign was observed; and a friction sound otherwise latent was also thus brought into play by pressure (3) at the time of the acme of the effusion in four patients whose cases have already been touched upon at page 359, and in one case during a second acme of the effusion.

1. *Friction Sound excited by Pressure during the onset and early period of the attack of Pericarditis.*—In eight cases, as has just been stated, the attack of pericarditis first declared itself by a friction sound induced by pressure over the region of the heart. As a rule this sound, so awakened, was smooth in character. In three instances it appeared as a single or double friction murmur, in one as a whiff, and in one as a soft to-and-fro sound. In the other three cases, however, the rubbing sound was more marked, being harsh and systolic in one, of a winnowing character in another, and creaking, in the third of those cases. In three of these eight cases, pressure was required to bring out the friction sound over the right ventricle during the advance of the effusion. The friction sound was excited by pressure made, in six cases over the sternum, in one over the fourth cartilage, and in one over the heart. As a rule the spontaneous friction sound partook somewhat of the character of the friction sound previously generated by pressure. Thus it was creaking in the case in which it was originally creaking; harsh in one of those (23) in which it was harsh; to-and-fro in that in which it was to-and-fro (56), rather smooth in the patient (28) with a systolic friction murmur; and a double friction murmur

---

[1] Prov. Med. Trans., xii. 540.
[2] Friedrich, Die Krankheiten des Herzens, page 229.

prevailed through the long history of the fatal case (49), in which a double friction murmur was originally aroused by pressure.

The acme of the pericardial effusion usually occurred in these cases very soon after the first appearance of the excited friction sound, or from the first to the third day, in six of the eight cases.

2. The four cases in which a friction sound, otherwise absent, was elicited by pressure during the acme of the disease have been already considered under their proper heading at page 359.

3. *Friction sound excited by Pressure during the decline of the effusion into the pericardium; and during the dying away of the attack.*—In the great majority of the cases in which pressure was required to elicit the friction sound during the period of the decline of the pericardial effusion, this sign was a prelude to the dying away of the friction sound. Thus in nineteen of the twenty-four cases that belong to this class the frottement never again appeared as an independent sound; and the attack of pericarditis was coming to an end. In three of the cases the friction sound, after being for a time only audible when excited by pressure, reappeared for from five to ten days as an independent to-and-fro sound. There was a complete suspension of the friction sound in connection with extreme general illness in two of these cases (45), and the return of the spontaneous friction sound was in both of them associated with improvement of health, and was preceded by the appearance of a pressure friction sound.

The friction sound became inaudible except on pressure in nearly one-half of the cases under examination during the first four days after the acme of pericardial effusion (11 in 24); and in more than one-half of them this sign came into play from five to twenty-one days after the occurrence of the acme (13 in 24).

The character of the spontaneous friction sound last observed before the pressure friction sound was called forth was, with few exceptions, decidedly of a subdued tone.

The lower two-thirds of the sternum was the favourite seat of the pressure friction sound which was heard in eleven of the cases over that bone, including two in which it was heard over the ensiform cartilage. In seven of the cases the rubbing sound was excited by pressure over the cartilages from the third to the fifth, in one other instance over the second space, and in one over the fourth space. Besides these cases the pressure friction sound was heard over the heart in one case, the right ventricle in three, and the apex in three.

II. *Influence of Pressure over the Region of the Heart in intensifying a Friction Sound already present* (see Table II. page 328).—Pressure exercised a marked influence on the friction sound in all but one of the forty-four cases under inquiry, and in that single exception there is no mention of the employment of pressure over the region of the heart during the attack of pericarditis. Pressure, therefore, as a means of diagnosis, and of illustrating the clinical conditions of the friction sound in pericarditis, is essentially interwoven into every part of what has gone before in relation to friction sound in that affection;

and one part has been devoted to the study of cases in which a soft friction sound audible over the heart at the time of the acme of the effusion into the pericardium, was converted by pressure into a harsh rubbing noise (see page 359). It is not, therefore, needful to give here again in a detached form what has already appeared distributed naturally through the preceding pages.

In four instances or observations, an endocardial murmur was masked on pressure by the occurrence of a friction murmur or friction sound. A friction murmur was modified by pressure in fifteen instances: a systolic murmur being intensified (in 3), rendered double (in 1), or transformed into a double friction sound (in 1), by the employment of pressure; and by the same means a double friction murmur was intensified in five and converted into a double friction sound in four instances. In a few instances (3) a friction sound resembling a murmur acquired its complete frictional character by pressure; and in a greater number a systolic friction sound was thus intensified (in 4), or rendered double (in 5). An ordinary friction sound usually double, sometimes soft or grazing (in 18), sometimes of the usual to-and-fro character (in 38), sometimes harsh (in 18), was intensified, or altered in tone, or rendered more harsh in seventy-four instances or observations. As a rule a succession of observations was made upon each case, and the same patient often reappears again and again under the varying phases of the friction sound, and of the influence of pressure upon that sound.

I have not, as a rule, illustrated in this summary the various transformations that the friction sound may undergo under the touch of pressure; but those two remarkable noises, the grating and the creaking friction noises, have been separately analysed, and all the instances in which either of those sounds replaced another character of friction sound, or was strengthened by pressure, are given in the summary at page 328, and in this place.

INFLUENCE OF PRESSURE IN INTENSIFYING A PERICARDIAL FRICTION SOUND.—*Continued from* p. 328.

Friction Sound rendered Creaking by Pressure.

Friction sound rendered almost creaking by pressure.	Systolic friction sound rendered almost creaking by pressure, 31, acme, 3rd space. Soft double friction sound (bellows murmur) almost creaking on pressure, 26, acme. Double friction sound rendered almost creaking by pressure, 6, acme, 3rd space, 40, acme, 39, after acme, 123, acme?
Friction sound rendered creaking by pressure.	Systolic friction murmur rendered creaking by pressure (diastolic rub), 33, acme, 4th cart. 33, 3 days later. Musical friction sound, changed to creak on pressure, 30, acme, 3rd space, (30, 2 days later, systolic creak produced by pressure). Friction sound like sand-paper rubbing, creaking on pressure, 30, after acme, 22, acme? double friction sound. Grating sound changed to creaking by pressure, 45, after acme. Harsh double brush, replaced by double creak on pressure, 30, before acme. Friction sound rendered creaking by pressure, 33, after 2nd acme, 33, ditto, 44, second acme.
Creaking friction sound increased by pressure.	To and fro sound partly creaking, increased by pressure, 40, after acme. Creaking systolic friction sound, increased by pressure, 34, acme, 42, acme, 42, after acme. Systolic creaking friction sound, double creak on pressure, 7, acme, 4th space, 122, acme?

A friction sound of indefinite quality was rendered grating by pressure in six instances, and in two a grating friction sound was intensified or rendered more harsh by pressure. A creaking friction sound was in an especial manner the offspring of pressure when applied over the seat of an ordinary friction sound, since in six instances a friction sound, double in all but one, was rendered almost creaking by pressure, and in twelve instances, various kinds of friction noise, grating, harsh, smooth, and murmuring, were transformed by pressure into a creaking sound; while in two others, pressure converted a systolic creaking sound into a double creaking sound. These eighteen instances occurred in fourteen different cases. In each of two of these patients a creaking sound was excited by pressure four different times in the course of the clinical history of the case; showing a strong tendency to the repeated recurrence of this sign when it has been once excited. In six cases a creaking friction sound was rendered more intense by pressure, and only one of these cases appears also among those just spoken of in which an ordinary friction sound was converted by pressure into a creaking sound.

Although I have only noticed in the summary those two more striking noises, the grating and the creaking, as being excited by pressure, yet there are many other friction sounds of a definitely individual character that are thus brought into existence. These sounds differ in no essential respect from those that are spontaneously excited from within by the simple rubbing of the heart against the pericardium, when their opposing surfaces are covered with roughened lymph. Pressure over the heart affected with pericarditis excited—either originally or by transformation, among my various cases—a single and a double friction murmur; a whiff; a single, and more often a double brush; rustling, grazing, scraping, scratching, and sawing friction sounds; a double sound like that made by rubbing with sand-paper; and a peculiar double sound, broken during the diastole, that brings to my ear a noise like that made by sharpening a scythe. A to-and-fro sound was not unfrequently excited by pressure. I again and again noticed that under the influence of pressure the two friction sounds, and especially the diastolic one, became more continuous.

Owing to the increased intensity and continuousness of the friction sound caused by pressure over the heart in pericarditis, the natural sounds of the heart which were previously audible side by side with the friction sound, but were not strictly rhythmical with it, were frequently silenced under the influence of pressure.

The Movements of Respiration in Pericarditis.

In the Cases included in the following Table the movements of respiration were observed with the aid of the chest measurer.

TABLE SHOWING THE MOVEMENTS OF RESPIRATION IN PERICARDITIS.

I.—CASES IN WHICH THE RESPIRATORY MOVEMENTS OF BOTH THE CHEST AND THE ABDOMEN WERE OBSERVED.

* EXPLANATION.—These figures indicate the movements of respiration in hundredths of an inch. For explanation of Symbols, see page 226.

15 (See p. 326). Female, æt. 16. ➨

	Rib.	*Rt.*	*Lft.*		*Rib.*	*Rt.*	*Lft.*		*Rib.*	*Rt.*	*Lft.*
1st day. Friction whiff on pressure, pain left side.	2nd	15°	8.°	4th day. Acme of pericardial effusion.	2nd	25°	15.°	5th day. Pain in epigastrium.	2nd	9°	12.°
	5th	5	2.		6th	6	5.		6th	3	3.
	9th	9	7.		9th	14	6.		9th	5	5.
	abdom.	5	9.		abdom.	6	5.		abdm.	3	3.
	abd. below ens. cartil. } −10.				abd. below ens. cartil. } −8.				abd. below ens. cartil. } −6.		

	Rib.	*Rt.*	*Lft.*		*Rib.*	*Rt.*	*Lft.*			
7th day. Better, pericardial effusion less.	2nd	15	12.	19th day. No friction sound, better.	2nd	9	7.	20th day. {	abd. below ensiform cartil.	10.
	5th	6	5.		6th	3	2.		abd. at navel	15.
	9th	9	7.		abd. below ens. cartil. } −4.					
	abdom. −10	3.			abdomen at navel	7.				
	abd below ens. cartil. } −3.									

36 (See p. 316). Female, æt. 20. ➨

	Rib.	*Rt.*	*Lft.*		*Rib.*	*Rt.*	*Lft.*		*Rib.*	*Rt.*	*Lft.*
9th day. Acme of pericardial effusion, less pain heart, resp. 52.	2nd	5	4.	10th day. Resp. 48.	2nd	5	4.	12th day. Feels better, Resp. 50.	2nd	18	12.
	5th	2	2.		6th	1	1.		6th	5	3.
	6th	3	3.		7th	7	3.		abdm.	3	2.
	9th	7	5.		9th	7	4.		abd. below ens. cartil. } 0.		
	abdm.	6	0.		abdm.	4	4.		abd. at navel 0.		
	abd. below ens. cartil. } −3.				bel. ens. car. −6.						
					abd. at navel 7.						

	Rib.	*Rt.*	*Lft.*		*Rib.*	*Rt.*	*Lft.*		*Rib.*	*Rt.*	*Lft.*
15th day. Friction sound more limited; feels better.	2nd	15	15.	18th day. Lying on right side, friction sound on pressure.	2nd	14	12.	21st day. Better, aspect good, resp. 30, no friction sound.	2nd	12-20	10-15
	6th	4	3.		6th	7	4.		6th	5	?
	9th	12	8.		9th	10	7.		9th	10	
	abd. below ens. cartil. } 0.				abdm.	3	5.		abdm.	3	10.
	abd. at navel 5.				abd. below ens. cartil. } 0.				abd. below ens. cartil. } 4.		
					abd. at navel 4.				do. deep breath 20		
									abd. at navel 5.		

22nd day. Weak.	below ens. cartil. } 5.		
	ditto, deep breath, } 25.		

33rd day.—Below ensiform cartilage, deep breath, 50.

27th day.—Below ensiform cartilage, deep breath, 90.

5 (See p. 324). Female, æt. 15. ➡

	Rib.	*Rt.*	*Lft.*		*Rib.*	*Rt.*	*Lft.*		*Rib.*	*Rt.*	*Lft.*
1st day. Pn. lft. side, ill a week. No friction sound.	2nd	20	15-20.	8th day. Acme, resp. 54, pain side.	6th	3	3.	12th day. Better, but resp. 55, no friction sound.	2nd	18	15.
	6th	6	3.		9th	9	4.		6th	6	3.
	9th	4	7.		abd. below ens. cartil. } −1.				9th	9	2.
	abd.	6	6.						abd.	1	−3.
									abd. b. ens. c. −2.		

4 (See p. 313.) Male, æt. 27. ➨

	Rib.	*Rt.*	*Lft.*		*Rib.*	*Rt.*	*Lft.*		*Rib.*	*Rt.*	*Lft.*
2nd day. Acme, very ill, resp. 36.	2nd	7-9	7-10.	3rd day. Better.	2nd	6	7.	7th day.	2nd	6	7.
	6th	4	4.		6th	6	3.		6th	4	2.
	1th	9	5.		9th	9.			9th	4	7.
	abd.	7	12.		abd. below ens. cartil. } 12.				abd. at navel 20.		

18 (See p. 323). Female, æt. 18. →

	Rib.	*Rt.*	*Lft.*
5th day.	2nd	30	20.
Acme,	6th	7	6.
pain over	9th	10	10.
heart.	abd. below		
	ens. cartil. } − 2.		
24th day.—Slight friction sound.			

	Rib.	*Rt.*	*Lft.*
8th day.	2nd	30	20.
Pain in	6th	6	5.
chest,	9th	15	7.
friction	abdm. − 8		−2.
sound.	abd. below		
	ens. cartil. } −4.		
	abd. at navel		0.

	Rib.	*Rt.*	*Lf*
11th day.	2nd	30	20.
Acme.	6th	6	3.
	9th	10	7.
	abd.	6	3.
	abd. below		
	ens. cartil. } −4.		
	abd. at navel		0.

19 (See p. 326.) Male, æt. 23. ↓↓

	Rib.	*Rt.*	*Lft.*
7th day.			
3 days af-	2nd	20	20.
ter acme,	6th	6	5.
very ex-	9th	5	7.
tensive			
friction			
sound.			

	Rib.	*Rt.*	*Lft.*
10th day.	2nd	25	20.
Improv-	6th	9	10.
ing, less	9th	13	10.
friction	abdm. 12		5.
sound;	abd. below		
left	ens. cartil. } . 1.		
pleurisy.			

	Rib.	*Rt.*	*Lft.*
13th day.	2nd	20	20.
Better,	6th	6	4.
very slight	9th	13	12.
friction	abdm.	6	10.
sound.	ab. b. ens. c.		2.
	abd. at navel		6.

26 (See p. 324). Male, æt. 25. →

	Rib.	*Rt.*	*Lft.*
6th day.	2nd	20	20.
Acme,	4th	16	10.
lessening	7th	9	10.
pain over	9th	9	10.
heart.			

	Rib.	*Rt.*	*Lft.*
	2nd	8	7.
10th day.	6th	16	8.
Resp. 22,	10th	9	9.
better,	abdm. 25		20.
friction	abd. below		
sound.	ens. cartil. } . 20.		
	abd. at navel		40.

	Rib.	*Rt.*	*Lft.*
13th day.	2nd	15	15.
better, sits	6th	10	10.
up in bed,	abdm. 30		35.
friction	abd. below		
sound on	ens. cartil. } 30.		
pressure.	abd. at navel		40.

49 (See p. 327). Male, æt. 17. ↓↓

	Rib.	*Rt.*	*Lft.*
8th day	7th	10	6.
before	abdm. 12		7.
acme pain			
in heart.			

12th day. Acme. } —abdomen below ensiform cartilage, −7.

II.—CASES IN WHICH THE RESPIRATORY MOVEMENTS OF THE CENTRE OF THE ABDOMEN WERE OBSERVED.

A.—*Cases observed*—(1) *below the Ensiform Cartilage, and* (2) *at the Navel.*

			Below ens. cartil.	at navel
25 (See p. 327). Male, æt. 17. ↓↓	12th day, second acme		−3,	4.
	21st day, no friction sound ...	,, ,,	*0	*12.
	35th day	,, ,,	18	20.
34 (See p. 316). Male, æt. 15. →↓↓	4th day, acme, pain epigast.	,, ,,	6	10.
	5th day, after acme	,, ,,	5	,,
	6th day, ,, ,,	,, ,,	4	,,
14 (See p. 315). Fem., æt. 17. →	2nd day, acme ?	,, ,,	0	10.
	1st day, acme	,, ,,	1	12.
40 (See p. 313). Male, æt. 17. →	7th day, after acme	,, ,,	5	,,
	15th day, friction sound ...	,, ,,	3	12.

B.—*Cases observed below Ensiform Cartilage.*

		Movement below ens. cartil.
51 (See p. 315). Male, æt. 22. →	4th day, acme	−2.
	7th day, decline of fld.	,, 6.
	9th day, second acme	,, 9.
	29th day, well. Deep breath	,, 110−170.
35 (See p. 327) Fem., æt. 21. ↷→	5th day, after acme	,, −2.
	11th day, improving	,, 3.
	32nd day, clothes on. Deep breath	,, 50.
56 (See p. 324.) Male, æt. 15. ↓↓	1st day before acme	,, 16.
	3rd day, acme	,, 6.
	11th day, well	,, 20.
36 (See p. 325). Fem., æt. 22 →	18th day, second acme ...	,, −2.
	22nd day, 3rd acme	,, 0.
28 (See p. 316). Fem., æt. 19. →	9th day, after acme	,, 1.
	11th day	,, −7.
30 (See p. 321). Fem., æt. 24. →	17th day, acme	,, −3.
	25th day	,, 17.
44a (See p. 323). Male, æt. 14. →	6th day, after first acme ...	,, 3.
13 (See p 314). Fem., æt. 25. →→	4th day, acme, or after ...	Mvt. bel. ens. cartil. or lower, 4.
58 See p. 323). Male, æt. 26. ↶→	5th day before friction sound ...	Movement below ens. cartil. 5.
54 (See p 320). Male, æt. 35. ↓↓	8th day, no friction sound ...	,, ,, 20.

The movements of respiration were affected in pericarditis in three different relations; (1) those of the ribs; (2) those of the abdomen on each side, just below the eighth cartilage; and (3) those of the centre of the abdomen.

(1.) The respiratory play of the upper ribs was more than doubled in extent in three-fourths of the cases observed (5 in 7), so that respiration was as a rule high.   This was due to the arrest or restraint of the action of the diaphragm caused by the extensive inflammation of the central tendon of the diaphragm, where it forms the floor of the pericardium.

In one (4) of the two exceptional cases, the movements of the second ribs were not at all or only slightly augmented throughout the whole period of the illness; but in the other case, in which the respiration was greatly accelerated, the action of those ribs, which was slight during the acme of the affection, was much increased during the decline of the effusion.

' The respiratory movement of the ribs on the left side of the chest was less than that of those on its right side, as might naturally be expected, in more than one-half of the cases (5 in 8); but in the remaining three patients the action of the two sides was nearly equal both during the acme and the decline of the pericarditis. The difference in the movement of the two sides of the chest was not, as a rule, limited to the ribs adjoining the pericardium, but extended along their whole range, from the second to the ninth. The study of the Table will show, however, that there were some exceptions to the rule that the play of the ribs was restrained throughout on the left side; since in two of the three cases in which the two sides of the chest moved with equal freedom, the ninth left rib was greatly restrained in its movements.

(2.) The lateral movements of the abdomen below the eighth cartilages were greatly restrained in three-fourths of the cases (6 in 8); and the respiratory play of the left side of the abdomen was much less than that of its right side in the same proportion of cases (6 in 8).

(3.) The inspiratory movement of the abdomen below the ensiform cartilage was either reversed (in 12), arrested (in 1), or restrained (in 6) in every case of pericarditis in which that sign was observed. This is at once accounted for by the inflammation, in that disease, of the central tendon of the diaphragm where it forms the floor of the pericardium, which leads to the virtual paralysis of the central portion of the diaphragm. This fact, that the anterior wall of the epigastric space, instead of advancing, recedes during inspiration, gives us a physical sign of great value in the diagnosis of pericarditis, and of the advance and decline of that disease. Thus in the first case in the Table (15), a girl, aged 16, the anterior wall of the abdomen below the ensiform cartilage fell backwards during inspiration for the tenth of an inch during the three early days, when the disease was at its acme; then, as the tide turned and the effusion diminished, the abdomen receded less and less up to the seventh day, when it did so for only the fiftieth of an inch ; after this it regained its natural forward movement, and on the twenty-sixth day the abdomen at the epigastric space advanced as much (the tenth of an inch) as it had receded on the day of admission. In the other case (56), the front of the abdomen advanced the sixth of an inch on the day of admission, when the pericarditis had scarcely pronounced itself; the sixteenth of an inch on the third day, when it had reached its acme ; and the fifth of an inch on the eleventh day, when it had declined and disappeared. In my paper on the movements of respiration I showed that in health the abdomen at the navel advanced during inspiration a quarter of an inch or a little more, but I did not ascertain the respiratory movement at the epigastric space. A short time ago I observed, with Mr. Rossiter, the respiratory movements of the abdomen in eleven patients in St. Thomas's Hospital, several of whom were convalescent, and one had pericarditis ; when we found that the inspiratory advance at the epigastric space varied from the sixth to the fifth of an inch. The latter was also the extent of the advance in two healthy men. I consider that this forward movement fairly represents the healthy respiratory play of the part in question ; that in pericarditis, as a rule, the whole of this advance is lost ; and that in addition the play is reversed to the extent of from the fiftieth to the tenth of an inch. It is worth noting, in conclusion, that in the case of pericarditis observed by Mr. Rossiter and myself in St. Thomas's Hospital, a boy, aged 12, in whom the disease was at its height, the wall of the abdomen receded during inspiration at the epigastric space from the sixteenth to the twentieth of an inch, and at the navel from the thirty-fifth to the fiftieth of an inch.

CONDITION OF KIDNEY.	CONDITION OF HEART.	Total Number.	Percentage to total number of cases in this class	Age.—Below 10 yrs.	Age.—10 yrs. to 20 yrs.	Age.—Above 20 yrs.	Male Patients.	Female Patients.	Fatal(?)	
Acute Bright's Disease following Scarlet Fever	Heart of natural size	2	40%	2	...	...	2	...	1	—
	Ditto with partial Pericarditis	1	50	1	...	...	1	...	1	—
	Heart rather large	1	20	1	...	...	...	1	1	—
	Heart large or very large	2	40	1	1	...	...	2	1	—
	Size of heart not described	1	16·6	...	1	...	...	1		—
Ditto. TOTAL		6	2·1%	4	2	...	2	4	3	—
Ditto with partial Pericarditis . . .		1	16·6	66·6% av. age 10·5	33·3% av. age 23	...	33·3%	66·6%	50%	—
Acute Bright's Disease	Heart of natural size	2	14·3%	1	1	...	1	1	...	—
	Heart rather large	4	28·6	...	2	2	1	3	...	—
	Heart large or very large, hyptrd.	8	57·1	...	4	4	7	1	1	—
	Ditto with general Pericarditis.	2	25	...	1	...	2	...	1	—
	Size of heart not described . .	1	6·6	...	...	1	1	...	...	—
TOTAL with Acute Bright's Disease		15	5·3%	1	7	7	10	5	1	2
Ditto with general Pericarditis		2	13·3	6·6% av. age 15	46·6% av. age 20·6	46·6% av. age 51	66·6%	33·3%	6 4/5%	13
Fatty Kidney . .	Heart small	14	25%	...	4	7	5	8	2	8
	Ditto with partial Pericarditis .	1	7·2	...	...	1	...	1	...	1
	Heart of natural size .	18	32	1	4	11	15	3	6	12
	Ditto with partial Pericarditis .	1	6	...	...	1	1	1	...	1
	Heart rather large	10	18	...	...	9	7	3	5	6
	Ditto with partial Pericarditis .	1	10	...	...	1	1	3	...	1
	Heart very large, hypertrophd.	14	25	1	3	9	14	...	2	12
	Size of heart not described .	6	9·6	...	1	3	3	3	1	1
	Ditto with general Pericarditis	1	16·6	...	...	1	1	...	...	1
	Ditto with partial Pericarditis.	2	33·3	...	1	...	...	2	1	1
TOTAL		62	21·7%	2	12	39	44	17	16	19
Ditto with general Pericarditis		1	1·6	3·7%	22·6%	73·6%	72%	28%	26%	30%
Ditto with partial Pericarditis		5	8·0	...	av. age 25	av. age 45	...	...	...	—
Granular Kidney. Kidney lessened in size	Heart small	4	3·5%	...	...	3	2	2	4	...
	Heart of natural size	24	20·5	...	5	18	10	13	5	2
	Ditto with general Pericarditis	5	20·8	...	2	3	3	2	1	1
	Ditto with partial Pericarditis .	2	8	...	1	1	...	1	1	1
	Heart rather large	20	17	...	4	16	10	10	2	1
	Ditto with partial Pericarditis	1	5	...	...	1	...	1	...	...
	Heart very large, hypertrophd.	69	59	...	8	55	48	21	16	9
	Ditto with general Pericarditis.	5	7·2	...	1	2	4	1	3	...
	Ditto with partial Pericarditis.	3	4·3	...	...	3	2	1	3	1
	Size of heart not described .	11	8·6	...	2	7	7	2	3	...
	Ditto with general Pericarditis .	3	27·2	...	2	...	1	2	...	...
	Ditto with partial Pericarditis.	1	9	...	...	1	1	...	...	...
TOTAL		128	45%	...	19	99	77	49	30	13
Ditto with general Pericarditis		13	10·1	...	16%	84%	51%	39%	28·4%	10%
Ditto with partial Pericarditis		7	5·5	...	av. age 26	av. age 51	...	...	...	—
Granular Kidney, Kidney of natural size, and larger than natural.	Heart of natural size . . .	8	16·6%	...	...	8	3	2	1	...
	Heart rather large, hypertrop.	4	13·3	...	...	3	3	2	2	...
	Ditto with general Pericarditis.	1	25	...	...	1	...	1	1	2
	Heart very large	21	70	...	3	16	6	3	2	—
	Ditto with general Pericarditis.	1	4·8	...	...	1	1	2	...	—
	Size of heart not described .	4	11·7	...	1	3	2	2	...	—
	Ditto with general Pericarditis.	1	...	...	...	...	1	...	...	—
TOTAL		84	12%	...	4	25	24	9	5	2
Ditto with general Pericarditis		3	8·8	...	14% av. age 28	86% av. age 46·3	72·7%	27·2%	14·7%	6%
Granular Kidney—GRAND TOTAL		162	57%	...	23 16%	194 84%	101 63·5%	58 36·5%	35 21·9%	15

Pleuro-pneumonia	Pulmonary Apoplexy	Pleuro-pulmonary Apoplexy	Purulent deposit or abscess in lung	Total attacks of inflam. of lungs (including Pulm. Apoplexy & Pleurisy)	Total cases with inflam. of lungs or pleura	Phthisis	General Pericarditis (Pus in pericardium included in General Pericarditis)	Partial Pericarditis	Adherent Pericardium	General Pericarditis	Total cases of Disease of Valve with incompetence	Total cases of Thickening of Valve, the Valve being competent	Atheroma or Dilatation of Aorta	Disease of Coronary Artery	Total cases with Affect. of Valves, with and without valvular incompetence, or with adherent pericardium	Cases with emaciation, great weakness, or exhausting disease?	Cases in good bodily condition
...	...	...	...	1	1	...	...	1	...	1	...	...	...	...	...	1	...
...	...	...	...	1	1	...	...	...	...	1	...	...	...	...	...	...	...
...	...	...	...	1	1	...	...	...	...	1	...	...	...	...	...	...	...
...	...	...	...	...	...	...	...	...	...	...	...	...	...	...	...	...	...
...	...	...	...	3 50%	3 50%	...	...	1 16·6%	...	33·3% 2	...	...	...	...	...	1	...
...	...	...	...	1	1	1	...	...	...	...	...	...	...	...	...	1	3
1	1	...	...	4	3	...	...	2	...	3	5	1	...	...	6	1	5
1	...	...	...	3	2	...	...	...	...	...	1	...	...	...	1	1	2
...	...	...	...	...	...	...	...	...	...	...	...	1	1	...	1	1	...
1 6·6%	2 13·3%	...	...	5 33·3%	4 26·6%	1 6·6%	2 13·3%	...	3 20%	...	5 33·3%	2 13·3%	1 6·6%	...	7 46·6%	3 27·2%	8 72·7%
...	...	...	...	4	4	7	...	1	...	1	...	3	...	...	3	12	1
4	1	...	2	16	12	1	...	1	...	...	1	1	...	...	4	9	2
2	1	1	1	9	7	2	...	1	...	...	2	4	2	...	6	2	4
2	3	...	1	8	6	...	...	...	5	1	6	3	2	...	12	1	4
...	...	...	1	4	3	...	1	2	1	...	2	1	1	...	3	1	...
...	...	...	...	1	1	...	...	...	...	...	...	...	...	...	...	...	...
...	...	...	2	...	...	...	...	...	...	...	...	...	...	...	...	...	...
8 12%	5 8%	1 1·6%	4 6·5%	41 66%	32 51·6%	10 16%	1 1·6%	5 8%	6 9·6%	2 3·4%	11 17·7%	12 19·4%	5 8%	...	28 45%	25 70%	11 30%
2	...	1	...	4	4	3	...	...	2	3	2	1	3	...	1	4	...
1	2	...	...	9	6	4	5	2	...	1	3	3	3	...	8	11	2
1	...	...	...	2	1	...	...	...	1	1	...	...	...	...	...	3	1
...	1	...	...	1	3	...	...	1	...	1	3	4	1	...	7	7	5
4	10	6	...	35	24	1	5	3	3	...	27	9	13	...	46	21	22
1	2	1	...	4	3	...	...	...	...	2	...	1	1	...	1	2	3
1	1	...	...	3	4	1	3	1	...	2	2	1	1	...	3	6	2
1	...	...	...	3	2	...	...	...	...	...	...	...	...	...	4	...	3
8 6·5%	14 11%	7 5·5%	...	57 44·5%	41 32·6%	10 7·9%	13 10%	7 5·5%	3 2·3%	6 4·7%	34 26·5%	18 14%	17 13·2%	...	66 51·5%	49 60%	32 40%
...	1	...	1	2	2	1	...	...	...	2	1	2	1	1	3	2	1
...	...	...	...	3	3	...	1	...	...	...	1	...	1	...	1	...	...
...	4	1	...	9	8	...	1	...	2	...	11	4	6	...	16	2	9
...	...	...	...	...	...	...	1	...	...	2	1	...	...	...	3	...	...
...	...	...	...	...	...	1	...	1	...	...	...	...	...	...	...	...	...
...	5 14·7%	1 3%	1 3%	14 41%	13 38·2%	1 3%	3 9%	...	3 9%	2 6%	14 41%	7 20·6%	7 20·6%	1 3%	23 64·7%	7 40%	10 60%
8 5%	19 11·7%	8 5%	1 ·6%	71 42·2%	54 32·6%	11 6·7%	16 9·9%	7 4·2%	6 3·7%	8 5%	48 29·6%	25 15·6%	24 14·6%	1 ·6%	88 54·3%	56 57%	42 43%

Condition of Kidney.	Condition of Heart.	Total number.	Percentage to total number of cases in this class	Age.	Age—Below 16 yrs.	Age—16 yrs. to 30 yrs.	Age—Above 30 yrs.	Male Patients.	Female Patients.	Pleurisy.	Peritonitis
Cases of actual and probable Lardaceous Disease.	Heart small	5	25%		..	4	1	5	...	...	..
	Heart of natural size	8	40		1	2	4	8	...	2	..
	Heart rather large	3	15		...	1	2	3	...	...	1
	Heart large or very large	4	20		...	...	3	3	1	...	..
	Ditto with general Pericarditis	1	25		...	...	...	1	1	...	..
	Size of heart not described	2	18·2		...	...	...	2	2	...	1
	Ditto with general Pericarditis	1	50		...	...	...	1	1	...	1
TOTAL of actual and probable Lardaceous Disease.		22	7.7%	...	1	7	12	21	1	3	1
Ditto with general Pericarditis		2	9%		5%	35%	60%	95%	5%	14%	14
					10	23·5	42				
1 Kidney large, 1 Atrophd.	Heart prob. of nat. size	1	...	...	...	...	1	1	1	...	..
Embolism of Kidney.	Heart very large	3	...	...	...	1	2	2	1	...	1
Obstr. Congesn. of Kidney.	Heart very large	3	...	...	...	...	3	1	2	1	1
Nature of Kidney, disease doubtful.	Heart of natural size	1	10%	...	...	...	1	1	...	...	..
	Ditto with general Pericarditis	1	...	...	...	...	1	1	...	...	..
	Heart rather large	4	40	...	...	...	4	1	3	...	..
	Ditto with general Pericarditis	2	50	...	...	...	2	1	1	...	..
	Ditto with partial Pericarditis	1	25	...	...	...	1	...	1	...	..
	Heart large or very large	5	50	...	...	...	4	3	2	1	2
	Ditto with general Pericarditis	1	20	...	...	...	1	1	...	1	1
	Ditto with partial Pericarditis	1	20	...	...	...	1	...	...	...	..
	Size of heart not described	1	9	...	...	...	1	...	...	...	..
Ditto. TOTAL		11	3·8%	...	...	...	10	5	5	1	...
Ditto with general Pericarditis		4	36·3	...	...	...	100 %	45%	45%	90%	13·7
Ditto with partial Pericarditis		2	18·1	...	...	av. age	49				
Total cases of Bright's disease; arranged according to the size of the heart.	Heart small	23	9 %	av. age below16 16 to 30 above30 35	...	8	11	12	6	6	2
	Ditto with partial Pericarditis	1	4·3	53	...	...	1	...	1	...	..
	Heart of natural size	61	23·0	37	5	12	37	40	20	15	11
	Ditto with general Pericarditis	6	10	43	...	2	4	4	2	1	1
	Ditto with partial Pericarditis	4	6·6	31	1	...	2	2	2	1	1
	Heart rather large	46	17·4	44	1	7	35	24	21	10	4
	Ditto with general Pericarditis	3	6.6	38	...	...	3	1	2	...	...
	Ditto with partial Pericarditis	3	6·6	56	...	...	3	1	2	1	...
	Heart large or very large, hypd.	120	50	45	2	19	99	94	34	24	19
	Ditto with general Pericarditis	10	8	41	...	2	6	7	2	5	4
	Ditto with partial Pericarditis	4	3·1	54	...	...	4	1	...	1	1
	Size of heart not described	26	10	47	...	5	18	15	11	5	4
	Ditto with general Pericarditis	6	23	58	...	2	2	4	2	3	3
	Ditto with partial Pericarditis	3	11·5	52	...	1	1	2	2	2	1
TOTAL		285	...	43 av. age	8 3%	51 19%	199 78%	185 66%	96 33%	60 22 %	44 14
Ditto with general Pericarditis		25	8·8%	...	...	...	...	16	8	9	8
Ditto with partial Pericarditis		15	5·3	...	...	...	...	6	9	6	2
Calculus in Kidney, &c. ; or dilated pelvis ; Hydronephrosis.[1]	Heart small	1	10 %	...	...	1	...	...	1	...	...
	Heart of natural size	3	30	...	...	2	...	3	...	1	1
	Heart rather large	4	40	...	...	1	2	2	2	1	1
	Heart large	2	20	...	...	...	2	1	1	...	...
	Size of heart not described	2	16·6	...	...	...	2	1	1	...	...
Ditto. TOTAL		12	...	...	...	4 40% av. age 23	6 60% av. age 54	7 60%	5 40%	2 16 0%	2 16·6
Suppurative nephritis from stricture, &c.[2]	Heart small	4	30·7%	...	...	1	2	4	...	...	...
	Heart of natural size	7	54	...	...	3	1	7	...	2	1
	Ditto with general Pericarditis	1	14·3	...	...	...	1	1	...	...	...
	Heart rather large	2	15·3	...	...	...	2	2	...	...	...
Ditto. TOTAL		13	...	...	...	4 44·4% av. age 20·5	5 16·4% av. age 50·8	13 100%	...	2 15 4%	2 15·4
Ditto with general Pericarditis		1	7·7%	...	...						
TOTAL NUMBER OF CASES		310									

[1] Calculus in kidney, pelvis, or ureter (4) : affection of bladder (3) : both affections (1).

	Pulmonary Apoplexy.	Pleuro-pulmonary Apoplexy.	Purulent deposit or abscess in lung.	Attacks of Inflam. of lung (inc. Palm. Apoplexy & Pleurisy)	Cases with Inflam. of lungs or pleura.	Phthisis.	Gen. Pericarditis (Peri in pericd. incl. in Gen. Pericard.)	Partial Pericarditis.	Adher. Pericarditis.	General Peritonitis.	Disease of Valve, with incompetence.	Thickening of Valve; competent Valve.	Atheroma or Dilatation of Aorta.	Dis. of Coron. Artery.	Affect. of Valve, with and without valvular increment or with adherent pericardium.	Dis. Heart & Aorta.	With emaciation, great weakness, or exhausting disease.	Cases in good bodily condition.
1	...	...	1	5	4	3	...	...	...	2	1	1	...	...	1	...	5	...
...	...	...	1	2	2	...	...	...	1	...	1	1	...	...	1	...	2	...
...	...	...	...	2	...	...	1	...	1	1	3	...	...	...	4	...	...	2
2	...	...	...	...	...	...	1	...	1	1	...	...	...	...	...	...	...	...
...	...	...	...	2	1	...	...	...	...	...	...	...	...	...	...	...	...	...
1	...	...	...	...	1	...	...	...	...	...	...	...	...	...	...	...	...	...
2 %/o	...	...	2 9°/o	9 41°/o	7 32°/o	3 14°/o	2 9°/o	2 9°/o	4 18°/o	5 33°/o	2 9°/o	...	...	7 32°/o	...	13 87°/o	2 13°/o	
...	...	...	...	...	1	...	...	...	...	...	...	...	...	...	...	...	...	...
1	...	...	...	3	2	...	...	2	...	3	...	...	...	3	...	2	...	
1	...	...	...	2	2	...	...	...	...	...	...	...	2	...	...	...	...	
...	...	...	...	...	...	...	1	...	...	...	...	...	...	...	...	...	...	...
...	1	...	...	1	1	...	2	1	1	4	...	...	...	4	...	2	...	
...	...	...	...	...	...	...	...	...	...	2	...	...	...	2	...	...	...	
1	1	...	...	4	3	...	1	1	1	1	1	...	...	2	...	2	2	
2	...	...	...	2	1	...	...	...	...	...	...	...	...	...	...	2	0	
...	...	...	...	...	...	...	...	...	...	...	1	...	...	...	...	1	...	
2 %/o	2 18°/o	...	...	5 45·4°/o	4 36·3°/o	...	4 36·3°/o	2 18°/o	1 9°/o	1 9°/o	5 45°/o	1 9°/o	...	...	6 54·5°/o	...	5 72°/c	2 28°/o
...	...	...	...	8	8	10	...	1	3	...	5	...	...	5	...	21	1	
...	...	...	...	1	1	10	...	...	...	...	...	...	...	...	...	...	...	
7	3	1	5	33	25	10	6	4	5	4	4	8	3	13	...	31	5	
1	...	...	2	2	1	...	...	...	1	...	...	...	...	2	...	...	1	
2	5	...	1	21	18	3	3	3	1	5	11	10	4	21	...	14	12	
...	1	...	...	1	1	...	...	...	...	1	1	...	1	2	...	1	...	
0	21	8	1	65	46	1	10	4	17	3	56	19	21	4	92	...	27	43	
3	2	...	...	11	6	...	...	1	...	...	1	...	1	...	2	...	1 or 2	3
2	...	1	...	2	2	...	...	1	...	2	1	1	...	3	...	1	2	
2	1	...	1	11	8	1	6	3	2	2	7	3	2	...	11	...	7	74
2	...	...	...	6	4	...	...	...	...	1	...	...	...	...	...	...	6	3
...	...	...	...	3	2	...	...	...	...	...	...	...	...	...	...	...	...	
1 40°/o	30 10·5°/o	9 3·1°/o	7 2·4°/o	136 48°/o	105 37°/o	25 9°/o	25 9°/o	15 5·20°/o	20 7°/o	19 6·7°/o	78 28°/o	41 14·4°/o	30 10·5°/o	7 2·4°/o	142 50°/o	...	100 60°/o	65 40°/o
6	3	...	...	20	12	...	...	...	1	2	2	...	...	2	...	5 or 6	7	
1	...	1	3	9	8	...	...	...	2	4	...	...	2	...	4	...	3	2
...	...	...	...	...	...	1	...	...	...	...	...	...	...	...	...	1	...	
1	...	...	...	2	1	...	...	...	...	...	...	...	...	...	...	1	...	
1	...	...	...	2	1	1	...	...	...	...	1	1	1	2	...	1	2	
...	...	...	...	...	...	...	...	...	...	...	1	...	1	...	...	...	...	
...	...	...	...	...	...	...	...	...	...	...	...	...	...	...	...	...	...	
2 60°/o	...	...	...	4 33·3°/o	2 16·6°/o	2 16·6°/o	...	...	...	1 8·3°/o	2 16·6°/o	...	8·3°/o	...	3 25°/o	...	3 60°/o	40°/o
...	...	...	...	3	3	2	1	...	...	...	1	1	...	1	...	4	...	
...	...	...	...	...	...	2	...	...	...	...	...	...	...	...	...	7	...	
...	...	...	...	1	1	...	...	...	...	...	...	...	...	...	...	1	...	
...	...	...	...	...	...	...	...	...	...	...	...	...	...	...	...	2	...	
...	...	...	...	4 31°/o	4 31°/o	4 31°/o	1 7·7°/o	...	...	...	1 7·7°/o	1 7·7°/o	...	1 7·7°/o	...	13 100°/o	...	

* Stricture, or affection of prostate or bladder (11) ; pyæmia (1) ; calculus in ureter (1).

COLLECTED CASES.]	Cases.	Pericar- ditis.	Pleurisy.	Perito- nitis.	Pneu- monia	Pulmon. Apoplx.	Partial Pericard.	Pur. dep. in lun...
CASES OBSERVED IN ENGLAND AND SCOTLAND.								
Dr. Bright (*Guy's Hospital Reports*, I.) . .	100	7 or 8	17	12	7	3	---	---
Ditto (*Guy's Hospital Reports*, V.) . .	8	0	1	1	1	...	---	---
Drs. Bright and Barlow (*Guy's Hospital Reports*, second series, I.) . . .	9	2	1	1	0	1	---	---
Dr. Gregory (*Edin. Med. Journ.*, vols. XXXVI., XXXVII.)	39	0	4	5	1	...	---	---
Dr. Christison (*On Granular Degeneration of Kidneys*)	15	0	2	0	1 ?	---	---	---
Dr. Johnson (*Diseases of Kidneys*) . .	11	1	2	2	0	---	---	---
Dr. Wilks (*Guy's Hosp. Rep.* new ser. VIII.)	76	6	12	7	6	---	---	---
Dr. Bashain (*On Dropsy*).	14	0	0	1	0	1	---	---
Dr. Dickinson (*On Albuminuria*) . . .	155	20	20	12	26	---	---	---
Dr. Miller (*Kidneys in Scarlet Fever*) .	10	1	5	2	5	---	---	---
Dr. Taylor (*Med. Chir. Trans.*, vol. XXIII.)	50	5	11	5	12	---	---	---
Dr. Roberts (*Urinary and Renal Disease*) .	8	0	0	0	0	---	---	---
Dr. Grainger Stewart (*Bright's Disease*) .	131	9	19	5	13	---	---	---
Dr. Greenfield (Table contributed to Author) . .	16	3	3	1*	4	1	---	---
The Author (*St. Mary's Hosp. Post-Mortem Records*, 1851–69)	285	{ 25 1 in 11 3; 8·8% }	60 1 in 4·8 21%	19 1 in 15 6·7%	39 { 1 in 6·4 15·5% }	30	14	---
TOTAL	927	80 { 1 in 11·6 : 8·6% }	157 1 in 5·9 17%	73 1 in 12·6 7·9%	115 1 in 8 12·4%	...	...	---
Dr. Chambers (*Decennium Pathologicum*) .	454	{ 36 or 37 1 in 12·5 8% }						
TOTAL	1381	116 { 1 in 11·9 8·4% }						
CASES OBSERVED IN GERMANY.								
Malmsten (*U. Brightsche Nierenkrank- heiten*)	33	3	2	0	3	...	---	---
Frerichs (*U. Brightsche Nierenkrankheiten*)	21	1	1	...	3	...	---	---
Bamberger (*Virchow's Archiv*)	48	8	9	2	11	1	---	---
Traube (various sources)	19	2	4	0	5	...	---	---
Wagner (*Virchow's Archiv*, III.)	8	0	0	0	0	...	---	---
Tüngel	19	2	1	0	0	...	---	---
Treitz (*Prager Vierteljahrschrift*, 1854) . .	5	0	3	1	0 ?	---	---	1 or 2
TOTAL	153	16 { 1 in 9·5 10·4% }	20 1 in 7·6 13%	3 1 in 51 2 %	22 1 in 7 14·4%	...	---	...
Rosenstein *Nierenkrankheiten*, p. 105) .	114	17 1 in 6·7 14·9%	22 1 in 5·1 19·2 %	13 1 in 8·7 11·4%	25 1 in 4·5 21·9%			
Ditto (ditto . . . . . p. 198) .	114	5 1 in 14 7%	19 1 in 6 16·6%	10 1 in 11·4 8·7%	20 1 in 5·7 17·5%			
(Second Summary of the same cases with different results.)								
Stein (*Myocarditis*)	10	1	...	...	1			
CASES OBSERVED IN FRANCE.								
Martin Solon (*De l'Albuminurie*) . . .	10	0	2	0	1 ?	...	---	---
Rayer (*Maladies du Rein*)	45	3	9	5	6	3	---	---
Becquérel (*Séméiotiques des Urines*, Adults)	45	1	7	6	8 ?	---	---	---
Ditto (ditto . . . . . Children)	17	0	3	6	6	---	---	---
Lanceraux (*Encyclop. des. Sc. Med.*) . .	14	0	...	...	...	..	---	---
TOTAL	131	4 { 1 in 33 3% }	21 1 in 6·2 16 %	17 1 in 7·7 13%	21 1 in 6·2 6·7%	...	---	...
CASES OBSERVED IN INDIA.								
Dr. Morehead (*On Diseases of India*) . .	17	0	3	2	4			
GRAND TOTAL	1228	100 { 1 in 12·3 8·1% }	201 1 in 6·1 16·4%	93 1 in 13 7·6%	162 1 in 7·6 13·2%	...	---	...
	*1682	136 { 1 in 12·3 8·1% }						

* With the addition of Dr Chambers's 454 cases.

	Cases.	Pericarditis.	Pleurisy.	Peritonitis.	Pneumonia.	Pulm Apop.	Part. Peric.	Absc. of lung.
ACUTE BRIGHT'S DISEASE FROM SCARLET FEVER.								
CASES BELOW 16 YEARS OF AGE.								
Dickinson (On Albuminuria, from Tables orally communicated to the Author) . .	21	1	4	2	6 or 7	...	...	...
Greenfield (from ditto)	4	1	0	0	0	...	...	...
Author (St. Mary's Hosp. Post Mort. Rec.)	4	0	2	2	0	...	1	...
. . . .	29	2 — 1 in 14 7%	6 — 1 in 5 20·7%	4 — 1 in 7 13·8%	6 or 7 — 1 in 5 21%	...	1	...
CASES ABOVE 15 YEARS OF AGE.								
Greenfield (loc. cit.)	3	0	0	0	2	...	...	...
Author (St. Mary's Hospital)	2	0	1	3	0	...	...	...
. . . .	5	0	1	0	2	...	...	...
ACUTE BRIGHT'S DISEASE, NOT FROM SCARLET FEVER.								
CASES BELOW 16 YEARS OF AGE.								
Dickinson (loc. cit.)	3	0	0	0	1	...	...	...
Greenfield (loc. cit.)	1	0	1	0	0	...	...	...
Author (St. Mary's Hospital)	1	0	0	0	0	...	...	...
L.	5	0	1	0	1	...	...	...
CASES ABOVE 16 YEARS OF AGE.								
Dickinson (loc. cit.)	4	0	1	1	1	...	...	...
Greenfield (loc. cit.)	8	2	2	1	2	1	...	...
Author (St. Mary's Hospital)	14	{ 2 — 1 in 7 14·8%	1 — 1 in 14 7%	0	2 — 1 in 7 14·4%	1	...	...
L.	26	4 — 1 in 6·5 15·4%	4 — 1 in 6·5 15·4%	2 — 1 in 13 7·7%	4 — 1 in 6·5 15·4%	2	...	...
CASES IN WHICH THE AGE WAS NOT SPECIFIED.								
Rosenberger, "first stage," (loc. cit.) . . .	8	1	1	1	3	1	...	...
L with Acute Bright's Disease, not from Scarlet Fever. All ages	39	5 — 1 in 7·8 13%	6 — 1 in 6·5 15·4%	3 — 1 in 13 7·7%	8 — 1 in 4·8 20·5%	...	...	...

Transitional Cases, passing from Acute Bright's Disease to the Fatty or Large White Kidney.

	Cases.	Pericarditis.	Pleurisy.	Peritonitis.	Pneumonia.	Pulm Apop.	Part. Peric.	Absc. of lung.
Dickinson (loc. cit.)	4	1	0	0	0	...	...	...
CASES WITH FATTY OR LARGE WHITE KIDNEY.								
Dickinson (loc. cit.)	6	0	2	1	0	...	...	...
Rosenberger, "second stage," (loc. cit.) . . .	23	1	4	1	5	...	...	...
Wilks (loc. cit.), "large white," 28 ; "coarse," 5 ; "fatty," 17, some with Waxy Kidney	45	3	8	5	2	...	...	...
Author (St. Mary's Hosp. P. M. Records)	62	{ 1 — 1 in 62 1·6%	16 — 1 in 4 25·8%	2 — 1 in 31 3·2%	16 — 1 in 4 25%	4	5	...
L with Fatty Kidney	136	5 — 1 in 27 3·7%	30 — 1 in 4·5 22%	9 — 1 in 15 6·6%	23 — 1 in 6 17%	...	...	...
GRANULAR KIDNEY, CONTRACTED.								
Wilks (loc. cit.)	31	3	4	2	1	...	...	...
Dickinson (On Albuminuria)	38	16	7	3	7	...	...	...
Grainger Stewart (loc. cit.)	13	1	2	0	1	...	...	...
Rosenberger, "third stage." (loc. cit.) . . .	16	5	4	0	3	1	...	...
Author (St. Mary's Hospital)	128	13 — 1 in 10 10%	30 — 1 in 4·3 23·4%	6 — 1 in 21·3 4·7%	13 — 1 in 10 10%	11	7	...
L with Contracted Granular Kidney . .	226	38 — 1 in 6 16·8%	47 — 1 in 4·8 21%	11 — 1 in 20·5 5%	25 — 1 in 9 11%	...	...	...
LARDACEOUS (AMYLOID) DISEASE OF KIDNEY.								
Dickinson (loc. cit., "depurative") . .	48	3	5	4	9	...	...	...
Grainger Stewart (loc. cit.)	50	4	3	3	2	...	...	...
Author (St. Mary's Hospital, Lardaceous disease actual and probable)	22	{ 2 — 1 in 11 9%	3 — 1 in 7 14·3%	4 — 1 in 5·2 19·4%	3 — 1 in 7 14·3%	...	...	2
L with Lardaceous Disease of Kidney .	120	9 — 1 in 13·3 7·5%	11 — 1 in 10·8 9·2%	11 — 1 in 10·8 9·2%	14 — 1 in 8·5 11·7%	...	...	...

PERICARDITIS IN BRIGHT'S DISEASE OF THE KIDNEYS.

Dr. Bright, in the first volume of Guy's Hospital Reports, gives 100 cases of albuminuria, seven of which, according to the tables, and eight according to his description, had pericarditis. Subsequently Dr. Gregory and Sir James Christison, in Edinburgh; Martin Solon, Becquerel and Rayer in France; and Malmsten in Germany, gave each of them a series or summary of cases of Bright's disease, in all of which cases, except those communicated by Malmsten, pericarditis was either infrequent or absent.

Dr. Taylor called attention, in 1845, to the large proportion in which cases of pericarditis are affected with Bright's disease, and to the frequency with which pericarditis occurs in cases of Bright's disease. He found that out of thirty-one patients with pericarditis, nine, if not eleven, had Bright's disease; and that of fifty post-mortem inspections of cases with Bright's disease, five, or one in ten, had pericarditis.

Several years later, or in 1851, Frerichs published his important work on Bright's disease, which contains a valuable table showing various conditions that existed in 292 cases collected by him from various sources, and including 21 observed by himself. He states that in 13 of those collected cases there was pericarditis; that is in only $4\frac{1}{2}$ per cent. or 1 in 22 of the cases. This return, which has been, and still is, much quoted, gives a lower proportion of attacks of pericarditis in Bright's disease than in the cases given or enumerated by Dr. Bright (7 or 8 per cent. or 1 in 14 or 12), Dr. Taylor (10 per cent. or 1 in 10), M. Rayer (5·4 per cent. or 1 in 18), and Dr. Gregory (5 per cent. or 1 in 20); and a higher proportion than in the cases observed by Becquerel (4·6 per cent. or 1 in 62). Frerichs appears to have overlooked some of the cases of pericarditis in his analysis. To test his figures, I examined as nearly as I could the same cases or tables given by the observers quoted by him, and I find that in a total of 326 cases, 17 or 19 had pericarditis, or about 5·5 per cent. or 1 in 18.[1]

During the nineteen years, ending in 1869, 285 cases of Bright's disease were examined after death in St. Mary's Hospital, and of these 25 or 1 in 11·3 or 8·8 per cent. were affected with pericarditis; which was present therefore somewhat more frequently in those cases than in 1,691 collected cases of Bright's disease, 136 of which, or 1 in 12·3 or 8·17 per cent. had pericarditis.

Besides the twenty-five cases of pericarditis noted in the records of St. Mary's Hospital, there were fifteen of partial or doubtful pericarditis; but these cases ought not, I think, to be taken into the general account.

If we separate the various forms of Bright's disease occurring in St. Mary's Hospital from each other we shall see the proportion in which each form was affected with pericarditis.

[1] *Frerichs.* Dr. Bright, 100 cases ; Sir James Christison, 14 ; Dr. Gregory, 37 ; Martin Solon, 8 ; Rayer, 48 ; Becquerel, 45 ; Bright and Barlow, 10 ; Malmsten, 9 ; Frerichs, 21 ; Total, 292. *Author.* The same authorities respectively ; 100, 14, 39, 10, 55, 45, 9, 33, 21 ; Total, 326.
Cases of pericarditis in the above, Frerichs, 13 ; Author, 17 or 19.

SUMMARY.

Acute Bright's disease, from scarlet fever, total number, 6; affected with pericarditis, 0; with partial pericarditis, 1.

Acute Bright's disease, *not* from scarlet fever, total number 15; affected with pericarditis, 2, or 1 in 7·5, or 13·3 per cent.; with partial pericarditis, 0.

Fatty or large white Kidney, total number, 62; affected with pericarditis, 1, or 1 in 62, or 1·6 per cent.; with partial pericarditis, 5.

Contracted Granular Kidney, total number, 128; affected with pericarditis, 13, or 1 in 10 or 10 per cent.; with partial pericarditis, 7.

Granular Kidney of natural or large size, total number, 34; affected with pericarditis, 3, or 1 in 11·3, or 8·8 per cent.

Granular Kidney, grand total number, 162; affected with pericarditis, 16, or 1 in 10, or 10 per cent.; with partial pericarditis, 7.

Lardaceous disease of Kidney, actual and probable, total number, 22; affected with pericarditis, 2, or 1 in 11, or 9 per cent.

Nature of Kidney disease doubtful, 11; affected with pericarditis, 4, or 1 in 2·7, or 36 per cent.; partial pericarditis, 2.

Total number of cases of Bright's disease, 285; affected with pericarditis, 25, or 1 in 11·3 or 8·8 per cent.; with partial pericarditis, 15.[1]

Calculus in kidney, pelvis, or ureter, or dilated pelvis (hydronephrosis), total number, 12; affected with pericarditis, 0.

Suppurative Nephritis from stricture, &c., total number, 13; affected with pericarditis, 1, or 1 in 13, or 7·7 per cent.

That I might enlarge the area of observation, I have brought together from various sources, including the returns from St. Mary's Hospital, in the accompanying Table, the number of attacks of pericarditis in 1,681 cases of Bright's disease; and the number of attacks of pleurisy, peritonitis, and pneumonia, in 1,228 cases (see p. 404).

I have also given in another and more extended table (see p. 400), the number of cases with pericarditis, pleurisy, and peritonitis, pneumonia, pulmonary apoplexy, and purulent deposit or abscess of the lung; and certain conditions of the heart and aorta in the various forms of Bright's disease among the 285 cases examined at St. Mary's Hospital; distinguishing also those cases in which the heart was small, of natural size, rather large, and large or very large, giving separately those various conditions as they appeared in the cases affected with pericarditis.

Among the cases of Bright's disease collected from various sources, 8·1 per cent. or 1 in 12·3 were attacked with pericarditis.

These cases are arranged in three sections devoted respectively to England, Germany, and France; and the occurrence of pericarditis

---

[1] For details of the cases of partial pericarditis see pages 411, 413.

in Bright's disease is here shown to be most frequent in Germany (1 in 9·5, or 10·4 per cent.), and least frequent in France (1 in 33, or 3 per cent.), while it is of medium or average frequency in England (1 in 11·9, or 8·4 per cent).

Comparative frequency of Pericarditis in the various Forms of Bright's disease.—I have added to the table of 1,682 cases collected from many sources, a series of secondary tables (see p. 405), showing the relative frequency of pericarditis, pleurisy, peritonitis, and pneumonia in the various forms of Bright's disease, in a certain number of the cases; and I shall here inquire into the frequency of pericarditis in the different forms of that disease.

Pericarditis is not frequent in cases of acute Bright's disease from scarlet fever in the young, since it only occurred in 1 in 14, or 7 per cent. of the patients under 16 years of age. The tendency to pericarditis in children in such cases is slight, as was pointed out to me by Dr. Dickinson, who kindly supplied me with the valuable tables of his cases of that class, amounting to 21. Pericarditis is on the other hand frequent in acute Bright's disease in the adult, since it was present in 1 in 6½ or 15·4 per cent. of those cases. The value of these returns has been greatly added to by the cases of acute Bright's disease kindly communicated to me by Dr. Greenfield.

During the transitional period, when acute Bright's disease slowly gives place to the fatty or large white kidney, pericarditis is probably frequent, since it occurred in one of Dr. Dickinson's four transitional cases.

When, however, acute Bright's disease instead of recovering passes into the second or chronic stage, in the form of large white kidney, the tendency to general pericarditis disappears, since it only occurred in 1 in 27 or 3·7 per cent. of the collected cases, and one in 62, or 1·6 per cent. of the St. Mary's Hospital cases, and the kidney in that single case was in the third or contracted stage of fatty disease. Five, however, of the St. Mary's Hospital cases with fatty kidney had partial pericarditis, showing that this affection, although still inherent, does not tend to develop itself in that form of the disease.

The two great and opposite forms of Bright's disease, the fatty kidney, or the chronic stage of acute Bright's disease, and the contracted granular kidney, show a marked difference in the proportion with which they were respectively affected with pericarditis; which attacked those with contracted granular kidney from six to four times as often (1 in 10 [1] and 1 in 6 [2]) as those with fatty kidney (1 in 62 [1] and 1 in 26·6 [2]).

Cases of lardaceous disease of the kidney have pericarditis with a moderate or average frequency (1 in 11, or 9 per cent.,[2] and 1 in 13·3, or 7·5 per cent.[2]).

Inquiry into the influence respectively of the fatty kidney, and the contracted granular kidney, in the production of pericarditis.—When inquiring into the influence of these two forms of Bright's disease in the production of pericarditis it may be well to consider two points

---

[1] In 285 cases examined after death in St. Mary's Hospital.
[2] In the collected cases.

which appear to be associated with the production of pericarditis, though for different reasons; (1) the proportion in which cases with fatty and contracted granular kidney were affected respectively with pleurisy, peritonitis, and pneumonia: and (2) the relative proportion in which the heart was enlarged and its left ventricle was hypertrophied in those two forms of disease; and the immediate relation, if any, that the enlarged heart may have had to the production of pericarditis.

1. Pleurisy attacked 60 of the 285 cases with Bright's disease occurring in St. Mary's Hospital (1 in 4·8 or 21 per cent.[1] and 1 in 6 or 16·4 per cent.[2]) It will thus be seen that in these cases of Bright's disease pleurisy was twice as frequent as pericarditis (1 in 11·3[1] and one in 12·3[2]). We have here a marked difference between the pericarditis of acute rheumatism and the pericarditis of Bright's disease, since while in the former disease, or acute rheumatism, the inflammation of the pericardium is much more common than that of the pleura; the pleurisy when present, being usually either due (1) to the spreading of the inflammation of the pericardium to the pleura, or (2) to pulmonary apoplexy which is the consecutive effect of the double inflammation of the heart, inside and out; in the latter affection, or Bright's disease, the pleurisy is an independent affection, and is, as we have just seen, twice as frequent as pericarditis in the cases under inquiry.

The same in principle may be said of peritonitis, which is practically unknown in acute rheumatism; while it occurs nearly as often as pericarditis in Bright's disease; the numbers being 93, or 1 in 13,[2] and 19, or 1 in 15[1] of peritonitis against 100 or 1 in 12·3[2] and 25 or 1 in 11·3[1] of pericarditis.

Two-fifths of the cases of pericarditis were also affected with pleurisy (10 in 25) and three-fifths were free from that affection (15 in 25); while only 2 in 25 of those cases had peritonitis.

The relative frequency of pleurisy and peritonitis on the one hand, and pericarditis on the other, varied much in the different forms of Bright's disease.

In acute Bright's disease from scarlet fever in the young, pleurisy occurs three times (1 in 5) and peritonitis twice (1 in 7) as often as pericarditis (1 in 14); but it is otherwise in acute Bright's disease in the adult, not from scarlet fever, since in such cases pericarditis is as frequent as pleurisy (each 1 in 6·5), while it is twice as frequent as peritonitis (1 in 11·5).

Pleurisy attacks many more cases (1 in 4[1] and 1 in 4·5[2]) with fatty kidney than pericarditis (1 in 62[1] and 1 in 27[2]); while in those with contracted granular kidney, pericarditis (1 in 10[1] and 1 in 6[2]) occurs, judging by the collected cases, nearly as often as pleurisy (1 in 4·3[1] and 1 in 4·8[2]). Although pleurisy is rather more frequent, pericarditis, as we have seen, is much less so in cases with fatty than in those with contracted granular kidney; and it is therefore evident

---

[1] In 285 cases examined after death in St. Mary's Hospital.
[2] In the collected cases.

that the causes producing the two inflammations have but little in common, and that the one rarely excites the other. Peritonitis occurred twice as often (1 in 31[1] and 1 in 15[2]) as pericarditis in cases with fatty kidney, while pericarditis attacked three times as many as peritonitis (1 in 21) in those with contracted granular kidney..

Pleurisy and peritonitis (each 1 in 10.8[2]) were both of them more frequent than pericarditis (1 in 13.3[2]) in cases of lardaceous disease of the kidney.

Pneumonia, which when it occurs by itself is an occasional cause of pericarditis, while it is less common (1 in 6.4[1] and 1 in 7.6[2]) than pleurisy (1 in 4.8[1] and 1 in 6[2]) is more common than pericarditis in cases of Bright's disease. Those two secondary affections, pneumonia and pleurisy, were of exactly equal frequency in cases of acute Bright's disease, whether from scarlet fever or not; so that what has been said with regard to the latter of those affections applies to the former.

Pneumonia was common (1 in 4[1] and 1 in 6[2]) and pericarditis was rare (1 in 62[1] and 1 in 27[2]) in cases with fatty kidney. It was almost the reverse in those with contracted granular kidney, in which pneumonia (1 in 10[1] and 1 in 9[2]) scarcely equalled pericarditis in number (1 in 10[1] and 1 in 6[2]). The proportion of pneumonia was, therefore, about twice as great in cases with fatty, as in those with contracted granular kidney, while pericarditis, rare in the former, was frequent in the latter form of the disease, making it evident that there was little in common between the production of pneumonia and that of pericarditis in these cases. Pneumonia was present in only one-third of the cases of Bright's disease that were affected with pericarditis (8 in 25).

2. Enlargement of the heart, usually with hypertrophy of the left ventricle, was present in one-half of the cases of Bright's disease under review (129 in 259) in which the size of the heart was described. The heart was large in more than half of the cases of pericarditis in which the size of the heart was defined (10 in 19[3]); or 10 in 129 of the total number of cases of Bright's disease with enlargement of the heart. Pericarditis occurred in six cases in which the heart was of natural size (or 6 in 61). It would thus appear that 1 in 10.1 of the latter in which the heart was natural in size, and 1 in 12.9 of the former, with hypertrophy of the heart, had pericarditis. This would seem to say that hypertrophy of the heart had no apparent influence in the production of pericarditis in these cases. If, however, we add the cases in which the heart was small (23), none of which had general pericarditis, to those in which it was natural in size (61), we find that 6 in 84 or 1 in 14 of those combined cases had that affection. If to these we join the cases in which the heart was rather large (45)[3] of which had pericarditis, the result is that 9 in 129 or 1 in 14.3 were thus attacked. From this analysis, it would appear that enlargement of the heart exercised a definite but not a predominant influence over the production of pericarditis in cases of Bright's disease.

[1] In 285 cases examined after death in St. Mary's Hospital. [2] In the collected cases.
[3] The size of the heart was doubtful in six cases with Pericarditis.

Although hypertrophy of the heart is absent in almost one-half of the cases of Bright's disease with pericarditis, we know that in every form and case of that disease, whether acute or chronic, fatty or granular, the action of the left ventricle is unduly strong; for it has to send the poisoned blood through vessels of great tension that oppose resistance to the onflow of the blood. The result is that in every case of Bright's disease, the left ventricle, whether hypertrophied or not, is beating with undue force; and thus tends, by the pressure of its walls with undue force against the pericardium, to induce pericarditis. The heart is prevented from becoming enlarged in many cases of Bright's disease by the exhausting loss of albumen, the general waste, and the lowering character of the disease. This especially applies to cases of fatty, lardaceous, and suppurative kidney. The left ventricle, notwithstanding the great waste of tissue that goes on in those cases, is actually hypertrophied in a certain proportion of them; and it is so in the greater number of those with acute Bright's disease, in spite of the waste of tissue entailed by the great loss of albumen and blood in such cases. We have already seen that in acute rheumatism, over action of the heart tends to induce pericarditis. It is, therefore, consistent with analogy, reason, and the clinical facts, that in Bright's disease over-action of the heart should increase the tendency to pericarditis, that tendency being already resident in the disease. May it not be that on the one hand, the lessened force of the heart, induced by the weeping of albumen, dropsy, and other secondary wasting diseases in cases with fatty disease of the kidneys, explains to some extent the rarity of general pericarditis (1 in 62[1] and 1 in 27[2]), and the comparative frequency of partial and undeveloped pericarditis (1 in 12·4), in that disease? and that on the other hand, the increased size and action of the heart in cases with granular kidney, which usually lose little albumen, are not dropsical, and are free from exhausting secondary disease, tend to increase the frequency of general pericarditis in that affection (1 in 10[1] and 1 in 6[2])?

Although the cases of partial pericarditis, which amounted to fifteen, cannot be classed rightly with those of general pericarditis; for the partial variety appears to have a tendency to remain partial, and those cases are not usually included among those with pericarditis, yet those cases ought to be studied. One of the fifteen cases of partial pericarditis had acute Bright's disease from scarlet fever (1 in 6 or 16·6 per cent.); five of them had fatty kidney (5 in 62, or 1 in 12·4, or 8 per cent.); seven of them had contracted granular kidney (7 in 129, or 1 in 18·3 or 5·5 per cent.); and in two the state of the kidney was not specified.

The proportion in which partial and general pericarditis respectively attacked the different forms of Bright's disease somewhat correspond.

In four of the cases of partial pericarditis the heart was very large, (1 in 32·2), and in three it was rather large (1 in 15); while in five of

---

[1] The cases of Bright's disease examined after death in St. Mary's Hospital.
[2] The collected cases.

them the heart was of natural size or small, (1 in 16·8) and in three the size of the heart was not described.

It thus seems that great enlargement of the heart does not favour the persistence of partial pericarditis, but rather tends to develop it into general pericarditis.

Amount of Fluid in the Pericardial Sac in Pericarditis from Bright's Disease.—The amount of fluid in the pericardial sac varied considerably in the twenty-five cases of pericarditis from Bright's disease, the smallest quantity being two drams, and the largest about a pint, in which case the contents of the sac were purulent.

In one-fifth of the cases (5) the contents of the pericardium are not described; and in one-fifth of them (5) there were recent adhesions. The sac contained only a small quantity of serum, or not more than one ounce in one-third (5) of the remaining cases (15); a moderate amount, or a few ounces, in another third of them (6); and much fluid, eight ounces in one instance, a pint in another, in the remaining third (4) of those cases. It is evident that the presence of adhesions, or of a small, a moderate, or an abundant amount of fluid in the pericardium, depends on the stage of the pericarditis at the time of death; and that in the several cases the fluid had either been removed, or was lessening, increasing, or at its height, when the final observation was made. It may, I think, be admitted that in the pericarditis of Bright's disease there is less effusion in the pericardium than in rheumatic pericarditis; but from the evidence here given it would appear that there is no very material difference in the amount of fluid in the sac at the time of death in the two classes of cases.

Character of the Exudation on the Surfaces of the Heart and Pericardial Sac in Pericarditis from Bright's Disease.—In a small proportion of cases the lymph covering the heart and lining the pericardium in case of pericarditis from Bright's disease presents the same pale and rough surface, firm to the finger, with "cat's-tongue"-like projections, so usual in pericarditis from acute rheumatism. It was thus in two of the twenty-five cases that were examined after death at St. Mary's Hospital. In two other cases also, both of acute Bright's disease, a rather firm layer of fibrin easily peeled off from the heart, leaving a finely-injected red surface underneath.

In the majority of cases of pericarditis from Bright's disease the exudation differs from that usual in rheumatic pericarditis. Universal adhesions of the heart, rare in the latter, are common in the former affection; the heart having been completely adherent in three instances, extensively so in one, and doubtfully so in another of those cases. There was pus in the sac in two cases. The lymph—was soft, granular, imperfectly organized, or in patches in six, in two of which the presence of pericarditis was perhaps doubtful; or was bloody or very red on the surface, or mixed with blood in three of the twenty-five cases of pericarditis from Bright's disease. These conditions, which affected nearly two-thirds of those cases, are rare or unknown in rheumatic pericarditis. The remaining cases were less definite in character, the heart in four of them having been covered by recent lymph, while in two the pericardium was affected with "recent pericarditis."

Appearances in Partial Pericarditis.—The cases of partial or doubtful pericarditis varied much in their features. In four of them flakes of lymph floated in the serum contained in the pericardial sac, the surfaces of the heart not being named. Pericarditis was limited, slight, or in traces or patches in seven other cases, and in two more it was highly vascular or congested. One case presented rough lymph easily detached, leaving an apparently healthy surface; and in the last instance there was a red fluid containing flakes of lymph in the sac, and lymph on the heart, the surface of which was healthy. These two cases, and the four in which flakes of lymph floated in the serum, were probably free from actual pericarditis.

Physical Signs of Pericarditis Occurring in Bright's Disease.—Dr. Taylor gives careful reports of nine cases of Bright's disease with pericarditis, in three of which there was a friction sound, while in six of them there was no definite sign of the affection. In three of these six cases there were complete recent adhesions, rendering friction sound impossible. In one of the three cases in which pericarditis was not discovered during life, a layer of soft lymph coated the heart, but there was no lymph on any part of the loose pericardium, and this appears to account for the want of friction sound. In one of the three cases that presented a friction sound, a double creaking noise was heard between the apex of the heart and the sternum; and the heart and sac were covered with soft, slightly rough lymph.

In two of the three cases without friction sound, excluding the three with complete adhesions, and in two of the three with friction sound, there was no adequate explanation, after death, of the absence of that sound in the two former cases, in which the opposed surfaces of the heart and sac were rough and scabrous; nor of its presence in the two latter cases in one of which there were extensive adhesions of the heart; while in the other the surface of the heart was simply red from fine injection, and there were but a few spots of lymph on the anterior coronary artery.

I possess notes of the symptoms during life, and the appearance after death of nine fatal cases of Bright's disease with pericarditis. I cannot find the notes of a tenth case with regard to which I find two lines of an abstract of symptoms. In seven of the cases immediate signs of pericarditis were observed, and in three of them the signs of pericarditis were not observed.

Cases in which the Signs of Pericarditis were not Observed.—In one patient, a man, aged 61, with granular kidneys, the heart, which was very fat, was covered and the sac was lined with recent lymph. On the third day after his admission, on which day he died, the heart's action to the left of the ensiform cartilage was loud; and loud mucous rattles were audible all over his chest. In the second case, a man, aged 47, the opposite surfaces of the pericardium, and the heart, at its base, and along the great vessels were rough with a deposit of fibrin. This patient was in the hospital fifty-two days, but there is only one note of the state of his heart, which was on the fifth day after his admission, when its sounds were rather loud.

I cannot find the notes of the remaining case with Bright's disease and pericarditis; but the following is the brief abstract preceding the notes of the examination after death. "At first, doubling of the first sound, afterwards systolic murmur after epistaxis," so that friction sound was evidently not observed in this case.

Cases in which the Signs of Pericarditis were Observed.—(1) A creaking noise with a thrill was present in three of the seven cases of pericarditis with friction sound; (2) a creaking sound without a thrill in two of them, and (3) in the remaining two there was a "friction sound."

(1.) *Cases with Thrill and a Creaking Friction Sound over the Seat of the Impulse, and Frottement extending far beyond and especially below the Region of the Pericardium.*—There were three cases of this class. One of them a woman, aged 32, who was in the hospital for a week, presented after death some fluid in the pericardium, and a rough deposit of recent lymph of a bright red colour, which covered the heart and lined the sac. On the day after her admission a systolic murmur was audible over the cardiac region. Two days later, when she complained of pain going across the chest, the upper border of cardiac dulness was situated at the third space; and a rasping, creaking friction sound, chiefly systolic, was heard all over the front of the chest, and down to the eighth and ninth costal cartilages, its maximum intensity being at the centre of the sternum, and during the middle of the systole. Next day a strong thrill extended over the heart from the right of the sternum to the nipple, and as high as the third cartilage; and the creaking sound was triple, being exactly like that made by the rise and fall and rise in the saddle. On the following day, the fifth, the thrill was less intense, and there was a triple creak at the apex, the friction sound being still audible over the lower cartilage; and two days later she died.

The second patient, a woman, aged 27, with contracted granular kidney, and pericarditis, had several patches of recent lymph on the surfaces of the heart and the free pericardium, and presented a double thrill, a double creak, and an extensive friction sound, which were all absolutely suspended for one day, under the influence of flooding.

The third case, a man, aged 33, had mitral-aortic incompetence, and highly albuminous urine. The heart and pericardium were greatly increased in size, and the right ventricle was covered with a white fibrinous structure, rough to the finger, like a cat's tongue. On admission he had pain over the heart; and for two days, mitral and double aortic murmurs were audible. He became worse, and on the fourth day the diastolic murmur disappeared. On the ninth day he was drowsy, a strong thrill was felt with each impulse from the third cartilage to the fifth; a loud grating double friction sound was present over the seat of the thrill, the rubbing noise radiating thence up to the top of the sternum, down to the eighth cartilages, and to the left and right; a leather creak was audible at the apex; and a sound of a friction character was heard behind, over the dorsal spine. On the next day, when he died, the vibration had increased, and extended from the third to the seventh cartilages; it lessened in extent above, on inspiration, below, on expiration; and was accompanied by a loud creak during systole, and a fainter creak during diastole, the sound spreading from the seat of the vibration over the front of the chest, and the upper third of the belly.

(2.) *Cases with a Creaking Friction Sound, no Thrill being Observed, over the Seat of the Impulse, and a Frottement extending beyond, and especially below the Region of Pericardial Dulness.*—One of the two cases of this class was a young married woman, with granular disease of the kidney. A firm coating partly in ridges and partly like a cat's tongue covered the heart and lined the sac. On her admission a creaking systolic friction sound was audible at the apex, in the fifth space. Four days later, when the pericardial dulness was at its acme, reaching up to the third cartilage, her respirations being fifty, the friction sound was no longer creaking but presented itself as an occasional brush; but three days after this, or on the eighth day, there was a loud leather creak over the whole region of the pericardium. After this the friction sound almost disappeared; but on the twelfth and preceding days it had again burst into full play as an extensive leather creaking noise, covering the whole pericardium, and extending down to the seventh cartilage; and eight days later she died.

In the second case, a man, aged 30, with small, probably granular, kidneys, recent, bloody, honey-combed lymph lined the pericardium and covered the heart. On the day of his admission the two sounds of the heart were indistinct. Next day the impulse was extensive, and a loud double creaking sound, more intense during systole, occupied the whole region of the heart, extending downwards to the seventh and eighth cartilages, and into the epigastrium. During the next few days the frottement was much smoother and more restricted in area. On the eighth day he was weak and in distress; the friction sound was audible over the whole pericardium, and beyond it, from the top of the sternum to the lower cartilage; and he could scarcely swallow or speak : and in the evening he died.

(3.) *Cases with " Friction Sound."*—One of the two cases of this class, a man aged 38, with granular kidney of full size, had recent lymph over the whole surface of the heart, and in some places the heart and pericardium were adherent by cord-like prolongations of lymph. On the fifty-seventh day there were doubling of the second sound, and a murmur over the third cartilage. On the seventy-fifth day, which was eight days before his death, " double friction sound over the pericardium," was noted for the first time. Three days later the pericardial friction sounds, which were scarcely audible without making pressure, were mingled with pleuritic friction sounds; but after this he was too ill for examination.

The other patient, an old woman, with contracted granular kidney and pericarditis, the whole surfaces of the heart and sac being covered by recent soft granular lymph, complained, on the twenty-first day after her admission, of great pain at the region of the heart. Next day there was pericardial dulness, and friction sound was present between the sternum and the left nipple; and three days later she died.

Several of these seven cases of Bright's disease and pericarditis presented certain broad features in common. In three of them a thrill or tactile vibration could be felt over the region of the heart's impulse, extending from the third to the fifth, the sixth, and in one instance the seventh cartilages. In one of those cases the thrill extended from the right border of the sternum across the chest to the nipple. In these three cases, and in two others in which a thrill was not observed, a loud sound like the creaking of new leather, usually double, but more intense and prolonged with the systole, was audible over the whole seat of the thrill, or when that was absent, over the region of the heart's impulse. The friction sound was, however, in none of the five instances restricted to the area of the thrill or impulse, or even of the distended pericardium; but extended upwards to the top of the sternum, downwards to the right and left along the seventh and eighth costal cartilages, and over and even below the ensiform cartilage. In these cases the wide-spread friction sound became softer in tone, and especially downwards, as it widened away from the focus of its greatest intensity. In two of these five cases with creaking and extended friction sound, the deposit of fibrin or lymph on the surface of the heart was firm and like a cat's tongue, in one of them it was rough, in one it was bloody and honey-combed, and in the fifth, patches of recent lymph were present on the heart.

In three of these cases there was a period of complete or partial suspension of the creaking and extensive friction sound; which after spreading with great intensity and over a large area, became silent or feeble and contracted in area for a time, and then suddenly burst forth again with full intensity, and over a wide space. It was evident that under these circumstances, some influences were at work exciting the heart at the time of the creaking and wide-spread friction sound, and depressing the heart when that sound ceased or became feeble. In one instance, the suspension of the thrill and creak was traced to the influence of flooding.

In the two other patients the surface of the heart is described as being covered with recent, and in one of them with soft, lymph. In neither of them is it noted that the coating of lymph was rough. In both of these cases it is simply stated that a "friction sound" was present over the region of the heart.

In all of these patients pressure intensified the friction sound.

Cases with a Friction Sound that were not Fatal, or not Examined after Death.—Besides these seven fatal cases of Bright's disease with pericarditis in which friction sound was observed during life, I find three other cases in which the signs of pericarditis were observed when the patients were in the wards.

One of these cases, probably fatal, admitted during the recess, very imperfectly recorded, presented a pericardial friction sound, which was chiefly present at and below the left nipple.

Another patient, a carpenter, aged 35, had Bright's disease and aortic regurgitation of some standing. On the eighty-second day he had great pain in the heart, and four days later a rough double noise resembling a friction sound was audible over the cardiac region. Four days after this there was dulness over the pericardium from the third space downwards, and pain over the heart, relieved by leeches; and next day a to-and-fro friction sound was audible over the heart, which continued for six days; after which, when he was in distress from aching over the heart, and sickness, the rubbing noise vanished, being replaced by the lost diastolic murmur of aortic regurgitation. This case left the hospital in improved health.

The last case of Bright's disease with friction sound, was one of great interest, a cab-driver, aged 45. His urine was loaded with albumen, and contained coarse granular and fatty casts. There was, on the fourth day, an extensive impulse, and a remarkable doubling of the first sound heard all over the region of the impulse, which was heard along with, but apart from, a peculiar pericardial friction sound chiefly systolic, which was audible for two inches below the nipple. This sound which was rasping at first, became creaking two days later, and five days after that, was only audible when pressure was made over the same spot, the sound being like that caused by rubbing together two pieces of emery paper. Next day there was great extension of the friction sound, which required no pressure for its production, over the whole region of the pericardium; and four days later, the seventeenth after admission, the friction sound was soft, double, and murmur-like, chiefly heard on pressure, and was accompanied by the natural heart sounds, with which it was not rhythmical. I could not make out which sound had the start of the other. For a few days a systolic friction murmur was audible on passing beyond the nipple line, and a double rustle was heard on pressure down to the twenty-eighth day. The extensive doubling of the first sound held its ground throughout, and on the forty-fourth and fifty-third days a little frottement was again present, produced by pressure. On the sixty-fifth day he felt lighter over the heart, and a tremor or thrill was perceived, extending over the cardiac region from the right to the left nipple. A loud double new-leather creak extended over the whole of this region, but the rubbing noise spread far and wide, being heard from axilla to axilla, and down the ensiform and seventh and eighth cartilages. The thrill and creak retained their intensity and area for five days, but on the 6th day the thrill was feeble, and the creak was replaced by a to-and-fro sound extending from the third to the sixth cartilage. Doubling of the first sound was mixed up with the friction sound, but pressure intensified the latter and extinguished the former. On the seventy-third day there was no thrill, and a systolic friction sound, double on pressure, was present between the fourth and sixth cartilages. Two days later the rubbing sound was no longer audible without pressure, and was quite lost on the seventy-ninth day. In this remarkable case the friction sound was present over a limited region near the apex, from the fourth to the twenty-eighth day; came into play slightly on the forty-fourth and fifth-third days; and on the sixty-fifth day burst out, with a thrill, with great intensity over the region of the impulse, and radiated thence as from a focus, all over the front of the chest, and down to the eighth costal cartilages, being audible with a lessening area and diminishing intensity to the seventy-fifth day. This long and intermittent duration of pericardial friction sound appears to me to be peculiar to the pericarditis of Bright's disease, and is certainly never found in rheumatic pericarditis.

These ten cases—which I have given with some detail, as, with the exception of Dr. Taylor's cases and two related, in this respect briefly, by Traube, I have found no cases of pericarditis from Bright's disease in which the signs are related—presented features that are common in them, but are comparatively rare in rheumatic pericarditis. A thrill was present, as we have just seen, in four of these cases or almost one-half (4 in 10); and a sound like the creaking of new leather was heard in six of those cases, or more than one-half (6 in 10), over the seat of the thrill or impulse; and that radiated thence as a softening sound over the front of the chest, beyond the region of the pericardium, and downwards over the ensiform cartilage and the seventh and eighth costal cartilages. These signs were much less frequent in rheumatic pericarditis, since a thrill was present in only one-fifth of those cases, or 13 in 63, and was distributed over the region of the impulse in only seven, was limited to the second space in two, to the apex in three patients, and to both those regions in one; and a creaking friction sound was present at or near the time of the acme of the pericardial effusion in about one-fourth of those cases, or about 18 in 63. The long duration of the friction sound, and its frequent suspension, observed in several of those cases of pericarditis from Bright's disease, likewise distinguish them from those with rheumatic pericarditis.

Calculus in Kidney, Pelvis, or Ureter; or Dilated Pelvis:—and Suppurative Nephritis from Stricture, &c.—I have added, in the Table of Pericarditis in Bright's disease, two sections of cases that, without ranking under that affection, float upon its borders; and substantially belong to the same disease in this respect, that the blood is poisoned, owing to the retention within it of the debris of the broken-up tissues of the body, owing to the imperfect action of the diseased kidney. In the first series, the secreting structure of the kidney is often atrophied by the backward compression of the organ, owing to the distension of the pelvis from the presence of calculus in the ureter, pelvis, or kidney. None of these cases, amounting to twelve, had pericarditis. In the second series of cases, numbering thirteen, there was suppurative disease of the pelvis or kidney, owing mainly to stricture, or disease of the prostate, or bladder (in 11 cases); in one case, to calculus in the ureter, and in another to pyæmia. One of these cases had pericarditis.

I refer to the table for the general condition of these two sets of cases.

PERICARDITIS, NEITHER RHEUMATIC NOR FROM BRIGHT'S DISEASE.

Rheumatic pericarditis, so common in the wards, is rare in the post-mortem room; and pericarditis, as we have seen, occurs in as many as eight or nine per cent. of all fatal cases of Bright's disease. Although uncomplicated pericarditis is a very rare affection, yet its association with other diseases when fatal, and generally as an effect of those diseases, is by no means rare. There is no single malady that is associated with pericarditis nearly so often as the two just mentioned; yet if we combine all the other fatal cases with that affection, except those with Bright's disease and acute rheumatism, we shall find that pericarditis is found on examination after death nearly twice as often in those combined affections as in Bright's disease, and three or four times as often as in fatal cases of acute rheumatism.

The records of the examinations made after death at St. Mary's Hospital during the nineteen years ending 1869-70 contain forty cases of pericarditis that were neither rheumatic nor from Bright's disease. The accompanying summary shows that thirty-nine of these cases of pericarditis were associated with some other disease, general or local, and that in only one case was the affection uncomplicated.

Besides these forty cases of pericarditis, there were sixteen with partial or slight pericarditis.

In addition to these cases I have analysed in one view (1) Dr. Chambers' complete and valuable table of the causes of pericarditis in 136 cases observed after death in St. George's Hospital during ten years; (2) thirty-seven cases with pericarditis published in the *Pathological Transactions;* and (3) seventy-nine cases collected from various sources.[1]

A. Three cases of pericarditis and three of slight pericarditis had pyæmia, one had scarlet fever, and in one the affection was associated with tubercular disease of the suprarenal capsule; B. twelve cases of pericarditis were associated with affections of the heart or aorta; C. fifteen with affections of the lungs or pleura; D. one with ulcer, and one with cancer of the œsophagus; E. five with affections of the abdomen; F. and besides these cases of secondary or associated pericarditis, there was,

[1] Corvisart (6); Bertin (5); Andral (9); Bouillaud (16); Dr. Stokes (13 including 4 from Testa); Dr. Law (2); Sir Thomas Watson (3); Tringel (13); Dr. Graves (5); Dr. Mayne (3); Dr. Green (1); Dr. Beattie (2); and Dr. Thwaites (1); Total, 79 cases.

CASES.	I. Not associated with Bright's Disease.					II. Associated with Bright's Disease.				
	Total	With Pericarditis	With slight Pericarditis	Pericardial adhesion. General	Pericardial adhesion. Partial	Total	Pericarditis. General	Pericarditis. Partial	Pericardial adhesion. General	Pericardial adhesion. Partial
A—Pericarditis, &c., associated with general or constitutional disease :—										
Secondary inflam. pyæmia, phlebit. erysip.	71*	3	3	2	...	12	...	1	...	...
With scarlet fever and mitral endocarditis	1	1	...	...	...	...	...	...	...	...
With disease of the supra-renal capsules .	1	1	...	...	...	...	...	...	...	...
With cancer, not including. †10 cancer of heart	63	...	1†	...	...	...	...	...	...	...
A—TOTAL	136	5	4	2	...	12	...	1	...	...
B—Pericarditis, &c. Associated with affections of the Heart :—										
Wound of the heart	2	1	...	...	...	...	...	...	...	...
Tubercular pericarditis (both had phthisis)	2	2	...	...	...	...	...	...	...	...
Aneurism of the heart	1	1	...	...	...	...	...	...	..	...
Aneurism of the ascending aorta.	25	...	1	3	—	..."	...	...	...	...
Cancer of heart (total cases of cancer 73) .	10	1	...	1	...	...	...	...	...	...
Heart enlarged without valvular incompetence or any other disease										
a. valves healthy in structure	9	1	..	6	—	54	3	3	4	...
b. with some thickening of mitral valve.	2	...	...	1	...	19	...	...	...	...
Mitral regurgitation	33	5	1	13‡	...	29	2	2	4	1
Mitral obstruction . . . .—*a.*	21	...	2	1	2	9	1	...	1	...
Aortic regurgitation—*a.* ascending aorta, not stated to be atheromatous . . .	13	...	1	..	1	15	...	...	3	1
b. aorta atheromatous, valve diseased .	14	..	...	1	...	5	1	...	...	...
c. aorta dilated, valve incompetent, flaps healthy.	5	...	...	1	...	1	...	...	...	...
Mitral-aortic valve-disease	31	1	...	11	2	20	1	...	...	1
Tricuspid valve-disease	1	...	...	1	...	...	...	...	..	...
Fatty disease of heart	11	...	...	1	...	...	...	...	...	...
B—TOTAL	180	12	5	40	5	152	8	5	13	3
Total with valvular disease .	118	6	4	38	5	79	5	2	8	3
Apoplexy	17	...	...	1	...	...	...	..	...	...
C—Pericarditis, &c. associated with Affections of the Lungs and Pleura :—										
Pneumonia.	49	8	3	2	1	40	7	1	2	...
Pleurisy, not with empyema or pneumonia.	22	3	2	...	...	39	3	4	1	...
Empyema, not including pneumonia . .	14	2	...	2	...	...	...	...	...	...
Pneumothorax	8	...	..	...	...	...	..	...	...	...
Phthisis, not including pneumothorax, 5 ; empyema, 2 ; tubercular pericarditis, 2 .	126	2†	1	3	...	25	...	...	...	...
Bronchitis, Emphysema	18	...	...	...	...	...	...	...	...	...
C—TOTAL	237	15	6	7	1	104	10	5	3	
D—Pericarditis, &c. associated with ulcer, 1, cancer, 1 of the Œsophagus. . . .	2	2	...	...	...	...	...	...	...	...
E—Pericarditis asso. with Affec. of the Abdo. :—										
Abscess of liver, 3a ; (of diaphragm, 1)	4	2a	...	...	...	...	...	...	...	...
Diaphrag. hernia, 1 ; tumr. con. with stom. 1	2	2	...	...	...	...	...	...	...	...
Peritonitis, including 6 tubercular peritonitis, not including 5 phthisis. TOTAL cases .	71	1	1	1	...	19	2	1	1	...
E—TOTAL	77	5	1	1	—	19	2	1	1	...
F—Pericarditis appar. not asso. with other affec.	1	1	...	...	...	9	5	4	...	...
Pericardial adhesion ; heart healthy, nat. in size	1	...	...	1	...	...	...	...	...	...
TOTAL	651	40	16	52	6	285‡	25	16	17	3

* Had also endocarditis. † One with tubercular pericarditis.

‡ In four of these cases the mitral-valve was thickened, but it was doubtful whether there was regurgitation through the mitral orifice.

§ In this column, the same case often reappears under different headings.

Cases with doubtful indications of Bright's disease, but without albuminuria or general dropsy :— Pyæmia, 6 ; mitral regurgitation, 1 ; mitral contraction, valve disease of aorta, 6 ; mitral aortic valve-disease, 5 ; pneumonia, 5 ; pleurisy, 4 ; phthisis, 10 ; peritonitis, 4.

SUPPLEMENTARY TABLE, *showing the Size of the Heart in the cases enumerated in the preceding Table, (1) in their total number ; (2) in those with Pericarditis, complete and partial; and (3) with Pericardial Adhesions.*

CASES.	Total Number.	Heart enlarged. Total	Pericarditis General	Pericarditis Partial	Pericardial Adhesions	Heart rather large. Total	Pericarditis General	Pericarditis Partial	Pericardial Adhesions	Heart of natural size, or "healthy." Total	Pericarditis General	Pericarditis Partial	Pericardial Adhesions	Heart small. Total	Pericarditis General	Pericarditis Partial	Pericardial Adhesions	Size of heart not described or known. Total	Pericarditis General	Pericarditis Partial	Pericardial Adhesions
—General Disease.																					
Pyæmia	71	8	...	...	1	9	...	...	...	44	...	3	...	4	...	...	...	11	3	...	1
Scarlet fever	1	...	1	...	...	...	...	...	...	...	...	...	...	...	...	...	...	...	...	...	...
Addison's disease	1	...	1	...	...	...	...	...	...	...	...	...	...	...	...	...	...	...	...	...	...
Cancer (not including 10 with cancer of heart)	63	1	...	...	...	3	...	...	...	48	...	1	...	3	...	...	...	8	...	...	...
A—TOTAL	136	4	2	...	1	12	...	...	...	92	...	4	...	7	...	...	...	19	3	...	1
—Diseases of Heart and Aorta.																					
Wound of heart	2	...	...	...	...	...	...	...	...	2	1	...	...	...	...	...	...	...	...	...	...
Tubercular pericarditis	2	1	1	...	...	1	1	...	...	...	...	...	...	...	...	...	...	...	...	...	...
Aneurism of heart	1	1	...	...	...	...	...	...	...	...	...	...	...	...	...	...	...	...	...	...	...
Aneurism of asc. aorta	25	7or8	...	...	2	8or9	...	1	...	2	...	...	..	...	...	...	...	7	...	...	1
Cancer of heart	10	3	1	...	1	...	...	...	...	2	...	...	...	2	...	...	...	3	...	...	...
Uncomplicated enlargement of heart, except with adhe. peri.	11	11	1	...	7	...	...	...	...	...	...	...	...	...	...	...	...	...	...	...	...
Mitral regurgitation	33	20	3	1	10	5	1	...	...	2	...	...	...	...	...	...	...	6	1	...	3
Mitral obstruction	21	8	...	2	1	6	...	...	1	5	...	...	...	...	...	...	...	2	...	...	1
Aortic regurgitation	32	25	...	1	2	2	...	...	...	1	...	...	...	1	...	...	...	3	...	...	1
Mitral-aortic valve dis.	31	26	1	...	11	1	...	...	...	...	...	...	...	...	...	...	...	4	...	..	2
Tricuspid valve disease	1	1	...	...	1	...	...	...	...	...	...	...	...	...	...	...	...	...	...	...	...
Fatty degeneration of the heart	11	...	..	...	...	4	...	...	1	5	...	...	...	...	...	...	...	2	...	...	...
Total affection of heart and pericardium.	180	104	6	4	35	27	3	1	2	19	1	...	...	3	...	...	...	27	1	...	8
Total with valvular disease.	118	78	4	4	25	14	1	...	1	8	...	...	...	1	...	...	...	15	1	...	7
Apoplexy	17	7	...	...	1	...	...	...	...	7	...	...	...	1	...	...	...	2	...	...	...
—Diseases of Lungs and Pleura.																					
Pneumonia	49	5	1	...	1	17	...	...	2	17	1	2	...	...	...	...	...	10	6	1	...
Pleurisy	22	1	..	...	...	3	...	...	...	13	...	1	...	...	...	...	...	5	3	1	...
Empyema	14	...	...	...	...	4	1	...	...	5	...	...	...	1	...	...	...	4	1	...	2
Pneumo-thorax	8	...	...	...	...	...	...	...	...	6	...	...	...	...	...	...	...	2	...	...	...
Phthisis	126	6	...	...	...	32	1	...	1	63	...	1	1	10	..	...	...	15	1	...	1
Bronchitis	8	1	...	...	...	6	...	...	...	1	...	...	...	...	...	...	...	...	...	...	...
Emphysema	10	7	...	...	...	1	...	...	...	...	...	...	...	...	...	...	...	2	...	...	...
C—TOTAL	237	20	1	...	1	63	2	...	3	105	1	4	1	11	...	...	...	38	11	2	3
—Ulcers, Cancers of Œsophagus.	2	...	...	...	...	...	...	...	...	...	...	...	...	...	...	...	...	2	2	...	...
—Diseases of Abdomen.																					
Peritonitis, inclu. 6 of tuberculr. peritonitis, not inclu. 5 of phthisis Abscess of liver, 8 ; of diaphr. 1 ; diaphr. hernia, 1 ; tumour connected with stomach, 1	71	3	1	...	1	5	...	...	...	45	...	...	...	6	...	...	...	12	...	1	...
	6	...	...	...	...	2	1	...	...	2	...	...	...	...	...	...	...	2	2	...	...
E—TOTAL	77	3	1	...	1	7	1	...	...	47	1	...	...	6	...	...	...	14	2	1	...
Uncomplic. pericard.	1	...	...	...	...	...	...	...	...	1	1	...	...	...	...	...	...	...	...	...	...
Uncomplicated pericardial adhesions	1	..	...	...	...	...	...	...	...	1	...	...	1	...	...	...	...	...	...	...	...
GRAND TOTAL	651	138	12	4	39	109	5	1	5	272	4	8	2	28	...	...	...	104	19	3	12
BRIGHT'S DISEASE.	285	129	10	4	17	46	3	3	1	61	6	4	...	23	...	1	..	26	6	3	2

C. PERICARDITIS IN ITS ASSOCIATION WITH OTHER DISEASES.
Cases collected from all Sources.

CASES.	A. Dr. Chambers' (Duceunium Pathologium) Pericarditis.	B. Post-mortem Record, St. Mary's Hospital Pericarditis. General	B. Partial	C. Pathological Transactions. Pericarditis. General	C. Partial	D. Various Authors. Pericarditis.
Pericarditis associated with acute Rheumatism	19	?	...	8	1	13
With Bright's disease	86	25	15	3	1	—
Dropsy	...	...	...	...	...	1
A—With general or Constitutional Diseases:—						
Pyæmia, secondary inflammation	18 or 17	3	3	5	1	5
Erysipelas (included with Pyæmia, St. Mary's Hospital)	4	...	...	...	...	1
Small-pox	...	...	...	...	...	1
Fever	4	...	...	...	...	1
Scarlet Fever	...	1	...	...	—	...
Cutaneous eruption	...	...	...	...	...	1
Tubercular disease, supra-renal capsule	...	1	...	...	...	...
Tubercle	...	...	...	1	...	...
Cancer	...	...	1?	1	...	...
Syphilis	...	...	...	...	...	1
A—TOTAL	**26 or 27**	**5**	**4**	**7**	**1**	**8**
B—With Affections of the Heart and Aorta:—						
Wound of the heart	...	1	...	...	...	...
Blow over the heart (1), fracture of the sternum (1)	1	...	...	...	...	1
Tubercular Pericarditis	...	2	...	1	...	1
Cancer of heart, pericardium or neighbourhood	3 or 4	1	...	1	...	1
Neighbouring abscess (2 in heart)	2	...	...	...	...	2
Fibroid disease of walls of heart	...	...	...	2	...	...
Aneurism of heart	...	1	...	...	...	...
Aneurism of ascending aorta	2	...	1	3	...	2
Enlargement of heart, without assigned complications	...	1	...	...	...	...
"Diseased heart" and "dropsy"	18	...	...	...	...	...
Valvular disease of heart	...	6	4	3	1	3
Cyanosis, malformation	...	...	...	1	...	...
B—TOTAL	**26**	**12**	**5**	**11**	**1**	**15**
C—With Affections of the Lungs and Pleura:—						
Pneumonia (generally with pleurisy)	10	8	3	...	...	11
Pleurisy (including empyema)	5	5	2	1	...	12
Phthisis	8	2	1	...	...	3
Communication between pericardium and abscess of 'ung	1	...	...	...	...	1
Indefinite affection of the chest	...	...	...	...	...	...
C—TOTAL	**23**	**15**	**6**	**1**	**...**	**28**
D—With wound (1); slough (1); ulcer (1); and cancer (1) of œsophagus	1	2	...	1	...	...
E—With Affections of the Abdomen, including the Diaphragm:—						
Diaphragmatic hernia (1); tumour connected with stomach (1)	...	2	...	...	...	...
Abscess of liver (3); one communicated with pericardium	...	2	...	...	...	1
Peritonitis	3	1	1	...	...	...
E—TOTAL	**3**	**5**	**1**	**...**	**...**	**1**
Pericarditis, not associated with other affections	2?	1	...	1	1	13
GRAND TOTAL	**136**	**40***	**16***	**33**	**5**	**79**

* Not including those from Bright's disease.

as I have just said, one in which the affection appeared to be primary, or uncomplicated.

A. *General Diseases.*—One of the three cases of pyæmia was a school-boy whose leg was doubled up under him five days before his admission. He came in with hurried breathing, blue lips, and tenderness over the chest and abdomen; on placing the hand over the heart a sense of friction was felt, and a loud pericardial friction sound was heard all over the cardiac region. He had delirium, and died during the night. The surfaces of the heart and sac were covered with recent lymph in ridges, and connected by threads; and the muscular substance of the heart was firm, and contained numerous minute purulent dots scattered through the fibres of the left ventricle. Dr. Trotter observed this patient.

This case is typical of a frequent method in which pyæmia induces pericarditis. In such cases the inflammation does not at once attack the surface of the heart, but spreads to it from the points of suppura-tive inflammation minutely scattered through the muscular walls of the organ, just as pleurisy is caused by the masses of suppurative inflamma-tion spread through the lungs. Dr. Moxon [1] has seen several cases of pyæmic abscesses of the heart, mostly in youths with suppurative periostitis, or acute necrosis of the long bones, in which pericarditis was often caused by the bursting of small abscesses into the pericar-dium. This is not however the invariable mode in which pericarditis is caused by pyæmic abscesses of the heart, since in my case, just given, and in Mr. Stanley's,[2] there was evidently no rupture of the minute collections of pus in the walls of the heart. Dr. Moxon finds that in cases with pyæmic inflammation of the lung near its surface the pleura becomes involved, and thus every diseased portion of tissue is covered with a layer of lymph; and that when general pleurisy takes place, the abscess has generally burst into the pleura, and so caused the serous inflammation (p. 328). This well represents the parallel condi-tions in cases of pericarditis caused by pyæmic abscesses in the heart.

Another case may be named, a man, who had rigors on the day after being operated upon for perineal fistula, and was seized on the follow-ing day with violent pain in the region of the heart, the sounds of which were natural. Next day there was a distinct pericardial fric-tion sound, which was feeble in the evening, and was not again dis-tinctly audible. He died on the twelfth day after the operation, and the pericardium was found to be adherent to the heart by a thick layer of recent lymph. In this case, unlike that related above, the pyæmic inflammation evidently struck directly at the pericardium, since violent pain seized the heart the day after the operation, and next day there was a pericardial friction sound. These two cases show the rapidity with which the processes of inflammation pass through their stages in pyæmia.

Pyæmia, including with it erysipelas, was a much more frequent

---

[1] *Lectures on Pathological Anatomy*, by Dr. Wilks and Dr. Moxon, p. 122.
[2] *Medico-Chirurgical Transactions*, vii. 323.

cause of pericarditis in Dr. Chambers' cases observed in St. George's Hospital (22 or 23 in 81 or 1 in 3·8 of the cases of pericarditis that had neither acute rheumatism nor Bright's disease) than in those recorded in St. Mary's Hospital (3 in 46 or 1 in 13·6; or including partial pericarditis 6 in 56 or 1 in 9·5).

Fever, in which the serous inflammations are rare, was only associated with pericarditis in six instances among those from every source. This does not include one of small-pox, properly pyæmic, nor one of scarlet fever.

Those constitutional diseases, tubercle, cancer, and syphilis, were very rarely complicated with pericarditis, or in only one each among the whole of the combined cases, not including however tubercular pericarditis or cancer of the heart, in which the action of the disease was strictly local.

One single instance of chorea, which is so closely connected with acute rheumatism, had pericarditis. This occurred among the collected cases.

The case of pericarditis associated with disease of the suprarenal capsules is figured at page 307. This man could not lie down, his chest was universally dull on percussion in front and at the left side, and the sounds and impulse of his heart were absent. Upon these grounds Sir James Alderson, under whose care he was, correctly inferred that he had pericarditis.

B. *Affections of the Heart and Aorta.*—In one case, a man, pericarditis was caused by a wound of the heart. The right ventricle was penetrated by a wound about half an inch long, and the surface of the heart, and that of the pericardial sac were covered with recent lymph, stained red in many places. He survived the injury nearly five days. The left ventricle was penetrated by a wound half an inch long. In another patient who survived nearly two days, fibrinous coagula were found on either side of the wound, but there was no definite note of pericarditis. Pericarditis was caused by an injury inflicted over the region of the heart in two of the collected cases.

Local affections of the pericardium itself, and of the immediately adjoining structures, whether bearing upon it from within, and occupying the walls of the heart or ascending aorta; or from without, and seated in the neighbouring tissues, all tend to produce pericarditis. Tubercular pericarditis occurred in two instances; and as tubercular disease of the pericardium is rare, it is evident that this affection has a strong tendency to inflame the surface of the heart.

Among the affections of the structure of the heart that excited pericarditis by bearing outwards upon the pericardial surface of the heart, there were four cases with cancer of the heart; two with fibroid disease of the heart, in which the disease extended to the surface of the organ; and two of abscess of the heart, in one at least of which, described by Dr. Graves, there was no pyæmia, and in which instance the abscess contained two ounces of pus, and did not therefore cause pericarditis by bursting into the sac. These cases are derived from all sources.

Aneurism of the heart was the cause of pericarditis in another patient, a well-formed woman, aged 53. The pericardium was distended with about eight ounces of fluid, and was adherent in front to the right ventricle, and behind to the left ventricle by quite recent attachments. The mitral valve was thickened and incompetent. An aneurism was discovered, on examination, in front of the left ventricle about the size of a small orange. The walls of the left ventricle were thickened, but in the position of the sac there was not a trace left of muscular tissue, and the wall was only formed by the parietal layer.

In all these cases, whether of cancer, fibroid disease, abscess, or aneurism of the heart with pericarditis, the inflammation of the surface of the heart is excited in the same manner. The new mass, projecting into the pericardium, and bearing upon it during the active contraction of the organ with a rude and unaccustomed force, excites inflammation in the opposite surfaces of the heart and the pericardial sac, and so establishes pericarditis.

Aneurism of the ascending aorta excited pericarditis in eight of the cases derived from all sources; and three of the twenty-six cases of that affection observed in St. Mary's Hospital, presented evidence of previous pericarditis in the form of pericardial adhesion. In these cases the pericarditis is excited by the constantly enlarging aneurism bearing upon the pericardium, in the same manner that it is excited by cancer, abscess, fibroid disease, and aneurism of the heart.

Cases with valvular disease of the heart, including all its varieties, without Bright's disease, were attacked with pericarditis in definite, but by no means frequent numbers, since that affection appeared in only 6 of the 117 fatal cases in which the valves of the heart were incompetent (1 in 20). These proportions are increased if we strike out the thirty cases of the class under examination in which there were complete adhesions of the heart, and in which pericarditis was therefore forbidden. Thus corrected, the attacks of pericarditis number 6 in 87 (or 1 in 14·5). It will be interesting to ascertain whether valvular incompetence with Bright's disease was more frequently visited with pericarditis, than when it existed free from that affection. In 78 cases of Bright's disease with imperfection of the valves, 5 had pericarditis (1 in 15·6), or, deducting nine in which the heart was completely adherent, the numbers stand 5 in 69 or 1 in 14. From these comparative results it would seem that Bright's disease scarcely increases the tendency to pericarditis in valvular disease of the heart, for the proportion is almost identical in the two sets of cases. Partial pericarditis was present in 4 of the 117 cases with valvular insufficiency that were free from Bright's disease; and in three of the 78 cases of that class in which the kidneys were affected.

The six cases of pericarditis have been just distributed over the whole series of cases with valvular disease, the varieties of the affection being merged under one common title. If, however, we distinguish the different affections of the valves from each other, we find a remarkable difference in the proportion in which they were respectively attacked with pericarditis. The cases of mitral incompetence included all but one of those attacks of pericarditis, or 5 in 32; or, deducting 12 with complete adhesions of the heart, 5 in 20 or 1 in 4 of those cases were thus affected. The remaining instance of pericarditis appeared in one of the thirty-one cases of mitral-aortic insufficiency, or, deducting fourteen with complete pericardial adhesions, 1 in 17 of those cases. Not one of 32 cases with aortic valve-disease, or of 20 cases with mitral obstruction, had pericarditis.

Pericarditis in cases of valvular disease had a strong but not exclusive preference for mitral incompetence among the collected cases, including those in the *Pathological Transactions*, for among eleven cases in which the affection of the valve was specified, eight had mitral insufficiency, while two had mitral-aortic, and one had aortic valve-disease. May not the comparative frequency of pericarditis in mitral valve-disease be due to the resistance to the flow of blood through the lungs, and the consequent distension of the right ventricle with blood; the powerful action of that ventricle, which presses so strongly upon the walls of the chest in front; and the fulness of the coronary veins—which occur in the final stage of that affection?

The cases of pericarditis in Bright's disease, with valvular insufficiency, were equally distributed over the whole series; two with mitral incompetence, one with mitral contraction, one with aortic, and one with mitral aortic valve-disease being thus affected.

Pericarditis attacked one case in which there was hypertrophy of the heart without valvular disease, or any other complication except pericardial adhesion. There were altogether eleven cases of hypertrophy of the heart thus circumstanced, and as in six of them the heart was adherent, rendering pericarditis impossible, that affection attacked one in five cases of this class.

It will be well to inquire as to the proportion in which pericarditis attacked cases with and without hypertrophy of the heart. The heart was enlarged in 130 out of 655 cases of all the kinds enumerated in the supplementary table at page 421, that were free from Bright's disease, and among these 130 cases, 12, or 1 in 11, had pericarditis. The heart was diseased in 86 of those cases in which the organ was enlarged, excluding eleven without other complications except adhesion; and including those cases with adherent pericardium, the heart was not diseased in 45 instances. Of the cases just referred to, 26 of the 86, and 9 of the 45, had pericardial adhesions, and could not therefore have pericarditis. After deducting the cases with adhesions, 7 in 60 (or 1 in 8·6), with disease of the heart, and 5 of the 36 (or 1 in 7), without other affection than hypertrophy of that organ, had pericarditis. Without going into detail it may be briefly stated that of the rest of the cases, after deducting those with adherent pericardium, 6 in 104 (or 1 in 17) of those in which the heart was rather large, 4 in 267 (or 1 in 66) of those in which that organ was natural in size, and 1 of the 26, in which it was small, had pericarditis.

These returns make it evident that enlargement, or hypertrophy of the heart exercises a powerful influence on the production of pericarditis. Besides the cases enumerated, there were 107 (or 1 in 6) in which the size of the heart was not described, and of these sixteen (or 1 in 6·7) had pericardial adhesions, and nineteen (or 1 in 4, excluding those with adhesions) had pericarditis. It thus appears that the size of the heart was not described in nearly one-half of the cases with pericarditis, owing evidently to the mind of the reporter being preoccupied by the morbid anatomy of the inflamed organ. One of the cases in which the size of the heart is not noted had mitral incompetence, and may therefore be ranked with those in which the organ was enlarged; and ten of them had pneumonia (in 6), pleurisy (in 3), or empyema (in 1). In these ten cases the labour of the right ventricle must have been increased and prolonged, with the effect of enlarging the right side of the heart. This would tell more on the cases with pleuro-pneumonia than in those with simple pleurisy or empyema, but in such cases, with much effusion into one side of the chest, the obstacle to the stream of blood through the lungs is often great. This was well evidenced in a case, already alluded to at page 140, of extensive effusion into the right side of the chest which I saw through the kindness of Dr. Wane. Mr. James Lane drew off a large quantity of fluid from the affected side. Before its removal there was a mitral murmur and doubling of the second sound. The doubling disappeared when the fluid was being extracted, and after a time the murmur vanished. In these cases, therefore, the prime effect of the spreading of inflammation from the pleura to the pericardium was heightened by the added secondary influence of the increased size and labour of the right ventricle.

C. Eight patients with pneumonia (8 in 46), three with pleurisy (3 in 26), and two with empyema (2 in 17) had pericarditis. In all these cases (13 in 89), whether the primary affection was pneumonia or pleurisy, it was the pleurisy affecting the outer surface of the pericardium, and spreading thence to its inner surface, that immediately kindled the pericarditis.

Three of the eight cases with pneumonia and pericarditis were under my care, but in none of them did I detect a friction sound.

Two of the three cases with pleurisy and pericarditis were my patients, and in both of them friction sound was heard. One of these was a little girl, who had been attacked a fortnight before with pain in the left side and over the heart, and was brought to the hospital in the mother's arms, in distress, pale, and breathing hurriedly. There was extensive pleurisy of the left side, and next day there was dulness on percussion, and a double, rather smooth friction sound over the whole pericardium. Chorea soon appeared, and on the seventh day, when there was a mitral murmur, the effusion had reached its acme. Two days later, when the friction sound was limited to the lower sternum, she died. The other case was a man who had been ill six months with pleurisy of the left side. On the eleventh day after admission double pericardial friction sound came into play, and continued to the nineteenth day. After two days it vanished from over the heart, and was only audible at the apex; it was thus ten days later, and on the following day he died. The heart was almost universally adherent by yellow lymph.

Although in these thirteen cases the pleurisy excited inflammation of the exterior of the pericardial sac, which travelled through its fibrous structure to its interior, and then attacked the surface of the heart; yet in many of the seventy-six other cases with pleuro-pneumonia or pleurisy the exterior of the pericardium was inflamed, and yet the sac proved to be a barrier to the inflammation, which did not extend inwards so as to excite pericarditis. We have seen that in rheumatic pericarditis the inflammation habitually travels through the fibrous walls of the sac, and attacks its exterior, or pleural surface, exciting pleurisy; so that pericarditis tends to pass from within outwards much more than pleurisy of the pericardium does so from without inwards.

A case of pleurisy with pericarditis, under my care, that recovered presented a peculiar pericardial friction sound on pressure, to the left of the lower sternum, that lasted about three weeks.

I have just alluded to the important secondary influence which the increased size and force of the right ventricle exercises in reinforcing the primary influence of the extension of the inflammation from the pleura to the pericardium in cases of pneumonia and pleurisy.

Pericarditis attacked two cases of phthisis out of a total number affected with that disease amounting to 12. This does not include the two cases of tubercular pericarditis with phthisis already spoken of. Dr. Stokes gives an important case communicated to him by Dr. McDowell in which pneumo-pericarditis was caused by a fistulous communication between the pericardium and a small cavity at the summit of the right lung; the apices of both lungs were healthy, but the bases of both lungs were solidified from a deposit of miliary tubercle and from pneumonia.[1]

D. Two cases were attacked with pericarditis owing to disease of the œsophagus where it passes behind the pericardium. In one of these patients, who was under the care of Dr. Chambers, the œsophagus was ulcerated from the bifurcation of the trachea to half an inch above the diaphragm. The ulcer gave way into the pericardium, which was filled with fluid from the stomach, and the interior of the sac was lined, and the heart was covered with recent fibrin.

The other patient, with cancer of the œsophagus behind the pericardium, a woman, aged 47, a cook, under my care, complained of slight difficulty in swallowing, referred to the fauces. A to-and-fro friction sound, louder with the diastole than the systole, was audible over the cardiac region, being most intense over the sixth cartilage, and heard from thence to the ninth cartilage. Pleural friction was also present. This patient died on the fifth day after admission.

[1] Dr. Stokes, On Diseases of the Heart and Aorta, p. 25.

E. There was a small and remarkable group of cases, in which pericarditis was caused by affections involving the diaphragm. One of them had diaphragmatic hernia; two others had abscess of the liver involving the diaphragm; and another had a tumour connected with the pericardium, and communicating with the stomach.

In the case of diaphragmatic hernia which was under the care of Sir James Alderson, the stomach, omentum, spleen, and transverse colon were forced through an opening into the left side of the chest, which contained six pints of liquid, partly digested blood, partly food. The heart was displaced to the right of the sternum, and there was pericarditis.

In one of two other cases an abscess, with thickened walls, containing several ounces of greenish pus, was situated between the pericardium and the liver, involving the diaphragm, and communicating with a small abscess in the liver. The pericardium contained many ounces of puriform fluid, and its lining membrane and the surface of the heart were "hyperæmic," the latter being very red and velvety. In the other case, the diaphragm was pushed up by the liver in a conical projection, which was formed by an abscess occupying the interior portion of the left lobe of the liver, and the contiguous part of its right lobe. The pericardium contained two or three ounces of turbid fluid, and the surface of the heart was roughened by a recent deposit of lymph. Dr. Graves gives an important case in which pneumo-pericarditis was caused by a hepatic abscess which communicated with the pericardium and the stomach.

In the fourth case the pericardium was full of thick yellow fluid and there were some nodules on the aorta; a dense white tumour which was interposed between the pericardium and the diaphragm was softened in the middle, and formed a cavity which communicated with the stomach and spleen, and resembled an ulcer.

One case of peritonitis out of a total of 64 had general, and another had partial pericarditis.

F. There remains one fatal case of pericarditis in which there was no evidence that the affection was secondary to, or associated with, any other disease.

In this patient, a woman, aged 44, the pericardium was nearly the eighth of an inch thick, and its sac contained a large quantity of sero-purulent fluid. The surfaces of the heart and the sac were covered with recent layers of plastic deposit, which was arranged at the base in a honeycomb shape, and was lengthened out at the apex into bands. The heart was small, hard, and contracted; the lungs were congested behind; and there was a quarter of a pint of brown fluid in each lateral cavity of the chest.

Two cases of pericarditis, under my care in St. Mary's Hospital, presented no other definite affection. One of these, a schoolboy, aged 12, was attacked, eighteen days before his admission, with pain in both sides of the chest, worse in the left. On admission the impulse of the heart was in the fifth space, there was fulness over the pericardium, dulness from the second cartilage to the sixth, and a loud to-and-fro sound, which was intensified by pressure, over the same region and up to the top of the sternum. Next day the dulness had lessened, but the friction sound was strong and grating, and extended beyond the region of dulness. For several days it was more feeble and limited; on the fourteenth, and two days later, it was again louder, but on the nineteenth day it had vanished. The other patient, a pregnant woman, took cold six weeks before admission. The heart's action was tumultuous, and on the third day the impulse extended from the sternum to two inches and a half beyond the left nipple, a to-and-fro sound appeared over and below the region of the heart, and a mitral murmur at the apex. Next day an impulse of a grating character, almost a thrill, extended over the region of the friction sound. These signs continued with variations, but lessening, and on the fourteenth day the impulse had shrunk inwards for two inches and a half, being bounded by the nipple line. Three days later a systolic murmur was converted by pressure into a friction sound, which disappeared on the eighteenth day.

THE TREATMENT OF PERICARDITIS.

Pericarditis, as we have just seen, is so rarely met with except as a combination of, or associated with, some other disease, that in the treatment of such cases we have to consider mainly the primary affection, and along with this the local management of the secondary inflammation of the pericardium. I shall of course here practically limit myself to this latter and local point. It will be important, however, to touch upon the measures, in the treatment of the main disease, that may tend to prevent the occurrence of pericarditis. I shall briefly consider (1) the preventive treatment of acute rheumatism, in relation to the possible occurrence of pericarditis and (2) the local treatment that the presence of pericarditis may render desirable in those diseases which are more or less frequently complicated with that affection.

(1) The chief objects to be kept in view in the treatment of *acute rheumatism* are (1) the mitigation of the endocarditis that is the usual and natural effect of that disease, and (2) the prevention of pericarditis, which, though the frequent, is not the customary complication of that disease. Fortunately the measures that tend to palliate the inflammation of the interior of the heart, tend also to prevent the inflammation of the exterior of that organ. The Address in Medicine, given at the meeting of the British Medicine Association in Newcastle-on-Tyne, was devoted to the treatment of acute rheumatism by rest and the relief of local pain, with a view to prevent pericarditis and lessen the severity and permanent ill effects of endocarditis. The publisher of this work will supply the reader, if he desire it, with a copy of that Address. The absolute rest of every limb and joint; and the soothing

application of the belladonna and chloroform liniment, sprinkled on cotton wool, to the affected joints, supported by flannel, applied over the seat of pain with uniform and comfortable pressure, are the most important measures in the treatment of acute rheumatism for the prevention of pericarditis. The rest and support of the affected joints should be strictly maintained for several days after the disappearance of the local inflammation; for the too early use of an affected joint or limb, after the relief of pain and swelling, often leads to a relapse, first attacking the joints of the over-used limb, extending to other joints, and often producing endocarditis and pericarditis. I have given, at pages 210, 211, brief notes of six cases in which a relapse of the joint affection, usually thus occasioned, induced endocarditis and pericarditis.

2. The employment of a few leeches, and the application of cotton wool or a poultice, sprinkled with the belladonna and chloroform liniment, over the region of the heart during the early and painful period of an attack of pericarditis, are the means that I have for a long time employed in the treatment of that affection.

I have before me the collected notes of 36 cases of pericarditis, in which several leeches were applied over the region of the heart. In 29 of these cases there was pain over the region of the inflamed pericardium, and in 7 of them there was no note of the presence of pain. In 24 of the cases suffering from pain, marked relief, sometimes complete, followed upon the application of the leeches; and this relief in a fair proportion of the cases so speedily followed the local bleeding that the relief must be attributed to the leeching. Brief notes of cases in which the application of leeches relieved the pain over the region of the inflamed pericardium will be found in the preceding pages (211, 219, 231, 238). The local bleeding, besides assuaging the local pain, lessened the oppression in the chest and the difficulty of respiration in many cases.

In one instance leeches were applied over the seat of pain five times; although on each occasion relief seemed to follow, yet the pain soon again increased.

In five cases leeches gave little or no relief. Although in these cases pain was not materially lessened by the local bleeding, yet in every instance but one, its action on the patient's state seemed to be favourable. In that patient (17), whose case has been already referred to at pages 219, 232, 235, and 237, there was pain over the heart, the action of which was very tumultuous at the time of admission. Leeches were applied with great relief, but unfortunately the bleeding from one of them could not be stopped, and she lost much blood. After this the action of the heart was irregular and intermittent, and she was evidently weakened by the hæmorrhage. She finally died after a long and severe illness, which was closed by an·attack of small-pox.

The employment of leeches produced a definite but very variable effect on the friction sound, and tended to lessen the force and extent of the impulse. Sometimes the friction sound was lessened in intensity (in 8), but as often it became more intense (in 8) after the local bleeding. In one patient (35, pp. 327, 360) its effect was to suspend the rubbing sound, which had been previously extensive and rough, for one day; but in the evening pain returned, and with it the frottement over the region of the heart. Another patient (16) on admission had excessive pain across the heart, where there was a double thrill, and a double harsh scraping friction sound; four leeches were applied; and next morning there was scarcely any pain, no friction sound, and no note of thrill. The friction sound returned on pressure that afternoon, and was again present on the following day. In one instance—I speak from memory—I examined a patient with pericarditis immediately after the withdrawal of leeches, and found that the friction sound that had been previously audible was entirely abolished. This disappearance of the friction sound in such a case is evidently not due to any change in the character of the lymph on the surfaces of the heart and sac, although their vascularity may be lessened, but to the diminished force of the action of the organ. In direct confirmation of this, we have already seen that in several cases friction sound was abolished, suspended, or softened, by the weakening of the action of the heart (see pages 235, 360).

The effect of leeching the region of the heart on the amount of effusion in the pericardium in cases of pericarditis was not very marked. The leeches were applied at the time of the acme of the effusion in ten cases, and in all of them but two the amount of effusion had lessened on the following day, and in the remaining two on the third day after the local bleeding, which lessened local pain in eight of these cases. To balance these instances, in eight others the effusion increased after the application of the leeches, and attained its acme in a day or two; at the same time, however, the pain over the region of the heart was relieved in six of those cases, but was not so in two of them.

Blisters applied over the heart are frequently employed in the treatment of pericarditis. I resorted to them occasionally up to the year 1856. I cannot, however, find any instance in which they appeared to be of service, and they were certainly, in some cases, a source of discomfort. It is evident that a blister over the region of the heart adds a second and outward inflammation to the primary and inward inflammation, and it therefore, unless there is a counter-balancing gain, increases the evil. Blisters were the definite cause of mischief in a case that I shall have occasion to quote when I speak of the removal of the fluid from the distended pericardium. In that instance they were applied seven times in succession over the præcordial region. A blister cannot alter the lymph covering the heart and lining the sac; and cannot directly lessen the amount of fluid in the pericardium, which as we have again and again seen, tends of itself to diminish rapidly when it has reached its acme. It appears to me that a blister over the distended pericardium would rather increase than lessen the morbid supply of blood to those inflamed parts to which it is so contiguous. Blisters, besides inflicting local injury, taint the blood by increasing its fibrin, and are apt to lead to a secondary and low kind of inflammation in distant parts, and perhaps even to degrade the character of the pericardial inflammation itself, and to prolong its existence.

It may be said that exciting pain at the surface of the chest in these cases lessens the severity of the internal pain. This is true, but this effect may be induced innocuously, by the application of chloroform over the seat of suffering, combined with belladonna liniment, sprinkled on cotton wool, and covered with oiled silk.

Paracentesis of the Pericardium.—We have seen again and again that when the fluid in the pericardium has reached its acme, it very soon begins to diminish. It is therefore evident that puncture of the pericardium is very seldom called for. In some rare instances, however, the quantity of serum in the sac is so great as to interfere seriously with the action of the heart, breathing, swallowing, and speech; owing to the compression of the auricles and venæ cavæ, the trachea and left bronchus, the œsophagus and the descending aorta; and the inflammation of the recurrent nerve. Generally the fluid of itself lessens so quickly that these threatening symptoms pass by without real danger to life. In some rare instances, however, life is in danger owing to the distension of the pericardium, and then paracentesis of the pericardium may become urgently called for.

Riolan,[1] in 1649, proposed that in dropsy of the pericardium, the sac might be opened by trephining the sternum an inch from the ensiform cartilage. Senac,[2] and Laennec,[3] at long intervals, both gave the same advice, the point selected by Laennec being immediately above the ensiform cartilage. Desault[4] attempted to open the pericardium between the sixth and seventh ribs, and Larrey,[5] between the fifth and sixth ribs; but they both evidently failed to enter the pericardium. Romero[5] opened the pericardial sac in three cases of " hydro-pericardium," twice with success, through an incision made in the fifth space, near the junction of the cartilages to the ribs, this wound being made, partly to explore, partly to open the pericardium or the pleura. The first circumstantial account of tapping the pericardium was in a patient of Skoda's, with pericarditis from cancer of the heart, operated upon by Schuh in 1840,[4] who first inserted a trocar by a perpendicular puncture through the third space close to the sternum over the great arteries, and failing to get fluid, penetrated the sac through the fourth space and obtained a certain amount of reddish serum. This patient lived for nearly six months, and died with extensive cancer of

---

[1] *Encheiridium Anatomicum et pathologicum*, p. 213.
[2] Senac, *de la Structure du Cœur*, ii. 369.
[3] Laennec, *Traité de l'Auscultation Mediate*.
[4] Trousseau et Lasègue, *Arch. Gen. de Med.* Nov. 1854.
[5] *Dict. des Sc. Médicales*, v. xl, p. 370. These cases are given imperfectly.

the chest.[1] In 1841 Heger performed paracentesis of the pericardium in another patient of Skoda's, with pericarditis. He entered the pericardium through the fifth space, two inches from the left border of the sternum. Altogether 1500 grammes (about 48 ounces) of a brownish serum, finely flocculent, escaped, and nineteen days later, the fluid having reaccumulated, he again punctured the pericardium at the same place, and 500 grammes (about 16 ounces) of a reddish troubled fluid escaped in the course of four hours. This patient died 51 days after the second operation. The pericardium was in great part adherent, and there were nine and five pints respectively in the two sides of the chest, and a tubercular cavity of the left lung. These two patients died from the primary diseases, cancer, and tubercle; but both operations were successful.

Behier thought that he punctured the pericardium through the sixth left space in a case related by him in 1854; the patient died twenty-six days afterwards, but there was no pericarditis, and no mark of puncture in the walls of the sac. Jobert,[2] in 1854, after cutting the skin punctured the pericardium with a trochar, in a case of pericarditis, a patient of M. Trousseau's, through the fifth left space, 1·2 inch from the edge of the sternum. The cannula was agitated by the beating of the heart—the fluid came at first in drops and then very slowly, and altogether 400 grammes (about 13 ounces) of liquid flowed in the course of an hour-and-a-half. The patient left the hospital eleven weeks after the operation, suffering from phthisis. Trousseau,[3] in 1856, operated on another case, and opened the chest with a bistoury below the nipple through the nearest intercostal space, and penetrated into the pericardium, from which flowed nearly 100 grammes (about three ounces) of a red serosity; and twice as much yellow serum came from the pleura. The patient died five days after the operation. The last of the French operators that I shall name was M. Aran,[4] who in 1855, after cutting through the skin, penetrated the pericardium with a trochar through the fifth space, about an inch from the extreme limit of pericardial dulness, and withdrew about 350 grammes (fully 11 ounces) of reddish transparent fluid, and then injected a solution of iodine.[1] Twelve days later he tapped a second time and withdrew 1,350 grammes (about forty ounces) of albuminous liquid. This patient recovered from the operation, but three months later presented signs of phthisis.

I have now to speak of two important cases of pericarditis with symptoms threatening life, in which Dr. Clifford Allbutt resolved with his colleagues on the performance of paracentesis of the pericardium.

---

[1] Trousseau and Laségue publish this case at length in the *Archives*, but in his *Clinique Médicale* Trousseau states that Schuh penetrated in his first puncture a mass of cancer, altogether of a thickness of six inches, which had invaded the sternum. It was not, however, until more than a month after the operation that this tumour showed itself. *Arch. G. de Med.*, 1854, p. 520.

[2] Trousseau et Laségue, *Arch. G. de Med.*, 1854.

[3] Trousseau, *Clinical Medicine. New. Syd. Soc.*, iii. 365.

[4] *Bulletin de l'Academie Royale de Médicine*, xxi. 142.

One of these cases was operated upon by Mr. Wheelhouse, who vividly describes the condition of the patient and the steps of the operation. He found the patient sitting up in bed, his head resting on his hands, his elbows on his knees, struggling for breath. I quote the following from his description, and refer to his paper for the full details of the operation; and the precautions adopted during its performance :—" I chose for my purpose a small trochar. This I placed on the upper margin of the fifth rib, half an inch to the left of the sternum; and inclining it upwards and inwards, thrust it steadily forwards through the intercostal space towards what I believed to be the centre of the ventricle. I pushed it onwards until I could distinctly feel the movements of the heart with the instrument; and then, sheathing the point, I advanced the cannula well up to the heart, until I could feel and see, and demonstrate to those around, the impulse of the heart as communicated to the instrument. The trochar was then withdrawn, and the fluid allowed to escape. This it did at first in a steady stream, which soon subsided into a saltatory flow coincident with the heart's contractions. The fluid consisted of a pale pink coagulable serum, and, upon the whole, about three ounces escaped. During the operation the patient gradually obtained relief; and after the cannula was withdrawn, the bed-rest was removed, and he was able to lie down."[1] This patient completely recovered, and was in perfect health the other day when Mr. Wheelhouse, in reply to my inquiries, kindly informed me as to the state of the patient. In the second of Dr. Clifford Allbutt's patients Mr. Teale drew off, as Mr. Wheelhouse had done, through a fine cannula five ounces of fluid which gave the patient great relief. The reaccumulation of the fluid called for a second operation, which was performed with considerable relief. Finally, however, this patient, a girl, died of bronchitis.[2]

The operation has been performed within the last three years on three occasions, and I owe the references to these cases to the kindness of Mr. Holmes. M. Villeneuve, in 1873, operated by means of the aspirator, on a child with arching and fluctuation over the præcordial region. He punctured the tumour at its most prominent part, and removed two syringe-fulls of serum. On withdrawing the cannula a jet of liquid spirted out of the wound, which remained open owing to the internal wall of the cavity having been very much thinned by the repeated application of blisters, seven of them having been placed one after another, without any improvement, on the same place. A pericardial fistula, yielding pus, was established and did not heal up until the sixth month after the operation.[3] In the other case, a man in whom paracentesis of the chest and abdomen had already been performed, Dr. Valtosta, in 1874, opened the pericardium by making an incision over the fifth space, commencing about half an inch from the sternum. The layers of muscles were then carefully divided and an

---

[1] See *British Medical Journal*, Oct. 10, 1868, p. 385.
[2] See Dr. Clifford Allbutt's important paper, *Lancet*, 1869, i. 807.
[3] *London Medical Record*, iii. p. 532.

elastic dilatation was felt. A puncture was made in this, the point
of a small trochar was introduced, and about ten ounces of fluid was
removed with immediate relief. This patient died four weeks after
the performance of the operation.[1] M. Chairon contributed a third
case in 1875, in which more than 1000 grammes (about 33 ounces) of
liquid were removed from the pericardium. The result is not given.
With reference to the method of operation, he says the spot to be
preferred is the fifth intercostal space, at an intermediate point between
the nipple and the sternum, rather nearer to the former, always being
guided by the apex of the heart. The aspiratory method should, he
considers, be preferred.[2]

Proposed Operation for Paracentesis of the Pericardium.—This
operation cannot well be called for unless the amount of effusion into
the pericardium be so great as to compress the venæ cavæ and the
auricles, the œsophagus, trachea, and left bronchus, and the descending
aorta, so as to interfere with the action of the heart, swallowing,
breathing, and the supply of blood to the abdomen and lower limbs.
Under these circumstances the pericardial sac is greatly distended
downwards towards the abdomen, and the heart itself is elevated. The
result is that the mass of the fluid occupies a large space below the
heart, measuring between one and two inches from above downwards,
between the lower surface of the ventricles and the floor of the pericardium, where it is formed by the central tendon of the diaphragm ;
which is depressed downwards almost or quite to the level of the
upper border of the sixth space, in the manner represented in the
figures at pages 311, 338, 340, and 378, and also, in principle, in
Pirogoff's important work.

When it is considered that in these serious cases the lower border
of the heart is above, while the mass of the fluid is below the level of
the lower edge of the fifth cartilage, I advise that the fine trochar,
such as that used by M. Aran, Mr. Wheelhouse, Mr. Teale, and M.
Chairon, should be inserted into the distended pericardium at a point
just above the upper edge of the sixth cartilage at the lowest part of
its curve, more than an inch within the mammary line ; and that the
instrument should penetrate gently inwards with a direction slightly
downwards, so that it may advance into the collection of fluid below
the level of the heart ; and that the liquid should be slowly and gently
extracted by the use of a syringe or the aspirator. By this proceeding
the collected fluid will be alone penetrated and the heart will be quite
untouched. Extensive incisions, and the injection of irritating fluids
should be of course avoided.

In every case in which the heart has been previously healthy, and
is of the natural size, its lower border is elevated above the level of
the fifth space when the effusion into the pericardium is at its height,
so that in such cases the procedure I have advised, which has the
sanction of Aran's and Chairon's operations, can be performed with
ease and safety.

[1] *London Medical Record*, iii. p. 275, 532.   [2] *Ibid*, p. 691.

When, however, the heart is enlarged owing to the existence of valvular disease of some standing, the heart is sometimes, as in the cases spoken of at page 336, to be felt beating in the fifth or even the sixth space at the time of the acme of the effusion, when the urgent distress and danger of the patient may demand paracentesis of the pericardium. Under such circumstances, which can be readily discovered by ascertaining the position of the impulse—which should always be some distance above the point of penetration, for a thin layer of fluid interposes itself between the surface of the heart above its lower border, and the front of the chest—another point than that just indicated in the fifth space must be chosen for the operation. This point should then be selected at the space between the left edge of the ensiform cartilage and the right border of the seventh cartilage in the epigastric region; or, if needful, owing to its margin being covered by the seventh costal cartilage, the ensiform cartilage, at its left border, may itself be perforated, first with the point of a bistoury, and then with the fine trochar. Trousseau states that Larrey advised that the puncture of the pericardium should be made through this space; but in the operation which he performed with a view—erroneous in this instance—to enter the pericardial sac, that great surgeon, as we have seen, entered the cavity of the chest between the fifth and sixth ribs. The lower border of the fully-distended pericardium is usually a little above, and sometimes even below, the lower end of the ensiform cartilage, as in figure 42, page 342; which is from a case, exactly in point, with mitral regurgitation and enlargement of the heart; and the pericardium may therefore be safely punctured through a point corresponding to the middle or the lower portion of that cartilage. The presence or absence of the impulse of the right ventricle in the epigastric space, and the position of the lower border of the pericardial dulness in that space, must be previously ascertained. Those two important points of diagnosis, which can be readily made, will prove a safe guide to the surgeon as to the place which he should select for the operation, which he will rightly fix sufficiently below the seat of the impulse, so as to avoid the heart; and sufficiently above the lower border of pericardial dulness, so as to prevent the cannula being tilted upwards when the floor of the pericardium elevates itself as the sac is being emptied. When he pushes the trochar onwards he must use all the precautions so clearly described by Mr. Wheelhouse, so that if the point of the instrument comes upon the front of the heart, he may withdraw the trochar at the same time that he gently presses the cannula forwards and downwards.

In the great majority of cases the fluid, after it has reached its acme, soon begins to lessen, and continues to do so steadily from day to day. Under these circumstances I do not advise the use either of aperients, which tend to disturb and lower the patient, or of diuretics. If, however, the quantity of the fluid is stationary, or lessens very slowly, then diuretics may sometimes be of use.

ADHERENT PERICARDIUM.

BY FRANCIS SIBSON, M.D. F.R.S.

THE discovery of adherent pericardium during life is in some cases impossible, and in some, doubtful or difficult; but in others, and these are amongst the most important cases, its existence may be ascertained during life on reasonable and well-ascertained grounds.

When the adhesions are partial, or when the heart, though completely adherent, is small, is not bound by external adhesions to the anterior walls of the chest, and is covered to the natural extent by the lungs, their expansion being free and unconstrained, then the varying relation of the heart and lungs to the chest is quite natural, and the diagnosis of the adhesions is impossible. If the adherent heart be enlarged, and is not attached to the lower half of the sternum and the cardiac cartilages by combined pericardial and pleural adhesions, so that the active or automatic and the passive or respiratory movements of the heart are scarcely or but little interfered with, the inspiratory expansion of the lungs is freely permitted, and the diagnosis of the adherent pericardium may be difficult, obscure, or even impossible.

When, however, the heart is, as usual, enlarged, being often affected with valvular disease, the adhesions may be short, fibrous, and binding; and the front of the organ may be fixed to the two lower thirds of the sternum and the adjoining cartilages by pleuro-pericardial adhesions, so that the automatic and respiratory movements of the heart, and the inspiratory expansion of the lungs are restrained : thus the discovery of the adhesions during life may generally in such cases be made by a careful study of the physical signs; its diagnosis being the more certain and easy in proportion as the heart is more enlarged, and more firmly fixed to the anterior walls of the chest.

ANATOMICAL DESCRIPTION OF ADHERENT PERICARDIUM.

Partial Adhesions.—Pericardial adhesions vary greatly in firmness of tissue and length of fibre, and when they are partial they are usually longer than when they are general.

Four conditions seem to regulate the position, extent, and firmness of partial adhesions of the heart. (1.) The amount of movement of the various parts of the heart and arteries; for it is evident that the more limited the movement of any part, the greater must be its tendency to adhesion: the relation of the surrounding sac (2) to the heart; and (3) to the outer borders of the pericardium, which are close to the heart, and are therefore more often adherent: (4) the gravitation of the heart in the fluid, since the posterior or depending parts of the heart, when the patient lies on the back, attach themselves readily to the parts on which they rest.

Partial adhesions take place most frequently near the apex and along the line of the ventricular septum; at the outer border of the left ventricle and the outer side of the right auricle, where the movements of those cavities are most limited, and to which parts the outer borders of the sac cling; the posterior surfaces of the left auricle and of the ventricles which rest upon the sac; and the great arteries at their higher parts, where the extent of their movement is least, and where they are most contiguous to the pericardium. The visible commencement of the ascending aorta is often free from adhesions, owing to the hollow, containing liquid, formed in front of that part of the vessel, between the appendix of the right auricle and the origin of the pulmonary artery. In several instances a patch of the right ventricle, to the right of the septum, and midway between the pulmonary artery and the lower border of the ventricle, was adherent when the rest of the ventricle was free; and it is to be remarked that this patch is the part of least movement, or stable equilibrium, of the walls of the right ventricle (see fig. 16, page 66). A frequent seat of partial adhesions is a point a little above and to the left of the apex of the heart. These adhesions near the apex frequently become stretched and attenuated, and at length give way. Several pendulous, filamentous, fibrous bands often hang from this point, near the apex, on the surface of hearts that are free from internal disease; but which display white fibrous patches on their surface; the filaments and the patches being evidently alike the result of a previous attack of pericarditis.

The parts of the surface of the heart and arteries that are usually not adherent when other parts are so, are the front of the right ventricle, especially in the neighbourhood of the right auricle and pulmonary artery, and above its own lower border; the appendix and ventricular border of the right auricle; and the parts of the aorta and pulmonary artery nearest to the heart, those being the parts that have respectively the greatest extent of movement during the action of the heart, as may be seen in the figures at page 66.

General Adhesions.—The adhesions are formed of fibrous threads of variable and often of considerable length, and they usually allow of a fair amount of movement of the heart. Long and loose adhesions interfere but little with the free play of the heart; but short, close, and firm attachments embarrass the action of the organ. The length of the fibres of adhesion varies over the different parts of the heart; their length usually corresponding to the amount of movement, and the power exercised by the respective parts during the action of the organ. The adhesions are generally longer at the apex than elsewhere: those over the left ventricle are longer than those over the right ventricle ; those over the auricular portion of the right ventricle are longer than those over its body and near the septum, and I believe that the same applies to the left ventricle also. The adhesions over the right auricle are much shorter than those over the right ventricle; and the auricular appendix is contracted in size by the fibrous covering. The attachments of the left auricle, the aorta, and the pulmonary artery are generally closer than those of the right auricle.

When the adhesions are long and loose, and the heart is free from valvular disease, and from any other influence tending to cause enlargement of the organ, the size of the heart is usually natural. It was thus in two of the cases examined after death at St. Mary's Hospital, in four cases that I observed at Nottingham, in many of those referred to by Dr. Stokes, in ten briefly described by Dr. Gairdner, and in 34 out of 90 cases collected by Dr. Kennedy.

When pericardial adhesions are associated with valvular disease, the heart is always enlarged. It was so in 25 out of 26 cases, and in the remaining instance, a case with mitral contraction, the heart was rather large. I have compared a double series of cases of valvular disease side by side, in one series with, and the other without adherent pericardium, and, not going here into details, I may say that the cases with adhesions were on an average five and a half ounces heavier than those in which there were no adhesions, an increase that was to a considerable extent accounted for, in many instances, by the augmented thickness and weight of the pericardial sac. The increased size of the heart would seem,·therefore, in such cases, judging by this analysis, to be traceable more to the affection of the valves, than to the adherent pericardium. We find, however, that in two-thirds of the cases without valvular disease in which the pericardium was adherent, the heart was enlarged (12 in 19) ; and in one-fifth of them it was rather large (5 in 19); while in only one-tenth of them the organ was of natural size (2 in 19). These proportions are borne out by Dr. Kennedy's important analysis of collected cases of adherent pericardium, who found that in fifty instances the heart was enlarged, in thirty-four it was of natural size, while in five it was atrophied. We may therefore conclude that in cases with the double affection of valvular disease and adherent pericardium, the valvular disease is the essential cause of the enlargement of the heart; yet that the adhesions, by giving an additional spur to the action of the organ, add to the more important enlarging effect of the valvular disease of the organ.

It is the natural effect of pericarditis for the inflammation to spread from the pericardial to the pleural surface of the fibrous sac. When, therefore, the pericardium becomes adherent to the heart in those cases, it becomes adherent also to the walls of the chest in front of the pericardium. These pleural adhesions often occupy an extensive space in front of the chest, and may extend from the second left cartilage to the sixth; from the manubrium to the upper half of the ensiform cartilage ; and from the right border of the sternum to the apex of the heart, to the left of the nipple line, as in the cases referred to in former pages, and there described. Though these are extreme instances, yet they are typical of many cases with pleuro-pericardial adhesions.

When the adhesions are short and powerful, and when, being pleuro-pericardial, they bind the walls of the heart extensively to the walls of the chest in front of them, a great and constant strain is put upon the ventricles; for they cannot contract upon themselves to expel their contents until they have dragged the sternum and cartilages powerfully inwards. The ventricles thus expend their force in two directions, one towards the interior to expel their contents, resisted in doing so by valvular incompetence; the other from the exterior, to compel the front of the chest, which is united to them like a solid buckler, to share in their contraction. Under these influences the ventricles tend to undergo a change in form, and to become flattened out, the one in front of the other. Two cases observed by me in Nottingham were thus influenced. The enlarged and thickened right ventricle, instead of sweeping half round the left ventricle, usually cone-shaped, lay directly in front of it; and the septum between the ventricles, instead of bulging forwards into the right cavity, became flattened.

When the adhesions, being extensive and pleuro-pericardial, are not short and close, but of moderate length, and do not, therefore, bind the sternum and cartilages to the heart like a buckler, they do not seriously embarrass the commencing action of the ventricles; but during their contraction, the ventricles at length begin to draw upon the walls of the chest; and in the course of the systole they drag those walls inwards.

When the adhesions are, as usual, longer and less solid, the ventricles contract more after their wont, and retain more or less perfectly their power. The right ventricle is usually enlarged as well as the left, but not always, for the size of the ventricles is necessarily influenced by the valvular affection. When that affection is mitral or mitral aortic, the right ventricle shares the labour and the enlargement with the left ventricle; when the aortic valve is alone affected, the left ventricle is often alone enlarged; and when there is mitral obstruction, the enlargement may mainly affect the two auricles, that of the ventricles being somewhat moderate.

The ventricles, when the pericardium is adherent, tend to enlarge outwards in every direction, and especially upwards to the manubrium, as well as downwards, into the epigastric space, to the right, and to the left. The great arteries are lifted up on the top of the ventricles into an unusually high position, and are crowded into the narrowed space at the top of the chest, almost as high as the root of the neck.

When the adhesions are dense, strong, and contracted they sheathe the whole heart in a tight, tough envelope, which grasps the auricles and ventricles, prevents their free expansion, and forcibly lessens the organ.

PHYSICAL SIGNS OF ADHERENT PERICARDIUM.

Clinical History. (A) *From a succession of Observers.*—Dr. Burns, in 1809, gave cases to show that when the pericardium is adherent, pulsation is felt in the epigastrium—a sign that had been previously observed by Korner—caused, he says, by the repercussions of the heart affecting the liver, which is the immediate seat of the pulsation.[1]   He gives a case of adherent pericardium in which Dr. Rutherford found a strong pulsation of the heart, accompanied by a jarring motion, most remarkable at the contraction of the ventricles.   Heim, according to Kreysig,[2] observed that a hollow appeared under the ribs during each systole when the pericardium was adherent.   Sander[3] found, in a case of adherent pericardium with great enlargement of the heart,

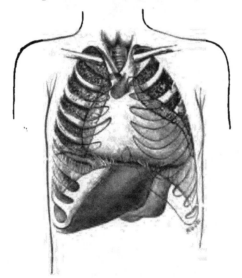

FIG. 49.

deepening of the space on the left side of the ensiform cartilage, followed quickly by a shock, perceptible to the hand; fulness over the cardiac cartilages; and extensive impulse over the front of the chest.

Corvisart[4] noticed that in these cases respiration is high, and this he connects with the trouble of the whole heart caused by the laborious action of the diaphragm, to which it is attached by the adhesions.

Dr. Hope,[5] in 1839, observed that pericardial adhesions sometimes

[1] Burns, on the *Diseases of the Heart*, p. 62.
[2] Kreysig, *Die Krankheiten des Herzens*, ii. 625.
[3] *Hufelunand Bibliothek d. p. Heilkunde*, Bd. 51, 120.
[4] Corvisart, *Sur les Maladies du Cœur*, p. 35.
[5] Dr. Hope, on the *Diseases of the Heart*, p. 194.

caused a prominence of the cardiac cartilages, sometimes an abrupt
jogging motion of the heart, corresponding with the systole and the
diastole, that with the diastole having the character of a receding
motion suddenly arrested. In the recital of four of his cases, to which
his general account does little justice, he states that they presented a
second or diastolic shock or back-stroke.

Dr. Williams,[1] in 1840, remarked that when the pericardium adheres
both to the heart when enlarged, and to the walls of the chest, the
heart pulsates in close contact with those walls; so that the pulsations
are felt very widely, extending upwards as well as downwards,
drawing in the intercostal spaces at each systole; and that respiration

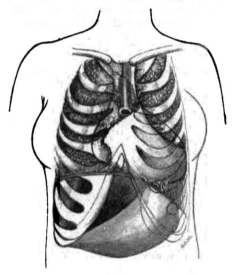

Fig. 50.

does not lessen the region of cardiac dulness on percussion, and of
impulse. Dr. Law, in a communication that I have not been able to
find, states that change of posture does not alter the position of the
impulse.

In my paper on the situation of the internal organs, I, in 1844,[2]
described four cases of adherent pericardium, and gave figures showing
the position of the internal organs after death, two of which figures
I reproduce here (see Figs. 49, 50). In one of these cases, a young
woman, the heart was small in size, and presented during life no
physical sign of disease of the heart, but the pulse was very feeble;
she had palpitation, dyspnœa, and anasarca; and her lips were blue.

[1] Dr. Williams, on the *Diseases of the Chest*, p. 24.
[2] *Prov. Med. Trans.*

The heart was very large in the three remaining cases, two of which had mitral regurgitation, and the third had narrowing of the mitral, aortic, and tricuspid orifices. One of the two cases with mitral disease has been already described, and is figured at page, 350. In the other case of the same class, the impulse was very strong and jogging; shaking and heaving the whole chest. The apex protruded strongly; the lower half of the sternum advanced firmly at the beginning of the systole, and fell back gradually and firmly during its continuance. The lower end of the ensiform cartilage receded during the systole ; the impulse was irregular, 140 to 160 (see figure 49, page 442).

The remaining case with adherent pericardium presented physical signs that differed materially from those observed in the two other cases. The obstructed, mitral, and aortic apertures tested by the cone, each measured half an inch, and the tricuspid orifice three-quarters of an inch. The heart was very large, weighing thirty-two ounces ; and all its cavities, and especially the ventricles, shared in the enlargement. The following were the physical signs :—" Strong protruding impulse at the apex between the sixth and seventh ribs. During the systole, the sternum and the left and right costal cartilages over the right ventricle became steadily depressed; immediately after the systole they advanced with a shock." [1] (See Fig. 50, p. 443.)

In the general description I thus defined the character of the impulse in the two classes of cases just given : " The sternum, costal cartilages, and xiphoid cartilage are heaved forward firmly and steadily at the beginning of the systole ; and during its continuance those parts fall back steadily and quickly, coinciding with the mode of systolic contraction of the right ventricle. In some cases the sternum and costal cartilages spring forward with a jerk during the diastole."

M. Bouillaud,[2] in 1846, described a sign by which he had been able to announce the existence of adherent pericardium in six or seven cases. ·It consisted in evident retraction of the pericardial region; the movements of the heart not being free, but embarrassed or curbed. He does not state during what period in the revolution of the heart's action the depression of the pericardial region took place.

Skoda,[3] in 1852, published an important paper on the diagnosis of adherent pericardium, in which he gives a critical account of most of the communications just analysed, and reports of three cases observed by himself. In the first case, a youth, there was dulness on percussion, equal in extent during inspiration and expiration, from the second left space to the ensiform cartilage, and from the middle of the sternum to the left nipple ; and fulness over the second space, which advanced during the systole and sank in during the diastole ; the third, fourth, and fifth spaces deepened with the systole and filled out with the diastole ; the heart's impulse was feeble, and the apex-beat

[1] Loc. cit. p. 562.
[2]. Traité de Nosographie Médicale, i.
[3] Zeitschrift der Gesellschaft der Aerzte zu Wien, 152, i. 306.

was imperceptible. The heart sounds were natural, but the second sound was split over the pulmonary artery. The pericardium was tied to the walls of the chest by filamentous bands, and was universally adherent to the heart, which was natural in position; the right ventricle was enlarged, the right auricle was changed into a stiff-crumbling tuberculous mass, and the conus arteriosus was widened, its walls being only a line in thickness.

The second case, which passed through all its stages under Skoda's eye, a youth, was admitted with pericarditis. The friction sound, then loud and extensive, became feeble and limited to the apex on the 15th, and was lost on the 19th day. On the 37th day there was a systolic deepening of the third, fourth, and fifth spaces, and the apex-beat was imperceptible. A month later, when he left the hospital, during each systole, besides the indrawing of the spaces, there was indrawing of the lower half of the sternum, which sprang forward after the systole with a perceptible shock. He was admitted ten weeks later with pneumonia, when the heart-signs were unchanged, and he died fully six months after his first admission. The right ventricle was enlarged; the valves were healthy; the heart, which lay in the middle of the chest, was firmly adherent to the pericardium, which was, in turn, strongly glued to the walls of the chest by a tuberculous exudation.

Skoda's third case was a man, with narrowing of the mitral orifice, ascites, and œdema. The region of cardiac dulness remained unchanged during inspiration and expiration. There was a considerable deepening of the fifth space during the systole, after which the hollow quickly disappeared, and a shock was perceived there at the beginning of the diastole. After his death, five months later, the pericardium and pleura were found to be universally adherent, and the right side of the heart was considerably enlarged.

These cases, published by Skoda, form a valuable addition to the clinical history of adherent pericardium, for the true points of diagnosis have here been clearly observed, stated, and confirmed; and are given with force, and as the effects of the central cause, the doubly adherent pericardium. They do not, however, present any new points of diagnosis, for it will have been seen, in the previous narrative, that he has been anticipated by one or more authors in the observation of each diagnostic sign. Thus the systolic deepening of the intercostal spaces had been observed by Heim and Dr. Williams, the return shock over the previously retracted space by Sander, and the great extent of the cardiac space upwards, and the non-diminution of that space, by Dr. Williams and myself; while the retraction during the systole of the lower half of the sternum, and its advance with a shock immediately after the systole, was observed by myself in the case already given.

Great diagnostic value is to be attached to the principal points specially illustrated by Skoda's paper, namely: the systolic indrawing of the lower sternum or intercostal spaces by the contraction of the adherent heart; and the diastolic shock or back-stroke that immediately follows, given by the return elasticity of the chest-walls.

Cejka,[1] in 1855, published four cases of adherent pericardium, three of which confirm, with more or less precision, the points illustrated in Skoda's paper. In one of them, with contraction of the aortic orifice, there was systolic indrawing of the third, fourth, and fifth spaces, and so strong a blow was given by the return elasticity of the chest walls that it was like the impulse of the heart. In another instance, an old man with adherent pericardium, a chronic affection of the lungs, dilatation of the aorta, and thickening of the mitral valve, the fifth and sixth spaces were drawn inwards with each systole, and became quickly even with each diastole. The impulse was not perceptible, and there is no note of diastolic backstroke. In the third patient, with aortic aneurism, the vaulting of the sixth left space, caused by the systole, gave place towards the end of the case to a slight drawing inwards of the corresponding region. Cejka's fourth case of adherent pericardium, also with aneurism of the aorta, presented no impulse and no apparent drawing inwards during the systole.

Clinical History. (B) *Cases observed in St. Mary's Hospital and at Nottingham.*—1. *Cases examined after Death.*—The pericardium was completely adherent in fifty-one, and partially so in nine of the cases free from Bright's disease, recorded after death in St. Mary's Hospital up to the year 1870. (See the table at p. 420.) Besides these, seventeen of the cases with Bright's disease had universally, and three of them had partially, adherent pericardium.

Rheumatic pericarditis had evidently been the cause of the adhesions in more than one-half of the cases, since of those with complete adhesions, 29 in 51 that were free from Bright's disease, and 9 in 17 with Bright's disease, had valvular disease of the heart; while the valves were affected in 7 out of 8 of those with partial adhesions that were free from Bright's disease, and the three cases of that class with that affection.

General adhesion of the pericardium was rarely associated with disease of the aortic valve (2 in 32), and with mitral obstruction (1 in 21), in cases free from Bright's disease, while that affection was very frequent in such cases with mitral and mitral-aortic valve disease (13 in 33 of the former and 11 in 31 of the latter affection). Adherent pericardium was present in one case with disease of the tricuspid valve. Partial adhesions of the pericardium were noted in one case with aortic regurgitation, in two with mitral obstruction, in none with mitral, and in two with mitral-aortic regurgitation, without Bright's disease; since the aortic valve was affected in 1 in 4 of the cases, while only two had mitral and two had mitral-aortic disease. Among the cases of complete (17) and partial (3) adhesions with Bright's disease, 4 (in

[1] *Vierteljahrschrift für die praktische Heilkund,* 1855, 128.

21) had aortic valve-disease, 5 (in 29) had mitral and 2 (in 20) had mitral-aortic valvular disease, and 1 (in 9) had mitral contraction.

Aneurism of the ascending aorta was the evident cause of adherent pericardium in three instances (3 in 25), and cancer of the heart in one (1 in 10).

There was no other affection of the heart or aorta, excepting enlargement of the organ itself, in more than one-third of the cases with complete adhesions (19 in 52). The adhesions were not accompanied by any other affection in less than one-half of these cases (7 in 19), and they were complicated in more than one-half of them with pyæmia (in 2), apoplexy (in 1), pneumonia (in 3), empyema (in 2), phthisis (in 3), or peritonitis (in 1). All those affections, excepting the last two, were acute; and they could not, therefore, have given rise to the adhesions. Phthisis, and especially empyema, which is so often associated with phthisis, may, owing to the duration of those diseases, have induced first pericarditis and then adhesions. Notwithstanding this, the whole of those cases may be taken into account when considering the effect of pericardial adhesions on the size of the heart, for none of them by themselves cause enlargement of that organ, excepting pneumonia, and, less often, phthisis, both of which affections tend to increase the right ventricle in size.

The heart was enlarged, its valves being thickened but competent in one instance, in fully two-thirds of the cases with adherent pericardium that were free from any other cardiac disease, and in which the size of the heart is mentioned (11 in 16); it was rather large in three of them; and in only two instances was the heart of its natural size. We may however, I think, estimate that in one-third of these cases the adhesions did not cause an increase in the size of the heart. These results do not differ materially from those arrived at by Dr. Kennedy,[1] who found that in 90 cases of adherent pericardium in which valvular disease was not present, the heart was of natural size—" healthy "—in 34, or fully one-third, hypertrophied in 51, or three-fifths—being dilated also in 26—and atrophied in 5.

It is proved that pericardial adhesions do not necessarily cause enlargement of the heart. I saw four cases in Nottingham in which the heart was of natural size and one in which it was lessened; Dr. Gairdner[2] gives brief notes of ten cases in which the heart was not morbid, and by inference was not affected in size; and Dr. Stokes[3] informs us that Professor Smith found that general adhesions of the pericardium corresponded with atrophy or with hypertrophy of the heart in nearly equal proportions.

We may, I think, safely conclude from what has gone before that adherent pericardium may, and often does, exist without influencing the size or healthy function of the heart; that in a few rare instances it may induce atrophy of that organ; and that in nearly two-thirds of

---

[1] *Edinburgh Medical Journal*, iii. 986.
[2] *Ibid*, Feb. 1851.
[3] Dr. Stokes, *Diseases of the Heart*.

the cases it tends to cause an increase in the size of the heart, both as regards the thickness of its walls and the capacity of its cavities.

We have just seen that the heart was enlarged in the majority of the cases of adherent pericardium that were free from any other affection of the heart itself. When we take this into account it is natural to expect that the heart should be more enlarged in cases with valvular disease when they are affected with adherent pericardium than when they are not so; and the analysis of the cases of this class that were recorded at St. Mary's Hospital by taking a simple average of the weights of the hearts with valvular disease, with or without pericardial adhesions, gives some support to this anticipation, as will be seen by the examination of the following summary of the average weight of the heart in those cases.

Average weight of the heart in cases of valvular disease with and without adherent pericardium. The cases were not affected with Bright's disease except where specified.

Mitral regurgitation, pericardium adherent (4) . average weight, 21 ounces.
Ditto, pericardium not adherent (14) . . . ,, ,, 16·6 ,,
Ditto, with Bright's disease, pericardium adherent (3) ,, ,, 25 ,,
Ditto, pericardium not adherent (19) . . . ,, ,, 19·4 ,,
Mitral obstruction, pericardium adherent (1) . . ,, ,, 21 ,,
Ditto, pericardium not adherent (14) . . . ,, ,, 14 ,,
Aortic regurgitation, pericardium adherent (2) . ,, ,, 26·7 ,,
Ditto, pericardium not adherent (23) . . . ,, ,, 22 ,,
Mitral-aortic regurgitation, pericardium adherent (6) ,, ,, 26·3 ,,
Ditto, pericardium not adherent (12) . . . ,, ,, 22 ,,
TOTAL of combined valvular diseases, without
  Bright's disease, pericardium adherent (13) . . ,, ,, 23·3 ,,
TOTAL of combined valvular diseases, without
  Bright's disease, pericardium not adherent (63) ,, ,, 19 ,,

This method is far from doing scientific justice to the question before us; for cases of all ages, both sexes, and various degrees of disease, are brought together under one common heading, although in reality many of these cases differ materially from each other. Notwithstanding this, a rough and ready answer is given to us that is probably not far from the scientific truth. We find, then, that the average weight of the heart in the thirteen cases of valvular disease, with adherent pericardium, was 24½ ounces, while its weight in sixty-three cases of a like kind, in which the pericardium was not adherent, was 19 ounces, or 5½ ounces less than the first series. It is to be kept in view that the pericardium was included with the heart in the first set of cases, and what its average weight may be under the varying circumstances I do not know. It may, however, I think, be concluded that in the cases of valvular disease of the heart the existence of adherent pericardium tended to increase the size and weight of the heart, but not to a great extent.

The size of the heart, as we have seen, has been usually described;

its weight being often given, in the cases with adherent pericardium observed in St. Mary's Hospital. The relative size of the different cavities of the heart has, however, only been described in 11 of these cases. I have, therefore, with a view to discover the influence that the presence of adherent pericardium may have on the size of the various cavities of the heart and the thickness of their walls, brought together 18 additional cases from various sources—or 29 in the whole—in which the general condition of the various cavities of the heart was described, and which are given in the following summary :—

Cases with adherent pericardium in which the size of the different cavities of the heart was described :—

1.—Cases in which both ventricles were enlarged (hypertrophy and dilatation) 16

    Of these, 6 were free from valvular or other heart disease (1 had Bright's disease) ; 10 had valvular disease (3 aortic, 2 mitral, 3 mitral-aortic, regurgitation, 2 mitral contraction).

2.—Cases in which the right ventricle was enlarged, the left being not so (in 1), or small (in 1), or not described (in 3) 5

    Of these, 3 were free from valvular disease, 1 had mitral regurgitation, and 1 aneurism of the aortic sinuses.

3.—Cases in which the left ventricle was enlarged, the right being small (in 1), or not described (in 7) 8

    Of these 3 had no valvular disease, 1 had aortic, and 3 mitral, regurgitation, and 1 had aneurism of the apex of the left ventricle.
                                                                            ——
TOTAL 29

There was valvular disease of the heart (15), or aneurism of the heart (1) or aorta (1) in 17 of these cases, and as those affections exercise a definite influence of their own on the size of the cavities of the heart, they must be left out of view in considering the direct effect of adherent pericardium on those cavities. The same must be said of one instance with Bright's disease among the remaining 12 cases in which there was no valvular or other affection of the heart or aorta. Hypertrophy and dilatation of both ventricles existed in 5; of the right ventricle in 3; and of the left ventricle in the remaining 3, of these 11 cases. From this it would appear that adherent pericardium, when it produces enlargement of the heart, tends to affect both ventricles to an equal but varying degree.

    2. *Physical signs observed during life in cases with adherent pericardium admitted into St. Mary's and the Nottingham Hospitals.* —I have observed nine cases with adherent pericardium in St. Mary's Hospital, and have added one recorded there by Dr. Markham ; and have examined seven such cases at Nottingham, four of which I published in 1844, and have given briefly above. There was no valvular disease of the heart in three of these seventeen cases, while in the remaining fourteen, one or more of the valves was affected, mitral regurgitation being present in nine of them, mitral-aortic regurgitation in three, and mitral obstruction in two, of those cases.

In one of the three cases in which the valves were healthy, in which case Bright's disease was present, the sounds of the heart were natural but weak, and the presence of impulse was not noted. In another of them, a man, with empyema and lardaceous disease of the kidney, the heart being only slightly enlarged, the impulse was at one time imperceptible, but afterwards, when it could scarcely be felt over the ribs, it was perceived over the ensiform cartilage. In these two cases, and in that of the same class already alluded to at page 439, in which the heart was small, the presence of adherent pericardium could not, I think, have been discovered during life.

The signs of the heart were not noticed in one of the cases in which adherent pericardium was associated with mitral regurgitation, an old man who presented various sonorous noises over the lungs. In one of two cases, both men, with mitral disease, observed at Nottingham, in which the heart was very greatly enlarged, the left ventricle was greatly hypertrophied and dilated, the right being so to a minor degree; and the impulse was feeble, the second sound, distinct over the sternum, was scarcely audible at the apex, and the lungs were œdematous. In the other case, with hypertrophy of both ventricles, the impulse was inconsiderable, but was diffused over the whole left mammary region.

The next case is an important one, reported by that careful and accurate observer, Dr. Markham, for it shows that the apex-beat may be strong, and far to the left, in some unusual cases of adherent pericardium. In this patient, a girl, the impulse was heaving and extensive, and was violent far to the left of the nipple line, and beneath the sixth rib. The second sound was very loud over the pulmonary artery, but was absent at the apex. M. Aran likewise describes a case of adherent pericardium, in which the apex-beat was present in the sixth space, three-and-a-half inches from the sternum, and the systolic impulse was strong and progressive, and was not followed by a diastole impulse. Skoda takes exception to my observation that the apex protruded extensively to the left in two of my cases published in 1844, given briefly above at pp. 439, 440. We shall see that the apex-beat is usually feeble, and does not often extend far to the left in cases of adherent pericardium; but it was certainly otherwise in this case of Dr. Markham, in that of M. Aran, and, I would say, also in my two published cases. It appears to me that in this patient, and in the other cases just given, there was no sign characteristic of adherent pericardium.

The next instance was too ill for careful physical examination, and presented a feature unusual in cases with pericardial adhesions. The healthy impulse was much more diffused than natural, being present in the epigastric space and four or five intercostal spaces, and the lower ribs retracted during the diastole, which is a rare occurrence. The apex-beat, which was felt in the fifth and sixth spaces, did not extend outwards so far as the nipple line. The two following instances present features that were sufficient to characterize them during life as being affected with adherent pericardium. In the first of these cases, the left ventricle was hypertrophied, the right ventricle was small, and both the auricles were very large. The apex-beat was seated in the sixth space, an inch to the left of the nipple line, and 5½ inches from the sternum, and in spite of the great and extensive hypertrophy of the left ventricle, was feeble. The second sound, which was heard over the right ventricle, was faint at the apex. There was, on the 54th day after admission, a diffused impulse chiefly over the cardiac cartilages, extending down to the seventh costal cartilage, and to the ensiform cartilage. The impulse advanced quickly and fell back suddenly during the systole, and was followed with a sharp sudden shock or jerk over the whole region of the impulse. There was slight pulsation of the liver below the ensiform cartilage. Breathing was rather high, the movement being chiefly at the upper part of the chest, with retraction at its lower part. The other case, equally remarkable, and the last of the series with mitral incompetence, had points of close resemblance to the last, with points of marked difference. In this case the front of the heart adhered strongly to the inner surface of the sternum through the medium of the pericardium. The walls of the right ventricle and auricle were much hypertrophied, while the left ventricle was only somewhat thickened; thus reversing the conditions that were present in the former case. There was some fulness over the region of the heart. The impulse over the heart, and especially over the right ventricle, was very extensive, spreading from the third to the seventh cartilage; and from the right cartilages, across the sternum and ensiform cartilage, to the sixth left space, an inch-and-a-half beyond the nipple line. The impulse was peculiar, and told remarkably on the sternum, first heaving that bone forwards with sudden force, and then drawing it backwards with great strength. "The heart" (or rather the front of the chest) "seemed to be dragged backwards during each systole. The apex-beat was feeble, low down, and far to the left, in the sixth space, an inch-and-a-half beyond the nipple line. There was some pulsation of the liver in the epigastric region. The second sound was loud and plunging over the right ventricle, and feeble at the apex, where a mitral murmur was loud and extensive. Afterwards the fulness over the heart, and the extent and force of the impulse lessened, but the beat of the heart retained its remarkable character, first advancing, and then forcibly retracting, during the systole. Later still the apex-beat, which was very weak, extended only a very little beyond the nipple line. Notwithstanding this contraction of the region of the impulse, it extended from right to left over a width of six inches. A deep inspiration caused a marked lowering of the upper and lower borders of the region of the impulse, in spite of its great extent. After a few days he became drowsy, felt tight in the chest, and died three weeks after his admission." It is to be remarked that while in the previous case a diastolic shock or back-stroke followed the systolic retraction, which was preceded by a systolic advance; in this case there is no note of back-stroke, though I cannot vouch for its absence; but the sudden systolic heave followed by a forcible systolic retraction of the sternum and cartilages, as if those parts were dragged backwards by the heart clinging, as it were, to its buckler, pointed definitely to adherent pericardium as the cause of the chain of signs.

The two cases of adherent pericardium with mitral-aortic incompetence present, like the last two cases, physical features that denote the presence of the adhesions, though not perhaps with the same emphasis as the two first related. In the first case, a youth, the heart was of very great size, so as complétely to cover the left lung. On his admission, three months before his death, the impulse was gradual, but ended abruptly with a shock; and extended from the third cartilage to the sixth, but scarcely beyond the nipple line; there was also a marked general pulsation over the whole liver, both in front and at the right side. A month later the impulse had extended itself to the left, being diffused, and shaking the whole of that side of the chest, the apex-beat being an inch-and-a-half to the left of the nipple line. Afterwards the impulse extended more to the right and was felt in the epigastrium, but its characteristic features are not again described. The other instance was a boy, and in him the heart, which was considerably enlarged, clung so close to the sternum and cartilages that it was found best to remove the viscera *en masse* from behind. There was fulness over the cardiac region, and the beat of the heart, which was extensive, reaching down to an inch-and-a-half below the sternum, and extending thence to the seventh cartilage, was of a peculiar character, beginning with a diffused heaving impulse, which gave way to a sudden and sharp retraction. He always said, after this examination, that he felt better, though he really was not so, and eight days later he died.

The two remaining cases with adherent pericardium had mitral contraction. In one of them, a young woman, the heart was very large; the impulse extended from the second space to the seventh costal cartilage and the ensiform cartilage, and, even when she lay on the left side, the apex beat was feeble. As in the last case, there was strong pulsation over the whole liver, extending from the front to the back. The remaining case with adherent pericardium and mitral contraction was observed by me in Nottingham in 1835, and although it presents no signs characteristic of the adhesions, is perhaps of interest, as being, so far as I know, the earliest case in which the so-called presystolic murmur was described. The size of the heart is not given, but there was no hypertrophy of either ventricle. The mitral opening was half an inch in diameter. A thrill, extending over a large space, was communicated to the hand when applied over the apex, which was terminated by a jerk. A peculiar purring sound was heard at the apex, the vibrations being longer and louder as the time progressed, the sound ending in a strong loud clear jerk, synchronous with the pulsation. The sound occupied two-fourths of the time, no other being audible at the apex.

Résumé of the Physical Signs observed in Cases of Adherent Pericardium.—The steady retraction of the lower half of the sternum during the whole of the systole of the ventricles, and the sudden starting forwards of the lower half of the sternum at the beginning of the diastole with a return shock or blow, was observed in my own case, published in 1844, and in one of Skoda's given in 1852.

The drawing inwards of the cardiac intercostal spaces during the systole was first observed by Heìm, and afterwards by Dr. Williams, by Skoda in three cases, and by Cejka in three more.

This sign, which is sometimes present in other cases, renders the existence of adherent pericardium probable, and especially if this sign is still present when the patient draws a deep breath; but if it is followed by a diastolic shock the diagnosis of that affection is certain. The existence indeed of a diastolic back-stroke taken by itself pronounces that the heart is adherent. This sign, which generally gives the impression of a double impulse, was first noticed by Sander; afterwards by Dr. Hope in four cases of adherent pericardium; in the two typical instances just given and described respectively by myself and by Skoda, who observed it in another instance; by Cejka in one, and by myself in two others given above.

A double movement of the systolic impulse, first forwards with a heaving motion, then backwards with a forcible retraction, was observed by myself in a case in the Nottingham Hospital, to the description of which Skoda takes exception, and afterwards in three other cases in St. Mary's Hospital. The outward pressure, equal in every direction, of the blood contained in the ventricle during its contraction naturally forces forwards the walls of the chest in front of it at the beginning of the systole. During the continuance of the systole, the adherent sternum resists the contraction of the heart, but in the struggle the bone yields, and is drawn forcibly inwards by the active ventricle.

The non-diminution of the region of pericardial dulness and of the impulse was observed by Dr. Williams; and the absence of change in the position of these signs when the patient lay on the left side was noticed by Dr. Law.

The non-diminution of the area of pericardial dulness and impulse is undoubtedly a valuable sign of adherent pericardium; in one of my cases, however, the impulse below was unusually strong at the end of expiration, and in another of them the upper and lower borders of the impulse palpably descended during a deep inspiration. This is indeed different from the diminution of the extent of dulness and impulse, and, what is still more important, from the bodily transfer during a deep breath of the seat of the dulness and impulse from the cardiac cartilages and the fifth space near the nipple, to the epigastric region, including the ensiform cartilage and the adjoining seventh costal cartilage. One of my cases illustrates in its own manner the other point just referred to—the non-shifting of the seat of the impulse when the patient turns on the left side. In that case, when the patient lay on the left side, the apex-beat, which was an inch and a half to the left of the nipple line, and in the sixth space, was very feeble. This is very different from the great transfer of the position of the apex-beat from the fifth space, a little lower than the nipple, and within the mammary line, to the sixth or seventh space, two inches to the left of that line, which was observed to be the case in several patients, in whom the chest was healthy, by Dr. Humphreys, Dr. Coupland, and myself, in the Middlesex Hospital.

These, so far as I know, are the only signs that are characteristic of adherent pericardium; but there are certain other signs that, without ranking in precision with those just named, have their significance.

The drawing inwards during the systole of the space between the ensiform cartilage and the seventh costal cartilage, was noticed by Sander in a case of adherent pericardium; and in another case, I observed that the tip of the ensiform cartilage was retracted during the contraction of the ventricle.

There was pulsation of the liver in four of my cases, which was limited to the epigastric space in two of them, but in the two others extended over the whole organ, in front, at the side, and in one even behind. Burns ˙ considered that the impulse so often present in the epigastric space in cases of adherent pericardium is due not immediately to the heart itself, but to the pulsation of the liver.

It is evident, from the brief recital of the cases that has just been given, that a great variation in the extent, force, character, and position of the impulse exists in cases of adherent pericardium.

The impulse was imperceptible in one of Cejka's, and at an early period in one of my own cases of adherent pericardium; and it was feeble in one of Skoda's and two of my own, cases; it was heaving during the systole and very extensive in one of Dr. Markham's cases, and in one of my own; it was tumultuous and very irregular in one of my cases; it was strong and very greatly extended, both upwards to the second space, and downwards to the epigastric space and the seventh cartilage, and to the right and left, across the chest, from a full inch to the right of the lower half of the sternum, to a full inch to the left of the nipple line in the sixth space, in cases observed by Dr. Hope, Dr. Markham, and myself; and in two of Dr. Hope's cases the violent action of the heart was observed over the whole front of the chest.

The apex-beat is, as a rule, feeble, even when it extends from an inch to an inch and a half to the left of the nipple line, being felt in the sixth space. Sometimes indeed, as in one of Skoda's cases, it is imperceptible; and at others it is situated, even when there is general enlargement with hypertrophy of the ventricles, to the right of the nipple line, as occurred in one of M. Aran's cases, in which the apex-beat was in the fifth space, two and a half inches from the sternum; and in two of the cases given by Dr. Gairdner, who points to this restraint of the apex as a probable element in the diagnosis of adherent pericardium.

There are, however, important exceptions to the rule that the apex-beat is usually restrained in its action and sometimes in its position by adherent pericardium, for in two cases published by me in 1844, the apex-beat was far to the left and low down, strong, gradual, and protruding; and as we have seen, the apex-beat presented the same condition in Dr. Markham's, and to a less degree in M. Aran's important cases.

The impulse was found in the epigastrium in Mr. Burn's cases, in two of Dr. Hope's, and in four of my own.

M. Aran, in 1844, gave the extinction of the second sound as the unique sign of adherent pericardium, on the strength of the absence or great feebleness of that sound in those cases reported by him. He does not distinguish between the second sound over the pulmonary artery and right ventricle, and that over the left ventricle. Dr. Markham describes the second sound as being, in his case with mitral incompetence, very loud, heard like a beat, over the pulmonary artery, while there was no second sound over the apex. In one at least of my cases observed in Nottingham the second sound was loud or natural over the right ventricle, while it was indistinct and dull at the apex, and in two of the cases given above the second sound, loud over the pulmonary artery and right ventricle, was feeble at the apex of the heart.

The last physical sign that I shall consider is the movement of respiration in relation to adherent pericardium. In two cases of adherent pericardium observed by myself in Nottingham, the inspiratory movement of the abdomen at its centre was equal to that at its sides : although in health, the central movements are from two to three times as great as the lateral movements of the abdomen. At the same time in both those cases the lower half of the sternum fell inwards, or was drawn backwards, and the left ribs, from the fourth to the sixth, either retracted or were stationary, or had much less movement during inspiration, than the corresponding right ribs. The retraction of the sternum was caused by the forcible displacement downwards of the central tendon of the diaphragm, where it forms the floor of the pericardium ; and as under these circumstances the lungs could not interpose themselves between the heart and the sternum, that bone was partly forced backwards by atmospheric pressure, and partly dragged backwards by the adherent heart, when drawn somewhat downwards by the diaphragm.

ENDOCARDITIS.

BY FRANCIS SIBSON, M.D., F.R.S.

ENDOCARDITIS, to a greater extent even than pericarditis, is chiefly associated with acute rheumatism. The extent to which this is the case will be seen by the study of the accompanying table, at page 461, from which it may be seen that endocarditis without pericarditis was established in one-third of the cases, or in 107 out of a total number of 325. If to these we add those cases with pericarditis that were also affected with endocarditis, amounting to 54, we find that endocarditis attacked one-half of the cases of acute rheumatism, or 161 in 325. In addition to these cases, in which the presence of endocarditis was rendered certain by the character of the signs and symptoms observed during the attack, there was a considerable proportion of the cases, amounting to one-fourth of the whole (76 in 325), in which endocarditis was either threatened (in 63) or very probable (in 13). Endocarditis is not however limited to acute rheumatism, being also present in a considerable proportion of cases affected with chorea, and in a small but uncertain number of those with pyæmia and Bright's disease. Cases, also, of established valvular disease of the heart are subject to intermitting attacks of endocarditis affecting the diseased valves.

I shall, in this article, (1) first give a brief account of the anatomical appearances that present themselves after death in endocarditis, and then (2) a clinical history of rheumatic endocarditis, as it presented itself in the cases with acute rheumatism under my care in St. Mary's Hospital, during the years 1851 to 1869-70 ; those cases being divided into two series, an earlier series from 1851 to 1866, and a later series, treated by means of rest, from 1867 to 1869-70.

I.—THE ANATOMICAL APPEARANCES OBSERVED IN CASES OF ENDOCARDITIS.

The anatomical appearances found after death in cases of endocarditis have been well described from actual observation in the excellent and readily available works of Rokitansky,[1] Hasse,[2] and Rindfleisch,[3]

---

[1] Rokitansky, *Pathological Anatomy*, Syd. Soc. iv. 175.
[2] Hasse, *Pathological Anatomy*, Syd. Soc. 124.
[3] Rindfleisch, *Pathological Histology*, New Syd. Soc. i. 279.

which have been well translated ; and in the original and interesting lectures of Dr. Moxon [1] and manual of Dr. Payne.[2]

The inflammation of the interior of the heart is as a rule limited to the left ventricle, this being evidently due to the great labour to which that ventricle is subjected when it drives the blood into the arteries of the system, and to the comparatively slight effort with which the right ventricle sends its blood through the vessels of the lungs. In the fœtal state, the right side of the heart, which is then the most powerful side, and has the greatest amount of work to do, is subject to endocarditis, judging by the frequency with which the pulmonary valves are adherent, so as to contract the orifice of the pulmonary artery. Dr. Norman Cheevers finds that sixty such cases have been observed by various authors. The mitral and aortic valves are the chosen seat of endocarditis, and especially the mitral valve. It is not, however, the whole of either valve that is the immediate seat of the inflammation ; which, as a rule, is limited to the lines and surfaces of contact of the valves, close to the edges of their flaps where they come together and press against each other so as to close their respective apertures. The aortic valve is shut by the blood quietly filling the sinuses towards and at the end of the systole and during the diastole. The blood, when the sinuses are filled, presses the sides of the flaps against each other with a diffused and equal but firm pressure. This pressure is made on the first closure of the valve at the end of the systole, by the blood filling the sinuses ; but this pressure is suddenly reinforced by the back-stroke or return wave of blood, caused by the recoil of the distended aorta and arteries, which propels the blood equally in every direction, forwards and sideways, as well as backwards with a return stroke, which beats on the aortic valve sinuses, and the ascending aorta, and which causes the second sound, which follows the closure of the valve by the tenth of a revolution of the heart's action. Afterwards the pressure of the aortic flaps upon each other is kept up during the diastole by the pressure of the blood, due to the steady contraction of the coats of the aorta and its branches. The pressure upon the aortic flaps bears, not upon their exact margins, but upon their surfaces of contact, a little within those margins, and upon the sesamoid bodies ; and the endocarditis affects, not the exact margins of the flaps, but their surfaces of contact.

The mitral valve is shut on exactly the same principle as the aortic valve, by the pressure of the blood driven during the systole into the small open cells on the under or ventricular surface of the valve, in the manner described and figured at page 51. The force with which the blood presses upon the closed mitral valve, owing to the contraction of the ventricle, is much greater than the force with which the blood presses upon the aortic valve, owing to the recoil of the previously distended walls of the aorta. The flaps of that valve are pressed

---

[1] Dr. Wilks and Dr. Moxon, *Pathological Anatomy*, 125.
[2] Dr. Jones, Dr. Sieveking, and Dr. Payne, *Pathological Anatomy*, 348.

together by the backward portion only of the effect of the recoil of the aorta walls, which expands itself in every direction; and that force of recoil is itself but a portion of the original propulsive force of the left ventricle, which presses with its full power upon the closed mitral valve. The surfaces or lines of contact and closure of the mitral valve extend along and just within the borders of its two flaps. This border of contact is not a mere edge, but a surface or line of adaptation, made up of the small bead-shaped cells, that dove-tail into each other along the margins of the flaps; those flaps being held in their place by the simultaneous contraction of the papillary muscles, acting on their tendinous cords; the result is that the margins of contact of the mitral flaps press against each other when the valve is shut with much greater tension, force, and concentration, than the margins of contact of the aortic valve; under the triple agency of a finer margin of contact, greater pressure of blood, and the muscular force and tendinous traction proper to the valve. The mitral valve, which is situated in the muscular centre of the ventricle and in the focus of its internal inflammation, is more immediately and frequently subjected to endocarditis than the aortic valve, which has broader surfaces of contact, less pressure of blood, and no muscular and tendinous traction.

Endocarditis, as I have said, does not therefore attack the very rim of the flaps of the mitral valve at the attachment of their out-spreading tendinous cords, but the line or margin of contact just within the edges of the valves. When the mitral valve is inflamed, a frill of small bead-like granulations lines the whole proper border of contact and closure of the valve; and tends to prevent their perfect adaptation, and to cause regurgitation through the valvular aperture when the ventricle contracts. These prominences consist of a swelling and granular disintegration of the connective tissue, with softening of the intercellular structure. Each of these prominences is covered by a cap of fibrin deposited from the blood in the manner well represented by Rindfleisch.[1] Endocarditis affects the surfaces of contact of the aortic valve in the same way that it affects those of the mitral valve.

This is the usual manner in which endocarditis affects the mitral and aortic valves, whether the parent affection, rendering those parts prone to inflammation, be acute rheumatism, chorea, or pyæmia. Sometimes, however, the inflammation deepens at its original seat on the surfaces of contact of the mitral valve, and extends beyond those surfaces, so as to affect a large portion of the flaps of the valve on their ventricular surface. Under these circumstances, the inflamed, softened, and thickened structures may undergo granular degeneration, and its ventricular layer may become broken or ulcerated. The auricular layer of the valve thus tends to yield before the pressure of the blood, which forces its way through the breach in the ventricular

---

[1] *Loc. cit.* p. 281, fig. 87.

layer, and to form pouches or aneurisms protruding into the left auricle. The auricular layer may then be involved in the inflammation, and become in turn subjected to granular disintegration and breaking up of tissue, so that the flap of the valve may become perforated. The fibrin of the blood deposits itself everywhere on the inflamed surfaces, often in the form of vegetations, which may become extensive; and thus the fibrin often lines, closes, and conceals the perforation.

We have already seen how many points in its favour, as regards its tendency to endocarditis, the aortic valve presents over the mitral; and it presents another in this respect—that while the pressure of the blood bears directly upon the inflamed surface of contact of the mitral valve during its closure at the time of the systole, the pressure of the blood does not bear upon the inflamed ventricular surface of contact of the aortic valve when it is closed at the time of the ventricular diastole, but upon the uninflamed upper or aortic surface of the valve. Although this condition, favourable to the aortic valve, exists, I have seen preparations in which a small aneurism, or aneurisms, of one or more of the flaps of the aortic valve protruded downwards into the ventricle.

The advantages are not, however, entirely on the side of the aortic valve when it is affected with endocarditis; for a serious counterbalancing disadvantage exists under such circumstances, as I shall now mention. The sesamoid body, and the margin or surface of contact of the valve on each side of the sesamoid body, which are the seat of endocarditis when it affects the aortic valve, receive the direct pressure of the column of blood in the aorta; and those parts, which are softened by the inflammation, tend therefore to be pushed downwards towards the ventricle during the ventricular diastole; with the effect of sometimes pro-ducing retroversion of the sesamoid body, and to a greater or less extent of the softened flap, of which it is the centre. We here see the great disadvantage in which the inflamed aortic valve is placed from the want of tendinous cords and papillary muscles to support its flaps when rendered soft and yielding by endocarditis.

Another special evil accruing to the aortic valve from a similar class of cause, is the tendency of the sesamoid body, and the adjoining portion of the flap affected with endocarditis, to lay hold of deposits of fibrin from the regurgitating stream of blood, with the effect of establishing a chain of fibrinous vegetations, which form one upon another, and which hang pendant into the left ventricle, being forced in that direction by the return current of blood. When this chain of fibrinous concretions forms upon either the right or the left posterior flap of the valve, it is driven down-wards and backwards by the stream of regurgitation, so as to beat against and rest upon the anterior flap of the mitral valve, with the effect of causing ulcerative endocarditis of that flap. As the blood regurgitating from the aorta into the ventricle beats upon that flap, it parts with its fibrin which clings to the inflamed surfaces of the mitral valve, and forms on these a second chain of fibrinous concretions.

The flaps of the mitral valve are, as we have seen, the principal seat of endocarditis, but inflammation may also attack the papillary muscles, and especially where they are brought into contact with each other towards the end of the systole, and cause fibroid degeneration of those muscles. The tendinous cords may also sometimes become inflamed, softened, and disintegrated, when the grave result of rupture of the cord may ensue.

I have just given a series of notable instances of the occurrence of endocarditis, locally excited by the contact with each other of the two opposing surfaces of the valve; of two adjoining papillary muscles; and of a pendant chain of fibrinous concretion beating against the anterior flap of the mitral valve. These are not the only parts of the interior of the heart that may be inflamed from this cause, for wherever two surfaces of the endocardium come into contact with and rub against each other, endocarditis may be excited in both of those surfaces. The influence of the labour of the left ventricle and the mutual contact of its internal surface in tending to produce endocarditis is illustrated in an original and able manner by Dr. Moxon. I would refer to his work and to the others already named for the study of the various effects of endo-carditis.

Among the effects of endocarditis, I would here simply name the formation of vegetations on the inflamed valves, already in part illustrated; the production of embolism by the washing away from the vegetations of fibrin into the current of the blood; the ulceration of the surface of the endocardium; the establishment of valvular disease from the thickening and enlargement of the valves; the contraction, adhesion, or retroversion, and perforation of their flaps; the rupture of the tendinous cords; the formation of aneurisms of the valves; the fibroid and atheromatous degeneration of the fibrous and muscular structures of the ventricle; the production of aneurisms of the heart; and other effects that will be found described in the works to which I have referred.

II.—CLINICAL HISTORY OF RHEUMATIC ENDOCARDITIS.

The accompanying analytical tables of 325 cases of acute rheumatism under my care in St. Mary's Hospital during the years 1851-66, show the proportion in which those cases were free from endocarditis, and were threatened with or attacked by that affection; and the number that were attacked by pericarditis, distinguishing those with established endocarditis; also those in which endocarditis was doubtful, and those in which it was absent.

The analyses contained in the tables sufficiently indicate the reasons for arranging the cases in the manner adopted.

TABLE SHOWING THE CONDITION OF THE CASES OF ACUTE
RHEUMATISM, WITH ESPECIAL RELATION TO THE ABSENCE OR
PRESENCE OF ENDOCARDITIS.

I.—Cases of Acute Rheumatism in which there was no Endocarditis.

Affection of joints somewhat severe or moderate, no general illness, no palpitation, signs over heart not named	2
Joint affection slight, some general illness, heart not named	13
Joint affection not, or scarcely severe, some or little general illness, heart sounds healthy	10
Joint affection not, or somewhat severe, some or considerable general illness, heart not named	5
Joint affection not severe, some or considerable general illness, heart sounds healthy	10
Joint affection severe, some general illness, heart not named	6
Joint affection somewhat severe, considerable general illness, heart sounds healthy, or loud and ringing	7
Joint affection severe, some general illness, heart sounds healthy	11
No description of state of joints, or general illness, heart sounds feeble	1
Joint affection not, or rather severe, slight or no general illness, slight prolongation of first sound	7
Joint affection rather severe, slight or no general illness, doubtful occasional obscure murmur	1
Previous valve-disease, mitral regurgitation ⇒	2
Death, delirium	4
I.—TOTAL	79

II.—Cases of Acute Rheumatism in which Endocarditis was threatened.

Some general illness, pain over the cardiac region, heart not named	1
Great general illness, pain left side, or region of heart, signs of heart not named	2
Great general illness, pain left side, heart sounds healthy	3
Great general illness, pleurisy, heart sounds healthy	1
Great or considerable general illness, pain left side, or region of heart, heart sounds healthy	8
Great general illness, delirium, pain left side	1
Considerable general illness, first sound very loud	3
Considerable general illness, doubling of first sound	1
Considerable general illness, first sound or heart sounds feeble or indistinct	3
General illness, pain over region of heart or left side, first sound indistinct or muffled	2
Slight general illness, prolonged first sound	13
Great general illness, prolonged first sound	3
Great general illness, lung affection, prolonged first sound	4
General illness, pain in region of heart or chest, prolonged first sound	10
Little general illness, faint or obscure murmur early or late in the attack	5
Considerable general illness, obscure murmur after cessation of attack (endocarditis probable)	1
Previous valve disease, considerable general illness	2
II.—TOTAL	63

III.—Cases of Acute Rheumatism in which Endocarditis was probable.

Great general illness, pulmonary apoplexy in 1, prolonged first sound (situation unknown), almost a murmur in 1, a pulmonic murmur in 1	2
Great general illness, severe cough in 2, prolonged first sound at apex, almost a mitral murmur in 2, almost a tricuspid murmur in 1, a pulmonic murmur in 3	4
Great general illness, prolonged first sound at right ventricle, almost a tricuspid murmur, and a pulmonic murmur	1
Slight general illness, tricuspid murmur ⇐, ending in prolonged first sound in 1	2
Slight general illness, previous or established mitral regurgitation ⇒ murmur did not vary materially in 1, murmur became louder in 1	2
Considerable general illness, previous or established mitral-aortic regurgitation ⇒ ⇓, aortic murmur absent at first in 1, mitral murmur became musical in 1	2
III.—TOTAL	13

IV.—Cases of Acute Rheumatism in which ENDOCARDITIS *was present without Pericarditis.*

Prolongation of first sound, almost a murmur, pain in heart 1, in chest 1, extreme general illness	2
Tricuspid murmur ←, murmur absent on recovery←o	7
Tricuspid murmur ←, murmur lessening on recovery←	6
Tricuspid murmur ←TOTAL	13
Mitral murmur →, murmur disappearing on recovery o→	27
Mitral murmur →, murmur lessening on recovery →	10
Mitral murmur →, murmur established on recovery →	14
Inflammation of mitral valve →, died, murmur in 1, no note of murmur in 1	2
Mitral endocarditis → TOTAL, mitral murmur in 50, no note of murmur in 1	51
Aortic murmur ↓ murmur disappearing on recovery↓	5
Aortic murmur ↓ aortic regurgitation established on recovery ↓	5
Aortic murmur ↓ TOTAL	10
Mitral-aortic murmur ↓→ murmurs disappearing on recovery o→↓	3
Mitral-aortic murmur, mitral murmur established, aortic murmur disappearing →↓	2
Mitral-aortic murmur, mitral-aortic regurgitation established →↓	4
Mitral-aortic murmur,→↓TOTAL	9
Previous valvular-disease, mitral regurgitation ⇒	6
Previous valvular-disease, mitral and tricuspid regurgitation ⇒	3
Previous valvular-disease, mitral regurgitation, adherent pericardium aortic regurgitation ⇒↓ 1	
Previous valvular-disease, aortic regurgitation ⇓	3
Previous valvular-disease, mitral-aortic regurgitation (tricuspid murmur 2) ⇒ ⇓	9
Previous valve-disease.—TOTAL	22
IV.—Total cases of Endocarditis	*107

V.—Cases of Acute Rheumatism with Endo-Pericarditis.

Heart previously healthy, 46.	Tricuspid murmur ← 3	Murmur disappearing on recovery ←o 1⎫3 / Murmur established on recovery ← 2⎭
	Mitral murmur → 36	Murm. disappearing on recov., mitral o→ 17, ⎫31⎫ / aortic o↓ 1, mitral-aortic o→ ↓ 1 = ⎭ ⎬43 / Murmur lessening on recovery, mitral → 8⎭
	Aortic murmur ↓ 1	
	Mitral-aortic murmur →↓6¹	Mur. estb. on rec., mitral →11, mit.-aor. →↓5⁷=16⎭

Total cases of endocarditis in which the heart was previously healthy . 46

Cases of endocarditis, with prev. valv. disease, mitral ⇒ 5, mitral-aortic ⇒ ⇓ 3 .

    Total cases with endo-pericarditis . 54

    IV., V.—Total with Endocarditis . 161

VI.—Cases of Acute Rheumatism with Pericarditis; Endocarditis being doubtful . 1

VII.—Cases of Acute Rheumatism with Pericarditis in which there was no Endocarditis . 6

    V., VI., VII. Cases of acute rheumatism with Pericarditis.—TOTAL . 13

    GRAND TOTAL of Cases of Acute Rheumatism . 325

* 108 cases of Endocarditis appear in the Tables at pages 187-188. I find that one of those cases has been accidentally enumerated twice over, a woman, aged 23.

Correct errors of press in the Table at page 216 thus— (1) line 9, for 1 read 6; (2) line 12, for mitral-aortic read mitral-aortic 5; (3) line 16, for total 19 read 13.

I have considered the cases of endocarditis according to the character of the valvular affection of the heart due to the inflammation of the interior of the ventricle, and have arranged these cases into those (I.) with an uncomplicated tricuspid murmur; (II.) with mitral regurgitation; (III.) with aortic regurgitation, (1) not accompanied by a mitral murmur, and (2) accompanied by a mitral murmur; (IV.) with prolongation of the first sound without a murmur; (V.) with endocarditis supervening upon previous valvular disease.

I.—CASES OF RHEUMATIC ENDOCARDITIS WITH AN UNCOMPLICATED TRICUSPID MURMUR. *Symbol* ←

In a moderate proportion of the cases of rheumatic endocarditis under my care in St. Mary's Hospital during the fifteen years ending 1866—amounting to 13 out of a total number of 107, or one in eight —there was a murmur over the right ventricle from regurgitation through the tricuspid valve, without a mitral murmur. In nearly all of these cases there was a greater or less amount of general illness, and in one-third of them (4) there was pain in the region of the heart. A tricuspid murmur was present also in 2 cases, in which endocarditis was probable, and in 2 that have been included, with a little doubt, among the cases of pericarditis.

In the majority of these cases the murmur had disappeared when recovery was established; and in the remainder the murmur was then diminishing in loudness, extent, and clearness.

This tricuspid murmur is usually present over the body of the heart, or, in other terms, over the right ventricle; and extends from the lower half of the sternum to a line a little within the left nipple, which line corresponds with the ventricular septum, and from the third to the sixth cardiac cartilage. The presence of this murmur in these cases over the right ventricle in the early stage of endocarditis, and that, too, when no other murmur prevails, naturally suggests to the mind at first sight that it is due to endocarditis affecting the right ventricle and the tricuspid valve.

This inference is, however, forbidden by the following considerations.

(1) Endocarditis, and disease the result of endocarditis of the tricuspid valve, are very rarely discovered on dissection in those who have died from rheumatic inflammation of the interior of the heart, or from valvular disease, the effect of such inflammation.

(2) The tricuspid murmur, when uncomplicated with disease of the mitral valve, was not established in any of my cases, but had either ceased altogether, or was steadily declining on the recovery of the patient.

(3) The tricuspid murmur was frequently associated with a mitral murmur, and less often with a mitral-aortic or an aortic murmur of recent origin.

A tricuspid murmur was present over the right ventricle in one-half, or 27 in 50, of the cases with recent mitral murmur. In 7 of those 27 cases the presence of a tricuspid murmur was somewhat doubtful. In eight of those cases the mitral was preceded by the tricuspid murmur, and in six of these the tricuspid murmur had ceased to be audible when the mitral came into play. In thirteen other cases both murmurs were present when they were first noticed, which was at the time of admission, in fully one-half of those patients. The mitral murmur appeared before the tricuspid in five cases. The tricuspid murmur disappeared when the mitral murmur was still audible in two-thirds of the cases (16 in 27); both murmurs ceased at the same time in seven instances; and in four the tricuspid murmur outlived the mitral. A tricuspid murmur was also present in one-third, (3 in 10), of the cases of endocarditis with mitral disease of old standing.

A tricuspid murmur was present in two or three of the eight cases of mitral-aortic, and in about four of the ten cases of aortic, regurgitation of recent origin; and in two of the five cases with aortic, and none of the seven instances with mitral aortic valvular disease of old standing affected with endocarditis.

(4) I have observed tricuspid regurgitation as a marked and lasting feature in a case of button-hole contraction of the mitral valve; in several instances in which the tissue of the lung was permanently condensed, owing to repeated attacks of bronchitis; in patients affected with contracted granular kidney, in whom obstruction of the pulmonary circulation, with enlargement of the right ventricle, had followed upon obstruction of the systemic circulation, with its attendant tension, dilatation, and thickening of the systemic arteries, and hypertrophy of the left ventricle.

These circumstances point irresistibly to the conclusion that the tricuspid regurgitation is usually due to the so-called "safety-valve" function of that valve, and not to endocarditis of the right side of the heart. In all these cases resistance to the flow of blood through the lungs has induced tension of the pulmonary artery, and distension of the right ventricle and auricle, with, as a result, incomplete closure of the tricuspid valve. The pent-up blood flows back through that aperture, and upon the veins of the system; with the effect of distending those veins, and of giving proportionate relief to the blood gathered up in excess in the pulmonary vessels. At each contraction of the right ventricle, indeed, instead of the whole of the blood flowing forwards into the over-charged pulmonary artery, a portion of it flows backwards into the right auricle, and venæ cavæ.

Inflammation of the left side of the heart, even when there is no regurgitation through the mitral orifice, impedes the flow of blood from the lungs into that side of the heart; and the accumulation of the blood in the pulmonary vessels, thus caused, induces and is relieved by the tricuspid regurgitation.

The tricuspid murmur was present on admission in two of the thirteen cases of endocarditis in which that murmur existed without mitral regurgitation. In nine of the remaining cases, the tricuspid murmur was not observed until from two 'to seven days after admission, and generally on the fourth or fifth day. In one case the murmur did not appear until the 26th day after admission.

In nine of these instances the duration of the illness before their admission is stated. In one of them the murmur appeared on the 7th day; in five, from the 10th to the 12th; and in two, from the 14th to the 16th day after the beginning of the attack of acute rheumatism; and we may therefore infer that the tricuspid murmur generally comes into play about the 10th or 12th day of the primary attack.

In four instances the murmur was preceded by a prolonged first sound over the right ventricle, and in one by a very loud, and in another by a peculiar booming first sound.

In five of the cases there was direct evidence of endocarditis at the time of admission, in the shape of pain in the heart, and a prolonged first sound; although the murmur did not pronounce itself fully until several days had elapsed. In two of them, indeed, the murmur did not appear until there was a marked improvement in the general symptoms.

The duration of the tricuspid murmur in these cases was very variable. In two instances it was only observed once, and in eleven it disappeared in from two to nineteen days; in eight the murmur when last noticed had become much more feeble, and in three of these the first sound became prolonged at the apex, at the time that the tricuspid murmur was diminishing. In three cases a pulmonic murmur, which indicates lessened tension of the pulmonary artery, appeared when the tricuspid murmur was lessening.

From these observations we are entitled, I consider, to infer:—
1. That the appearance of a tricuspid murmur over the body of the heart, extending from the sternum to the nipple, and limited to that region, which corresponds to the right ventricle, is usually the effect and the evidence of endocarditis affecting the left side of the heart.
2. That when this murmur is neither coupled with nor replaced by a mitral murmur, we may safely foretell that when the inflammation leaves the heart, the valves will be perfect and the organ free from disease.

A tricuspid murmur, as I have already remarked, is often the prelude, and for a time the accompaniment, of mitral murmur in cases of rheumatic endocarditis. The latter murmur, however, in two-thirds of the cases (16 in 27) outlives the former, which is essentially a transient murmur. I have already given the proportion in which mitral regurgitation is accompanied, preceded, or followed by a tricuspid murmur (see p. 463).

The duration of the tricuspid murmur in these cases, in which it was associated with a mitral murmur, though variable, was usually short. In ten instances it was only heard once, and that generally on the day of admission, but in one half of these the existence of the murmur was doubtful; in six cases it was audible for from two to seven days, and in seven from nine to sixteen days; while in three, after a short duration, it vanished and reappeared after about twenty days, and in another case after a much longer period.

The tricuspid murmur appeared much earlier in a large proportion of those cases in which it was associated with mitral regurgitation than in those in which it was the only murmur audible. The murmur was present at the time of admission, or on the second day—in two-thirds of the cases (19 in 27), in which there was both a tricuspid and a mitral murmur, and in only one-sixth (2 in 13) of those in which the tricuspid murmur was alone audible. This contrast between the two sets of cases is more striking if we date the murmur from the beginning of the attack. The tricuspid murmur appeared on or before the eighth day in at least nine cases in which there was both tricuspid and mitral regurgitation; and in one only in nine of the cases in which the tricuspid murmur was alone audible. In one of the cases in which both murmurs were in full play on the day of admission, the patient had been ill only two days, in two others four days, and in three others a week. These cases of combined mitral and tricuspid regurgitation, in respect to the more rapid development of the murmur, and not in that respect only, present greater intensity, energy, and rapidity of inflammation in the left cavities of the heart, than in the cases in which the tricuspid murmur was alone audible. In almost all the cases of tricuspid incompetence there was at the time of admission great general illness; but this and other points of clinical interest must be reserved until mitral regurgitation is specially considered. In four of these cases the tricuspid murmur was replaced on its disappearance by a transient prolonged first sound over the right ventricle. The tricuspid regurgitation reappeared after being absent for a longer or shorter period in five of the patients. In four of these the renewed tricuspid murmur was conjoined with mitral murmur, but in the remaining one it cropped up alone 47 days after it had disappeared, and 34 days after the cessation of the mitral murmur.

The tricuspid murmur is easily recognized by its position and character. It is distributed over the right ventricle from the sternum to the nipple and from the 3rd cartilage to the 6th, it usually stops at the septum, occasionally extends over the right auricle, to the right of the lower sternum, and is sometimes audible over the epigastrium below the lower boundary of the heart. The tricuspid murmur is usually grave or even vibrating in tone, and superficial, and it begins with an accent or shock, and ends with the second sound.

In cases of extensive mitral regurgitation without tricuspid murmur, the first sound is feeble while the second is intensified over the pulmonary artery, owing to the tension of that artery, the second sound being usually loud over the right ventricle, and sometimes even at the apex.

When, however, mitral is coupled with tricuspid regurgitation, the blood is thrown back upon the right auricle and the venæ cavæ, the tension of the pulmonary artery is relieved, and the first sound over that artery is moderately loud, or prolonged, or even murmuring; and the second sound, though perhaps rather loud, ceases to be intensified.

The mitral murmur is usually softer and less grave in tone than the tricuspid, being more like a bellows sound; it appears also to be deeper; and its point of greatest intensity is situated to the left of the nipple, and, in endocarditis, towards the axilla. When the mitral murmur is loud and vibrating, and especially if accompanied by a thrill over the apex, perceptible to the finger, it is heard very extensively, radiating in every direction. It then becomes audible over the right ventricle. This transmitted mitral murmur over that ventricle is readily distinguished from the tricuspid murmur originating within the right ventricle itself; for the transmitted or mitral murmur is accompanied and more or less masked by the normal first sound of the right ventricle; while the immediate or tricuspid murmur, besides being grave and shallow, begins with an accent, and is inseparably incorporated with the first sound of the right ventricle.

When the mitral and tricuspid murmurs coexist, it is usually easy to distinguish them from each other upon the principles just stated; for the tricuspid murmur over the right ventricle is then palpably more superficial than the apex murmur, instead of being less so, as it is when the mitral is alone audible; the first sound of the right ventricle does not mask or muffle the murmur; and the difference in tone of the two murmurs is perceptible, the mitral being soft and smooth, the tricuspid grave or vibrating. Two cases were typical instances of this difference in tone of the two murmurs when thus coexisting; in one of them the mitral murmur was a soft bellows sound, while the tricuspid murmur was grave; and in the other the tricuspid murmur was harsh and grating, while the mitral was soft. When the mitral murmur is rasping and vibrating in character, the difficulty of distinguishing the presence of a conjoint tricuspid murmur is increased. An instance of this was presented by a patient in whom the apex murmur was short and rasping, while there was a bellows sound over the right ventricle. Here the rasping mitral murmur might have become softened by its transmission through that ventricle.

It is sometimes difficult to distinguish between a tricuspid murmur and a friction sound, especially when the latter is murmur-like in character, as it frequently is at the beginning and towards the end of an attack of pericarditis. The chief points of distinction are—that the friction sound is usually double or to-and-fro in character; the tricuspid murmur being single: the friction sound is not exactly rhythmical with the heart sounds, those sounds being readily heard distinct from the friction sound when that sound is not loud and grating, so as to extinguish every other noise; the tricuspid murmur is incorporated with the heart sounds; the friction sound starts off without a shock, and retains the same tone throughout; the tricuspid murmur begins with an accent or shock. The pressure test usually clears up every doubt. When the stethoscope is applied over the right ventricle with increased force, the tricuspid murmur may be intensified, but is not materially changed in character; while the friction sound is usually both intensified and changed in tone, it ceases to be murmuring, and becomes grazing, rubbing, grating, or creaking in character.

When pericarditis supervenes upon a tricuspid murmur, the pressure test is sometimes in the early stage almost essential to the discovery of the friction sound; sometimes, however, the patient under these circumstances is so ill that you cannot make pressure. Local pain will then usually guide the treatment, and time will clear up the obscurity.

In five of my cases, aortic regurgitation was accompanied by a tricuspid murmur; and in two of these by a mitral murmur also.

Cases of endocarditis with aortic regurgitation present obstruction to the flow of blood through the lungs, and so may cause tension of the pulmonary artery and tricuspid regurgitation; more, however, owing to the inflammation of the interior of the left cavities and the mitral valve itself, than to the aortic regurgitation, which is rarely sufficient in volume to induce congestion in the lungs. This is shown by the clinical fact that there were four instances with tricuspid murmur in the sixteen cases of endocarditis in which there was recent aortic regurgitation, in seven of which there was mitral regurgitation also; while there was no instance of tricuspid murmur in the fourteen cases of endocarditis in which there was aortic regurgitation owing to the previous disease of the valve, in one-half of which cases there was mitral regurgitation also.

A tricuspid murmur was present in three cases of endo-pericarditis; and in two of those cases the murmur was persistent; while in one of them it disappeared, after the recovery from acute rheumatism.

I will give here the proportion in which a tricuspid murmur was present in cases of acute rheumatism with endocarditis under my care from October, 1866, to 1869, treated by means of rest.

There were altogether 31 cases of endocarditis in a total of 74 of acute rheumatism, and in none of those thirty-one cases was one tricuspid murmur present without a mitral or other murmur.

While the tricuspid murmur unaccompanied by another murmur was absent in those cases; although it was present in the proportion of one in eight of such patients treated during the previous fifteen years; the proportion in which the conjoint tricuspid and mitral murmurs were present was fully maintained in the cases treated by rest. Mitral regurgitation was present without aortic regurgitation in twenty of those cases, and of these, tricuspid murmur was present in nine, or, if we add two doubtful cases, in eleven instances.

In none of these instances did the tricuspid murmur precede the mitral; in four the two murmurs appeared at the same time; in four the mitral preceded the tricuspid murmur by from one to three days, and in one (45) by nine days.

In three of these cases the mitral murmur outlived the tricuspid; in two it was the reverse; in three they were combined to the last, and in the remaining case the mitral murmur probably lasted beyond the tricuspid.

The relation of prolongation of the first sound over the right ventricle to tricuspid murmur will be considered at pages 473, 492.

II.—Cases of Rheumatic Endocarditis with a Mitral Murmur.
Symbol →

The mitral and the tricuspid valves, while they correspond in general structure and function, differ essentially in the construction and arrangement of their flaps and in the whole setting of the valve.

The tricuspid valve, as I have already stated, is composed of three great flaps and several intervening small ones, which meet somewhere about the centre of the valve; and the aponeurotic ring which forms the base of those flaps is surrounded on all sides by muscular walls. (See figs. 1, 2, pp. 40, 41; and figs. 13, 14, 15, pp. 55—57.)

In health, when the ventricle is not over-distended, the flaps of the valve adapt themselves to each other perfectly, and close the tricuspid aperture completely during the contraction of the ventricle.

When, however, the cavity is over distended, as it is under the various circumstances which I have already described, the flaps of the valve adapt themselves only partially to each other, especially, so far as I have observed, at the meeting-point of the three great flaps, and regurgitation ensues. The so-called "safety-valve" function of the valve is thus brought into play, with the effect of relieving the tension of the vessels of the lungs, and throwing the blood backwards upon the veins of the system.

The result is that the tricuspid murmur is, with rare exceptions, not a sign of inflammation of that valve, but of the over distension of the right ventricle, caused by obstruction to the flow of blood through the lungs.

The mitral valve is formed of one great semilunar or convex flap, the base of which is incorporated with the powerful aponeurotic structure that is continuous with the two posterior sinuses of the aorta; and of a crescentic or horse-shoe flap, complex in structure, being formed of three segments, set in the muscular walls at the base of the left ventricle. The setting of the base of the valve is therefore two-thirds muscular and one-third aponeurotic. There is no tendency in the aperture to widen outwards at the base of the valve equally in all directions, for the aponeurotic structure, when healthy, though elastic, is practically unyielding. The single anterior semilunar flap, held in check by its proper chords and fleshy columns, fills up the posterior crescentic flap with perfect adaptation. The edges of the opposed flaps press against each other with increasing force in proportion to the increasing pressure of the blood on their under surfaces; and the over distension of the left cavity does not, owing to the structure to which I have alluded, readily tend to widen the orifice and open up the valve. The healthy mitral valve, therefore, when the left ventricle is not greatly enlarged, possesses only under circumstances of extreme backward pressure or forward resistance a function like the "safety-valve" function of regurgitation with which the tricuspid valve is endowed. Such a function of the mitral valve would indeed be the opposite of a "safety" valve function, for it would immediately endanger the lungs by throwing the blood backwards upon their vessels. (See figs. 1, 2, pages 40, 41 ; and figs. 7—12, pp. 50—52.

The result is that when the right ventricle is over distended, it relieves itself backwards through the tricuspid aperture upon the veins of the system ; and that when the left ventricle is over-distended, it, with rare exceptions, relieves itself directly forwards upon the arteries of the system, and so the lungs are spared in both instances.

I derive the more important evidence of the correctness of this view from the well-understood pathological history of aortic regurgitation from widening of the orifice of the aorta, owing to atheroma of its walls. In those cases the cavity of the left ventricle becomes greatly, sometimes enormously, enlarged, and yet I know of comparatively few instances of this kind in which the mitral valve was therefore incompetent.

Mitral regurgitation, without disease of the structure of the valves, occurs most frequently among cases in which there is great arterial tension owing to Bright's disease, and great consequent distension of the left ventricle ; in which cases there is often also an atheromatous or thickened state of the mitral valve, with, as an effect, widening of the fibrous portion of that aperture, and possible regurgitation.

Mitral murmur is, as a rule, neither a sign of over-distension of the left ventricle, nor of a supply of blood to that cavity too small in amount, or too thin in quality.

The existence then of a mitral murmur in a first attack of acute rheumatism is a direct sign of inflammation affecting the left side of the heart.

Mitral regurgitation, not connected with previous disease of the valve, and without aortic regurgitation, was present in 50 out of 107 cases of rheumatic endocarditis under my care in St. Mary's Hospital from 1851 to 1866, and in 20 of 31 such cases treated by rest from 1866 to 1869. In twenty-five of the earlier series of cases the murmur had disappeared, and in ten others it was lessening at the time of the patient's recovery, while in fourteen of them the murmur seemed to be established ; and it was absent in one and present in the other of two fatal cases of mitral endocarditis at the time of death. In the cases of the later series the corresponding numbers were thirteen, four, and three, the latter being the only cases in which the murmur was established at the time of the patient's recovery.

In one-half of the cases of both sets the mitral murmur was heard on the day of admission or the next day ; the numbers being 28 in 50 of the first set, and 9 in 20 of the second set. The murmur presented itself within six days of admission in three-fourths of the remainder, or seventeen of the earlier and nine of the later series, and from 8 to 17 days after admission in the remaining cases, amounting to one-seventh of the whole.

Among the thirty-seven cases of endocarditis, combining the two series, admitted with mitral murmur, one-third, or eleven, had been ill from 2 to 7 days, nearly one-half, or fifteen, from 8 to 14 days, six from 2 to 4 weeks, two for a longer time, and three for an unknown period.

The mitral murmur became audible after admission in thirty-six cases, and of these the murmur appeared in six during the first 7 days, in eleven from 8 to 14 days, and in eight from 15 to 28 days after the beginning of the attack of acute rheumatism ; in six at a later period ; and in three at a time unknown.

The mitral murmur may be present in full force on the third day of the attack, or its appearance may be delayed until the fortieth day. In a fair proportion of the cases, amounting to one-fourth, it is developed during the first week, and in the larger number, or two-thirds, before the end of the second week.

General illness.—In nearly every case of endocarditis the patient presents great or considerable general illness. Thus in sixty-two of the seventy-one cases of mitral endocarditis the illness was great or considerable, in two it was definite, and in five it was slight ; while in two there is no description of the general state of the patient.

In most of the few exceptions to this rule of the presence of great general illness in these cases, the murmur was established at the time of their admission, and the severity of the attack was already mitigated or passing away.

Those cases in which there was no endocarditis, present a very different aspect, since in scarcely one-third of them was there considerable general illness.

As might be expected, constitutional illness was more severe and frequent in those instances in which there was a threat of endocarditis, though its existence was not actually demonstrated by valvular incompetence, since in nearly two-thirds of them the general illness was either great or considerable.

The illness in cases of endocarditis is peculiar. It differs from and is superadded to that due to simple rheumatic inflammation of the joints, and is such as to call the attention of the physician to the state of the heart.

The face may be flushed all over, the forehead, nose, lips and chin being of as high a colour as the cheeks, a state that is usually associated with profuse perspiration, drops of sweat standing in beads on the surface—a condition, however, that may be present in cases with severe affection of the joints without endocarditis. Thus when endocarditis exists the face loses the brightness, glow, and smoothness, and the variety of hue and tone of health, and becomes clouded, being dusky, dull, or ashy in hue, or glazed, or unduly white, or even of a bluish tint. The countenance, no longer expressive of interest in things and persons around, or even of pain in the limbs, is marked by internal trouble. The aspect of the patient is altered, often profoundly so, being anxious, depressed, or indifferent. The eye loses its lustre and expression, and becomes heavy and dull.

Sleep is often absent, the nights being restless ; but this is perhaps more often due to the inflammation of the joints than to that of the interior of the heart.

The nervous system is often gravely affected. Delirium at night, the patient wandering, muttering, and complaining, is occasional, but rare; it occurred in two instances, in which the affection of the heart was evidently the primary exciting cause of the mental trouble. In another patient the head was confused on the third day.

Choreal movements, as we have seen, are in some instances a definite effect of endocarditis, especially of the non-rheumatic kind, traceable frequently to cerebral embolism; but choreal movements, and indeed embolism, were of very rare occurrence in my cases of rheumatic endocarditis uncomplicated with pericarditis. In one instance the patient, previously anxious, and with sordes on his teeth, was nervous and fidgetty; and in another, starting appeared on the 6th day, having been preceded on the 4th day by pain in the heart.

Sickness is occasionally present. It was so in four of my cases. These cases, however, point not to the stomach as the cause of sickness, but rather and usually to the state of the nervous system, and more immediately to that of the brain itself; as in a case in which giddiness and sickness appeared together, and in another in which sickness was preceded by restlessness.

Failure in the power of the heart is an occasional occurrence in cases of endocarditis. Thus, two of my patients were attacked with fainting. One of these fainted on the day of admission, and again on the thirteenth, and on the following day was sick, so that failure of the heart may be a cause of sickness. In the other case pain in the heart and fainting appeared on the seventeenth day after admission. We may fairly attribute the fainting in these cases to the actual failure of the heart itself, caused by the internal inflammation of that organ.

The pulse is often quick, feeble, and fluctuating. I believe that it is dichrotous, but I have not employed the sphygmograph in any case of endocarditis, being perhaps deterred by the state of the wrist.

Perspiration is often especially profuse and of long continuance; sudamina being also present in some of the more severe cases.

The breathing is usually affected, being more or less quickened. In rare instances pulmonary apoplexy or extravasation is the result of the difficulty to the flow of blood through the lungs, which is the general effect, varying in degree, of endocarditis.

The chain of symptoms here described points mainly to the affection of two great functions. The nervous power is lowered; and the circulation of the blood through the fine vessels of the lungs and the body is enfeebled.

Pain in the Region of the Heart.—Pain in the region of the heart, sometimes severe and lasting, sometimes slight or transient, amounting perhaps only to uneasiness, was present in about one-fourth of the cases of tricuspid and of mitral murmur belonging to the earlier series, and in one-half of the later series, treated by rest. If to these we add other cases having mitral or tricuspid murmur in which there was pain in the left side, or in the chest; the proportion thus affected reaches to nearly one-half in the first series, and to fully one-half in the second.

The pain in the heart was sometimes, but not generally, severe. In a few instances the pain was increased or excited by pressure. We may fairly infer that in those cases pericarditis was imminent or was actually present, though not, except in rare instances, with such intensity as to cause even a transient friction sound.

Palpitation was very rarely complained of, but fainting, as I have already stated, occurred in two instances.

Prolongation of the First Sound occurring during the Early Period of Mitral Endocarditis.—In one-half of my patients affected with mitral regurgitation, as we have just seen, a murmur was established at the time of admission. In one-half of the cases in which the murmur was not thus established, prolongation of the first sound preceded, and was merged into, the murmur. In all but one of those cases the first sound was prolonged at the time of admission, and in that case and two others a tricuspid murmur was then in full play.

The tricuspid murmur was likewise heralded by prolongation of the first sound in one-half of the cases in which that murmur was not already present at the time of admission.

In a number of the cases, the exact position of the prolongation of the first sound was not defined; but wherever it was so, the mitral murmur was preceded by prolongation of the first sound at the apex; and the tricuspid murmur by prolongation of the first sound over the front of the heart, or the right ventricle.

I think that no cardiac sign is more readily recognized than prolongation of the first sound, and yet there is none so difficult to define. That this is so, however, is natural, for it is a transition sound. It forms, as we have just seen, the transition from a clear healthy first sound to a murmur; and as we shall see, at a later period, in a large proportion of the cases, it forms a transition between a mitral or tricuspid murmur when dying out, and the restoration of the healthy first sound. In one-half of the cases in which the prolongation preceded the murmur, there was a double transition, the murmur being both preceded and followed by prolongation of the first sound. This prolongation is sometimes so like a murmur that it is difficult to make the distinction, and this is especially the case just before the time of transition, when the prolongation precedes the murmur; and just after that time, when it follows the murmur.

Prolongation of the first sound is the absence of silence and the presence of a wavering, grave, feeble sound during the interval between the first and second sounds. It is not the prolongation of the shock of the first sound which is itself significant, being sometimes a precursor of the more telling signs of endocarditis. The prolongation of the first sound is not the same as the natural loud vibrating character of that sound over the superficial cardiac region which is almost always present in cases of anæmia, when the muscular force of the ventricles is maintained, and even in excess, but when the blood is scanty and thin, being deficient in red corpuscles.

Prolongation of the first sound is, I repeat, a feeble, indeterminate, wavering sound, that fills up the space between the first and second sounds, which space is silent in health. It presents every gradation, from a sound so feeble that it is with difficulty discovered, to a sound so murmurlike that it can scarcely be distinguished from the murmur into which it so often ripens. Prolongation of the first sound was noticed on the first day of observation in fourteen cases; the prolongation developed into a murmur in two-thirds or nine of those cases before the seventh day after admission; and in the remaining third, or five, between the seventh and fourteenth days. In two other instances the prolongation, absent on the day of admission, appeared on the following day, and in the other after a lapse of four days.

It is evident that in all these cases the endocarditis was present before the appearance of the murmur for a period of time at least as long as the previous period of duration of the prolongation of the first sound.

There are other modifications of the first sound, besides its prolongation, that point to endocarditis, if they do not indicate it, which have been, in a few instances, the precursors of murmur. It will be sufficient if I simply name them. They are—1. Loud heart sounds, the first being sharp, the second ringing; or both sounds may be ringing. 2. Healthy sounds with powerful action of the heart. 3. Roughness of the first sound. 4. A humming noise over the right ventricle, and in one case at the apex, where it was associated with murmur. 5. Doubling of the first sound (over the ventricle), which occurred in two cases associated with a prolonged first sound, which was not followed by a murmur in one of those cases. 6. Feeble first, loud second sound, followed by tumultuous action of the heart and mitral and aortic murmurs. 7. Extensive presystolic murmur ($rrrp$) present in one case for five days, followed in succession by loud heart sounds (6th day), doubling of the second sound (15th day), and a faint mitral murmur, not limited to the apex. 8. Loud "plunging" first sound over both ventricles, present on the 4th day, followed by prolongation of the first sound on the 6th, and mitral murmur on the 8th; and 9. muffling of the first sound, which in one case succeeded the murmur, which was extinguished by an attack of pain in the heart, followed by fainting.

All the above varieties in character of the first sound were, in the instances referred to, followed within a very few days by a mitral murmur.

· The only one of these varieties of the first sound that I would speak of is the last: the peculiar "plunging" sound. I call it so for want of a better name. The sound is something like what I have heard in the working of a steam-engine. It was as if the piston made a peculiar plunging sound when it dipped down and reached the bottom of its play. I have heard this sound in at least three cases. One of them was attacked afterwards with delirium, long torpor, almost coma, extreme depression, and pericarditis, but no murmur. In all the cases, the constitutional symptoms more or less threatened endocarditis.

Besides these peculiarities of the first sound preceding mitral murmur, there is one other affection of the sounds of the heart that I would name; and that is a complete silence of both sounds; which occurred in one case threatened with endocarditis, in which a mitral murmur did not appear. In that case there was tenderness over the heart, fighting for breath, a piercing pain between the chest and back, and great depression, lasting for some days. On the 8th day she looked more bright, on the 9th the sounds of the heart were audible, on the 14th its impulse had returned and was gaining power, and on the 26th day the sounds were of natural loudness, and there was no murmur.

In most of the cases of endocarditis with mitral murmur there is undue, but not great, strength of the impulse of the right ventricle, which may be seen and felt between the cardiac cartilages to the left of the lower sternum. This is found even in the earlier stages, and before the appearance of the mitral murmur.

It is evident from what has just been stated, that while in some cases that murmur bursts into full play at the commencement of the attack, being audible on admission, and on the 3rd, 4th, 5th, 6th, or 7th days after the seizure; in others it is not audible until a period varying from the 8th to the 30th day, although there is unequivocal evidence that the inflammation in the left side of the heart was present before and at the time of admission. This evidence consists in the existence of a tricuspid murmur, or a prolonged first sound, or pain in the region of the heart or in the chest, with great or considerable general illness.

The inflammation of the valve cannot cause regurgitation until perfect adaptation is prevented by the formation of small prominences, covered with a deposit of fibrin upon the surfaces or lines of contact of the margins of the valve, or by the softening and yielding of its flaps.

In three of the cases tricuspid or mitral murmur became audible after admission, when the patient's illness increased. In ten other cases, however, it was the reverse, for in all of them the murmur came into play when the patient's health began to improve.

We are therefore, I conceive, warranted in assuming that in a considerable number of the cases, the active stage of the endocarditis is passing away at the time of the appearance of the murmur.

Progress of Cases of Endocarditis with a Mitral Murmur.—Cases with a mitral murmur from endocarditis affecting a valve previously healthy, may usually be readily distinguished from those in which the murmur is due to established disease of the mitral valve by the character, seat, and area of the murmur, its changes, duration, and transition, its cessation or establishment; by the size of the heart and the force, extent, and position of its impulse; and by the nature of the first and second sounds over the right ventricle, the pulmonary artery, the aorta and great arteries in the neck. The mitral murmur is always situated over the apex and body of the left ventricle, and the ventricular septum. The centre of the murmur and its point of greatest intensity and purity is usually just below the left nipple. Sometimes it is limited to this point, but in general it covers a larger area, spreading inwards towards the right ventricle, outwards and upwards towards the axilla and over the lung, and downwards over the stomach. This area is rarely extensive, being usually limited by a diameter of from two to three inches.

When the heart is high, owing to the elevation of the diaphragm, and when the left ventricle is exposed in consequence of the shrinking of the overlapping portion of the left lung, the murmur extends upwards towards the axilla, and even above the mamma, and a little outwards, rather than downwards. The direction of the murmur upwards towards the axilla is peculiar to the mitral murmur of endocarditis, for when disease of the valve is established, the lungs expand downwards to an unusual extent, and so muffle or arrest the murmur in its course towards the axilla.

The extent of the area of the murmur depends much upon its character. A smooth, soft, bellows-murmur, especially if it is rather feeble, is in general limited to the apex and left ventricle; so also is a weak, grave murmur. But when it is vibrating, loud and almost musical, and especially if a thrill is felt by the finger over the apex—then the area of the murmur is extensive. Sometimes, indeed, it is so all-pervading that it may be heard over the whole cage of the chest, front and back, and even upwards into the neck and downwards over the abdomen.

It is only in established mitral disease, or in very rare cases of endocarditis with extensive mischief to the valve, that we find this pervading vibrating murmur with perceptible thrill.

In cases of established mitral disease the murmur is usually audible to a greater or less extent over the region of the stomach, often coming quite down to its lower boundary. The vibration in the left ventricle, which rests immediately upon the stomach, the diaphragm alone interposing, awakens a corresponding vibration in the stomach, and as this takes place in a hollow sac, its tone is often metallic, and it thus sometimes imparts a musical character to the murmur at the apex.

In cases of endocarditis with mitral regurgitation, the murmur is often so feeble that it is limited to its birthplace, and is unable to generate corresponding vibrations in the adjoining organs. In these patients the murmur is inaudible over the stomach; but in other cases of endocarditis, according to the loudness and penetrating quality of the tone, the murmur makes itself heard over a greater or less portion of the stomach, at that part of it nearest to the apex of the heart.

The murmur was heard over the lower part of the back of the chest in only two of the fifty cases of endocarditis with mitral murmur of the first series, and in one of the twenty cases of the second series. In one of these cases the murmur was audible over the lower part of the back, the lungs being condensed, on the 4th day, but it was not again heard in that position. In another such case the murmur was heard over the back of the chest from the 27th to the 34th days after admission, but ceased to be so on the 30th; and in the third case the murmur was heard below the shoulder blades for the first time on the 18th, and for the last time on the 42nd day. After that date the murmur was less loud, and its area was correspondingly lessened.

I have to add to these, one case of death with inflammation of the mitral valve; the anterior flap was softened and enlarged, its edge and that of the posterior flap were covered with lymph or fibrine, and the valve permitted extensive regurgitation through the mitral aperture. The patient, a young man previously in good health, had been ill a fortnight with acute rheumatism; when admitted, he had an anxious expression, hurried and difficult breathing, and sickness. A loud mitral murmur, beginning with a sharp shock and followed by the second sound, extended forwards almost to the sternum, where the heart sounds were healthy, and backwards to below both shoulder blades. From the 9th day to the 11th he raised phlegm tinted with blood, he was propped up in bed, and there was dulness and fine crepitation over the left lower lobe. On the 14th he sat forward in bed in great distress, breathing with difficulty. In the course of that day he died, and on dissection he presented the inflammation of the mitral valve and the extensive pulmonary apoplexy that were evidenced during life.

The patients usually lay flat in bed, their pain being increased by movement, and as the back was not examined, some of these might have presented a murmur over the lower lobes of the lungs behind; but when we regard the limited area over which the murmur was usually heard in front and at the side, it is evident that it could scarcely have been audible behind. I think it probable that three cases, in addition to those just named, may have been exceptions to this rule, and perhaps two others, for in them the murmur was loud, while in the first three it was vibrating in tone.

The mitral murmur at the time of its first appearance, or of its transition from prolongation of the first sound, is as a rule either weak and grave; or it is a soft, feeble, bellows murmur, and is therefore limited in area.

The mitral murmur invariably begins with an accent or shock, which corresponds with the shock of the impulse, and it generally ends with the second sound. It fills up, in fact, the space between the first and second sounds, that space being often lengthened so as to admit of greater prolongation of the murmur, with the effect of altering the rhythm of the heart. Sometimes the murmur does not quite fill up this space, so that there is a distinct silent pause between the end of the murmur and the second sound. The presence of the accent or shock at the beginning of the first sound distinguishes an endocardial murmur from an exocardial or friction murmur.

The pressure test comes in to settle the difficulty of distinguishing one condition from the other. If the noise be endocardial, the sound may become louder from the closer application of the stethoscope, when pressed upon the walls of the chest; but the quality of the noise is unaltered, it is rhythmical with the heart sounds, it retains its accent or shock, it fills up the space between the first and second sounds, and it ends exactly with the second sound.

But if the noise be frictional, it usually loses its murmur-like tone when the pressure is made—and becomes rustling or grazing, grating or creaking in character; it extinguishes the first and second sounds of the heart, which were previously heard side by side, but not incorporated with the murmur; it brings out a double sound where there was but a single one before, a sound to-and-fro in character, or a noise not unlike that made by the sharpening of a scythe, with a single down-stroke during the beat of the heart, and a double up-stroke during its pause. Sometimes the mitral murmur is masked or confused at the apex by the co-existence of a vibrating systolic noise. The interposition of a piece of paper or cloth between the stethoscope and the surface of the chest annihilates this vibrating noise, and the mitral murmur is then heard with perfect purity and clearness. The interposition of the lung effects the same end—for this vibratory noise is heard only where the heart is in direct contact with the walls of the chest; and hence, when using the naked stethoscope, we meet with cases in which the murmur is more smooth and bellows-like just to the left of the apex or towards the axilla, than it is over the apex itself. For this effect, however, the layer of lung must be thin and the tone of the murmur must be penetrating. In cases of endocarditis with mitral regurgitation, the murmur is often muffled by a rumble, or a comparatively feeble vibration. The interposed paper or the intervening lung extinguishes this vibrating noise, and brings a pure, soft, bellows murmur into play.

The changes that the mitral murmur of endocarditis undergoes during the progress of the case are remarkable, and they vary in almost every instance. These changes consist in alterations of its tone, loudness, and area; in its transition from a true murmur to prolongation of the first sound; in the substitution of a tricuspid for a mitral murmur, or the reverse, or the companionship of the two murmurs; in the suppression and reawakening of the murmur; and frequently in its final extinction, either directly or by passing again into prolongation of the first sound, which precedes the restoration of the healthy sounds of the heart.

In one-fourth of the cases (18 in 70) the mitral murmur was only heard on one occasion.

Of 50 cases, in all of which the mitral murmur was heard more than once, that murmur was of equal loudness during the successive observations in one-fifth (11); became gradually weaker in one-third (17), but in six of these it passed through a double oscillation and increased and lessened a second time; became gradually stronger in one-fifth of the cases (11), in one-half of which it again gradually declined; was suspended and then renewed for a time in one-fourth of the cases (12), when the murmur again faded away; and it sometimes yielded to the healthy sounds of the heart, and sometimes to prolongation of the first sound. In two instances, already included in the abstract just given, there was a double disappearance and reawakening of the mitral murmur, which in one of them met with final extinction, while in the other it became established.

The changes in the area of the murmur corresponded in a considerable degree to the changes in its loudness, the former widening as the latter increased and narrowing as it diminished.

In the great majority of the cases, and especially in those in which the murmur disappeared, the tone of the murmur underwent but little change. It became progressively louder and feebler, more clear and more obscure in almost every instance, but it usually retained its original character.

The murmur was observed to be soft and smooth, approaching to the character of a bellows sound, in less than one-half of the first series of the cases of endocarditis with mitral regurgitation, and in less than one-third of the second series; the cases in each series in which the murmur was not characterized amounting to fully one-third of the whole.

In a small proportion of the first series and a large proportion of the second series of cases, the murmur was grave in character, being in some of them feeble, and in a few, loud and almost vibrating.

Musical, sawing, and rasping murmurs formed but a small proportion of the total number of cases, and these were they that passed through a series of changes in tone and character.

One case, a youth, was a notable and rare instance of the variety of changes in tone through which the mitral murmur may pass. He had been ill a fortnight and had suffered from pain in the heart. On admission he presented a tricuspid murmur. To this a loud mitral murmur was added on the 3rd day, when he was very ill. On the 8th he was better, and from that day to the 15th the murmur was weak, soft, and smooth. On the 21st it was louder and on the 29th it altogether changed its tone and became musical. After this, without apparent cause, it underwent two variations, having first the character of a sawing and then of a bellows sound. The tone of the murmur then again altered, and it became grave, and finally on the 52nd day it had regained its lost musical character.

We must now answer the important practical questions suggested by these observations, what are the character and progress of the murmur, when the attack tends to end in perfect restoration of the efficiency of the valve? and what, when it tends to become permanently incompetent, owing to the establishment of mitral disease?

The answer may be already almost gathered from what has gone before. When the murmur is permanently feeble, soft, and smooth, with an approach to, or even the formation of, a gentle bellows sound;

or when it is feeble and grave, the complete restoration of the efficiency of the valve may be anticipated. In illustration of this statement we find that the murmur was feeble, soft, and approaching to a bellows sound in 14 of the 25 cases of the first series that ended in recovery of the valve; and in 4 of the 10 that left with a lessening murmur, the corresponding number in the two like classes of cases of the second series being 5 in 17, while of the 17 cases that ended in established valve disease out of a total of 71, the murmur was feeble in none, and was smooth or soft in 6, most of which presented a definite bellows murmur.

The feeble grave murmur was more frequently developed in the later than in the earlier series of cases, but in both its presence was almost always followed by the restoration of the function of the valve.

When the loudness of the murmur steadily diminished, or when it first rose and then fell, or when after disappearing it reappeared and again faded away, the integrity of the valve was generally regained.

When the murmur was loud, its area being extensive; when it presented a sharply-defined loud, bellows, musical, sawing, or rasping sound; when it was vibrating in tone; when it steadily increased in loudness, or only slightly rose and fell to rise and fall again, without a temporary disappearance; then valvular disease was, as a rule, though not invariably, permanently established. One patient, a nurse in the Hospital, left with a loud mitral murmur, but after a time, when she resumed her work, the murmur had given place to healthy heart sounds.

Condition of the Heart and the Great Vessels in Cases of Endocarditis affecting the Mitral Valve.—In these cases there are, as I have already illustrated, many affections of the heart besides imperfection of the mitral valve with its attendant murmur. When inflammation affects the great central cavity of the heart, the pivot of its action, the whole organ is involved, and every part of it becomes, in succession, modified in its action; and in the force, movement, and sounds by which it makes that action known.

Inflammation of the fibrous structure of the left side of the heart is as essentially a part of acute rheumatism, as is inflammation of the fibrous structure of the joints. The inflammation may commence in the heart at the same time that it commences in the limbs. It attacks that part of the heart that is working with the greatest force, just as it attacks those parts of the limbs that are subjected to the greatest labour. The increasing inflammation of the joints calls forth increasing force in the action of the left ventricle, and so stirs up and adds to the inflammation that may have already existed in that cavity from the commencement of the attack.

This inflammation of the ventricle, like the inflammation of every other organ, lessens the power of the muscular cavity to expel its contents, and to propel the blood round the vessels of the system. This imperfect transmission of blood to the system, the demand for which is increased by the inflammation in the limbs, causes distension of the left auricle, and impedes the transmission of the blood through the lungs. This induces distension of the pulmonary artery and its branches, with, as its effects, accentuation—or loudness and sharpness, or shock—of the second sound, with relative feebleness, or even absence, of the first sound over that artery; and distension of the right ventricle, with increase in the action of its walls and in the force and extent of its impulse.

We have, thus, two ventricles beating side by side, the left one, the seat of the inflammation, beating with lessened power; the right one, with increased force.

The increased fulness and force of the right ventricle tend, when they pass certain limits, to reverse the flow of a portion of the blood, and to send it from the right ventricle back into the right auricle; with the effect of relieving the distension of the arteries of the lungs, increasing the fulness of the veins of the system, and producing a tricuspid murmur.

After a time, the whole volume of the blood is diminished, and the proportion of its red corpuscles is lessened; and then appear as later and secondary effects, a murmur over the pulmonary artery, and sometimes a murmur over the aorta and its great branches—murmurs that are due to the lessening of the contents, and relaxation of the walls of those vessels.

Such murmurs in the great arteries appear, however, also in the early stages of the affection, in the aorta more frequently, owing evidently to the lessened power of the inflamed left ventricle, and the diminished supply of blood that is therefore sent into the aorta, the walls of which are thus relaxed; and in the pulmonary artery occasionally, for reasons that have yet to be ascertained.

The close study of the condition of the heart and great vessels generally throws more light upon the degree of the inflammation of the heart, and its effect on the vital powers of the organ, than does the simple observation of the mitral murmur.

I shall now rapidly review the conditions of the heart and great vessels as they presented themselves in the cases of endocarditis with incompetence of the mitral valve—that valve being previously in the virgin state and uninjured.

The Impulse of the Heart.—I find that I have taken notes of the state of the impulse in one half of the cases with mitral incompetence, or in 25 out of 50 of the first series, and 9 out of 20 of the second.

The beat of the heart was, as a rule, not extensive or strong. It showed itself rather in the higher than the lower cardiac intercostal spaces, being present in only one instance below the fifth space, less frequently in that space than in the fourth, and sometimes even in the third space. While the impulse at the apex was in general feeble or absent; that of the right ventricle, though rarely powerful, was usually somewhat increased in strength, being present in the third and fourth, and even the fifth spaces between the cartilages. This impulse of the right ventricle was not as a rule marked or strong, but it could be felt diffused over those spaces when the ball of the palm of the hand was applied over them, or when the fingers were pressed gently into the spaces.

In a few instances the action of the heart, and especially the impulse of the right ventricle, was strong and diffused or powerful, or even tumultuous and violent, soon after admission; and then the size of the heart, which was not in general notably affected, became enlarged, the chest over the cardiac region being more prominent than over the corresponding space on the right side.

In one or two patients the impulse presented a peculiar shock.

But the distinctive feature with regard to the impulse in a fair proportion of the cases was its variation during the successive periods of the disease. Thus, in one instance, it was feeble on the 1st day in the fourth space, very strong on the 3rd day, moderate in strength in the fifth space on the 8th day, and in the third and fourth spaces on the 12th day. In another patient the impulse was felt in the second and third spaces on the 2nd day, when there was pain in the heart; on the 5th, the pain still continuing, the heart beat violently; from the 6th to the 18th the pulsation was strong in the second space, and from the 28th to the 34th it was diffused from the third to the fifth spaces. In this case mitral disease was established, and the gradual extension of the impulse of the right ventricle told with precision the story of the increasing valvular disease in the left ventricle.

The study of the impulse conveys the most important lesson in all cases of endocarditis. Its absence may tell of the want of vital power; and its excess in the right ventricle, while it is wanting in the left, shows lessened power from inflammation in the latter cavity, and consequent increased labour in the former. Its gradual increase in force, and enlargement in area, with persistence of mitral murmur towards the period of the termination of the attack of endocarditis, and after its cessation, mark advancing and established valvular disease: and its extent and force point out the amount of the back-flow of blood from the left ventricle into its auricle, and the obstacle to the on-flow of blood through the lungs induced thereby. The impulse of the right ventricle is, in short, a measure of the extent of the injury to the mitral valve, and of the consequent resistance to the circulation through the lungs.

The impulse of the right ventricle was diffused and strong, extending out to the nipple, in a considerable proportion of the cases in which there was a tricuspid murmur.

In a few instances the impulse of the right ventricle was so high as to be present in the second space; but generally the pulsation felt in that space was due to the presence there of the distended pulmonary artery, when that pulsation was double, the second impulse being more smart and shock-like than the first. In these cases the pulmonary artery was distended, the first sound was feeble or absent, while the second was unusually loud and strong, penetrating the ear with a shock.

The apex beat is, in cases of endocarditis with mitral regurgitation.

usually slight, sometimes absent—during the early period, before the mitral murmur is developed, owing to the weakened muscular power of the inflamed left ventricle; and—after the appearance of the murmur, owing to the relief afforded to the organ by the greater ease with which its surcharge of blood is sent backwards into the auricle than forwards into the aorta.

There are, however, certain exceptional cases of great interest, several of which have come under my observation, in which the left ventricle beats with great force, and unduly to the left.

In three of these cases there was extensive pulmonary apoplexy, or pneumonia of that type, in the lower portion of the left lung.

One was a youth, with hurried and difficult breathing, tinted phlegm, and dulness over the lower portion of the left lung, which was solid and lessened in size owing to pulmonary apoplexy. The condensed and solidified lung shrank away from its natural position between the walls of the chest and the apex of the heart; and the apex was therefore completely exposed, beating with all its force upon the fifth space more than an inch beyond the left nipple. At that time there was no mitral murmur, but as soon as the lung began to recover itself, the murmur came into full play. When the lung again expanded, it covered the apex of the heart, and its beat was no longer perceptible. The whole heart in this case was displaced to the left; and its displacement was still greater in the sister case, in which the apex beat was situated three inches beyond the nipple line; the impulse of the right ventricle was placed to the left of the costal cartilages; and the double pulsation of the pulmonary artery, with a strong second shock, was present in the second space above the mamma.

A fourth case, when admitted, had pain in the region of the heart, and the apex beat was situated an inch and a half to the left of the nipple. Five days later the extreme limit of the impulse had shrunk one inch, being seated half an inch to the left of the nipple.

Accentuation of the Second Sound, with Silence, Feebleness, or Prolongation of the First Sound over the Pulmonary Artery.—Accentuation of the second sound over the pulmonary artery, in the left second space, is a well established sign attendant upon mitral regurgitation, and it may be present in every degree.

The second sound may be more or less loud and sharp or ringing—or it may penetrate and strike the ear with a loud shock; when a double impulse is to be felt over the pulmonary artery, the first being gentle and gradual, while the second gives to the hand a smart shock.

This increase in loudness and sharpness of the second sound is due to distension of the pulmonary artery, owing to the difficulty with which the blood travels through the vessels of the lungs.

Whenever the blood thus accumulates in the lungs, whatever be the cause, the same effect is induced. In cases of phthisis, and notably when there is hæmorrhage from the lung and shrinking of its tissue, the pulmonary artery, enlarged and tense, displaces the lung superficial to it, and presses against the second space ; where there is a double impulse the first gentle, the second felt and heard as a shock. In bronchitis, emphysema and pneumonia, there is the same distension of the pulmonary artery, but greater in degree. The interposition of the lung, enlarged owing to the disease, screens the pulmonary artery from the hand and the ear, so that over it the second sound is often not unduly loud ; but it is so in some instances over the right ventricle.

Whenever the tension of the pulmonary artery is thus so great as to cause a strong and loud shock with the second sound, the first sound is either almost silent, or feeble, or faintly prolonged.

When the blood is sent into a tight and full artery, it makes but little, often no sound, either in the shape of shock or murmur ; but the second sound caused by the smart and strong reflux of the blood upon the walls and closed valves of the artery, makes a loud, sometimes a ringing or metallic sound. The same occurs in the aorta when it is enlarged and rendered tense owing to the difficulty with which the blood leaves the arterial system in advanced cases of contracted granular kidney. When you listen over the aorta a single sound is often heard, a loud ringing metallic second sound, the first being almost or absolutely silent. Sometimes in these cases the artery is so large and tense that it presses against the second right intercostal space, producing there a double pulsation, the first gentle and gradual, the second smart and with a shock.

I find that I have described the second sound as being loud or sharp or ringing in about one-half of the 50 cases of the first series and 9 of the 20 of the second series of cases of endocarditis with mitral murmur, and in 5 of 13 of those of the first series with an uncomplicated tricuspid murmur. This does not of course include all of this class.

It was noticed that the second sound was sharp or loud in the early period in a large proportion of the cases in which that sign was observed, or in 13 out of 25 of the first series, and 7 out of 9 of the second series.

In all but six of the patients in whom it was noticed that the second sound was intensified, it continued to be loud down to a late period, to the time in fact of approaching recovery.

Loudness of the second sound may be associated with each of the signs, singly or in combination, that are habitually found in cases of endocarditis with inflammation of the mitral valve. It accompanied a mitral murmur, either alone or in combination with a tricuspid murmur in 22 of the cases ; in about 15 cases it was allied with prolongation of the first sound over the left and sometimes the right ventricle ; and in 8 cases it was joined to tricuspid regurgitation, which was however combined with other important signs in every instance but one. The first sound of the pulmonary artery was affected, when the second sound over that artery was loud or sharp, on ten occasions, in different patients : in 4 of these there was a pulmonic murmur, in 4 the first sound was prolonged, being generally free from shock, and in 2 it was silent or scarcely audible.

These numbers, however, taken by themselves give a very inadequate idea of the relation of the first to the second sound of the pulmonary artery in cases when that second sound is intensified. Thus, as we have just seen, pulmonic murmur was followed by a sharp second sound in four instances, but there were altogether 32 cases in which a pulmonic murmur was heard, and in only four of them was it stated that the second sound was thus affected at the time when the pulmonic murmur was audible. In one of the cases in which there was a pulmonic murmur on admission, the second sound was free from accent; while on the 3rd when the pulmonic murmur had disappeared, that sound was slightly accentuated over the pulmonary artery. Again, in only two of the cases is it noted that the first sound of the pulmonary artery was silent or scarcely audible when the second sound was loud. Since, however, my attention has been drawn to the relation of the first to the second sound of the pulmonary artery, in every instance that I have observed accentuation of the second sound, especially with, but even without shock, the first sound has been either very feeble, being occasionally prolonged, or almost or even quite silent. This condition was signally marked in a case of chorea under my care in the hospital, a boy, who on admission, presented no mitral or other murmur over the heart. After gaining ground steadily he became rather worse, his temperature rose, he had pain in his chest, and the second sound was loud, the first feeble over the pulmonary artery; and six days later a mitral murmur came into play. At the same time the right ventricle, previously quiet, beat with great force, and a strong shock was felt over the pulmonary artery with the second sound. On listening over that vessel, a loud second sound penetrated the ear and struck it as it were with a shock, and the first sound was silent, the second sound being alone audible to all who listened. After a short time he became very ill, and for two days he passed his evacuations involuntarily in bed. He kept both hands fixed on his wrists, and his fingers on his hands. He soon began to improve, and gradually as this boy gained strength, speech, power to move, and freedom from irregular movements; and as his lungs enlarged, the mitral murmur being still audible, the second sound though still loud lost its shock, the second impulse ceased to be felt over the pulmonary artery, and the first sound, though feeble, became more and more audible.

In a fair proportion of the cases in which the second sound was sharp and loud at the early period of the disease, that sound retained its character unaltered through all the surrounding changes in the sounds of the heart. Let us take one case. At first there was a tricuspid murmur, the second sound being sharp; on the 6th day there was a mitral murmur, and the second sound was loud; next day the murmur was less marked, but the second sound was still loud; and on the 11th the murmur had given place to prolongation of the first sound over the right ventricle, and yet the second sound still remained loud. In another instance on the 9th day there was an obscure mitral murmur, on the 16th there was mitral, tricuspid and direct aortic murmurs, on the 19th these had all vanished, and on the 23rd the tricuspid and direct aortic murmur had returned ; and yet on each occasion there was the same sharp second sound over the pulmonary artery. I could give several instances of this kind and would refer to four cases. In these instances the sharp second sound went on drumming, like the tom-tom in the streets, whatever was the variety of the surrounding noise, or even when there was freedom from murmur or prolongation of the first sound.

The intensified second sound is, however, by no means always so unvarying in its note. Thus, in one very interesting case on the 11th day the second sound was very loud over the pulmonary artery, the first being scarcely audible ; on the 34th both sounds were loud over the ventricles, the second being very loud ; and next day all the sounds were natural.

I must refer to one other case, in which on admission the first sound was faint, the second loud over the pulmonary artery, the first sound being prolonged over the ventricles ; on the 13th day the two sounds were equal over the artery and there was a feeble murmur at the apex ; on the 27th the second sound was again louder than the first ; and on the 40th a singular change took place, the first sound being louder than the second over the pulmonary artery—while over the aorta it was the reverse, and on the 50th day the natural standard was regained, the second sound being louder than the first.

The close study of the second sound and of its relation to the first over the pulmonary artery, is of practical importance in cases of endocarditis affecting the mitral valve. It may foretell the coming murmur in the early, and betray the recently extinct murmur in the later, period of the disease ; and during its progress, it points by the degree and force of its accent to the amount of the resistance to the pulmonary circulation, the intensity of the internal inflammation of the ventricle, and the extent to which the function of the ventricle is impaired. It is, in short, a tell-tale sound pointing to the agency in the central cavity of the heart which gives it birth. The intensified second sound of the pulmonary artery, or that of the aorta, is associated as we have seen with a corresponding feebleness. or even silence, of the first sound of each of the vessels respectively. The observation of the one sound demands a corresponding observation of the other sound. When the artery is distended, it enlarges, lengthens, and advances, and comes gradually into contact with the second intercostal space, displacing the intervening lung from before it. You can then feel the double pulsation of the great artery ; the first move-ment is gentle, gradual, barely perceptible to the touch ; the second strikes the walls of the chest and the applied hand with a sudden smart shock or tap. When you listen to it the ear takes in the same effect through another sense ; the first sound is in extreme cases silent, or is soft and gentle, feeble and perhaps somewhat prolonged; while the second penetrates and strikes the ear with a loud shock, often ringing and metallic. Over the pulmonary artery, as I have just said, that subdued sound or even silence, and this shock, betoken tension of the artery, and obstacle to the flow of blood through the vessels of the lungs; whether that obstacle be caused by a back flow, due to inflammation or disease, with incompetence, of the mitral valve; or directly to disease of the lung itself, whether from phthisis, contracted lung, pneumonic bronchitis, or emphysema; the shock being in these last cases shielded from the hand and muffled to the ear by the interposition of a couch of lung, thickened by the undue expansion of the air cells induced by the disease.

When the aorta is thus distended, pushing aside the lungs, beating with a double pulsation upon the second right intercostal space, over the ascending aorta, the first gentle and gradual, the second, a smart shock, the first feeble or even silent, the second, a loud ringing, metallic shock, you know that the blood forces its way with difficulty through the fine vessels of the system, and that the cause of this is the contamination of the blood, induced by advanced granular contraction of the kidney.

Two conditions are needed for the production of this double effect, one, that just spoken of, the obstacle to the onflow of the blood; the other, the force with which the pulsating ventricle sends its blood into the artery. Lessen that force, and the supply of blood is lessened, the proportion of blood in the vessels and the power to pass it on is brought more into equipoise; the tension of the blood being relieved, the first sound becomes again audible, and the shock of the second sound is subdued, so that it becomes merely unduly sharp or loud.

Additional observations are wanted on this important practical point of the relative loudness of the first and second sounds over the pulmonary artery and aorta; combined with information as to the poisoning and accumulation of the blood, structural change in the walls of the arteries, and vital power. The two sounds must be listened to, and their relative intensity noted, which I do by the ready method of figures of varying size written on a diagram of the body on which the outline of the ribs is traced. The size of each figure denotes the relative intensity and actual loudness, judged of by the ear, of the two sounds. When the first sound is silent, and the second is loud and with a shock, I mark it thus, $^{\circ}/2$; when two sounds are equal, thus, $1/2$; when the first is louder than the second, thus, $1/_2$; and when the second is louder than the first, thus, $^1/2$. Every shade can be thus rendered. Combined sphymographic and cardiographic tracings, some of which I have made, in these cases, will give positive and scientific accuracy to our knowledge.

Doubling of the Second Sound.—In two of the cases of endocarditis with mitral murmur, there was doubling of the second sound. One of these came in with doubling of the first sound, or almost a murmur at the apex, on the 4th day a peculiar plunging first sound, with scarcely any second sound, appeared over the ventricles. On the 6th day there was doubling of the second sound. On the 8th day mitral and pulmonic murmur appeared, followed by a tricuspid murmur, and on the 10th these murmurs had all vanished. In the other case the doubling of the second sound appeared late and was very tenacious. There was a mitral murmur up to and on the 23rd day, when the second sound was prolonged over the pulmonary artery. On the next day there was doubling of the second sound over that artery. The second second sound was louder than the first—and this proved that the later sound was the pulmonic, the earlier the aortic sound. In this instance the doubling of the second sound, which lasted to the 60th day, disappearing on the 69th, was due, I consider, to the longer time occupied by the right ventricle than the left in emptying itself, owing to the resistance to the flow of blood through the lungs.

Pulmonic Murmur.—Symbol ↖.—A systolic murmur over the pulmonary artery, at the second left space, was heard in a considerable number of the cases of endocarditis with mitral murmur. This number amounted to one-third of the first series, or seventeen in fifty-two, and to one-half of the second series, or ten in twenty. This murmur was present also in one-third of those cases of endocarditis affecting the left side of the heart, in which there was tricuspid, but not mitral, murmur. In more than one-half of those cases the pulmonic murmur appeared towards the close of the attack, when all the acute symptoms had gone by, when the period of convalescence was approaching or established, when the patient was pale and thin, having lost a large proportion of the red corpuscles from the blood, and was weak from the exhausting nature of the disease. In nearly one-half of the remaining cases this murmur appeared at the middle period, and in one in four of the whole number it was audible soon after the admission of the patient.

The murmur almost always occupied a well-defined limited area at the edge of the sternum in the second space, just over the pulmonary artery. It never extended as far as the right edge of the sternum, but it could be heard very feebly in the first space, and occasionally in the third. When the position of the pulmonary artery was unusually low, the murmur moved downwards, being then heard strongly over the third space, and feebly over the second and fourth spaces.

The pulmonic murmur rarely presents a smooth soft bellows sound, but is usually grave and superficial, without however being large in character or very loud. The murmur appeared as a peculiar scratching noise in one-half of the cases, or 4 out of 8, in which the sign appeared soon after admission, and besides these in one on the 8th and in another on the 21st day. The scratching nature of the sound when I first observed it (I found it noticed in one case as early as the year 1852) was very puzzling. It strongly suggested friction sound. But it differed in these respects : it was always systolic, being never to-and-fro ; pressure sometimes highly intensified, but never altered it in tone ; it clung to one spot; and it gradually disappeared without passing into a wide-spread double friction sound. Its noise was exactly like that made by scratching slowly and gently with a pin on a deal table.

The cause of the pulmonic murmur is exactly the same as that of the aortic "anæmic" murmur, which is audible only during the systole. It is due to the blood being very thin and lessened in quantity, and propelled into the vessel when its walls are relaxed, with undue force, by the ventricle.

- When the pulmonary artery is flaccid, its contents have free room to vibrate as they move onwards in the current of the circulation, and therefore pulmonic murmur is engendered. The pulmonic murmur thus indicates that there is relaxation of the pulmonary artery, or a condition the opposite to that of tension of the artery. The second sound following the murmur may be loud, but it is usually feeble. It is loud if, during and towards the end of the contraction of the right ventricle, the pulmonary artery becomes tense; its walls then recoil with force upon their contents and propel them with equal pressure in two directions, forwards into the vessels, and backwards upon the ascending pulmonary artery, its sinuses, and valve, where the back-stream strikes with a sudden shock, the shock of the loud second sound. The second sound is, on the other hand, feeble if the flaccid artery does not become distended during the systole; when the recoil of the walls is therefore weak, and when the back-wave breaks with only moderate force upon the roots of the artery.

Silence or feebleness of the first sound is the opposite in character and cause to pulmonic murmur. If the artery is distended when the ventricle begins to contract, the column of blood moves steadily forwards, the walls of the vessel and its contents are not thrown into vibration, and the first sound is either absent or feeble. The extreme tension of the pulmonary artery thus induced, leads, when the blood has ceased to enter it, to the recoil of its walls with excessive force upon their contents, which are driven with a strong back-stroke or shock upon the walls, sinuses, and valve of the artery. When the lung is displaced from before the pulmonary artery, thus distended, this shock is felt by the hand and heard striking against the ear with a loud metallic sound.

Pulmonic murmur, as we have just seen, came into play most frequently when the disease was passing away. It was therefore rarely, or only once or twice, associated with a mitral murmur when at its zenith, and uncomplicated with other murmurs. In fully one-half of the cases (13 in 24) it accompanied prolongation of the first sound, or a feeble mitral murmur; in nearly one-half of them (9) it appeared with a conjoint mitral and tricuspid murmur; and in one-fourth with a simple tricuspid murmur, a companion sign that was therefore present in three-fourths of the cases. In one-fourth of the cases (6) it was traced side by side with an anæmic murmur over the aorta or carotid artery; and thrice it was unaccompanied by any murmur. Nearly all these instances point to a state in which the tension of the pulmonary vessels was either not yet established or was passing away.

A pulmonic murmur was audible in a large proportion (or 5 in 13) of those cases that I have classed as being probably affected with endocarditis. In all of these cases there was prolongation of the first sound. In three of them it was noticed soon after admission, and in the two others at a late period of the illness.

A pulmonic murmur was heard in a small proportion of the cases in which endocarditis was either threatened or only transient, amounting to 7 in 63 of the first series, and 2 in 22 of the second, or one-tenth of the cases. In all of these but one it appeared at a late period, when the intensity of the disease was passing away.

Pulmonic murmur is not then a direct sign of endocarditis Its presence, however, in the early period of acute rheumatism usually points to endocarditis, and to the actual or approaching presence of a mitral or tricuspid murmur.

Its existence at a late period in a case of endocarditis generally points to relief in the severity of the disease, to the cessation of the inflammation of the heart, to a definite removal of the tension of the pulmonary artery, due to congestion in the lungs, and to the establishment, for a time, of the opposite state of that vessel, its walls being relaxed and the quantity of its blood diminished.

The pulmonic murmur, then, while it is a sign threatening inflammation of the interior of the left side of the heart in the early stage of acute rheumatism, is a sign of the passing away of endocarditis when it appears at a time when that affection has been established. Pulmonic murmur never becomes permanent. It generally diminishes rapidly when the patient leaves the bed, and gains colour and strength, and in the convalescent patient it is often inaudible when standing or after walking, when it may be still heard if the patient is lying down.

I have heard the pulmonic murmur in several cases of enteric fever, when it indicates the condition of which I have just spoken, or relaxation of the pulmonary artery.

The pulmonic murmur usually, I believe, tends to become less vibrating and more feeble during the progress of the systole, when the artery is becoming less relaxed, and to die out at the end of the systole when the vessel is becoming tense, and the stream of blood is being gradually brought to a stand-still.

Tricuspid Murmur in Cases of Endocarditis with a Mitral Murmur. —I have already illustrated this sign when I described tricuspid murmur in cases of endocarditis of the left side of the heart without mitral murmur. I refer to that part at pages 463—467, and shall here therefore only state generally the conditions under which this murmur is found.

A tricuspid murmur is not, as we have already seen, a sign of inflammation of the right side of the heart, and of the tricuspid valve; but of inflammation of the left side of the organ and of the mitral valve. When the left ventricle is weakened by that inflammation, it sends less blood into the vessels of the system, and an undue amount of blood therefore accumulates in the vessels of the lungs. The pulmonary artery is over-filled, and the left ventricle is distended. The " safety-valve" function of the tricuspid valve is then brought into play, regurgitation takes place, and by throwing a portion of the blood backwards upon the veins of the system, it lessens the pressure of the blood forwards upon the arteries of the lungs.

Tricuspid regurgitation, then, while it declares the presence of inflammation of the left ventricle and the mitral valve, relieves the congestion in the lungs, which is one of the worst effects of that inflammation.

A tricuspid murmur is present in nearly one-half of the cases of endocarditis with mitral murmur. A tricuspid murmur may precede a mitral murmur, accompany it, alternate with it, or waken up after it has disappeared. A tricuspid murmur, then, is a friendly sign—it warns you of inflammation elsewhere, and relieves the ill effects of that inflammation. It is a danger signal, and a brake, lessening the mischief.

Aortic Systolic Murmur (Anæmic).—A direct aortic murmur was noticed in twelve of the seventy cases of endocarditis with mitral murmur, and there were others in which its presence was doubtful. This murmur appeared in the early period of the disease in eight of the cases, and in the later period in four. In three of the patients in whom the murmur appeared early, it lived through the whole of the attack; and in one other of them, after vanishing for a time, it again appeared when the patient was recovering.

In all the cases but one, the aortic murmur was associated with conjoint mitral and tricuspid murmurs, and in fully one-half of them, seven, the aortic was coupled with a pulmonic murmur, usually at a late period of the disease. These twin murmurs, the aortic and pulmonic, are due to the same cause, a deficient supply of blood in the great arteries, which are therefore imperfectly filled. Their walls are consequently flaccid, and their contents have free room to vibrate as they move onwards in the current of the circulation.

The direct aortic murmur is much less frequent than the pulmonic murmur in cases of mitral endocarditis. But the aortic murmur appears early in the attack much more frequently in proportion than the pulmonic murmur. The reason of this would appear to be that in the early stage the inflamed left ventricle sends its blood with insufficient force and volume into the aorta, and vibrations with their consequent murmur therefore ensue. At a later period, the lessened volume of the blood circulating through the body, and the diminution of its red particles, lead to the formation of the murmur.

The question is an interesting one, and is not easy to answer, why the pulmonic murmur is so much more frequent than the aortic at the later period of the affection? May it not arise from two influences? (1) The increased size to which the pulmonary artery has attained during the period of its tension, when the disease was approaching to and at its acme; and (2) the greater relative influence that the diminished supply of blood has upon the comparatively restricted area of the arteries of the lungs, when compared with the much larger area of those of the body ?

Prolongation of the First Sound occurring at a late Period in Cases of Endocarditis with Mitral Regurgitation.—We have already seen that in a considerable proportion of those cases of endocarditis that are admitted before the appearance of a mitral murmur, that murmur is preceded by prolongation of the first sound.

Prolongation of the first sound (as we have seen at page 473) may develop into a tricuspid or mitral murmur, and when the murmur fades away, it may give place to a renewal of the prolongation of the first sound. This was precisely what occurred in one case, a patient in whom, when admitted, the first sound was prolonged; on the 10th day a tricuspid murmur was audible, which was replaced on the 19th by prolongation of the first sound. In another case the sounds were at first healthy, but the first sound was prolonged at the apex on the 4th day, a tricuspid murmur appeared on the 6th, which yielded on the 9th to prolongation of the first sound over the right ventricle, and on the 48th day the sounds were again healthy. In five cases with mitral murmur a similar chain of transformations took place. In one of these a mitral murmur, which appeared on the 5th day, superseded prolongation of the first sound at the apex; that murmur became weaker on the 10th, and was joined on the 12th by three other grave feeble murmurs, a tricuspid, a pulmonic and an aortic. On that day the murmurs were audible when the patient lay down —but they passed into prolongation of the first sound when he stood up—and on the 20th day that prolongation was only audible when he lay down, the sounds being healthy when he stood up; owing evidently to the greater amount of blood that was then demanded by the body and the lungs, and was consequently supplied to the aorta and pulmonary artery.

In a few of the patients the murmur during the illness yielded for a time to prolongation of the first sound, and then reappeared. One case, a female patient, was a notable instance of the variety of trans- formation sounds that may occur in this disease. When admitted, she presented a mitral or tricuspid murmur; on the 3rd day the first sound was prolonged, and on the 6th the sounds were natural. But on the evening of that day a mitral murmur set in which remained for several days, being joined by other murmurs. On the 14th those had vanished, the first sound being prolonged. On the 16th a tricuspid murmur appeared, which was exchanged for a mitral murmur on the 27th, which from that date became permanently established.

In many instances the position of the prolongation of the first sound is not specified, but when it is, the situation of the murmur as a rule corresponded with that of the prolongation of the first sound out of which it grew and into which it faded—both being present at the apex when the murmur was mitral, and over the right ventricle when it was tricuspid.

The passage from murmur to prolongation and the reverse was often very gradual; they often each glided insensibly into the other. The prolongation was often murmurlike in character, and the murmur was often so obscure as to be quite as fitly ranked with prolongation.

In several of the patients, prolongation of the first sound over one ventricle was accompanied by a murmur over the other. Thus in three cases a tricuspid murmur was associated with prolongation of the first sound at the apex; and in another instance a mitral murmur was coupled with prolongation over the right ventricle. One case is an example of both kinds in succession. At the time of admission, when the patient was very ill, the sounds were loud, the first being sharp. From the 2nd day to the 7th there was a tricuspid murmur with prolongation of the first sound at the apex; and on the 21st there was a double exchange, a mitral murmur being joined by prolongation of the first sound over the right ventricle. Sometimes there was a double prolongation of the first sound, at the apex, and over the right ventricle, as occurred in four cases. I have noticed this coupling of the sign only in cases observed at a later period, and I am certain that it occurs much more frequently than my earlier notes would indicate. In a large proportion of the cases the murmur passed into prolongation of the first sound towards the period of convalescence. This was noticed in six of the thirteen cases of endocarditis with tricuspid murmur; in sixteen of the forty-one cases of endocarditis with mitral murmur of the first series, in one of which that sign gave place finally to a permanent mitral murmur; and in twelve of the twenty of the same class of the second series.

Prolongation of the first sound is the first whisper of an approaching murmur, the last of a departing one. It is a sign of coming danger, and it usually betokens, towards the conclusion, a favourable issue.

Prolongation of the first sound, or an obscure murmur, was heard in seven of the seventy-nine cases of the first series, and in none of the fourteen cases of the second series that were classed as having had no endocarditis.

Of those patients in whom endocarditis was threatened or probable, the first sound was prolonged, or there was a doubtful murmur, in forty-three of the seventy-six cases of the first series, and eighteen of the twenty-six of the second series. In more than one-half of the cases thus affected there was great general illness (35 in 61), and of these in fifteen there was pain in the region of the heart.

We must look then upon prolongation of the first sound as a sign of actual, or probable, or threatened, inflammation of the heart; whether we regard its presence in those cases of pronounced endocarditis with a mitral or a tricuspid murmur, or in those of probable or threatened endocarditis, in which the murmur was not declared.

The duration, the degree, and the progress of endocarditis is not to be estimated by the presence of a mitral murmur alone, but by the effects also of the inflammation upon the body, the lungs, and the heart. The face is anxious and dusky; there is sometimes pain in the heart; the breathing is quickened and oppressed; the impulse of the left ventricle is weak, while that of the right is unduly strong; the circulation through the lungs is impeded; the pulmonary artery is distended, its first sound is silent or feeble, and its second is accentuated; a tricuspid murmur is often present, sometimes alone, sometimes conjointly with a mitral murmur; prolongation of the first sound precedes and follows the mitral and tricuspid murmurs; and anæmic murmurs are often heard both over the pulmonary artery and the aorta, during the early and also the late period of the disease, but rarely during its acme; the pulmonic murmur being more frequent at the period of convalescence, the aortic murmur during the early stage of the disease.

III. Cases of Rheumatic Endocarditis with Aortic Regurgitation. (1) Not Accompanied by Mitral Murmur. (2) Accompanied by Mitral Regurgitation.

Symbol ↓.

(1) *Aortic Regurgitation, not accompanied by Mitral Regurgitation.* —Incompetence of the aortic valve is much less frequent in rheumatic endocarditis than incompetence of the mitral valve. There was a diastolic aortic murmur not accompanied by a mitral murmur in ten; and there was a mitral murmur without a diastolic murmur in fifty of the first series of cases—while there was mitral regurgitation in twenty, and aortic regurgitation in none of the later series of cases. This brings up the cases of mitral in relation to aortic regurgitation to the proportion of seventy of the former to ten of the latter. Besides these, eight of the first series and one of the second presented both mitral and aortic incompetence. This makes the total number of cases in which there was aortic regurgitation eighteen, and the total number in which there was mitral regurgitation seventy-nine.

In more than one-half of the cases of endocarditis with aortic regurgitation, there was no mitral murmur (10 in 18). The mind naturally infers that in these patients the inflammation was limited to the aortic valve, and did not extend to the mitral. The close examination of the cases, however, leads I consider to the conclusion that in all of them there was inflammation of both the mitral and the aortic valves.

A mitral murmur appeared in one of the ten cases for a single day and was not again heard. That was the only case in which this, the central and immediate sign of mitral endocarditis, was noticed. In the others, however, the more important secondary signs of inflammation of the interior of the left ventricle were present.

In five of the cases a tricuspid murmur was audible over the right ventricle. In three of these that murmur was heard before the murmur of aortic regurgitation came into play; in one, the two murmurs were present on the day of admission; and in the fifth case, the tricuspid murmur appeared a week later than the aortic, but the aortic murmur was preceded by prolongation of the first sound, which was present on the day of admission.

The first sound was prolonged over one or both of the ventricles in six of the cases; in three of which there was, and in three there was not a tricuspid murmur. In two of the three in which there was no tricuspid murmur, prolongation of the first sound preceded the aortic murmur.

Thus eight of the ten cases of endocarditis with aortic incompetence, without mitral murmur, presented either a tricuspid murmur, or prolongation of the first sound over the ventricles, or both signs. In six of them, one or other of those signs preceded the appearance of the aortic incompetence; in one other the patient came in with both aortic and tricuspid regurgitation murmurs; and in the remaining one only did the aortic murmur precede by three days the prolongation of the first sound. The ninth case was admitted with aortic regurgitation, and he suffered from pain in the region of the heart.

The tenth case, a female patient, was an anomalous and doubtful one. She was very ill when admitted, when she had pain in the left side, and the sounds of her heart were rough. On the 12th day a soft double murmur was audible in the second left space which was probably due to aortic incompetence.

(2) *Cases of Rheumatic Endocarditis with Aortic Regurgitation accompanied by Mitral Regurgitation.*—In eight cases mitral and aortic incompetence were combined, and in six of these the mitral murmur preceded the aortic. Both murmurs were present on admission in one of the two remaining cases, and they appeared together in the other one on the seventh day after admission.

These illustrations, and the considerations that I have just advanced, appear to me to render it conclusive, that the inflammation always commences in the interior of the left cavities, affecting primarily the mitral valve; and that it extends at a later period, and in a limited number of cases to the aortic valve.

These facts lead us to expect that in cases of endocarditis the aortic diastolic murmur appears at a later period than the mitral murmur. In two only of the cases was the aortic murmur heard on the day of admission. One of these had been ill a week, and that was the earliest date of the appearance of the murmur. In three of the patients the aortic murmur appeared from the 7th to the 10th days, in one-fourth of them (5) from the 10th to the 15th days, and in more than one-half (10) from the 22nd to the 88th days, after the beginning of the attack of acute rheumatism.

We have seen that aortic regurgitation is preceded with rare exceptions by a mitral or tricuspid murmur, or a prolonged first sound over the ventricle, or in other words by evidence, immediate or secondary, of inflammation of the left cavities of the heart and the mitral valve.

In a small proportion of the cases, amounting to three in eighteen, the murmur of aortic regurgitation was preceded by prolongation of the second sound over the aorta or the carotid artery. This prolongation of the second sound over the aorta before the appearance of the aortic diastolic murmur, has evidently the same relation to that murmur, that prolongation of the first sound has to a mitral or tricuspid murmur. It is a transition sound, and is the immediate herald of the coming complete murmur of regurgitation.

An anæmic systolic aortic murmur sometimes precedes the appearance of the diastolic murmur made by aortic regurgitation; but it more often comes at the same time or later, when the two sounds combine to form a true double murmur. This double murmur was present in eleven of the eighteen cases of endocarditis with aortic regurgitation, in four of which the systolic murmur was audible before the diastolic murmur, in five they appeared together, and in two the latter murmur came first into play.

The situation of the aortic diastolic murmur of endocarditis is ruled by the position of the aperture of the aorta, and the direction of the back current flowing through it into the left ventricle.

The murmur is more loud and intense to the left of the middle of the sternum, just over the root of the aorta, than elsewhere. It takes there a direction downwards and to the left, and is audible to the left of the lower three-fifths of the sternum, becoming feebler as it descends, and is lost usually before it reaches the limit of the lower end of the sternum. The murmur was heard also in five cases as high as the lower end of the manubrium, and indeed over that portion of the sternum. In rare cases it is audible at the apex.

In my cases of endocarditis with aortic regurgitation, the most frequent position of the murmur was to the left of the lower portion of the sternum, a space that extended from the middle of the sternum to its lower end, and from the third left costal cartilage to the sixth; a space that is immediately in front of the right ventricle, where it is denuded of lung. The murmur was audible over this space in thirteen of the eighteen cases. In four others it was heard at or to the left of the mid-sternum, a position that is included in the space noted as being to the left of the lower sternum, and which is, therefore, the position at which the aortic diastolic murmur of endocarditis is heard most frequently and with the greatest intensity.

In two of the cases the murmur was audible just below, and in one of these over the manubrium. In none of them is it stated that the murmur was heard to the right of the upper portion of the sternum, a position in which the direct aortic murmur was audible in five of the cases. In the exceptional and doubtful case, the double murmur was restricted to the left second space. There was certainly no regurgitation in that case from the pulmonary artery into the right ventricle, and we are therefore, I think, entitled to consider that it was, like the others, a case of aortic endocarditis, with regurgitation. In a patient under my care in St. Mary's Hospital an exquisite musical plaintive diastolic murmur sprang up at a late period just over and below the lower portion of the manubrium, and over the pulmonary artery in the second space, and was limited to that region. In this case the position of the heart was high and the murmur was heard over a correspondingly high and limited area.

In four, and in four only, of the cases the diastolic murmur was heard at the apex.

When we consider that the current of blood flows from the aorta back into the left ventricle, it seems natural to expect that the murmur of aortic regurgitation should be heard over the left ventricle, into which the stream of blood falls ; and not over the right ventricle, which, with its double wall and its full contents, is interposed between the stream of return-blood and the ear. But the fact is the reverse of this. The murmur is always heard in front of the heart, over the right ventricle, and rarely over the left ventricle, to the left of the septum.

After a little reflection, the reason of this curious deviation of the direction of the sound becomes apparent.

When the aortic valve is incompetent, two streams pour side by side into the left ventricle. One of these comes down, in a large volume of blood, from the left auricle, through the mitral orifice, into the left ventricle ; and this large living stream of blood occupies and completely fills the whole of the outer portion of that cavity, which is the part that is in contact with the walls of the chest at and beyond the septum, and at the apex. The other stream is that of regurgitation from the aorta. It is a small and an active stream which plays downwards into the innermost portion of the cavity, or that portion of it which lies immediately behind the right ventricle. The large living stream of blood that pours down from the left auricle into the outer part of the left ventricle, through the mitral orifice, cuts off the inner, deeper, and finer current flowing back from the aorta into the left cavity, and so silences it. This answers the question, why do you not hear the murmur of aortic regurgitation at the apex and over the left ventricle ? The answer, however, to the second question is still to seek, why do we hear that murmur through the right ventricle, with its double walls, and its large volume of blood entering freely through the tricuspid orifice ? When thinking out the answer to this question, we must steadily come back upon the facts as to the position of the aortic orifice, the nature of that part of the ventricle immediately in front of the aortic aperture, the direction of the return-current of blood into the right ventricle, the point of the greatest intensity of the murmur, and the bearing of the fading away of the murmur.

The aortic valve lies behind the middle of the sternum, at its left edge ; in front of it is the conus arteriosus, which is the shallowest part of the right ventricle, its cavity being there wider than it is deep, and its posterior wall being there pushed forwards by the left ventricle and the root of the aorta and the aortic orifice through which this back-current flows; the walls of the conus arteriosus are here thin, especially the front wall; the blood contained in this part of the right ventricle is not in lively motion during the diastole, for it is above the current of blood from the right auricle into the right ventricle; and that current pours across from right to left, low down into the larger, deeper, and lower portion of the ventricle behind the lower part of the sternum and upper part of the ensiform cartilage. The murmur rapidly loses loudness and intensity as it approaches the lower part of the sternum in front of the tricuspid current, and it is lost before we reach the top of the ensiform cartilage.

We now see that the murmur of aortic regurgitation has a shorter way to travel, and passes through a less troubled blood, by passing straight through the arterial cone of the right ventricle, immediately in front of the aortic aperture; than it would if it were to force its way through the large and deep living current of blood that flows from the left auricle, through the mitral orifice, into the left ventricle, and that completely occupies the body and outer or left side of that cavity, where it presents itself at and beyond the septum and at the apex.

When active endocarditis passes away and leaves the aortic valve permanently incompetent, the murmur becomes more intense, and its area more extensive. The diastolic murmur may then be present over the whole length of the sternum, extending to the right of that bone at its upper portion; and slightly to the right, and to a great extent to the left of that bone at its lower portion; the area of the murmur sometimes extending as far outwards as the region of the apex of the heart.

The murmur of aortic regurgitation in cases of endocarditis is usually soft, smooth, and like a bellows sound. Sometimes it is musical, the note being fine and plaintive, limited in area to the middle of the sternum, or a little above that point, not penetrating, and easily obscured by the other sounds of the heart, and by respiration. It was thus in one case—a very pale woman aged 49. On her admission she presented tricuspid, carotid, and loud mitral systolic murmurs, and a musical diastolic murmur over the middle of the sternum. On the fourth day she was better, and all the murmurs were less marked; and on the sixth they were gone. Next day there was an obscure musical diastolic murmur, which also disappeared in a few days. In one case, on the 101st day after admission there was a double musical murmur to the left of the lower sternum. In another case, already alluded to, an exquisite musical murmur appeared just below the manubrium, extended to the left during the time of convalescence, was limited in area, and disappeared in about a week.

In another patient, a man, who came in with a mitral murmur, which established itself, a distinct double murmur appeared for the first time on the 69th day. Six days later the diastolic murmur appeared as a long whistle, but it resumed its usual character on the following day. One other patient that presented a peculiar musical

diastolic murmur was a woman, aged 40, ill with acute rheumatism for
four days, who came in with a faint blowing tricuspid murmur, which
went on the third day, when she had pain in the heart. On the tenth she
was better in every respect, but a peculiar diastolic murmur appeared to
the left of the lower sternum, like the twang of a harp-string, which was
still audible next day; but this was soon replaced by an ordinary short
diastolic murmur to the left of the mid-sternum, which ceased after a
few days, when both sounds were a little prolonged. Dr. Broadbent
observed this case with me.

In another patient, a man affected with acute rheumatism and
endo-pericarditis, a loud, grave musical murmur sprang up in the
course of the illness, a vibrating murmur, with a perceptible thrill over
the aorta, in the second right space, where the murmur was most
intense; but the sound was heard to a great extent over and even
below the chest. This murmur became established.

Of the remaining cases (14), in nearly one-half (6) the murmur was
soft, or like a bellows sound, and this was undoubtedly its predominant character in the rest, although in them the precise nature of
the murmur is not stated.

In about one-half of the cases of rheumatic endocarditis with aortic
regurgitation, the murmur disappeared when the patients were under
observation; while in the greater proportion of the remaining half, the
murmur became fixed, being associated with established mitral regurgitation in two-thirds of those cases.

It was interesting and a source of anxiety to watch the progress of
the murmur, dwindling and disappearing in the former set of cases,
and ripening into permanent valvular disease in the latter set.

We have already seen that the fine musical diastolic murmurs with
a limited area disappeared, while the louder ones of that class became
established.

The character of the early murmur of aortic regurgitation gave
little ground for foreseeing whether the incompetence would be permanent or transient. Thus in three, if not four, instances, a diastolic
murmur, obscure, faint, feeble or confused at first, ripened later into
an established aortic valve disease.

The history of the murmur, its development or decay, the widening
out or contraction of its area, and the presence or absence, the increase
or diminution of the characteristic signs of aortic regurgitation
attendant upon the murmur; give more information as to the actual
state, progress, and probable future of the patient than the exact
character of the murmur on any particular day.

A statement of the duration of the murmur, and of the attendant
secondary signs in the cases in which the valve completely regained
its function; and a brief recital of the leading points in one or two of
the cases that ended by producing aortic valve disease, will illustrate
practically the probable future prospect of the affection in these
important cases.

The diastolic murmur was short-lived in all but three of those cases that ended in restoration of the function of the valve, its duration being from one to eight days. In the three others the murmur, which diminished steadily in loudness, or sometimes remitted, lasted from fifteen to fifty days.

We shall be the better able to understand the extent to which these cases depart from health, and approach to disease, of the aortic valve with regurgitation, by rapidly reviewing the characteristic signs of the established disease, so as to obtain a standard of comparison.

The characteristic signs of permanent aortic regurgitation are— enlargement of the left ventricle, fulness over that ventricle, and undue force of the apex-beat, which extends beyond and below the left nipple; strong visible pulsation of the carotid arteries; sudden hammering stroke and collapse of the pulse, especially when the arm is raised, when the pulse is visible, and is audible with a loud shock that gradually lessens and disappears when the arm is lowered beneath the level of the heart; diastolic bellows murmur over the whole sternum, its maximum intensity being to the left of the middle of the bone; the murmur extending to its left at the lower portion of the sternum, becoming more feeble downwards, and to its right at the upper portion becoming more feeble upwards; a direct aortic murmur, generally audible over the manubrium, and to its right, where there is a true double aortic murmur; and a grave vibrating systolic murmur in the neck, over the visibly pulsating carotid artery, which is not followed either by a second sound or a diastolic murmur.

When the patient sits up, the extent of regurgitation and the collapse of the artery increases; and as a consequence, the diastolic murmur often becomes louder and more intense and extensive over its proper region; and the systolic murmur becomes more grave over the aorta and carotid artery, or is replaced there by a local and sudden shock when the regurgitation is very great so as to empty the ascending aorta during the diastole, the shock being occasioned by the blow with which the advancing column of blood is impelled by the stroke of the left ventricle upon the walls of the empty aorta and carotid artery.

If the incompetence of the aortic valve is caused by great enlargement of the aperture of the aorta, owing to dilatation of the vessel from atheroma, the artery extends to the right of the upper sternum, displacing the lung, and may present there a thrill and a loud vibrating musical murmur, heard, perhaps, at some distance from the surface, and extending over the whole chest, front and back, the neck, and even the abdomen.

My cases of endocarditis with aortic regurgitation ending in complete restoration of the valve, presented, with the exception of the double murmur, to a very slight degree the characteristic signs of disease with incompetence of the aortic valves. The diastolic murmur was present at the mid-sternum, and a little higher, and extended downwards, and to the left, becoming gradually feeble; but it was never heard upwards, over and to the right of the upper sternum, unless it was joined to a mitral murmur. The area of the diastolic murmur was thus limited; and it was feeble, very soft, and like a bellows-sound, or plaintively musical.

A systolic murmur was present over the aorta, or the carotid artery, or both, in two-thirds of the cases, this being an anæmic murmur, and not one caused by obstruction. It was due, in fact, to the flaccid state of the aorta, caused primarily by the comparatively small amount of blood sent into it by the inflamed and weakened'left ventricle, and increased by the reflux of a portion of that blood sent back again into the left ventricle through the inflamed and insufficient aortic valve. This flaccid state of the aorta allowed the blood contained in it to play freely to and fro in a series of noisy vibrations, with the effect of inducing a grave systolic aortic murmur.

The impulse was rarely notably strong. It was observed in four of the nine cases of this class. The apex-beat was felt close to the nipple in one of these patients; and in another, in whom the murmur lasted long, it was present on admission in the fifth space, outside the mammary line, and was stronger than usual on the 7th day; but it retreated within the nipple line from the 12th day, varying in position from the fourth to the fifth space.

The second sound, which is usually lost over the carotid artery in disease of the aortic valve, was audible in the neck in seven out of the nine cases of endocarditis in which the incompetence of the aortic valve was only temporary. In several of these cases the second sound was at one time or other less clear than natural over the neck, being feeble in two, grave in a third, and in a fourth, first prolonged, then silent, and afterwards natural, but feeble.

Although, then, in these cases, the second sound is still audible, perhaps, over the aorta, and certainly over its branches, the innominate and carotid arteries, it is often palpably modified in character. The presence of a second sound over the great arteries at the root of the neck, and over the ascending aorta, where it is, however, rendered doubtful by being blended with the transmitted presence of the pulmonic second sound, is due to the slight degree of the imperfection of the aortic valve. The shock of the second sound is therefore caused over those parts by the recoil of the walls of the distended arteries after the end of the systole, which sends the blood not only forwards into the arteries, but with a pressure equal in every direction, also backwards with a return-stroke upon the inner walls of the ascending aorta, including its sinuses, and slightly imperfect valve. The aortic second sound, although present, is often modified in tone and blunted, owing to the force of the back-stroke of the blood being impaired; (1) by the reflux of a small portion of the blood into the left ventricle through the inflamed and slightly insufficient valve; and (2) by the lessened supply of blood to the aorta and arteries from the left ventricle, the action of which is weakened by the inflammation of its inner surface. The degree to which the second sound over the neck is rendered feeble, blunted, prolonged, or almost or quite silenced, is a key to the knowledge of the amount of regurgitation, and of the defective supply of blood from the left ventricle. This important element of diagnosis is farther illustrated by what is found in cases of Bright's disease with contracted granular kidney, when the aortic valve is rendered slightly insufficient by the great distension and enlargement of the aorta. Here the blood is sent by the powerful left ventricle into the aorta and the arteries, already rendered tense by the difficult onflow of the poisoned blood through the small vessels; and the relief afforded to the tension by the reflux through the insufficient valves is so slight, that the back-stroke of the blood caused by the recoil of the arterial valves is still made with so much force, that the second sound usually retains the metallic ring, and the first sound the feeble note, so characteristic of aortic tension from Bright's disease.

Some of the cases of endocarditis with aortic regurgitation, ending in disease of the aortic valve, acquired step by step the characteristic signs of the permanent affection.

One case of this class, a man, ill a week, came in with quick breathing, a slightly prolonged second sound, and a rather extensive impulse. On the 5th day a soft mitral murmur appeared, which was loud on the 7th, when a diastolic murmur was also audible over the sternum, which extended next day slightly both to the apex and the neck. A week later there was a combination of mitral, tricuspid, and double aortic murmurs, and an obscure second sound was heard in the neck. At the end of the third week the disease was settling into its permanent form, the impulse being extensive, the carotid pulsation visible, and the second sound absent from the neck. The diastolic murmur, feeble on the 24th day, was loud on the 34th, when it was combined with a mitral murmur, and the apex-beat was strong.

Another patient, a labourer, ill eight weeks, was admitted with profuse perspiration, tremulous hands, rather quick breathing, and a double murmur to the right of the upper half of the sternum. On the 4th day the murmur was louder, and was audible over the right ventricle; but on the 6th he was faint, and the murmur was again limited to the aorta. On the 8th day he felt better, and the aortic murmur was again audible to the left of the lower portion of the sternum, as well as to the right of its upper portion. Variations followed, renewed diminution of the aortic murmur over the right ventricle being joined to renewed illness; but after this the systolic murmur became rasping, especially over the third right cartilage, and the diastolic bellows sound became again widened in area.

The third case of this class, a woman, ill a week, came in with prolongation of the first sound, but no murmur. On the 3rd day an obscure diastolic murmur was audible at the left nipple, and on the 7th this murmur was present along the whole sternum, especially from below the manubrium, and to the right of its upper portion. The second sound was heard in the neck, and the pulse was not distinctly audible at the wrist. On the 15th the diastolic murmur, smooth and prolonged, was more extensive downwards; the second sound, feeble at the apex, was audible in the neck; and a mitral murmur was present for the only time. On the 29th day the pulse was visible at the wrist, and on the 52nd, when she was almost well, there was some fulness over the region of the heart, its impulse being stronger over both ventricles, and especially at the apex. The diastolic murmur was most intense at the fourth cartilage, but was audible along the whole sternum, except its summit. The second sound was still present in the neck, and the pulse was not audible.

In these three cases of endocarditis, the affection of the aortic valve advanced steadily, but with variations, under my notice, and during the evolution of the disease its characteristic signs came into play one by one.

The next case, a man, stands alone; the aortic regurgitation, after being suspended for a time, returned, and again lessened, without disappearing.

In the last group of four cases of endocarditis with aortic regurgitation, ending in disease of the aortic valve, the murmur appeared at a late period of the disease.

In one of these patients, a man, the murmur appeared suddenly without warning and in full force on the 88th day, being heard loud along the lower sternum. He had previously presented a variable mitral and an occasional tricuspid murmur. This mitral murmur was suspended during a period when the patient was ill with enteric fever, and when prolongation of the first sound was its temporary substitute.

A second case of this class, a boy, ill a week, came in with pain in the heart, a friction sound, and a mitral murmur, which was still present on the 5th day. After this there is a gap in the narrative until the 49th day, when there was still a mitral murmur. On the 69th day a double aortic murmur suddenly appeared for the first time, and already the pulse at the wrist was audible when the arm was raised. This diastolic murmur varied, increased, and extended to below the ensiform cartilage, but not to the top of the sternum; was once a long whistle, but generally a bellows sound; was accompanied by a mitral murmur at the apex, probably by a tricuspid, and certainly by a direct aortic murmur, there being no aortic second sound. The impulse of both ventricles became extensive, strong, and peculiar, pointing to adherent pericardium; it presented a double shock, one during the systole, and the other at the commencement of the diastole.

In the third case, a woman, one of remarkable interest, a faint diastolic murmur appeared to the left of the lower sternum on the 47th day, having been preceded and accompanied by varying mitral and tricuspid murmurs. In this case the thyroid gland became very large on the 64th day; was a good deal smaller on the 74th, and finally resumed its natural size. There was a distinct double murmur on the 101st day.

The last case presented healthy heart-sounds on the 17th day after admission, and on the 22nd a soft diastolic murmur came into play to the left of the lower sternum, and a double aortic murmur just below the manubrium. The pulse was audible when the arm was raised, and the impulse was normal in extent.

These interesting cases of aortic regurgitation, coming on by surprise at a late period in cases of endocarditis, usually with a persistent mitral murmur and extensive and deep-seated inflammation of the interior of the left cavities; show that the aortic valve, though it suffers rarely and slightly when compared with the mitral valve, may silently and without warning, and when the patient appears to be well, break down in its functions by the steady and long advance of a latent inflammation.

When we consider how remote the aortic valve is from the focus of the inflammation, how passive and rigid the structures at the outlet of the left ventricle are in which that valve is embedded, how gently the flaps of the valve come together, how comparatively slight is the force exerted upon the valve by the back-flow of the blood in the artery, due to the recoil of the walls of the aorta—that vessel being imperfectly supplied with blood by the inflamed and weakened left ventricle—a force that spends itself mainly in driving the blood forwards, and secondarily in impelling it backwards on the valve, it is only natural that the aortic valve should be rarely incompetent during the attack of endocarditis, and more rarely permanently crippled. These cases perhaps point to a gradual extension of the inflammation on the ventricular surface of the valve, and to the gradual yielding of the inflamed and softened valve; which at length gives way suddenly at its margin, and so admits of regurgitation from the aorta into the left ventricle.

IV.—CASES OF RHEUMATIC ENDOCARDITIS WITH PROLONGATION OF THE FIRST SOUND.

The examination of the cases of endocarditis in which there was tricuspid, mitral, or aortic murmur, alone or in combination, show, I think conclusively, that prolongation of the first sound at the apex or over the right ventricle points to actual or imminent endocarditis.

Thus prolongation of the first sound both preceded and followed a temporary tricuspid murmur in three cases, preceded the appearance of that murmur in two other cases, and followed its disappearance in two additional ones. The first sound was therefore prolonged in one half of the cases (7 in 13) in which a tricuspid murmur was present without a mitral murmur.

Again, a mitral murmur when present without aortic regurgitation was preceded and followed by prolongation of the first sound in seven cases; and was preceded by it in nine, and was followed by it in twenty other instances. The first sound therefore was prolonged in fully two-thirds (36 in 50) of the cases of endocarditis with mitral murmur in which there was no aortic regurgitation.

Finally, the first sound was prolonged in six of the ten cases of endo-carditis with aortic regurgitation in which there was no mitral murmur; and in four of the nine in which there was both aortic and mitral regurgitation, or in more than one-half (10 in 19) of the cases of endocarditis with aortic diastolic murmur.

If we combine the three series of cases with tricuspid, mitral, and aortic regurgitation, we find that in a little more than three-fifths of the whole number (53 in 82) the first sound was prolonged over one or other or both of the ventricles, and that this proportion held its ground in each of the three classes of valvular murmur from endo-carditis. If we deduct from the 29 patients in whom there was no prolongation of the first sound, those who both came in and went out with tricuspid or mitral murmur, amounting to fully twelve cases, and who could not therefore present prolongation of the first sound preceding or following a murmur, we naturally increase the proportion in which the first sound was prolonged; and this proportion would necessarily be still further increased if we could deduct the unknown quantity of cases in which the prolongation of the first sound escaped observation.

It is evident then that prolongation of the first sound is a sign of transition; that it tends to expand into a mitral murmur when situated over the apex, into a tricuspid murmur when over the right ventricle, and occasionally into a systolic aortic murmur when situated over the aorta; and that when either of these murmurs passes away, it naturally glides into prolongation of the first sound over the region of the lost murmur.

Prolongation of the first sound over one or both of the ventricles in a case of acute rheumatism is in itself then a sign, actual, probable, or threatening, of endocarditis affecting the left cavities of the heart. If it is present when the face is covered with a diffused flush, or is dusky and anxious, when the breathing is quickened or oppressed, or when pain is seated in the region of the heart, and the second sound is intensified over the pulmonary artery, we may at once conclude that the patient is affected with endocarditis.

I have included among the cases of endocarditis two of the patients affected with acute rheumatism, who had prolongation of the first sound without murmur, but in both of whom that sound was murmur-like; and who had also several important symptoms pointing to internal inflammation of the heart, including pain over the heart in one, pain in the chest in the other, and very great general illness. I have ranked seven of these cases with prolongation of the first sound apart, among a class in which endocarditis was probable, and I may say almost certain.

In more than one-half, or five, of these nine cases, including both those in which endocarditis was present, and those in which it was probable, the prolongation of the first sound was murmur-like in character. In six of these cases there was a pulmonic murmur; in four the face was dusky; in three there was restlessness or delirium; in two others the sleep was bad; in three there was pulmonary apoplexy, or cough, with phlegm ; in one there was pain in the heart; and in two there was pain in the chest.

It is more difficult to settle the exact position of those cases with prolongation of the first sound that I have ranked among those threatened with endocarditis.   Among the cases of this class belonging to the first series, amounting in the whole to 63, almost one-half (30) presented prolongation of the first sound; and in five more there was a double murmur; while in nine others the sounds of the heart were affected, the first sound being very loud in three, and doubled in one ; while both sounds were feeble or indistinct in five.

Of the 30 patients in whom there was prolongation of the first sound, in one half (14) there was great or considerable, and in 16 there was slight, general illness.   I think that we may consider that the fourteen patients with great or considerable general illness, nine of whom had pain in the region of the heart, were probably, or almost certainly, affected with endocarditis.   To these perhaps may be added the four patients who presented an obscure murmur.   Three of these, however, had but slight general illness.   If we add to the fourteen with great general illness and prolongation of the first sound, the case with an obscure murmur and also with great general illness, we may conclude that fifteen of those who were threatened with endocarditis were almost certainly attacked with that affection.

Among the 79 cases that are ranked among those who had no endocarditis, seven had prolongation of the first sound, and one had an obscure murmur.   All of these had but slight general illness, and I think that they have been properly assigned to their present place.

If we examine the cases of the second series, or those treated by means of rest, we find that out of twenty-two cases threatened with endocarditis fourteen presented prolongation of the first sound.   Of these nine had pain in the region of the heart, or great general illness, or both, while in one of them the general illness was slight.   Eight of these cases may therefore, I think, be almost ranked with the cases of endocarditis.

In two of the remaining cases threatened with endocarditis there was a transient murmur.

V.—Cases of Rheumatic Endocarditis with previous Valvular Disease of the Heart.

Previous valvular disease of the heart was present in 22 of the 107 cases of endocarditis of the first series, and in 7 of the 28 of the second series of cases admitted into St. Mary's Hospital under my care during the years 1851—1869-70. Among the cases of the first series, ten had mitral, five had aortic, and seven had mitral-aortic regurgitation, and the seven of the second series had mitral incompetence.   Sixteen additional cases with previous valvular disease appear among my 325 cases with acute rheumatism of the first series; and of these eight had endocarditis combined with pericarditis, four had " probable " endocarditis, two were "threatened" with that affection, and only two presented no sign or symptom of endocarditis. We thus see that of the total number of cases of acute rheumatism with established valvular disease (amounting to 38),30(or 79 per cent.)had endocarditis; in 6 (or 16 per cent.) endocarditis was probable or threatened ; and 2 (or 5 per cent.), had no endocarditis. Compare these cases broadly with the rest of the cases of acute rheumatism in which there was no previous valvular disease. Of the total number, amounting to 287, 161 (or 56 per cent.), had endocarditis, of which 54 had pericarditis also ; in 73 (or 25 per cent.) endocarditis was probable or threatened, including 3 with pericarditis; and in 83 (or 29 per cent.) there was no endocarditis, including 6 with pericarditis. We thus see that previous valvular disease of the heart, in cases of acute rheumatism, exercised an all-powerful influence in exciting endocarditis. Nor can we wonder at this important result. It has been the key-note, underlying the whole of this long clinical history of pericarditis and endocarditis, that whatever part, liable to be affected by the disease, was exposed to the burden of labour, was exposed, in exact proportion to that labour, to the attack of inflammation, the severity and extent of the inflammation being proportioned to the amount of labour.

The presence, then, of established valvular disease, which adds very seriously to the labour of the heart in cases of acute rheumatism, adds very seriously to the probability, the almost certainty, of endocarditis in such cases. We have just seen that the influence of valvular disease, which tells with such force in the production of endocarditis, has but little effect in exciting pericarditis. The reason is, I think, obvious. The great extra work is thrown upon the interior, and not upon the exterior, of the left ventricle, and especially upon its mitral valve. A second local influence, in the altered apertures and roughened surfaces of the mitral and aortic valves, and especially at their margins, comes in to heighten the effect of the local labour in the production of endocarditis.

The two conditions that prevailed through the whole series of cases of established valvular disease with endocarditis are—the variability of the murmur from day to day ; and great general illness. That chain of signs distinguished every case, and that chain of symptoms affected all but two of the whole series of instances of endocarditis with disease of one or more of the valves of the heart.

The variability of the murmurs showed itself not only in their greater or less loudness during the successive phases of the disease, but also in their transformation from one tone to another quite different ; their extinction, suspension, and reappearance ; and their extended, contracted, and shifted areas. This variation in the nature, character, and field of the murmur, is governed mainly by three leading influences :—(1) the changes to which the valves themselves and the interior of the heart are subjected by the inflammation ; (2) the varying power of the heart under the influence of increasing general weakness, and returning strength ; and (3) the tumultuous action of the heart owing to local pain, or the struggle to pass the blood onwards through the obstructed orifices ; or its intermission and failure from the exhaustion of previous overwork.

I shall illustrate the variable character of the murmur in these cases of endocarditis with previous valvular disease by the brief notes of a few cases, first selecting from among those with mitral regurgitation, then those with aortic, and finally those with mitral-aortic valvular disease.

The first instance with *mitral* disease that I shall quote was a young woman who had left the hospital four days previously with a mitral murmur, due to a primary attack of acute rheumatism. She came in suffering from a fresh attack, with a distressed, anxious look, a dusky face, rather livid lips, and accelerated breathing. She had pain over the heart, its action being rapid and tumultuous, and an indistinct murmur. On the 3rd day there was a loud systolic murmur at the apex, and the second sound was sharp over the pulmonary artery : and on the 4th she had agonizing pain in the heart, its action was tumultuous, and its sound could not be defined ; she struggled violently and perspired profusely. Next day a loud systolic murmur, tricuspid as well as mitral, was audible over the whole region of the heart. On the 10th day the tricuspid murmur was audible along the sternum, and a second impulse, with a loud second sound, were present over the pulmonary artery in the second left space. On the 18th she was bright and cheerful, but a cough was still present, and the murmur was softer. On the 23rd day she walked about the ward, but on the 29th there was a return of pain on movement, and the murmur was louder. After this she did well, there was a thrill over the heart, the murmur was loud over the apex, and was heard over the left scapula. Here the mitral murmur was obscured when the heart was tumultuous ; and was loud and smooth, and joined by a tricuspid murmur, when the health improved and the heart was steady in its action. Another case, with previous mitral regurgitation, had, when admitted, tightness of the chest, pain over the heart, and a loud systolic murmur. Three days later, with less pain, the murmur was almost musical at the apex, and quite so below it over the stomach ; two days later she looked better, and the murmur presented a third change, being not nearly so loud ; but next day, with returning tightness of the chest, there was a fourth transformation of the murmur, which was rasping or almost musical over the heart ; the 10th day, however, with renewed improvement, showed a fifth variation in the murmur, which was no longer rasping ; but on the following day there was a sixth change, and the murmur was musical around the apex ; after this, on the 13th day, the murmur was grave, this being its seventh variation ; its eighth occurring on the 18th day, when it was again musical over the stomach, and when it was joined by a systolic murmur over the aorta. After this, with steady improvement, the murmur was no longer variable. A third case illustrates the variations of the murmur during the convalescent period.

These two cases are typical, but their successive snatches of ever-varying murmur, contrast with the murmur, now swelling, now dwindling, that is found in other and more simple cases. I will just quote one of these. A youth, a carpenter, came in with pain in the chest and a prolonged musical systolic murmur at the apex. This murmur was persistent, but it varied in tone, being grave on the 8th day, when pain was present. The heart's beat was strong.

Each of the remaining seven cases presented features of its own; the variations of the murmur being great and complicated in four of them, and in three of them comparatively simple. In four cases, if not five, the mitral murmur was associated with a tricuspid murmur, in one with a pulmonic, and in one with a direct aortic murmur; while in one the first sound was prolonged over the right ventricle. In one of the cases just enumerated, a diastolic aortic murmur appeared and disappeared, reappeared, and was finally extinguished, the mitral murmur being permanent throughout.

The *aortic* murmurs of established valvular disease scarcely vie with the mitral murmur in variety of tone, loudness and area, and alternate extinction and return, in cases of rheumatic endocarditis; but I may state that the study of the five cases that I can cite shows that in all these points the diastolic-aortic murmur presents frequent variation; though the systolic murmur of aortic contraction is much less subject to change.

In one case with aortic regurgitation, probably of some standing, tricuspid and mitral murmurs were added temporarily to the diastolic murmur, which varied much and was not always audible during the attack of endocarditis. At the cessation of the illness a double aortic murmur was alone audible. In the other case a double aortic murmur, which went and came again during the illness, was apparently joined on the 28th day by a tricuspid murmur, which had departed on the 34th, leaving a double aortic murmur.

The remaining seven instances had previous *mitral-aortic* valvular disease. Two of the cases belonging to this last group were admitted twice with mitral aortic endocarditis, so that the actual number of patients belonging to it is reduced to five. One of those two patients that were thus admitted twice with endocarditis, had left the hospital six months previously, after an attack of rheumatic endocarditis, and came in with double aortic, and mitral murmurs; which varied somewhat in loudness and extent, but were substantially unchanged during this illness. Four years later she returned with severe acute rheumatism and endocarditis, and died after a very long illness, albuminuria having been finally added to her ailments. The murmurs underwent several oscillations, sometimes the mitral, sometimes the aortic diastolic murmur, being very loud, while at other times one or other of those murmurs was almost or quite extinguished at the heart; the mitral murmur being however generally distinctly though feebly audible over the back of the chest.

In the three remaining cases the variations in the murmurs were rather in loudness and extent of area, than in the tone and character of the sounds.

The extent and strength of the impulse, and their variation during the attack, are among the most decisive tests of the previous presence of valvular disease in cases of rheumatic endocarditis. As a rule, the impulse in such cases is unduly diffused, strong, and propulsive; and this applies more in degree to cases with mitral aortic, than to those with simple mitral regurgitation. The extent of the impulse in a case of valvular disease without endocarditis, is a test of the undue amount of labour to which the heart has been put to overcome the obstacle to the circulation of the blood caused by the affection of the valves. The supervention of endocarditis sometimes, by rendering the heart's action tumultuous, increases the impulse; but sometimes its effect is the reverse, and by lowering the power of the heart, it lessens the impulse.

Among the ten cases of endocarditis with previous mitral incompetence, including one in which aortic incompetence sprung up temporarily during the attack, in five the impulse was strong, in one it was diffused, in two it was moderate, in one it was feeble, and in one it was not described. In three of those cases the impulse was stronger during the attack of endocarditis than after it, and in two it was the reverse. The impulse of the left ventricle was usually increased in the cases of established mitral incompetence, but that of the right ventricle was, in proportion, more affected in those cases.

Among the five cases of previous aortic incompetence with endocarditis, including the two that were joined during the attack, one by mitral, the other by tricuspid incompetence, in three the impulse was strong and extensive, especially towards the apex; in one it was diffused but rather feeble; and in one it was of moderate force and extent. The impulse was more extensive during the attack of endocarditis than after it in one case. The impulse was strong, extensive, and unduly far to the left, in five of the seven cases of previous mitral-aortic incompetence with endocarditis; it was diffused but rather feeble in one; and in one it was feeble. The impulse appeared to be strengthened during the period of the endocarditis in four instances, while in one case it was the reverse.

Pain was present over the region of the heart in four of the ten cases of endocarditis with previous mitral incompetence, in four of the five with aortic incompetence, and in four of the seven with mitral-aortic incompetence. There was pain in the side or chest, or tightness of the chest, not including those with pain in the heart—in four of the ten with mitral; in one of the four with aortic; and in three of the seven with mitral-aortic valvular disease. There was no pain either in the heart, chest, or side, in two of the ten cases with mitral; in none of the five with aortic; and in one of the seven with mitral-aortic valvular disease, or in only three of the twenty-two cases under consideration. We have seen that pain in the heart, side, or chest, occurs in by far the largest proportion of such cases; and that pain in the parts named is much more frequent in cases of endocarditis in which the heart was previously affected with valvular disease, than in those cases of endocarditis in which the heart was previously healthy.

The respiration was seriously affected in a very large proportion of the cases of valvular disease with endocarditis. This condition in such cases is inevitable, for the effect of all the diseases of the valves is to interfere with the efficient onflow of the blood towards the system, and therefore to throw the blood backwards upon the lungs. This applies of course with primary and immediate force to incompetence of the mitral valve, which throws a portion of the blood just received back again upon the lungs, with the effect of overcharging the pulmonary vessels. The return of the blood back again from the aorta, owing to aortic incompetence, into the left ventricle from which it has just been sent, is, however, only one short stage forwards from the seat of mitral incompetence; and the almost immediate effect of the aortic incompetence is to produce a back-flow of blood upon the pulmonary vessels, and to delay the blood in those vessels and congest them. The presence of this surplus amount of blood in the lungs, which upsets the healthy balance of the circulation through the lungs and the body, compels the respiratory organs to exert themselves to the top of their power, so that they may, if possible, expel forwards into the body the weight of blood that oppresses them. Hence result laborious, difficult, and rapid breathing, pulmonary apoplexy, pleurisy, catarrh, and bronchitis.

The respiration was rapid in four, the chest was painful or tight in two, and cough with pulmonary apoplexy occurred in another of the cases with mitral valve-disease; while in two of those cases there is no note of the state of the lungs, and in one they were healthy in function. The breathing was quick, or there was cough, or pain in the chest, in four of the five cases with aortic, and in six of the seven with mitral-aortic valvular disease. More than three-fourths, therefore, of the cases of valvular disease with endocarditis had serious disturbance of the respiratory functions.

CLINICAL HISTORY OF ENDOCARDITIS IN CASES OF CHOREA.

The association of chorea with endocarditis has long been known, both clinically and from examination after death; and it has already received illustration in this volume, at pages 290, 291, where two important cases of chorea are alluded to that have been published by Dr. Broadbent and Dr. Tuckwell, in both of which there was endo-carditis, and minute cerebral embolism; and in one of which there was acute rheumatism as well as chorea. I had also occasion, in this article on endocarditis, to give at page 485 a case which illustrates the association of chorea with endocarditis. I shall now give a brief account of the cases of chorea treated by me in St. Mary's Hospital, with especial relation to their association with endocarditis.

Clinical History of the Cases of Chorea, in relation to the presence of Endocarditis, observed by the Author in St. Mary's Hospital.—I find notes of 40 cases of chorea that were under my care in St. Mary's Hospital, and in 34 of them the signs of the heart are noted, while in 6 of them they are not so.

CASES OF CHOREA IN RELATION TO THE PRESENCE OR ABSENCE OF ENDOCARDITIS.

1.—Cases in which there was no endocarditis, heart sounds healthy   .   10

2.—Cases in which there was probably no endocarditis :—
    a. Slight prolongation of the first sound   5
    b. Anæmic murmur over the pulmonary artery   .   .   1
                                               6

3.—Cases in which there probably was endocarditis :—
    a. Prolongation of the first sound.   3
    b. Murmur, tricuspid or pulmonic   2
                                             5

4.—Cases in which there was endocarditis :—
    a. With mitral regurgitation →
       Ending in restoration of valve   2
       Lessening of murmur on recovery   .   .   .   2
       Mitral regurgitation established on recovery   .   .   8
                                           12

    b. ↓↓ With aortic regurgitation ↓   1
                                         13

                                         34

Cases in which the heart was not observed   6

                 TOTAL   40

Association of the Cases of Chorea with Rheumatism.—The well-established association of chorea with articular rheumatism, renders the study of the connexion of rheumatism with these cases of chorea necessary before we consider the occurrence of endocarditis in chorea. Acute rheumatism, as we have just seen, is so very frequently accompanied by endocarditis that we must be careful, when ascertaining the frequency of endocarditis in chorea, not to attribute the internal inflammation of the heart too readily to chorea, when it may be caused by the rheumatism associated in certain cases with that affection.

Articular rheumatism, in a subacute form, was definitely present during the attack in six of the forty cases of chorea. In five of these cases the rheumatic affection immediately preceded the occurrence, and continued for a short time after the supervention of the attack of chorea. In one of the cases, in which there had been no previous rheumatic attack, the joints became inflamed in the course of the choreal affection.

In addition to these six cases of chorea with pronounced articular rheumatism, there were five cases of chorea in which there was pain in all the limbs (in 1), or in the shoulder and hips (in 1), or in the legs (in 1), or in the hands (in 1), or there was stiffness of the arms and legs, and of the left ring-finger (in 1). In none of these cases, however, was there swelling or redness over the joints; but this does not apply to the redness which affected the wrists, elbows, and face in one patient from violent friction. There were also five cases of chorea that were free from rheumatism during the attack, that gave a history of antecedent acute rheumatism, occurring from two years to two or three months, and in one instance for an uncertain period, before the occurrence of the chorea.

The proportion in which endocarditis appeared in those cases will be given presently.

Proportion of Cases of Chorea in which Endocarditis was present.— In nearly one-third (10 in 34) of the cases of chorea in which the sounds of the heart were observed, those sounds were healthy; in one-sixth of them (5) there was slight prolongation of the first sound, and in one case there was a pulmonic murmur. I have classed the six latter cases among those in which there was probably no endocarditis, and I think we may infer that those sixteen cases, amounting almost to one-half of the whole, were free from inflammation of the interior of the heart.

In three cases in which there was marked, almost murmur-like, prolongation of the first sound, and in two with a tricuspid or pulmonic murmur, amounting to almost one-sixth of the whole (5 in 34), the presence of endocarditis was probable.

The remaining cases, amounting to fully one-third of the whole (13 in 34), gave complete evidence of the existence of endocarditis, in the presence of a mitral murmur in twelve instances, and of a diastolic-aortic murmur in one.

I think it probable that the majority of the six cases of chorea in which the heart was not observed, ought to be added to those in which there was no endocarditis.

Cases of Endocarditis with a Mitral Murmur.—The cases of choreal endocarditis with mitral regurgitation, considering the comparatively small number of those cases, offered as great variety in character, mode of commencement, course, and result, as the cases of rheumatic endocarditis with mitral regurgitation.

Endocarditis with mitral regurgitation ended more than twice as often in established mitral disease in chorea, than in acute rheumatism. Mitral regurgitation became permanently established in two-thirds of the cases of chorea with mitral murmur (8 in 12); and in less than one-third of the cases of acute rheumatism with mitral murmur of the first series (14 in 49), and in only one-sixth of those of the second series treated by rest (3 in 20). The integrity of the valve was restored in one-sixth of the cases of chorea with a mitral murmur (2 in 12), and in another sixth of them, the murmur was becoming feebler when the patient left the hospital (2 in 12).

The mitral murmur in fully one-half of the cases (7 in 12) was situated in the region of the apex, and was not described as extending beyond that region; but was simply entered as a systolic mitral murmur, or a systolic murmur at the apex.

The five remaining cases, compared with those just dismissed, presented greater breadth of area; variety in intonation and volume of sound; and individual life.

In two of these cases the mitral murmur was very extensive, being audible over the back of the chest, above and below the scapulæ, and the greater part of the left side. One of them, when admitted, had been ill with chorea in a severe form for some weeks, but the affection was now but slight. A loud systolic murmur centred itself at the apex; and was audible along the sternum, and far to the right of its lower portion, though feeble at its upper part; from the third to the seventh left costal cartilages; in front of the epigastrium and the liver; and all over the dorsum, especially on the left side. The impulse of both ventricles was immoderately strong and extensive, the apex-beat being present an inch to the left of the nipple-line. These signs underwent little change after the admission of the patient, and it was evident that the endocarditis had ceased.

The other case came in with acute endocarditis, a mitral murmur being audible at the apex and over the right ventricle. A few days later it could be heard towards the axilla, and over the back, as high as the upper part of the scapula. At the end of the seventh week the murmur was grave and musical, and a fortnight later it appeared as a prolonged bellows sound. After this it was hardly so loud, but towards the end of the fourth month after admission it was grave and vibrating.

This case had an interest much broader than the simple relation of chorea to endocarditis; for it had interwoven with it from its commencement, and throughout an important part of the early period of its course, the relation of acute rheumatism to chorea, and of acute rheumatism to endocarditis also. It began with inflammation of the ankle, conjoined with chorea. Six weeks later, when admitted, the knee was inflamed, chorea being the most pronounced disease, and the two affections being accompanied by endocarditis. Was this endocarditis the direct offspring of the subdued attack of acute rheumatism, or of the chorea, or of the two conjoined affections, each taking its part in giving a combined birth to endocarditis?

During the third week the arms were slightly rheumatic, as well as the lower limbs, and the patient lay motionless in bed, apparently stilled by the affections of the limbs and joints, the chorea being almost or quite latent. After this the rheumatism insensibly disappeared, the chorea insensibly reasserted itself, and for the remainder of the patient's long history, the chorea, modified in form and severity, was the only apparent affection; accompanied throughout, however, by endocarditis.

The other three instances of which I have to speak were cases of chorea, unalloyed, during the attack, by rheumatic arthritis; but two of them had suffered some time before from acute rheumatism.

One of them, a girl, had been long ill with chorea, and had gone through a rheumatic attack two years before. She came in with a loud, smooth, systolic murmur at the apex, which was audible over the right ventricle. After this the murmur underwent minor transformations, being like a bellows sound on the 4th day, and almost musical on the 8th, when the apex-beat extended further outwards, the murmur being faintly, if at all, audible below the angle of the left scapula. The apex-beat extended a little beyond the nipple. This case came in with endocarditis, which was evidenced by the varying character of the murmur; but there is nothing to show whether or not this patient had acquired mitral disease from the old attack of acute rheumatism.

This last question does not complicate the next case, for though this patient, a girl, had twice been affected with acute rheumatism, yet she had no murmur, but a prolonged first sound, on admission. A murmur, however, appeared at the apex on the 4th day, which was grave on the 6th and the 8th, and was loud on the 14th day, when it extended towards the axilla. The apex-beat was strong on the 6th day, three-and-a-half inches from the sternum; but on the 8th it could scarcely be felt.

The last case, a boy, was free from rheumatic taint, and presented no murmur during the first six weeks; but at the end of that time he had pain in the chest, and a week later a smooth bellows murmur appeared at the apex, which three weeks later spread upwards towards the axilla, and downwards over the stomach. After this, during a long period, extending from first to last over five months, the murmur underwent various changes, being a very smooth bellows murmur on the 62nd day, audible upwards towards the axilla, and downwards over the stomach. On the 76th the murmur was very loud and superficial, being heard towards the axilla, but for a very short way below the heart. The first sound was very feeble, while the second was very loud over the pulmonary artery, in the manner already related at page 464. After this the mitral murmur underwent various modulations, being moderately loud on the 102nd day, very loud at the apex on the 105th, but scarcely audible over the lung to the left, or towards the axilla; much weaker on the 126th; but on the 135th day it was loud below, especially on expiration, and was not heard outwards during inspiration. On the 146th day, and the last report, there was very slight fulness over the heart, the impulse of the right ventricle, which seven weeks previously was strong, extending from the third cartilage to the sixth, and from the sternum to the nipple, was on the last observation less strong to the right of the lower sternum, and extended from the second to the fourth cartilages. The mitral bellows murmur was not so smooth as before, and was again heard up to the axilla. The double impulse of the pulmonary artery, previously marked, was no longer perceptible. There was no murmur over the back. He went out comparatively well, being free from choreal movements.

In this case, as in that just related, during the attack of endocarditis, when the patient lay speechless in bed, the heart became enlarged, and the lung shrank away from before the heart, exposing its increased impulse over a large area; and the mitral murmur was heard extensively over the region of the contracted lung, and that of the stomach. At a later period, however, with returning health, strength, and exercise, the lung expanded freely, and interposed itself between the greater part of the heart and the walls of the chest, so as to cut off the extended border of the area of impulse, and to lessen that of the murmur by damping and silencing its sound.

Case of Endocarditis with a Diastolic-Aortic Murmur.—This patient, a boy, came in with a second attack of chorea, which began three weeks previously with pain in the legs of a rheumatic character, followed, a week later, by choreal symptoms, which became gradually more severe. On his admission the heart sounds, so far as they could be made out, were healthy, but on the 3rd day a diastolic murmur was audible over the centre of the sternum. Ten days later this murmur was heard, very prolonged and loud, over the whole length of the sternum; being audible to the right of the upper part of the bone, and to the left of its lower portion, but becoming weaker towards the apex of the heart. On the 86th day the diastolic murmur was still loud, and maintained its ground everywhere; and it was joined by a systolic murmur, loudest at the sternum and not mitral. Three weeks later the diastolic murmur was inaudible at the middle of the sternum, and was feeble at its upper and lower portions; but on the 79th day, the last observation, it had apparently resumed much of its loudness and extent, and the systolic murmur was silent.

In this case, as in one of those just told, the question must be put, Was the endocarditis caused by the primary articular rheumatism, or by the resulting chorea, or by the combined influence of the two affections?

ENDOCARDITIS IN PYÆMIA.

There was only one instance among the 71 cases of pyæmia or secondary inflammation examined after death in St. Mary's Hospital in which the appearance of endocarditis was observed and reported. That case, a man, who was under my care, presented a spot in the right lung, an inch long, consisting of pus, and apparently broken down lung-tissue, and superficial to this a patch of dry fibrinous deposit on the pleura; and numerous spots, similar but smaller, through the back of the middle and lower lobes of that lung. There was also a large globular and fluctuating tumour on the upper and inner part of the left kidney three inches in diameter. On cutting into it highly offensive blood-like fluid escaped, and on laying it freely open there was a clot of blood and a little pus. The sac was lined with a delicate, highly organised, chorion-like membrane, with numerous prominent blood-vessels ramifying on its surface. There was a large black spot of apoplectic effusion in the substance of the kidney near the membrane. The structure of the kidney was healthy.

The heart was of natural size, and there was a patch of recent roughness on the surface of the left auricle. Several nodules, from the size of a split pea to that of a millet-seed, were situated on the free margin of the mitral valve. The corpora Arantii of the aortic valve were enlarged. The patient was admitted in a state of great depression, his mind wandered, and mucous and sonorous noises were audible over the chest. The state of the heart was not observed.

The attack of endocarditis was in this case the marked secondary effect of the pyæmia, but the solitary occurrence of this instance with endocarditis in 71 cases of pyæmia shows that the inflammation of the interior of the heart, so common, as we have seen, in acute rheumatism and chorea, is rare in pyæmia, though less so, as we shall see, than in the fatal stage of Bright's disease.

The signs of the heart affection were not observed in this case of pyæmic endocarditis. I have had, however, frequent opportunities of examining a patient affected with pyæmia, in the course of whose very serious illness the signs of endocarditis appeared and held their ground. Pleurisy first showed itself, and the evidence of inflammation in both lungs; and after a time a systolic murmur became audible at the apex. This murmur was constant, but it varied in loudness, tone, and area during the course of the illness. After this patient's recovery a mitral murmur was established.

ENDOCARDITIS IN BRIGHT'S DISEASE.

I have only been able to find one instance with evidence after death of endocarditis in the whole of the cases of Bright's disease described in the post-mortem records of St. Mary's Hospital, amounting to 207, excluding those in which there was regurgitation through the mitral or the aortic valve, or through both valves, or obstruction of the mitral orifice. That case was one of fatty disease of the kidney in a man, aged 41, who was under my care. His heart was rather large, weighing 12¼ ounces, and was dilated and flabby. The structure of the valves was healthy, with the exception of a patch of white deposit on the anterior flap of the mitral valve, which did not appear, after death, to interfere with the function of the valve.

This man, when admitted, presented a yellowish pallor and puffiness of face. He had been a healthy man until he took cold, nine months previously, after which he became gradually weak and pale, and had palpitation and frequent vomiting, symptoms with which he was still troubled. There was some albumen in his urine. The right veins of his neck was rather swollen and pulsating, and there was pulsation of the temporal artery. The heart's impulse was very feeble, and diffused over the cardiac space during expiration only, but it could be felt between the ensiform cartilage and the left seventh costal cartilage. The liver was firm and low, and presented a diffused pulsation in the epigastric space.

A soft systolic bellows murmur was audible at the apex, and a peculiar short double murmur between the nipple and the sternum, which was obscured by the natural heart sounds. These murmurs varied considerably from day to day, but they were generally audible, though the diastolic noise was more or less obscure. About a week after his admission a peculiar humming venous murmur was heard to the right of the sternum when he sat up, but not when he lay down, which, sometimes, disappeared without apparent cause, when it could be brought back by pressure over the jugular vein.

On the 42nd day he presented considerable general dropsy, and for the first time the murmurs were very faint and obscure, and two days later they were lost. After this the mitral murmur was sometimes audible, but was generally not so, and the diastolic murmur was only heard once, corresponding with a thrill near the apex. The last observation was made on the 77th day, when a faint systolic murmur was heard over the seventh cartilage, and feeble doubling of the first sound over the sixth cartilage. The urine was then scarcely albuminous, and it had been so during a considerable period of the history of this patient, who died on the 98th day.

I have ranked this case as one of endocarditis, because of the presence of a white deposit on the mitral valve, which was otherwise healthy, and of the history of varying murmurs, pointing to changing affection of the mitral and aortic valves. The long duration of the case, and the small amount of change to which the valve had been subjected, make it doubtful whether the endocarditis was present in more than its effect, the white deposit on the mitral valve, at and before the time of death; but if we take that appearance, and the varying signs of double regurgitation into account, I think we may infer that this case was one of endocarditis. It is true that both mitral and aortic regurgitation may be present in Bright's disease when there is very great tension of the arteries, and great hypertrophy, with dilatation of the left ventricle; that in such cases those murmurs usually vary in character, according to the varying intensity of the causes that gave them birth; that they may be suspended, restored, and again lost, even permanently; but this case did not present those conditions, for the heart, though dilated, was not greatly enlarged, and was not hypertrophied, since it only weighed 12½ ounces.

Admitting, then, that this was a case of endocarditis occurring in a patient affected with Bright's disease, it is evident, that as this was the solitary instance of that kind that was noticed among so many cases of Bright's disease without disease of the valves, that although endocarditis may occur in that disease, yet that it is rare. This becomes more marked when we compare the cases of acute rheumatism, and of chorea, with those of Bright's disease; for in the two former affections, from one-half to one-third of the cases were affected with inflammation of the interior of the heart.

The frequent presence of thickening of the mitral valve, and occasionally of the aortic valve ; and the large proportion of cases of valvular disease without a previous history of acute rheumatism ; perhaps point to the occurrence of endocarditis in those cases during the earlier period of their history. If so, endocarditis, and pericarditis, behave very differently from each other in Bright's disease, for while pericarditis is common towards the fatal period of this disease, especially when the kidney is granular, and is rare during its earlier history, endocarditis is very rare towards its fatal period, but is not very infrequent during its earlier history ; that is—if the thickening of the valves, and especially of the mitral valve, and complete valvular disease, have their origin in the Bright's disease itself.

CLINICAL HISTORY OF ENDOCARDITIS OCCURRING IN CASES OF VALVULAR DISEASE OF THE HEART.

The influence of previous valvular disease in rendering endocarditis more frequent and severe in cases of acute rheumatism has been already seen at page 507. We then observed that the presence in that affection of disease in the valves of the heart, by adding to the labour of that organ, and by rendering its internal apertures more rough and irregular, increased the danger of the occurrence of internal inflammation of the heart, and intensified that inflammation when established.

So great, indeed, is the influence of valvular disease in exciting and intensifying inflammation of the diseased valve, that we find that endocarditis is apt to occur in such cases, even when free from acute rheumatism, chorea, or any other general disease.

I would refer here to some interesting remarks by Dr. Moxon on this important subject.

The accompanying table (p. 520) will show at a glance the proportion in which endocarditis was present at the time of death in the cases of valvular disease of the heart treated in St. Mary's Hospital.

PATHOLOGICAL EVIDENCE OF ENDOCARDITIS IN CASES OF VALVULAR DISEASE OF THE HEART.

It is difficult, even impossible, in every case to say, from the appearances presented after death, whether or not endocarditis is present on the affected valves, and the adjoining surfaces of the ventricle and auricle. This is due to the readiness with which, in certain cases, a deposit of fibrin from the blood as it streams backwards and forwards through the mitral and aortic apertures, attaches itself to the surfaces of the imperfect valves, roughened by disease. This is equally the result, whether those surfaces be roughened by the slow degeneration of the diseased fibrous tissues, which, although they may have been generally inflamed at the starting point of the disease, yet they may have long ceased to be so ; or whether the surfaces of the valve be inflamed by a recent and renewed attack of local endocarditis. In many instances, however, it is self-evident that inflammation actually affects the valve, for the appearances presented are precisely those that are found in cases of recent endocarditis, owing to acute rheumatism, chorea, or pyæmia. Those appearances in these cases are to be confided in, for the diseased valves have been described, without, however, as a rule being defined as being inflamed, by a succession of able and careful pathologists, including the distinguished names of Dr. Markham, Dr. Burdon Sanderson, Dr. Murchison, Mr. Gascoyne, Dr. Charlton Bastian, and Dr. Payne.

Table showing the number of cases with established valvular disease, among those not affected with acute rheumatism, in which endocarditis was present at the time of death.

		Affected with Bright's disease.
I.—Cases with established mitral regurgitation :—		
a. Cases with endocarditis, not affected with Bright's disease	9	5
b. Cases with fibrinous concretions on the valve, probably not affected with endocarditis	2	3
c. Cases in which no description of the valve was found	1	2
d. Cases without endocarditis or concretions	22	19
I.—TOTAL	34 [1]	29 [1]
II.—Cases with aortic regurgitation : (A)—from disease of the aortic valve :—		
a. Cases with endocarditis, not affected with Bright's disease	5	1
b. Cases with fibrinous concretions, endocarditis doubtful or absent	5	5
c. Cases in which there was no description of the valve	2	2
d. Cases without endocarditis or concretions	13	12
TOTAL	25	20
(B)—From great dilatation of the aorta, the flaps of valve being healthy but insufficient	5	1
II.—TOTAL with aortic regurgitation	30	21
III.—Cases with mitral-aortic regurgitation:—		
a. Cases with endocarditis, not affected with Bright's disease	5	3
b Cases with fibrinous concretions, endocarditis doubtful or absent	4	0
c. Cases in which there was no description of the valve	3	0
d. Cases without endocarditis or concretions	16	16
III.—TOTAL	28	19
IV.—Cases with obstruction of the mitral orifice :—		
a. Cases with endocarditis, not affected with Bright's disease	1	1
b. Case with roughness and ulcer at edge of valve	0	1
c. Cases with vegetations or concretions on valve, endocarditis doubtful or absent	2	1
d. Cases without endocarditis or concretions	18	6
IV.—TOTAL	21 [2]	9 [2]

[1] I am not certain that these numbers include the whole of the cases with mitral regurgitation, since most of the original copies of those cases have been lost or misplaced, and I have taken them from a detached tabulated abstract of those cases. This note applies also to the cases of mitral regurgitation given in the Table at page 512.

[2] In 5 of these cases the size of the mitral aperture is not described; in 5 it was contracted to a moderate extent, and in 19 to a great extent; and in 1 it was almost closed by a ball of organised fibrin.

Among the cases of *mitral regurgitation*, five presented "fringes" and one a ring of small papillary elevations or granulations around the free edges of the valve, and two others had warty or rough excrescences, and another had nodules of lymph on those free edges; and in one of these, the auricular surface of the valve was roughened. One of those instances described, I think, by Dr. Payne, presented also yellow succulent elevations, almost resembling a false membrane, but seated under the epithelium. I have also included among the cases of endocarditis four instances with vegetations on the auricular surface of both flaps of the mitral valve, and one with extensive ulceration of its anterior flap, in which case the adjoining surface of the ventricle was inflamed; five other cases presented large excrescences, or concretions and smaller vegetations, but these I have not included among those with endocarditis, although some of them may have had that affection. This may be said also of a doubtful case in which the posterior flap of the valve was attached to the wall of the ventricle by adhesions readily separated.

Five of the fourteen cases that I have classed among those with endocarditis were affected with Bright's disease, and nine of them were not so.

Forty-one cases with mitral regurgitation were free from vegetations, and of these, nineteen had Bright's disease, and twenty-two were free from that affection.

The cases with *aortic regurgitation* presented comparatively few instances or severe, with endocarditis, but these presented great variety in their features. One of them showed deposits of red vegetations towards the edge and centre of each flap of the aortic valve. In another, the flaps of the valve were cemented together, and then free margins were roughened, by fibrinous deposit. In a third the aortic aperture was converted into a mere chink by adhesions; and there was an irregular deposit of lymph, forming vegetations, about the basis of the conjoined flaps, some being hard, some cheesy, and others apparently quite recent. The united flaps projected like a funnel into the aorta in the fourth instance, and a little above the valve, and therefore on the inner surface of the aorta, was an oval patch, half an inch long, with a red highly vascular flocculent surface. The aortic valve, in the fifth case, was enlarged but soft. One of the flaps had ulcerated away at the sides, and a large nodular mass was appended to its sesamoid body. The sixth case was one of great interest, with contraction of the descending aorta below the subclavian artery so as scarcely to admit a probe, and embolism, blocking up the left brachial artery. The valve was universally red, soft, pulpy, and formless, and the aperture was contracted. I had originally only ranked five of these cases as being affected with endocarditis, but I think that the whole six may safely be so classed. Only one of these six cases with endocarditis had Bright's disease, the remaining five being not so affected. Ten other cases presented concretions of various size, some being large, one like an alpine strawberry, attached to the aortic valve;

these cases being affected, and unaffected, by Bright's disease in equal numbers. Twenty-five of the cases with aortic regurgitation were free from concretion, and of these, thirteen had Bright's disease, and twelve were free from that affection. In six cases, aortic regurgitation was due to great enlargement or dilatation of the ascending aorta, the flaps of the aortic valve being healthy in structure, but of insufficient size to close the widened orifice of the aorta.

It will I think be sufficient if I state the proportions in which the cases with *mitral aortic regurgitation* were affected with endocarditis, presented concretions, without distinct evidence of endocarditis, and were free from concretions, without entering into details. I consider that eight of those cases had endocarditis, five being free from, and three being affected with, Bright's disease; four of them had concretions on the valves, none of which had Bright's disease; and in thirty-two there was no concretion on the valves, one half of these being free from, and the other half affected with, Bright's disease.

I shall deal with the cases with *obstructed mitral orifice* in the manner that I have just dealt with those having mitral-aortic regurgitation. Two of them had endocarditis, one being free from, and one affected with, Bright's disease, and another case having that disease presented roughness and ulceration of the edge of the contracted mitral valve; three had vegetations, one of those only having Bright's disease, and twenty-five of them had neither endocarditis nor concretions in any form on the obstructed mitral orifice, only seven of which cases had Bright's disease.

It is evident that while cases with mitral regurgitation are affected in a rather large proportion, or nearly one-fourth (14 in 63), with endocarditis, only one, or at most two, in twenty-nine of the cases with obstruction of the mitral orifice gave evidence after death of that affection. Cases with aortic regurgitation occupy a middle position between the two classes just considered, 6 in 51 (or 1 in 9) of these cases being affected with endocarditis. The cases of aortic regurgitation that were free from Bright's disease were much more frequently affected with endocarditis (5 in 30 or 1 in 6) than those that were affected with that disease (1 in 21).

Cases with mitral-aortic regurgitation have endocarditis rather more frequently (8 in 47 or 1 in 6) than those with aortic regurgitation (6 in 51 or 1 in 9), and less frequently than those with mitral regurgitation (14 in 63 or 1 in 4½).

Valvular disease was less frequently attacked with endocarditis in those cases that were affected with Bright's disease (11 in 78 or 1 in 7) than those that were free from that affection (20 in 105 or 1 in 5·2); and, as we have seen, this tendency in Bright's disease to lessen the frequency of the occurrence of endocarditis in cases affected with valvular disease, prevailed through the whole of the varieties of disease of the valves that we have been investigating, excepting in cases with mitral obstruction.

The Signs and Symptoms of Endocarditis affecting Cases with Valvular Disease.

The signs and symptoms of endocarditis when it occurs in cases of valvular disease of the heart, not affected with acute rheumatism, do not differ essentially from the signs and symptoms of endocarditis, when it attacks cases of acute rheumatism affected with valvular disease of some standing. I have already given a brief clinical history of a series of cases of that class at pages 507-511, and it will, I think, be sufficient if I here refer to the narrative and *résumé* of those cases. As in those cases so in these, the two great distinguishing features of the supervention of endocarditis upon valves already affected with regurgitant or obstructive disease are (1) the great variability of the valvular murmurs, and of the size of the heart, as indicated by the alternate extension and contraction of the area of the impulse, and the alternate increase and diminution of its force; and (2) the great general illness with which the patient is affected, an illness not marked by dropsy, but by elevation of temperature, over-action or failing power of the heart, and pain in the cardiac region, side, or chest, hurried, difficult, and laboured respiration, connected often with a congestive affection of the lungs, showing itself sometimes in the form of bronchitis or of pulmonary apoplexy with its attendant pleurisy. I would again refer to the illustrations I have given with regard to those vital symptoms in a previous part of this article.

I would here remark that the occurrence of a special fever, such as enteric fever, may, as we have already seen, suspend a mitral or an aortic regurgitant murmur for a time; but this occurrence proclaims itself by its own distinctive symptoms.

I have not given any account of the temperatures of the body in the above clinical histories of pericarditis and endocarditis; for the thermometer was only employed in the later cases, and therefore in an insufficient number to enable us to arrive at general results.

Endocarditis affecting the Tricuspid Valve.

Endocarditis and structural disease of the tricuspid valve are admitted to be so rare in the adult, that there are few clinical or pathological records describing affections of that valve.

I have examined the whole of the cases of valvular and other diseases of the heart, and of Bright's disease, contained in the post-mortem records of St. Mary's Hospital, from 1851 to 1869-70, with the special object of ascertaining the frequency, extent, and character of any affection of the tricuspid valve that might occur in those cases, and the result is given in the accompanying Table.

M M 2

CASES WITH AFFECTION OF THE STRUCTURE OF THE TRICUSPID VALVE, not including instances in which the valve was incompetent owing to the great size of the tricuspid aperture; but including all those in which the edges of the valve were thickened, but the function of the valve was unaffected.

		Affected with Bright's disease
a. Cases with endocarditis, not affected with Bright's disease .	1	1
b. Case with fibrinous concretion on valve	0	1
c. Case with contraction of mitral valve	0	1
d. Cases with thickening and corrugation, or roughness of valve (1 with mitral-aortic reg., 1 with mitral obstr.) . . .	2	0
e. Cases with thickening of valve, valve not incompetent . .	11[1]	7[2]
	14	10

The tricuspid valve was affected with endocarditis in two instances; one of these patients was a woman, aged 40, who had been subject to acute rheumatism when a child, and had palpitation on slight exertion. She had been a patient in the hospital ten months previously with dropsy, ascites, albuminuria, and a mitral murmur. The ascites and dropsy disappeared, but they were greater than before when she was readmitted, when the lips and nose were blue; and the urine was scanty and very albuminous. The mitral murmur was louder than before, and dyspnœa appeared in paroxysms. The heart was rather large (12 inches), and presented patches of lymph on its surface; the walls of the right ventricle were half an inch thick, being thicker than those of the left ventricle. Warty, rough, irregular fibrous excrescences were present around the margin of the mitral orifice; looking towards, and being entirely in, the left auricle; the ventricular surface being free from deposit: and there was a smooth fibrinous deposit on the (auricular) surface of the tricuspid valve.

The other case with endocarditis of the tricuspid valve, was a woman aged 42, who had contraction of the mitral orifice, which allowed of the passage of but one finger. The heart was of very great size, and its cavities contained twenty ounces of blood, although it only weighed 13¼ ounces. The tricuspid valve had all its flaps thickened with excrescences along their margins, but the valve itself was competent. She became subject to palpitation twelve months previously after a shock or fright. Three days before admission, she raised half a pint of bright blood. The legs and feet were swollen, she had pain in the chest, the heart's action was violent, and there was a confused rumbling sound at the apex. There was no albumen in the urine. She became gradually worse, and finally palpitation and dyspnœa were superseded by drowsiness.

In both of these cases, the right side of the heart was excited to

---

[1] O the 11 without Bright's disease, 2 had mitral, 2 aortic, 3 mitral-aortic regurgitation; 2 mitral obstruction, and 1 had no valvular disease.

[2] Of the 7 with Bright's disease, 2 had aortic regurgitation, and 5 had no valvular disease.

excessive and continuous labour by the diseased condition of the mitral valve, which in one instance was affected with regurgitation, and in the other with great obstruction.

In one remarkable case a large concretion was attached to the tricuspid valve. This patient was a man, aged 69. The heart was large, weighing 16 ounces, the tricuspid valve was universally thickened, and a fibrinous deposit, the size of a nut, was present on the anterior surface of one of the flaps. The tendinous cords were hypertrophied and atheromatous. One of the valves of the pulmonary artery was converted into a hard concrete mass. There is no account of the left side of the heart.

These were all the instances that I can find in which there was endocarditis of the tricuspid valve, or the presence of concretions on its flaps; but the inquiry into the number of other cases in which the tricuspid valve was affected may throw some light on the probable frequency of antecedent endocarditis of the tricuspid valve, as a probable cause of disease of the valve.

I may briefly state that in one case there was contraction of the tricuspid orifice, so as barely to admit two fingers; and thickening round the margins of the valve; and although the other valves were stated to be healthy, a mitral murmur was audible during life. In another case, with mitral obstruction, the edges of the tricuspid valve were thick and corrugative; and in a third patient, who had been affected with acute rheumatism six months previously, which was followed by mitral-aortic regurgitation, the tricuspid valve, which was not seen, felt rough and thick. These are the only cases that permit definite evidence that in them the tricuspid valve had been previously affected with endocarditis. There were however eighteen other cases, as may be seen in the Table, in which there was some thickening of the tricuspid valve, in two of which it was stated to be atheromatous; but in none of these cases did it appear that the tricuspid valve was incompetent. Twelve of those cases had mitral, aortic, or mitral-aortic regurgitation or mitral obstruction; and of the remaining six cases that were free from valvular disease, five had Bright's disease.

It does not appear to me that any of these cases present definite evidence of the previous existence of endocarditis of the tricuspid valve as the cause of the thickening of its flaps, although it is probable that in some of them the valve had been originally inflamed and especially in those cases that presented aortic, mitral, or mitral-aortic regurgitation, or mitral obstruction.

TREATMENT OF ENDOCARDITIS.

Endocarditis is so completely an affection associated with those important diseases, acute rheumatism and chorea, in which it is rare, with pyæmia and Bright's disease, in which it is common, and with established valvular disease, that the proper treatment of the parent affection must in all such cases be the proper treatment of the associated inflammation of the valvular structure of the heart. The treatment of those diseases, however, should be modified in the form of additional precautions when endocarditis appears; and the general treatment of acute rheumatism and chorea must, from the first, be mainly governed by the consideration that in both of them endocarditis is the most serious natural complication of the general disease. What I have said with regard 'to the treatment of acute rheumatism in relation to the prevention of pericarditis, applies also to the treatment of acute rheumatism in relation to the prevention, if possible, and the alleviation of endocarditis. We have already seen that one-half of the first series of cases of acute rheumatism are affected with endocarditis (165 in 325); and that in one-half of the remainder (79 in 164) the occurrence of endocarditis is either threatened (in 63) or probable (in 13). This treatment may be summarized in the brief but effectual rules of (1) the absolute rest of every limb and joint, and of the whole body, during the attack of acute rheumatism ; and the maintenance of this absolute rest, especially in the limbs and joints that have been most recently affected, for a period of several days after the complete disappearance of the local inflammation ; and (2) the application of the belladonna and chloroform liniment, sprinkled on cotton-wool, over the affected joints, and the support of those joints by the application of flannel over the affected parts so equally adjusted as to give relief and comfort to the patient. We have already seen that the great cause of the inflammation affecting the interior of the left ventricle is the powerful exercise and over-work of that ventricle in maintaining the circulation through the vessels of the inflamed parts, which at the same time call for a greater supply of blood. The fibrous structures of the heart, in common with the fibrous structures of the joints, are prone to inflammation in acute rheumatism ; and in the struggle to which the left ventricle is subjected, the valves of that ventricle readily become inflamed at their surfaces and lines of contact. When endocarditis threatens, or first discloses itself, and especially if there be pain in the region of the heart, the application of three or four leeches over that region may be of essential service in lessening the inflammation, and so perhaps permanently saving the valve. It will be well also to cover the region of the heart with cotton-wool, sprinkled with the belladonna and chloroform liniment.

The influence of the treatment of acute rheumatism by means of rest, and the employment of soothing applications and comfortable support to the joints, on the occurrence, severity, and permanent ill effects of endocarditis, will be best illustrated by comparing the clinical history of the 74 cases treated by rest,[1] with that of the 325 cases not so treated.

There was endocarditis alone, or combined with pericarditis, in one-half (161 in 325) of the first series of cases that were not treated

[1] See the Author's Address on Medicine ; a copy of which will be given by the Publisher of this work to any reader applying for it.

upon a system of absolute rest; and in two-fifths (34 in 74) of the series that were so treated.

Valvular disease became established in 43 of the 127 cases (or 1 in 3·1, or 34 per cent.) of endocarditis, with a cardiac murmur, including those with pericarditis also (18 in 46), but excluding all those that had previous valvular disease, of the series not treated by rest; and in 3 of the 24 (or 1 in 8, or 12·5 per cent.) of the same kind of cases, of the series that were treated by rest. If we extend the comparison to the whole of both series of cases, excluding those that had previous valvular disease, we find that 43 in 281, or 1 in 6·6, of the series that were not treated by rest, and 3 in 61, or 1 in 20, of the series that were treated by rest, had established valvular disease, indicated by a permanent murmur after their recovery from acute rheumatism, and at the time of their last examination.

There was no murmur, and therefore no valvular disease, when the patient recovered from the attack of acute rheumatism, in 60 of the 127 cases with endocarditis, and without previous valvular disease (or 1 in 2·1, or 44·4 per cent.), that were not treated by rest; and in 17 of the 24 (or 1 in 1·4, or 71 per cent.) of the cases of the like kind that were so treated.

The murmur was lessening in intensity at the time of the last observation, when the patient had recovered from acute rheumatism, in 24 of the 127 cases just spoken of (or 1 in 5·4) that were not treated by rest; and in 4 of the 24 (or 1 in 6) of the analogous cases that were treated by rest.

We here find that, in the series of cases of acute rheumatism that were treated by a system of absolute rest, the proportion of those that were attacked with endocarditis was slightly less than that of those that were not so treated. Thus far the comparison is but slightly in favour of the treatment of acute rheumatism by a rigid system of rest; and this would seem to suggest that a certain, and a very large proportion of cases of acute rheumatism are habitually and intrinsically attacked by endocarditis. When, however, we extend the comparison, and ascertain the proportion in which those cases of endocarditis, not previously so affected, acquired permanent valvular disease, so as to injure health during the remainder of life, and to shorten life itself, we discover that the series of cases not treated by a system of absolute rest were thus permanently injured in a far larger proportion of cases, amounting to more than twice as many, or in the ratio of 8 to 3, than in those that were treated by rest.

If we pursue the inquiry further, so as to discover the relative extent to which the interior of the heart was inflamed in the two series of cases, we discover that there was but one instance, or 1 in 24, of those with endocarditis and without previous valvular disease, of the series treated by a rigid system of rest, that gave definite evidence of inflammation of both the aortic and mitral valves; while in 19 instances in 127, or 1 in 6·7, of the same kind of cases that were not treated by a rigid system of rest, there was direct evidence of aortic regurgitation. In nine, or rather ten, of those cases that were not treated by rest, there was a mitral murmur, and therefore direct evidence of inflammation of the mitral valve; but in the remaining nine cases there was also evidence of mitral endocarditis in the shape of a tricuspid murmur, or prolongation of the first sound, with intensification of the pulmonic second sound, and obstacles to the flow of blood through the lungs. The whole chain of evidence points then, I think, irresistibly to the conclusion that the extent, severity, and permanent ill effects of the endocarditis were much greater in the series of cases that were not rigidly treated by rest than in the series that were so treated.

Pericarditis, also, attacked a much larger proportion of the cases not treated by a system of rest, or 63 in 325, or 1 in 5·2, than of those that were treated by rest, or 6 in 74, or 1 in 12·2. Thus more than twice as many of the former series of cases, that were not treated by a rigid system of rest, were attacked with pericarditis, than of the latter series of cases that were treated by a rigid system of rest.

I am of opinion, however, from a careful revision of the clinical history of those cases, that the treatment by opium, which was pursued in a considerable proportion of the first series of cases that were not treated by rest, had some influence in increasing the frequency and severity of inflammation of the heart, and especially of its exterior. Taking this into account, however, I consider that the clinical evidence here afforded shows, that the severity and permanent ill effects of endocarditis, and the frequency and severity of pericarditis, are greatly lessened by a system of treatment by rest absolutely maintained; and combined with the use of local means in the shape of the application of the belladonna and chloroform liniment, and of equal and comfortable support to the affected joints, and the employment of leeches applied over the region of the heart, when that organ was attacked by inflammation, and especially on its exterior, and when accompanied by pain.

The clinical evidence in favour of the treatment of acute rheumatism by rest is conclusively supported on the pathological grounds stated at the commencement of this article (see page 457), and in Dr. Moxon's very striking, important, and convincing lecture on endocarditis, to which I have there referred. We have there seen that the surfaces or lines of contact, pressure, and friction of the valves, and chiefly of the mitral valve, are the parts that are especially affected with endocarditis. Thus the over-work of the left ventricle of the heart, and the resulting friction, pressure, and tension of its valves, in cases of acute rheumatism and chorea, tend to augment the primary influence of the parent disease, and to excite and intensify the inflammation of the interior of the heart, and especially of the mitral valve.

CARDITIS.

By W. R. Gowers, M.D.

SYNONYMS.—Myocarditis; Interstitial Myocarditis.

DEFINITION.—An acute affection of the walls of the heart, consisting in interstitial serous exudation or cell-infiltration, and degeneration of the muscular fibres. The latter may occur without any change in the interstitial tissue. This has been regarded as a "parenchymatous myocarditis." But this change, when general throughout the heart, occurs as the result of some general blood state, and is unassociated with other evidence of inflammation in the heart or remaining organs. Without denying the possibility of the occurrence of a general parenchymatous inflammation of the heart, it seems more consistent with the relations of the process to consider these cases as examples of acute degeneration. (See Art. "Fatty Degeneration.")

VARIETIES.—The inflammation may be general, affecting all parts of the heart; or it may be partial, being limited to a small area. When general it may be diffused uniformly through the heart; it may affect the superficial layers only (when secondary to pericarditis); or it may result in scattered foci of suppuration. Circumscribed inflammations may result in the formation of an abscess in the wall of the heart. Lastly, the varieties have been distinguished of primary and secondary inflammation; the former occurring apart from, the latter in consequence of, pre-existing disease, general or local.

ETIOLOGY.—In the consideration of the causes of the disease, the variety which is due to the extension of inflammation from the pericardium may be excluded from consideration, since it owns the same causes as the pericarditis to which it is due, and is commonly the consequence of acute rheumatism. Other forms of carditis occur in the male much more frequently than in the female sex; and at all ages, but rather more frequently before than after thirty years of age. As a primary affection, carditis is extremely rare: a few of the recorded cases have been ascribed to exposure to cold after severe exertion, or to blows on the precordial region. In other cases no exciting cause could be discovered. As a secondary affection it has occurred in a few cases of acute rheumatism, apart, it is said, from endo- or peri-carditis, and also in various septicæmic affections. Its chief local causes are peri-carditis, endocarditis in rare cases, embolism, and growths in the heart.

PATHOLOGICAL ANATOMY.—The inflamed muscular substance is at first injected, and then swollen and softened. Points of extravasation are scattered through it; the tissue becomes paler, of a reddish-grey tint, and may break down into a pulpy mass, partly from

the acute degeneration and destruction of the muscular fibres, and
partly owing to their separation by an interstitial infiltration of serum,
blood-corpuscles, and corpuscular inflammatory products, derived from
the interstitial connective tissue-elements or from the blood. These
may be in the form of pus cells, which may be disseminated through
the heart in the tracts of connective tissue, or may be aggregated in
minute abscesses. In the localised form of inflammation, softening
and breaking down of tissue may occur without actual pus formation,
and a pseudo-abscess may result. If pus cells are formed, a true
abscess of the heart is the consequence, and the destruction of the
muscular fibres may be so complete that only pus may be found in
the cavity. The adjacent tissue is, however, softened and degenerated.
Such an abscess may attain the size of a hazel-nut. This local
inflammation is much more common in the wall of the left than in
that of the right ventricle, and is very rare in the auricles. It is most
common in the left ventricle near the apex, in the posterior wall,
or in the septum. When softening, purulent or non-purulent, has
occurred, the wall is bulged at the spot, and secondary pericarditis
may be produced. When the inflammation is adjacent to the inner
surface, it may invade the endocardium, and spread to an adjacent
valve. Ultimately, in most cases, the outer or inner wall of the abscess
or pseudo-abscess gives way, and the contents escape into the pericardial cavity or into the ventricle; causing, in the former case, purulent
pericarditis, in the latter, an " acute aneurism of the heart " and septicæmia, usually fatal in a few hours. Both walls have given way at
the same time, and " rupture of the heart " has occurred. An abscess
in the septum has burst into both ventricles; from the upper part of
the septum it has burst into the aorta behind the aortic valves, or into
the right auricle. In this way a fistulous communication has been
established between the two ventricles, between either or both ventricles and the aorta, or between the left ventricle and the right
auricle. If the inflammation subsides without the formation of pus,
the cellular products may develop into fibrous tissue. This often occurs
in the superficial layers of the heart after pericarditis, and it may
occur in the localised form of carditis, a circumscribed patch of fibrous
tissue resulting. Less commonly caseation takes place, even after pus
has been formed, and the caseated mass may shrink and calcify.

SYMPTOMS.—The symptoms of acute inflammation of the heart are
sometimes distinct enough, but are in other cases obscure or misleading. The local signs are those of cardiac weakness, suddenly
developed, after, it is said, a transient stage of excitement. The impulse
is weakened or imperceptible; the first sound toneless. A systolic
murmur has been heard in some cases, due, perhaps, to incapacity of
the papillary muscles. The cardiac dulness is normal, or sometimes
widened, from acute dilatation. The pulse is feeble, frequent, and may
be irregular. Uneasiness about the sternal or cardiac region has
been an early symptom in several cases, increasing in some to acute
pain. The general symptoms are those of heart failure, and those

which depend on cerebral anæmia may be so pronounced as entirely to obscure the real nature of the case. Dyspnœa is the most constant symptom, continuous or felt on the slightest exertion. Nausea and vomiting, collapse, with coldness of extremities, and clammy perspiration occur. Convulsions, delirium, and coma have been prominent symptoms in several cases. The central temperature is raised ; in one recorded case it reached 107°. The symptoms of collapse rapidly increase, and death occurs usually in a few days. Friedreich found the average duration to be four days, the minimum being a few hours, the maximum a week.

Localised inflammation of the heart may be attended by similar but less urgent symptoms, or may run an entirely latent course until the occurrence of the grave symptoms which proclaim the rupture of an abscess, such as, on the one hand, those of acute pericarditis, or, on the other, those of systemic or pulmonary embolism. In one case a pustular rash occurred, it is conjectured from embolism of the cutaneous arteries.

DIAGNOSIS.—The diagnosis is a question rather of theory than of practice, for the disease is extremely rare, and its symptoms are produced by many other causes. The sudden onset of symptoms of cardiac weakness and failure, less sudden than in cases of rupture, more sudden than in cases of acute degeneration, if coupled with considerable elevation of temperature, and especially if occurring in the course of a disease such as pyæmia, may give rise to a suspicion of the existence of carditis. Abscess of the heart is even more equivocal in its symptoms. The rupture of an abscess may be suspected if sudden symptoms of systemic or pulmonary embolism or of pericarditis, supervene on less urgent symptoms of cardiac failure.

PROGNOSIS. —General carditis has hitherto only been diagnosed after death, and it is doubtful whether recovery has ever taken place. In the circumscribed form it is probable that subsidence of the inflammation has, in a few cases, permitted the continuance of the heart's action and the disappearance of the symptoms. The prognosis in the form which is secondary to pericarditis is much less grave, since a large proportion of the muscular tissue is not damaged, and, with the subsidence of the adjacent inflammation, recovers good functional power.

TREATMENT.—The treatment of carditis is necessarily symptomatic. Its existence can rarely be ascertained, and, if known, no means of direct treatment exists. Rest to the heart is the first point to be secured. Cold to the precordial region has been recommended ; warm poultices would perhaps give more relief. Warmth should be applied to the extremities, to equalise the circulation and lessen the tendency to correlated congestion of internal organs. The heart's action must of necessity be sustained by stimulants which, with the recumbent posture, constitute the best treatment for the cerebral symptoms. For the cardiac failure in septicæmia, full doses of the perchloride of iron have seemed to the writer to be of distinct service.

HYDROPERICARDIUM.—HYDROPS PERICARDII.

By J. Warburton Begbie, M.D.

The occupation of the pericardial sac to a greater or less extent by serous fluid, a condition known under both of the terms mentioned above, or simply as Dropsy of the Pericardium, is not of unfrequent occurrence. Laennec indeed speaks of this condition as being very common. " L'hydro-péricarde," he says, " ou l'accumulation d'une quantité plus ou moins grande de sérosité dans le péricarde, est un cas extrêmement commun;"[1] but he qualifies this statement by the remark, that idiopathic effusion into the pericardium is very rare, that ordinarily but a few ounces of serum are found in the sac, and that this quantity is effused shortly before death, sometimes at the very moment of dying, or even immediately thereafter. The causes of dropsy of the pericardium are various, and some of them most obscure. Dr. Walshe recognises an *Active* and *Passive* Hydropericardium; also, a third form dependent on *mechanical obstruction.*[2] The first of these three varieties is very rare. Dr. Walshe, however, refers to certain instances of Bright's disease, in which he has known the pericardium fill with fluid, the symptoms indicating an irritative state, while the signs of pericarditis were wanting. Examples of a precisely similar kind are familiar to the writer, in connection with the dropsy of scarlet fever. He has seen a sudden and copious effusion into the pericardium occur at the same time that dropsical swelling manifested itself in the more ordinary situations, and in such cases, found no evidence whatever of plastic formations either upon or within the heart.

Passive Hydropericardium is seen in connection with other dropsies, with anasarca and ascites, but especially with hydrothorax. The relation of the latter, however intimate, as in some cases it is, to pleural dropsy, is by no means constant. On two occasions we have found a very large Hydropericardium in cases of primary cardiac disease with great anasarca, but with little, if any, hydrothorax.

Mechanical Hydropericardium.—An effusion of serous fluid into the cavity of the pericardium has been found in connection with aneurism of the aorta, with cancerous disease seated in the anterior mediastinum, exerting injurious pressure on the great venous trunk, and thus preventing the due return of blood through the coronary and pericardial veins, and certain morbid states of the heart itself, in

[1] Traité de l'Auscultation.—Des Maladies du Cœur, chap. xxii.: De l'Hydro-péricard
[2] Diseases of the Heart, p. 266.

which the venous circulation is greatly embarrassed. In such instances the dropsy, evidently due to direct obstructions near its seat, may with great propriety be called mechanical.

The serous fluid which occupies the pericardial sac is sometimes colourless; at other times, although quite limpid, and without any admixture of albuminous floculi, it presents a lemon yellow, or even rose-coloured tints; rarely is it sanguinolent. The quantity of fluid varies greatly. Usually it is not excessive, but, on the contrary, moderate. In Passive Hydropericardium, Dr. Walshe has stated the amount to be from eight to twelve ounces; more than the latter quantity he has never seen. Instances, however, are on record in which a very large accumulation of serous fluid has been found in the pericardium. Benisart has related one, in which there existed four pints, or eight pounds (*huit livres*). From twelve to eighteen ounces of fluid can be injected into the healthy pericardium of an adult, but there can be no doubt that the pericardium, contrary to what is stated in certain anatomical treatises,[1] is extensible; the fibrous, as well as serous nature of the membrane may impair, but does not prevent its extensibility. In all probability, those cases of enormous distension of the sac by fluid, which are described by Corvisart, Avenbrugger, and others, were examples of pericarditis. It is apparently when altered by inflammation that the pericardium becomes most capable of distension.

Dr. Stokes refers to a case published by Sir Dominic Corrigan, in which the heart was covered with a pulpy lymph, and there was a vast effusion of liquid into the sac,[2] and Dr. Graves, in describing a most interesting case of Hydropericardium, connected with malforma-tion of, and recent deposition of lymph upon the pulmonary valves, makes the remark, " the pericardium was distended with straw-coloured fluid, so abundant that we expected to find pericarditis; "[3] implying that this distinguished physician regarded pericarditis as the usual determining cause of *large* pericardial effusions.

The most important and reliable indications of the existence of Hydropericardium are furnished by percussion and auscultation, but independently of these, there are other particulars, the value of which is by no means small. A sensation of discomfort in the region of the heart is frequently complained of, and even a sense of weight—a symptom of pericardial effusion to which Lancisi attached great sig-nificance. Senac describes the undulatory movement of the fluid as visible between the third, fourth, and fifth ribs; and Corvisart, the sense of fluctuation in the same situations, as distinguished by touch. Dyspnœa, more or less urgent, is usually present in cases of Hydro-pericardium. It must, however, be admitted that there exists no small amount of difficulty in assigning the true share in the production of this symptom to the effusion within the pericardium, seeing that it may

[1] *E.g.* Holden's Illustrated Manual of Anatomy, p. 98.
[2] Diseases of the Heart, p. 20.
[3] Clinical Lectures : Pericarditis, p. 578.

in most cases be in part likewise attributed to the visceral disease, on which this form of dropsy depended, or possibly to the hydrothorax, by which it is so likely to be accompanied. A feebleness of the pulse, and, not unusually, an intermittent or irregular condition of the pulse exists. By auscultation, the heart-sounds are feebly audible, and appear to be distant or remote. On percussion there is extended pericardial dulness, for the most part not rising so high, nor passing to the same limits laterally, as is the case in chronic, and even in some instances of acute inflammatory effusion within the pericardium. The dilatation of the precordial region, or even of the left lateral region, as noticed by Louis, the epigastric tumour described by Corvisart, and the extension of the left lung upwards, of which Dr. Graves and Dr. Stokes have written, are rare but striking phenomena connected with large pericardial effusions, dependent, however, on inflammatory action. Besides the general symptoms to which reference has been made, it must be held in view that others of the same nature will be likely to show themselves, the latter, however, having a more distinct relationship with the visceral disease on which the dropsy depends. The Hydropericardium, moreover, will in all probability be connected with some other dropsical effusion, hydrothorax or anasarca, or it may be ascites.

The remedies most useful in the treatment of dropsies are seldom effectual in relieving the dropsy of the pericardium. The writer has known the repeated application of blisters over the region of the heart to produce a decided impression in one case. The stronger diuretics and hydrogogue cathartics, "will," as Dr. Walshe observes, "be tried, were it only for the removal of the usually concomitant dropsies." Paracentesis pericardii, which has been repeatedly performed in the treatment of pericarditis attended by large effusion, and in some instances successfully performed, is of course an available means for affording temporary relief in the truly dropsical affection, temporary because, although the heart be freed by the operation from the surrounding fluid, unless the disease giving rise to the dropsy be removed, the fluid must necessarily re-accumulate.

ANGINA PECTORIS AND ALLIED STATES; INCLUDING CERTAIN KINDS OF SUDDEN DEATH.

By Professor Gairdner, M.D.

THE phenomena of the disease, or group of symptoms, termed Angina Pectoris by Heberden, are perhaps the most interesting in themselves, and the most deserving of study in relation to other forms of cardiac disorder, of any which we shall have to consider in this section. In treating of this difficult subject we must separate with great care the essential facts of the disease from the various speculations, or associated ideas, that almost inevitably force themselves into the mind in considering the facts. And this separation is by no means easy; for in this instance the facts themselves are apt to be more or less withdrawn from exact observation; the phenomena characteristic of the disease being mostly *subjective*, i.e. present to the consciousness of the patient only, and only through his description of them made known to the physician. It may even be said with truth, that no one fact in a typical case of angina pectoris is necessarily other than subjective, with the exception of the awful terminal fact of sudden death. And when this is wanting, or when it is delayed, there is hardly any combination of the remaining symptoms that may not vary in individual cases, or be differently presented by the sufferer, according to the exactness and concentration of his habits of thought, the vividness and power of his imagination, or the degree and kind of his individual sensitiveness to morbid impressions.

Still, the fact of sudden death, superadded to the evidence of certain sensations preceding death, may be considered to afford the nearest approach we have to an accurate definition of this disease. What these sensations are we shall endeavour to indicate, in so far as the inadequacy of language will allow, from the consideration of such individual instances as have been minutely and carefully recorded either by the sufferers themselves, or by physicians simply giving expression to the spontaneous testimony of their patients. By following the ideal descriptions of those who have allowed themselves to be guided by theories of the disease rather than by the facts, we might easily add to the fulness, without increasing the value, of our description.

First on the list of symptoms, according to Heberden and the majority of authors who have followed him, is *pain*.[1] How far pain,

---

[1] In his Commentaries (1796), Heberden treats of this disease under the general title "De dolore pectoris" (Sec. lxx.). In his first communication on the subject to the College

in the ordinary sense of the word, is essential to the idea of angina pectoris, we shall afterwards consider; for the present it may be sufficient to observe that pain, or at least a sensation of local distress amounting in certain cases to pain of a peculiarly overwhelming character, is in this disease closely associated with the symptoms immediately preceding death.

This peculiar anguish, or, as it might justly be called, agony of suffering, is paroxysmal; it frequently reaches its climax within a few minutes, and is relieved or disappears entirely within a like period of time, or at most within an hour or two; it recurs at uncertain intervals, sometimes without any obvious exciting cause, at others manifestly determined by exertion, and especially by too rapid walking up-hill, in which case it often ceases, especially in the earlier attacks, almost immediately on standing still: it is instinctively associated in the mind of the patient with the idea of a particularly severe form of oppression or suffocation; or rather, to be more exact, with some indefinable sense of impending danger, to which he is unable to give expression, and which he endeavours to convey to others by similitudes that do not satisfy his own mind. A frequent expression is that recorded by Dr. Latham in the case of a very eminent man of the highest intellectual power; after an attack he said he "could scarcely bear it if it were as severe as it had been;" and shortly afterwards, "One can bear outward pain; but it is not so easy to bear inward pain."[1] This essential *unbearableness* of the suffering is most characteristic of angina pectoris, and it is quite independent of the degree of severity of the pain in other respects. And further, it is to be observed that the intolerance here alluded to is not the mere impatience of the nerves, which can be mastered by a strong will and a calm heroic self-restraint; it is the sense that the very springs of life are implicated, and that under a prolongation or increase of the pain the whole machine must suddenly give way.[2] It is from this sense of impending death (rarely thus expressed in words by the patient), and from the fact that sudden death actually occurs during the paroxysm in a certain number of cases, that the pain, or special sensation, of angina pectoris derives almost all that it has of a distinctive character; and therefore Dr. Latham has justly elevated this most important but almost indescribable symptom to a co-ordinate rank with the pain itself, in his description of the disease as a whole. Angina pectoris, according to his admirably succinct definition, "consists essentially of pain in the chest and a sense of

of Physicians in 1768 (Medical Transactions, vol. ii. p. 59), he merely terms it "A Disorder of the Breast." The two descriptions do not differ in essentials, but a few details of difference which seem to be of more or less importance will be noticed below. The eminently careful and exact use of language by Heberden in his singularly condensed clinical studies, whether in Latin or in English, tends to invite attention to even the minutest discrepancies between his earlier and later statements.

[1] Latham, "Diseases of the Heart," vol. ii. pp. 375-6. It is no secret, that the case was that of the late Dr. Arnold, of Rugby.

[2] "Qui hoc morbo tenentur, occupari solent . . . ingratissimo pectoris angore, vitæ extinctionem intentante, siquidem augeretur, vel perseveraret."—HEBERDEN, *Comm.* loc. cit

approaching dissolution." " The subjects of angina pectoris report that it is a suffering as sharp as anything that can be conceived in the nature of pain, and that it includes, moreover, something which is beyond the nature of pain, a sense of dying." [1]

Such, then, are the most important or essential facts which clinical observation teaches in reference to angina pectoris. Let us now consider them separately, and more in detail.

The *pain* of angina is usually felt at the lower sternum, but sometimes also under the middle or upper sternum, inclining, however, towards the left side.[2] Sometimes the pain extends to both sides of the chest in front, and perhaps more frequently into both shoulders, and into the back. Very specially characteristic is a " pain about the middle of the left arm,"[3] sometimes present in the right, or in both arms, which, according to Dr. Heberden, occasionally precedes,[4] but more commonly follows the pain in the chest. This, together with a degree of numbness of the left arm, may be described as present in the majority of cases in which the pain extends beyond the thorax.[5] The pain and numbness together, or the pain alone, may extend down to the fingers, or may stop short at the elbow, usually at the inner side of the arm; and painful sensations, more or less definite in character, may be felt also in the neck, or in one or both lower extremities; but these are exceptional, and there is reason to think that in some cases the local symptoms connected with aneurismal tumours implicating the nerves may have been confounded with those more specially characteristic of angina pectoris.[6] At all events, these local varieties of pain are not to be regarded as essential

---

[1] Op. cit. pp. 366, 364.

[2] "*Always* inclining more to the left side." (Heberden, *Med. Trans.*) "*Non raro* inclinatior ad sinistrum latus."—*Comment.*

[3] Heberden, *Med. Trans.* uti supra. " Dolor sæpissime pertinet a pectore usque ad cubitum lævum. . . . In nonnullis vero . . . ad dextrum pariter ac lævum cubitum pertigit, atque etiam usque ad manus; sed hoc rarius evenit; rarissimum autem est, ut brachium simul torpeat ac tumeat."—*Comm.* loc. cit.

[4] *Med. Trans.* vol. iii. p. 3.

[5] The group of symptoms here alluded to, though first clearly indicated by Heberden as characteristic, was described long before by Morgagni in the case of a woman, forty-two years of age, who died suddenly during a paroxysm, and was found to have a dilated and ossified aorta. The description is worth quoting, from the fact that it is probably one of the first clinically exact records existing in medical literature of a case of this kind. The patient had been "diu valetudinaria, diuque obnoxia paroxysmo cuidam ad hunc modum se habenti. A concitatis corporis motibus ingruebat molestus quidam angor intra superiorem thoracis sinistram partem, cum spirandi difficultate, et sinistri brachii stupore: quæ omnia, ubi motus illi cessarent, facile remittebant. Ea igitur mulier, cum circa medium Octobrem A. 1707 Venetiis in continentem trajecta, rheda veheretur, lætoque esset animo, ecce tibi ille idem paroxysmus; quo correpta, et mori se, aiens, ibi repente mortua est." The examination after death showed disease of the aortic orifice and aorta, and Morgagni regards the sudden death as due to the sudden excitement of carriage exercise ("insolitum in Veneta fœmina rhedæ motum ") operating upon a circulation weakened and obstructed by chronic disease, as to lead to ultimate failure in the power of the heart to propel the blood ("ut sanguis restitans promoveri amplius non poterat ").—*De Sedibus et Causis Morborum,* ii. *Epist.* xxvi. 31 et seq.

[6] As, for instance, in several of the cases recorded by M. Trousseau in his interesting chapter on the subject. (Clinique de l'Hôtel-Dieu, vol. ii. p. 434 *et seq.* deuxième édition ; Paris, 1865.) English Translation, 1868, vol. i. p. 596, *et seq.*

elements of the disease, although from their occurrence and their distribution they may lead to more defined conceptions of the nervous plexuses involved, and thus occasionally to the detection of an organic cause, or of something tending to throw light upon the peculiarities, or to guide the treatment of an individual case.[1]

Local tenderness on pressure is an occasional but by no means a constant symptom of angina pectoris. Sometimes, on the other hand, the pain is decidedly relieved by pressure, or by rubbing, as well as by counter-irritation of the parts affected. The pains are aggravated by movement of the whole body, and especially by severe or even moderate exertion in walking, which indeed becomes impossible during a severe paroxysm. Very marked relief is often afforded by the eructation of wind from the stomach, whether spontaneously or under the influence of carminatives. Rest of body, and warmth to the extremities, are among the more obvious of the physiological conditions which have been observed to have a well-marked effect in relieving the pains of angina, in their less extreme varieties.

The *peculiar sensation which culminates in the sense of impending death*, has been very variously described,[2] and indeed seems from its very nature to be almost indescribable. Among the uninstructed, or in the case of persons unaccustomed to observe and analyse their own sensations, nothing is more common than to find the term "breathlessness," or "want of breath," applied to every kind of thoracic oppression, and the sense experienced in angina pectoris of constriction, or in other cases of repletion in the chest, accompanied as it usually is by gasping or irregular respiration, is undoubtedly often called a "want of breath," or "suffocation," by persons who are simply feeling about, as it were, for an expression whereby to represent an uncommon and intensely oppressive sensation. A similar confusion

[1] In one very exceptional case, recorded by Heberden in the "Commentaries," there was no pain complained of in the chest, but only in the left arm, having, however, in other respects the characters of angina. After fifteen years of occasional and increasing suffering, the patient died suddenly at seventy-five years of age.

[2] It is difficult to judge from Heberden's descriptions how far the "angor pectoris, intentans vitæ extinctionem," was regarded by him as a simple pain. In his first memoir he speaks of the "sense of strangling, and anxiety with which it (the disorder of the breast) is attended," and applies the name Angina Pectoris on account of these characters rather than on the ground of pain. The anonymous patient who described his own case in the third volume of the "Medical Transactions," apparently discriminates very sharply, on the one hand between the pain in the left arm and chest, coming on "when walking, always after dinner, or in the evening;" and on the other, the "sensations which seem to indicate a sudden death;" which he describes as being like "a universal pause within me of the operations of nature for perhaps three or four seconds," and afterwards "a shock at the heart, like that which one would feel from a small weight fastened to a string to some part of the body, and falling from the table to within a few inches of the floor." This distinction of the sensation of impending death from the pain was unfamiliar to Heberden, who says he does not remember to have heard it mentioned by any other patient; and thinks that the sudden death of this patient, which came to his knowledge afterwards, was connected more with the pain than with this peculiar sensation. Dr. Parry speaks of the first symptom in angina pectoris as "an uneasy sensation, which has been variously denominated a stricture, an anxiety, and a pain." Dr. Latham was probably among the first to define the sense of impending death as being distinct from the pain.

lies latent even under the more technical language of Heberden, in his use of the Greek term Angina,[1] which, according to its etymology, signifies a *strangling*, and according to its actual and primitive use was applied chiefly to certain affections of the throat, occasionally leading to sudden death by laryngeal suffocation, and giving rise to a sense of choking, or of constriction in the fauces. Yet Heberden, in using this term, had thoroughly realised the fact that angina pectoris is not really a suffocation or a breathlessness, in the ordinary acceptation of these terms. At most it is a sensation which by its urgency and oppressiveness recalls the impression of suffocation, and which may in certain cases be associated with true dyspnœa, or still more frequently with orthopnœa. In many instances, however, careful examination shows, and the patients themselves may be easily convinced, that respiration is really not impeded; that inspiration and expiration are alike free and noiseless; that the air is taken into the chest in full measure, and (in so far as the evidence of stethoscopic examination goes to prove the fact) that the mechanical renewal of the air in the vesicles of the lungs is perfectly accomplished. In this sense, the observation of Heberden is profoundly exact, that in the beginning of this distemper the patients "nulla tenentur spirandi difficultate, a qua hic pectoris angor prorsus est diversus." [2] And yet it might possibly be maintained that in a more transcendental sense respiration, *i.e.*, the chemistry of respiration, is usually impeded; that the transit of the blood through the pulmonic capillaries is for the time suspended or impaired, that the right heart is perhaps unduly loaded, and that the sensation of "breathlessness" is therefore not without a physical equivalent in the state of the blood, for the time restricted in its supply of oxygen. In the more advanced stages of angina pectoris, indeed, especially when in connection with organic disease, it rarely happens that some positive evidence of real dyspnœa does not exist, at least as a complication, if not as a part of the disease. Even in such complicated cases, however, it is usually easy for the experienced clinical observer to detect a difference of habit and aspect from cases in which the breathing is primarily impaired, *e.g.* as in aggravated cases of emphysema with bronchitis, or of double pneumonia, or extensive pleuritic effusion unconnected with a cardiac cause.

We are obliged, therefore, under these circumstances, to accept the necessary limitations of ordinary language in conveying extraordinary or almost indescribable impressions. It is certain that the patient in angina pectoris has a sense of obstruction in the thorax so overwhelming and so full of apparently imminent danger that he instinctively likens it to a suffocation;[3] yet it is equally certain that in

---

[1] From ἄγχω, *strangulo*, whence also the compound words Cynanche and Synanche, and the Latin verb *angere*, which acquired the secondary sense of undefinable distress conveyed also by *anxietas*, and still more by our English word *anguish*.

[2] Heberden, *Comment.* loc. cit. "Have no *shortness of breath.*" (*Med. Trans.* uti supra.)

[3] "A *sense* of dissolution, not a fear of it," said one of the most gifted men I ever knew, and one most competent to analyse sensations.—J. F. R. EDITOR.

many cases impeded respiration, in the ordinary sense of the term, is not present. This remarkable sensation, which is sometimes represented as a tightness or constriction, sometimes, on the other hand, as a fulness or over-distension of the chest, contributes even more than the pain to the indescribable *anguish* of angina pectoris; and it is this sensation especially which gives to the pain its peculiar character of "unbearableness" already noticed; this also, which carries with it in its graver forms that impress of immediately inpending death, by which the real danger, and the ultimate probable event, are rendered so vividly present to the consciousness of the patient.[1]

The other symptoms of angina pectoris have been variously described; so variously, indeed, as to lead to a suspicion of inaccuracies of detail on the part of individual observers of the paroxysm. On all hands it is agreed that in the intervals the patient may have all the appearances of perfect health; his colour may be good, his appetite unimpaired, his breathing apparently natural, the action and sounds of the heart perfectly normal. It is equally certain that the paroxysm itself is unattended by fever, and that in uncomplicated cases it has none of the characters, as it has none of the consequences, of an inflammatory seizure.[2] But it is difficult to accept without hesitation the statement of some authorities, that throughout the attack the pulse may be entirely undisturbed either as to its rate of frequency, or as to its characters.[3] In most of the cases in which details have

[1] A recent medical observer, himself a sufferer from angina, whose case will be referred to again in the section on treatment, has contributed what is perhaps the only really exact description in medical literature of one form of the constrictive sensation: "The front of the chest seemed to be bulged out in a convex prominence, which suddenly terminated at the lower end of the sternum in a sharp and deep depression towards the spine. This was a purely subjective phenomenon. There was no contraction of the diaphragm, and no retraction of the abdominal walls. But though the hand laid upon the parts convinced my mind of their normal condition, it in no way modified the sensation." (Dr. W. Herries Madden, in the *Practitioner*, vol. ix. 1872, p. 334.) In the case of John Hunter, to be cited below (a case full of instruction in detail as to many phases of disease included in the present article), the sense of thoracic constriction in one attack was preceded for a fortnight by symptoms of "nervous irritation" in the left side of the face and head, as well as down the left arm. The special sensation in the chest in this case was a "feeling of the sternum being drawn backwards towards the spine, as well as of oppression in breathing; *although the action of breathing was attended with no real difficulty.*" (See *infra*, p. 563.) The special character of the breathing in Hunter's case, elsewhere alluded to, will be found to be a most exact anticipation of what has since been called "ascending and descending," or by some, "suspirious" repiration; a form of disturbance frequent in cases of angina, though it seems to have escaped Heberden's observation. See also the remarks on the case of Seneca, below: and at page 563, *note*.

[2] Dr. Latham has admirably *modernised* Heberden's arguments on this point. (Op. cit. vol. ii. p. 383.)

[3] "The pulse is, *at least sometimes*, not disturbed by this pain." (Heberden, *Med. Trans.*) "Arteriæ eorum, qui in hoc dolore sunt, naturaliter prorsus moventur. . . . In ipsa accessione pulsus non concitatur." (*Comment.* loc. cit.) Several authors have followed Heberden here without observing that his real meaning is not that there is no alteration of the pulse, but that there is no excitement of it, *i.e.* that the pulse is not *quickened* ("non concitatur") as in inflammation. Dr. Parry, regarding the disease as a *syncope*, speaks from another point of view, and has no difficulty in showing that the pulse, though not always greatly disturbed, "becomes more or less feeble according to the violence of the paroxysm." Such personal experience as I have on the point leads me to

been carefully given, the pulse, at the height of the seizure, has been found small, often imperceptible or irregular in rhythm, but not necessarily accelerated, and sometimes morbidly slow; the countenance has been pale as death, the features pinched and anxious, the extremities cold; there has been often a cold sweat on the brow, sighing or interrupted respiration, and other signs of approaching syncope. On the other hand, it must be admitted that in a few instances the heart has been heard beating in the very midst of a paroxysm without appreciable alteration in the character of the sounds and impulse, and the pulse has been also said to be regular, and neither rapid nor weak. The senses and the consciousness have also been observed to be frequently quite entire in the midst of the paroxysm, though this fact also, like some of the others above mentioned, must be held as subject to numerous exceptions. On the whole, the strict analogy between the phenomena of angina pectoris and ordinary syncope cannot be unreservedly maintained, notwithstanding the arguments of Dr. Parry,[1] who, however, has undoubtedly marshalled a strong array of facts and reasonings in favour of this view of the case. The paroxysm of angina pectoris remains, after all, a mode of morbid function *sui generis*, although in some instances the manner of death in the paroxysm is more or less allied to syncope.

The condition of the nervous system, and especially of the brain and spinal cord, in angina pectoris, opens up many very difficult, and at present even insoluble problems connected with its ultimate pathology. For practical purposes it is sufficient to state the facts established by clinical observation. While it is quite certain, as stated above, that integrity (in a practical sense) of the nervous functions may be maintained up to the very instant of death in certain cases of angina, it is equally well ascertained that in other instances giddiness, vertigo, disorders of the special senses, spasms, tonic and clonic, and almost every kind of disorder of the general sensibility and consciousness, may occur, and may also be the distinguishing features of particular paroxysms in persons in whom at other times paroxysms may occur devoid of all such phenomena. It is probable that in some of these forms of the disease the cerebro-spinal complications may be determined by special derangements of the circulation within the

agree with Dr. Parry. The recent experiments and sphygmographic tracings of Dr. Lauder Brunton will be discussed in connection with the pathology of the disease further on.

[1] His expressions are as follows :—"From the preceding observations, I think it evidently appears that the Angina Pectoris is a mere case of syncope or fainting, differing from the common syncope only in being preceded by an unusual degree of anxiety, or pain in the region of the heart, and in being readily excited during a state of apparent health, by any general exertion of the muscles, more especially that of walking." (Inquiry into the Symptoms and Causes of the Syncope Anginosa, commonly called Angina Pectoris, &c. p. 67). To the points of difference here noted must be added the persistence of the sensibility up to the very instant of death in many cases of angina pectoris, and the incomplete extinction of the pulse; while in ordinary syncope (as for example from emotion, or from hot rooms) the most absolute temporary insensibility, with a radial pulse which cannot be felt, and respiration just sufficient to maintain life, may occur as symptoms and be maintained for some minutes, with almost no danger to life.

cranium, or even by disease of the arterial system extending to the brain; but there are very rarely any permanent changes, either of structure or of function, tending to throw light on these attacks. On the other hand, it seems premature to infer, with Trousseau, the existence of any distinct relation between epilepsy as a predisposing cause, and angina pectoris; still more premature to affirm that "in certain cases, and perhaps in a considerable number, the *angor pectoris* is one expression of this formidable and cruel disease, a phase of its vertiginous form, or in two words an *epileptiform neuralgia*."[1] The extreme rarity, on the one hand of true angina pectoris among the countless multitudes of confirmed epileptics, on the other of genuine and well-formed epileptic attacks among the subjects of angina pectoris, seems to oppose a considerable difficulty in the way of accepting M. Trousseau's hypothesis. That the relation, however, between the occasional cerebro-spinal symptoms in these cases, and the cardiac disorder, is more than a coincidence, is shown by the fact that a very similar series of symptoms is observed in some cases of fatty heart; and the author of this article has in more than one instance observed like phenomena in connexion with large aneurisms within the thorax.

In certain cases of angina pectoris, more especially when perfect rest cannot be obtained during the attacks, they are apt to be attended by more or less of sickness, and even of vomiting; but these symptoms are rarely obstinate. Flatulence has been already noticed as a frequent accompaniment of the paroxysm, the discharge of the imprisoned air by the mouth usually giving marked relief. In some instances the close of the paroxysm is accompanied or followed by a copious discharge of watery urine, as in hysteria. In one case Dr. Walshe has observed tetanic spasms, with complete opisthotonos, followed by local tonic spasms continuing for some hours after the paroxysm.

The *diagnosis* of angina pectoris is not very difficult in severe cases, except in so far as difficulties may arise from the inability of the patient to express his sufferings in words, or on the other hand from the too fluent and misleading descriptions of comparatively insignificant pains referred to the heart, by persons either unduly frightened or unduly sensitive. Persons who have lost near relatives or even intimate friends, by sudden death of cardiac origin, are extremely apt to be terrified by nervous symptoms of this kind; gouty and rheumatic sufferers are frequently a prey to flying pains which now and then occupy the habitual seats of angina pectoris, and which sometimes give rise to alarms not justified by the event, all the more when suspicion has been once aroused, and when, as happens not unfrequently, the physician as well as the patient may be for some time in doubt as to the cause of the symptoms. Disorders

[1] Clinique Méd. de l'Hôtel-Dieu, t. ii, p. 444. Paris, 1865; and in the English translation, vol. i. p. 692.

of the stomach, and still more notably of the uterus, frequently
lead to pains in the left side, which may pass for cardiac angina.
Intercostal neuralgia may have many causes, and not unfrequently
radiates towards the left arm. In hysterical and romantic girls, pains
about the heart are often associated with palpitation and irregular
sighing respiration, sometimes also with well-marked irregularities of
cardiac rhythm, or with murmurs requiring care in their discrimination, though not, on the whole, very apt to lead into serious error.
Each of these cases requires its own special diagnosis, with reference
to the cause of the symptoms ; and it should always be remembered
that the number of persons presenting themselves on account of such
symptoms immensely exceeds that of the sufferers from genuine and
dangerous angina pectoris. Moreover, the urgency of the symptoms
is usually far less in these affections than in the true angina. The
pains, in the milder disorders, are usually much less defined in
character, and are never, or hardly ever, accompanied by so grave a
sense of impending dissolution. The diagnosis requires tact and
judgment rather than any elaborate rules of investigation, to save
the physician from error.

A much more difficult diagnosis, and one in which in many cases it
is impossible to arrive at more than a proximate conclusion, is the
determination of *how far* any organic disease, and *what kind* of
organic disease, may have had to do with the symptoms present in any
particular instance of angina pectoris. Clinically speaking, it may
be said that, as a question of pure experience in the living patient, the
formidable prognosis of true angina is not necessarily relieved by the
knowledge that after careful examination no organic disease can be
discovered; for, in the first place, organic disease may exist without the possibility of discovery ; and, secondly, they are precisely the
forms of organic disease most difficult of discovery that have been
shown to be most frequently associated with death from angina
pectoris. Given, therefore, a very perfectly characterised instance of
angina in repeated paroxysms *nearly* fatal, and tending to increase in
severity, it cannot be said that the special diagnosis of organic
associated lesions has any very immediate practical significance.
The prognosis in such cases is emphatically grave in the highest
degree, and remains so even after the most careful examination of the
organs of circulation has given only a negative result. In cases of
minor urgency, however, and in cases where the diagnosis of the
angina paroxysm is not perfectly clear and well defined, or where one
or two such paroxysms only have occurred at long intervals, it
becomes a very important question for the physician, and still more
for the patient, whether or not there is any organic lesion of the chest
forming a barrier to ultimate recovery, and in case any such lesion
exists, whether it is of a kind likely to be rapidly and inevitably
fatal, or the contrary. These considerations give an importance to the
details of diagnosis in angina pectoris which at first sight they might
not seem to possess, as bearing on prognosis and treatment.

Dr. Latham has very truly said that in this respect at least the paroxysm of angina bears a certain resemblance to the paroxysm of epilepsy. In the attack itself we are obliged to act by routine, and are unable to discriminate. It is in the intervals that the physician tries to advance beyond the mere name that has guided him in dealing with the most urgent symptoms, and by careful examination of every organ and every function to discover how the whole organisation can be most effectually strengthened against the enemy that is at the gates—nay, that is threatening the very stronghold of life itself. Such a complete investigation, and no other, constitutes *diagnosis.*

It needs scarcely be said that in the first instance the attention of the physician must be concentrated upon the heart, arteries, and great veins. He will inquire with the utmost care into the whole details connected with the circulation, both during the paroxysm and during the intervals. He will carefully look for evidences of hypertrophy, dilatation, valvular disease. But above all, and even in the absence of these, he will endeavour to estimate the probabilities of structural disease in the fibre of the heart itself, or of disease in the coats of the arteries leading, it may be, to induration and obstruction. or to aneurism.

Dr. Jenner, the discoverer of vaccination, was the first to make a decided advance in the pathology of angina pectoris. He did not himself publish anything on the subject, but communicated his information to Dr. Parry,[1] by whom his views were substantially adopted and brought before the public. A very remarkable series of facts appeared to these observers to show conclusively that angina pectoris was dependent in many, if not in most cases, on "ossification," or some other form of obstruction by disease, of the coronary arteries of the heart. Subsequent researches have proved that this view cannot be exclusively maintained, although according to Lussana[2] this condition has been found present in twenty-one out of thirty-six fatal cases. The statistics adduced by Sir John Forbes[3] show that in twenty-four out of forty-five cases examined after death there were found diseases and degenerations of the aorta; in sixteen cases the coronary arteries were diseased, and in a like number the valves of the heart; while in ten cases there was positive disease, and in twelve cases preternatural softness, of the heart itself. Many authors, from Morgagni downwards, have recorded cases of thoracic aneurism having in a more or less perfectly developed form the characteristic symptoms of angina pectoris; and we have already alluded to M. Trousseau as confirming by his large and carefully-watched experience the view that such cases may very closely resemble, and may, in fact, for a lengthened period, and after careful observation, be undistinguishable from what he regards as the truly idiopathic

[1] Op. cit. p. 8.

[2] Gazzetta Med. Lombard. 1858-9 (ref. by Friedreich in Virchow's Handbuch, vol. ii. p. 422).

[3] Cyclop. of Pract. Med. ; art. Angina Pectoris.

forms of angina. The author of this article is able from personal experience to say that no organic disease has appeared to him more frequently to assume the symptomatic characters of angina than aneurism; and he is also prepared to state as the general result of inquiries pursued over many years, and particularly directed to this subject, that even small aneurisms, arising very near the heart, and especially such as project into the pericardium, or compress in any degree the base of the heart itself, are much more apt to give rise to angina-like symptoms than much larger tumours in more remote positions. The attention of the physician in cases of supposed angina pectoris should therefore always be very minutely directed to the state of the arterial system as a whole, and more especially to any evidences that may exist of irregularities in the sounds or impulse of the arteries near the heart, or of the aorta in its ascending portion. The careful examination by percussion of the substernal region, and especially of the upper sternum; the comparison of the sounds of the heart with the arterial sounds, as heard at different points of this region; the detection of even slight traces of abnormal impulse, or of evidences of arterial obstruction at the root of the neck; the comparison of the radial pulses, and the thorough investigation even of remote parts of the arterial system, may lead to inferences favourable, or the contrary, to the idea of an organic cause for the symptoms of angina pectoris.

Not less important, could it be obtained with reasonable precision, would be the evidence, in any case of angina, of a permanently weakened or disorganised state of the muscular fibre in the heart itself. We have seen that in twelve of the forty-five dissections collected by Sir John Forbes, there was found preternatural softness, and in ten positive disease of the heart, apart from valvular lesions. That many of these must have been cases of fatty degeneration of the ultimate texture of the organ is rendered extremely probable, if not absolutely certain, by the results of later inquiries,[1] which show that in a large proportion of cases of sudden death such changes in the tissue of the heart have been revealed by the microscope. On the other hand, it must be admitted that fatty heart has been often observed to be present to a very great degree when no symptoms at all resembling angina pectoris have been recorded during life, and when death, too, has not been sudden, but has occurred in the course of ordinary and sometimes of acute disease, having no apparent connexion with the state of the heart. This subject will come under consideration hereafter, but in the meantime it may be stated in general terms that while a degenerated state of the cardiac muscular fibre is with great probability to be inferred in angina pectoris, there are few positive criteria which can be applied so as to ascertain the fact of the degeneration, much less its pathological character, or the

---

[1] Dr. Quain has stated the argument with reference to the older observations of soft flabby heart, with great force and conciseness in his paper on "Fatty Diseases of the Heart;" Medico. Chir. Trans. vol. xxxiii. p. 129.

extent of fibre involved in any particular case. Only after careful and repeated examination of the heart under various conditions of activity and comparative repose, will a careful physician venture an opinion as to the soundness of the organ in this respect, and even then it will be prudent to express his opinion with some degree of reserve. The practical inferences, moreover, which can be safely founded on such an opinion, either in relation to prognosis or treatment, are far from being clearly established.

Having as far as possible investigated the condition of the heart and arteries, it will be the duty of the physician to complete his diagnosis by a survey of the condition of the other organs and functions. Although in many of the most extreme cases of angina pectoris the lungs seem to be perfectly healthy, yet a certain amount of pulmonary congestion or obstruction may attend the disease in particular cases, especially in those complicated with dilatation of the heart, or with valvular disease. Such cases usually present more or less alteration of the complexion in the direction of lividity, and are also attended by cough, or by true dyspnœa. And it must not always be concluded that the effect of a pulmonary or bronchial complication is to give a more dangerous or hopeless character to the symptoms of angina. On the contrary, the pulmonary disease being frequently of a manageable kind, the application of the proper treatment will sometimes extricate the patient from a state of the greatest apparent danger, and allow of the return of the heart to a state either apparently normal, or nearly so. The author has a most vivid recollection of one case in particular, where, on numerous occasions during five or six years, he had to attend a patient manifestly suffering under complex diseases of the heart and lungs, with distinct paroxysms of angina, and physical signs of dilatation of the heart. In the worst attacks there was always a nearly or absolutely complete disappearance of the pulse at the wrist; the complexion was livid, and the expectoration was of the character usual in hæmorrhagic condensation of the lungs, which was also indicated by dull percussion at both bases; yet from this formidable state the patient again and again rallied under careful treatment of the pulmonary disease, and although the state was evidently one of hopeless character as regards the ultimate termination, he was able in the intervals to pursue a rather laborious occupation. In other instances, the symptoms of angina pectoris are associated with enlargement or disease of the liver, and it is not easy to say whether the hepatic disorder is of primary or of secondary origin; but here also the cautious use of remedies is often very effective in removing the obstruction to the portal circulation, and thereby in restoring the heart to a comparatively sound condition, in which the threatening symptoms of angina may disappear.[1] Renal disease forms

---

[1] It occasionally happens that the very intense and sickening pain of biliary calculus presents a degree of resemblance to angina in its accessories; and the author has even observed cases in which the diagnosis remained doubtful until the yellow tinge of the conjunctiva, appearing after an interval of hours, relieved the apprehensions of the

a very serious and often unmanageable complication, attended by most distressing sickness, or by violent dyspnœa or orthopnœa, and requiring great caution in the use of internal remedies, but perhaps not altogether beyond the scope of treatment. Dyspeptic complications are usually of secondary importance, and cannot be said to be characteristic. They are most frequently associated with gouty angina.

Among constitutional states, gout is unquestionably the one which is most frequently related to angina pectoris; indeed, it would scarcely be too much to say that a large proportion of the suddenly fatal endings of gout in its irregular and atonic forms, more especially in the forms popularly termed "gout in the stomach," or "gout in the heart," are of this character.[1] No doubt the pathology of the states indicated by these terms is very uncertain, and the terms themselves vague and unsatisfactory to the last degree; but enough remains after every deduction to show—1. That gouty persons, and especially those who have had regular gout, degenerating after repeated attacks into the irregular and atonic forms, are subject, in an unusual degree, to the causes of sudden death; 2. That not only is death in such persons apt to be extremely sudden, but, further, the course of the disease is apt to be disturbed by violent paroxysms of internal pain; 3. That in certain cases the pain has distinctively the character of angina, while in other instances it seems to be associated with dyspeptic suffering, and with disorders of the liver and kidneys—the latter, at least, distinctly represented by a special form of disorganisation which can be discovered and recognised after death; 4. That in gouty subjects the heart and arteries are very prone to become disorganised, and that the disorganisation is specially apt to assume the form which other observations show to give a predisposition to angina, viz., calcareous degeneration of the aorta, especially of its commencement, and of the coronary arteries; 5. That cerebral disorders of various kinds in the gouty have often a like origin in disease of the arteries of the brain. From these various observations, which will be found amply supported by the experience of physicians, and illustrated in the treatises of best authority upon gout, it may be inferred that the so-called metastasis of gout to the heart is the result of gradual degenerative changes operating more or less throughout the organism, which, if not so distinctly related as has sometimes been supposed to the gouty paroxysm in its ordinary form, are at all events closely associated with the causes of gout, and therefore form part of its history as a disease of the constitution. So much may be fairly asserted here, without involving us in this article in a discussion of the complicated

physician. The remarks in the text, of course, apply not to this condition of pseudo-angina, but to the combination of true angina with hepatic congestion. But the admission of the existence of such a combination is not to be taken as a confirmation of the view of Brera, and of the elder Latham, that angina pectoris may be simply a disorder of the liver and nothing more.

[1] On this subject see Dr. Brinton's thoughtful dissertation on "Gout in the Stomach," in the second edition of his work on Diseases of the Stomach, p. 354, 1864.

questions of pathology and diagnosis, as well as of treatment, which arise out of the general question of gouty metastasis.

As regards other constitutional states associated with, or tending to produce, angina pectoris, nothing is known of sufficient importance to find place here. But the careful physician will always endeavour in each case to discover all the causes of deranged general health which may be interfering with the normal state of the functions; and thus, with each new observation thoroughly and scientifically recorded, the diagnosis of the disease, and with this many questions bearing on its pathology and treatment, will probably be rescued from the obscurity that at present surrounds the whole subject.

What has to be said here about the *causes* of angina has been to a considerable extent anticipated in the preceding sketch of the diagnosis. All the associated diseases may be regarded as causes or on the other hand, and sometimes with greater probable truth, as conjoined effects of one or more common causes. Thus, to take the last-mentioned instance, gout may be more or less directly a cause of the angina paroxysm; or gout and angina pectoris, each of them separately considered in relation to previously existing states of the constitution, may have grown out of like proclivities in respect of age, sex, inheritance, habits of life, &c. In following out this obscure subject, there is great danger of running into over-refinements, which may mislead, and at all events may not be supported by sound practical observation. A few facts, however, remain to be stated as to the predisposing causes.

In his classification of cases according to age, Sir John Forbes found that only one-seventh of the cases recorded (12 out of 84) were below the fiftieth year of age; and in respect of sex, only one-eleventh (8 out of 88) were in women. It is just possible, indeed, that these apparent facts may be greatly biased by the mode of collection of the instances.[1] In a disease the symptoms of which are so purely subjective, the deaths of men of eminence, or men of a certain force and decision of character, leading to clear and precise statements as to their symptoms and morbid history, will culminate, as it were, in the minds of physicians, and will be recorded prominently when others would pass unobserved, or at least unrecorded; and in this point of view it is worth while to remark that the Registrar-General's returns, bearing on sudden death, do not show anything approaching to this remarkable disparity

---

[1] Sir John Forbes, in giving the numbers in the text, expressly states that it is necessary to "make some allowance for circumstances connected with these recorded cases, before they can be received as grounds for fixing the statistics of the disease, taken without reference to its degree of severity." His idea is that the "more severe cases, particularly such as depend on organic disease of the heart and great vessels," occur chiefly in males; the milder in females. "The very severe cases naturally attract more attention, more particularly if they have been terminated by a sudden death, and followed by a dissection; and these are the cases that are usually recorded and published." Art. Angina Pectoris, Cyclop. of Medicine. vol. i. p. 88.)

of males and females, nor even the marked if not exclusive proclivity of the advanced ages to this form of death. On the other hand, the Registrar's returns no doubt include under the term " sudden death " a great mass of utterly heterogeneous cases, some of which have no natural alliance with the disease now under consideration; and the convictions of individual physicians of large experience tend more or less in the direction of Sir John Forbes's averages.[1] Another fact, of importance if correct, and so far corroborated by Dr. Walshe, is to be found in certain tables by Sir Gilbert Blane,[2] showing the rarity of Angina Pectoris in hospital practice. Both in hospital and private practice, however, perfectly typical instances of the angina of Heberden are rather rare; and Sir G. Blane's figures, supported as they seem to be by an appeal to so large a number of miscellaneous cases (3,835 hospital, 3,813 private), probably mean only that Sir G. Blane was too busy to know much about the internal sensations of his hospital patients, and knew only a little about a very few of his more distinguished private patients. Medical statistics are altogether perverted from their legitimate use when statements of this kind are put forward without qualification, as if numerically exact. It is certain that conditions at least closely allied to angina pectoris are not very rare in hospital practice, and the author of this article has seen enough even of typical instances in hospitals to neutralise the force of Sir G. Blane's remark. Still, it may be conceded as at least probable, that in the higher ranks of society cases of extremely sudden death, associated with the symptoms described by Heberden, and not of aneurismal origin, or connected with valvular disease of the heart, bear numerically a higher proportion to the whole field of disease than among the classes usually treated in hospital. The subject, however, is one still open to investigation, and one on which a really adequate contribution of carefully and impartially observed facts would be of great advantage to science. The facts above recorded, so far as they may be trusted in leading towards a conclusion, tend to support the theory of the gouty origin of true angina pectoris. It cannot fail to be remarked that the disease seems to be dominated by the same proclivities of age, sex, and condition in life as gout. And there is further a very general impression among physicians and among the public, not supported by exact statistical evidence, but not on that account to be disregarded, that sudden death from heart disease is frequently hereditary, or at least is found to cling as a tolerably well-marked characteristic to certain families, sometimes for several generations. On the other hand, it should be stated, in qualification of this impression, that there are numerous instances of eminently gouty families in which no such tendency has been observed.

---

[1] Among authorities of the first class, Trousseau is almost singular in disputing this position. "I do not think it proved," he says, "that males are more subject than females to this singular affection." Op. cit., Eng. Transl. p. 603.

[2] Med. Chir. Trans. iv. 133.

The general result of the inquiry into predisposing causes has been stated by Sir John Forbes in terms which may well receive the assent of physicians, at least as a provisional conclusion, till further and more exact analysis of the facts becomes possible. "Like many other diseases," he writes, " angina is the attendant rather of ease and luxury than of temperance; on which account, though occurring among the poor, it is more frequently met with among the rich, or in persons of easy circumstances."[1] To this it must be added, that the influence of sedentary occupations is remarkably apparent in Dr. Quain's collection of cases of fatty heart, in many of which the death was sudden, and with symptoms more or less allied to angina. Thus, in twenty-four of the cases in Dr. Quain's memoir,[2] in which the habits of life were noted, they were found to be "sedentary" in twenty-two, "active" only in two cases; and in several cases the sedentary habits were obviously determined by injuries which had restricted the power of exercise, or by accumulations of external fat amounting to excessive corpulency. In some cases also, the disease itself has produced an aggravation of the tendency, by still further limiting the capacity for physical exertion, and thus allowing of fatty accumulation. Thus, in the well-known case of John Hunter, who certainly was not chargeable with any original sins of laziness, and who died of angina, it is recorded that after the tendency had been clearly declared, "the want of exercise made him grow unusually fat."

Thus far we have treated of Angina Pectoris as a distinct morbid form or group of phenomena, in which disorders of the circulation tending to sudden death are associated with local pain and other symptoms in the chest of a more or less definable character. But it must be added that many cases of sudden death, in which there is reason to attribute the ultimate result to disease of the heart, have occurred apparently without pain, sometimes without any, even the slightest, previous evidence of cardiac uneasiness, and certainly without any of the more characteristic and special symptoms of angina pectoris. It remains to consider these cases before proceeding to discuss the pathology of the whole subject.

Dr. Latham has justly remarked, in reference to the present subject, that "cases of sudden death often present themselves as mere fragments to our observation. Individuals are found dead. The mode of their dissolution and the circumstances preceding it are unknown." It can only be inferred remotely, as it were, and that only in some instances, from some casual and often very imperfect observation, that in these individuals the symptoms might possibly have been shown, had they been fully ascertained, to "hold a pathological kindred" with angina pectoris.

[1] Loc. cit., vol. i. p. 83.
[2] Med. Chir. Trans., vol. xxxiii. p. 194.

But again: cases not infrequently occur in which the symptoms observed during life resemble angina pectoris, but where certain of the characters attributed to that disease are either entirely wanting or imperfectly developed. It may be the pain that is wanting to the completion of the picture; it may be the sense of impending death, or it may be that sudden death does not actually occur, although most of the other symptoms of angina are present. Can we, with any degree of security, bring out of these nosological "fragments" such new combinations as may tend still further to throw light on the pathology of angina?

In this difficult inquiry, in which we are reduced to the study of " broken lights" and "fragments" of truth, we feel more strongly than ever the inadequacy of language, as between man and man, in treating of the mysteries of life. We are engaged upon what ought to be a strictly inductive clinical investigation; but the very elements of the induction are in great part withheld. Many patients, when threatened with death, refuse to speak about it, and remain, up to the very last, silent as to what is passing within. Many other patients throw out hints and indications, but are either unable or unwilling to enter into a detailed analysis of their sensations. A few describe their sensations with great minuteness, but in terms which are almost sure to mislead.

From these various causes it happens that sudden death may appear to occur absolutely without previous warning, or with very imperfect previous warning, and yet there may have been in reality a very decidedly abnormal state, fully present to the consciousness of the patient, but not *spoken out* by him; either because the symptoms were *unspeakable*, or because from one cause or other he was indisposed to speak. On the other hand, sudden death may not occur, and yet a patient may have lived days, or months, or even years, in the apprehension of sudden death, being warned by such internal sensations as have been described in reference to the paroxysm of angina. When, indeed, *pain* is the culminating symptom, the patient rarely omits, or refuses to speak out; he is then sufficiently explicit as regards the pain, but in many cases he leaves the other and less definable sensations to be inferred. But where pain is not the culminating symptom, we are often reduced to inference altogether; and it is only in the case of persons whose outward lives and inner thoughts are much before the public, that an inferential diagnosis can be arrived at. Two cases of this kind, occurring in different ages of the world, and under very different circumstances, appear to afford in some degree the means of access to some of the information we are in quest of. One of these is the case of the Roman philosopher Seneca; the other that of the Christian divine Dr. Chalmers. The former case has been often referred to (though with some hesitation, the source of which will be immediately apparent) as one of angina pectoris; the latter has been recorded expressly as a case of sudden death from fatty heart.

The case of the philosopher Seneca was as follows :—

In early life he was apparently of delicate constitution. It is
recorded of him by Dio, that but for the apparent probability of his
early death spontaneously, Caligula would have had him destroyed.
The supposed disease at this time was a *tabes*. He himself records
that he was nursed with difficulty through a long illness by his aunt
(*Consolatio ad Helviam*, 16). He further speaks in one of his epistles
of having been extremely subject to catarrhal fluxes (destillationes), and
in another he says that almost every form of bodily disturbance had
affected him at one time or other.[1] It seems, therefore, extremely
probable that Seneca was one of those martyrs to tubercular disease
in early life, who, after a more or less protracted period of ill-health
became somewhat more robust in constitution towards the middle
term of life. He was, however, to the last more or less delicate, and
at the time of his violent death at the instigation of Nero, he is said
by Tacitus to have been "emaciated in body from scanty nourishment."[2] The peculiar symptoms, however, which have specially
attracted the attention of writers as indicating angina pectoris, seem
to have been confined to the last two years of his life, according to the
opinion of Lipsius, who considers the epistles to Lucilius as having
been written when he was sixty-one or sixty-two years of age. What
gives a peculiar interest to the description, and at the same time may
possibly make necessary a qualification of some of its expressions, is
the somewhat affected and pretentious tone in which in these letters
Seneca, a disciple of the Stoic philosophy, congratulates himself on
the ease and freedom with which he could look death in the face, and
maintain under severe illness, and in the prospect of sudden death,
the calm, self-possessed, and cheerful spirit of the sage. His philosophy, under these circumstances, has in its details no important
relation to the present inquiry; but the fact that his mental condition
was such as is here described is important.

After a long truce from suffering, he says,[3] his bad health has
returned upon him suddenly. He is as if given over to one disease,
as regards which he adds: "I know not why I should give it a Greek
name, for it may fitly enough be called *Suspirium*—a sighing, or want
of breath." The attack is very brief and like a hurricane—it is over
almost within an hour. As compared with any other disease it is like
the difference between *being sick* merely, and *giving up the ghost*—so
that the physicians themselves call this disease *meditatio mortis;* and
sometimes death, which is always threatening in it, actually occurs.
Knowing these things Seneca adds that he is by no means confident
of recovery, even when relieved from severe symptoms. He considers only that he has got a respite; he is perfectly prepared for

[1] *Omnia corporis aut incommoda aut pericula per me transierunt.* Epist. ad. Lucilium,
54.
[2] The scanty nourishment here spoken of was not starvation, but probably deficient
power of assimilation; for Seneca, as is well known, was enormously rich, and there is
no reason whatever to suppose that his stoicism ever took the form of asceticism, or of
voluntary fasting such as to injure bodily health.
[3] Epist. ad Lucilium, 54.

death; he does not at any time count even upon seeing out the day. He is, however, buoyant and cheerful, entertains himself with gladsome and strong thoughts, even in the midst of the stifling (*in ipsa suffocatione*). Death is, after all, not to be dreaded by the wise man; death may take him unawares, but he is nevertheless always ready to go. Even at the best, he adds, reverting to his own precarious condition, his state is not one of entire comfort; the breathing[1] is not quite natural; he feels always a degree of impediment (*hæsitationem quandam ejus et moram*). " Be that as it may be," he adds, " provided my sighing is not in sad earnest " (*dummodo nisi ex animo suspirem*). He holds himself as in the condition of one likely to be soon ejected, but yet not to be *ejected*, inasmuch as he is willing to go. ' *Nihil invitus facit sapiens; necessitatem effugit quia vult quod ipsa coactura est.*'[2]

In this case of Seneca we have, in a highly developed form, the sense of impending death, associated wth something which he himself calls a " suffocation," occurring in paroxysms, and causing daily and hourly uncertainty as to his tenure of life. But we have not the severe and peculiar pain of the angina of Heberden, nor have we the actual fact of sudden death, at least in the usual sense of the word; for, as is well known, Seneca was put to death by Nero, or rather was invited to put himself to death; and what we are able to gather from contemporary history as to his last moments would lead us to infer that death came by no means easily, but after a rather long and tedious struggle. Much doubt has been expressed accordingly, since this narrative was suggested to Dr. Parry by "a learned physician" as a case of angina pectoris, whether the symptoms will bear that construction. Dr. Parry himself inclines to consider it " rather a disorder of respiration than angina pectoris."[3] Sir John Forbes, on the other hand, says that "the case of Seneca, as described by himself, has been generally considered a case of angina, and we think most justly."[4] It

---

[1] " Non ex naturâ fluit spiritus." The double sense of *spiritus* in Latin, as of the Greek πνεῦμα, must be kept in view in interpreting this expression.
[2] Loc. cit. Compare also Epist. 61.
[3] Op. cit. p. 36.
[4] Loc. cit. p. 81. The opinion of Dr. Stokes, published in 1854, and founded mainly on the character of the respiration as implied in the word "suspirium," (which, as we shall hereafter see, he had himself occasion to describe as characteristic of fatty degeneration of the heart) is too important for its details to be omitted here. We therefore give it entire, as it occurs in " The Diseases of the Heart and Aorta," p. 530. " We must agree with Dr. Parry in the opinion that the symptoms here detailed are not those of angina pectoris. It is remarkable that the occurrence of pain is not alluded to. But their similarity to that abnormal respiration, already described as the attendant on the fatty heart, is too obvious to be overlooked. For in this affection we see that special form of dyspnœa which may be described as a paroxysm of sighing. Seneca's words, ' Satis enim apte dici suspirium potest,' and again ' Brevis autem valde, et procellæ similis, impetus est,' are singularly expressive of a severe case of the cardiac sighing observed in persons labouring under fatty heart, for which, when the highest point of suspirious breathing has been reached, we can have no better comparison than that of a storm. And the words ' Deinde paullatim suspirium illud quod esse jam anhelitus cœperat, intervalla majora fecit et retardatum est et remansit,' well expresses the gradual ascent from what we may term the apnœal period to the extreme point of the paroxysm, and its subsequent decline." It is important to observe, that Dr. Stokes, in the chapter on Deranged Action of the Heart, expresses himself as follows with regard to angina pectoris in general :—" The respiratory

is evident that materials fail us in attempting to decide the question; and they fail precisely at the very point where materials always must fail, unless the fact of actual death, and of sudden death with symptoms and signs referrible to the heart, comes in to decide the point in favour of angina. True, the absence of recorded pain on the one hand, and the presence of something like a record of dyspnœa on the other, have been regarded as additional circumstances in favour of the view that Seneca's disease was spasmodic asthma. But in spasmodic asthma, however severe, there is rarely that vividly present sense of impending death so much dwelt upon by Seneca. Moreover, the noisy paroxysms of asthma would probably have provoked some more distinct allusion to the wheezing as a feature of the attack. Having regard to the idiom of the Latin language, indeed, the question as between some form of cardiac suffering and asthmatic dyspnœa must remain doubtful; but while the allusions to the breathing are of a very indefinite character, it must be remarked that the sense of impending death is the one obvious fact in the description.[1]

Turning now to the case of Dr. Chalmers, we find in almost every point the converse of that of Seneca. We have here the awful fact of sudden death in all its solemnity and mystery—not only without any adequate clinical history of chronic disease, but without any evidence of angina, or any other form of acute attack preceding the fatal event. And what adds to the mysteriousness of the result is, that the death took place, not amid any exciting crisis of passion, or of physical exertion, but in the darkness and stillness of the night, when body and mind alike had been undisturbed for hours. One indeed, who knew him,[2] has said of his conversation and manner the evening before his death:—"I had seen him frequently in his most happy moods, but I never saw him happier." But this is not all. The narrative of Dr. Chalmers's death, and of the last weeks of his life, has reached us from two particularly well-informed sources. Dr. Hanna, who was his son-in-law and perhaps his most intimate friend,

---

phenomenon which belongs to angina is some form of the sighing respiration so important a symptom in the fatty or weakened heart. . . . Upon the whole we may conclude that the special group of symptoms described as angina pectoris by Heberden, Parry, Percival, and Latham, is but the occurrence, in a defined manner, of some of the symptoms connected with a weakened heart." *Op. cit.*, p. 487. These remarks of one of the greatest masters of modern medical observation will be found to have a very special importance in connection with what we have ventured to call, in a subsequent paragraph, *Angina sine Dolore.*

[1] Seneca particularly notes that the physicians called his disease *meditatio mortis;* a very unlikely and unusual form of medical expression for a disease so well-known as ordinary spasmodic asthma. On the other hand it must be admitted that *suspirium* was sometimes used as synonymous with asthma. Compare Cael. Aurel. Morb. Chronic. L. iii. 1; and Plin. Nat. Hist. xxiii. 7, 63, § 121. Celsus makes use of *difficultas spirandi*, and *spiritus difficultas*, but not of *suspirium.* The noise of the breathing is specially noticed by Celsus—"spirare aeger sine sono et anhelatione non possit" (L. iv. 8); and also by Cael. Aurel. "stridor, atque sibilatio pectoris." Loc. cit.

[2] The Rev. Mr. Gemmel who was living in his house at the time. See Hanna's Life of Chalmers, edition of 1854, vol. ii. p. 775.

has given us the facts as known to his domestic circle. Dr. Begbie, who was his medical attendant, has recorded them with special reference to the observation, made after death, that the heart was in an advanced state of fatty degeneration, soft and friable, the muscular fasciculi barely traceable, without visible striae, and everywhere containing fatty granules; the ventricles unusually thin, the "coronary artery loaded with calcareous deposit, much contracted, and in one place obliterated, presenting considerable resistance to the knife."[1] It is in the presence of these pathological data (given on the authority of Dr. Bennett) that we have to explain, if we can, the known facts of Dr. Chalmers's later life, and of its sudden and mysterious close. And the peculiar interest and value of the case in relation to our present inquiry consists in the following statements, which are carefully condensed from the two narratives above referred to.

Dr. Chalmers was a man not only of great genius and devotion; but of the most incessant and absorbing occupations. During a life extending nearly to the term of "threescore years and ten," he was scarcely ever withdrawn from public observation. He was eminently, in the highest and best sense, ἄναξ ἀνδρῶν—a leader and ruler of men; the "care of all the churches" was upon him, as on St. Paul, and the earnest and ceaseless labours of a life devoted to noble ends, were continued up to the very day before his death, in 1847, in his sixty-eighth year. In 1834, it is true, on the 23rd of January, he had suffered a rather alarming attack of hemiplegia, from which, however, he soon recovered; and in June of the same year there was again a threatening; but with these exceptions his health appeared to have been always good, and equal to every ordinary exertion whether of mind or body. "He was hardly ever incapacitated by infirmity or loss of health, from prosecuting his enterprise; and from early manhood to green old age, even up to his latest hour, he toiled, and spent his energies and strength." Probably no man in Scotland in the present century, with the doubtful exception of Sir Walter Scott, had led a life of such persistent literary activity, combined with so much and so various intercourse with men of all ranks in society. In his later years he retired more than previously from public business, but, as Dr. Begbie writes, "he was firm and robust. With accumulating years came a disposition to obesity; and with the silver-grey on the massive forehead came also the pallid and somewhat sickly look of fading health. Yet he seldom complained; or, if indisposed, it was only by some trivial ailment arising from indigestion. He was sometimes sick at stomach, but he was never faint, nor ever swooned away. . . . He had no præcordial pain, or distress in breathing; no palpitation of the heart, or intermission of the pulse. He ascended heights with wonderful facility; he slept on either side, and

---

[1] *Edinburgh Monthly Journal of Medical Science,* vol. xii. 1851, p. 205. There were also traces of very chronic disease of the membranes of the brain, but probably not of such amount and character as to have much clinical importance as regards the fatal event.

his rest was calm and refreshing." Such was his state apparently, according to his physician, up to a period indefinitely near the fatal close.

It so happens that of the last month of Dr. Chalmers's life we have very exact records, including many memoranda, letters, &c., from his own hand. It was a month fraught with unusual excitement and exertion for a man in his sixty-eighth year. On Thursday the 6th of May, 1847, he set out for London to attend a committee of the House of Commons on a subject in which he was very deeply interested. He preached [1] in Marylebone Church on the 9th, and on the 12th submitted to a long, searching, and fatiguing examination, wherein Sir James Graham tried to "heckle" him (as he expresses it) for an hour together; but, he writes at the close of a lengthened description of the day's proceedings, "we concluded in a state of great exhaustion, but with an erect demeanour and visage unabashed." Such was his own humorous account of an event which obviously gave him much anxiety. In London, also, he made many visits and saw many sights, not sparing himself at all, or complaining in any way. On the 15th he went to Brighton, where he preached on the 16th, returning to London on Monday. On Tuesday he went to Oxford, seeing the sights of the place and then going on to Bristol: the remainder of the week he spent there in excursions with great enjoyment, and among friends. He preached on Sunday at Bristol, and on Tuesday the 25th was at Darlington. In this interval he wrote a long and carefully considered note on the Education Question for Mr. Fox-Maule; and took a most affectionate leave of his sister, Mrs. Morton, with many effusions of pious feeling, but apparently without any despondency or personal misgiving as to the future; on Friday the 28th he returned home, as Dr. Hanna records, "bearing no peculiar marks of fatigue or exhaustion."

The next day (Saturday) was fully occupied in preparing a Report for the General Assembly, which he was to read on the following Monday. On Sunday morning (30th of May) he did not rise to

---

[1] It may be worth while to remark here that *preaching*, with Dr. Chalmers, was something very different from the mere delivery of written words in an audible tone of voice. It was, in truth, a work into which he threw all his great energy of mind and body, and in its effect fully justified the remark of the old Scotchwoman who found it necessary to apologise for her favourite preacher *reading* his sermon, "Ay, but its *fell reading then.*" That Dr. Chalmers preached on every Sunday during this excursion is therefore a noteworthy fact, and the more so as he appears at this time to have been little in the habit of preaching when at home.—In a more recent case, where death from heart disease was not sudden, but on the contrary very lingering, and where the very earliest symptoms, twenty-seven years before, had been such as to give warning of an impending danger, preaching had to be abandoned almost from the first; and although afterwards resumed, it became, in a second attack of ill health, the first duty that had to give way, from its manifest tendency to overstrain the weakened organ. (See the Autobiography and Memoir of the Rev. Dr. Guthrie, recently published; especially vol. ii. pp. 201-41, 215, 16, 18, 406-11.) It is to be observed that a very active use of the pen, and a great deal of work and enjoyment of life, continued possible to Dr. Guthrie for eight or nine years after the formal closure of his career as a preacher. He died in 1873, in his seventieth year.

breakfast, but, in answer to inquiries, said—"I do not by any means feel unwell; I only require a little rest." He conversed "with the greatest clearness and vigour;" attended church, and walked some distance afterwards with a friend on his way homewards; spent the evening in apparent good health and spirits, and among other occupations wrote to his sister at Bristol a hopeful and affectionate letter, expressive of perfect contentment and satisfaction. He retired to rest at the usual time, and next morning was discovered dead and cold.

The separate accounts given by Dr. Hanna and Dr. Begbie leave no doubt that death took place long before the morning light, but at what exact period it was impossible to say. The body had an attitude of calm repose. "The bed-clothes were scarcely disordered; on them rested a basin which had received the contents of the stomach."[1] This was the only evidence of anything like a death-struggle. Had it not been for this, it might have been supposed that Dr. Chalmers died in his sleep.

Cases like that of Dr. Chalmers (in respect to the suddenness of the fatal close) have often been recorded; but in very few of those in which the fatal result has been most sudden and startling have there been any such records of the incidents preceding death as are given above. In not a few of the cases observed personally by, or more or less intimately known to, the author of this article, there has been reason to believe that considerable suffering, or sense of disability, though not always of one and the same character, has been present; and in some of these it might easily, perhaps, have escaped attention had the individual been extremely reticent, or not surrounded by anxious friends, intent upon everything that appeared to affect the comfort of one dear to them, or the well-being of a family. In several instances, the first note of real alarm has been sounded on the discovery of an irregularity in the pulse; in one such case, sudden death took place within a fortnight, or at most three weeks, after this discovery.[2] In other cases there has been an indefinite distress felt on exertion, or on going up a hill; in a few, the more regular form of angina pectoris. One patient, who had more or less of angina-like pain and (so-called) breathlessness on exertion for at least some years, died at the last in bed, in the night, and at the side of his wife, who was not even awakened, or in any way made aware of his being at all uneasy, but found her husband motionless and half-cold, probably some hours after the event.[3] It therefore becomes exceedingly probable that the

---

[1] *Monthly Journal,* ubi supra, p. 205.

[2] In the case of Dr. Guthrie, above mentioned, a similar irregularity, with symptoms not very dissimilar in other respects, appeared to threaten sudden death in 1846, while death did not actually take place till 1873.

[3] This case was recorded with additional details, in Gout : Its History, Causes, and Cure, by William Gairdner (first edit. 1849, pp. 38—42), as a case of fatty degeneration of the heart, liver, and kidneys. The narrative there given of the symptoms is by my father, but I have a most distinct personal recollection, even at this distance of time, of all the essential facts, which both from intimate friendship, and from early professional studies, had more than usual interest for one who was just then engaged for the first time

actual death was either painless, or at least that the duration of the suffering was so brief, as not to have given an opportunity for any expression of it. Thus a person may have been affected with angina pectoris once or oftener, and he may die suddenly, and yet it may not be at all clear that he has died in a paroxysm of angina. On the other hand, symptoms of a different order from the genuine, painful, angina pectoris, may become associated with angina-like paroxysms at a subsequent period; and yet, even then, the death may not be strictly sudden (in the sense above described), or even unexpected as to its occurrence, but rather the gradual culmination of days or weeks of sleepless agony. It is notorious among physicians that in valvular diseases of the heart, and even in aneurisms, in which the popular impression, derived from a few startling instances, is to the effect that sudden death is always to be expected, this mode of termination is in fact exceptional. One or two cases, widely reported, and taking possession of the imagination by their peculiar and mysterious close, become the types of a whole series, in which the incidents are only slightly or not at all removed from the ordinary course of fatal disease, as to the fact of the end being to a certain extent expected and foreseen. But even here we are beset by anomalies of experience arising from the extreme difficulty of realising facts depending so much upon subjective impressions. For example, a young man intimately known to the author of this article went to Edinburgh many years ago to study medicine, it being known to himself and some of his friends that there was some internal flaw or weakness, in regard to the precise nature of which he always maintained a strict reserve. It was reputed (as in the case of Seneca) to be more or less of the character of "asthma;" but no regular asthmatic paroxysm was ever brought under notice. This young man pursued all his medical studies and took his degree without apparent difficulty; living in the main carefully, but often visiting the hospital at night and doing all the miscellaneous work of a hardworking student. He afterwards went to the Crimea and served through the whole campaign, up to the taking of the Redan fort, as an assistant-surgeon attached to a regiment; his letters at this time giving most minute descriptions of all his personal impressions of the scenes and great events around him, but being almost entirely silent as to his own physical sensations, if he had any, of chronic disease. He was afterwards affected with some of the current diseases of the service, and had also an attack of rheumatic fever, after which he was sent home, but continued with his regiment on its return, and finally died at Chichester in a time apparently of profound tranquillity, and with such startling suddenness that he had barely time to use some of the most familiar remedies

in minute pathological research; especially as occurring only a few months after the death of Dr. Chalmers. The patient became subject to the first symptoms of cardiac disease in 1841; had a smart attack of regular gout in 1846, followed by giddiness and cardiac pains, which were rarely altogether absent afterwards. He died suddenly, as described, in September 1847, in the 63rd year of his age.—W. T. G.

and common external appliances before he was called away, his fellow-officers having had no previous note of warning whatever. A subsequent inquiry led to the discovery that the local applications which he had himself - directed in the moment preceding his death were precisely those which he had learned in the Edinburgh Royal Infirmary to apply in several cases of angina pectoris, in the study of which he had interested himself. He had also, it appeared, confided to his mother the idea that he might possibly die suddenly, owing to some imperfection of which he was sensible at the heart. He died in his twenty-seventh year. The pericardium was found to be firmly adherent, and the heart rather small, its muscular fibres pale, and apparently altered in texture. In this instance it would seem probable that symptoms of an appreciable, but still of a tolerable kind, may have existed for many years, unreported, undescribed, and perhaps not even distinctly realised by the patient himself, though he was one carefully instructed in all that relates to this subject, and known to have taken a special interest in it from the point of view of medical observation.[1]

The cases adverted to above have been, with one or two exceptions, cases of sudden death in which the symptomatic history of the facts leading up to the fatal result is either imperfect, or altogether mysterious; and in which also the picture of angina pectoris as drawn by Heberden fails at some point or other to apply to the facts. But in cases of true angina of the most typical kind, and especially in those associated with a distinct organic lesion, such as calcification or other disease of the coronary arteries or fibre of the heart, it might easily be argued that the fact of a *sudden*, as opposed to a more ordinary mode of death, is not less mysterious than in any of those cases in which it has been preceded by no such typical symptoms. For, after all, what we know in cases of true Angina is simply the fact that pain of a certain order and of a certain degree of severity often brings death in its train; how the death occurs, and what precise conjunction of phenomena or pathological causes determines its occurrence at a particular moment, we know as little apparently in the painful as in the comparatively painless cases. It is plainly out of the question to suppose that a chronic, and in its very nature

---

[1] For additional details see the Edinburgh Medical Journal, vol. v. 1859, p. 25. Heberden's remarks in his first paper (1768) as to the association of angina with sudden death are important. He had at that time seen about twenty cases (four years later he notes fifty, and in his Commentaries about a hundred cases); of the twenty cases first observed he had *known* six to have died suddenly; and perhaps more may have so perished, without the fact being known. "But," he argues, "though the natural tendency be to kill suddenly, yet some of those afflicted may die in another manner" (unless such persons could be considered as exempt from all the other diseases proper to advancing age) "since this disorder will last, as I have known it more than once, near twenty years." Heberden had first become aware of the tendency to sudden death in angina, on mentioning the peculiar symptoms to a physician of great experience, who had told him that most of these cases had in his experience been suddenly fatal. The careful manner in which Heberden's own experience had been *matured* (so to speak) for publication appears very clearly in these incidental remarks.

gradually advancing lesion, like fatty degeneration or disease of the
coronary vessels is the direct and immediate determining cause of
a death which occurs in a moment, or of spasmodic seizures which
come on in the midst of comparative health, and pass away in many
instances in a few minutes, or at most in an hour or two, leaving the
patient with a quiet pulse, free from serious complaint, and (apart
from certain forms of exertion) able for many of the ordinary duties
of life. The cardiac fibre which carried Dr. Chalmers safely over the
last three weeks of his life, with its harassing duties and active exertions in various places, cannot be reasonably supposed to have become
suddenly so much more diseased (physically speaking) that it must
needs be disabled to the extent of ceasing to act altogether, in the
absolute quiet of an undisturbed night, after a day peacefully and
happily spent in his own home, and an evening closed in a state of
radiant satisfaction and joy, without any apparent trace of morbid
misgivings. A like argument would probably apply to many or most
of Dr. Heberden's cases of angina pectoris ; to all cases, indeed, in
which the element of spasm (so-called) is a prominent feature; and in
the elaborate argument, so well rendered and modernised by Dr.
Latham, in which Heberden vindicates for his "dolor pectoris" a
place among the spasms, as opposed to inflammation or organic disease,
we are only seeking, with him, for a mode of reasoned description or
of generalisation for facts which are confessedly mysterious. The
whole of the argument that has been raised since Heberden's time as
to whether death in these cases is caused by *spasm* or by *paralysis* of
the heart, and the small amount of actual information or real science
which has emerged from the somewhat fruitless controversy, shows
strongly how much we may deceive ourselves with the idea that in
describing a mere association of symptoms with certain pathological
lesions, we have fully explained the nature of the connection of the
one group of facts with the other. From this point of view one more
instance of sudden death, with all its preceding life-history, may be
regarded as having a sufficient interest for us to be cited here with
some detail.

The great comparative anatomist and profound physiologist John
Hunter died, as is well known, with startling suddenness in the year
1793 ; and from all that has been transmitted to us of the circumstances of his fatal illness, and of the symptoms from which he
suffered for twenty years before his death, it is evident that the
opinion of one, at least, of his most intimate and confidential friends,
as well as probably the secret convictions, in the end, of the distinguished sufferer himself, pointed in the direction of the angina
pectoris of Heberden as the true nosological interpretation of his
morbid state. The detailed posthumous narrative of the symptoms,
coming as it does, almost from the very lips of Hunter,[1] and charac-

---

[1] "Each symptom," writes Sir Everard Home, "was described at the time it
occurred, and either noted by himself, or dictated to me when Mr. Hunter was too ill to

terised by all his restless activity of mind in the search after truth, forms unquestionably one of the most instructive chapters in the whole history of medicine. There is hardly a sentence in this wonderful narrative which will not repay the careful study of the physician; and although the substance of the whole is here faithfully preserved, the need for condensation will compel the sacrifice of many of the vivid touches which reveal the mind of genius intent, even amidst physical suffering, upon the mysteries of its own being.

How far these descriptive touches had been reasoned out into clear conceptions in the mind of Hunter himself does not appear from the narrative; it is certain, however, that his most intimate and congenial friend, Edward Jenner, postponed for many years the publication of certain highly original observations on angina pectoris (afterwards adopted and in part published by Dr. Parry), from the fear of compromising the feelings of John Hunter by a too obvious reference to his case.[1] It is well established, also, that the case, did, in fact, fulfil the anticipations of Jenner, both as to the fatal event, and as to the appearances observed after death. It has rarely happened, surely, that two minds so keenly alive to theoretic truth, and yet so observant of detail, have been applied to any, even the most indifferent obscure case in medicine; for in this instance it is the author of the "Treatise

---

write . . . As the statement is made up from detached notes which were not written with a view to publication, it will appear in point of language extremely deficient; it was thought, however, best to leave it in its present form, lest by altering the language the effect of some of the expressions might be diminished, or misunderstood."—*Life of Hunter, prefixed to the Treatise on Inflammation*, 1794, p. xlv.

[1] The circumstances, as delivered in writing by Jenner to Dr. Parry, are curious, and specially interesting as bearing on the early symptoms in John Hunter's case. "The first case I ever saw," writes Jenner, "of angina pectoris was that in the year 1772, published by Dr. Heberden, with Mr. Hunter's dissection. There, I can almost positively say, the coronary arteries were not examined. Another case of a Mr. Carter, at Dursley, fell under my care" (date not given); but in this case "the coronary arteries were become bony canals." "Soon afterwards Mr. Paytherus met with a case" . . . "At this very time, my valued friend Mr. John Hunter began to have the symptoms of angina pectoris too strongly marked upon him; and this circumstance prevented any publication of my ideas upon the subject, as it must have brought on an unpleasant conference between Mr. Hunter and me. I mentioned both to Mr. Cline and Mr. Home my notions of the matter; but they did not seem to think much of them. When however Mr. Hunter died, Mr. Home very candidly wrote to me, immediately after the dissection, to tell me I was right." In 1778, Jenner wrote a distinct statement of his fears about Hunter's case, and of his views on the pathology of angina pectoris, intending it as a communication in private to Dr. Heberden; but, probably from the fear that it might lead to publication, the letter never was sent (See *Life of Edward Jenner*, by Dr. Baron, vol. i. p. 39). It is, moreover, certain that Hunter, in a fatal case recorded by Dr. Fothergill ("Medical Observations and Inquiries," vol. v. p. 254), had actually observed disease of the coronary arteries in connection with sudden death from angina pectoris as early as March, 1775; so that the presumption is exceedingly strong that Hunter not only was intimately acquainted with Jenner's views on the subject, but also had in part suggested them. There is thus a chain of evidence of no ordinary consistency tending to show that Hunter, who never formally identified his own symptoms with those of the angina pectoris of Heberden, was nevertheless cognisant of their real nature and probable termination, at least as early as Jenner's suspicions took origin, which, as we shall afterwards see reason to believe, was in 1777. The death of Hunter, in 1793, was in fact almost an exact reproduction of the very circumstances of Fothergill's case, viz. "in a sudden and violent transport of anger;" and the appearances on dissection were also strikingly similar.

on the Blood, Inflammation," &c., who is both sufferer and narrator, while it is the clear-sighted and eminently truth-loving discoverer of vaccination who forms and announces to us the diagnosis.

John Hunter "was a very healthy man for the first forty years of his life, if we except an inflammation of his lungs in the year 1759. In the spring of 1769, in his forty-first year, he had a regular fit of the gout, which returned in the three following springs, but not in the fourth." In the spring of 1773 (rather more than twenty years before his death) he had the first appalling attack of what..may, from our present point of view, be fairly regarded as angina pectoris, though the pain (perhaps from some association of ideas with "gout in the stomach," the regular attack having, as stated above, not appeared at the expected time) was in this instance referred to the region of the pylorus. "While he was walking about the room, he cast his eyes on the looking glass, and observed his countenance to be pale, his lips white, giving the appearance of a dead man; this alarmed him, and led him to feel for his pulse, but he found none in either arm; the pain continued, and he found himself at times not breathing. Being afraid of death soon taking place if he did not breathe, he produced the voluntary act of breathing by working his lungs by the power of the will."[1] The "sensitive principle" was not affected; for three quarters of an hour he continued in this state, when the pain gradually lessened, and in two hours he was completely recovered.

The next attack was in 1776;[2] it was distinguished,. however, by a very decided amount of vertigo, which was not present, apparently, in the first attack; he felt as if he had drunk too much, and was a little sick; on lying down it seemed as if he was suspended in the air; motion in a carriage gave the uneasy "sensation of going down, or sinking;"[3] motion, either of the head or foot, was insufferable, from the idea it gave of ranging through vast distances. "The idea he had of his own size was that of being only two feet long." The special senses were extremely acute; the appetite indifferent; the pulse about

---

[1] In this and other passages the mind of Hunter is very apparent. The speculations which follow may possibly be those of Sir Everard Home, and at all events they are not of much value as regards the present narrative.

[2] This date is probably a mistake, either of Hunter or the copyist; the true date was 1777, as appears from a letter to Jenner on May 11th, in which Hunter writes—"Not two hours after I saw your brother, I was taken ill with a swimming in the head, and could not raise it off the pillow for ten days; it is not yet perfectly recovered." During his convalescence Hunter went to Bath for three months, on the advice of his friends, who took a much more serious view of his case than he himself appeared to do. It was during his residence at Bath, apparently, that Dr. Jenner saw Hunter personally, and formed the strong views as to the character and probable issue of the case which he ever afterwards retained, and which he wrote out, as above mentioned, for Dr. Heberden in 1778.

[3] There is a characteristically Hunterian note here given in Home's narrative, which is valuable as showing how much these details of subjective phenomena interested John Hunter as a physiologist, while as mere personal matters he gave all his own sufferings extremely little consideration, "It is very curious that the sensation of sinking is very uneasy to most animals. When a person is tossed in a blanket, the uncomfortable part is falling down; take any animal in the hand and raise it up, it is very quiet, but bring it down, and it will exert all its powers of resistance, every muscle in its body is in action; this is the case even with a child as early as its birth."

sixty, and weak.   In this state he continued for about ten days; bleeding was of no service, purging and vomiting (by medicine) "distressed him greatly;" nothing appeared to be of the least use.   From this severe illness he gradually recovered, but only after a long con-valescence; and he does not seem to have been ever again perfectly well, having, it is said, grown much older looking in the interval between this and his next severe attack, which was in 1785.

The illness of April 1785 may be said to have commenced with an ordinary attack of gout, followed by a great variety of anomalous nervous sensations which are minutely described, but over which it is not necessary to detain the reader.[1] Suffice it to say, that from this time onwards Hunter became increasingly subject to paroxysmal attacks, which assumed more and more the characters of typical angina pectoris.   The nervous disturbance appears to have been at first peripheral, e. g., " a sensation of the muscles of the nose being in action," an unpleasant sensation in the left side of the face, jaw, and throat, which seemed to extend into the head on that side, and down the left arm as low as the ball of the thumb, where it terminated all at once."   After a fortnight these symptoms of nervous irritation " extended to the sternum, producing the same disagreeable sensations there, and giving the feeling of the sternum being drawn backwards towards the spine, as well as that of oppression in breathing, although the action of breathing was attended with no real difficulty ; at these times the heart seemed to miss a stroke, and upon feeling the pulse, the artery was very much contracted, often hardly to be felt, and every now and then the pulse was entirely stopt."   He had also pains in the heart itself, as well as the diaphragm and stomach, attended with considerable eructations of wind, " a kind of mixture of hic-cough and eructation."   In the most severe attacks " he sunk into a swoon or doze, which lasted about ten minutes, after which he started up, without the least recollection of what had passed, or of his preceding illness."   The agonies he suffered were dreadful,[2] and when he fainted away he was thought to be dead.

As in other instances of angina, these attacks were at first brought on chiefly by motion, " especially on an ascent, either of stairs or of rising ground."   The affections of the mind that were chiefly injurious were anxiety and anger ; " it was not the cause of the anxiety, but the quantity of it, that affected him ; the anxiety about the hiving of

---

[1] Dr. Pitcairn elicited on this occasion, by special inquiries, that Hunter's mind had been much harassed, in consequence of his having opened the body of a person who had died of the bite of a mad dog, about six weeks before ; in doing which he had wounded his hand.   For a fortnight, it is added, his mind had been in continual suspense, from the idea that he might be seized with symptoms of hydrophobia ; and it certainly seems very probable, as it was supposed, that the nervous symptoms alluded to may have been in some measure, at least, determined or produced by this accident.

[2] This is the personal testimony of Sir Everard Home, who witnessed this attack, having become Hunter's regular assistant in his practice, and acted for him during his illness.   It is probable, but not expressly stated, that Home also was a witness to the first attack of illness in 1773, as he was then a young man living in Hunter's house.

a swarm of bees, the anxiety lest an animal should escape before he could get a gun to shoot it," brought on an attack ; " anger brought on the same complaint, and he could conceive it possible for that passion to be carried so far as to deprive him of life; but what was very extraordinary, the more tender passions of the mind did not produce it ;" compassion, admiration, &c. might be carried to the extent of tears, " yet the spasm was not excited." " He ate and slept as well as ever, and his mind was in no degree depressed ; the want of exercise made him grow unusually fat."

Mrs. Hunter, in writing to Jenner, called the disease, even at this stage, " flying gout."[1] We have already seen what Jenner thought of it several years before. Hunter himself was probably familiar with Heberden's description, and at all events had assisted in Heberden's inquiry by performing the examination of the very remarkable case recorded in the " Medical Transactions " in 1772. He himself began to suffer in 1773. That he had realised in some degree the danger of his position, therefore, can scarcely be doubted. He had indeed no unmanly fear of death, and was far too busy to occupy himself with what he would have regarded as weak sentimentalisms about himself. He probably avoided the subject deliberately,[2] and felt himself able to pursue all his various occupations with the same ardour as ever, in the intervals of suffering. But he was deeply sensible of the risk to which he was sometimes exposed by over-exertion, and still more by his uncontrollable temper; he was accustomed to say, that " his life was in the hands of any rascal who chose to annoy and tease him ; "[3] a remarkable expression, and a sad anticipation of the actual ending.

The close of 1789 brought with it a new set of complications, which may be briefly summarised as loss of memory, and various kinds of visual disturbance, especially the apparent deflection of objects from their true direction ; some of the former subjective sensations, mentioned in the attack of 1776, returned upon him. " Dreams had the strength of reality, so much so as to awaken him ; the disposition to sleep was a good deal gone, an hour or two in the twenty-four being as much as could be obtained. Neither the mind, nor the reasoning faculty, however, were affected ;" indeed he reasoned most acutely in regard to his own visual derangements, and pursued the questions suggested by them in physiology with a keenness, which was quite characteristic.

At last the busy, ever active mind was to cease from its labours, and the strong, much-enduring bodily frame, wearied out and spent in the service, was to give way. His recovery from this indisposition was much less perfect than from any of the others; he never lost entirely the oblique vision ; his memory was in some respects evidently impaired, and the spasms became more constant ; he never went to

[1] Palmer's Life of John Hunter, p. 96.
[2] In all his published correspondence there is only one brief allusion to his own illnesses, the one given above from a note to Jenner.
[3] Palmer, *ut supra*, p. 119.

bed without their being brought on by the act of undressing himself; they came on in the middle of the night; the least exertion in conversation after dinner was attended by them. Even operations in surgery if attended with any nicety, now produced the same effects.

The end is well known. There is reason to think it was almost foreseen by himself. A dispute of a painful, but not, after all, of a very serious or overwhelming character, had embittered his relations with the governors of St. George's Hospital. On the 16th of October, 1793, he determined to be present at a meeting, where, however, he apprehended a personal dispute. He expressed to a friend the feeling that such a dispute might be fatal to him, but went nevertheless. Something that he said in the Board-room was noticed, and flatly contradicted. He stopped, left the room in a silent rage, and had just time to gain the next room, when "he gave a deep groan, and fell down dead."

The appearances in the dead body were complex. The pericardium was very unusually thickened; the heart very small, its muscular substance pale; the coronary arteries were converted into open bony tubes; the valves of the left side of the heart also were involved in a similar degeneration; the aorta was dilated, in its ascending part, to the extent of one-third. The carotid and vertebral arteries within the cranium were also bony, and the basilar artery "had opaque white spots very generally along its coats." The structure of the brain itself was normal.

To these observations of what may be almost called historical cases, bearing upon the fact of sudden death and its associated symptoms, I will add only a few details gathered from a long and close observation of cardiac diseases in general.

Apart from what has been variously termed cardiac asthma, dyspnœa, or orthopnœa, which in many cases receives its clear explanation from the associated states either of the pulmonary circulation, or of the lungs, bronchi, and pleuræ, as disclosed by physical signs, there is often an element of subjective abnormal sensation present in cardiac diseases which, when it is not localised through the coincidence of pain, is a specially indefinable and indescribable sensation, almost always felt to be such by the patient himself. I make this remark deliberately, as the result of experience, and well knowing that it is liable to be brought into question in particular instances; that, in fact, a large part of what has been described under the titles given at the commencement of this paragraph, has been inextricably confounded by systematic writers with the sensation, or group of sensations, to which I refer.[1] To this group of sensations, when not distinctly accompanied by local pain, I have, in various instances, given the

[1] "In considering this subject we must not forget," writes Dr. Stokes, "that under the name angina pectoris, physicians have included, and still include, many examples of diseases which vary in their nature and combinations. Well marked instances of the affection as described by Dr. Latham, are rarely met with; and the same may be said of

name of *Angina sine dolore*, recognising, thereby, what I believe to be
its true diagnostic and pathological significance, and its alliance with
the painful angina of Heberden; the pain in which, however, as we
have already seen, is an exceedingly variable element, both in degree
and in kind. This painless, or at least not definitely and locally
painful, angina, is found in connection with every kind of cardiac
lesion which ends in death (whether sudden or not) in varying proportions; often associated with the other phenomena which make up
the picture of a confirmed case of organic heart disease tending to
death, but not rarely also under circumstances which admit of its
being separately described. Among the valvular lesions of the heart,
incompetency of the aortic valves is the one which most frequently
gives rise characteristically to this peculiar form of suffering; and in
the majority of the cases in which it arises early in the course of
aortic valvular disease there is neither dropsy, or lividity, nor hæmoptysis; very often there is no disease of the lungs ascertainable by
physical signs, and in particular no wheezing, even in very severe
paroxysms of this truly cardiac anguish or indefinable distress. But
there is, in variable degrees, a sensation which can only be called
anxiety, or *cardiac oppression;* the patient acquires a haggard, almost
a frightened look, and from his habitual attitude and manner, as much
as from anything he distinctly declares in words, it becomes evident
that he is suffering from a sense of insecurity which he cannot possibly express. In the more aggravated cases the loss of sleep is a
serious part of the suffering, and patients will sometimes declare that
they are afraid to sleep, lest some other and greater evil than the loss
of sleep should come upon them; obviously an experience actually
acquired, that sleep is, in this state, sometimes the precursor, and
apparently the cause, of a formidable increase in the symptoms. An
intelligent patient in this condition recently put the question to his
medical attendant, with respect to a very moderate dose of hydrate of
chloral, proposed to be given after many sleepless nights, whether it
would not be "dangerous," *i.e.* (as he afterwards explained to me),
whether the sleep artificially induced might not be the means of
determining an attack which might prove ·fatal. When sleep is
obtained, it is brief and easily disturbed, often by frightful dreams:
and when these occur they are mixed up with the sensations of an approaching paroxysm, so that the dream may appear to be the actual
cause of the paroxysm. An assertion of the patient just alluded to
was that he "woke up with the peculiar sensation on him, and
it was too late to check it." In very extreme cases, which are often,
however, complicated with true orthopnœa, dropsy, and other more
recognised cardiac and respiratory symptoms of secondary origin, the
patient may for weeks together be unable to lie down or to take

the purely nervous cases noticed by Laennec. *I have never seen either of these forms.*
The disease which in this country" (Ireland?) "most often gets the name of angina
pectoris might be more properly designated as cardiac asthma." *Op. cit.* p. 488.

ordinary rest, and on the other hand may be almost continually *half-asleep*; in such cases accidents are apt to occur, from the patient falling forwards in a fit of sheer exhaustion, or getting burned or otherwise injured while in a state of insensibility. Nor are more distinctly cerebral symptoms wanting. In some of these cases I have seen attacks closely resembling epilepsy, without any subsequent paralysis; when however, hemiplegia or aphasic symptoms occur, it is most probable that they are due to more distinctly organic changes in the nervous centres; and usually to cerebral embolism. It would be vain to indicate the verbal expedients by which patients endeavour to describe their sensations, when found in an attack of this paroxysmal suffering. Palpitation, and breathlessness are often alluded to, separately or together; but still more often it is a sense of "oppression," or of "pressure," which is sometimes described as if the chest were actually being compressed from before backwards; one patient described it as a "kind of surging up," which came, as he thought, from the bowels, and was attended with the feeling of wind, and also, I suspect, with a degree of hysteric globus, rising, as he described it, to his throat, and causing him to pant for breath. The respiration is by no means necessarily or invariably disturbed in these cases, though it is frequently more or less quickened, and sometimes the opposite; in certain cases the respiration is alternately frequent and infrequent; several rapid panting or gasping respirations are continued over half-a-minute together, and are gradually succeeded by a corresponding period of comparative quiescence, which at times culminates in a positive arrest or suspension, for a time, of a respiratory act (see the narrative of John Hunter's case above cited).[1]

This peculiar type of "suspirious," or irregularly sighing, respiration (as it has been termed), is so far characteristic of the "angina

[1] It is very remarkable that Dr. Stokes, who is undoubtedly entitled to the credit of having first distinctly realised, and clearly stated, the importance of this type of respiration as indicating cardiac disease (especially weakened action, or fatty degeneration, of the fibre of the heart) should have so completely overlooked the case of John Hunter, while fixing upon the symptoms described in Seneca's case as characteristic (see *note*, p. 553). The same remark applies to all the now numerous dissertations, in Germany as well as in this country, on the "Cheyne-Stokes respiration," as it has been called on the continent. "It consists," says Dr. Stokes (*op. cit.* p. 324), "in the occurrence of a series of inspirations, increasing to a maximum, and then declining in force and length, until a state of apparent apnœa is established. In this condition the patient may remain for such a length of time as to make his attendants believe that he is dead, when a low inspiration, followed by one more decided, marks the commencement of a new ascending and then descending series of inspirations." Probably the first really exact description of this phenomenon was by Dr. Cheyne, in 1818 (Dublin Hospital Reports vol. ii.; p. 216). The peculiar interest and value of Hunter's case, however, for us consists in its giving the personal impressions, or subjective sensations, of that great physiologist in a way that no merely objective description could effect, and wholly apart from hypothesis. It is curious to observe how completely Hunter's description of his own sensations corresponds with Galen's commentary on a notable passage in Hippocrates, where a certain kind of "rare and large" respiration is described as "like a person who forgot for a time the need of breathing, and then suddenly remembered." See the very interesting account of the most ancient observations on this subject by Dr. Warburton Begbie, in his recent Address in Medicine (*British Medical Journal*, August 7, 1875, p. 166) in which there will also be found a brief but exact account of the more modern theories as to this kind of respiratory disorder.

sine dolore," that I cannot but regard it as being in some way related to lesions involving the respiration through the cardiac nerves. Whether dependent necessarily on cardiac causes or not, however, it is certainly not necessarily associated with any organic lesion of the lungs or air-passages; it occurs, as Dr. Stokes has recorded, " without any *râle* or sign of mechanical obstruction." Frequently the irregularities of respiration do not go beyond a few quick gasps, or deep sighing inspirations, at a time, and the period of apnœa, or of rare and slow respiration, is correspondingly shortened; but when this condition of the respiration, even in its minor degrees, is associated with the peculiar look of indescribable *anguish*, the head thrown back, the arms extended or tossed about, and the whole frame showing by sheer muscular restlessness the terrible character of the *agony* (indicated óften by cries, even when without local or positive pain), it scarcely requires the aid of a verbal description to make the diagnosis of angina clear to the observer. It is, however, important to remark that the character and peculiarly altered rhythm of the breathing are essentially distinct from the laborious but more regular and at the same time noisy respiration of true spasmodic asthma and of asthmatic bronchitis. I have also observed that organic and valvular deformities of the right side of the heart, even when complicated with great cyanosis, are only slightly characterised by the symptoms I have now endeavoured to indicate; and, on the whole, the diseases of the mitral valve are less apt to be accompanied by this form of angina than those of the aortic, and the obstructive lesions less than the regurgitations. Dilatation of the heart in its more aggravated forms, however caused, and aneurisms (as already indicated) arising very near the heart, or projecting into the pericardium, are apt to be accompanied by considerable degrees of angina, as above described. And some of the worst cases I have seen have been those, in which the only lesion that could be fairly presumed to exist was fatty or other degeneration of the fibre of the heart, sometimes with, sometimes without, direct evidence of moderate or slight dilatation of the left ventricle.[1] As in the case of the locally painful, or neuralgic

[1] In one case of this kind, a much valued friend and a distinguished clergyman of the Church of Scotland, who died at the age of forty-one, after a gradually progressive illness watched with the greatest anxiety, and with full fore-knowledge of its character and probable termination, the beats of the heart frequently numbered as low as 22-24 in the minute; and I have counted them as low as 18, without any marked irregularity. The radial pulse was at these times exceedingly soft and small, but although the suffering was at times intense, it was not usually accompanied by positive definable pain, at least until the last few days or weeks of the disease, when (the patient not being at the time under my own immediate observation) I had the testimony of a well-informed medical friend as to the really angina-like character of the paroxysms. The suspirious respiration was always present in the more considerable paroxysms of suffering, and was usually not altogether absent. There were on several occasions very alarming pseudo-apoplectic or slight epileptic attacks, without permanent disorder either of the intellectual functions or of voluntary movement. Although this truly noble-minded and self-denying man pursued the work of his life up to the very verge of sudden fainting or death in the pulpit, yet his death in the end was by no means sudden, but rather a lingering agony. The entire duration of his fatal illness was under two years, and he continued at his post, with some interruptions, until about eight months before his death, which happened in

angina, the relation of the symptoms to the organic lesion is by no means constant, even when the latter can be shown to be present, and to be presumably, in a certain sense, the cause of the symptoms. And it may further be affirmed, that the essentially paroxysmal character of this angina is such as to lead us inevitably to look for an explanation of it beyond the positive and permanent organic lesion of the heart or aorta, whatever that may be in the particular case.

We are now in a position to discuss, with such assistance as can be had both from clinical observation and from physiological pathology, the extremely obscure subject of the mode in which the innervation of the heart is affected in Cardiac Angina—in other words, the *ultimate pathology or pathogeny of the affection.* We have seen that the dolor pectoris, or angina pectoris, of Heberden was specially distinguished by him from all those pains in the chest which were regarded as due to inflammation, accompanied or followed by organic changes corresponding with the extent and severity of the inflammatory process. In other words, the essential pathology of angina, according to Heberden, was that of a *neurosis.* This we believe to be the only just rendering of the argument of this great physician, when he assigned to angina pectoris a place among the *distensiones,* or spasms. Later observers and pathologists have been much exercised in the attempt to resolve the question, whether sudden death, occurring under such circumstances, is from spasm, or from paralysis, of the heart; but we may safely conclude that no such question was, otherwise than remotely, involved in Heberden's argument. That argument was directed towards a very practical and real conclusion, and was not at all, we may well suppose, intended to foreclose questions of physiological pathology, which, according to all the evidence before us, were not before his mind, or, at least, not matured for discussion at the time at which he wrote. Angina pectoris had to be placed carefully apart from the *pyrexiæ* and the *phlegmasiæ;* had any doubt been left open on this subject, the *dolor pectoris* would have been considered as demanding the treatment of all so-called inflammatory pains in that day—large and repeated bleedings, vomitings, purgings, &c.[1] Hence the anxious care with which Heberden insisted on the paroxysmal and non-febrile character of the pain, and on the collateral circumstances which led him to bring it into the great group of the spasms; *e.g.* " *subito accedit, et recedit* "—" *in ipsa accessione pulsus non concitatur,*" &c. It is needless to pursue the argument in detail; possibly, indeed, the details

January, 1865. Up to a few days before death he maintained his pastoral connection with his congregation by means of letters, some of which have been published, and show all the power of a robust mind under the guidance of Christian principle and hope. Dr. Walshe, who saw this case with me in consultation, agreed with me in considering it one probably of fatty degeneration of the heart; but there was no *post-mortem* examination.

[1] Angina pectoris, quantum adhuc illius naturam intellexi, ad distensionem, non autem ad inflammationem, videtur pertinere. . . . . Sanguinis missio, vomitus, et purgantia mihi visa sunt aliena.—*Comm. uti supra.*

might be open to question in some instances. But on endeavouring, as Dr. Latham has done, to grasp the essential principles of the argument, as seen through a somewhat obsolete phraseology, we may readily assent to them, even if we should suppose that Heberden, in his desire to prove angina pectoris a *neurosis*, may have somewhat neglected the evidence of its being often associated with organic disease.[1] He found in the suddenness of the paroxysms, in the apparent good health of the intervals, in the relief often afforded by stimulants and by opium, the basis of his pathology of angina ; and we may easily admit that some cases, at least, of the typical angina of Heberden must have been fairly open to the construction of being cases of spasm, and nothing more. But we now know that this typical angina is only the culminating form of a group of symptoms, which, in their less pronounced, less definitely painful, and more complicated forms, are found to permeate the whole field of cardiac pathology and diagnosis. The angina which consists purely of a paroxysm of pain, and of a paroxysm which kills suddenly and instantaneously, is rare ; but the angina which consists of a tendency to paroxysmal aggravations (not always purely of pain), superinduced upon, and complicating, the other symptoms and sequelæ of cardiac organic diseases, is matter of every-day experience. In both forms there occurs occasionally a paroxysm which ends in death ; but in the second form death is less frequently instantaneous and unexpected, both because the paroxysms are individually less intense, and because the fatal result, when it arrives, is brought about in part by other causes than the immediate causes of the paroxysm. And even if we should maintain that *fatal* angina is always more or less dependent upon organic changes,[2] there would still remain to be explained these unquestionable facts, viz :—1. Pain, suddenly coming and going ; 2.

[1] He refers, however, to several cases which seemed to him to imply the existence of organic change; and to one only, in which "a very skilful anatomist could discover no fault in the heart, in the valves, in the arteries, or in the neighbouring veins, excepting some small rudiments of ossification in the aorta. Nor were any indications of disease found in the brain." There is no doubt that Heberden's personal experience of angina was almost purely clinical, not pathological ; but it has the advantage, for us, of being stated in language singularly terse, exact, and free from the suspicion of prejudice. Heberden claims, in his Commentaries, to have seen nearly a hundred cases of angina pectoris, of which three were in women. One was a boy twelve years old, "who had something resembling this affection." All the rest were in men near or past the fiftieth year of their age. At the time of his first paper, in 1768, Heberden had "never seen one opened, who had died of it. Most of those," he adds, "with whose cases I had been acquainted were buried before I heard that they were dead." The case specially alluded to above was almost certainly that of the "Unknown," who, in April 1772, wrote to Heberden a minute account of his symptoms, and dying suddenly about three weeks thereafter, was found to have left in his will express instructions that Heberden should be informed of his death, with the view of having his body examined. This was accordingly done by John Hunter, and it is this case to which Dr. Jenner alludes, when he says that he can almost certainly affirm that the coronary arteries were not examined. The case was recorded in the third volume of the Medical Transactions.

[2] Eulenburg refers to Desportes, in Lartigue—"De l'Angine de Poitrine," p. 78, Paris, 1846 ; Surmay, L'Union Médicale, XXXI, No. 80, p. 34 ; for evidence of angina without disease of the heart. Anstie, in his Treatise on Neuralgia, pp. 69, 70, details, briefly, a fatal case, in which "not the slightest organic heart mischief could be detected, either during life or after death." Latham has also recorded cases where the appearances.

The paroxysmal character of the symptoms, other than pain; 3. Absolutely sudden death in a few cases. On these grounds, now as in the time of Heberden, we may assuredly claim for angina pectoris a place among the *neuroses*, even while the admission is freely made that the element of *neurosis* is often superinduced upon organic, too often indeed incurable, disease in the heart itself, or in its nutrient vessels, or in the first part of the aorta.

Certain authorities have treated of angina pectoris as a form of visceral neuralgia, or "hyperæsthesia"[1] (Romberg) of the cardiac plexus. The latter term (as Dr. Anstie has well pointed out) is essentially a bad one; the former, in the case of typical angina, is perhaps admissible, viewing the disease from the side of the pain alone; but it errs both by excess and by defect, inasmuch as, on the one hand, pain of the severe form implied in the term neuralgia is not always the central or exclusive phenomenon, even of the cases ending in sudden death; while, on the other hand, a form of cardiac pain, or *pseudo-angina*[2] (as it has been termed) is not infrequent, which has most of the attributes of a neuralgia in the highest possible degree, and which, though eminently paroxysmal, is by no means apt to lead to sudden death, or to any grave consequences whatever. This admission, which is very candidly and fully made by the late Dr. Anstie[3] in his interesting dissertation upon the subject, appears to me a very cogent reason for maintaining, rather than consenting to forego, the now well-known term angina pectoris, for which he entertains so strong an aversion, but which is, nevertheless, quite indispensable to us, as carrying the impress of a long line of personal observations, extending back to that "molestus quidam angor," which Morgagni has described as having suddenly terminated the life of a Venetian woman in 1707. And if it must be admitted that the name "angina pectoris" has sometimes been used in ignorance, or rather (from disregard of purely clinical experience) in a way really objectionable and tending to confusion, it is equally certain that the term "neuralgia" is beset with theoretical interpretations which tend to bias both.

after death were, at least, of very questionable and doubtful character. But it is difficult to prove a negative by isolated instances which are opposed to the general results of pathological research.

[1] "Pain has been described by some of the most distinguished writers on nervous diseases as a *hyperæsthesia*. Yet there is really very little difficulty in convincing ourselves, if we institute a thorough inquiry into the matter, that pain is certainly *not* a hyperæsthesia, or excess of ordinary sensory function, but something which, if not the exact opposite of this, is very nearly so."—Anstie on Neuralgia, p. 2, *et. seq.*

[2] "Genuine angina pectoris is undoubtedly a very rare affection. On the other hand, I *almost daily* meet with a form of complaint combining in a minor degree many of the characters of angina; and to this imitation of the true disease I propose to give the name of pseudo-angina. I believe that herein lies the explanation of Laennec's notion (so discordant with the experience of English observers) that angina pectoris is of very frequent occurrence."—Walshe, Diseases of the Heart and Great Vessels, 4th edit., 1873, p. 208. Compare the observations on Diagnosis in p. 542, of present chapter.

[3] On Neuralgia, and the Diseases that resemble it, by F. E. Anstie, M.D., 1871; pp. 63, 64. The first sketch of this most valuable treatise, contributed by the much-lamented author to the present work in 1868, contains no detailed reference to angina pectoris.

clinical and pathological research. We have endeavoured in the preceding pages to give an impartial statement of a wide range of phenomena, into which a neuralgic element enters in various proportions. A consistent theory must take account of that element, but will not allow it to take possession of the entire field.

Another question that requires consideration is, the nature of the disorders in connection with motor nerves which unquestionably occur in angina pectoris. Here, again, we find ourselves in the presence of vague and often quite fruitless discussions, indicated by the general terms spasm, paralysis, hyperkinesis, &c., and, among the older authors, asthma convulsivum, stenocardia, syncope anginosa, &c.

A third department of the inquiry, less generally entertained, inasmuch as the phenomena to which it refers are less constant, is the nature of the connection between the cardiac symptoms in angina pectoris, and those cerebro-spinal manifestations which sometimes occur, and which we saw well illustrated in the case of John Hunter.

Is it possible to give any account of these three orders of phenomena which shall be consistent and intelligible, which shall be founded on positive facts and well-ordered experiments, and shall thus fulfil the purposes, even provisionally, of a reasonable theory of angina pectoris? In endeavouring to answer this question, it will be necessary to refer to physiological researches which are still very incomplete, and even to clinical facts which have not as yet been tested by a sufficient number of independent observers. But it certainly seems as though some large and fruitful lines of research had recently been opened up amid much darkness and confusion.

We owe to Dr. Lauder Brunton [1] the clinical observation of a fact which, besides its therapeutic consequences (to be afterwards considered), may be regarded as shedding a new light upon the pathology of angina pectoris. In investigating a case of rheumatic disease of the aortic valves (obstruction and regurgitation), with dilatation of the aorta, and considerable hypertrophy of the heart, he found that during the angina-like paroxysms of pain to which the patient was subject, the sphygmograph invariably showed a great diminution in the amplitude of the pulse-wave, with blunting of the apex, slow or greatly postponed recoil, and obliteration of the dicrotic wave; the ordinary pulse of the individual (at least in the right radial artery) being characterised by a very ample and instantaneous upstroke, a pointed apex, a rapid recoil, and a distinct though not exaggerated dicrotic wave. Repeated experiments convinced Dr. Brunton that

[1] Lancet, July 27, 1867, p. 97; Journal of Anatomy and Physiology, vol. v. p. 92; Trans. of the Clinical Society of London, vol. iii. p. 191. The case, which is fully recorded in the Clinical Society's Transactions, was that of a man aged twenty-six, admitted into the Royal Infirmary of Edinburgh under Professor Maclagan, on Dec. 7, 1866; and sphygmographic observations, begun at his instance, were continued under Prof. Bennett, to whom the case was transferred on Feb. 1, 1867. There were palpitation of the heart, and violent throbbing of the carotids, besides the angina-pain. The aconite and digitalis were ordered by Professor Maclagan; the small bleedings by Professor Bennett.

these altered characters of the pulse were due to an increased tension in the systemic arteries during the paroxysm, and that this increased tension was chiefly, if not solely, owing to " contraction of the small systemic vessels, so sudden and so great as to deserve the name of spasmodic."[1] Following up this line of observation, and being aware that Dr. B. W. Richardson [2] and Dr. Arthur Gamgee [3] had performed numerous experiments which showed that nitrite of amyl, when inhaled in small quantities, had the effect of remarkably lessening arterial tension by diminishing the contraction of the arterioles, Dr. Brunton was led to employ this substance for the purpose of relieving the symptoms in this case, and had the great satisfaction not only of finding that almost immediate ease was given in the severer paroxysms, but that the observations previously made on the relation of the paroxysm to increased vascular tension, were *emphasised* (so to speak) by the action of the nitrite of amyl. For when in the severest paroxysms the pulse was almost annihilated to the finger (though still regular and somewhat accelerated), thirteen drops of the nitrite of amyl inhaled from a cloth produced, in one minute and twenty seconds, a decided effect at once on the sphygmographic tracing and on the pain; while one or two smaller doses, repeated over sixteen minutes, restored the amplitude of the pulse-wave, and entirely removed the pain. It is, perhaps, unnecessary to multiply details, especially as regards doubtful points.[4] The experiment was repeated sufficiently often to show that, in this patient at least, increased arterial tension and angina-spasm were constantly associated, and that agents which produced diminution of the arterial tension always relieved the paroxysms. Among these agents, it is to be noted (though none was nearly so powerful as nitrite of amyl), small blood-lettings (of four ounces) were found to exercise a notable influence. Digitalis, on the other hand, appeared rather to aggravate the pain, and both digitalis and aconite made the pulse intermit, which was never the

[1] Clin. Soc. Trans., *ubi supra*, p. 199. A lithograph, with eleven tracings in different states of the patient, is given, on which the description in the text is founded.

[2] Dr. Richardson's numerous and valuable reports of experiments on anæsthetic vapours, and on nitrite of amyl, from 1863 onwards (brought in successive years before the Brit. Association of Science), determined the power of this substance as an anti-spasmodic and paralysing agent, and made numerous suggestions as to its probable curative value in tetanus, asthma, and other spasmodic diseases. Dr. Richardson also repeated, and investigated scientifically, Guthrie's accidental observation in 1859, as to its effect in dilating the capillaries ; and he inferred that this effect was due to its paralysing the arterioles through the vaso-motor nerves.

[3] Dr. Gamgee's (unpublished) experiments were made with the sphygmograph and hæmodynamometer, and led directly to Dr. Brunton's trials of the nitrite of amyl in angina, by demonstrating in animals and in man its action in lessening arterial tension.

[4] There is an ingenious attempt to show that a partial restoration of the original form of the pulse-tracing, which was shown to correspond to a remission, but not cessation, of the paroxysm under nitrite of amyl, was due to the persistence of abnormal tension in the pulmonary circulation, after the systemic had been relieved. The pain, under such circumstances, " disappeared from the greater part of the cardiac region, the neck, and the arm, but remained persistent at a point about two inches to the inside of the right nipple . . . . So long as this condition remained the pain was almost certain to return."—Clin. Trans. iii. p. 199.

case with the nitrite. On the whole, it must be admitted, that not-withstanding certain unavoidable deficiencies, the experiment is as complete as can reasonably be expected in the evidence it affords of a correlation of some kind between angina-paroxysms and increased arterial tension, in at least one clearly-defined case of organic cardiac disease.[1]

Many other experiments, both on man and on animals, have been performed, which amply confirm the action attributed to the nitrite of amyl in this case. The therapeutical part of the subject will receive consideration afterwards ; in the meantime it is sufficient to say, that the relaxing effect of the vapour on the arterioles, and its efficacy, in some cases at least, in greatly and instantly relieving the breast-pang, have been placed beyond reasonable doubt.

The points still open to further investigation seem to be these :—It is as yet not *proved* that all the forms, and all cases of angina, are characterised by increased arterial tension during the paroxysm. If, indeed, there be cases corresponding exactly with the original descrip-tion of Heberden, cases in which (the heart being to stethoscopic and physical examination normal) "the pulse is not disturbed by the pain," it would be extremely desirable to have sphygmographic observations of such apparently uncomplicated angina-paroxysms. But we have already expressed doubts of the existence of such cases; at all events, the one recorded by Dr. Brunton is not such a case, but rather one in which the phenomena of the arterial tension must be regarded as wholly abnormal, being influenced by the fact of aortic regurgitation, a strictly mechanical cause of permanently and morbidly lowered blood-pressure in the arteries.

But again : Supposing it proved that a suddenly-developed and decided increase in the arterial tension is a characteristic, or even an essential feature of the true angina-paroxysm, we may still regard it as an open question whether the change in the blood-pressure is to be attributed entirely in such cases to contraction of the arterioles, or partly also to changes in the innervation of the heart itself, which would account at once for the pain and for the sudden death which sometimes occurs during the attack ? Dr. Brunton has himself pointed out a fact which tells in this direction, notwithstanding the elaborate reasonings by which he supports the theory of vaso-motor derangement ending in spasm of the arterioles as the starting-point of the paroxysm. The experiments of Marey and others have shown that the effect of high blood-pressure in the arteries, *per se*, is to retard the pulse ; while diminished arterial tension arising from relax-ation of the arterioles (as in fever, or in capillary congestion from the

---

[1] It is to be observed, that although the diagnosis actually made was that of aortic obstruction and regurgitation *without aneurism*, and although this was quite in accord-ance with the physical signs, and particularly the murmurs, described in the report, the remarkable difference in the sphygmographic tracings of the two radial pulses cannot but be regarded as leaving a doubt open as to the negative part of the diagnosis. On the other hand, aneurism, if present, may have been responsible in part for the definite character of the pain, which is usually not so well-marked in cases of aortic regurgitation simply.

effect of external warmth) increases the frequency of the heart's contractions. Now in the case alluded to, what actually took place was exactly the reverse of what might have been expected on the theory above mentioned. During the severest paroxysms, when arterial tension was at its height, the pulse was *small and rapid*, and when the pain and spasm had been subdued by the inhalation of the nitrite, the pulse diminished in frequency while regaining strength and volume. Dr. Brunton considers these phenomena as indicating " a derangement of the cardiac regulating apparatus, producing quickened instead of slowed pulsation." Further observations, therefore, seem to be required before it can be safely assumed that either vaso-motor derangement on the one hand, or disorder of the cardiac innervation on the other, is the primary or *essential* phenomenon of true angina pectoris; although we may probably take it as provisionally established that some law of intimate relation exists between increased blood-pressure in the arteries and certain forms, at least, of the angina-paroxysm.

The peculiar interest of Dr. Brunton's observations, for us, consists not in his having finally settled the *nature* of this relation, but in his having shown that a remedy which has the remarkable power of instantly diminishing arterial tension has also a corresponding and almost equally instantaneous control over those paroxyms of angina in which increased arterial tension is known to occur. We shall recur to this subject when speaking of treatment.

Meantime it seems necessary to observe that Dr. Brunton had been anticipated, in several quarters, in the merely speculative attempt to connect the symptoms of angina pectoris with vaso-motor changes. Thus Traube[1] had argued that the diminished volume and increased tension shown in the arteries in many attacks of stenocardia are to be viewed, in connection with the increased rate of the pulse and the feeling of anxiety (angstgefühl), as related to an increased stimulation of the nerve-centre of the vaso-motor system. Cahen[2] had treated at length of various neuralgic affections (including trifacial neuralgia, and various painful affections of the pelvic organs) as affections of the vaso-motor system of nerves attended by congestion; and he referred angina pectoris to the same category, and indicated arsenic as a valuable remedy for such cases, without, however, adding anything important to the symptomatology of angina. Landois[3] had made a somewhat similar generalisation as to some cases of excessive nervous palpitation, which he regarded as being a vaso-motor angina pectoris. Finally, Nothnagel, in a very ingenious and interesting contribution to the clinical study of the " vaso-motor neuroses," devotes an entire article[4] to the special consideration of "Angina Pectoris

[1] Die Symptome der Krankheiten des Respirations-und Circulations-apparatus, p. 41. (Ref. in Nothnagel's article, *infra.*)

[2] Archives Générales de Médecine, 1863, vol. ii. p. 564.

[3] Correspondenz-Blatt für Psychiatrie, 1866 (quoted by Nothnagel).

[4] Deutsches Archiv. für Klinische Medizin, vol. 3, xiv. p. 309. Compare also vol. 2, p. 190, Case VII.

vaso-motoria," upon the basis of five detailed cases (without special sphygmographic observations). But the details of Nothnagel's cases will show that, however closely some of the subjective symptoms of angina pectoris may be simulated by a purely vaso-motor lesion, there are some very striking differences between the disease so induced and the true angina pectoris of Heberden. For—1st, in the greater number of Nothnagel's cases the disease yielded easily to very simple treatment, and in none was there a fatal issue, or even, apparently, much real apprehension of immediate or urgent danger; 2ndly, the sensations in the extremities (deadness, coldness, formication, *not* pain) were usually present in *all* the extremities indifferently, and *preceded* the palpitations and the cardiac uneasiness by some minutes; 3rdly, the specially cardiac or other internal sensations were, a very distressing sense of palpitation, attended by anxiety, and sometimes by vertigo, or incipient faintness; 4thly, in one of these cases only was the pulse-rate decidedly altered, and in that case it was diminished from 84 to 64 — 60 during the attack; 5thly, pain was either absent, or assumed little prominence among the symptoms; 6thly, the sensation of impending death was evidently *connected with, and probably caused by, the palpitation* (in Heberden's most characteristic case above quoted,[1] as also probably in John Hunter's case, the very opposite of this was the fact; the feeling was of "a pause in the operations of nature for perhaps three or four seconds"). 7thly, Several of the cases recorded were below the typical age (30, 38, 39, 46), and one only above it (63); that one being a woman. The lesson, therefore, taught by Nothnagel's cases is not, properly speaking, that typical, still less that fatal, angina pectoris is always to be regarded as due to vaso-motor spasm, but rather that, under certain peculiar conditions of the system, a sudden check to the circulation in the extremities, determined by vaso-motor spasm, may become the cause of an increased action of the heart, palpitation, and *pseudo*-angina; the disease so induced, however, being devoid of the characteristic pains and the more aggravated phenomena of fatal angina; and that in such cases heat, and mild counter-irritation of the surface, have almost complete power to control both the external and internal manifestations; the prognosis being (according to N.) entirely favourable. At the same time, although we cannot admit that Nothnagel's cases were genuine cases of Heberden's angina, they are very instructive, and may, no doubt, afford some insight into the pathology of the true disease.

Leaving, for the moment, the line of inquiry suggested by these observations, we may revert to the *pain* of angina, which has been commonly regarded as a neuralgia of the cardiac plexus; the impressions of pain in the severer cases being radiated outwards through the numerous connections which are known to exist between the special ganglionic system of the heart, and the spinal nerves entering into the cervical and brachial plexuses through the cervical ganglia. It

[1] See page 538, note 2.

is difficult, from the very nature of the case, to prove this proposition ; but there is no inherent improbability in it, unless, indeed, we should assume that the cardiac nerves of the ganglionic system are incapable of giving rise to acute pain ; an assumption not in accordance with the facts of medical experience in the cases of gallstone, colic, &c. Holding in view, moreover, the proved association of angina pectoris in many cases with disease of the coronary arteries of the heart, and with other lesions exclusively within the range of the ganglionic system of the heart and aorta, it is difficult to resist a bias in favour of the view that the nervous system of the heart itself is the origin or the chief seat of the pain, in the great majority of the cases. To these arguments it may be added that in most cases the internal sensations (whether distinctly referred to the heart or not by the patient) are obviously first in the order of time and of degree ; the brachial, intercostal, or cervical pains being sometimes altogether absent, and usually present only in the more severe and protracted attacks. It has, however, been plausibly maintained, notwithstanding these facts, that the spinal nerves are the true seats of the apparently cardiac pains of angina, and that all the apparently reflected sensations in the limbs, &c., are transmitted, like the external neuralgiæ, through a spinal centre. Dr. Anstie, who holds this view, adduces the unilateral character of the brachial pain in at least four cases out of five (?), as an almost irresistible argument against the radiation of pain outwards from the cardiac ganglia, through the peripheral nerves of communication. "It appears greatly more probable," he writes, "that angina is essentially a *mainly unilateral morbid condition of the lower cervical and upper dorsal portion of the cord ;* liable of course to be seriously aggravated by such peripheral sources of irritation as would be furnished by diseases of the heart, and especially by diseases of the coronary arteries." The question is one which can scarcely be made less obscure by any arguments falling within the scope of this article.

We have already indicated some of the difficulties that have to be encountered in extending the group, or order, of the *neuralgiæ* so as to include angina pectoris ; meaning by that term, of course, the formidable and fatal disease we have been chiefly describing, and not the very numerous, or rather innumerable, instances of pains referred to the heart, by hysterical women and others, which have no such significance. Referring chiefly to fatal cases of angina pectoris, Sir John Forbes and all the more considerable authorities from Heberden downwards concur in giving an immense preponderance to the male sex. Without insisting too much on the numerical details, which for reasons formerly indicated may perhaps be considered as somewhat biased by the mode of collection, it may be well to compare this overwhelming proportion of males who fall victims to cardiac angina (an excess on the male side greatly exceeding the greater proclivity of males to organic disease of the heart in general) with the numerical statements given incidentally in Dr. Anstie's work as regards the liability of the two sexes to neuralgiæ in general. "Eulenburg saw a hundred and six cases of neuralgia of all kinds, of which seventy-six were in women, and only thirty in men: my own experience is very similar; viz., sixty-eight women and thirty-two men out of a hundred hospital and private patients."[1]   A difference so extreme as this is not to be accounted for "by supposing that as men take a much larger amount of strong physical exercise than women, they will furnish a much larger proportion of subjects in whom an ill-nourished heart will break down under its work, and be seized either with paralysis or cramp;"[2] and it seems scarcely necessary to do more than place these facts before the reader, in order to make it apparent that many of the arguments by which analogies drawn from the study of neuralgia in its more familiar forms are applied to angina pectoris, are questionable, if not altogether unsound.   And yet I would by no means be understood to deny that persons hereditarily predisposed to neurotic diseases, and especially to those of advanced life, may be specially liable, *cæteris paribus*, to angina in its more painful forms.   Much care, however, is necessary in sifting facts and details of symptoms when recorded with a view to make good a general theory of this kind; and when we are called upon to accept a narrative of *epidemic angina pectoris* in a ship's crew, in which "numbers of men were simultaneously affected," while others were seized with "other forms of neuralgia, and severe colics,"[3] I cannot but infer that the limits of a safe induction have been considerably exceeded.   In like manner, "remarkable" cases of "hysteria, the paroxysms of which were always accompanied by stenocardiac attacks," can only serve to give a doubtful character to the theoretic interpretations which Eichwald has obtained from such a field of experience.[4]   And even Eulenburg, notwithstanding the sobriety of his tone in general, and the great importance of his work as a magazine of valuable information and research, has shown how much a sound clinical observation has been subordinated to theoretical ideas, when he pronounces dogmatically that the disorders of respiration in angina are merely "consequences of the pain; the patient is afraid to inspire deeply, but if induced to do so, can generally accomplish it."[5]   It may be doubted, I think, on the whole, whether

---

[1] Op. cit. p. 158.

[2] Ibid. p. 72. This might be a valid hypothesis were it possible to affirm that the subjects of fatal angina are chiefly drawn from the class of men that take the greatest amount of strong physical exercise. The opposite, however, is notoriously the fact.   We have already alluded to the generally received statement of Sir John Forbes, that angina pectoris is "the attendant rather of ease and luxury than of temperance;" and that it is comparatively rare (in its simple and typical form), among the laborious classes.

[3] Ibid. p. 74.   The authority given is Guélineau, Gaz. des Hopitaux, 1862.

[4] See Eulenburg, *infra*, p. 483. Perhaps the same remark applies to the presumed relationship between angina pectoris and spasmodic asthma, as indicated by Kneeland, Amer. Journal of Med. Science, Jan. 1850, and Anstie, op. cit., p. 68.   It is to be remarked that Trousseau, in his vast and varied experience, has not recorded anything tending to confirm the relationship of these two neuroses, except in a case where both of them were dependent on aneurism of the aorta.   See his Clin. Med., English translation, vol. i. p. 634.

[5] Med. Times and Gazette, March 26, 1870, p. 329. We have seen how emphatically this idea is contradicted by the specific statements in John Hunter's case, as well as by all the most exact clinical observations from Heberden downwards.

much real knowledge has been gained by the classification of angina pectoris among the neuralgiæ; to which, nevertheless, the character of its pain shows a remarkable affinity.

Proceeding now to consider the motor derangements which form a part of the angina-paroxysm, and especially those which, affecting the heart itself, determine the fatal termination, it is impossible to overlook the facts brought to light by physiology as regards the influence of certain nerves on the movements of the heart. In particular, the remarkable inhibitory influence of the efferent nerves proceeding to the heart through the pneumogastrics, demonstrated by the brothers Weber [1] in 1846, and in 1856 shown by Waller [2] to be due to filaments from the spinal accessory nerves joining the pneumogastrics near their origin, has a peculiar interest for us in connection with this subject. It has been conclusively shown that by a galvanic current transmitted outwards through these filaments, or by galvanisation of the centre in the medulla from which they are derived, the heart's action may be controlled, or even stopped, so that a true cardiac paralysis is the result of a strong current, while weaker galvanic action produces an indefinite retardation in the rate of the cardiac pulsations. Whatever theory be adopted as regards the so-called inhibitory influence, its results are too closely allied to the phenomena of syncope, pure and simple, to escape attention in treating of sudden death from angina. But it has been further shown by Cyon and Ludwig,[3] that a reflex influence may be so transmitted through nerves arising from the pneumogastrics, (viz., the so-called depressor-nerves), as at once to control the cardiac pulsations through the inhibitory efferent nerves, and to diminish muscular tension through the vaso-motor system. As we have already seen reason to believe that in angina pectoris the vascular tension is usually increased rather than diminished, it may be inferred with great probability that if the pneumogastric nerve be implicated at all in the angina-paroxysm, it is probably more as an inhibitory or efferent, than as a reflex or afferent nerve. It must not be forgotten, however, that paralysis of the sympathetic nerve has the effect also of enfeebling and retarding, though not, apparently, of stopping, the heart's action; which, in a certain sense, may be regarded as not essentially dependent upon influence transmitted from any nerve-centre, though subject, as we have just seen, to control through the inhibitory or efferent cardiac filaments of the pneumogastric.

If we endeavour now to determine, in the light of these facts, what is the particular mode in which the heart's action is suddenly arrested in a paroxysm of angina, it must be confessed that no ultimate decision seems possible. Almost all the vague and unsatisfactory speculations formerly alluded to, as to whether *spasm* or *paralysis* is the prevailing condition in the fatal paroxysm, have proceeded on the assumption that these two conditions are essentially contrasted, or

[1] Wagner, Handwörterbuch der Physiologie, Bd. iii., 2te Abtheilung, S. 42.
[2] Gazette Médicale, Paris, 1856, t. xi. p. 420.
[3] Journal de l'Anatomie, Paris, 1867, t. iv. p. 472.

rather opposite to, and inconsistent with, one another; the former representing undue strength, the latter undue weakness, or absolute annihilation of contractile energy. Now this assumption can by no means be regarded as a legitimate, or even a probably correct one. At least it may be fairly affirmed, as a probable result both of physiological and pathological inquiries, that spasm (*i.e.*, irregular or abnormal contraction, whether painful or not) in a voluntary muscle is much more allied to weakness, or to deficient innervation, than to absolute excess of normal energy. And the frequency of the association of rigid or tonic spasm with paralysis, in the voluntary muscles, would tend to show that there is no absolute inconsistency, at least, in the supposition that *both* spasm and paralysis may, in varying degrees, be present in the heart's arrested action which leads up to sudden death in the angina-paroxysm. As far as observation goes, in the case of spasm of the involuntary muscles (other than the heart), it seems as though abnormal, or painful, disturbances of rhythmic action were almost always an indication of weakened innervation, rather than of superfluous energy in the contractile apparatus as a whole. The spasm of colic, for instance, is associated with constipation, or deficient peristaltic action of the intestines; the false pains, or painful spasms, of the uterine muscles retard, instead of expediting, the process of delivery. We might, therefore, not unfairly argue from these analogies, that a painful spasm of the heart might be expected to interfere with its rhythmic or normal action quite after the manner of a paralysis, the abnormal being substituted for the normal action, and the whole sum of disordered effort being less than the sum of normal energy expended in healthy cardiac action. So that it might very well be presumed that painful spasm is by no means unlikely to be associated with a tendency to sudden stoppage of the heart's action, or virtual paralysis, whether from inhibitory nervous irritation through the pneumogastrics, or from disorders originating in the cardiac ganglia themselves, and allied in character to true paralysis of muscular energy. It must, however, be conceded to the advocates of the theory of paralysis, pure and simple, that nothing but the presence of severe pain in the angina-paroxysm, and the absence of this symptom, as a rule, in purely paralytic affections, tends to support the spasm-theory of angina. Post-mortem examinations have generally shown that the heart is found flaccid, rather than rigidly contracted; and the lesions found in the muscular substance of the heart itself are usually such as would confirm the idea of decidedly and permanently weakened energy, rather than a disposition to abnormal contraction. Rupture of the muscular bundles, so commonly observed in tetanus and other severe spasms of voluntary muscles, has never been recorded in sudden deaths from angina pectoris; while anæmia, fatty degeneration, and fibro-tendinous substitution, have been the predominating lesions of the muscular fibre itself. The question as between spasm and paralysis, therefore, is one of great difficulty, if not indeed practically insoluble in the present state of our knowledge.

While dealing with hypotheses of which no absolute or experimental proof can be obtained, we may remark that vaso-motor spasm, operating indirectly through the smaller arteries upon the muscular fibre of the heart itself, may possibly give a clue to some of the pathological changes which attend the paroxysm, and especially those which precede dissolution. Both Erichsen[1] and V. Bezold[2] have shown that as a result of deligation or occlusion of the coronary arteries, the heart's contractions become feeble or irregular, and ultimately cease; the normal action being restored again on removal of the ligature or of the compression. Now apart from the obvious bearing of these facts upon the case of organic obstruction or constriction of the coronary vessels (perhaps the most clearly established of all the permanent organic changes in connection with fatal angina pectoris), is it not extremely probable that a similar effect, or an aggravation of a pre-existing tendency to interrupted cardiac action, might occur, if in a case of disease of the aorta or coronary arteries, cardiac anæmia were aggravated for the moment by vaso-motor spasm of the smaller arteries within the heart itself? Even without such preceding organic disease it is conceivable that extreme vaso-motor spasm might affect the cardiac circulation directly through its smaller arteries, and so produce changes more or less similar to those observed in the experiments above mentioned. What has been already stated, however, in regard to Nothnagel's observations would seem to show that really fatal angina does not occur in this way; and that the first effects of general vaso-motor spasm upon the heart are more of the nature of palpitation, or excited action, than of interrupted or suspended pulsation.

On the whole, it must be admitted that the ultimate pathology of the angina paroxysm does not admit of being reduced to any very precise expression or definition; but various more or less probable conjectures may be made, in accordance with known facts and experimental researches, as well as with clinical and pathological observation, to account for the facts. Viewing the paroxysm as a *neurosis*, we might attribute its phenomena partly to vaso-motor spasm, and partly to inhibitory influence transmitted through the vagus nerve from the medulla oblongata. This latter influence would account more reasonably and probably than any other for those cases of angina in which mental causes and sudden shocks of any kind are known to influence the production of the paroxysm, without the intervention of peripheral changes such as can be attributed to vaso-motor spasm. In cases, again, resembling in their symptoms those described by Nothnagel, whether accompanied by organic disease or not—cases in which coldness of the surface, deadness of the extremities, and perhaps palpitation or increased rate of the pulse can be ascertained to precede the cardiac pain, there would be reasonable ground for presuming that the vaso-motor nerves were the earliest involved in the

[1] London Medical Gazette, July 8, 1842,
[2] Centralblatt für die Med. Wissenschaften, 1867, No. 23.

morbid circle, though it is still probable that, if such cases ever end in sudden death, it is through some more direct impression on the cardiac nerves, or on the coronary circulation. It is very doubtful, however, whether under any circumstances fatal angina pectoris can be viewed as a pure *neurosis*. Much more probably, the paroxysm is the expression in symptoms of sudden changes arising, indeed, from neurotic accidents, but only assuming grave importance in respect of their coincidence with a permanent cause of detriment to the circulation. Either the heart's fibre is permanently weakened, or its arteries are obstructed and diseased, or the general arterial circulation is disturbed through disease in the first part of the aorta, aneurismal or other. In certain cases it may be that the innervation of the heart is directly implicated in organic disease; at least in two cases of this kind[1] the cardiac plexus and cardiac branches of the vagus were found to be compressed in connection with angina-paroxysms which proved fatal; though probably the inferences which have been drawn from these rare instances may not be applicable to the general pathology of the subject. But whatever be the nature of the permanent change underlying the disease, its effect in the most characteristic cases is not much felt when the circulation is in a moderately tranquil state. In some of the very worst cases, indeed, it has been clearly ascertained that very shortly before a fatal paroxysm the patient has been in a state of entire comfort and tranquillity, with a regular and normally acting heart, and all the functions apparently so well-adjusted as to involve no appearance of any disease tending to shorten life. Usually there is an incapacity for sudden or severe exertion, and a liability to grave disturbance under strong emotion; but on the other hand, a patient has been known to say, *within three days of his death in a paroxysm*, "I can walk with ease ten or fifteen miles, after I have been stopped three or four times at intervals of a hundred yards."[2] In such cases the paroxysms are plainly neurotic; but the disease is nevertheless not a pure neurosis. It is, on the contrary, obviously of a complex character, involving a permanent nucleus, so to speak, of organic change, together with a neuralgic element, more or less pronounced, and, connected with this, perhaps as a reflected neurosis in some cases, an element of motor disturbance in the heart's action, which may in some cases be of vaso-motor origin, while in others it may be more directly determined through the inhibitory filaments of the vagus. It is probably in the former

[1] Heine, in Müller's Archiv. 1841, p. 236; and Lancereaux, in Gazette Médicale. 1867, p. 432. In the former case the heart was at times observed to cease beating for several seconds, and at these times there was a feeling of indescribable anxiety, like that of angina pectoris; in the intervals of the paroxysms the patient felt perfectly well. The right phrenic nerve, the nervus cardiacus magnus, and the pulmonary branches of the left vagus were all involved in, or compressed by, calcareous deposits. In Lancereaux's case, the cardiac plexus was found vascular, and compressed by exudation; but the coronary arteries were also obstructed, and the aorta was diseased. The patient died of angina pectoris, in a paroxysm.

[2] Walshe, Diseases of Heart and Aorta, 4th edit., p. 199, *note*.

class of cases that the action of nitrite of amyl is most immediately and surely productive of benefit.

There remains for remark only one obscure, and apparently non-essential, part of the pathology of angina pectoris, viz., the nature of the cerebral accidents we have indicated in the description of the disease as sometimes coinciding, sometimes alternating; with the more decidedly cardiac attacks. It is to be observed that among these accidents spasms, giddiness, temporary attacks of coma, associated with, or followed by, various disorders of the special and general sensibility, are common; while on the other hand, paralysis, either spinal or cerebral, is rare. These facts point strongly in the direction of a neurosis, and very probably a vaso-motor neurosis, of the cerebral circulation; and we know that in animals most of the symptoms above referred to may be induced artificially, by cutting off the arterial vascular supply of the brain and medulla-oblongata, as in the well-known experiments of Sir Astley Cooper.

The *Prognosis* of angina pectoris is difficult to realise in individual cases, in proportion to the absence of clear lines of distinction between this and the various affections resembling Heberden's angina, which we have discussed in various parts of this article. Probably a critically exact, or absolute, prognosis, could only be founded on a knowledge of the nature and extent of the organic changes underlying the paroxysmal neurosis; and although we have already indicated a doubt as to whether the latter ever terminates fatally in the absence of such organic changes, yet it is beyond all question that the amount of organic disease which can be detected in any given case during life is a most insecure guide in estimating the probabilities of death during a paroxysm in that particular case. "It is accordant with my experience," says Dr. Walshe, "that fatal angina is more to be dreaded in association with organic defects, either difficult or impossible to diagnose (such as slight fatty metamorphosis and calcified coronary arteries), than with those grave forms of structural mischief that are readily discoverable by physical examination."[1] Add to this that the mere inference from symptoms as to the gravity of the prognosis is likewise extremely open to fallacy; inasmuch as a series of comparatively mild or lessening attacks may sometimes (under apparently unchanged conditions) be succeeded by the most violent or dangerous, even fatal, paroxysms; while on the other hand, one or more attacks, very nearly fatal, may be followed by a long interval of comparative, or nearly complete, freedom. From this dilemma there is, in the present state of our knowledge, no escape; and all that we can do, therefore, towards the establishment of a guarded and limited prognosis in any case, is to study carefully its individual features, and particularly the relation of the symptoms to particular causes of aggravation, or of relief. Generally speaking, a form of disease which yields, gradually, to carefully pursued hygienic

[1] Op. cit. p. 201.

treatment, and in which the paroxysms are obviously under the control of the remedies about to be discussed, is relatively favourable; while the opposite indications justify the gravest prognosis. An absolutely favourable prognosis could only be justified by circumstances tending to place the disease in the category of pseudo-angina, as above indicated; and indeed it may be generally observed that the gravity of cases of angina in the experience of individual observers is often found to be in an inverse proportion to their estimated frequency, cases of hysteria, intercostal neuralgia, spasmodic dyspnœa, &c., being admitted by some more freely than others into the category of angina. There seems no reason to doubt, however, that a person affected with absolutely typical angina pectoris may survive for years, even after repeated paroxysms; and in some cases, apparently of the most threatening kind at one stage of their progress, the disease has been so far reduced in its frequency and severity that we may even, perhaps, speak of such cases as cured, in a practical sense. But cures of this kind are rarely, if ever, recorded with such minute attention to details as to inspire confidence, apart from the credit due to the reporters; and perhaps even the statements of Heberden as to the long survival of some of the cases mentioned in his first paper (see p. 559, *note*) may require qualification on the ground that clear evidence is wanting as to the absolutely typical character of the symptoms referred to.[1] Among cases actually ending by a fatal paroxysm, it has not occurred to me personally to have been informed of a longer duration than six or seven years, counting from the first well-defined seizure; but I have known more than one instance of survival for much longer periods, after attacks bearing so much resemblance to true angina as only to have required death to have occurred in a paroxysm, as a conclusive argument for considering them to be typical instances of the disease. In John Hunter's case, as we have seen (assuming the first attack of supposed gout in the stomach to have been really identical in character with succeeding seizures) a duration of rather more than twenty years, with numerous intervals of tolerable health and great mental activity, may be regarded as well established. Dr. Walshe has "met with an instance in which there was the strongest evidence that the first paroxysm had occurred *twenty-four* years prior to my interview with the patient."[2] And, in the general experience of physicians who have had occasion to see much of cardiac disease, it is by no means uncommon to find cases of valvular or other very positive and well-defined organic disease, in which symptoms of a dangerous or proximately fatal kind, probably

[1] It is at least worth noting (though the omission may be accidental) that in the Commentaries these statements are not repeated: and perhaps the language, though carefully guarded, admits of the inference that thirty years of additional experience had rather increased than diminished Heberden's sense of the gravity of the prognosis. "*Exitus hujus affectus est perquam memorabilis. Qui enim eo tenentur, siquidem, nullo casu interveniente, angina pectoris ad axμην pervenerit, omnes repente corruunt, et ferè momento pereunt.*" . . . "*Unicum vidi (ægrum), in quo hoc malum sponte sud finitum est.*"   [2] Op. cit., p. 200.

more or less allied to angina, have preceded the fatal issue by an interval of very many years; sometimes, indeed (as in the case of the Rev. Dr. Guthrie, already referred to[1]) for more than a quarter of a century. Such cases, however, are rarely quite typical instances of Heberden's angina, and accordingly only a small proportion of them are characterised by the very sudden ending proper to the disease as described in the "Commentaries." It is difficult to obtain exact clinical histories of cases extending over so many years, but in one, in which I was consulted in 1872, and which terminated fatally some months ago, there was reason to suppose that the foundations of the aortic valvular lesion of which the physical signs were apparent, and of which the obvious symptoms had certainly existed many years before 1872, had been laid as early as 1852, when the patient had suffered from pulmonary hæmorrhage. The threatening symptoms present on that occasion had been popularly attributed to a consumptive tendency, but Dr. Christison, who was consulted, had evidently detected some valvular lesion of the heart, and had carefully questioned the patient as to its possible rheumatic origin. It is not, indeed, certain, or even perhaps very probable, that well-marked and considerable aortic regurgitation existed at this period, nor is it possible now to ascertain at what precise interval after the first commencement of the disease the angina-like symptoms, which were notably present when I saw the patient, first became apparent. What I can personally affirm is, that in 1872 the symptoms and physical signs were those of old-established aortic regurgitation, with very considerable hypertrophy of the left ventricle, and all the usual concomitants; and notwithstanding this, the patient assured me that so late as 1870 he had explored the Aletsch glacier, and on other occasions, from about 1865 onwards, had been able to carry out walking tours in Switzerland, the Tyrol, and the Dolomite country, the character of which may be inferred from his having walked over the Monte Moro pass and the Gemmi, visited the Mer de Glace, and gone nearly to the Jardin, in addition to all the usual excursions about Chamounix. Moreover, this gentleman was in 1872 performing the duties of a parish clergyman in a populous place, sparing himself somewhat, indeed, in visiting, but preaching often more than once a day, and, as he affirmed, without any apparent injury or physical exhaustion; and the question most urgently and repeatedly pressed upon his medical advisers was as to his carrying out an engagement of marriage, entered into several years before, and maintained with full knowledge on both sides of the precarious condition of his bodily health. I need not say that no medical encouragement to this step could be obtained; but the marriage, nevertheless, took place in about a year after I was first consulted, and the death of this patient not long ago shows how real was his danger, and at the same time what a terrible burden of positive organic disease may be borne without apparently "giving in," by one whose objects in life are of sufficient importance to induce him

[1] See *ante*, p. 568, *note*.

to disregard the silent warnings of internal suffering. In yet another case known to me, in which, however, the symptoms were far more decidedly and typically those of angina pectoris, while the physical signs were much less manifest than in the preceding case, the patient was able to make numerous long journeys to the Holy Land, Egypt, &c., and always felt himself the better for them. This patient in the end perished suddenly.

The TREATMENT of angina pectoris resolves itself naturally into two departments, viz., that of the paroxysm, and that of the intervals. The former treatment is essentially palliative, and directed exclusively to the urgent symptoms then existing: the latter aims at being founded, in a wider sense, upon the diagnosis and prognosis of the individual case, after a complete examination into the state of all the bodily functions.

Heberden's views of treatment were limited to the first indication —the control of the paroxysm. "Wine and cordials taken at going to bed will prevent, or weaken, the night fits; but nothing does this so effectually as opiates. Ten, fifteen, or twenty drops of the tinctura Thebaica taken at lying down will enable those to keep their beds till morning who had been forced to rise, and sit up, two or three hours every night for many months." [1] We have already seen that Heberden altogether repudiated the (so-called) antiphlogistic treatment as inapplicable to this disease, which he considered as belonging to the order of spasms, not of inflammations. In his later work he repeats in general terms the above recommendations, and adds to them a single phrase in favour of rest and warmth. He has seen an approach to a cure in one case, where the patient prescribed to himself the labour of sawing wood for half an hour every day. Beyond this, he has little or nothing to tell, and does not profess to have greatly advanced the cure of a disease, "qui vix ad huc locum, aut nomen in medicorum libris invenit." It may be fairly inferred from these expressions, that Heberden's views of the treatment of angina remained almost stationary for at least thirty years; and that here, as in the matter of prognosis, he does not appear to have gained confidence with his advancing experience. The treatment of the paroxysm by opiates and stimulants of various kinds has in fact been repeated by almost all the leading authorities, and is even now the only medical treatment which can be said to have received general assent. Latham, Stokes, and Walshe, among our more modern authors, concur in recommending from forty to sixty drops of laudanum, together with wine, brandy, or aromatic spirits of ammonia, repeated according to the violence of the paroxysm. Hoffmann's anodyne, or sulphuric ether in half-drachm doses, has been a favourite remedy with many; and musk, camphor, and other anti-spasmodics, have also been employed, though confessedly of less value than ether, which has also been followed by good results when administered by inhala-

[1] Med. Trans., vol. ii., ut supra.

tion. Of late years, opium has been given hypodermically, and, it is stated, with more immediate as well as more successful results than when administered by the mouth. In so far as the principle of the treatment can be inferred from the success that has attended those remedies in some cases, it would appear that a rapidly induced narcotism, benumbing the sensory nerves and extending, perhaps, to the centre through which painful sensory impressions are reflected in the form of a paralysing or inhibitory influence on the heart, by the motor fibres of the pneumogastric, is the first object to be accomplished in the presence of overwhelming pain, while the second and not less important object is to stimulate the heart's action by all the known excitants of the circulation. Warmth to the extremities and to the epigastrium, sinapisms to the thorax, and sometimes between the shoulders or at the back of the neck, may be regarded also as additional means of fulfilling the latter indication, and of assisting the cardiac contractions by their influence on the vaso-motor nerves. In my own experience, no remedial agencies have appeared more powerful than warm pediluvia with mustard, and fomentations applied at the same time to the arms and thorax, as hot as they can well be borne. With these, and with ether and other diffusible stimulants, I have often been able to dispense with the use of large opiates, in doubtful cases, or in cases where they seemed to be in some respects contra-indicated. It is well, if possible, to be informed of the condition of the kidneys, and of the lungs before prescribing opiates. Dr. Stokes [1] evidently looks upon large opiates as unsafe where fatty degeneration of the heart's fibre is suspected ; and Niemeyer [2] discountenances narcotics altogether. The use of opium, however, is too valuable in typical cases of Heberden's angina, when apparently uncomplicated, to be readily given up. It should be given with discretion, its effects being carefully watched ; and it should probably be withheld, or given in extremely moderate doses, wherever there is risk of uræmia, or of bronchial and pulmonary sudden congestion or œdema, or of the cerebral accidents that accompany angina in certain cases, especially those in which the cardiac fibre is the seat of degeneration. In these cases, too, it is not usual for the mere pain of angina to be so threatening, *per se*, as to suggest opium in the same high doses as in the more typical instances where the paroxysm occurs in the midst of apparent good health.

Hydrate of chloral, from its well-marked sedative and anodyne powers, has been suggested as a substitute for opium in cases of painful angina ; [3] but on the other hand, the depressing action of chloral-hydrate in large doses has been supposed to be a fatal objecttion to its employment in cases of weakened cardiac action. My experience of this remedy in severe cases resembling angina pectoris is limited to one case, but it is so remarkable as to deserve notice here. John McN., æt. 35, was subject to paroxysms of intense cardiac

---

[1] Diseases of the Heart and Aorta, p. 489.
[2] Text-book of Practical Medicine, American translation, vol. i., p. 371.
[3] Strange, Medical Times and Gazette, Sept. 4, 1870.

suffering, of a rather obscurely painful character, but with considerable orthopnœa, palpitation, sleeplessness, and frightful dreams. His symptoms are more particuiarly referred to in an earlier part of this article, and from a very careful consideration of them I arrived at the conclusion that they were essentially of the character there described as *angina sine dolore*, with slight bronchitic complication, and slightly albuminous urine—sp. gr. 1013—20. The heart's action was irregular, and the physical signs pointed unmistakably to hypertrophy of the heart and liver, with valvular and (probably) arterial disease. The details are too complicated to be introduced here, but my diagnosis was—Aortic insufficiency, with aneurism. The case was certainly not one in which extreme doses of any narcotic would have been regarded as expedient; but, guided by experience acquired before he applied to me, I allowed this patient to have thirty grains of hydrate of chloral to obviate the sleeplessness, and if possible to ward off the attacks. It answered well the first night, and on a succeeding occasion the same dose was ordered, and was to be given a little before midnight. By a misunderstanding of the directions three drachms of hydrate of chloral were sent instead of a like quantity of the usual syrup, and this being in one dose, apparently to be given as a draught, the patient took 180 grains at once of chloral-hydrate, from the hands of a night-nurse, after a restless and disturbed evening, at 11.30 p.m. Next morning I found him very drowsy, but not quite comatose, as he could be roused to give rational answers as to his own condition; the breathing was quiet, and only slightly stertorous. The pupils were, on the whole, contracted, but variably so; the pulse, which had been irregular in rhythm, was decidedly more natural than before; the face was a little congested, and the eyelids puffy, but the surface generally warm, and the whole appearances not such as to justify any very great alarm, especially as at the time it was supposed that only thirty grains of chloral-hydrate had been given, the mistake being found out afterwards. The patient gradually recovered from the effects of the overdose, and it is very remarkable that he always continued to attribute to this happy accident (as it might be called, speaking of the result only) a comparative immunity afterwards from the angina-like symptoms. The irregularity of the pulse recurred after the effects of the overdose of chloral had passed off, but under repeated doses of from thirty to sixty grains he became much better in all respects, and a course of iodide of potassium, with careful hygienic management, accomplished what, so far as the more immediately urgent symptoms are concerned, may almost be called a temporary cure of a very perilous condition. This man is now performing regulated duties as a railway servant, and is still occasionally taking hydrate of chloral, though warned not to allow it to become a regular habit. It is clear, therefore, that in some cases, at least, of angina pectoris chloral-hydrate might probably with advantage replace opium in the treatment, and that irregularity of the heart's action does not always prove a contra-indication to its use.

Inhalations of chloroform have been proposed, and in some cases employed, for the relief of painful angina; but, from the supposed tendency of deep chloroform-anæsthesia to paralyse the heart, this remedy has never been warmly supported or largely employed by physicians in such cases. The inhalation of ether seems preferable as attended with less risk; and chloroform, if given at all, should be in doses short of complete anæsthesia, whether by inhalation or by the mouth.

Of all the more modern additions, however, to the resources of the physician in the angina-paroxysm, the most important by far appears to be the employment by inhalation of nitrite of amyl, as first recommended by Dr. B. W. Richardson, and successfully carried out on a basis of careful clinical and experimental observation in angina by Dr. Lauder Brunton. We have already indicated in this article the nature of the scientific evidence on which this therapeutic suggestion rests, and have now only to consider the details of purely clinical experience in relation to this remedy, and the qualifications and cautions required in its employment. On this subject our knowledge is still very incomplete, but it is none the less necessary to place on record here whatever can be said to be well established as a guide to the practitioner.

My own experience, I may remark in passing, is certainly favourable to the use of this remedy, not only in positive angina pectoris, but also in many cases of cardiac asthma, and even of true spasmodic asthma without cardiac complication. In the very few cases of typical angina in which I have prescribed it, I have had distinct testimony as to the relief afforded, although my opportunities of close observation of the actual paroxysms have not been such as to enable me to add anything of real value to the statements of other observers. Looking to the practical aspects of the question, there is probably no single observation hitherto made which, as a simply clinical narrative, can rank beside the history of his own case by Dr. W. Herries Madden of Torquay.[1] We shall therefore give here some details of this remarkable personal experience.

Dr. Madden seems to have suffered from a temporary break-down in health at 24 years of age, " with obscure heart-symptoms, and threatened lung mischief." His father had died shortly before from angina pectoris—"the organic cause in his case being atheromatous obstruction of the coronary arteries." In the winter of 1859, at about 44 years of age, Dr. Williams detected slight mitral incompetency. In the spring of 1871, Dr. Madden records that he suffered from an attack of bronchitis, with great nervous prostration, but recovered in autumn, and was able to perform all his usual duties during the next winter and spring, in the midst of " a good deal of professional anxiety and much painful worry of a different nature." On July the 8th, 1872 (at 57 years of age), he had his first attack of angina, which occurred " suddenly, without the slightest warning," and was charac-

[1] The Practitioner, vol. ix. 1872, p. 331.

terised by "pain extending across the front of the chest, along the inside of the left arm, and across the chin." In about ten days the frequent recurrence and increased severity of the attacks compelled him to desist from all professional duty. Notwithstanding the repose so obtained, the attacks, after a few days' interval, continued to increase in violence, lasting, for the most part, for a quarter of an hour or twenty minutes, and recurring frequently at intervals of about three hours. " Various remedies were tried, but with little or no benefit. Hypodermic morphia was the most useful, but it was impossible to employ it often enough without producing dangerous narcosis." At this period Dr. Madden was led, after considerable hesitation, to give a trial to the nitrite of amyl, which he had previously supposed to be suitable only for those cases in which the face was pallid during the paroxysm. "As mine was flushed," he writes, "I dismissed from my mind all thoughts of trying it, and paid the penalty of hasty conclusions in the shape of a large amount of acute suffering." The result of the first trial of five drops, inhaled during a severe attack in the night, "was truly wonderful. The spasm was, as it were, strangled at its birth. It certainly did not last *two* minutes, instead of the old weary *twenty*. And so it continued. The frequency of the paroxysms was not diminished for some time ; but then they were mere bagatelles as compared with their predecessors. Under these improved circumstances, strength gradually returned ; the attacks became less and less frequent, and finally ceased. At the time of writing these lines (October 11, 1872) I have not had an attack for five weeks, and have resumed my ordinary duties, of course with care." It is most satisfactory to be able to add, from a private letter with which the author has been favoured, from Dr. Madden, that his confidence in the remedy continues unabated, but that at this date (August 1875) he has not required to use it for a considerable time.

As regards the more obvious effects of the inhalation of nitrite of amyl, Dr. Madden records that "the first effect was often bronchial irritation, causing cough ; then quickened circulation ; then a sense of great fulness in the temples, and burning of the ears ; then a violent commotion in the chest, tumultuous action of the heart, and quick respiration. The angina pain died out first in the chest, next in the left upper arm, and last of all in the wrist, where it was usually extremely severe. . . . When the pain had ceased there was generally for some time a strong involuntary tendency to suspension of breathing, each prolonged pause being followed by a very deep inspiration. There was not at any time the slightest confusion of thought, or disturbance of vision, but occasionally slight and transient headache." The physical signs in Dr. Madden's case seem to have varied somewhat, and latterly had more the characters of aortic than of mitral disease. The description of the peculiar subjective sensations connected with the heart-pang in this case has been already quoted at p. 540, note 1.

It can be but rarely that, in a disease so paroxysmal and uncertain in its characters as angina pectoris, the conditions of a therapeutical experiment can be so perfectly attained as in this case. The hereditary predisposition, the age and sex of the patient, the proved existence of positive cardiac disease, and the vivid and personal narrative of the symptoms, combine in assuring us that the angina was of the most formidable kind, and all but typical, if not indeed absolutely so, in character. On the other hand, the relief was so marked, so strikingly instantaneous, and so frequently observed in repeated paroxysms, as to leave no doubt of the control exercised by the remedy. And further, the ultimate relief amounts to something more than a palliative remedial action; something, indeed, closely approaching the character of a cure. Further, as Dr. Madden has remarked, the relief is shown not to have been contingent upon the external evidences of vaso-motor disturbance during the paroxysm, although closely associated (as in Dr. Brunton's case) with the physiological action of the remedy in relaxing arterial tension. It is to be remarked, however, that beyond the more obvious facts, no very exact observations were made in Dr. Madden's case as to the connection between the attacks of angina and vaso-motor changes. "The presence of intense pain," he says, " is not favourable to the exercise of calm, philosophic analysis, and I can only tell what I felt."

But although this case, and others more or less resembling it which have been published, give the utmost assurance of the beneficial action of nitrite of amyl in the angina-paroxysm as a fact ascertained by experience, yet the moment we proceed beyond the mere fact, we find the question of the *modus operandi*, indications, and contra-indications of the remedy surrounded with difficulties which have not as yet been resolved by scientific observation. It has been commonly supposed that the action of the amyl-nitrite is purely peripheral, *i.e.*, on the vaso-motor nerves of the vessels only, apart from the vaso-motor nervous centre; and that the relief caused in angina is in direct relation with the previously increased vascular tension, as suggested by Dr. Lauder Brunton in his first experiment. We had occasion to point out, however, when speaking of that remarkable case in its relation to the theory of the angina-paroxysm, that the state of the heart's action corresponding with the period of increased vascular tension on the one hand, and with the relief through amyl-nitrite on the other, was different from what could be attributed to vaso-motor spasm and paralysis alone; and that there remain phenomena of the paroxysm which can be explained, in all probability, only through the innervation of the heart itself. A like difficulty still surrounds the explanation of the physiological and therapeutic action of the nitrite of amyl. Though unquestionably producing some of its well-known effects through vaso-motor paralysis, we are not quite able to affirm with confidence that its action is purely peripheral, or even that it is quite uniform in all cases of angina. Thus in Dr. Madden's case it seems to have produced, as a primary result, "quickened circulation, tumultuous action of the heart, and quick respiration." This is, in fact, the usual effect of amyl-nitrite on healthy persons, in whom the pulse-rate may be raised in a few seconds from a normal state of about 70 to 120 or 140 pulsations in the minute; the flushing of the face, and the other distinctly vaso-motor effects following the rise in the pulse-rate. In Dr. Brunton's case, on the other hand, the pulse became slower when the spasm was being relieved. In a case published by Dr. Haddon, which, though rather imperfectly reported, appears to have been one of aortic incompetency with angina-like pain, the pulse was jerking, and 80 per minute at the commencement of the inhalation, and after only three drops were inhaled "the pulse lost its jerking character and became gradually slower," but the face did not become flushed, and the pain was not relieved. In the course of a minute, "the pulse beat so slowly that I thought the heart would stop altogether; while the patient raised himself on his elbow, and with a pale face moved his head about, as if for breath. At the same time he seemed confused, and did not answer questions."[1] Under brandy and free ventilation the pulse recovered its former character and frequency, and the patient fell asleep in half an hour. In another case, which proved on post-mortem examination to be one of aneurism of the first part of the aorta, pressing on the right ventricle and pulmonary artery, and with universal adhesion of the pericardium, besides a degree of compression of the left phrenic nerve by a diseased bronchial gland, the paroxysms of coughing, which were among the most apparently dangerous symptoms in the case, were greatly aggravated on one occasion by the inhalation of five drops of amyl-nitrite, and a critical state of apnœa was induced. It is obvious that neither of these cases was one of typical angina, and it is quite possible that the phenomena may have been only accidentally connected with the inhalation; but Sander has recorded two cases, and Samelsohn one case,[2] in which alarming symptoms of collapse followed closely on the inhalation of amyl-nitrite. In the latter case there was not even a suspicion of internal disease, the inhalation being done experimentally, with a view to test its effects upon spasmodic closure of the eyelids in an anæmic young woman. The usual flushing occurred, but was in an instant "replaced by a deadly pallor; the pulse became thread-like and slow, the skin cold and clammy, respiration difficult, and gasping; consciousness was retained." These symptoms recurred again and again at intervals for an hour, and even up to next day the patient complained of feeling very cold. It is stated that she was menstruating at the time, and that on subsequent occasions she inhaled the nitrite without any such alarming incidents. It is quite possible that the effects of fright, or agitation, or some other accidental disturbing cause, may in these cases have complicated the action of the amyl-nitrite; but still they form a warning, not only that dangerous results may in certain circumstances follow its

[1] Edin. Med. Journal, July 1870, p. 46.
[2] London Medical Record, March 17, 1875, p. 168; and Aug. 16, 1875, p. 479.

inhalation, but that the theory which regards its action as purely vaso-motor, and still more that which considers the vaso-motor nervous centres, and the brain and spinal cord generally, as not within the range of its direct influence, must be held in the meantime as subject to reservations to be afterwards ascertained by experience.

Generally speaking, the administration of nitrite of amyl in angina has been found to be free from danger, when used in doses of from two or three up to ten minims on a cloth or handkerchief, abundant access of air being allowed at the same time. The first effects of the remedy in healthy persons are, as stated above, increased frequency of the cardiac pulsations, with a feeling of palpitation, and throbbing of the carotids, followed in the course of thirty to forty seconds after the commencement of the inhalation by flushing of the face, warmth of the head, face, and neck, with perspiration; the latter symptoms being often general. Breathlessness and disposition to cough, giddiness, headache, slight indistinctness of vision, lassitude, and a feeling of intoxication, are among the variable after-effects. The actual thermometric temperature of the body does not appear to be much, if at all, affected; and consciousness is always preserved.[1] When given in angina the effects are similar, with the exception of the discrepancy formerly alluded to as regards the cardiac pulsations. The flushing of the face must be fully developed, in severe attacks of angina, before any relief is to be obtained; but in minor attacks the pain and sense of constriction give way before a very few drops; almost immediately on the first inhalations, or even after merely applying a bottle containing a little of the remedy to one nostril. Three to five drops on a small piece of lint, or on a handkerchief, may be said to be an ordinary, or experimental dose, as a commencement. When the patient has become thoroughly familiar with the effects of the remedy he may, if intelligent and conscientious, be entrusted with a quantity sufficient for ordinary use at his own discretion. One patient mentioned by Dr. Jones[2] had used about thirty ounces in six months; but the large quantity was accounted for by his belief that the remedy when kept in the pocket in a small stoppered bottle, became "flat," and required to be renewed. Dr. Jones believes that he was right in this impression. This patient discarded the lint, and always inhaled directly from the bottle, which he always carried about with him, containing about half a teaspoonful of the remedy. "One night his father found him sound asleep, with his

---

[1] Compare Goodhart, Practitioner, vol. vi. 1871, p. 12; and Talfourd Jones, ibid. vol. viii. 1872, p. 213. Dr. Wood (Amer. Journal of the Med. Sciences, new series, vol. lxi. 1871, p. 422) found that by poisonous doses in animals temperature was lowered "to a degree which is almost unheard of in the history of drugs." He also found that this substance has "the curious chemical property of checking oxidation." It prevents the change of venous into arterial blood, produces gradual paresis, depresses the action of the heart, and yet fails to affect consciousness and sensibility almost to the very last. Some of these results appear to require confirmation.

[2] The Practitioner, vol. viii. p. 219.

hand hanging over the bed, and the bottle held firmly in its grasp." He declared that " he would not be without ' his bottle of drops ' for a hundred pounds." This was a most remarkable case of relief, in what seems to have been aortic regurgitation, in a man of twenty-one years of age. It shows, however, that this remedy, like all others of the same class, is liable to abuse.

The remaining remedies of the angina-paroxysm are probably of small account in comparison with those already mentioned ; but it is desirable to add a few words with respect to some of them. Notwithstanding the opinion of Heberden, blood-letting has been recommended, and in some cases, perhaps, successfully practised ; the cases being probably those in which evident signs of cardiac venous congestion existed. In Dr. Brunton's case *small* blood-letting, of a few ounces only, appeared to give relief. Dry cupping between the shoulders is a more reasonable, or, at all events, less spoliative method of unloading the heart, and might in some cases co-operate advantageously with the use of warm stimulation of the surface as above recommended. Laennec first suggested the transmission of a magnetic current through the chest ; but this suggestion may be said to have had no practical result, and the first apparently effective use of electrical or galvanic currents in angina pectoris is due to Duchenne, of Boulogne,[1] who professes not only to have relieved, but to have cured a typical case of severe angina of five months' duration, in a currier, aged fifty, " of a stout build and sanguine temperament, rather fat, and with a short neck," by treatment for a fortnight only with a strong faradic current passed through the skin of the nipple and upper region of the sternum. The description of the case is extremely striking, but its phenomena being purely subjective, there is not any absolute guarantee for its being more than a severe case of intercostal neuralgia, in which the extremely violent action of the " induction-apparatus graduated to maximum intensity, and working with very rapid intermissions," produced the effect of a strong and sudden counter-irritation. On any other supposition, indeed, the results are almost too wonderful for belief. The first shock produced excruciating pain, so that the patient uttered a loud shriek, and the current had to be arrested. This artificial pain, however, completely and immediately removed the angina pain, as well as the sensations of numbness and formication which accompanied it ; and " the patient felt at once in his normal condition." Succeeding paroxysms were similarly arrested, and in a fortnight the patient was able to resume his employment. Another case, communicated by Aran to Duchenne, is specially cited by Trousseau (who records both cases in great detail) as " giving more value to the preceding considerations ;" but this will probably not be the judgment of the reader of the preceding pages,

[1] De l'électrisation localisée et de son application à la pathologie et à la thérapeutique. 3ᵉᵐᵉ. edit. Paris, 1872, p. 808. See also note Sur l'influence thérapeutique de l'excitation électro-cutanée dans l'angine de poitrine, *Bulletin de Thérapeutique*, 1853 ; and compare note on next page.

when he learns that the subject of Aran's therapeutical experiment was a woman of thirty-two, who had been extremely hysterical, if not cataleptic, from intense grief, and had been for a long time a prey to a multitude of nervous disorders, the result of violently disturbing emotions.[1] Eulenburg has employed 'the constant current, up to a strength represented by thirty elements of Siemen's battery, applying the positive pole with a large surface for contact to the sternum, and the negative to the side of the lower cervical vertebræ; the successes which he claims, however, are rather equivocal, and it may be inferred from the method of his reasoning that he only employed the remedy in cases regarded as of vaso-motor origin.[2] I am not aware of any case in which angina pectoris of obviously organic origin has been, even temporarily, relieved by any form of electrical or galvanic application; but possibly further trials may still be desirable. Digitalis, aconite, and veratrum, have all proved either useless or injurious.

The *treatment of the inter-paroxysmal state* in angina pectoris depends essentially on the careful application to the individual case of all the practical suggestions arising from a very complete diagnosis, and from a consideration of the causes which have been observed or supposed to be chiefly at work in predisposing to, or in actually bringing on, the paroxysms. Generally speaking, tranquillity, both of body and mind; especially the suspension of all occupations, or even amusements, that tend to overstrain the heart, or hurry the breathing; very moderate daily exercise on level ground, and only to such an extent as is requisite for preserving the bodily tone, or for good digestion; the avoidance of all manner of food tending to flatulence, and the regular, but strictly moderate evacuation of the bowels, either spontaneously or by the mildest laxatives, are measures of hygiene so obviously suggested by simple prudence as hardly to require more than a passing allusion. It is not by any means certainly ascertained whether the subjects of angina ought to use alcoholic stimulants in any measure *habitually*, or to reserve them for the critical period of the attack. I incline to the latter opinion. Venereal excitement is probably in all cases an unfavourable influence. The use of tobacco

---

[1] It is, perhaps, worthy of remark, that the experience of twelve years after his first acquaintance with the facts of Duchenne's and Aran's cases had not enabled Trousseau to add anything of a more personal kind to his long citation from Duchenne's narrative, first published in 1853. See the 2nd edition of Trousseau's "Clinique de l'Hotel Dieu" (vol. ii. pp. 453-7), published in 1865, not long before his death. Duchenne himself, in the 3rd edition of his well-known work (referred to above) published in 1872, and called in the preface "presque un nouveau livre," gives only one new case, with scanty and unsatisfactory details, in which, moreover, after "partial amelioration" under the method of electro-cutaneous excitation previously described, the patient died suddenly when entering M. Duchenne's consulting-room. He refers, however, to a case of cure by M. Boullet, and to "several cases of cure" communicated to the Academy of Sciences, in February 1869, by M. Ed. Becquerel. These last I have not been able to discover. M. Becquerel simply reports M. Boullet's case without commentary, and with such brevity and want of essential details as to deprive it of all real clinical value. Evidently there is great inexactitude here, as well as a "plentiful lack" of trustworthy facts.

[2] Med. Times and Gazette, May 7, 1870, p. 490.

in great excess has been specially investigated as a cause of angina by M. Beau;[1] but although I have frequently observed palpitation and intermission of the heart's action in smokers, it has not occurred to me to observe true angina pectoris thus produced. It will be obviously right, however, to discountenance any indulgence of this kind which is even doubtful as to its effects upon the heart's action. Beyond these simple measures of precaution, the treatment must vary according to the circumstances observed in each case, and it may even be said that there are cases in which no clear indication exists for any treatment beyond that of the paroxysm. But if it be discovered that gout, or congestion of the liver or lungs, or well-marked dyspeptic symptoms, or renal derangement, has concurred with, or alternated with, the paroxysms, or even that any of these disorders has been a marked feature of the case, without any obvious relation to the angina, it may be found that in undertaking the treatment of these apparently intercurrent disorders the cure or alleviation of the paroxysms may follow in due course. It is said, indeed, by some that gouty angina is peculiarly amenable to treatment, and therefore less formidable in its prognosis than other kinds; and although this is probably only an imperfect statement of the fact that cures of angina-like symptoms are sometimes obtained by remedies in the gouty habit,[2] yet as a practical question of duty there can be no doubt that we are bound to treat the constitutional disease, as the best means known of influencing the local symptoms. It will therefore be expedient to use all possible means for eradicating, or at least diminishing, the gouty predisposition, in cases of angina so characterised, by careful regulation of the diet and the use of anti-arthritic remedies, such as the carbonates of potash and lithia, or even in some cases small doses of colchicum; though it is very doubtful how far a well-marked attack of gout in the foot ought to be checked, either by colchicum or any other disturbing remedy, in those who have had angina and other internal manifestations of the disease. A holiday at Carlsbad, Vichy, or Töplitz, or, according to the fashion of last century, at Bath, may help to dispose of the remains of gout when its regular form threatens to pass into irregular manifestations. Fothergill and others have affirmed the cure of angina pectoris in this way.[3] If the urine shows persistently, or even frequently, a

---

[1] De l'influence du tabac à fumer sur la production de l'angine de poitrine.—*Gazette des Hôpitaux*, 1862.

[2] On the other hand, a large proportion of the fatal cases of angina pectoris has been, as already shown, connected with gout, and between these two opposite sides of the question it is not easy to find a secure basis for the alleged relatively favourable prognosis of gouty angina.

[3] The case here specially referred to was mentioned by Fothergill in 1773, incidentally, in a paper on angina pectoris, as "the first case apparently of this nature that occurred to me, above twenty years ago." He adds, "the person is now, or lately was, living, and is good health . . . He was at that time about thirty years of age, and the youngest subject I have ever seen affected with this disorder." The symptoms are fairly described, considering the early date, and long interval between their occurrence and the publication, but can scarcely be looked upon as thoroughly characteristic. He "went to Bath

tendency to deposit lithic acid crystals, the treatment will of course
be guided by this indication : and if acid dyspepsia is present, it will
be necessary to use remedies at once antacid and tonic. If, on the
other hand, the neuralgic element is highly pronounced, more especially if it is hereditary, or has been manifested in the individual
patient in other forms, the angina pectoris being presumably a mere
form of a more extended constitutional neurosis ; we may probably
look in such cases for relief to nervine tonics, but especially to iron,
strychnine, and arsenic. I have seen in one or two cases very decided
good results from the last of these remedies, given in the form of
the ordinary Fowler's Solution, ℳ v. for a dose, two or three times a
day over a considerable period ; and I can to this extent support the
statements of Dr. Anstie, who in this country has chiefly advocated
the use of arsenic in angina pectoris, and who refers to a case published by Philipp,[1] as having first strongly directed his attention to
the subject. Anstie begins with three minims, and increases the dose
gradually, if well tolerated, up to eight or ten minims three times a
day ; he has found, however, that some neurotic patients cannot tole-
rate arsenic from the irritability of their alimentary canal, and in such
cases it must be discontinued, or perhaps some other form of administration might be devised. Anstie gives several striking cases, in one
of which, at least, there had been a few slight attacks of gout, and
a few small calculi ; another was that of a woman, aged forty-six,
who was still menstruating, though irregularly, and who certainly
seems to have had extremely severe symptoms of the order of angina ;
she was cured by a six months' course of arsenic in doses gradually
mounting to 21 minims daily ; after eight weeks the patient
abandoned the remedy, supposing herself cured, but had to recur to it
from experiencing a renewal of her sufferings, which again yielded to
a precisely similar treatment.[2] Arsenic is specially adapted for
anæmic cases, and often exercises a favourable influence over the
function of hæmatosis ; but in cases where anæmia is well-marked it
may be combined with iron, or the latter may be given with

several successive seasons, and acquired his usual health. This is the only instance that
has occurred to me," writes Fothergill, " of a perfect recovery from this obscure, and too
often fatal malady." We have seen that Heberden's experience also yielded only one
case of apparently perfect recovery. In one other case, with distinct gouty complications,
Fothergill prescribed Bath waters, with good results as regards the gout, but with no
favourable effect on the angina. In another case the Buxton water appeared to be of
temporary service. Fothergill seems to have been strongly impressed with the necessity
of reducing exuberant fatty deposition in angina pectoris, and for this purpose recommended vegetable diet ; though he did not anticipate in any respect later observations as
to the connection of sudden death with fatty degeneration of the fibre of the heart itself.
See Medical Observations and Inquiries, vol. v., 1776, p. 223, " Case of an Angina
Pectoris, with Remarks ; " and p. 252 of " Farther Account of the Angina Pectoris, by
J. Fothergill, M.D., F.R.S."

[1] Berliner Klin. Wochenschrift, 1865. See, however, Cahen (*ut supra*) Archives
Générales, 1863 ; and a much older case by Alexander, of Halifax, 1790 (History of a
case of Angina Pectoris cured by the Solutio arsenici), Medical Commentaries, vol. xv., p.
373. This last case has, apparently, had very little effect on English practice, but is
referred to by Desgranges, Trousseau, and other continental authorities.

[2] Anstie, op. cit. Compare pp. 78, 182-4, 226-7.

strychnine (ten minims of the sesquichloride tincture with $\frac{1}{30}$ gr. strychnine three times a day). Phosphorus has lately been recommended by Dr. Broadbent, in doses of from $\frac{1}{50}$ to $\frac{1}{16}$ gr. twice daily, but has not as yet been adequately tested. Zinc, silver, and most of the older remedies of this class, have been, on the whole, found wanting in true angina pectoris, though sometimes useful in pseudo-angina. A remarkable experience was that of Bretonneau (detailed by Trousseau),[1] who, following out a very crude chemical theory of the calculous origin of angina, professed nevertheless to have stumbled upon the practical result of treating cases of angina successfully by large doses of bicarbonate of soda, combined in certain cases with belladonna. The directions given are very complicated, but the essential part of the treatment seems to be as follows: The alkaline treatment is begun with two scruples of the bicarbonate of soda, daily, in divided doses, rising gradually to eight or ten scruples, increasing and diminishing the dose alternately over intervals of ten days, and then suspending the treatment for fifteen or twenty days together; these various processes are repeated up to the end of a year or more, after which a pause of several months is allowed. At all stages of this lengthened treatment, belladonna may be given in gradually increasing doses, up to the point of relief to the spasms, or until symptoms of incipient poisoning occur, viz., "unpleasant dryness of the mouth, marked disturbance of vision, accompanied by a very striking dilatation of the pupils." Notwithstanding the great therapeutic reputation of Bretonneau, I have not been able to learn that anyone else in France has personally succeeded with this treatment, and even M. Trousseau, his most distinguished pupil and follower, does not profess to do more than record his master's opinions. The facts as stated may therefore probably remain among the curiosities of medical experience; but as they have been generally referred to, it is necessary to make brief allusion to them here.

In cases of angina connected with positive organic disease, the treatment must follow the lines of that of the cardiac or vascular lesion which is discovered to be the cause of the symptoms. It is very doubtful, however, whether in cases of fatty heart, or of calcareous and other degenerations of the vessels, there is any positive special treatment which can be recommended with confidence. In cases of aneurism, on the other hand, the iodide of potassium, in large doses of 20 to 30 grains and upwards, will be found of great value in checking all the painful sensations, and even, in some cases, arresting or suspending the disease; and the bromide of potassium, or of ammonium, may be given in some cases along with the iodide, as a palliative. A late American writer[2] specially commends the bromide of ammonium, and gives two cases in which, in doses of 15 to 20 grains, it seems to have averted the paroxysms.

---

[1] Op. cit., Eng. transl., vol. i. p. 610.
[2] Dr. Rufus K. Hinton, Philadelphia Medical and Surgical Reporter, March 6, 1875.

Note on the Literature of Angina Pectoris.—The leading authorities
have been mostly referred to in the preceding pages, and will be
found quoted much more numerously and in chronological order in
the two great French dictionaries mentioned below,[1] under the head
" Angine de poitrine." I have not in the text of this article referred
to the letter of M. Rougnon to M. Lorry, in 1768,[2] which has been
set forth by M. Jaccoud and others as constituting a claim on the part
of France to priority, or at least to a simultaneous discovery of angina
pectoris with that of Heberden. From the accounts given of this
letter, as I have been able to read them, it is manifest that M.
Rougnon is in no just sense of the words a rival or competitor of
Heberden ; he is, however, probably entitled to the credit of having
independently described a single case of sudden death, with symptoms
more or less resembling Heberden's angina, as we have seen that
Morgagni had done a century before. Without in the least degree
desiring to detract from what is due on this account to Rougnon, it
must be here pointed out that Heberden's position is entirely different. Instead of describing only one case, and reasoning inaccurately
as to its pathology, Heberden founded a minute and exact clinical
description upon the observation of not less than twenty cases, of
which, he informs us, six had been known to him as having perished

---

[1] Nouveau Dictionnaire de Médecine et de Chirurgie pratiques, tome 2ᵗᵉᵐᵉ. 1865, p. 509
(Art. by Jaccoud). Dictionnaire Encyclopédique des Sciences Médicales, tome 5ᶦᵉᵐᵉ
1866, p. 65 (Art. by Parrot). Consult also the Bibliography in Forbes, Cyclopædia of
Practical Medicine, vol. iv. ; the essay of Wichmann, Ueber angina pectoris und polypus
cordis (Ideen zur Diagnostic, vol. ii. 1801); Brera (Della stenocardia ; saggio patologico-
clinico, Modena, 1810) ; Desportes (Traité de l'angine de poitrine, Paris, 1811) ; Zecchi-
nelli (Sull' angina del petto e sulle morte repentine, Padova, 1814); Jurine (Mémoire sur
l'angine de poitrine, Paris et Genève, 1815) ; Lartigue (De l'angine de poitrine, Paris,
1846) ; Lussana (Intorno all' angina pectoris, Gazetta Medica Lombarda, 1858-59),
besides the great and well-known works of Senac, Corvisart, Laennec, Testa, Kreysig,
Bouillaud, Hope, Latham, Stokes, Walshe, Friedreich (in Virchow's Handbuch), Bamberger, and others on Diseases of the Heart, the most recent being that of Dr. Hayden,
Dublin (1875), which reached me after the first part of this article was written, but to
which I have been indebted for several suggestions in the latter part of it, and some
valuable references. The works of Romberg and Eulenburg, on Diseases of the Nerves,
should also be consulted ; and the articles in all the older systematic treatises and dictionaries, whether British or continental. With the exception of Rougnon, all the
authorities quoted in any of these sources up to 1778 are English. In that year Elsner
published at Königsberg a monograph, entitled, "Abhandlung über die Brustbraune,"
which was followed in 1782 by Grüner (Spicilegium ad anginæ pectoris . .), and
Schäffer (Dissertatio de angina pectoris, 1787). Several articles or treatises soon followed in Germany, Denmark, and Holland ; but I do not know if angina pectoris is even
mentioned by name in French medical literature prior to the paper of Baumés in 1808,
"Récherches sur cette maladie à laquelle on a donné les noms d'angine de poitrine
et de syncope angineuse," (Annales de la Société de Médecine pratique de Mont-
pellier, 1808). The first Italian monograph was that of Brera in 1810, cited above.
After this, the literature becomes much more copious ; but the well-known article of Dr.
Forbes, in the first volume of the Cyclopædia of Practical Medicine, 1833, will always
remain, especially for the English reader, the chief source of exact information down to
a comparatively recent date.

[2] Lettre à M. Lorry touchant les causes de la mort de M. Charles, ancien capitaine
de cavalerie, arrivée à Besançon le 23 février, 1768 (Besançon, 1768, 8vo.) Rougnon
described the paroxysms of pain, and ascribed these and the sudden death to ossification of the costal cartilages. He did not give any name to the disease, or indicate
otherwise its pathological and clinical relations.

suddenly. Heberden's account of the "Disorder of the Breast,"
accordingly, soon became known to medical men in various countries
as an accurate and comprehensive sketch of a new disease, while
Rougnon's case passed into oblivion, without even in France exciting
the attention that was perhaps due to it as an isolated observation.
The claim advanced on behalf of Rougnon is evidently an after-
thought, and cannot now be admitted. If sudden death from angina
is to be recognised in any sense at all as a discovery on the strength
of an individual case, the credit undoubtedly belongs to Morgagni
rather than to Rougnon. It is right, however, to add that I make
these remarks without having personally read Rougnon's letter,
which I have inquired for in vain in the medical libraries of this
country.

DISEASES OF THE VALVES OF THE HEART.

By C. HILTON FAGGE, M.D., F.R.C.P.

THE literature of diseases of the valves of the heart, as of all other thoracic diseases, is necessarily divided into two periods; that before, and that after, the discovery of auscultation. The earlier period, however, contains very few observations. Burns[1] quotes two cases of aortic obstruction, briefly related by Riverius and Willis respectively, towards the end of the seventeenth century. Dr. Gee[2] points out that Vieussens in 1715 recorded a case of disease of the aortic valves, in which the pulse was "*fort vîte, dur, inégal, et si fort que l'artère de l'un et de l'autre bras frappait le bout de mes doigts autant que l'auroit fait une corde fort tendue et violemment ébranlée.*"

Friedreich[3] is therefore not quite accurate in heading his list of papers and works on affections of the endocardium with Meckel's essay in the Mém. de l'Acad. Roy. des Sciences, published in Berlin in 1756. But it is in the second half of the eighteenth century that we find the first detailed observations of diseased cardiac valves. Among the most striking of these is one recorded by John Hunter, in his "Treatise on the Blood, &c.," which originally appeared in 1794. It is that of a Mr. Bulstrode,[4] who had "almost throughout his life had an irregular pulse and upon the least increase of exercise a palpitation at his heart, which was often so strong as to be heard by those who were near him. . . . He of late years (about the age of thirty), took to violent exercise such as hunting; and often in the chase he would be taken ill with palpitations and almost a total suffocation. Some of these fits continued several days: at such times he became black in the face. Sometimes an universal yellowness took place; and then he could not lie down in his bed, but was obliged to sit up for breath. He consulted Dr. Heberden and Sir George Baker; the palpitation I

---

[1] "Observations on some of the most frequent and important Diseases of the Heart." Edinburgh, 1809, pp. 175, 176.

[2] "Auscultation and Percussion," 1870, p. 260.

[3] "Krankheiten des Herzens," Virchow's Handbuch der speciellen Pathologie und Therapie, 1867, p. 198.

[4] The preparation from this case is still in the Hunterian Museum of the Royal College of Surgeons, which also contains several other specimens of diseased cardiac valves, preserved by Hunter himself. The passages cited in the text are from the "Catalogue of Path. Specimens," vol. iii. p. 197.

suppose they thought either arose from spasm or was nervous, for they ordered cordials. I was sent for on the same day to give a name to the disease. My opinion was that there was something very wrong about the heart, that the blood did not flow freely through the lungs. . . That the means to be practised were rest, bleed gently, eat moderately, keep the body open and the mind easy. . . Eight ounces of blood were taken from him that day which relieved him. . . At last he became yellow, and his legs began to swell with water. . . and he died. The heart was very large . . . the valves of the aorta shrivelled up, thicker and harder than common. The diseased structure of the valves accounts for every one of what may be called his original symptoms; the blood must have flowed back into the cavity of the ventricle again at every systole of the artery. . . . We can easily trace the effects of this retrograde motion, which would only be a stagnation of the blood beyond the left ventricle, first in the left auricle, then the pulmonary veins, then the pulmonary arteries, next the right auricle, and in all the veins of the body; producing that darkness in the face, &c." Even earlier than this, Senac, in his Treatise on the Heart (the second edition of which appeared in 1783) had related a case in which the auriculo-ventricular valves were ossified, and remarked that the pulse was necessarily small, because the blood did not all pass into the aorta, but some of it flowed back into the auricle. Soon after the commencement of the present century, three works on diseases of the heart were published, in which valvular affections are treated of with considerable detail: that of Corvisart,[1] in 1806; that of Allan Burns,[2] in 1809; and that of Kreysig,[3] in 1815.

The study of these works is of considerable interest. Corvisart gives an admirable account of the anatomical appearances exhibited by diseased valves, which he distinguishes as undergoing calcareous or osseous induration, or as presenting excrescences (vegetations[4] It is remarkable, however, that he seems to have had no conception of these diseases as causing regurgitation, or imperfect closure of the valves.[5] The tendency of valvular affections to cause dilatation of

---

[1] "Essai sur les Maladies et les lésions organiques du Cœur et des Gros Vaisseaux." So far as diseases of the heart are concerned, however, this writer (who will always be remembered as having popularized Avenbrugger's discovery of percussion) is better known by his second edition, which appeared in 1811, and was translated into English by Mr. Hebb in 1813. [2] Op. cit.

[3] "Die Krankheiten des Herzens." Berlin.

[4] The word "vegetation" is now commonly used in this country, but it may be interesting to note that Mr. Hebb, the translator of Corvisart, never employs it as an English term, but always incloses it between brackets, and uses "wart" or "excrescence" as its equivalent.

[5] This must be borne in mind in estimating the claims of different writers to priority in regard to the discovery of the presystolic thrill and bruit. Corvisart first mentioned the sign afterwards known as *frémissement cataire*. He speaks of it as "a particular rustling, difficult to describe, perceptible to the hand when it is placed over the præcordial region, and which doubtless proceeds from the difficulty which the blood experiences in passing through an aperture no longer proportionate to the amount of fluid to which it has to give vent." It might thus appear that Corvisart associated thrill with mitral stenosis. But it must be recollected that he summed up the effects of all valvular

the heart (or, as he terms it, "aneurism of the heart") was well known to Corvisart. By Burns and Kreysig considerable advances were made. Both these writers recognize valvular lesions as producing two distinct effects, "obstruction" and "regurgitation," and trace many of the consequences of the latter condition. Kreysig lays special stress on inflammation of the endocardium as causing the lesions in question. Burns may even be said to hint at the occurrence of cardiac murmurs, for he speaks of regurgitation from the ventricle into the auricle as producing not only a jarring sensation but also "a hissing noise, as of several currents meeting. In all probability" (he goes on to say) "it is something of this kind which is described as audible palpitation in some diseases of the heart."

The history of the subsequent literature of valvular affections is involved in that of the auscultatory phenomena which they produce; and hereafter, when these are under consideration, I must endeavour to deal with the most important parts of it.

DESCRIPTION AND ANATOMY.—The pathological changes met with in the valves of the heart are naturally divisible into two groups; 1. Those which are acute: 2. Those which are chronic.

1. The acute affections are of an inflammatory nature, and come under the general head of endocarditis. Indeed, it has long been known that the membrane forming the valves is more liable to inflammation than any other part of the endocardium. And, as we shall presently see, recent observations have shown that this is true in a more absolute sense than had been imagined: and that when inflammation of the linings of the heart's cavities is met with, it has almost always been set up by a similar affection of one of the valves.

The microscopical anatomy of inflammation of the valves may, therefore, be dismissed in a very few words, as being the same as that of endocarditis in general. The minute blood-vessels, which recent observers have shown to exist in the valves, become gorged with blood, and the cells of the external tunic of these vessels undergo proliferation.[1] But this change is quite subordinate to that which occurs in the proper substance of the valve itself: in the connective tissue of which young cells are formed in large numbers, while the intercellular material becomes softened. The tissue is thus much swollen; and as the change in question is not at first general, but is confined to certain spots, the result is the formation of a number of small granulations, projecting from the surface of the valve. These granulations are very commonly limited, in the first instance, to a particular region in each valve, namely, that which lies immediately behind the line of closure. Thus, in a cuspid or auriculo-ventricular valve, the earliest swelling is found on the auricular surface, and a little above

diseases in the contractions of the corresponding orifices which he supposed them to cause. He had no conception that the presence of thrill was of any value as regards a *differential diagnosis* of valvular affections.

[1] Rindfleisch, "Lehrbuch der pathologischen Gewebelehre." Leipzig, 1871, p. 205.

the free edge ; in the case of the semilunar valves, it is on the ventricular surface, and along the delicate curved line, limiting the apposition of the valves, that stretches on either side of the corpus Arantii. In these positions the granulations are often pretty uniformly arranged, like a row of minute beads. The remembrance of their seat may be facilitated by imagining the valves to have been coated on their apposed surfaces with a layer of some soft substance (such as butter), which during closure of the valves would be forced into precisely the positions that the granulations occupy. And according to the view formerly entertained, that the granulations were formed of an exudation of plastic lymph, it was easy (with Sir Thomas Watson)[1] to refer their arrangement to this cause. But, as we have seen, the microscope shows that they are swellings of the tissue of the valve itself, and this explanation is, therefore, untenable. The granulations vary in appearance ; being sometimes colourless, sometimes red (the latter perhaps from imbibition). Their consistence is different in different cases: sometimes they are so soft as to be detached from the valve by the slightest touch ; sometimes they are so hard as to resist all attempts to remove them. They are much more often seen on the valves of the left, than on those of the right side of the heart: the former being in fact much more subject to endocarditis than the latter.

When acute endocarditis occurs as part of a rapidly fatal general disease, the presence of such a line of minute granulations is generally the only sign that inflammation of the valves had existed: and if (as is often the case) the affection be confined to the auricular surface of the edge of the mitral valve, it may be entirely overlooked, unless attention be specially directed to this spot.

But in certain cases, the changes are far more considerable. The granulations are very much larger, and become confluent, so as to form masses, which fairly deserve the name of vegetations. These bodies, projecting into the stream of the blood, necessarily offer a favourable surface for the reception of coagula ; and thus colourless fibrin of firm consistence is deposited upon them, often in large quantity. This so closely resembles in appearance the swollen tissue of the valve itself, that it may be impossible to say where the one begins and the other ends. Indeed (as has already been mentioned) the older theorists (who thought that the valves, which were then supposed to be non-vascular, were incapable of inflammation) believed even the smallest granulations to have been thus deposited from the blood. When this opinion was shown to be incorrect, its opposite prevailed: and it is only after repeated and prolonged discussions that pathologists have come to the conclusion that the larger masses have the double origin just attributed to them. These, again, are often found to be still further increased in size by the deposition of dark red clots upon them, while the patient is in the act of dying, or during the post-mortem coagulation of the blood.

These vegetations necessarily float to and fro with the valve to which

[1] "Princ. and Pract. of Physic," 4th edition, vol. ii. p. 294.

they are attached, and thus they are almost always brought into contact with the surface of another valve opposed to them, or with some
part of the endocardial lining of the heart's chambers. For it must
be added that they are not always sessile, but are often suspended by a
pedicle of some length, allowing them to swing backwards and forwards
through a considerable range of movement. The result is that they
frequently set up inflammation in the parts against which they rub.
This fact was, I believe, first pointed out by Dr. Moxon, who, in 1868
and 1869 exhibited to the Pathological Society several illustrative
specimens.[1] My own observations have convinced me that his statements are perfectly correct. A vegetation hanging from an aortic
valve is often thrown upon the wall of the aorta during the ventricular
systole, and sets up there a little ulcer, penetrating into the middle
coat, or even down to the adventitia : during the diastole the same
vegetation is carried downwards, and touches the anterior surface of
the mitral valve, or the endocardial lining of the ventricle, and the
spot touched is found, after death, to be precisely indicated by the
presence of a little fresh mass of vegetations. The opposed surfaces of
the aortic valves are often seen to be coated with vegetations, in such
a way as to suggest that the one was affected secondarily to the
other, although it may not be possible to say which was primarily
diseased. Or, again, a button-like mass of vegetations projecting from
one aortic valve has been seen to bore a hole right through the substance of the valve opposed to it. A cluster of vegetations growing
from the auricular surface of the mitral valve often sets up inflammation in the base of the opposed segment of the valve, where the
vegetations meet it during closure of the valve : and from this spot
the inflammation spreads into the auricle.[2] Dr. Moxon has even
expressed the opinion that vegetations attached to the lining membrane
of the heart's cavities are scarcely met with, except as the result of
friction, in the way just described, the valves being first diseased.
And I would add my belief that there are few cases of acute inflammation of the valves, in which secondary effects of this kind may
not be traced.

The rapid and extensive movements performed by these floating
vegetations have probably much to do with the frequency with which
portions of them become detached and carried with the blood-stream to
distant parts, producing effects which we shall hereafter have to consider.
But it must be added that they are also very liable to undergo a
finely granular metamorphosis (according to Rindfleisch, not fatty),
which renders them still softer than they originally were. In this
softening process the inflamed tissue of the valve itself takes part :
so that large portions of it often become disintegrated, and an ulcer is

[1] Path. Trans. xix. p. 148, xx. p. 156. It will be shown further on that Dr.
Hodgkin long ago described the effects of friction in the case of valves affected with
chronic disease.

[2] These statements are derived from the detailed reports of the post-mortem examinations at Guy's Hospital during the last few years, most of which were made by Dr.
Moxon, but some by myself.

produced, which may destroy the whole thickness of the valve and perforate it. Such ulceration, for instance, may separate one or both edges of an aortic valve from attachment to the arterial wall; or eat away a large part of its substance. In the mitral valve, it is not uncommon for a hole to be pierced right through its substance. In this case, however, the edges of the aperture are always thick and raised, and covered with large vegetations; and these generally meet across it, so that there is no reason to suppose that by such a perforation the physiological action of the valve is in any way impaired. Indeed, these vegetations are often so massive, that the existence of a perforation, and even of an ulcer, may escape notice unless it be specially looked for. The records of post-mortem examinations at Guy's Hospital contain only one notice of such a perforation in the course of six years; but I have little doubt that it had really occurred more often. It must be added that the ulceration not rarely extends from the valves themselves into the adjacent parts of the muscular substance of the ventricle.

The same process of softening and ulceration, occurring in the chordæ tendineæ of the cuspid valves, leads to their rupture. This is by no means infrequent; in six years I find it recorded sixteen times in the reports of post-mortem examinations just referred to. Clinically it would appear to be of far greater importance than perforation of the valve: I imagine that it must invariably render the valve incompetent. The changes which precede rupture of the chordæ would appear to consist in a swelling and thickening of their substance. Generally they give way in about the middle of their length; but sometimes they are torn away from the musculus papillaris, which may then exhibit no trace of their original insertion into it. The left and the right chordæ of the mitral valve appear to be equally liable to rupture. Sometimes the laceration is confined to a single chorda; sometimes it affects nearly all those that arise from one musculus papillaris. The ruptured chordæ float to and fro with the stream of blood, which necessarily regurgitates freely into the auricle at each systole. Once I saw such a loose end tied neatly into a knot, which took some time to undo. In another instance three or four broken chordæ were twisted up spirally into a body resembling an uvula, being matted together by a deposit of fibrin. In a third case, recorded by Dr. Moxon, the free extremities of two such chordæ seemed to have become adherent to the surface of the mitral valve above, forming loops, beneath which a probe could be passed. Large masses of fibrin are whipped out from the blood, and deposited on the sides and extremities of ruptured chordæ, and often unite them together, so that it is impossible to say how many of them may have been torn through, until the superjacent mass of coagulum is removed.

Another effect of this process of ulceration, especially in the mitral valve, is the formation of a so-called "aneurism of the valve." An ulcer having formed on its ventricular surface, the base of this yields before the pressure of the blood, and a pouch is formed, projecting from

he auricular face of the valve. Such an aneurism is generally very
small : I lately saw one which was of about the size of a percussion
cap ; it had on its summit a mass of small vegetations. This form of
aneurism must be distinguished from that described by Dr. Thurnam,[1] which arises in the gradual yielding of all the coats of the valve,
and which may attain a much larger size.

2. In *chronic* diseases of the valves the appearances vary greatly,
not only in individual cases, but also according as one or another
valve is affected. But they may generally be summed up as dependent on the growth of a firm connective tissue, which thickens the
substance of the valve, and by its contraction leads to great alteration in its form, and more or less seriously impairs its functions.
Calcareous matter also is often deposited.

This "*sclerotic*" change,—if we may adopt the term sclerotic as
equivalent to the *chronische sclerosirende Endocarditis* of German
authors,—may either be primarily chronic, or arise out of an acute
inflammation of the valve. In the latter case, vegetations are sometimes found, showing that endocarditis had once occurred ; and these
may even be calcified. But they are not necessarily present. In
several cases of valvular disease, that had, in each instance, doubtless
arisen in attacks of acute rheumatism which the patient had had some
years previously, I have, on post-mortem examination, found that the
mitral valve exhibited no trace of vegetations : it was simply thickened,
with its chordæ ; and its orifice was narrowed. Here the affection had
been of acute origin : but the appearances were undistinguishable
from those which are met with in disease that has from the first been
chronic. The difficulty of determining the way in which valvular
changes arise is further increased by the fact that thickened valves
are very liable indeed to the supervention of an acute process, identical
with that already described as belonging to acute endocarditis. It
would appear that the elements of the morbid tissue in chronically
diseased valves are apt to undergo a fatty change, analogous to that
which gives rise to atheroma in chronic arteritis. The result is that
the structure of the valves becomes softened and gives way, and thus
that a process of ulceration is set up, precisely as in acute endocarditis.
A very large proportion of the cases in which the autopsy shows the
chordæ tendineæ of the mitral valve to have been freshly ruptured
are cases of long-standing valvular disease, in which inflammation
has thus supervened. Another common result is that masses of
calcareous deposit, evidently of old formation, are found lying loose
in the floor of recent ulcers.

a. In the cuspid valves the effect of chronic disease is generally to
produce a stenosis or narrowing of the aperture. The wall of the
valve, especially towards its free edge, becomes greatly thickened, and
its segments cohere together. The morbid tissue is exceedingly dense
and hard, so that by the older writers such valves were described as
cartilaginous : it often contains masses of calcareous deposit, and

[1] Med. Chir. Trans., ser. ii. vol. iii. p. 250.

these sometimes attain a very considerable size. The chordæ tendineæ undergo a similar change and coalesce, so that sometimes each musculus papillaris gives origin only to a single massive column, which may be more or less fluted, or pierced with one or two slits, indicating the lines of separation between the chordæ of which it was made up; at the same time the chordæ generally become much shortened, so that the edge of the valve is drawn down; and thus with its small aperture it has very much the appearance of a funnel, projecting far into the cavity of the ventricle. Dr. Douglas Powell,[1] has endeavoured to distinguish two forms of stenosis of the mitral orifice, in one of which the valve presents this funnel shape, while in the other it is stretched horizontally, like a diaphragm, between the auricle and the ventricle. But it appears to me that no such distinction can be fairly drawn, and that in all cases a narrowed mitral valve tends more or less to assume the form of a funnel, although this is no doubt much more marked in some instances than in others. The orifice at the bottom of the funnel is sometimes circular: but in the case of the mitral valve it more often resembles a slit, of which the axis corresponds with the line uniting the meeting angles of the original segments of the valve. The latter variety has long been known as the button-hole mitral. In either form the aperture may be so contracted as hardly to admit the tip of the little finger; and cases are often met with in which only two fingers can be introduced, instead of the three which can be passed through the healthy valve.

But the effect of chronic disease of the mitral valve is not always to produce stenosis. It may be the very reverse. It is said that sometimes one of the flaps of the valve becomes adherent to the ventricular wall, and so is rendered incapable of meeting its fellow. But this is a very rare occurrence; indeed I doubt whether it is ever met with. At any rate I have not been able to find a single instance of it in the recent records of post-mortem examinations at Guy's Hospital. These records, however, contain one case in which Dr. Moxon found the edge of the anterior curtain of the valve turned up on its ventricular surface, and adherent there, so as to form a ridge on this surface,[2]—a change by which the depth of the curtain must of course have been diminished. It might be thought that the same process of contraction which ordinarily causes stenosis of a thickened valve might (if acting in a direction at right angles to that in which it usually acts) draw up and shorten the valve without narrowing its orifice. Writers have in fact described such an appearance. But it is one which I have never myself seen, nor have I met with any recorded instance of it: and I am not sure that it ever occurs. Not uncommonly, however, some of the chordæ tendineæ become elongated,

---

[1] Med. Times and Gaz., 1871, vol. i. p. 395.

[2] This condition is analogous to one which is commonly seen in cases of perihepatitis, where the anterior thin edge of the liver is neatly folded over on to the convex surface, and bound down beneath the thickened capsule, the apparent rounded margin of the liver being thus really derived from the under surface of the organ.

and do not properly tether the membranous part of the valve, which therefore becomes inverted into the auricle during the ventricular systole; and this result is often favoured by the conversion of the corresponding muscularis papillaris into a dense fibrous tissue. Sometimes those chordæ which are inserted nearest the centre of the valve alone undergo this process of lengthening, and this part of the curtain is then found after death to be bent on itself and flaccid, having evidently been accustomed to yield before the pressure of the blood. Sometimes, again, the chordæ become shortened by disease, instead of being elongated, and thus tether the valve too closely, and prevent the apposition of its segments.

I believe that the preceding paragraph includes descriptions of all the chronic changes in the cuspid valves, by which regurgitation is produced, without obstruction to the onward current of blood. Each of these, however, is of infrequent occurrence. In six years, during which period sixty-seven cases of mitral stenosis presented themselves in the post-mortem theatre of Guy's Hospital, I find only twelve recorded instances of what I may term pure regurgitant disease of the same valve; in six of which the edge of the valve is stated to have been inverted into the auricle, in the manner above described.

The fact just stated will doubtless surprise many readers, who are aware of the frequency with which mitral regurgitant disease is clinically spoken of. The question must be discussed in detail further on; but it may be well here to state that, in a large proportion of cases, a reflux of blood into the auricle during the ventricular systole is probably independent of disease in the valve itself, and due to changes in the walls and cavity of the ventricle, destroying the due proportion between the auriculo-ventricular orifice and the valve by which it should be closed. It must be added that many cases are placed after death under the head of mitral stenosis, which had before been regarded as examples of regurgitant disease. For when moderate obstruction and regurgitation co-exist, the latter is often clinically more noticeable, and (as I believe) is often alone discoverable before death; while at the autopsy the appearance of the valve may be exactly similar to that which is found in another case, in which during life obstruction had been the main feature.

β. In the semilunar valves the morbid appearances resulting from chronic disease vary much more than in the cuspid valves. First may be mentioned the adhesion of the valves together. This begins at the point where the corners of adjacent valves are inserted into the aortic wall, and gradually creeps along their free edges, uniting them together. All three valves may thus be fused into a single mass, projecting into the arterial channel in the form of an inverted funnel, with a central aperture, which is often of very irregular form, and may be extremely small, being, in most cases, further narrowed by the presence of rough calcareous nodules of greater or less size, deposited in the substance of the altered valves. While this process is going on, the natural attachment of the corners of the valves to the aorta often gradually becomes obliterated ; two of the pouches, or even all three of them, become thrown into one; and three slight projections in the floor of the resulting funnel-shaped mass are often all that is left to indicate the original lines of separation between the different valves.

In other cases the effect of chronic disease of the semilunar valves is, that they become puckered and shrivelled. Instead of forming pouches, they often rather resemble flat, narrow shelves, projecting a little way from the wall of the artery, the mouth of which they are quite unable to close. The corpus Arantii, with the thin curved borders on either side of it, disappears entirely ; and all that is left is a thick, shapeless body, often with its rounded edge retroverted, and perhaps torn away from its aortic attachment on one side, so as to hang down like the lip of a jug, or a dog's ear. Or, again, the valve may contract, and its free border thus become tightly drawn across between its points of attachment, so that the open pouch is converted into a deep pocket with a narrow entrance, into which the tip of the finger cannot be made to enter. This result, however, is not always due to changes in the valves themselves. Sometimes it depends on chronic disease in the coats of the base of the aorta, attended with yielding and dilatation of its walls, by which the valves, although healthy, are unduly stretched. So considerable may this yielding be, that in one case recorded in the reports of post-mortem examinations at Guy's Hospital, the corners of adjacent valves had become distant from one another a quarter of an inch at their points of attachment.

When a valve, thickened or retroverted by chronic disease, comes into contact with any part of the lining of one of the heart's cavities during the movements of that organ, further morbid changes are produced by the friction, as is the case in acute affections. There is, however, this difference, that the endocardium does not become ulcerated or covered with vegetations, but is thickened, opaque, and slightly roughened. This was pointed out by Dr. Hodgkin as far back as the year 1829.[1] In the case of Dr. Cox, one of aortic disease, in which a valve was stretched to upwards of an inch in length, "the coats of the aorta for about an inch and a half above the retroverted and distended valve, and against which it must have been carried during the systole of the heart, were considerably thickened, and presented an uneven surface. On the inner surface of the heart there were some irregular spots of opacity at the part where the diseased valve would have struck during the diastole." Dr. Hodgkin adds that " the partial thickening on the internal surface of the heart and vessels, in consequence of some unusual contact, is a morbid appearance, which has not been particularly pointed out by pathological anatomists, yet it does not appear to be a rare occurrence." Except Dr. Moxon, I do not find that any writer

[1] "On Retroversion of the Valves of the Aorta," Lond. Med. Gaz. vol. iii. p 439.

has since alluded to the appearance in question. But in another respect our knowledge has advanced greatly since the publication of Dr. Hodgkin's paper; for we find him relying on these effects of contact as proving that the blood had been subjected to two motions— the one progressive, and the other retrograde—a fact with which, of course, everyone is now familiar. According to Dr. Peacock and Dr. Bristowe,[1] it is not uncommon, in cases of disease of the aortic orifice, for the endocardium below the valves to present a fibroid thickening in the form of bands or reticulations, due probably to the impact of the regurgitant stream of blood on that part. Of this I have lately seen a striking instance. The same thing may also occur in the auricle, as the result of mitral regurgitation.

It will be observed that in the semilunar, as in the cuspid, valves the effects of chronic disease are twofold. It may either cause obstruction to the onward flow of blood, or give rise to regurgitation and to a backward current. All writers, in fact, insist on this distinction, while admitting that both effects often exist together. Dr. Moxon, therefore, rather surprised me a short time ago by stating that in his experience the occurrence of aortic obstruction, apart from regurgitation, has been extremely rare. I at first supposed that he was referring to fatal cases only, among which pure aortic stenosis would naturally be infrequent, since this is generally said to affect the prospect of life less than any other form of valvular affection, and since, moreover, it is very apt to become complicated sooner or later by the development of regurgitation. Thus, in looking through the records of post-mortem examinations for the last six years—during which time there have occurred sixty-eight fatal cases of aortic regurgitant disease—I find only two, or perhaps three, of pure aortic stenosis; and in at least one of them the patient's death was due not to this affection, but to co-existing mitral stenosis. But I afterwards ascertained that Dr. Moxon believed aortic obstruction, independent of regurgitation, to be rare clinically, as well as in the dead-house; and this opinion certainly appears to be confirmed by the fact that, during part of the period in which I acted as Medical Registrar at Guy's Hospital (within which period seventy-one cases of aortic regurgitation came under observation) I find only two recorded instances of pure stenosis of the orifice in question; and in one of these regurgitation became developed before the patient's death.

The changes to which the aortic valves are liable are not all included in the thickenings, and adhesions, and puckerings that have hitherto been described. In some cases the tissue of the valves undergoes atrophy; and they become so thin, that it is difficult to believe that they were capable of sustaining a column of blood. A striking example of this came lately under my notice. A young man, æt. thirty-two, had long suffered from asthma, and becoming anasarcous was admitted into Guy's Hospital under the care of Dr. Wilks. After death the aortic valves were found to be most remarkably thinned;

[1] Path. Trans. xxi. p. 105.

they had no more substance than the most delicate tissue-paper, and no corpora Arantii could be felt in them. One of them was slightly fenestrated near its margin. They were very small, and, when left to themselves, fell back into the Sinuses of Valsalva. The pulmonary valves presented the same change in a minor degree ; and the mitral valve was likewise unusually thin. The heart was much enlarged. The lungs were emphysematous , and it appeared to me that the thinning of the heart's valves was due to a process of atrophy, perhaps related pathologically to that which caused the pulmonary emphysema. I have since found, in the records of post-mortem examinations at Guy's Hospital, a similar case, observed by Dr. Moxon. It is that of a man, aged fifty-six, whose lungs are stated to have been senile and a little emphysematous, and to have contained much black matter. The heart was small ; the right side was dilated, forming the apex ; the pericardium was everywhere adherent ; the mitral and aortic valves were very delicate in appearance.[1] This atrophy of the aortic valves is probably rare, and has not yet been shown to have any clinical significance. But there would certainly appear to be danger of the rupture of such thin structures, when strained in an effort of coughing or in any other way.

I have still to mention another abnormal appearance in the aortic valves, formerly supposed (by Corrigan) to render them incompetent, but now known to interfere in no way with their functions. I refer to the small openings which are sometimes found in the thin, crescent-shaped borders which extend on either side of the corpora Arantii. By some writers analogies have been found for such a fenestrated condition of the aortic valves in the normal state of the same valves in some of the lower animals ; while others have regarded it as exhibiting an identity of structure between the semilunar and the cuspid valves ; the filaments which remain above the apertures being supposed to answer to the chordæ of a mitral or tricuspid segment. It has also been doubted whether this fenestration of the aortic valves is the result of a slow atrophic change, or whether it is simply a defect of original development. And with reference to this point Dr. Wilks [2] states that he has seen it in young people, and has therefore always regarded it as congenital.

ETIOLOGY.—Before passing to the consideration of the other causes of disease of the cardiac valves, it may be convenient to discuss the views of certain writers, who have attributed to congenital malformation (or to intra-uterine disease) some affections that, as it appears to me, may arise at any period of life. These views are of considerable antiquity. In his account of Mr. Bulstrode's case, already referred to, John Hunter expresses a doubt whether the shrivelled appearance

---

[1] Since this was written I have (in November 1874) met with a third instance of extreme thinning of the aortic valves, in another patient, who died of the effects of pulmonary emphysema.

[2] Pathological Anatomy, p. 93.

of the valves of the aorta was " a natural formation, or a disease." And of another specimen, in which there were two valves only instead of three, one of which had a kind of frænum or cross-bar attaching its middle to the side of the artery,—the catalogue of the Hunterian Museum says, " this malformation was in all probability congenital." Early in the present century, Mr. Burns described as a " species of mal-conformation of the heart," that condition in which the mitral valve, instead of being formed of two flaps, presents the appearance of a septum, with an aperture in its centre, stretching across the opening. More recently several observers have expressed similar opinions. Dr. Conway Evans,[1] in recording a case in which the mitral valve was funnel-shaped, says this condition was "evidently of congenital origin." Dr. Kelly has recently maintained the same view.[2] And Dr. Peacock devoted to this question a part of his first Croonian Lecture, delivered before the Royal College of Physicians in 1865.

The arguments for and against the opinion that certain affections of the valves are congenital require to be taken separately for the different valves.

And, first, with regard to the *mitral* valve. Great stress has been laid on the fact that mitral stenosis is very frequently associated with tricuspid stenosis. It is generally said that all the valves on the right side of the heart, which are so rarely subject to disease in after life, are much more liable to intra-uterine disease and to malformation than the valves on the left side. And congenital union of the pulmonary valves is really common, being indeed the most important malformation of the heart, and being generally attended with other evident malformations, such as an aperture in the septum, &c. Now, since the relatively higher function of the right side of the heart during fœtal life is supposed to be the cause of the greater liability to congenital disease in the pulmonary (as compared with the aortic) valves, writers have assumed that this liability must be shared by the tricuspid valve also. But, as a matter of fact, there is no proof that disease of the tricuspid valve before birth is otherwise than an exceptional occurrence, like disease of the aortic valves, or of the mitral valve at the same period. Friedreich,[3] indeed, says that in newly-born infants minute soft granulations are not rarely found on the auricular surface of the tricuspid valve; but, as they do not generally disturb the functions of the valve, he hardly regards them as morbid, considering them rather to stand on the border between physiological and pathological appearances. Dr. Peacock, however, has related[4] a case in which there was a thick exudation of recent lymph on the auricular surface of the tricuspid valves, in a cyanotic child, who died when about seven months old. It is stated that the cusps were thickened and adherent at their angles, so as to contract

[1] Path. Trans. xvii. p. 90.   [2] Path. Trans. xxi. p. 91
[3] Op. cit., p. 216.   [4] Path. Trans. v. p. 64.

the dimensions of the orifice: but this still admitted a ball twenty-four lines in circumference, while the mitral aperture had a circumference of only eighteen lines. Friedreich has related a similar instance. Now it is certainly possible that tricuspid stenosis may have its origin in the inflammatory process described by these writers, as occurring in certain infants at or soon after birth. But in that case it might fairly be expected that the mitral valve, if affected at all, should be so in a slighter degree. Now I believe that it is invariably the case, that when both the valves in question are stenosed, the mitral is much thicker and much narrower than the tricuspid. For instance, it was so in Mr. E. Pye Smith's [1] case, which Dr. Peacock cites as of congenital origin.

Another argument in favour of the view that mitral stenosis may be due to malformation is based upon the fact that the patient has sometimes been in bad health for many years, or even from birth. Thus, in Mr. Pye Smith's case, the patient had been ailing all his life; and, although thirty-seven years of age, did not appear more than fifteen or sixteen, and had never presented any signs of puberty.[2] In 1870, Dr. Kelly exhibited to the Pathological Society [3] a heart with a button-hole mitral valve, taken from a woman aged thirty-three, who, even when a child, "could not run about well or indulge in any severe exertion on account of great shortness of breath and palpitation of the heart." But, so far as I can learn, such cases are quite exceptional. Patients affected with mitral stenosis generally state that they have had perfect health until a few months, or at most two or three years, before they first came under medical observation for their heart-disease. Moreover those who are practically conversant with the routine of morbid anatomy will, I think, agree with me, that in the bodies of those who have had rheumatic fever some years before death, the mitral valve is very frequently found presenting appearances which clearly indicate the gradual development of stenosis. In such cases the inferior edge of the valve is thickened, and harder than natural; its orifice no longer admits three fingers readily; its chordæ are beginning to cohere. Every stage of transition may be seen between a healthy valve and one presenting the most extreme degree of stenosis. My belief, therefore, is that it is needless to refer this affection of the mitral valve further back than a past attack of acute rheumatism, if the patient has had such an attack. And even when shortness of breath and other symptons of cardiac defect have existed from childhood, it appears to me more likely that the stenosis is due to morbid changes arising in the years that may have elapsed since birth, than to malformation or disease occurring in the short period of intra-uterine life; especially since in the fœtus the left side of the heart is so situated as to be very little susceptible of morbid action.

[1] Path. Trans. iii. p. 283.
[2] Dr. Peacock, "Malformations of the Heart," 2nd ed., 1866, p. 132.
[3] Path. Trans. xxi. p. 91.

Secondly, as concerns the *aortic* valves. Adhesion of two or more of these valves sometimes occurs in very young children. Thus Dr. Lloyd[1] exhibited to the Pathological Society the heart of an infant thirteen months old, in which there were only two aortic valves, and these were very red, rough, hard, cartilaginous on their surface and puckered: one of them was twice as large as the other, and had an indistinct ridge intersecting its centre. Dr. Workman,[2] again, showed to the same Society the heart of a little girl, only four years old at the time of death, in which the aortic orifice was much contracted, and its valves thickened and fused together. Again, adhesion of the aortic valves has sometimes been found in young persons, associated with the similar change in the pulmonary valves which is believed to be invariably of congenital origin. Thus Dr. Wilks[3] has recorded the case of a girl, æt. eighteen, in whom the pulmonary valves were adherent, and the aortic valves were two in number, the larger of them having in its interior a raised line indicating the point of union of two former valves. Dr. Ogle[4] saw another instance of the same kind, in a girl, fourteen years old, in whom "two contiguous aortic valves had their adjoining angles torn away from their attachment to the aorta, and subsequently united to each other at a lower level." It is no doubt probable that in all these cases the union of the aortic valves occurred before birth: but such cases are extremely rare, and surely afford no ground for supposing that the adhesions which are so commonly found at an advanced age are also congenital.

I must next insist on the fact, that the cases last referred to have characters which distinguish them in a very important way from those in which the union of the valves is known to be congenital. In the first place, *partial* adhesions of the aortic valves are very commonly met with in older subjects, especially when the coats of the aorta are also diseased. The adjacent edges of the valves are found to have grown together for one or two lines, the rest remaining free. There can be no question of any congenital defect, since I am not aware that such partial adhesions are ever observed at an early period of life:[5] yet it is obvious that the continuation of the same process would lead to the complete fusion of the valves, after which the line of union might be expected to gradually waste and disappear. Again, when the aortic valves are adherent, the orifice is generally irregular, and the substance of the valves greatly puckered and often deformed by large masses of calcareous deposit. Of this several capital illustrations are given in Dr. Peacock's published Croonian Lectures. He supposes that in these cases the union of the valves took place before birth. But the appearance is very different from that which is seen in the affection of the pulmonary valves which (as has already been stated) is known to be congenital.

[1] Path. Trans. i. p. 60.　　　　　　　　[3] Ibid. xviii. p. 55.
[2] Ibid. x. p. 80.　　　　　　　　　　　[4] Ibid. v. p. 70.
[5] Since this was written I have met with an instance, in which a partial adhesion of two of the aortic valves was found in the body of a boy, æt. 16, who had been drowned.

In that case the united valves form a smooth, dome-shaped body, with a regular orifice in its centre, and three small ridges or fræna on its upper surface, placed at equal distances from one another.

An argument in favour of the view that adhesions of the aortic valves are congenital has been found in the fact that, when there are only two valves, they are sometimes of equal size. It is supposed that the union must have taken place while the valves were in course of development. In reality, however, this fact merely proves that adhesion occurred before they were fully grown. A case in point recently came under my notice. A man, æt. twenty-three, died in Guy's Hospital of febrile delirium in the course of acute rheumatism. There was no recent valvular disease : but two of the aortic valves were adherent, and the resulting valve was scarcely larger than the third valve, which was itself much thickened along its whole edge, and also contracted, so that it lay flat against the aortic wall. The pericardial sac was universally closed by old adhesions. Now this patient was said to have had chorea and rheumatic fever in childhood, and afterwards to have suffered from distinct symptoms of heart-disease, dyspnœa, palpitation, &c. His illness at that time was doubtless the cause of the morbid changes both outside his heart and in its interior.

Two points remain to be considered, which afford powerful, and to my mind convincing, arguments against the view that adhesions of the aortic valves are always, or even frequently, of congenital origin. The first is the extreme frequency with which such adhesions are found in the later periods of life. Thus, according to Dr. Peacock,[1] " of forty-three cases in which the aortic valves were diseased, either alone or in conjunction with the mitral valve, in eleven (or 25·5 p.c.) there was malformation of the valves, which probably laid the foundations of the subsequent disease." Dr. Peacock goes on to say that this proportion is much larger than would à priori have been expected. I think that it shows clearly how untenable is his position. It is scarcely conceivable that a congenital malformation, which we have seen to be extremely rare in infants, should be so commonly found in adults. Again, the duration of life in the cases under consideration is altogether adverse to the opinion that the valvular disease had existed from the time of birth. Congenital malformations may, of course, be found in the bodies of those who have lived long, provided these malformations were not such as to interfere with the functions of any vital organ : and in exceptional cases, even when they did so interfere. But, if we average a considerable number of cases, we may surely assert with confidence that a congenital adhesion of the aortic valves, greatly narrowing the aperture, must inevitably tend to shorten life. Yet we find Dr. Peacock deducing from his statistical inquiries that " in cases of aortic valvular disease assigned to malformation, the age of all the patients averaged 42·3 years, and the extremes of ages were eighteen and seventy-six : while the mean age of the patients in whom aortic valvular disease originated in other ways was only

[1] Croonian Lectures.

slightly greater, or 47·4 years, and the extremes of age were twenty-one and sixty-two."

The influence of congenital defect in the causation of diseases of the cardiac valves is perhaps not limited to the cases which we have hitherto been considering. According to Virchow,[1] who has recently devoted much attention to the defective development of the aorta that is found in patients affected with chlorosis, inflammation of the mitral or aortic valves is found with disproportionate frequency in these cases. He thinks that the congenital narrowness of the aorta impedes the outflow of blood from the left ventricle, and so increases the strain to which the valves are exposed. In connection with this subject, the late Dr. Barlow[2] must be mentioned. He believed that in certain young subjects the trachea failed to undergo due development. This, he thought, led to imperfect expansion of the chest, and consequently the supply of blood to the left side of the heart was impeded; and not only the aorta, but likewise even the orifices of the heart's chambers, were prevented from attaining their proper size. Dr. Wilks has put up in the museum of Guy's Hospital[3] a specimen illustrative of Dr. Barlow's theory. I find, however, that in this, as in both Dr. Barlow's cases, mitral stenosis existed in a degree quite disproportionate to that of the other changes; and I must confess that I am inclined to think that this was the primary lesion, that it arose in childhood (as seems often to be the case), and that the smallness of the trachea was but a part of a defective development of the body generally, consequent on the imperfect state of the circulation caused by the valvular disease.

We have now to ask, what *are* the causes by which diseases of the valves of the heart are generally produced? And the answer to this question is, that by far the most common cause is an attack of "rheumatic fever," or "articular rheumatism," as it is termed in Dr. Garrod's article in the first volume of this work. Dr. Garrod has there pointed out that as far back as 1788 Dr. Pitcairn had noticed that persons subject to rheumatism were attacked more frequently than others with symptoms of heart disease; and that other writers at the commencement of the present century mentioned the same fact. But they were exceptions. Few things in medical literature are more curious, than to read the works of Burns and Kreysig and Corvisart on diseases of the heart, and to find that they had not the slightest suspicion of the rheumatic origin of these affections. So late as the year 1835, indeed, Bouillaud[4] was able to claim for himself the discovery that rheumatic pericarditis (a disease at that time generally recognized), is frequently accompanied by inflammation of the lining membrane of the heart—for which disease he then proposed the name of endocarditis.

[1] "Ueber die Chlorose, und die damit zusammenhängenden Anomalien im Gefässapparatus," Berlin, 1872, p. 18.
[2] Guy's Hospital Reports, 1st series, vol. vi. p. 235.
[3] Prep. 1412³³. Catalogue, vol. i p. 31.
[4] "Traité Clinique des Maladies du Cœur," Paris, tom. i. p. 275.

After this I suppose that the occurrence of valvular disease of the heart in the course of rheumatic fever soon became universally known; and several writers have published numerical statements with regard to its frequency. In these there is a fair general agreement. Dr. Peacock[1] quotes Dr. Fuller as stating that in his cases of acute rheumatism some cardiac complication was present in 49·3 per cent.; while Dr. Barclay found that in his cases the proportion was 39 per cent. Dr. Peacock gives 42·4 per cent. as the corresponding proportion in the cases which came under his care from 1846 to 1868.

It is to be observed that, in these figures, pericarditis is included as well as endocarditis; and also that in many cases there was old disease of the heart from former attacks of acute rheumatism. Both Dr. Fuller and Dr. Peacock have attempted to distinguish these cases, and to determine the exact frequency of recent endocardial mischief; but I doubt whether much reliance can be placed upon their results, which are based upon stethoscopical evidence only. Indeed, it is questionable whether we can trust to auscultation for determining the presence or absence of early endocarditis. I believe that at Guy's Hospital it has been found that in fatal cases of acute rheumatism (and still more of chorea) there has been by no means a close correspondence between the observation of a murmur during life and the detection of vegetations on the valves after death. Sometimes, when a systolic murmur has been present, the valves have been healthy; and, on the other hand, when no murmur could be detected they have been found to be diseased.

On the other hand, objections of at least equal force may be urged against the use of pathological observations to determine the question as to the numerical frequency of endocarditis in acute rheumatism. As far as I know, no series of unselected cases of fatal acute rheumatism has as yet ever been published. But I find that at Guy's Hospital, in a period of rather more than twenty years, there have been thirty-two such cases, in most of which the disease was a first attack. Now in twelve of these cases the valves were perfectly healthy; in twenty cases one or more of them was diseased. Six times the mitral valve was alone affected; three times the aortic valves alone: in ten cases both the mitral and the aortic valves were diseased; and in one other case, both these and the tricuspid also. This would give 62·5 per cent., as the proportion of cases of acute rheumatism in which acute endocarditis occurs.

Now I shall presently show that in all these cases the changes in the valves were slight, and that they were not at all concerned in causing death. The fatal termination was doubtless generally due to hyperpyrexia, which (as is well known) often comes on in cases that had previously appeared to be of a mild character. Still I think it cannot be denied that the thirty-two fatal cases were on an average cases of excessive severity; for in twenty-one of them there was

[1] Clinical Society's Transactions, ii. p. 222.

recent pericarditis. Probably, therefore, we cannot accept these cases as showing that 62·5 per cent. is really the proportion of cases of acute rheumatism in which endocarditis occurs. Indeed, if the cases could be regarded as average ones, we should have to suppose the proportion to be really higher still, for in many of them death occurred at a very early stage.

After all, it may perhaps be said that the exact determination of the frequency of endocarditis in acute rheumatism is of less consequence than has been supposed : for Dr. Peacock's observations render it probable that this may vary considerably at different periods and among different classes of the population. For practical purposes we may perhaps take it at from 40 to 50 per cent.

Next to acute rheumatism, chorea is the disease which most frequently gives rise to disease of the cardiac valves. I believe that this fact was first pointed out by Dr. Hughes in a paper in the Guy's Hospital Reports.[1] He found that out of 14 fatal cases of chorea, in which the state of the valves of the heart is mentioned, there were only two in which these structures were reported to be healthy. .In the last twenty years we have had at Guy's Hospital sixteen other fatal cases of chorea, in which post-mortem examinations have been made ; and in only two of these were all the valves perfectly healthy. Nine times there were vegetations on the mitral valve alone ; twice on the aortic valves alone ; three times on both the mitral and the aortic valves. Probably, however, these figures must not be taken as indicating the liability to the occurrence of cardiac disease in non-fatal cases of chorea, since severe forms of the disease are at once more likely to destroy life than mild ones, and more likely also to be complicated with valvular inflammation.[2] Thus it would not be safe to infer (as might at first be supposed) that disease of the cardiac valves is absolutely of more constant occurrence in chorea than in acute rheumatism itself.

Even in protracted fatal cases of chorea, I believe that the cardiac affection is always slight in degree ; not going beyond the presence of a row of minute granulations on the edge of one or more of the valves, which might easily escape notice, if not specially looked for. Pericarditis, again, scarcely ever occurs as a result of chorea apart from rheumatism ; having, in fact, been present in only one of the thirteen cases that I have collected. It is, I think, generally supposed that acute rheumatism differs from chorea, not only in the liability to pericarditis, but also in the much greater severity and extent of the endocarditis which attends it. It was, therefore, with some surprise that I found that in each of the fourteen cases of fatal acute rheumatism, which I have already mentioned as having presented valvular disease, the affection consisted merely in the presence of a row of minute

[1] Series ii. vol. iv. p. 360 ; and Series iii. vol. i. p. 217.
[2] I may mention, however, that in one of the fatal cases of chorea under consideration the girl's death was accidental, having been due to diphtheria, which she caught from another patient. In this instance vegetations were found in the aortic valves.

granulations, precisely like those seen in chorea. In no instance were those larger vegetations present that are so commonly found under other conditions, nor was there ever any ulceration.

A third disease, which may also lead to changes in the valves, exactly like those which occur in acute rheumatism and in chorea, is pyæmia. In 1865 I exhibited to the Pathological Society two specimens in which there were well-marked vegetations on the mitral valve, in pyæmia after surgical operations. Similar cases have since been recorded by other observers. In six years (from 1866 to 1871 inclusive) I find that the records of post-mortem examinations at Guy's Hospital contain twelve cases of pyæmia in which one or more of the cardiac valves has been found diseased. In two or three of these cases, however, the affected valve has been found ulcerated. This has sometimes been observed, when the pyæmia was evidently of external origin. Thus in 1867 I find a case of pyæmia recorded, in which part of the flap of the mitral valve was found ulcerated away from its chordæ. The point is of some importance, because (as I have shown elsewhere)[1] it suggests a doubt as to the interpretation of some of the cases in which ulcerative endocarditis has been believed to have been the *cause* of blood-poisoning by Dr. Kirkes and others.

Another, but an indirect, cause of endocarditis is, I believe, the existence of chronic spinal deformity. I have recently[2] recorded several cases of this kind in which death took place from pulmonary obstruction and dropsy. In one of them the aortic valves were found to be retroverted and covered with vegetations. This at first seemed to be difficult of explanation : but I subsequently found reason to attribute it to the increased tension within the aorta that must have resulted from the sharp bend in its descending part where it was tied by its intercostal branches into the very acute angle formed by the diseased vertebræ. Since then I have seen acute endocarditis affecting the aortic and the mitral valves in a man who died of bronchitis and dilatation of the bronchial tubes, consequent on anchylosis of all the vertebræ together, and of the ribs to the vertebræ. But in this case I did not discover any evidence that the aorta had been compressed or interfered with. A somewhat analogous case to the first one mentioned in this paragraph has, however, occurred to me, in which the aorta was compressed by large masses of caseous glands, and in which the aortic valves were affected with acute endocarditis. And Dr. Goodhart lately met with a case of congenital stenosis of the descending part of the arch of the aorta in which there was a similar affection of the valves.

There are still some other diseases in which similar minute granulations on the cardiac valves have been occasionally found in the post-mortem theatre of Guy's. Thus in six years (1866–71) I find their presence recorded in three cases of cancer (of the uterus, the liver, and the gall-bladder respectively), in one case of phthisis, in

[1] Path. Trans. xvii. p. 60.
[2] Guy's Hospital Reports, series iii. vol. xix. p. 199.

one case of lobular pneumonia, in one case of Bright's disease, in one case of puerperal peritonitis, in one case of syphilitic disease of the liver, twice in cases of dilated heart, and once when there was old adhesion of the two surfaces of the pericardium. They were also found in one case of cholera; but as the disease proved fatal in 12 hours, it must be supposed that they existed before the attack commenced.

It has been stated that in all the fatal cases of rheumatic fever that have come under observation at Guy's Hospital within the last few years the changes in the valves have been slight, and in fact identical with those which are well known to occur in chorea. But I must not omit to mention that writers have recorded instances in which the valves have been much more severely attacked. Thus Sir Thomas Watson[1] relates two cases, in which death is stated to have occurred in a first attack of rheumatic fever, complicated with acute pleurisy, three weeks and four weeks respectively after admission of the patients into hospital. In neither instance was any trace of pericarditis discovered after death. In each, one of the aortic valves was a mass of ragged ulceration; and the adjacent portions of the two other valves were in a slighter degree implicated. In one of the cases the ulcerating process had penetrated through the valve into the muscular substance beyond, and eaten a hole completely through the septum. In the other case an abscess as large as a hazel-nut was found in the muscular substance of the septum, immediately opposite the disorganized valve. Now the occurrence of such an abscess is so rare in acute rheumatism, that I almost think it is permissible to express a doubt whether the case was not rather one of pyæmia, or of primary ulcerative endocarditis, with articular pains : for such cases have often been mistaken for cases of rheumatic fever. Sir Thomas Watson goes on to remark that these were the only instances of the kind which he had seen. In the other fatal cases of acute rheumatism related in his book only slight changes in the cardiac valves were found after death.

It may be convenient here to complete all that has to be said in reference to the general etiology of the acute destructive disease of the valves, which has recently attracted so much notice, under the name of Ulcerative Endocarditis—a name first given to it, I believe by Charcot and Vulpian in 1861. Besides its occasional origin in pyæmia and perhaps in acute rheumatism (as just mentioned), this affection has often been found to occur in the latter months of pregnancy, or a few weeks after delivery. Virchow[2] says that in the Charité at Berlin there is never a year in which several instances of this do not occur. It is true that in the majority of these cases inflammation of the uterus is present, so that the endocarditis might be supposed to be simply a manifestation of pyæmia, but occasionally the pelvic organs are quite healthy. Very often, however, ulcerative endocarditis can be traced to none of these conditions, and may be

---

[1] Lectures on the Principles and Practice of Physic, 4th edition, 1857, p. 315.
[2] " Ueber die Chlorose . . . . Endocarditis Puerperalis," Berlin, 1872, p. 20 ; see also Trousseau, "Lectures on Clinical Medicine," New Sydenham Society's Trans. vol. iv. p. 459.

said to arise spontaneously, so far as our knowledge at this time extends. The patient may have previously been a healthy subject, and the disease may arise suddenly with shivering, so that it is often mistaken for enteric fever or some other acute disease. But such cases are exceptional; much more commonly ulcerative endocarditis attacks valves which were previously unsound, and its effects overlie and are blended with those of chronic valvular disease.

We may now pass to consider the causation of chronic affections of the cardiac valves; and of these a large proportion, probably the majority, arise out of the acute affections already described as occurring in the course of acute rheumatism and of chorea (for pyæmia, being itself almost always fatal, can hardly be credited with a share in the production of these more remote changes). With regard to the details of the processes by which these results are brought about, it may be said that at the present time we know scarcely anything. We do not even know whether an acute affection, once developed, ever subsides entirely, and leaves the valve perfectly healthy. I think that this must not infrequently occur, especially after chorea, for we have seen that the valves are very often affected in this common malady, and yet it has in my experience comparatively seldom happened that patients labouring under valvular disease have stated that they had previously had chorea. Another argument to the same effect may perhaps be found in the comparative rarity of chronic rheumatic disease of the aortic valves in women. We have seen that the aortic valves were found to be affected in thirteen out of twenty cases of acute rheumatic endocarditis. Now of these cases at least seven occurred in females. But in the years 1867-71, for 23 cases of chronic aortic disease with history of previous acute rheumatism in males, only 6 cases in females came under observation in the post-mortem theatre at Guy's. It would seem to follow that in women rheumatic inflammation of the aortic valves must often subside entirely, without leading to chronic disease. If this be true, it is of very great importance, for it may teach us a most valuable lesson. We shall presently see that the aortic valves are in men liable to strain. and pressure, from which in the other sex they are free; and that in consequence non-rheumatic disease of the aortic valves is in men very common, in women comparatively rare. It appears very probable that the same freedom from strain and pressure may also enable these valves in women to recover from rheumatic inflammation more perfectly than in men. And, if so, we may learn how to obviate the ill-effects of such inflammation in both sexes, and in the case of all the valves, by keeping the patients at rest, and making them abstain from work and exertion of every kind, for a long period after an attack of endocarditis.

It is at any rate certain that the granulations, which appear to be constantly present in acute affections of the valves, have generally but a transitory existence. Sometimes, indeed, they become calcified. and can thus be recognized long after all acute disease has passed away. But more often they disappear, and thus in chronic rheumatic disease the surface of the thickened and calcified valves is often found to be perfectly free from them. When uncalcified granulations or vegetations are found in cases of long standing, I believe that they are always of rather recent formation, and due to the supervention of an acute inflammation, to which (as we have seen) valves already diseased are particularly liable.

In a considerable proportion of cases, however, chronic valvular disease can be traced to none of the conditions that have as yet been mentioned. And its etiology appears then to be different in the case of different valves. Affections of the aortic valves often accompany similar morbid changes in the walls of the base of the aorta itself, changes often spoken of as "atheromatous," but really dependent on a chronic inflammation of the arterial coats, or (as it is termed by Virchow and others) an arteritis deformans. This disease occurs especially in men (as for example, sawyers, smiths, strikers and riveters, bricklayer's labourers, and hodmen) whose occupations involve great muscular efforts, by which the arterial pressure and the strain on the aortic coats are increased. Writers have generally stated that persons of rather advanced age are more liable to it, but Dr. Allbutt says that it is very common in Leeds among quite young men.[1] According to Peacock, a similar affection is not infrequently observed to occur in girls engaged as nursemaids, and in other servants, who are subjected to straining efforts before they have attained their full strength. It is further to be noted that, although the affection of the valves in all these cases appears to be identical in nature with that which occurs in the walls of the aorta, the two are by no means invariably affected in an equal degree. Dr. Allbutt has suggested the opinion that continuous labour, such as hammer-work, is more injurious to the aorta itself, and that sudden strains, like the lifting of weights, tell rather upon the valves. The relative frequency with which valvular disease is thus due respectively to mechanical strain or injury and to the effects of antecedent acute disease, probably differs greatly among different classes of the population, and in different localities, according to the occupations of the lower orders in them. Dr. Allbutt tells us that in Leeds, in hospital practice, heart diseases due to acute rheumatism are among young men fewer than those which he has learnt to attribute to over-exertion of the body. In this statement, however, no account is taken of the affections of different valves separately. I believe that in hospital practice in London one fails to obtain a history of a past attack of rheumatic fever in at least half the cases of chronic regurgitant disease of the aortic valves that are met with in adults, and that in almost all these cases the changes in the valves are associated with similar changes in the walls of the aorta, and are the result of habitual or repeated straining efforts of one kind or another.

[1] "The Effects of Overwork and Strain on the Heart and Great Blood-vessels," St. George's Hospital Reports, v. p. 23.

It is far otherwise in the case of the mitral valve. In this structure atheroma appears only in the form of slight cream-coloured patches, placed near the base of the valve, and therefore incapable of impeding its closure. Nor can any morbid change in the mitral valve be traced in association with the disease of the aortic valves just described as due to arteritis deformans. Still, there are a large number of cases of mitral stenosis in which no previous attack of acute rheumatism or chorea seems to have occurred, and the subjects are many of them children, in whom no definite illness could have been overlooked or for-gotten. Such cases have been by some writers attributed to congenital malformation, a view which I have already endeavoured to disprove. Other observers have supposed them to be due to latent rheumatism : that is, to manifestations of the rheumatic state, which has for some reason failed to display itself in the characteristic articular malady. On closer inquiry it may sometimes be elicited that such patients have formerly suffered from "growing pains" or "rheumatic pains" of greater or less severity, and certain observers, among whom may be mentioned no less an authority than the late Dr. Addison, have pressed these into service as affording evidence of the existence of a consti-tutional state. It must be admitted that rheumatic pericarditis often precedes any affection of the joints, and that in young people already suffering from valvular disease of the heart without any history of previous rheumatism, the joints sometimes become swollen and painful, or chorea is developed. I have therefore no doubt that many of these cases of mitral stenosis are really the results of a rheumatic tendency. But it is still a question whether they are not too frequent for such an explanation to be applicable to all of them in which no history of previous rheumatism can be traced.

It would appear, therefore, that the mitral valve is very liable, even in children and young subjects, to undergo those changes which lead to stenosis, either as the result of a spontaneous chronic morbid process, or else as the consequence of some disease (other than rheumatism or chorea), the tendency of which to produce endo-carditis is as yet unknown. Can this disease be scarlatina or diph-theria ? I have read (but I do not know where) that M. Bouchut has recently brought forward diphtheria as often leading to the formation of granulations on the mitral valve, but in the few autopsies that I have made these have been absent. As is well-known, scarlatina is often followed by acute rheumatism, or an articular disease allied to it : and this may be complicated with endocarditis, as has been shown by Trousseau and others. Nay, in cases of chronic valvular disease it is not very uncommon for the patient's illness to be referred back to an attack of scarlatina. But I am nevertheless very doubtful whether this disease can be called in to account for the cases that now need explanation, for I fail to find any evidence that scarlatina in itself is capable of setting up endocarditis. So far as I am aware, when a child dies of scarlatinal dropsy, or of any one of its other sequelæ, the valves are constantly found healthy.

Within the last few years it has been a matter of frequent discussion among pathologists whether syphilis is ever a cause of disease of the cardiac valves. The idea is indeed no new one ; for Corvisart [1] long ago suggested that vegetations of the valves were of venereal nature. No less an authority than Virchow [2] has since stated his readiness to admit the possibility that this may sometimes be the case : but he has given no case in proof. When Mr. Myers [3] and other army surgeons recently showed the frequency of heart-disease in soldiers, and attributed it to the faulty clothing and accoutrements which they are made to wear, or to the exercises they are called upon to perform, it was objected that soldiers are very subject to syphilis, and that this was really the cause of the cardiac affections to which they are liable. But to that argument a rejoinder was made that sailors are equally apt to have venereal disease, while they are not found to suffer in the same proportion from morbus cordis. For my own part, I confess that I have met with no facts, either by observation or by reading, that would lead me to believe that syphilis has anything to do with the diseases under consideration.

The effects of sudden violence in injuring the cardiac valves still remain to be considered. Corvisart appears to have been the first writer who reported a case in which the valves of the heart were clearly shown to have been injured during muscular exertion. Since that time several instances of the kind have been placed on record : and in 1865 Dr. Peacock [4] collected seventeen cases, four of which had come under his own observation.

It has already been stated that in advanced valvular disease softening and laceration are very apt to occur, whether as a result of slight muscular efforts, or independently of any such cause. . But symptoms of heart disease have then generally existed for a long time. The peculiarity of the cases now under consideration is, that the subjects of them are apparently in perfect health when the injury arises, and have never had rheumatism, or been suspected of any cardiac disease. It is indeed true that such accidents have been observed chiefly in adult men, whose occupations had long been such as are known to carry with them the liability to induce chronic changes in the heart and great vessels: and some have therefore argued that the lacerated valve might not have been in a healthy state at the time of the injury, but might have previously undergone degeneration. And this supposition is very difficult to negative, since death seldom occurs in such cases until after the lapse of a considerable interval, when of course the state of the valves before their rupture cannot be determined. But in this, as in so many other instances, the maxim may be applied, "*De non apparentibus et de non existentibus, eadem est ratio.*" For practical purposes it is more important to remember that a valve may rupture in a man who has hitherto been active and robust, and free from the slightest symptom of cardiac disease, than

[1] Op. cit. p. 194.   [3] Path. Trans. xx. p. 141.
[2] Arch. f. Path. Anat. xv. 1858, p. 288.   [4] Croonian Lectures.

to discuss whether the valve has or has not previously undergone slight degenerative changes, which no one could have discovered or suspected.

Perhaps the most striking example that could be quoted, in which mechanical injury led to the rupture of a previously healthy valve, is recorded by Dr. Wilks in the sixteenth volume of the Pathological Transactions (p. 77). The patient, a youth aged nineteen, fell from a height, and alighting on a stone struck his left side violently, so as to lacerate a portion of the intestine, as a consequence of which peritonitis arose, and proved fatal on the third day. It had been observed that he had considerable oppression at the chest, and much distress in breathing after the accident; but unfortunately no stethoscopical examination was made. At the post-mortem examination it was found that the most posterior of the aortic valves was torn through, from its free margin to its base, a little on one side of its attached edge. Only a ragged portion remained attached to the aorta, while the bulk of the valve was free to flap backwards and forwards. A small deposit of fibrin had already commenced to form on the ragged edges.

In this case there was no mark of bruising on the chest, nor any sign of injury external to the heart. But I think it can hardly be doubted, from the history of the accident, that the cause of the laceration was the blow on the side, rather than any muscular effort made by the youth at the moment. The case would then be strictly parallel to those which are not unfrequently met with, in which an accident gives rise to severe laceration of some one of the abdominal viscera, or of the interior of the brain, without there being any bruise on the surface, or visible track by which the vibrations had passed to the deeper structures.

In this respect, however, Dr. Wilks' case would appear to be exceptional, if the conclusions of Dr. Peacock are to be relied on in reference to the question at issue. The last-named observer collected seventeen cases of rupture of a valve from injury. In three or four of them the patient had sustained direct injuries at the same time; but Dr. Peacock was nevertheless of opinion that in all of them the immediate cause of the rupture was the violent effort made at the same moment. "In one case the patient had made a long and rapid journey on horseback: two men were pulling or loading heavy casks, two were running violently, one was rowing, another was striking with a heavy sledge, a third was endeavouring to force open a door, and others were climbing rapidly, endeavouring to leap over a fence, and carrying heavy deals. In others, violent coughing appears to have been the cause of the rupture."

The comparatively small number of cases which Dr. Peacock could collect is in itself a sufficient proof that rupture of a valve in a previously healthy subject is after all a decidedly rare occurrence; and this conclusion is confirmed by the fact that few cases of the kind are recorded in the Pathological Transactions, which are generally particularly rich in examples of the more striking forms of disease. Among the different valves, those of the aorta are the most liable to injury, having probably been ruptured in ten out of Dr. Peacock's seventeen cases. Laceration of the columns of the mitral valve seems to have occurred in four instances, and of the tricuspid in the remaining three. In the aortic valves the part torn appears to be usually the attached margin or angle.

Effects.—Diseases of the cardiac valves produce serious effects of various kinds, by which the patient's health is disturbed and his life often endangered. In these are to be found the "*symptoms*" of the diseases in question. But before entering upon their consideration it will be convenient to discuss first another class of effects also resulting from such diseases, and in the eyes of the physician no less important, although to the patient himself they are of but little direct concern. I refer to the altered sounds, accompanying the heart's action, that are heard by the ear or stethoscope applied to the patient's chest—the "*auscultatory signs*" of valvular lesions.

In England these altered sounds are termed indifferently "*murmurs*" or "*bruits.*" The latter term is of course a relic of the French influence that predominated in this country for many years after the discovery of auscultation. But it may be worth while to note that French writers themselves apply the word "*bruit*" indifferently to the natural heart sounds, and to the murmurs heard in disease, adding the epithet "*anormal*" when a murmur is to be referred to, or else designating it a "*bruit de souffle,*" from the blowing character which generally belongs to such morbid sounds.

Numerous theories have been formed to explain the production of cardiac murmurs; but they have attracted more attention abroad than in this country, English writers having generally passed them by, as of theoretical rather than of practical importance. One of the earliest of such theories was, however, originally propounded by Sir Dominic (then Dr.) Corrigan, in the year 1829; and, quite recently, the labours of certain French observers have gone far towards establishing the correctness of this view, to the exclusion of all others.

It must be remarked that murmurs are by no means confined to the heart, but may arise in almost any part of the circulatory system ; and this fact has to be taken into account by any theory that would explain their production. Laennec had ascribed the *bruit de souffle* to "a special vital state—a sort of spasm or tension of an artery."[1] Corrigan[2] easily showed that this opinion was untenable. "Apply," he says, "the stethoscope under the outermost third of the clavicle, not allowing it to pass (? press) on the subclavian. In a strong

[1] "Traité de l'auscultation médiate," seconde édition, 1826. In his first edition Laennec had described the *bruit de souffle* as occurring when the heart was too full of blood, and as caused by contraction of one of the heart's orifices. But afterwards, finding that there was no organic lesion which coincided constantly with the *bruit*, he expressed the opinion cited in the text.

[2] Lancet, 1829, vol. ii. p. 1.

healthy man, not agitated, the mere impulse of the diastole of the vessel is felt. Now compress the artery *above* the clavicle, so as to diminish the current of blood through it: a loud *bruit de souffle* is heard. Make strong pressure, so as to stop the flow of blood: no sound is heard. If the sound in this experiment arose from the arterial tube being excited into muscular action by the stimulus of the pressure, why does it cease when the stimulus is increased!" And he goes on to give the following explanation of the *bruit de souffle* :—"When an artery is pressed upon, as in the experiment above related, the motion of the blood in the artery immediately beyond the constricted part (looking from the heart) is no longer as before. A small stream is now rushing from a narrow orifice into a wider tube, and continuing its way through surrounding fluid. The rushing of the fluid is combined with a trembling of the artery, and the sensation to the sense of hearing is the *bruit de souffle*." Further on he applies the same theory to the murmurs heard in aneurisms and in narrowing of the auriculo-ventricular orifices of the heart, &c.; and he proves that the condition supposed to produce murmur may be imitated by passing a forcible current of water through a portion of small intestine. In this experiment, as soon as constriction was made on any part, a very loud *bruit de souffle* immediately became evident just below the narrowed part, where no sound had been previously heard.

The writers who followed Corrigan dealt with the causation of cardiac murmurs from an entirely different point of view. By Gendrin (1841-2) they were placed in the same category with the morbid sounds heard in pericardial inflammations; and since the latter are due to friction between the two serous surfaces, he naturally attributed the former, which he termed "*bruits de frottement endocardiaques*," to friction between the blood and the surface over which it passes. This *friction theory* has since been generally adopted.[1]

But in the year 1858, Chauveau, of Lyons, published an important memoir, in which he endeavoured to show that the friction theory was untenable, while he revived Corrigan's views, and placed them on a firmer physical basis.[2] In the first place, he proved that roughening the interior of an artery does not cause a bruit. Thus he exposed the carotid artery of a horse, and tore through the internal and middle coats, at four or five points near one another. The tube was, of course, greatly roughened, but no bruit was produced. On the other hand, whenever a dilatation was placed in the course of an artery, the blood entering the dilated part gave rise to a *bruit de souffle*. This Chauveau ascribed to the fact that under such circumstances a sonorous jet is formed, such as Savart studied experimentally under the name of the "*veine fluide*." He even laid bare the pulmonary artery of a horse (in which artificial respiration was kept up after *pithing*),

[1] See Walshe, "A Practical Treatise on Diseases of the Heart and Great Vessels," 1862, p. 86.
[2] Gazette Médicale de Paris, 1858, p. 247.

and introduced his finger into the artery through a slit in its wall. When the vessel was narrowed by tightening a thread round its base, he could feel the vibrations of the *veine fluide* which was generated, whereas the flow of the blood had previously been scarcely perceptible.

Chauveau therefore sums up the results of his experiments in the statement that "the *bruit de souffle* is produced by the vibrations of the *veine fluide*, which is always formed when the blood passes into a part of the circulating apparatus actually or relatively dilated."

Very soon after the discovery of auscultation, it was found that a *bruit de souffle* could sometimes be heard even in persons in whom the heart was perfectly healthy, especially in those who were chlorotic or anæmic. Such a bruit has been generally attributed to the thin and watery state of the blood, rendering it liable to be thrown into vibrations while flowing through the vessels. This explanation, however, is far from satisfactory, and has indeed been rendered untenable by the experiments of Chauveau and others, who have shown (in opposition to some earlier experiments of De la Harpe) that the production of murmurs in general is altogether independent of the nature of the fluid in which they are formed.

It would seem, however, that the theory of Chauveau, just stated, is applicable to such anæmic murmurs. As is well known, these are of two kinds—the arterial, and the venous, or "*bruit de diable.*" The former is audible chiefly at the base of the heart, along the aorta, or the pulmonary artery. Now, Chauveau has shown that in anæmic horses the arteries generally are one-third smaller than in healthy animals; the mass of blood is greatly reduced; the heart and its orifices become diminished in size, so as to adjust themselves to the altered volume of the blood; but the great arteries, being comparatively inelastic, retract less perfectly. The conditions for the production of a murmur are thus satisfied. Moreover, the arterial pressure during the cardiac diastole is found to be very much lower than usual; hence, when the artery becomes distended by the heart's contraction, the force with which the blood enters is far greater than in health. In other words, the *range* of pressure within the arterial system is greatly increased.

The venous anæmic murmur, or *bruit de diable*, receives a very similar explanation. As Hamernyk long ago showed, it is met with only at the root of the neck; and the cause of this lies in the anatomical fact (first pointed out by Bérard) that in this region the lower ends of the jugular and subclavian veins on each side are adherent to the deep cervical fascia, and therefore cannot collapse. This venous ampulla, as it has been termed, evidently affords the conditions necessary for the generation of a *veine fluide*, whenever the blood-stream in the jugular vein above is narrowed, whether by simple adjustment of its calibre to the diminished volume of the blood in anæmia, or by the pressure of the stethoscope, or by both combined. Thus, as might be expected, in some healthy subjects a *bruit de diable* can be generated by nice compression of the jugular vein with the stethoscope; and, on the other hand, even in those who are anæmic a certain amount of pressure is required to develop the murmur, unless the morbid state is present in an extreme degree.

Since the publication of Chauveau's essay, this subject has been studied by several French writers, especially by Marey, Luton,[1] and Bergeon,[2] who have expressed their general adhesion to his views. And for my own part I think that they have proved that a *bruit de souffle* occurring in an artery or vein at a distance from the heart is invariably caused by the generation of a sonorous *veine fluide*, and due to the passage of a narrow jet of blood into a wider cavity or part of the vessel.

But this explanation is certainly not applicable to all cardiac murmurs. The bruit caused by a sonorous *veine fluide* is heard only in the dilated part of the channel, and not at all (or very faintly) in the narrowed part behind it. In other words, it is propagated in the direction of the stream of fluid. Now, as we shall see presently, some cardiac murmurs obey this law; among which are those of mitral and aortic stenosis. But in mitral and in aortic imperfection this is not the case: the murmur is audible, not only in the direction of the regurgitant blood-stream, but also on the other side of the orifice (over the left ventricle in the case of the mitral valve; along the aorta in the case of the aortic valves). Now Bergeon has given a complete explanation of this, and has shown that it may be easily imitated in experiments (such as have several times been referred to), in which water is made to traverse tubes narrowed at a certain point. One has only to provide the tube at the seat of constriction with a lip or rim projecting backwards into the stream, and a second murmur is at once generated, which is heard behind the obstruction. A *cul de sac* is formed, and the fluid which occupies this receives the shock of the onward current, and is thrown into sonorous vibrations. It is evident that this experiment exactly meets the case. The incompetent valves, whether mitral or aortic, project backwards into the blood-stream, exactly like the lip or rim employed by Bergeon.

But I think that the very success of this attempt to enlarge the range of conditions to which Chauveau's narrow theory would limit the production of a cardiac *bruit de souffle*, shows how cautious we ought to be in assuming that we are now perfectly acquainted with all these conditions. In expressing my belief that *vascular* murmurs have always such an origin as Chauveau supposes, I am mainly influenced by the consideration that the circulation of a stream of fluid through a tube is a very simple physical matter, the phenomena of which have been thoroughly studied experimentally. But it is far

[1] " Nouveau Dictionnaire de Médecine et de Chirurgie Pratiques," art. Auscultation.
[2] "Des Causes et du Méchanisme du Bruit de Souffle," Paris, 1868, p. 108. In this essay will be found a detailed investigation into the physical cause of cardiac and vascular bruits.

otherwise in the case of the heart. In the left ventricle we have a contracting chamber, with projections of various kinds from its inner surface. During its systole, in particular, the mitral valve with its tendons and columns must tend to project into its cavity, with a space between it and the posterior wall of the ventricle. Under normal conditions the chamber empties itself completely during its systole, and this space can hardly be said to exist. No murmur is then generated. But let the ventricle be dilated, and let its contraction be imperfect and incomplete—as we must necessarily suppose it to be, if the quantity of blood poured into the aorta be not greater than in health, and if there be no mitral regurgitation (of which there is certainly in many cases no evidence). Is it not very probable that under such circumstances the blood in the space behind the mitral valve may be thrown into vibrations, and so a *bruit de souffle* be generated, exactly as in the *cul de sac* employed in Bergeon's experiments? Such a bruit would be heard at the heart's apex, and nowhere else. We shall hereafter see that precisely such a bruit is very frequently heard, in various diseases, and that its interpretation is still open to very great doubt.

Now, cardiac murmurs, instead of being soft and blowing, are sometimes very rough and harsh. The older French auscultators laid stress on such varieties, and gave them special names, as "*bruit de râpe*," "*bruit de scie*," "*bruit d'étrille*," devoting great pains to the determination of their precise physical causes. Little success, however, appears to have attended their efforts: as might indeed be expected from the erroneous views that they entertained concerning the origin of murmurs in general. The rough and harsh murmurs in question are very generally accompanied with a thrill that can be felt if the hand be placed on the surface of the body at the spot where the murmur is audible: and to this Laennec gave the name of *frémissement cataire.* Now, according to Bergeon, murmurs are rough and attended with frémissement, when they are intense, and when the tube (he is speaking of simple physical experiments) is thin and elastic. It might, therefore, be thought that such murmurs owe their peculiar quality to the fact that the walls of the orifice take part in their production, and that they are not produced by the vibrations of the fluid alone. Such a view, however, is entirely inconsistent with Savart's experiments already referred to. And clinical facts are equally adverse to it. As we shall presently see, no murmur is so generally harsh, and so commonly attended with thrill, as the so-called presystolic murmur of mitral stenosis. But in this affection, the margin of the orifice, far from being thin and elastic, is almost always thick and hard, and often contains much calcareous matter. The peculiar quality of the murmur in this case is evidently not due to the fact that the orifice itself, as well as the fluid, vibrates. What, then, is its cause? There can, I think, be hardly any doubt that it depends upon the circumstance that the jet of blood in which the murmur is generated, entering the flaccid empty ventricle, impinges on its inner surface at a point which must be very close indeed to the part of the ventricle which strikes the chest-wall and produces the heart's impulse. The physician may thus almost be said to receive with his finger the full shock of the sonorous jet propelled into the left ventricle through the narrowed mitral orifice. It would be interesting to determine whether similar conditions are traceable in other cases in which similar murmurs occur: for instance, in cases of aneurism. For the present it must, I think, be concluded that the harsh rasping quality of a bruit, and the accompanying thrill, are not due to any peculiar state of the orifice at which the bruit is produced, but rather to the intensity of the murmur itself, and to the fact that the jet of blood which generates it is directed towards the surface of the patient's body.

Another modification of murmurs is that in which they are high-pitched and resemble the note of a musical instrument, or a whistle, the cooing of a dove, the puling of a chicken, or the mewing of a cat. These are generally spoken of as " *musical* " murmurs ; and according to Bergeon, they may arise in either of two ways. Sometimes they are due to the fact that the channel into which the *veine fluide* passes is not straight but bent, so that the *veine* impinges on its wall on one side. This is the case, for instance, in the jugular fossa at the base of the skull ; where (according to this writer) a musical bruit is often generated, which gives rise to an intolerable singing in the ears. More frequently such a bruit is due to the presence of a thin membranous flap or valve, vibrating in the stream of blood which flows over its surface ; the musical character of some cardiac murmurs appears generally to be due to something of this kind. But the subject is one still admitting of further elucidation. In vol. vi. of the Pathological Transactions, Dr. Peacock has recorded a case in which a musical murmur, exactly resembling the sound of a cuckoo-clock, was audible at the distance of some feet from the patient : after death no special morbid appearance was discoverable in explanation of it.

But the differences in the *quality* of cardiac murmurs, which we have hitherto been considering, are of trifling consequence (so far as the interpretation of their cause is concerned) in comparison with two other points, to which we must now turn our attention. The first of these is their *rhythm*, or relation to the movements and natural sounds of the heart ; the second their *seat*, or capability of being heard at different parts of the surface of the chest.

The passage of the blood through the heart and arteries is effected by three successive movements, each of which may, under certain circumstances, cause a bruit. (1.) The most important of these is the ventricular systole: and since the contraction of one or other ventricle is invariably the cause of any murmur that coincides with it in time, such murmurs are very fitly termed *systolic* (or, sometimes, *ventricular-systolic*). They, of course, take the place of, or follow, the first sound: they coincide with the closure of the auriculo-ventricular valves, or at least occur when these ought to close. (2.) After the ventricular systole comes the elastic recoil of the aorta and pulmonary artery. This, again, may generate a bruit, which coincides with (or replaces, or follows) the second sound, and occurs at the moment when the sigmoid valves should fall together. It would have been better that the name given to such a murmur should have indicated its origin: but no convenient title suggests itself, and since the ventricle is dilating at the time, the bruit in question has always been termed *diastolic*. This is unfortunate, for the ventricular diastole is only very indirectly concerned in its production, and may indeed have nothing at all to do with it. (3.) Moreover, there is a third movement, which likewise occurs during the ventricular diastole, and generates a third kind of bruit. This is the auricular systole. In health, it produces no sound; but in disease it may give rise to a very loud murmur: the best name for this would undoubtedly be that of *auricular-systolic* (proposed for it by Dr. Gairdner); but in practice it is generally called *presystolic*, because it more or less closely precedes the ventricular systole.

Thus it is usual to designate the rhythm of a bruit by indicating its relation to the contraction of the ventricles; a murmur that is synchronous with this contraction is called systolic : one that follows it is called diastolic; one that precedes it is called presystolic. Now, when the heart is beating slowly, it is generally easy to distinguish which of the cardiac sounds or murmurs is systolic, from the fact that the pause before the first sound is very much longer than that which follows it. But when the pulsations are more rapid, this criterion is lost, for the increased pace is gained at the expense of the period of rest, and the one pause may then be as short as the other. The well-known difference in quality between the first sound and the second may then enable the rhythm to be detected; but this again often fails; and one is driven to determine the ventricular systole by noting at what period the heart's apex strikes the chest or (which is to me more easy) by feeling the carotid pulse with the finger while one is listening to the heart.

A systolic sound or murmur having been thus identified, it remains to consider whether any other bruit that may be audible is diastolic or presystolic. And here, again, all depends on the rate of the heart's beats. When these are infrequent, and the diastolic pause is prolonged, the so-called *diastolic* murmur, occurring at the commencement of this pause, is easily differentiated from the *presystolic* murmur that occupies its termination, and runs up to the following ventricular systole. But it is quite another case when the heart's action is rapid, and the pause proportionately shortened. The distinction between a presystolic and a diastolic murmur may then, as I believe, become quite artificial, so far as their mere rhythm is concerned. But there still remain differences of quality and seat, which usually enable the nature of the murmur to be determined without much difficulty.

We will now consider the three kinds of bruits in the order of their occurrence: I. the Presystolic; II. the Systolic; III. the Diastolic. And since each of these may be developed on either the right or the left side of the heart, it will be necessary to mention two varieties of each. But, as has already been stated, disease of the left valves is greatly more common than of the right.

I. A presystolic murmur, due to the auricular systole, is never produced unless the auriculo-ventricular orifice is narrowed. And practically it is almost always indicative of that chronic change in the corresponding valve that has been described under the name of stenosis.[1]

a. When developed at the mitral orifice, this murmur is much louder at the heart's apex than anywhere else. It is also remarkably local, being sometimes audible only at a single spot, and not being traceable round the side of the chest towards the left scapula, as is the case with the systolic murmur of mitral regurgitation.

The quality of a presystolic, or (as it is sometimes called) " *direct*," mitral murmur is in most cases peculiarly harsh, and it is often accompanied by a thrill perceptible to the touch. It is generally spoken of as having a "churning" or "grinding" character; and this may enable a practised ear to distinguish it at once from other bruits. I think I have never yet heard a direct mitral murmur which has been soft or musical. There is, however, an important modification of the presystolic murmur, which, I believe, I first described in a paper on this subject in the Guy's Hospital Reports for 1870–71. Such a murmur is often very short; and it may be so short as to resemble a tone, and thus to be hardly distinguishable from the natural first sound of the heart. Now, it happens that in cases of this kind the real first sound is commonly peculiarly sharp and clear, and so resembles the second sound; while the second sound is itself inaudible at the heart's apex. Thus the sounds heard at this spot may at first appear to be normal; while on closer examination it may be discovered that their rhythm is entirely different from that of the healthy sounds; and that one of them is in fact an abbreviated presystolic bruit. In the paper above referred to, I have described a case in which this observation led to the confident assertion that mitral stenosis existed in the case of a woman who had no other sign or symptom of cardiac disease, having been admitted into a surgical ward for gangrene of the leg. She died six weeks later; and the mitral orifice would admit only one finger-point.

It is only within the last few years that presystolic murmurs have been rightly interpreted. The name was invented by Gendrin.[2] He did not, however, attach any special importance or diagnostic value to such murmurs. But in 1843, Fauvel communicated to the *Archives Générales* a paper in which he showed by the narration of four cases (three of them fatal) that a presystolic murmur was indicative of

---

[1] It is indeed possible that a mass of vegetations, formed upon the surface of the valve during acute disease, might so obstruct the channel as to lead to the development of such a murmur; but (so far as I am aware) no case of the kind has as yet been placed on record. I have always believed hypertrophy of the auricle to play an important part in the development of a presystolic murmur; and this implies the existence of chronic disease.

[2] Leçons sur les Maladies du Cœur, &c., 1841-2.

mitral stenosis. Subsequent French writers, however, have thrown very little light on this subject. For many years the Paris School of Medicine was divided into two camps with regard to the rhythm of the heart's impulse, which Beau would have to be synchronous with the ventricular diastole. Agreement on minor points was therefore out of the question ; and Hérard,[1] Bouillaud,[2] and Durosiez,[3] may be mentioned as having written on the subject of mitral stenosis, and expressed views opposed to those of Fauvel. Durosiez, in 1862, thought it sufficient to make a passing reference to "ce fameux bruit présystolique, dont tout le monde a parlé, sur lequel personne ne s'entend, que Hope lui-même avoue n'avoir jamais entendu, que M. Bouillaud enfin neglige et même nie." Racle, again, in his " Traité de Diagnostic médical," published in 1859, speaks of it as " une distinction plus subtile que réelle."

In Great Britain the first writer who alluded to this subject was, I believe, Dr. Gairdner of Glasgow,[4] who expressed views precisely similar to those of Fauvel, except that he preferred to term the murmur auricular-systolic, rather than presystolic. Subsequently papers on the same subject were published by Dr. Wilks, Dr. Gull, Dr. Hayden (of Dublin), Dr. Peacock, Dr. Sutton, Dr. Simpson (of Manchester), and Dr. Hyde Salter.[5]

Thus in my communication to the Guy's Hospital Reports I was able to refer to twenty-eight cases (seven contributed by myself), in each of which a post-mortem examination proved the existence of mitral stenosis, and in which this condition had been diagnosed from a presystolic murmur heard during life. Since then the subject has been taken up by Dr. Douglas Powell and Dr. Silver. Even now, however, there are observers who deny that the rough grinding murmur heard in cases of mitral obstruction is really presystolic in rhythm. In the year 1872 Dr. Barclay contributed to the *Lancet*[6] a series of papers in which he endeavoured to prove that the peculiarity in the rhythm of this murmur really depends on the circumstance that the closure of the mitral valve is delayed. Instead of this closure occurring at the commencement of the ventricular systole, he believes it to take place only when the systole is nearly completed ; the first sound being of course postponed likewise. Dr. Barclay thus regards the murmur as really regurgitant and not obstructive, although he does not deny its constant association with mitral stenosis. But it appears to me that no one who has studied the relation between the murmur and the heart's beat or the carotid pulse can admit that Dr. Barclay's hypothesis is tenable. Neither beat nor pulse can be felt while the bruit is audible ; they both follow it.

It is important here to mention that the presystolic bruit by no

[1] Arch. génér. de Méd., sér. v., tom. ii. p. 543. 1853.
[2] Traité clinique des Maladies du Cœur, 1836.
[3] Arch. génér. de Méd., sér. v., tom. xx. p. 385.
[4] Edinburgh Medical Journal, vol. vii., part 1, p. 438. 1861.
[5] In my paper in the Guy's Hospital Reports, I have gone into the literature of this question in much greater detail than is possible here.
[6] Vol. i., pp. 283 *et seq.*

means always merges gradually into the heart's first sound, as would appear from the accounts given of it by some writers. Much more often it is separated from the first sound by a distinct interval, which seems to me sometimes as long as that which separates the natural first from the second sound. The murmur, too, is often prolonged through a period much exceeding that of the natural auricular systole. This has been explained in two different ways. The late Dr. Salter supposed that the first part of the murmur is generated while blood is flowing passively from the auricle into the ventricle. I have argued that the auricle begins to contract earlier, and goes on contracting longer than in the healthy heart, and that the whole of the bruit is thus due to the auricular systole. This view has since been established by the cardiographic observations of Mr. Mahomed.[1] I append copies of two of his tracings, taken from the heart's apex

Fig. 1.　　　　　　　　Fig. 2.

in the same patient at an interval of seven months. It will be observed that the slight elevation which Marey proved to be due to the auricular contraction takes place very soon after the preceding ventricular systole, and is succeeded by a gradually ascending line, throughout the whole duration of which the auricular systole is sustained. The figures seem to speak for themselves: and unless it can be shown that their peculiarities are capable of some different interpretation, it appears to me that they not only establish the point now under consideration, but also give the *coup de grâce* to Dr. Barclay's hypothesis.

It is the more necessary to insist on the fact that the presystolic murmur is often separated from the following first sound of the heart by a distinct interval, because I believe that this fact has had much to do with the impression that so long prevailed as to the real rhythm of such murmurs. The old view was that the murmur caused by mitral obstruction should be diastolic in rhythm: and with the single exception of Dr. Markham all writers were agreed that diastolic apex murmurs were very rare. Evidently, therefore, those observers mistook for systolic the murmurs which they heard: and collateral evidence of this is further afforded by the fact that they described as systolic the *frémissement* which we know to go with the murmur. Nor did the mistake end here. I have shown in my paper that the real first sound of the heart at the apex was mistaken for the second sound, which it resembles so closely in character. It might appear

[1] Med. Times and Gazette, 1872, vol. i. p. 569.

needless to discuss the errors of a bygone period. But a little experience in clinical teaching shows that these very errors are still committed by every student, who has not had his attention specially drawn to them. And it appears to me that some of the most recent German writers have not yet extricated themselves from the same pitfall. Dr. P. Niemeyer, of Magdeburg, in an elaborate work on " Percussion and Auscultation," published in 1870, gives as diagnostic of mitral stenosis "a loud long systolic apex murmur and strong *frémissement cataire;* in rare cases, also, a short diastolic murmur." But Traube, Felix von Niemeyer (of Tübingen), and Friedreich, describe the direct mitral murmur as presystolic.

I have already remarked that presystolic murmurs are often of long duration, and thus commence very soon after the second sound has completed the previous cardiac movement. It must be added that when the heart-sounds are traced downwards from the base, these murmurs have sometimes an apparent relation to the second sound, which is very apt to mislead the student, and which I cannot altogether explain. At the base, the second sound is clear and single; lower down, it appears to be reduplicated; still lower, the presystolic murmur seems to grow out of it. In my paper in the Guy's Hospital Reports I have discussed this subject at some length, and quoted the statements of Hamernyk, Drasche, and Guttmann, in regard to it. Here I must limit myself to a simple statement of the fact.

An objection frequently made to the view that these long murmurs are due to a prolonged auricular systole—and indeed to the view that they are due in any way to mitral obstruction—is, that since the pulmonary veins are unprovided with valves, blood would be forced back into them during the whole duration of the auricular systole, and the circulation through the lungs would be brought to a standstill. But it is forgotten that, in cases of mitral stenosis, the tension in the pulmonary vessels is very high—much higher than under normal conditions; whereas the left ventricle is in the condition of an empty flaccid sac, and thus readily receives the blood expelled by the contraction of the auricle. This objection, therefore, appears to have but little weight.

b. When developed at the tricuspid orifice, and due to stenosis of the corresponding valve, a presystolic murmur is heard, according to Dr. Hayden,[1] principally over the fifth left costal cartilage, and the fourth intercostal space, close to the sternum. Dr. Hayden has lately recorded a case of this kind, in which, between the area over which the tricuspid presystolic murmur was audible and that over which a coexistent mitral presystolic murmur was audible, there was a space in which neither could be distinctly heard. Both lesions, therefore, were diagnosed; and after death the right auriculo-ventricular orifice would admit only the point of the middle finger; and the left one was smaller still. The tricuspid murmur was even harsher in quality than the mitral one, and began earlier in the ventricular

[1] Dublin Journ. of Med. Science, May 1874.

diastole. As far back as 1864, Dr. Haldane[1] related a similar case, in which the tricuspid orifice was found after death to admit only the point of the forefinger. But it must be added that a mitral presystolic murmur was at the same time audible; and the mitral was in fact much the narrower of the two valves. Indeed, although tricuspid stenosis in moderate degree is common enough when mitral stenosis is considerable or extreme, I am not aware that it is ever clinically met with apart from such an association.[2]

II. A systolic (ventricular-systolic) murmur may have various origins. As we shall presently see, it has not always anything to do with the valves. And when it is due to valvular disease or imperfection, it may be formed at any one of the orifices into either ventricle; namely, either the mitral, the aortic, the tricuspid, or the pulmonary. Evidently a mitral or tricuspid systolic murmur must be due to regurgitation: an aortic or pulmonary systolic murmur must be obstructive or direct. These four varieties of systolic murmurs may be in part distinguished by their seat.

a. A mitral systolic murmur is loudest at or near the heart's apex; that is, if the left ventricle be of normal size, about the fifth costal cartilage, and a little internal to the nipple; if the heart be enlarged, further downwards and outwards. It is not heard over the base of the heart, nor near the ensiform cartilage; or, if it can be heard there, it is much less loud than at the heart's apex. It can very generally be traced along the left ribs (or, to use a common expression, *into the axilla*), and is audible at the angle of the left scapula. The question will hereafter be discussed whether it is not invariably heard in these positions when of sufficient intensity.

b. An aortic systolic murmur is most plainly heard in the *second* right interspace, and is traceable over the ascending arch, that is, towards the inner end of the right clavicle; and often also along the arteries of the neck, or even of other parts of the body.

c. A tricuspid systolic murmur is heard over the ensiform cartilage, and sometimes to the right of it. It is also (according to Gairdner and Sutton[3]) heard over the surface of the right ventricle; that is to say, a little to the left of the sternum; but it "is little audible above the level of the third rib." I should myself have fixed its upper limit at a much lower point. In some rare cases it is very loud, and may then be heard over a wide area; but most commonly it is a faintly

---

[1] Ed. Med. Journ., vol. x., 1864, p. 271.

[2] An exception must be made for a very remarkable case which occurred to Dr. Gairdner, and in which a rounded tumour projected into the interior of the right auricle, in such a way that it formed a kind of ball-valve to the tricuspid orifice. In that case a tricuspid presystolic murmur was heard several years (I think, ten years) before death by Dr. Gairdner, who published his diagnosis in his work on Clinical Medicine. I am not aware that he has yet placed the result of the post-mortem examination formally on record. I saw the preparation of the heart, with the tumour, at the meeting of the British Medical Association in 1873. One remarkable feature about the specimen was that there was no marked hypertrophy of the right auricle. This certainly throws some doubt on the opinion which I have expressed in a note to p. 34.

[3] London Hosp. Reports, iv. 1867–8, p. 288.

audible bruit; and I think it is then generally discoverable at one spot only. Indeed this appears a principal reason for its presence being often overlooked.

d. A pulmonary systolic murmur is loudest about the third left costal cartilage, and is transmitted upwards and to the left, towards the middle or inner end of the left clavicle.

The *clinical significance* of these four murmurs varies widely in different cases. They must, therefore, be discussed separately ; and it will be convenient to take the two *basic* murmurs first.

As we have seen, the pulmonary valves are scarcely liable to any disease beyond congenital malformation. In practice, therefore, a pulmonary systolic murmur, if due to change in the valves, almost always indicates a congenital defect, and needs no further discussion here. An aortic systolic murmur, on the other hand, is frequently caused by acquired stenosis of the orifice in question. But, as has already been stated, such stenosis is (far more constantly than is generally supposed) accompanied by regurgitation ; and the systolic murmur, therefore, is followed by one which is diastolic.

A systolic murmur, however, audible at the base, and traceable along the aorta, is by no means limited to cases in which there is actual stenosis. Formerly it was held that any roughening of the orifice, or of its valves, or even of the lining membrane of the vessel, would suffice to generate it. But even then it was recognized that such a murmur was frequently heard under various conditions, when after death no morbid change in any of these parts was discoverable. This led to the theory that the murmur was due to an altered state of blood ; at first, that an anæmic state only could produce it ; but afterwards, that various changes in the composition of the blood might generate it. I have already, in discussing the physical theory of murmurs, mentioned the ingenious explanation given by Chauveau of some of the more striking of these anæmic murmurs, as they have been called. This explanation, indeed, hardly covers the whole range of the bruits that have been regarded as hæmic, in the wider sense of the term. And it must be admitted that the precise significance of many basic murmurs has still to be determined. It is important to note that many undoubtedly anæmic murmurs appear to be seated rather in the pulmonary artery than in the aorta ; and that they are sometimes of a harsh quality, such as might *à priori* have been supposed to belong rather to murmurs due to some very definite organic cause.

It must be added that the so-called hæmic murmurs are believed to arise in many acute diseases, including not only fevers, but also those affections in which endocarditis is apt to occur, as, for instance, acute rheumatism. In this disease there is a further ground for uncertainty as to the cause of a basic murmur, in the fact that a similar sound may probably be caused by the presence of lymph in small quantity outside the heart, round the bases of the great vessels.

In this connexion I must not omit to mention the fact that in children (even when in good health) a murmur over the pulmonary valves may be generated by the pressure of the stethoscope, as is shown by the fact that it disappears when the instrument is lightly applied. . It is said that a similar murmur has sometimes been observed even in adults, when the chest-walls are thin and yielding. And consolidation of the anterior edge of the left lung appears sometimes to cause pressure on the trunk of the pulmonary artery, and consequently a systolic murmur. Yet another suggestion with regard to these basic pulmonary murmurs has recently been made by Quincke; and Dr. Balfour [1] has adopted it. It is that they sometimes depend upon the edge of the left lung being retracted, in consequence of which the heart, during its systole, compresses the pulmonary artery against the parietes of the thorax, instead of merely pushing aside this edge of the lung. In support of this it is asserted that the murmur disappears when the diminution of the cardiac dulness shows that the lung has recovered its normal dimensions. Dr. Balfour even relates a case in which the murmur ceased whenever the patient inspired deeply and held his breath. But I must confess that I see little probability in this explanation.

This is perhaps the most convenient place for noticing the suggestion of another German writer (Naunyn), which is also quoted with approval by Dr. Balfour; namely, that the systolic murmur of mitral regurgitation is sometimes heard an inch or two to the left of the sternum, between the second and third ribs. The seat of such a murmur is supposed to be in the appendix of the left auricle. I must confess that when I read Naunyn's paper on the subject I thought there must be some mistake: and this suspicion is not removed by Dr. Balfour's remarks on the subject, for I find him saying that this remarkable modification of the mitral regurgitant murmur is almost invariably present when the insufficiency is dependent upon anæmia and chlorosis!

Passing on to consider the clinical significance of *apical* systolic murmurs, we may take first that which is audible near the ensiform cartilage, and which is referred to the tricuspid valve; and of this murmur the interpretation is seldom difficult. According to universal belief, it is always due to regurgitation through the tricuspid orifice. In some cases this is the result of primary disease of the valve itself, which (as we shall see further on) is occasionally affected with an acute ulcerative change. In such cases a bruit would doubtless be heard by any physician sufficiently acute to search for it. Most commonly, however, there is no actual change in the valve itself; its segments are kept apart by the dilatation and distension of the right ventricle, while at the same time its orifice is greatly widened. The distension of the ventricle may result either from disease of the valves on the left side of the heart, or from some chronic affection of the lungs, such as emphysema or fibroid disease. The cases in which I have heard the loudest tricuspid regurgitant murmurs have been those in which there was cirrhosis of one lung.

[1] Med. Times and Gaz., 1874, ii. p. 556.

Two good examples of this are recorded in Dr. Bastian's table in the third volume of this work (cases vi. and xiii.). I well remember the second of these cases, which occurred in the practice of the late Dr. Addison, when I was his clinical clerk. The murmur was so loud that it was heard over the heart's apex, as well as over the ensiform cartilage; and Dr. Addison, although repeatedly pressed upon the point, would not admit that the case was other than one of primary mitral regurgitation. Indeed, as Dr. Wilks has pointed out, cases of cirrhosis of the lung are often so like those of primary heart disease in their general aspect and symptoms as to be mistaken for examples of such disease.

There might, indeed, well be the same uncertainty about the theoretical significance of tricuspid, that we shall see to prevail in regard to the corresponding mitral, murmurs. But in practice such doubts have not arisen, since tricuspid systolic murmurs are not very often heard, and they are perhaps never heard unless those conditions of obstructed pulmonary circulation are present which most physiologists regard as readily capable of inducing regurgitation through the orifice in question. Physicians, therefore, have been more disposed to admit the occurrence of regurgitation when murmur is absent than to doubt its existence when murmur is present.

It is very different with those systolic murmurs which are audible at the apex of the heart, and which (if of valvular origin at all) must be referred to the *mitral* orifice. They are perhaps the commonest of all murmurs, and their significance is the most uncertain.

There are, in the first place, certain sounds which an inexperienced auscultator may easily mistake for endocardial murmurs, but which really arise not in the heart, but in that little flap or tongue-like process of the lung which commonly projects forwards over the apex of the heart, just below the seat of its visible impulse. The contraction of the ventricle, altering the form of the heart, causes a movement of air into or out [1] of this portion of the lung, and thus produces a murmur which, though of respiratory origin, is distinctly systolic in rhythm. The sound in question is generally soft and blowing; but I have several times known it to be of distinctly musical quality. Its most important peculiarity is that it is not constant, but accompanies only those beats of the heart which occur at a particular period of the respiratory act, this period being generally that of inspiration. Thus, when the patient breathes out, the first sound may be quite natural; but when he draws in his breath, a systolic murmur may be audible, which acquires its maximum intensity when the cardiac beat happens to coincide with the acme of the inspiratory effort. When the patient is made to hold his

[1] According to certain modern views on the theory of the respiratory murmur (of which a full account is to be found in the Med. Chir. Review for July 1873), a sound within the lung can be generated only by the entrance of air into that portion of lung, and not by its exit. We must therefore suppose that when the heart assumes a globular form during its systole, air is sucked into the flap of lung in question.

breath, the murmur in question is often, but not always, suppressed for the time.

A little care, however, excludes this source of fallacy. If the murmur be heard uniformly with every ventricular systole without exception, we may conclude that it arises within the heart itself.[1] And the same conclusion may also be arrived at, even when the murmur fails to accompany certain beats, provided that its absence depends not upon any relation to the respiratory rhythm, but upon the circumstance that the corresponding heart-beats are feeble and imperfect. How, then, is such a systolic apex murmur produced?

Now, if after death some of the tendinous cords of the mitral valve be found softened and ulcerated through by disease,—or if the edge of the valve have become turned inwards towards the auricle,—or even if the orifice be so thick and hard that it obviously must have remained patulous:—if any one of these conditions should be present, we may be sure that regurgitation occurred during life, and we have good grounds for inferring that any systolic apex murmur that may have been audible was due to regurgitation.

The conditions just mentioned are, however, comparatively seldom met with. But it is to be observed, that, if we exclude these conditions, we can never with certainty determine, when we are examining the heart after death, whether the mitral valve was or was not competent. We have no means of testing satisfactorily the action of the valve. We may, indeed, tie the base of the aorta; and having cut open the apex of the left ventricle, may hold the heart upside down, and pour water into the cavity to see whether it runs out. But in such an experiment the conditions are very different from those which obtained during life. Then, the base of the muscular columns was moved towards the orifice by the ventricular contraction: while those columns at the same time underwent shortening, so as to keep the tendinous cords stretched to the proper degree. Now, ventricular wall and fleshy columns are alike relaxed. Errors may thus arise in either direction. When the muscular columns are converted into non-contractile fibrous tissue, the valve may have been very imperfect in the living body, and yet may close well enough when tested after death. Conversely, when the ventricle is dilated, without the the tendinous chordæ being increased in length, it may happen that the valve allows reflux to occur after death, although it had before been efficient.

This deficiency in the proof of mitral regurgitation, when a case has reached the dead-house, would be of but little consequence, if the orifice or its valve were constantly found to be obviously diseased in those cases in which a systolic apex murmur had been heard during life. But all who have worked at the subject know that this is not so. To quote the words of Dr. Bristowe,[2] "In a large pro-

[1] Evidence is, I think, wanting to show that a white patch on the serous surface of the apex, or any like condition, can generate the murmur in question.
[2] Med. Chir. Review, 1861, July, p. 215.

portion" of such cases "the mitral valve and the orifice it protects are found to present a perfectly healthy appearance." Now Dr. Bristowe has proposed a very ingenious solution of the difficulty. He believes that valvular incompetence exists whenever a systolic apex murmur is heard; and in the cases now under consideration he attributes this incompetence to "disproportion between the size of the ventricular cavities and the length of the chordæ tendineæ and musculi papillares." He has shown in fact that while the former are found after death to be dilated, the latter are often small and seem to be on the stretch. But these observations are exposed to the full force of the objections already made to the post-mortem evidence of mitral regurgitation. The appearance of the mitral cords and columns in a dilated ventricle relaxed by death can surely afford no proof that these parts were too short to allow the valve to close, when the ventricle itself was shortened by its own systole.

Dr. Bristowe regards it "as an axiom, that the existence of a systolic murmur at the apex of the heart is a sure indication of incompetence of one or other of the auriculo-ventricular valves." And he deems it unnecessary to offer any evidence in support of this position, beyond the fact that in all the cases recorded in his paper the general symptoms and the condition of internal organs (lungs, liver, spleen, &c.) were such as are found in this form of disease. Subsequent writers, however, have dealt with this question in a different way. Both Dr. Austin Flint[1] and Dr. Andrew[2] have expressed the opinion that the murmur by no means necessarily indicates such regurgitation: according to the latter observer, indeed, regurgitation is absent in 34 per cent. of the cases in which the murmur is audible.

These authorities believe that there are two criteria which may be applied to the determination of the fact, that in a particular case a systolic apex murmur is really due to mitral regurgitation. The criteria are: 1, That the murmur should be audible in the left side of the back, about the inferior angle of the scapula; 2, That the pulmonary second sound should be intensified.

1. A good illustration of the fact that the murmur caused by mitral regurgitation is heard in the left side of the back is afforded by cases in which the tendinous cords are ruptured or ulcerated through. It has been so in the cases which I have seen, and I have not met with any recorded instance to the contrary. But in such cases the murmur is generally loud, and the amount of regurgitation probably large. I am not sure that when the murmur is feeble one can fairly expect that it should always be carried backwards: for one must remember that, though the direction of the blood-stream is towards the vertebral column, the auricle is not itself in any close relation with the part of the chest-wall at which one looks for the murmur. Consequently, although I am prepared to admit that whenever a systolic murmur is heard in the back, it is caused by mitral regurgitation,

[1] Am. Med. Times, 1862. Quoted in Braithwaite's Retrospect, xlvii. (1863, p. 69.
[2] St. Bartholomew's Hospital Reports, 1865, i. p. 13.

I cannot regard the fact that a feeble murmur is not heard in that position as conclusive against its being so caused.

2. Intensification of the pulmonary second sound (that is, of the second sound heard at the second left, as compared with the second right costal cartilage [1]) is undoubtedly present in many of the most marked cases of mitral regurgitant disease. Its cause is evidently the increased tension of the blood within the pulmonary system of vessels. But this (as I shall endeavour to show further on) may arise from any cause which prevents the left side of the heart from emptying itself. I cannot see, therefore, how intensification of the second sound can be indicative of regurgitation through the mitral orifice, rather than of other conditions which will then be mentioned. Moreover, I believe that intensification of the pulmonary second sound requires, as a condition of its occurrence, that the right ventricle should be powerful, and that the tricuspid valve should be efficient. I think I have observed that this sign is present chiefly in the early stages of mitral regurgitant disease, before it has begun to tell upon more distant parts.

My own views with regard to the interpretation of systolic apex murmurs may therefore be summed up as follows :

1. If such a murmur be audible in the back, it indicates mitral regurgitation.

2. If such a murmur be heard only at the heart's apex, we are unable at the present time to pronounce any positive opinion as to its cause. Should the murmur be loud, we may probably conclude that it is not due to mitral regurgitation : since really regurgitant murmurs, when loud, are, perhaps, always audible in the back, though for slight murmurs the same statement may not be tenable.

The question still remains, How is a systolic apex-murmur produced when it is not caused by mitral regurgitation ? I have already (vide p. 631) suggested that it may be due simply to dilatation of the left ventricle, as was long ago supposed by many of the earlier writers on auscultation.

III. A " diastolic" murmur, as has been stated, accompanies the elastic recoil of the aorta and pulmonary artery. It almost invariably indicates regurgitation, through the space that should be closed by one or other set of sigmoid valves, into the ventricle ; and in the immense majority of cases the valves affected are those of the aorta.

The quality of the diastolic murmur of aortic regurgitation varies greatly in different cases ; it may be soft and blowing, rough, and attended with thrill, or even musical. It may be so loud as to be audible at some little distance from the patient ; or so slight as to require the utmost vigilance for its detection.

The seat of this murmur is somewhat variable. As a rule, it is

---

[1] Dr. Andrew has shown that it is necessary, in instituting this comparison, to remember that the same difference may be due to enfeeblement of the aortic second sound, while the pulmonary second sound is natural ; and also that an emphysematous lung overlapping the heart on one side may modify the intensity of the sound.

very plainly audible over the base of the heart; its point of maximum intensity is generally stated to be at the sternal end of the second right costal cartilage, or in the second right interspace; and it is carried downwards along the length of the sternum (apparently in consequence of the fact that osseous substance is a good conductor of sound), so that it may often be loudly heard near the ensiform cartilage. This fact has been especially insisted on by Dr. Gairdner.[1] Again, this murmur is frequently plainly audible at the heart's apex, and sometimes it is louder there than at the base. Lastly, it may be conducted along the arteries, sometimes, to a surprising distance: according to Dr. Gee, as far as the radial arteries.

In discussing the theory of murmurs in general, I have pointed out the conditions upon which some of the varieties in the seat of this bruit appear to depend (see p. 630). If the views there stated are correct, the fact that in a particular case an aortic diastolic murmur is transmitted upwards along the aorta may be interpreted as indicating that the valves are so far free from serious damage that, although they do not meet, they nevertheless project inwards into the aorta to a greater or less extent; while in those cases in which the murmur is solely carried downwards it may be concluded that the valves are more completely destroyed.

A further refinement in regard to diastolic murmurs has lately been suggested by Dr. Balthazar Foster[2] of Birmingham. He believes that when such a murmur is heard at the apex of the heart it is due to incompetency of the left aortic segment, so that the regurgitant blood-stream falls upon the mitral curtain and is carried downwards; and, on the other hand, that a similar murmur propagated towards the ensiform cartilage indicates defect in the right and posterior segments, by which the blood is thrown upon the septum. He alludes to cases corroborative of his views, to which he further attaches considerable importance as regards prognosis. He thinks that incompetency of an aortic segment must specially interfere with the flow of blood into the coronary artery contained within the corresponding sinus (which flow he, in common with many other authorities, believes to occur during the recoil of the aorta), and so must tend to impair the nutrition of the heart. Now the left aortic segment has no coronary artery in relation with it. Dr. Foster therefore infers that, cæteris paribus, life is more likely to be prolonged when this segment is affected, or (in other words) when the murmur is audible at the apex. But my belief has hitherto been that the murmur is propagated in this direction especially when the regurgitant stream is large: and if so, one would suppose that the prognosis must be particularly unfavourable. I think that the point is one which needs further observations.

It has been stated that in the immense majority of cases a regurgitant murmur has its seat at the aortic orifice. In fact a pulmonary regurgitant bruit is so rare as scarcely to need consideration. In

[1] Clinical Medicine, p. 587.
[2] Med. Times and Gazette, 1873, ii. pp. 658, 686.

1865 Dr. Wilks exhibited to the Pathological Society[1] a specimen of disease of the valves in question, in which a double bruit had been heard during life: and one or two other cases are recorded in medical literature. In Dr. Wilks's case the question of disease of the pulmonary artery was considered during the patient's life, for the pulse gave no indication of aortic regurgitation, and the bruit became less marked towards the right, and in the course of the aorta, but was equally distinct, or even somewhat more intense, towards the left clavicle. But the great rarity of such disease led to its rejection as a diagnosis. Indeed, one can hardly expect in future to attain to greater accuracy: for (as we shall presently see) the pulse may fail to be characteristic of aortic regurgitation even when this disease exists: and the tendency of aortic diastolic murmurs to be transmitted downwards along the sternum must always prevent a pulmonary regurgitant murmur from being identified by its being heard over the right ventricle. Still, acquired disease of the pulmonary valves is so exceedingly rare (and in congenital disease I do not know that marked regurgitation ever occurs), that one hardly needs to make a reservation on account of it in attributing a diastolic murmur to aortic regurgitation. The real necessity for reservation lies in the fact that aortic aneurism sometimes causes such a murmur, probably because it receives blood during the elastic recoil of the aorta, as well as during the ventricular systole. It is only when an aneurism arises from the commencement of the arch that its murmur could be mistaken for one of regurgitation through the valves: and even then the former would perhaps never be transmitted to the heart's apex, as is so generally the case with the latter. Very frequently, indeed, the two conditions are combined.

Another infinitely rare condition, in which a diastolic murmur, not due to regurgitation through the aortic valves, may be heard at the base of the heart, is that in which the aorta communicates with the pulmonary artery, either by a patent ductus arteriosus, or through an aneurismal sac. Of the former affection I have recorded a remarkable instance.[2] The murmur (which was in part musical) was audible at the second left costal cartilage, and was transmitted to the left along this cartilage, but not downwards along the sternum. It was not everywhere continuous with the second sound. It had a wavy character, quite unlike anything that I had ever heard before. It was clearly distinguished (during the patient's lifetime) from an aortic regurgitant murmur; and it was thought not unlikely to be due to an opening from the aorta into the pulmonary artery. A case in which an aortic aneurism was correctly diagnosed to open into the pulmonary artery has been related by Dr. Wade,[3] of Birmingham. The diastolic murmur was prolonged, and of a hissing character with distinct purring tremor. It was audible over the cartilage of the fourth left rib, and in the neck, back, and upper part of the chest.

[1] Path. Trans. xvi. p. 74.
[2] Guy's Hospital Reports, 1872-3, series iii., vol. xviii. p. 23.
[3] Med. Chir. Trans. vol. xliv.

With these exceptions, a diastolic murmur (as I believe) invariably indicates regurgitation through the aortic orifice into the left ventricle.

It may be expected that something should be said as to the not infrequent coexistence of two or more of these murmurs in the same case. I have already remarked on the rarity of systolic murmurs indicating actual obstruction of the aortic orifice, unless a diastolic murmur be also present, and discoverable on careful examination. It may be added that in disease of the aortic valves the tendency is for regurgitation to follow obstruction. In the case of the mitral valves the opposite is observed. Commencing disease appears to produce a regurgitant murmur: and it is only as the orifice becomes more and more contracted that an obstructive murmur is heard. There is this further peculiarity, that when mitral stenosis causes a marked presystolic murmur, it rarely happens that any systolic murmur is at the same time audible. I have scarcely ever heard a systolic murmur in association with the rough grating bruit, attended with thrill, that is so characteristic of the more extreme degree of constriction of the mitral valve. A more or less distinctly double murmur at the apex is not, indeed, very uncommon: but in this case both portions of the murmur are rather of a soft and blowing quality: and the inference probably is that the stenosis is moderate in degree.

With regard to the coexistence of murmurs developed at different orifices I have nothing particular to say. Their determination must be based on the principles which regulate the diagnosis of each murmur separately: guided, of course, by the known liability of particular valves to undergo simultaneous or consecutive changes.

The other effects of disease of the cardiac valves—those which affect the patient's health, and are consequently commonly called the *symptoms* of such disease—are divisible into three distinct classes.

I. We may take first a class of effects, which are of great importance, but which have only recently attracted notice, and probably do not yet receive a due share of attention. The valves of the heart are bathed on all sides by the circulating fluid. When they are inflamed or ulcerated, the blood flows directly over the diseased surface. When any portion of their substance, or of the products of inflammation, becomes disintegrated, the detached fragments necessarily pass into its stream. This is so obvious, that we may well be surprised to find that no one had recognized it until Dr. Kirkes pointed it out in the year 1852.[1] And as he showed, the phenomena attendant on this process are divisible into two distinct groups :—

(*a.*) *Embolism.*—In the first place, a mass of some size may be detached, which, passing into the arterial system, sooner or later reaches a vessel which it cannot traverse, and which it consequently plugs. The result is that the circulation is entirely arrested in the region supplied by the artery, unless indeed blood from collateral arteries enters the obstructed vessel beyond the seat of the

---

[1] Med. Chir. Trans. xxxv. p. 281.

obstruction. It might have been expected that the region in question would become anæmic. Recent observations, however, have shown that such is not the case. Prévost and Cotard,[1] and afterwards Lefeuvre,[2] have studied this question experimentally. They injected foreign bodies (especially the seeds of tobacco) upwards into the abdominal aorta of dogs, and exposed the kidneys and spleen by opening the abdomen, so as to make apparent the earliest effects of obstruction of the arteries of those viscera. They found that the regions supplied by the blocked arteries instantly became of a dark purple colour, and in the spleen were distinctly raised above the level of the rest of the region. This state of engorgement is believed to be due to a paralysis of the muscular coat of the vessels. They become unable to resist the pressure of the blood in the veins, which consequently flows back into the capillaries and arteries, and distends them up to the point of obstruction. Hæmorrhage then takes place. After a time the effused blood and the elements of the tissue undergo fatty degeneration: and the affected part acquires a characteristic yellow colour. This always extends to the surface of the organ, and penetrates more or less deeply towards its interior in the form of a wedge or cone, which is generally surrounded by a red halo of congestion. Still later, absorption takes place: and in the end nothing is left beyond a deep fissure or puckering. It must be added that sometimes, instead of the whole mass undergoing fatty degeneration and conversion into the peculiar yellow matter, a part of it sloughs: in other cases it breaks down into pus.

The changes just described do not occur in all organs alike. They are especially well marked in the spleen and kidneys.[3] The reason appears to be that the branches of the splenic and renal arteries anastomose but little or (in the case of the splenic artery) not at all. In the liver, on the other hand, a true infarctus is, perhaps, never met with, apparently because its lobules do not derive their supply of blood entirely from a single source. The mesenteric arteries occasionally become the seat of embola. This occurred in one of Lefeuvre's experiments with tobacco seeds. The affected part became first pale and afterwards of a livid purple colour. Embolism of a mesenteric artery has also sometimes been observed as a result of disease in the human subject. The cerebral arteries are very liable to embolism; this is believed to occur more frequently in the left middle cerebral than in any other artery, apparently because its course in some way favours the entrance of a detached mass. In the brain, the result of arterial plugging is generally white softening of the corresponding part of the brain; but sometimes a firm yellow infarctus is produced. When embolism occurs in one of the arteries of the

[1] Gaz. Méd., 1866, p. 202.
[2] Étude physiologique et pathologique sur les Infarctus Viscéraux, Thèse de Paris, 1867. A review of these observations will be found in the Med. Chir. Review for October 1871, p. 368.
[3] According to Sperling, (Inaug. Diss., Berlin, 1872; London Med. Record, Jan. 1573) the kidney is more frequently the seat of embolism than the spleen, in the proportion of 75 to 51.

extremities, the tendency is for the limb beyond the seat of obstruction to mortify. The gangrene is not then always of the dry variety, as was formerly taught. It 'may be moist, and attended with the formation of bullæ. This is doubtless preceded by an hyperæmia, like that which we have seen to follow plugging of an artery in the spleen or kidneys, except that as the veins of the limbs are provided with valves, the blood probably comes from the collateral arteries of the limb. In the arteries of the extremities, and indeed in all arteries, embola are especially apt to be arrested at those points where the vessel is dividing, or where a large branch is given off, so that the calibre of the channel is suddenly diminished. Thus in the upper limb, they are most commonly found in the axillary artery, and at the bifurcation of the brachial artery: in the lower limb, at the points of division of the common femoral and the popliteal arteries respectively. The left lower limb is decidedly more subject to embolism than the right: and by Virchow[1] this is attributed to the fact that the left common iliac artery comes from the abdominal aorta in a more direct line than the right. The peculiar wedge-shaped masses in the abdominal viscera appear to have been described independently by Hodgkin,[2] Cruveilhier, and Rokitansky. Their association with heart-disease was first noticed by the last-named observer, and has been admitted by all modern writers on morbid anatomy. It is, however, only within the last few years that they have been regarded as possessing any clinical interest, or that their formation has been supposed to be attended with any symptoms affecting the health of the patient. Following Kirkes, Virchow[3] is the writer to whom credit is especially due for having drawn attention to this subject: and recently several French memoirs and papers have been written on it, in which the affection is described as a special disease, under the title of "Ulcerative Endocarditis."

The clinical features observed in these cases are of two kinds. In the first place, there are the direct efforts of intercepted blood-supply to the part served by the obstructed vessel. Thus, as we have seen, a limb may mortify as the result of embolism of its main artery. Many of the cases of spontaneous gangrene in young subjects that come under the care of the surgeon are of this kind; and, with the stethoscope, the existence of disease of the valves of the heart may often be recognized without difficulty. It may be worth while to note that the embolism in these cases is not always derived from the diseased valve itself; sometimes it comes from the auricle or ventricle, having been one of the little rounded ante-mortem clots which are so apt to form in the heart's chambers behind any obstruction.[4]

Embolism of the cerebral arteries, again, may give rise to a great variety of symptoms, according as one or another part of the brain

---

[1] Gesammelte Abhandlungen, p. 444.   [2] Med. Chir. Trans. xxvi.
[3] Gesammelte Abhandlungen, pp. 636—729.
[4] Such an ante-mortem clot may, when a valve is stenosed, be the direct cause of sudden death : getting washed into the blood-current, it may completely occlude the narrowed orifice. See a case recorded by Dr. Van der Byl, Path. Trans. ix. p. 91.

is deprived of its due supply of blood. The most frequent effect is the production of right hemiplegia, with or without aphasia. This corresponds with the fact that the left middle cerebral artery is especially apt to become plugged. Embolism of the retinal arteries leads to changes which can be studied with the ophthalmoscope.

It has already been stated that in the viscera, instead of the usual yellow wedge-shaped masses or infarctus being formed, suppuration, or even sloughing, sometimes occurs in the regions supplied by an artery that has become the seat of embolism. It is perhaps doubtful whether these changes ever in themselves produce any appreciable influence on the patient's health, or on the symptoms from which he suffers. But they may set up a peritonitis, and this will usually be attended with a great aggravation of his complaint, and even with danger to his life; and embolism of a mesenteric artery may cause severe enteritis, which may be quite capable of clinical recognition.

(b.) *Infection.*—But in almost all these cases the effects of the occurrence of embolism in particular arteries are complicated with, and probably overpowered by, those which depend upon a general contamination of the blood, as it passes over the surface of the diseased valve. This was clearly pointed out by Dr. Kirkes, in his classical paper already more than once referred to ; and of late years many observers have worked at the subject, in the hope of explaining it more fully. So severe and rapidly fatal are some of these cases, that Virchow has given them the designation of *Endocarditis Maligna.*

A principal symptom in these cases is the presence of *fever.* The temperature is raised two or three degrees, or more, above the normal standard. Dr. Goodhart [1] mentions one case in which it was several times noted at 104° ; and in a case which I recently examined it reached 105·8°. Not rarely there are repeated attacks of shivering: indeed, the illness is often ushered in by a sudden rigor. The pulse is quickened; the tongue is often dry. Extreme prostration, delirium, and somnolence, are occasionally present. According to Dr. Wilks, articular pains are often complained of. Vomiting and diarrhœa are common. The spleen is greatly enlarged, and is sometimes tender on pressure. The skin has an icteroid tinge, and there may even be jaundice, of which Lancereaux [2] has recorded several examples. Petechiæ may be present, or even distinct purpuric blotches.[3] Ecchymotic spots may also be found on the surface of the pleura and pericardium, and on the mucous membranes lining the larynx, stomach, intestines, and urinary bladder. The liver after death is found to be pale, supple, and flabby. The tissue of the spleen (which is many times larger than natural) is soft and pulpy.

When a patient is known to be suffering from disease of the cardiac valves, there is but little difficulty in assigning to their true

---

[1] Guy's Hosp. Reports, xv. p. 415.   [2] Gaz. Méd., 1862, p. 662.
[3] Path. Trans. xxi. p. 109.

cause the symptoms just enumerated. By carefully examining the heart several times at short intervals, one may be able to detect such variations in the physical signs as may demonstrate the fact that acute changes in the valves are going on. Charcot and Vulpian [1] mention one case in which the most marked signs of aortic insufficiency became prominently developed within a week.

But in many instances there is nothing to draw the physician's attention to the state of the valves; and the real nature of the case may then be easily overlooked. The valves may previously have been quite healthy. And since palpitation, præcordial pain, and oppression of the breathing may all be absent, there may be nothing to suggest the necessity of examining the heart. The case is thus very likely to be mistaken for one of enteric fever, or, if there be much shivering, of idiopathic pyæmia, or even ague; or again, if there be marked jaundice, for one of pylephlebitis. The relation to purulent infection has been especially insisted on by Dr. Wilks, and he has proposed to designate the affection an " arterial pyæmia."

In the previous paragraphs it has been taken for granted that the diseased valves are those on the left side of the heart, and that the phenomena of embolism or of infection therefore show themselves in the course of the distribution of the systemic arteries. However, when the tricuspid valve is diseased, or the pulmonary valves, precisely similar effects show themselves; but, of course, within the lungs. A striking case of this kind has been recorded by Charcot and Vulpian,[2] which was diagnosed during life. One flap of the tricuspid valve was softened and perforated, and presented numerous vegetations. The lungs contained scattered abscesses. Other instances have been related by Dr. Kirkes and Dr. Moxon.[3] Dr. Moxon's case occurred in a woman, within a month after her delivery.

The precise nature of the process of *Infection* in the cases under consideration has been much discussed of late years, and even now it has not been fully ascertained. In almost his earliest paper on the subject, Virchow related some experiments that he had made of injecting different substances into the jugular veins of dogs. And he proved that while portions of caoutchouc simply produced obstruction of branches of the pulmonary artery into which they were carried, animal substances (pieces of muscle, fibrin, &c.) set up severe inflammation of the corresponding tracts of lung tissue, leading to suppuration or even to sloughing. Hence he concluded that the phenomena of infection are not merely of *mechanical* origin, but must result from some *chemical* action. The same fact has since been insisted on by Feltz[4] of Strasburg, who maintains that solid elements by themselves

[1] Gaz. Méd. 1862, p. 388.   [2] Gaz. Méd., 1862, p. 423.
[3] Path. Trans. xxi. p. 107.
[4] Traité clinique et expérimentale des embolies capillaires. 2ème éd., Strasbourg, 1870.

never carry infection: this is always propagated by septic fluids. Another writer, Panum of Kiel,[1] endeavoured to show that the immediate cause of irritant effects is the decomposition, *within the bloodvessels*, of the masses by which they are plugged. By Lancereaux, again, stress was laid on the opinion that the poisoned state of the blood in these cases is due to the alteration and transformation of the connective tissue of the valves themselves, and never to the mere disintegration of fibrinous concretions.

These speculations have, however, been almost superseded by observations of a different order. As far back as 1855, Virchow[2] found that a small coagulum upon the mitral valve (in a case of erysipelatous perimetritis with a diphtheritic inflammation of the large intestine) contained a number of small white miliary bodies, which consisted almost entirely of fine closely aggregated granules, embedded in a gelatinous substance. These granules were insoluble in potash, acetic acid and hydrochloric acid, but were dissolved by chloroform, so that he regarded them as probably of a fatty nature. Charcot and Vulpian[3] afterwards insisted on the peculiar micro-chemical relations of the detritus of diseased valves, shown in their power of resisting strong acids and alkalies. But still more recent observations have tended to show that the properties of these minute granules are not due merely to their chemical constitution, and that they are in fact living organisms. Prof. Winge, and Prof. Heiberg,[4] of Christiania, appear to have been the first writers to express this view in a decided form: it has since been adopted by no less an authority than Virchow himself. It is proposed by these writers to give to the affection in question the name of *Mycosis Endocardii.* Winge's case, which occurred in 1869, was that of a man, æt. 44, who died with symptoms of bloodpoisoning apparently dependent on a suppurating corn. On the aortic valves there were certain greyish masses, the size of peas or beans, which could be easily picked off, leaving the surface slightly uneven and ulcerated. The tricuspid valve presented similar masses. With a microscope of moderate power these appeared to consist of a fine network of fibrin threads. But under a higher objective these threads were seen to be made up of rod-like or spherical bodies, arranged in chains, and thus resembling leptothrix. There were also a number of fine rounded or rod-shaped bodies, some of which were probably bacteria, others fat granules. Similar bodies were found in the cylindrical plugs in the smaller arteries of the kidney, corresponding to infarctus. Heiberg's case was that of a girl, æt. 22, who died six or seven weeks after delivery, with symptoms of blood-poisoning. The mitral valve was perforated by a recent ulcer, the margins of which and the chordæ were coated with vegetations. These contained numerous minute granules, apparently simple detritus: and in addi-

---

[1] Experimentelle Untersuchungen zur Physiologie und Pathologie der Embolie, &c., Berlin, 1864.
[2] Op. cit., p. 709.   [3] Gaz. Méd., 1862, p. 385.
[4] Virchow's Arch. lvi., 1872, p. 409.

tion, many rod-shaped bodies resembling bacteria, and a considerable number of rows of granules, of uniform size, arranged in chains of greater or less length, which Heiberg therefore regarded as leptothrix. These, and many of the isolated bodies, resisted the action of even boiling caustic potass. Specimens from both these cases were forwarded to Virchow, who confirms the accuracy of the accounts given by the Swedish writers, and states that he has no doubt as to the parasitic nature of the bodies in question. He is not yet prepared, however, to admit the propriety of using the name leptothrix for them. Eberth,[1] of Zürich, has since recorded another case of the same kind, which differs from those previously referred to, in the fact that there was no evident external source of blood-poisoning. He entitles it "Diphtheritic Endocarditis." [2] It occurred in a young man, previously healthy, who died after little more than two days' illness. Two of the aortic valves were ulcerated through, and the disease extended into the muscular substance of the heart, penetrating almost to the endocardium lining the right auricle. The margins of the affected valves were covered with soft vegetations. These consisted mainly of a finely granular substance: and the individual granules were shining spherical bodies of uniform size, some of which exhibited slight movements, the majority being motionless and embedded in a gelatinous material. Neither boiling alcohol nor boiling alkalies affected these granules, beyond making them slightly paler. Tincture of iodine and sulphuric acid gave them a yellow colour. It is therefore almost certain, says Eberth, that they were really spherical bacteria.

So far as I am aware, no similar observations have as yet been published in this country. But my colleague, Dr. Goodhart, informs me that he has in three instances detected minute organisms in the fungating masses attached to ulcerated valves. In each case he found, besides innumerable spheroids, rod- and dumb-bell-shaped bacteria, as well as some which formed beaded strings. Most of these had feeble oscillatory movements. Vertical sections of the deepest part of the diseased valves showed a cell growth, to a small extent, such as is described at page 603. On this was deposited a hyaline clot in small rounded masses: and upon these, and in the crevices between them, the bacteria clustered. Dr. Goodhart, however, considered that the appearances which he observed were strongly suggestive of the view that the bacteria were derived from the elements of disintegrating blood-clot.

The precise scope and bearing of these observations are, as yet, imperfectly understood; but I think there can be little doubt that

---

[1] Virchow's Arch. lvii., 1873, p. 228.

[2] This designation has also been frequently used by Virchow. It is important for English readers to remember that German writers use the term diphtheritic in a sense very different from that to which we are accustomed in this country, applying it to inflamed structures of which the most superficial layers, infiltrated with inflammatory materials, are gangrenous.

they will hereafter be found to play an important part in the explanation of the phenomena of blood-poisoning now under consideration.
Heiberg, indeed, expressly states that he does not attribute all cases
of ulcerative endocarditis to a Mycosis, since he has failed to find any
parasitic organisms in specimens of this disease preserved in the
Museum of Christiania. And when bacteria are present in the tissues
of diseased valves, it is as yet quite impossible to say what relation
they bear to the processes of embolism and infection to which the
disease gives rise. This question is in fact only a part of the much
wider one which concerns the relations of these minute organisms
to pyæmia, septicæmia, and allied processes. The theory advocated by
Eberth[1] is that the bacteria originally enter the blood from without,
and then become aggregated together into a sticky mass, which adheres
to the surface of the cardiac valves, when it is brought to them in the
stream of the circulation. In confirmation of this opinion, he appeals
to observations showing that the ante-mortem coagula in the appendices of the auricles are likewise often coated with a complete layer of
bacteria. The valves and chambers of the heart thus form a kind of
halting-place for the microphytes, which multiply, and subsequently
distribute to all the arteries of the body masses of bacteria in the form
of embola, which set up suppuration wherever they are deposited. In
the arteries of the kidneys especially, agglomerations of this nature
have been demonstrated: and also within the glomeruli and the
uriniferous tubules of the affected parts of these organs.

II.—Another series of effects produced by diseases of the cardiac
valves consist in the modifications that they tend to induce in the circulation of the blood, and in the consequent morbid changes which arise
in the several cavities of the heart, in the blood-vessels, and in distant
organs. To these effects we must now turn our attention, and as they
are both numerous and varied, it is needful that we should arrange
them in as orderly a manner as possible.

Each of the cardiac valves may be viewed as separating from one
another two of the chambers of the circulatory system, and when any
one of the valves is diseased, we may consider that (1) the *primary*
effect of the disease is exerted upon that chamber which lies immediately behind the valve in the order of the circulation, and which was
protected by the valve when in its normal state. From the chamber
in question, again, disturbance of the circulation is, or may be, propagated in two directions:—(2) *forwards*, or with the blood-stream;
and (3) *backwards*, or against the blood-stream. The effects of disease
of the several valves have, therefore, to be considered under these
three heads.

A. It will be found convenient that we should begin with diseases
of the *aortic valves*. These, as we have seen, may be of two kinds,

---

[1] In a large number of recent cases of pyæmia Eberth has constantly found microphytes, not only on the surface of the wound, but also in the subjacent tissues, sometimes to a considerable depth.

obstructive and regurgitant; but in the immense majority of cases, obstruction and regurgitation coexist.

(1.) The primary effect of diseases of the aortic valves may be said to occur in the left ventricle, which is of course the chamber that lies behind the valves in the order of the circulation. Now in aortic stenosis or obstruction the blood cannot be forced into the aorta so easily nor so quickly as in health. The ventricle, therefore, tends to be overloaded with blood, and its walls become stretched or dilated; at the same time it has to exert increased force to propel its contents onwards; and it consequently becomes hypertrophied. In aortic regurgitation the ventricle may empty itself readily enough during its systole, but in its diastole it not only has to receive the blood flowing onwards from the auricle, but also that which is poured back into it from the aorta; it therefore becomes both dilated and hypertrophied. The changes which occur in the left ventricle are thus the same in the two conditions of stenosis and regurgitation respectively. They constitute the *compensation* by which these several morbid changes are more or less completely prevented from further disturbing the circulation. But there is a distinction of some importance, which has not, I think, been noticed by writers on this subject. In aortic stenosis, hypertrophy of the ventricle is all that is needed to restore the balance; dilatation is directly injurious, tending to impair the power of the chamber, and to render still more hypertrophy necessary. But, in aortic regurgitation, dilatation is the main requirement, since the ventricle has to accommodate the blood that enters it from both sides during its diastole; hypertrophy is needed only secondarily, and because a dilated ventricle has to exert more force than one of normal size, in order to propel its contents onwards.

The dilatation and hypertrophy of the left ventricle in cases of aortic disease may be extreme in degree. The heart then acquires a peculiar pointed form, the right ventricle often looking like a mere appendage. The organ often weighs between 20 and 30 ozs., and many instances have been observed in which it has been even heavier. In one case which I have myself examined—that of a young man, æt. 26—the heart weighed 48 oz. I am not sure whether this is not the largest heart on record; the next largest being one weighing 46½ oz., which Dr. Bristowe exhibited at a meeting of the Pathological Society.

These changes, of course, require time for their development; but Dr. Peacock has adduced evidence to show that they may take place more quickly than might have been expected. Valvular affections themselves often arise gradually; and the compensatory processes are induced *pari passu* with the disease. On the other hand, when the valves give way or are lacerated suddenly, time may not be allowed for the ventricle to become dilated and hypertrophied; and this is probably one of the main reasons why in such cases the fatal termination is often rapid. Again, either obstruction or regurgitation may of course be so extreme as to render compensation impossible. Lastly, when perfect compensation has existed for a

considerable time, it may begin to fail; and then further effects arise
which will be considered hereafter. It is generally supposed that
this is due, either to the progressive increase in the valvular changes
(with which the compensatory processes are unable to keep pace),
or to the occurrence of fatty degeneration in the hypertrophied
ventricular wall.[1]

(2.) The onward effects of disease of the aortic valves consist in
changes in the blood current in the aorta and its branches; in other
words, in changes in the arterial pulse. These are not the same in
aortic obstruction, as in regurgitant disease; and the two affections
must therefore be considered separately.

In aortic stenosis the character of the pulse appears to be but little
altered, unless the obstruction to the blood current is extreme, in
which case Walshe says that "the pulse, though regular in force and
rhythm, is small, hard, rigid, and concentrated." Dr. Wilks has
mentioned to me that in certain cases he has observed the number
of pulsations of the heart, per minute, to be greatly reduced. In
illustration of this fact, I find in the notes of post-mortem examinations at Guy's Hospital two cases recorded by Dr. Wilks himself.
One[2] is that of a man, æt. 68, in whom "two of the aortic valves were
adherent and bony; the aperture was reduced to a very narrow
chink; the edge of one valve slightly overlapped the bony margin
of the other, and thus no doubt prevented regurgitation. The pulse
during life had been 40 per minute, very small, and sometimes hardly
perceptible." The other[3] is that of a youth, æt. 19, in whom the
pulse was said to have been "small and slow. The aortic orifice would
only admit a catheter; all the valves were adherent together, leaving
only a small rounded hole in the middle." Such cases are doubtless
exceptional; but, as has already been stated, aortic stenosis, without
regurgitation, is decidedly a rare affection.

In regurgitant aortic disease the pulse presents characters so
remarkable that they have led to its receiving several special
designations, and that they often enable the physician to diagnose
the nature of the case without aid from any other source. A passage
has already been quoted from Vieussens (1715)[4] in which the peculiar
character of pulse that is now known to belong to this affection is
clearly indicated. So far as I am aware, the next writer to mention
it was Dr. Hodgkin, who, in his paper on "Retroversion of the Aortic
Valves,"[5] published in 1829, says that in one case there was "inordi-
nately violent arterial action, which was very rapid and frequent,

[1] Dr. Allbutt has recently given another explanation of loss of compensation, which
is certainly of great interest. It was first suggested to him by Mr. Busk, who compared the change in question to that which occurs in the arms of file-cutters. These
men constantly practise rapid flexions of the elbow-joint, and the biceps enlarges
greatly. But after a few years the muscle again wastes, and falls far below the normal
value. This is so certain a consequence, that the file-cutters receive high wages, calcu-
tated upon the average duration of an hypertrophied biceps. ("On the Effects of Overwork and Strain upon the Heart and Great Vessels," p. 43, Macmillan and Co., 1872.)
[2] Inspection 109, in the year 1859.   [3] Inspection 72, in the year 1862.
[4] Œuvres Françoises.   [5] London Med. Gaz. vol. iii. p. 433.

although regular, there was a remarkable thrill in the pulse, and the carotids were seen violently beating on both sides." But it was Sir Dominic Corrigan,[1] who in 1832 first laid stress on the peculiarity of the pulse in this disease, a fact commemorated in the designation of " Corrigan's pulse," which is commonly applied to it both on the Continent and in this country.

The feature on which Corrigan especially insists, as indicating " inadequacy of the aortic valves," is the existence of visible pulsation in the arteries of the head and superior extremities. He describes the subclavian, carotid, temporal, brachial, and even palmar arteries as being " suddenly thrown from their bed, and bounding up under the skin." In the arteries of the lower extremities, even of larger size than those which present it about the head and neck, pulsation is not (he goes on to say) seen to any comparative degree, and generally not at all, while the patient is sitting or standing. The pulsation of the brachial and palmar arteries is increased in a most striking degree by merely elevating the arm above the head: and the same effect is produced in the lower limbs by lying down and elevating them on an inclined plane.

In addition to these points, it may be added that, in aortic regurgitation, the arteries are elongated during their pulsations much more than in health, and can be seen in many positions to become distinctly flexuous with each beat of the heart. Consequently, one name for the pulse in question is that of the " locomotive " pulse.

But these visible characters of the pulse of aortic regurgitant disease are after all of little consequence in comparison with those which can be felt. To the touch, the pulse in question gives a sensation of peculiar largeness or fulness, immediately followed by an equally peculiar collapse. Instead of the artery slowly receding beneath the finger, it falls as rapidly as it rose. The pulse is, therefore, often spoken of as "jerking," "splashing," or "collapsing;" or as the " water-hammer" pulse, from the well-known scientific toy of that name.

Lastly, the pulse of aortic regurgitation differs from that of health in travelling along the arteries much more slowly. Normally, even the radial pulse follows very quickly upon the ventricular systole; in the disease under consideration, it may almost be synchronous with the second sound of the heart.

There is little difficulty in explaining the peculiarities that have been enumerated. We have seen that when the aortic valves allow of regurgitation, the ventricle is greatly, often enormously, dilated and hypertrophied. The quantity of blood injected into the aorta is, therefore, much increased. No wonder that the pulse feels full and large, that the arteries lengthen, and seem to bound from their seats, beating much more plainly than in health. Then comes the elastic recoil of the larger arteries. Under normal conditions, this is gradual. The aortic valves are closed, and the blood moves slowly onwards.

[1] Ed. Med. and Surg. Journal, April 1, 1832, p. 225.

into the small arteries and capillaries, meeting considerable resistance. But when the valves in question are diseased, and allow reflux to take place through them, there is nothing to support the column of blood in the aorta and its branches during their recoil ; the blood is rapidly driven out of them, part one way and part another ; and the pulse as suddenly collapses.

Since the invention of the sphygmograph, no description of the peculiarities of the pulse in any morbid state can be regarded as complete unless full reference is made to the results obtained with that instrument. And probably diseases of the aortic valves were among the first in which the sphygmograph was applied. It cannot, indeed, be said that those who have specially devoted themselves to this subject have as yet come to a complete agreement in reference to the indications which it affords. But I believe that the existing state of our knowledge is fairly expressed in the following account of the matter :—

In aortic stenosis, one might expect that, in proportion as the aortic orifice is obstructed, the exit of blood from the ventricle would be impeded. The upstroke of the sphygmographic tracing should, therefore, be oblique, or sloping. According to Mahomed, this is the case. I append (Figs. 3 and 4) copies of two tracings given by this observer in the *Medical Times and Gazette* for 1872,[1] which show well the sloping upstroke and the rounded summit, indicative of the fact that " the influence of percussion is lost ; the tidal wave alone remains."

FIG. 3.　　　　　FIG. 4.　　　　　FIG. 5.

Very similar to this is another diagram (Fig. 5), which is a copy of one given by Jaccoud.[2] According to Mahomed, however, another very different form of pulse may accompany aortic obstruction. It is illustrated in the following diagrams (Figs. 6, 7, 8,) which are copied from those given by him.[3] It will be observed that there is a marked separation between the percussion and tidal waves. It ought perhaps to be mentioned that, in the case from which the tracing No. 8 was taken, there was a double murmur over the aorta, but the existence of considerable aortic obstruction was made out, not only from the characters of the pulse, but also from the fact that a tracing obtained from the heart showed the contractions to be very slow and gradual. It is to be borne in mind that only extreme degrees of aortic stenosis can be expected to affect the pulse in the ways described by Mr. Mahomed. He himself

[1] Plate V., Figs. 12 and 13, p. 142.
[2] Traité de Pathologie Interne, quatrium Ed. tome i. p. 676.
[3] Loc. cit., Pl. V., Figs. 17, 18, 19.

gives a tracing from a case in which "considerable obstruction was produced by the adherence of two of the aortic valves;" in this tracing no sign of the obstruction is apparent.

In aortic regurgitation, the sphygmographic tracings of the pulse present peculiarities which correspond in a very striking way with what might theoretically have been expected. The percussion-wave is strongly marked, and the upstroke is therefore high. On the other

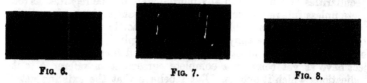

FIG. 6.   FIG. 7.   FIG. 8.

hand, the dicrotic wave (or "diastolic expansion") is wanting, in consequence of the aortic valves failing to support the column of blood in the aorta during its recoil. Lastly, a high pressure is required to bring out the characters of the pulse fully; this being the result of the hypertrophy of the left ventricle, which is constantly present in cases of aortic regurgitation.

The three following figures, which are copies of tracings given by Mr. Mahomed,[1] illustrate these points. It ought perhaps to be added that Marey originally laid great stress on a little peak or point at the

FIG. 9.   FIG. 10.   FIG. 11.

summit of the long upstroke, as indicative of aortic regurgitation ; bu this was soon shown to be a mistake. At the present time, there seems to be a fair agreement among different observers as to the characters in a sphygmographic tracing which point to the disease in question.

In some cases of aortic regurgitation the pulse does not present its peculiar characters in any marked degree, whether to the touch or to the sphygmograph ; and this, although the diastolic murmur may be loud and prolonged. This may be due either to the circumstance that the reflux of blood is really small in amount, or to the fact that mitral regurgitation is also present. Mr. Mahomed gives in his papers in the *Medical Times and Gazette* some very valuable illustrations of the way in which the sphygmograph may be used in cases of this kind, both to determine the degree of valvular incompetency, and to gauge the amount of compensatory hypertrophy of the left ventricle ; and

[1] Loc. cit., Plate V., Figs. 7, 4, 6 respectively. In Fig. 10 (Fig. 4 in Mr. Mahomed's plate) there are also indications that the arteries are atheromatous.

also to decide which of two coexistent affections—mitral and aortic—is of preponderating importance. It is in the solution of such questions as these that the great value of the instrument appears to lie, so far as diseases of the cardiac valves are concerned. The mere detection of valvular incompetency can be effected more easily, and perhaps as surely, by the stethoscope ; but in prognosis the sphygmograph seems to lend great assistance.

The onward effects of diseased conditions of the aortic valves are not necessarily confined to the arterial system. The capillaries may be imperfectly supplied with blood, and both the nutrition and the functions of the different organs may in consequence be greatly impaired. This is perhaps especially marked in the case of the brain. Attacks of giddiness are far from uncommon in aortic regurgitation, and are ascribed to failure in the due supply of arterial blood to the nervous centres. Anæmia and wasting of the whole body are also frequent symptoms : the former being in fact so constantly present as to be a marked feature in the physiognomy of the disease.

(3.) *Backward* effects of aortic disease are absent, so long as the changes in the left ventricle above described enable the heart to do its work efficiently, even though this result should be attained at the expense of increased labour and friction, and under augmented frequency of beats. And since patients with aortic regurgitation very often die suddenly while these conditions are fulfilled, backward effects are not rarely wanting to the last. But whenever the compensatory processes fail, so that the arteries no longer receive for transmission onwards their full supply of blood per minute, the necessary result is that the quantity discharged into the ventricle by the left auricle must also be deficient. The inevitable consequence of this, again, is the development of a fresh series of changes, which we are about to study in detail, as the effects of primary disease of the mitral orifice. It is often stated that in affections of the aortic valves these changes occur only when the mitral valve has been stretched, so as to allow of regurgitation through it,—this being probably a common result of the dilatation of the left ventricle. But I conceive that the statement in question is an error, and that backward effects must necessarily arise in the way I have indicated, even though the closure of the mitral valve may still remain perfect.[1]

B. Diseases of the *mitral* valve, again, are of two kinds—obstructive and regurgitant : which will to some extent require to be considered separately from one another.

(1.) The *primary* effect of diseases of the mitral valve may be said to be exerted upon the left auricle. In mitral stenosis the effect in

[1] So far as post-mortem evidence can be brought to bear upon this question, I believe that such evidence is favourable to the view expressed in the text. Thus I find in my notes one case (in which I made an autopsy in July 1873) of aortic disease with retroversion of one of the valves. Dropsy occurred before death, and the lungs contained apoplectic patches. The mitral valve appeared to be quite healthy : and, after death, it did not allow regurgitation to occur. The left auricle was dilated and hypertrophied, and the right auricle was still more so.

question is well marked. The cavity becomes dilated, often enormously so.[1] The appendix is elongated,—in one instance I find it noted as 2¾ inches long by Dr. Moxon,—and acquires a peculiar curved form ; and its aperture of communication with the auricle is much wider than natural. The walls of the auricle also become much hypertrophied; they no longer collapse when the cavity is cut open, but support themselves stiffly : the muscular substance may in places be from ⅛ to ¼ of an inch thick. The endocardial lining is said to be more opaque than usual.

These changes are almost constantly met with in cases of mitral stenosis. And were the current doctrines in regard to mitral regurgitation true, they would doubtless be found no less uniformly in cases of the latter affection;—just as dilatation and hypertrophy of the left ventricle occur equally in aortic obstruction and in aortic incompetency. However, this is not so. Definitely marked hypertrophy of the muscular wall of the left auricle is seldom present in cases of so-called mitral regurgitant disease. It is true that the cavity in question is often found to be dilated ; but then all the other cardiac cavities are generally enlarged at the same time. I shall endeavour to explain these facts further on.

(2.) The *onward* effects of diseases of the mitral valve are of course seen first in the left ventricle. In mitral stenosis this chamber is very generally found to be small, and its muscular substance is no thicker, and may perhaps even be thinner, than under normal conditions. The aorta too is often small and thin-walled. But in some cases of mitral stenosis and in almost all cases of " mitral regurgitation " the left ventricle is large and fleshy; and not infrequently it is as much dilated and hypertrophied as in aortic regurgitation. Various explanations of this have been given. By Friedreich[2] it is supposed that the augmented tension in the systemic venous system (which we shall presently show to be one of the consequences of mitral diseases) causes an increased resistance in the systemic arteries likewise. But, apart from the difficulty of admitting that the effects of obstruction thus traverse the complete circuit of the circulation, a fatal objection to this theory is that it would require dilatation of the left ventricle to be the rule in fatal cases of mitral stenosis, instead of its being quite exceptional. Another view is that when the ventricle is enlarged in mitral disease, this is not really due to the valvular affection, but depends upon some other cause. Thus, in rheumatic cases many other conditions generally exist (such, for example, as diseases of other orifices, or thick pericardial adhesions) to which the change in the ventricle may be ascribed. Indeed,

[1] This condition was long ago described as "true aneurism of the left auricle" by Dr. Thurnam (Med. Chir. Trans., ser. ii., vol. iii., 1838, p. 244), who expressly insists on its association with contraction of the mitral orifice, and mentions that the lining membrane is opaque and rough, and in some cases even ossified, and that it is lined with fibrinous layers very similar to those met with in arterial aneurisms.
[2] Op. cit., pp. 161 and 227.

according to some observers, primary dilatation of the left ventricle commonly occurs in the course of acute rheumatism, and may persist after the subsidence of that disease. But, again, in very many cases of so-called "mitral regurgitant disease" the valve is itself healthy: and the imperfection in its working (if we are to assume that it does close imperfectly) is itself the result of ventricular dilatation. There is, however, one class of cases in which it certainly appears that mitral imperfection leads to enlargement of the left ventricle:—I refer to those cases in which rupture of the tendinous cords of the valve occurs in persons who had not previously exhibited any symptoms of cardiac disease.[1] It may indeed be objected that both the ventricle and the valve were possibly affected with latent disease before the sudden rupture took place: but of such disease there is no evidence, and to suppose its existence is to abandon in favour of an arbitrary hypothesis the direct interpretation of the facts observed. The explanation, indeed, seems to be sufficiently easy. In such cases, the ventricle has greatly increased labour; a good deal of the blood which enters it having to be expelled twice over from its cavity. On the other hand, in cases of uncomplicated mitral stenosis, the work thrown upon the left ventricle is in no way augmented, if it be not even less than under normal conditions: and as I have already stated, I believe that in such cases the left ventricle is always small, and its muscular substance no thicker than natural.

The arterial pulse in mitral diseases may present very varied characters, the variations depending not merely upon the nature of the valvular lesion, but also upon the changes secondarily induced by it in the heart's chambers. Formerly it was supposed that in mitral stenosis the pulse is always small; but since the presystolic murmur has enabled this condition to be diagnosed before severe symptoms set in, it has been found that the pulse is often perfectly natural. Indeed, there is no reason why it should be otherwise, so long as the hypertrophied auricle keeps the ventricle duly supplied with blood. In a very large proportion of cases in which a presystolic murmur is audible, the pulse is perfectly regular, and has ample volume and force. Accordingly, Mr. Mahomed says [2] that "in this disease the sphygmographic tracing does not necessarily present any diagnostic characteristics." I have already quoted this writer as having demonstrated that cardiographic tracings, taken at the heart's apex, often afford proof of the existence of mitral stenosis (or, at least, of hypertrophy of the left auricle), by showing that the auricular systole commences at an earlier period in the ventricular diastole than is

[1] Thus in Dr. Dickinson's case (Path. Trans. xx. p. 150) the heart weighed 20 oz.: all the cavities were dilated to at least three times their natural capacity; the auricles and right ventricle were thinned. The left ventricle was hypertrophied to such an extent as to retain, notwithstanding its dilatation, about its normal thickness. And in the report of the post-mortem examination of a similar case that occurred in Guy's Hospital under Dr. Habershon's care, Dr. Moxon states that "all the cavities were dilated."

[2] Op. cit., No. 6, p. 569.

normal. He further maintains that in some cases this premature contraction of the auricle stimulates the ventricle to contract likewise; and that in this way the tracing of the pulse at the wrist may indicate a second ventricular systole, alternating with the main beat, but very much less forcible. The accompanying diagram is

FIG. 12.

copied from one of Mr. Mahomed's tracings, taken from a patient of mine who was suffering from mitral stenosis, and in whom the double ventricular systole was made very marked by the administration of digitalis. Both contractions were felt in the pulse at the wrist, the beats of which were alternately strong and feeble. I have observed a similar double rhythm in several other instances of valvular disease; but I am unable to say whether they were or were not all of them cases of mitral stenosis.

In the later stages of the disease—when the peculiar murmur can often be no longer detected—the pulse assumes very different characters. It is now rapid, soft, small, and very irregular, both in volume and force.

The accompanying tracings (Figs. 13, 14, 15) copied from Jaccoud,[1] show the sphygmographic character of a pulse of this kind; they are very much what might have been expected from the impression

FIG. 13.   FIG. 14.

which it gives to the touch. It has long been known as the *mitral* pulse; and, in fact, it is met with, not only in the advanced stages of mitral stenosis, but also in those cases which are commonly grouped under the heading of "regurgitant mitral disease." Whether it is of any diagnostic value, as indicating that the valve in question is impaired in structure or function, is a very difficult question to answer. I have already stated more than once that "regurgitant mitral disease" has no constant pathological appearances, but that it includes a variety of conditions, in some of which the valve certainly admits of regurgitation, while in others there is doubt whether this occurs. I must now add my belief that for the production of the so-called "mitral pulse" the mitral valve need not be

[1] Op. cit., No. 21, p. 678; No. 9, p. 616; No. 7, p. 615.

either narrowed or incompetent. The same kind of pulse probably arises whenever the ventricle does not empty itself completely during its systole, so that the stream of blood projected into the aorta is greatly diminished. Now it would appear that such a perversion of the heart's action is far from being uncommon, being liable to occur

FIG. 15.

in the course of various cardiac and pulmonary diseases without presenting any characters peculiar to one rather than to another of these diseases. The condition in question was first described by Beau, who gave to it the name of *asystolie;* and most recent French writers have adopted this designation. Dilatation of the heart appears to be the morbid change which is most constantly present in cases of this kind; but very frequently valvular disease also exists. The sphygmographic tracings (Figs. 13 and 14), which I have copied from Jaccoud as illustrative of the "mitral pulse," are given by that writer as indicating the existence of a condition of "*asystolie.*"

(3.) *Backward Effects.*—So long as the left auricle can duly empty itself, and receive its full supply of blood from the pulmonary veins, the parts of the circulatory apparatus behind the auricle are in no way affected by the existence of mitral disease, whether obstructive or regurgitant. But, except in the earlier stages or slighter degrees of such disease, the compensatory action of the auricle is very seldom thus complete; and whenever it fails, the necessary consequence is an augmented tension in the pulmonary system of vessels and in the chambers of the right side of the heart. It has already been stated that the same result occurs also in diseases of the aortic valves, as soon as compensatory changes fail to enable the left ventricle to carry on the circulation properly.

This increase of tension in the pulmonary vessels soon leads to changes in their walls, which become thickened, or hypertrophied. In the main trunk of the pulmonary artery this is particularly noticeable. The records of post-mortem examinations at Guy's Hospital contain notes by Dr. Moxon of the case of a boy, æt. ten years, in whom the coats of the pulmonary artery were nearly twice as thick as those of the aorta at its thickest part; and less striking examples of the same kind are very commonly met with. The artery also becomes greatly dilated.

Another result of the increased tension of blood within the pulmonary artery is the fact that in these cases the branches of the vessel are very apt to become atheromatous, although under normal changes they are but little liable to such a change. Perhaps the most striking instance of this that could be quoted is one which Dr.

Conway Evans [1] has recorded, and which occurred in a boy, who died
of dropsy, consequent on mitral stenosis, at the age of fourteen years.
It would appear that Dittrich [2] was the first to point out the frequency with which atheroma of the pulmonary artery is found in cases
of this kind, and that he described it as occurring especially in the
smaller branches, and as being the immediate cause of the patches of
" pulmonary apoplexy " which are so commonly met with under such
conditions. The explanation of pulmonary apoplexy, however, is
still open to doubt. The branch of artery leading to an apoplectic
patch is generally, perhaps always, plugged with fibrin; and this
has led many modern observers to regard the affection as of
embolic origin. In the first volume of the " System of Medicine,"
at p. 201, Dr. Bristowe has discussed this question at considerable
length.

The pulmonary tissue is also liable to assume a peculiar appearance, which is generally known to German pathologists under the
name of " brown induration." In the third volume of the present work,
at p. 800, Dr. Wilson Fox has given a detailed account of this affection; but he seems to have laid hardly enough stress on the dilated
and varicose state of the pulmonary capillaries, which Buhl has
shown to be present, and which is so striking a proof of the increased
pressure upon these vessels. I have found that this dilated state of
the capillaries is recognizable without difficulty, even in uninjected
specimens.

Before leaving the subject now under consideration, I must not
omit to mention another way in which the left lung suffers from
cardiac disease—namely, from the dilated left auricle pressing
directly upon the bronchus. Mr. Wilkinson King [3] first pointed this
out, in the year 1838, and his preparations, which are now in the
museum of Guy's Hospital, show that the anterior surface of the tube
may in this way be rendered quite flat, and its calibre diminished by
one-half. But the most remarkable instance is one recorded by
Friedreich, [4] in which narrowing of the left bronchus was diagnosed
four years before the patient's death, from the presence of a loud
humming sound accompanying both the inspiration and the expiration, heard most plainly over the root of the left lung, near the
spine, but also audible over the whole left side of the chest. There
was extreme stenosis of the mitral orifice with enormous dilatation
of the left auricle. Virchow made the autopsy; and the left main
bronchus was found to be compressed, so that only a small narrow
channel was left.

The cavities of the right side of the heart also become greatly
dilated and hypertrophied under the conditions now being considered.
The muscular tissue of the right ventricle grows much harder than

[1] Trans. of the Path. Soc., xvii. p 90.
[2] Ueber den Laennec'schen Lungen-Infarktus. Erlangen, 1850.
[3] Guy's Hospital Reports, series i, vol. iii. p. 178.
[4] Op. cit., p. 30.

natural—indeed, it is peculiarly hard, in comparison even with the substance of an hypertrophied left ventricle. The tricuspid orifice is stretched.

C. & D.—It is at this point that we ought to consider the effects of primary disease of the pulmonary and the tricuspid valves respectively. But such diseases are so rare (excepting malformations, which are treated of separately) that they need scarcely interrupt us in tracing out the backward effects of diseases of the valves of the left side of the heart. It will suffice to state that (1) the *primary* effect of disease of the pulmonary valves is to cause dilatation and hypertrophy of the right ventricle; and that that of disease of the tricuspid valve (if primary chronic disease of this valve ever occurs) would probably be to cause dilatation and hypertrophy of the right auricle; (2) Concerning *forward* effects of the diseases in question, no definite statements could perhaps be made; (3) Their *backward* effects must be the same as those which more remotely arise from uncompensated diseases of the mitral and aortic orifices, and to these our attention may now be directed.

Taking first the vena cava superior and the veins from which it arises, we find that they are enlarged and gorged with blood. Hence the livid countenance, the turgid cheeks, the purple ears, cheeks, and lips, that are so commonly seen in patients suffering from affections of the cardiac valves. The veins of the upper limbs are also distended; the hands and nails acquire a livid purple colour, and the hands, and often even the arms, become œdematous. The lividity may approach, if it may not even equal, that which is seen in cases of malformation of the heart, in the condition known as *cyanosis.* A further consequence of the congestion of the upper limbs which exists in these cases, is that the finger-ends often become enlarged, or (as it is usually termed) " clubbed." Dr. Dobell [1] has recently stated that the clubbing of the fingers from heart disease differs from that which is due to phthisis, in the circumstance that the sides and tips of the nails are not at the same time incurved; the reason for this difference being, that in heart disease wasting of the adipose tissue is absent, which wasting he believes to be the cause of incurvation.

At the root of the neck the jugular veins, besides being enlarged and unnaturally full, present another phenomenon which requires further consideration—they can often be seen to pulsate with each beat of the heart. This seems to have been first noticed by Lancisi. [2] Jugular pulsation is commonly taken as a certain indication of regurgitation through the tricuspid orifice; and the frequency of its occurrence, when the circulation through the right side of the heart is impeded, is supposed to bear out Mr. Wilkinson King's views of the existence of a physiological safety-valve action by which reflux is allowed whenever the right ventricle becomes

[1] On Affections of the Heart and in its neighbourhood, 1872, p. 17.
[2] De motu Cordis et aneurysmatibus. Rom. 1728, Lib. ii., Propos. 57.

unduly charged with blood. It has, however, been shown by Friedreich that the matter is by no means so simple. In the first place, when the jugular veins are distended they often exhibit rhythmical movements synchronous with the respiratory acts. Each expiration causes an increased pressure upon the large venous trunks within the thorax ; and even though the valves at the root of the neck may close perfectly, the blood that is pouring in from the veins of the head and upper limbs is stopped, and accumulates behind the obstruction. An apparent pulsation may thus occur without any blood really regurgitating into the jugular veins from below. So, again, it is possible that when these veins are very full, variations in their size may occur, synchronously with the heart's movements, from the temporary arrest of the onward flow of blood during the closure of the tricuspid valve, quite independently of reflux. In this case, however, compression of the veins in the middle of the neck will at once stop the apparent jugular pulsation.

When jugular pulsation is really due to regurgitation of blood, it is of course necessary that the valves at the junction of the subclavian and jugular veins should be incompetent. Dr. Parkes[1] is said to have taught that this is due to rupture of these valves : but as Dr. Walshe points out, it is doubtless sufficient that the veins should be greatly distended, so as to prevent the edges of the valves from touching one another. According to Friedreich it is possible for a true jugular pulsation to be produced by the pressure of the ascending aorta, when dilating during the ventricular systole, upon a distended vena cava superior. But this explanation appears farfetched, and unnecessary. Friedreich will not allow that tricuspid regurgitation is present, unless a systolic murmur is audible. I shall presently show, however, that almost any kind of valvular defect may exist, without the corresponding murmur : and my belief at present is that regurgitation through the tricuspid orifice exists in all cases in which the jugular veins really pulsate. Indeed, I cannot even agree with Friedreich that if pulsation disappears when the vein is compressed higher up, the existence of regurgitation is absolutely disproved : for this procedure may simply prevent the wave being transmitted upwards in the empty vessel. The most that can be said is that it renders the occurrence of reflux doubtful.

Friedreich gives sphygmographic tracings of the jugular pulse, which appears to be dicrotic, the beat due to the ventricular systole being preceded by a smaller elevation accompanying the contraction of the auricle.

It must be added that pulsation is generally more distinct in the right than the left jugular vein. In exceptional cases the veins of the face, arms, and hands have been seen to pulsate: and also the thyroid and mammary veins.

Turning now to the vena cava inferior and its tributaries, we find that these veins become greatly dilated as a consequence of distension

[1] Walshe, op. cit., p. 138.

of the right auricle. Senac [1] mentioned a case in which the cava itself was as thick as an arm. The hepatic veins also become much enlarged, running as wide open channels through the substance of the liver, and opening into the cava by orifices much larger than natural. These facts are of some importance, as throwing light on the epigastric pulsation, which is often observed in cases of chronic disease of the heart. It was long ago suggested by Allan Burns [2] that this is due to regurgitation of blood along the inferior cava, and into the vessels of the liver. And Friedreich at the present time maintains the same view.[3] English writers in general, however, describe the dilated right ventricle as giving a shock to the neighbouring parts which can be felt in the substernal notch: and some have even spoken of the heart as " beating in the epigastrium," the impossibility of which it did not need the labours of Hamernyk to point out.

The probability that epigastric pulsation is often due to reflux into the hepatic veins is increased by the fact that the liver itself is greatly enlarged under these conditions. It is also much congested and fatty, presenting a peculiar mottled appearance, which has gained for it the name of the nutmeg liver. At the same time it is very liable to a chronic inflammatory process, attended with an increase in its connective tissue, approaching that which occurs in cirrhosis. The congestion is transmitted through the liver to the portal vein and its radicles. The spleen becomes enlarged and its tissue very hard, in this respect contrasting with the still larger but soft spleen which is found in association with ulcerative disease of the cardiac valves. The veins of the omentum and mesentery are gorged with blood. The stomach has its lining intensely reddened and coated with mucus: hæmorrhage takes place into its submucous tissue, and the ecchymosed spots often become exposed by solution of the mucous membrane over them, forming the so-called " hæmorrhagic erosions." The intestines are also greatly congested and lined with mucus: and hæmorrhoids are often developed. These changes in the digestive organs are attended with more or less marked symptoms: partial jaundice; dyspepsia, nausea, sickness, even hæmatemesis; constipation. The engorgement of the veins lying beneath the peritoneum leads to ascites, often of considerable amount.

Nor do the other veins that open into the inferior vena cava escape. Thus the renal veins become distended; and the kidneys are deeply congested, a condition which easily passes into one of chronic inflammation, and often leads to the presence of albumen in the urine. The return of blood from the lower limbs is impeded; the veins are gorged, and very often thrombosis of the femoral veins arises, which, as has already been stated, is perhaps the remote cause of the development of pulmonary apoplexy.

[1] Friedreich, p. 41.   [2] Op. cit., p. 265.
[3] My colleague, Dr. Frederick Taylor, has observed distinct pulsation of the liver in four cases of chronic cardiac disease. When one hand was placed in the epigastrium and the other in the right loin, the organ could be felt to expand with each beat of the heart. Guy's Hosp. Rep. (vol. xx. 1875).

This engorgement of the veins of the lower limbs, although we mention it last in tracing backwards the consequences of disease of the cardiac valves, is in fact often one of the first effects of such disease to be observed; manifesting itself by the transudation of serum through the walls of the most distant venous radicles, and the production of œdema of the ankles and feet. The anasarca, slight at first, may increase until the whole of the lower extremities, the abdominal parietes, and even the genital organs, have become dropsical in the highest degree. As a rule, however, the genital organs remain comparatively free: and in this respect cardiac dropsy differs from that which occurs in renal disease, and the distribution of which is not in the same way dependent upon simple mechanical conditions. On the other hand, the icteroid tinge of the skin, which is generally present in cases of heart disease, is wanting in other forms of dropsy.

III. A third series of effects, produced by diseases of the cardiac valves, consist in sensations of various kinds experienced by the patient. These are the *subjective symptoms* of the diseases in question. They may present all degrees of intensity: they may even be entirely absent.

Pain may be felt either over the heart itself, or in the left shoulder; or it may extend down the inner side of the left arm to the elbow, or even to the fingers. It may either be a constant aching, or have a " shooting" or "stabbing" character. It is often distinctly paroxysmal, especially in cases of aortic regurgitation, in which it frequently assumes all the features of true angina pectoris. Pain in the arm and hand is sometimes accompanied with numbness: and sometimes (according to Dr. Dobell) these parts are deadly white while the numbness lasts. In some cases the pain is limited to the little and ring fingers, following the distribution of the ulnar nerve to these fingers: but in other cases it affects all the fingers, and even the thumb. Sometimes the pain also passes from mid-sternum to the right shoulder and down the right arm: but when pain occurs in these parts earlier than in the cardiac region, Dr. Dobell thinks that the presumption is in favour of disease of the aorta rather than of the heart.

A very important character of the reflected pains due to cardiac disease is that they are generally aggravated by anything which disturbs the heart's action, and especially by muscular exertion. Not unfrequently, pain is absent so long as the patient is at rest, but comes on at once as soon as he attempts to walk.

Another point, on which Dr. Dobell has particularly insisted, is that the pain of heart disease is often greatly increased by distension of the stomach with food or gas. Hence, when dyspepsia is present, it may easily be regarded as the cause of pain really due to heart disease; and relieving the indigestion may prevent the return of the pain.

Not infrequently, instead of pain, the patient speaks rather of a fluttering sensation in the præcordial region: or simply of palpitation. But it is to be observed that a spontaneous complaint of palpitation is heard far more often when the patient is suffering from one of its indirect causes, than when any of the cardiac valves are diseased. Indeed, as a rule, the subjective symptoms of valvular affections are subordinate to the other symptoms. And it may be said that when a patient comes to the physician complaining of pain in the heart, and fearing that he has heart disease, the great probability is that that organ is perfectly healthy.

Another morbid sensation, belonging to the diseases under consideration, is dyspnœa. Very often, indeed, the first thing that suggests a suspicion that there is anything wrong with the patient is that he is conscious of shortness of breath after mounting stairs, or making some moderate muscular effort. When he is at rest, he may be able to breathe comfortably enough; but this freedom from distress often continues only so long as he sits up. As soon as he lies down on an ordinary bed or couch, he becomes aware of unpleasant feelings, which compel him to change his posture. Thus, even in the slighter forms of cardiac valvular disease, it will generally be found that the patient lies at night with his head raised, employing two or three pillows, whereas a man in health would only require one. And in the more severe degrees of such disease, the patient is often utterly unable to lie down, or even to recline backwards. This condition has received a special name, that of Orthopnœa. It doubtless depends upon the circumstance that in the recumbent posture the diaphragm is pressed upwards by the contents of the abdomen (themselves greatly augmented in size), so that the enlarged heart is embarrassed in its movements.[1] Orthopnœa is in many respects a serious symptom. By preventing sleep, it greatly taxes the patient's strength, and diminishes his power of resisting the disease. Moreover, as Dr. Dobell has pointed out, it fatigues the lumbar muscles, and makes the back ache. It keeps the lower limbs at right angles with the trunk, and so, leading to compression of the veins and lymphatics in the groins, increases the œdema of the legs. Scarcely any condition is, in fact, more pitiable than that of a patient in this plight; and any mechanical appliance by which it can be remedied must certainly be an unspeakable boon. For this purpose Dr. Dobell has contrived a "Heart Bed," of which he has given a description and a figure in his book; and from his account it seems to be well worthy of trial in these distressing cases.

There are other subjective symptoms, belonging to the various secondary effects of diseases of the cardiac valves; but space fails me to describe them in detail; most of them have been incidentally referred to in other parts of this article.

DIAGNOSIS.—Under this heading I do not propose simply to recapitulate facts that have already been stated in previous paragraphs;

[1] Even when the heart is healthy, the position of its impulse may be higher or lower, according as the patient sits up or lies down, if there be an enlargement of the liver.

nor shall I attempt to construct any tables which might aid the student in distinguishing diseases of the cardiac valves from other affections with which they may be confounded. In my opinion such tables are scarcely ever made use of in practice; indeed, I do not think that they are applicable to really doubtful cases, in which the difficulty of diagnosis most commonly depends upon either a deficiency of symptoms, or their ambiguity: their being, in fact, such as might belong indifferently to any one of several maladies; or else their being in part such as commonly occur in one disease, in part such as belong rather to another disease. In cases of this kind, diagnostic skill is a matter of judgment and experience; and all that could be said under the present heading could do but little to further it.

There are, however, some important questions in reference to the detection of affections of the valves of the heart which have not yet been touched upon. In discussing each kind of murmur, I have endeavoured to indicate all the causes to which it may be due, and to point out how these may be distinguished from one another. But of the absence of murmur I have as yet said nothing. I now propose to consider this question, and to discuss whether abnormal sounds or bruits are constantly present in the various diseases of the different cardiac valves.

And first, with regard to the aortic valves. It may almost be said that in practice the diagnosis of aortic regurgitation depends wholly upon the discovery of a diastolic murmur, audible at certain parts of the thoracic parietes. If such a murmur is heard, the stethoscopist regards it as certain that regurgitation exists. If no such murmur can be detected, there is perhaps no combination of symptoms (unless it be by the aid of the sphygmograph) that would justify the physician in asserting that the aortic valves fail to close. It is therefore a most important question whether a diastolic bruit can always be detected in those persons in whom after death the valves are found to have been incompetent. Now, on looking through the records of post-mortem examinations at Guy's Hospital, I have found that this condition was discovered in 40 cases during the years 1870-71. And on referring to the clinical reports attached to these cases, it appears that in 26 of them regurgitation was positively diagnosed during life; and that in 11 out of the remaining 14 cases the patients came from the surgical division of the hospital, or were less than seven days in the wards (some having been dying at the time of admission, or brought in dead), or had no notes taken of the auscultatory signs which they presented. Thus the proportion of cases of this disease that may be said to have resisted diagnosis was very small.

It has been stated that several of the cases in which the aortic valves were found incompetent after death during the period named were cases of surgical disease or injury, in which one may presume that there were no obvious symptoms of cardiac disease. This accords well with the fact that aortic regurgitation is more frequently than any other valvular affection discovered by the auscultator when the patient's history and symptoms had not previously suggested any suspicion of its existence. Dr. Walshe relates the case of a man, about 35 years old, the very picture of robust health, who had never had a symptom of disease connected with any organ in his body, and who presented himself for life insurance. Almost as a matter of form, Dr. Walshe put his stethoscope to the chest; his attention was at once arrested by a loud diastolic murmur. The man dropped dead in the street within a fortnight. I lately saw a bank clerk, aged 32, whose sole complaint was a pain in the chest about the ensiform cartilage, with occasional pain in the back, such as might have been due to any trifling cause. On listening to his chest I heard a well-marked diastolic bruit.[1]

It might be supposed that there would often be a difficulty in distinguishing between the to-and-fro sounds of pericarditis and those of disease at the aortic orifice. And for my own part I believe that this difficulty would arise oftener than it does, were it not for the very different clinical history and course and other symptoms belonging severally to these two diseases. The comparatively superficial seat of pericardial friction-sounds, their want of definite localization at the spots where valvular murmurs are most marked, their intensification by pressure with the stethoscope, and their failing to correspond accurately with the cardiac rhythm, are all valuable points of distinction; but as a matter of pure auscultation, I think that doubt would sometimes be admissible; and as a matter of fact I have occasionally experienced this difficulty, especially when (as in cases of Bright's disease at an advanced age) the presence of either chronic pericarditis or disease of the aortic coats would accord with the other features of the case.

The diagnosis between a presystolic and a diastolic murmur is not generally difficult to those who are well acquainted with the seat and quality of these murmurs respectively. But I have sometimes found

---

[1] A very striking instance, in which the patient discovered the murmur, has just come under my notice in a young medical man, a friend of my own. On January 23rd, 1875, he had gone to his brother's for a day's shooting; and while at lunch, he noticed a strange noise, which he thought came from his stomach. He forgot all about it, as he went out shooting for two hours. After dinner he heard the noise again. On the next day, while standing in his dining-room, he became conscious of a loud sound in his chest: and his wife, who was three or four feet off, heard it also. During four days it remained audible at a distance. He consulted a medical friend, who discovered valvular disease. Dr. Wilks saw him two weeks afterwards, and kindly sent him to me. His health remained perfectly good. He would not have known that anything was the matter with him, except that when he made any exertion he could feel a vibration in his chest. A loud diastolic murmur was audible over an extensive area. There was no excessive impulse: but the apex beat was situated below the sixth rib; and the heart's dulness extended downwards and outwards for six inches. In this case I think it is clear that, whatever may have been the original cause of the sudden development of the transitory murmur heard at a distance from the patient's body, the valve had previously been diseased. He had, however, been apparently in perfect health: able to ride, shoot, and run as well as ever. The only sudden effort that he remembered making on the day when he first noticed the murmur was that he had lifted his wife out of a high dog-cart: but this he had done many times before.

it to be far from easy; and a distinguished physician, who has himself written much on the subject of heart disease, has informed me of one case in which he confidently asserted the existence of a presystolic murmur, but in which the aortic valves proved to be unsound, while the mitral valve was healthy. The mistake most likely to happen to the unpractised or careless auscultator is that of supposing the murmur of aortic regurgitation, when it happens to be loud at the apex of the heart, to be a mitral regurgitant bruit. To commit this error is completely to misunderstand the rhythm of the heart in the patient under examination. But I have nevertheless seen it committed more than once. Either no pains at all were taken to determine the period of the ventricular systole; or the radial pulse was employed as a guide to it. Now it has been already stated that in aortic incompetency the radial pulse is often delayed, so as to be almost synchronous with the recoil of the aorta; or, in other words, with the regurgitant bruit. Hence by feeling the wrist in cases of this kind one may easily mistake a diastolic for a systolic murmur.

It still remains to be mentioned that an aortic regurgitant murmur is sometimes hard to detect. I well remember that, when I was a student, I had very great difficulty in hearing the murmur in more than one case in which my teachers spoke confidently of its presence. And I now find that I in my turn discover murmurs which my pupils cannot hear, even when I tell them what to listen for. When such a murmur is once heard, it often seems so distinct that one wonders that one could have overlooked it. In other instances the sound is really very slight, and it is thus drowned by any little noise, although plainly audible at night, or when a ward is very quiet. Lately I had a patient under my care, in whom the existence of an aortic regurgitant murmur was matter of the most lively discussion. I was sure that I had heard it two or three times, but on every other occasion I failed to detect it. After death the valves were found to be obviously incompetent. There is of course no relation between the amount of reflux and the loudness of the murmur.

The diagnosis of mitral disease is far from resting on so satisfactory a footing as that of aortic obstruction and regurgitation. We may first take the comparatively simple case of mitral stenosis. I have already said that a presystolic murmur, when heard at the heart's apex, is pathognomonic of this affection. But we have now to approach the subject from the opposite point of view, and to inquire in what proportion of cases such a murmur is audible. Some years ago I collected for the Guy's Hospital Reports all the instances in which mitral stenosis was found after death during a period of some years. They amounted to forty-seven; and in only seven (or perhaps six) of them had a presystolic murmur been detected during life. It is true that from them a considerable number (fifteen or twenty) had to be subtracted, as having proved fatal soon after admission, or as having been cases of surgical disease or injury, or as having in some other way failed to afford an opportunity for diagnosis. But there still remained at least three cases of mitral stenosis without presystolic murmur, to one in which such a murmur was recognized.

At that time the whole question of prosystolic bruits was comparatively a new one; and I thought that, with further experience, the number of undiagnosed cases of mitral stenosis would diminish. I am bound to say that this appears not to be the case. I have not indeed submitted to numerical analysis the observations that have been made since my paper was written; but my impression is that, in the very large majority of the cases in which mitral stenosis is found after death, there is no record of the presence of a presystolic murmur during life. Some observers, I know, hope to reduce this proportion of failures in diagnosis, by the more frequent detection of a short presystolic murmur preceding the systolic murmur of mitral regurgitation. I must confess that my own experience in this direction has not hitherto been very encouraging. In more than one instance in which I thought I had detected such a second murmur, the mitral orifice has been found after death of its natural size.

It remains to add that, even when a presystolic murmur has once been detected, it may often cease for a time to be audible, or even altogether disappear. In the later stages of the disease, when the heart is beating quickly and irregularly, it is almost always absent. Thus, at first there was some difficulty in verifying the correctness of the modern view with regard to the rhythm of presystolic murmurs by post-mortem evidence; and in the majority of cases that have terminated fatally soon after the diagnosis of mitral stenosis, some accidental complication has been the cause of death. Again, when the patient is prostrated by any depressing intercurrent disease, the murmur may become temporarily inaudible, returning with convalescence. Of this Dr. Sutton has related a capital instance.[1] In other cases, no murmur can be heard as long as the patient remains perfectly quiet; but muscular exertion or effort soon makes it audible. Sometimes even making the patient sit up in bed will bring out a presystolic murmur that had a moment before been absent; sometimes it is necessary that he should walk two or three times the length of a ward, or even go quickly upstairs. One can never safely assert the absence of a presystolic murmur when one has examined the patient only in a recumbent posture. It may be added, parenthetically, that in aortic stenosis (the chief other form of obstructive disease at a cardiac orifice), a loud murmur may sometimes be brought out by making the patient run upstairs, although none had previously been audible. I state this on the authority of Dr. Wilks.[2]

From the remarks that have already been made with regard to the so-called mitral regurgitant disease, it will be evident that there can be no question here as to the frequency with which its diagnosis is effected during life. I believe that a systolic murmur, louder at the apex

[1] Lond. Hosp. Rep., vol. iv., 1867-8. The patient was very much weakened by frequent vomiting during the time when the murmur disappeared.

[2] Dr. Walshe taught this clinically twenty-five years ago. See his "Diseases of the Lungs and Heart," 1851, p. 217.—EDITOR.

than elsewhere, and audible at the angle of the left scapula, proves the existence of mitral regurgitation ; but it is certainly present in comparatively few of the cases that are commonly placed in this category.

There is, in fact, a large residue of cases of valvular disease in which either no murmur is audible at the time of observation, or only a systolic murmur, confined to the apex. These cases constitute the sandy desert of cardiac pathology—not, indeed, unexplored, but with a surface so precarious and shifting as to have hitherto prevented the laying down of roads across it, much less the division of it into territories by fixed boundary lines. As we have seen, the cases in question do not differ at all, so far as stethoscopical evidence goes, from others in which the presence of valvular disease is altogether doubtful. It may be true that, since advanced organic changes in the mitral valve almost always lead to stenosis, the diagnosis of stenosis becomes exceedingly probable in any case which can be shown to be primarily one of organic disease of this valve. But it is precisely here that the difficulty arises; and for such cases I think that the diagnosis of " morbus cordis " is often the most exact that can be given.

I may refer, for example, to a series of cases of fibroid disease of the heart that I have recorded in the Pathological Transactions for 1874, vol. xxv. p. 64. In several of these cases there was a systolic apex murmur; and it is probable that, at least in some of them, the mitral valve was really inefficient, since the fibroid change often invaded one of its fleshy columns. Now, during life, there was nothing to distinguish these cases from those of ordinary " mitral regurgitant disease," and even in the other cases, in which no murmur existed, valvular disease might really have existed, and been latent. Since my cases were published, it has occurred to me that perhaps one positive indication of the presence of fibroid disease of the heart, rather than of any affection of the valves, may be found in its resisting treatment with greater obstinacy. When a considerable part of the wall of the left ventricle has had its muscular substance replaced by fibrous tissue, it appears reasonable to suppose that the remedies which would be useful in a case of valvular disease should prove to be altogether powerless.

I have still to lay stress on the importance of watching, with great care, for the occurrence of those changes in valves already diseased which have already been described, and the recognition of which is so important for purposes of prognosis. The development of incompetency in aortic valves that had hitherto simply obstructed the onward current, the production of stenosis in a mitral valve previously the seat of regurgitation alone, the rupture of the chordæ of a diseased mitral valve, the tearing down of a softened aortic segment, the supervention of acute inflammation in valves long thickened, atheromatous, or calcified,—all these might probably be discovered much oftener than is now the case, were the physician to pay more regard to the probability of their occurrence. Nor should the liability to intercurrent pericarditis, and to the development of changes in the heart's muscular tissue, ever be forgotten by those who would have their diagnosis complete for the post-mortem examination.

PROGNOSIS.—To determine the probable duration of life in a patient affected with valvular disease of the heart, and the chance that existing symptoms may be relieved or removed, is generally very difficult; and it can hardly be discussed systematically in an article of this kind, since it requires that all the circumstances of the case should, one after another, be taken into consideration. But some leading points may be briefly stated.

And in the first place, can a diseased valve ever recover its normal structure and functions? In reference to the acute affections of the valves, arising in rheumatic fever or in chorea, some facts have already been adduced which indicate that this is possible. And a further argument in favour of the same view may perhaps be found in the circumstance that in each of the diseases in question a systolic murmur is heard, which in many cases disappears after recovery. If such a murmur, when audible at the heart's apex, be regarded as proof that the mitral valve is affected, it would seem to follow that endocarditis is curable. Such an opinion has, in fact, been recently maintained by Dr. Peacock, who, in an analysis[1] of 146 cases of acute rheumatism that had been under his care, found that "the proportion of cases of recent cardiac complication (which he states to have consisted in endocarditis more frequently than in pericarditis) entirely cured was 41·5 per cent." But the conclusion, of course, depends for its validity upon the question whether the determination of the cause of the murmur is accurate. And this I am not prepared to admit unreservedly.

A valve once affected with chronic disease is no doubt almost always damaged beyond possibility of repair. Thickened and calcified aortic valves can never again become thin and supple.[2] Nor is it probable that a stenosed mitral orifice can become widened. Friedreich has indeed suggested that in young subjects this may not be impossible: but in proof of it he can only refer, in general terms, to cases in which there were at one time symptoms of extreme stenosis, but in which these gradually diminished, and after death the mitral orifice was found capable of admitting two fingers.

There is, however, no doubt that thirty years ago the most practised auscultators of the day condemned, as the victims of organic valvular disease that would soon destroy them, children who have since grown up to be men and women, and who to all appearance enjoy excellent health. It is probable that they attached too absolute an importance to the existence of a murmur, and that they also committed the error of supposing that the louder the murmur, the worse the disease. One cannot insist too strongly on the fact that between these two things there is no relation whatever. The prognosis in the cases under consideration

[1] Clinical Society's Transactions, ii. p. 221.
[2] The analogy of scleroderma, however, perhaps suggests that even this is not absolutely out of the question.

must be based not upon the physical qualities of the murmur, but upon a determination of the degree to which the disease disturbs the circulation; or, if compensation be complete, upon the degree of increased strain thrown upon the heart.

I have already pointed out how compensation is in many cases effected by dilatation and hypertrophy of certain of the heart's chambers. According to Jaksch there is another kind of compensation, consisting in conservative changes in the valves themselves, which absolutely prevent diseases of the valves from producing their natural consequences. When one cusp of the mitral valve is diseased, he imagines that the other may grow broader, and its chordæ may lengthen until it meets its fellow. When one aortic valve is puckered up, the others may gradually become deeper and wider, so as to fill up the gap. The change last mentioned is one which I have myself seen; but it doubtless occurs only in very young patients.

It has already been stated more than once that in valvular diseases of the heart the development of serious symptoms is often very long delayed. Dropsy may first show itself in a person advanced in years, and destroy life in a few months: but the mitral disease which is rightly regarded as the cause of the dropsy may be traceable to an attack of rheumatic fever twenty or thirty years back: and in the interval the patient may either have had excellent health, or may always have suffered more or less from dyspnœa on exertion, which has shown that the heart was defective.

It is a question discussed by almost all writers on Heart Diseases, whether a prolonged existence, and delay in the development of serious symptoms occur in all forms of valvular disease alike, or belong especially to any one group of cases. Considerable interest would indeed attach to the determination of the relative prognosis of the various affections of different valves: and, although statistical accuracy is not to be looked for, a general concurrence of opinion on the subject might fairly be expected. The case is not so, however. According to one of the most recent French writers, Jaccoud,[1] stenoses in general are more serious than regurgitations: and mitral stenosis is more so than aortic stenosis. Again, Friedreich, the author of perhaps the latest German monograph,[2] says that "as a rule the prognosis in obstructive forms of valvular disease is less favourable, and the duration of life shorter, in obstructive than in regurgitant affections." Now, according to all English writers this is absolutely incorrect. Walshe places "the chief valvular derangements in the following descending series on the basis of their relative gravity,—that is, estimating this gravity not only by their ultimate lethal tendency, but by the amount of complicated miseries they inflict:—Tricuspid regurgitation: mitral constriction and regurgitation: aortic regurgitation; pulmonary constriction; aortic constriction." Thus Dr. Walshe regards aortic stenosis as admitting of a far better prognosis than aortic regurgitation:

[1] Traité de Pathologie Interne, tome i. p. 657.
[2] Krankheiten des Herzens, Handbuch der spec. Path. und Ther., 2te Aufl. 1867, p. 282.

and Dr. Peacock agrees with him, stating that in the former disease life may be prolonged for many years, and a large amount of health and vigour be enjoyed ; whereas in aortic incompetency it is very rare to find life sustained for a considerable period. Dr. Peacock, indeed, differs from Dr. Walshe and from most other English writers in believing the prospects of longevity to be actually less in persons who labour under aortic regurgitation than in those who have mitral disease. I confess that I am unable to reconcile these conflicting statements. It is evident that the discrepancy is in great part due to the uncertainty which still attaches to the interpretation both of auscultatory phenomena and of morbid appearances. I have shown that, according to experience at Guy's Hospital, aortic stenosis, without regurgitation, is far more rare than has generally been supposed; and certainly it would not within the last few years have been possible to make any observations that would have allowed of a numerical comparison between its mortality and that of regurgitant disease of the same orifice. The latter disease, however, is undoubtedly a very fatal one. I find from the clinical records at Guy's, that from 45 to 50 per cent. of the patients who have aortic regurgitation die within the comparatively short period during which (under ordinary circumstances) they are allowed to remain as in-patients. But then it is to be observed that the fact of their admittance implies the existence of severe symptoms at the time : and the observations in question are not incompatible with the fact that the disease often exists for a lengthened period before such symptoms show themselves. I have already remarked that changes in the aortic valves, allowing regurgitation, have often been found in persons who have presented themselves for life assurance, or in the dead bodies of those who have been killed by accident. Instances of this kind appear to be fairly comparable with the case, on which Dr. Peacock lays so much stress, of a woman, æt. 76, who died of strangulated hernia, and in whom two of the aortic curtains were completely blended into one, and the orifice reduced to a mere slit, although she was not known to have had any symptoms of disease of the heart. Unless we agree with Dr. Peacock in supposing that disease of this kind always originates in congenital malformation, there is no proof whatever that in the case in question the disease had existed longer than in the examples of unsuspected regurgitant aortic disease which are so common. But while thus criticising some of the evidence brought forward in proof that aortic stenosis is a less serious disease than aortic regurgitation, I nevertheless believe that this is really the case.

Again, it is very difficult to institute a comparison between the duration of life in mitral stenosis and mitral regurgitation respectively. For, as we have seen, the cases included under the latter designation present no one pathological lesion, but rather a variety of more or less allied conditions. Many cases of mitral stenosis, with marked presystolic murmur, remain under observation for some years, and are admitted into the wards again and again, without the symptoms undergoing any great increase of severity, and without there being at any time reason to apprehend an immediately fatal issue. And on the other hand, it is well known that the systolic murmur of mitral regurgitation may be detected by auscultation for years before any serious symptoms show themselves.

Lastly, I doubt whether any data exist from which one could accurately determine the relative gravity of regurgitant aortic, and of regurgitant mitral disease. For, in addition to other points that have already been noticed, there is between these two affections an important distinction in the fact that one of them is far more constantly traceable to a past attack of rheumatic fever than the other. Hence, while one can often with confidence say, in the case of mitral regurgitation, that the cardiac affection began years before, when the patient had acute rheumatism, one is commonly obliged to refer the commencement of aortic disease to the date when the patient first began to suffer from definite symptoms of heart-disease. Now it is certain that aortic disease sometimes exists for a long time without any symptoms at all: but whether this is the rule or the exception we have no means of knowing.

There is, however, one particular mode of death which appears beyond doubt to occur in regurgitant aortic disease far more frequently than in any other affection of the cardiac valves: and it is one which for many persons has especial terrors,—namely, that in which the fatal termination is sudden. It is a curious circumstance that the contrary is stated by Corrigan, in the interesting paper which is almost the first that was written on this subject. In permanent patency of the mouth of the aorta, he says, "*the fatal result is never sudden.*" "Under proper restrictions the patient is not only able to lead an active life for years, but is actually benefited by doing so." All recent writers, however, recognize the tendency to the occurrence of sudden death in the disease in question. Thus Dr. Walshe says:[1] "Taken as a group, valvular impediments cannot fairly be cited as frequent causes of sudden death: but there is one among the number, of which the tendency to kill instantaneously is so strong that the fact must always be borne in mind in estimating its prognosis, and that is aortic regurgitation. . . . The manner of death is clearly syncopal: but the immediate mechanism, whether mechanical or dynamic, is difficult enough of comprehension. I have known death take place during the act of walking, of eating, of speaking,—while the patient was emotionally excited, and, *per contra*, at a moment when he was perfectly calm." Further on, Dr. Walshe appears to imply that the liability to sudden death is greater when the heart itself is perfectly healthy than when it presents dilatation and hypertrophy of the left ventricle or other morbid changes. But in this he differs from Dr. Peacock, who says[2] that "in cases in which the heart is most remarkably enlarged, sudden death is yet of common occurrence," and who cites two instances of the kind, in which the hearts weighed 40 oz. and 46 oz. respectively.

[1] Op. cit., p. 390.   [2] Croonian Lectures, p. 108.

With regard to the prognosis of the diseases of the valves believed to originate in injury, all that can be said is that in recorded cases the duration of life has been very variable. Dr. Peacock states that the period of death in the different cases of injury to the aortic valves collected by him was "twenty-one days, three months and a half, thirteen months, two years, twenty-seven months, and three years and a half: and two persons were still surviving after five months and five years had elapsed" in their respective cases. "In the cases of rupture of the mitral valve, the patients lived nine days, and twenty months: and two still survived eighteen months, and two years, after the occurrence of the accident."

TREATMENT.—The prophylaxis of acute affections of the cardiac valves belongs to the treatment of those diseases in which such affections are most apt to arise; and if endocarditis can really be prevented by medicine, this is, in fact, the most important part of the treatment of the diseases in question. But at present I do not know that one can really say any more about it than that rest should be strictly enforced, and that the chest should perhaps be protected from cold by a layer of cotton-wool.

Scarcely less important is the prevention of the development of chronic disease in valves that have once been damaged by acute inflammation. I have already adduced facts which tend to prove that endocarditis not rarely subsides without leaving any injurious effects behind it; in particular, that a large proportion of the cases of rheumatic inflammation of the aortic valves in women must terminate in the restoration of the normal structure of the valves. The comparative immunity of the female sex from the more remote changes which so frequently arise in the male sex can only be ascribed to the fact that women lead less active lives than men, and are not compelled to endure such continuous exertion, or to make such violent muscular efforts. The plain inference is, that in either sex the way to prevent chronic disease of the valves, after endocarditis in rheumatism or chorea, is to keep the patient for many months—or even some years —as perfectly as possible at rest; to insist on abstention from violent exercise, athletic sports and games, of all kinds; to direct the choice of a light, sedentary employment, and to urge the avoidance of all emotional excitement. General hygienic conditions should at the same time be carefully attended to. I think, too, that it may hereafter be shown that medicines are useful. I have pointed out how the anatomical characters of chronic disease of the valves differ from those of acute endocarditis; that the vegetations disappear, but that the edges of the valves become thickened and fused together. Surely it is possible that iodide of potassium, mercury, or arsenic, may be able to arrest or prevent these changes, as much as those which belong to certain skin diseases, or the chronic inflammations of parts accessible to the sight or touch of the surgeon.

Similar principles must be applied in the endeavour to prevent those forms of valvular disease which are from the first of gradual origin. A very large proportion of the cases of aortic regurgitant disease that occur so commonly in labouring men past middle life, are due to the fact that these men have gone on with work involving straining efforts, which can with safety be made only by younger individuals, whose tissues are still elastic and supple. Dr. Peacock and Dr. Allbutt have indeed shown that such diseases of the cardiac valves frequently occur at an earlier period of life than has generally been supposed; but even then they are perhaps favoured by some particular diathetic condition, or by habitual excessive indulgence in alcoholic drinks, which promotes degenerative changes in the tissues. It may hereafter be possible for the physician to select certain individuals as especially liable to suffer from the harder kinds of labour, and to recommend for them less arduous employments. Among the higher classes, again, chronic disease of the cardiac valves appears very frequently to be due to men forgetting that they are advancing in years, and to their continuing to take violent exercise long after they have ceased to be fit for it. This is especially apt to occur in professional men, whose habits are generally sedentary, and who, during an occasional holiday, often run great risks. The physician should always be on the look-out for the earliest signs of tissue-degeneration in such persons, and should be ready to warn them of the necessity that they should avoid too great exertions or straining efforts. It is no longer believed that the signs in question are an early arcus senilis, and the fact that the hair has turned prematurely grey; and I am myself inclined to doubt whether tortuosity of the temporal arteries, or an apparent rigidity of the radial arteries to the touch, is to be much relied on, as indicative of degeneration of those vessels; but, taken with other points, they are probably of value; and it seems that the sphygmograph may here lend very valuable assistance.

Even when valvular disease is fairly established, the prophylactic measures already referred to by no means cease to be applicable. Probably such disease is almost always *progressive*; and it is, moreover, liable to become complicated at any period of its course by the supervention of acute endocarditis.

But the treatment of diseases of the cardiac valves, properly so-called, reduces itself to the treatment of their effects. To these we must therefore refer in brief detail.

1. Very little, and perhaps nothing, is known of any effectual treatment for the contamination of the blood with morbid materials, which is so apt to occur in the more acute forms of valvular disease, or for the occurrence of embolism in the larger vessels. Quinine would seem to be indicated in the former condition, and may perhaps be of some service; but Lancereaux observes that its failure has often been demonstrated in cases that had been mistaken for ague, and had therefore been treated with this drug. The mineral acids are recommended by Friedreich. I am not aware that any evidence is to be obtained as to the use of the sulphites or hyposulphites, as recommended

by Polli in septic conditions, but I should conceive that there is, at any rate, more chance that they might be useful in the cases under consideration than in the specific fevers against which they have chiefly been employed. Cases in which "typhoid" symptoms occur, with hæmorrhages into the skin and mucous membranes, &c., are probably of necessity fatal; and it is almost useless to administer the ammonia, ether, and musk, which are generally recommended, and which at once suggest themselves to the mind as the drugs that can be most appropriately given.

When there is evidence of the occurrence of embolism in any particular artery, it is possible that the administration of ammonia, as suggested by Dr. Richardson,[1] may favour the solution of the co-agulum—if indeed he is right in attributing success to this treatment in cases of fibrinous deposition within the heart. The plan which he recommends is the administration of ten-minim doses of the liquor ammoniæ in iced water, every hour, with three to five-grain doses of the iodide of potassium every alternate hour.

2. The changes which diseases of the cardiac valves induce in the circulation of the blood, and in the several chambers of the heart, are capable of being modified in a very remarkable degree by various medicines and modes of treatment; and to these we must now turn our attention, following as far as possible the same order which was adopted in the account of these changes given in pages 55 to 69.

In cases of aortic regurgitation, so long as the state of the ventricle is such as perfectly to compensate for the valvular defect, medicinal treatment is scarcely applicable. Patients admitted into an hospital sometimes lose all their symptoms as a consequence of the rest which they obtain, and which is so essential to them. The avoidance of all violent or straining efforts should in fact be insisted on in this, even more than in other forms of cardiac disease, on account of the marked tendency to sudden death, which must always be borne in mind.

For the less severe effects of aortic regurgitant disease, the slighter degree of malaise and discomfort caused by it, senega is the common remedy. It is difficult to say how this drug acts; and as ammonia is generally given with it, this has been supposed to be the really efficient remedy. I have, however, repeatedly prescribed it alone, and patients have sometimes declared that it has given them distinct relief. I am therefore disposed to believe that it is of value, and the more so, as the late Dr. Barlow (a physician of much experience in such matters) used to teach that in many cases only moderate doses could be borne. The dose usually given is half an ounce to an ounce of the infusion, with or without half a drachm or a drachm of the tincture, and perhaps the same quantity of the aromatic spirits of ammonia, or five grains of carbonate of ammonia.

When compensation fails in aortic regurgitant disease, we have seen that effects are developed which are identical with those that

---

[1] Med. Press and Circular, Nov. 20, 1872.

occur in mitral disease. They require the same treatment, which I shall describe in the next paragraph.

In the treatment of a case of "mitral disease,"—using that term for the moment in its widest sense,—the primary point is the due regulation of the contractions of the left ventricle, for which we have in *digitalis* a remedy of wonderful power. Within the last few years a great change has taken place in our views as to the action of this herb, and our knowledge is very much more accurate than it formerly was. The older opinion was that it enfeebled the power of the heart,[1] and therefore that dangerous effects might in certain cases follow its administration, from its tendency to cause fatal syncope. It is true that Dr. Withering in the last century stated it to be most useful in those cases of dropsy in which the pulse was feeble or intermitting, declaring also that it seldom succeeded in men with a tight and cordy pulse. But its good effects in such cases were attributed to its diuretic action, not to its having any power of strengthening a feeble heart.

Within the last few years, however, it has been demonstrated that the action of digitalis on the heart is in fact that of a tonic. The proofs of this are varied. In cold-blooded animals, in which the cardiac pulsations can be watched after exposure of the organ, digitalis causes spasm of the left ventricle, beginning at isolated points in its wall, and finally affecting its whole substance, so that its beats cease, and it remains rigidly contracted and white. In conjunction with Dr. Stevenson, I some years ago performed a number of experiments on frogs, in which this result was uniformly observed.[2] In the higher animals it is less easy to study directly the action of digitalis on the heart, but according to Fothergill,[3] Handfield Jones and Fuller have noticed similar effects as regards the state of the heart after death in mammals.

The present doctrine with regard to digitalis, then, is that it strengthens the heart's contractions. It is true that when very large doses are given, the pulse may become weak, frequent, and intermittent; but this is supposed to be due to the fact that the ventricle is in a state of spasm, and therefore that its beats are imperfect, and throw but a small quantity of blood into the arteries.

Thus the cases of heart disease in which digitalis is most useful are those in which the organ beats feebly and irregularly, in which a condition of "asystolie" exists, and in which the pulse presents the sphygmographic characters indicated at p. 63. In such cases the action of the remedy is to diminish the frequency of the cardiac pulsations, to make them regular, and to increase their force.

Among affections of the cardiac valves, "mitral regurgitant disease" is that one which most commonly presents the indications for the administration of digitalis; and in a large proportion of cases of this

[1] Pereira's Mat. Med., 4th ed., 1855, vol. ii., p. 536.
[2] Proc. of the Roy. Soc., 1865 ; Guy's Hosp. Rep., 1866.
[3] "Digitalis: its mode of action and its use," 1871.

kind, great relief is afforded by the remedy; the symptoms may for a time be entirely removed, and the patient restored to a state of apparent health. On the other hand, it is often useless and perhaps injurious in cases of mitral stenosis; for the left ventricle in the earlier stages of this affection generally contracts regularly and with due force, as is apparent from the normal character of the pulse. At a later period in the course of mitral stenosis, digitalis is often very useful; but the physical characters of the disease are then less distinctive; it is often difficult or even impossible to determine its exact nature. Again, in aortic regurgitation, when the hypertrophied ventricle is carrying on the circulation vigorously, digitalis often aggravates all the symptoms; and if the patient should die suddenly, it is liable to the charge of having caused the fatal result, a charge which cannot be refuted, and is probably often justly made against the drug. But Dr. Ringer has shown that the existence of aortic disease does not contra-indicate the use of digitalis, if the symptoms suggest its administration. When there is dilatation of the heart (rather than hypertrophy), and the pulse is feeble, frequent, fluttering, and (above all) irregular, it may be given with a fair expectation that it will afford relief.

The dose of digitalis is a matter of some importance; a drachm of the infusion is enough to begin with, or five or ten minims of the tincture. According to Dr. Fothergill, the injurious effects of digitalis in aortic disease, with hypertrophy of the left ventricle, may be avoided by employing very minute doses, which will in such cases do as much good as is produced under ordinary circumstances by larger quantities of the remedy.

It is doubtful whether any other remedies are capable of exerting the same action as digitalis on the diseased human heart. Dr. Stevenson and I found that squill and two species of helleborus (*H. viridis* and *niger*) produced the same peculiar effects in the healthy frog. *Veratrum viride* is often supposed to resemble digitalis in this respect; and in America it has been largely used to diminish the frequency of the heart's beats. But in frogs its action is the very opposite of that of digitalis; it rather resembles aconite, paralyzing the heart, which, when it stops, is dilated and of a deep purple colour.

The treatment for the *backward* effects of diseases of the valves of the heart must of course aim at reducing the increased tension in the pulmonary and venous systemic vessels, upon which these effects depend. And there are two principal ways in which this can be done. The first is the removal of a portion of the venous blood by venesection, leeches, or cupping. Now, if we take into consideration the fact that blood is forced into the veins from the capillaries in a continuous stream, we shall not at first suppose that much benefit is likely to accrue from the abstraction of a few ounces of blood from one part of the venous system. It seems like taking a cupful of water from a pail that is running over with the supply from a spring. We cannot help imagining that the veins will almost instantly become again distended. But there is abundant evidence to show that such a supposition is erroneous. Thus the hæmoptysis which accompanies pulmonary apoplexy often relieves the patient's breathing for several days or even weeks ; and nausea and vomiting, due to congestion of the stomach, are frequently removed for a considerable time by an atttack of hæmatemesis. It is clear that the relations, as regards tension, of the different parts of the circulating system can be much more steadily maintained than one would at first sight have imagined. Equally decided are the therapeutical proofs of the same fact. The withdrawal of a small quantity of venous blood is often attended with the most beneficial results in cases of heart disease. Perhaps the most striking example that I can cite is one, recorded by Dr. Dickinson,[1] of a man who had ruptured almost all the chordæ of the posterior flap of the mitral valve. " This patient was frequently relieved temporarily by the abstraction of blood. He was frequently cupped, always with apparent relief of the dyspnœa and distress. Towards the close of his sufferings, when, though there was much cardiac action, the pulse was nearly imperceptible, and the patient was approaching a condition of collapse, with much dyspnœa and blueness of the face, eight ounces of blood were taken by venesection, with immediate and decided relief, the pulse recovering itself as the blood flowed, while the distress of the patient was much lessened. The improvement, however, was only temporary. The patient died the following night."

The extreme gravity of the lesion in this case seems to render it worthy of being quoted. If the removal of blood could give relief when one-half of the mitral valve "had lost all valvular action, and swung uselessly from its base," there is hardly any case in which one need despair of its doing good. In the ordinary forms of valvular disease it is often useful, and the relief afforded by it is sometimes maintained for several days, or even weeks, so as to allow time for the operation of other remedies. The application of leeches to the epigastrium relieves the sickness and nausea due to congestion of the stomach; probably they would be still more useful if applied near the anus.

The other method of relieving the engorged pulmonary and venous systemic circulation is by removing, not blood itself, but its watery part alone ; in other words, by giving purgatives and diuretics. Among the former remedies, the hydragogues are of course to be preferred ; jalap, or even elaterium, scammony, salines, &c. As regards diuretics, it has already been observed that one of the principal indications of the favourable action of digitalis is its increasing the flow of urine, sometimes to an enormous extent. Whatever view may be taken of the theory of its action, there is no doubt about the fact. Other remedies which are supposed to act as diuretics in the diseases under consideration are squill, juniper, broom, and cream of tartar. Copaiba is sometimes very useful. I have notes of one case of mitral disease which had previously resisted various kinds of treatment, and in which ascites and anasarca rapidly vanished under the administration of a

[1] Path. Trans. xx. p. 151.

simple copaiba mixture. I shall never forget the gratification of the patient as the loops of string that held his trousers together soon became unnecessary, and the buttons themselves had to be moved again and again, in adaptation to the rapidly-decreasing girth of his belly. Dr. Wilks has recently found the resin of copaiba no less effectual, as it is certainly more pleasant.

3. The third group of effects of disease of the cardiac valves —the symptoms subjectively experienced by the patient—are frequently capable of great relief by medical treatment, but too often resist all the physician's efforts, and make the termination of a case of this kind almost more distressing and painful than that of any other disease.

The obvious remedies for dyspnœa, palpitation, and the sense of pressure and weight in the epigastrium, are the ethers and ammonia, especially when combined with digitalis, if the nature of the disease should be such as to indicate its employment. The application of a large belladonna plaister to the cardiac region often gives considerable relief to local pain and to palpitation.

Hyoscyamus is commonly given as an anodyne in these cases; but I have not seen it do very much good. Opium is generally said to be inadmissible, or to be used only with great caution. On the other hand, it would appear that the subcutaneous injection of morphia may be employed with safety, and with the most marked results. Its use has been especially advocated by Dr. Allbutt.[1] He uses the hydrochlorate, in doses of one-tenth to one-third of a grain. It is especially useful, he says, in cases of mitral regurgitation, "when the head is full of venous blood, and distress and stupor seem striving together. An injection of morphia three or four times a week, by tranquillizing the heart, and allowing the circulation to recover its freedom, sets free also the organs that are oppressed. . . . . Directly and immediately the injection seems to affect the chest almost alone. The face generally becomes less turgid, and its expression calmer. The heart becomes tranquil and rhythmical. . . . . The insufferable præcordial distress ceases. . . . . The quick, shallow, anxious, cardiac dyspnœa gives way to a deeper, slower, and easier movement. . . . . The patient, who has been tossing in misery, feels the first tranquil sleep he has enjoyed for weeks."

The attacks of angina-like pain, which form so important a part of the symptoms in many cases of aortic regurgitation, require essentially the treatment of neuralgias. I have more than once found the regular administration of arsenic able to prevent their recurrence. The paroxysms themselves are often arrested by the inhalation of ten drops of nitrite of amyl, or of a few whiffs of chloroform; or again by the subcutaneous injection of morphia. In one case that I saw—in which all these were used in succession—the patient preferred the morphia, as giving him the highest amount of relief.

---

[1] Practitioner, iii. p. 342.

ATROPHY OF THE HEART.

By W. R. Gowers, M.D.

Synonym.—Phthisis of the Heart (old writers).

Definition.—Diminution in the size and weight of the heart, consequent on diminution in the amount of muscular tissue contained in its walls. Of these characters the diminution in weight is the most important. An atrophied heart, according to the common use of the term, is one the weight of which is less than the average weight for a person of the same stature. It is said that, in very rare instances, a heart, the total muscular tissue of which is lessened, and the weight below the normal, may be larger than natural, owing to the dilatation of its cavities. The occurrence of such instances is, by some authorities, denied. If they occur, dilatation is their conspicuous feature, and they come more accurately under that head. Diminished bulk remains a character of those forms of atrophy which may most conveniently be considered under this designation. On the other hand, the muscular tissue of the heart may be lessened in quantity, may have undergone atrophy, when there is increase of other elements in the cardiac wall. In such cases the weight of the heart is, as a rule, not diminished, and these instances are considered under the head of the special degenerations. Only those rare examples will be here alluded to in which the weight of a heart so changed is less than normal.

History.—The important functions always attributed to the heart rendered its atrophy a more anomalous condition, in the eyes of the earlier observers, than its enlargement. Accordingly we find that this condition early attracted attention. Pliny states that the kings of Egypt noted its occurrence. Riolanus alluded to it, and ascribed it to deficiency of the pericardial fluid. A well-marked case was recorded by Soumain at the beginning of the last century.[1] Senac, in 1749, described it carefully in his treatise on the heart,[2] which probably

---

[1] Relation de l'ouverture d'une femme presque sans cœur. Paris, 1728.
[2] Traité de la Structure du Cœur, de son action et de ses maladies. Paris, 1749, tom. ii., p. 393.

remains the longest monograph yet written on cardiac anatomy and pathology. Allan Burns, in 1809, described some very characteristic examples.[1] It is not mentioned by Corvisart, who wrote nearly at the same time. Mérat, in 1813,[2] alluded to several instances which he had seen, and Bertin, in 1824, gave a full account of it, while by his editor, Bouillaud,[3] varieties were subsequently discriminated, which have since been recognised by most writers on the subject.

VARIETIES.—Forms of cardiac atrophy have been distinguished corresponding to the varieties of cardiac hypertrophy. Thus, reduction in the weight of the heart due to mere attenuation of the walls, the cavities remaining of normal size, was termed by Bouillaud, *simple atrophy*.

Reduction in size of the heart, with diminution in the size of its cavities, so that they still bear the normal proportion to the heart, is the *concentric atrophy* of Bouillaud and Walshe,[4] the *simple atrophy* of Hayden.[5]

Attenuation of the cardiac walls and diminished weight of the heart, with increase in the size of the cavities, is the *eccentric atrophy* of Bouillaud, Förster, Walshe, and others. These cases, as just stated, come more properly under the head of dilatation. Hayden applies the term "eccentric atrophy" to a condition of heart, examples of which must be very rare, in which the walls are attenuated, the whole heart smaller, but the cavities larger than normal. As "concentric atrophy" he classes hearts which are smaller than normal, have the walls relatively thickened, and the cavities reduced in capacity. This variety was described by Mérat in 1813. It may be doubted whether either of these two varieties has any real existence; they probably represent only states of contraction or relaxation in atrophied hearts. Chomel distinguished two varieties according to the cause of the atrophy—the *congenital* and *accidental*.[6]

CAUSES.—Smallness of heart may be a congenital or an acquired condition.

A. *Congenital* atrophy is usually well marked. The heart of an adult otherwise free from disease may not exceed that of a child six or seven years old, as in an example mentioned by Allan Burns. The immediate causes of this condition are unknown. Hereditary influence has not, hitherto, been traced. It is said to be more common in women than in men. The subjects of it may be in other respects well formed, but sometimes it has appeared to be part of a more general arrest of development, shown by a childish aspect and defective development of the sexual organs. Parrot[7] doubts the

[1] Allan Burns, Observations on Diseases of the Heart. Edinburgh, 1809, p. 110.
[2] Dictionnaire des Sciences Médicales, Art. Cœur.
[3] Traité clinique des Maladies du Cœur. 2ième. edition. Paris, 1841.
[4] Diseases of the Heart and Great Vessels Fourth edition. London, 1873, p. 274.
[5] Diseases of Heart and Aorta, 1875, p. 585.
[6] Dictionnaire en 30 volumes.
[7] Dictionnaire Encyclopédique des Sciences Médicales, 1876, art. Cœur.

congenital nature of these cases, and believes them to be due to a simultaneous arrest of the growth of the heart and of the sexual organs, occurring at puberty.

B. *Acquired* atrophy may be the result of general or local causes. The chief *general* causes are *chronic wasting diseases*, in which the heart frequently undergoes diminution in size. This may occur in cancer, phthisis, syphilis, chronic suppuration, diabetes. According to the statistics of Quain,[1] the heart is small in about half the cases of phthisis, and the diminution in size is rather more frequent in women than in men. Out of 171 cases, it was small in 53 per cent. of the males, in 67 per cent. of the females. There is no evidence of any special influence exercised by these diseases on the heart. The organ apparently wastes in common with the rest of the body, in consequence of the defective nutrition.

The *local* causes are such as influence directly the nutrition of the heart. *Narrowing of the coronary arteries* is said to be an occasional cause. The influence of this condition is to be more distinctly traced in the production of local degeneration. Walshe, however, regards the influence of pressure in causing local atrophy as due to its effect on the blood supply.

Compression of the heart is apparently, in some cases, a cause of its atrophy. The heart has been found small in long-continued *pericardial effusion*, and the condition has been compared to the contraction of a lung in long-continued effusion into the pleura. *Pericardial adhesions* have been supposed in some cases to have caused cardiac atrophy. The association of the two conditions was first pointed out by Chevers.[2] Hypertrophy and dilatation are more frequent consequences. Kennedy[3] found atrophy in only five out of ninety cases of pericardial adhesion without valve disease. The contraction of tough lymph, resulting from pericarditis, has in some cases been associated with very distinct atrophy of the subjacent portion of the heart.[4] Walshe corroborates this, but believes that the effect is due to pressure upon the arteries. *Compression by fatty tissue* sometimes leads to atrophy of the muscular fibres, especially when the fat is infiltrated among them. The instances of this change in which the heart is smaller than the normal are very rare. Wilks and Moxon mention such a case as an example of "fatty atrophy." The heart weighed only 5½ oz.

Local atrophy, affecting one part of the heart, is due most commonly to the last-described condition, to local infiltration with fat. Occasionally, the limited position of contracting lymph, or narrowing of one coronary artery, may have the same effect.

PATHOLOGICAL ANATOMY.—A heart the subject of atrophy is, as already stated, lessened in weight. The heart of an adult may weigh

---

[1] Lumleian Lectures, 1872. Abstract in Lancet, vol. i., p. 426.
[2] Guy's Hosp. Reports, vol. vii.   [3] Edin. Med. Journal, 1858.
[4] An observation of this kind was recorded by Malpighi.

only six, five, or even four ounces. Quain mentions an instance of the heart weighing only 1 oz. 14 drs. in the case of a girl aged fourteen, who died of phthisis.[1] Its size is also lessened. The circumference at the base may be only six inches. Chomel has recorded an instance in which the heart of an adult did not exceed in size a hen's egg. The thickness of the walls depends chiefly on the condition of the heart, whether contracted or relaxed. The degree of contraction may be estimated by the size of the cavity. In cases of acquired atrophy almost all the adipose tissue has disappeared from the surface, on which the vessels stand out conspicuously. There is often serous infiltration of the fibrous tissue from which the fat has been removed. The texture of the heart may be little changed, or it may be pale in colour and softer than natural. On the other hand, it may be dark, dense, and tougher than natural. The change depends on the presence and form of degeneration, whether fatty or fibroid, partly also on the accumulation of pigment granules within the fibres. The microscope shows the primitive bundles to be lessened in size. The fibres are often fattily degenerated; their striation is lessened, sometimes indistinguishable.[2] The fibrous tissue between the bundles may be increased in quantity. Occasionally, especially in the old, brownish pigment may encircle the nuclei of the fibres, or be uniformly distributed through their substance. When it occurs, the pigmentation is usually generally distributed through the heart, and gives its substance a reddish-brown tint. Rindfleisch[3] has described it as a special form of atrophy—"brown atrophy." Friedreich believes that the pigment is derived from the colouring matter of the muscle.

Associated conditions, causing the atrophy, may coexist. The various general conditions, cancer, phthisis, &c., may be present. Pericardial changes, effusion, lymph, plates of calcification, fatty accumulation, may compress the heart, or there may be from some cause obvious reduction in size of the coronary artery. The pericardial fluid is, according to Bamberger, often increased in quantity as a consequence of the cardiac atrophy.

SYMPTOMS.—The physical signs of atrophy depend on the lessened bulk and diminished force of the heart. The extent of dulness, especially the deep dulness, is smaller than normal. To be significant the diminution must be independent of emphysema or any lung condition obscuring the cardiac dulness. The impulse is weak, and felt over a small area. The sounds may be lessened in intensity, or they may be unchanged. The latter has been the case in Walshe's experience. The pulse is small, the patient weakly. When due to a local cause the symptoms of the local causative condition,

---

[1] Lumleian Lectures, loc. cit.
[2] The "yellow atrophy" of Rindfleisch is fatty degeneration.
[3] Pathologische Gewebelehre, 1875, p. 126.

pericardial effusion, &c., are often present. Palpitation, dyspnœa, and dropsy, are said to occur in cases of acquired atrophy from local malnutrition. The quantity of blood remains unchanged, and the small heart obstructs the circulation. When due to a general state, the heart suffers in common with the blood and the rest of the system, so that the special failing is unnoticed.

The general conditions associated with atrophy of the heart were, in part at least, attributed by the earlier writers to the influence of the cardiac state. Phthisis especially was believed to be entirely due to the small size of the heart, so often found associated with it. It is customary now, as already stated, to regard the small size of the heart as secondary to the general state, and to attribute to it no causative influence.

DIAGNOSIS.—In determining, post mortem, the existence of atrophy, weight should be taken as the test. The error of mistaking contraction for atrophy will thus be avoided. Burns suggested, as a means of avoiding the same error, a comparison between the size of the heart and of the pericardium. The size of the body should always be taken into consideration. It is rarely that atrophy of the heart can be diagnosed during life. It may be suspected when a weak impulse and diminished dulness coincide with signs of cardiac failure and with some recognised causal condition.

PROGNOSIS.—Little can be done to remedy the condition, even when its existence is recognised. The prognosis is therefore unfavourable, but it is always subordinate to that of the condition to which the atrophy is secondary.

TREATMENT.—The treatment is in the main that of the causal state. In general wasting diseases the atrophy of the heart corresponds to its diminished use, and needs no special treatment beyond general tonics, cod-liver oil, nux vomica, &c. When secondary to local changes, little can be done by treatment beyond the removal as far as possible of the fluid pressing on the heart, or the diminution, by dietetic management, of accumulations of fat.

HYPERTROPHY OF THE HEART.

By W. R. Gowers, M.D.

SYNONYMS.—Enlargement of the Heart, Dilatation of the Heart (old writers); Active Aneurism (Corvisart); Uniform Enlargement of the Heart, distinguished from dilatation (Allan Burns); Hypersarcosis Cordis (Lallemand).

DEFINITION.—An overgrowth of the muscular tissue which forms the walls of the heart. Besides muscular tissue the heart contains connective tissue and adipose tissue. An increase in either of these constituents may be, and has been, spoken of as an element in cardiac hypertrophy. Thus "fatty hypertrophy" and "connective tissue hypertrophy," or "false hypertrophy," of the heart have been described. It seems more in accordance with the nomenclature applied to other organs to consider these changes as allied to degenerations, and to confine the term "hypertrophy" to increase in the muscular tissue of the heart. Increased thickness of the endocardium and pericardium, which often coexists with muscular hypertrophy, and is sometimes regarded as part of it, is described separately in the articles "Endocarditis" and "Pericarditis."

HISTORY.—The earliest allusions to enlargement of the heart appear to be those of Nicolaus Massa in 1559[1] and of Vesalius. Enlargement with thickening of the walls was described in the seventeenth century by Albertini, by our own countryman Mayow, and by Blancard. Its origin in overwork due to obstruction in the circulation was clearly pointed out by Mayow, who in 1674 described the dependence of hypertrophy of the right ventricle on mitral constriction.[2]

Vieussens[3] in 1715 alluded to the origin of hypertrophy of the left ventricle in the overwork caused by constriction of the aortic

---

[1] Nicolaus Massa, Anatomiæ Liber Introductorius. Venice, 1559, p. 56.

[2] "Inasmuch as the blood, on account of the obstruction, could not pass freely into the left ventricle, it necessarily happened that the vessels of the lungs, and also the right ventricle, were distended with blood; as a consequence the heart, particularly the right ventricle, would have to contract more violently, in order that it might as far as possible propel the blood through the lungs on to the left ventricle. This again explains why the walls of the right ventricle were so strong and dense, since this chamber, being submitted to more violent action, would be enlarged beyond the rest." Mayow, Tractatus medico-physici, Oxonii, 1674. De Motu Musculari, cap. vii. The translation is that of Cockle, On Insufficiency of the Aortic Valves. London, 1861.

[3] Traité du Cœur, 1715.

orifice, and the effect of obstruction in causing enlargement was systematically described by Senac in his treatise published in 1749.[1]

Enlargement from overgrowth without dilatation was mentioned by Morgagni[2] in 1779, by Burserius in 1798,[3] and later by Corvisart in 1806, and distinguished by Allan Burns in 1809, who recorded an example of a heart "weighing several pounds, in which the cavities were not more capacious than natural." Corvisart gave a clear description of the various forms of hypertrophy with dilatation, and recognised the frequency with which the left ventricle is affected. Although he mentioned the occurrence of hypertrophy without dilatation, he did not include it in his account of the forms of enlargement,[4] but described all enlargements of the heart as "aneurisms," classifying them as "active" or "passive," according as there was or was not hypertrophy. Bertin, in a memoir read before the Académie des Sciences in 1811,[5] pointed out the special character of hypertrophy and its isolated occurrence. It was also carefully distinguished by Kreysig in 1816.[6] But in France the nomenclature of Corvisart continued in use by Mérat, Cloquet,[7] and Cruveilhier until, and indeed long after, the publication of Bertin's treatise on diseases of the heart[8] in 1824 gave currency to his distinction of the "concentric," "simple," and "eccentric" forms of hypertrophy. Bertin also demonstrated by microscopical examination that the increase of the heart's substance in hypertrophy depends on an overgrowth of muscular tissue, and also endeavoured to show, by a chemical examination of the tissue of the two ventricles, that the quantity of fat in the hypertrophied muscle was less than in the normal portion.[9] He also ably vindicated hypertrophy from some of its supposed consequences.

Avenbrugger in 1763 first employed percussion as a means of ascertaining and estimating enlargement of the heart. The example was followed by Corvisart, who translated Avenbrugger's work. Bertin advocated auscultation as a means of distinguishing the "concentric" and "eccentric" forms. The alterations in the heart-sounds in hypertrophy were, however, first accurately stated by Laennec.[10]

---

[1] Traité de la Structure du Cœur, de son action et de ses maladies, par M. Senac. Paris, 1749. Tom. ii., p. 408.

[2] "Ventriculus dexter corveam quidem secundum naturam, sed crassissimas parietes habebat." De sedibus et Causis morborum. Epist. xvii., art. 22. See also Epist. xxix., art. 20.

[3] The Institutions of the Practice of Medicine, by J. Baptist Burserius, of Kamfeld, 1798. Translated by Cullen Brown. Vol. v. p. 312. Edinburgh, 1803.

[4] This accounts for Laennec's assertion that the occurrence of hypertrophy without dilatation escaped the notice of Corvisart. Bertin pointed out that the condition is described by Corvisart in a case of aneurism of the aorta. "The left ventricle, without being so dilated, had much stronger and thicker parietes than usual." On Diseases of the Heart, Hebb's Translation, p. 283.

[5] Mem. de l'Académie Royale des Sciences, 1811.

[6] Die Krankheiten des Herzens, Theil ii., Abt. i., p. 460.

[7] Dict. des Sciences Médicales, art. Cœur. 1813.

[8] Traité des Maladies du Cœur et des Gros Vaisseaux, by R. J. Bertin. Rédigé par Bouillaud. Paris, 1824. [9] Loc. cit., p. 300.

[10] A Treatise on Diseases of the Chest, Forbes' Trans. 1821, p. 372.

VARIETIES.—The hypertrophy may be *general,* when each portion of the heart is affected, or *local,* when only part of the heart is changed. When the result of the change is a simple increase in the thickness of the wall, without any change in the size of the cavity, the hypertrophy is called "*simple;*" when there is dilatation of the cavity as well as hypertrophy of the walls, the hypertrophy has been termed "*eccentric.*" "Hypertrophy with dilatation," or "dilated hypertrophy" are other names which have been applied to this condition. If, on the other hand, the cavity is lessened in size, the hypertrophy has been termed "*concentric.*" The existence of this form is doubtful; it is probable that the supposed permanent reduction in the size of the cavity is merely the result of a strong contraction. "Mixed" hypertrophy was the designation given by Bertin to the condition in which one part of a ventricle is thinned and another thickened.

CAUSES AND PATHOLOGY.—A. *Predisposing Causes.*—Strictly speaking, hypertrophy of the heart cannot be said to have any morbid predisposing causes. It is a healthy reaction against a morbid influence, and the conditions which permit its occurrence are those of health. Every divergence from a state of health, which does not immediately excite hypertrophy of the heart, tends to hinder its occurrence. The only general or distant morbid states which are concerned in its production are the antecedents of its exciting causes, and these cannot, strictly, be regarded as "predisposing." Hereditary taint, sex, and age influence the occurrence of the exciting causes of hypertrophy, and render the condition twice as frequent in males as in females (Walshe), and frequent in proportion to age, because men are by occupation and exposure liable to the causes of hypertrophy more than women, and hypertrophy is frequently the result of degenerative changes, the tendency to which increases with age.

Four conditions of health may be considered as especially predisposing to hypertrophy.

(1) General nutritive energy of the system. This influence is shown in the tendency of the normal tissue elements to increase, under certain local stimuli; its defect by their tendency to waste, to degenerate, and give place, under the local nutritive stimulus, to tissue elements of lower vital capacity. This influence is greater in the young than in the old. Its effect in determining the occurrence or the degree of hypertrophy is masked by the greater frequency and greater force of the causes of hypertrophy in later life. It is seen, however, in the rarity with which considerable hypertrophy is developed in old age.

(2) Nutritive quality of blood. The influence of this condition is obvious, and is seen in the distinct increase in hypertrophy which often follows the administration of hæmatinics, as iron, and a good supply of food.

(3) The supply to the cardiac walls of a due quantity of blood. The force of the circulation within the cardiac walls is proportioned

to the distension of the aorta.[1] Hence, whatever interferes with the quantity of blood entering the aorta lessens, *cæteris paribus*, the capacity of the heart for overgrowth; whatever increases the quantity of blood sent into the aorta, and increases the tension of the blood in it, increases the blood-supply to the heart, increases its capacity for overgrowth. This is no doubt one of the conditions which determines the great hypertrophy so common in aortic regurgitation. The distension of the aorta at the end of the ventricular systole, when the coronary arteries are being filled, is, in that disease, extreme.[2]

(4) The greater (within limits) the proportional amount of rest of the heart, the more perfect is its nutrition. The period available for nutrition is greater when the contractions are infrequent than when they are frequent. The systole is nearly of the same duration at different frequencies; increased frequency in contraction is at the expense of the diastole. Hence infrequent contraction favours the development of hypertrophy when its exciting cause exists. The actual influence of this condition is obscured by the increase in the exciting cause, overwork, which frequency of action involves.

B. *Exciting Causes.*—As far as is at present known muscular hypertrophy has but one immediate cause—increase of work. . The operation of this cause, the " physiological stimulus," as it has been termed, may be traced in almost every instance in which hypertrophy is found. Each apparent exception becomes conformable to the rule when the conditions under which the hypertrophy began are accurately known. The over-action of the heart is the cause of its overgrowth. Such over-action may be primary, or it may be secondary to an increased resistance to its action. Primary over-action commonly takes the form of increased frequency of contraction. Secondary over-action is in the form of increased force of contraction. But the distinction is not absolute, as will appear immediately.

Other causes have been assumed to account for hypertrophy in cases in which the influence of increased work could not be clearly traced. An irritative influence of the blood on the heart, leading directly to its overgrowth, has been assumed in order to account for some cases of hypertrophy. But there are at present no facts to support the idea that any blood state, any nutritive influence other than the physiological stimulus, ever leads to overgrowth of muscular tissue.[3]

I. *Simple Over-action of the Heart*, the conditions of the circula-

[1] This was very clearly taught by Corvisart. " The heart . . . will have to drive forward, through the narrow artery, too great a column of blood . . . which will necessarily react upon the agent which impels it. . . . Finally, the coronary arteries as well as the capillaries of the heart, remaining in a permanent state of fulness, will supply more nourishing matter to the fleshy substance of this organ ; whence arise, without doubt, the increase, at least in part, of its vital energy . . . the greater consistence of the parietes, and the more vigorous action of the organ."—Loc. cit., p. 60.

[2] Milner Fothergill (Diseases of the Heart, p. 65) maintains that the blood-supply to the heart walls is deficient in aortic regurgitation, because the tension in the aorta so soon falls. But, from the short course of the coronary arteries, their distension must be rapid, and related, in degree, to the degree of the tension of the aortic blood, rather than to the duration of the tension.

[3] The conditions of overgrowth in different tissues no doubt vary widely. In some,

tion and heart entailing no increased resistance, *i.e.* no primary increase of work—is always the consequence of deranged innervation. Its nervous mechanism is at present ill-understood. It is extremely doubtful whether a simple increase in the force, without change in the frequency, of the heart's action, ever results from this influence. Increased frequency is the common result. The more frequent contractions are often apparently more forcible. Such over-action of the heart is well seen in simple nervous palpitation, and most strikingly in exophthalmic goitre. Continuous emotional excitement is a powerful cause of it. It is produced also by the influence of many agents, such as alcohol, tea, and coffee. It is produced also by general muscular effort. Effort acts, it must be remembered, in another way, by causing increased resistance to the movement of the blood.[1]

Such increased frequency of contraction tends to cause hypertrophy only in so far as it increases the total work of the heart. It does this, however, in more than one way. (1) Part of the work of the heart consists in the movement of its own mass. No doubt this is but a small fraction of its total labour, but it is a definite quantity, and increases directly as the frequency of contraction. (2) Although simple increase in the frequency of contraction of the heart does not necessarily increase that part of the heart's work which consists in the propulsion of the blood, it does practically effect such an increase. If a heart contracts at twice the normal frequency, and the blood enters the heart at the normal rate, only, say, one-half of the normal quantity of blood will at each diastole enter, and at each systole be discharged. The work of the heart in propelling the blood would thus remain the same. Practically, however, increased frequency of contraction tends to quicken the whole circulation, so that under the circumstances assumed, more than half the normal quantity of blood would at each contraction enter and leave the heart.

hyperplasia of the proper tissue-elements is induced by any local irritant. This has suggested a generalisation which asserts a common basis for hypertrophy and inflammation. The conclusion, true of some tissues, is quite inapplicable to muscular fibres. (*Vide* Moxon, Med. Times and Gazette, Nov. 26, 1870.) But the theory has obtained in Germany wide currency and application, so that a recent writer (Zielonko, Virchow's Archiv, 1872) gives, as an example of hypertrophy of the heart, the enlargement which resulted from the insertion of a seton in its substance, although microscopical examination showed only ordinary inflammatory products as the cause of the enlargement. Henry Green (Clin. Soc. Trans., vol. ii.) has suggested that hypertrophy of the heart may sometimes be due to the irritative influence of the blood in rheumatism, but the evidence which he has adduced is chiefly clinical, and possesses little weight in comparison with the almost uniform significance of pathological facts.

[1] Les mouvemens violents donnent souvent plus de masse au cœur de même que les maladies : nous réduirons ces mouvemens aux exercises fatiguants, à l'agitation qui suit les excès du vin, et à celle qui causent les passions (Senac, loc. cit., tom. ii., p. 400). Corvisart recorded his conviction that the passions were the most powerful cause of organic diseases of the heart, and instanced the influence of the French revolution in causing the malady (loc. cit., pp. 322 and 323). Statistics furnished by Parr, and given by Quain in his Lumleian Lectures, show that the deaths of males at all ages from heart disease have increased fifty per cent. on the increase in population, and that this increase affects adult life almost exclusively (Lancet, 1872, vol i. p. 392).

Hence the tension of the arterial blood becomes increased, and the pulse fuller and less compressible. Reflex relaxation of the peripheral arterioles, the natural effect of increased tension, relieves, but often incompletely, this increased tension. Thus the intra-ventricular pressure and the work of the heart are increased. (3) The heart, acting thus with excessive frequency, may act also with excess of force. The increased force may be felt under such circumstances. The heart "thumps" against the ribs. In the pulse the increased force often is unnoticed on account of the smaller quantity of blood which leaves the left ventricle at each contraction. It should be remembered that many circumstances which increase the frequency, also, at the same time, increase the force of the heart's action. Muscular effort is one of these.

This then is the mechanism by which increased frequency of contraction may cause hypertrophy. Its total influence is not, however, great. Increase in frequency of contraction is rarely of long duration under circumstances of due nutritive energy, and it is not often that hypertrophy can be ascribed with probability to simple primary overaction of the heart.

II. *Increased Resistance to the Action of the Heart* is unquestionably the chief cause of its hypertrophy. Such resistance may be in the form of (1) traction from without, or of (2) pressure within the contracting organ.

(1) As a matter of fact pericardial adhesions are frequently associated with cardiac hypertrophy;[1] and, according to Wilks,[2] with hypertrophy of the right ventricle much more frequently than of the left. It is easily conceivable that such adhesions may oppose the diminution in size, and change of shape, which the heart undergoes during its contraction. But for such adhesions to hinder a contracting heart, the external surface of the pericardium must be connected with more than usual firmness to the adjacent structures. It is not certain, moreover, that resistance to contraction applied from without has the same effect as resistance applied within the heart, and the conditions are so complex that it is impossible to trace the direct influence of the adhesions in causing the hypertrophy. Dilatation is invariably, under such circumstances, associated with the hypertrophy of the heart. It would seem to be a more direct result of the pericardial adhesion than the hypertrophy, both as the simple effect of the external traction, and as the result of the weakening of the wall of the heart by the sub-pericardial changes. But dilatation tends in itself, as will be shown immediately, to produce hypertrophy, and the hypertrophy in an adherent heart, without other cause of hypertrophy, is commonly not more than the dilatation might account for. The effect of pericardial adhesions is considered at greater length, in the article on Dilatation of the Heart. Their direct influence in causing hypertrophy must be regarded as possible, but unproved.

[1] As Morgagni, Beau, Hope, and others have especially noticed.
[2] Guy's Hosp. Reports, vol. xvi., p. 202.

(2) Increased blood-pressure within the heart during its systole is the common cause of its muscular over-growth. This is the element which underlies most of the conditions capable of giving rise to hypertrophy. This increased pressure may be due to one of two causes; (*a*) the mass of blood to be moved may be abnormally large; (*b*) there may be an abnormal obstruction to the movement of the blood. The effect of each condition is to augment the resistance to be overcome by the contracting fibres—to increase the work of the heart.

(*a*) The mass of blood to be moved may be abnormally large. This condition exists in all forms of over-distension of the heart. Dilatation cannot exist without an increase in the work of the heart. Hence hypertrophy is its almost invariable concomitant—invariable when the nutritive conditions are such as to render growth of muscular fibre possible.

The mechanism of over-distension is considered fully in the article on Dilatation of the Heart. It may be direct or indirect. It is direct when a cavity is over-filled by the contraction of an over-distended chamber behind it. Thus in mitral regurgitation the left ventricle is over-filled by the contraction of the over-distended left auricle, and becomes dilated and hypertrophied; or the over-distension may be indirect, the result of a supply of blood to the chamber from a double source— the regurgitation of blood into the chamber and its supply in the normal course of the circulation. Thus the left ventricle becomes over-distended, dilated, and often enormously hypertrophied in aortic regurgitation; and the left auricle becomes dilated and hypertrophied in mitral regurgitation. So, too, in dilatation from the weakening of the wall consequent on pericarditis, hypertrophy commonly ensues. No doubt in these conditions of dilatation the whole of the blood is not always expelled from the ventricle at each systole, but the intra-cardiac pressure during the systole is still increased, and with it the work of the heart.

Plethora has been supposed to cause cardiac hypertrophy. Niemeyer points out that the transient plethora induced by a hearty meal with much fluid may, if habitually repeated, have such an influence. The action of the kidneys commonly prevents any permanent distension of the vessels from this cause.

(*b*) There may be an obstruction to the movement of the blood superadded to that which exists in health. This obstruction may be situated within or without the heart. Within the heart, it may be at the orifice by which the blood leaves the chamber affected. Thus an obstruction at an auriculo-ventricular orifice will cause hypertrophy of the corresponding auricle; obstruction at the orifice of the pulmonary artery will cause hypertrophy of the right ventricle; obstruction at the aortic orifice will cause hypertrophy of the left ventricle. In all these cases dilatation may be conjoined with the hypertrophy, and increase its amount.

The obstruction may be outside the heart. It may be in the larger arteries, the aorta and pulmonary artery. Their calibre may be reduced by pressure upon them (as by an aneurism of another vessel), or by constriction due to changes in their walls.[1] The hypertrophy which occasionally occurs in long-continued displacement of the heart, whether from pleural effusions or deformities of the thorax, consequent on curvatures of the spine, &c., is probably due chiefly to the increased obstruction in the great vessels from their displacement and altered course.[2]

Aortic aneurism has been regarded as a cause of hypertrophy of the left ventricle since the days of Corvisart. The association of the two has frequently been noted, and has been referred by Niemeyer to the law in physics according to which the resistance encountered by a liquid moving through a tube is increased if the tube be suddenly expanded, just as if it be contracted. But it is a matter of considerable doubt whether hypertrophy does occur as a simple consequence of aortic aneurism. Senac long ago expressed a doubt upon the subject.[3] Stokes affirmed that "we have no reason to believe that the existence of aneurism in any portion of the aorta throws additional labour on the heart, and hence we commonly find a small heart co-existing with "a vast aneurism."[4] Walshe also regarded the hypertrophy as an occasional consequence, and not invariable even when the sac of the aneurism was situated near the sigmoid valves. The observations of Axel Key,[5] indeed, suggest the question whether hypertrophy of the heart is not more common when the aneurism is far from, than when near the heart. He has recorded eighteen cases of aneurism near the heart, in not one of which was there hypertrophy of the left ventricle. In most of the cases, indeed, the muscle was more or less thinned, with or without slight dilatation, especially of the lower part of the cavity. Considerable dilatation seemed related to disease of the aortic valves, not to the aneurism. In several cases the cavity of the ventricle was positively diminished in capacity, although the walls were thinned. In some instances the muscle of the conus arteriosus was thick, while the rest was thin. The atrophy of the muscular tissue was most marked in some cases in which the aneurism lay near the heart. He suggests as an explanation of this singular atrophy of the left ventricle, the pressure of the aneurism on the pulmonary artery, lessening the amount of blood reaching the left ventricle, and the withdrawal from the circulation of the blood contained in the sac of a large aneurism.

[1] Hypertrophy of the left ventricle has been produced artificially by Zielonko, in the guinea-pig by tying a ligature round the aorta, and thus reducing its calibre. Virchow's Archiv, Bd. 62, Heft I. p. 22.

[2] See Hilton Fagge, Path. Traus., vol. xvii.

[3] "It is certain that the dilatation of these vessels (aorta and pulmonary artery) have not always the consequence (of causing enlargement of the heart)." He goes on to describe a case in which the aorta was dilated to the size of a head, from the arch to the diaphragm, in which the volume of the heart was normal. Senac, Traité, &c., 1749, tom. ii., p. 407.

[4] Diseases of the Heart and Aorta, p. 579.

[5] Nord. Med. Ark. 1869, I. 4, Nr. 22, and Schmidt's Jahrbuch, vol. 150, p. 21.

Degenerative changes in the arteries cause a considerable increase in the total work of the heart, and are effective causes of hypertrophy. The increased resistance which they produce is due to the loss of elasticity in the vessels, their more tortuous course, and the increased friction from roughening of their inner surface. In health the elastic vessels yield before the blood which is thrown into them. When elasticity is lost the vessels approximate to rigid tubes, and the resistance they present is consequently increased. By the increased tortuosity of the vessels, due to the loss of elasticity, their absolute length becomes greater, and the friction of the blood against the wall of the vessel is also increased. These degenerative changes are usually found, in greater or less degree, after middle life, and are probably the cause of the increase in the thickness of the left ventricle, which has been said by Bizot[1] to occur during the later period of life. Degenerative changes may be a consequence as well as a cause of cardiac hypertrophy, the result of the increased strain to which the vessels are exposed. This fact, which will be considered presently, must not be forgotten in estimating the significance of the association.

The obstruction may be situated in the minute arterioles and capillaries. In certain diseases of the lungs obstruction from this cause may be traced. In emphysema many vessels are destroyed, and those which remain are elongated and narrowed by the over-distension of the air-cells. The obstruction to the passage of the blood through the lungs is thus very much increased, and hypertrophy and dilatation of the right ventricle result, and may be carried to a high degree. Hypertrophy of the heart is not infrequent in phthisis; Quain states that in 171 cases it was present in 25 per cent. of the males, 7 per cent. of the females. The conditions of lung to which it is related have not yet been ascertained, but in cirrhosis of the lung it is especially frequent; the compression and destruction of the minute vessels by the contracting tissue produce the obstruction. Compression of the lung tissue by pleural effusion is said to have a similar effect. In all these conditions, if long continued, hypertrophy of the right ventricle may occur.

Long-continued muscular effort entails cardiac hypertrophy. As Clifford Allbutt and Myers have shown, the influence of this cause can often be distinctly traced, especially (Milner Fothergill says) among those who work with the arms. Animals frequently afford instances of the remarkable effect which this cause is capable of producing. The most celebrated instance is that of the Irish greyhound "Master Magrath," the heart of which bore three times its normal proportion to the body-weight, and no cause for the enlargement but extreme and long-continued exertion could be discovered.[2] The increased work in which the hypertrophy arises is probably in part the result of the increased frequency and force with which, in

[1] Mémoirs de la Société Médicale d'Observ. de Paris, 1836.
[2] Haughton, British Medical Journal, Jan. 20, 1872.

consequence of the respiratory needs, the heart acts. But it is in part the result of the compression of the capillaries of the muscles by the contracting fibres, and also the result of the compression of the arterial trunks by the rigid muscles. The total resistance to the action of the heart is thereby considerably increased. This resistance is not a matter of conjecture. Increase in arterial pressure during general muscular contraction has been demonstrated experimentally by Traube.

During pregnancy the addition of the placental to the systemic circulation involves a considerable addition to the work of the heart. Larcher [1] found, on examination of the hearts of 100 women who died in child-birth, that the wall of the left ventricle was invariably thickened. The average thickness was ·015 m. (about $\frac{5}{8}$ inch). His observations have been confirmed by the clinical investigations of Duroziez, who found that the greater the number of pregnancies the more permanent is the enlargement. He asserts that the enlargement continues through the whole of the lactation period. Friedreich, however, expresses some doubt on the subject.[2]

The remarkable hypertrophy of the heart which is met with in Bright's disease must be considered among those which result from obstruction to the flow through the minuter vessels. It occurs in all forms of chronic kidney disease, most frequently in the contracted kidney, least frequently in the lardaceous form. According to Grainger Stewart, it is invariable in the last stage of the acute inflammatory affection, in which, the disease having assumed a chronic form, the kidney undergoes reduction in bulk.

The hypertrophy which occurs in this condition is confined to the left ventricle, and is often uncomplicated by dilatation. It is frequently considerable in amount. Among such hearts the best examples of simple hypertrophy are met with. After death the heart often remains firmly contracted, and the characters of a concentric hypertrophy are simulated. Dilatation may co-exist with the hypertrophy in consequence of coincident degeneration.

The association of this hypertrophy of the heart with kidney disease was first pointed out by Bright in 1827[3] as so remarkable that some causal connection between the two must exist, and he afterwards, in 1836,[4] expressed his opinion "either that the altered quality of the blood affords irregular and unwonted stimulus to the organ immediately, or that it so affects the minute and capillary circulation as to render greater action necessary to send the blood through the distant subdivisions of the vascular system." The latter theory is that which has obtained general acceptance, with certain modifications to be alluded to more fully. Modern investigation, while it has extended our knowledge of the conditions under which

---

[1] Archives Gén. de Méd., Mars 1859, and note by Larcher appended to a paper by Menière, *Ibid*, tom. xvi 1828, p. 521.
[2] Herzkrankheiten, p. 288. [3] Med. Reports, p. 23.
[4] Guy's Hosp. Reports, vol. i. p 397.

the hypertrophy arises, has scarcely carried us further in our explanation.

The most important addition to our knowledge is certainly the fact that increased tension of the arterial blood commonly occurs in those cases of Bright's disease in which hypertrophy of the heart is so often found. The hardness of the pulse in such cases had long been remarked, but its significance was not generally recognised until the sphygmograph, by supplying a measure of its degree, drew attention to its importance as supplying independent evidence of an obstruction to the movement of the blood through the smaller vessels.

Traube,[1] who first called attention to the significance of the increased arterial tension, assumed, in effect, that the increased resistance within the kidney was the cause of the obstruction. The theory has been largely accepted in Germany, but its manifest inadequacy has prevented it from meeting even partial acceptance in this country. It is said[2] that Traube himself before his death ceased to hold it in its original form.

In the smaller arteries a remarkable change of structure was pointed out by George Johnson in 1850· as hypertrophy of the muscular coat.[3] First discovered in the kidney, the change was soon found to be general throughout the system. The occurrence of such increased thickness of the walls of the arteries is now generally admitted, and the view that the thickening is due to hypertrophy of the muscular coat has received very wide confirmation. Muscular over-action being the only known cause of muscular hypertrophy, Johnson at first ascribed the vascular change to the same cause as the hypertrophy of the heart—the resistance to the movement of the blood through the capillaries. It was assumed that the arteries by their contraction aided the circulation of the blood, and over-acted to overcome the increased resistance. But with the fall of the theory of arterial propulsion, this explanation became untenable. The function of the muscular coat of the vessels being, as far as is known, the adjustment of the calibre of the vessel, permanent spasmodic contraction became the only explanation of the hypertrophy, and has been for many years ably maintained by Johnson. That such spasm exists is, on Johnson's facts, highly probable, and may, the writer believes, be actually seen in the arteries of the retina in most cases of Bright's disease in which a high arterial tension exists. The effect of such spasm must be an increased resistance to the movement of the blood in the arteries, an augmentation of its tension. Instead of aiding, it thus directly opposes the action of the heart. That it is the sole cause of the increased resistance may be doubted. Even if it

---

[1] Zusammenhang zwischen Herz u. Nierenkrankheiten, Berlin, 1856.

[2] By Milner Fothergill, Diseases of the Heart, p. 286. The inadequate character of Traube's theory led Bamberger into a denial of Traube's facts, relative to the increased obstruction to the movement of the blood, and consequently increased arterial pressure. But these facts may now be considered to be established, and the details of the controversy between Traube and Bamberger have ceased to be instructive.

[3] Med.·Chir. Trans., vol. xxxiii., 1850, p. 107.

were the only cause, the difficulty is not lessened, for we arc almost as ignorant of its origin as we are of the nature of any obstruction due to the changed composition of the blood. The natural effect of increased arterial tension, increased endocardial pressure, is immediate relaxation of the minute arteries, and freer circulation. The spasm of the vessels under these circumstances is therefore a phenomenon very difficult to explain. Ludwig asserts on experimental grounds that it is due to the action of the retained urinary salts on the vaso-motor centre.

The existence of the hypertrophy of the muscular coat of the arteries has, however, been denied by Gull and Sutton,[1] who ascribe the thickening to a "fibrosis," and attribute the resistance to the movement of the blood to the obstruction in the vessels due to the inelasticity of this tissue. They do not regard the fibrosis as the consequence of the renal disease, but as a primary general change, of which the affection of the kidney is only one local instance. This theory of the primary general character of Bright's disease accords very well with the phenomena of some cases, but as an explanation of all cases of contracting kidneys it is open to some objections apart from the weight which must be attached to Johnson's observations. In many cases of contracting kidney there is certainly fibroid over-growth to be found widely distributed, but the degree of change in the kidney is incomparably greater than that in other organs, so as to suggest strongly the idea of a primary affection of the kidney. Another fact to be taken into consideration is that, whatever be the cause of the hypertrophy of the heart in the contracted kidney, a similar hypertrophy results as a remote consequence of kidney disease unquestionably local in its origin. In later stages of an acute nephritis, hypertrophy of the heart is even more frequent than in the primary contracting kidney, and is associated with the same increased arterial tension.

The conclusion then seems to be that hypertrophy of the heart occurs in kidney diseases as a result of increased arterial blood-pressure, the result of some obstruction to the movement of the blood in the minute vessels; that such obstruction is in many cases the indirect consequence of the kidney disease; that it is accompanied in most cases with a morbid state of the smaller arteries, to which it is in part to be ascribed.

Lastly, in some cases, the obstruction causing the hypertrophy of one ventricle may be situated, not in the vessels, large or small, but beyond them, in the other side of the heart. Thus in mitral obstruction, the right ventricle is very constantly hypertrophied; in obstruction in the pulmonary system and right side of the heart, the left ventricle may become hypertrophied. The obstruction may even be on the same side of the heart, and act through both systems of vessels, the pulmonary and the systemic. Thus mitral regurgitation

---

[1] Med.-Chir. Trans vol. lv. 1872,

may, as Friedreich has remarked, cause not only congestion of the lungs, distension of the right side of the heart, over-filling of the systemic venous system, but increase on the tension of the arterial blood, and thus cause an increase in the work of the left ventricle, and an increase in its hypertrophy. It is not easy to understand the mechanism by which this arterial distension is effected, but as a clinical fact it is unquestionable, and occurs especially in cases of mitral regurgitation, in which the left ventricle is greatly dilated and hypertrophied. It is perhaps to be ascribed to the effect of the secondary dilatation of the right side of the heart in augmenting the mechanical obstruction. A tracing from a pulse in such a condition is shown in Fig. 1, p. 714.

It may be convenient to group the causes of hypertrophy which have been described, first, according to their position (Table I.), secondly, according to their effect (Table II.).

TABLE I.

EXCITING CAUSES OF CARDIAC HYPERTROPHY.

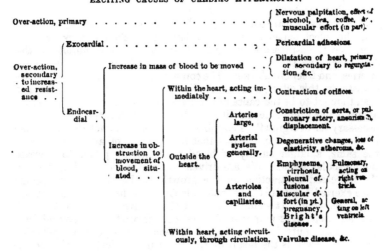

TABLE II.

CAUSES OF HYPERTROPHY.

AFFECTING—
 ALL PARTS OF HEART—
  Over-action from nervous and toxic influences.
  Dilatation of cavities.
  Displacement of heart.

LEFT VENTRICLE—
  Mitral regurgitation.
  Constriction and regurgitation at aortic orifice.
  Constriction or compression of aorta.
  Aneurism of aorta (?).
  Degeneration of arterial system.
  Renal disease.
  Pregnancy.
  Muscular efforts.
  Valvular disease of right side of heart, and all causes of dilata-
    tion of right ventricle.

LEFT AURICLE—
  Mitral constriction and incompetence.

RIGHT VENTRICLE—
  Constriction or regurgitation at pulmonary orifice.
  Constriction of or pressure on pulmonary artery.
  Degeneration of pulmonary arteries.
  Lung diseases, obstructing, compressing, and destroying vessels.
    Chronic bronchitis.
    Emphysema.
    Cirrhosis.
    Pleural effusion.
  Affections of mitral orifice.

RIGHT AURICLE—Regargitation and constriction at tricuspid orifice.

By what mechanism the increased work leads to muscular overgrowth we have little knowledge. The theory has been put forward
that the effect depends on reflex dilatation of the coronary arteries.
Increased blood-pressure within the heart is known to inhibit, by the
depressor nerve, the vaso-motor system, causing dilatation of the minute
arteries, and freer circulation. The coronary arteries are believed to participate in this effect, and the readier circulation through them has
been thought to be the cause of the hypertrophy. That such an action
occurs is most probable, and it is probable that thus the nourishment
necessary for overgrowth is supplied. But that it is not the sole cause
is almost certain, from the fact that if the work of a muscle remains
the same, a larger supply of blood to it has no power to increase
the muscular tissue. We are driven to assume a direct influence of
the increased contraction on the growth of the fibre. The average
force exerted habitually by a muscle is far below its possible maximum
at any moment. It would seem as if this average force, and the bulk
of the muscle, were proportioned, that an increase in the habitual force
leads, in due nutritive conditions, to muscular over-growth. Whether
this over-growth is the result of the direct mechanical stimulus to the
contracting fibre, or whether it is the result of a reflex influence exerted
through the nervous system, and excited by the increased pressure on
the endocardium or by the increased tension on the contracting fibres,
we do not know.

One condition is, however, essential for the development of hypertrophy—time. A certain period is necessary for growth of old, or
for the development of new tissue. Dilatation may occur quickly;
hypertrophy can only take place slowly. Hence the rapidity with
which an increased resistance is developed largely influences the

resulting condition of heart. Obstruction is usually slowly developed, regurgitation may occur rapidly, and this is one reason why the former entails so much simpler an hypertrophy than the latter.' So, too, in the obstruction which is developed in the most gradual manner, that of Bright's disease, uncomplicated hypertrophy is commoner than in any other morbid state. The related conditions of origin of hypertrophy and dilatation are considered more fully in the article on Dilatation.

A few cases of hypertrophy have been recorded in which no mechanical cause for the hypertrophy could be discovered. Their proportion to the cases of hypertrophy in which a mechanical influence can be traced is very small, so small that it is probable that some such cause may have existed and have escaped observation. Some of the cases were recorded before the relation of hypertrophy of the heart to kidney disease was well known, and the existence of the latter may easily have been overlooked. In Bristowe's case of "hypertrophy without sufficient cause," recorded in the Path. Trans., vol. v., p. 82, the heart, which weighed twenty-seven ounces, was uniformly enlarged and hypertrophied without local disease, but the kidneys were reduced in size, and granular, and presented atrophy of the Malpighian bodies. In other cases the increased bulk of the organ is due to an increase in the fibrous, as well as in the muscular tissue. Such was the case in a heart weighing forty ounces, preserved in St. George's Hospital Museum, and supposed to be an example of true hypertrophy, until Quain examined it, and discovered its real nature.

PATHOLOGICAL ANATOMY.—Hypertrophy may occur in each division of the heart, but varies in different parts, both in the frequency of its occurrence and in the degree commonly attained. The comparative affection of the different parts of the heart depends partly on the frequency and degree with which the causes of hypertrophy affect the different portions, and partly on the amount of muscular tissue each part possesses, and by which it is enabled to resist rather than yield to the internal pressure, which is the cause of the hypertrophy. The left ventricle is that affected most frequently, and in the greatest degree. Next in frequency and degree comes the right ventricle; then the left auricle; lastly, the right auricle. It is rare for the hypertrophy to be general, and to affect all parts of the heart. More commonly it is partial, affecting one part only. The increase in the weight of the heart is the invariable characteristic of hypertrophy. Since the healthy heart consists almost exclusively of muscular tissue, over-growth of that tissue cannot occur at the expense of any other constituent, and must result in an absolute increase in the weight of the heart, proportioned to the hypertrophy.

There is also in most cases an increase in the size of the heart. If the cavities of the heart are unaltered, the increase in its size is proportioned to the hypertrophy. This is the case in the so-called "simple" hypertrophy. The cavities rarely, however, remain unchanged. They are believed by some authorities to be occasionally diminished in size. The heart then may be of normal size, or may be very slightly enlarged. The increased thickness of the walls is at the expense of the cavity, which may become reduced to very small dimensions, it is said incapable of containing a walnut. This constitutes the concentric hypertrophy of Bertin. Lastly, the cavity is, in the majority of cases, dilated, and the dilatation adds greatly to the size of the heart. This constitutes the eccentric variety of Bertin.

Concentric hypertrophy of the heart has, in most recorded examples, been local, and confined to the left ventricle. Its existence has, however, been the subject of much discussion. It was thought to be common until Cruveilhier, in 1833,[1] pointed out how perfectly its characters were simulated by hearts the subjects of simple hypertrophy and post-mortem contraction. When the heart is at the time of death in systole, the final contraction is fixed by the rigor mortis, the thickened walls are, by their contraction, further increased in thickness, and so remain, and the cavity is reduced to very small dimensions. The resemblance of such a heart to "concentric hypertrophy" is admitted by all authorities. Cruveilhier maintained that all cases of the supposed change are thus explicable, that the cavity of such a ventricle can always be opened out with the fingers, and in this he has been followed by Budd[2] and many later pathologists, who urge further that the contraction of the cavities supposed to occur is incompatible with the absence of symptoms of impeded circulation of the blood. Other authorities believe that concentric hypertrophy does rarely occur. Skoda, Rokitansky, Bamberger, Förster, Walshe are all of this opinion. They assert that hearts are occasionally met with, the cavities of which are so small that the hypothesis of mere contraction is untenable, and is not verified by the effect of post-mortem decomposition, which should relax completely the contraction of rigor mortis. Dechambre and Forget maintained that such hearts could not be expanded, as simply contracted hearts can be.

The balance of recent pathological evidence is certainly opposed to the occurrence of concentric hypertrophy. It is to be noticed that the careful pathological observation of recent years has brought to light few supposed examples of this change. One specimen only has been brought before the Pathological Society.[3] There is in the museum of University College a specimen (No. 2,140) which has been described as itself establishing the existence of the change. But on close examination its characters are far from satisfactory evidence—it is obviously merely an example of the permanent contraction of a heart the subject of simple hypertrophy.[4] The known

---

[1] Dict. de Méd. et de Chir. Prat., art. Hypertrophie.
[2] Med.-Chir. Trans., 1838.
[3] By Wickham Legg. Trans. Path. Soc. vol. xxv., p. 105. The specimen presented contraction of the mitral orifice. Details of the measurement and weight of the heart are not given.
[4] The specimen in question has been appealed to as so decisive, and illustrates so well

mechanism of hypertrophy renders the origin of this form of over-growth scarcely conceivable. If hypertrophy is the result of increased work, increased intra-ventricular pressure, the volume of the blood within the ventricle can scarcely have been lessened ; but without such lessening, reduction in the size of the cavity cannot have occurred. Thus the increased thickness of the wall and lessened size of the cavity are, on etiological grounds, almost incompatible. Moreover, post-mortem decomposition relaxes hearts, firmly contracted, in a very imperfect manner.

Concentric hypertrophy of the right ventricle has been described as an occasional consequence of some congenital malformations of the heart.

Eccentric Hypertrophy.—The thickening of the wall in eccentric hypertrophy is not always conspicuous. The cavity is dilated, and the superficial area of the wall increased, and the increase in tissue may be only enough, or even not enough, to maintain the normal thickness of the wall. Thus the wall of the left ventricle may be so hypertrophied as to lead to a considerable increase in the weight of the heart, and yet may be only of the average thickness. In estimating the presence and amount of hypertrophy, therefore, the size of the cavity must always be taken into consideration. In one of the heaviest hearts recorded, a heart much dilated, the thickness of the wall of the left ventricle was not more than is common in less dilated hearts of only half the weight.

The increase in the size and weight of the heart is often very considerable. In estimating them it should be remembered that the normal average weight varies according to the sex, age, size of the individual. These are considered elsewhere (art. " Size and Weight of the Heart.") A heart which exceeds 9 oz. in a man or 8 oz. in

the characters which have led to the establishment of this variety, that it is worth detailed description. In the circular glass jar in which it had been preserved for many years it certainly had striking proportions. The walls appeared of great thickness, and the cavity "scarcely capable of containing a hazel nut." When removed from the jar it appeared considerably smaller. Its weight, with the root of the aorta, is 11½ oz., but it has been kept for many years in spirit. The external length of the ventricle is 4 inches. The heart has been divided transversely midway between the base and apex of the left ventricle. The diameters of the section are antero-posterior 2½ inches, lateral 3 inches. It is evidently a firmly contracted heart, for the cavity of the right ventricle is a mere curved line. The cavity of the left ventricle is, on close examination, stellate ; from the centre three linear branches radiate, and can be opened up. Between them lie the enlarged papillary muscles. On measurement with a wire, the circumference of this stellate cavity, following its branches but excluding the loose papillary muscles, is 4½ inches. But the most conclusive evidence is afforded by the thickness of the walls measured at the extremities of the radii of the cavity. On the left side the wall measures ⅝ of an inch, in front and behind just ½ inch in thickness. After every allowance has been made for the effect of the spirit, it seems clear that the thickness of the wall is only a little above the normal. The increased weight is proof that the extent of the wall cannot have been below the normal. It is clear also, from the state of the right ventricle, that the heart is firmly contracted, and also that the circumference of the inner surface of the left ventricle—the test of the actual reduction in size of the cavity—is little, if any, less than the normal. It seems, therefore, to be merely an example of firm contraction in a heart the subject of moderate simple hypertrophy. The history of the specimen is not known.

a woman, probably possesses an excess of some constituent, in most cases of muscular tissue. A common weight for hypertrophied hearts is 12–16 oz. Hearts are occasionally seen of much greater weight, especially when dilatation extends the area, and hypertrophy the thickness of the cardiac walls. Under these circumstances the enormous "bovine" hearts are met with. Walshe has met with one weighing 40 oz.; Lancisi mentions one which weighed, emptied of blood, two pounds and a half; Croker King one of $44\frac{1}{2}$ oz.; Austin Flint one of 46 oz., while hearts weighing $46\frac{1}{2}$ oz. have been shown by Bristowe and by Dávid at the Pathological Society. The enormous weight of five pounds, mentioned by Lieutaud, must be regarded as doubtful. How much more then the "quinze livres" of Marchetis![1]

The shape of the heart is altered according to the part affected. If one ventricle is more affected than the other, that which is the more hypertrophied forms a larger share of the apex than in health, and the chief enlargement of the heart is on the side of the affected ventricle. Thus in simple hypertrophy of the left ventricle, the extremity of that ventricle extends beyond the other, so as alone to constitute the apex, while increased width results from the lateral enlargement. The resulting shape resembles an obtuse-angled triangle when the heart is relaxed, an elongated ovoid when partially contracted. In hypertrophy of the right ventricle the extremity of that ventricle extends to the apex of the heart, but does not usually pass beyond the other. Hence the apex is much rounder than in health, and may be indistinguishable. When dilatation is joined to the hypertrophy, the width of the heart is much increased, and the transverse may exceed the vertical diameter. This is especially the case when the right ventricle is affected, when the heart may assume an almost spherical shape. Hypertrophy of the auricles is never sufficient to alter the shape of the heart; the effect of their dilatation is considered elsewhere.

The increase in the thickness of the wall is in direct proportion to the amount of hypertrophy, but in inverse proportion to the amount of dilatation. The hypertrophy is usually so much in excess of the dilatation as to cause an absolute increase in the thickness of the wall. This is commonly greater in the outer wall than in the septum. In the ventricles the trabeculæ and papillary muscles usually participate in the hypertrophy, and, it is said, to a greater extent in the right than in the left ventricle. Sometimes they are thinned, when the heart is dilated.

In health the thickness of the ventricular wall varies considerably

---

[1] Quoted by Senac, loc. cit., tom. ii., p. 408. Bellingham is said, by several writers, to have met with a heart weighing 80 oz. The only ground for the assertion seems to be that Bellingham states that he had seen a heart preserved in the museum of St. George's Hospital which was said to weigh five pounds. This seems to refer to the large heart alluded to by several writers and mentioned above (p. 706) as lately examined by Quain and found to weigh 40 oz.

in different parts.   The average thickness of the wall of the left ventricle is about half an inch in men, rather less in women. The measurement should be always exclusive of the papillary muscles, and the place at which the measurement is made should always be specified. The increase is usually greater towards the base than towards the apex.   Hope pointed out that the greatest thickening is a little above the middle of ventricle, at the place where the columnæ carneæ are inserted.   Thence it decreases suddenly towards the aortic orifice, gradually towards the apex of the heart, Occasionally the reverse obtains, especially in aortic regurgitation (Walshe), and the wall is thicker towards the apex than towards the base.

When the wall of the left ventricle measures three-fifths of an inch in thickness it may be considered hypertrophied. An increase in the average thickness to three-quarters of an inch, or an inch, is not uncommon. An inch and a quarter is occasionally reached, and it is said, an inch and a half, or even two inches.   The larger dimensions were probably in cases in which there was little dilatation, and the heart was contracted.   In the large heart described by Bristowe, the weight of which was forty-six and a half ounces, the wall of the left ventricle was only ⅗ths of an inch in thickness at the base; the length of the cavity of the ventricle being six inches.

The right ventricle yields readily to internal pressure, and presents a marked increase in the thickness of the wall much less frequently than the left; simple hypertrophy is very rare. The average normal thickness of the wall is two-and-a-half lines in men, two lines in women. When hypertrophied it is often a third, or half an inch in thickness, and even in rare instances three-quarters of an inch, an inch, and even, it is said, an inch and a quarter (Bertin, 88th case, "eleven to sixteen lines.") The numerous columnæ carneæ are commonly much thickened. The cavity is usually enlarged, but may be lessened in rare cases; probably, however, only in cases of malformation. When the ventricle is thus hypertrophied, and the left ventricle is dilated, the two may, as Morgagni and Bertin remarked, seem to have become transposed.

The left auricle is not unfrequently hypertrophied. The average normal thickness of its wall is one line and a half; where hypertrophied it may reach two to three lines.   The right auricle is rarely hypertrophied, and always in least degree. The average thickness of its walls is one line; when hypertrophied it may attain one-and-a-half or two lines.   The auricles have never been found to present contraction of their cavity.

In pure hypertrophy the part changed is of firm consistence, firmer than the normal heart, so that the walls do not collapse when cut across. It presents little deviation from the normal colour, it is sometimes a little darker. Such unmixed hypertrophy is rare. More commonly the tissue has undergone degeneration, and is paler and softer than normal, sometimes generally, sometimes partially. Rokitansky points out that in the hypertrophy of the ventricles the changed wall of the right ventricle is always tougher than that of the left.

The hypertrophied wall of the heart usually contains more fibrous tissue than the healthy wall. The tissue lies between the primitive bundles, separating them, and here and there forms more extensive tracts. This change, when more considerable, is considered as " fibroid degeneration." It is more abundant in the wall of the right ventricle than in that of the left, and doubtless is the cause of its greater consistence.

The nature of the change in the muscular fibre in hypertrophy has been the subject of much discussion. Does the increase in the size of the heart depend on an increase in the size, or in the number of fibres ? The evidence, in some degree conflicting, is on the whole strongly in favour of the view that the increased thickness of the wall is due solely to increase in the number of the fibres constituting it, *i.e.* to the formation of new fibres. The chief evidence of an increase in the size of the fibres is obtained from the measurements of Hepp,[1] still quoted as authoritative, and who asserted, and gave measurements to show, that the average thickness of the fibres in hypertrophy is about four times the thickness of the fibres in health. This conclusion, however, by itself suggests a fallacy, since the average thickness of the wall in hypertrophy is less than double the average normal thickness. Vogel and Henle, Rindfleisch and Walshe conclude that there is no increase in the size of the fibres, while Robin thinks that there is a slight increase, although not enough to account for the increased size of the heart. Wilks and Moxon are convinced that the chief share in the increase in size is due to increase in number. Considerable weight must be attached to the careful observation of Zielonko,[2] who finds that the average of a large number of measurements of the fibres of hypertrophied hearts is a little *less* than the average of the normal fibre. His observations also corroborate the fact (long before stated by Förster) that the normal fibres are smaller in early than in later life, and are increased in size by good general nutrition. The writer has found on direct enumeration of the fibres in a transverse section of the wall that their number is in the main proportioned to its thickness. The conclusion appears justified that there is no increased size of the fibres in hypertrophy, that the over-growth of the heart is entirely dependent on the development of new and less perfectly nourished tissue elements. Rindfleisch suggests that they may arise by fissuring of the pre-existing fibres. He has observed that the square cells, of which the muscular fibres of the heart have been shown to consist, contain several nuclei, instead of a single nucleus, as in health.[3]

[1] Zeitschrift für rat Méd. 1854, p. 257.
[2] Virchow's Archiv, Bd. 62, Heft I. p. 29.
[3] Pathologiste Gewebelehre, Vierte Aufl. 1875, p. 193.

SYMPTOMS.—Cardiac hypertrophy gives rise to certain distinctive physical signs, and may be accompanied by certain definite symptoms. These signs and symptoms depend on the increased size of the heart, and on the increased force with which it acts. They vary according to the part of the heart which is affected, and according to the amount of dilatation which is associated with the hypertrophy. It will be convenient to consider separately the symptoms of the change in each division of the heart, beginning with the left ventricle. In it the change is carried to the greatest degree, and gives rise to the signs and symptoms commonly understood as those of hypertrophy of the heart.

Whenever hypertrophy is considerable, the heart, unless fixed by adhesions, lies, in consequence of its greater weight, lower in the thorax than in health. The weight of the base is said to increase the natural obliquity of the organ, so that it may assume a nearly transverse position.

LEFT VENTRICLE.—*Physical Signs.*—The increased bulk of the heart may cause precordial bulging, noticeable chiefly in the area between the nipple and the left edge of the sternum. The intercostal spaces are widened, and the surface of the chest is more prominent than is the corresponding part on the opposite side. This bulging is most marked in hypertrophy occurring in early life.

The area of dulness is increased. The superficial dulness is usually more extensive, the deep dulness invariably larger, and the increase is chiefly to the left. The left edge of the deep dulness, instead of passing from the middle of the third left cartilage to the apex, extends from the inner extremity of the third rib to the nipple, or even to the anterior axillary line, one, two, or even three inches outside the nipple. It may also, although less commonly, extend upwards to the second interspace. Its shape is thus usually more oval than in health.[1] Resistance on percussion is greater than in health. In extreme enlargement the resonance in the left back is defective, and Walshe has even known the dulness to be so marked, and respiration so weakened by pressure upon the lung, that pleural effusion was simulated. The apex-beat, marking approximately the limit of the heart, is moved outwards and downwards, with its enlargement, into or outside the vertical nipple line, and into the sixth or seventh interspace, into the latter probably only in dilated hypertrophy (Walshe).

The increased force of action manifests itself by increased impulse.[2]

---

[1] The deep cardiac dulness is, except in the presence of extreme emphysema, an accurate and convenient measure of the enlargement of the heart. By many authorities it has been strangely undervalued. Niemeyer's assertion that percussion often fails to reveal hypertrophy of the left ventricle is comprehensible only in consequence of the guide employed being the superficial dulness, which depends much more on the state of the lung than on the state of the heart. For a very full and clear account of the relations and significance of the diminished resonance caused by the heart in its various conditions, see Balfour, Clin. Lect. on Diseases of the Heart, 1876, Lect. 1.

[2] According to old writers, Fernel, &c., the impulse of a hypertrophied heart had been known to fracture the ribs! All the instances, however, seem to have occurred in con-

The area of impulse is increased; it may be felt in the fourth, fifth, and sixth interspaces. A larger portion of heart comes in contact with the chest wall, and the increased force aids also in producing a more extensive impulse. In pure hypertrophy a maximum apex-beat is still perceptible, bearing a normal proportion to the rest of the impulse. But the impulse is not only more forcible, it presents a special change; it is slower, more deliberate, as well as more forcible, and hence has been for long termed "heaving." In dilated hypertrophy the impulse is more abrupt than in simple hypertrophy, in which the slow heave is carried to its greatest degree. The extension of the impulse is often visible, and the whole left front of the chest may be raised by it. It was spoken of as "jarring" by old writers, and still is occasionally so described. But a "jar" implies vibration, and although a vibratory character is often felt in the impulse of a hypertrophied heart, it is due to co-existing valvular disease, not to the over-action of the heart itself. Occasionally a double impulse can be felt with each beat of the heart. Rarely it is a double systolic impulse (Walshe), the origin of which is obscure. More commonly the second and slighter impulse corresponds with the commencement of diastole, at the end of the "sinking back," as Hope expressed it, who first pointed out the phenomenon. He explained it as due to the sudden filling of the ventricles with blood. Hayden, who adopts a similar explanation, has pointed out the coincidence of this second impulse with the second sound. Walshe remarks that the movement is rather a succussion than an impulse against the chest walls. This character, and the obvious coincidence with the second sound, have, in several cases, suggested to the writer the probability that the impulse is really due to the shock communicated to the whole heart by the closure of the aortic valves, a closure rendered more forcible by the greater distension of the aorta. It is in accordance with this explanation that, as Hope and Walshe both point out, this second impulse may occur in simple hypertrophy, but is most marked in dilated hypertrophy (in which the distension of the aorta is greatest), and that it is absent in simple dilatation.

The sounds of the heart are altered. The first sound is rendered less loud, but longer, the change being especially marked over the ventricle. The sound may be normal at the base and ensiform cartilage (Walshe). Sometimes the muffling of the sound amounts almost to extinction. The second sound is usually loud. When dilatation is added to the hypertrophy the first sound becomes louder and clearer. The post-systolic silence is shortened, as Laennec noted, in consequence of the lengthening of the first sound. Laennec thought that this lengthening may amount to a faint murmur, apart from valve disease or hæmic state, and Walshe corroborates the opinion. During attacks of palpitation the first sound may be much more distinct than when the heart is acting uniformly.

vents or monasteries. Cæsalpinus and others assert that two ribs of St. Philip de Neri were torn from their cartilages by the palpitation of his heart. Senac wisely doubted the occurrence of such fractures, unless the ribs had been previously weakened by disease.

Reduplication of the first sound is occasionally met with in hypertrophy: rarely according to Walshe; almost invariably in eccentric hypertrophy, according to Hayden. It is certainly frequent in some forms of hypertrophy, especially in that due to Bright's disease (Sibson). Irregularity in force is not common, in frequency very rare, except in association with dilatation and degenerative changes.

Symptoms, proper.—A great number of morbid phenomena have been ascribed to the influence of cardiac hypertrophy. The list, however, has been shortened according as the symptoms of the causes of hypertrophy and of the other associated consequences of those causes, are distinguished from the symptoms directly due to the hypertrophy itself.[1] Almost all the consequences of dilatation of the heart were formerly ascribed to the conjoined hypertrophy. The credit belongs to Bouillaud of having first vindicated hypertrophy from its supposed influence in causing dropsy and other consequences of cardiac failure.

Subjective symptoms of cardiac hypertrophy may be absent, when the hypertrophy is moderate, with little or no dilatation, and is adequate to overcome the obstruction which has produced it. In such cases, however, the varying force of the heart's action, the varying amount of the obstruction, and the common conjunction of relative weakness with absolute strength, lead to sensible evidence of derangement.

Fig. 1.—Tracing from pulse in great hypertrophy and dilatation of left ventricle in a case of mitral regurgitant disease, with general venous distension and ultimate increase in arterial tension. Artery large and incompressible. Tracing taken at very high pressure, which did not modify its character.

Consciousness of the increased force with which the heart acts is a more or less frequent symptom in all except the slightest forms of hypertrophy. Under excitement the conscious beating may amount to "palpitation." Slight irregularity may increase the discomfort, but much irregularity or considerable palpitation is rare, except in dilatation, and to that the symptom is to be ascribed. Pain, as Walshe points out, is extremely rare in simple hypertrophy, and anginal attacks are almost confined to cases in which the dilatation is considerable. The force with which the left ventricle contracts has an immediate effect on the arterial pulsations. The carotids throb

---

[1] Senac, in speaking of this subject, says:—"Rien n'est plus ordinaire que les erreurs des observateurs dans la recherche des causes ; tout ce qu'ils trouvent dans les cadavres ils attribuent souvent à la dernière maladie, ou à celle qui a attiré leur attention." *loc. cit.*, tom. ii., p. 398.

visibly. The pulse is large, full, hard, sustained. When dilatation is conjoined with the hypertrophy, the pulse is still full, but is softer and more compressible and less sustained. The sphygmogram shows these characters in a sudden and high rise, and, where the hypertrophy is simple, there is a high and often sustained tidal wave. Where there is coexisting dilatation, the tidal wave may not be sustained in consequence of the imperfect emptying of the ventricle (Fig. 1.) Aortic obstruction may, however, modify considerably these characters, rendering the pulse smaller, while it remains hard, sustained, and incompressible. If considerable, it also renders the contraction slow, and the percussion stroke may be lost in a slowly rising tidal wave, as in the accompanying tracing :—

Fig. 2.—Tracing from infrequent and slow pulse of aortic obstruction, with coexisting mitral disease, and hypertrophy of the left ventricle. The slowness of the contraction had been increased by the administration of digitalis. Taken at a high pressure ; pulse small but almost incompressible.[1]

The force with which the blood is driven into the smaller vessels may modify the function of certain tissues and organs. The face is often flushed. Tinnitus aurium, flashes of light, and muscæ volitantes may be complained of. Headache and mental dulness are sometimes observed, but as a rule the intellect is unaffected. The general nutrition also suffers little. Organic functions are little interfered with. Increased arterial pressure might be supposed, as Walshe remarks, to modify considerably the urinary secretion, increasing the quantity of water. The urine presents, however, no distinctive change. Swelling of the bronchial mucous membrane, and increased secretion are connected by Niemeyer with the active distension of the bronchial arteries. Shortness of breath on exertion is common, and is by Walshe connected directly with the hypertrophy. True cardiac dyspnœa is rare ; and any considerable shortness of breath is probably to be ascribed to the cause of the hypertrophy, or to concurrent dilatation. The pressure exerted on the lungs by an enlarged heart may cause some interference with their function and increase the dyspnœa.

Consequences of Hypertrophy.—A long train of evils which are met with in more or less frequent association with hypertrophy, were formerly regarded as its consequences. Many of them are in no way related to its occurrence, but are the result of the dilatation, or remotely of the cause of the hypertrophy. Such are œdema, capillary engorgement, venous congestions, passive hæmorrhages. These were enumerated by Hope as consequences of hypertrophy. Bertin

[1] These two tracings were taken for me by Mr. H. R. O. Sankey.

long before taught clearly that they cannot be regarded as such, since they are absent when hypertrophy exists in its most simple form, and occur in proportion as the hypertrophy is complicated by other conditions, such as valvular disease, dilatation of the ventricle, &c., themselves capable, without hypertrophy, of causing the symptoms.

Not only does hypertrophy not produce these effects, but its tendency is to prevent their occurrence. Its power of arresting the mechanical effects of its causes is very great, and proportioned to its degree. Disease of the aortic orifice, for instance, as long as the hypertrophy is great and unweakened by degeneration, produces no backward effect. So in mitral obstruction, hypertrophy of the left auricle may for a long time save the lungs from passive congestion. So, too, hypertrophy of the right ventricle may prevent any over-distension of the venous system from obstruction to the circulation through the lungs or the left side of the heart.

The only morbid effects of hypertrophy which can accurately be thus regarded, are those which result from the greater force with which the blood is driven into the arterial system. These consequences are seen best when there is no impediment to the escape of blood from the ventricle, and especially when the cause of the hypertrophy is occasional or is situated in front of the arterial system. The tendency is for the due proportion between the contents of the arteries and the veins to be disturbed, for the arteries to become over-filled, the veins and the pulmonary system under-filled with blood. It has been said that the whole circulation is accelerated, but this can only be the case when the action of the heart is for the time being more than enough to overcome the resistance which has evoked it.

It has been supposed that the increased supply of arterial blood may lead to the overgrowth of organs, but the conjecture is unsupported by observation.

A more direct effect upon the vessels may often be traced. When the obstruction is situated beyond the arteries, their walls are exposed to a greatly increased pressure. The same effect occurs when the obstruction is at the aortic orifice, and the action of the heart is from any cause (as dynamic excitement, or the cessation of another cause) in excess of the obstruction. Both the large and small arteries suffer under these circumstances. The increased pressure on the aorta may cause its dilatation, although, as Senac observed, the enlargement from this cause is not often considerable. A more frequent consequence of the pressure to which the arteries are exposed is seen in the degeneration of the vessels.[1] Modern observation has established the frequent association of so-called endarteritis deformans (atheroma) with increased strain. The change is seen in the aorta, in the pulmonary artery, and in the smaller vessels, especially in those in which the relative pressure is the greatest, as in those at the base of the brain.

[1] Pointed out by Kirkes in 1857, Med. Times and Gaz., No. 370, 371.

But degeneration is not the only effect of the increased strain upon the vessels; they not unfrequently give way, and hæmorrhage results. Hæmorrhage into the brain is, on account of its frequency, magnitude and importance, that form to which attention has been chiefly directed. The frequent association of apoplexy and enlargement of the heart led Corvisart first to assume a causal relationship between the two.[1] In this he has been followed by most subsequent writers—Bertin, Hope, Bouillaud, Andral, Burrows, and others. But the conclusions of the earlier observers require some abatement in the light of modern knowledge of the frequency with which apoplectic attacks result, by another mechanism, from cardiac disease. Embolism may give rise to symptoms not unlike those of cerebral hæmorrhage, and embolism is almost constantly associated with hypertrophy of the heart. But even when these cases are eliminated from the discussion, the pathological evidence of the association of apoplexy and hypertrophy of the heart is still unimpeachable. In sixty-five cases of apoplexy collected by Quain[2] the heart was enlarged in two-thirds, and in one-half there was no valve disease. The significance of the latter fact is that in these cases the cause of the hypertrophy was probably situated away from the heart, in or beyond the arterial system, which would thus have to bear the whole force of the over-acting heart. But this is the condition in which arterial disease is produced; the small vessels degenerate, and, becoming weaker, are less able to bear the increased pressure to which they are exposed. This is the case, notoriously, in Bright's disease, especially in the contracted kidney, with which cerebral hæmorrhage and cardiac hypertrophy are so constantly associated. In primary degenerative changes in the smaller vessels the same result is seen—a like obstruction may cause hypertrophy, and a like weakness yield before the increased pressure. The same sequence is sometimes seen when the cause of the obstruction is situated beyond the arteries and capillaries, and acts, it may be, through both systems of the circulation. Mitral disease may lead to extreme blood tension in the arterial system, as the sphygmographic tracing on page 714 shows. Cerebral hæmorrhage sometimes occurs in such cases, even in the young, from the rupture of an overstrained artery.

All authorities are agreed as to the causal relationship between hypertrophy of the heart and the rupture of diseased vessels. But to this some, as Watson, Eulenberg, Rokitansky, would limit the connection. It must be considered still doubtful whether an over-acting heart can rupture a healthy artery. It is true the large arteries of the

---

[1] "Where apoplexy takes place in a person in whom there is an excess of muscular substance and strength in the heart, it is easy to conceive that the resistance of the vessels of the brain is not in unison with the extraordinary impetus which the heart impresses on the blood ; it necessarily follows that the smaller vessels of the brain become more permeable to this fluid, or that they give way and cause effusion and apoplexy." Corvisart, l. c., p. 164. It, however, would seem to have been first suggested by the death of Malpighi, who died from cerebral hæmorrhage, and whose heart was found greatly hypertrophied, "the parietes of the left ventricle were two fingers in thickness." (Baglivi.)   [2] Lumleian Lectures, loc. cit.

brain are often found healthy in cases of cerebral hæmorrhage, but this affords only slight evidence of the condition of the smaller vessels of the cerebral substance. These are frequently diseased when the vessels at the base of the brain appear healthy.

Statistics on this point corroborate, but do not extend, the conclusion from isolated observations. Quain found that diseased vessels are more common in cases of cerebral hæmorrhage when the heart is healthy than when it is hypertrophied. They are present in two-thirds of the former, and only in about half of the latter. The inference suggested is that, since extensive disease of vessels shown by the implication of the larger trunks is less common, in cerebral hæmorrhage, when the heart is hypertrophied than when it is healthy, an over-acting heart needs less diminution in the strength of the vessels, in order to effect their rupture, than a healthy heart.

The occasional, though rare, occurrence of cerebral hæmorrhage in the young does not help to decide the question. Disease of the cerebral vessels is now known to be not uncommon in early life, and some of the cases occur in the subjects of heart disease, in whom there exists circuitous increase of arterial tension, just described. Moreover in such subjects cerebral aneurisms, perhaps from imperfect embolism, are frequent, and in many cases it has certainly been by the rupture of such an aneurism that cerebral hæmorrhage has occurred.

Concentric Hypertrophy of the Left Ventricle.—The symptoms are as uncertain as the existence of the malady. Theoretically, the signs of simple hypertrophy might be expected, and with them some dyspnœa in consequence of the impediment which must be presented to the passage of blood through a heart so much lessened in capacity.

RIGHT VENTRICLE.—Considerable increase in the size of the right ventricle causes prominence of the lower part of the sternum, epigastric fulness, and often bulging of the lower left cartilages adjacent to the sternum. The superficial cardiac dulness is little changed, but the deep dulness extends further to the right than normal, the right edge being one or two fingers' breadth to the right of the sternum. This dulness is partly dependent on the enlargement of the ventricle, partly on over-distension of the auricle, which always accompanies the change in the ventricle. Pulsation may be felt at the epigastrium. The apex-beat is in its normal situation, or moved a little to the left, extended as far as, but not beyond, the nipple line. It is frequently changed, being obscured and diffused when the right ventricle lies in front of it. A distinct impulse may be felt over the right ventricle, *i.e.*, over the lower part of the sternum,[1] and in the adjacent left interspaces. In health a distinct impulse is very rarely to be felt in this situation. In hypertrophy the impulse may have considerable strength, but it is generally quick, rarely of the slow, heaving character which hypertrophy of the left ventricle

---

[1] This was pointed out by Burggrave in 1754 (Act. Acad. Nat. Cur. vol. x. p. 140.)

produces. It may sometimes be felt as far as the base. Little alteration in the sounds of the heart is caused by hypertrophy of the right
ventricle. The pulmonary second sound is usually intensified by the
increased tension within the pulmonary artery. Sometimes the second
sound is reduplicated. Jugular pulsation has been associated with
hypertrophy of the right ventricle by Lancisi, Laennec, Hope, and
others. It is doubtless due to actual regurgitation through the
tricuspid orifice, and coexisting dilatation of the ventricle is necessary
for its production.

Few symptoms proper can be associated with the condition. The
pulse is natural. The venous system shows no sign of engorgement.
It is remarkable how completely hypertrophy of the right ventricle
will prevent the development of dropsy, and other signs of venous
stagnation, by an obstacle in front of it. The lungs or left side of
the heart usually present evidence of the condition causing the
hypertrophy, emphysema, disease of the mitral orifice, &c. Dyspnœa
is common, as Walshe points out, but is more frequently the
result of the cause of the hypertrophy, than of the hypertrophy
itself.

Consequences of Hypertrophy of the Right Ventricle.—The immediate
effect of over-action in the right ventricle is to over-distend that part
of the pulmonary vascular system which lies between the ventricle
and the obstruction which has caused the hypertrophy—the pulmonary
arterial system, when obstruction is in the tissues of the lung, the pulmonary veins also, when the obstruction is on the left side of the heart.
Atheroma of the pulmonary artery frequently exists in conjunction with
this condition, and has been regarded as causal, but in few cases have the
two been observed except in conjunction with some other recognised
cause of such hypertrophy, and it seems more reasonable to conclude
that the degeneration is the result of the increased strain to which
the pulmonary artery is exposed. Where the degeneration is considerable and of old standing, as in cases in which the artery is found
calcified, it may be the only discoverable cause of a moderate
hypertrophy of the ventricle.

Pulmonary congestions, œdema, and especially pulmonary apoplexy,
have, since the days of Bertin, been commonly ascribed to hypertrophy
of the right ventricle. Where the obstruction causing the hypertrophy
is situated on the left side of the heart, the increase in the strength
of the right ventricle will add considerably to the strain upon the
distended pulmonary vessels, and may constitute the efficient cause
of their rupture. Modern pathological research, however, has shown
that diseases of the right side of the heart frequently cause pulmonary
apoplexy in another way, by leading to pulmonary embolism. We are
only beginning to learn how large a proportion of pulmonary apoplexies
is due to this cause. When such embolism occurs, hypertrophy
of the right ventricle will increase very much the strain on the
collateral circulation, and, in consequence, will augment the amount
of hæmorrhage.

AURICLES.—*Hypertrophy of the Left Auricle* is usually attended with evidence of its enlargement, *i.e.* dulness, commonly relative only, in the inner part of the second left interspace. Less frequently a distinct impulse is to be recognised in this situation, preceding in time the ventricular impulse and due to the auricular systole. Evidence of mitral disease is commonly present, a systolic or presystolic murmur. Dilatation of the auricle invariably coexists. No symptoms are known to be associated with the hypertrophy. Its tendency is to prevent the mitral mischief from influencing the pulmonary circulation.

Hypertrophy of the Right Auricle is very rare, and is always associated with dilatation. Its signs are dulness to the right of the sternum in the third and fourth interspaces, and, in very rare cases, an impulse, presystolic in rhythm, in this situation. It is often attended with marked jugular pulsation, and with the evidence of disease of the right ventricle or of the tricuspid orifice.

DIAGNOSIS.—The diagnosis of hypertrophy depends on the recognition of increased force of impulse, and especially, in the case of the left ventricle, by the deliberate heaving character which indicates the contraction of a large mass of muscle. In the case of right ventricular and of auricular hypertrophy, the increased force is indicated by impulse, where in health none is present. Evidence of enlargement of the heart, by percussion dulness, or by movement of the apex-beat, or by extension of the impulse, is usually also obvious. In left ventricular hypertrophy the character of the pulse assists the diagnosis. Where doubt remains, the presence of a morbid state, capable of causing the hypertrophy, may afford evidence of its probable existence.

In judging of the existence and degree of hypertrophy the condition of the lungs must always be taken into consideration. Considerable emphysema may conceal all the signs of a hypertrophy of high degree. The impulse may be imperceptible, the dulness masked, and the heart-sounds weakened. The existence of hypertrophy must then be inferred from the condition of the arterial system.

There are certain conditions from which hypertrophy has most frequently to be distinguished.

Undue Exposure of the Heart in very flat- or narrow-chested persons, with small lungs, may simulate hypertrophy. The heart comes into more extensive contact with the anterior wall of the chest than in health. Its impulse is felt over a larger area, and may appear to have undue force. A maximum apex-beat is still preserved. The superficial dulness is more extensive than in health. The distinction from hypertrophy rests on the absence of a heaving character in the impulse, on the normal or nearly normal position of the apex-beat (it is never outside, though it may be in the nipple-line), on the natural extent of the deep dulness, on the unchanged pulse, on the absence of any causal condition, and on the recognition of the short antero-posterior or transverse diameter of the chest. The difficulty of diagnosis in such cases is sometimes increased by the presence of an exocardial murmur, produced by the undue friction of the heart against the bony chest wall, and, by the circumstance, that patients with very flat chests are often weakly and anæmic, and suffer from shortness of breath and extreme consciousness of any dynamical heart-disturbance.

Dynamical Disturbance of the Heart may be mistaken for hypertrophy. Under excitement the heart may beat with apparently increased force, and be brought into abnormal contact with the wall of the chest, so that there is an increase in the area as well as in the force of the impulse. Sometimes the increase in force is more apparent than real, and the pulse is small and weak. Frequently, however, the rapidly-acting heart distends the arteries, and the pulse becomes hard and full. There is an entire absence of the deliberate heave of hypertrophy, and of evidence of permanent change in the form of the heart; there is no bulging, no increased dulness. Rest in the recumbent posture soon reduces the impulse to the normal. It must not be forgotten that an hypertrophied heart readily palpitates under excitement, and any irregularity in the excited action is ground for suspicion.

Displacement of the Heart may lead to an apparent extension (really a movement) of the impulse and dulness in a given direction. Displacement to the left, moving the apex outside the nipple line, may simulate hypertrophy of the left ventricle; and displacement downwards, rendering the impulse of the right ventricle perceptible at the epigastrium, may resemble dilated hypertrophy of the right ventricle. But under these circumstances there is no alteration of the character of the impulse as there is in hypertrophy; the opposite boundary of the heart may be found to have undergone a corresponding change of position, and a cause of the displacement will be discoverable.

Dilatation of the Heart resembles hypertrophy in causing increase in size, shown by extension of dulness and increased area of impulse. The impulse is, however, diffuse and weak; the proportional intensity of the apex-beat is lost, the pulse is soft, and the action of the heart often irregular. The distinction between the two conditions can rarely be absolute, since they are usually, in varying degree, conjoined.

Pericardial Effusion may cause bulging and an increase in the area of dulness. The impulse, however, is less, instead of more forcible; and the apex is raised, instead of being moved outwards or downwards. The dulness extends upwards in the pyramidal form, and its left boundary is beyond, instead of corresponding to, the left limit of the impulse. Apart from auscultatory signs, the acuteness of the symptoms in pericarditis, sudden pain, dyspnœa, fever, will usually prevent an error in diagnosis. In auricular hypertrophy, the extension of dulness above the normal limits of the cardiac dulness is usually slight. If sufficient to simulate pericardial effusion, a presystolic impulse will, in most cases, be detected.

Aneurism has been confounded with hypertrophy, but the conditions under which such a mistake could arise must be very rare. The double centre of pulsation usually affords a sufficient distinction.

Local diagnosis of the part of the heart affected with hypertrophy has been alluded to in describing the symptoms produced by the change in the several chambers of the heart. The chief difficulty arises in some cases of ventricular hypertrophy. In hypertrophy of the right ventricle, slight hypertrophy of the left ventricle may be concealed or simulated by the strong impulse of the anterior right ventricle and the displacement outwards of the apex-beat consequent on the enlargement of the right side. The diagnosis of the state of the left ventricle must then depend on the character of the apex-beat —on the presence or absence of a distinct heaving impulse. On the other hand, considerable hypertrophy of the left ventricle may cause an impulse over the position of the right ventricle. In such a case the impulse of the left ventricle possesses great force, and the diagnosis must be based on the relative proportion of the impulse over the two ventricles.

In all cases a comparison of the extent of causal lesion, with its mechanical effects, will often suggest an accurate opinion as to the existence and degree of hypertrophy when the part affected is not accessible to physical examination. For instance, congestion of the lungs is the necessary mechanical effect of mitral constriction. The absence of such congestion, when considerable mitral constriction exists, is valid ground for suspecting compensatory hypertrophy of the left auricle. So too we sometimes find that such compensation has not occurred—that the lungs are constantly overloaded with blood, but that the general venous system has not suffered; the jugular veins are undistended; there is no anasarca or albumen in the urine. In such a case we may be sure that there is hypertrophy of the right ventricle.

PROGNOSIS.—The difficulty of extricating hypertrophy from the various conditions with which it is associated has led authorities to entertain very different opinions regarding its influence on the life and well-being of the patient. The gravest consequences of hypertrophy (as formerly described) are now known to be those of its attendant conditions; the "conservative" character of hypertrophy, as a healthy reaction against a morbid influence, is generally recognised, and its prognosis is admitted to be, as a rule, favourable; any unfavourable element being due rather to coexisting dilatation, or to other effects of the cause of the hypertrophy, than to that condition itself.

It is rarely that evil results can be traced directly to the overgrowth of the heart. The unpleasant sensations attending the action of a hypertrophied heart suggest many possible evils which experience rarely justifies. It may produce hæmorrhage, especially into the brain, when vessels are rotten, but probably does not rupture healthy vessels; it may render inflammations more severe, but never initiates them. Most observers will share Walshe's profound doubt whether in its most extreme forms, hypertrophy can ever *per se* lead to death.

Does hypertrophy ever diminish or disappear? It is probable that hypertrophy lasts as long as its cause exists. Many facts on record support the opinion that, if the cause of simple hypertrophy cease to act, the heart gradually resumes its normal size. Atrophy may occur in an hypertrophied as readily as in a normal heart. Whether a heart the subject of dilated hypertrophy ever regains its normal volume is doubtful. The occurrence of the so-called concentric atrophy, in which the size of the cavities lessens, and also the disappearance of the dilatation of atony, support the idea that a moderately-dilated heart may regain its normal size.

The prognosis in hypertrophy must, therefore, largely depend on the extent to which its cause is removable. For practical purposes the work of the heart in these cases may be divided into three categories :—(1) that which is required to carry on the healthy circulation, the body being at rest; (2) superadded work, temporary and variable, such as is involved in muscular exertion, emotional excitement, local inflammation, pregnancy, &c.; (3) some permanent abnormal resistance to the movement of the blood, increasing the pressure within the cavity affected. The second of these is alone amenable to treatment. The chance of removing or curing hypertrophy depends on the extent to which causes of this class constitute the work of the heart. Where hypertrophy is developed when the work of the second class is as slight as possible, where no avoidable exertion is made, and where no occasional causes of obstruction exist, the chance of removing or lessening hypertrophy is small. In the rare cases in which the whole increase over the normal work of the heart depends on causes of the second class, the prognosis is the most favourable. Such cases are sometimes met with among athletes, as in an instance Walshe records.

The probable permanence of the hypertrophy on the one hand, the likelihood that it may give place to dilatation on the other hand, must influence the prognosis in any individual case. This probability must be estimated by the degree to which the causes of dilatation are, or are likely to be, in operation. Impaired general health, or the presence of degenerative tendencies, local or general, render the prognosis less favourable.

Where the cause of hypertrophy is permanent, the influence of the hypertrophy varies, and with it the prognosis. In certain conditions the increased force with which the heart acts may lead, directly or indirectly, to evil consequences, and in such cases the presence and degree of the hypertrophy may entail, *per se,* a corresponding increase in the gravity of the prognosis. In all forms of valvular disease in which the hypertrophy depends on direct obstruction to the escape of blood from the cavity, the hypertrophy is purely beneficial in its effect; it secures a due supply of blood to the parts beyond the obstruction; it saves the vessels and organs behind from suffering from the impediment. It is only when hypertrophy is due, in part, to a variable cause beyond the obstruction, that it may be occasionally in sufficient excess to produce prejudicial arterial distension.

In cases of regurgitation, in which the heart has to exert undue force in the propulsion of an undue quantity of blood, the hypertrophy is less simply beneficial in its influence. The muscular force with which the ventricle contracts tends to increase the amount of blood regurgitated, and so increase its own repletion. This is the case directly in aortic regurgitation, indirectly in mitral regurgitation. The degeneration of the arteries is hastened by the strain to which they are exposed by the action of the hypertrophied ventricle in aortic regurgitation; while in mitral regurgitation, although the stronger action of the ventricle may drive a larger quantity of blood into the aorta, it also increases the amount regurgitated through the incompetent valves. But it must be remembered that in these cases the hypertrophy is a substitute for dilatation, and may be accepted as the less of the two evils; or it counteracts the influence of dilatation which coexists.

When the obstruction causing the hypertrophy is situated in the vascular system, pulmonary, or systemic, whether the consequence of degeneration, Bright's disease, &c., the hypertrophy is also less simply beneficial, since the increased strain to which the vessels are subjected increases their liability to degeneration and to rupture.

In Bright's disease this danger reaches its height, since degeneration of the strained vessels is very apt to occur and renders their rupture easy. In senile changes cardiac and vascular degeneration often correspond, and the hypertrophy which at first is evoked by the change in the vessels yields to dilatation, by which the blood-tension is lessened. But this retro-compensation is not without new risks.

In all cases, however, it is still true that the prognosis of the hypertrophy is subordinate to that of the lesion causing it, and also to that of co-existing dilatation. Once established as the result of a permanent cause, it usually increases, and bears a simple proportion to its cause. It is extensively employed in prognosis, but is used rather as an indication of the extent and gravity of the lesion causing it than as affording in itself much information. As far as it goes, its presence renders the prognosis of the causal lesion better. Compensatory in its action, it wards off evil and promotes health.

TREATMENT.—Current opinion as to the treatment of hypertrophy has undergone great changes, in accordance with the altered ideas of its relation to the common consequences of organic heart disease. When most of these were considered to be the direct effects of the over-acting heart, every effort was made to diminish its over-action and to lessen its over-growth. Low diet and frequent bleedings are the measures which Albertini and Valsalva handed down to a long series of their successors; and the effects of their doctrine is even now to be traced, although perhaps rather in the pages of text-books than in practice. Even after the purely consecutive nature of hypertrophy was clearly recognised by Bertin, the same treatment was advocated.

. The judicious management of hypertrophy depends on the recognition of the fact that it is sometimes purely beneficial, usually welcome as a substitute for its too frequent associate, dilatation, and rarely directly prejudicial. No universal rule for the treatment of hypertrophy can therefore be laid down, since the proper course may be sometimes to foster its occurrence, sometimes to lessen its excess, or, failing that, to prevent its increase.

Hypertrophy of the heart being the result of two factors, nutritive activity and increased work, its increase may be to some extent prevented, and its amount diminished, by lessening each factor in its production. The nutritive activity of the heart can be lessened only by diminishing that of the general system by low diet, bleeding, &c. But to attempt this while the causes of hypertrophy continue, is to substitute dilatation for hypertrophy. The system has been advocated, however, in conjunction with causal treatment, from the time of Bertin. It may be questioned whether the causes of established hypertrophy can ever be sufficiently reduced to permit the safe employment of "antiphlogistic" measures. Moreover they can rarely be necessary. We see in the voluntary muscles that reduction of work is invariably followed by reduction in size of muscle. Every analogy suggests that cardiac hypertrophy will rapidly subside when the condition which excited it has lessened or has ceased. It is not often that this result can be proved to occur in the case of the heart, but instances are not infrequent in which it seems to take place. The reduction of the causes of hypertrophy, *i.e.* the work of the heart, to a minimum, constitutes, then, the main object in the treatment of hypertrophy. This work is partly of a constant, partly of an occasional nature. The normal work of the circulation must be carried on; the permanent organic cause of the hypertrophy can rarely be lessened; but the occasional addition to the heart's work involved in violent muscular exercise, increased frequency of contraction from alcohol or emotion, increased obstruction from remediable states of blood or local inflammations, may all be to a large extent removed. Rest of body and mind is therefore the first and most essential element in treatment. All exercise which quickens the pulse must be absolutely forbidden.[1] Emotional tranquillity must be as far as possible secured. The utmost temperance in food and alcohol should be enforced. A fair amount of nitrogenous food, and a very little light wine with it, constitute the best diet. If food is well taken without alcohol, the latter may often with advantage be prohibited. The digestive organs should be carefully attended to. Nothing disturbs the action of the heart so readily as a distended stomach. Food must be moderate in amount, and every cause of transient plethora avoided. The secretions must be carefully regulated, and

[1] "On doit regarder le repos comme un remède préservatif; mais ce repos n'exclut pas un exercice modéré, lorsque les grands accidents sont calmés."—Senac, l. c., p. 419.

impaired action of the kidneys or the skin must be supplemented by mild purgation or diuresis. Local inflammations, bronchitis, &c. must be carefully guarded against, and when they occur, removed as speedily as possible.

Too often, however, the amount of obstruction which can by these means be removed bears but a small proportion to the total against which the heart has to contend. Can this permanent obstruction be further reduced ? To some extent the work of the heart can always be lessened by reduction in the total quantity of the blood. This formed an important element in the old system of treatment, and it was partly with this object that frequent and repeated bleedings were recommended. Their condemnation in the present day is superfluous. It may be doubted whether occasional leeching, which still finds advocates, is justified by its ultimate results, although its immediate effect is to give relief to the heart. Restriction of fluids has been suggested. It is at any rate a harmless measure; but the rapidity with which urinary secretion regulates the volume and density of the blood renders it doubtful whether more than a very transient effect is produced.

It will be gathered from these statements that the conditions under which an attempt at the removal of hypertrophy is indicated are very rare. Whenever the hypertrophy can act immediately on the causal resistance, its influence is always, on the whole, and sometimes entirely beneficial. Only when the over-action of the heart is primary, or is due to a cause which has ceased to operate, is it to be attacked directly. In the rare instances in which violent exercise has called out persistent hypertrophy, or some obstruction has been removed, the condition may call for immediate treatment to reduce its effect. Where the obstruction is situated far from the heart, and degenerated vessels are interposed which have to bear the full force of an over-acting ventricle, as in Bright's disease, the question also sometimes arises of the chances of evil from vascular rupture, on the one hand, and from a weakened heart on the other. The certain, slow, but sure evil of a weakened heart will generally counterbalance the possible catastrophe, and any attempt to lessen the cardiac strength will be avoided.

The use of drugs in hypertrophy is a subject on which various opinions have been held.[1] Most observers agree with Walshe, that the reduction of the bulk of the heart is beyond the direct power of any drug. The chief *rôle* of medicine lies in regulating the cardiac contractions and in freeing the circulation from removable causes of embarrassment. Frequent action involves a great increase in the work of the heart. Force is needed, it has been stated already, to move the heart, apart from the movement of the blood. The minimum frequency consistent with the due supply of blood to the system gives

---

[1] Their possible use seems not to have occurred to the French school of physicians at the beginning of this century, although the chief cardiac medicine, digitalis, had long before been employed in this country.

he heart its best conditions of action. Moreover, very frequent action nay fill the arteries to repletion, and so increase their distension as reatly to augment the intra-cardiac pressure. Lastly, frequent action essens the total rest of the heart, and favours degeneration. No remedy ias been discovered which lessens the undue frequency of the action f the heart so effectually as digitalis. But digitalis strengthens the ardiac action, and hence its use in hypertrophy has been dis- :ountenanced by most modern writers, and by some strongly condemned.

The experience of clinical observers is not, however, in complete ιccord with theoretical conclusion. By many the value of digitalis in ιypertrophy is strongly asserted. One explanation for this may lie n the fact that hypertrophy is so rarely simple. Almost invariably, lilatation is conjoined with it. In dilatation, digitalis is of extreme ralue, and its use in hypertrophy is to a great extent proportioned :o the existence and amount of dilatation. Moreover all irregular ιction of the heart involves waste of force, involves useless work. Γoo frequent contraction does the same. Each may generally be :ontrolled by digitalis. Even where there is no irregularity and little dilatation, the cardiac action may be below the actual needs of the system; the compensation is insufficient, and the additional strength of contraction imparted by digitalis is purely useful. The dose of digitalis needed in these circumstances is smaller than that required in dilatation. Five minims of the tincture, or a drachm of the infusion, three times a day, will usually effect all that is required. A larger dose, is, as Milner Fothergill states, much more frequently deleterious than in dilatation, in which large doses are borne, not only with impunity, but with advantage. In pure hypertrophy, digitalis is rarely necessary. Veratrum viride has been used, especially in America, to reduce the strength of the heart, when in hypertrophy its force appears beyond the present need of the system. Doses of five minims of the tincture may be given three times a day. Both the force and frequency of the heart's action are reduced. Inunction of Ung. Veratriæ has also been employed for the same purpose.

Where hypertrophy is not pure but is great, and acts directly on the vascular system, or tends to increase its cause (as in aortic regurgi- tation), it may be necessary, by similar measures, to reduce the force of the heart to a minimum necessary for the work of the circu- lation. Digitalis has been employed in small doses and recommended strongly by B. Foster, but most authorities discountenance its use under these circumstances, and Ringer[1] points out that the same end may be attained by small doses of aconite. A combination of aconite and veratrum is recommended by H. C. Wood.[2]

The consciousness of the cardiac contractions, which constitutes so troublesome a symptom of hypertrophy, is only in part due to the force with which the heart acts. It is much more frequently the result

[1] Handbook of Therapeutics, fifth edition, p. 427.
[2] Philadelphia Med. Times, 1874, Nov. 14 and 21.

of irregular or too sudden contractions, and related to coincident dilatation rather than to hypertrophy. It is commonly controlled by rest and digitalis.

For the relief of cardiac pain, direct sedatives may be needed. Opium, or morphia, is very effectual. Aconite is strongly praised by Walshe. Belladonna, Indian hemp, hydrocyanic acid are also useful in some cases. The Virginian prune bark, which contains hydrocyanic acid, is sometimes useful, but its tonic properties render it more suitable for dilatation. Cold locally applied to the cardiac region is strongly recommended by Niemeyer.

The treatment of hypertrophy of the right ventricle must be conducted on the same general principles as that of the left. It is almost always united with dilatation, and is never excessive. Hence it needs as far as possible to be strengthened, both absolutely by tonics, digitalis, &c., and relatively by diminishing its work, by lessening as far as possible the obstruction to the movement of blood through the lungs, and by the avoidance of over-exertion, &c. Hypertrophy of the auricles rarely calls for special treatment. Never simple, the conjoined dilatation always predominates.

The more detailed treatment of dilated hypertrophy is described in the next article, on Dilatation of the Heart.

DILATATION OF THE HEART.

By W. R. GOWERS, M.D.

SYNONYM.—Enlargement of the Heart (old writers); Aneurism of the Heart (Baillou; Lancisi); Passive Aneurism, or Passive Dilatation (Corvisart); Herzerweiterung (Freysig); Cardiectasis (Jaccoud).

DEFINITION.—Increase in the size of one or more of the cavities of the heart. Such increase in size may or may not be attended with obvious thickening or thinning of the cardiac walls.

HISTORY.—Dilatation of the heart received much attention from the earlier pathologists, being rightly regarded as the chief cause of its enlargement. In the middle of the sixteenth century, Vesalius gave an account of a heart, the left ventricle of which contained two pounds of blood, and Baillou[1] mentioned one that equalled in size a man's head. Harvey[2] also in 1628 alluded to this condition. Dilatation of the auricles was described by Willis. Dilatation of the right ventricle and left auricle, as the result of mitral constriction, was described by Mayow in 1674. Vieussens,[3] in 1715, described a case, observed in 1695, of extreme dilatation of left ventricle, the consequence of aortic regurgitation. Peyer, Lancisi, and all successive writers alluded to, or related instances of the condition. The first systematic account of its mechanism and causes was given by Senac[4] in 1749, who distinguished dilatation with and without thickening of the walls. Morgagni,[5] in 1779, described very clearly its origin, and effect on the circulation. Several cases were related by Ferriar,[6] in 1792, and the general causes and symptoms of dilatation were described by Allan Burns, in 1809. In France, after the writings of Lancisi had given the word currency, Baillou's term " aneurism," had been used to designate enlargements of the heart, as

---

[1] Epidemies et Ephemerides, 1574. Yvaren's Trans., Paris, 1858, p. 289.
[2] De motu cordis et sanguinis.
[3] Traité du Cœur.
[4] Traité de la Structure du Cœur, &c., tom. ii.
[5] De Sed. et Caus. Morb., Epist. xxvii.
[6] Medical Histories and Reflections, by John Ferriar, M.D., vol. i., 1792, p. 144.

well as of the great vessels. Corvisart, in his description of dilatation in his work, published in 1806, designated the two varieties described by Senac, "active" and "passive" aneurism, with a subprotest against the application of the term to conditions with such different tendencies. He described accurately, as far as the description went, the different symptoms and tendencies of the two conditions, and pointed out the association of dropsy, or the "serous diathesis," with dilatation, rather than hypertrophy. A further account of dilatation of the left auricle as a mechanical consequence of mitral constriction was given by Abernethy in 1806.[1] Dilatation consequent on carditis, and associated with adherent pericardium, was described, as the result of articular rheumatism, by Sir W. Dundas in 1808.[2] Its varieties were recognised a little later by Kreysig. Bertin, in 1811, distinguished the conditions and processes of dilatation and hypertrophy (in the sense in which the words are now used), and Laennec's work on Auscultation, published in 1819, gave the terms authoritative use. In Bertin's systematic treatise, edited by Bouillaud in 1824, the chief varieties were distinguished which have since been generally recognised.

The detection, by percussion, of enlargement of the heart, of which dilatation is the chief cause, is due to Avenbrugger (1763) ; that of the altered impulse by palpation, to Corvisart (1806); that of the auscultatory signs, to Laennec (1820).

VARIETIES.—From the condition of the cardiac walls, their increase or diminution in thickness, certain varieties have long been distinguished.

(1). *Dilatation with Hypertrophy* (active aneurism of Corvisart), in which the walls are increased in thickness, as well as the cavities in size.

(2). *Dilatation with Attenuation* (passive aneurism of Corvisart), in which the cavities are increased in size, while the walls are reduced in thickness. To these Bertin proposed to add that of *simple dilatation*. in which the dilated walls preserve their normal thickness, and *mixed dilatation*, in which the walls are in one place increased, in another diminished, in thickness. These varieties have been adopted by most subsequent writers. The name, "simple dilatation," cannot, however, be considered an accurate designation of the condition which it denotes, dilatation without hypertrophy of tissue. If a heart be dilated only, its walls, extended in area, are necessarily lessened in thickness. For the normal thickness of the walls to be preserved when the cavity is dilated, overgrowth of tissue must occur. Thus the condition of "simple dilatation" necessarily produces dilatation with attenuation, while the state to which the term is applied is really dilatation with moderate hypertrophy : this was shown clearly by Stokes. Forget applied to the condition the term *hypertrophie dilatoire*. Many writers have suggested, and Wilks and Moxon maintain, that pure dilatation

---

[1] Med.-Chir. Trans., vol. i., p. 27.
[2] Ibid., p. 37.

never occurs, that hypertrophy is the invariable accompaniment, as the increased weight testifies, and that recorded examples of hearts dilated and not increased in weight have been examples only of relaxation. They prefer the simple distinction into dilatation with thickening, and dilatation with thinning.

Other varieties which have been distinguished are those of *general dilatation*, in which all four cavities of the heart suffer, and *partial dilatation*, in which the change is confined to one or some of them. It has also been proposed by Hayden[1] to designate those cases in which an obvious active cause of dilatation can be distinguished, *consecutive*, and those in which no such causes exists, *primary*. Lastly, dilatations have been classified as *temporary* or *permanent*. Bertin suggested that the latter only should be included under the term, the temporary forms being rather examples of distension than of dilatation.

CAUSES.—The maintenance of the normal size of the heart ultimately depends on the existence of a due proportion between its elastic and contractile force, and the blood-pressure to which it is exposed in passive resistance and active contraction. A disproportion between these two forces is the ultimate cause of its dilatation ; such disproportion may result from a change in the amount of either factor, an increase in the blood-pressure, a decrease in the cardiac strength. Often the two conditions are conjoined : a weakened heart yields before an increased pressure, and thus becomes over-distended ; and, the conditions being permanent, becomes permanently dilated. To these two causes must, probably, be added the effect of traction from without, which acts by lessening the effect of the contractile force of the heart, and so corresponds in its action with the weakening of the wall.

Thus diminished strength of the walls of the heart constitutes a predisposition to dilatation, and the causes of that weakening may be considered as the *predisposing causes* of dilatation ; the increased endocardial pressure being regarded as the *exciting cause* of the dilatation. But, as is the case with many predisposing causes of disease, the weakness of the wall of the heart may be the only morbid antecedent. Moreover, the action of these two causes of dilatation is not simply predisposing and exciting. It will be convenient, however, to consider the mechanism of their action after they have been described in brief detail. The antecedents of the predisposing and exciting causes may be spoken of as the *remote causes* of dilatation.

It must be remembered also, that increased endocardial pressure is the immediate cause, not only of dilatation, by its mechanical effect, but of hypertrophy, by the vital reaction which it induces. Its effect in producing dilatation is influenced in part by the existence of the predisposition (weakness of the cardiac wall), in part by the conditions under which it acts, and which may be regarded as *determining causes*. Commonly, however, the double tendency of the increased

[1] Diseases of Heart and Aorta : Dublin, 1875, p. 558.

3 B 2

pressure results in the double effect, and hypertrophy and dilatation are conjoined. We have thus four classes of causes to consider, the remote, predisposing, exciting, and determining causes.

(A.) *Remote Causes.*—The general conditions of hereditary influence, age, sex, occupation, previous illness, &c., enter largely into the causation of dilatation of the heart, as the antecedents of the conditions on which it immediately depends. They can only be fully understood when the immediate causes are known. *Hereditary taint* has a powerful influence in disposing to special degenerations and to certain diseases, such as acute rheumatism, on which the immediate causes largely depend. *Age* has a similar influence. Degenerative changes are concerned in the production of both causes of dilatation, and hence the disease increases in frequency with advancing years. *Sex* influences the occurrence of dilatation by determining exposure to one of the commonest causes of increased endocardial pressure, muscular exertion. Degenerative changes in the vascular system are largely due to the same influence, and are causes of dilatation. Hence the disease is more frequent in men than in women. *Occupation* has a similar influence; all those occupations which involve considerable effort tend to cause dilatation of the heart.

(B.) *Predisposing Causes.*—Conditions of weakness of the cardiac walls may consist in acute or chronic changes in the muscular fibres, or in destruction of those fibres and their replacement by tissue elements which yield more readily to the pressure of the blood. Morbid states of the muscular fibres are, (1.) Atony, in which the relaxation of the fibres at rest is more absolute, their contraction less complete. (2.) The granular degeneration of acute disease. (3.) Fatty degeneration, resulting ultimately in the actual destruction of fibres. (4.) Fatty overgrowth, in which the muscular fibres undergo secondary atrophy. (5.) Fibroid degeneration, the sequel to an acute inflammatory change or the result of a chronic perversion of nutrition. (6.) Special degenerations and growths. (7.) Weakening of the fibres due to the state of dilatation. Beau pointed out that the fibres common to the two ventricles may be so weakened by dilatation of one, as to lessen considerably the contractile force of the other ventricle, and so to aid its dilatation. (8.) Lastly, it has been stated by Niemeyer[1] that the muscular fibres may so lose their contractile power as to permit dilatation when no structural change in the cardiac wall, or in the fibres themselves, can be detected by the microscope. Seitz[2] has lately advocated the same view. In all the recorded examples, however, over-exertion has been the exciting cause of the dilatation, and the cases appear to have been characterised rather by insufficient power to react against the augmented pressure, than by any primary degeneration.

The conditions by which these pathological processes are produced

[1] Text book of Practical Medicine, American Trans., vol. ii. p. 320.
[2] Zur Lehre von der Ueberanstrengung des Herzens. Deutsches Archiv für klin. Med. 1873, xi., xii.

constitute the predisposing causes of dilatation. The most important of these conditions are: (1.) Anæmia and chlorosis, in which the general mal-nutrition results in atony, and, it may be, granular degeneration of muscular fibre throughout the body. (2.) Acute febrile diseases, especially rheumatism, erysipelas, pyæmia, typhus, typhoid fever, &c., having a similar effect. (3.) Inflammation, primary or secondary to endo- or peri-carditis, the inflammation in the latter case invading the adjacent layer of the heart. (4.) Obesity, with local overgrowth of fatty tissue. (5.) Chronic degenerative changes in the system, as yet ill-defined, but often due to chronic alcoholism, and causing fatty and fibroid degeneration of various organs, including the heart. (6.) Derangements of the blood-supply to the walls of the heart. Chronic and intermitting passive congestions cause, as Sir William Jenner points out,[1] degeneration of the heart, toughening its walls and lessening its contractile power. Diminished blood-supply is a common cause of fatty and granular degeneration. It may be due to imperfect distension of the coronary arteries in consequence of the defective distension of the aorta, or it may result from narrowing of those vessels by the contraction of lymph outside the heart, or by degeneration, atheromatous and calcareous, of their walls. (7.) Defective nerve-power probably in some cases leads to inefficient contraction and dilatation of the heart. Dr. Dobell believes that sexual excesses are powerful causes of cardiac weakness.

Traction from without, the result of pericardial adhesions, is sometimes a cause of dilatation of the heart. The two conditions are constantly found associated, but in the majority of cases there exists also endocardial mischief sufficient to account for the dilatation. Hence, Morgagni and many subsequent writers doubted whether the state of the walls was not always the consequence of the coexisting valvular disease. But cases are not infrequent in which dilatation exists, and no morbid condition can be found to explain its occurrence except an adherent pericardium. Beau,[2] arguing from a small number of such cases, inferred that dilatation was the invariable result of pericardial adhesion. The same view was very strongly maintained by Hope.[3] Wider observation showed, however, that adhesions were frequent enough with no morbid state of the heart's walls. Laennec, Bouillaud,[4] Barlow, Stokes, and others maintained, therefore, that pericardial adhesions have no direct effect in causing dilatation. The same view has been still more recently maintained by Hayden.[5] Gairdner,[6] however, emphasized the fact that in a minority of cases no other cause can be discovered for the changes in the walls of the heart. At the same time he showed that, in other cases, the adhesions not only do not tend to cause dilatation, but they do not prevent the reduction in size which

[1] On Congestion of the Heart, Med.-Chir. Trans., vol. xliii.
[2] Arch. Gén. de Méd., ser. ii., tome x., 1837, p. 425.
[3] Diseases of the Heart, p. 192.
[4] Traité Clinique, &c., 1835, p. 454.
[5] Diseases of the Heart and Aorta, p. 363.
[6] Edin. Med. Journal, February 1851.

accompanies chronic wasting diseases. The most extensive statistical evidence on the question is that furnished by Kennedy,[1] of Dublin. who collected ninety cases of adherent pericardium without valve disease, and found that the heart remained healthy till death in thirty-four, and was enlarged in fifty-one. But some of his cases were from museums, into which hearts of the normal size would be little likely to find their way, and it is probable, therefore, that his proportion of healthy hearts is too small. Dr. Hayden has collected twenty-three cases of adherent pericardium, without valve disease, and found that in seven there was enlargement without any other discoverable cause.[2] Putting together these facts, and those recorded by other authorities, it seems fair to conclude that adherent pericardium causes enlargement of the heart in one-third of the cases.

The difference in the effect of the adhesion is not to be explained by difference in its extent. The most marked hypertrophy and dilatation was due, in one of Gairdner's cases, to a firm adhesion of very limited extent, near the apex of the left ventricle. In other cases in which no influence was exerted, the adhesion was universal. Dr. Wilks[3] has pointed out that, when general adhesion is associated with dilatation, the effect is more marked on the right ventricle than on the left. This is no doubt due to the thinness of the muscular wall of the right ventricle. In estimating the effect of pericardial adhesions it must be remembered how frequently they are associated with another cause of dilatation, the damage to the subjacent portion of the cardiac wall by the extension to it of the pericardial inflammation. For the settlement of the question of their influence more facts are needed which shall embrace not only the state of the heart's walls. and the fact of adhesions, but the extent, firmness, and probable duration of the latter, the extent to which the pericardium is connected with parts around, and the extent to which the muscular fibres of the heart have suffered from the inflammation.

Dr. Gairdner[4] has maintained that when the expansion of the lungs is interfered with by their atrophy, the inspiratory efforts to distend them, which he regards as the great cause of emphysema, may lead to over-distension of the heart. He believes that it is by this mechanism that emphysema is associated with dilatation of the heart, and appeals in support of the theory, to the fact that the dilatation is not confined to the right side but affects in slighter degree and a little later in time the left side also. This view depends for its probability on the inspiratory theory of emphysema. If, with Sir William Jenner and most modern authorities, emphysema is believed to arise chiefly, not from primary atrophy of the lung, but from its over-distension during expiratory efforts, this explanation of the origin of dilatation of the heart falls to the ground. No dilating influence by traction can result from

[1] Edin. Med. Journal.
[2] Loc. cit., table on p. 362.
[3] Guy's Hosp. Rep., vol. xvi., p. 202.
[4] British and Foreign Medico-Chirurg. Rev., July 1853, p. 212.

violent expiratory efforts, and when emphysema is once established the inspiratory effort which can be made is far less than in health. If the dilatation of the right ventricle in these cases is referred, as is generally taught, to obstruction to the flow through the lungs, the simultaneous affection of the left side can be explained in another way.

(C.) *Exciting Causes.*—Increase in the endocardial blood-pressure has been mentioned as the chief exciting cause of dilatation of the heart. Such increased pressure opposes the contraction of the heart, and leads, by a mechanism to be presently described, to its dilatation. It depends on increased resistance to the movement of the blood, the result of an increase in its mass, or an obstruction in the orifices or vessels through which it flows. This increased pressure leads to two results, directly to dilatation, indirectly to hypertrophy. The causes of the increased pressure, which are more fully considered in the article on hypertrophy, are as follow :—

(1.) Increase in the mass of blood to be moved, consequent on over-distension of the heart. Thus, regurgitation through an orifice causes dilatation of the chamber behind. Thus, too, the dilatation tends to its own increase, a process which is only arrested by the occurrence of hypertrophy.

(2.) Resistance to the movement of the blood in consequence of narrowing of the orifice by which it leaves the affected chamber. The influence of this condition in causing dilatation is not great. The obstruction is gradually developed, and unless associated with weakness of the cardiac walls, the latter become hypertrophied to overcome the increased resistance. In aortic obstruction, for instance, dilatation is rare.

(3.) Resistance to the movement of the blood through the vascular system is a powerful cause of dilatation, and is most effective when suddenly developed or intermitting, and especially when the condition in which it arises is such as to impair the nutrition of the walls of the heart. Disease of the large vessels, aorta and pulmonary artery, rarely causes dilatation. Obstruction of the smaller vessels is a more effective cause, and especially those forms of obstruction which affect the pulmonary circulation alone, or in conjunction with the systemic vessels.

Long-continued and severe muscular efforts are, as Ferriar [1] pointed out, a powerful cause of dilatation and hypertrophy. The resulting condition of heart depends largely on the existence of the conditions which favour the occurrence of one or the other state. The effect of effort is to obstruct the circulation through both the general and pulmonary system. Its influence on the left ventricle has been described in relation to hypertrophy. Clifford Allbutt has especially pointed out the direct effect on the right ventricle and the influence of undue smallness of lungs on its occurrence. The obstruction to the pulmonary circulation by the pressure of the air on the inner surface of the air cells obstructs the escape of blood from the right

[1] Med. Hist. and Ref., vol. i. 1792.

side of the heart. The compression of the heart itself interferes with the entrance of blood from the veins, tends to their over-distension, and when the pressure is removed, to the over-distension of the right auricle and ventricle. Thus the intermitting obstruction causes intermitting over-distension of the right side of the heart, and that intermitting congestion of the walls of the heart which leads to the degeneration of its substance and renders dilatation permanent.

It is by a similar mechanism, according to the views generally accepted, and fully stated by Sir William Jenner in the third volume of this work, that emphysema of the lungs causes dilatation of the heart. Intermittent distension results, as just described, from the violent expiratory efforts with closed glottis, which constitute the efficient cause of emphysema; and as the latter condition is developed, degeneration, elongation, and destruction of capillaries render the obstruction permanent, which before was occasional. The right side of the heart undergoes dilatation, sometimes to an extreme degree. Hypertrophy is usually also produced. The congestion of the cardiac wall disposes the left ventricle to yield before the increased pressure of the aortic blood, which is an ultimate effect of the venous distension acting through the capillary system.

Other forms of pulmonary change have a slighter tendency to cause dilatation of the heart than emphysema. An exception must, however, be made for cirrhosis of the lung, which produces, in a large number of cases, hypertrophy and dilatation of the right side. Such a change was present in one-third of the cases of cirrhosis collected by Bastian.[1]

Mechanism.—The consideration of the mechanism by which dilatation is effected is necessarily, in the main, theoretical. It has, perhaps on this account, received little attention, and has even been sometimes dismissed as useless. But any clear conception of the way in which a morbid state is related to its causes, if correct, must afford a clearer view of its pathological significance, and of the way in which by treatment it may best be met.

The dilatation of the heart is produced, in every case, by its over-distension with blood. Just as the various causes of hypertrophy involve, as the efficient cause, overwork, so the various causes of dilatation involve over-distension. The immediate cause of this over-distension is, in each case, the existence at the end of the diastole of an endocardial pressure disproportioned to the resisting power of the wall of the heart, and before which the wall yields. The act of dilatation thus occurs during the diastole of the heart. This circumstance lessens the simplicity of the relative action of the exciting and predisposing causes of dilatation, since, as will be immediately explained, each may act by producing a similar effect.

Three sources of over-distension may thus be recognised. (1.) The mass of blood entering in the normal course of the circulation may be abnormally large; *simple over-distension.* (2.) Blood may enter the cavity from an abnormal source (regurgitation), and being added

[1] Art. Cirrhosis of Lung, vol. iii.

to that entering it in the normal course of the circulation, increases the mass of blood and so the distension of the chamber; *over-distension from regurgitation.* (3.) The whole of the blood previously in the chamber may not be expelled from it during contraction, the residual blood being added to that entering from behind increases the distension of the chamber; *over-distension from imperfect contraction,* or *residual over-distension.*

(1.) *Simple over-distension* is the result of over-distension of the source from which the blood enters the affected chamber. It is well seen in the effect of mitral regurgitation on the left ventricle. The over-distended auricle drives an abnormal quantity of blood into the ventricle, into which probably an increased quantity has already passed in consequence of the heightened tension of the blood within the auricle. It is probable that a large quantity of blood enters the ventricle during diastole, enough to equalise, or almost to equalise, the pressure within the ventricle and within the auricle,[1] before the auricular contraction effects the actual distension or over-distension of the ventricle. The pressure to which the inner surface of the ventricle is exposed at the end of the auricular systole is very great, for in accordance with the well-known law of hydrostatics it is multiplied directly as the area of the inner surface of the ventricle exceeds that of the auriculo-ventricular orifice. Simple over-distension may occur, especially in the auricles, in conditions of acute weakening of the cardiac walls. The lessened tone of the muscular fibres allows them to yield unduly before the pressure of the incoming blood, and as the current is continuous, they thus become directly over-distended. Similarly the flaccid ventricles may yield unduly before the current which enters during diastole, and the systole of the auricles may over-distend the ventricles. This mechanism has been described by Beau[2] as *dilatation sans asystolie.* But the conditions are those under which contraction is imperfect, and the small pulse renders it probable, in many cases, that such imperfection occurs. Residual over-distension will then increase the dilatation.

(2.) *Over-distension from regurgitation* is one of the most efficient causes of dilatation. The cavity is filled with blood from a double source. That which enters in the normal course of the circulation is added to that which has regurgitated into the cavity, and over-distension results. In aortic regurgitation, for instance, it is the addition of the contents of the auricle to the blood regurgitating into the ventricle from the aorta, which actually distends the chamber and dilates it until, ultimately, the dilating process is met by compensating

---

[1] That this is the case is highly probable, from a phenomenon sometimes to be observed in cases of mitral constriction. When diastolic and presystolic murmurs are both present, the former due to the slow passage of blood through the orifice in consequence of the tension of the blood within the auricle, the latter due to the contraction of the auricle, there may be, during an occasional prolonged diastole, an interval of silence between the two murmurs. When the diastolic murmur is loud, this silence can only be explained by a cessation, or almost cessation, of the flow of blood, which means, of course, an equalisation of the pressure in the two cavities.

[2] Beau, Traité d'Auscultation. Paris, 1856.

hypertrophy. In permanent patency of the semilunar valves the intra-ventricular pressure at the end of the auricular systole must be very great, since the pressure of the aortic blood will be added to that produced by the contraction of the auricle.

(3.) *Over-distension from imperfect contraction; residual over-distension.*—Whenever, from any cause, systole is incomplete, blood must remain in the chambers and render the entrance of the normal quantity of blood an over-distending agent. Incompleteness of contraction is theoretically possible from two causes, diminished contractile force, and increased resistance to contraction. It is probable that each of these does actually prevent complete contraction, since each is found to be an efficient cause of dilatation.

(*a*) The various conditions which weaken the cardiac walls, already considered, must tend to render the heart incapable of overcoming all the resistance that is opposed to it, whether that be normal or increased. Hence the contraction is imperfect and the residual blood is the ultimate cause of over-distension. To this condition Beau gave the name of *asystolie.* This weakening of the wall not only leads to over-distension, it also renders the effect of the over-distending force greater in degree and in duration, for the weak wall yields more to the increased pressure, and the yielding of the degenerated wall is permanent. Among the conditions weakening the heart must also be reckoned the state of dilatation. The dilated heart has increased work, for it has to move an increased mass of blood, to overcome a greater pressure. To this it is even less competent than a healthy heart. Hence the dilatation itself renders the contraction additionally incomplete, and is thus perpetuated and increased. The influence of dilatation is of course here considered apart from that of the hypertrophy commonly conjoined with it, and to some extent counteracting its effect.

It is by interfering with contraction that pericardial adhesions must be considered to exert whatever influence they possess in causing dilatation of the heart. Connections of the pericardium with parts around, consequent on the extension of inflammation to its outer surface, may cause the adhesions to the heart to oppose considerably the reduction in size during systole, and thus to render the contractions incomplete.[1] Moreover, a similar effect may be produced by the interference with the approximation of different parts of the surface during contraction, which must occur if a thick inelastic membrane covers the heart. Such an influence will interfere chiefly with the contraction of the thin-walled right ventricle, and this may be one reason why it suffers most. The effect will be to cause a residual over-distension, just as does the simple weakening of the cardiac wall with which the adhesions are so often associated.

(*b*) Increased resistance from some obstruction to the circulation is

---

[1] Thus in Gairdner's case, already mentioned, in which marked hypertrophy and dilatation of the left ventricle were associated with, as the only discoverable cause, a local adhesion near the apex, a corresponding adhesion connected the other side of the pericardium with the left lung.

another cause of incomplete contraction. Such increased resistance may interfere with the contraction of a healthy heart, but probably rarely does this unless great and suddenly developed. The reserve of power usually prevents imperfect contraction, and compensating hypertrophy gradually renders the heart efficient. But when suddenly developed, or when the nutrition of the heart is interfered with, the chamber dilates. This dilatation was formerly, and is still by some, ascribed to the direct effect of the increased pressure on the contracting fibres.[1] It was compared by Senac to the effect of an extending force in elongating a cord.[2] Niemeyer[3] pointed out that such an explanation is entirely inapplicable to the conditions of the phenomenon. Increase in the capacity of a contracting chamber from increased pressure within it during contraction is inconceivable. Such increased capacity can only be explained by an increased quantity of blood entering it under a pressure sufficient to overcome the resistance of its walls. The influence of increased resistance to contraction may be to weaken the muscular fibres, to lessen the elasticity of the walls, and to render over-distension easier, but more than this it cannot directly effect.

(D.) *Determining Causes.*—The exciting causes of dilatation and hypertrophy are thus to some extent the same; the occurrence of the result is influenced not only by the predisposition already described, but also by certain determining conditions.

(1.) The rapidity of the development of the increased blood-pressure, *i.e.*, the rapidity with which the valvular disease, or the systemic or pulmonary obstruction is produced. Time is necessary for the production of that hypertrophy which alone can prevent dilatation, and a suddenly-developed obstruction invariably leads to dilatation.

(2.) The small amount of muscular tissue normally existing in the wall of the affected chamber of the heart. This is naturally proportioned to the work of each segment of the heart, *i.e.*, to the blood-pressure, to be by it passively resisted and actively overcome. The extra pressure induced by the abnormal obstruction or regurgitation bears no necessary proportion to the normal blood-pressure, and before absolute equal increments of pressure, the smaller the normal amount of muscular tissue, the more readily does dilatation occur, because the systole is the more readily rendered imperfect, and residual over-distension produced.

Each cavity of the heart affords an illustration of these influences,

[1] Lately by Chirone in Lo Sperimentale, August 1874.
[2] "La contraction qui resserre les ventricules est peut-être l'instrument qui augment les dimensions, que le sang soit en trop grande quantité dans ces réservoirs ; qu'il trouve quelque barrière que l'empêche d'en sortir avec la liberté qu'il a ordinairement, l'action des fibres sera plus forte : or cet excès de force doit nécessairement les allonger : un raccourcissement forcé produit le même effet qu'une action qui tire et qui tend une corde, ses éléments doivent nécessairement s'ecarter, et même se séparer, s'ils sont tirés avec trop de violence."—Senac, Traité, &c., 1749, tom. ii., p. 397.
[3] Loc. cit., vol. ii. p. 316.

and although our knowledge is still very imperfect, we can understand something of the origin of the condition found in each instance, and it is worth while to recapitulate briefly the way in which the different results are brought about.

In aortic obstruction the left ventricle is commonly hypertrophied, less commonly dilated. The left ventricle, containing the greatest amount of muscular tissue, possesses a large reserve of force, and can overact so as to overcome a moderate increase in resistance, and so prevent residual over-distension and dilatation. The development of obstruction is usually slow, and thus there is time for hypertrophy to occur. In aortic regurgitation there is always dilatation, and usually much, often very much, hypertrophy. The regurgitant blood causes the ventricle to be overfilled, and the patent aortic orifice transmits to the interior of the ventricle, during its passive state, the intra-aortic pressure. The regurgitation is usually slowly developed, and the muscular tissue of the ventricle considerable, and hence hypertrophy occurs. This is favoured by the abundant blood supply to the heart, consequent on the great distension of the aorta.

In mitral disease, obstructive and regurgitant, the left auricle undergoes dilatation and hypertrophy, the former predominating in regurgitation, from the direct over-distension and frequently rapid development of the pathological state. Hypertrophy of the auricle is usually more frequent in obstruction, from the slowness with which the lesion is developed. Dilatation is always, however, conjoined, from the ease with which the contraction of the weak auricle is rendered imperfect by obstruction. In mitral regurgitation, the left ventricle is hypertrophied and dilated, and the dilatation is usually considerable, in consequence of the direct over-distension of the chamber, and perhaps also of the imperfect distension of the coronary arteries and consequent damaged cardiac nutrition.

The right ventricle, in disease of the left side, usually undergoes dilatation, from its small amount of muscular tissue, but often is also hypertrophied, in consequence of the slowness with which the obstruction in the left side tells back upon the right. The hypertrophy is usually less and the dilatation as much marked, when the obstruction is situated in the pulmonary system, in consequence of the directness with which such obstruction affects the ventricle, the rapidity with which it is frequently developed and increased, and the damage to the cardiac nutrition, which results from the extreme and sudden passive congestion to which the heart is, in these cases, very often liable.

In obstructions to the systemic circulation, hypertrophy is the common change in the left ventricle, and often, especially in Bright's disease, is wholly unattended with dilatation. The extreme slowness with which the obstruction is developed is, no doubt, a chief factor in determining the occurrence of hypertrophy rather than dilatation. Occasionally, however, dilatation occurs instead of hypertrophy. Such cases are perhaps instances of simultaneous cardiac and vascular degeneration, in which the increased blood tension is the result of the latter, and the damaged heart is incapable of resisting the abnormal pressure.

The sequence of the conditions of hypertrophy and dilatation varies under different circumstances. It is certainly not uniform, as has been maintained by some writers. When an increased resistance or a cause of over-distension is suddenly developed, dilatation results at once, and hypertrophy slowly, when time allows overgrowth to occur. This is frequently seen in aortic and mitral regurgitation. The order is the same when the initial state is one of defective power in the walls of the heart; dilatation precedes and is the cause of hypertrophy —as in that which results from carditis. On the other hand, dilatation may be secondary. Degeneration occurs in the hypertrophied tissue more readily than in the healthy heart. Nutritive influences fail from impaired health or advancing years.[1] Again, the coronary vessels suffer from undue strain, degenerate, and lessen the blood supply. This, as pointed out by Mauriac, is a frequent occurrence in aortic regurgitation. Under all these conditions the degeneration weakens the cardiac wall, and dilatation occurs at a later period than the hypertrophy.

PATHOLOGICAL ANATOMY.—Dilatation may affect all the chambers of the heart or only some of them. It has been a subject of rather unprofitable discussion whether general or partial dilatation is the more common. It is rare for one chamber to suffer considerably alone. When the cause of the dilatation is disease of an orifice, the chambers behind the orifice are usually alone affected. An exception is mitral regurgitation, in which the cavity in front of the orifice is dilated also. The chamber immediately behind the diseased orifice commonly suffers more than the others. In mitral constriction, for instance, the left auricle is most dilated. In all diseases of the left side of the heart, the right side may ultimately become dilated. Hence the most widely distributed change occurs when the obstruction is in front of the left ventricle, and affects each part of the heart successively. In aortic regurgitation, for instance, enormous hearts are met with, in which every cavity is dilated. Occasionally a similar result follows obstruction in the aortic system.

The dilatation, as already stated, is rarely simple. Hypertrophy is usually present, and varies in amount according to the conditions described in the last article. From the variations in the amount of dilatation and associated hypertrophy very different effects on the form and size of the heart are produced.

The amount of dilatation is estimated by comparison with the normal capacity, by measurement of the external size of the heart, the thickness of the walls, and the length and mid-circumference of the cavity. In estimating it, regard must be had to the age of the

---

[1] Niemeyer pointed out how frequently from this cause the hypertrophy which results from senile vascular degeneration gives place to dilatation.

patient, and to the state of the body. The capacity of the heart naturally increases with age. In decomposition the relaxation of the heart is extreme, the cavities present their maximum capacity, the walls their minimum thickness. The existence of decomposition which in some cases is very rapid, must therefore induce caution in inferring actual dilatation from a flaccid and apparently dilated state of the heart.

A heart, the subject of general or partial dilatation, is increased in size and altered in shape. The increase in size may be considerable: the circumference being two, three, or four times the normal. Occasionally the left ventricle is so large as to be "capable of containing another heart"—a favourite comparison since the time of Malpighi. The left auricle may be dilated, in disease of the mitral orifice, to very large dimensions. In a case recorded by Cruveilhier, it had four times its normal dimensions. The greatest dilatation, however, occurs on the right side. Both ventricle and auricle may be very large. The right auricle, as Burserius[1] remarked, may undergo greater dilatation than any other part of the heart. Stokes[2] mentions a case in which the auricle was so capacious as to contain a pound of blood.

The shape is altered according to the part of the heart affected. In general dilatation the heart is increased in width, so that it has a more globular shape. This depends especially on the dilatation of the right chambers, and is marked when these alone are affected. Considerable dilatation of the auricles may alter considerably the normal shape' of the heart. Thus in the case mentioned by Stokes, the dilated right auricle "formed a vast purple tumour, which concealed the whole of the anterior portion of the right lung."

In pure dilatation the weight of the heart is normal. Instances of this are, however, to say the least, very rare. As a rule the weight of the dilated heart is greater than normal, in consequence of the almost invariable coexistence of hypertrophy.

The walls of the heart the subject of simple, or nearly simple, dilatation are flaccid, and collapse when cut across. They are thinner than normal in proportion to the amount of dilatation, and to its freedom from accompanying hypertrophy. In most cases the attenuation, however considerable, is the result of the extension of the wall. In rare cases the wall may actually be atrophied. In the ventricles the thinning is most marked towards the apex. The wall of the left ventricle may be reduced to one-sixth of an inch at the middle and one-twenty-fifth of an inch at the apex. The walls of the auricles may, in extreme dilatation, be reduced to an almost membranous condition. Very frequently, coexisting hypertrophy prevents noticeable diminution in the thickness of the walls, even when the dilatation is very great. The thickness of the wall may even be above the

[1] The Institutes of the Practice of Medicine, 1798. Cullen Brown's Trans., vol. v., p. 312.
[2] Diseases of Heart and Aorta, p. 275.

normal, notwithstanding the dilatation, especially when the latter is moderate in degree.

The muscular tissue is sometimes normal in appearance, sometimes pale or mottled. Under the microscope it usually presents evidence of degeneration, especially when the dilatation is comparatively pure. The muscular fibres present indistinct striation, or granular or actual fatty degeneration. The connective tissue between the fibres is often increased, and may also present granular degeneration. The endocardium may be thicker or thinner than normal; it is often irregularly thickened and opaque, especially in the auricles. The pericardium is stretched in proportion to the dilatation, and is also often unduly opaque.

The orifices participate in the dilatation of the cavities of the heart. The auriculo-ventricular orifices undergo the greatest extension, especially when the cavities on each side of them are dilated. The ultimate result is that the valves become incompetent to close the orifice, in consequence of the disproportion between their area and that of the enlarged orifice. This effect is increased by the removal of the bases of the papillary muscles to a greater distance from the orifice, in consequence of the extension of the wall. For a time the incompetence may be averted. The segments of the valves may undergo some amount of dilatation so as to close the enlarged orifice, and the papillary muscles may undergo at their apices transformation into fibrous tissue, which, being incapable of contraction during the systole, effects a practical elongation of the muscle, and so helps to counteract the effect of the removal of their points of attachment. Ultimately, however, the dilatation of the orifice exceeds the influence of these compensations, and incompetence of the valves results. This is the case especially in the right side of the heart, in which the dilatation of the two cavities is usually simultaneous and considerable, and is the common cause of tricuspid incompetence.[1]

In dilatation of the auricles, the large venous trunks opening into them, unprotected by valves, commonly participate in the dilatation, and may be greatly enlarged, so that their openings into the auricle may be hard to determine. The auricular appendices are also much dilated.

Certain associated conditions are commonly met with in cases of dilatation. Some of these are causal, such as valvular disease, pericardial adhesions, emphysema of the lungs, kidney disease. Others are sequential, such as passive congestion of organs, and its consequences in alteration in their texture.

CONSEQUENCES.—From the incompetence of the valves due to the dilatation of the orifices, regurgitation of blood with all its consequences, results. Before, however, sequential regurgitation is developed, the same consequences, although in less degree, may result from the diminished power of propelling the blood. The resistance of a larger quantity of blood has to be overcome, and the power of moving it is absolutely

[1] This was first insisted on by Forget, Gazette Médicale de Paris, 1844, p. 657. The dilatation of the orifice was pointed out by Corvisart, loc. cit. p. 154.

diminished by the dilatation. Hence, unless compensatory hypertrophy assist, less blood leaves the dilated chambers at each systole. The amount of residual blood may be so large that the quantity which can enter in the normal course of the circulation is less than in health. Hence, as Morgagni pointed out,[1] the dilatation acts as an obstruction to the onward movement of the blood, the vessels behind (venous system) become overfilled, the vessels in front (arterial system) underfilled.

The effect of dilatation of a cavity may thus come to be the same as that of obstruction at the orifices of the heart by which the blood should enter the chamber. If the chamber affected be a ventricle, the first effect is the over-distension of the corresponding auricle, and its consequent dilatation and perhaps hypertrophy. The veins by which the blood enters the auricles are over-distended, and when valvular incompetence is added, the pulmonary and larger systemic veins may be enormously dilated. I have known the right internal jugular to be so large, in dilatation of the right side of the heart, as to be mistaken for an aneurismal dilatation of the common carotid artery. Pulsation may be communicated to the veins as a result of the valvular incompetence (see article on Diseases of the Valves). The venous congestion affects alike the general tissues, causing various dropsies into the cellular tissue and serous cavities, and the organs, especially the lungs, brain, liver, portal system, and kidneys. Lastly, the other side of the heart may be overloaded and dilated, and ultimately even the side of the heart first affected, by the transmission of the influence through both systems of circulation. The last effect, which occurs only when the primary disease is at the mitral orifice, is perhaps due to the secondary dilatation of the right side. The effect of this venous congestion is to overload the venous radicles of the organs with blood, and cause their permanent dilatation. The proper tissue-elements of the organs undergo atrophy, or it may be granular, or fatty degeneration, partly in consequence of the pressure upon them of the distended veins, partly from the imperfect supply of arterial blood. Lastly, the connective tissue of the organs overgrows, and their consistence is thereby increased. The effect of these changes is somewhat modified by the characters of the organ affected.

The heart itself may suffer from the mechanical congestion of its walls, the consequences of which have been already pointed out. The mechanical congestion, however, it is believed, affects the heart later and less than the other organs, in consequence of the obliquity of the opening of the cardiac veins which produces a valve-like effect.

[1] Morgagni, speaking of a case of aortic regurgitation, says :—"Some portion of (the blood) returned into the left ventricle of the heart when the ventricle ought to receive the blood that was coming in from the lungs, it would necessarily happen that the returning portion, as well as the portion which had not been extruded just before, must occupy some part of that space which, from the design of nature, was entirely due to the blood that was coming in from the lungs, which circumstance finally could not but overload the lungs and heart." De Sedibus et Causis Morborum, 1779, letter 23, art. 12. As translated by Cockle, loc. cit.

The lungs are overloaded with blood, and serosity exudes from their walls into the air-cells and minute bronchi, and probably blood corpuscles migrate into the parenchyma. Ultimately the capillaries become varicose,[1] the blood-pigment collects in the cellular elements of the lung, giving it a brown colour, and the connective tissue is increased in quantity,[2] augmenting considerably the consistence and to a slighter extent the size of the lung, and producing ultimately the condition of " brown induration."

The brain undergoes slighter changes, no doubt in consequence of the effect of gravitation in opposing the movement of the blood. Its venules are enlarged and the distension of the surface veins may be very great. The pressure of the distended vessels in the interior may lead to their rupture into the perivascular sheaths, or to atrophy of the adjacent brain substance. The consistence of the brain is often lessened. Induration does not result. Corvisart maintained that rupture of large vessels and cerebral hæmorrhage might result from venous congestion, but his opinion has not received much confirmation.

The liver is congested, in a very high degree, from the directness with which the hepatic vein suffers from increased distension of the inferior vena cava. The organ becomes uniformly enlarged, first and mainly from the distension of the radicles of the hepatic vein, and afterwards by fatty degeneration of the liver tissue, or by fibroid overgrowth around the vessels and between the lobules, by which the organ may become indurated. On section, the distended venules are very conspicuous, and their enlargement is such that the hepatic tissue is compressed between them, and the appearance is produced of lobules lying between the distended venules, and thus a portal congestion is simulated. The liver tissue is frequently pale from fatty or fibroid degeneration, and, contrasting with the dark vessels, the so-called " nutmeg liver " is produced. Ultimately the liver may undergo reduction in size from atrophy of the proper elements and contraction of the fibrous tissue (Murchison).[3]

The flow through the liver capillaries is necessarily impeded, and thus the obstruction is transmitted to the portal system. The spleen is enlarged, and, like the liver, may be the seat of fibroid overgrowth, causing its induration. The peritoneal and intestinal vessels are distended, and fluid may be effused into the peritoneal cavity. The fibroid overgrowth in the liver may ultimately lead to compression of the portal venules, and consequent portal congestion, out of proportion to the congestion which results simply from the cardiac state.

The kidneys suffer similar congestion, and present the appearance which was produced artificially by ligature of the hepatic vein, by

---

[1] Buhl, quoted by Wilson Fox, vol. iii., art. Brown Induration of the Lung, p. 801.

[2] Rokitansky, Wilson Fox, loc. cit.

[3] Clinical Lectures on Diseases of the Liver, 1868, p. 120.

Robinson.[1] They are enlarged, smooth, and dark in colour from the venous distension. The cortical and pyramidal portions preserve their relative proportions.   At first their consistence may be lessened, and the capsule separate readily; after a time fibroid overgrowth occurs and the kidneys become indurated. Ultimately this tissue may contract, the organs becoming smaller and harder, their surface slightly granular, and the capsule unduly adherent.

The veins of the body generally are also over-distended. Serum escapes from them into the connective tissue and accumulates in the more depending parts.   Usually the condition comes on gradually, and the œdema commences in the legs.   It is first noticed in the evening and disappears during the night, when the legs are raised; but it continues increasing, until, although lessened, it is not removed by the horizontal posture.   If the patient be in bed it may be first noticed in the lower part of the back.   It may increase until the distension of the legs is extreme, and the skin, if not relieved, may slough.   Lastly, coagulation may occur in the distended veins, but this accident is not common.   The amount of congestion varies from time to time in dependence upon accidental causes of increased obstruction, due sometimes to variable cardiac strength, more frequently to variations in the cause of the dilatation in the lungs, &c.   Again, the manifestations of venous congestion are not uniform in different cases. An accidental cause, a local inflammation, may determine a large effusion of serum in some special position, as the pleural or peritoneal cavity. Some accidental obstruction may lead to local œdema. A special predisposition to disease in some one organ, as the liver or the kidney, may cause that organ to suffer in undue degree and give a special character to the symptoms.   Moreover a vicarious action is often observable between the vessels of the organs and of the limbs and cellular tissue.   The extreme affections of organs, the very large livers, the extreme albuminuria, are often seen where the general œdema is slight; whereas when the anasarca is extreme there may be even to the last only a trace of albumen in the urine, and the enlargement of the liver may be trifling.   Fibroid overgrowth in organs may hinder the distension of their vessels, and so throw an additional strain upon those of the general system.

The over-distension of the venous system, on which so many of the symptoms depend, can only be in part ascribed to the dilatation of the heart.   It is in large part due to the cause of the dilatation. Dilatation of the right ventricle permits the obstruction in the lungs which exists in emphysema, to tell back upon the venous system. But it also adds to the obstruction.   When due to no increased resistance but to muscular degeneration, it will give rise to similar symptoms. So in the latter case, degeneration of the cardiac wall, the weakness in its contractile power which permits dilatation, is itself, as Niemeyer pointed out, a cause of the impaired circulation. The resulting

[1] Med. Chir. Trans., 1843, p. 51

dilatation, by its mechanical influence, intensifies what may be called the potential obstruction which results.

SYMPTOMS.—The existence of dilatation is declared by certain symptoms and physical signs. Some difficulty in their determination has arisen from the circumstance that pure dilatation is so rarely met with; dilatation is usually accompanied by hypertrophy. But pure hypertrophy is not uncommon, and by comparison of these cases with those in which dilatation co-exists, and especially with those in which dilatation predominates, the symptoms of the latter condition have been ascertained. They are most marked and characteristic in general dilatation.

The *Physical Signs* depend on the increased size and lessened strength of the heart. The area of dulness, both deep and superficial, is increased. The deep dulness may extend from the anterior axillary line, to two fingers' breadth to the right of the sternum, even in rare cases as far as the right nipple; upwards it may reach to the first rib, and downwards to the seventh rib. It inclines to squareness of outline, in consequence of the lateral increase in the size of the heart. The greater the dilatation, the greater is the lateral increase in the dulness. The impulse is perceptible over an abnormally large area. It may be felt from the epigastrium to the axilla. It is also diffused. A maximum apex-beat may or may not be perceptible. It is always less distinct than in health. When it cannot be felt it may sometimes be seen (Walshe). The impulse is weak and sudden in proportion to the amount of dilatation and to its purity, *i.e.* its freedom from associated hypertrophy. It may be somewhat undulatory in character, in consequence of different parts of the heart striking the chest wall successively, not simultaneously. Successive beats may be unequal in strength, and may also strike the chest-wall at different points. Bulging of the chest-wall is slight in dilatation, and is said to be always absent when there is no hypertrophy; now and then in a large dilated and slightly hypertrophied heart it is very distinct. Displacement of organs occurs in the hypertrophied form, the lungs are pushed out of the way, the liver may be displaced downwards, so that its rounded upper surface is visible beneath the ribs.

The sounds of the heart are weakened, the first sound is shortened and its tone raised. As Flint,[1] puts it, the valvular element in the sound predominates. When there is co-existing hypertrophy, the first sound may be clear and ringing, but the sound becomes weaker in proportion to the amount of dilatation. The shortening may cause the first sound to resemble in its characters the second sound, so that, as Stokes[2] pointed out, it may not be easy to distinguish between them. Laennec taught that clearness of the first sound is a sign of dilatation. Stokes and Gairdner[3] showed that this clearness

[1] On Diseases of the Heart, second edition, p. 86.
[2] Op. cit., p. 260.
[3] Edinburgh Medical Journal, July 1856, p. 56.

exists only when hypertrophy is combined with the dilatation. Reduplication has been noticed in some cases, and may be due to the asynchronous contraction of the two ventricles.

In dilatation of the ventricle, especially of the left ventricle, a systolic apex murmur is frequently heard. In a large number of cases it depends on incompetence of the auriculo-ventricular valves, primary (in the case of the mitral valve), or due to the extension of the orifice in the dilatation of the heart. In many cases, however, no incompetence can be discovered after death although a systolic apex murmur was heard during life. But the post-mortem tests for incompetence of the mitral valve are not very satisfactory. Slight inefficiency may remain undetected, and on the other hand, slight regurgitation cannot be accepted as conclusive evidence of functional incompetence. In each case the action of the papillary muscles during life may vitiate the post-mortem conclusion. Hence some authorities believe that such a murmur, when heard in dilatation of the ventricle, is always due to auriculo-ventricular regurgitation. Others, among whom are Stokes [1] and Walshe, believe that a murmur is occasionally to be heard in cases in which the post-mortem evidence of valvular competence is so conclusive that regurgitation is a very improbable explanation. They consider that the contraction of the ventricle alone may throw the blood into audible vibrations. The conditions are certainly such as to render the result conceivable. It is probable that the systole of a dilated ventricle is never complete. A considerable amount of blood remains in its cavity. The spaces between the various projections into the cavity,—the trabeculæ, papillary muscles, the cuspid valves,—are larger than in health, and remain unobliterated at the end of the ventricular contraction, and the eddies into which the blood is thrown must be considerable. Moreover, the irregularity of the blood current is no doubt sometimes increased by irregularity in the contraction of the ventricles. By these means it seems probable that a murmur may be produced within the ventricle, the consequence and the sign of dilatation only.

The *pulse* is weak in proportion to the amount and purity of the dilatation. It is sometimes of moderate size, sometimes small; its size is largely influenced by the condition of heart to which the dilatation is secondary. It is often quick, and is unduly quickened by exertion. Sometimes it is infrequent, either because the heart's action is infrequent, or because the irregularity in force is so great that every systole does not influence the pulse. Thus the effect of intermission is produced. Actual intermissions may also occur.

Dilatation of the *left ventricle* alone, is attended by the changes in the impulse which have been already described as among the most conspicuous signs of general dilatation. The impulse is diffused, and both impulse and dulness are extended to the left. The first sound is weak; the pulse presents the characters just described. Sooner

---

[1] Diseases of the Heart and Aorta, p. 261.

or later the mitral orifice is stretched to incompetence of the valves ; then general dilatation, with all its symptoms, quickly follows.

Dilatation of the *left auricle* may lessen the resonance at the inner end of the second left interspace, and a feeble presystolic impulse may be perceptible there. Pressure on the left bronchus may interfere with the expansion of the left lung (Barlow).

Dilatation of the *right ventricle* causes pulsation to be transmitted to the epigastrium, and extension of dulness to the right of the sternum in the fifth and sixth interspaces ; the apex of the heart is in the normal position. Jugular fulness is common, and pulsation consequent on tricuspid incompetence is not rare, and, as tricuspid incompetence is rarely due to any other cause, it affords additional evidence of the existence of dilatation of the right ventricle. The pulse may, as Lancisi pointed out, be little changed.

Dilatation of the *right auricle* causes dulness to the right of the sternum, where pulsation may sometimes be detected, generally presystolic, rarely systolic in consequence of the tricuspid insufficiency (as in a case of Dr. Stokes,[1] in which an aortic aneurism was simulated). Jugular pulsation, systolic in rhythm, occurs, and may be in rare cases diastolic also.

Symptoms.—Dilatation of the heart affects, secondarily, almost every organ in the body, and its symptoms, direct and indirect, are very numerous. They vary widely, however, in distribution and degree, in different cases.

Cardiac discomfort is frequently present ; it varies from mere uneasiness to acute pain, constant or paroxysmal (pseud-angina). Palpitation is very common. The sudden contraction of the enlarged heart is perceived unduly by the patient, especially when irregularity in force or rhythm is superadded. The heart is easily excited to frequent contraction by slight causes—muscular exertion, emotional excitement, or mechanical disturbance, as by a distended stomach.

The general strength is always lessened. The patient complains of lassitude and languor, and faints easily.

All parts of the general system present evidence of passive congestion. The venous stasis is seen in the distended superficial veins and the cyanotic tint. Subcutaneous œdema is often present and may be considerable. Its occurrence is influenced, not only by the cardiac obstruction, but by the state of the blood. In anæmic persons the normal blood-pressure may suffice to cause slight œdema of the feet, and a similar state of blood assists very much the effect of the increased venous pressure in cardiac dilatation. The local dropsies, effusions into the pleural, pericardial, or peritoneal cavities are attended by their special symptoms. Their occurrence may alter the character, and add much to the gravity of the symptoms present in a given case.

Special symptoms result also from the congestion of organs. The

---

[1] Diseases of the Heart and Aorta, p. 275.

congestion of the lungs is indicated by cough, dyspnœa, cyanosis. Cough is often a very troublesome symptom. It may be paroxysmal and independent of any bronchial secretion, or a small amount of mucus may excite an excessive cough. Secretion is often, however, abundant enough from the congested vessels, and the sputa may be abundant, watery, or mucous, often stained with blood. The congested bronchi are liable to inflammation, by which all the symptoms are increased.

Dyspnœa is a very constant symptom, due chiefly to the imperfect pulmonary circulation and deficient aëration of the blood. At first it is slight, and is felt only when exertion increases the need for oxygen ; especially on ascending a hill or stairs. Later on it may be constant, and be increased when the body is recumbent (probably because the descent of the diaphragm is impeded by the weight of the abdominal viscera). Respiration may be quickened to thirty or forty acts per minute, and is panting in character, with noisy expiration. It varies in intensity, sometimes in correspondence with cardiac failure, sometimes without apparent cause. The patient, never free from a sense of want of breath, may from time to time start up in an agony of dyspnœa, undo the clothes upon his chest, and grasp convulsively at any object within his reach. Often even the reclining posture with the head backwards cannot be borne, and the sufferer can only rest or sleep sitting up with his forehead supported. Sometimes a rhythmical character may be observed in the dyspnœa, analogous to, though not identical with, the Cheyne-Stokes breathing. Brief attacks of panting dyspnœa commence suddenly, and gradually subside to comparative, perhaps dozing, calm, with which they alternate. These spasmodic forms of dyspnœa may be singularly out of proportion to the interference with the aëration of the blood, as estimated by the amount of cyanosis.

The congestion of the brain causes frequent headaches. Vertigo is common. The patient sleeps and dreams much. He dozes during the day, and at night is disturbed by restless starts. Corvisart pointed out that the passive congestion sometimes causes a " subapoplectic " state during the last hours of life. Delirium is not uncommon, and may be violent ; a state of approaching chronic mania sometimes results.

The congestion of the liver is indicated by an icteric tint of skin, by pain and weight in the right back, right shoulder, or hepatic region, and by abdominal discomfort due to the increased size of the organ. Frequently the enlargement can be both seen and felt. Pulsation may be felt in it, either communicated to it directly by the heart, or, it is said, transmitted through the venous system. The liver is very constantly depressed as well as enlarged. More urgent symptoms result from the transmitted obstruction in the portal system. The functions of the stomach and intestine are interfered with by the mechanical congestion of their walls. Vomiting is a common, and often a most troublesome, symptom. It is probably due to the mechanical congestion of, and direct pressure upon, the stomach. Possibly, in some cases, it may, as Walshe suggests, be the reflex result of an irritation of the pneumogastric nerve. It sometimes results from a catarrhal condition, which is easily excited in the congested organ. The distended vessels may give way, and hæmatemesis result. Piles are common. The hæmorrhage from them may relieve the congestion and prevent other symptoms. In other cases, from the mechanically congested vessels, serum escapes into the intestinal canal, or the peritoneal cavity, causing diarrhœa or ascites. In the former the stools are copious and watery, and give little pain. Such diarrhœa may constitute the earliest symptom of cardiac mischief. All these symptoms of portal congestion may, in the later stages, be intensified by an increase in the obstruction due to secondary changes in the liver itself.

The mechanical congestion of the kidneys produces changes in the urine, which becomes scanty, dense, high-coloured, often loaded with lithates, and may contain albumen. The quantity of albumen varies, and does not always correspond, as might be expected, with the amount of venous congestion. Roberts[1] suggests that it depends on the pressure to which the arteries are exposed in the congested state, and he points out that it is often greater, the stronger the force with which the heart acts. Tube-casts are frequently present in the urine, and are generally hyaline or slightly granular, and of medium size.

The ultimate effect of general dilatation is to act through the venous and capillary system on the arteries and the left ventricle, increasing the tension of the pulse and the effect on the left side of the heart. The variation in the amount of obstruction at different times produces great alterations in the organic symptoms. As Stokes pointed out, attacks of dyspnœa due to cold, &c., may be accompanied with a rapid increase in the size of the liver, which will descend in a short time far into the abdomen, partly from the enlargement, partly from displacement, and on the subsidence of the attack will return to its ordinary volume. The albumen in the urine may undergo a similar modification, although in less simple dependence on the venous stasis.

DIAGNOSIS.—The essential sign of dilatation, by which its existence and degree may best be ascertained, is the diffusion of the cardiac impulse, its comparative uniformity over the whole area in which it can be felt. In proportion to the purity of the dilatation the first sound is toneless, high pitched, and short and weak; the pulse is small and feeble, and the lungs and general system suffer from the secondary consequences of the cardiac failure.

Obscuration of impulse may simulate diffusion, and thus lead to a mistaken diagnosis of dilatation. A thin layer of over-distended lung may intervene between the heart and the chest-wall, and so

[1] On Urinary and Renal Diseases, third edition, p. 356.

render the apex-beat indistinct and apparently diffused. The increased resonance over the cardiac area will indicate the cause of the indistinctness. Dilatation may also be simulated, as Niemeyer pointed out, when the apex strikes against a rib, and the impulse is felt equally in the interspace above and below the point of contact. This is most frequent in narrow-chested persons, whose ribs are near together. A mistake may be avoided by noticing this conformation of thorax, and by observing that the apex-beat is nearly in the normal situation, and that the apparent diffusion is vertical only; there is no lateral extension of the impulse.

From *hypertrophy* the diagnosis can rarely be one of absolute distinction. Some hypertrophy usually coexists with dilatation, and often confers on the diffused impulse increased force, and sometimes the pathognomonic "deliberate," heaving character. In proportion to the predominance of the dilatation, the impulse is weak and sudden, the precordial region is not bulged, the cardiac dulness is increased laterally rather than vertically, the impulse is extended laterally rather than lowered, and the pulse is weak rather than strong.

From *pericardial effusion* dilatation is principally to be distinguished by the direction of the increase in dulness which occurs in each condition—in dilatation laterally, in pericardial effusion upwards. The pyramidal apex of the latter, when distinct, is not simulated by the dulness of the dilated heart. The impulse of the heart and the dulness are conterminous, to the left at all events, in dilatation; while the dulness of pericardial effusion may extend beyond the impulse. The apex-beat is not raised in dilatation, and the sounds of the heart are as loud over the precordial region as at the top of the sternum, where in effusion they are most distinct (Walshe). Lastly, there is no friction-sound, and far less displacement of organs or precordial bulging, than in pericardial effusion. But precordial bulging and obliteration of intercostal spaces may be present in dilated hypertrophy, and in extreme dilatation the sounds may be much weakened. In a case recorded by Evans the right ventricle was actually tapped under the idea that it was a pericardial effusion.[1]

From *fatty degeneration* dilatation may be distinguished by the evidence of enlargement of the heart, by the diffusion of its impulse, and by the proportion between its diffusion and its weakness. In fatty degeneration, when it exists alone, there is no enlargement of the heart, and the change in the impulse is a simple weakening without diffusion. Often the two conditions are conjoined.

PROGNOSIS.—The prognosis in dilatation of the heart is always grave. Unless compensated for by hypertrophy, its direct effect is to interfere with the function of the heart, and to lead to those serious results to which death is often due. Hence the gravity of the prognosis is proportioned (1) to the purity and extent of the dilatation; (2) to the existence of a tendency to degeneration rather than to

[1] Clin. Soc. Trans., 1874-5.

growth, and of states of general malnutrition, defective food-supply, &c., which interfere with the occurrence of hypertrophy ; (3) to the extent to which the dilatation is due to causes beyond control, to the amount of irremovable work which the heart has to perform.

Must the state, once established, be regarded as permanent ? The *relative* amount of dilatation may certainly be lessened by the development of hypertrophy. There is some reason to believe that apart from the development of hypertrophy a dilated heart may lessen in size. It was long ago asserted by Beau and Larcher that dilatation is sometimes temporary when due to a temporary cause, and it has been said that a similar diminution may occur when, by absolute rest, the work of a recently dilated heart is reduced to a minimum. Individual cases have conveyed this idea very strongly to careful and unbiased observers. Milner Fothergill has lately brought forward strong evidence to show that such reduction in size may occur. He has shown that diminution in the cardiac dulness may correspond with the disappearance of the symptoms of dilatation, and afford evidence that the condition is itself diminished. The same conclusion is indicated by the completeness with which the acute dilatation of adynamic diseases, such as fever, may pass away.

TREATMENT.—The object of treatment in dilatation of the heart must be to restore as far as possible the disturbed balance between the cardiac work and the cardiac strength. The increased blood pressure, to which the dilatation may be primarily due, must be reduced to the minimum compatible with the work of the circulation. Accidental causes of obstruction must be removed. Bronchitis must be got rid of as soon as possible. Especially, exertion must be avoided. Rest, mental, moral and physical, is of the greatest importance. Muscular exertion involves a large increase in the work of the heart, and its cessation will often suffice to restore the disturbed balance. In extreme dilatation, confinement to bed or the couch for a time is a wise measure, and will not seldom remove most of the troublesome subjective symptoms, and even some grave objective signs of dilatation. Where this cannot be secured, or is unnecessary by reason of the moderate degree of the dilatation, the rigid avoidance of all needless and severe exertion should be enforced.

The blood-pressure may also be lessened by the reduction of the total volume of the blood. This may be accomplished in more than one way. The most ready method is by the abstraction of blood by venesection or cupping. The relief which it affords is often immediate and striking. The ultimate effect, however, is that the volume of the blood is soon reproduced, while the heart is permanently weakened. Hence it must only be employed when the need for immediate relief is paramount, and renders the danger of the ultimate damage a secondary consideration,—that is to say, when the patient is in imminent danger of death. It is especially useful when the right heart and venous system are overloaded. The quantity of blood taken need not be large. In less urgent cases the same end may be obtained by other means, by purgation and diuresis. The former must not be severe, or the subsequent depression is not easily rallied from Diuresis is often of great service in these cases, even where there is no dropsy.[1] The amount of fluid taken as drink should be small.

The power of the heart should be increased so that it may resist the blood-pressure, and may contract completely, so as to expel the whole of its contents. To this end the general nutrition must be, as far as possible, improved. A dry bracing air is useful, and gentle exercise should be taken which does not increase materially the work of the heart; food must be nutritious and easily digested. Iron is of great service, and seems to aid directly the production of the needful hypertrophy.[2]

Excited action of the heart must be calmed by avoiding the causes of excitement, and by sedative medicines. Moral emotion must, as far as possible, be avoided, and the sources of gastric disturbance guarded against or relieved. A distended stomach easily excites an attack of palpitation.

Of drugs having a direct action on the heart, none is so useful as digitalis, which increases the tone of the heart, lessens the frequency and increases the force of the contraction. There has been much discussion as to the action of digitalis, and the condition of heart in which it is of most service, but there is at present a consensus of opinion that its action is tonic and that in dilatation its most marked beneficial effect is produced.[3] The heart's action is reduced in frequency and increased in force; irregularity in force and rhythm is lessened or removed. The sphygmographic tracing shows this effect. The grave consequences of dilatation are lessened, venous congestion, dyspnœa, and œdema, general or local, are all diminished.[4]

Concerning its *modus operandi*, there is still some difference of opinion. The lessened frequency of contraction probably lessens the work of the heart by diminishing that part which consists in moving its own mass, and at the same time the longer periods of rest probably conduce to the perfectness of the cardiac nutrition. Frequency of

---

[1] "In morbis pectoris, semper ducendum esse ad vias urinæ." Baglivi, quoted by Ferriar.

[2] Chalybeate waters were recommended by Senac in commencing dilatation (Traité, 1769, t. ii., p. 330), and his recommendation was endorsed by Ferriar (Med. Hist. an. Ref., vol. i., 1792, On Dilatation of the Heart, p. 168).

[3] Withering pointed out that digitalis "seldom succeeds in men of great natural strength," but does much good "if the pulse be feeble or intermitting, the countenance pale, the lips livid, the skin cold." An Account of the Foxglove, &c. Birmingham, 1785.

[4] "I do not intend to say how this medicine (digitalis) acts, but I can, from observation, declare, that it has a very powerful effect in obviating the urgency of the symptoms in dilatation of the heart" (Allan Burns, 1809, loc. cit., p. 57). Ferriar had previously largely used digitalis in dilatation. The verbal accord between these writers and those of the present day is more complete than is that of their meaning. Dilatation of the heart was to the former synonymous with its enlargement and over-action, and they valued digitalis for (and believed that it did good by) its supposed power of lessening such over-action, when it was really strengthening the heart's defective power.

action is at the expense of rest, for the length of the systole remains nearly the same at various degrees of frequency of contraction, increased frequency being obtained at the expense of the diastole. It has been calculated that the time of rest to the heart which is contracting 144 times per minute, is increased by one-third if the pulse is reduced to 72.[1] Moreover, the smaller cardiac vessels, arteries, and veins, as well as capillaries, must be emptied of blood during the cardiac systole.[2] A certain time must elapse on each diastole before the capillaries can be filled with blood and transudation of nutritive fluid through their walls can take place. This period will be nearly the same in every diastole, and hence the total period of rest available for cardiac nutrition will on this account also be greater the less frequent the contraction.[3]

Digitalis appears to act also by increasing the completeness of the contraction of the heart. Under its influence the heart of an animal becomes firmer at the end of systole. Such contraction ensures the expulsion of the whole of the blood contained in the chamber. Every approximation to this is, in dilatation, a direct gain. It not only assists directly the circulation, but it arrests a process which is probably the main mechanism of the origin and increase of dilatation, viz., the over-distension of the chamber in consequence of the addition of residual blood to that which enters it from the ordinary source. Increased firmness of contraction will not only lessen the tendency to further dilatation, but will improve the condition of the cardiac walls,[4] and increase the tendency to compensatory hypertrophy.

Digitalis acts also by steadying the heart, diminishing its irregularity. Dr. Ringer [5] suggests that its main effect in dilatation of the left ventricle accompanying mitral regurgitation is thus produced. By preventing irregular contraction it arrests that part of the regurgitation which depends on the irregular action of the papillary muscles, and so relieves the over-distension of the auricle, and indirectly of the ventricle.

Five to fifteen drops of the tincture of digitalis may be given with advantage three times a-day. Most observers have found the tincture convenient and reliable, but the infusion is believed by Ringer to be a surer preparation, in doses of one or two drachms. Much larger

---

[1] Milner Fothergill, Diseases of the Heart, p. 4.

[2] Harvey observed that the substance of the heart becomes pale during its contraction.

[3] Assuming, for instance, that the period required for the vascular distension of the heart, and not available for nutrition, to be uniform at different frequencies of contraction, and to amount at each contraction to one-tenth of a second, the total period then available for nutrition would be increased about three per cent. from this cause only, by a reduction in the frequency of the pulse from 100 to 80. But it is probable that the time needed for the vascular distension of the heart is shorter the greater the distension of the aorta, and hence that it is shorter the less frequent the contraction, and the actual increase in the period available for nutrition will be rather greater than is represented by the above estimate.

[4] Partly, no doubt, by rendering perfect the expulsion of the blood from the cardiac veins, as Dr. H. C. Wood points out (Phil. Med. Times, 1874, Nov. 14, 21).

[5] Handbook of Therapeutics, 5th ed. p. 421.

doses have been given, but these should be employed with caution. Ringer recommends strongly that the minimum effectual dose should be employed in the first instance, since an increase after a time is often necessary.

The Virginian prune has been long employed as a cardiac tonic in America, and was introduced into this country by Clifford Allbutt,[1] who has found it very useful in cardiac dilatation. I have found its power as a tonic, although marked, inferior to digitalis; but it is of much value for the relief of continuous cardiac discomfort, and may with advantage be given for a time, while digitalis is omitted. Twenty or thirty minims of the tincture may be given three times a-day. Nux vomica and strychnia are also useful in improving the cardiac tone. Arsenic has been recommended for the same purpose.

Treatment of Special Symptoms.—Cardiac discomfort, in various forms, whether as pain or palpitation, is the source of much distress. The tranquillising influence of digitalis on the heart relieves much of the pain. Aconite is of use in the same way, and is of most service when "extreme irritability of contraction coincides with great weakness of beat" (Walshe). Half a minim or a minim may be given; its effects being watched. Drawing a few deep breaths will often arrest an attack of palpitation (Brown-Séquard). Belladonna may be given internally in doses $\mathfrak{m}$ v. to $\mathfrak{m}$ xv. three times a-day, and is often of much service. Belladonna plasters have been condemned by some authorities as useless, but they certainly give relief to the cardiac discomfort. Patients constantly ask for their repetition. The tincture of the Virginian prune sometimes gives very marked relief to continuous pain, and will sometimes stop for a time slight pseud-anginal seizures. Opium has the same power over cardiac as over other pains. Hypodermic injections of morphia give quick relief, but their use has been discountenanced in grave heart diseases, on account of the fear of too profound a sedative influence on the heart. But Clifford Allbutt and Ringer have employed them extensively, and assert that $\frac{1}{10}$th or $\frac{1}{8}$th of a grain may be injected with perfect safety, even in grave dilatation. The relief to the patient is certainly in many cases most striking. A very small quantity will sometimes procure sleep, in cases of cardiac insomnia, when sedatives given by the mouth fail altogether. Tolerance of sedatives by the mouth in these cases does not always imply a corresponding tolerance of the hypodermic injection, and the first injection should therefore always be very small.

For paroxysmal pains, antispasmodics may also be given. Nitrite of Amyl in inhalation, so useful in true angina, also gives relief to the pseud-anginal seizures, and to the sense of suffocation, which is sometimes troublesome. If necessary, it may be employed diluted with spirit. A few drops of chloroform, or what is more convenient, half a teaspoonful of chloric ether, inhaled with steam, is also useful.

Attacks of increased cardiac failure need general stimulants and

[1]. Medical Times and Gazette, Feb. 16 and March 2, 1867.

antispasmodics. Alcohol, given with hot water, is one of the most rapidly diffusible stimulants. Sal-volatile and ether, with tincture of lavender, are the most convenient and most effective drugs. Stimulation of the ends of the pneumogastric nerve in the stomach seems to have some influence in exciting the heart's action, and effervescing drinks and carminatives are useful in that way.

In syncopal seizures the head should be placed low, and the remedies just enumerated should be employed. Active respiratory movement should be restored as quickly as possible. It is thus, and by arousing consciousness and will, that cold affusions and stimulating applications to the nostrils are of service.

The lung complications of dilatation of the heart, bronchitis, œdema, congestion, need the most stimulating special treatment for each variety. Stimulating expectorants, as ammonia, are necessary for the bronchitis; and congestion is best relieved by the cardiac tonics and stimulants already described, and by mild counter-irritation.

Cough is often an exceedingly troublesome symptom in these cases, it may be paroxysmal or constant, and out of all proportion to the expectoration. Morphia is generally necessary to control it; one-twelfth of a grain may be given by the mouth, and with it a few minims of the tincture of belladonna.

Dyspnœa is among the most obstinate, as well as the most distressing, symptoms of dilatation. Its chief treatment is that of the cardiac failure, and the same diffusible stimulants are needed. The paroxysmal form is relieved most effectually by more direct sedatives: opium, Indian hemp, belladonna, lobelia inflata. Dry-cupping, and a few leeches to the precordial region, are recommended by Walshe when there is palpitation as well as dyspnœa. Posture is important; the head should be well raised, and Walshe recommends an attitude leaning forward, with the forehead supported by a sling. When the dyspnœa is dependent on pulmonary œdema, relief is often only to be obtained in the sitting posture.[1]

Headache is not often a troublesome symptom except in dependence on the cough. It is best relieved by posture, and by bathing the forehead with hot water. Sleeplessness is often a distressing symptom. Rest is disturbed by sudden starts, or the patient wakes up in a sudden fright with a sense of great distress. Such symptoms may usually be removed by the administration of the third dose of digitalis at bedtime in combination with bromide of potassium. Indian hemp (gr. $\frac{1}{2}$ of the extract or ℥x. of the tincture), will also, though less uniformly, give relief. Actual insomnia may be relieved by chloral, chloral and bromide, and morphia by the mouth or skin, employed with caution.

The congestion of the liver may be lessened to a marked extent by

---

[1] A reclining-chair, with a cross rest on which the forehead can be supported, has been for some years in use at University College Hospital, and a " heart-bed " for the same purpose is described and recommended by Dobell.

mercurials. Every relief given to the portal congestion no doubt lessens immediately the pressure upon the hepatic lobules.

Vomiting is sometimes a very troublesome symptom. Effervescing ammonia, with bismuth and hydrocyanic acid or morphia, is the most useful. The amount of ammonia need not be large; gr. x. of the carbonate with gr. xi. of citric acid is sufficient. Ice should be sucked, and food given in small quantities. Counter-irritation to the epigastrium is sometimes useful. Any portal congestion must be relieved the bowels being kept open. Diarrhœa sometimes demands treatment, and should be moderated rather than restrained. If constipation is present, moderate doses of hydrogogue purgatives are most useful, as Püllna or Hunyädi Janos water, colocynth, or podophyllin. Flatulence is often very troublesome, and adds much to the cardiac and general distress. Hot fomentations externally and carminatives internally give most relief; sal-volatile, peppermint, chloric ether, spirit of horse-radish, are all useful. The relief which is afforded to the sufferers from dilatation of the heart by the removal or diminution of their gastric troubles is often very great. Dobell has lately drawn attention specially to this subject.[1]

The scanty urine consequent on the kidney congestion may call for treatment. Mild diuretics, with digitalis for its double action, often suffice to relieve the kidneys. Often, however, this long-continued congestion induces tissue changes in them, and dry-cupping to the loins, or stronger diuretic treatment—broom, juniper, &c.—may be necessary. Stokes[2] remarks that diuretics often succeed after a mercurial, where they have previously failed.

Dropsy is almost invariably a troublesome symptom in the later periods of a case. It is dependent partly on the blood-state, favouring osmosis, partly on the mechanical congestion, increasing the pressure of the blood in the small vessels, and increasing it to the greatest extent in the most depending parts, where gravitation aids the cardiac failure. It can only be effectually combated by treating each of these causes, first by strengthening the heart, and secondly by improving the blood-state. Hæmatinic and cardiac tonics are needful for this. But it may be lessened by other measures. No remedy can promote, directly, the absorption of the effused fluid from the cellular tissue back into the blood-vessels, but reduction in the volume of the blood exercises a marked influence. The abstraction of blood will be necessary only when acute pulmonary œdema threatens life, and then cupping on the chest is preferable to venesection. Often purgation is sufficient, and hydrogogue cathartics, bitartrate of potash, elaterium, jalap, are the most effectual. Where there is evidence of enlargement of the liver, a dose of a mercurial is stated by Hayden to increase the

---

[1] On Affections of the Heart, 1872. The value of carminatives has long been known Albrecht relates that Sylvius removed all symptoms in a case of cardiac dilatation by their use. According to Pliny, the Egyptians believed the juice of horse-radish to be the only cure for atrophy of the heart.

[2] Loc. cit., p. 263.

effect of the purge upon the dropsy. Diuresis occupies a position hardly second to purgation for the removal of dropsy; copaiba, iodide of potassium, nitrate of potash, juniper, broom, nitric ether, and especially digitalis, may be given. The dose of digitalis for the removal of dropsy by its diuretic action needs to be larger than when its tonic action alone is needed; ʒij. or ʒiv. of the infusion, or ♏x. or xx. of the tincture, may be given twice a day. Dry-cupping over the kidneys sometimes, it is said, increases the effect of the diuretic.

In severe cases all these means, successful at first, may ultimately fail to remove the dropsy, and it becomes necessary to relieve the distended limbs, or sloughing will occur. It is necessary to anticipate this and to scarify or puncture the skin, and allow the limb to drain. Scarification is the more effectual, but is said to be attended with greater risk of erysipelas. Erysipelas will rarely occur when the precaution is taken to wrap up the limbs in flannel, wrung out of warm water, immediately after the scarification, renewing it every two hours during the first two days. A harelip pin is a convenient instrument for the punctures.

Jaccoud[1] recommends, as a substitute for punctures, friction each day with croton oil: in a day or two the characteristic eruption is produced, and from it the serum escapes abundantly. The frequency with which a slight inflammation is the starting-point of a slough makes it difficult to believe that the risk of gangrene is lessened by this method.

In all cases of dropsy, as little fluid as possible should be taken. When the kidneys are underacting from congestion, its effect is, as Milner Fothergill[2] has insisted, only to throw an increased strain upon the heart.

[1] Pathologie interne, 4th ed. vol. i. p. 621.
[2] The Progress of Heart Disease, Lancet, vol. i., 1875.

FATTY DISEASES OF THE HEART.

By W. R. Gowers, M.D.

FATTY degeneration of the heart consists in the substitution of fat for its muscular substance. This result may be reached by two processes of different pathological and clinical relations. The one process effects simply the molecular substitution of fat for the proper substance of the muscular fibres. The other consists in the overgrowth of the normal fatty tissue of the heart among the muscular fibres, so as to compress, and ultimately to destroy and replace them. The former process needs the microscope for its demonstration; the latter is obtrusively conspicuous to the naked eye. The one is an indication of diminished vitality, and may be its initial stage, a necrosis; the other is at first a growth. Some varieties of the two processes present common pathological features, and their effect on the function of the organ is the same; but their diverse conditions of origin and anatomical characters need separate description. In pursuing this course the example is followed which was set by Dr. Quain [1] in a memoir on the subject, which has served as a model for most subsequent writers. The hypertrophic form of " fatty infiltration " will first be described, and then the " necrobiotic " process of fatty degeneration.

FATTY OVERGROWTH.

SYNONYMS.—Fatty Infiltration (Rokitansky); Fatty growth, Fatty Hypertrophy (Quain); Adipose Cardiaque, Surcharge Graisseuse. Obésité du Cœur (French writers).

DEFINITION.—An abnormal development of adipose tissue on and in the substance of the heart. Fatty tissue is always present on the surface of the heart, and varies in amount according to the age, and the nutritive conditions and tendencies of the individual. In abnormal development this fat may become so excessive that mechanical interference with the function of the organ is the result. It is a

---

[1] On Fatty Diseases of the Heart, Med. Chir. Trans., vol. xxxiii.

local "instance of the extension into the domain of disease of the physiological process of growing fat."[1]

HISTORY.—Some of the symptoms of obesity, which are in part cardiac, were among the earliest medical observations. Hippocrates noticed the tendency of fat persons to earlier death than others, and both he and Celsus observed the dyspnœa which is associated with obesity. Harvey described an excess of fat around the heart of Old Parr. Since that time almost every writer on diseases of the heart has alluded to or described a similar condition. Kerkering,[2] in 1717, noted its occurrence at so early an age as two years. Senac[3] in 1749 described carefully the normal variations in the quantity of fat according to time of life, &c. Morgagni[4] recorded examples of hearts so loaded with fat that no muscular tissue could be seen. Portal[5] noted the concurrence of fatty overgrowth in the heart with a similar condition in the voluntary muscles. The state was fully described by Corvisart, who suspected that it might be a cause of sudden death. Morgagni thought that the muscular fibres of the heart suffered in this condition of fatty growth. The microscope, long after, showed that this is actually the case. It was inferred, however, from the apparent substitution of the fatty for the muscular tissue, and from the evidence of cardiac weakness. Hearts subject to this mixed change were described, and the disease ably discussed, by Duncan (1816), Cheyne (1818), Townsend (1832), and R. W. Smith (1838).[6]

CAUSES.—Excess of adipose tissue on the heart is usually associated with excess of adipose tissue elsewhere, and is due to the same causes. Quain found that in almost every case of fatty growth about the heart there was general obesity. The converse holds good to a less extent. King Chambers[7] records that of thirty-six corpulent persons a considerable excess of fat at the base of the heart was found in twelve. On the other hand, in 165 bodies not remarkable for fat, there was excess of fat about the heart of four only.

Hereditary predisposition exercises a marked influence on the occurrence of obesity, and no doubt also on the occurrence of fatty infiltration of the heart. In two-thirds of the cases of general obesity it is found that hereditary or collateral obesity exists. Sex also influences its occurrence. If the statistics of Quain[8] be combined with the cases of fatty growth contained in the valuable tables of Hayden,[9] we have thirty-five cases of this condition of which twenty-five were men and ten women. The condition is

---

[1] Hayden, Diseases of Heart and Aorta, p. 596.
[2] Opera Omnia Anat., 1717, p. 134. [3] Traité, &c., vol. i. p. 187.
[4] De Sed. et Caus. Morb. Ep. iii. Obs. 20 ; xxvii. 2 ; xxx. 18.
[5] Mém. de l'Acad. des Sciences, 1784. [6] See Fatty Degeneration—History.
[7] On Corpulence, 1850, p. 92. [8] Loc. cit.
[9] Diseases of the Heart and Aorta, p. 648, et seq. These tables are compiled from the Transactions of the Pathological Societies of London and Dublin, and from Dr. Hayden's own case-books.

therefore more than twice as common in the male as in the female sex. Age also exercises a distinct influence. At birth, as Senac pointed out, the heart is free from fat, and the amount increases as years go on. After six years fat is always present between the auricles and the ventricles. Fatty infiltration follows the same law and commonly occurs after middle life.[1] The combined cases of Quain and Hayden illustrate this very clearly. Under 20 there was but one case, between 20 and 30, three cases; between 30 and 40, none; between 40 and 50, four; between 50 and 60, eleven; between 60 and 70, nine; and over 70, seven cases. Sedentary habits increase the tendency to this condition. Food is an effective agent if the disposition to grow fat exists. Starchy, saccharine, and fatty foods are the chief fat-forming elements. Their effect is the supply to the system of a quantity of carbon in excess of the respiratory needs, and this carbon is stored up as fat. But if the oxygen supplied be in considerable deficiency, nitrogenous food may yield fat by its imperfect oxidation. Alcoholism also exercises a remarkable influence. Malt liquor seems to be more effective in causing fatty growth than spirits, but any form of alcoholism conduces to it; the blood in chronic alcoholism has been found to contain far more fat than in health. Sudden changes in the conditions of the system seem sometimes to determine the overgrowth of fat, general and local. An acute illness, and confinement to bed owing to an accident, are among the causes which Chambers mentions as having set the obese tendency in operation which has continued after the cause ceased to act.

PATHOLOGICAL ANATOMY.—The fat normally present on the heart exists chiefly in the auriculo-ventricular and inter-ventricular sulci, extending thence on to the ventricles, especially on to the surface of the right ventricle. When excessive it may conceal from view almost the whole of the muscular tissue of the heart. It may remain confined to the surface, but when considerable it usually invades the substance of the heart, passing in between the muscular fibres. On section the muscular substance appears narrowed, its junction with the surface fat being much nearer to the inner surface of the wall than in health. Streaks of fat may extend into the muscular tissue. Sometimes the latter is reduced to a thin endo-cardial layer, and even, as Laennec pointed out, the papillary muscles may appear to arise from a mass of fat. The muscular fibres are not really destroyed so completely as they appear to be: under the microscope they may still be seen in considerable number among the fatty tissue by which they are separated and displaced, and often pressed upon. Fatty degeneration of the fibres does, however, occur in a very large majority of the cases. Of the twenty cases contained in Hayden's table, in two only were the muscular fibres stated to be healthy.

[1] The case which is described by Kerkering stands almost alone.

The fat does not, however, always form such extensive and continuous layers. A follicular variety of fatty overgrowth was described by Laennec, and has since been generally recognised. In it the fatty tissue occurs in minute areas, which can be seen as specks in the substance of the heart, especially beneath the endocardium. In all conditions of fatty growth the fat is contained in oval and round cells, having an average diameter of $\frac{1}{100}$th inch, and very similar to those which contain fat elsewhere. In cases of fatty overgrowth upon the heart there is usually also an excess of fat outside the pericardium.

SYMPTOMS.—A considerable increase in the amount of fat upon the surface of the heart may be unattended by morbid signs. This was remarked by Corvisart and Laennec, and their observations have since been abundantly confirmed. Where the fat has invaded the substance of the heart, is infiltrated in the muscular tissue, the effect is a simple weakening of the heart, identical with that presently to be described as the result of the fatty degeneration, which is so frequently combined with the fatty growth. The impulse and sounds of the heart are weakened. The apparent weakening is greater than that which actually exists, because the subcutaneous and mediastinal fat obscures the impulse and dulls the sound. From the same cause the slight increase in the size of the heart which commonly exists is rarely to be detected. The actual diminution in the strength of the heart is often considerable. The pulse is weak, but may be perfectly regular even to the last. Dyspnœa is frequent, and syncope, and even rupture of the heart, may occur. The tendency to sudden death is very marked. Out of thirty-four cases in which the character of the death was noted it was sudden in twenty-four. Of these a third died from rupture of the heart, and another third from syncope. In every case of rupture, and in most of those in which syncope occurred, there was fatty degeneration of the remaining muscular fibres.

DIAGNOSIS.—The diagnosis of fatty overgrowth in this condition depends on the recognition of the association of cardiac weakness and general obesity. The signs and symptoms are those of fatty degeneration. With such signs, if general overgrowth of fat is present, we are justified in suspecting the existence of fatty overgrowth and infiltration of the heart.

TREATMENT.—The treatment is essentially that for the general obesity of which the local overgrowth is but a part. The main object is to lessen the supply of the fat-forming hydrocarbons, and to increase their consumption in the system. The amount of food taken, if excessive, should be restricted; and fat, starch, and sugar should be, as far as possible, excluded from the diet. As much exercise should be taken as is practicable without putting undue strain upon the weakened heart. It is doubtful whether drugs

3 D 2

possess any power of lessening the local accumulation of fat. Alkalies are believed by Chambers to diminish general obesity : whatever beneficial influence -they exercise on general obesity they will also exert on the local state.

In other respects the treatment of fatty overgrowth is the same as that of fatty degeneration of the heart presently to be described.

FATTY DEGENERATION.

SYNONYMS.—Ramollissement (Corvisart, Laennec), Softening of the Heart ; Carditis (Bouillaud) ; Greasy Degeneration (Hope) ; Fatty Metamorphosis (Rokitansky) ; Atrophie Graisseuse (Parrot) ; Steatose Parenchymateuse (Blachez).

DEFINITION.—A change in the muscular fibres of the heart, by which the transverse striæ are at first obscured, and afterwards disappear, being replaced by granules and globules of fat. This granular and fatty degeneration of the heart, as far as we at present understand it, has nothing in its nature of specific character, but is simply the expression of defective nutrition of the proper substance of the fibre. Hence, as might be expected. the conditions with which it is associated, and to which, directly or indirectly, it is due, are widely different in their nature and mode of action. So diverse are they that it is evident that the condition of the heart is rather a common consequence, than a special disease. It has, however, its own symptoms and its own consequences, and so needs special description.

HISTORY.—Fatty degeneration was a late discovery in cardiac pathology. Morbid appearances, such as are now known to result from fatty degeneration, were mentioned by Robert Fludd [1] in the beginning of the seventeenth century, and by Lancisi a hundred years later, but received little attention. Overgrowth of the surface fat, and its invasion of the muscular tissue, were indeed described by Morgagni and many other writers, as has been already stated, and there can be little doubt that, in some of the instances recorded, true fatty degeneration of the remaining fibres was present. Such a change in voluntary muscles was discovered by Haller and Vicq d'Azyr; and some French pathologists at the beginning of the present century suspected that a similar process might be the cause of some morbid appearances in hearts which did not present the ordinary characters of fatty growth. Corvisart,[2] who was perfectly familiar with the latter, had heard of this opinion, and considered the explanation plausible, although he had not himself seen the change referred to. In 1816, Andrew Duncan [3] described a heart which was probably an

[1] Senac quotes from Fludd an account of a heart so soft and brittle that the finger could be placed in its substance. It is said that the man from whom it was taken had played at cards two days before his death. (Senac, Traité, &c., vol. ii. pp. 332, 339.)
[2] Diseases of the Heart, Hebbs' Translation, p. 168.
[3] Edinburgh Medical and Surgical Journal, 1816.

example of the mixed change, fatty growth and degeneration, and a similar case was recorded by Cheyne[1] in 1818. The naked eye characters of the simple degeneration were first accurately distinguished by Laennec[2] in 1819, who described the change in a limited area in very exact terms, recognised its identity with the degeneration described by Haller and Vicq d'Azyr, and gave to it the definite name of "fatty degeneration of the heart."[3] Bertin,[4] quoting Laennec's description, believed he had noticed the change in question, but admitted that he had confounded it with chronic softening, "of which," he said, "it is perhaps only a variety." General softening of the heart was described by Bertin as the effect of carditis.[5] It was thus described also by Bouillaud.[6] The combination of fatty overgrowth with softening and degeneration of the remaining fibres was especially noted by Adams[7] in 1827, Elliotson[8] in 1830, Townsend[9] in 1832, and Latham in 1839. Simple fatty degeneration was described and distinguished from fatty growth by Hope[10] in 1839, and by Williams[11] in 1843, who compared it to the formation of adipocere.

Fresh interest was given to the subject in 1844 by the publication of Rokitansky's observation of the microscopical characters of the degenerated fibres.[12] In 1845 Peacock[13] published similar observations, made apparently in 1843, independently of Rokitanksy's discovery. In 1847 a very clear description of the process in its wider associations was given by Paget,[14] and of its chemical pathology by Virchow.[15] In 1849 a series of cases illustrating the facts previously ascertained, were published by Ormerod[16] and by Kennedy,[17] and in 1850 Quain[18] contributed the very full account of the whole subject of fatty diseases of the heart, which has been already mentioned.

VARIETIES.—According to the appearance of the fibres, whether they contain granules or globules of fat, the two stages have been distinguished of *granular* and *fatty* degeneration, and it has been held that these two varieties are sometimes distinct forms of degeneration. There are, however, reasons for regarding them as stages of the same process, and both forms will be considered here. For con-

[1] Dublin Hosp. Rep., vol. ii. 1818, p. 216.
[2] On Diseases of the Chest, Forbes' Translation, 1821, p. 229.
[3] It is difficult to believe that Laennec did not recognise the identity of "softening and fatty degeneration, for he described the two conditions in identical terms.
[4] Traité des Maladies du Cœur, 1824, p. 431.
[5] Bertin noted (p. 400) as symptoms of "softening" many which are now ascribed to fatty degeneration, such as weakened or inappreciable impulse, dulness of sound, and extreme frequency or slowness of the pulse.
[6] Traité Clinique des Maladies du Cœur, Ed. Quinzième, tome i. p. 615.
[7] Dublin Hosp. Rep. vol. vi. 398.   [8] Lumleian Lectures, p. 32.
[9] Dublin Journal of Medicine, 1832, p. 165.   [10] Diseases of the Heart, p. 348.
[11] Principles of Medicine, 1843, p. 304.
[12] Handbuch der Path. Anat. Bd. ii. 1844, p. 463.
[13] Monthly Journal of Medical Sciences, Jan. 1845, p. 20.
[14] London Med. Gazette, 1847 (lect. vi.).
[15] Virchow's Archiv, Bd. i. p. 152.   [16] London Med. Gazette, 1849.
[17] Dublin Med. Press, vol. xxi.   [18] Med.-Chir. Trans. vol. xxxiii.

venience' sake the single term " molecular degeneration " may be used to denote them. "Primary" and "secondary" degenerations were distinguished by Quain, the former occurring without, the latter dependent on, preceding inflammation. Ponfick[1] would divide the degeneration into two forms, according as the muscular tissue of the heart was or was not in a preceding abnormal condition, and would further divide the cases in which the muscular tissue presents no other change than the degeneration, into "toxæmic," "senile," and " anæmic " varieties, according to their supposed causes.

ETIOLOGY.—(A) PREDISPOSING CAUSES.—*Hereditary Influence.*— A few facts are on record which suggest that fatty degeneration of the heart may own an inherited cause, and thus be transmitted. The cause may be a tendency to early decay of the muscular fibres, due to their defective vitality, or it may be a predisposition to one or other of the exciting causes of fatty degeneration, to be immediately described, especially to fatty overgrowth or arterial disease.

Sex has a marked influence. This is established by all the statistics which have been collected. The disease is at least twice as frequent in men as in women. Quain found the proportion 4 to 1, Ormerod about 3 to 1, Hayden more than 2 to 1. Ponfick states that the fatty degeneration which results from general anæmia is an exception to the rule, and is more common in women than in men.

Age.—Fatty degeneration of the heart may occur at any age. It has been found in the fœtus, and has been met with at every period of life from infancy to old age. But it is much more common in the second than in the first half of life. It is itself a degeneration, and it owns, as its frequent exciting causes, other degenerations, and is thus most frequent during the degenerative period. About three-quarters of the cases occur after forty years of age.

Habits of Life have probably less influence in causing fatty degeneration, than on the occurrence of fatty growth. The condition is more common among the lower classes than among the upper—the reverse of the proportion that obtains in cases of fatty growth. Sedentary habits predispose to imperfect nutrition of the muscular fibres, and some occupations act also by rendering the individuals liable to the exciting causes.

Depressing Emotions are believed by Quain to predispose, in some cases, to fatty degeneration. Moral emotion or long-continued physical pain is said to have such an influence.

Nutritive Influences.—The tendency to the formation of fat, which has so marked an influence on fatty growth, has apparently much less effect in causing fatty degeneration. Quain found that the disease occurred with almost equal frequency in fat and in thin persons.

---

[1] Berlin Klinische Wochenschrift, 1873, Nos. 1 and 2.

(B) EXCITING CAUSES.—The exciting causes of fatty degeneration of the heart comprehend all those conditions which can interfere directly with the nutrition of its fibres. They are very diverse in character, but fall naturally into the two groups—general and local. They may act in conjunction with, or apart from, the predisposing causes.

I. *General Conditions* causing molecular degeneration of the heart are numerous, and various in their character. The tendency to degeneration may (1) be primary, or (2) it may be secondary to other morbid states, of which the most important are certain causes of general impairment of nutrition, certain states of poisoned blood, and certain poisons introduced from without.

(1). Fatty degeneration of the heart may own as its only cause the tendency to general degeneration which is natural to old age and which may occur at a much earlier date. This constitutional tendency is undoubtedly one of its chief causes. The degeneration is rarely confined to the heart ; it is in most cases more widely spread and is seen in the inelastic skin, the rigid vessels, the white hair, the arcus senilis. But the tendency of such degeneration to unequal distribution is well known and may be manifested by disproportionate degeneration of the heart, especially when the conditions of life are such as to put an undue strain upon the organ. This degenerative tendency may or may not be associated with overgrowth of fatty tissue, and thus two types of degeneration are met with, the pathological tendencies of which Paget long ago pointed out.

(2). Fatty degeneration may be the result of some general condition of imperfect nutrition.

Anæmia both quantitative and qualitative may cause it. The influence of repeated losses of blood in causing this degeneration has long been observed as a clinical fact,[1] and it has been recently studied experimentally by Perl.[2] It can be readily produced in dogs by repeated bleedings, but much more readily by occasional large bleedings than by more frequent smaller bleedings. It was especially marked when the loss of blood amounted to three per cent. of the weight of the body. The papillary muscles of both ventricles are said to suffer first, then the walls of the left ventricle, and lastly the walls of the right ventricle. Stokes pointed out that depressing treatment may act in a similar manner. In idiopathic anæmia fatty degeneration of the heart also occurs. Biermer[3] has remarked that fatty degeneration of the blood-vessels often coexists. In pregnancy, intense anæmia sometimes occurs, and in such cases fatty degeneration of the heart has been found.[4]

Wasting Diseases were noticed first by Ormerod, to have as one of their consequences fatty degeneration of the heart. Those in which it is most frequently met with are phthisis, cancer, and chronic suppura-

[1] Ormerod, loc. cit. p. 832.
[2] Virchow's Archiv, lix. 1. Similar experiments had also been made by Tschudnowsky. Botkin's Archiv, Bd. ii. 1866—7.
[3] Bericht über der 42en Versammlung deut. Naturforscher u. Aerzte. Dresden, 1868.
[4] Gusserow, Archiv für Gynækologie, 1871, ii. 2, p. 218.

tion. In each condition the amount of degeneration may be considerable. In cancer it has seemed to the writer to be sometimes associated in degree with the degree of the fatty degeneration in the new growth. In Addison's disease it has also been met with.[1]

Toxæmic Influences constitute another group of causes. Fatty degeneration may result from many acute and some chronic blood changes. These include the various acute febrile conditions, specific and non-specific, and certain chronic diseases which alter the constitution of the blood.

In acute febrile diseases, molecular degeneration of the heart has been noticed by a large number of observers. Its naked-eye characters were distinguished by Laennec, and its conditions of origin and consequences were carefully studied by Louis and Stokes. Laennec pointed out that it occurred especially in those cases in which marks of "putridity" were present. By most writers the change has been regarded as inflammatory, as due to "myo-carditis." It is certain that actual inflammation, as by extension from the pericardium, causes a similar degeneration. But in most of these cases, as Louis and Stokes pointed out, other evidence of inflammation is wanting; there is no purulent infiltration, no effusion of lymph on the pericardium; and Stokes pointed out that local inflammations are rare in the conditions in which this change occurs.

Moreover, identical changes may occur from other influences with equal rapidity, in which there is no suspicion of inflammation, but proof of a profound alteration in the state of the blood—as for example in phosphorus poisoning. Simple elevation of the temperature of the body has been shown capable of producing a similar degeneration.[2]

Many acute diseases are attended with this molecular degeneration. In acute rheumatism the condition is usually associated with undoubted inflammation outside or inside the heart, and is confined to the adjacent fibres, and other evidence of inflammation is to be found where the change is most intense. But in other cases in which the blood-change is profound, a simple degeneration may extend through the whole thickness of the wall and be apparently related to the pyrexia or to the degree of the blood-change, as in other febrile diseases, rather than to the special form of the toxæmia.

The other diseases in which the change occurs are the various febrile affections, and especially those in which any pyogenic influence is at work. It is common, for instance, in erysipelas, puerperal fever, and small-pox. In the last it has been found to be very frequent.[3] It occurs also in yellow-fever,[4] and malarial fevers.[5] In

[1] E. Wagner, Die fette Metamorphose des Herzfleisches. Leipzig, 1865.
[2] Iwaschkewitsch, Journal für Militärärzte, 1870, and Virchow's Jahresb, 1870, i. 179. Wickham Legg, Path. Trans. vol. xxiv. 1873, p. 226.
[3] P. Sick quoted in Canstatt's Jahresbericht, 1866, ii. 39. Desnos and Huchard. Senac noted the frequency of syncopal death in this disease. Traité, &c. 1749, ii. 551.
[4] Bat. Smith, quoted in London Med. Record, 1874, p. 517.
[5] Ponfick, loc. cit. ; Vallin, l'Union Méd. 1874, No. 23.

typhus and typhoid fevers,[1] it is also common, although other forms of degeneration are also found in the heart as well as in the voluntary muscles in these diseases. In typhus Stokes found that it marked some epidemics much more than others, and that it generally commenced about the sixth day. In typhoid, Wagner[2] found extensive fatty degeneration in nine cases out of fifty-nine. In diphtheria the change is also common. G. Homolle found it in six out of fourteen cases which he examined, and Parrot found it in almost as large a proportion.[3]

In measles also Parrot found it present in about one-fourth of fifty-four fatal cases. In one case it was extreme. Extreme degeneration of the heart has also been met with in acute atrophy of the liver.

Chronic alterations in the blood may cause fatty degeneration of the heart. It occurs in gout, as Charcot has pointed out.[4] At first it is slight, but as the disease progresses it may become very considerable and become a cause of sudden death. In the altered state of blood, which results from chronic renal diseases, it also occurs. It has also been found in purpura, scurvy, and the hæmorrhagic diathesis;[5] in the latter perhaps as a result of the loss of blood. It has also been seen in trichinosis.

Certain poisons possess a remarkable power of inducing fatty degeneration of the heart in common with that of other parts. Foremost among these must be placed phosphorus, which has a very rapid action on the heart, liver, kidneys, and other organs, causing marked fatty degeneration in a few days. In a case recorded by Habershon, on the fifth day after a dose of five grains of phosphorus all the organs were the seat of fatty degeneration. The heart becomes yellowish or reddish-grey, soft, and friable, the fibres being filled with fat drops. According to Schraube[6] the affection of the heart is almost invariable in phosphorus poisoning. Arsenious acid, lead, and antimony[7] are said to cause a similar molecular degeneration. In poisoning by sulphuric and other acids it has also been found; and it occurs in greater degree the more readily the acid can get into the blood.[8]

Alcohol is, if not the most powerful, at any rate the most frequent toxic cause of fatty degeneration. In chronic alcoholism the blood is loaded with fat. The habitual use of ether and chloroform is said to have a similar effect.

II. *Local Causes.*—All local causes of atrophy of the heart (q.v.)

[1] Stokes, Diseases of the Heart, p. 366 ; Murchison, On Fever, pp. 256, 631.
[2] Loc. cit.
[3] Dict. Encyclopédique des Sciences Méd., vol. xviii, 1876, art. Cœur. It has also been observed in diphtheria by Bengelsdorf (Berl. Klin. Wochenschrift, 1871), and Bouchut (Gaz. des Hôp. 1872, p. 117).
[4] Maladies des Vieillards et Maladies Chroniques. Paris, 1868.
[5] Wagner, loc. cit.   [6] Schmidt's Jahrb. 1867, 209.
[7] Salkowsky, Virchow's Archiv, xxxiv. 1 and 2.
[8] Munk and Leyden, Berlin Klin. Wochenschrift, 1865, Nos. 49 and 50.

may also cause the fatty degeneration of its fibres. This is, indeed, partly the mechanism by which the atrophy is produced.

External pressure may have this effect. Compression by fluid rarely causes molecular degeneration, but pressure by the contraction of lymph, limited in area, or by the pressure of calcified plates, may produce it. It is possible that the effect is in many cases produced, not by the direct pressure on the muscular fibres, but, as Walshe suggests, by the compression of the arteries and consequent defective supply of blood, a powerful cause of fatty degeneration.

Interstitial pressure on the muscular fibres may certainly, however, be an immediate cause of this fatty degeneration. It is seen in fibroid and fatty overgrowth. It is well seen in the effects of syphilitic and other growths in the heart. In each condition the fibres are compressed directly by the new tissue which is developed between them. In fatty overgrowth they may be little changed, but they frequently suffer, presenting narrowing and indistinctness of striation, sometimes simple atrophy, sometimes very distinct fatty degeneration. This latter occurs especially when any predisposing cause of fatty degeneration coincides in operation, such as congestion of the heart in fibroid overgrowth, sedentary habits, degenerative tendencies, or alcoholism in fatty overgrowths.

Local Anæmia from vascular obstruction is a frequent cause of extreme fatty degeneration. The obstruction is usually gradual, and due to atheromatous changes in the walls of the coronary arteries, calcification, &c.; sometimes it is sudden from thrombosis, or less frequently embolism. The left coronary artery is said to be affected more frequently than the right. The degeneration is limited to that part of the heart to which the diseased vessel is distributed. This connection was noticed by Quain, and his observations have since been abundantly confirmed. He found diseased coronary vessels present in thirteen out of thirty-three cases, and pointed out that the effect depends on the absence of anastomoses with other vessels, by which a collateral circulation could be established, the "terminal character" of the arteries, as it would now be termed, first demonstrated by Swan.[1]

Congestion of the walls of the heart is, as Jenner[2] pointed out, a cause of fatty degeneration of the muscular fibres. The degeneration is rarely simple, more or less fibroid growth is usually conjoined. The chief cause of such congestion is dilatation of the right side of the heart and obstruction, consequent on the distension of the auricle to the escape of the blood from the coronary sinus. Hence fatty degeneration of the heart is frequent in emphysema, long-continued pleural effusion, and diseases of the left side of the heart, which overload the right chambers.

Inflammation of the substance of the heart, "carditis," is also attended with molecular degeneration of the fibres. The effect is

---

[1] Med. Gazette, xlii. 751.   [2] Med.-Chir. Trans. vol. xliii.

clearly seen in cases of pericarditis in which the inflammation invades the subjacent layer of muscular tissue. The depth to which the change extends varies according to the degree and duration of the inflammation. Sometimes only a sixteenth, sometimes a quarter, or more, of the whole thickness of the heart is thus damaged. Wagner found fatty degeneration of muscular fibres present in seventeen out of thirty-five cases of severe pericarditis which he examined. In other forms of carditis the muscular fibres suffer in the same way. In the rare cases of suppurative carditis the degeneration proceeds to the complete destruction of the fibres. It has been already stated that inflammation has been regarded as the mechanism by which the heart suffers in the acute febrile diseases, and that these cases cannot justly be regarded as inflammatory.

Defective vitality of the muscular fibres of the heart has already been described as part of a general proneness to degeneration; it may also occur as a local condition. This influence is seen in the proneness of the fibres of certain individuals to undergo such degeneration, apart from any other exciting cause. It is seen also in the tendency of hypertrophied hearts to undergo this change. Other hypertrophied muscles have been said, after a certain period of use, to fail and undergo degeneration.[1] Fatty degeneration occurs with undue readiness in the newly-formed fibres, and in the majority of cases hypertrophied hearts present degeneration of some of the fibres. This is the case especially in conditions of valvular disease which entail venous congestion of the walls of the heart, but it is also found in other conditions of hypertrophy. In that which occurs in Bright's disease, for instance, E. Wagner found fatty degeneration in one-third of the cases (twelve out of thirty-five).

PATHOLOGICAL ANATOMY.—In considering the pathological anatomy of fatty degeneration it will be convenient to reverse the usual order and to describe first the microscopical changes in the fibres, and afterwards the alterations in the naked-eye characters which result from the minute changes.

The first indication of the degeneration is the appearance of minute black granules within the substance of the fibres. At first they may co-exist with the normal transverse striation and seem to lie in rows between the primitive fibrillæ. As they increase they appear to replace the transverse striæ, which diminish in distinctness and finally cease to be recognisable. Often from the first no regularity can be observed in the disposition of the granules; they are scattered uniformly through the primitive bundle.

As the degeneration progresses the granules increase in size, and become translucent in the centre, being, in fact, globules of fat. These become larger, but rarely, as Quain observed, exceed the size of a blood-corpuscle. A linear arrangement of these fat

---

[1] The hypertrophied biceps of the file-cutter is said by Clifford Allbutt, on the authority of Busk, to waste after a certain time.

globules is frequently to be observed: some are scattered throughout the substance of the fibre, while others are arranged in rows. Ultimately they may occupy the whole area of the fibre: sometimes they are aggregated in one part of it, and the remaining space is clear, free from granules or striæ. The globules constantly appear to accumulate outside the primitive bundles; whether by the coalescence of granules formed there, or by migration from within the fibres, is not clear. The appearance is too constant to be accounted for by the accidental escape of globules when the section is being made. The muscular fibres are ultimately left clear ; empty fibre sheaths appear to remain in their place. The existence of a sarcolemma to the muscular fibres of the heart has been denied : if absent, the appearance of the empty sarcolemma is simulated by the unchanged fibrous tissue between and separating the primitive bundles.

The affection of different fibres is rarely uniform. Some may contain many fatty globules, and others only minute granules, while others are still healthy. Similar degrees of affection may be observed in the course of the same fibre : one part may be healthy, in another part the granular stage may be present, and in another there are only globules of fat.

The globules and larger molecules of fat are soluble in ether and resist acetic acid. It is necessary to rupture the fibre in order to apply this test. There is some doubt whether the finer molecules at the earliest stage of the degeneration are all soluble in ether. It has been affirmed by some writers, but lately denied by Rindfleisch,[1] who maintains that at the commencement of a true fatty degeneration the granules are insoluble in ether. The point will be alluded to in its bearing on the pathology of the process. To the last the molecules and globules of fat maintain their appearance. They never blend into uniform masses such as occupy the cells in fatty overgrowth.

The effect of this molecular degeneration is to modify considerably the naked-eye characters of the affected part. It is changed in colour. The granules and globules reflect light strongly, and render the tint paler. It becomes grey, ashy-grey or greyish-yellow. Laennec aptly compared the colour often seen to that of a faded leaf. In the degeneration which occurs in acute diseases, the substance of the heart may be dark in colour, from the rapid staining of the tissues consequent on the decomposition of the blood-corpuscles, and the escape and transudation of their colouring matter.

At the same time the consistence is changed. The affected part is soft and flabby. The fibres become brittle and break up easily into short pieces, so that a scraping from a cut section shows much shorter fragments of fibres under the microscope, than does that from a healthy heart. The effect of this brittleness of the fibres is to render the tissue friable and easily broken under the finger, and sometimes the change is so great that the tissue softens and breaks down

[1] Path. Gewebelehre, 1875, p. 16.

in a limited portion, or the substance may be torn by a violent contraction of the heart. This diminished consistence may be the most conspicuous feature, and hence the change was described as " pale softening."

The part so changed may have a greasy aspect and feel, and may actually grease paper which is applied to it. The increase in the quantity of fat contained in the tissue is, however, smaller than might be expected. Hermann Weber indeed affirmed that there was no increase; and it has been established by other investigators that in slight fatty degeneration only the same amount of fat is to be obtained from a heart fattily degenerated as from a healthy heart. But it has been shown that in more considerable fatty degeneration, the amount of fat is increased from two or three per cent., to four or five per cent. over the quantity contained in a healthy heart.[1]

The distribution of the change varies. In the form which is secondary to acute diseases, the degeneration is often distributed uniformly through the whole heart. But frequently, as Louis and Stokes pointed out, the left ventricle is affected much more than the right. When secondary to pericarditis only the superficial layer is affected, adjacent to the inflamed pericardium. Occasionally, in fever, according to Stokes, the change may affect only the superficial layer. When arising from a chronic process it may be confined to the inner layer beneath the endocardium, or may be greater in that than in the superficial layer.[2] More commonly it is widely distributed through the heart, generally in the form of minute foci of degeneration, pale spots, lines, crescents, in apparent isolation, or connected, and forming, as has been said, a plexus of degenerated areas throughout its substance. The resulting mottling appears on section or may be visible through the endocardium. This form is often presented by the degeneration which succeeds hæmorrhage. Lastly, a limited area of the heart's wall, generally near the apex, may be affected intensely and uniformly; the affected region is sometimes sharply limited. It was this variety which first attracted the attention of Laennec. This form commonly results from vascular disease. Not rarely a diseased vessel may be traced passing directly into the area, as in cases which have been described by Quain and others.

When degeneration affects part of the heart the frequency varies with which different portions suffer. The ventricles are affected much more frequently than the auricles. Indeed, Ormerod doubted whether the auricles are ever affected : they are certainly occasionally the seat of this degeneration, and their wall may be affected in a limited area through its entire thickness. Quain found that in about half the cases both ventricles are affected, and that where one ventricle only is affected the left is diseased twice as frequently as the right.

The size of a heart the seat of fatty degeneration may seem to be

[1] Böttcher, Virchow's Archiv, xii.; Krylow, *ibid.* 1868, xliv. 4. Stevenson, quoted in Wilks' and Moxon's Pathological Anatomy, p. 119.
[2] Ormerod, loc. cit. p. 832, case vii.

increased, but this is due to the diminished firmness of the organ, in consequence of which it does not maintain its shape when placed on a table. In pure fatty degeneration the size of the heart is normal or only increased slightly by the occurrence of secondary dilatation, and not rarely it is diminished. A wall partially degenerated may be bulged out so as to cause a local dilatation of the cavity. Fatty degeneration, however, may and often does occur in hearts previously enlarged. Hypertrophied tissue, as already stated, undergoes degeneration more readily than healthy fibres.

Associated changes may be found in other organs, especially those which are causes of this condition or are other results of a common cause. Those most frequently met with are degenerated vessels, and fatty degeneration in other organs. Ormerod thought the fatty degeneration in other organs was more commonly associated with fatty degeneration of the right than of the left ventricle.

It has been already stated that hearts, the subject of fatty growth, frequently present fatty degeneration of the remaining fibres.

In all seats of fatty degeneration calcareous salts are apt to be deposited, but this seems to occur less frequently in the substance of the heart than in some other seats of degeneration. Most cases of "ossification of the heart" are cases of calcareous deposits in subpericardial inflammatory tissue. (See "Adherent Pericardium.") The papillary muscles are occasional seats of calcification of degenerated tissue. In rare cases calcareous deposits are found in the substance of the heart. In a case mentioned by Renauldin[1] the substance of the left ventricle of a man, aged 33, was infiltrated with grains of calcareous matter, larger towards the cavity of the ventricle. Some of them were as large as the tip of the finger. Two remarkable forms of calcification have been described by Coats:[2] in one the fibres were dotted with spherules of calcareous matter like globules of oil; in the other the process had resulted in a "petrifaction" of the fibres without change of form.

The blood has been said to contain fat in some cases of fatty degeneration. R. W. Smith stated that he had seen globules of fat visible to the naked eye in the blood after death, and Stokes noted the same thing. Some doubt attaches to these observations from the difficulty of avoiding the escape of fat from the divided tissues into the blood. Dumenil and Pouchet,[3] however, state that they found a considerable quantity of fat in the blood of a person, the subject of chronic alcoholism, who, on subsequent death, was found to have fatty degeneration of the heart and liver. Magnus Huss also affirmed that he had seen fat in the blood of drunkards.

PATHOLOGY.—The significance of this molecular degeneration is clear; it is a sign of lessened vitality, sometimes of actual death. But

[1] Journal de Méd., Jan. 1816. Quoted by Laennec, p. 231.
[2] Glasgow Med. Journal, August 1872.
[3] Gazette Hebd. de Méd. et Chir. 1862, p. 32.

the nature of the process has been the subject of much discussion, and is still, to a considerable extent, obscure.

It seems probable that the first step in fatty degeneration is a molecular change in the muscular fibre, by which the fat which exists within it in an invisible form, combined with the protein constituent, is separated and precipitated in visible granules and globules. Invisible fat, to be detected by chemical analysis only, exists in the blood, the heart, and, in fact, all the animal tissues,[1] and is believed to be combined with the nitrogenous material, because it is found that the different nitrogenous substances have their own special forms of fat; that the fat of fibrin, for instance, is different from the fat of serum.[2] In the healthy heart the fat thus combined amounts to about two or three per cent. In moderate fatty degeneration, even when granules and some globules of fat are visible under the microscope, chemical analysis shows that there is no increase in the total quantity of fat.[3] It would thus appear that the first step of the degeneration is a separation and precipitation of the combined fat. It is probable also that the granules, which constitute the first stage of degeneration, are not all of a fatty character; that some of them are of protein nature. Virchow suggested that the protein material may ultimately be changed to a soluble extractive and pass away, leaving the precipitated fat.

But in more advanced fatty degeneration the quantity of fat is greater than this explanation will account for. Fibres are seen to be filled with globules of fat, and analysis shows that the amount of fat in the tissue is actually considerably increased, often to double the normal quantity. What is the source of this additional quantity of fat? It must be either formed in the fibre or introduced from without. The former is the simpler explanation; by it the fat is supposed to arise by a chemical change, an imperfect oxidation, of the nitrogenous constituent of the fibre. This is the explanation which harmonises well with the visible characters of the change, since the transverse striation disappears as the fat is formed. Rindfleisch[4] points out that the stage of "cloudy swelling" of cells, in which they are filled with minute granules soluble in acetic acid, if it does not resolve, passes into one in which the granules resist acetic acid and dissolve in ether. This view was suggested by Fick[5] and Rokitansky,[6] and has been adopted by Virchow, Paget, Quain, and others. It is certain that fat may be formed from nitrogenous material. The vegetable world affords many instances of this. Butyric acid, a fatty acid, may be formed by the decomposition of fibrin (Wurtz). Chemistry supplies other examples of the same class. If the fat, in molecular degeneration, is not formed by a change in the protein matter, it must be introduced from without. But the

---

[1] Virchow, in his Archiv für Path. Anat. i. 1847, p. 156.
[2] Lehmann, Physiological Chemistry; Virchow, loc. cit.
[3] Hermann Weber, Ormerod.   [4] Pathologische Gewebelehre, p. 16.
[5] Müller's Arch. 1842, p. 19.   [6] Path. Anat.

increase in the fat is sometimes found in situations in which it cannot have been introduced from without. Prolonged maceration in dilute nitric acid, for instance, will produce such a degeneration in healthy muscular fibres; a similar change is often seen in preparations preserved in dilute alcohol. Doubtless this is chiefly due to the separation of the combined fat, and it has accordingly been found that there may be no increase in the total quantity of the fat contained in the fibre before and after the occurrence of the degeneration. In some cases, however, a considerable increase in the amount of fat has been found; that is to say, there has been a considerable formation of fat. Handfield Jones[1] found the increase of fat to amount to nearly fifty per cent., and as any accession of fat from without is impossible it can have arisen only by the decomposition of the protein material. The formation of adipocere is another illustration of the same process, but this substance seems somewhat variable in its character and mode of formation. Ormerod, indeed, maintained that its composition always agrees with the composition of the fat of the animal, and that its fatty element is due to a change in, and infiltration of, the normal fat into the muscular and other tissue. But he found that one specimen consisted of at least half pure fat, and Quain found that adipocere from the muscle of a horse was almost entirely soluble in ether.

Other evidence, although less conclusive, of the origin of the fat from the protein matter, is drawn from the occurrence of extreme fatty degeneration in parts to which the blood cannot gain access. It is seen, for instance, in "infarctions." The area from which the blood-supply is cut off by embolism is the seat of intense fatty degeneration. It is seen also in the experiments (performed first by Wagner) in which portions of animal tissue have been inclosed in the peritoneal and other cavities of living animals, and have become changed to masses of fat. But these experiments are deprived of some of their significance by the fact that the inclosure of the fragments in an impermeable coating prevents any increase in the fat beyond that present in the healthy tissue (Burdach). Inorganic substances permeable to the animal fluids become charged with fat in just the same way as the organic tissue. These facts, indeed, negative all the significance of these experiments as proof of the transformation of protein substance. They do not, however, exclude the possibility that some of the fat may have arisen in this way, since an impermeable coating will prevent the access of oxygen, without which the oxidation of the protein material, imperfect though it be, cannot occur.

The fatty degeneration found in phosphorus poisoning, in poisoning by acids, and intense anæmia, has been regarded as further evidence of the formation of fat by imperfect oxidation of nitrogenous material, since it is believed that all these conditions act by a common mechanism, the diminished supply of oxygen to the tissues consequent

[1] British and Foreign Medico-Chirurgical Review, July 1853, p. 59.

on the diminished number of blood-corpuscles. The diminished oxidation is also indicated by the fall in the temperature of the body.

These facts prove that in fatty degeneration some of the excess of fat present in the fibres may be, and probably is, due to a chemical change in the protein constituent of the fibre. They do not, however, exclude the entrance of some of the fat into the fibre from without. It has been argued, indeed, by Robin[1] and Ormerod,[2] and the view is supported by Walshe, that all the fat seen in the fibres in fatty degeneration enters them from without, that it is essentially an infiltration of the fibres with fat, derived directly from the blood, and replacing the protein constituent of the fibres, which has been removed by a process of atrophy. There are two ways in which such infiltration of fat is conceivable. Minute fatty globules may enter the fibre from the blood, passing through its wall as fat, just as the fatty molecules of the portal blood pass into the liver cells adjacent to the portal canals.[3] Or the fat may enter the fibre in invisible combination with the liquid protein material which must, in the normal course of nutrition, always permeate the fibres. Within the fibre this fat may be separated and precipitated by a process similar to that concerned in the separation and precipitation of the fat contained originally in the muscular tissue, the nitrogenous material passing out as "extractive." The constant repetition of such a process may fill the fibre with fat globules. There is some reason, as just stated, to believe that most of the fat which is found after a time in pieces of tissue inclosed in the peritoneal cavity of another animal passes in from without. If this is so with regard to substances separated from all structural continuity with the living tissues, it may be the same with the fat which is found in such excess in areas in which, in consequence of arrest of blood-supply, necrosis has occurred. The permeation of these areas with fat-containing plasma, from the adjacent healthy region, must constantly go on. The analogy of calcification, which often succeeds fatty degeneration, affords some support to this theory. Normally, the blood, heart, and other organs contain a small proportion of calcareous salts, probably combined with the protein substance. No transformation of the other elements can produce the lime salts which are found in the calcified tissue. They must enter the tissue from without, with the blood plasma, from which they are separated and deposited, while the nitrogenous element passes away. This process, continuing during a long time, ultimately effects a complete infiltration of the tissue with calcareous matter.

A consideration of all the facts of fatty degeneration make it probable, then, that, as Handfield Jones suggested, each process may be concerned in the production of the excess of fat which is found in advanced fatty degeneration; that the fatty material at first seen in

[1] Chimie Anatomique.
[2] Brit. Med. Journal, 1864, ii , p. 152; St. Barth. Hosp. Rep., vol. iv. 1868, p. 30.
[3] Fatty "degeneration" (infiltration) of the liver was produced artificially by Magendie and Gluge injecting fat into the portal vein.

the fibre is merely separated and precipitated in visible form, and that the subsequent excess arises in part by a transformation of the protein material, and in part by the entrance of fat from without.

CONSEQUENCES.—The effect of fatty degeneration on the function of the heart is to lessen its propulsive power, and thus to lead to imperfect filling of the arterial system, and consequent visceral anæmia. This effect is much more marked than is the correlative venous distension, which is so prominent an effect of dilatation of the heart. The relative defective supply to the arterial system is recognisable in the symptoms which it causes during life, rather than by any pathological consequences which can be observed after death. These symptoms are described further on.

The fatty degeneration of the fibres may not only affect the function of the heart, it may lead to changes in its condition which have their own results. The weakened walls may yield unduly before the pressure of the blood, and the heart may become dilated. Such dilatation is rarely very great. Its mechanism and conditions have been already considered (Art. "Dilatation"). But the weakness which fatty degeneration produces may have a much graver result. The brittleness of the fibres may lead to their rupture, and when the degeneration extends through the whole thickness of the wall of the heart, the whole wall may give way. This accident, "rupture of the heart," is of such gravity and importance as to need detailed consideration, and it is therefore described at the end of this article.

SYMPTOMS.—The physical signs and the symptoms which attend fatty degeneration of the heart are usually indistinct and never distinctive. All are common to other morbid states. They depend on the diminished power of the heart, which modifies the signs of its action, and affects the function of other organs.

As the size of the heart in simple fatty degeneration is little changed, the area of dulness presents no alteration. The slight dilatation, which is the consequence of the fatty degeneration, rarely leads to the signs of enlargement of the heart. In a considerable number of cases the dulness is increased, but this increase depends rather on pre-existing hypertrophy or dilatation, or else it is due to concurrent fatty growth.

Diminished force of impulse is the most important physical sign of cardiac degeneration. The area of impulse, like the area of dulness, is only increased by coexisting conditions. As long as the impulse is perceptible, the apex-beat may, in most cases, still be felt. When dilatation has occurred in consequence of the weakening of the cardiac wall, the impulse may be diffused and peculiar in character, resembling, as Stokes remarked, rather the slight, general impulse of an aneurism than the normal impulse of the heart. When the patient is thin, and the lungs are small, so that the impulse of the heart can be well felt, a partial change in impulse may be observed to correspond to a partial degeneration. Stokes, for instance, observed that in fever, when the left ventricle was much more degenerated than the right, while an apex impulse might be lost, an impulse in the lower sternal region, due to the right ventricle, might be still perceptible.

The sounds of the heart are weakened in correspondence with the weakness of the impulse. The first sound, to which the contraction of the heart directly contributes, is that which presents the greatest change. It is usually toneless, shorter, and relatively high-pitched, and may become almost or even quite inaudible at the apex, only the second sound remaining. The first silence is longer than normal in consequence of the shortening of the first sound. The second sound is also weakened in consequence of the deficient distension, and therefore deficient recoil, of the aorta and pulmonary artery. When the first sound is shortened and raised in pitch it may resemble the second. The sounds of the foetal heart are then very closely simulated, especially if the heart acts rapidly. When the degeneration is local, the sounds may be modified locally, just as the impulse. In the acute degeneration of fever, Stokes observed that the first sound might be lost over the left ventricle when it was still audible over the right, in cases in which the post-mortem examination showed the left ventricle to be the more affected. Walshe has observed a similar alteration of intensity in chronic disease under similar circumstances. According to Stokes, if, after ceasing to be heard for a time, the first sound reappeared, it was heard first over the right ventricle and afterwards over the left. In one case both sounds were inaudible for thirty-six hours before death.

Stokes believed that a systolic basic murmur might exist during the early stage of the degeneration. Other observers have noted the occurrence of an apex murmur due to regurgitation, and have ascribed it to fatty degeneration of the papillary muscles.

The rhythm of the heart's action varies much. It may be regular throughout, but is often irregular, chiefly, Walshe thinks, when dilatation coexists; sometimes it is frequent, even to an extreme. It may be slower than natural, and the diminution in frequency may proceed to a degree met with in no other affection. This was first pointed out by Adams. It may fall to forty, thirty, or twenty beats per minute. In rare cases it has sunk as low as eight or ten beats per minute for hours before death.[1] The pulse is weak and small, in proportion to the cardiac failure. Its rhythm, as a rule, corresponds with that of the heart; rarely it is less frequent than the heart's contractions, in consequence of the weaker beats of the heart failing to send a wave along the vessels sufficient to be felt.

Pain is not a common symptom, but now and then is complained of, and is sometimes very troublesome. It may be confined to

---

[1] Ormerod thought that infrequency was associated rather with fatty infiltration than with fatty degeneration. Lond. Med. Gaz. 1849, p. 917.

the cardiac region, may be referred to the sternum, or may extend down the arm. It may be paroxysmal, and simulate angina pectoris in its characters. Occasionally true anginal seizures occur, but no direct relation is known between their occurrence and the fatty degeneration of the heart.

Syncopal attacks, as might be expected from the nature of the disease, are not rare; they are usually produced by some effort. They vary in intensity, sometimes amounting only to a sense of faintness, sometimes to loss of consciousness. They may be accompanied by a sense of great distress, as if death were impending. Death does not unfrequently occur in such an attack. Often in this condition cerebral symptoms are associated with those of cardiac failure. Convulsions may occur. Vertiginous sensations are not unfrequent. Walshe mentions a case in which loss of memory for recent events preceded each attack of syncope. Or the loss of consciousness commencing as apparent syncope, may continue, and deepen, slowly or rapidly, to coma, with stertorous breathing. These "pseudo-apoplectic" seizures, as they have been termed, are usually brief, and leave no paralysis. They have, however, a great tendency to recur. They were referred by Adams and R. W. Smith to congestion of the brain, but Stokes pointed out that their association is with a deficient supply of arterial blood, and that they are probably due to cerebral anæmia, the immediate cause of the syncopal seizures. In confirmation Stokes mentioned a case in which they could be averted at their onset by hanging down the head so that it nearly touched the floor. When death has occurred in these attacks, the brain has appeared free from organic disease. It is needless to remark that apoplexy from actual organic changes in the brain may occur in subjects of fatty degeneration of the heart. Other occasional symptoms on the part of the nervous system are numbness and formication, such as have been attributed to anæmia of the spinal cord.

Dyspnœa is a common symptom. It may be slight, felt only on exertion, especially on ascending an incline or on making some other effort. Or the dyspnœa may be severe, constant, amounting to a continuous sense of suffocation. Considerable dyspnœa is said to be present in one half of the cases of pronounced fatty degeneration. Occasionally it has a special form. Sometimes frequent sighing is observed, as Stokes pointed out. Sometimes the dyspnœal breathing possesses a peculiar rhythm of striking character, which has attracted much attention since it was first described by Cheyne.[1] It was very carefully studied by Stokes,[2] and by him especially associated with fatty degeneration of the heart, although further observation has shown that it is by no means confined to that affection.

This form, which has been termed the "Cheyne-Stokes dyspnœa" or "ascending and descending respiration," is characterised by recurring series of respiratory acts, first increasing and then decreasing in

---

[1] Dubl. Hosp. Rep., 1818, p. 216.
[2] Dubl. Journal of Med. Science and Diseases of the Heart, August, 1846, p. 324.

intensity. In the intervals breathing seems to have almost or entirely ceased; then slight respiratory movements are noticeable, which gradually become deeper and deeper, until an acme of very deep and laboured breathing is reached, after which the respirations gradually become shallower until they subside into the same apparent apnœa, which is again broken by the gradual onset of another series. In the classical case recorded by Cheyne, the cycle included about thirty respirations and lasted a minute. In most of the other cases recorded it has occupied a shorter time. Hayden has found the pulse unchanged during the paroxysms.

As just stated, this form of dyspnœa is by no means confined to fatty degeneration of the heart. It has been seen in other forms of heart disease, especially in valvular disease with dilatation [1] and in atheroma of the aorta.[2] It has been met with even more frequently and at all ages in affections of the nervous system, in cerebral hæmor-rhage,[3] in tumours of the brain, uræmia, and tubercular meningitis.[4] It has frequently been seen in cases in which affections of the heart and brain coexist. It has been produced artificially in animals by Filehne[5] by the injection of morphia and subsequent inhalation of ether and chloroform. It has also been observed in a case of fatty degeneration of the heart, during the narcosis which followed a fatal injection of morphia, and also in chloral narcosis. Its probable explanation lies in a lowered sensibility of the respiratory centre in the medulla oblongata, as was suggested first by Walshe,[6] and after him by Laycock and Traube.

A form of dyspnœa which has in several instances been described as that of Cheyne, is that in which the dyspnœa subsides slowly into dozing apnœa, to be broken after a few seconds by a sudden rouse to conscious, or half-conscious, dyspnœa, which, after a few seconds, slowly subsides. This occurs rather in dilatation than in fatty degeneration of the heart. It seems readily explicable on the theory of diminished sensitiveness of the respiratory centre which requires a voluntary or half voluntary reinforcement. The latter is only excited by a stronger degree of the physiological stimulus ("anoxæmia") than the former; the blood, when well aërated by the dyspnœal respirations, ceases to excite it; sleep gradually withdraws the reinforcement, and the respiratory centre ceases to act; the apnœal venosity of blood increasing, at last awakes the higher mechanism to renewed action. But the true Cheyne-Stokes breathing differs from this in the very gradual in-crease in the breathing, from shallow to deep, as the dyspnœa comes on.[7]

---

[1] Seaton Reid, Dub. Hosp. Gaz. 1860.
[2] Hayden, loc. cit. p. 632.
[3] Laycock, M Fothergill, &c. The writer has also seen it in one case of cerebral hæmorrhage, and has been informed of two other cases in which it was marked.
[4] Traube, Roth.
[5] Berlin. Klinische-Wochenschr., 1874, No. 13, 14, 32, 35.
[6] Diseases of the Heart and Aorta. Third Ed. 1862, p. 345.
[7] Several theories have been framed to explain the details of the phenomena. Traube accounted for the slow accession of the dyspnœa by supposing that the venosity of the

In some cases there may be from first to last no embarrassment of the breathing. Walshe has pointed out that this freedom from dyspnœa may accompany even the syncopal and apoplectic seizures. Cough is sometimes present without bronchitic or other cause.

The other symptoms referable to the general system are in the main those of defective blood supply. The skin is pale, the muscular power deficient, the surface and extremities cold; the mind is weak, often depressed. The digestive organs suffer; anorexia is common. Symptoms of over-distension of the venous system are rare. Slight œdema may occur, but marked dropsy probably never occurs as a consequence of the fatty degeneration. It sometimes results from coexisting dilatation, especially when primary. It is only under such a condition that the urine contains albumen. In simple fatty degeneration of the heart the urine presents no deviation from the normal. Coexisting degeneration of other organs often modifies the general characters of the symptoms of fatty degeneration.

COURSE AND TERMINATIONS.—The course of molecular degeneration of the heart varies according to the circumstances under which it arises, and especially as it occurs gradually as a slow degeneration, senile or premature, or acutely in consequence of blood-poisoning.

In senile degeneration the symptoms are gradual in onset, and may be marked, or may be very obscure. The duration of the affection may be long, sometimes twelve to fifteen years. In these cases other causes often increase the effect of age, and may be to some

---

blood first excites the terminal branches of the vagus in the lungs, which, it is known, can liberate only slight reflex respiratory movements, too slight to prevent accumulating venosity and general stimulation of the afferent nerves, producing the intenser dyspnœa. The gradual onset of the returning respiration is not, however, difficult to explain, for it is the natural form in which the physiological stimulus manifests its returning action after it has been withdrawn by the abundant aëration of the blood in the dyspnœal breathing. A state of apnœa may easily be produced in health by a series of very deep respirations. The highly oxygenated blood no longer stimulates the respiratory centre; no *besoin d respirer* is felt, and, except by a voluntary effort, no respiratory movement is made, until, after a few seconds, the slowly increasing state of blood causes respiratory movements, slight at first, afterwards deeper, until the normal respiration is reached. To explain the degree and duration of the dyspnœa, as well as its gradations, Filehne assumed that vaso-motor spasm causes continued stimulation of the respiratory centre, until that spasm is slowly relaxed by a degree of aëration of the blood which ceases to stimulate the respiration, and thus the slow relaxation of the spasm causes a slow diminution, and finally cessation, of the respiratory movement. He found that by simple alternate compression and relaxation of the arteries in a guinea-pig (right innominate and left subclavian) he could produce perfect Cheyne-Stokes respiration. In further confirmation of his theory he states that he has arrested the characteristic breathing by inhalation of nitrite of amyl.

It is not difficult to understand the origin of this form of respiration in cerebral diseases, in which the lowered sensitiveness of the respiratory centre is likely, as the withdrawal of higher influence may leave its tendency to rhythmical action free to modify a series of its actions. Its connection with cardiac diseases is less easy to understand. Little's theory of unequal action of the ventricles is certainly unsupported. Hayden suggests that the etiological condition is atheroma of the aorta interfering with the supply of arterial blood to the peripheral vessels. This explains the occurrence of dyspnœa better than its rhythmical cessation. Long-continued over-stimulation of the respiratory centre may possibly lead to its diminished sensitiveness.

extent removable, and the extension of the degeneration may be arrested for a considerable time. Sooner or later the cardiac failure comes; late, if the conditions of a tranquil unemotional existence can be secured; soon, if the sufferer has still to face the storms of life, physical and moral. In an acute illness, preceding degeneration of the heart prejudices very much the patient's state. The pulse becomes weak and irregular, often, as Kennedy showed, extremely frequent; and, if the acute disease be at all severe, syncopal failure occurs. Under other conditions the end may come as slow failure, or sudden stoppage from loss of power, or from rupture. The latter occurs in a considerable proportion of the cases in which the disease is well marked. When the coronary vessels are diseased and the heart degenerated, the sudden complete obstruction of a large branch will stop the damaged heart.[1] The more acute degeneration commonly occurs in the course of some pyrexial affection. It is characterised by more or less sudden failure of the heart's action, out of proportion to the other evidences of intensification of the general disease. The condition usually corresponds with a high temperature, and often occurs before the primary disease has begun to subside. When the patient recovers, and the pyrexial stage is over, the action of the heart may become very infrequent or may remain unduly frequent.

The form of degeneration which succeeds a hæmorrhage is marked by more gradual sinking, the patient becomes weaker and weaker, and dies asthenic at the end of a few days or a week or two from the loss of blood.

DIAGNOSIS.—It will be gathered from the preceding remarks that the diagnosis of fatty heart is never easy and is often difficult or impossible. The opinion of Latham that the existence of the disease does not admit of positive recognition, only of probable conjecture, is that of most later authorities. Many of the symptoms which are the most uniformly connected with fatty degeneration of the heart, are also due to so many other conditions, that they have not, even conjointly, much significance. The diagnosis, as far as it can be made, depends on the following points :—

(1). *On the Simple Loss of Power.*—A very similar loss of power may be due to dilatation, but dilatation diffuses the impulse and enlarges the heart; neither effect belongs to degeneration, unless dilatation is associated with it, and then the muscular degeneration can rarely be detected. Such simple loss of power may, however, occur in either a normal or a hypertrophied heart. In each it has the same significance, but in the latter the weakness is commonly relative only. It needs in all cases to be carefully distinguished from concealment of impulse in consequence of over-distension of the lung. A mistake may be avoided by attention to the other signs of emphysema, and especially to diminution or obliteration of the superficial cardiac

[1] Payne, Brit. Med. Journal, Feb. 5th, 1870.

dulness, which always occurs when a distended lung pushes the heart away from the chest wall. Weakness of the first sound of the heart is also most valuable, in the absence of emphysema, as concurrent evidence of the diminished force of its contraction. Other symptoms of fatty degeneration are of less significance, except perhaps slowness of pulse, which is, however, rare ; the special forms of dyspnœa are also too rare, and they are also too equivocal, to be of much value. Some weight has been attached to the syncopal seizures which occur in this disease, and especially to the mixture of syncopal and cerebral symptoms. Mental depression has also received attention as adding weight to other symptoms. Pallor of the surface has a similar significance.

(2). *On the Presence of Similar Degeneration elsewhere.* — Senile degeneration is in some persons local, much more commonly it is general, and its wider manifestation may give significance to cardiac symptoms, which alone would be of little import. Of these degenerations the most important are those of the vascular system, of which the heart is part. The smaller vessels are accessible to direct examination, and their degeneration is manifested by hardness and tortuosity. Perhaps of next significance is the change in the cornea known as "arcus senilis," and which, since it was shown by Canton to depend on fatty degeneration, has attracted much attention as convenient indication of a diathetic tendency to such a change. That it has such significance in some cases is unquestionable,[1] and it has been thus accepted by Quain, Barlow, Paget, and others. But its value may easily be over-rated. Like every other local degeneration, it may be part of a similar widely-spread change or it may be an isolated phenomenon. The latter is the case perhaps, more frequently than the former, and has led many observers to deny that any weight can be attached to it as evidence of fatty degeneration of the heart. Haskins[2] has recorded twelve cases with no affection of the heart. A wider observation has shown that the truth lies between the two extremes, and that the arcus senilis, as already stated, may give weight to other characters but alone is of little significance. Other evidences of degeneration are of still less value ; but greyness of hair is probably a stronger evidence of degenerative tendencies than is its loss.

(3). *The existence of a recognised cause* of fatty degeneration is also of considerable value as an aid to diagnosis. Of the various causes, chronic alcoholism is that which is most frequently associated with the degeneration ; and most frequently assists the diagnosis.

PROGNOSIS.—Molecular degeneration of the heart is always serious, but its gravity varies much under different circumstances. The condition to which danger is especially related is the persistence of the cause of the degeneration. As long as the cause lasts, the degeneration

[1] Luithlen, Virchow's Archiv, 1871, p. 91.
[2] Ann. Jour. Med. Sciences, January, 1853.

continues and increases. Life depends on the maintenance of the functional power of the walls of the heart, and progressive degeneration must sooner or later produce death. If the cause of the degeneration ceases to act, the disease ceases to progress, and if moderate in degree, may, it is probable, even be recovered from. When a certain point of damage has been reached, the condition seems to preclude more than partial restoration of structure.

The forms of degeneration which occur in acute diseases are those in which the immediate danger is greatest, but at the same time the ultimate prognosis is usually favourable. It is immediately grave, because the heart is often unable to resist the prostrating influence of the general disease. It is ultimately good, because the causal disease soon ceases, and often before the change in the heart has reached an irreparable degree. After the acute illness is over, the patient may die from the subsequent slow failure of the heart, but frequently he recovers, sometimes completely, sometimes with some permanent damage to the substance of the heart.

In chronic degeneration the immediate prognosis is less grave, but the ultimate prognosis is worse than in the acute cases. Those are the most hopeful in which there exists a removable cause of degeneration, such as the consumption of alcohol. Where the malady has arisen as a senile degeneration, or as a widely-spread idiopathic change, and the conditions of life are unalterable for good, the prognosis is very unfavourable. It is worse also the earlier in life the patient is attacked, since, as Quain pointed out, early age often entails an inability to obtain that rest which alone can ward off the consequences of the disease.

The fatty degeneration of the heart which coexists with a like degeneration in the vessels has been regarded as being not without advantages: adapted, in senile atrophy, to the lessened mass of blood,[1] and diminishing, by the lessened strength of contraction, the strain to which rotten vessels are exposed.[2]

TREATMENT.—Advanced fatty degeneration of the heart is generally an irremediable condition. Something may be done to ward off its effects, but little to restore the heart to its normal state. In slight degeneration, improvement, even perhaps recovery, may take place. The great end to be aimed at is the removal of the cause. In the acute degeneration of pyrexia there is, as stated, every reason to believe that a state of granular degeneration may be recovered from, when the cause has ceased to act. A chief object in treatment must therefore be to maintain the strength of the patient, to keep his heart going by judicious stimulation until the disease is over. General tonics will then aid recovery. Strychnia has been thought by many to be of great use.

In the chronic forms of degeneration there is frequently little room

---

[1] Crisp, Treatise on the Blood-vessels, 1851, p. 363.
[2] Sir W. Jenner, Address to the British Med. Association, 1869.

for therapeutics. The change is too often due to conditions beyond the influence of any means at our disposal. All removable causes, however, such as chronic alcoholism and gout, must be carefully searched for, and their influence, if possible, removed or neutralised. A fair amount of nitrogenous food is necessary. Restriction of fat is of more doubtful benefit. Tonics are useful—iron, quinine, or strychnine. Digitalis has been recommended to strengthen the fibres which are weakened but not destroyed. Walshe says it is most useful where the pulse is frequent and dilatation coexists. If the degeneration can be arrested, hypertrophy of the remaining fibres may occur, and help to restore the functional power of the heart.

In every form of degeneration care must be taken not to overtax the heart. Its weakened texture is easily damaged still further, and approximate health depends on the avoidance of exertion, &c. Effort with closed glottis must be especially avoided, such as pulling on boots, lifting weights, straining at stool; the latter has in several instances been the immediate cause of cessation of the heart's action. All causes of syncope must also be carefully avoided. In acute illness, the horizontal posture must be carefully maintained as long as the cardiac failure continues, and it must be left off with caution. The general health must be carefully attended to. A life in the open air is strongly praised for such cases by Stokes. The digestive organs must be put right, and the heart preserved from every cause of embarrassment to its action.

Stimulants are needful for the cardiac failure, and a diffusible stimulant may be kept at hand for the syncopal attacks. Coffee has been strongly praised by Desnos and Huchard in the degeneration of small-pox.

Hayden has found the nitrite of amyl of service in the paroxysms of rhythmical dyspnœa. It is equally useful in the attacks of suffocative oppression or anginal pain.

Pain may be relieved by sedatives such as have been recommended for the pain in dilatation of the heart. But equal caution is needful respecting the use of opiates, especially by hypodermic injection. I have known half a grain of morphia, injected hypodermically, followed by death, of which there was no premonition. Ormerod relates a case in which the same quantity was taken by the mouth, and death occurred during the ensuing sleep. Chloroform should not be inhaled; ether should be employed instead. In a large majority of cases of death while under the influence of chloroform, fatty degeneration of the heart has been found.

Rupture of the Heart.

This accident occurs in a considerable proportion of the cases of fatty degeneration, both simple and associated with overgrowth of fat. Conversely, fatty degeneration is by far the most common cause of rupture. Spontaneous rupture never occurs in a healthy heart, and the number of cases due to any other cause, as abscess, or aneurism, or deep endocardial ulceration, is very small. Out of one hundred cases of rupture collected by Quain,[1] in seventy-seven fatty degeneration was detected by the microscope, and of the remaining cases, in all but two either softening was noticed, or the state of the heart was not mentioned. It is thus probable that in at least nine-tenths of the cases of rupture fatty degeneration is the condition of the cardiac wall to which the accident is due.

The degeneration which permits rupture is rarely uniform throughout the whole of the cardiac walls. Uniform degeneration causes uniform weakening; the force of contraction is lessened, and there is no spot specially incompetent to bear the lessened strain. It is when the degeneration, as is so commonly the case, is unequal, and especially when the degeneration in a limited area reaches a high degree, that rupture takes place. The contraction of the more healthy portions of the cardiac wall puts upon the more rotten portion a strain which the former can bear, but which the latter is quite unable to bear. This unequal change is the form which is associated, as its immediate cause, with local and degenerative, rather than with general or inflammatory causes. It rarely, for instance, results from the damage to the cardiac wall, from endo- and peri-carditis, or from pyrexia; whereas it is common in the degeneration secondary to unequal fatty growth and infiltration, and still more frequent in that which results from vascular obstruction, chronic or acute. It is not uncommon to find a degenerated or thrombosed branch of the coronary artery going straight into a patch of intense fatty degeneration in which the rupture has occurred.[2] The sudden occlusion of a vessel by embolism may cause a similar patch of softening.

There is another way in which rupture has sometimes been produced by the association of diseased vessels and fatty change. The degenerated vessels may give way; the resulting extravasation readily tears its way in the softened tissue, and may reach the surface, being assisted, no doubt, by the contractions of the heart. The systole of the heart empties its vessels of blood, and when a hæmorrhage has occurred into the substance of the wall, the contraction must compress the effused blood, and force it in the direction of least resistance. It is not uncommon to find more than one extravasation in the wall of the heart.[3] Such hæmorrhages are said to be sometimes the result of embolism.

The chief other causes of rupture, aneurism of the heart, cysts in its walls, &c., are considered elsewhere.

The influence of the degenerative conditions is seen in the effect of age on the occurrence of rupture of the heart. The accident occurs chiefly in the old. Of the cases collected by Quain, two-thirds were over 60. The mean of forty-eight cases has been

[1] Lumleian Lectures, Lancet, 1872.
[2] Quain, Path. Trans. iv. 80. Simon, Berl. Klin. Wochenschrift, 1872, No. 45.
[3] Colin, Gaz. des Hôpitaux, 1867, p. 104.

found to be 68 years.[1]　Most collections of cases have shown the accident to be more frequent in the male sex, but Quain's statistics give an equal number of cases in each sex. Occasionally, hereditary predisposition has appeared to influence the occurrence, and even the seat of rupture, perhaps by similarity of vascular distribution. A classical instance is the death of George II. and his relation, the Princess of Brunswick, of rupture of the right ventricle.

In primary rupture of the heart the immediate cause of the tear is probably a contraction of undue strength, the strain upon the fibres being greater than the degenerated texture can resist. Thus the accident has commonly occurred during conditions of excited action of the heart, during unusual effort, such as running to catch a train, lifting a weight, cough, straining at stool,[2] or during emotional excitement. Of twenty-four cases collected by Barth, in five death occurred during the act of defæcation. Sometimes no undue exertion can be traced, the symptoms come on suddenly while the patient is at rest, even during sleep.[3]

All parts of the muscular substance of the heart are liable to rupture. It has occurred in the walls of each ventricle, of each auricle, in the septum between the ventricles, and in the papillary muscles. It is however far more frequent in the left ventricle than elsewhere. All statistics agree in showing that the left ventricle is the seat of rupture in three-quarters of the cases, and that it is at least twice as frequent in the anterior as in the posterior wall. The usual seat is near and parallel to the septum, and not far from the apex. About twelve per cent. of the cases occurred in the right ventricle, about six per cent. in the right auricle; while only two or three per cent. have occurred in the wall of the left auricle and in the septum.

The size of the rupture varies from a point scarcely recognisable to an inch in length. It may be larger on the inner surface than on the outer surface. Sometimes it is larger outside, and the inner opening may be small, and concealed among the columnæ carneæ. When the latter is the case, Blaud thought that the rupture had occurred from without inwards. The course of the rent is often oblique, so that inner and outer openings do not correspond. It is usually parallel to the muscular fibres, less frequently across them. The rupture is usually single; sometimes there are several partial ruptures, and one complete. A coagulum usually lies between the lips of the rent, and the cavity of the pericardium is usually filled with clot.

A morbid state of the heart, to which the rupture may be ascribed, is always present. In the rare cases in which fatty degeneration or

---

[1] In the few cases on record of rupture of the heart at earlier ages, most were due to other causes than fatty degeneration. In rupture of the left ventricle, for instance, in a woman aged 49, described by Gregorie (Virchow, Jahresb. 1870), the cause was the perforation of a circular ulcer, probably, since the woman was the subject of constitutional syphilis, due to a softened gumma.

[2] Arch. Gén. de Méd. 1871.

[3] Quain, Path. Trans. i. 62.

softening, or other change, has not been detected, degeneration of the coronary arteries has been found when looked for, and the rupture has probably been produced by interstitial hæmorrhage.

SYMPTOMS.—Sudden, intense pain usually marks the occurrence of the rupture. The pulse becomes at once extremely weak and irregular, and soon imperceptible. There is pallor and coldness of the surface, consciousness is lost, the patient may vomit, respiration ceases, and death occurs in a few moments. Sometimes consciousness is lost before any manifestation of pain can be made. The person falls, pallid and unconscious, a few breaths are drawn, and he is dead. In seventy-one out of one hundred cases of rupture, collected by Quain, death was thus rapid. Occasionally the patient lives for several hours, even for a few days, with intense cardiac distress, and evidence of cardiac failure. The pain may extend down the left arm, sometimes down the right arm also. Vomiting is troublesome, and has been referred to the irritation of the fibres of the pneumogastric by the slowly progressing rent. It may be accompanied by diarrhœa so intense that an attack of cholera is simulated.[1] In a few cases the course of the symptoms is less regular. Some improvement takes place, and then the symptoms recur. Walshe believes these stages represent the rupture of successive layers of the cardiac wall. In a case recorded by Crisp[2] vomiting and pain for several hours were followed, before death, by the cessation of the pain. Five cases out of one hundred collected by Quain lived forty-eight hours. One lived a week. In some of the cases in which the patient lived for a few days the rupture was through the septum only.[3] A case is on record of rupture through the posterior wall, in which the patient lived for six days.

When the patient lives sufficiently long to allow a physical examination of the chest to be made, the pulsations of the heart are found to be imperceptible, increase in the cardiac dulness may be recognised just before death, or for some hours previously.[4] Probably in such a case the rupture is at first small, blood escapes into the pericardium, slowly, and chiefly at the period of complete distension of the heart, and the accumulation of blood in the pericardium lessens the degree of diastolic distension of the heart, and of the escape of blood. A fall of temperature of 3½° C. was observed in Liouville's case.

Rupture of the papillary muscles and chordæ tendineæ give rise to sudden but less urgent symptoms, and are described in the article on Diseases of the Valves of the Heart.

DIAGNOSIS.—From simple syncope, and from all forms of cerebral loss of consciousness, rupture of the heart is distinguished by the

[1] Land, Norsk Maga. fur Laegevidsk, bd. 23, p. 103. Virchow, Jahresb. 1870, ii. 96.
[2] Path. Trans. i. 62.
[3] De Barry, Arch. f. Klin. Med. vii. 152.
[4] Liouville, Gaz. de Paris, 1868, No. 50. Simon, Berl. Klin. Wochenschrift, 1872, No. 45.

sudden, intense pain. Where pain is absent death is usually too rapid
to permit diagnosis. The cessation of the pulse is peculiar to rupture,
and distinguishes it from other less grave causes of cardiac pain, as
angina pectoris. From rupture of an aneurism, that of the heart may
be distinguished only by the rapidity of the symptoms, and by the
absence of the physical signs of pericardial effusion. The pain and
vomiting may cause a slow case to be mistaken for gastric disturbance;[1] the profound syncopal symptoms, and the seat of the pain,
should prevent such an error.

PROGNOSIS.—Complete rupture of the heart is of necessity fatal.
It is rarely, indeed, that the occasion for a prognosis presents itself.
In cases of slower rupture, where the tear is at first incomplete, the
prognosis is scarcely less certain. No case is on record in which a
spontaneous rupture has been shown to have healed. The manner
in which wounds of the heart sometimes heal suggests the possibility
of a like result in rupture ; but the diseased state of the walls
which permitted the rupture seems to preclude any attempt at
cicatrisation. It is just possible, however, that a partial rupture of
a comparatively healthy heart, by interstitial hæmorrhage, may, with
careful treatment, heal. One or two cases are on record in which
the symptoms of partial rupture passed away, and it is possible
that they may have been of this character.

TREATMENT.—In complete rupture death is too speedy to permit
treatment. Where the symptoms are of slower progress, and
the rupture partial only, an attempt may be made to prevent its
extension. The tearing force being, in all probability, due to the
contractions of the heart, these must be reduced to a minimum.
Absolute rest should be secured. Aconite may be given for the
double purpose of thus lessening the force of the heart and of
relieving pain. No stimulants should be given. Ice should be sucked,
and stimulating applications to the epigastrium, such as chloroform, or
spongo-piline, or camphor liniment, may lessen the vomiting and
afford some relief to the pain. There is only too certain reason to
fear a steady increase in the symptoms.

---

[1] Thompson, Lancet, 1871, ii. 635.

FIBROID DISEASE OF THE HEART.

By W. R. Gowers, M.D.

SYNONYMS.—Fibroid Infiltration; Fibroid Transformation (Ormerod); Connective Tissue Hypertrophy (Quain); Cirrhosis of the Heart; Induration of the Heart; Chronic Myocarditis; Schwielen des Herzfleisches.

DEFINITION.—Fibroid disease of the heart, cardiac fibrosis, as it may be termed, consists in an increase in the interstitial connective tissue, without, or more commonly with, a secondary atrophy of the muscular fibres.

The change may affect the whole heart in slight degree, or a limited portion in a high degree. Increase in the interstitial fibrous tissue of the heart may result from chronic inflammation, and all forms of fibroid disease are, therefore, by some authorities, regarded as forms of myocarditis. But the condition may certainly arise by a slow chronic process, in which no characteristic of inflammation can be traced.

HISTORY.—Induration of the heart, when considerable, is so obvious a morbid state that it early attracted attention. It is said to have been described in 1529 by Benivenius, a Florentine physician. Senac and Morgagni noticed its occurrence. Fothergill recorded a case in which the heart was examined by John Hunter.[1] Corvisart described an example in which the ventricles sounded like horn when struck, and grated under the knife. Laennec, Bertin, Bouillaud, Hope, all described it, and the last three observers regarded it as an effect of chronic inflammation. Rokitansky described it in its relation to aneurism of the heart. Many cases have been brought before the Pathological Society, and the disease has been the subject of special study in this country by Quain[2] and Hilton Fagge,[3] in Germany by Skoda,[4] Dittrich,[5] and Skrzeczka,[6] and in France by Pelvet.[7]

[1] Med. Obs. and Inq. v. 1774, p. 252.
[2] Lumleian Lectures, 1872; Lancet, 1872, vol. i.
[3] Path. Trans. 1874, p. 64.
[4] Wiener Wochenschrift, 1856. Med. Zeitung, 1869.
[5] Prager Vierteljahreschrift, 1852.
[6] Virchow, Archiv, 1857, xi. 176.
[7] Des Anévrysmes du Cœur. Paris, 1867.

ETIOLOGY.—The causes of fibroid degeneration are still little known. It is certainly more frequent in men than in women, and chiefly occurs during or after middle life. The right side of the heart is said to be affected occasionally in fœtal life. It is not commonly associated with fibroid degeneration of other organs, and it seems not specially related to the habits or conditions of life of the individual. Walshe believes, however, that it is sometimes due to chronic alcoholism. Its occurrence is chiefly influenced by local causes. Long-continued intermitting congestion of the heart causes, as Jenner [1] showed, toughening and induration of the organ, with increase in the interstitial tissue. The frequent existence of fibroid overgrowth in hypertrophy of the heart is probably due to the congestion which results from the cause of the hypertrophy. Local inflammation may result in fibroid change, as in the superficial layers of the heart after pericarditis. Where the fibrosis is limited in area, it has also been ascribed to an extension to the wall of adjacent endo- or peri-carditis, but Hilton Fagge has suggested that the traces of inflammation which are found may be secondary to the fibroid change, and cannot be taken as proof of such an origin. Injuries, blows on the precordial region, have been assigned, in some cases, as the cause of the symptoms. Lastly, there is clear evidence that syphilis is capable of causing local indurations of the heart; most probably by the transformation into fibrous tissue, of gummatous growths.

PATHOLOGICAL ANATOMY.—The slighter diffused form of fibrosis may affect the whole heart, or only one chamber. The intenser form is usually limited to a portion of one chamber. Occasionally a high degree of fibroid growth may extend around the heart, and has been described as a true "stenosis of the heart.[2]" In the fibroid change secondary to pericarditis the outer layers of the heart are most affected, and sometimes one-half of the thickness of the wall may be transformed into fibrous tissue.

The local forms of fibrosis affect the papillary muscles more frequently than any other parts. These may be entirely transformed into fibrous tissue of tendinous aspect. More rarely the wall of the heart is the seat of circumscribed changes, especially the neighbourhood of the apex. They are also found in the septum, and in the posterior wall at the base. In the right ventricle the degeneration is usually near the base. The local forms are commonly most marked towards the inner surface of the wall. If the whole thickness of the wall is affected, it is rendered thinner, even apart from aneurismal bulging. The endocardium over the degeneration is often thickened.

The diffuse fibrosis renders the wall of the whole heart tougher, more resistant to the fingers and knife. Sometimes, when the new tissue is soft, and the muscular fibres are degenerated, the consistence may

---

[1] Med. Chir. Trans. xliii.
[2] Dittrich, loc. cit.

not be increased, may even be diminished. The change may alter very little the naked-eye appearances, or the enlarged intermuscular septa may be visible in the cut section. The localised change usually presents a glistening fibrous appearance, grey or white, sometimes of a greenish or bluish tint. The section may have a spongy appearance. (Hilton Fagge.) Where less advanced, whitish bands and tracts of fibrous tissues may be seen in the muscular substance. In some cases several separate areas are affected. Occasionally calcareous deposits have been found in the changed tissue.

Under the microscope the localised forms present well-developed fibrous tissue with nuclei. In more recent cases a fusiform cell-growth has been found, developing into fibres. It is said to begin around the blood-vessels, in the intermuscular septa, with an infiltration of nuclei and leucocyte-like cells. Sometimes, it is said, the new substance appears very obscurely fibrillated or amorphous, and may undergo fatty degeneration. Pelvet has seen much elastic tissue in some specimens. Through the fibrous tissue the muscular fibres may be seen passing, lessened in number, sometimes narrowed by pressure, or the seat of fatty degeneration. It is rare for them to disappear entirely. Occasionally the degeneration is in excess of the development of fibrous tissue, and the affected area softens.

CONSEQUENCES.—The effect of fibrosis on the form and size of the heart varies. Hypertrophy and dilatation usually co-exist with the diffuse change, and sometimes the overgrowth of the muscular and fibrous tissues, advancing *pari passu*, may enlarge the heart to vast dimensions, as in the specimen preserved in St. George's Hospital and described by Quain.[1] The increase in the fibrous tissue which results from congestion is commonly greater in the right ventricle than the left. Localised fibrosis also often occurs in hypertrophied hearts, although it may be found in hearts which are normal in size. The cavity may present little change, or it may be generally dilated. More commonly the wall of the affected spot is bulged out into an aneurism. (See Aneurism of the Heart.)

SYMPTOMS.—The necessary effect of fibrosis of the heart will be, as Corvisart clearly taught, to lessen its contractile power. The diffused form, therefore, promotes dilatation or lessens the effects of the hypertrophy which it accompanies. The symptoms of the localised form, in marked cases, have commonly been those of cardiac weakness. Dyspnœa and dropsy have been the chief troubles, and in their general character the symptoms resemble those of dilatation of the heart. The impulse is weakened.[2] The first sound is weak and toneless, and it has been noticed to be much weaker over the

---

[1] Lumleian Lectures, loc. cit.
[2] Laennec taught that induration increases the firmness of the heart's contraction ; but this was probably a hasty conclusion from the firmness of hypertrophied and strongly-contracted hearts.

left than over the right ventricle, when the former was most affected. A systolic murmur has been present in many cases, due, in some, to regurgitation from fibrosis of papillary muscles. The pulse is weak, and has been, in some cases, very infrequent; only thirty beats per minute have been noted. Cardiac pain is present in a considerable number of the cases. In many instances, however, the symptoms have been entirely latent. These differences depend no doubt partly on the extent and position of the fibrosis, affecting the action of the rest of the muscular tissue more in some cases than in others. Death in many instances has been sudden, apart from the rupture, or even the existence of an aneurism.

DIAGNOSIS.—Fibroid degeneration of the heart is at present hardly more than a pathological curiosity, for it is doubtful whether it has ever been recognised during life. Its detection, apart from the signs of aneurism of the heart, must depend on the symptoms of cardiac dilatation without its physical signs.

TREATMENT.—The treatment needed is that for cardiac weakness— for the dilatation which it resembles in its effects. Rest, the avoidance of all strain on the circulation, and the administration of digitalis, to strengthen the remaining fibres, are the chief measures. If there is any suspicion of syphilis, iodide of potassium should be given, although it is doubtful whether the stage of induration can be modified by that drug.

INDEX.

INDEX.

ABDOMEN, tympanitic distension of the, a cause of displacement of the heart, 15, 27, 130 ; collapse of the, also affects the position of the heart, 127.

Abscess of the heart, 530 ; a cause of aneurism of the heart, 155 ; of rupture of the heart, 787.

Abscesses, multiple, in the lungs, from embolism, 651.

Aconite, value of, in the treatment of hypertrophy of the heart, 727, 728 ; of dilated heart, 756.

Adherent pericardium, article on, 438 ; including,—pathological anatomy, 438 ; physical signs, 442.

Adventitious products in the heart, article on, 165.

Age, predisposing to aneurism of the heart, 162 ; to angina pectoris, 548 ; to dilatation of the heart, 732 ; to fatty overgrowth of the heart, 761 ; to fatty degeneration of the heart, 766 ; to fibroid disease of the heart, 792 ; to hypertrophy of the heart, 694 ; to rheumatic pericarditis, 187 ; to renal pericarditis, 408 ; to tubercular pericarditis, 168 ; to rupture of the heart, 787.

Age, influence of, on the position of the heart, 89 ; on the weight of the heart, 6 ; on the area of pericardial dulness, 331.

Albuminuria, see Bright's disease.

Alcoholic excess, habitual, a cause of dilatation of the heart, 733 ; of fatty heart, 762, 769 ; of fibroid disease of the heart, 792 ; of valvular disease of the heart, 681 : predisposes to the occurrence of delirium in rheumatism, 273, 285.

Ammonia, value of, in the treatment of angina pectoris, 586 ; of dilated heart, 757 ; of chronic valvular disease of the heart, 682, 686.

Amyl, nitrite of, value of, in the treatment of angina pectoris, 573, 589, 686 ; of dilated heart, 756 ; of fatty heart, 786 ; occasional alarming effects of, 592 ; mode of administration, 593.

Anæmia, predisposes to dilatation of the heart, 733 ; to fatty degeneration of the heart, 767.

Anæmic measures, so-called, mode of production, 629, 639.

Anasarca, see Dropsy.

Aneurism of the aorta, a cause of displacement of the heart, 129, 148 ; of angina pectoris, 544 ; of hydrops pericardii, 532 ; of hypertrophy of the heart, 699 ; of pericarditis, 425.

Aneurism of the heart, 729 ; acute, 530 ; false consecutive, 151, 154.

Aneurism, lateral or partial, of the heart, article on, 149 ; including,—aneurism of the left ventricle, 150 ; of the left auricle, 162 ; of the valves, 163.

Aneurism of the cardiac valves, 163 ; mode of origin of, 458, 606 ; of the mitral valve, 163 ; of the aortic valve, 164.

Angina pectoris, article on, 535 ; including, —symptoms, 535 ; diagnosis, 542 ; etiology, 548 ; pathology, 569 ; prognosis, 583 ; treatment, 586.

Angina pectoris, relation of, to the neuralgiæ, 577, 582.

Angina sine dolore, 566.

Aorta, aneurism of the, see Aneurism.

Aorta, arch of the, anatomical relations of, in front, 80 ; at sides, 90 ; at back, 99, 106, 122 ; variations in the position of, 18, 111 ; position of the, affected by respiration, 73, 81 ; by shape of chest, 86.

Aorta, the ascending, variation in the position of, 37 ; in the length of, 22.

Aorta, the, descending, relations of, in the chest, 107.

Aorta, root of the, connections of, in the chest, 84, 116, 123 ; variations in the position of, 37, 39.

Aortic aperture, the, size of, in health, 5 ; extreme enlargement of, 8.

Aortic murmurs, diagnosis of, from pericardial friction, 346, 672 ; systolic anæmic murmur occurs in rheumatic endocarditis, 491, 496.

Aortic obstruction, characters of murmur, 638 ; rarely uncomplicated by regurgitation, 611 ; effects of, on the heart,

740; a cause of hypertrophy, 655; prognosis of, 677.

Aortic regurgitation, a consequence of rheumatic endocarditis, 494; early characters of murmur, 496, 498; signs of established disease, 500, 644; late appearance of, 504; effects of, on the heart, 740; a cause of dilatation of the heart, 655; of angina pectoris, 566; diagnosis of, 671, 673; prognosis of, 677, 679; treatment of, 682; use of digitalis in, 684.

Aortic sinuses, the, position, 41, 45.

Aortic stenosis, see Aortic obstruction.

Aortic valves, the, relations of, 41, 45, 117; mode of action of, 457; aneurism of, 164; atrophy, 611; congenital disease of, 615; endocardial inflammation of, 459; chronic changes in, 609.

Aortic valves, diseases of the, due to atheroma, 623; to rheumatic endocarditis, 212, 213; effects of, on the heart, 655; a cause of hypertrophy of the heart, 9; predisposes to endocarditis, 521.

Aortic vestibule, the, 42.

Apex of the heart, the, position of during life, 79; after death, 17, 36, 110; a common seat of aneurismal dilatation, 155; change in the position of, caused by respiration, 73; by habit of body and nature of occupation, 86; by pericardial effusion, 218, 366; by hypertrophy of the heart, 712.

Apex-beat of the heart, changes in, caused by rheumatic endocarditis, 483; by adherent pericardium 450, 454; by dilatation of the heart, 747.

Apex murmurs, systolic, clinical significance of, 640, 675; a sign of dilatation of left ventricle, 748; sometimes present in fibroid disease of the heart, 675, 794.

Apoplexy, cerebral, a consequence of hypertrophy of the heart, 717; pulmonary, connection of, with embolism, 719.

Arcus sinilis, value of, in diagnosis of cardiac degeneration, 784.

Arterial pyæmia of Wilks, 651.

Arterial tension, increase of, during the anginal paroxysm, 573.

Arteries, thickening of the walls of, in Bright's disease, 702.

Arteritis deformans of Virchow, 623.

Arsenic, value of, in the treatment of angina pectoris, 597, 686.

Ascites, a cause of displacement of the heart, 133; a consequence of chronic heart disease, 668.

Aspirator, use of the, for tapping the pericardium, 435.

Asthma, spasmodic, a cause of vertical displacement of the heart, 127.

Asystolie of the heart, 664, 738; treatment of, 683.

Atheroma, a cause of incompetence of the cardiac valves, 623; a consequence of hypertrophy of the heart, 716, 719; of the coronary arteries, a cause of dilatation of the heart, 733; of fatty degeneration of the heart, 770; of the pulmonary artery, a consequence of mitral stenosis, 664.

Atrophy of the heart, article on, 687; including,—definition and history, 687; varieties and causes, 688; pathological anatomy, 689; symptoms, 690; treatment, &c., 691.

Auricle, the left, position of, 94; movements of, during life, 80; aneurism of 162; signs of dilatation of, 749; of hypertrophy of, 710, 720; hypertrophy of, a consequence of mitral stenosis, 661.

Auricle, the right, position of, 25; dimensions of, 31, 114; movements of, 77; signs of dilatation of, 749.

Bacteria, found in the heart in acute ulcerative endocarditis, 652; relation of, to embolism, 654.

Bath, use of the, in rheumatic hyperpyrexia, 255, 262, 266.

Belladonna, value of, in the treatment of angina pectoris, 598; of dilated heart, 756; external application of, in rheumatic endocarditis, 526, 528; in pericarditis, 431; in chronic valvular disease of the heart, 686.

Blisters, value of, in the treatment of hydrops pericardii, 534; of pericarditis, 432.

Blood-letting, for the relief of angina pectoris, 594; in dilatation of the heart 753; in hypertrophy of the heart, 724, 726; in chronic valvular disease, 684.

Brain, the, changes in, caused by dilatation of the heart, 745; by embolism due to valvular disease, 648; by capillary embolism due to endocarditis, 291, 292.

Bright's disease, effects of, on the heart, 740; a cause of endocarditis, 456, 517, of pericarditis, 406; of hypertrophy of the heart, 7, 701; complicating angina pectoris, 547; predisposes to hydrops pericardii, 532.

Bronchitis, a cause of displacement of the heart, 127; of hypertrophy of the heart, 7.

Bronchus, the left, partial obstruction of by the left auricle from extreme mitral stenosis, 665.

Calcification of the walls of the heart, 179 a mode of cure of aneurism of the heart 161; of the valves of the heart, 607; of the coronary arteries, see Atheroma.

Cancer of the heart, 169

Cancer, a cause of fatty degeneration of the heart, 767 ; of hydrops pericardii, 532; of pericarditis, 424.

Cardiac asthma of Stokes, 565 ; treatment of, 589.

Cardiograph, the, indications of, in mitral stenosis, 636, 662 ; in aortic stenosis, 658.

Carditis, article on, 529 ; including,—etiology, 529 ; pathological anatomy, 530; symptoms, diagnosis, &c., 531.

Carotid artery, the left, position of, in the chest, 80.

Chalmers, Dr., sudden death of, 554.

Chest, pain in the, a symptom of angina pectoris, 537 ; of pericarditis, 234 ; of chronic valvular disease, 669 ; shape of the, affects the position of the heart, 86, 97.

Cheyne-Stokes, respiration, or rhythmical dyspnœa, 567 (note), 780.

Chloral-hydrate, value of, in the treatment of angina pectoris, 587 ; in dilated heart, 757.

Chloric ether, inhalation of, for the relief of pseudo-angina, 756.

Chloroform, use of, in the treatment of angina pectoris, 589 ; danger of, in fatty heart, 786 ; external application of, in rheumatic pericarditis, 433 ; in endocarditis 526.

Chordæ tendineæ of the heart, rupture of the, 606.

Chorea, complicating rheumatic pericarditis, 292 ; with non-rheumatic pericarditis, 298 ; numerical summary, 301 ; connection of, with cerebral embolism, 291 ; relation of, to endocarditis, 456, 511, 619.

Cirrhosis of the heart, 791.

Cirrhosis of the lung, a cause of displacement of the heart, 141 ; of dilatation of the right ventricle, 736 ; of tricuspid regurgitation, 640.

Coma, occurrence of, in carditis, 531 ; in rheumatism with endocarditis, 263 ; with pericarditis, 255, 282; without heart affection, 265, 283.

Concentric hypertrophy of the heart, 694, 707.

Congenital atrophy of the heart, 688.

Congenital disease of the valves of the heart, 613.

Conus arteriosus, position of the, 34, 41, 43 ; relation of, to the lungs, 64.

Convulsions, a symptom of carditis, 531 ; of pericarditis, 300.

Copaiba, value of, in dropsy from chronic heart disease, 685, 759.

Coronary arteries, origin of the, 45 ; atheroma of, a cause of dilatation of the heart, 733 ; of fatty degeneration of the heart, 770 ; embolism of, a cause of rupture of the heart, 787 ; ossification of, a cause of angina pectoris, 544, 547, 561 (note).

Corrigan's pulse, 657.

Cough, a troublesome symptom in dilated heart, 750.

Cupping, value of, in the treatment of angina pectoris, 594 ; of dilated heart, 753, 758 ; in chronic valvular disease, 685.

Cysts in the heart, 171.

DEATH, mode of, affects the size of the heart, 4, 707 ; the position of the heart, 15, 28.

Death, sudden, in cases of angina pectoris, probable cause of, 579 ; from aneurism of the heart, 161; from aortic regurgitation, 679; from fatty heart, 763, 783; from fibroid disease of the heart, 794 ; from " heart disease " generally, 550 ; from rupture of the heart, 789.

Delirium, a symptom of carditis, 531 ; of endocarditis, 472 ; of dilated heart, 750 ; occurs in rheumatism with pericarditis, 256, 283 ; with endocarditis, 263, 284 ; without heart affection, 265, 284 ; melancholic, 288 ; in non-rheumatic pericarditis, 296.

Delirium tremens, complicating rheumatism, 257, 273, 285.

Delusions, occurrence of, in rheumatic patients, 286.

Diaphragm, the, movements of, affect the position of the heart, 69 ; affections of, causing pericarditis, 429.

Diarrhœa, in rheumatic hyperpyrexia, 270 ; in dilated heart, 751, 758.

Diastole of the heart, *see* Heart, movements of.

Diastolic murmurs, causes of, 633, 644.

Digitalis, value of, in the treatment of chronic valvular disease of the heart, 683 ; in dilated heart, 754 ; in fatty heart, 786 ; in hypertrophy of the heart, 727.

Dilatation of the heart, article on, 729 ; including,—definition and history, 729; etiology, 731 ; pathological anatomy, 741 ; consequences, 743 ; symptoma, 747 ; diagnosis, 751 ; prognosis, 752 ; treatment, 753.

Dimensions of the heart, in health, 5 ; in disease, 8.

Diphtheria, a cause of endocarditis, 624 ; of acute fatty degeneration of the heart, 769.

Diphtheritic endocarditis of Eberth, 653.

Diseases, constitutional, influence of, on the size of the heart, 6 ; acute febrile, a cause of fatty degeneration of the heart, 768.

Diuretics, value of, in the treatment of dilated heart, 759 ; of hydrops pericardii, 534 ; of pericarditis, 437 ; of valvular disease of the heart, 685.

Dropsy, a consequence of aneurism of the heart, 159 ; of dilated heart, 744, 749 ; of fatty heart, 782 ; of chronic valvular disease, 669 ; symptoms of, 746 ; treatment, 758.

Dropsy, ovarian, effect of, on the action of the heart, 134.

Ductus arteriosus, patent, a rare cause of cardiac murmurs, 646.

Dulness on percussion, area of, from dilatation of the heart, 747, 752 ; from hypertrophy of the heart, 712, 721 ; from pericardial effusion, 329.

Duration of angina pectoris, 584 ; of fatty degeneration of the heart, 782 ; of dilatation of the heart, 753 ; of hypertrophy of the heart, 723 ; of rheumatic pericarditis, 207 ; of effusion into the pericardium, 218, 309.

Dysphagia, caused by pericardial distension, 239.

Dyspnœa, a symptom of heart disease, 670; of angina pectoris, 539 ; of carditis, 531 ; of dilated heart, 750 ; of fatty heart, 567, 763, 780 ; of hydrops pericardii, 533 ; of hypertrophy of the heart, 715 ; causes of, in pericarditis, 237 ; treatment of, 757.

ECCENTRIC hypertrophy of the heart, 694 ; pathology of, 708.

Electricity, use of, in the treatment of angina pectoris, 594.

Embolism, a consequence of valvular disease of the heart, 647 ; pathology of, 605, 648 ; a cause of pulmonary apoplexy, 665, 719 ; of the cerebral arteries, a probable cause of chorea and rheumatic insanity, 290, 291 ; connection of, with hypertrophy of the heart, 717 ; of the coronary arteries, a cause of rupture of the heart, 787.

Emphysema, pulmonary, a cause of displacement of the heart, 125 ; of dilatation of the heart, 736 ; of hypertrophy of the left ventricle, 700.

Empyema, a cause of displacement of the heart, 135.

Endarteritis deformans, 716 ; *see* Atheroma.

Endocarditis, article on, 456 ; including,—pathological anatomy, 456 ; physical signs and symptoms, 460 ; prognosis, 499 ; diagnosis, 505 ; treatment, 525.

Endocarditis diphtheritica, 653 ; maligna, of Virchow, 650 ; secondary to acute rheumatism, 456 ; to Bright's disease, 517 ; to chorea, 511 ; to pyæmia, 516 ; to chronic valvular disease of the heart, 506, 519, 607.

Endocarditis, rheumatic, comparative frequency of, in relation to joint affection, 186, 526, 618 ; increased liability to,

after first attack, 208, 216 ; relation of, to pericarditis, 212 ; predisposes to aneurism of left ventricle, 149, 152.

Endocarditis, recurrent, pathology of, 519; symptoms of, 523 ; diagnosis of, in cases of old valvular disease, 507.

Endocarditis, ulcerative, etiology of, 621. pathology of, 458, 605 ; symptoms, 650; diagnosis, 651 ; treatment, 681 ; relative of, to pyæmia, 620.

Entozoa in the heart, 172.

Epigastrium, pulsation at the, causes of, 126, 668 ; a sign of dilatation of right ventricle, 749 ; of hypertrophy of right ventricle, 718 ; of adherent pericardium, 451, 454 ; pain at the, a symptom of pericarditis, 230.

Erysipelas, a cause of acute fatty degeneration of the heart, 768.

Ether, value of, in the treatment of angina pectoris, 586 ; of dilated heart, 757 ; in chronic valvular disease of the heart, 686.

Exercise, beneficial in cases of fatty heart, 763 ; an aid to diagnosis of heart disease, 674.

Expiratory type of chest, 87.

FACE, the, expression of, in angina pectoris, 541 ; in endocarditis, 471, 494 ; in rheumatic pericarditis, 243 ; cyanosis of, from dilated heart, 749 ; from distended pericardium, 248 ; from chronic valvular disease, 666 ; flushing of, in hypertrophy of the heart, 715.

Fainting, *see* Syncope.

Fatty degeneration of the heart, article on, 764 ; including definition and history, 764 ; varieties, 765 ; etiology, 766 ; pathological anatomy, 771 ; symptoms, 778 ; diagnosis, 783 ; prognosis and treatment, 785.

Fatty overgrowth of the heart, article on, 760 ; including,—causes, 761 ; pathological anatomy, 762 ; symptoms and treatment, 763.

Fibrinous deposits in the heart, 176 ; on the cardiac valves, 604.

Fibro-cartilage, the central, of the heart, 44.

Fibro-cartilaginous degeneration of the walls of the heart, 177.

Fibroid disease of the heart, article on, 791 ; including,—definition and history, 791 ; etiology and pathology, 792 ; symptoms, &c., 793.

Fifth left costal cartilage, variations in relative position of, 17.

Fingers, clubbing of the, a result of chronic heart disease, 666.

First sound of the heart, *see* Sounds of the heart.

Fluid in the pericardium, physical signs of, 329 ; effects of, on neighbouring organs, 306 ; on the heart itself, 307 ; diagnosis of, from dilated heart, 752 ; from hypertrophy of the heart, 330 ; characters of the, in hydrops pericardii, 533.

Fremitus, the friction, of pericarditis, *see* Thrill.

Friction-sound, the, of pericarditis, time of its appearance in acute rheumatism, 209, 348 ; auscultatory signs of, 345 ; area of, 352, 361 ; spots of greatest intensity, 364, 381 ; varieties, 353 ; decline and disappearance of, 375, 384; diagnostic characters of, 388 ; effects of pressure on, 391 ; diagnosis of, from endocardial murmurs, 346, 672 ; relation of, to amount of effusion, 329, 349 ; characters of, in pericarditis from Bright's disease, 413.

Friction, pleuritic, complicating pericarditis, 232.

Furrow, the interventricular, 33, 104 ; the auriculo-ventricular, 34, 58, 101.

Gangrene of the limbs from embolism, 649.

Granulations on the cardiac valves, in endocarditis, 458, 603 ; further changes in, 622.

Gout, chronic, a cause of fatty degeneration of the heart, 769 ; predisposes to angina pectoris, 547, 596.

Hallucinations, occurrence of, in rheumatic patients, 286, 289.

Headache, from dilated heart, 750 ; treatment of, 757.

Head, oscillatory movements of the, a rare symptom in pericarditis, 302.

Heart, the, abscess of, 530 ; acute aneurism of, 530 ; lateral or partial aneurism of, article on, 149.

Heart, adventitious products in the, article on, 165 ; including,—tubercle in the heart, 165 ; cancer, 169 ; cysts, 171 ; entozoa, 172 ; fibrinous deposits, 176 ; fibro-cartilaginous or osseous degeneration, 177 ; polypoid growths, 179.

Heart, atrophy of the, article on, 687.

Heart, dilatation of the, article on, 729 ; a cause of angina pectoris, 568 ; a consequence of aortic regurgitation, 655 ; diagnosis of, from pericardial effusion, 752.

Heart, dimensions of the, in health, 5 ; in disease, 8.

Heart, displacement of the, due to, abdominal distension, 15, 27 ; to angular curvature of the spine, 699 ; to ascites, 133 ; to asthma, 127 ; to aortic aneurism, 129, 148 ; to bronchitis, 127 ; to cirrhosis of the lung, 141 ; to diaphragmatic hernia, 429; to deformities of the thorax, 699; to pulmonary emphy-

sema, 125 ; to empyema, 135 ; to hypertrophy of the heart, 712 ; to enlargements of the liver, 29, 135 ; to mediastinal tumours, 130, 144 ; to pericardial effusion, 218, 308 ; to pleuritic effusion, 130, 136, 141 ; to pneumothorax, 141 ; to distension of the stomach, 130; *see* also Heart, position of.

Heart, fatty diseases of the, article on, 760; including,—fatty overgrowth, 760 ; fatty degeneration, 764.

Heart, fatty degeneration of the, a cause of angina pectoris, 545, 568 ; of sudden death, 763 ; predisposes to rupture of the heart, 786.

Heart, fibroid disease of the, article on 791 ; a cause of mitral regurgitation, 675.

Heart, gout in the, 547.

Heart, hypertrophy of the, article on, 692 ; effects of, on size and weight of the heart, 8 ; a consequence of aortic stenosis, 655 ; relation of, to pericarditis in Bright's disease, 410 ; predisposes to pericarditis in acute rheumatism, 426 ; relation of, to dilatation of the heart, 739.

Heart, impulse of the, *see* Impulse, cardiac.

Heart, movements of the, described, 65 ; relation of, to the normal sounds and to abnormal bruits, 632.

Heart, ossification of the, 774.

Heart, malpositions of the, article on, 125 ; including,—vertical displacements, 125; lateral, 135 ; forward, 148 ; backward, 148.

Heart, pain in the region of the, *see* Pain.

Heart, position of the, during life, 73 ; variations in the, vertical, 14 ; lateral, 28 ; due to age, 89 ; to position of patient, 29 ; to respiration, 69, 97 ; to sex, 89, ; to state of health and nature of occupation, 86 ; to shape of thorax, 97 ; to mode of death, 15, 28.

Heart, rapid enlargement of the, 10 ; relation of, to spinal column, 94, 100, 122.

Heart, rupture of the, article on, 786 ; a result of carditis, 530 ; of fatty degeneration of the heart, 779.

Heart, state of the, after death from angina pectoris, 544, 580.

Heart, syphilitic affections of the, 176.

Heart, weight of the, in health, 4 ; in general diseases, 7 ; when itself diseased, 8 ; when atrophied, 689 ; when hypertrophied, 655, 709.

Hemiplegia, right, a common result of cerebral embolism, 650.

Hereditary predisposition to dilatation of the heart, 732 ; to fatty heart, 761, 763 ; to rupture of the heart, 788.

Hunter, John, illness and sudden death of, 560.

Hydatid cysts in the heart, 173.

Hydropericardium, hydropericarditis, 532.
Hydro-pneumo-pericarditis, diagnosis of, 185.
Hydrops pericardii, article on, 532; including,—etiology and pathology, 532; symptoms, 538; treatment, 534.
Hyperæsthesia, local cutaneous, in rheumatic pericarditis, 224.
Hyperpyrexia, occurrence of, in cases of rheumatism with pericarditis, 254; with endocarditis, 262; without heart affection, 264; without delirium, 266; general summary, 270, 284: occurs also in sunstroke, &c., 271.
Hypertrophy of the heart, article on, 692; including,—definition and history, 692; causes, 694; pathological anatomy, 706; symptoms, 712; diagnosis, 720; prognosis, 722; treatment, 724.

IMPULSE, the, of the heart, character of, in carditis, 531; in dilated heart, 747, 751; in fatty heart, 778, 783; from hypertrophy of left ventricle, 712; of right ventricle, 718; changes in, caused by adherent pericardium, 342, 385; by endocarditis affecting mitral valve, 481; by pericarditis with effusion, 334, 371, 380; value of, in diagnosis, 720, 752.
Injury, local, a cause of acute rheumatism, 221.
Innominate artery, position of, in the chest, 80.
Insanity, temporary, a sequela of acute rheumatism, 286.
Insomnia, from heart disease, treatment of, 757.
Inspiration, effect of, on the heart, 72; see Respiration.
Inspiratory type of chest, 86.
Intra-thoracic tumours, a cause of displacement of the heart, 144.
Iodide of potassium, value of, in the treatment of angina pectoris, 598; of chronic valvular disease of the heart, 680, 682.
Iron, value of, in the treatment of carditis, 531; of dilated heart, 754.

JACTITATION, muscular, in pericarditis, 302.
Joints, the, first affected in acute rheumatism, 221.
Jugular veins, pulsation in the, a sign of tricuspid regurgitation, 666; fulness of the, from distended pericardium, 242, 248; from dilatation of right ventricle, 749.

KIDNEYS, congestion of the, due to dilated heart, 745, 751; to chronic valvular disease of the heart, 668; treatment of, 758.
Kidneys, chronic disease of the. see Bright's disease.

LARYNGITIS, a cause of displacement of the heart, 127.
Leeches, use of, in the treatment of dilated heart, 757; of endocarditis, 526, 528; of pericarditis, 431; in chronic valvular disease of the heart, 685.
Liver, changes in the, caused by chronic valvular disease, 668; by dilatation of the heart, pathology of, 745; symptoms, 750; treatment, 757; enlargement of, a cause of displacement of the heart, 29, 135, 146.
Lungs, the, relations of, to the heart, 60, 82; relative size of, 62, 113; relative size of, affects the position of the heart, 28; abscesses in, from embolism, 651; brown induration of, a consequence of mitral stenosis, 665, 745; embolism of, 665, 719.
Lungs, cirrhosis of the, a cause of displacement of the heart, 141; of dilatation of the right ventricle, 736; of tricuspid regurgitation, 640

MEDIASTINUM, tumours in the, affect the position of the heart, 130, 144.
Melancholia, following acute rheumatism, 286.
Microscopical appearances in endocarditis, 603; in fatty degeneration of the heart, 771; in fibroid disease of the heart, 793.
Mitral orifice, the, circumference of, in health, 5; in disease, 8; variations in the position of, 53; anatomical relations of, anterior, 85; posterior, 103.
Mitral valve, the, description of, 49; relations of, 85, 118, 124; action of, 68, 457; aneurism of, 164; endocardial inflammation of, 458; frequently attacked by rheumatic endocarditis, 212.
Mitral disease, chronic, causes of, 624; pathology of, 608; rarely congenital, 613; due to chorea, 513; a cause of hypertrophy of the heart, 10; effect of, on the cardiac impulse, 342; predisposes to secondary endocarditis, 521.
Mitral regurgitation, characters of murmur, 467, 476, 638; causes of, 641; diagnosis of, 643, 674; diagnosis of murmur from pericardial friction, 347, 478; not always audible at back, 104; effects of, on the heart, 740; guides to prognosis in early stage, 479; relation of, to pericarditis, 426; treatment of, 682.
Mitral stenosis, frequency of, 609; characters of murmur, 634; effects of, on the heart, 740; diagnosis of, 673, prognosis, 678; treatment, 684; see also Presystolic murmurs.
Morphia, hypodermic injection of, in angina pectoris, 590; in dilated heart, 756; in late stages of mitral disease, 686; caution necessary, 786.

Movements, involuntary muscular, in pericarditis, 300.

Murmurs, endocardial, mode of production, 627, 630; variability of, a sign of endocarditis, 507; pericardial, characters of, 345, 386.

Muscular fibres of the heart, anatomical arrangement of, 44.

Muscular strain, habitual or long-continued, a cause of dilatation of the heart, 735; of hypertrophy of the heart, 700; of chronic valvular disease, 623.

Mycosis endocardii, 652.

Myocarditis, acute, 529; chronic, 791; a cause of fibrinous deposits in the walls of the heart, 176; of irregular action of the heart, 236; relation of, to fatty degeneration, 768.

Nervous system, symptoms affecting the, in angina pectoris, 541; in endocarditis, 472; in non-rheumatic pericarditis, 296; in rheumatism with pericarditis, 249, 281; with endocarditis, 262, 282; without heart affection, 264, 282; connection of, with high temperature, 254, 270; with remission of joint affection, 259, 285; with suppression of perspiration, 259, 263; with alcoholism and nervous exhaustion, 273.

Nutmeg liver, the, a result of chronic heart disease, 668, 745.

Obesity, effects of, on the action of the heart, 133; predisposes to dilatation of the heart, 733; to fatty heart, 761.

Occupation, influence of, on the position of the heart, 86; on the joints first affected in acute rheumatism, 220; predisposing to angina pectoris, 549, 550; to dilatation of the heart, 732; to fatty heart, 762, 766; to hypertrophy of the heart, 700; to acute rheumatism, 189, 220; to rheumatic pericarditis, 189, 200; to chronic valvular disease of the heart, 623.

Œsophagus, disease of the, a cause of pericarditis, 428; perforation of the, a cause of pneumo-pericardium, 183, 184.

Opiates, value of, in the treatment of angina pectoris, 586, 587; of dilated heart, 756; of rheumatic endocarditis, 528; see also Morphia.

Opisthotonos, in angina pectoris, 542; in pericarditis with nervous complications, 303.

Orthopnœa, from chronic valvular disease of the heart, 670; from dilated heart, 750; see Dyspnœa.

Ossification of the heart, 177, 774; of the coronary arteries, 544, 561.

Over-exertion, a cause of hypertrophy of the heart, 8, 700; of chronic valvular disease, 623, 681.

Pain, the, of angina pectoris, characters of, 535; seat of, 537; causes of, 576.

Pain in left arm and shoulder, a symptom of chronic valvular disease of the heart, 669.

Pain in the region of the heart, a symptom of carditis, 531; of dilatation of the heart, 749; of endocarditis, 472, 510; of fatty degeneration of the heart, 779; of fibroid disease, 794; rare in hypertrophy, 714; of rheumatic pericarditis, 210, 223, 231; sudden, from rupture of the heart, 789, 790.

Palpitation of the heart, in rheumatic pericarditis, 219; in dilatation of the heart, 749; in hypertrophy, 714; value of, as a sign of heart disease, 669.

Papillary muscles, the, of the heart, arrangement of, 52, 55; relations of, 84, 85; action, 67.

Paracentesis pericardii, in acute pericarditis, 433; in pericardial dropsy, 534; mode of performing the operation, 436; precautions, 437.

Patches, white, on the heart, origin of, 439.

Pericardial sac, the average capacity of, 305, 533.

Pericardial friction, see Friction.

Pericarditis, article on, 186; including rheumatic pericarditis, 186; renal, 400; due to other causes, 295, 419.

Pericarditis, rheumatic, article on, 186; including,—etiology, 187; relation of, to other symptoms of rheumatism, 202; to endocarditis, 212; pathological anatomy, 217; symptoms,—pain, 223; changes in pulse, respiration, &c., 235; in expression and general appearance, 243; symptoms affecting the nervous system and hyperpyrexia, 249; physical signs, 304; percussion, 309; inspection and palpation, 332; auscultation, 345; diagnosis, 330, 346, 388; relapses, 370; treatment, 430.

Pericarditis, relative frequency of, in acute rheumatism, 186; relation of, to the severity of the joint affection, 203; a cause of aneurism of the heart, 152, 154; of carditis, 529; of fatty degeneration of the heart, 771; of fibroid disease of the heart, 178, 792; of adherent pericardium, 342.

Pericarditis, tubercular, 165.

Pericardium, adherent, article on, 438; a cause of atrophy of the heart, 689; of dilatation of the heart, 733, 738; of hypertrophy, 10, 440, 447, 697 ; effect of, on the cardiac impulse, 342, 385.

Pericardium, distension of the, a cause of dyspnœa, 237 ; of dysphagia, 239 ; of cardiac syncope, 236, 242 ; of lividity of the face, 248.

Pericardium, dropsy of the, 532.

Pericardium, effusion into the, physical signs of, 218, 309, 329, 345 ; process of absorption and cure, 382 ; diagnosis of, from dilatation of the heart, 752 ; from hypertrophy of the heart, 721 ; relation of, to joint affection in acute rheumatism, 205 ; amount of, in pericarditis from Bright's disease, 412.

Perspiration, profuse, a symptom of rheumatic endocarditis, 472 ; suppression of, in rheumatic hyperpyrexia, 259, 263, 268, 288.

Phthisis, pulmonary, effects of, on the size of the heart, 6 ; a cause of atrophy of the heart, 689 ; of hypertrophy, 700 ; of fatty degeneration of the heart, 767.

Phosphorus, use of, in the treatment of angina pectoris, 598 ; chronic poisoning by, a cause of fatty degeneration of the heart, 769.

Pleurisy, a cause of pericarditis, 427 ; relation of, to pericarditis in Bright's disease, 409.

Pleuritic pain, occurrence of, in pericarditis, 224, 232.

Pneumonia, relation of, to pericarditis in Bright's disease, 410.

Pneumo-pericardium, article on, 182 ; diagnosis of, 184.

Pneumothorax, a cause of displacement of the heart, 141.

Polypi in the heart, 179.

Position of the patient, the, affects the position of the heart, 29 ; characteristic of pericardial effusion, 334 ; of chronic heart disease, 670, 750, 757.

Pregnancy, a cause of hypertrophy of the heart, 701 ; predisposes to ulcerative endocarditis, 621.

Pressure of stethoscope, effect of, on pericardial friction sound, 357, 359, 391 ; a cause of pulmonary murmur in children, 640.

Presystolic murmurs, explanation of 635 ; relation of, to first sound of the heart, 636; to second sound, 637 ; diagnosis of, 672, 673 ; variable character of, 674.

Prognosis, in rheumatic endocarditis, as to mitral disease, 479 ; as to aortic disease, 499.

Pseudo-angina pectoris, 571, 576.

Pulmonary apoplexy, pathology of, 665, 668 ; a consequence of pericardial distension, 242 ; relation of, to embolism, 719.

Pulmonary artery, the, relations of, 81, 90, 96 ; to vertebral column, 123 ; to the aorta, 22, 96 ; variations in position of, 19, 21, 34, 111 ; in the length of, 20, communication of, with the aorta, a rare cause of murmur, 646 ; hypertrophy of, a consequence of mitral stenosis, 664.

Pulmonary artery, orifice of the, size of in health, 5 ; in disease, 8 ; congenital contraction of, 10.

Pulmonary artery, valves of the, anatomical relations of, 83 ; results of disease of, 666.

Pulmonary artery, the, regurgitant murmur in, 646 ; systolic murmur in, 368 . characters of, 488, 639 ; causes of, 489. clinical significance of, 490 ; diagnosis of, from pericardial friction, 347.

Pulmonary veins, anatomical relations of the, 95, 101.

Pulsation, epigastric, see Epigastrium.

Pulse, characters of the, in aortic stenosis, 656 ; in aortic regurgitation, 657 ; in angina pectoris, 540 ; in carditis, 531 ; in dilated heart, 748 ; in fatty heart, 763, 779 ; in fibroid disease of the heart, 794 ; in hypertrophy of the heart, 715, 719 ; in hydrops pericardii, 534 ; in mitral stenosis, 662 ; in mitral regurgitation, 663 ; rheumatic endocarditis, 472; in rheumatic pericarditis, 241.

Pulse, the radial, an unsafe guide in the diagnosis of cardiac murmurs, 673 ; carotid pulse useful, 633.

Purgatives, value of, in chronic valvular diseases of the heart, 685 ; in dilated heart, 758.

Pyæmia, a cause of dilatation of the heart, 733 ; of simple endocarditis, 456, 516, of ulcerative endocarditis, 621 ; of pericarditis, 423.

Relapses, occurrence of, in rheumatic pericarditis, 370 ; symptoms of, 373 ; effect of, on prognosis, 374.

Respiration, characters of the, in angina pectoris, 539 ; in rheumatic endocarditis, 472, 494 ; in endocarditis complicating old valvular disease, 511 ; in pericarditis, 237, 396 ; in adherent pericardium, 455 ; in rheumatic hyperpyrexia, 269 ; see also Dyspnœa.

Respiration, influence of, on the position of the heart, 69 ; on pericardial friction sound, 391 ; ratio of, to the pulse in rheumatic pericarditis, 241.

Rest, importance of, in the after-treatment of endocarditis, 622 ; in the treatment of angina pectoris, 595 ; of dilated heart, 753 ; of endocarditis, 526, 683 of hypertrophy of the heart, 725 ; of pericarditis, 430.

Rheumatism, acute articular, a cause of dilatation of the heart, 733 ; of chronic valvular disease, 617 ; relation of, to chorea, 512, 514.

Risus sardonicus, occurrence of, in rheumatic pericarditis, 253, 260, 303.

Rupture of the heart, article on, 786 ; including,—etiology and pathology, 786 ; symptoms and diagnosis, 789 ; treatment, 790.

Rupture of aneurism of the heart, 161 ; of the valves of the heart, 625 ; of the aortic valves, 9.

SCARLATINA, a cause of endocarditis, 624.

Sclerosis, chronic, of the valves of the heart, 607.

Sedentary habits predispose to angina pectoris, 550 ; to fatty heart, 762, 766.

Seneca, description of angina pectoris by, 552.

Senega, value of, in aortic regurgitation, 682.

Septum, the fibrous, of the heart, 43 ; the interventricular, 44, 45.

Septicæmia, a cause of carditis, 530 ; of acute fatty degeneration of the heart, 768 ; *see* Pyæmia.

Servants, domestic, very liable to rheumatic pericarditis, 189, 198.

Sex, influence of, on the size and weight of the heart, 5 ; on the position of the heart, 89 ; on the area of pericardial effusion, 331.

Sex, the, predisposing to aneurism of the heart, 162 ; to angina pectoris, 548 ; to dilatation of the heart, 732 ; to fatty heart, 761, 766 ; to fibroid disease of the heart, 792 ; to hypertrophy of the heart, 694 ; to rheumatic pericarditis, 187, 200 ; to tubercular pericarditis, 169 ; to rupture of the heart, 788 ; to valvular disease of the heart, 622.

Sound of the heart, the first, prolongation of, an early symptom of endocarditis, 473 ; also a sequela of endocarditis, 492 ; diagnostic value of, 504.

Sound of the heart, the second, modification of, in aortic regurgitation, 501 ; accentuation of, in mitral regurgitation, 483 ; character of, a valuable guide in mitral disease, 486 ; reduplication of, a consequence of mitral disease, 487.

Sounds of the heart, the, relation of, to the movements of the heart in health and disease, 632 ; changes in, caused by dilatation of the heart, 747, 752 ; by fatty degeneration, 779 ; by fibroid disease, 793 ; by hypertrophy, 713, 719 ; by pericarditis, 345.

Spasm, cardiac, a cause of the sudden death in angina pectoris, 580.

Spasms, muscular, tetanic or choreic, occurrence of, in angina pectoris, 542 ; in rheumatism with pericarditis, 260, 285 ; with endocarditis, 263, 472 ;

without heart affection, 267 ; with delirium or mania, 287, 292 ; in non-rheumatic pericarditis, 298.

Sphygmograph, indications of the, in angina pectoris, 572 ; in aortic stenosis, 658 ; in aortic regurgitation, 659 ; in hypertrophy of the heart, 715 ; an aid to prognosis in valvular disease, 660.

Spine, angular curvature of the, a cause of endocarditis, 620.

Spleen, state of the, in acute ulcerative endocarditis, 650 ; in chronic valvular disease of the heart, 668.

Stenocardia, *syn.* for angina pectoris, 572, 575.

Stenosis of the heart, 792.

Sternum, relation of the, to the arch of the aorta, 22 ; to the heart, 22, 26, 109 ; to the pulmonary artery, 21 ; to the vertebral column, 121.

Stimulants, value of, in the treatment of angina pectoris, 586, 595 ; in dilated heart, 757 ; in fatty heart, 786.

Stomach, collapse of the, a cause of displacement of the heart, 127 ; distension of the, also causes displacement, 130.

Strain, long-continued muscular, a cause of dilatation of the heart, 735 ; of hypertrophy of the heart, 700 ; of chronic valvular disease, 623.

Subclavian artery, the left, position of, in the chest, 80.

Suspirious respiration, the, characteristic of heart disease, 553 (note), 567.

Syncope, from fatty heart, 763, 780 ; from dilated heart, 749 ; in rheumatic endocarditis, 472 ; in pericarditis, 235.

Syphilitic affections of the heart, 176.

Syphilis, a cause of fibroid disease of the heart, 792 ; of valvular disease of the heart, 625.

Systole, the, of the heart, described, 65, 95, 103.

Systolic endocardial murmurs, causes of, 638.

Swallowing, difficulty in, caused by pericardial effusion, 239.

TEMPERATURE, elevation of, in carditis, 531 ; in acute ulcerative endocarditis, 650 ; in acute fatty degeneration of the heart, 783 ; *see* also Hyperpyrexia.

Tension, arterial, increase of, during the anginal paroxysm, 572, 591 ; in Bright's disease, 702.

Tetanus, a rare complication of pericarditis, 299, 303.

Thickness of the parietes of the heart, 5, 8, 710.

Thrill, characters of the, due to pericardial friction, 343, 414, 418 ; relative frequency of, 353 ; late appearance of, 371 ; causes of, in chronic valvular disease, 631.

Tricuspid orifice, the, relations of, 58, 84; circumference of, in health and disease, 5, 8.

Tricuspid regurgitant murmur, characters of, 463, 466, 638; causes of, 464, 640; diagnosis of, from pericardial friction, 347, 467; clinical significance of, in cases of rheumatic endocarditis, 490.

Tricuspid stenosis, characters of murmur, 637.

Tricuspid valve, the, description of, 54; relations of, 84, 119, 124; variations in the position of, 59; action of, 68; incompetence of, a result of endocarditis, 212, 213; not often thus diseased, 523.

Trismus, in rheumatic pericarditis, 261, 303.

Tympanitic distension of the abdomen, a cause of displacement of the heart, 15, 27.

Typhus, a cause of acute fatty degeneration of the heart, 769.

Tubercle in the heart, 165.

Tumours, abdominal, effect of, on the action of the heart, 134; mediastinal, a cause of displacement of the heart, 144; cancerous, also causing displacement, 138.

Urine, state of the, in rheumatic hyperpyrexia, 269; in dilated heart, 751; in fatty heart, 782; in hypertrophy of the heart, 515; in chronic valvular disease, 668.

Valves, the, of the heart, aneurism of, 163, 458, 606; atheroma of, 623; calcification of, 607; rupture of, 625.

Valves of the heart, diseases of the, article on, 601; including,—pathological anatomy, 603; etiology, 612; physical signs, 627; symptoms, 647; diagnosis, 670; prognosis, 675; treatment, 680.

Valvular disease of the heart, chronic, a frequent complication of cardiac aneurism, 158; predisposes to recurrent endocarditis, 519, 607; to ulcerative endocarditis, 622; comparative frequency of, after acute rheumatism, 212; influence of, on prognosis in rheumatism, 216; predisposes to endocarditis, 606; to pericarditis, 425; effect of, on area of pericardial effusion, 332; on the position of the impulse, 336; relation of, to adherent pericardium, 446, 448.

Valvular disease of the heart, chronic, guides to prognosis of, 675; relative importance of the different forms, 677.

Vegetations on the cardiac valves, mode of origin of, 459, 603.

Veins, the cervical, fulness of, from pericardial effusion, 242, 248; from chronic heart disease, 749; pulsation of, from tricuspid regurgitation, 666.

Vena cava, inferior, relations of, in the chest, 104; superior, relations of, 81, 99, 107; dilatation of, a consequence of mitral disease, 666, 668.

Venesection, *see* Blood-letting.

Venous murmurs, in the neck, causes of, 629; varieties of, 632.

Ventricle, the left, dimensions of, in health and disease, 5, 8; breadth of, 35; thickness of parietes, 710; relations of, in the chest, 94, 101; movements of, 79.

Ventricle, the left, aneurism of the, article on, 150; including,—nature and mode of origin, 151; seat of the disease, 155; form and size, 157; state of other parts of the heart, 158; of other organs of the body, 159; symptoms and cause of death, 160.

Ventricle, the left, dilatation of, 748; hypertrophy of, 712; most liable to rupture, 788; changes in, caused by mitral stenosis, 661; simple dilatation of, may cause a murmur, 748.

Ventricle, the right, dimensions of, 5, 8; breadth of, 32, 114; length of, 20, 25; thickness of wall, 710; position of, 92, 95; action of, described, 79; not liable to aneurismal dilatation, 149; signs of dilatation of, 749; of hypertrophy of, 718; changes in, caused by mitral stenosis, 665.

Ventricles, the, systole of, 65, 95, 108.

Veratrum viride, use of, in hypertrophy of the heart, 727; in chronic valvular disease, 684.

Vertigo, a symptom of aortic regurgitation, 669; of dilated heart, 750.

Vestibule, the aortic, 42.

Virginian prune, bark of the, useful in dilated heart, 728, 756.

Voice, loss of, in rheumatic pericarditis, 240.

Vomiting, a symptom of rheumatic endocarditis, 472; of rupture of the heart, 789; of dilated heart, 750; treatment of, 756.

Weight of the heart, normal, 4; affected by general diseases, 7; by local diseases, 8; when atrophied, 689; when hypertrophied, 655, 709; general remarks on, 11.

LIST OF CHIEF AUTHORS REFERRED TO IN
EACH ARTICLE.

LIST OF THE CHIEF AUTHORS REFERRED TO IN EACH ARTICLE.

ADHERENT PERICARDIUM, ARTICLE ON, BY FRANCIS SIBSON M.D., F.R.S., p. 438.

AUTHORS REFERRED TO.

Bouillaud, on the diagnosis of adherent pericardium, 444.
Hope, on the physical signs of adherent pericardium, 442.
Kennedy, on adherent pericardium as a cause of hypertrophy of the heart, 440, 447.
Skoda, description of the physical signs of adherent pericardium by, 444.
Stokes, on the effects of adherent pericardium on the heart, 447.

ANGINA PECTORIS AND ALLIED STATES, ARTICLE ON, BY PROFESSOR GAIRDNER, M.D., p. 535.

AUTHORS REFERRED TO.

Anstie, on the relation of angina pectoris to the neuralgiæ, 571 ; on the value of arsenic in the treatment of angina, 597.
Brinton, on gout at the heart, a form of angina, 547.
Brunton, L., on the character of the pulse in angina, as indicated by the sphygmograph, 572.
Forbes, Sir J., on the connection between angina pectoris and heart disease, 544 ; on the etiology of angina, 548.
Heberden, angina pectoris first described by, 535, 537 ; on sudden death in angina, 559 his treatment, 586.
Latham, on the pain of angina pectoris, 536.
Parry, on the pathology of angina pectoris, 541, 561.
Seneca, description of angina pectoris by, 552.
Stokes, on the peculiarity of the respiration during the anginal paroxysm, 567.
Trousseau, on thoracic aneurisms as a cause of anginal symptoms, 537, 544 ; on the relation between angina pectoris and epilepsy, 542.
Walshe, on pseudo-angina, 571 ; on the influence of evident disease of the heart on the prognosis of true angina, 583 ; on the duration of angina pectoris, 584.

ANEURISM OF THE HEART, LATERAL OR PARTIAL, ARTICLE ON, BY THOMAS BEVILL PEACOCK, M.D., F.R.C.P., p. 149.

AUTHORS REFERRED TO.

Breschet, on the origin of aneurisms of the left ventricle, 149, 150 ; on the situation of aneurisms of the left ventricle, 155, 156.
Cruveilhier, on fibroid degeneration as a cause of aneurism of the heart, 151 ; on the cure of aneurism of the left ventricle by calcification, 161.
Hope, on aneurisms of the base of the left ventricle, 156.
Rokitansky, on endocarditis as a cause of aneurism of the left ventricle, 149, 151, 152 ; on aneurism of the mitral valve, 163.
Thurnam, on the pathology of aneurismal dilatations of the heart, 149, 150, 152 ; on the size of aneurisms of the left ventricle, 157 ; on aneurisms of the left auricle, and of the mitral valve, 163.

ENDOCARDITIS, ARTICLE ON, BY FRANCIS SIBSON, M.D., F.R.S., p. 456.

AUTHORS REFERRED TO.

Cheevers, Norman, on endocarditis in the foetus, 457.
Hasse, on the pathological anatomy of endocarditis, 456.
Moxon, on the pathological anatomy of endocarditis, 457, 460, 528 ; on endocarditis secondary to chronic valvular disease, 519.
Payne, on the pathological anatomy of endocarditis, 457, 521.
Rindfleisch, on the pathological anatomy of endocarditis, 456, 458.
Rokitansky, on the pathological anatomy of endocarditis, 456.

HEART, ADVENTITIOUS PRODUCTS IN THE, ARTICLE ON, BY THOMAS BEVILL PEACOCK, M.D., F.R.C.P., p. 165.

AUTHORS REFERRED TO.

Andral, on hydatid cysts in the heart, 173, 174.
Aran, on polypi of the heart, 180.
Baillie, description of tubercular growths in the pericardium by, 165.
Bouillaud, on tubercle in the heart, 166.
Cobbold, on entozoa in the heart, 175.
Corvisart, on tubercular pericarditis, 166 ; on syphilitic growths in the heart, 176 ; on fibro-cartilaginous degeneration of the heart, 177.
Cruveilhier, on tubercular pericarditis, 166, 167 ; on fibro-cartilaginous degeneration of the heart, 178.
Jenner, Sir Wm., on fibro-cartilaginous degeneration of the heart, 178, 179.
Laennec, on tubercles in the heart, 165 ; on syphilitic disease of the heart, 176.
Louis, on tubercle in the heart, 165 ; in the pericardium, 167.
Rilliet and Barthez, on tubercular pericarditis in children, 166.
Rokitansky, on the rarity of tubercle in the heart, 165 ; on hydatid cysts in the heart, 173, 174.
Virchow, on syphilitic degeneration of the heart, 177.
Walshe, on tubercular pericarditis, 167 ; on cancer of the heart, 169.

HEART, ATROPHY OF THE, ARTICLE ON BY W. R. GOWERS M.D., p. 687.

AUTHORS REFERRED TO.

Bouillaud, on the varieties of cardiac atrophy, 688.
Burns, Allan, description of atrophy of the heart by, 688.
Chomel, on atrophy of the heart, 688, 690.
Hayden, on atrophy of the heart, 688.
Quain, on atrophy of the heart in phthisis, 689, 690.
Rindfleisch, on the pathological anatomy of cardiac atrophy, 690.
Senac, on phthisis of the heart, 687.
Walshe, on the varieties of atrophy of the heart, 688 ; on the symptoms, 690.

HEART, DILATATION OF THE, ARTICLE ON, BY W. R. GOWERS, M.D., p. 729.

AUTHORS REFERRED TO.

Beau, on asystolie of the heart, 738.
Bouillaud, on the pathology of dilatation of the heart, 730
Corvisart, on aneurism of the heart, 730.
Gairdner, on adherent pericardium as a cause of dilatation of the heart, 733 ; on chronic pulmonary emphysema as a cause of dilatation, 734.
Hayden, on the varieties of cardiac dilatation, 734 ; on the influence of adherent pericardium on the production of dilatation, 733, 734.
Laennec, description of the physical signs of dilatation by, 730.
Niemeyer, on the pathology of cardiac dilatation, 732, 739, 741.
Stokes, on the pathology of dilatation of the heart, 730 ; on adherent pericardium as a cause of dilatation, 733 ; on dilatation of the auricles, 742 ; on alterations of the heart sounds from dilatation, 747, 748.
Walshe, on the physical signs of dilatation of the heart, 747, 748, 752.
Wilks, on the pathology of cardiac dilatation, 730, 734.

HEART, FATTY DISEASES OF THE, ARTICLE ON, BY W. R. GOWERS, M.D. p. 760.

AUTHORS REFERRED TO.

Hayden, on predisposition to fatty hypertrophy of the heart, 761 ; to fatty degeneration of the heart, 766.
Laennec, on the pathological anatomy of fatty hypertrophy or the heart, 762, 763 ; of fatty degeneration, 765.
Louis, on acute molecular degeneration of the heart, 768, 773.
Ormerod, on wasting diseases as a cause of fatty degeneration of the heart, 767.
Paget, Sir James, on the pathological anatomy of fatty degeneration of the heart, 765, 767.
Quain, on the causes of fatty hypertrophy of the heart, 761, 762 ; on the pathology of fatty degeneration of the heart, 769, 770, 773 ; on fatty degeneration as a cause of rupture of the heart, 787.
Rindfleisch, on the pathological anatomy of fatty degeneration of the heart, 772, 775.

Rokitansky, on the microscopical appearances of fatty degeneration of the heart, 765, 775.
Stokes, on acute molecular degeneration of the heart, 768, 773 ; on the physical signs o. fatty degeneration of the heart, 779 ; on peculiarities of the respiration during anginal paroxysms, 780.
Walshe, on the symptoms of fatty degeneration of the heart, 779 ; on the use of digitalis in treatment, 786.

HEART, FIBROID DISEASE OF THE, ARTICLE ON, BY W R GOWERS, M.D., p. 791.

AUTHORS REFERRED TO.

Corvisart, on the pathology of fibroid disease of the heart, 791, 793.
Hilton Fagge, on the pathology of fibroid disease of the heart, 792, 793.
Pelvet, on fibroid disease as a cause of dilatation of the heart, 791, 793.
Quain, on connective tissue hypertrophy of the heart, 791, 793.

HEART, HYPERTROPHY OF THE, ARTICLE ON, BY W. R GOWERS, M.D., p. 693.

AUTHORS REFERRED TO.

Birtin, on the pathology of cardiac hypertrophy, 693, 707, 710.
Bright, on chronic renal disease as a cause of hypertrophy of the heart, 701.
Corvisart, on cardiac hypertrophy as a cause of aneurism of the aorta and of cerebral apoplexy, 699, 717.
Cruveilhier, on the real nature of concentric hypertrophy, 707.
Laennec, on the physical signs of cardiac hypertrophy, 693, 713.
Quain, on hypertrophy of the heart in phthisis, 700 ; on hypertrophy of the heart as a cause of apoplexy, 717.
Rindfleisch, on the pathological anatomy of cardiac hypertrophy, 711.
Senac, on the connection between hypertrophy of the heart and arterial degeneration, 716 ; on the importance of rest in treatment, 725.
Walshe, on the physical signs of hypertrophy of the heart, 712, 713.

HEART, MALPOSITIONS OF THE, ARTICLE ON, BY FRANCIS SIBSON, M.D., F.R.S., p. 125.

AUTHORS REFERRED TO.

Bennett, on displacement of the heart by intra-thoracic tumours, 130, 135, 144.
Gairdner, on the displacement of the heart in pleurisy, 140.
Hope, on displacement of the heart by aneurism of the aorta, 148.
Stokes, on epigastric pulsation in bronchitis and emphysema, 126 ; on cancer of the lung without displacement of the heart, 145.
Townshend, on displacement of the heart by empyema, 138, 140.
Walshe, on displacement of the heart by pleuritic effusion, 137.
Wintrich, on displacement of the heart by pleuritic effusion, 138, 139, 148 ; in pneumo-thorax, 141.

HEART AND GREAT VESSELS, Position and Form of the, Article on, by Francis Sibson, M.D., F.R.S., p. 14.

AUTHORS REFERRED TO.

Braun, on the relative position of the thoracic viscera, 92, 109.
Haller, on the valves of the heart, 37, 47.
Heath, description of the aortic sinuses, 48.
Le Gendre, on the anatomy of the thorax, 109.
Pirogoff, on the anatomy of the heart, 48, 84 ; on the relative position of the thoracic viscera, 92, 109.
Reid, on the anatomy of the heart, 46.
Sibson, on the medical anatomy of the thorax, 50, 89, 91.
Thurnam, on the aortic sinuses, 46.

HEART, WEIGHT AND SIZE OF THE, Article on, by Thomas Bevill Peacock, M.D., F.R.C.P., p. 3.

AUTHORS REFERRED TO.

Bouillaud, on the variations in the weight of the heart, 3, 4, 11.
Bright, on hypertrophy of the heart from chronic renal disease, 8.
Glendinning, on the weight of the heart in health and disease, 3, 4, 6.
Laennec, on the size of the heart, 3.
Reid, on the weight and dimensions of the heart, 3, 4.
Cases by Bristowe, Vanderbyl, Church, &c., in the Pathological Transactions.

HYDROPERICARDIUM, Article on, by W. R. Gowers, M.D., p. 532.

AUTHORS REFERRED TO.

Corvisart, on the physical signs of pericardial dropsy, 533, 534.
Graves, on effusion into the pericardium without evidence of inflammation, 533, 534.
Laennec, on the occurrence of pericardial effusion during the last hours of life, 532.
Stokes, on pericardial dropsy, 533, 534.
Walshe, on the causes of hydro-pericardium, 532.

PERICARDITIS, Article on, by Francis Sibson, M.D., F.R.S., p. 186.

AUTHORS REFERRED TO.

Allbutt, Clifford, on paracentesis pericardii, 434.
Burdon-Sanderson, on the distribution of the nerves of the heart, 236 ; on the influence of the sympathetic nerves on the circulation, 247.
Bouillaud, on pericarditis with nervous complications, 289, 296, 297.
Fuller, on delirium in pericarditis, 294.
Fox, Wilson, on the treatment of hyperpyrexia, 255, 257, 261.

Frerichs, on pericarditis from renal disease, 406.
Laennec, on paracentesis pericardii, 433.
Moxon, on pericarditis from pyæmia, 423.
Trousseau, on delirium in rheumatism, 285 ; on paracentesis pericardii, 433.
Watson, Sir Thomas, on nervous complications of acute rheumatism, 286, 295.

PNEUMO-PERICARDIUM, Article on, by J. Warburton Begbie, M.D., p. 182.

AUTHORS REFERRED TO.

Bouillaud, on the diagnosis of pneumo-pericardium, 182.
Laennec, on the frequency of pneumo-pericardium, 182, 183 ; on the physical signs of, 184.
Stokes, on a case of pneumo-pericardium, 182 ; physical signs of, 185.
Walshe, on the diagnosis of pneumo-pericardium, 183, 185.

VALVES OF THE HEART, DISEASE OF THE, Article on, by C. Hilton Fagge, M.D., F.R.C.P. p. 601.

AUTHORS REFERRED TO.

Allbutt, C., on overwork as a cause of valvular disease, 623, 681.
Bouillaud, on the rheumatic origin of valvular disease of the heart, 617.
Corrigan, Sir D., on the mode of production of cardiac murmurs, 627 ; on the peculiar pulse of aortic regurgitation, 657.
Chauveau, on the cause of blood murmurs, 628, 639.
Corvi-art, on the pathological anatomy of valvular disease, 602 ; on rupture of the cardiac valves, 625.
Friedreich, on endocarditis in infants, 613 ; on hepatic pulsation, 668 ; on the prognosis of valvular disease, 677.
Gairdner, on auricular systolic murmurs, 635.
Hayden, on the murmur of tricuspid stenosis, 637.
Moxon, on endocarditis secondary to valvular disease, 605.
Peacock, on congenital valvular disease, 613, 615 ; on rupture of cardiac valves, 625, 626.
Rindfleisch, on the pathological anatomy of endocarditis, 603.
Walshe, on the relative importance of the different forms of valvular disease, 677, 679.

LONDON :
R. CLAY, SONS, AND TAYLOR, PRINTERS,
BREAD STREET HILL,
QUEEN VICTORIA STREET.

J. B. LIPPINCOTT & CO.'S

CATALOGUE

OF

MEDICAL AND SURGICAL

WORKS.

AGNEW.—Hand-book of Practical Anatomy. By D. Hayes Agnew, M.D. With Illustrations. Second edition, revised. 12mo. Cloth. $2.00.

AITKEN.—Outlines of the Science and Practice of Medicine. By William Aitken, M.D. (Edin.), F.R.S., Professor of Pathology in the Army Medical School; Corresponding Member of the Imperial Society of Physicians of Vienna, etc. 8vo. Cloth. $5.00.

"The book cannot fail to become a popular one, and we cordially recommend it to the notice of teachers and students."—*London Lancet.*

"It is, we believe, destined to as great a popularity as the larger works of the same author. It is well digested, clear, well written, and the work of a man who is conversant with every detail of his subject, and a thorough master of the art of teaching."—*British Med. Journal.*

"While intended chiefly for students, there is a great deal in it which it would profit most practitioners to read, and we can assure them that it is widely different from the superficial compends put into the hands of American students."—*Phila. Med. and Surg. Reporter.*

ALLEN.—Outlines of Comparative Anatomy and Medical Zoology. By Harrison Allen, M.D. Second edition. 8vo. Cloth. $2.00.

——Studies in the Facial Region. By Harrison Allen, M.D. Illustrated. 8vo. Cloth. $2.00.

ANSTIE.—Notes on Epidemics. For the Use of the Public. By Francis E. Anstie, M.D. Edited, with American Notes, by William A. Hammond, M.D. 12mo. Cloth. $1.00.

ARTHUR.—Treatment and Prevention of Decay of the Teeth. By Robert Arthur, M.D., D.D.S. Illustrated. 16mo. Cloth. $1.50.

1

ASHHURST.—On Injuries of the Spine, their Pathology and Treatment. By JOHN ASHHURST, JR., A.M., M.D. 12mo. Cloth. $1.50.

With special reference to the propriety of Spinal Resection. Also, an Appendix giving Analyses of 394 cases of Injury to the Spine; the Age of Patient; Mode of Injury; Progress of Case; Time under Observation; Result; Remarks; Author and Reference.

ATLEE.—General and Differential Diagnosis of Ovarian Tumors, with Special Reference to the Operation of Ovariotomy. By WASHINGTON L. ATLEE, M.D. Illustrated. 8vo. Cloth. $5.00.

"As regards matter, from title-page to colophon, we have hardly turned a leaf without finding something new, something interesting, something of value."—*Phila. Med. Times.*

"In this work we have an unusual amount of *original* matter; in fact, it is altogether drawn from the author's long and carefully studied experience. In this respect it is almost unique, and is an honor to independent American Surgery."—*Phila. Med. and Surg. Reporter.*

BANTING.—A Lecture on Corpulence. Addressed to the Public. Eighth edition. By WILLIAM BANTING. 18mo. Paper. 25 cents.

BARTHOLOW.—A Manual of Hypodermic Medication. By ROBERTS BARTHOLOW, A.M., M.D. Second Edition, revised and enlarged. Illustrated. 12mo. Cloth. $1.50.

BECK.—Beck's Medical Jurisprudence. Elements of Medical Jurisprudence. By T. R. and J. B. BECK, M.D. With Notes by an Association of the Friends of the Drs. Beck. New and thoroughly revised edition, with Additions, by Dr. CHAS. H. PORTER. 2 vols. 8vo. *In press.*

BENNETT.—Text-Book of Physiology: General, Special, and Practical. By JOHN HUGHES BENNETT, M.D., F.R.S.E., Professor of the Institutes of Medicine or Physiology, and Senior Professor of Clinical Medicine in the University of Edinburgh. Illustrated. Crown 8vo. Cloth. $3.50.

"It is undoubtedly a work of great value, and will be highly appreciated by all students."—*Pacific Med. and Surg. Journal.*

"For a compact, highly scientific, and complete text-book of physiology, we have met no superior to this work of Prof. Bennett's. His experience of nigh thirty-five years as a teacher and practical worker in the department renders him a master of instruction."—*Phila. Med. and Surg. Reporter.*

BERNARD and ROBIN.—Notes on M. Claude Bernard's Lectures on the Blood, and of M. Charles Robin's Lectures on the Minute Anatomy of the Blood, and concerning Circulation. By WALTER F. ATLEE, M.D., Philadelphia. 12mo. Cloth. 75 cents.

BLACK.—The Ten Laws of Health; or, How Disease is Produced and can be Cured. By J. R. BLACK, M.D. 12mo. Cloth. $1.75.

CALKINS.—Opium and the Opium-Appetite: with Notices of Alcoholic Beverages, Cannabis Indica, Tobacco and Coca, and Tea and Coffee, in their Hygienic aspects and Pathological Relations. By ALONZO CALKINS, M.D. 12mo. Cloth. $1.75.

CAMPBELL.—Essays on the Secretory and the Excito-Secretory System of Nerves, in their Relation to Physiology and Pathology. By Henry Fraser Campbell, A.M., M.D. 8vo. Cloth. $1.50.

CHAPMAN.—Diarrhœa and Cholera: Their Origin, Proximate Cause, and Cure through the Agency of the Nervous System by Means of Ice. By John Chapman, M.D., etc. 16mo. Paper. 25 cents.

----Diarrhœa and Cholera: Their Nature, Origin, and Treatment through the Agency of the Nervous System. By John Chapman, M.D., etc. Second edition. 8vo. Cloth. $3.75.

CHAVASSE.—Advice to a Wife on the Management of her own Health; and on the Treatment of some of the Complaints incidental to Pregnancy, Labor, and Suckling. By Pye Henry Chavasse, F.R.C.S. Thirteenth edition. 12mo. Cloth. $1.50.

"A little book so well known and appreciated by the public as not to stand in need of any further assistance on our part than the announcement of a new edition."—*London Lancet.*

----Advice and Counsel to a Mother on the Management of her Children. Ninth edition, greatly enlarged. By Pye Henry Chavasse, F.R.C.S. 2 vols. in one. 12mo. Cloth. $2.00.

COOLEY.—Hand-book of Compound Medicines; or, The Prescriber's and Dispenser's Vade-Mecum. By Arnold J. Cooley. 12mo. Cloth extra. $1.25.

COPEMAN.—Cerebral Affections of Infancy. A report on the Cerebral Affections of Infancy, with a few Comments and Practical Remarks. By Edward Copeman, M.D., Senior Physician to the Norfolk and Norwich Hospitals. 12mo. Extra cloth. $2.00.

DA COSTA.—Medical Diagnosis, with Special Reference to Practical Medicine. A Guide to the Knowledge and Discrimination of Diseases. By J. M. Da Costa, M.D., Lecturer on Clinical Medicine, and Physician to the Pennsylvania Hospital; Fellow of the College of Physicians of Philadelphia, etc., etc. Illustrated with numerous Engravings. Fourth edition. 8vo. Cloth, $6.00. Sheep, $7.00.

"Da Costa's work is well known and highly and justly esteemed in England as in America. It is too firmly established, and its value too thoroughly recognized, to need a word *pro* or *con.*"—*London Med. Times and Gazette.*

"The book before us is the work of the first diagnostician in America. It is the best book on diagnosis extant."—*The Amer. Practitioner.*

"It has been prepared with careful research among books, at the bedside, and in the autopsy; and it is made available by a good arrangement, and a style of unusual case, clearness, and finish. To digest and memorize the matter of all its pages will well repay the labor it costs."—*Amer. Journal of Med. Sciences.*

"We cannot too highly commend it to our readers. We believe it is destined to hold a permanent place in American medical literature."—*Boston Med. and Surg. Journal.*

"The execution in detail is very intelligent, and exhibits, wherever we turn to it, always all that is essential, judged according to the more recent standpoint of European Medicine."—*Schmidt's Jahrbucher der Medicin.*

"It is sufficient to say that we believe it the best and safest authority which can be selected for the guidance of the student or young practitioner, and cordially commend it to them as such."—*Phila. Med. Times.*

DAMON.—The Neuroses of the Skin: their Pathology and Treatment. By HOWARD F. DAMON, A.M., M.D. 8vo. Cloth. $2.00.

——The Structural Lesions of the Skin: their Pathology and Treatment. Illustrated. By HOWARD F. DAMON, A.M., M.D. Cloth. $3.00.

DIEULAFOY.—Pneumatic Aspiration. A Treatise on the Pneumatic Aspiration of Morbid Fluids. A Medico-Chirurgical Method of Diagnosis and Treatment of Cysts and Abscesses of the Liver, Strangulated Hernia, Retention of the Urine, Pericarditis, Pleurisy, Hydarthrosis, etc. By Dr. GEORGES DIEULAFOY, Gold Medallist of the Hospital of Paris. Crown 8vo. Extra cloth. $4.00.

"It is but just to the author to admit that his numerous carefully conducted and conclusive experiments have supplied all the evidence which the most incredulous could demand, and mark the introduction of pneumatic aspiration as the beginning of a new era in rational medicine, constituting a new triumph of logical induction from observed phenomena to a scientific principle entitled to take rank with vaccination and auscultation."—*Chicago Med. Journal.*

DRAKE.—A Systematic Treatise: Historical, Etiological, and Practical, of the Principal Diseases of the Interior Valley of North America, as they appear in the Caucasian, African, Indian, and Esquimaux Varieties. By DANIEL DRAKE, M.D. Edited by S. HANBURY SMITH, M.D., and FRANCIS G. SMITH, M.D. 8vo. Sheep. $5.00.

DUTCHER.—Pulmonary Tuberculosis. Its Pathology, Nature, Symptoms, Diagnosis, Prognosis, Causes, Hygiene, and Medical Treatment. By ADDISON P. DUTCHER, M.D. Illustrated. Crown 8vo. Extra cloth. $3.00.

"Few men in our country have given the subject under consideration more thought than Dr. Dutcher, and his experience has been ample. While we object to portions of the treatment recommended in the book, we are bound to give the author credit for furnishing the profession with one of the best, if not the very best, work extant on this subject."—*St. Louis Amer. Med. Journal.*

EBERLE and MITCHELL.—A Treatise on the Diseases and Physical Education of Children. By JOHN EBERLE, M.D.; late Professor of the Theory and Practice of Medicine in Transylvania University. Fourth edition. With Notes and large Additions. By THOMAS D. MITCHELL, A.M., M.D. 8vo. Sheep. $3.50.

EVE.—A Collection of Remarkable Cases in Surgery. By PAUL F. EVE, M.D. Sheep. $5.00.

EYRE.—The Stomach and its Difficulties. By SIR JAMES EYRE, M.D. Sixth edition. 16mo. Cloth. 75 cents.

FARABEUF.—Ligation of Arteries. An Operative Manual. By Dr. L. H. FARABEUF. With Forty-three fine Engravings. Translated by JOHN D. JACKSON, M.D. 12mo. Cloth limp, red edges. $1.75.

"The translator has done a good service in placing this useful little work before the profession in excellent English. As a manual or handbook of the ligation of arteries the work admirably fulfills the purpose of its author. The descriptions of the various operations are so clear and full as to render the manual one of much practical value."—*N. Y. Med. Journal.*

GARRETSON.—A System of Oral Surgery : being a consideration of the Diseases and Surgery of the Mouth, Jaws, and Associate Parts. By JAMES E. GARRETSON, M.D., D.D.S., late Lecturer on Anatomy and Surgery in the Philadelphia School of Anatomy, etc. Illustrated with Steel Plates and numerous Wood-cuts. New and enlarged edition. 8vo. Extra cloth, $10.00. Sheep, $11.00.

" For accurate description, skillful arrangement, and thoroughness of detail, it has no equal. As a text-book for the mechanical and surgical dentist, it is invaluable."—*N. Y. Med. Record.*

" A glance at the headings of the chapters of this work will abundantly convince the reader of the great importance of the several subjects treated, and reading of the text will demonstrate that the author has accomplished the task proposed with consummate ability and fidelity."—*Chicago Med. Journal.*

" There is no work of the kind which bears comparison with it."—*Pacific Med. and Surg. Journal.*

GERHARD.—The Diagnosis, Pathology, and Treatment of the Diseases of the Chest. By W. W. GERHARD, M.D. Fourth edition. Revised and enlarged. 8vo. Sheep. $4.00.

GETCHELL.—The Maternal Management of Infancy. For the Use of Parents. By F. H. GETCHELL, M.D. 18mo. Cloth. 75 cents.

GORTON.—Mental Hygiene. An Essay on the Principles of Mental Hygiene. By D. A. GORTON, M.D. 12mo. Cloth. $1.75.

——The Drift of Medical Philosophy. An Essay. By D. A. GORTON, M.D. 12mo. Cloth, limp, 75 cents. Paper cover, 60 cents.

GROSS.—A Manual of Military Surgery ; or, Hints on the Emergencies of Field, Camp, and Hospital Practice. Illustrated with Wood-cuts. By S. D. GROSS, M.D. 18mo. Cloth. 63 cents.

HAMMOND.—Lectures on Venereal Diseases. By WILLIAM A. HAMMOND, M.D. 8vo. Cloth. $3.00.

——Military, Medical, and Surgical Essays. Prepared for the United States Sanitary Commission. By WILLIAM A. HAMMOND, M.D. 8vo. Cloth. $5.00.

——Physiological Memoirs. By WILLIAM A. HAMMOND, M.D. 8vo. Cloth. $2.00.

——Sleep and its Derangements. By WILLIAM A. HAMMOND, M.D. Second edition, revised. 12mo. Cloth. $1.75.

" When the original monograph appeared, it received our careful attention and commendation ; and now we have only to repeat our good words, and express our gratification that the work has undergone such careful revision."—*Cincinnati Lancet and Observer.*

HARTSHORNE.—Cholera : Facts and Conclusions as to its Nature, Prevention, and Treatment. By HENRY HARTSHORNE, A.M., M.D. 18mo. Paper cover. 25 cents.

——The Family Adviser and Guide to the Medicine Chest. A concise Handbook of Domestic Medicine. Revised and enlarged. By HENRY HARTSHORNE, A.M., M.D. 18mo. Cloth. 75 cents.

——Glycerin and its Uses. A Monograph. By HENRY HARTSHORNE, A.M., M.D. 18mo. Cloth. 60 cents.

HANCE.—The Physician's Medical Compend and Pharmaceutical Formulæ. By EDWARD H. HANCE. 16mo. Tuck. $1.00. 12mo. Cloth. $1.50.

HOPPE.—On Percussion and Auscultation as Diagnostic Aids. By Dr. CARL HOPPE. A Manual for Students and Practitioners of Medicine. Translated by L. C. LANE, M.D. 12mo. Cloth. $1.50.

"This little book of 152 pages, as the translator remarks, is a model of conciseness and completeness; for it will be found, on examination, to contain in a compendious form every point of importance bearing upon this branch of medicine. . . . The medical student will find this one of the best text-books in the English language."—*Pacific Med. Journal.*

HORNER.—The United States Dissector: Lessons in Practical Anatomy. By WILLIAM E. HORNER, M.D. Illustrated with 177 Wood Engravings. Fifth edition, carefully revised and entirely remodeled. By HENRY H. SMITH, M.D. 12mo. Sheep. $2.00.

KEEN.—Early History of Practical Anatomy. Being the Introductory Address to the Course of Lectures on Anatomy at the Philadelphia School of Anatomy. By WILLIAM W. KEEN, M.D. Cloth limp, 50 cents. Paper cover, 30 cents.

"This lecture embraces so much that the wonder to us is how Professor Keen managed to deliver it to his class at one time. The lecture gives in terse English just what its title indicates, together with incidents connected with the early anatomists."—*Lancet and Observer.*

KÖLLIKER.—A Manual of Human Microscopical Anatomy. By A. KÖLLIKER, Professor of Anatomy and Physiology in Würzburg. Translated by GEORGE BUSK, F.R.S., and THOMAS HUXLEY, F.R.S. Edited, with Notes and Additions, by J. M. DA COSTA, M.D., and illustrated with over 300 Wood Engravings. 8vo. Sheep. $3.50.

"The reputation of Professor Kölliker will be enhanced by this text-book; for such it is destined to be pre-eminently. We commend it to the profession, and to students especially, as worthy of their patronage."—*N. Y. Med. Gazette.*

LEE.—The Correct Principles of Treatment for Angular Curvature of the Spine. By BENJAMIN LEE, A.M., M.D. Illustrated. Second edition. 12mo. Cloth. $1.00.

LEIDY.—An Elementary Treatise on Human Anatomy. By JOSEPH LEIDY, M.D. With 392 Wood Engravings. 8vo. Sheep. $5.00.

MACLEOD.—Notes on the Surgery of the War in the Crimea. With Remarks on the Treatment of Gunshot Wounds. By GEORGE H. B. MACLEOD, M.D., F.R.C.S. 12mo. Cloth. $1.50.

"I regard it as one of the best of the modern works on military surgery. Its publication at the present moment is a valuable contribution for our army surgeons, all of whom should have it."—HENRY H. SMITH, *Surgeon-General of Pennsylvania.*

MALGAIGNE.—A Treatise on Fractures. With 106 Illustrations. By J. F. MALGAIGNE, Membre de l'Académie Royale de Médecine. Translated from the French, with Notes and Additions, by JOHN H. PACKARD, M.D. 8vo. Sheep. $4.00.

McCLELLAN.—The Principles and Practice of Surgery. By the late GEORGE McCLELLAN, M.D., and JOHN H. B. McCLELLAN, M.D. With Illustrations. Demi 8vo. Sheep. $2.00.

" The work is worthy of strong commendation."—*N. Y. New Remedies.*
" Containing much valuable information."—*Pacific Med. and Surg. Journal.*
" The very best work for practitioners before the profession."—*Georgia Med. Companion.*

MEDICAL TIMES.—A Weekly Journal of Medical and Surgical Science. Vols. I., II., III., and IV. Imperial 8vo. Fine cloth. Each. $5.00.

MEREDITH.—The Teeth, and How to Save Them. By L. P. MEREDITH, M.D., D.D.S. Illustrated. 16mo. Cloth. $1.25.

MITCHELL.—Five Essays on the Cryptogamous Origin of Malarious and Epidemic Fevers; Animal Magnetism, or Vital Induction; the Penetrativeness of Fluids; the Penetrativeness of Gases; and a new Practice in Acute and Chronic Rheumatism. By JOHN KEARSLEY MITCHELL, M.D., late Professor of the Practice of Medicine in Jefferson Medical College of Philadelphia. 12mo. Cloth. $1.25.

MITCHELL.—Injuries of the Nerves, and their Consequences. By S. WEIR MITCHELL, M.D. 8vo. Cloth. $3.00.

" Dr. Mitchell's well-earned reputation as an experimental physiologist of the highest order has been admirably maintained by the manner in which he has executed his task. . . . A volume which they can refer to now, and will be able to refer to in the future, with the utmost confidence and satisfaction."—*British and Foreign Medico-Chirurgical Review.*
" It is certainly one of the most valuable contributions to modern medical science."—*Pacific Med. Journal.*
" The work is evidently a contribution of great value to the profession. We know of no other in the English language at once so complete, so original, and so readable."—*Detroit Review of Medicine and Surgery.*

——Wear and Tear: or, Hints for the Overworked. By S. WEIR MITCHELL, M.D. 16mo. Paper, 30 cents. Cloth, 50 cents.

MITCHELL.—Materia Medica and Therapeutics; with ample Illustrations of Practice in all the Departments of Medical Science, and Copious Notices of Toxicology. The whole adapted to the wants of Medical Pupils and Practitioners. By THOMAS D. MITCHELL, M.D. New edition, revised and corrected. 8vo. Sheep. $4.00.

MORGAN.—Practical Lessons in the Nature and Treatment of the Affections produced by the Contagious Diseases, with Chapters on Syphilitic Inoculation, Infantile Syphilis, etc. By JOHN MORGAN, M.D. Sixty Colored and Plain Illustrations. 12mo. Cloth extra. $1.75.

MORRIS.—A Practical Treatise on Shock after Surgical Operations and Injuries: with special reference to Shock caused by Railway Accidents. By EDWIN MORRIS, M.D., F.R.C.S. 12mo. Cloth. $1.25.

MORTON.—An Illustrated System of Human Anatomy; Special, General, and Microscopical. By the late SAMUEL GEORGE MORTON, M.D. With 391 Engravings on Wood. 8vo. Sheep. $4.50.

NÉLATON.—Clinical Lectures on Surgery. By M. NÉLATON. From Notes taken by WALTER F. ATLEE, M.D. 8vo. Sheep. $3.00.

NELIGAN.—A Treatise on Materia Medica. By J. M. NELIGAN 12mo. Cloth. $2.00.

PACKARD.—Lectures on Inflammation. By JOHN H. PACKARD, M.D. Being the First Course delivered before the College of Physicians of Philadelphia, under the Bequest of Dr. Mütter. 12mo. Cloth. $2.50.

——A Manual of Minor Surgery. By JOHN H. PACKARD, M.D. Illustrated with 145 Wood Engravings. 12mo. Cloth, limp. $1.25.

——Handbook of Operative Surgery. By JOHN H. PACKARD, M.D., Secretary of the College of Physicians of Philadelphia, etc. With 54 Steel Plates and Numerous Illustrations on Wood. 8vo. Extra Cloth, $5.00. Sheep, $5.75.

"Its distinguishing feature is abundant illustration, and in this respect is unequaled by any handbook with which we are acquainted. . . . To students and practitioners who have not the frequent opportunity of witnessing practical surgery, the volume before us will prove of unquestionable value."—*N. Y. Med. Record.*

PELOUZE and FREMY.—General Notes on Chemistry. Translated from the French by EDMUND C. EVANS, M.D. With 27 Illustrations. 12mo. Cloth. $1.75.

PHARMACOPŒIA of the United States of America. Fifth Decennial Revision. Published by authority of the National Convention for Revising the Pharmacopœia, held at Washington in 1870. 12mo. Cloth, $1.75. Sheep, $2.25. Sheep, interleaved, $3.25.

POWER.—Anatomy of the Arteries of the Human Body, Descriptive and Surgical, with the Descriptive Anatomy of the Heart. By JOHN HATCH POWER, M.D. Authorized and adopted by the Surgeon-General of the United States Army, for Use in Field and General Hospitals. Illustrated with numerous Wood Engravings. 12mo. Cloth. $2.50.

RAND.—Elements of Medical Chemistry. By B. HOWARD RAND, M.D., Professor of Chemistry in the Jefferson Medical College. New edition, carefully revised, with Additions. Illustrated. 12mo. Cloth, $2.00. Sheep, $2.50.

"We consider that the profession are deeply indebted to Dr. Rand for the labor and research expended in preparing so useful a volume in so neat and acceptable a form."—*The Journal of Applied Chemistry.*

READ.—Placenta Prævia: its History and Treatment. By WILLIAM READ, M.D. 340 pp. 8vo. Paper cover. $2.00.

REEVES.—A Practical Treatise on Enteric Fever: its Diagnosis and Treatment: Being an Analysis of one hundred and thirty consecutive Cases derived from Private Practice, and embracing a Partial History of the Disease in Virginia. By JAMES E. REEVES, M.D. 12mo. Cloth. $1.00.

REESE.—A Manual of Toxicology. A Practical Treatise on the Properties, Modes of Action, and Means of Detection of Poisons. By JOHN J. REESE, M.D., Professor of Medical Jurisprudence and Toxicology in the University of Pennsylvania. 8vo. Cloth, $5.00. Sheep, $6.00.

"Dr. Reese's book should be sure of a welcome on our tables, presenting, as it does, the practical essentials of toxicology in a compact and accessible form. The sections on therapeutics are brief, but the latest discoveries in the line of treatment of poisonings are carefully given."—*Amer. Jour. of the Med. Sciences.*

RICHARDSON.—A Handbook of Medical Microscopy. By JOSEPH G. RICHARDSON, M.D., Microscopist to the Pennsylvania Hospital; Lecturer on Pathological Anatomy in the University of Pennsylvania, etc., etc. With numerous Illustrations. 1 vol. 12mo. Extra cloth. $2.25.

"As a whole, we have not seen a work of its sort that in completeness and practical utility can rival it or compare with it."—*N. Y. Med. Record.*

"Comprehensive as regards its subject-matter, concise in style, and explicit in statement."—*Chicago Med. Journal.*

RICHARDSON.—Elements of Human Anatomy: General, Descriptive, and Practical. By T. G. RICHARDSON, M.D., Professor of Anatomy in the Medical Department of the University of Louisiana. Second edition. Carefully revised, and illustrated with nearly 300 Engravings. 8vo. Sheep. $6.00.

REYNOLDS.—A System of Medicine. Edited by J. RUSSELL REYNOLDS, M.D., F.R.C.P., London, and contributed to by the most eminent Physicians in England. New edition, thoroughly revised and enlarged. Three volumes now ready. 8vo. Price per volume, Cloth, $9.00. Sheep, $10.00.

In a review of the first edition, the London *Lancet* said, "It is unnecessary to say a word in favor of the high claims of all these gentlemen to speak with authority on the subjects which they respectively handle; and we congratulate the editor on his distinguished success in securing the services of such a staff."

RILEY.—A Compend of Materia Medica and Therapeutics. For the Use of Students. By JOHN C. RILEY, A.M., M.D., Professor of Materia Medica and Therapeutics in the National Medical College, etc. 8vo. Cloth. $3.00.

"Prof. Riley has done his work very well. . . . The descriptions of the various articles of the Materia Medica are very concise and remarkably accurate."—*N. Y. Med. Journal.*

SANSOM.—The Antiseptic System. A Treatise on Carbolic Acid and its Compounds, with an Inquiry into the Germ-Theories of Putrefaction, Fermentation, and Infection, the Theory and Practice of Disinfection, and the Employment of Antiseptics in Practical Medicine and Surgery. By E. A. SANSOM, M.D., London, M.R.C.P. With forty-two Illustrations. 8vo. Cloth extra. $5.00.

SEATON.—A Handbook of Vaccination: Adapted to the American Profession. By EDWARD C. SEATON, M.D., Medical Inspector to the Privy Council, London. Illustrated. Cloth. $1.25.

"Dr. Seaton's 'Handbook of Vaccination' may be regarded as a boon not only to the medical profession, but to the public at large."—*Saturday Review.*

SHAW.—Odontalgia, commonly called Toothache: its Causes, Prevention, and Cure. By S. PARSONS SHAW. 16mo. Extra cloth. $1.75.

"The anatomical points in regard to the structure of the teeth ought to be familiar to every physician, but it will not hurt to remind afresh; while the differential diagnosis of different forms of toothache and the proper treatment is a knowledge with which physicians are not generally familiar."—*Lancet and Observer.*

SIAMESE TWINS.—Report of the Autopsy of the Siamese Twins, together with other information concerning their Life. 16mo. Paper. 25 cents.

SIMPSON.—The Obstetrical Memoirs and Contributions of James Y. Simpson, M.D., F.R.S.E., Professor of Midwifery in the University of Edinburgh, etc. Edited by W. O. PRIESTLEY, M.D., and HORATIO R. STORER, M.D. With Illustrations. Two vols. 8vo. Cloth, $7.50. Sheep, $9.00.

SMITH.—The Common Nature of Epidemics, and their Relation to Climate and Civilization. Also, Remarks on Contagion and Quarantine. By SOUTHWOOD SMITH, M.D., Physician to the London Fever Hospital. Edited by J. BAKER, Esq., author of "Laws Relating to Public Health, Sanitary, Medical, and Protective." 12mo. Cloth. $1.50.

STILLÉ.—Epidemic or Malignant Cholera. By ALFRED STILLÉ, M.D., Professor of the Theory and Practice of Medicine in the University of Pennsylvania. 16mo. Paper cover. 30 cents.

STROMEYER and ESMARCH.—Gunshot Fractures and Resection in Gunshot Injuries. By Dr. LOUIS STROMEYER and Dr. FRIEDRICH ESMARCH. Translated by S. F. STATHAM. 12mo. Cloth. 75 cents.

SYME.—The Principles of Surgery. By JAMES SYME, F.R.S.E., Surgeon in Ordinary to Queen Victoria, in Scotland. To which are appended Treatises on the Diseases of the Rectum; Stricture of the Urethra and Fistula in Perineo; The Excision of Diseased Joints; and numerous Additional Contributions to the Pathology and Practice of Surgery. Edited by DONALD MACLEAN, M.D., L.R.C.S.E. 8vo. Cloth. $7.00.

TANNER.—A Handbook of Practical Midwifery and Obstetrics (Including Anæsthetics). By JOHN TANNER, M.D., M.A., LL.D., Member of the Royal College of Physicians; Obstetric Physician to the Farringdon Lying-in Charity; etc., etc. With 150 Illustrations. 16mo. Fine Cloth. $2.00.

"Clear and exact, profusely and excellently illustrated, we take pleasure in commending this little book as a companion both for students and 'busy practitioners.'"—*Chicago Med. Journal.*

TAYLOR.—Infantile Paralysis, and its Attendant Deformities. By CHARLES FAYETTE TAYLOR, M.D., Resident Surgeon New York Orthopedic Dispensary. Illustrated with numerous Engravings. 12mo. Paper cover, 75 cents. Cloth, $1.00.

THOMAS.—A Comprehensive Pronouncing Medical Dictionary: Containing the Etymology and Signification of the Terms made use of in Medicine and the Kindred Sciences. With an Appendix comprising a complete list of all the more important articles of the Materia Medica, arranged according to their medicinal properties. Also an explanation of the Latin terms and phrases occurring in Anatomy, Pharmacy, etc., together with the necessary directions for writing Latin prescriptions. By J. THOMAS, M.D. 8vo. Cloth, $3.25. Sheep, $3.75.

TURNBULL.—A Clinical Manual of Diseases of the Ear, including the Anatomy, Physiology, Pathology, and Treatment. By LAURENCE TURNBULL, M.D., Physician to the Department of the Eye and Ear, Howard Hospital, Philadelphia. 8vo. 500 Pages. 106 Illustrations. Extra cloth. $5.00.

"It might almost be called an aural encyclopædia."—*Amer. Jour. of the Med. Sciences.*

"Sound, clear, and eminently practical in all its parts."—*Boston Med. and Surg. Journal.*

"Dr. Turnbull proves himself thoroughly acquainted with the literature of the subject, and employs it very promptly."—*Monatsschrift für Ohrenheilkunde, Berlin, May,* 1873.

TYSON.—Practical Histology. An Introduction to the study of Practical Histology. By JAMES TYSON, M.D. For Beginners in Microscopy. 12mo. Cloth, $1.00. Cloth, interleaved with blank paper for notes, $1.50.

"It would be difficult to find elsewhere such a simple statement of what can be done by any and all who may possess even a slight active interest in the subject of histology."—*Boston Med. and Surg. Journal.*

——Transactions of the Pathological Society of Philadelphia. Vol. IV. Containing the Report of the Proceedings for the Years 1871, 1872, 1873. Edited by JAMES TYSON, M.D., Recorder of the Society. Illustrated. 8vo. Cloth. $4.00.

"By pathological students this will be welcomed as an invaluable addition to their libraries, and all physicians ought to be students of pathology to a certain extent. It will throw light on many obscurities in practice."—*Phila. Med. and Surg. Reporter.*

WOOD.—A Treatise on the Practice of Medicine. By GEORGE B. WOOD, M.D., LL.D. Sixth edition. 2 vols. Thick 8vo. Cloth, $9.00. Sheep, $10.00.

———A Treatise on Therapeutics and Pharmacology, or Materia Medica. By GEORGE B. WOOD, M.D., LL.D. Third edition. 8vo. Cloth, $9.00. Sheep, $10.00.

——Introductory Lectures and Addresses on Medical Subjects. Delivered chiefly before the Medical Classes of the University of Pennsylvania. By GEORGE B. WOOD, M.D., LL.D. Second edition. 8vo. Cloth. $3.00.

WOOD and BACHE.—The Dispensatory of the United States of America. By GEORGE B. WOOD, M.D., and FRANKLIN BACHE, M.D. Thirteenth edition, carefully revised. Large 8vo. Sheep. $10.00.

WOOD.—Treatise on Therapeutics. Comprising Materia Medica and Toxicology, with Especial Reference to the Application of the Physiological Action of Drugs to Clinical Medicine. By H. C. WOOD, JR., M.D. Second Edition. Revised, with important additions. 8vo. Cloth, $6.00. Sheep, $6.50.

"It is a sort of work on materia medica and therapeutics that has been long needed both by the practitioner and student, and we congratulate the author upon his success in carrying out a most difficult undertaking. Only those who have worked among the tangled heaps of wheat and weeds that encumber the therapeutics even of the last half century, and tried to sift the grain from the chaff, can appreciate the difficulty of producing a work like the one before us."—*Amer. Jour. of the Med. Sciences.*

"We warmly congratulate Dr. Wood on the ability, energy, and careful research, of which every page in the book bears evidence. . . . The industry displayed by Dr. Wood in collecting information from every available source is very great, and the references which he constantly gives enable any one desirous of further information to consult the original papers on the subject without losing time in a search after them. . . . Altogether, this work stands by itself as the only complete treatise on the physiological action of drugs in the English language, and no student of scientific therapeutics should be without it."—*London Practitioner.*

———Thermic Fever, or Sunstroke. By H. C. WOOD, JR., M.D. Awarded the Boyleston Prize of Harvard University. 12mo. Cloth. $1.25.

"We know of no work which gives so full an exposition of this affection. The profession are under many obligations to Dr. Wood for his excellent monograph."—*Buffalo Med. and Surg. Journal.*

"We know no account of the subject at once so clear and so free from one-sidedness."—*N. Y. Nation.*

WOODWARD.—Outlines of the Chief Camp Diseases of the United States Armies as observed during the War. A Practical Contribution to Military Medicine. By JOSEPH JANVIER WOODWARD, M.D., Member of the Academy of Natural Sciences of Philadelphia. 8vo. Cloth. $2.50.

———

The works on this list are for sale by Booksellers generally, or will be sent, free of charge, upon receipt of the price by

J. B. LIPPINCOTT & CO.,

PUBLISHERS, BOOKSELLERS, AND IMPORTERS,

715 AND 717 MARKET STREET, PHILADELPHIA.

www.ingramcontent.com/pod-product-compliance
Lightning Source LLC
Chambersburg PA
CBHW071353050326
40689CB00010B/1624